ENGLAND TEST CRICKETERS

ENGLAND TEST CRICKETERS

The complete record from 1877

BILL FRINDALL

Sponsored by
THE CARPHONE GROUP

WILLOW BOOKS
COLLINS
8 GRAFTON STREET LONDON W1

Willow Books
William Collins Sons & Co. Ltd
London · Glasgow · Sydney · Auckland
Toronto · Johannesburg

First published 1989

British Library Cataloguing In Publication Data
Frindall, Bill, 1939–
England test cricketers 1876/7 1988/9
1. Cricket. English teams. Test matches, to 1988
I. Title
796.35'865

ISBN 0-00-218339-0

Editorial planning by Jollands Editions
Designed by Humphrey Stone
Set in Palatino
by Ace Filmsetting Ltd, Frome, Somerset
Printed and bound in Great Britain by
Butler and Tanner Ltd,
Frome, Somerset

CONTENTS

PREFACE & ACKNOWLEDGEMENTS

This volume was conceived by Tim Jollands when, during his days as a commissioning editor for Queen Anne Press and then Collins, he discovered that no publication had ever featured match-by-match breakdowns of individual Test careers. When he found that I had compiled such statistics on every post-war Test cricketer using a loose-leaf system of sheets specially designed for the BBC's *Test Match Special* commentaries, the die for this work had been cast. Like Topsy it grew, with profiles, illustrations and lists of notable feats being added for each of the 536 cricketers who represented England in the 651 matches which have come to be universally accepted as official Tests.

The term 'Test match' was coined during the first cricket tour to Australia when, in 1861–62, games between H.H. Stephenson's team and each of the colonies were described as 'Test matches'. Those early contests were played against odds with the opposition batting and fielding more than eleven men. Not until the fourth expedition to Australia, by James Lillywhite's professionals in 1876–77, did an English team play on level terms overseas. That initial encounter, against a combined eleven from Melbourne and Sydney, has become accepted as the first official Test match.

The first list of Test matches was published in 1894 by Mr Clarence Moody (*Australian Cricket and Cricketers*) and it was adopted the following year by Mr John Pentelow in the first book of Test cricket (*England v Australia – the Story of the Test Matches*). Although there must be considerable doubt concerning the inclusion of matches in which England was represented by privately arranged teams in Australia and South Africa (prior to the first official MCC tours to those countries in 1903–04 and 1905–06 respectively), I have resisted the temptation to meddle with their status. That has become sanctified by time and the same must apply to the coincidental England rubbers in New Zealand and the Caribbean during the early months of 1930.

The International Cricket Conference controls the title 'Test match' and they ruled that England's matches against the Rest of the World in 1970 were unofficial and should not be included in Test match records. Those games, substituted for a cancelled series against South Africa, were played with the full panoply of Test matches and against considerably stronger opposition than most of England's official adversaries have provided. It is an unfortunate but essential anomaly that, although he is the proud and rightful owner of an England cap for appearing at Lord's in the opening match of that rubber, Alan Jones of Glamorgan is not included in this directory because he alone of the players representing England in those five encounters was never selected for an official Test. It is ironical that he should possess a full England cap, awarded only for appearing in a home Test match, whereas a substantial number of cricketers qualifying for this volume played only in Tests overseas and had to be content with the MCC touring cap.

England's Test cricketers are arranged in alphabetical order and are listed in an Index of photographs at the back of this volume. That section shows the page or pages where they are illustrated (with the exception of Reginald Wood) and the seasons in which their first-class career started and finished.

Each player's section includes his full given (and acquired) names, his major first-class teams with the dates of his first and last appearances, his place and date of birth (and, where appropriate, death), his inclusion among *Wisden*'s Cricketers of the Year, and his major tours. To economise on space, the venues of those tours have been abbreviated (A – Australia, SA – South Africa, WI – West Indies, NZ – New Zealand, I – India, P – Pakistan, SL – Sri Lanka/Ceylon, Z – Zimbabwe/Rhodesia), as have the titles of private tours:

Cahn	Sir Julian Cahn's XI	Norfolk	Duke of Norfolk's XI
Cav	Cavaliers	Pres XI	President's XI
Cwlth	Commonwealth XI	PM XI	Prime Minister's XI
Eng Co	English Counties XI	Robins	D.H. Robins's XI
Howard	C.G. Howard's XI	RW	Rest of the World
Int W	International Wanderers	SAB	South African Breweries XI
Int XI	International XI	Swanton	E.W. Swanton's XI
Joel	S.B. Joel's XI	Tennyson	Lord Tennyson's XI

Again to preserve space, private tours prior to the first official MCC tour to a particular country are not shown as such. Only tours on which the player appeared in first-class matches are given and those to North and South America and East Africa are omitted.

The reference numbers in the match-by-match tables are those which appear in my *Wisden Book of Test Cricket* (published by Macdonald Queen Anne Press in 1979 and 1985). The matches are arranged in chronological order by rubber. The suffix of each match number refers to England's chronological order; for example, 467/350 is the 467th official Test match listed and the 350th involving England. As the four-match series in New Zealand in January and February 1930 began one day before England's simultaneous rubber in the West Indies, those four Tests are listed first. Only the prefix of the reference is given in the profiles, notable feats and Test notes.

An asterisk immediately after the reference number denotes that the player in question was captain. Asterisks elsewhere in the tables, profiles and notable feats denote either a 'not out' innings or an unfinished partnership. A dagger after the reference number denotes that the player in question was wicket-keeper.

Venues of Test matches have been listed according to centre, apart from the two London grounds, Lord's and The Oval, which are treated as separate centres. The following key has been used where more than one ground in a city has played host to a Test match:

Bombay[1]	Gymkhana Ground	Durban[2]	Kingsmead
Bombay[2]	Brabourne Stadium	Johannesburg[1]	Old Wanderers
Bombay[3]	Wankhede Stadium	Johannesburg[2]	Ellis Park
Brisbane[1]	Exhibition Ground	Johannesburg[3]	Wanderers Stadium
Brisbane[2]	Woolloongabba	Lahore[2]	Gaddafi Stadium
Colombo SO	Saravanamuttu (Colombo) Oval	Madras[1]	Chepauk Stadium
Durban[1]	Lord's	Madras[2]	Corporation (Nehru) Stadium

'Rate' in the bowling sections of the career tables denotes the players' striking rate in terms of balls per wicket. As in the case of W.G. Grace, total wickets in a career are occasionally given as '2864+12', denoting that full bowling analyses are not available for the extra wickets. Balls rather than overs are listed because the number of deliveries in an over has varied from four to eight. Since 1979–80 the six-ball over has been universally used in Test cricket. Prior to that season the following exceptions were in use:

In England: 1880 to 1888 – 4; 1890 to 1899 – 5; 1939 – 8.
In Australia: 1876–77 to 1887–88 – 4; 1924–25 – 8; 1936–37 to 1978–79 – 8.
In South Africa: 1888–89 – 4; 1891–92 to 1898–99 –5; 1938–39 to 1957–58 – 8.
In New Zealand: 1968–69 to 1978–79 – 8.
In Pakistan: 1974–75 to 1977–78 – 8.

Tests in the West Indies, India and Sri Lanka have all involved the six-ball over. 'Balls' in the wicket-keeping analysis denotes the number of legitimate deliveries bowled during that innings; no-balls and wides are excluded. Where a player has kept for only part of an innings it has not always been possible to ascertain exactly where a change of 'keeper occurred. In those instances the complete number of balls in that innings has been charged against the official custodian.

Test match statistics have been taken from details recorded in official scorebooks. Where that document no longer survives, research has turned to contemporary match reports preserved with impressive efficiency at The British Library. Catches held as a substitute fielder are not included in the individual records.

In compiling the individual first-class records, only matches considered first-class by the Association of Cricket Statisticians (ACS) or, since 1947, accorded such status by the MCC and ICC, have been included, with a few exceptions in order to bring the figures in line with those in *Wisden Cricketers' Almanack* and the *Playfair Cricket Annual*. This means that there are a few discrepancies between the figures given in this book and those produced in some of the publications of the ACS. The following players are those affected:

W.G. Grace, whose figures are those originally detailed in *Wisden* 1916 by F.S. Ashley-Cooper.

J.B. Hobbs and H. Sutcliffe, whose figures exclude the Maharaja of Vizianagram XI matches in India in 1930–31.

M.C. Bird and H.W. Lee, whose figures exclude some matches played in India in 1917–18 and 1918–19.

R. Kilner and W. Rhodes, whose figures exclude matches played in India in 1922–23.

M.C. Bird, C. Blythe, C.P. Buckenham, D. Denton, F.L. Fane, J.B. Hobbs, W. Rhodes, G.H.T. Simpson-Hayward, H. Strudwick, N.C. Tufnell and F.E. Woolley, whose figures include the match MCC v The Reef in 1909–10.

J.T. Brown, Lord Hawke, G.H. Hirst, A.C. MacLaren, R. Peel, A.G. Steel, G. Ulyett and E. Wainwright, whose figures exclude matches played between Yorkshire and Liverpool & District in 1889, 1891, 1892, and 1893.

Economy of space has demanded that only players scoring 1000 runs, taking 50 wickets or making 50 dismissals qualify for a series-by-series survey.

The profiles are not intended to be a complete survey of each career; their inclusion is an attempt to add a little flesh to the bare bones of the statistics. Having watched Test cricket only since 1950, I have had to rely on the assessments of contemporary writers and players for the earlier cricketers.

Thanks to the demonic activities of various politicians, this volume will be up to date at the time of its publication, England's scheduled 1988–89 tour to India – and a subsequent replacement to New Zealand – having been cancelled. Hopefully the ICC agreement of January 1989 concerning cricketers' links with South Africa will prevent further tours being aborted. Having been privileged to attend the SACU's centenary celebrations and seen at first hand the considerable progress in coaching non-white cricketers throughout the Republic, I fervently hope that the readmittance of South Africa to the Test match fold is not too distant. That England's representative's have not been able to test their skills against South Africa's leading cricketers since 1965 has been one of sport's greatest tragedies.

This volume, inspired and master-minded by Tim Jollands, has been very much a team effort and it would not have been completed without the considerable assistance and expertise of Philip Bailey. For many years he has been a leading member of the ACS and his comprehensive research and dutiful checking has greatly enhanced the accuracy of these statistics. The task of typesetting over three million characters fell on Jim Henretty and his colleagues at Ace Filmsetting who, despite being set an almost impossible deadline, remained calm and supportive to the end. A special tribute is due to Humphrey Stone whose skill as a designer has overcome immense problems imposed by the variable shapes and sizes of tables, text and photographs. The experience gained in grappling with these posers must surely qualify him for the next world jigsaw puzzle championships. Nor would by own contributions have been possible without the assistance of many friends, particularly Debbie Brown and Alison Mitchell. It was Tim Jollands who conceived and planned this work, who secured the generous sponsorship of The Carphone Group from their supreme cricket enthusiast, Ted Markwick, and who has undertaken the monumental task of picture research.

I am most grateful to Michael Doggart and his colleagues at Collins Willow and even more indebted to the 536 England cricketers who made it all possible.

BILL FRINDALL
London
March 1989

Photographic Acknowledgements

Our special thanks go to Patrick Eagar who has supplied photographs of all but a handful of the modern players. For earlier players we have drawn extensively on the archives of Central Press, owned at the outset of our research by Visual Communications Limited but purchased at a critical time in proceedings by the Hulton Deutsch Collection. We are grateful to their respective managers, Mike Watson and Roger Wemyss Brooks, for giving us priority treatment during the transition period; and to Siobhan Hewitt and Bill Hulme at The Keystone Collection for their help in actual research. The Hulton Deutsch Collection – which includes the archives of the BBC Hulton Picture Library, Central Press, Fox Photos, Keystone Press Agency – is now the single most important source of cricket photographs and we are grateful to the Collection for allowing us to reproduce some 150 of them in this book. We are also grateful to the authorities at Lord's, in particular Stephen Green and his staff at the MCC Library, for allowing us to reproduce photographs from the MCC Collection. Further acknowledgements are due to the following individuals and organisations: George Beldam Collection, David Frith Collection, Guinness Superlatives Ltd, Ken Kelly, Roger Mann Collection, Nottinghamshire CCC, Press Association-Reuter, Bill Smith and Sport & General Press Agency.

W.H.F. & T.W.J.

ABEL, Robert

Surrey (1881 to 1904)

Wisden 1890
TOURS
A 1887–88, 1891–92; SA 1888–89
Born Rotherhithe, Surrey 30 Nov 1857
Died Stockwell, London 10 Dec 1936

Bobby Abel, at 5ft 4in one of the most diminutive cricketers to represent England, was the forerunner of an outstanding lineage of Surrey opening batsmen which includes Tom Hayward, Jack Hobbs, Andy Sandham and John Edrich. Known as 'The Guv'nor' and accorded folk-hero status by The Oval crowds, he was instantly recognizable with his slow waddle to the wicket, upright stance and shrunken, faded chocolate cap. He mastered all types of bowling much as he was to dominate the output of Craig, Surrey cricket's poet. An outstanding slip catcher and useful right-handed round-arm slow bowler, Abel sired two Surrey cricketers. Appropriately his signed photo adorns the collection of Victorian entertainers at London's only surviving music hall, The Players' Theatre.

Bobby Abel after his historic innings of 357 for Surrey against Somerset in 1899.*

NOTABLE FEATS

- Top-scored with 46 in South Africa's inaugural Test (and first-class) match (Test *31*). A fortnight later, he recorded the first hundred in South African first-class cricket (*32*).
- The first of only 4 players to carry their bat through an England innings (*36*).
- Exceeded 1000 runs 14 times, including 2000 in each of 8 successive seasons from 1895, becoming the second after K.S. Ranjitsinhji to reach 3000 (3309 in 1901).
- In 1899, at the age of 41, he set world records which still survive by carrying his bat for the highest score (357*) throughout the largest completed innings total in which this feat has been achieved: 811 by Surrey v Somerset at The Oval. That total still represents the most runs added during any batsman's innings in all first-class cricket. Abel batted just over 8½ hours, hitting 1 six, 7 fives, 38 fours, 11 threes, 23 twos and 85 singles. That same season he shared with T.W. Hayward in Surrey's highest partnership for any wicket: 448 v Yorkshire at The Oval.
- When Surrey required 346 runs for victory in 170 minutes against Kent at The Oval in 1900, Abel (120*) and W. Brockwell (132*) scored 270 to establish the highest fourth-innings total in Britain without the loss of a wicket.
- Scored 12 first-class hundreds in 1900 to eclipse W.G. Grace's world record by two.
- His 9 double centuries include the second-highest score (247) in the history of Gentlemen v Players matches.

						Batting 1st			Batting 2nd			
Ref	Series	V	T	Venue	Result	No	R	HO	No	R	HO	Ct
28/28	1888	A	1	Lord's	L-61	2	3	b	2	8	c	1
29/29			2	Oval	W-I & 137	5	70	ro	–	–	–	1
30/30			3	Manchester	W-I & 21	2	0	b	–	–	–	1
31/31	1888–89	SA	1	Port Elizabeth	W-8w	1	46	c	1	23	*	3
32/32			2	Cape Town	W-I & 202	1	120	b	–	–	–	1
35/35	1891–92	A	1	Melbourne	L-54	2	32	b	5	28	c	1
36/36			2	Sydney	L-72	1	132	*	1	1	c	2
37/37			3	Adelaide	W-I & 230	2	24	st	–	–	–	1
50/50	1896	A	1	Lord's	W-6w	3	94	b	2	4	c	–
51/51			2	Manchester	L-3w	4	26	c	4	13	c	–
52/52			3	Oval	W-66	4	26	c	4	21	c	1
72/72	1902	A	3	Sheffield	L-143	2	38	b	2	8	c	1
73/73			4	Manchester	L-3	2	6	c	5	21	b	–

Career	M	I	NO	HS	R	Avge	100	50	Ct	St	Balls	R	W	Avge	BB	5w	10w	Rate
Test	13	22	2	132*	744	37.20	2	2	13	–	–	–	–	–	–	–	–	–
F/c	627	1007	73	357*	33124	35.46	74	145	586	–	14421	6314	263	24.00	6-15	3	–	54.83

ABSOLOM
Charles Alfred

Cambridge University (1866 to 1869)
Kent (1868 to 1879)

TOUR A 1878–79
Born Blackheath, Kent 7 Jun 1846
Died Port-of-Spain, Trinidad 30 Jul 1889

Charlie Absolom could well have been a prototype for Ian Botham. A well-built natural athlete who excelled at the long jump, shot-putting and soccer, he batted, bowled and fielded at a lively pace. Dubbed 'The Cambridge Navvy', he was swarthy with a long black beard and his training schedule largely involved hay-making and beer. In an age dominated by fashionable headgear he always remained bare-headed and, in 1866, on his first appearance at Lord's, he created a sensation by wearing a red shirt. In his only Test he contributed England's highest score of the match. He made the last of his 57 appearances for Kent the following summer before roving North America and communing with the Spokabe tribe. He met an agonizing and bizarre end as purser of the SS *Muriel* in Port-of-Spain when a crane loading sugar crushed him. [*Illus. p.* 222]

Ref	Series	V	T	Venue	Result	Batting 1st			Batting 2nd			Ct
						No	R	HO	No	R	HO	
3/3	1878–79	A		Melbourne	L-10w	9	52	c	8	6	c	–

Career	M	I	NO	HS	R	Avge	100	50	Ct	St	Balls	R	W	Avge	BB	5w	10w	Rate
Test	1	2	0	52	58	29.00	–	1	–	–	–	–	–	–	–	–	–	–
F/c	99	178	11	94	2515	15.05	–	4	127	–	13082	5471	281+1	19.46	7-45	19	3	46.55

AGNEW
Jonathan Philip

Leicestershire (1978 to date)

Wisden 1988
TOURS
I 1984–85; SL 1985–86 (Eng B);
Z 1980–81 (Leics)
Born Macclesfield, Cheshire 4 Apr 1960

Jon Agnew is a classic example of a consistently successful county cricketer failing to make the grade at Test level. Although unsuccessful during his three opportunities, this tall (6ft 3½in), exceedingly slim right-arm fast bowler with a fine, high action capable of extracting awkward bounce was unlucky to be ignored in 1987 and 1988 when, employing a reduced run, he took 101 and 93 wickets respectively. A useful tail-ender and a product of Uppingham School, Jon Agnew is currently developing a career in local radio.

Jon Agnew

Ref	Series	V	T	Venue	Result	Batting 1st			Batting 2nd			Ct	Bowling 1st			Bowling 2nd		
						No	R	HO	No	R	HO		Balls	R	W	Balls	R	W
993/605	1984	WI	5	Oval	L-172	11	5	b	11	2	*	–	72	46	0	84	51	2
994/606	1984	SL		Lord's	D	11	1	*	–	–	–	–	192	123	2	66	54	0
1020/615	1985	A	4	Manchester	D	11	2	*	–	–	–	–	84	65	0	54	34	0

Career	M	I	NO	HS	R	Avge	100	50	Ct	St	Balls	R	W	Avge	BB	5w	10w	Rate
Test	3	4	3	5	10	10.00	–	–	–	–	552	373	4	93.25	2-51	–	–	138.00
F/c	172	175	36	90	1582	11.38	–	2	31	–	27341	14967	537	27.87	9-70	29	5	50.91

ALLEN, David Arthur

Gloucestershire (1953 to 1972)

TOURS
A 1962–63, 1965–66; SA 1964–65; WI 1959–60; NZ 1960–61, 1965–66; I 1961–62; P 1961–62, 1967–68 (Cwlth); SL 1961–62
Born Horfield, Bristol 29 Oct 1935

From a deceptively lazy four-pace amble, this trim, dark-haired off-spinner combined subtle variations of flight with substantial degrees of turn and could bowl accurately for long spells – as he proved on his fiery baptism against the powerful West Indies batsmen on shirt-front Caribbean pitches. Although frequently overlooked in favour of Titmus and Illingworth for home Tests, David Allen was an automatic selection overseas for six years after Laker's retirement and toured all England's opponent countries at least once. Operating in harness with Fred Titmus, he bowled England to victory on responsive pitches at Durban and Sydney. A doughty lower-order batsman who delighted in the cut, he was at his best against the fastest bowling – as he showed in fending off Wes Hall's final two balls to draw the 1963 Lord's Test with the injured Colin Cowdrey (fractured arm) as his last partner. He was also a quality outfielder with a powerful flat throw.

NOTABLE FEATS

- 50 wickets in 17th Test (*517*); 100 wickets in 33rd Test (*598*).
- Shared in 2 surviving England record stands against Pakistan with P.H. Parfitt in 1962: 153* (6th wkt) at Birmingham and 99 (8th wkt) at Leeds.
- Achieved 'double' (1001 runs and 124 wickets) in 1961.

						Batting 1st			Batting 2nd				Bowling 1st			Bowling 2nd		
Ref	Series	V	T	Venue	Result	No	R	HO	No	R	HO	Ct	Balls	R	W	Balls	R	W
487/359	1959–60	WI	1	Bridgetown	D	10	10	lbw	–	–	–	–	258	82	0	–	–	–
488/360			2	Port-of-Spain	W-256	10	10	*	10	16	c	1	30	9	0	186	57	3
489/361			3	Kingston	D	10	30	*	10	17	*	–	168	57	1	54	19	0
490/362			4	Georgetown	D	9	55	c	8	1	*	–	252	75	3	–	–	–
491/363			5	Port-of-Spain	D	9	7	c	3	25	ro	–	144	61	2	90	57	0
495/367	1960	SA	4	Manchester	D	9	0	lbw	8	14	*	–	119	58	4	42	5	0
496/368			5	Oval	D	8	0	lbw	8	12	*	1	168	36	0	12	2	0
507/369	1961	A	1	Birmingham	D	9	11	ro	–	–	–	–	144	88	2	–	–	–
509/371			3	Leeds	W-8w	10	5	*	–	–	–	–	168	45	1	84	30	2
510/372			4	Manchester	L-54	8	42	c	8	10	c	–	–	–	–	228	58	4
511/373			5	Oval	D	9	22	*	9	42	*	–	180	133	4	–	–	–
512/374	1961–62	P	1	Lahore[2]	W-5w	3	40	lbw	–	–	–	1	198	67	2	132	51	3
513/375	1961–62	I	1	Bombay[2]	D	8	0	c	–	–	–	2	234	54	3	66	12	0
514/376			2	Kanpur	D	9	12	c	–	–	–	–	258	88	1	–	–	–
515/377			3	Delhi	D	–	–	–	–	–	–	–	282	87	4	–	–	–
516/378			4	Calcutta	L-187	8	15	b	8	7	c	–	204	67	5	260	95	4
517/379			5	Madras[2]	L-128	8	34	b	8	21	c	1	309	116	3	198	64	1
518/380	1961–62	P	2	Dacca	D	9	0	b	–	–	–	1	243	94	2	139	30	5
519/381			3	Karachi	D	8	1	c	–	–	–	–	162	51	1	210	42	0
530/382	1962	P	1	Birmingham	W-I & 24	7	79	*	–	–	–	–	192	62	2	216	73	3
531/383			2	Lord's	W-9w	6	2	lbw	–	–	–	–	–	–	–	90	41	1
532/384			3	Leeds	W-I & 117	9	62	c	–	–	–	–	54	14	0	144	47	3
534/386			5	Oval	W-10w	–	–	–	–	–	–	–	132	33	1	162	52	1
539/391	1962–63	A	5	Sydney	D	10	14	c	–	–	–	1	344	87	2	152	26	3
543/395	1963	WI	1	Manchester	L-10w	8	5	c	9	1	b	–	342	122	2	1	1	0
544/396			2	Lord's	D	10	2	lbw	10	4	*	–	60	35	1	126	50	1
561/405	1964	A	1	Nottingham	D	9	21	c	8	3	lbw	–	96	22	1	–	–	–
571/410	1964–65	SA	1	Durban[2]	W-I & 104	–	–	–	–	–	–	–	119	41	5	282	99	2
572/411			2	Johannesburg	D	9	2	lbw	–	–	–	–	234	45	1	294	87	4
573/412			3	Cape Town	D	9	22	c	–	–	–	–	240	79	2	102	27	0
575/414			5	Port Elizabeth	D	10	38	*	–	–	–	1	264	80	3	–	–	–
597/421	1965–66	A	1	Brisbane[2]	D	8	3	c	–	–	–	–	312	108	0	–	–	–
598/422			2	Melbourne	D	10	2	c	–	–	–	1	160	55	2	144	48	1
599/423			3	Sydney	W-I & 93	10	50	*	–	–	–	–	152	42	2	160	47	4
600/424			4	Adelaide	L-I & 9	9	2	c	9	5	*	–	168	103	0	–	–	–
602/426	1965–66	NZ	1	Christchurch	D	8	88	c	–	–	–	–	240	80	0	114	8	1
603/427			2	Dunedin	D	9	9	b	–	–	–	–	166	68	2	198	46	4
604/428			3	Auckland	D	7	7	*	–	–	–	–	287	123	5	141	34	1
605/429	1966	WI	1	Manchester	L-I & 40	8	37	c	8	1	c	–	187	104	2	–	–	–

Career	M	I	NO	HS	R	Avge	100	50	Ct	St	Balls	R	W	Avge	BB	5w	10w	Rate
Test	39	51	15	88	918	25.50	–	5	10	–	11297	3779	122	30.97	5-30	4	–	92.59
F/c	456	641	147	121*	9291	18.80	1	29	252	–	77619	28586	1209	23.64	8-34	56	8	64.20

David Allen ends Richie Benaud's final Test innings in England at The Oval, 1961. John Murray is behind the stumps; the non-striker is Ken Mackay.

D. A. ALLEN – TEST BOWLING SUMMARY

Series	V	M	Balls	R	W	Avge	BB	5w	10w	Rate
1959–60	WI	5	1182	417	9	46.33	3-57	–	–	131.33
1960	SA	2	341	101	4	25.25	4-58	–	–	85.25
1961	A	4	804	354	13	27.23	4-58	–	–	61.84
1961–62	P	3	1084	335	13	25.76	5-30	1	–	83.38
1961–62	I	5	1811	583	21	25.85	5-67	1	–	86.23
1962	P	4	990	322	11	29.27	3-47	–	–	90.00
1962–63	A	1	496	113	5	22.60	3-26	–	–	99.20
1963	WI	2	529	208	4	52.00	2-122	–	–	132.25
1964	A	1	96	22	1	22.00	1-22	–	–	96.00
1964–65	SA	4	1535	458	17	26.94	5-41	1	–	90.29
1965–66	A	4	1096	403	9	44.77	4-47	–	–	121.77
1965–66	NZ	3	1146	359	13	27.61	5-123	1	–	88.15
1966	WI	1	187	104	2	52.00	2-104	–	–	93.50
	A	10	2492	892	28	31.85	4-47	–	–	89.00
	SA	6	1876	559	21	26.61	5-41	1	–	89.33
	WI	8	1898	729	15	48.60	3-57	–	–	126.53
	NZ	3	1146	359	13	27.61	5-123	1	–	88.15
	I	5	1811	583	21	25.85	5-67	1	–	86.23
	P	7	2074	657	24	27.37	5-30	1	–	86.41
Home		14	2947	1111	35	31.74	4-58	–	–	84.20
Overseas		25	8350	2668	87	30.66	5-30	4	–	95.97
Totals		39	11297	3779	122	30.97	5-30	4	–	92.59

ALLEN
Sir George Oswald Browning CBE

Middlesex (1921 to 1950)
Cambridge University (1922 to 1923)

TOURS
A 1932–33, 1936–37; WI 1947–48;
NZ 1932–33, 1936–37
Born Bellevue Hill, Sydney, Australia
31 Jul 1902
Knighted for services to cricket 1986

As a high-class all-rounder, captain, selector and adminsitrator, Sir George 'Gubby' Allen must be ranked alongside W.G. Grace, Lord Harris and Sir Pelham Warner as one of the game's most powerful influences. A clear-minded, forthright, shrewd traditionalist, for more than 60 years he has been a major force at Lord's. The nephew of R.C. Allen, who played for Australia in the Second Test of 1886–87, 'Gubby' was a magnificent right-arm fast bowler whose galloping, rhythmic approach and compact sideways-on action extracted maximum pace from any surface. A brave, orthodox, stylish, hard-hitting batsman, superb close fielder and highly astute leader, he was the complete all-rounder. Although business interests reduced his county career to a spasmodic 146 matches between 1921 and 1950, he twice toured Australia. Refusing to resort to 'bodyline' he took 21 wickets in the 1932–33 series and captained the following mission which restored friendly relations. He served as MCC president (1963–64) and treasurer (1964–76) after seven seasons (1955–61) as a most successful chairman of selectors who backed class against averages.

						Batting 1st			Batting 2nd				Bowling 1st			Bowling 2nd		
Ref	Series	V	T	Venue	Result	No	R	HO	No	R	HO	Ct	Balls	R	W	Balls	R	W
195/181	1930	A	2	Lord's	L-7w	7	3	b	7	57	lbw	–	204	115	0	–	–	–
209/190	1931	NZ	1	Lord's	D	9	122	c	–	–	–	–	90	45	1	150	47	2
210/191			2	Oval	W-I & 26	–	–	–	–	–	–	1	78	14	5	78	23	0
211/191			3	Manchester	D	–	–	–	–	–	–	–	–	–	–	–	–	–
220/194	1932–33	A	1	Sydney	W-10w	8	19	c	–	–	–	3	90	65	0	54	13	1
221/195			2	Melbourne	L-111	8	30	c	8	23	st	1	102	41	2	72	44	2
222/196			3	Adelaide	W-338	8	15	lbw	4	15	lbw	2	138	71	4	104	50	4

Ref	Series	V	T	Venue	Result	Batting 1st No	R	HO	Batting 2nd No	R	HO	Ct	Bowling 1st Balls	R	W	Bowling 2nd Balls	R	W
223/197			4	Brisbane[2]	W-6w	7	13	c	–	–	–	–	144	83	2	102	44	3
224/198			5	Sydney	W-8w	9	48	c	–	–	–	1	150	128	1	70	54	2
225/199	1932–33	NZ	1	Christchurch	D	–	–	–	–	–	–	–	120	46	2	25	5	0
226/200			2	Auckland	D	6	12	b	–	–	–	–	30	11	0	18	4	0
227/201	1933	WI	1	Lord's	W-I & 27	8	16	ro	–	–	–	–	78	13	2	66	33	1
235/209	1934	A	3	Manchester	D	9	61	b	–	–	–	–	186	113	0	36	23	1
237/211			5	Oval	L-562	8	19	b	7	26	st	2	204	170	4	96	63	0
252/221*	1936	I	1	Lord's	W-9w	8	13	c	–	–	–	–	102	35	5	108	43	5
253/222*			2	Manchester	D	7	1	c	–	–	–	–	84	39	2	114	96	0
254/223*			3	Oval	W-9w	7	13	c	–	–	–	1	72	37	1	120	80	7
255/224*	1936–37	A	1	Brisbane[2]	W-322	9	35	c	7	68	c	–	128	71	3	48	36	5
256/225*			2	Sydney	W-I & 22	6	9	lbw	–	–	–	2	47	19	3	152	61	1
257/226*			3	Melbourne	L-365	9	0	*	7	11	c	2	96	35	1	184	84	2
258/227*			4	Adelaide	L-148	8	11	lbw	8	9	c	2	128	60	2	112	61	0
259/228*			5	Melbourne	L-I & 200	8	0	c	8	7	c	–	136	99	0	–	–	–
296/259*	1947–48	WI	2	Port-of-Spain	D	5	36	c	6	2	c	1	96	82	2	26	21	1
297/260*			3	Georgetown	L-7w	11	0	*	5	20	lbw	2	16	5	1	–	–	–
298/261*			4	Kingston	L-10w	6	23	c	6	13	lbw	–	120	83	1	12	14	0

Career	M	I	NO	HS	R	Avge	100	50	Ct	St	Balls	R	W	Avge	BB	5w	10w	Rate
Test	25	33	2	122	750	24.19	1	3	20	–	4386	2379	81	29.37	7-80	5	1	54.14
F/c	265	376	54	180	9232	28.67	11	47	131	–	36367	17518	788	22.23	10-40	48	9	46.15

'Gubby' Allen bowling to Stan McCabe in the Adelaide Test of 1936–37.

NOTABLE FEATS

- 50 wickets in 16th Test (*253*).
- Shared Test cricket's longest surviving partnership world record of 246 for the 8th wkt with L.E.G. Ames (Test *209*).
- Bowled a 13-ball over (3 wides, 4 no-balls) in Test *235*.
- Ended career at the age of 45 years 245 days – the second-oldest Test captain after W.G. Grace.
- Returned record Middlesex analysis of 10 for 40 (8 clean-bowled) v Lancashire at Lord's in 1929.

G. O. B. ALLEN – TEST BOWLING SUMMARY

Series	V	M	Balls	R	W	Avge	BB	5w	10w	Rate
1930	A	1	204	115	0	–	–	–	–	–
1931	NZ	3	396	129	8	16.12	5-14	1	–	49.50
1932–33	A	5	1026	593	21	28.23	4-50	–	–	48.85
1932–33	NZ	2	193	66	2	33.00	2-46	–	–	96.50
1933	WI	1	144	46	3	15.33	2-13	–	–	48.00
1934	A	2	522	369	5	73.80	4-170	–	–	104.40
1936	I	3	600	330	20	16.50	7-80	3	1	30.00
1936–37	A	5	1031	526	17	30.94	5-36	1	–	60.64
1947–48	WI	3	270	205	5	41.00	2-82	–	–	54.00
	A	13	2783	1603	43	37.27	5-36	1	–	64.72
	WI	4	414	251	8	31.37	2-13	–	–	51.75
	NZ	5	589	195	10	19.50	5-14	1	–	58.90
	I	3	600	330	20	16.50	7-80	3	1	30.00
Home		10	1866	989	36	27.47	7-80	4	1	51.83
Overseas		15	2520	1390	45	30.88	5-36	1	–	56.00
Totals		25	4386	2379	81	29.37	7-80	5	1	54.14

ALLOM
Maurice James Carrick

Cambridge University (1926 to 1928)
Surrey (1927 to 1937)

TOURS
A 1929–30; SA 1930–31;
WI 1927–28 (Tennyson); NZ 1929–30
Born Northwood, Middlesex
23 Mar 1906

NOTABLE FEATS
- Took 4 wickets in 5 balls, including the hat-trick, on his Test debut.

Swerving the ball sharply in a buffeting wind, Maurice Allom enjoyed an extraordinary introduction to Test cricket when his eighth over brought him the wickets of Dempster, Lowry, James and Badcock in the space of five balls: (W.WWW). A tall (6ft 3in), right-handed, fast-medium swing bowler, who could bat usefully, his amateur appearances for Surrey were curtailed by business commitments to 100 matches in 11 seasons. Allom wrote, in collaboration with Maurice Turnbull, humorous accounts of his two major tours, and served as president of MCC (1969–70) and Surrey (1971–79). In 1927 he played tenor and baritone saxophone in Fred Elizalde's jazz band at The Savoy.

Maurice Allom

Ref	Series	V	T	Venue	Result	Batting 1st No	R	HO	Batting 2nd No	R	HO	Ct	Bowling 1st Balls	R	W	Bowling 2nd Balls	R	W
186/172	1929–30	NZ	1	Christchurch	W-8w	11	4	*	–	–	–	–	114	38	5	90	17	3
187/173			2	Wellington	D	11	2	c	–	–	–	–	168	73	1	36	21	0
188/174			3	Auckland	D	–	–	–	–	–	–	–	36	3	0	–	–	–
189/175			4	Auckland	D	11	8	*	–	–	–	–	157	42	4	–	–	–
206/187	1930–31	SA	3	Durban[2]	D	–	–	–	–	–	–	–	150	44	0	66	27	1

Career	M	I	NO	HS	R	Avge	100	50	Ct	St	Balls	R	W	Avge	BB	5w	10w	Rate
Test	5	3	2	8*	14	14.00	–	–	–	–	817	265	14	18.92	5-38	1	–	58.35
F/c	179	203	51	64	1953	12.84	–	5	83	–	34022	14291	605	23.62	9-55	30	3	56.23

ALLOTT
Paul John Walter

Lancashire (1978 to date)
Wellington (1985–86 to 1986–87)

TOURS
WI 1982–83 (Int XI), 1986–87 (Lancs);
I/SL 1981–82, 1984–85
Born Altrincham, Cheshire 14 Sep 1956

NOTABLE FEATS
- Shared with R.G.D. Willis in record England 10th-wicket stand of 70 v India (Test *928*).

A strapping 6ft 4in, right-arm fast-medium swing bowler whose career has been interrupted by back injuries. Paul Allott's high action and strong build have brought consistent performances at county level but he lacked sufficient movement and variety to become a dangerous force against Test batsmen on good pitches. The mainstay of Lancashire's new-ball attack throughout the 1980s, he is a handy lower-order batsman who celebrated his arrival on the Test scene by contributing a fifty to England's retention of the Ashes. A contact-lens-wearing Durham graduate with a dry sense of humour.

Paul Allott

Ref	Series	V	T	Venue	Result	Batting 1st			Batting 2nd			Ct	Bowling 1st			Bowling 2nd		
						No	R	HO	No	R	HO		Balls	R	W	Balls	R	W
907/571	1981	A	5	Manchester	W-103	10	6	*	10	14	c	–	36	17	2	102	71	2
916/577	1981-82	I	5	Madras[1]	D	10	6	c	–	–	–	–	186	135	0	–	–	–
921/579	1981-82	SL		Colombo SO	W-7w	9	3	c	–	–	–	–	78	44	0	–	–	–
928/580	1982	I	1	Lord's	W-7w	10	41	*	–	–	–	1	24	15	0	102	51	1
930/582			3	Oval	D	10	3	c	–	–	–	1	144	69	1	24	12	0
991/603	1984	WI	3	Leeds	L-8w	9	3	b	10	4	lbw	1	161	61	6	42	24	0
992/604			4	Manchester	L-I & 64	8	26	c	7	14	b	–	168	76	3	–	–	–
993/605			5	Oval	L-172	10	16	b	9	4	c	1	102	25	3	156	96	2
994/606	1984	SL		Lord's	D	9	0	b	–	–	–	–	216	89	1	6	2	0
1017/612	1985	A	1	Leeds	W-5w	10	12	c	–	–	–	–	132	74	2	102	57	0
1018/613			2	Lord's	L-4w	11	1	*	4	0	b	–	180	70	1	42	8	1
1019/614			3	Nottingham	D	11	7	b	–	–	–	–	108	55	1	–	–	–
1020/615			4	Manchester	D	10	7	b	–	–	–	–	78	29	0	36	4	0

Career	M	I	NO	HS	R	Avge	100	50	Ct	St	Balls	R	W	Avge	BB	5w	10w	Rate
Test	13	18	3	52*	213	14.20	–	1	4	–	2225	1084	26	41.69	6-61	1	–	85.57
F/c	206	223	54	88	2963	17.53	–	9	93	–	33336	14310	578	24.75	8-48	29	–	57.67

AMES
Leslie Ethelbert George CBE

Kent (1926 to 1951)

Wisden 1929

TOURS

A 1928–29, 1932–33, 1936–37; SA 1938–39; WI 1929–30, 1934–35; NZ 1932–33; I/SL 1950–51 (Cwlth)

Born Elham, Kent 3 Dec 1905

Les Ames behind the stumps for Kent against Surrey in 1932. The batsman is F.R. Brown.

Les Ames was probably the greatest batsman/wicket-keeper the game has known. A powerfully built, hard-hitting strokemaker who excelled at cutting and hooking, his orthodox method brought him 102 first-class hundreds, including 9 double-centuries, 3058 runs in 1933 and over 2000 runs in five other seasons. He was a 'keeper of the highest class, equally proficient against the leg-spin and googlies of 'Tich' Freeman as he was against the fiery pace of Larwood and Voce. England's first professional to be appointed a selector (1950–56 and 1958), Ames was Kent's secretary/manager (1960–74) during their most triumphant years and was president in 1976. He managed three MCC tours, including the riot-torn 1968–69 mission to Pakistan, with cheerful calm and great diplomatic skill. An outside-left for Folkestone, Clapton Orient and Gillingham, he is now a youthful octogenarian addicted to gardening and golf.

NOTABLE FEATS

- 1000 runs in 17th Test (*227*) (25 inns); 2000 runs in 41st Test (*263*) (62 inns). 50 dismissals in 24th Test.
- Shared Test cricket's longest surviving partnership world record of 246 for the 8th wkt with G.O.B. Allen (*209*). With W.R. Hammond shared England record stands of 242 in 144 min (5th wkt v New Zealand – Test *225*) and 197 in 145 min (4th wkt v South Africa – Test *268*).
- First wicket-keeper to score a hundred for England (*193*).
- Holds world Test record for most runs in a pre-lunch session: 123 in Test *246*.
- First England wicket-keeper to make 8 dismissals in a Test (*229*).
- Only wicket-keeper to score a century in E v A Tests (*234*) until A.P.E. Knott in 1974–75.
- Exceeded A.F.A. Lilley's England record of 92 dismissals (*270*).
- Holds world first-class records for most dismissals (128 in 1929) and most stumpings (64 in 1932) in a season.
- First to achieve wicket-keepers' 'double' of 1000 runs and 100 dismissals (1928); repeated feat in 1929 and 1932.
- Exceeded 1000 runs in a season 17 times, including 2000 on 6 occasions (most: 3058 in 1933).
- Won Lawrence Trophy for fastest first-class 100 in 1936 (68 min) and 1939 (67 min).

TEST NOTES

- *229* Strained back – F.E. Woolley kept throughout 2nd inns.
- *264* Fractured finger – E. Paynter kept for part of 2nd inns.

Ref	Series	V	T	Venue	Result	Batting 1st No	R	HO	Batting 2nd No	R	HO	Fielding 1st Ct	St	Byes	Balls	Fielding 2nd Ct	St	Byes	Balls
185/171†	1929	SA	5	Oval	D	8	0	c	–	–	–	2	–	4	1032	–	–	–	–
190/176†	1929–30	WI	1	Bridgetown	D	6	16	b	5	44	*	–	–	6	685	1	–	20	916
191/177†			2	Port-of-Spain	W-167	6	42	c	5	105	c	1	–	4	524	2	1	8	674
192/178†			3	Georgetown	L-289	5	31	c	5	3	c	2	2	3	888	–	1	9	765
193/179†			4	Kingston	D	5	149	b	5	27	c	1	–	19	671	–	1	17	987
209/190†	1931	NZ	1	Lord's	D	7	137	c	6	17	*	1	1	2	447	–	–	23	946
210/191†			2	Oval	W-I & 26	5	41	c	–	–	–	3	–	2	571	–	–	6	507
211/192†			3	Manchester	D	–	–	–	–	–	–	–	–	–	–	–	–	–	–
219/193†	1932	I		Lord's	W-158	7	65	b	7	6	b	–	–	5	558	–	–	5	357
220/194†	1932–33	A	1	Sydney	W-10w	9	0	c	–	–	–	3	–	12	614	1	–	12	381
221/195†			2	Melbourne	L-111	7	4	b	6	2	c	–	–	5	519	2	–	3	341
222/196†			3	Adelaide	W-338	4	3	b	7	69	b	1	–	2	574	–	–	4	416
223/197†			4	Brisbane	W-6w	6	17	c	5	14	*	1	2	5	726	–	–	13	411
224/198†			5	Sydney	W-8w	7	4	ro	–	–	–	–	–	13	650	–	–	4	328
225/199†	1932–33	NZ	1	Christchurch	D	6	103	b	–	–	–	–	–	3	697	–	–	0	97
226/200			2	Auckland	D	5	26	b	–	–	–	–	–	–	–	–	–	–	–
227/201†	1933	WI	1	Lord's	W-I & 27	7	83	*	–	–	–	–	–	3	353	–	–	1	367
228/202†			2	Manchester	D	6	47	c	–	–	–	1	–	0	814	1	1	8	361
229/203†			3	Oval	W-I & 17	7	37	c	–	–	–	2	2	1	179	4	–	0	428
233/207†	1934	A	1	Nottingham	L-238	7	7	c	7	12	b	2	–	4	914	2	–	22	540
234/208†			2	Lord's	W-I & 38	7	120	c	–	–	–	1	–	1	654	1	–	6	321
235/209†			3	Manchester	D	7	72	c	–	–	–	1	–	20	1143	–	–	1	162
236/210†			4	Leeds	D	7	9	c	7	8	c	1	–	8	1103	–	–	–	–
237/211†			5	Oval	L-562	7	33	*rh	–	–	–	2	–	4	1026	–	–	–	–
238/212†	1934–35	WI	1	Bridgetown	W-4w	5	8	lbw	–	–	–	–	2	0	282	–	–	4	114
239/213			2	Port-of-Spain	L-217	4	2	c	8	6	c	–	–	–	–	1	–	–	–
240/214†			3	Georgetown	D	8	0	c	8	5	*	1	–	4	558	–	1	9	144
241/215†			4	Kingston	L-I & 161	6	126	c	5	17	c	–	–	8	1008	–	–	–	–
242/216†	1935	SA	1	Nottingham	D	6	17	c	–	–	–	1	–	4	701	–	–	0	54
243/217			2	Lord's	L-157	5	5	b	5	8	lbw	–	–	–	–	1	–	–	–
244/218†			3	Leeds	D	7	0	b	7	13	b	–	–	8	526	–	1	14	572
246/220†			5	Oval	D	6	148	*	–	–	–	3	–	6	874	–	2	6	438
255/224†	1936–37	A	1	Brisbane	W-322	6	24	c	6	9	b	2	–	4	686	–	–	0	99
256/225†			2	Sydney	W-I & 22	5	29	c	–	–	–	–	–	1	191	1	–	0	775
257/226†			3	Melbourne	L-365	6	3	b	5	19	b	1	2	2	523	1	–	6	1199
258/227†			4	Adelaide	L-148	6	52	b	7	0	lbw	2	–	0	622	3	–	10	986
259/228†			5	Melbourne	L-I & 200	7	19	b	7	11	c	3	–	1	1125	–	–	–	–
260/229†	1937	NZ	1	Lord's	D	7	5	b	5	20	c	1	–	4	668	1	–	4	461
261/230†			2	Manchester	W-130	6	16	*	6	39	lbw	–	2	4	646	1	–	7	322
262/231†			3	Oval	D	7	6	*	–	–	–	1	–	2	499	1	–	4	412
263/232†	1938	A	1	Nottingham	D	7	46	b	–	–	–	2	–	10	783	–	–	5	1104
264/233†			2	Lord's	D	7	83	c	8	6	c	–	–	1	730	–	–	–	–
267/236†	1938–39	SA	1	Johannesburg	D	5	42	c	5	3	*	–	1	5	1081	–	–	0	408
268/237†			2	Cape Town	D	5	115	b	–	–	–	–	1	2	950	1	–	1	424
269/238†			3	Durban	W-I & 13	5	27	*	–	–	–	1	–	1	365	3	–	7	914
270/239†			4	Johannesburg	D	5	34	b	5	17	b	1	–	5	813	–	–	–	–
271/240†			5	Durban	D	5	84	c	6	17	*	2	–	2	1622	–	–	5	1137

Career	M	I	NO	HS	R	Avge	100	50	Ct	St	Balls	R	W	Avge	BB	5w	10w	Rate
Test	47	72	12	149	2434	40.56	8	7	74	23	–	–	–	–	–	–	–	–
F/c	593	951	95	295	37248	43.51	102	176	703	418	1400	801	24	33.37	3-23	–	–	58.33

L. E. G. AMES – TEST SUMMARY

Series	V	M	I	NO	HS	R	Avge	100	50	Ct	St	Byes	Balls
1929	SA	1	1	0	0	0	0.00	–	–	2	–	4	1032
1929–30	WI	4	8	1	149	417	59.57	2	–	7	5	86	6110
1931	NZ	3	3	1	137	195	97.50	1	–	4	1	33	2471
1932	I	1	2	0	65	71	35.50	–	1	–	–	10	915
1932–33	A	5	8	1	69	113	16.14	–	1	8	2	73	4960
1932–33	NZ	2	2	0	103	129	64.50	1	–	–	–	3	794
1933	WI	3	3	1	83	167	83.50	–	1	8	3	13	2502
1934	A	5	7	1	120	261	43.50	1	1	10	–	66	5863
1934–35	WI	4	7	1	126	164	27.33	1	–	2	3	25	2106
1935	SA	4	6	1	148*	191	38.20	1	–	5	3	38	3165
1936–37	A	5	9	0	52	166	18.44	–	1	13	2	24	6206
1937	NZ	3	5	2	39	86	28.66	–	–	5	2	25	3008
1938	A	2	3	0	83	135	45.00	–	1	2	–	16	2617
1938–39	SA	5	8	3	115	339	67.80	1	1	8	2	28	7714
	A	17	27	2	120	675	27.00	1	4	33	4	179	19646
	SA	10	15	4	148*	530	48.18	2	1	15	5	70	11911
	WI	11	18	3	149	748	49.86	3	1	17	11	124	10718
	NZ	8	10	3	137	410	58.57	2	–	9	3	61	6273
	I	1	2	0	65	71	35.50	–	1	–	–	10	915
Home		22	30	6	148*	1106	46.08	3	4	36	9	205	21573
Overseas		25	42	6	149	1328	36.88	5	3	38	14	239	27890
Totals		47	72	12	149	2434	40.56	8	7	74	23	444	49463

AMISS
Dennis Leslie MBE

Warwickshire (1960 to 1987)

Wisden 1975

TOURS

A 1974–75, 1976–77; SA 1981–82 (SAB); WI 1973–74; NZ 1974–75; I/SL 1967–68 (Int XI), 1972–73, 1976–77; P 1966–67 (MCC U-25), 1967–68 (Int XI), 1970–71 (RW), 1972–73

Born Harborne, Birmingham 7 Apr 1943

A phlegmatic, determined opening batsman, Dennis Amiss was a patient accumulator with massive powers of concentration and an insatiable appetite for large scores; on only two of the 11 occasions when he registered a century in Tests was he dismissed for under 150. Of average height (5ft 11in), strongly built with massive forearms, he favoured the front foot, his most productive strokes being the cover-drive and leg-glance. After a rocky beginning – 348 runs, avge 18.31, in his first 12 Tests – he amassed over 2000 runs, avge 71, with 8 hundreds in his next 20 matches, his advance coinciding with his elevation to opener. From 1972 to late 1974 he was England's outstanding run-getter, scoring 1379 runs in a single year, including his marathon match-saving career-best innings of 262* in Jamaica. In 1974–75 he was completely overwhelmed by the formidable Australian pace attack and thereafter lost his wicket to Dennis Lillee on numerous occasions, suffering several blows on the head. But he managed a remarkable double century against a rampant Michael Holding in 1976 and enjoyed a successful tour of India before joining the Packer bandwaggon. Although this effectively ended his Test career, he treated Warwickshire followers to another decade of fine batting, his confidence reinforced by protective headgear which he first marketed in Britain.

NOTABLE FEATS

- 1000 runs in 18th Test (*724*) (32 inns); 2000 runs in 27th Test (*739*) (49 inns); 3000 runs in 42nd Test (*781*) (72 inns).
- Scored 262* in 570 min, facing 563 balls and hitting a six and 40 fours in Test *732*. Had R.G.D. Willis not survived for 53 min during an unbroken last-wicket partnership, Amiss would have become only the fourth to carry his bat through a completed innings for England and his would have been the highest such score in Tests.
- His aggregate of 1379 runs in 1974 was just 2 short of R.B. Simpson's record (subsequently beaten).
- Reached his hundred with a six and recorded England's highest score (179) in a Test in India until 1984–85 (Test *788*).
- 21st batsman to score 100 first-class hundreds (1986).
- Holds Warwickshire records for most runs (35,146) and hundreds (78).
- Scored 1000 runs in each of 23 consecutive seasons (1965–87), including 2000 three times.

Dennis Amiss during his double century against West Indies at The Oval in 1976.

Ref	Series	V	T	Venue	Result	Batting 1st No	R	HO	Batting 2nd No	R	HO	Ct
609/433	1966	WI	5	Oval	W-I & 34	5	17	lbw	–	–	–	–
619/435	1967	I	2	Lord's	W-I & 124	3	29	b	–	–	–	2
620/436			3	Birmingham	W-132	5	5	c	5	45	c	2
623/439	1967	P	3	Oval	W-8w	5	26	c	4	3	*	–
637/445	1968	A	1	Manchester	L-159	5	0	c	5	0	b	–
687/467	1971	P	1	Birmingham	D	4	4	b	4	22	c	–
688/468			2	Lord's	D	4	19	*	–	–	–	1
689/469			3	Leeds	W-25	4	23	c	4	56	c	–
690/470	1971	I	1	Lord's	D	4	9	c	4	0	ro	2
703/478	1972–73	I	1	Delhi	W-6w	2	46	st	2	9	c	–
704/479			2	Calcutta	L-28	2	11	c	2	1	c	1
705/480			3	Madras[1]	L-4w	2	15	c	2	8	c	–
719/483	1972–73	P	1	Lahore[2]	D	2	112	b	2	16	c	–
720/484			2	Hyderabad	D	2	158	st	2	0	c	–
721/485			3	Karachi	D	2	99	c	2	21	*	2
722/486	1973	NZ	1	Nottingham	W-38	2	42	c	2	138	*	–
723/487			2	Lord's	D	2	9	c	2	53	c	–
724/488			3	Leeds	W-I & 1	2	8	lbw	–	–	–	–
725/489	1973	WI	1	Oval	L-158	2	29	b	2	15	c	–
726/490			2	Birmingham	D	2	56	c	2	86	*	1
727/491			3	Lord's	L-I & 226	2	35	c	2	10	c	1
731/492	1973–74	WI	1	Port-of-Spain	L-7w	2	6	c	2	174	lbw	–
732/493			2	Kingston	D	2	27	c	2	262	*	–
733/494			3	Bridgetown	D	2	12	b	2	4	c	–
734/495			4	Georgetown	D	2	118	c	–	–	–	–
735/496			5	Port-of-Spain	W-26	2	44	c	2	16	b	–
739/497	1974	I	1	Manchester	W-113	2	56	c	2	47	c	–
740/498			2	Lord's	W-I & 285	1	188	lbw	–	–	–	–
741/499			3	Birmingham	W-I & 78	1	79	c	–	–	–	–
742/500	1974	P	1	Leeds	D	1	13	c	1	8	lbw	–
743/501			2	Lord's	D	1	2	c	1	14	*	1
744/502			3	Oval	D	1	183	c	–	–	–	–
750/503	1974–75	A	1	Brisbane[2]	L-166	1	7	c	1	25	c	1
752/505			3	Melbourne	D	1	4	c	1	90	c	–
753/506			4	Sydney	L-171	1	12	c	1	37	c	–
754/507			5	Adelaide	L-163	1	0	c	1	0	c	–
755/508			6	Melbourne	W-I & 4	1	0	lbw	–	–	–	2
758/509	1974–75	NZ	1	Auckland	W-I & 83	1	19	c	–	–	–	3
759/510			2	Christchurch	D	1	164	*	–	–	–	–
760/511	1975	A	1	Birmingham	L-I & 85	2	4	c	4	5	c	–
761/512			2	Lord's	D	4	0	lbw	4	10	c	1
781/519	1976	WI	5	Oval	L-231	2	203	b	2	16	c	–
788/520	1976–77	I	1	Delhi	W-I & 25	1	179	c	–	–	–	–
789/521			2	Calcutta	W-10w	1	35	c	1	7	*	–
790/522			3	Madras[1]	W-200	1	4	lbw	1	46	c	–
791/523			4	Bangalore	L-140	1	82	c	1	0	c	1
792/524			5	Bombay[2]	D	1	50	c	1	14	c	–
803/525	1976–77	A		Melbourne	L-45	5	4	c	4	64	b	1
804/526	1977	A	1	Lord's	D	1	4	b	1	0	b	1
805/527			2	Manchester	W-9w	1	11	c	1	28	*	1

TEST NOTES

- *744* Retired hurt when 178* at 305–4; resumed at 539–9.
- *760* Retired hurt when 2* at 7-0; resumed at 100-6.

Career	M	I	NO	HS	R	Avge	100	50	Ct	St	Balls	R	W	Avge	BB	5w	10w	Rate
Test	50	88	10	262*	3612	46.30	11	11	24	–	–	–	–	–	–	–	–	–
F/c	658	1139	126	262*	43423	42.86	102	212	418	–	1153	718	18	39.88	3-21	–	–	64.05

D. L. AMISS – TEST BATTING SUMMARY

Series	V	M	I	NO	HS	R	Avge	100	50
1966	WI	1	1	–	17	17	17.00	–	–
1967	I	2	3	–	45	79	26.33	–	–
1967	P	1	2	1	26	29	29.00	–	–
1968	A	1	2	–	0	0	0.00	–	–
1971	P	3	5	1	56	124	31.00	–	1
1971	I	1	2	–	9	9	4.50	–	–
1972–73	I	3	6	–	46	90	15.00	–	–
1972–73	P	3	6	1	158	406	81.20	2	1
1973	NZ	3	5	1	138*	250	62.50	1	1
1973	WI	3	6	1	86*	231	46.20	–	2
1973–74	WI	5	9	1	262*	663	82.87	3	–
1974	I	3	4	–	188	370	92.50	1	2
1974	P	3	5	1	183	220	55.00	1	–
1974–75	A	5	9	–	90	175	19.44	–	1
1974–75	NZ	2	2	1	164*	183	183.00	1	–

Series	V	M	I	NO	HS	R	Avge	100	50
1975	A	2	4	–	10	19	4.75	–	–
1976	WI	1	2	–	203	219	109.50	1	–
1976–77	I	5	9	1	179	417	52.12	1	2
1976–77	A	1	2	–	64	68	34.00	–	1
1977	A	2	4	1	28*	43	14.33	–	–
	A	11	21	1	90	305	15.25	–	2
	WI	10	18	2	262*	1130	70.62	4	2
	NZ	5	7	2	164*	433	86.60	2	1
	I	14	24	1	188	965	41.95	2	4
	P	10	18	4	183	779	55.64	3	2
Home		26	45	6	203	1610	41.28	4	6
Overseas		24	43	4	262*	2002	51.33	7	5
Totals		50	88	10	262*	3612	46.30	11	11

ANDREW
Keith Vincent

Northamptonshire (1953 to 1966)

TOURS

A 1954–55; WI 1959–60; NZ 1954–55; I 1964–65 (Cwlth); P 1963–64 (Cwlth)

Born Greenacres, Oldham, Lancashire 15 Dec 1929

It was to the detriment of Test cricket that only twice did the selectors choose the most talented wicket-keeper of his generation rather than fall into the trap of picking inferior glovemen who could bat. A brilliant unobtrusive wicket-keeper, he was a natural timer of the ball but his lower-order batting returned only a modest average. Northamptonshire's captain during five seasons (1962–1966) when they frequently mounted a rare championship challenge, Keith Andrew is now the NCA's chief executive.

NOTABLE FEATS

- Held 7 catches in an innings, a tally only twice exceeded in first-class cricket, for Northamptonshire v Lancashire at Manchester in 1962.

Keith Andrew and Bob Appleyard with some of the 1954–55 MCC team bound for Australia in their successful defence of the Ashes: standing *R. Appleyard, J.V. Wilson, T.W. Graveney, J.E. McConnon, M.C. Cowdrey, P.J. Loader;* kneeling *J.H. Wardle, P.B.H. May, F.H. Tyson, K.V. Andrew.*

						Batting 1st			Batting 2nd			Fielding 1st				Fielding 2nd			
Ref	Series	V	T	Venue	Result	No	R	HO	No	R	HO	Ct	St	Byes	Balls	Ct	St	Byes	Balls
391/315†	1954–55	A	1	Brisbane[2]	L-I & 154	9	6	b	9	6	b	–	–	11	1032	–	–	–	–
543/395†	1963	WI	1	Manchester	L-10w	10	3	*	3	15	c	1	–	3	1176	–	–	0	1

Career	M	I	NO	HS	R	Avge	100	50	Ct	St	Balls	R	W	Avge	BB	5w	10w	Rate
Test	2	4	1	15	29	9.66	–	–	1	–	–	–	–	–	–	–	–	–
F/c	390	476	160	76	4230	13.38	–	3	723	181	49	31	2	15.50	2-9	–	–	24.50

APPLEYARD, Robert

Yorkshire (1950 to 1958)

Wisden 1952
TOURS A 1954–55; NZ 1954–55
Born Wibsey, Bradford, Yorkshire
27 Jun 1924

Tall, strong-shouldered, with a high, easy action, Bob Appleyard was a medium-fast, right-arm bowler who could deliver inswingers and off-breaks with subtle variations of pace. Remarkably accurate, his unusual bounce and deceptive flight made him a devastating prospect on drying pitches. After three matches for Yorkshire in 1950, he struck gold the following year at the fairly late age of 27, claiming an astonishing haul of 200 wickets in his first full season and heading the national averages. Prolonged illness restricted him to one match in the next two seasons but he made a spectacular return in 1954. Coming second in the averages with 154 wickets at 14.42, he won his first England cap and took a wicket with his second ball in Test cricket. [*Illus. p.* 11]

NOTABLE FEATS
- Took 200 wickets (avge 14.14) in 1951 to establish a record for any bowler in his first full season.
- Took 3 wickets in 4 balls in Test *402* as New Zealand were dismissed for the lowest total in Test history (26).
- Hat-trick for Yorkshire v Gloucestershire at Sheffield in 1956.

						Batting 1st			Batting 2nd				Bowling 1st			Bowling 2nd		
Ref	Series	V	T	Venue	Result	No	R	HO	No	R	HO	Ct	Balls	R	W	Balls	R	W
388/312	1954	P	2	Nottingham	W-I & 129	–	–	–	–	–	–	–	102	51	5	184	72	2
392/316	1954–55	A	2	Sydney	W-38	10	8	c	10	19	*	–	56	32	0	48	12	1
393/317			3	Melbourne	W-128	11	1	*	11	6	b	–	88	38	2	32	17	1
394/318			4	Adelaide	W-5w	10	10	*	–	–	–	2	184	58	3	96	13	3
395/319			5	Sydney	D	–	–	–	–	–	–	2	128	54	1	–	–	–
401/320	1954–55	NZ	1	Dunedin	W-8w	10	0	*	–	–	–	–	42	16	0	42	19	2
402/321			2	Auckland	W-I & 20	10	6	c	–	–	–	–	96	38	3	36	7	4
408/322	1955	SA	1	Nottingham	W-I & 5	11	0	*	–	–	–	–	168	46	2	114	32	0
425/327	1956	A	1	Nottingham	D	10	1	*	–	–	–	–	66	17	2	114	32	0

Career	M	I	NO	HS	R	Avge	100	50	Ct	St	Balls	R	W	Avge	BB	5w	10w	Rate
Test	9	9	6	19*	51	17.00	–	–	4	–	1596	554	31	17.87	5-51	1	–	51.48
F/c	152	145	54	63	776	8.52	–	1	80	–	30026	10965	708	15.48	8-76	57	17	42.40

ARCHER Alfred German

Worcestershire (1900 to 1901)

TOUR SA 1898–99
Born Richmond, Surrey 6 Dec 1871
Died Seaford, Sussex 15 Jul 1935

Alfred Archer played in his only Test by accident and before he had made any of his four appearances for Worcestershire. A wicket-keeper who did not even aspire to the Haileybury XI and a lower-order batsman, he gained unexpected international status when Bromley-Davenport was injured. He batted at ten and did not keep. [*Illus. p.* 196]

						Batting 1st			Batting 2nd			
Ref	Series	V	T	Venue	Result	No	R	HO	No	R	HO	Ct
59/59	1898–99	SA	2	Cape Town	W-210	10	7	c	10	24	*	–

Career	M	I	NO	HS	R	Avge	100	50	Ct	St	Balls	R	W	Avge	BB	5w	10w	Rate
Test	1	2	1	24*	31	31.00	–	–	–	–	–	–	–	–	–	–	–	–
F/c	12	24	3	43	231	11.00	–	–	10	2	–	–	–	–	–	–	–	–

ARMITAGE, Thomas

Yorkshire (1872 to 1879)

TOUR A 1876–77
Born Walkley, Sheffield, Yorkshire
25 Apr 1848
Died Pullman, Chicago, USA
21 Sep 1922

A tall, robust Yorkshire all-rounder who toured Australia with James Lillywhite's team and played in cricket's first two Test matches. Tom Armitage was a dual purpose bowler; a useful round-arm medium pacer, he could also bowl underarm lobs with such devastating accuracy that on 15 June 1872 he took 18 wickets in a club match for Keighley. Four years later he took 13 for 46 against Surrey, hugely impressing James Southerton who recommended him to Lillywhite. He spent the latter half of his life near Chicago [*Illus. p.* 278]

					Batting 1st			Batting 2nd				Bowling 1st			Bowling 2nd		
Ref	Series	V	T Venue	Result	No	R	HO	No	R	HO	Ct	Balls	R	W	Balls	R	W
1/1	1876–77	A	1 Melbourne	L-45	6	9	c	8	3	c	–	12	15	0	–	–	–
2/2			2 Melbourne	W-4w	9	21	c	–	–	–	–	–	–	–	–	–	–

Career	M	I	NO	HS	R	Avge	100	50	Ct	St	Balls	R	W	Avge	BB	5w	10w	Rate
Test	2	3	0	21	33	11.00	–	–	–	–	12	15	0	–	–	–	–	–
F/c	56	92	8	95	1122	13.35	–	3	23	–	4197	1699	119	14.27	7-26	12	3	35.26

ARNOLD Edward George

Worcestershire (1899 to 1913)
London County (1900)

TOUR A 1903–04
Born Exmouth, Devon 7 Nov 1876
Died Worcester 25 Oct 1942

NOTABLE FEATS

- Took V.T. Trumper's wicket with his first ball in Test cricket.
- Achieved the 'double' in 4 consecutive seasons (1902–05), 1157 runs and 143 wickets in 1903 being his best.
- Took 4 for 8 for MCC at Melbourne in 1903–04, sharing with W. Rhodes (5 for 6) in Victoria's dismissal for 15 – the lowest total in Australian first-class cricket.
- Contributed 200* to a 5th-wkt stand of 393 with W.B. Burns v Warwickshire at Birmingham in 1909 which remains the record for any first-class match in Britain.

An outstanding all-round cricketer, Ted Arnold did much to earn Worcestershire first-class rank in 1899 and remained the lynchpin of their team until the Great War. Tall, lean and loose-limbed, he spun the ball from a pace which he varied up to a lively right-arm medium-fast. He could extract bounce from the most placid surface and was a masterly exponent of the art of bowling on drying pitches. A powerful, fluent strokemaker with a good defence and a competent slip fielder, he took part in three of England's triumphant Ashes campaigns.

Ted Arnold

					Batting 1st			Batting 2nd				Bowling 1st			Bowling 2nd		
Ref	**Series**	**V**	**T Venue**	**Result**	**No**	**R**	**HO**	**No**	**R**	**HO**	**Ct**	**Balls**	**R**	**W**	**Balls**	**R**	**W**
78/75	1903–04	A	1 Sydney	W-5w	4	27	c	–	–	–	1	192	76	4	168	93	2
80/77			3 Adelaide	L-216	9	23	*	3	1	b	–	162	93	3	114	74	0
81/78			4 Sydney	W-157	9	0	lbw	3	0	c	1	93	28	4	72	42	2
82/79			5 Melbourne	L-218	3	0	c	10	19	c	2	108	46	1	48	23	2
83/80	1905	A	1 Nottingham	W-213	11	2	*	–	–	–	1	66	39	1	24	7	0
84/81			2 Lord's	D	11	7	*	–	–	–	–	42	13	1	–	–	–
86/83			4 Manchester	W-I & 80	8	25	ro	–	–	–	1	84	53	2	90	35	2
87/84			5 Oval	D	8	40	c	1	0	b	–	54	50	0	54	17	1
93/90	1907	SA	1 Lord's	D	9	4	b	–	–	–	–	132	37	5	78	41	0
94/91			2 Leeds	W-53	8	0	b	8	12	c	2	24	11	0	78	10	1

Career	M	I	NO	HS	R	Avge	100	50	Ct	St	Balls	R	W	Avge	BB	5w	10w	Rate
Test	10	15	3	40	160	13.33	–	–	8	–	1683	788	31	25.41	5-37	1	–	54.29
F/c	343	592	62	215	15853	29.91	24	76	187	–	55170	24763	1069	23.16	9-64	63	13	51.60

ARNOLD Geoffrey Graham

Surrey (1963 to 1977)
Sussex (1978 to 1982)
Orange Free State (1976–77)

Wisden 1972

TOURS

A 1974–75; WI 1973–74; NZ 1974–75; I 1972–73; P 1966–67 (MCC U-25), 1972–73; SL 1969–70, 1972–73

Born Earlsfield, Surrey 3 Sep 1944

In favourable conditions Geoff Arnold was the most dangerous new-ball bowler of his era. A tall, strong-shouldered right-hander, he seamed the ball prodigiously either way at fast-medium pace and moved his outswinger devastatingly late. Dubbed 'Horse' (GG), his promising batting talent was never developed at county level. After ending his career with Sussex, he returned to The Oval as Surrey's coach.

NOTABLE FEATS

- 50 wickets in 16th Test (*724*); 100 wickets in 29th Test (*753*).
- Only bowler to take a wicket with the first ball of a Test on 2 occasions: S.M. Gavaskar (*741*) and J.F.M. Morrison (*759*).
- Hat-trick for Surrey v Leicestershire at Leicester in 1974.

					Batting 1st			Batting 2nd				Bowling 1st			Bowling 2nd		
Ref	**Series**	**V**	**T Venue**	**Result**	**No**	**R**	**HO**	**No**	**R**	**HO**	**Ct**	**Balls**	**R**	**W**	**Balls**	**R**	**W**
622/438	1967	P	2 Nottingham	W-10w	9	14	lbw	–	–	–	1	102	35	3	30	5	0
623/439			3 Oval	W-8w	9	59	c	–	–	–	–	174	58	5	102	49	0
658/458	1969	NZ	3 Oval	W-8w	8	1	b	–	–	–	2	48	13	0	60	17	0
698/473	1972	A	1 Manchester	W-89	11	1	c	11	0	*	–	150	62	4	120	59	1
701/476			4 Leeds	W-9w	11	1	*	–	–	–	–	59	28	2	36	17	2
702/477			5 Oval	L-5w	10	22	b	10	4	lbw	–	210	87	3	90	26	1
703/478	1972–73	I	1 Delhi	W-6w	8	12	c	–	–	–	–	142	45	6	124	46	3
705/480			3 Madras[1]	L-4w	9	17	c	9	0	c	–	139	34	3	24	11	0
706/481			4 Kanpur	D	9	45	b	–	–	–	–	210	72	1	42	15	1
707/482			5 Bombay[2]	D	10	27	lbw	–	–	–	–	126	64	3	18	13	0
719/483	1972–73	P	1 Lahore[2]	D	9	0	c	9	3	*	–	258	95	2	24	12	0
720/484			2 Hyderabad	D	8	8	c	8	19	*	–	144	78	1	–	–	–
721/485			3 Karachi	D	10	2	c	–	–	–	–	114	69	0	90	52	0
722/486	1973	NZ	1 Nottingham	W-38	10	1	c	10	10	*	–	108	23	2	318	131	5
723/487			2 Lord's	D	10	8	*	10	23	*	–	246	108	1	–	–	–
724/488			3 Leeds	W-I & 1	10	26	c	–	–	–	–	162	62	3	132	27	5
725/489	1973	WI	1 Oval	L-158	10	4	c	10	4	c	–	234	113	5	109	49	3
726/490			2 Birmingham	D	10	24	c	–	–	–	1	222	74	3	120	43	4
727/491			3 Lord's	L-I & 226	9	5	c	9	1	c	1	210	111	0	–	–	–
733/494	1973–74	WI	3 Bridgetown	D	9	12	b	9	2	*	1	156	91	1	–	–	–

Ref	Series	V	T	Venue	Result	Batting 1st			Batting 2nd			Ct	Bowling 1st			Bowling 2nd		
						No	R	HO	No	R	HO		Balls	R	W	Balls	R	W
734/495			4	Georgetown	D	10	1	ro	–	–	–	–	60	17	0	–	–	–
735/496			5	Port-of-Spain	W-26	9	6	ro	10	13	b	–	48	27	0	33	13	1
740/498	1974	I	2	Lord's	W-I & 285	9	5	b	–	–	–	1	149	81	1	48	19	4
741/499			3	Birmingham	W-I & 78	–	–	–	–	–	–	–	84	43	3	114	61	2
742/500	1974	P	1	Leeds	D	9	1	c	–	–	–	–	191	67	3	139	36	3
743/501			2	Lord's	D	9	10	c	–	–	–	–	48	32	0	90	37	1
744/502			3	Oval	D	10	2	c	–	–	–	1	222	106	1	36	22	2
751/504	1974–75	A	2	Perth	L-9w	10	1	ro	10	4	c	–	216	129	2	15	15	1
753/506			4	Sydney	L-171	11	3	*	11	14	c	–	232	86	5	176	78	1
754/507			5	Adelaide	L-163	10	0	b	10	0	b	–	98	42	1	160	71	1
755/508			6	Melbourne	W-I & 4	10	0	c	–	–	–	–	48	24	0	184	83	3
758/509	1974–75	NZ	1	Auckland	W-I & 83	–	–	–	–	–	–	–	160	69	1	48	31	0
759/510			2	Christchurch	D	–	–	–	–	–	–	–	200	80	3	–	–	–
760/511	1975	A	1	Birmingham	L-I & 85	11	0	*	11	6	*	1	198	91	3	–	–	–

Career	M	I	NO	HS	R	Avge	100	50	Ct	St	Balls	R	W	Avge	BB	5w	10w	Rate
Test	34	46	11	59	421	12.02	–	1	9	–	7650	3254	115	28.29	6-45	6	–	66.52
F/c	365	379	90	73	3952	13.67	–	7	122	–	61028	24761	1130	21.91	8-41	46	3	54.00

Geoff Arnold

G. G. ARNOLD – TEST BOWLING SUMMARY

Series	V	M	Balls	R	W	Avge	BB	5w	10w	Rate
1967	P	2	408	147	8	18.37	5-58	1	–	51.00
1969	NZ	1	108	30	0	–	–	–	–	–
1972	A	3	665	279	13	21.46	4-62	–	–	51.15
1972–73	I	4	825	300	17	17.64	6-45	1	–	48.52
1972–73	P	3	630	306	3	102.00	2-95	–	–	210.00
1973	NZ	3	966	351	16	21.93	5-27	2	–	60.37
1973	WI	3	895	390	15	26.00	5-113	1	–	59.66
1973–74	WI	3	297	148	2	74.00	1-13	–	–	148.50
1974	I	2	395	204	10	20.40	4-19	–	–	39.50
1974	P	3	726	300	10	30.00	3-36	–	–	72.60
1974–75	A	4	1129	528	14	37.71	5-86	1	–	80.64
1974–75	NZ	2	408	180	4	45.00	3-80	–	–	102.00
1975	A	1	198	91	3	30.33	3-91	–	–	66.00
	A	8	1992	898	30	29.93	5-86	1	–	66.40
	WI	6	1192	538	17	31.64	5-113	1	–	70.11
	NZ	6	1482	561	20	28.05	5-27	2	–	74.10
	I	6	1220	504	27	18.66	6-45	1	–	45.18
	P	8	1764	753	21	35.85	5-58	1	–	84.00
Home		18	4361	1792	75	23.89	5-27	4	–	58.14
Overseas		16	3289	1462	40	36.55	6-45	2	–	82.22
Totals		34	7650	3254	115	28.29	6-45	6	–	66.52

ARNOLD, John

Hampshire (1929 to 1950)

Born Cowley, Oxford 30 Nov 1907
Died Southampton, Hampshire
4 Apr 1984

A mainstay of Hampshire's batting from 1930 to 1950, Johnny Arnold was an aggressive opener with a partiality for inswing and off-spin bowling. His only Test opportunity provided his first appearance in any match at Lord's and occurred when Hobbs had retired and Sutcliffe was injured. Fleet of foot as befits a soccer international, he was an outstanding cover-point with a powerful throw and an occasional right-handed slow bowler. A warm-hearted man with a fruity Oxfordshire accent, he was probably the only first-class umpire (1961–74) to use cob nuts as counters. A double international, he gained an England soccer cap v Scotland in 1932–33 (outside left for Oxford City, Southampton and Fulham).

NOTABLE FEATS
• Exceeded 1000 runs in a season 14 times, including 2261 in 1934.

						Batting 1st			Batting 2nd			
Ref	Series	V	T	Venue	Result	No	R	HO	No	R	HO	Ct
209/190	1931	NZ	1	Lord's	D	2	0	c	2	34	c	–

Career	M	I	NO	HS	R	Avge	100	50	Ct	St	Balls	R	W	Avge	BB	5w	10w	Rate
Test	1	2	0	34	34	17.00	–	–	–	–	–	–	–	–	–	–	–	–
F/c	402	710	45	227	21831	32.82	37	117	184	–	1531	1182	17	69.52	3-34	–	–	90.05

Johnny Arnold

The 1925–26 MCC team touring the West Indies with Lord Harris on his 75th birthday: back *P. Holmes, F.B. Watson, E.J. Smith, L.G. Crawley, R. Kilner;* standing *C.T. Bennett, G.C. Collins, H.L. Dales, W.R. Hammond, T.O. Jameson, C.F. Root;* seated *H.D. Swan, G. Challenor (West Indies), Hon. F.S.G. Calthorpe (captain), Lord Harris, H.B.G. Austin (West Indies), Lord Tennyson;* front *T.H.C. Levick (manager), W. Williams, W.E. Astill.*

ASTILL
William Ewart

Leicestershire (1906 to 1939)

Wisden 1933
TOURS
SA 1924–25 (Joel), 1927–28;
WI 1925–26, 1928–29 (Cahn), 1929–30, 1930–31 (Tennyson); I/SL 1926–27
Born Ratby, Leicestershire 1 Mar 1888
Died Stoneygate, Leicester 10 Feb 1948

Ewart Astill was for many years one of England's finest all-rounders and yet never gained selection against Australia. Of medium height and slightly built, he was an extremely crafty, medium-pace, right-arm bowler who could spin the ball sharply either way. As a batsman he graduated from tail-ender to a solid, orthodox, middle-order player who mustered 1000 runs in a season 11 times. A delightful and popular man, he served as an Army officer in both world wars. A champion billiards player (BAOR once, Leicestershire thrice), he was also a notable vocalist and capable musician whose talents with the piano, banjo and ukulele were in constant demand on tour. He spent his final years coaching, briefly at Tonbridge School.

NOTABLE FEATS
• Achieved the 'double' 9 times between 1921 and 1930, a tally exceeded only by W. Rhodes, G.H. Hirst and V.W.C. Jupp.
• Holds Leicestershire's career wicket-taking record: 2130.
• First professional to be appointed Leicestershire captain (1935).
• With P. Holmes shared in a stand of 327 for MCC v Jamaica at Kingston in 1925–26 which remains the 5th-wkt record for West Indies first-class cricket.

						Batting 1st			Batting 2nd				Bowling 1st			Bowling 2nd		
Ref	Series	V	T	Venue	Result	No	R	HO	No	R	HO	Ct	Balls	R	W	Balls	R	W
168/154	1927–28	SA	1	Johannesburg[1]	W-10w	8	7	c	–	–	–	–	48	11	0	36	17	0
169/155			2	Cape Town	W-87	7	25	lbw	7	9	c	1	48	32	1	174	48	3
170/156			3	Durban[2]	D	7	40	c	–	–	–	2	18	8	0	144	41	2
171/157			4	Johannesburg[1]	L-4w	7	3	c	7	17	c	1	66	55	2	20	10	1
172/158			5	Durban[2]	L-8w	8	1	lbw	8	0	c	–	216	99	3	12	9	0

Ref	Series	V	T	Venue	Result	Batting 1st No	R	HO	Batting 2nd No	R	HO	Ct	Bowling 1st Balls	R	W	Bowling 2nd Balls	R	W
190/176	1929-30	WI	1	Bridgetown	D	8	1	c	–	–	–	1	54	19	1	180	72	0
191/177			2	Port-of-Spain	W-167	8	19	c	8	14	c	1	146	58	4	120	34	0
192/178			3	Georgetown	L-289	8	0	ro	8	5	hw	–	168	92	0	258	70	4
193/179			4	Kingston	D	9	39	b	9	10	b	1	198	73	3	276	108	1

Career	M	I	NO	HS	R	Avge	100	50	Ct	St	Balls	R	W	Avge	BB	5w	10w	Rate
Test	9	15	0	40	190	12.66	–	–	7	–	2182	856	25	34.24	4-58	–	–	87.28
F/c	733	1153	145	164*	22731	22.55	15	107	464	–	138485	57783	2431	23.76	9-41	140	22	56.96

ATHEY
Charles William Jeffrey

Yorkshire (1976 to 1983)
Gloucestershire (1984 to date)

TOURS
A 1986-87, 1987-88; WI 1980-81; NZ 1979-80 (Robins), 1987-88; P 1987-88; SL 1985-86 (Eng B)
Born Middlesbrough, Yorkshire
27 Sep 1957

A prolific scorer in county cricket, particularly after escaping to Bristol from his strife-torn native county, Bill Athey all too frequently failed at the highest level. Promoted to open in Australia in 1986–87, he enjoyed his one successful series but, that mission and a subsequent hundred against Pakistan excepted, he managed only one other fifty in 31 innings. Of average height (5ft 9½in) and wirily built, his fielding, particularly in the short mid-wicket area, was outstanding. Possibly the only Test cricketer to sport a tattoo (on his upper arm).

NOTABLE FEATS
- Shared opening stand of 223 with B.C. Broad (Test *1059*) – England's highest for any wicket at Perth.
- Scored 4 hundreds in successive first-class innings in 1987.

Bill Athey

Ref	Series	V	T	Venue	Result	Batting 1st No	R	HO	Batting 2nd No	R	HO	Ct
885/562	1980	A		Lord's	D	3	9	b	3	1	c	1
898/565	1980-81	WI	4	St John's	D	3	2	c	3	1	c	1
899/566			5	Kingston	D	3	3	b	3	1	c	–
1047/624	1986	I	2	Leeds	L-279	6	32	c	6	8	c	–
1048/625			3	Birmingham	D	3	0	c	3	38	c	–
1049/626	1986	NZ	1	Lord's	D	3	44	c	3	16	b	–
1050/627			2	Nottingham	L-8w	3	55	lbw	4	6	c	2
1051/628			3	Oval	D	2	17	lbw	–	–	–	1
1058/629	1986-87	A	1	Brisbane[2]	W-7w	2	76	b	2	1	c	–
1059/630			2	Perth	D	2	96	b	2	6	c	1
1060/631			3	Adelaide	D	2	55	b	2	12	c	–
1061/632			4	Melbourne	W-I & 14	2	21	lbw	–	–	–	1
1062/633			5	Sydney	L-55	2	5	c	2	31	b	1
1075/634	1987	P	1	Manchester	D	1	19	b	–	–	–	–
1076/635			2	Lord's	D	3	123	b	–	–	–	–
1077/636			3	Leeds	L-I & 18	3	4	c	3	26	lbw	2
1078/637			4	Birmingham	D	3	0	b	6	14	*	–
1084/639	1987-88	P	1	Lahore[2]	L-I & 87	5	5	lbw	5	2	c	–
1085/640			2	Faisalabad	D	3	27	c	3	20	b	–
1086/641			3	Karachi	D	3	26	b	3	12	c	–
1090/642	1987-88	A		Sydney	D	5	37	c	–	–	–	2
1091/643	1987/88	NZ	1	Christchurch	D	5	22	c	5	19	c	1
1101/649	1988	WI	4	Leeds	L-10w	3	16	lbw	3	11	c	–

Career	M	I	NO	HS	R	Avge	100	50	Ct	St	Balls	R	W	Avge	BB	5w	10w	Rate
Test	23	41	1	123	919	22.97	1	4	13	–	–	–	–	–	–	–	–	–
F/c	293	490	47	184	14978	33.81	31	70	281	2	3018	1706	37	46.10	3-3	–	–	81.56

ATTEWELL, William

Nottinghamshire (1881 to 1899)

Wisden 1892
TOURS A 1884–85, 1887–88, 1891–92
Born Keyworth, Nottinghamshire
12 Jun 1861
Died Long Eaton, Derbyshire
11 Jun 1927

NOTABLE FEATS

- Recorded the most economical career figures in Test cricket (21.96 runs/100 balls) by a bowler delivering at least 2000 balls.
- Took all 10 wickets for MCC v Worcestershire in 1883 before that county attained first-class status.
- Scored 200 for MCC v Northumberland at Lord's in 1887 sharing in a stand of 419 with W. Gunn.

'Dick' Attewell, an outstanding member of Nottinghamshire's attack for 16 seasons, was a right-handed medium-pace bowler of exceptional accuracy. A cunning exponent of flight and spin, he could, like Alfred Shaw, sustain a perfect length for long periods without tiring – as in 1887 when he returned figures of 52.2–42–19–4 against Kent. Although he exceeded 100 wickets in a season ten times, he was only once selected for a home Test. A handy lower-order batsman and sprightly fielder, usually at cover-point, he was an exceptionally good-natured man and an extremely popular cricketer. A butcher by trade, he stood as a first-class umpire from 1902 to 1907.

'Dick' Attewell

						Batting 1st			Batting 2nd				Bowling 1st			Bowling 2nd		
Ref	Series	V	T	Venue	Result	No	R	HO	No	R	HO	Ct	Balls	R	W	Balls	R	W
17/17	1884–85	A	1	Adelaide	W-8w	9	12	*	–	–	–	1	200	48	1	72	26	0
18/18			2	Melbourne	W-10w	9	30	c	–	–	–	–	244	54	2	20	7	0
19/19			3	Sydney	L-6	9	14	b	9	0	ro	1	284	53	4	232	54	2
20/20			4	Sydney	L-8w	9	1	b	9	1	*	2	72	22	0	12	4	0
21/21			5	Melbourne	W-I & 98	9	0	c	–	–	–	1	20	18	1	145	24	3
27/27	1887–88	A		Sydney	W-126	10	7	*	10	10	*	1	–	–	–	18	4	1
33/33	1890	A	1	Lord's	W-7w	11	0	*	–	–	–	2	160	42	4	212	54	1
35/35	1891–92	A	1	Melbourne	L-54	9	8	c	10	24	c	–	127	28	1	366	51	2
36/36			2	Sydney	L-72	10	0	b	10	0	c	1	186	25	1	276	43	1
37/37			3	Adelaide	W-I & 230	11	43	*	–	–	–	–	–	–	–	204	69	3

Career	M	I	NO	HS	R	Avge	100	50	Ct	St	Balls	R	W	Avge	BB	5w	10w	Rate
Test	10	15	6	43*	150	16.66	–	–	9	–	2850	626	27	23.18	4-42	–	–	105.55
F/c	429	644	68	102	8083	14.02	1	27	364	–	108263	29896	1950	15.33	9-23	134	27	55.51

BAILEY, Robert John

Northamptonshire (1982 to date)

Born Biddulph, Staffordshire
28 Oct 1963

A tall (6ft 3in), middle-order batsman who deputised for the injured Allan Lamb in the final Test against West Indies in 1988 and was selected for the following winter's aborted tour of India. Rob Bailey is an imposing, upright, fierce striker of the ball, who uses his height to counteract short-pitched bowling and has a penchant for driving on the up. A product of Staffordshire cricket, he is a useful change bowler (right-arm seam or off-spin) and dependable slip fielder.

						Batting 1st			Batting 2nd			
Ref	Series	V	T	Venue	Result	No	R	HO	No	R	HO	Ct
1102/650	1988	WI	5	Oval	L-8w	3	43	c	3	3	b	–

Career	M	I	NO	HS	R	Avge	100	50	Ct	St	Balls	R	W	Avge	BB	5w	10w	Rate
Test	1	2	–	43	46	23.00	–	–	–	–	–	–	–	–	–	–	–	–
F/c	134	218	35	224*	7346	40.14	15	37	90	–	894	462	14	33.00	3-27	–	–	74.50

BAILEY
Trevor Edward

Essex (1946 to 1967)
Cambridge University (1947 to 1948)

Wisden 1950
TOURS
A 1950–51, 1954–55, 1958–59; SA 1956–57; WI 1953–54, 1963–64 (Cav), 1964–65 (Cav); NZ 1950–51, 1954–55; I 1963–64 (PM XI)
Born Westcliff-on-Sea, Essex 3 Dec 1923

Trevor Bailey

England's outstanding all-rounder of the 1950s, Trevor Bailey will be remembered as the tenacious master of the forward defensive block who revelled in his sobriquet, 'The Barnacle'. A quick-scoring, fluent strokemaker for Essex, he readily adopted a contrasting role for England, particularly against the 'old enemy'. His massive concentration and astringent competitive spirit, allied to an excellent technique and keen appetite for a good crisis, rescued the side from disaster on numerous occasions during Len Hutton's two successful Ashes campaigns, his last-ditch stand with Willie Watson at Lord's in 1953 being one of Test cricket's most heroic feats. Enduring 257 minutes, the pair survived from 12.42 until 5.50pm – 40 minutes from the close. As a right-arm, fast-medium bowler with a beautifully high action which added bounce to his ability to swing and cut the ball, he enjoyed a formidable new-ball partnership with Alec Bedser before becoming the main support bowler to Tyson and Statham. A brilliant close catcher, he was an astute county captain who managed to combine that task with the post of secretary. Only a controversial newspaper article published under his name prevented his supreme tactical acumen from being channelled into Test captaincy. His talents on the soccer field earned him a blue and an FA Amateur Cup winners' medal with Walthamstow. 'The Boil's' cricketing knowledge and insight have produced a wealth of literature and, in his role of the BBC's *Test Match Special* guru, hours of devoted listening.

NOTABLE FEATS

- 1000 runs in 22nd Test (*384*) (33 inns); 2000 runs in 48th Test (*438*) (72 inns). 50 wickets in 21st Test (*383*); 100 wickets in 47th Test (*437*) to complete the Test 'double', the third to do so for England after W. Rhodes and M.W. Tate.
- Took a wicket with his eighth ball in Test cricket and returned a 6-wicket analysis in his first innings.
- Shared match-saving 5th-wkt stand of 163 with W. Watson (Test *373* – see above).
- After defending for 262 min in 2nd inns he seized the ball and prevented an Australian victory by bowling leg theory (Test *375*).
- Returned then record England analyses against West Indies for all Tests (7 for 34 in *386*) and in home Tests (7 for 44 in *440*).
- Scored 50 in 357 min (Test *464*), still the slowest recorded fifty in all first-class cricket. He batted 438 minutes for 68 scoring off only 40 of the 425 balls bowled to him.
- Having allowed himself to be bowled to give R.R. Lindwall his 100th wicket against England (Test *395*), in his final Test (*468*) he was dismissed for a 'pair' by that bowler.
- Took a hat-trick for Essex v Glamorgan at Newport in 1950 and claimed 7 wickets in 29 balls in the return fixture at Brentwood.
- Took all 10 Lancashire wickets for 90 at Clacton in 1949.
- His seasonal aggregates netted 1000 runs 17 times (including 2011 in 1959), 100 wickets 9 times and the 'double' on 8 occasions (a tally exceeded only by W. Rhodes, G.H. Hirst, V.W.C. Jupp and W.E. Astill), including the only post-war instance of 2000 runs and 100 wickets (1959).

TEST NOTES

- *436* Retired hurt when 15* at 48–1 (2nd inns); resumed at 167–5, surviving 55 min with hand in plaster.

Rob Bailey

						Batting 1st			Batting 2nd				Bowling 1st			Bowling 2nd		
Ref	Series	V	T	Venue	Result	No	R	HO	No	R	HO	Ct	Balls	R	W	Balls	R	W
314/272	1949	NZ	1	Leeds	D	7	12	c	–	–	–	–	195	118	6	54	51	0
315/273			2	Lord's	D	7	93	c	7	6	*	–	198	136	0	–	–	–
316/274			3	Manchester	D	6	72	*	–	–	–	–	182	84	6	96	71	1
317/275			4	Oval	D	5	36	c	–	–	–	–	157	72	3	66	67	0
323/276	1950	WI	1	Manchester	W-202	7	82	*	6	33	ro	1	60	28	1	18	9	0
326/279			4	Oval	L-I & 56	6	18	c	6	12	lbw	–	206	84	2	–	–	–
327/280	1950–51	A	1	Brisbane[2]	L-70	9	1	*	4	7	c	2	96	28	3	56	22	4
328/281			2	Melbourne	L-28	4	12	b	3	0	b	2	137	40	4	120	47	2
329/282			3	Sydney	L-I & 13	7	15	c	8	0	*	–	–	–	–	–	–	–
331/284			5	Melbourne	W-8w	9	5	c	–	–	–	–	72	29	0	120	32	1
332/285	1950–51	NZ	1	Christchurch	D	5	134	*	–	–	–	–	180	51	2	–	–	–
333/286			2	Wellington	W-6w	7	29	st	–	–	–	1	66	18	2	86	43	3
334/287	1951	SA	1	Nottingham	L-71	9	3	c	6	11	c	–	270	102	0	12	10	0
337/290			4	Leeds	D	6	95	b	–	–	–	–	102	48	0	6	8	0
372/301	1953	A	1	Nottingham	D	7	13	lbw	–	–	–	1	264	75	2	30	28	0
373/302			2	Lord's	D	6	2	c	6	71	c	1	96	55	0	60	24	0
374/303			3	Manchester	D	8	27	c	–	–	–	1	156	83	1	–	–	–
375/304			4	Leeds	D	7	7	ro	7	38	c	–	132	71	3	36	9	1
376/305			5	Oval	W-8w	6	64	b	–	–	–	–	84	42	1	–	–	–
382/306	1953–54	WI	1	Kingston	L-140	6	28	*	6	15	*	1	96	36	0	120	46	1
383/307			2	Bridgetown	L-181	7	28	c	7	4	c	–	132	63	1	72	48	0
384/308			3	Georgetown	W-9w	7	49	c	–	–	–	–	30	13	0	132	41	2
385/309			4	Port-of-Spain	D	2	46	c	–	–	–	1	192	104	0	72	20	2
386/310			5	Kingston	W-9w	2	23	c	–	–	–	–	96	34	7	150	54	1
387/311	1954	P	1	Lord's	D	8	3	b	–	–	–	–	18	1	0	36	13	1
388/312			2	Nottingham	W-I & 129	6	36	*	–	–	–	–	18	18	0	–	–	–
389/313			3	Manchester	D	2	42	ro	–	–	–	–	–	–	–	–	–	–
391/315	1954–55	A	1	Brisbane[2]	L-I & 154	6	88	b	6	23	c	1	208	140	3	–	–	–
392/316			2	Sydney	W-38	2	0	b	2	6	c	–	140	59	4	48	21	0
393/317			3	Melbourne	W-128	6	30	c	6	24	*	–	72	33	0	24	14	0
394/318			4	Adelaide	W-5w	6	38	c	6	15	lbw	1	96	39	3	–	–	–
395/319			5	Sydney	D	6	72	b	–	–	–	–	–	–	–	–	–	–
401/320	1954–55	NZ	1	Dunedin	W-8w	6	0	lbw	–	–	–	–	74	19	2	48	9	0
402/321			2	Auckland	W-I & 20	6	18	c	–	–	–	2	78	34	0	–	–	–
408/322	1955	SA	1	Nottingham	W-I & 5	6	49	lbw	–	–	–	1	30	8	0	102	21	2
409/323			2	Lord's	W-71	6	13	lbw	6	22	c	–	96	56	1	–	–	–
410/324			3	Manchester	L-3w	6	44	c	7	38	*	–	222	102	1	–	–	–
411/325			4	Leeds	L-224	1	9	lbw	6	8	c	–	96	23	1	245	97	3
412/326			5	Oval	W-92	7	0	c	7	1	lbw	–	30	6	1	36	15	0
425/327	1956	A	1	Nottingham	D	6	14	c	–	–	–	2	18	8	0	54	16	0
426/328			2	Lord's	L-185	6	32	b	6	18	c	3	204	72	2	149	64	4
427/329			3	Leeds	W-I & 42	8	33	*	–	–	–	1	42	15	0	42	13	0
428/330			4	Manchester	W-I & 170	5	20	c	–	–	–	–	24	4	0	120	31	0
434/332	1956–57	SA	1	Johannesburg[3]	W-131	2	16	c	2	10	c	1	120	33	3	124	20	5
435/333			2	Cape Town	W-312	2	34	c	2	28	b	1	88	13	0	–	–	–
436/334			3	Durban[2]	D	2	80	c	2	18	c	–	136	38	1	–	–	–
437/335			4	Johannesburg[3]	L-17	2	13	c	2	1	c	1	168	54	3	104	12	2
438/336			5	Port Elizabeth	L-158	2	41	b	2	18	c	–	200	23	3	199	39	2
439/337	1957	WI	1	Birmingham	D	6	1	b	–	–	–	1	204	80	0	–	–	–
440/338			2	Lord's	W-I & 36	6	1	b	–	–	–	2	126	44	7	132	54	4
441/339			3	Nottingham	D	8	3	*	–	–	–	–	168	77	1	72	22	0
443/341			5	Oval	W-I & 237	6	0	ro	–	–	–	–	–	–	–	–	–	–
454/342	1958	NZ	1	Birmingham	W-205	6	2	c	6	6	*	2	120	17	2	120	23	2
455/343			2	Lord's	W-I & 148	6	17	c	–	–	–	1	6	4	0	30	7	1
456/344			3	Leeds	W-I & 71	–	–	–	–	–	–	–	18	7	0	18	3	0
458/346			5	Oval	D	6	14	c	–	–	–	–	84	32	2	–	–	–
464/347	1958–59	A	1	Brisbane[2]	L-8w	6	27	st	3	68	b	–	104	35	3	40	21	0
465/348			2	Melbourne	L-8w	2	48	c	2	14	c	–	128	50	0	–	–	–
466/349			3	Sydney	D	1	8	lbw	1	25	c	–	40	19	0	–	–	–
467/350			4	Adelaide	L-10w	2	4	b	6	6	c	1	176	91	1	–	–	–
468/351			5	Melbourne	L-9w	2	0	c	2	0	b	–	112	43	0	–	–	–

Career	M	I	NO	HS	R	Avge	100	50	Ct	St	Balls	R	W	Avge	BB	5w	10w	Rate
Test	61	91	14	134*	2290	29.74	1	10	32	–	9712	3856	132	29.21	7-34	5	1	73.57
F/c	682	1072	215	205	28641	33.42	28	149	428	–	116898	48170	2082	23.13	10-90	110	13	56.14

T. E. BAILEY – TEST SUMMARY

Series	V	M	I	NO	HS	R	Avge	100	50	Balls	R	W	Avge	BB	5w	10w	Rate
1949	NZ	4	5	2	93	219	73.00	–	2	948	599	16	37.43	6-84	2	–	59.25
1950	WI	2	4	1	82*	145	48.33	–	1	284	121	3	40.33	2-84	–	–	94.66
1950–51	A	4	7	2	15	40	8.00	–	–	601	198	14	14.14	4.22	–	–	42.92
1950–51	NZ	2	2	1	134*	163	163.00	1	–	332	112	7	16.00	3-43	–	–	47.42
1951	SA	2	3	–	95	109	36.33	–	1	390	168	0	–	–	–	–	–
1953	A	5	7	–	71	222	31.71	–	2	858	387	8	48.37	3-71	–	–	107.25
1953–54	WI	5	7	2	49	193	38.60	–	–	1092	459	14	32.78	7-34	1	–	78.00
1954	P	3	3	1	42	81	40.50	–	–	72	32	1	32.00	1-13	–	–	72.00
1954–55	A	5	9	1	88	296	37.00	–	2	588	306	10	30.60	4-59	–	–	58.80
1954–55	NZ	2	2	–	18	18	9.00	–	–	200	62	2	31.00	2-10	–	–	100.00
1955	SA	5	9	1	49	184	23.00	–	–	857	328	9	36.44	3-97	–	–	95.22
1956	A	4	5	1	33*	117	29.25	–	–	653	223	6	37.16	4-64	–	–	108.83
1956–57	SA	5	10	–	80	259	25.90	–	1	1139	232	19	12.21	5-20	1	–	59.94
1957	WI	4	4	1	3*	5	1.66	–	–	702	277	12	23.08	7-44	1	1	58.50
1958	NZ	4	4	1	17	39	13.00	–	–	396	93	7	13.28	2-17	–	–	56.57
1958–59	A	5	10	–	68	200	20.00	–	1	600	259	4	64.75	3-35	–	–	150.00
	A	23	38	4	88	875	25.73	–	5	3300	1373	42	32.69	4-22	–	–	78.57
	SA	12	22	1	95	552	26.28	–	2	2386	728	28	26.00	5-20	1	–	85.21
	WI	11	15	4	82*	343	31.18	–	1	2078	857	29	29.55	7-34	2	1	71.65
	NZ	12	13	4	134*	439	48.77	1	2	1876	866	32	27.06	6-84	2	–	58.62
	P	3	3	1	42	81	40.50	–	–	72	32	1	32.00	1-13	–	–	72.00
Home		33	44	8	95	1121	31.13	–	6	5160	2228	62	35.93	7-44	3	1	83.22
Overseas		28	47	6	134*	1169	28.51	1	4	4552	1628	70	23.25	7-34	2	–	65.02
Totals		61	91	14	134*	2290	29.74	1	10	9712	3856	132	29.21	7-34	5	1	73.57

BAIRSTOW
David Leslie

Yorkshire (1970 to date)
Griqualand West
(1976–77 to 1977–78)

TOURS
A 1978–79, 1979–80;
WI 1980–81, 1986–87 (Yorks)
Born Horton, Bradford, Yorkshire
1 Sep 1951

Ginger-haired, sturdily built, ebullient and pugnacious, David Bairstow combined live-wire wicket-keeping with gutsy, hard-hitting batsmanship to become a lynchpin of the Yorkshire team for almost two decades. Making his debut whilst still at Bradford's Hanson Grammar School and immediately after sitting an A-level exam, he made over 10,000 runs and 1000 dismissals for the County, captaining them for three seasons. A soccer professional (Bradford City), he always exuded enthusiasm, relished a crisis and was unlucky not to establish an England place.

NOTABLE FEATS

- Equalled the world first-class record by holding 11 catches for Yorkshire v Derbyshire at Scarborough in 1982.

David Bairstow appeals as Venkataraghavan is run out near the end of India's epic run chase at The Oval in 1979.

						Batting 1st			Batting 2nd			Fielding 1st				Fielding 2nd			
Ref	Series	V	T	Venue	Result	No	R	HO	No	R	HO	Ct	St	Byes	Balls	Ct	St	Byes	Balls
854/552†	1979	I	4	Oval	D	8	9	c	8	59	c	3	–	2	477	–	–	11	905
884/561†	1980	WI	5	Leeds	D	8	40	lbw	8	9	*	2	–	2	509	–	–	–	–
885/562†	1980	A		Lord's	D	8	6	lbw	–	–	–	1	1	1	804	1	–	1	320
897/564†	1980–81	WI	3	Bridgetown	L-298	8	0	c	8	2	c	4	–	4	541	1	–	3	654

Career	M	I	NO	HS	R	Avge	100	50	Ct	St	Balls	R	W	Avge	BB	5w	10w	Rate
Test	4	7	1	59	125	20.83	–	1	12	1	–	–	–	–	–	–	–	–
F/c	442	624	116	145	13455	26.48	9	71	926	137	582	308	9	34.22	3-25	–	–	64.66

BAKEWELL Alfred Harry

Northamptonshire (1928 to 1936)

Wisden 1934
TOUR I/SL 1933–34
Born Walsall, Staffordshire 2 Nov 1908
Died Westbourne, Dorset 23 Jan 1983

Fred Bakewell

The car smash which ended Fred Bakewell's career was as disastrous for cricket as that which effectively terminated Colin Milburn's. One of the most exciting batsmen of his generation, he overcame the apparent handicap of an exaggeratedly square-on, crouching stance with a separated grip to become one of the most spectacular drivers and cutters ever seen. Nimble-footed and naturally strong on the leg side, he worked assiduously to improve his off-stump defence. A useful change bowler and brilliant short-leg fielder, he played for a very weak Northamptonshire side which, during his nine-season career, finished bottom five times. He had just scored 241* at Chesterfield when his car overturned on its homeward journey, severely fracturing his right arm.

NOTABLE FEATS

- Made double centuries in successive innings in 1933 (246 and 257) – both then record scores for Northamptonshire.
- Scored 1000 runs in each of his full seasons (1929 to 1936), setting the then record Northamptonshire aggregate of 1952 runs in 1933 when he scored 2149 in all first-class matches.
- His match aggregate of 8 catches for Northamptonshire v Essex at Leyton in 1928 has been bettered only by W.R. Hammond in all first-class cricket.

TEST NOTES

- *245* Bowled in 2nd inns: 0 for 8 (18 balls).

						Batting 1st			Batting 2nd			
Ref	Series	V	T	Venue	Result	No	R	HO	No	R	HO	Ct
209/190	1931	NZ	1	Lord's	D	1	9	lbw	1	27	c	–
210/191			2	Oval	W-I & 26	1	40	ro	–	–	–	–
229/203	1933	WI	3	Oval	W-I & 17	2	107	c	–	–	–	2
232/206	1933–34	I	3	Madras[1]	W-202	1	85	c	1	4	c	–
245/219	1935	SA	4	Manchester	D	2	63	b	2	54	b	1
246/220			5	Oval	D	1	20	c	–	–	–	–

Career	M	I	NO	HS	R	Avge	100	50	Ct	St	Balls	R	W	Avge	BB	5w	10w	Rate
Test	6	9	0	107	409	45.44	1	3	3	–	18	8	0	–	–	–	–	–
F/c	250	453	24	257	14570	33.96	31	74	225	–	1607	1271	22	57.77	2-17	–	–	73.04

BALDERSTONE
John Christopher

Yorkshire (1961 to 1969)
Leicestershire (1971 to 1986)

TOUR Z 1980–81 (Leics)
Born Longwood, Huddersfield, Yorkshire 16 Nov 1940

NOTABLE FEATS

- With D.I. Gower shared Leicestershire record 2nd-wkt stand of 289* v Essex at Leicester in 1981.
- Hat-trick for Leicestershire v Sussex at Eastbourne in 1976.
- On 15 September 1975 played cricket for Leicestershire v Derbyshire at Chesterfield (11.30am to 6.30pm) and soccer for Doncaster Rovers v Brentford at Doncaster (7.30pm to 9.10pm).

As a dependable right-handed opening or middle-order batsman, flighty slow left-arm orthodox spin bowler and specialist gully fielder, Chris Balderstone was an important and highly professional member of Ray Illingworth's successful Leicestershire team of the 1970s. His two England caps were gained against the West Indies at their peak. Professional commitments for, successively, Huddersfield Town, Carlisle United, Doncaster Rovers and Queen of the South limited his cricket career and once compelled him to play a league soccer match at the end of a full day of championship cricket.

Chris Balderstone

					Batting 1st			Batting 2nd				Bowling 1st			Bowling 2nd		
Ref	Series	V	T Venue	Result	No	R	HO	No	R	HO	Ct	Balls	R	W	Balls	R	W
780/518	1976	WI	4 Leeds	L-55	4	35	c	4	4	c	–	–	–	–	–	–	–
781/519			5 Oval	L-231	4	0	b	4	0	b	1	96	80	1	–	–	–

Career	M	I	NO	HS	R	Avge	100	50	Ct	St	Balls	R	W	Avge	BB	5w	10w	Rate
Test	2	4	0	35	39	9.75	–	–	1	–	96	80	1	80.00	1-80	–	–	96.00
F/c	390	619	61	181*	19034	34.11	32	103	210	–	19338	8160	310	26.32	6-25	5	–	62.38

BARBER
Robert William

Lancashire (1954 to 1962)
Cambridge University (1955 to 1957)
Warwickshire (1963 to 1969)

Wisden 1967
TOURS
A 1965–66; SA 1964–65;
WI 1960–61 (Swanton); 1966–67 (RW);
NZ 1960–61; I/SL 1961–62; P 1961–62
Born Withington, Lancashire
26 Sep 1935

An adventurous left-handed opening batsman with a full repertoire of strokes, Bob Barber realised his full potential only after moving to Edgbaston following nine seasons at Old Trafford. Previously a careful, introverted player, he suddenly blossomed into an aggressive and richly entertaining strokemaker. He reached his peak on Mike Smith's tour of Australia's fast, bouncy pitches, going on the rampage from the start of every innings to total 1001 runs, avge 50.05, in all first-class matches. A fearless short-leg and a self-underrated leg-break and googly bowler, he enjoyed an outstanding career at Ruthin School, achieving the rare feat of the 'double' in 1953. Highly intelligent and independent, he sacrificed cricket for a business career while still in his batting prime.

NOTABLE FEATS

- 1000 runs in 20th Test (*596*) (31 inns).
- With G. Pullar shared a record England opening partnership v Pakistan: 198 in Test *518*.
- Scored 185 in 296 min off 255 balls in Test *599* – the highest individual England score on the first day of a Test v Australia.
- Hat-trick for Warwickshire v Glamorgan at Birmingham in 1963.

Ref	Series	V	T	Venue	Result	Batting 1st No	R	HO	Batting 2nd No	R	HO	Ct	Bowling 1st Balls	R	W	Bowling 2nd Balls	R	W
492/364	1960	SA	1	Birmingham	W-100	8	5	lbw	7	4	c	–	36	26	0	60	29	1
512/374	1961–62	P	1	Lahore[2]	W-5w	7	6	st	7	39	*	–	240	124	3	125	54	3
513/375	1961–62	I	1	Bombay[2]	D	6	19	st	2	31	ro	3	132	74	1	78	42	0
514/376			2	Kanpur	D	6	69	*	6	10	ro	–	–	–	–	–	–	–
515/377			3	Delhi	D	–	–	–	–	–	–	–	150	103	1	–	–	–
516/378			4	Calcutta	L-187	6	12	b	5	6	c	1	18	17	0	12	9	0
517/379			5	Madras[2]	L-128	2	16	lbw	2	21	b	–	84	70	2	–	–	–
518/380	1961–62	P	2	Dacca	D	2	86	lbw	–	–	–	–	66	12	0	–	–	–
519/381			3	Karachi	D	6	23	st	–	–	–	1	84	44	1	246	117	3
565/409	1964	A	5	Oval	D	2	24	b	2	29	lbw	–	36	23	0	–	–	–
571/410	1964–65	SA	1	Durban[2]	W-I & 104	2	74	b	–	–	–	2	84	48	2	36	8	0
572/411			2	Johannesburg[3]	D	2	97	b	–	–	–	–	84	33	1	12	12	0
573/412			3	Cape Town	D	2	58	lbw	–	–	–	2	–	–	–	6	2	0
574/413			4	Johannesburg[3]	D	2	61	lbw	–	–	–	2	–	–	–	–	–	–
591/415	1965	NZ	1	Birmingham	W-9w	2	31	b	2	51	c	1	18	7	2	270	132	4
592/416			2	Lord's	W-7w	2	13	c	2	34	b	–	48	24	0	168	57	3
593/417			3	Leeds	W-I & 187	1	13	c	–	–	–	1	12	2	0	84	14	0
594/418	1965	SA	1	Lord's	D	2	56	b	2	12	c	1	63	30	2	150	60	1
595/419			2	Nottingham	L-94	2	41	c	2	1	c	1	54	39	0	18	20	0
596/420			3	Oval	D	1	40	st	1	22	c	–	–	–	–	78	44	0
597/421	1965–66	A	1	Brisbane[2]	D	1	5	c	1	34	c	–	40	42	0	–	–	–
598/422			2	Melbourne	D	2	48	c	2	0	*	1	48	24	0	136	87	1
599/423			3	Sydney	W-I & 93	2	185	b	–	–	–	2	17	2	1	40	16	0
600/424			4	Adelaide	L-I & 9	2	0	b	2	19	c	–	32	30	0	–	–	–
601/425			5	Melbourne	D	2	17	ro	2	20	b	1	128	60	1	–	–	–
608/432	1966	WI	4	Leeds	L-I & 55	2	6	c	2	55	b	–	84	55	1	–	–	–
609/433			5	Oval	W-I & 34	2	36	c	–	–	–	2	90	49	3	133	78	2
637/445	1968	A	1	Manchester	L-159	6	20	c	6	46	c	–	66	56	2	60	31	1

Career	M	I	NO	HS	R	Avge	100	50	Ct	St	Balls	R	W	Avge	BB	5w	10w	Rate
Test	28	45	3	185	1495	35.59	1	9	21	–	3426	1806	42	43.00	4-132	–	–	81.57
F/c	386	651	52	185	17631	29.43	17	90	210	–	31596	16176	549	29.46	7-35	12	–	57.55

R. W. BARBER – TEST BATTING SUMMARY

Series	V	M	I	NO	HS	R	Avge	100	50
1960	SA	1	2	–	5	9	4.50	–	–
1961–62	P	3	4	1	86	154	51.33	–	1
1961–62	I	5	8	1	69*	184	26.28	–	1
1964	A	1	2	–	29	53	26.50	–	–
1964–65	SA	4	4	–	97	290	72.50	–	4
1965	NZ	3	5	–	51	142	28.40	–	1
1965	SA	3	6	–	56	172	28.66	–	1
1965–66	A	5	9	1	185	328	41.00	1	–
1966	WI	2	3	–	55	97	32.33	–	1
1968	A	1	2	–	46	66	33.00	–	–
	A	7	13	1	185	447	37.25	1	–
	SA	8	12	–	97	471	39.25	–	5
	WI	2	3	–	55	97	32.33	–	1
	NZ	3	5	–	51	142	28.40	–	1
	I	5	8	1	69	184	26.28	–	1
	P	3	4	1	86	154	51.33	–	1
Home		11	20	–	56	539	26.95	–	3
Overseas		17	25	3	185	956	43.45	1	6
Totals		28	45	3	185	1495	35.59	1	9

Bob Barber

BARBER, Wilfred

Yorkshire (1926 to 1947)

TOURS A 1935–36; NZ 1935–36
Born Cleckheaton, Yorkshire 18 Apr 1901
Died Bradford, Yorkshire 10 Sep 1968

A product of Yorkshire Council cricket, Wilf Barber contributed text-book opening batsmanship to eight of the County's championship titles. A strong off-side player with a sound defence, he was a first-rate outfielder but a very occasional bowler. One of six Yorkshire cricketers to represent England in 1935, he took a wicket with his second (and last) ball in Test cricket. He became coach and groundsman at Ashville School, Harrogate. [*Illus. p.* 498]

NOTABLE FEATS

- Shared record Yorkshire 2nd-wkt stand of 346 in 4 hours with M. Leyland v Middlesex at Sheffield in 1932.
- Exceeded 1000 runs in a season 8 times, including 2147 in 1935.

						Batting 1st			Batting 2nd				Bowling 1st			Bowling 2nd		
Ref	Series	V	T	Venue	Result	No	R	HO	No	R	HO	Ct	Balls	R	W	Balls	R	W
244/218	1935	SA	3	Leeds	D	3	24	c	3	14	c	1	–	–	–	2	0	1
245/219			4	Manchester	D	3	1	c	3	44	b	–	–	–	–	–	–	–

Career	M	I	NO	HS	R	Avge	100	50	Ct	St	Balls	R	W	Avge	BB	5w	10w	Rate
Test	2	4	0	44	83	20.75	–	–	1	–	2	0	1	0.00	1-0	–	–	2.00
F/c	373	526	49	255	16402	34.38	29	78	182	–	657	419	16	26.18	2-1	–	–	41.06

BARLOW Graham Derek

Middlesex (1969 to 1986)

TOURS A 1976–77; I/SL 1976–77
Born Folkestone, Kent 26 Mar 1950

Graham Barlow

A dependable, cheery and whole-hearted cricketer, Graham Barlow was a determined left-handed batsman with a fine array of strokes and a quite outstanding cover fielder. Although he scored consistently in county cricket, he failed totally on his three appearances for England but created a memorable impression with some brilliant work in the field.

NOTABLE FEATS

- With W.N. Slack shared record Middlesex opening stand of 367* v Kent at Lord's in 1981.

						Batting 1st			Batting 2nd			
Ref	Series	V	T	Venue	Result	No	R	HO	No	R	HO	Ct
788/520	1976–77	I	1	Delhi	W-I & 25	3	0	c	–	–	–	–
789/521			2	Calcutta	W-10w	2	4	c	2	7	*	–
804/526	1977	A	1	Lord's	D	6	1	c	5	5	lbw	–

Career	M	I	NO	HS	R	Avge	100	50	Ct	St	Balls	R	W	Avge	BB	5w	10w	Rate
Test	3	5	1	7*	17	4.25	–	–	–	–	–	–	–	–	–	–	–	–
F/c	251	404	59	177	12387	35.90	26	58	136	–	115	68	3	22.66	1-6	–	–	38.33

BARLOW
Richard Gorton

Lancashire (1871 to 1891)

TOURS A 1881–82, 1882–83, 1886–87
Born Barrow Bridge, Bolton, Lancashire 28 May 1851
Died Blackpool, Lancashire 31 Jul 1919

A stonewalling opening batsman and an excellent judge of length, Dick Barlow employed forward play for purposes of defence to an extent unknown in his era. He combined his role as opening partner to his Lancashire captain, the more flamboyant A.N. Hornby, with extremely accurate, probing, left-handed medium-pace bowling to develop into an outstanding all-rounder. A superbly fit and zealous worker, he was a county soccer goalkeeper and an award-winning sprinter. At 64 he challenged anyone of his age to a single-wicket contest. Cricket was his all-consuming passion from early boyhood and he became a highly respected Test umpire. A friendly, chatty character and a model professional, he once expressed his utter contentment by remarking: 'I don't think any cricketer has enjoyed his cricketing career better than I have done'.

NOTABLE FEATS
- With G. Ulyett shared the first century opening partnership in Test cricket (122 in Test 6).
- Carried his bat through a completed first-class innings 11 times, his 5 (out of 69 in 2 hours) v Nottinghamshire in 1882 being the lowest score by anyone achieving this feat.
- Bowled J. West of Yorkshire with his first ball in first-class cricket (Sheffield 1871).
- Four hat-tricks, 3 for Lancashire and 1 for the Players v the Gentlemen.

Dick Barlow

						Batting 1st			Batting 2nd				Bowling 1st			Bowling 2nd		
Ref	Series	V	T	Venue	Result	No	R	HO	No	R	HO	Ct	Balls	R	W	Balls	R	W
5/5	1881–82	A	1	Melbourne	D	1	0	c	1	33	st	–	92	22	0	–	–	–
6/6			2	Sydney	L-5w	2	31	b	2	62	c	1	32	8	0	16	6	0
7/7			3	Sydney	L-6w	2	4	c	2	8	c	–	–	–	–	–	–	–
8/8			4	Melbourne	D	2	16	c	2	56	ro	1	60	25	0	–	–	–
9/9	1882	A		Oval	L-7	1	11	c	3	0	b	–	124	19	5	52	27	0
10/10	1882–83	A	1	Melbourne	L-9w	1	10	st	1	28	b	2	80	37	0	16	6	0
11/11			2	Melbourne	W-I & 27	1	14	b	–	–	–	–	88	9	1	124	67	3
12/12			3	Sydney	W-69	1	28	c	3	24	c	1	189	52	1	138	40	7
13/13			4	Sydney	L-4w	1	2	c	1	20	c	3	192	88	3	149	44	0
14/14	1884	A	1	Manchester	D	9	6	c	7	14	*	–	32	18	0	–	–	–
15/15			2	Lord's	W-I & 5	7	38	c	–	–	–	1	80	44	0	84	31	1
16/16			3	Oval	D	7	0	c	1	21	*	–	200	72	0	–	–	–
22/22	1886	A	1	Manchester	W-4w	6	38	*	5	30	c	3	92	19	1	208	44	7
23/23			2	Lord's	W-I & 106	7	12	c	–	–	–	–	24	7	0	100	12	2
24/24			3	Oval	W-I & 217	7	3	c	–	–	–	1	–	–	–	56	13	0
25/25	1886–87	A	1	Sydney	W-13	4	2	b	4	4	c	1	140	25	3	52	20	0
26/26			2	Sydney	W-71	5	34	c	3	42	*	–	–	–	–	36	12	0

Career	M	I	NO	HS	R	Avge	100	50	Ct	St	Balls	R	W	Avge	BB	5w	10w	Rate
Test	17	30	4	62	591	22.73	–	2	14	–	2456	767	34	22.55	7-40	3	–	72.23
F/c	351	608	64	117	11217	20.61	4	39	266	–	43468	13799	951	14.50	9-39	66	14	45.70

BARNES
Sydney Francis

Warwickshire (1894 to 1896)
Lancashire (1899 to 1903)

Wisden 1910
TOURS
A 1901–02, 1907–08, 1911–12;
SA 1913–14
Born Smethwick, Staffordshire
19 Apr 1873
Died Chadsmoor, Staffordshire
26 Dec 1967

Sydney Barnes

Regarded by many, particularly his contemporary players and observers, as the greatest of all bowlers, Sydney Barnes could change his mode of attack to suit any type of pitch. From a springy, modest run, his tall, erect figure would erupt into a bounding, high action; his long arms and large, strong fingers could extract maximum bounce and movement from the most placid of surfaces. He was a master of deception and flight and could turn or swing the ball either way. Usually he operated at a brisk medium pace but he could maintain the same control at slow-medium. At will he could bowl a late inswinging leg-cutter, pitched to hit the off stump. The arch-perfectionist, he never tired of experimenting with a variety of grips and seam positions. An aloof, austere, brooding character, he disliked the daily grind of county cricket and, apart from 50 matches spread over eight seasons for Warwickshire and Lancashire, he confined his bread-and-butter performances to minor counties matches for Staffordshire and Saturday appearances in the northern leagues. It was from such obscurity that A.C. MacLaren plucked him for his first tour of Australia after batting against him in the Old Trafford nets. He continued in league cricket until 1934 when, at the age of 61, his wickets cost under 11 runs apiece, and worked into his nineties, still maintaining a fastidious copperplate hand.

NOTABLE FEATS

- 50 wickets in 9th Test (*100*); 100 wickets in 17th Test (*120*); the first bowler to take 150 wickets – in 24th Test (*130*).
- *117* Aged 38, and unwell before play began, he dismissed W. Bardsley (with his first ball), C. Kelleway, C. Hill and W.W. Armstrong for just 1 run in 5 overs, taking 5 for 6 in his opening spell of 11 overs.
- *120* Took 34 wickets in the rubber to set E v A record (passed by M.W. Tate in 1924–25).
- *128* Bowled unchanged through both inns to finish with 34 wickets v SA in 3 matches. His analysis of 8 for 29 (all taken pre-lunch) remains the record for Tests at The Oval.
- *131* His match analysis of 17 for 159 has been bettered only in Tests by J.C. Laker's 19 for 90 in 1956.
- *133* His match analysis of 14 for 144 (the Test record at Durban) took his aggregate for the rubber to the surviving world record of 49 wickets. He declined to play in the Fifth Test after a disagreement over his wife's accommodation.
- Took his last 100 Test wickets in only 11 matches (21 inns).
- In 133 first-class matches he took 5 or more wickets in an innings 68 times.
- In all cricket he took 6229 wickets, avge 8.33, and on 7 occasions claimed all 10 wickets in an innings.
- Hat-trick for England v The Rest at The Oval in 1912.
- First to take 100 first-class wickets in a season in South Africa (emulated only by R. Benaud in 1957–58): 104 wickets, avge 10.74, in 12 matches in 1913–14.
- Holds Minor Counties Championship record for most wickets in a season: 119 for Staffordshire in 1906.

						Batting 1st			Batting 2nd				Bowling 1st			Bowling 2nd		
Ref	Series	V	T	Venue	Result	No	R	HO	No	R	HO	Ct	Balls	R	W	Balls	R	W
65/65	1901–02	A	1	Sydney	W-I & 124	10	26	*	–	–	–	2	211	65	5	96	74	1
66/66			2	Melbourne	L-229	10	1	c	10	0	c	–	97	42	6	384	121	7
67/67			3	Adelaide	L-4w	10	5	c	–	–	–	–	42	21	0	–	–	–
72/72	1902	A	3	Sheffield	L-143	11	7	c	11	5	b	–	120	49	6	72	50	1
96/93	1907–08	A	1	Sydney	L-2w	9	1	b	9	11	b	–	132	74	1	180	63	2
97/94			2	Melbourne	W-1w	9	14	c	9	38	*	–	102	30	0	166	72	5
98/95			3	Adelaide	L-245	9	12	c	9	8	c	–	162	60	3	252	83	3
99/96			4	Melbourne	L-308	9	3	c	9	22	*	–	138	37	1	210	69	1
100/97			5	Sydney	L-49	11	1	ro	11	11	b	1	136	60	7	162	78	1
103/100	1909	A	3	Leeds	L-126	9	1	b	9	1	b	–	150	37	1	210	63	6
104/101			4	Manchester	D	10	0	b	–	–	–	1	162	56	5	135	66	1
105/102			5	Oval	D	10	0	c	–	–	–	–	114	57	2	162	61	2

Ref	Series	V	T	Venue	Result	Batting 1st No	R	HO	Batting 2nd No	R	HO	Ct	Bowling 1st Balls	R	W	Bowling 2nd Balls	R	W
116/108	1911–12	A	1	Sydney	L-146	10	9	b	10	14	b	1	210	107	3	180	72	1
117/109			2	Melbourne	W-8w	10	1	lbw	–	–	–	–	138	44	5	193	96	3
118/110			3	Adelaide	W-7w	10	2	*	–	–	–	1	138	71	3	280	105	5
119/111			4	Melbourne	W-I & 225	11	0	c	–	–	–	–	175	74	5	120	47	2
120/112			5	Sydney	W-70	10	5	c	10	4	b	–	114	56	3	234	106	4
122/113	1912	SA	1	Lord's	W-I & 62	10	0	*	–	–	–	1	78	25	5	204	85	6
123/114		A	1	Lord's	D	–	–	–	–	–	–	–	186	74	0	–	–	–
124/115		SA	2	Leeds	W-174	10	0	b	10	15	*	2	132	52	6	128	63	4
126/116		A	2	Manchester	D	10	1	*	–	–	–	–	–	–	–	–	–	–
128/117		SA	3	Oval	W-10w	10	8	c	–	–	–	–	126	28	5	100	29	8
129/118		A	3	Oval	W-244	10	7	c	10	0	c	1	162	30	5	24	18	0
130/119	1913–14	SA	1	Durban[1]	W-I & 157	10	0	ro	–	–	–	1	118	57	5	150	48	5
131/120			2	Johannesburg[1]	W-I & 12	11	0	*	–	–	–	–	161	56	8	232	103	9
132/121			3	Johannesburg[1]	W-91	10	5	b	10	0	b	–	96	26	3	228	102	5
133/122			4	Durban[1]	D	10	4	*	–	–	–	1	179	56	7	192	88	7

Career	M	I	NO	HS	R	Avge	100	50	Ct	St	Balls	R	W	Avge	BB	5w	10w	Rate
Test	27	39	9	38*	242	8.06	–	–	12	–	7873	3106	189	16.43	9-103	24	7	41.65
F/c	133	173	50	93	1573	12.78	–	2	72	–	31521	12289	719	17.09	9-103	68	18	43.84

S. F. BARNES – TEST BOWLING SUMMARY

Series	V	M	Balls	R	W	Avge	BB	5w	10w	Rate
1901–02	A	3	830	323	19	17.00	7-121	3	1	43.68
1902	A	1	192	99	7	14.14	6-49	1	–	27.42
1907–08	A	5	1640	626	24	26.08	7-60	2	–	68.33
1909	A	3	933	340	17	20.00	6-63	2	–	54.88
1911–12	A	5	1782	778	34	22.88	5-44	3	–	53.00
1912	SA	3	768	282	34	8.29	8-29	5	3	22.58
1912	A	3	372	122	5	24.40	5-30	1	–	74.40
1913–14	SA	4	1356	536	49	10.93	9-103	7	3	27.63
	A	20	5749	2288	106	21.58	7-60	12	1	54.23
	SA	7	2124	818	83	9.85	9-103	12	6	25.59
Home		10	2265	843	63	13.38	8-29	9	3	35.95
Overseas		17	5608	2263	126	17.96	9-103	15	4	44.50
Totals		27	7873	3106	189	16.43	9-103	24	7	41.65

BARNES, William

Nottinghamshire (1875 to 1894)

Wisden 1890
TOURS A 1882–83, 1884–85, 1886–87
Born Sutton in Ashfield, Nottinghamshire 27 May 1852
Died Mansfield Woodhouse, Nottinghamshire 24 Mar 1899

For 20 seasons Billy Barnes was a key all-rounder for Nottinghamshire. A tall, adventurous, hard-hitting batsman, particularly strong on the offside, he scored with devastating power between cover-point and mid-off. He was a leading batsman of the 1880s and a most valuable right-handed, fast-medium change bowler who made his debut in the first Test staged in England and became an automatic selection. Although he shared many long opening partnerships with his captain, Arthur Shrewsbury, he once quarrelled with him so severely that he refused to bowl on a pitch that was ideally suited to him (Test *19*). A boisterous character who enjoyed a drink, he once put himself out of action as a result of punching an Australian player and was constantly at odds with his County committee. When the latter eventually dispensed with his services he became a publican but died within five years.

NOTABLE FEATS

- 50 wickets in 20th Test (*20*).
- With A. Shrewsbury added 161 to register England's first hundred partnership for the 5th wkt (Test *23*).

Ref	Series	V	T	Venue	Result	Batting 1st			Batting 2nd			Ct	Bowling 1st			Bowling 2nd		
						No	R	HO	No	R	HO		Balls	R	W	Balls	R	W
4/4	1880	A		Oval	W-5w	4	28	b	5	5	c	2	–	–	–	35	17	1
9/9	1882	A		Oval	L-7	8	5	b	9	2	c	1	–	–	–	48	15	1
10/10	1882–83	A	1	Melbourne	L-9w	10	26	b	10	2	*	1	120	51	2	52	6	1
11/11			2	Melbourne	W-I & 27	6	32	b	–	–	–	2	92	32	2	12	4	0
12/12			3	Sydney	W-69	6	2	c	6	3	lbw	2	52	22	1	–	–	–
13/13			4	Sydney	L-4w	7	2	b	9	20	c	–	40	33	0	64	22	0
14/14	1884	A	1	Manchester	D	7	0	c	6	8	b	1	76	25	1	–	–	–
16/16			3	Oval	D	3	19	c	–	–	–	–	208	81	2	–	–	–
17/17	1884–85	A	1	Adelaide	W-8w	4	134	b	4	28	*	–	56	37	0	124	51	3
18/18			2	Melbourne	W-10w	3	58	b	–	–	–	5	200	50	3	155	31	6
19/19			3	Sydney	L-6	4	0	st	4	5	c	2	–	–	–	–	–	–
20/20			4	Sydney	L-8w	4	50	b	4	20	c	1	143	61	4	36	15	1
21/21			5	Melbourne	W-I & 98	2	74	c	–	–	–	–	112	47	2	–	–	–
23/23	1886	A	2	Lord's	W-I & 106	6	58	c	–	–	–	–	59	25	3	40	18	1
24/24			3	Oval	W-I & 217	5	3	c	–	–	–	–	–	–	–	28	10	0
25/25	1886–87	A	1	Sydney	W-13	3	0	c	3	32	c	1	89	19	2	184	28	6
28/28	1888	A	1	Lord's	L-61	3	3	c	9	1	st	1	24	17	0	–	–	–
29/29			2	Oval	W-I & 137	6	62	c	–	–	–	–	64	18	2	116	32	5
30/30			3	Manchester	W-I & 21	5	24	b	–	–	–	–	–	–	–	–	–	–
33/33	1890	A	1	Lord's	W-7w	8	9	b	–	–	–	2	30	16	1	30	10	1
34/34			2	Oval	W-2w	7	5	c	8	5	lbw	–	–	–	–	–	–	–

Career	M	I	NO	HS	R	Avge	100	50	Ct	St	Balls	R	W	Avge	BB	5w	10w	Rate
Test	21	33	2	134	725	23.38	1	5	19	–	2289	793	51	15.54	6-28	3	–	44.88
F/c	459	725	60	160	15425	23.19	21	69	342	3	42248	15548	902	17.11	8-64	45	11	46.83

Billy Barnes

W. BARNES – TEST BOWLING SUMMARY

Series	V	M	Balls	R	W	Avge	BB	5w	10w	Rate
1880	A	1	35	17	1	17.00	1-17	–	–	35.00
1882	A	1	48	15	1	15.00	1-15	–	–	48.00
1882–83	A	4	432	170	6	28.33	2-32	–	–	72.00
1884	A	2	284	106	3	35.33	2-81	–	–	94.66
1884–85	A	5	826	292	19	15.36	6-31	–	–	43.47
1886	A	2	127	53	4	13.25	3-25	–	–	31.75
1886–87	A	1	273	47	8	5.87	6-28	1	–	34.12
1888	A	3	204	67	7	9.57	5-32	1	–	29.14
1890	A	2	60	26	2	13.00	1-10	–	–	30.00
Home		11	758	284	18	15.77	5-32	1	–	42.11
Overseas		10	1531	509	33	15.42	6-28	2	–	46.39
Totals		21	2289	793	51	15.54	6-28	3	–	44.88

BARNETT
Charles John

Gloucestershire (1927 to 1948)

Wisden 1937
TOURS
A 1936–37; I 1933–34, 1953–54 (Cwlth); SL 1933–34
Born Fairview, Cheltenham, Gloucestershire 3 Jul 1910

Within five years of starting his career at the age of 16 as an amateur middle-order batsman, Charlie Barnett had turned professional and been promoted to opener. A natural timer of the ball with a wonderfully vertical arc to his strokes, he rapidly developed into one of the most entertaining and aggressive openers the game has ever seen. His strong wrists and fore-arms enabled him to drive even balls short of a good length and he was an excellent cutter. A fearless and dynamic destroyer of new-ball bowling, he completed his hundred off the first ball after lunch against an Australian attack which included McCormick and O'Reilly, the closest that any England batsman has come to achieving a pre-lunch century on the first day of a Test. The Second World War stole six of his prime seasons but, reverting to his mid-order role, he made four Test appearances afterwards. A handy medium-fast bowler who frequently took the new ball, and an outstanding outfielder, he returned to his own school, Wycliffe College, as coach.

Ref	Series	V	T	Venue	Result	Batting 1st No	R	HO	Batting 2nd No	R	HO	Ct	Bowling 1st Balls	R	W	Bowling 2nd Balls	R	W
229/203	1933	WI	3	Oval	W-I & 17	8	52	ro	–	–	–	2	–	–	–	–	–	–
230/204	1933–34	I	1	Bombay[1]	W-9w	3	33	c	3	17	*	–	12	1	0	–	–	–
231/205			2	Calcutta	D	3	8	lbw	2	0	c	1	–	–	–	12	7	0
232/206			3	Madras[1]	W-202	6	4	c	3	26	c	3	–	–	–	6	1	0
254/223	1936	I	3	Oval	W-9w	1	43	lbw	1	32	*	–	–	–	–	–	–	–
255/224	1936–37	A	1	Brisbane[2]	W-322	2	69	c	2	26	c	1	–	–	–	–	–	–
256/225			2	Sydney	W-I & 22	2	57	b	–	–	–	–	–	–	–	–	–	–
257/226			3	Melbourne	L-365	2	11	c	2	23	lbw	1	–	–	–	–	–	–
258/227			4	Adelaide	L-148	2	129	lbw	2	21	c	–	–	–	–	40	15	0
259/228			5	Melbourne	L-I & 200	1	18	c	1	41	lbw	–	–	–	–	–	–	–
260/229	1937	NZ	1	Lord's	D	6	5	b	4	83	*	–	–	–	–	–	–	–
261/230			2	Manchester	W-130	1	62	c	1	12	lbw	–	–	–	–	–	–	–
262/231			3	Oval	D	1	13	c	1	21	c	1	–	–	–	–	–	–
263/232	1938	A	1	Nottingham	D	1	126	b	–	–	–	–	–	–	–	6	10	0
264/233			2	Lord's	D	1	18	c	1	12	c	2	–	–	–	–	–	–
265/234			4	Leeds	L-5w	2	30	c	2	29	c	1	–	–	–	–	–	–
286/254	1947	SA	2	Lord's	W-10w	5	33	b	–	–	–	1	–	–	–	–	–	–
287/255			3	Manchester	W-7w	5	5	c	5	19	*	1	48	11	0	30	12	0
288/256			4	Leeds	W-10w	5	6	c	–	–	–	–	–	–	–	–	–	–
299/262	1948	A	1	Nottingham	L-8w	6	8	b	6	6	c	–	102	36	0	–	–	–

Career	M	I	NO	HS	R	Avge	100	50	Ct	St	Balls	R	W	Avge	BB	5w	10w	Rate
Test	20	35	4	129	1098	35.41	2	5	14	–	256	93	0	–	–	–	–	–
F/c	498	821	45	259	25389	32.71	48	113	319	–	28227	12207	394	30.98	6-17	12	2	71.64

Charlie Barnett square cuts Fleetwood-Smith during his meteoric innings at Trent Bridge against the 1938 Australians. The wicket-keeper is Ben Barnett.

C. J. BARNETT – TEST BATTING SUMMARY

Series	V	M	I	NO	HS	R	Avge	100	50
1933	WI	1	1	–	52	52	52.00	–	1
1933–34	I	3	6	1	33	88	17.60	–	–
1936	I	1	2	1	43	75	75.00	–	–
1936–37	A	5	9	–	129	395	43.88	1	2
1937	NZ	3	6	1	83*	196	39.20	–	2
1938	A	3	5	–	126	215	43.00	1	–
1947	SA	3	4	1	33	63	21.00	–	–
1948	A	1	2	–	8	14	7.00	–	–
	A	9	16	–	129	624	39.00	2	2
	SA	3	4	1	33	63	21.00	–	–
	WI	1	1	–	52	52	52.00	–	1
	NZ	3	6	1	83*	196	39.20	–	2
	I	4	8	2	43	163	27.16	–	–
Home		12	20	3	126	615	36.17	1	3
Overseas		8	15	1	129	483	34.50	1	2
Totals		20	35	4	129	1098	35.41	2	5

NOTABLE FEATS

- 1000 runs in 16th Test (*265*) (29 inns).
- Scored 98 before lunch on first day (England record), off-driving a boundary off the next ball (Test *263*).
- Exceeded 1000 runs in a season 12 times, including 2000 on 4 occasions, and scored 4 double centuries.
- Scored 194 in under 4 hours, hitting 11 sixes (Gloucestershire record), v Somerset at Bath in 1934.
- Was the first overseas player to score a hundred on his first-class debut in Ceylon – 116 in 125 min for MCC v Ceylon in 1933–34.

BARNETT, Kim John

Derbyshire (1979 to date)
Boland (1982–83 to 1987–88)

Wisden 1989
TOURS
NZ 1979–80 (Robins);
SL 1985–86 (Eng B)
Born Stoke-on-Trent, Staffordshire
17 Jul 1960

An attacking strokemaker with a sound defence, equally at home opening or in the middle order, Kim Barnett celebrated his Test debut with a mature innings of 66 and was selected for the following winter's aborted tour of India. A powerful striker of the ball, particularly square on either side of the wicket, he can also adopt a more defensive role. Appointed Derbyshire's youngest captain when only 22, he has become a sound tactician and popular leader who must be a strong contender for the England mantle. One criticism of his captaincy would be that he makes too little use of his ability as a leg-break and googly bowler. A fearless short-leg fielder.

Kim Barnett (right) with Neil Foster and two other players making their Test debuts for England against Sri Lanka at Lord's, 1988: 'Syd' Lawrence and 'Jack' Russell.

					Batting 1st			Batting 2nd				Bowling 1st			Bowling 2nd		
Ref	Series	V	T Venue	Result	No	R	HO	No	R	HO	Ct	Balls	R	W	Balls	R	W
1103/651	1988	SL	Lord's	W-7w	4	66	c	3	0	c	1	–	–	–	–	–	–

Career	M	I	NO	HS	R	Avge	100	50	Ct	St	Balls	R	W	Avge	BB	5w	10w	Rate
Test	1	2	–	66	66	33.00	–	1	1	–	–	–	–	–	–	–	–	–
F/c	241	384	33	239*	12850	36.60	25	68	153	–	6326	3367	75	44.89	6-115	1	–	84.34

BARRATT, Fred

Nottinghamshire (1914 to 1931)

TOURS A 1929–30; NZ 1929–30
Born Annesley, Nottinghamshire
12 Apr 1894
Died Nottingham 29 Jan 1947

A tall (6ft 1in), heftily built miner, Fred Barratt had a simple cricketing philosophy: to bowl as fast as humanly possible and to hit the ball out of the ground. From a modest 10-pace approach, his high, right-arm action made maximum use of his massive shoulders and once sent a bail 38 yards; and he developed into a powerful lower-order batsman. A strong driver, he was capable of despatching all types of bowling with great freedom. He twice hit three sixes off successive balls and his career-best 139* (v Warwickshire in 1928) included 7 sixes and took only 84 minutes. War interrupted his career immediately after he had become the only Nottinghamshire bowler to take 100 wickets in his first season. Although he passed the 100-mark four more times and once achieved the 'double', he met with scant success at Test level. He was a daunting full-back for Aston Villa and Sheffield Wednesday. [*Illus. p.* 459]

NOTABLE FEATS

- Took 8 for 91 on debut (v MCC at Lord's) and accounted for 115 wickets in his first season (1914), the fifth of 11 bowlers to achieve this feat.
- In 1928 (his benefit season), he achieved Nottinghamshire's first 'double' since 1906.

Ref	Series	V	T	Venue	Result	Batting 1st No	R	HO	Batting 2nd No	R	HO	Ct	Bowling 1st Balls	R	W	Bowling 2nd Balls	R	W
184/170	1929	SA	4	Manchester	W-I & 32	9	2	*	–	–	–	1	60	8	1	120	30	1
186/172	1929–30	NZ	1	Christchurch	W-8w	9	4	st	–	–	–	1	24	8	0	54	16	1
187/173			2	Wellington	D	9	5	b	–	–	–	–	198	87	0	–	–	–
188/174			3	Auckland	D	–	–	–	–	–	–	–	72	26	1	–	–	–
189/175			4	Auckland	D	9	17	c	–	–	–	–	222	60	1	–	–	–

Career	M	I	NO	HS	R	Avge	100	50	Ct	St	Balls	R	W	Avge	BB	5w	10w	Rate
Test	5	4	1	17	28	9.33	–	–	2	–	750	235	5	47.00	1-8	–	–	150.00
F/c	371	467	52	139*	6445	15.53	2	24	174	–	64803	27811	1224	22.72	8-26	69	11	52.94

BARRINGTON Kenneth Frank

Surrey (1953 to 1968)

Wisden 1960
TOURS
A 1962–63, 1965–66; SA 1960–61 (Cav), 1964–65; WI 1959–60, 1967–68; NZ 1962–63; I 1961–62, 1963–64; P 1955–56, 1961–62; Z 1959–60 (Surrey)
Born Reading, Berkshire 24 Nov 1930
Died Needham's Point, Bridgetown, Barbados 14 Mar 1981

Ken Barrington during his innings of 121 in the Second Test against West Indies on the 1959–60 tour.

Ken Barrington converted himself from a flowing front-foot strokemaker into a solid batting fortress, his immense patience and intense determination enabling him to become one of the most prolific and consistent of post-war batsmen. Five years elapsed between his arrival at The Oval as a bowler and his first-class debut as a front-line batsman. Then there was a four-year hiatus between his premature introduction to Test cricket and the start of his long and productive tenure as the backbone of England's batting; a period spent in eliminating risky strokes and tightening up his defence. A shade above average height at 5ft 10½in, he was stockily built with powerful arms and abundant courage; a technically sound middle-order batsman who evolved a highly effective back-foot method founded on a square-shouldered stance. Apart from the cut, this method restricted his off-side strokes but it produced a powerful on-side repertoire and a virtually impregnable defence. The price he had to pay was a reputation as a slow scorer and as a saver of matches rather than a winner of them. He was a right-arm leg-break and googly bowler with good control who spun the ball sharply; although he often headed the bowling averages on overseas tours, he was given few bowling opportunities on the slow pitches at home. A capable fielder, he was originally an expert slip but his later years in the deep revealed a powerful and accurate throwing arm. A mild heart attack compelled his premature retirement and was a prelude to the fatal one that befell him in Barbados when he was England's assistant-manager; he had been a Test selector since 1975. A kind, cheerful and humorous man, his skill at clowning and mime, discouraged by the Surrey committee, made him a great favourite with overseas crowds. His technical knowledge and abiding interest in cars found a perfect outlet when he invested in a motoring business at Great Bookham.

NOTABLE FEATS

- 1000 runs in 15th Test (*495*) (22 inns); 2000 runs in 25th Test (*515*) (41 inns); 3000 runs in 38th Test (*540*) (61 inns); 4000 runs in 51st Test (*565*) (82 inns); 5000 runs in 61st Test (*596*) (97 inns); 6000 runs in 72nd Test (*621*) (116 inns).
- *513* Batted over 9 hours in the match without being dismissed.
- *517* Record series aggregate of 594 runs in E v I Tests.
- *538* Second batsman after J. Darling (1897–98) to complete 100 in E v A Tests with a six.
- *543* For the first time in England, 3 players from the same county occupied the first 3 places in E's batting order: M.J. Stewart, J.H. Edrich and Barrington of Surrey.
- *564* His 10th Test 100 was his first in England; his score of 256 remains England's highest at Manchester and his batting time of 683 min the second-longest first-class inns by an Englishman.
- *571* First to score 100 in all 7 current Test-playing countries; shared record 6th-wkt E v SA stand of 206* with J.M. Parks.

TEST NOTES

• *490* Retired hurt at 161–3 (1st inns); resumed at 219–7.

• *491* Retired hurt when 23* at 256–3 (1st inns); resumed at 268–4.

• *598* Deputised as wicket-keeper for J.M. Parks on fourth day from start of Australia's 2nd inns until tea and caught R.B. Simpson.

• *638* Retired hurt when 61* at 271–4; resumed at 330–6.

NOTABLE FEATS *cont.*

• *573* 'Walked' after being given 'not out' in response to appeal for a catch by the wicket-keeper.

• *591* His 137 occupied 437 min and resulted in him being dropped for the next Test; his score remained on 85 for 62 min while 20 overs were bowled.

• *593* Shared record stand for any wkt in E v NZ Tests with J.H. Edrich: 369 in 339 min.

• *600* Scored his 10th consecutive 50 in first-class matches at the Adelaide Oval: 104, 52, 52*, 63, 132* (in 1962–63); 69, 51, 63, 60, 102 (in 1965–66).

• *601* First to reach 100 with a six twice in E v A Tests.

• *621* Shared record E v P 3rd-wkt stand of 201 in 223 min with T.W. Graveney.

• *623* First to score a Test 100 on each of England's 6 current Test grounds.

• *628* Completed his fourth 100 in successive Tests (with a six) and surpassed L. Hutton's world Test record of 52 fifties.

• Exceeded 1000 runs in a season 12 times, including 2000 on 3 occasions.

						Batting 1st			Batting 2nd				Bowling 1st			Bowling 2nd		
Ref	Series	V	T	Venue	Result	No	R	HO	No	R	HO	Ct	Balls	R	W	Balls	R	W
408/322	1955	SA	1	Nottingham	W-I & 5	5	0	c	–	–	–	–	–	–	–	–	–	–
409/323			2	Lord's	W-71	5	34	b	5	18	c	–	–	–	–	–	–	–
474/354	1959	I	1	Nottingham	W-I & 59	5	56	b	–	–	–	1	–	–	–	–	–	–
475/355			2	Lord's	W-8w	5	80	c	–	–	–	–	–	–	–	–	–	–
476/356			3	Leeds	W-I & 173	5	80	c	–	–	–	1	–	–	–	–	–	–
477/357			4	Manchester	W-171	5	87	lbw	6	46	lbw	2	84	36	3	162	75	2
478/358			5	Oval	W-I & 27	5	8	c	–	–	–	1	36	24	0	–	–	–
487/359	1959–60	WI	1	Bridgetown	D	3	128	c	–	–	–	–	108	60	1	–	–	–
488/360			2	Port-of-Spain	W-256	3	121	c	3	49	c	2	96	15	0	155	34	2
489/361			3	Kingston	D	3	16	c	3	4	lbw	–	126	38	1	24	0	0
490/362			4	Georgetown	D	4	27	c	7	0	c	–	36	22	0	–	–	–
491/363			5	Port-of-Spain	D	5	69	c	6	6	c	–	48	21	0	48	27	1
493/365	1960	SA	2	Lord's	W-I & 73	4	24	lbw	–	–	–	–	–	–	–	–	–	–
494/366			3	Nottingham	W-8w	4	80	c	4	1	*	–	–	–	–	18	5	0
495/367			4	Manchester	D	5	76	b	7	35	c	–	–	–	–	–	–	–
496/368			5	Oval	D	4	1	lbw	4	10	c	–	–	–	–	–	–	–
507/369	1961	A	1	Birmingham	D	5	21	c	5	48	*	1	–	–	–	–	–	–
508/370			2	Lord's	L-5w	6	4	c	6	66	lbw	2	–	–	–	–	–	–
509/371			3	Leeds	W-8w	6	6	c	–	–	–	–	–	–	–	–	–	–
510/372			4	Manchester	L-54	6	78	c	6	5	lbw	1	–	–	–	–	–	–
511/373			5	Oval	D	6	53	c	6	83	c	–	–	–	–	–	–	–
512/374	1961–62	P	1	Lahore[2]	W-5w	3	139	ro	3	6	lbw	–	36	25	0	–	–	–
513/375	1961–62	I	1	Bombay[2]	D	3	151	*	3	52	*	1	–	–	–	18	18	0
514/376			2	Kanpur	D	3	21	b	3	172	ro	–	–	–	–	–	–	–
515/377			3	Delhi	D	3	113	*	–	–	–	–	54	39	0	–	–	–
516/378			4	Calcutta	L-187	3	14	b	3	3	c	1	–	–	–	–	–	–
517/379			5	Madras[2]	L-128	3	20	c	3	48	lbw	–	–	–	–	–	–	–
518/380	1961–62	P	2	Dacca	D	3	84	b	–	–	–	1	66	39	0	126	17	0
530/382	1962	P	1	Birmingham	W-I & 24	5	9	lbw	–	–	–	1	12	0	0	–	–	–
531/383			2	Lord's	W-9w	5	0	c	–	–	–	–	–	–	–	6	8	0
532/384			3	Leeds	W-I & 117	5	1	c	–	–	–	2	–	–	–	6	4	0
534/386			5	Oval	W-10w	4	50	*	–	–	–	–	–	–	–	12	10	0
535/387	1962–63	A	1	Brisbane[2]	D	5	78	c	5	23	c	1	96	44	1	–	–	–
536/388			2	Melbourne	W-7w	5	35	lbw	5	0	*	2	48	23	0	40	22	0
537/389			3	Sydney	L-8w	5	35	lbw	5	21	b	1	64	43	0	–	–	–
538/390			4	Adelaide	D	3	63	b	3	132	*	2	–	–	–	–	–	–
539/391			5	Sydney	D	3	101	c	3	94	c	–	–	–	–	64	22	0
540/392	1962–63	NZ	1	Auckland	W-I & 215	3	126	c	–	–	–	1	72	38	0	–	–	–
541/393			2	Wellington	W-I & 47	3	76	c	–	–	–	3	15	1	1	66	32	3
542/394			3	Christchurch	W-7w	3	47	lbw	1	45	c	1	30	18	0	–	–	–
543/395	1963	WI	1	Manchester	L-10w	3	16	c	4	8	b	–	–	–	–	–	–	–
544/396			2	Lord's	D	4	80	c	4	60	c	1	–	–	–	–	–	–
545/397			3	Birmingham	W-217	4	9	b	3	1	b	1	–	–	–	–	–	–
546/398			4	Leeds	L-221	4	25	c	4	32	lbw	1	–	–	–	–	–	–
547/399			5	Oval	L-8w	4	16	c	4	28	b	–	–	–	–	–	–	–
553/400	1963–64	I	1	Madras[2]	D	5	80	c	–	–	–	–	24	23	0	12	6	0

Ref	Series	V	T	Venue	Result	Batting 1st No	R	HO	Batting 2nd No	R	HO	Ct	Bowling 1st Balls	R	W	Bowling 2nd Balls	R	W
561/405	1964	A	1	Nottingham	D	5	22	c	4	33	lbw	2	–	–	–	–	–	–
562/406			2	Lord's	D	4	5	lbw	–	–	–	–	–	–	–	–	–	–
563/407			3	Leeds	L-7w	4	29	b	4	85	lbw	1	–	–	–	–	–	–
564/408			4	Manchester	D	4	256	lbw	–	–	–	–	–	–	–	6	4	0
565/409			5	Oval	D	5	47	c	6	54	*	–	–	–	–	–	–	–
571/410	1964–65	SA	1	Durban[2]	W-I & 104	4	148	*	–	–	–	1	–	–	–	–	–	–
572/411			2	Johannesburg[3]	D	4	121	c	–	–	–	–	24	29	0	–	–	–
573/412			3	Cape Town	D	4	49	c	2	14	*	–	–	–	–	19	4	3
574/413			4	Johannesburg[3]	D	4	93	c	4	11	c	–	–	–	–	–	–	–
575/414			5	Port Elizabeth	D	5	72	c	–	–	–	2	–	–	–	–	–	–
591/415	1965	NZ	1	Birmingham	W-9w	4	137	c	–	–	–	1	–	–	–	30	25	0
593/417			3	Leeds	W-I & 187	3	163	c	–	–	–	2	–	–	–	–	–	–
594/418	1965	SA	1	Lord's	D	4	91	ro	4	18	lbw	3	–	–	–	–	–	–
595/419			2	Nottingham	L-94	3	1	b	5	1	c	–	–	–	–	–	–	–
596/420			3	Oval	D	3	18	b	4	73	lbw	2	–	–	–	–	–	–
597/421	1965–66	A	1	Brisbane[2]	D	4	53	b	4	38	c	1	–	–	–	–	–	–
598/422			2	Melbourne	D	4	63	c	–	–	–	2	–	–	–	60	47	2
599/423			3	Sydney	W-I & 93	4	1	c	–	–	–	–	–	–	–	–	–	–
600/424			4	Adelaide	L-I & 9	4	60	lbw	4	102	c	–	–	–	–	–	–	–
601/425			5	Melbourne	D	4	115	c	4	32	*	–	–	–	–	–	–	–
605/429	1966	WI	1	Manchester	L-I & 40	3	5	c	3	30	c	–	–	–	–	–	–	–
606/430			2	Lord's	D	4	19	b	3	5	b	–	–	–	–	–	–	–
618/434	1967	I	1	Leeds	W-6w	3	93	ro	2	46	c	1	–	–	–	54	38	0
619/435			2	Lord's	W-I & 124	2	97	b	–	–	–	–	–	–	–	–	–	–
620/436			3	Birmingham	W-132	3	75	c	3	13	c	1	–	–	–	–	–	–
621/437	1967	P	1	Lord's	D	3	148	c	3	14	b	2	66	29	1	78	23	2
622/438			2	Nottingham	W-10w	3	109	*	–	–	–	1	–	–	–	–	–	–
623/439			3	Oval	W-8w	3	142	c	3	13	*	–	–	–	–	48	29	0
628/440	1967–68	WI	1	Port-of-Spain	D	4	143	c	–	–	–	–	108	44	1	90	69	1
629/441			2	Kingston	D	4	63	c	4	13	lbw	–	–	–	–	36	14	0
630/442			3	Bridgetown	D	4	17	c	–	–	–	1	48	29	1	24	17	0
631/443			4	Port-of-Spain	W-7w	4	48	lbw	–	–	–	1	60	41	1	–	–	–
632/444			5	Georgetown	D	5	4	c	5	0	c	–	108	43	1	–	–	–
638/446	1968	A	2	Lord's	D	5	75	c	–	–	–	–	–	–	–	12	12	1
639/447			3	Birmingham	D	4	0	lbw	–	–	–	1	–	–	–	–	–	–
640/448			4	Leeds	D	5	49	b	5	46	*	2	–	–	–	36	14	0

Career	M	I	NO	HS	R	Avge	100	50	Ct	St	Balls	R	W	Avge	BB	5w	10w	Rate
Test	82	131	15	256	6806	58.67	20	35	58	–	2715	1300	29	44.82	3-4	–	–	93.62
F/c	533	831	136	256	31714	45.63	76	170	515	–	17083	8907	273	32.62	7-40	8	–	62.57

K. F. BARRINGTON – TEST BATTING SUMMARY

Series	V	M	I	NO	HS	R	Avge	100	50
1955	SA	2	3	–	34	52	17.33	–	–
1959	I	5	6	–	87	357	59.50	–	4
1959–60	WI	5	9	–	128	420	46.66	2	1
1960	SA	4	7	1	80	227	37.83	–	2
1961	A	5	9	1	83	364	45.50	–	4
1961–62	P	2	3	–	139	229	76.33	1	1
1961–62	I	5	9	3	172	594	99.00	3	1
1962	P	4	4	1	50*	60	20.00	–	1
1962–63	A	5	10	2	132	582	72.75	2	3
1962–63	NZ	3	4	–	126	294	73.50	1	1
1963	WI	5	10	–	80	275	27.50	–	2
1963–64	I	1	1	–	80	80	80.00	–	1
1964	A	5	8	1	256	531	75.85	1	2
1964–65	SA	5	7	2	148*	508	101.60	2	2
1965	NZ	2	2	–	163	300	150.00	2	–
1965	SA	3	6	–	91	202	33.66	–	2
1965–66	A	5	8	1	115	464	66.28	2	3
1966	WI	2	4	–	30	59	14.75	–	–
1967	I	3	5	–	97	324	64.80	–	3
1967	P	3	5	2	148	426	142.00	3	–
1967–68	WI	5	7	–	143	288	41.14	1	1
1968	A	3	4	1	75	170	56.66	–	1
	A	23	39	6	256	2111	63.96	5	13
	SA	14	23	3	148*	989	49.45	2	6
	WI	17	30	–	143	1042	34.73	3	4
	NZ	5	6	–	163	594	99.00	3	1
	I	14	21	3	172	1355	75.27	3	9
	P	9	12	3	148	715	79.44	4	2
Home		46	73	7	256	3347	50.71	6	21
Overseas		36	58	8	172	3459	69.18	14	14
Totals		82	131	15	256	6806	58.67	20	35

BARTON
Victor Alexander

Kent (1889 to 1890)
Hampshire (1895 to 1902)

TOUR SA 1891–92
Born Hound, Netley, Hampshire 6 Oct 1867
Died Belle Vue, Southampton, Hampshire 23 Mar 1906

An aggressive batsman and useful right-arm medium-pace bowler, Victor Barton was a bombardier when he scored 91 and 102 for the Royal Artillery against MCC at Lord's in 1889. Invited to play for Kent, he failed to gain a regular place but bought his discharge in 1891 and joined Hampshire. By the time they gained first-class status (after his third season), his powerful on-driving had become legendary: 'Fieldsmen who stood at mid-on had a wholesome dread of him.' – *Wisden*. Ill-health compelled his retirement at the age of 34 and he died barely four years later. [*Illus. p.* 201]

						Batting 1st			Batting 2nd			
Ref	Series	V	T	Venue	Result	No	R	HO	No	R	HO	Ct
38/38	1891–92	SA		Cape Town	W-I & 189	5	23	c	–	–	–	–

Career	M	I	NO	HS	R	Avge	100	50	Ct	St	Balls	R	W	Avge	BB	5w	10w	Rate
Test	1	1	0	23	23	23.00	–	–	–	–	–	–	–	–	–	–	–	–
F/c	157	282	15	205	6411	24.01	6	30	101	–	10071	4036	141	28.62	6-28	3	–	71.42

BATES, Willie

Yorkshire (1877 to 1887)

TOURS
A 1881–82, 1882–83, 1884–85, 1886–87, 1887–88
Born Lascelles Hall, Huddersfield, Yorkshire 19 Nov 1855
Died Lepton, Yorkshire 8 Jan 1900

Billy Bates was one of Yorkshire's finest all-rounders; a dynamic, hard-hitting middle-order batsman and a round-arm off-break bowler who spun the ball prodigiously from an immaculate length. The fact that his fielding, although enthusiastic, often involved his muffing the simplest of catches probably explains why, although he toured Australia five times, he was never selected for a Test at home. When only 33 and at the height of his powers, his career was terminated when he was blinded in one eye by a ball struck by a team-mate in the Melbourne nets. His son, W.E. Bates, scored nearly 16,000 runs for Yorkshire and Glamorgan.

Billy Bates

NOTABLE FEATS
- 50 wickets in 15th Test (*26*).
- Achieved the first hat-trick for England when he dismissed P.S. McDonnell, G. Giffen and G.J. Bonnor in the first innings of Test *11*. He went on to become the first player to score 50 and take 10 or more wickets in the same Test.

TEST NOTES
- *21* Retired ill when 54* at 214–4; resumed at 324–6.

						Batting 1st			Batting 2nd				Bowling 1st			Bowling 2nd		
Ref	Series	V	T	Venue	Result	No	R	HO	No	R	HO	Ct	Balls	R	W	Balls	R	W
5/5	1881–82	A	1	Melbourne	D	4	58	c	4	47	c	–	164	43	2	52	43	2
6/6			2	Sydney	L-5w	4	4	st	4	5	b	1	288	52	4	96	37	1
7/7			3	Sydney	L-6w	4	1	c	4	2	c	1	152	67	3	99	43	1
8/8			4	Melbourne	D	4	23	st	4	52	*	–	113	49	3	–	–	–

Ref	Series	V	T	Venue	Result	Batting 1st			Batting 2nd			Ct	Bowling 1st			Bowling 2nd		
						No	R	HO	No	R	HO		Balls	R	W	Balls	R	W
10/10	1882–83	A	1	Melbourne	L-9w	7	28	c	8	11	c	–	84	31	1	53	22	0
11/11			2	Melbourne	W-I & 27	9	55	c	–	–	–	1	106	28	7	132	74	7
12/12			3	Sydney	W-69	8	17	c	8	4	c	1	180	55	1	–	–	–
13/13			4	Sydney	L-4w	8	9	c	7	48	*	2	60	24	1	156	52	2
17/17	1884–85	A	1	Adelaide	W-8w	5	18	c	–	–	–	–	97	31	5	36	26	0
18/18			2	Melbourne	W-10w	4	35	b	–	–	–	1	68	17	0	–	–	–
19/19			3	Sydney	L-6	5	12	c	5	31	c	–	24	6	0	80	24	5
20/20			4	Sydney	L-8w	5	64	c	5	1	c	1	68	44	0	–	–	–
21/21			5	Melbourne	W-I & 98	6	61	c	–	–	–	1	–	–	–	–	–	–
25/25	1886–87	A	1	Sydney	W-13	1	8	c	1	24	b	–	84	19	1	68	8	0
26/26			2	Sydney	W-71	2	8	c	2	30	b	–	–	–	–	104	26	4

Career	M	I	NO	HS	R	Avge	100	50	Ct	St	Balls	R	W	Avge	BB	5w	10w	Rate
Test	15	26	2	64	656	27.33	–	5	9	–	2364	821	50	16.42	7-28	4	1	47.28
F/c	299	495	20	144*	10249	21.57	10	47	328	–	61033	14980	874	17.13	8-21	52	10	69.83

W. BATES – TEST BOWLING SUMMARY

Series	V	M	Balls	R	W	Avge	BB	5w	10w	Rate
1881–82	A	4	964	334	16	20.81	4-52	–	–	60.25
1882–83	A	4	771	286	19	15.05	7-28	2	1	40.57
1884–85	A	5	373	148	10	14.80	5-24	2	–	37.30
1886–87	A	2	256	53	5	10.60	4-26	–	–	51.20
Totals		15	2364	821	50	16.42	7-28	4	1	47.28

BEAN, George

Nottinghamshire (1885)
Sussex (1886 to 1898)

TOUR A 1891–92
Born Sutton in Ashfield, Nottinghamshire 7 Mar 1864
Died Mansfield, Nottinghamshire 16 Mar 1923

A fast-scoring middle-order or opening batsman, handy right-arm medium-pace change bowler and specialist cover-point, George Bean moved to Sussex after a single season with his native Nottinghamshire. At Hove his keen appetite for the cut was handsomely rewarded by the short pavilion boundary. He scored 145* and 92 against his original county at Hove in 1891, just failing to become only the second batsman after W.G. Grace to score a hundred in each innings of a first-class match. He spent his final years as a senior member of the MCC groundstaff.

Lord Sheffield's team to Australia, 1891–92: standing H. Philipson, O.G. Radcliffe, W. Attewell, G. Bean, A. Shaw (manager); seated A.E. Stoddart, G.A. Lohman, W.G. Grace (captain), R. Abel, J.M. Read; in front G. MacGregor, J. Briggs, J.W. Sharpe.

Ref	Series	V	T	Venue	Result	Batting 1st No	R	HO	Batting 2nd No	R	HO	Ct
35/35	1891–92	A	1	Melbourne	L-54	3	50	c	3	3	c	–
36/36			2	Sydney	L-72	3	19	b	3	4	c	1
37/37			3	Adelaide	W-I & 230	5	16	c	–	–	–	3

Career	M	I	NO	HS	R	Avge	100	50	Ct	St	Balls	R	W	Avge	BB	5w	10w	Rate
Test	3	5	0	50	92	18.40	–	1	4	–	–	–	–	–	–	–	–	–
F/c	247	438	21	186	8634	20.70	9	40	145	–	17076	7087	260	27.25	8-29	9	2	65.67

BEDSER
Alec Victor CBE

Surrey (1939 to 1960)

Wisden 1947
TOURS A 1946–47, 1950–51, 1954–55; SA 1948–49; NZ 1946–47, 1950–51; I 1956–57 (Howard); Z 1959–60 (Surrey)
Born Reading, Berkshire 4 Jul 1918

Alec Bedser

From an economic six strides and a bound, this tall (6ft 3in), massively built right-arm bowler extracted such control and varied late movement, all at fast-medium pace, that Sir Donald Bradman rates him as the most difficult he had to face. Alec Bedser ranks as one of the great bowlers: he had a perfect harmonious action, his left arm flung high, his powerful body pivoting on a firmly braced left leg, and a flowing follow-through. His huge hands commanded sensitive seam control; his stock ball was the inswinger but he could combine this with a lethal leg-cutter which turned like a fast bouncing leg-break in responsive conditions. For eight seasons after the Second World War he virtually carried the England new-ball attack on his broad shoulders, and he was a major contributor to Surrey's seven consecutive Championship titles in the 1950s. A steadfast batsman with method based on a straight-batted firm-footed defence, he was an extremely valuable nightwatchman. An intensely loyal man who enjoyed an exemplary playing career, he thrived on hard work and became very successful in commerce after his retirement. He continued to find time for cricket: appointed an England selector in 1962, he was chairman for a record term of 13 seasons (1969 to 1981); he managed the 1974–75 and 1979–80 tours of Australia and was assistant to the Duke of Norfolk on the 1962–63 visit; in 1987 Surrey accorded him its greatest honour and made him president. His confusingly identical twin brother Eric was an off-spinning all-rounder in Surrey's finest years and they remain inseparable.

NOTABLE FEATS

- 50 wickets in 12th Test (*299*); 100 wickets in 26th Test (*326*); 150 wickets in 36th Test (*336*); 200 wickets in 44th Test (*373*) – first to take 200 wickets for England.
- *277* Took 11 wickets for second match in succession – career figures of 22 wickets at 10.81 runs apiece after 2 Tests.
- *300* Dismissed D.G. Bradman for fifth time in successive Test innings.
- *372* Australia lost last 7 1st-inns wickets for 12 runs to Bedser, T.E. Bailey and the new ball. Bedser's match analysis of 14 for 99 remains the Test record for Nottingham and was the best by an England bowler since 1934.
- *375* Passed C.V. Grimmett's world record of 216 Test wickets.
- *376* Dismissed A.R. Morris for the 18th time in 20 Tests. Surpassed M.W. Tate's record by taking 39 wickets in an E v A rubber.
- Exceeded 100 wickets in a season on 11 occasions, including 150 twice.
- Hat-trick for Surrey v Essex at The Oval in 1953.

Ref	Series	V	T	Venue	Result	Batting 1st No	Batting 1st R	Batting 1st HO	Batting 2nd No	Batting 2nd R	Batting 2nd HO	Ct	Bowling 1st Balls	Bowling 1st R	Bowling 1st W	Bowling 2nd Balls	Bowling 2nd R	Bowling 2nd W
276/244	1946	I	1	Lord's	W-10w	9	30	b	–	–	–	–	175	49	7	193	96	4
277/245			2	Manchester	D	10	8	lbw	–	–	–	3	156	41	4	150	52	7
278/246			3	Oval	D	–	–	–	–	–	–	–	192	60	2	–	–	–
279/247	1946–47	A	1	Brisbane[2]	L-I & 332	10	0	lbw	10	18	c	1	328	159	2	–	–	–
280/248			2	Sydney	L-I & 33	10	14	b	10	3	*	–	368	153	1	–	–	–
281/249			3	Melbourne	D	10	27	*	8	25	lbw	–	248	99	3	275	176	3
282/250			4	Adelaide	D	9	2	b	9	3	c	2	240	97	3	120	68	0
283/251			5	Sydney	L-5w	10	10	*	9	4	st	–	216	49	2	176	75	2
284/252	1946–47	NZ		Christchurch	D	9	8	*	–	–	–	1	234	95	4	–	–	–
285/253	1947	SA	1	Nottingham	D	8	7	c	8	2	c	–	343	106	3	84	31	1
286/254			2	Lord's	W-10w	9	0	b	–	–	–	1	156	76	0	84	20	0
299/262	1948	A	1	Nottingham	L-8w	10	22	c	10	3	*	–	266	113	3	87	46	2
300/263			2	Lord's	L-409	10	9	b	10	9	c	1	258	100	4	204	112	1
301/264			3	Manchester	D	9	37	ro	–	–	–	–	216	81	4	114	27	0
302/265			4	Leeds	L-7w	4	79	c	9	17	c	–	188	92	3	126	56	0
303/266			5	Oval	L-I & 149	9	0	b	9	0	b	–	188	61	1	–	–	–
309/267	1948–49	SA	1	Durban[2]	W-2w	9	11	c	9	1	*	1	109	39	4	144	51	2
310/268			2	Johannesburg[2]	D	9	12	b	–	–	–	–	176	42	1	136	51	1
311/269			3	Cape Town	D	9	16	b	–	–	–	1	272	92	0	56	40	0
312/270			4	Johannesburg[2]	D	8	1	lbw	7	19	b	–	192	81	2	136	54	1
313/271			5	Port Elizabeth	W-3w	8	33	c	5	1	c	1	304	61	4	128	43	1
314/272	1949	NZ	1	Leeds	D	9	20	c	–	–	–	3	132	56	0	54	26	0
317/275			4	Oval	D	9	0	c	–	–	–	1	186	74	4	138	59	3
324/277	1950	WI	2	Lord's	L-326	10	5	b	10	0	b	–	240	60	3	264	80	1
325/278			3	Nottingham	L-10w	10	13	c	10	2	b	–	288	127	5	66	35	0
326/279			4	Oval	L-I & 56	9	0	lbw	9	0	c	–	228	75	2	–	–	–
327/280	1950–51	A	1	Brisbane[2]	L-70	–	–	–	5	0	c	1	133	45	4	53	9	3
328/281			2	Melbourne	L-28	10	4	*	10	14	*	1	152	37	4	131	43	2
329/282			3	Sydney	L-I & 13	9	3	b	9	4	b	2	344	107	4	–	–	–
330/283			4	Adelaide	L-274	8	7	lbw	7	0	c	1	208	74	3	200	62	0
331/284			5	Melbourne	W-8w	8	11	b	–	–	–	–	176	46	5	163	59	5
332/285	1950–51	NZ	1	Christchurch	D	8	5	c	–	–	–	–	246	83	1	–	–	–
333/286			2	Wellington	W-6w	9	28	b	–	–	–	1	114	21	0	144	34	1
334/287	1951	SA	1	Nottingham	L-71	10	0	*	10	0	b	–	378	122	3	136	37	6
335/288			2	Lord's	W-10w	9	26	*	–	–	–	–	48	7	0	144	53	2
336/289			3	Manchester	W-9w	9	30	*	–	–	–	–	195	58	7	146	54	5
337/290			4	Leeds	D	8	8	b	–	–	–	1	348	113	2	24	5	0
338/291			5	Oval	W-4w	9	2	c	–	–	–	–	117	36	2	119	32	3
351/297	1952	I	1	Leeds	W-7w	10	7	b	–	–	–	–	198	38	2	126	32	2
352/298			2	Lord's	W-8w	10	3	c	–	–	–	1	198	62	2	216	60	2
353/299			3	Manchester	W-I & 207	9	17	c	–	–	–	–	66	19	2	90	27	5
354/300			4	Oval	D	–	–	–	–	–	–	–	89	41	5	–	–	–
372/301	1953	A	1	Nottingham	D	10	2	lbw	–	–	–	–	231	55	7	104	44	7
373/302			2	Lord's	D	10	1	b	–	–	–	–	256	105	5	191	77	3
374/303			3	Manchester	D	11	10	b	–	–	–	–	270	115	5	24	14	2
375/304			4	Leeds	D	11	0	*	11	3	*	–	173	95	6	102	65	1
376/305			5	Oval	W-8w	11	22	*	–	–	–	1	174	88	3	66	24	0
388/312	1954	P	2	Nottingham	W-I & 129	–	–	–	–	–	–	–	126	30	2	180	83	2
389/313			3	Manchester	D	9	22	*	–	–	–	–	95	36	3	48	9	3
391/315	1954–55	A	1	Brisbane[2]	L-I & 154	8	5	b	8	5	c	1	296	131	1	–	–	–
410/324	1955	SA	3	Manchester	L-3w	11	1	lbw	10	3	c	–	186	92	2	60	61	2

Career	M	I	NO	HS	R	Avge	100	50	Ct	St	Balls	R	W	Avge	BB	5w	10w	Rate
Test	51	71	15	79	714	12.75	–	1	26	–	15918	5876	236	24.89	7-44	15	5	67.44
F/c	485	576	181	126	5735	14.51	1	13	289	–	106192	39279	1924	20.41	8-18	96	16	55.19

A. V. BEDSER – TEST BOWLING SUMMARY

Series	V	M	Balls	R	W	Avge	BB	5w	10w	Rate
1946	I	3	866	298	24	12.41	7-49	2	2	36.08
1946–47	A	5	1971	876	16	54.75	3-97	–	–	123.18
1946–47	NZ	1	234	95	4	23.75	4-95	–	–	58.50
1947	SA	2	667	233	4	58.25	3-106	–	–	166.75
1948	A	5	1647	688	18	38.22	4-81	–	–	91.50
1948–49	SA	5	1653	554	16	34.62	4-39	–	–	103.31
1949	NZ	2	510	215	7	30.71	4-74	–	–	72.85
1950	WI	3	1086	377	11	34.27	5-127	1	–	98.72
1950–51	A	5	1560	482	30	16.06	5-46	2	1	52.00
1950–51	NZ	2	504	138	2	69.00	1-34	–	–	252.00
1951	SA	5	1655	517	30	17.23	7-58	3	1	55.16
1952	I	4	983	279	20	13.95	5-27	2	–	49.15
1953	A	5	1591	682	39	17.48	7-44	5	1	40.79
1954	P	2	449	158	10	15.80	3-9	–	–	44.90
1954–55	A	1	296	131	1	131.00	1-131	–	–	296.00
1955	SA	1	246	153	4	38.25	2-61	–	–	61.50
	A	21	7065	2859	104	27.49	7-44	7	2	67.93
	SA	13	4221	1457	54	26.98	7-58	3	1	78.16
	WI	3	1086	377	11	34.27	5-127	1	–	98.72
	NZ	5	1248	448	13	34.46	4-74	–	–	96.00
	I	7	1849	577	44	13.11	7-49	4	2	42.02
	P	2	449	158	10	15.80	3-9	–	–	44.90
Home		32	9700	3600	167	21.55	7-44	13	4	58.08
Overseas		19	6218	2276	69	32.98	5-46	2	1	90.11
Totals		51	15918	5876	236	24.89	7-44	15	5	67.44

BENSON
Mark Richard

Kent (1980 to date)

Born Shoreham, Sussex 6 Jul 1958

Mark Benson is a comfortably built, 5ft 10in tall, left-handed opening batsman with a first-class career average approaching 40. A highly competent player of fast bowling, he can consider himself unlucky to have been given just one opportunity at Test level. That chance came when he was called up as a last-minute replacement for Wayne Larkins against India in 1986. Far from being a failure, he batted 235 minutes for a match aggregate of 51 runs.

Mark Benson

						Batting 1st			Batting 2nd			
Ref	Series	V	T	Venue	Result	No	R	HO	No	R	HO	Ct
1048/625	1986	I	3	Birmingham	D	2	21	b	2	30	b	–

Career	M	I	NO	HS	R	Avge	100	50	Ct	St	Balls	R	W	Avge	BB	5w	10w	Rate
Test	1	2	0	30	51	25.50	–	–	–	–	–	–	–	–	–	–	–	–
F/c	175	300	21	162	10754	38.54	24	65	90	–	275	312	3	104.00	2-55	–	–	91.66

BERRY, Robert

Lancashire (1948 to 1954)
Worcestershire (1955 to 1958)
Derbyshire (1959 to 1962)

TOURS A 1950–51; I 1953–54 (Cwlth)
Born West Gorton, Manchester
29 Jan 1926

NOTABLE FEATS

- Took all 10 Worcestershire wickets for 102 at Blackpool in 1953.

An orthodox left-arm slow bowler, Bob Berry utilised his diminutive stature (5ft 6in) to accentuate a full range of flight variations. In a sensational first Test, Berry (9) shared half the wickets to fall with another slow left-arm debutant, Alf Valentine (11). That was to be the pinnacle of his success; he failed to take a wicket in the next match and, being no great spinner of the ball, endured a disappointing tour of Australia. When he lost his Lancashire place to M.J. Hilton, he moved first to Worcestershire and then to Derbyshire, becoming the first cricketer to be capped by three counties. A left-handed lower-order batsman, he was a most capable outfielder with a strong return. He eventually became landlord of the Black Bull in Mansfield and established a reputation as a pigeon breeder.

Bob Berry

						Batting 1st			Batting 2nd				Bowling 1st			Bowling 2nd		
Ref	Series	V	T	Venue	Result	No	R	HO	No	R	HO	Ct	Balls	R	W	Balls	R	W
323/276	1950	WI	1	Manchester	W-202	11	0	b	11	4	*	2	191	63	5	156	53	4
324/277			2	Lord's	L-326	11	2	c	11	0	*	–	114	45	0	192	67	0

Career	M	I	NO	HS	R	Avge	100	50	Ct	St	Balls	R	W	Avge	BB	5w	10w	Rate
Test	2	4	2	4*	6	3.00	–	–	2	–	653	228	9	25.33	5-63	1	–	72.55
F/c	273	305	112	40	1463	7.58	–	–	138	–	50727	17389	703	24.73	10-102	34	5	72.15

BINKS James Graham

Yorkshire (1955 to 1969)

Wisden 1969
TOURS
I 1961–62, 1963–64; P/SL: 1961–62
Born Hull, Yorkshire 5 Oct 1935

An elegant, undemonstrative wicket-keeper, Jimmy Binks was extremely unlucky to be given so few opportunities at international level. He was a highly skilled technician, particularly impressive when standing up to spin bowlers. A lower-order batsman, he was employed as a makeshift opener during his two Test matches in India. He emigrated to America in the mid-1980s. [*Illus. p.* 329]

NOTABLE FEATS

- Made 107 first-class dismissals in 1960 (Yorkshire record), establishing world record of 96 catches in a season.
- Appeared in 412 consecutive County Championship matches between 1955 and 1969, missing only one of the 492 matches played by Yorkshire during his career.

						Batting 1st			Batting 2nd			Fielding 1st				Fielding 2nd			
Ref	Series	V	T	Venue	Result	No	R	HO	No	R	HO	Ct	St	Byes	Balls	Ct	St	Byes	Balls
554/401†	1963–64	I	2	Bombay[2]	D	7	10	b	2	55	c	3	–	2	681	–	–	0	690
555/402†			3	Calcutta	D	2	13	c	2	13	b	5	–	0	512	–	–	7	720

Career	M	I	NO	HS	R	Avge	100	50	Ct	St	Balls	R	W	Avge	BB	5w	10w	Rate
Test	2	4	0	55	91	22.75	–	1	8	–	–	–	–	–	–	–	–	–
F/c	502	598	129	95	6910	14.73	–	18	895	176	84	82	0	–	–	–	–	–

BIRD, Morice Carlos

Lancashire (1907)
Surrey (1909 to 1921)

TOURS SA 1909–10, 1913–14
Born St Michael's Hamlet, Liverpool, Lancashire 25 Mar 1888
Died Broadstone, Dorset 9 Dec 1933

Morice Bird was a tall, powerfully built, aggressive right-handed batsman who excelled in all the off-side strokes. An outstanding schoolboy cricketer at Harrow, he scored 100 and 131 against Eton at Lord's in 1907, and remains the only player to score two separate hundreds in that fixture (he also took five wickets with his bustling medium-pace bowling). Captain of Surrey (1911–13), he made all his ten Test match appearances on two tours of South Africa. The son and brother of first-class cricketers, he subsequently coached at Harrow School and The Oval. [*Illus. pp.* 113, 273]

						Batting 1st			Batting 2nd				Bowling 1st			Bowling 2nd		
Ref	**Series**	**V**	**T**	**Venue**	**Result**	**No**	**R**	**HO**	**No**	**R**	**HO**	**Ct**	**Balls**	**R**	**W**	**Balls**	**R**	**W**
106/103	1909–10	SA	1	Johannesburg[1]	L-19	7	4	c	7	5	c	–	6	0	0	24	11	3
107/104			2	Durban[1]	L-95	7	1	c	7	42	c	–	18	3	0	42	10	1
108/105			3	Johannesburg[1]	W-3w	5	20	b	8	45	ro	–	–	–	–	6	0	0
109/106			4	Cape Town	L-4w	7	57	c	7	11	c	–	6	3	1	6	5	0
110/107			5	Cape Town	W-9w	7	0	b	1	0	c	1	–	–	–	18	12	0
130/119	1913–14	SA	1	Durban[1]	W-I & 157	8	61	c	–	–	–	–	–	–	–	–	–	–
131/120			2	Johannesburg[1]	W-I & 12	8	1	c	–	–	–	–	24	15	0	–	–	–
132/121			3	Johannesburg[1]	W-91	9	1	st	9	20	*	–	–	–	–	12	2	0
133/122			4	Durban[1]	D	8	8	b	–	–	–	1	–	–	–	36	21	0
134/123			5	Port Elizabeth	W-10w	9	4	ro	–	–	–	3	–	–	–	66	38	3

Career	M	I	NO	HS	R	Avge	100	50	Ct	St	Balls	R	W	Avge	BB	5w	10w	Rate
Test	10	16	1	61	280	18.66	–	2	5	–	264	120	8	15.00	3-11	–	–	33.00
F/c	192	306	14	200	6928	23.72	7	34	110	–	7245	3836	149	25.74	5-48	2	1	48.62

BIRKENSHAW, Jack

Yorkshire (1958 to 1960)
Leicestershire (1961 to 1980)
Worcestershire (1981)

TOURS
WI 1969–70 (Duke of Norfolk), 1973–74; I 1967–68 (Int XI), 1972–73; P 1967–68 (Int XI), 1972–73; SL 1972–73
Born Rothwell, Yorkshire 13 Nov 1940

NOTABLE FEATS

- Two hat-tricks for Leicestershire: v Worcestershire at Worcester in 1967 and v Cambridge University at Fenner's in 1968.
- Shared in Leicestershire record 7th-wkt stand of 206 with B. Dudleston v Kent at Canterbury in 1969.

A 5ft 9in tall, right-arm off-spinner, left-handed middle-order batsman and close fielder, usually at slip, Jack Birkenshaw was an extremely handy and determined all-rounder who twice changed counties because of competition with Ray Illingworth. A considerable spinner of the ball, his light-footed, skipping approach enabled him to vary his deceptively dipping flight and made him a more dangerous proposition on a dry surface than on a drying one. His sound defence and competitive spirit made him difficult to dislodge and he was a fine player of spin. His dry humour made him a valuable touring companion. When all ten Northamptonshire wickets fell to catches by different fielders at Leicester in 1967, Birkenshaw was the only player to miss out.

Jack Birkenshaw

Appointed to the first-class umpires list in 1982, he officiated in his first Test match four years later.

Ref	Series	V	T	Venue	Result	Batting 1st No	Batting 1st R	Batting 1st HO	Batting 2nd No	Batting 2nd R	Batting 2nd HO	Ct	Bowling 1st Balls	Bowling 1st R	Bowling 1st W	Bowling 2nd Balls	Bowling 2nd R	Bowling 2nd W
706/481	1972–73	I	4	Kanpur	D	7	64	c	–	–	–	–	120	42	1	150	66	2
707/482			5	Bombay[2]	D	8	36	b	1	12	b	–	138	67	2	72	52	0
721/485	1972–73	P	3	Karachi	D	9	21	c	–	–	–	1	186	89	1	111	57	5
734/495	1973–74	WI	4	Georgetown	D	8	0	c	–	–	–	–	132	41	1	–	–	–
735/496			5	Port-of-Spain	W-26	8	8	c	9	7	c	2	48	31	0	60	24	1

Career	M	I	NO	HS	R	Avge	100	50	Ct	St	Balls	R	W	Avge	BB	5w	10w	Rate
Test	5	7	0	64	148	21.14	–	1	3	–	1017	469	13	36.07	5-57	1	–	78.23
F/c	490	665	123	131	12780	23.57	4	53	318	–	69193	29276	1073	27.28	8-94	44	4	64.48

BLIGH
Hon. Ivo Francis Walter

Kent (1877 to 1883)
Cambridge University (1878 to 1881)

TOUR A 1882–83
Born Westminster, London 13 Mar 1859
Died Puckle Hill, Cobham, Kent
10 Apr 1927

Ivo Bligh was a tall (6ft 3in), stylish opening batsman and a notable fielder in the deep or at point. He represented Cambridge in four University matches, gaining his blue as a freshman in 1878 and being a member of the team which gained victories in each of its eight matches, including an innings defeat of the Australians. From the age of 21 he was dogged by ill-health but, three weeks after a mock obituary following Australia's shock victory at The Oval in August 1882 had created 'The Ashes', he led a team to recover them. By winning the original three-match rubber 2–1 he succeeded, although a subsequent match (an afterthought) was lost. En route his team had become the first from overseas to play in Ceylon. Two days out of Colombo their ship had been rammed by a barque and forced to return to port for repairs, an enquiry, and a second game of cricket. A genial, kind-hearted man, he was president of Kent in 1892 and 1902, and of MCC in 1900 – the year in which he succeeded to the earldom of Darnley. After his death, his widow presented the famous 'Ashes' urn to the MCC.

Ivo Bligh and the team which recovered the Ashes on the 1882–83 tour of Australia: standing *W. Barnes, F. Morley, C.T. Studd, G.F. Vernon, C.F.H. Leslie;* seated *G.B. Studd, E.F.S. Tylecote, Bligh, A.G. Steel, W.W. Read;* in front *R.G. Barlow, W. Bates.*

Ref	Series	V	T	Venue	Result	Batting 1st No	R	HO	Batting 2nd No	R	HO	Ct
10/10*	1882–83	A	1	Melbourne	L-9w	2	0	b	5	3	b	–
11/11*			2	Melbourne	W-I & 27	8	0	b	–	–	–	2
12/12*			3	Sydney	W-69	10	13	b	9	17	*	3
13/13*			4	Sydney	L-4w	9	19	b	8	10	c	2

Career	M	I	NO	HS	R	Avge	100	50	Ct	St	Balls	R	W	Avge	BB	5w	10w	Rate
Test	4	7	1	19	62	10.33	–	–	7	–	–	–	–	–	–	–	–	–
F/c	84	143	11	113*	2734	20.71	2	12	81	–	–	–	–	–	–	–	–	–

BLYTHE, Colin

Kent (1899 to 1914)

Wisden 1904
TOURS
A 1901–02, 1907–08;
SA 1905–06, 1909–10
Born Deptford, Kent 30 May 1879
Died near Passchendaele, Belgium
8 Nov 1917

As a slow left-arm bowler, Colin ('Charlie') Blythe dominated Edwardian cricket and earned his place among the greatest bowlers of all time. Ranjitsinhji considered his deceptive flight made him more difficult to attack than Rhodes, his contemporary. Amongst an imaginative and varied armoury was an extremely swift and deadly inswinging 'arm' ball delivered without any discernible change of action. A master of flight, his sensitivity and command of rhythm as a violinist was revealed in his bowling. From a behind-the-back action balanced by a high right arm, he spun the ball considerably and could be virtually unplayable on a drying or slightly crumbling pitch. His bowling played a key role in Kent's first four Championship titles and he coached the redoubtable Frank Woolley. An epileptic who found Test cricket a severe strain, his death in action during the Great War, while serving as a sergeant in the Kent Fortress Engineers, is commemorated at the St Lawrence Ground.

NOTABLE FEATS
- 50 wickets in 13th Test (*94*); 100 wickets in 19th Test (*110*).
- The only bowler to take 15 South African wickets in a Test in England (Test *94*), his match analysis of 15 for 99 remains the record for a Test at Leeds.
- Shared all 20 Australian wickets with fellow left-arm bowler G.H. Hirst (9 for 86) in Test *101*.
- Bowled F. Mitchell of Yorkshire with his first ball in first-class cricket (Tonbridge 1899).
- The first bowler to take 17 first-class wickets in a day, his outstanding analysis of 17 for 48 (10 for 30 and 7 for 18 for Kent v Northamptonshire at Northampton in 1907) remains the best by anyone achieving this feat. He took 15 or more wickets in a match 5 times.
- Two hat-tricks for Kent in 1910: v Surrey at Blackheath (4 wickets in 5 balls) and v Derbyshire at Gravesend.
- Shared an unchanged bowling partnership throughout both innings of a completed match for Kent on 5 occasions.
- Took 100 wickets in 14 of his 15 full seasons (he was ill during the other), 7 times exceeding 150 wickets and once 200 (215, avge 14.54, in 1909).

Colin Blythe

Ref	Series	V	T	Venue	Result	Batting 1st No	R	HO	Batting 2nd No	R	HO	Ct	Bowling 1st Balls	R	W	Bowling 2nd Balls	R	W
65/65	1901–02	A	1	Sydney	W-I & 124	11	20	c	–	–	–	–	96	26	3	78	30	4
66/66			2	Melbourne	L-229	11	4	c	11	0	*	–	96	64	4	186	85	1
67/67			3	Adelaide	L-4w	11	2	c	10	10	*	1	66	54	1	246	66	0
68/68			4	Sydney	L-7w	11	4	b	11	8	c	–	222	57	1	36	23	1
69/69			5	Melbourne	L-32	11	0	*	11	5	*	–	54	29	1	78	36	2
85/82	1905	A	3	Leeds	D	11	0	b	–	–	–	–	48	36	1	144	41	3
88/85	1905–06	SA	1	Johannesburg[1]	L-1w	11	17	b	11	0	b	1	96	33	3	168	50	1
89/86			2	Johannesburg[1]	L-9w	11	12	b	11	0	b	–	150	66	1	29	7	0
90/87			3	Johannesburg[1]	L-243	11	3	*	11	7	c	–	156	72	2	186	96	1
91/88			4	Cape Town	W-4w	3	27	b	–	–	–	1	192	68	6	173	50	5
92/89			5	Cape Town	L-I & 16	11	1	b	11	11	*	1	210	106	2	–	–	–
93/90	1907	SA	1	Lord's	D	11	4	*	–	–	–	–	48	18	2	126	56	2
94/91			2	Leeds	W-53	10	5	*	10	4	*	–	95	59	8	136	40	7
95/92			3	Oval	D	10	10	b	10	0	b	1	123	61	5	75	36	2
96/93	1907–08	A	1	Sydney	L-2w	10	5	b	10	15	c	1	72	33	0	114	55	1
101/98	1909	A	1	Birmingham	W-10w	11	1	c	–	–	–	–	138	44	6	144	58	5
104/101			4	Manchester	D	11	1	b	–	–	–	–	123	63	5	144	77	2
109/106	1909–10	SA	4	Cape Town	L-4w	11	1	*	11	4	*	–	90	26	0	120	38	2
110/107			5	Cape Town	W-9w	11	2	*	–	–	–	–	108	46	7	180	58	3

Career	M	I	NO	HS	R	Avge	100	50	Ct	St	Balls	R	W	Avge	BB	5w	10w	Rate
Test	19	31	12	27	183	9.63	–	–	6	–	4546	1863	100	18.63	8-59	9	4	45.46
F/c	440	588	137	82*	4478	9.92	–	5	206	–	103585	42136	2506	16.81	10-30	218	71	41.33

C. BLYTHE – TEST BOWLING SUMMARY

Series	V	M	Balls	R	W	Avge	BB	5w	10w	Rate
1901–02	A	5	1158	470	18	26.11	4-30	–	–	64.33
1905	A	1	192	77	4	19.25	3-41	–	–	48.00
1905–06	SA	5	1360	548	21	26.09	6-68	2	1	64.76
1907	SA	3	603	270	26	10.38	8-59	3	1	23.19
1907–08	A	1	186	88	1	88.00	1-55	–	–	186.00
1909	A	2	549	242	18	13.44	6-44	3	1	30.50
1909–10	SA	2	498	168	12	14.00	7-46	1	1	41.50
	A	9	2085	877	41	21.39	6-44	3	1	50.85
	SA	10	2461	986	59	16.71	8-59	6	3	41.71
Home		6	1344	589	48	12.27	8-59	6	2	28.00
Overseas		13	3202	1274	52	24.50	7-46	3	2	61.57
Totals		19	4546	1863	100	18.63	8-59	9	4	45.46

BOARD, John Henry

Gloucestershire (1891 to 1914)
London County (1900 to 1904)
Hawke's Bay (1910–11 to 1914–15)

TOURS
A 1897–98; SA 1898–99, 1905–06
Born Clifton, Bristol 23 Feb 1867
Died on board SS *Kenilworth Castle*
en route from South Africa 15 Apr 1924

Jack Board

Jack Board was a robust, fearless wicketkeeper who played for Gloucestershire from 1891 until the outbreak of the Great War. A doughty batsman who combined sound defence with bold hitting, he exceeded 1000 runs in a season on six occasions and his sixth-wicket stand of 320 with G.L. Jessop against Sussex at Hove in 1903 remains the county record. He umpired first-class cricket from 1921 until his death from heart failure after an annual coaching engagement.

NOTABLE FEATS
- Established Gloucestershire records for most dismissals in a season (75 in 1895) and in a career (1016).

Ref	Series	V	T	Venue	Result	Batting 1st No	Batting 1st R	Batting 1st HO	Batting 2nd No	Batting 2nd R	Batting 2nd HO	Fielding 1st Ct	Fielding 1st St	Fielding 1st Byes	Fielding 1st Balls	Fielding 2nd Ct	Fielding 2nd St	Fielding 2nd Byes	Fielding 2nd Balls
58/58 †	1898–99	SA	1	Johannesburg[1]	W-32	9	29	c	10	17	c	1	1	5	421	1	–	4	386
59/59 †			2	Cape Town	W-210	9	0	b	9	6	b	–	1	4	287	–	–	5	114
88/85 †	1905–06	SA	1	Johannesburg[1]	L-1w	9	9	*	9	7	lbw	2	–	9	277	–	–	6	677
89/86 †			2	Johannesburg[1]	L-9w	9	0	b	9	2	b	–	1	9	602	1	–	2	65
91/88 †			4	Cape Town	W-4w	1	0	b	8	14	*	2	–	20	585	–	–	0	361
92/89			5	Cape Town	L-I & 16	7	20	c	6	4	b	1	–	12	664	–	–	–	–

Career	M	I	NO	HS	R	Avge	100	50	Ct	St	Balls	R	W	Avge	BB	5w	10w	Rate
Test	6	12	2	29	108	10.80	–	–	8	3	–	–	–	–	–	–	–	–
F/c	525	906	97	214	15674	19.37	9	64	852	355	63	46	0	–	–	–	–	–

BOLUS, John Brian

Yorkshire (1956 to 1962)
Nottinghamshire (1963 to 1972)
Derbyshire (1973 to 1975)

TOUR I 1963–64
Born Whitkirk, Leeds, Yorkshire
31 Jan 1934

A dependable opening batsman at his peak, Brian Bolus was a strong on-side player who, later in his career, stabilized the middle order. Usually he adopted a grafting role, being a particularly adept accumulator of leg-byes, but occasionally he revealed his full range of strokes during a prolonged attacking innings. Against the express bowling of Wes Hall, he on-drove his first ball in Test cricket to the boundary. A handy left-arm medium-pace bowler, he became the third player after Bob Berry and Roy Swetman to be capped by three counties, and was the first to captain two (Nottinghamshire and Derbyshire) in successive seasons.

NOTABLE FEATS
- Exceeded 1000 runs in a season 14 times, including 2000 twice.

TEST NOTES
- *557* Bowled in 2nd inns: 0 for 16 (18 balls).

Brian Bolus

Ref	Series	V	T	Venue	Result	Batting 1st No	Batting 1st R	Batting 1st HO	Batting 2nd No	Batting 2nd R	Batting 2nd HO	Ct
546/398	1963	WI	4	Leeds	L-221	2	14	c	2	43	c	–
547/399			5	Oval	L-8w	1	33	c	1	15	c	1
553/400	1963–64	I	1	Madras[2]	D	1	88	lbw	1	22	st	1
554/401			2	Bombay[2]	D	1	25	c	1	57	c	–
555/402			3	Calcutta	D	1	39	c	1	35	c	–
556/402			4	Delhi	D	1	58	lbw	–	–	–	–
557/404			5	Kanpur	D	1	67	c	–	–	–	–

Career	M	I	NO	HS	R	Avge	100	50	Ct	St	Balls	R	W	Avge	BB	5w	10w	Rate
Test	7	12	0	88	496	41.33	–	4	2	–	18	16	0	–	–	–	–	–
F/c	469	833	81	202*	25598	34.03	39	142	201	–	1736	886	24	36.91	4-40	–	–	72.33

BOOTH
Major William

Yorkshire (1908 to 1914)

Wisden 1914
TOUR SA 1913–14
Born Pudsey, Yorkshire 10 Dec 1886
Died near La Cigny, France 1 Jul 1916

Born in the cricket nursery of Pudsey, Major Booth was a tall, handsome all-rounder who was in his prime as a cricketer when he was killed in action whilst serving as a 2nd Lieutenant in the West Yorkshire Regiment. From an easy right-handed action he swerved the ball late at medium pace, made it appear to gather speed off the pitch, and commanded a vicious off-break. An extremely popular man, he was a dashing middle-order batsman. [*Illus. p.* 113]

NOTABLE FEATS

- Two hat-tricks for Yorkshire: v Worcestershire at Bradford in 1911 and v Essex at Leyton in 1912.
- With Alonzo Drake he bowled unchanged throughout consecutive matches v Gloucestershire at Bristol and v Somerset at Weston-super-Mare in 1914.
- Completed the 'double' in 1913 when his aggregate of 181 wickets was the highest of the season.

						Batting 1st			Batting 2nd				Bowling 1st			Bowling 2nd		
Ref	Series	V	T	Venue	Result	No	R	HO	No	R	HO	Ct	Balls	R	W	Balls	R	W
130/119	1913–14	SA	1	Durban[1]	W-I & 157	9	14	ro	–	–	–	–	60	38	2	–	–	–
134/123			5	Port Elizabeth	W-10w	10	32	b	–	–	–	–	108	43	1	144	49	4

Career	M	I	NO	HS	R	Avge	100	50	Ct	St	Balls	R	W	Avge	BB	5w	10w	Rate
Test	2	2	0	32	46	23.00	–	–	–	–	312	130	7	18.57	4-49	–	–	44.57
F/c	162	243	39	210	4753	23.29	2	21	120	–	25189	11953	603	19.82	8-47	43	9	41.77

BOSANQUET
Bernard James Tindal

Oxford University (1898 to 1900)
Middlesex (1898 to 1919)

Wisden 1905
TOURS
A 1902–03, 1903–04; WI 1901–02; NZ 1902–03
Born Bulls Cross, Enfield, Middlesex 13 Oct 1877
Died Ewhurst, Surrey 12 Oct 1936

A most remarkable cricketer and the acknowledged inventor of the googly (an off-break delivered with a leg-break action), Bernard Bosanquet was a tall, strong, medium-pace right-arm leg-break bowler and hard-hitting batsman. Coached at Eton by the Surrey professionals Read and Brockwell, he represented Oxford against Cambridge three times as a fast-medium swing bowler who gradually cultivated the leg-break. He devised the googly (also known as a 'Bosie') while playing 'Twisti-Twisti'; that game's object was to bounce a tennis ball on a table so that your opponent seated opposite could not catch it. His first attempt at bowling it in a first-class match resulted in Samuel Coe, the left-handed Leicestershire batsman, being stumped for 98 off a specimen that bounced four times. Six years after retiring from regular county cricket he scored a 75-minute hundred for the Gentlemen at Scarborough against a Players attack that included S.F. Barnes. He gained half-blues at billiards and hammer-throwing, was accomplished at ice-hockey, and sired the late Reginald Bosanquet of television fame.

Bernard Bosanquet hiding another mystery.

NOTABLE FEATS

- His spell of 5 for 12 in Test *81* enabled England to regain the Ashes.
- His figures of 8 for 107 (*83*) remain the best in Tests at Nottingham.
- His match analysis of 15 for 65 v Sussex in 1900 remains the record for Oxbridge.
- Hat-trick for R.A. Bennett's XI v Barbados at Bridgetown in 1901–02.
- Achieved the 'double' in 1904 with 1405 runs and 132 wickets.
- Was the first to complete the match 'double' of a hundred in each innings and an aggregate of 10 wickets: 103 and 100*, 3 for 75 and 8 for 53, for Middlesex v Sussex at Lord's in 1905.
- Scored 214 in 195 min for Rest of England v Surrey at The Oval in 1908.

						Batting 1st			Batting 2nd				Bowling 1st			Bowling 2nd		
Ref	Series	V	T	Venue	Result	No	R	HO	No	R	HO	Ct	Balls	R	W	Balls	R	W
78/75	1903–04	A	1	Sydney	W-5w	8	2	c	7	1	*	1	78	52	2	138	100	1
80/77			3	Adelaide	L-216	7	10	c	9	10	c	2	181	95	3	95	73	4
81/78			4	Sydney	W-157	8	12	b	8	7	c	–	12	5	0	90	51	6
82/79			5	Melbourne	L-218	10	16	c	7	4	c	1	24	27	0	–	–	–
83/80	1905	A	1	Nottingham	W-213	6	27	b	6	6	b	3	42	29	0	196	107	8
84/81			2	Lord's	D	7	6	c	7	4	*	1	–	–	–	–	–	–
85/82			3	Leeds	D	7	20	b	7	22	*	1	24	29	0	90	36	1

Career	M	I	NO	HS	R	Avge	100	50	Ct	St	Balls	R	W	Avge	BB	5w	10w	Rate
Test	7	14	3	27	147	13.36	–	–	9	–	970	604	25	24.16	8-107	2	–	38.80
F/c	235	382	32	214	11696	33.41	21	63	191	–	26558	14974	629	23.80	9-31	45	11	42.22

BOTHAM, Ian Terence

Somerset (1974 to 1986)
Worcestershire (1987 to date)
Queensland (1987–88)

Wisden 1978

TOURS

A 1978–79, 1979–80, 1982–83, 1986–87; WI 1980–81, 1985–86; NZ 1977–78, 1983–84; I 1979–80, 1981–82; P 1977–78, 1983–84; SL 1981–82.

Born Heswall, Cheshire 24 Nov 1955

A world-class all-rounder, undoubtedly the best to represent England in modern times, and an outstanding entertainer, Ian Botham is a most thrilling cricketer. His big-match temperament has produced a happy knack of consistently winning Test matches. A fine attacking bowler who swings the ball late either way, he commands an enticing bouncer and a useful slower ball. Tall (6ft 1in), broad-shouldered and deep-chested, he drives, cuts and hooks with vast power, and possesses a complete range of strokes based on a sound technique. A fierce and totally fearless competitor, he reached his peak against the 1981 Australians when with bat and ball he reshaped the destiny of a series which looked irretrievably lost halfway through the Third Test; it was then that his 149* blitzed England towards an incredible victory against bookmakers' odds of 500–1 after they had followed on. He has always relished fast bowling and his hundred against a rampant Dennis Lillee in the Fourth Test was a memorably dramatic affair. As a fielder he is outstanding, his electric reactions prompting and often achieving the improbable, usually at slip. The first to achieve the triple 'double' of 3000 runs and 300 wickets in Test cricket, he has extended it beyond 5000 runs and 370 wickets. Botham's one blatant failure involved his brief and premature flirtation with captaincy when he was slightly unfortunate that 9 of his 12 matches were against the might of the West Indies. His reign, which produced 4 defeats and 8 draws, adversely affected his form and he wisely resigned. His zest for life and new challenges has frequently resulted in spectacular conflict with authority; happily it found its more heroic outlet in two walking expeditions in aid of leukaemia sufferers, one a modest stroll from John o'Groats to Land's End, the second an interesting adaptation of Hannibal's crossing of the Alps.

Ian Botham appeals for lbw to dismiss Jeff Crowe during the Third Test against New Zealand at The Oval in 1986, thereby passing Dennis Lillee's world record of 355 Test wickets.

NOTABLE FEATS

- 1000 runs in 21st Test (*854*) (27 inns); 2000 runs in 42nd Test (*912*) (66 inns); 3000 runs in 55th Test (*938*) (83 inns); 4000 runs in 69th Test (*990*) (110 inns); 5000 runs in 94th Test (*1079*) (149 inns).
- 50 wickets in 10th Test (*829*); 100 wickets in 19th Test (*852*) – fastest 100 wickets (2 yrs 9 days) until Kapil Dev in 1979–80; 150 wickets in 29th Test (*883*) in record time of exactly 3 yrs; 200 wickets in 41st Test (*908*) in record time of 4 yrs 34 days and at (then) youngest age of 25 yrs 280 days; 250 wickets in 55th Test (*938*); 300 wickets in 72nd Test (*993*); 350 wickets in 83rd Test (*1041*).
- *854* 1000r/100w in 21 Tests – 2 matches fewer than M.H. Mankad's world record; 1500r/150w in fewest Tests (30) – first instance for E; 2000r/200w in fewest Tests (42), shortest time (4 yrs 126 days), and at (then) youngest age (26 yrs 7 days); 3000r/300w – first to complete triple 'double'.
- *826* First to score 100 and take 8 wickets in an inns of same Test: his analysis, which included a spell of 6 for 8 in 53 balls, remains the record for Tests at Lord's and for E v P.
- *853* Added 99 (9* to 108*) before lunch on fourth day.
- *876* First to score 100 and take 10 wickets in a Test.
- *905* 100 off 87 balls; second after J.M. Gregory to score 100 and take 5 wickets in an inns of an E v A Test.
- *906* Took 5 for 1 in 28 balls.
- *907* 100 off 86 balls; hit 6 sixes – record v A and in any Test inns in England.
- *930* 200 off 220 balls – fastest Test 200 in terms of balls.
- *940* 1000 runs v A; 1000 runs in Tests during year 1982.
- *941* 1000r/100w v A in 22 Tests – fourth to achieve that 'double'.
- *959* First to take 50 wickets in E v NZ Tests.
- *975* 100 and 5 wickets in an inns for fifth time – alone in achieving this feat more than twice.
- *978* Last of 65 consecutive Test appearances, equalling A.P.E. Knott's England record.
- *990* First bowler to take 8 wickets in an inns v WI in England.
- *1017* Second after W. Voce to take 3 wickets in 4 balls for E v A.
- *1018* 25th instance of 5 wickets in an inns – surpassing world record of S.F. Barnes. Overtook record England wicket total of 325 by R.G.D. Willis.
- *1021* Overtook E v A record wicket total of 128 in 35 Tests by R.G.D. Willis in his 28th Test v A.
- *1051* Surpassed D.K. Lillee's world record of 355 Test wickets. Scored 50 off 32 balls (Test record) in 48 min, including 24 (464604) off D.A. Stirling's ninth over to equal Test record.
- *1058* 1500 runs v A; his 138 is an England record at Brisbane.
- *1059* 100th catch in Tests.
- Hit 80 sixes in 1985 season – first-class record.
- Exceeded 1000 runs in a season 4 times and 100 wickets once.
- Scored 100 in 50 min off 48 balls for England XI v Central Zone at Indore in 1981–82.
- Hit 10 sixes and scored 100 in 52 min off 56 balls for Somerset v Warwickshire at Taunton in 1982.
- Hit 32 runs off one over (466466) off I.R. Snook for England XI v Central Districts at Palmerston North in 1983–84.
- Shared in Somerset record stands of 310 (4th wkt with P.W. Denning v Glos, Taunton, 1980) and 172 (8th wkt with I.V.A. Richards v Leics, Leicester, 1983).
- Hit 12 sixes in inns of 138* for Somerset v Warwickshire at Birmingham in 1985.
- Hat-trick for MCC v Middlesex at Lord's in 1978.

						Batting 1st			Batting 2nd				Bowling 1st			Bowling 2nd		
Ref	Series	V	T	Venue	Result	No	R	HO	No	R	HO	Ct	Balls	R	W	Balls	R	W
806/528	1977	A	3	Nottingham	W-7w	8	25	b	–	–	–	1	120	74	5	150	60	0
807/529			4	Leeds	W-I & 85	8	0	b	–	–	–	–	66	21	5	102	47	0
817/534	1977–78	NZ	1	Wellington	L-72	7	7	c	6	19	c	1	102	27	2	75	13	2
818/535			2	Christchurch	W-174	7	103	c	4	30	*	3	199	73	5	56	38	3
819/536			3	Auckland	D	6	53	c	–	–	–	1	272	109	5	104	51	0
825/537	1978	P	1	Birmingham	W-I & 57	7	100	c	–	–	–	1	90	52	1	102	47	0
826/538			2	Lord's	W-I & 120	7	108	b	–	–	–	2	30	17	0	125	34	8
827/539			3	Leeds	D	8	4	lbw	–	–	–	1	108	59	4	–	–	–

Ref	Series	V	T	Venue	Result	Batting 1st No	R	HO	Batting 2nd No	R	HO	Ct	Bowling 1st Balls	R	W	Bowling 2nd Balls	R	W
828/540	1978	NZ	1	Oval	W-7w	7	22	c	–	–	–	–	132	58	1	114	46	3
829/541			2	Nottingham	W-I & 119	6	8	c	–	–	–	2	126	34	6	144	59	3
830/542			3	Lord's	W-7w	6	21	c	–	–	–	–	228	101	6	109	39	5
834/543	1978–79	A	1	Brisbane[2]	W-7w	7	49	c	–	–	–	–	96	40	3	208	95	3
835/544			2	Perth	W-166	6	11	lbw	6	30	c	1	88	46	0	88	54	0
836/545			3	Melbourne	L-103	6	22	c	6	10	c	1	161	68	3	120	41	3
837/546			4	Sydney	W-93	6	59	c	6	6	c	5	224	87	2	–	–	–
838/547			5	Adelaide	W-205	6	74	c	6	7	c	–	92	42	4	112	37	1
839/548			6	Sydney	W-9w	6	23	c	–	–	–	4	79	57	4	–	–	–
851/549	1979	I	1	Birmingham	W-I & 83	6	33	b	–	–	–	3	156	86	2	174	70	5
852/550			2	Lord's	D	6	36	b	–	–	–	1	114	35	5	210	80	1
853/551			3	Leeds	D	6	137	c	–	–	–	2	78	39	0	–	–	–
854/552			4	Oval	D	6	38	st	6	0	ro	4	168	65	4	174	97	3
868/553	1979–80	A	1	Perth	L-138	7	15	c	6	18	c	–	210	78	6	275	98	5
870/554			2	Sydney	L-6w	7	27	c	8	0	c	1	102	29	4	141	43	0
872/555			3	Melbourne	L-8w	6	8	c	7	119	*	2	239	105	3	72	18	1
876/556	1979–80	I		Bombay[3]	W-10w	6	114	lbw	–	–	–	–	137	58	6	156	48	7
880/557*	1980	WI	1	Nottingham	L-2w	6	57	c	6	4	c	1	120	50	3	100	48	1
881/558*			2	Lord's	D	6	8	lbw	–	–	–	–	222	145	3	–	–	–
882/559*			3	Manchester	D	6	8	c	6	35	lbw	1	120	64	3	–	–	–
883/560*			4	Oval	D	8	9	lbw	7	4	c	–	110	47	2	–	–	–
884/561*			5	Leeds	D	6	37	c	6	7	lbw	–	114	31	1	–	–	–
885/562*	1980	A		Lord's	D	6	0	c	–	–	–	–	132	89	0	56	43	1
896/563*	1980–81	WI	1	Port-of-Spain	L-I & 79	6	0	lbw	6	16	c	2	168	113	2	–	–	–
897/564*			3	Bridgetown	L-298	6	26	c	6	1	c	2	151	77	4	174	102	3
898/565*			4	St John's	D	6	1	c	–	–	–	–	222	127	4	–	–	–
899/566*			5	Kingston	D	7	13	c	7	16	c	1	157	73	2	–	–	–
903/567*	1981	A	1	Nottingham	L-4w	7	1	b	7	33	c	1	101	34	2	60	34	1
904/568*			2	Lord's	D	8	0	lbw	6	0	b	1	156	71	2	48	10	1
905/569			3	Leeds	W-18	7	50	c	7	149	*	2	236	95	6	42	14	1
906/570			4	Birmingham	W-29	7	26	b	7	3	c	1	120	64	1	84	11	5
907/571			5	Manchester	W-103	7	0	c	7	118	c	4	38	28	3	216	86	2
908/572			6	Oval	D	7	3	c	7	16	lbw	3	282	125	6	252	128	4
912/573	1981–82	I	1	Bombay[3]	L-138	6	7	c	6	29	c	–	168	72	4	135	61	5
913/574			2	Bangalore	D	7	55	c	–	–	–	–	282	137	2	–	–	–
914/575			3	Delhi	D	6	66	c	–	–	–	–	246	122	2	–	–	–
915/576			4	Calcutta	D	6	58	c	5	31	c	1	162	63	2	66	26	0
916/577			5	Madras[1]	D	5	52	c	–	–	–	2	186	83	1	48	29	0
917/578			6	Kanpur	D	5	142	st	–	–	–	–	150	67	1	–	–	–
921/579	1981–82	SL		Colombo SO	W-7w	6	13	b	–	–	–	–	77	28	3	72	37	0
928/580	1982	I	1	Lord's	W-7w	5	67	c	–	–	–	–	118	46	5	191	103	1
929/581			2	Manchester	D	5	128	b	–	–	–	–	114	86	1	–	–	–
930/582			3	Oval	D	5	208	c	–	–	–	1	114	73	2	24	12	0
931/583	1982	P	1	Birmingham	W-113	5	2	b	6	0	lbw	–	144	86	2	126	70	4
932/584			2	Lord's	L-10w	5	31	c	5	69	c	–	264	148	3	42	30	0
933/585			3	Leeds	W-3w	6	57	c	6	4	c	1	149	70	4	180	74	5
938/586	1982–83	A	1	Perth	D	5	12	c	5	0	b	–	240	121	2	36	17	0
939/587			2	Brisbane[2]	L-7w	5	40	c	6	15	c	1	132	105	3	95	70	0
940/588			3	Adelaide	L-8w	5	35	c	5	58	c	3	221	112	4	60	45	1
941/589			4	Melbourne	W-3	6	27	c	6	46	c	–	108	69	1	151	80	2
942/590			5	Sydney	D	6	5	c	7	32	lbw	5	180	75	4	60	35	1
957/591	1983	NZ	1	Oval	W-189	5	15	b	5	26	ro	2	96	62	4	24	17	0
958/592			2	Leeds	L-5w	5	38	c	5	4	c	–	156	81	0	1	4	0
959/593			3	Lord's	W-127	6	8	lbw	6	61	c	1	124	50	4	42	20	1
960/594			4	Nottingham	W-165	6	103	lbw	6	27	c	–	84	33	1	150	73	0
975/595	1983–84	NZ	1	Wellington	D	6	138	c	–	–	–	1	166	59	5	216	137	1
976/596			2	Christchurch	L-I & 132	6	18	c	6	0	c	1	102	88	1	–	–	–
977/597			3	Auckland	D	7	70	ro	–	–	–	1	174	70	0	–	–	–
978/598	1983–84	P	1	Karachi	L-3w	6	22	c	6	10	b	4	180	90	2	–	–	–
989/601	1984	WI	1	Birmingham	L-I & 180	6	64	c	6	38	lbw	–	204	127	1	–	–	–
990/602			2	Lord's	L-9w	6	30	c	6	81	lbw	–	166	103	8	121	117	0
991/603			3	Leeds	L-8w	6	45	c	6	14	c	2	42	45	0	–	–	–
992/604			4	Manchester	L-I & 64	6	6	c	6	1	c	1	174	100	2	–	–	–

Ref	Series	V	T	Venue	Result	Batting 1st No	R	HO	Batting 2nd No	R	HO	Ct	Bowling 1st Balls	R	W	Bowling 2nd Balls	R	W
993/605			5	Oval	L-172	7	14	c	6	54	c	2	138	72	5	135	103	3
994/606	1984	SL		Lord's	D	6	6	c	–	–	–	–	174	114	1	162	90	6
1017/612	1985	A	1	Leeds	W-5w	6	60	b	6	12	b	2	175	86	3	198	107	4
1018/613			2	Lord's	L-4w	6	5	c	8	85	c	–	144	109	5	90	49	2
1019/614			3	Nottingham	D	6	38	c	–	–	–	1	206	107	3	–	–	–
1020/615			4	Manchester	D	6	20	c	–	–	–	1	138	79	4	90	50	0
1021/616			5	Birmingham	W-I & 118	6	18	c	–	–	–	1	162	108	1	85	52	3
1022/617			6	Oval	W-I & 94	7	12	c	–	–	–	3	120	64	3	102	44	3
1038/618	1985–86	WI	1	Kingston	L-10w	6	15	c	6	29	b	–	114	67	2	–	–	–
1039/619			2	Port-of-Spain	L-7w	6	2	c	6	1	c	1	58	68	1	–	–	–
1040/620			3	Bridgetown	L-I & 30	6	14	c	7	21	c	2	144	80	1	–	–	–
1041/621			4	Port-of-Spain	L-10w	6	38	b	6	25	c	1	145	71	5	18	24	0
1042/622			5	St John's	L-240	7	10	c	8	13	b	–	240	147	2	90	78	0
1051/628	1986	NZ	3	Oval	D	6	59	*	–	–	–	–	150	75	3	6	7	0
1058/629	1986–87	A	1	Brisbane[2]	W-7w	6	138	c	–	–	–	–	96	58	2	72	34	1
1059/630			2	Perth	D	6	0	c	6	6	c	4	132	72	1	44	13	0
1061/632			4	Melbourne	W-I & 14	6	29	c	–	–	–	3	96	41	5	42	19	0
1062/633			5	Sydney	L-55	6	16	c	6	0	c	3	138	42	0	18	17	0
1075/634	1987	P	1	Manchester	D	7	48	c	–	–	–	–	84	29	1	–	–	–
1076/635			2	Lord's	D	7	6	c	–	–	–	–	–	–	–	–	–	–
1077/636			3	Leeds	L-I & 18	6	26	c	8	24	c	–	–	–	–	–	–	–
1078/637			4	Birmingham	D	7	37	c	4	6	c	2	288	121	1	123	66	2
1079/638			5	Oval	D	6	34	b	6	51	*	1	312	217	3	–	–	–

Career	M	I	NO	HS	R	Avge	100	50	Ct	St	Balls	R	W	Avge	BB	5w	10w	Rate
Test	94	150	5	208	5057	34.87	14	22	109	–	20801	10392	373	27.86	8-34	27	4	55.76
F/c	329	509	37	228	16422	34.79	33	81	303	–	53821	26980	1005	26.84	8-34	53	7	53.55

I. T. BOTHAM – TEST SUMMARY

Series	V	M	I	NO	HS	R	Avge	100	50	Balls	R	W	Avge	BB	5w	10w	Rate
1977	A	2	2	–	25	25	12.50	–	–	438	202	10	20.20	5-21	2	–	43.80
1977–78	NZ	3	5	1	103	212	53.00	1	1	808	311	17	18.29	5-73	2	–	47.52
1978	P	3	3	–	108	212	70.66	2	–	455	209	13	16.07	8-34	1	–	35.00
1978	NZ	3	3	–	22	51	17.00	–	–	853	337	24	14.04	6-34	3	1	35.54
1978–79	A	6	10	–	74	291	29.10	–	2	1268	567	23	24.65	4-42	–	–	55.13
1979	I	4	5	–	137	244	48.80	1	–	1074	472	20	23.60	5-35	2	–	53.70
1979–80	A	3	6	1	119*	187	37.40	1	–	1039	371	19	19.52	6-78	2	1	54.68
1979–80	I	1	1	–	114	114	114.00	1	–	293	106	13	8.15	7-48	2	1	22.53
1980	WI	5	8	–	57	134	16.75	–	1	786	385	13	29.61	3-50	–	–	60.46
1980	A	1	1	–	0	0	0.00	–	–	188	132	1	132.00	1-43	–	–	188.00
1980–81	WI	4	8	–	35	108	13.50	–	–	872	492	15	32.80	4-77	–	–	58.13
1981	A	6	12	1	149*	399	36.27	2	1	1635	700	34	20.58	6-95	3	1	48.08
1981–82	I	6	8	–	142	440	55.00	1	4	1443	660	17	38.82	5-61	1	–	84.88
1981–82	SL	1	1	–	13	13	13.00	–	–	149	65	3	21.66	3-28	–	–	49.66
1982	I	3	3	–	208	403	134.33	2	1	561	320	9	35.55	5-46	1	–	62.33
1982	P	3	6	–	69	163	27.16	–	2	905	478	18	26.55	5-74	1	–	50.27
1982–83	A	5	10	–	58	270	27.00	–	1	1283	729	18	40.50	4-75	–	–	71.27
1983	NZ	4	8	–	103	282	35.25	1	1	677	340	10	34.00	4-50	–	–	67.70
1983–84	NZ	3	4	–	138	226	56.50	1	1	658	354	7	50.57	5-59	1	–	94.00
1983–84	P	1	2	–	22	32	16.00	–	–	180	90	2	45.00	2-90	–	–	90.00
1984	WI	5	10	–	81	347	34.70	–	3	980	667	19	35.10	8-103	2	–	51.57
1984	SL	1	1	–	6	6	6.00	–	–	336	204	7	29.14	6-90	1	–	48.00
1985	A	6	8	–	85	250	31.25	–	2	1510	855	31	27.58	5-109	1	–	48.70
1985–86	WI	5	10	–	38	168	16.80	–	–	809	535	11	48.63	5-71	1	–	73.54
1986	NZ	1	1	1	59*	59	–	–	1	156	82	3	27.33	3-75	–	–	52.00
1986–87	A	4	6	–	138	189	31.50	1	–	638	296	9	32.88	5-41	1	–	70.88
1987	P	5	8	1	51*	232	33.14	–	1	807	433	7	61.85	3-217	–	–	115.28
	A	33	55	2	149*	1611	30.39	4	6	7999	3852	145	26.56	6-78	9	2	55.16
	WI	19	36	–	81	757	21.02	–	4	3447	2079	58	35.84	8-103	3	–	59.43
	NZ	14	21	2	138	830	43.68	3	4	3152	1424	61	23.34	6-34	6	1	51.67

Series	V	M	I	NO	HS	R	Avge	100	50	Balls	R	W	Avge	BB	5w	10w	Rate
	I	14	17	–	208	1201	70.64	5	5	3371	1558	59	26.40	7-48	6	1	57.13
	P	12	19	1	108	639	35.50	2	3	2347	1210	40	30.25	8-34	2	–	58.67
	SL	2	2	–	13	19	9.50	–	–	485	269	10	26.90	6-90	1	–	48.50
Home		52	79	3	208	2807	36.93	8	13	11361	5816	219	26.55	8-34	17	2	51.87
Overseas		42	71	2	142	2250	32.60	6	9	9440	4576	154	29.71	7-48	10	2	61.29
Totals		94	150	5	208	5057	34.87	14	22	20801	10392	373	27.86	8-34	27	4	55.76

BOWDEN
Montague Parker

Surrey (1883 to 1888)
Transvaal (1889–90)

TOURS A 1887–88; SA 1888–89
Born Stockwell, Surrey 1 Nov 1865
Died Umtali, Mashonaland 19 Feb 1892

A stylish middle-order batsman and wicket-keeper, Monty Bowden deputized as captain for a fever-stricken C. Aubrey Smith in the second Test ever played in South Africa. At 23 years 144 days he remains the youngest to lead England. After that tour he remained in South Africa, forming a stock-broking firm with Smith, and both played for Transvaal in the inaugural Currie Cup Challenge match, Bowden scoring 63 and 126*. Later he travelled to Rhodesia with the Pioneer Column of Cecil Rhodes. After three years he fell from a cart and died in a glorified mud hut which served as Umtali Hospital; his body had to be protected from marauding lions by an armed guard before it was interred in a coffin made out of whisky cases.

TEST NOTES

• *31* Deputized as wicket-keeper after lunch on second day and caught W.H. Milton.

The 1888–89 England team prior to their departure for South Africa, where Monty Bowden was to become the youngest player to lead England: standing *B.A.F. Grieve, A.C. Skinner, A.J. Fothergill, J.M. Read, R. Abel;* seated *C.A. Smith, Major Warton (manager), Hon. C.J. Coventry, J.E.P. McMaster, M.P. Bowden;* in front *J.H. Roberts, H. Wood;* inset *J. Briggs, G. Ulyett, F. Hearne.*

Ref	Series	V	T	Venue	Result	Batting 1st No	R	HO	Batting 2nd No	R	HO	Ct
31/31	1888–89	SA	1	Port Elizabeth	W-8w	6	0	ro	–	–	–	1
32/32*			2	Cape Town	W-I & 202	7	25	c	–	–	–	–

Career	M	I	NO	HS	R	Avge	100	50	Ct	St	Balls	R	W	Avge	BB	5w	10w	Rate
Test	2	2	0	25	25	12.50	–	–	1	–	–	–	–	–	–	–	–	–
F/c	86	132	17	189*	2316	20.13	3	7	73	14	75	35	2	17.50	2-7	–	–	37.50

BOWES, William Eric

Yorkshire (1929 to 1947)

Wisden 1932
TOURS
A 1932–33; WI 1935–36 (Yorks); NZ 1932–33
Born Elland, Yorkshire 25 Jul 1908
Died Menston, Leeds, Yorkshire 5 Sep 1987

A gangling (6ft 4in), bespectacled figure, Bill Bowes was not readily identifiable as the most 'heady' new-ball bowler of his day but, in tandem with Hedley Verity's left-arm spin, he provided the basis of a Yorkshire attack which claimed seven Championship titles in the 1930s. Bowling right arm at a fast-medium pace from a ten-yard run, he swung the ball either way, had a sharp break-back, and memorized the technical defects of his opponents. His weak batting and modest fielding limited his Test appearances but he did have the unique satisfaction of bowling Bradman first ball (Test *221*). Converted into a wartime army officer and captured at Tobruk, he spent three years in Italy with his fellow POW, Freddie Brown. Afterwards he bowled at a substantially-reduced pace for two more seasons (and another title) before turning his attention to 40 years of notable cricket writing.

NOTABLE FEATS
- 50 wickets in 12th Test (*266*).
- Took 100 wickets in a season nine times, exceeding 150 on three occasions.
- Hat-trick for MCC v Cambridge U at Lord's in 1928 in his second first-class match.

Bill Bowes's first-ball dismissal of Don Bradman at Melbourne during the Second Test of the 1932–33 series.

						Batting 1st			Batting 2nd				Bowling 1st			Bowling 2nd		
Ref	Series	V	T	Venue	Result	No	R	HO	No	R	HO	Ct	Balls	R	W	Balls	R	W
219/193	1932	I		Lord's	W-158	11	7	c	–	–	–	–	180	49	4	84	30	2
221/195	1932–33	A	2	Melbourne	L-111	11	4	*	11	0	*	–	114	50	1	24	20	0
226/200	1932–33	NZ	2	Auckland	D	–	–	–	–	–	–	–	114	34	6	12	4	0
234/208	1934	A	2	Lord's	W-I & 38	11	10	*	–	–	–	–	186	98	3	84	24	1
236/210			4	Leeds	D	11	0	c	–	–	–	–	300	142	6	–	–	–
237/211			5	Oval	L-562	–	–	–	9	2	c	–	228	164	4	69	55	5
242/216	1935	SA	1	Nottingham	D	–	–	–	–	–	–	–	132	31	0	24	2	0
244/218			3	Leeds	D	11	0	*	–	–	–	–	174	62	2	114	31	2
245/219			4	Manchester	D	11	0	*	–	–	–	1	216	100	5	90	34	0
246/220			5	Oval	D	–	–	–	–	–	–	–	244	112	3	78	40	2
265/234	1938	A	4	Leeds	L-5w	11	3	b	11	0	lbw	–	214	79	3	66	35	0
266/235			5	Oval	W-I & 579	–	–	–	–	–	–	–	114	49	5	60	25	2
272/241	1939	WI	1	Lord's	W-8w	–	–	–	–	–	–	1	228	86	3	152	44	1
273/242			2	Manchester	D	–	–	–	–	–	–	–	140	33	6	40	13	1
276/244	1946	I	1	Lord's	W-10w	11	2	lbw	–	–	–	–	150	64	1	24	9	0

Career	M	I	NO	HS	R	Avge	100	50	Ct	St	Balls	R	W	Avge	BB	5w	10w	Rate
Test	15	11	5	10*	28	4.66	–	–	2	–	3655	1519	68	22.33	6-33	6	–	53.75
F/c	372	326	148	43*	1528	8.58	–	–	138	–	74124	27470	1639	16.76	9-121	116	27	45.22

W. E. BOWES – TEST BOWLING SUMMARY

Series	V	M	Balls	R	W	Avge	BB	5w	10w	Rate
1932	I	1	264	79	6	13.16	4-49	–	–	44.00
1932–33	A	1	138	70	1	70.00	1-50	–	–	138.00
1932–33	NZ	1	126	38	6	6.33	6-34	1	–	21.00
1934	A	3	867	483	19	25.42	6-142	2	–	45.63
1935	SA	4	1072	412	14	29.42	5-100	1	–	76.57
1938	A	2	454	188	10	18.80	5-49	1	–	45.40
1939	WI	2	560	176	11	16.00	6-33	1	–	50.90
1946	I	1	174	73	1	73.00	1-64	–	–	174.00
	A	6	1459	741	30	24.70	6-142	3	–	48.63
	SA	4	1072	412	14	29.42	5-100	1	–	76.57
	WI	2	560	176	11	16.00	6-33	1	–	50.90
	NZ	1	126	38	6	6.33	6-34	1	–	21.00
	I	2	438	152	7	21.71	4-49	–	–	62.57
Home		13	3391	1411	61	23.13	6-33	5	–	55.59
Overseas		2	264	108	7	15.42	6-34	1	–	37.71
Totals		15	3655	1519	68	22.33	6-33	6	–	53.75

BOWLEY
Edward Henry

Sussex (1912 to 1934)
Auckland (1926–27 to 1928–29)

Wisden 1930
TOURS
A 1929–30; SA 1924–25 (Joel);
WI 1931–32 (Tennyson); NZ 1929–30
Born Leatherhead, Surrey 6 Jun 1890
Died Winchester, Hampshire 9 Jul 1974

A technically-sound, stylish opening batsman, Ted Bowley was a magnificent strokemaker, especially off the back foot. His method of keeping the bat and left elbow high against the rising ball enabled him to drive straight and to the off with tremendous force, and he was an exceptional square-cutter. Competition from such great opening batsmen as Hobbs, Sutcliffe, Sandham and Holmes severely curtailed his international appearances and he was 39 before he made his debut. On his only MCC tour he scored a chanceless hundred in the first Test series played in New Zealand. A notable player of slow bowling, he was himself an extremely handy right-arm leg-spinner who once achieved a 9-wicket analysis and claimed 90 wickets in 1929. For 23 years he was coach at Winchester School.

NOTABLE FEATS

- Exceeded 1000 runs in each of 15 successive seasons (excluding Army service in the Great War), passing 2000 on 4 occasions.
- His partnerships of 490 (1st wkt) with J.G. Langridge v Middlesex in 1933 and 385 (2nd wkt) with M.W. Tate v Northamptonshire in 1921 remain Sussex records.

Ted Bowley

						Batting 1st			Batting 2nd				Bowling 1st			Bowling 2nd		
Ref	Series	V	T	Venue	Result	No	R	HO	No	R	HO	Ct	Balls	R	W	Balls	R	W
183/169	1929	SA	3	Leeds	W-5w	2	31	c	2	46	c	–	–	–	–	24	7	0
184/170			4	Manchester	W-I & 32	2	13	b	–	–	–	1	–	–	–	–	–	–
187/173	1929–30	NZ	2	Wellington	D	1	9	b	1	2	c	1	30	32	0	30	19	0
188/174			3	Auckland	D	1	109	st	–	–	–	–	–	–	–	–	–	–
189/175			4	Auckland	D	1	42	ro	–	–	–	–	168	58	0	–	–	–

Career	M	I	NO	HS	R	Avge	100	50	Ct	St	Balls	R	W	Avge	BB	5w	10w	Rate
Test	5	7	0	109	252	36.00	1	–	2	–	252	116	0	–	–	–	–	–
F/c	510	859	47	283	28378	34.94	52	147	373	–	40818	19257	741	25.98	9-114	28	2	55.08

BOYCOTT
Geoffrey OBE

Yorkshire (1962 to 1986)
Northern Transvaal (1971–72)

Wisden 1965
TOURS
A 1965–66, 1970–71, 1978–79, 1979–80; SA 1964–65, 1981–82 (SAB); WI 1967–68, 1973–74, 1980–81; NZ 1965–66, 1977–78; I 1979–80, 1981–82; P 1977–78; SL 1969–70
Born Fitzwilliam, Yorkshire 21 Oct 1940

Geoffrey Boycott

TEST NOTES

- *698* Retired hurt when 3* at 13–0 (1st inns); resumed at 118–4.
- *726* Retired hurt when 54* at 105–0; resumed at 249–7 but immediately retired again after being struck on arm first ball; resumed again at 299–8.
- *819* R.G.D. Willis led England on last 2 days after a contact lens had damaged Boycott's right cornea.
- *883* Retired hurt when 3* at 9–0 (1st inns); resumed at 155–1.

The most prolific, single-minded and controversial of post-war batsmen, Geoffrey Boycott combined immense powers of concentration and application with arguably the best defensive technique of all time. Although he commanded a full range of strokes and was especially adept at cover-driving off the back foot, he was seldom motivated to take an attack apart. He became an outstanding opening batsman, a clinical arch-perfectionist passionately obsessed with batting and his own performances. Although he was a devotedly successful accumulator of runs, his erratic judgement of what constituted a single made partnering him a cricketing form of Russian roulette. He fulfilled his ambition of scoring the record aggregate of runs in Test cricket but failed to disturb any of Herbert Sutcliffe's major Yorkshire records. His Test aggregate would have been extended substantially but for his self-imposed exile of 30 matches (1974–77) and three-year banishment for joining a rebel tour of South Africa. An occasional right-handed medium-pace inswing bowler who usually kept his cap on, he made himself into a sound outfielder. He was singularly unsuccessful as a captain, a hypersensitive and dictatorial man who sought too much from his players and for whom communication and working relationships were difficult. His four-match reign after Brearley's injury in 1977–78 was not a success and Yorkshire failed to gain a single honour under his leadership (1971–78). He became the centre of a traumatic schism in the Yorkshire Club; sacked as a player in 1983, he was reinstated after his supporters overthrew the committee and elected him on to its successor.

NOTABLE FEATS

- 1000 runs in 16th Test (*599*) (27 inns); 2000 runs in 32nd Test (*632*) (53 inns); 3000 runs in 44th Test (*676*) (76 inns); 4000 runs in 55th Test (*725*) (95 inns); 5000 runs in 66th Test (*808*) (115 inns); 6000 runs in 81st Test (*851*) (141 inns); 7000 runs in 94th Test (*885*) (165 inns); 8000 runs in 107th Test (*914*) (190 inns).
- *618* Scored 246* off 555 balls in 573 min – highest score in E v I Tests. First 100 took 341 min (316 balls) and he was excluded from next Test as disciplinary measure. Shared in 100 partnerships for 3 successive wickets.
- *678* With J.H. Edrich became third opening pair to share 100 partnership in both inns of a Test v A.
- *806* With A.P.E. Knott equalled E v A 7th-wkt partnership record of 215 – only E v A stand to be equalled or broken since 1938. Batted on each day of the 5-day Test (second after M.L. Jaisimha).
- *807* First to score his 100th first-class hundred in a Test; became the fourth England player to be on the field for an entire Test.
- *835* Eighth to score 2000 runs for E v A.
- *837* Out first ball for the only time in his 193 Test inns; first duck in 68 Test inns.
- *851* Emulated K.F. Barrington by scoring 100 on each of England's 6 current home grounds.
- *868* Became the fourth to carry his bat through a completed England inns and the first to do so without scoring 100. First to score 99* in a Test.
- *904* 100th Test for England – 2nd after M.C. Cowdrey (1968).
- Gained 3 Test records from M.C. Cowdrey: (*907*) exceeded England aggregate of 7624 runs in 11 fewer Tests; (*908*) 61st 50 – world record; (*913*) 189th innings – world record.
- *914* At 4.23pm on 23 December 1981, Boycott passed G.St A. Sobers's world Test record of 8032 runs having played 30 more inns and batted over 451 hours (cf 15 complete 5-day Tests). His 22nd hundred equalled England record. (S.M. Gavaskar gained the aggregate record on 13 November 1983.)

NOTABLE FEATS *cont.*
• His first-class aggregates of 48,426 runs and 151 hundreds are the eighth- and fifth-highest respectively.
• Only batsman to average 100 in an English first-class season twice: 2405, avge 100.12, in 1971; and 1538, avge 102.53, in 1979.
• Exceeded 1000 runs in a home season 23 times (plus 3 overseas), including 2000 3 times. Seven of his 10 double centuries were for Yorkshire.
• Shared Yorkshire 10th-wkt record stand of 149 with G.B. Stevenson v Warwickshire at Birmingham in 1982.

						Batting 1st			Batting 2nd				Bowling 1st			Bowling 2nd		
Ref	Series	V	T	Venue	Result	No	R	HO	No	R	HO	Ct	Balls	R	W	Balls	R	W
561/405	1964	A	1	Nottingham	D	1	48	c	–	–	–	–	–	–	–	–	–	–
563/407			3	Leeds	L-7w	1	38	c	1	4	c	–	–	–	–	–	–	–
564/408			4	Manchester	D	1	58	b	–	–	–	–	6	3	0	–	–	–
565/409			5	Oval	D	1	30	b	1	113	c	–	–	–	–	–	–	–
571/410	1964–65	SA	1	Durban[2]	W-I & 104	1	73	lbw	–	–	–	–	–	–	–	–	–	–
572/411			2	Johannesburg[3]	D	1	4	c	–	–	–	–	–	–	–	30	3	0
573/412			3	Cape Town	D	1	15	c	1	1	*	–	–	–	–	120	47	3
574/413			4	Johannesburg[3]	D	1	5	c	1	76	*	–	48	25	0	–	–	–
575/414			5	Port Elizabeth	D	1	117	c	1	7	c	2	156	69	1	12	13	1
591/415	1965	NZ	1	Birmingham	W-9w	1	23	c	1	44	*	–	–	–	–	–	–	–
592/416			2	Lord's	W-7w	1	14	c	1	76	lbw	–	–	–	–	–	–	–
594/418	1965	SA	1	Lord's	D	1	31	c	1	28	c	–	–	–	–	–	–	–
595/419			2	Nottingham	L-94	1	0	c	1	16	b	–	–	–	–	156	60	0
597/421	1965–66	A	1	Brisbane[2]	D	2	45	b	2	63	*	–	32	16	0	–	–	–
598/422			2	Melbourne	D	1	51	c	1	5	*	–	–	–	–	72	32	2
599/423			3	Sydney	W-I & 93	1	84	c	–	–	–	1	24	8	0	–	–	–
600/424			4	Adelaide	L-I & 9	1	22	c	1	12	lbw	–	56	33	0	–	–	–
601/425			5	Melbourne	D	1	17	c	1	1	lbw	–	–	–	–	–	–	–
602/426	1965–66	NZ	1	Christchurch	D	1	4	c	1	4	ro	–	72	30	0	–	–	–
603/427			2	Dunedin	D	1	5	b	–	–	–	2	–	–	–	–	–	–
606/430	1966	WI	2	Lord's	D	1	60	c	1	25	c	–	–	–	–	–	–	–
607/431			3	Nottingham	L-139	1	0	lbw	1	71	c	–	–	–	–	–	–	–
608/432			4	Leeds	L-I & 55	1	12	c	1	14	c	–	–	–	–	–	–	–
609/433			5	Oval	W-I & 34	1	4	b	–	–	–	–	–	–	–	–	–	–
618/434	1967	I	1	Leeds	W-6w	2	246	*	–	–	–	–	–	–	–	–	–	–
620/436			3	Birmingham	W-132	1	25	st	1	6	b	2	–	–	–	–	–	–
622/438	1967	P	2	Nottingham	W-10w	1	15	b	1	1	*	–	–	–	–	–	–	–
628/440	1967–68	WI	1	Port-of-Spain	D	1	68	lbw	–	–	–	–	–	–	–	–	–	–
629/441			2	Kingston	D	1	17	b	1	0	b	–	–	–	–	–	–	–
630/442			3	Bridgetown	D	1	90	lbw	–	–	–	–	–	–	–	–	–	–
631/443			4	Port-of-Spain	W-7w	2	62	c	2	80	*	–	–	–	–	–	–	–
632/444			5	Georgetown	D	2	116	c	2	30	b	1	–	–	–	–	–	–
637/445	1968	A	1	Manchester	L-159	2	35	c	2	11	c	1	–	–	–	–	–	–
638/446			2	Lord's	D	2	49	c	–	–	–	–	–	–	–	–	–	–
639/447			3	Birmingham	D	2	36	lbw	2	31	c	–	–	–	–	–	–	–
653/453	1969	WI	1	Manchester	W-10w	1	128	lbw	1	1	*	–	–	–	–	–	–	–
654/454			2	Lord's	D	1	23	c	1	106	c	–	–	–	–	–	–	–
655/455			3	Leeds	W-30	1	12	lbw	1	0	c	–	–	–	–	–	–	–
656/456	1969	NZ	1	Lord's	W-230	1	0	c	1	47	c	–	–	–	–	–	–	–
657/457			2	Nottingham	D	1	0	b	–	–	–	–	–	–	–	–	–	–
658/458			3	Oval	W-8w	2	46	b	2	8	b	–	–	–	–	–	–	–
674/459	1970–71	A	1	Brisbane[2]	D	1	37	c	1	16	c	1	–	–	–	–	–	–
675/460			2	Perth	D	1	70	c	1	50	st	–	8	7	0	–	–	–
676/461			4	Sydney	W-299	1	77	c	1	142	*	1	–	–	–	–	–	–
677/462			5	Melbourne	D	1	12	c	1	76	*	–	–	–	–	–	–	–
678/463			6	Adelaide	D	1	58	ro	1	119	*	2	–	–	–	–	–	–
688/468	1971	P	2	Lord's	D	1	121	*	–	–	–	–	–	–	–	–	–	–
689/469			3	Leeds	W-25	1	112	c	1	13	c	–	–	–	–	–	–	–
690/470	1971	I	1	Lord's	D	1	3	c	1	33	c	1	–	–	–	–	–	–
698/473	1972	A	1	Manchester	W-89	1	8	c	1	47	lbw	–	–	–	–	–	–	–
699/474			2	Lord's	L-8w	1	11	b	1	6	b	–	–	–	–	–	–	–
722/486	1973	NZ	1	Nottingham	W-38	1	51	lbw	1	1	ro	–	–	–	–	–	–	–

						Batting 1st			Batting 2nd				Bowling 1st			Bowling 2nd		
Ref	Series	V	T	Venue	Result	No	R	HO	No	R	HO	Ct	Balls	R	W	Balls	R	W
723/487			2	Lord's	D	1	61	c	1	92	c	–	–	–	–	–	–	–
724/488			3	Leeds	W-I & 1	1	115	c	–	–	–	1	–	–	–	–	–	–
725/489	1973	WI	1	Oval	L-158	1	97	c	1	30	c	1	–	–	–	–	–	–
726/490			2	Birmingham	D	1	56	*	–	–	–	1	–	–	–	–	–	–
727/491			3	Lord's	L-I & 226	1	4	c	1	15	c	–	–	–	–	–	–	–
731/492	1973–74	WI	1	Port-of-Spain	L-7w	1	6	c	1	93	c	1	–	–	–	–	–	–
732/493			2	Kingston	D	1	68	c	1	5	c	–	–	–	–	–	–	–
733/494			3	Bridgetown	D	4	10	c	4	13	c	–	–	–	–	–	–	–
734/495			4	Georgetown	D	1	15	b	–	–	–	–	–	–	–	–	–	–
735/496			5	Port-of-Spain	W-26	1	99	c	1	112	b	1	–	–	–	–	–	–
739/497	1974	I	1	Manchester	W-113	1	10	lbw	1	6	c	1	–	–	–	–	–	–
806/528	1977	A	3	Nottingham	W-7w	2	107	c	2	80	*	–	–	–	–	–	–	–
807/529			4	Leeds	W-I & 85	2	191	c	–	–	–	–	–	–	–	–	–	–
808/530			5	Oval	D	2	39	c	2	25	*	–	–	–	–	–	–	–
814/531	1977–78	P	1	Lahore[2]	D	1	63	b	–	–	–	–	24	4	0	–	–	–
815/532			2	Hyderabad	D	1	79	ro	1	100	*	–	–	–	–	–	–	–
816/533*			3	Karachi	D	1	31	b	1	56	c	–	–	–	–	–	–	–
817/534*	1977–78	NZ	1	Wellington	L-72	2	77	c	2	1	b	2	–	–	–	–	–	–
818/535*			2	Christchurch	W-174	2	8	lbw	2	26	ro	–	–	–	–	–	–	–
819/536*			3	Auckland	D	1	54	c	–	–	–	–	–	–	–	–	–	–
829/541	1978	NZ	2	Nottingham	W-I & 119	2	131	c	–	–	–	–	–	–	–	–	–	–
830/542			3	Lord's	W-7w	2	24	c	2	4	b	–	–	–	–	–	–	–
834/543	1978–79	A	1	Brisbane[2]	W-7w	1	13	c	1	16	ro	–	–	–	–	–	–	–
835/544			2	Perth	W-166	1	77	lbw	1	23	lbw	1	–	–	–	–	–	–
836/545			3	Melbourne	L-103	1	1	b	1	38	lbw	–	–	–	–	–	–	–
837/546			4	Sydney	W-93	1	8	c	1	0	lbw	–	–	–	–	–	–	–
838/547			5	Adelaide	W-205	1	6	c	1	49	c	–	–	–	–	–	–	–
839/548			6	Sydney	W-9w	1	19	c	1	13	c	1	8	6	0	–	–	–
851/549	1979	I	1	Birmingham	W-I & 83	2	155	lbw	–	–	–	–	30	8	0	–	–	–
852/550			2	Lord's	D	2	32	c	–	–	–	1	–	–	–	–	–	–
853/551			3	Leeds	D	1	31	c	–	–	–	–	12	0	0	–	–	–
854/552			4	Oval	D	1	35	lbw	1	125	b	–	–	–	–	–	–	–
868/553	1979–80	A	1	Perth	L-138	2	0	lbw	2	99	*	1	–	–	–	–	–	–
870/554			2	Sydney	L-6w	2	8	b	2	18	c	–	–	–	–	–	–	–
872/555			3	Melbourne	L-8w	2	44	c	2	7	b	1	–	–	–	–	–	–
876/556	1979–80	I		Bombay[3]	W-10w	2	22	c	2	43	*	–	–	–	–	–	–	–
880/557	1980	WI	1	Nottingham	L-2w	2	36	c	2	75	b	–	–	–	–	–	–	–
881/558			2	Lord's	D	2	8	c	2	49	*	–	42	11	0	–	–	–
882/559			3	Manchester	D	2	5	c	2	86	lbw	–	–	–	–	–	–	–
883/560			4	Oval	D	2	53	ro	2	5	c	–	–	–	–	–	–	–
884/561			5	Leeds	D	2	4	c	2	47	c	–	–	–	–	–	–	–
885/562	1980	A		Lord's	D	2	62	c	2	128	*	–	–	–	–	–	–	–
896/563	1980–81	WI	1	Port-of-Spain	L-I & 79	2	30	c	2	70	c	–	–	–	–	–	–	–
897/564			3	Bridgetown	L-298	2	0	b	2	1	c	1	–	–	–	–	–	–
898/565			4	St John's	D	2	38	c	2	104	*	1	18	5	0	–	–	–
899/566			5	Kingston	D	2	40	c	2	12	c	–	–	–	–	–	–	–
903/567	1981	A	1	Nottingham	L-4w	2	27	c	2	4	c	2	–	–	–	–	–	–
904/568			2	Lord's	D	2	17	c	2	60	c	–	–	–	–	–	–	–
905/569			3	Leeds	W-18	2	12	b	2	46	lbw	–	18	2	0	–	–	–
906/570			4	Birmingham	W-29	1	13	c	1	29	c	–	–	–	–	–	–	–
907/571			5	Manchester	W-103	2	10	c	2	37	lbw	–	–	–	–	–	–	–
908/572			6	Oval	D	1	137	c	1	0	lbw	–	–	–	–	–	–	–
912/573	1981–82	I	1	Bombay[3]	L-138	2	60	c	2	3	lbw	1	–	–	–	–	–	–
913/574			2	Bangalore	D	2	36	c	2	50	b	1	–	–	–	–	–	–
914/575			3	Delhi	D	2	105	c	2	34	*	–	–	–	–	–	–	–
915/576			4	Calcutta	D	2	18	c	2	6	lbw	–	–	–	–	–	–	–

Career	M	I	NO	HS	R	Avge	100	50	Ct	St	Balls	R	W	Avge	BB	5w	10w	Rate
Test	108	193	23	246*	8114	47.72	22	42	33	–	944	382	7	54.57	3-47	–	–	134.85
F/c	609	1014	162	261*	48426	56.83	151	238	264	–	3641	1459	45	32.42	4-14	–	–	80.91

G. BOYCOTT – TEST BATTING SUMMARY

Series	V	M	I	NO	HS	R	Avge	100	50
1964	A	4	6	–	113	291	48.50	1	1
1964–65	SA	5	8	2	117	298	49.66	1	2
1965	NZ	2	4	1	76	157	52.33	–	1
1965	SA	2	4	–	31	75	18.75	–	–
1965–66	A	5	9	2	84	300	42.85	–	3
1965–66	NZ	2	3	–	5	13	4.33	–	–
1966	WI	4	7	–	71	186	26.57	–	2
1967	I	2	3	1	246*	277	138.50	1	–
1967	P	1	2	1	15	16	16.00	–	–
1967–68	WI	5	8	1	116	463	66.14	1	4
1968	A	3	5	–	49	162	32.40	–	–
1969	WI	3	6	1	128	270	54.00	2	–
1969	NZ	3	5	–	47	101	20.20	–	–
1970–71	A	5	10	3	142*	657	93.85	2	5
1971	P	2	3	1	121*	246	123.00	2	–
1971	I	1	2	–	33	36	18.00	–	–
1972	A	2	4	–	47	72	18.00	–	–
1973	NZ	3	5	–	115	320	64.00	1	3
1973	WI	3	5	1	97	202	50.50	–	2
1973–74	WI	5	9	–	112	421	46.77	1	3
1974	I	1	2	–	10	16	8.00	–	–
1977	A	3	5	2	191	442	147.33	2	1
1977–78	P	3	5	1	100*	329	82.25	1	3
1977–78	NZ	3	5	–	77	166	33.20	–	2
1978	NZ	2	3	–	131	159	53.00	1	–
1978–79	A	6	12	–	77	263	21.91	–	1
1979	I	4	5	–	155	378	75.60	2	–
1979–80	A	3	6	1	99*	176	35.20	–	1
1979–80	I	1	2	1	43*	65	65.00	–	–
1980	WI	5	10	1	86	368	40.88	–	3
1980	A	1	2	1	128*	190	190.00	1	1
1980–81	WI	4	8	1	104*	295	42.14	1	1
1981	A	6	12	–	137	392	32.66	1	1
1981–82	I	4	8	1	105	312	44.57	1	2
	A	38	71	9	191	2945	47.50	7	14
	SA	7	12	2	117	373	37.30	1	2
	WI	29	53	5	128	2205	45.93	5	15
	NZ	15	25	1	131	916	38.16	2	6
	I	13	22	3	246*	1084	57.05	4	2
	P	6	10	3	121*	591	84.42	3	3
Home		57	100	10	246*	4366	48.51	14	15
Overseas		51	93	13	142*	3758	46.97	8	27
Totals		108	193	23	246*	8114	47.72	22	42

BRADLEY Walter Morris

Kent (1895 to 1903)
London County (1903)

Born Sydenham, Kent 2 Jan 1875
Died Wandsworth Common, Surrey 19 Jun 1944

NOTABLE FEATS

- The first to take a wicket (F. Laver) with his first ball for England, he returned a 5-wicket analysis in his first Test innings.
- Twice took 100 wickets in a season, including a remarkable 156 in 1899.
- Three hat-tricks for Kent: v Essex and Yorkshire in 1899, and v Somerset in 1900.

Bill Bradley was a tall, hard-working, right-handed fast bowler who possessed such stamina that he could maintain considerable pace for long periods from an exceptionally long approach. After captaining Alleyn's School and once taking six Mitcham wickets with consecutive balls for Lloyd's Register, he was taken under Lord Harris's wing and played for Kent as an amateur. His action with arms flung high and head thrown back epitomized aggression. Essentially an attacking bowler, he aimed at the stumps and seldom bowled short. Although very definitely in the rabbit class as a batsman, he surprised even himself by scoring 67* out of 95 in 45 minutes against Yorkshire at Canterbury in 1897.

'Bill' Bradley

Ref	Series	V	T	Venue	Result	Batting 1st No	Batting 1st R	Batting 1st HO	Batting 2nd No	Batting 2nd R	Batting 2nd HO	Ct	Bowling 1st Balls	Bowling 1st R	Bowling 1st W	Bowling 2nd Balls	Bowling 2nd R	Bowling 2nd W
63/63	1899	A	4	Manchester	D	11	23	*	–	–	–	–	165	67	5	230	82	1
64/64			5	Oval	D	7	0	ro	–	–	–	–	145	52	0	85	32	0

Career	M	I	NO	HS	R	Avge	100	50	Ct	St	Balls	R	W	Avge	BB	5w	10w	Rate
Test	2	2	1	23*	23	23.00	–	–	–	–	625	233	6	38.83	5-67	1	–	104.16
F/c	144	216	57	67*	956	6.01	–	1	80	–	28340	14341	633	22.65	9-87	44	10	44.77

BRAUND
Leonard Charles

Surrey (1896 to 1898)
Somerset (1899 to 1920)
London County (1900 to 1904)

Wisden 1902
TOURS A 1901–02, 1903–04, 1907–08
Born Clewer, Berkshire 18 Oct 1875
Died Putney Common, Surrey
23 Dec 1955

NOTABLE FEATS

- Shared 6th-wkt stand of 145 in 75 min with G.L. Jessop in Test *93*.
- Achieved the 'double' 3 times, exceeding 1000 runs on 6 occasions and 100 wickets 4 times (172 in 1902).
- Shared record Surrey 9th-wkt stand of 204 with T.W. Hayward v Lancashire at The Oval in 1898.
- Carried his bat through a completed Somerset innings on 4 occasions.
- Returned match figures of 15 for 71 v Yorkshire at Sheffield in 1902.
- Hat-trick for Somerset v Worcestershire at Worcester in 1906.

Len Braund was an outstanding lithe and athletic all-rounder: an accomplished middle-order batsman in all conditions, a high-class leg-break bowler who extracted exceptional turn and bounce, and a phenomenal slip-catcher. Discarded by Surrey, a lapse equal almost to that involving Essex and Jack Hobbs, he was the pillar of Somerset teams for two decades. A big match player who remained calmly determined in any crisis, he was an automatic selection for England during the first seven years of the century, his Test career comprising an unbroken sequence of 23 matches. He held several unbelievable catches, including one when, anticipating a leg-glance, he darted from slip to hold an astonishing leg-side chance. On retiring, he coached Cambridge University and became a first-class umpire who stood in three Tests. One of cricket's gentlemen, he retained his enthusiasm and innate cheerfulness despite having both legs amputated.

Len Braund

						Batting 1st			Batting 2nd				Bowling 1st			Bowling 2nd		
Ref	Series	V	T	Venue	Result	No	R	HO	No	R	HO	Ct	Balls	R	W	Balls	R	W
65/65	1901–02	A	1	Sydney	W-I & 124	8	58	c	–	–	–	2	90	40	2	172	61	5
66/66			2	Melbourne	L-229	9	2	*	7	25	c	3	–	–	–	320	114	1
67/67			3	Adelaide	L-4w	7	103	*	6	17	b	2	276	143	3	150	79	0
68/68			4	Sydney	L-7w	6	17	lbw	6	0	b	2	360	118	4	90	55	0
69/69			5	Melbourne	L-32	6	32	c	6	2	c	3	60	33	1	157	95	5
70/70	1902	A	1	Birmingham	D	9	14	b	–	–	–	2	6	1	0	30	14	1
71/71			2	Lord's	D	–	–	–	–	–	–	–	–	–	–	–	–	–
72/72			3	Shefield	L-143	7	0	st	8	9	c	5	78	34	2	72	58	0
73/73			4	Manchester	L-3	7	65	b	7	3	st	1	54	37	0	66	22	0
74/74			5	Oval	W-1w	6	22	c	6	2	c	–	101	29	2	54	15	2
78/75	1903–04	A	1	Sydney	W-5w	6	102	b	5	0	c	1	156	39	0	72	56	0
79/76			2	Melbourne	W-185	5	20	c	4	3	b	3	30	20	0	–	–	–
80/77			3	Adelaide	L-216	5	13	c	6	25	b	1	78	49	0	126	57	2
81/78			4	Sydney	W-157	6	39	c	6	19	c	1	66	27	2	96	24	0
82/79			5	Melbourne	L-218	8	5	c	1	0	c	3	173	81	8	24	6	1
93/90	1907	SA	1	Lord's	D	5	104	c	–	–	–	–	42	10	1	24	26	0
94/91			2	Leeds	W-53	5	1	lbw	5	0	c	2	–	–	–	–	–	–
95/92			3	Oval	D	5	18	b	5	34	c	–	–	–	–	6	5	0
96/93	1907–08	A	1	Sydney	L-2w	5	30	b	6	32	*	4	102	74	2	42	14	0
97/94			2	Melbourne	W-1w	5	49	b	5	30	b	1	96	41	0	108	68	0
98/95			3	Adelaide	L-245	5	0	b	5	47	c	–	54	26	1	138	85	2
99/96			4	Melbourne	L-308	5	4	ro	5	10	b	2	72	42	0	42	48	0
100/97			5	Sydney	L-49	7	31	st	6	0	c	1	–	–	–	120	64	0

Career	M	I	NO	HS	R	Avge	100	50	Ct	St	Balls	R	W	Avge	BB	5w	10w	Rate
Test	23	41	3	104	987	25.97	3	2	39	–	3803	1810	47	38.51	8-81	3	–	80.91
F/c	432	752	57	257*	17801	25.61	25	75	545	1	53792	30388	1114	27.27	9-41	80	16	48.28

BREARLEY
John Michael OBE

Cambridge University (1961 to 1964)
Middlesex (1961 to 1983)

Wisden 1977

TOURS

A 1976–77, 1978–79, 1979–80; SA 1964–65; I 1976–77, 1979–80, 1980–81 (Overseas XI); P 1966–67 (MCC U-25), 1973–74 (Int XI), 1977–78; Z 1980–81 (Middx)

Born Harrow, Middlesex 28 Apr 1942

Mike Brearley was an outstanding captain whose batting never quite fulfilled its early promise. During four years as a Cambridge blue (two as captain) he recorded a record aggregate, hit ten hundreds and gained a first in Classics. Although eventually successful as an opening batsman for Middlesex, his limited range of strokes and dominant right hand restricted his contributions at Test level. Academically brilliant, his tactical acumen, charm and training in psychology made him a notable manipulator of cricketers, especially his bowlers and particularly Ian Botham in 1981. In that year against Australia, England, 1–0 down after two Tests, recalled Brearley, who rallied the side to an epic 3–1 victory. His great strength was as a communicator who could establish a rapport with each member of his team. Formerly a wicket-keeper, he became a specialist slip and very occasional right-arm seamer. Since retiring he has concentrated on psychotherapy, writing and teaching.

NOTABLE FEATS

- 1000 runs in 27th Test (*839*) (45 inns). 50 catches in 39th Test (*908*).
- Only the second captain after L. Hutton to regain and then successfully defend the Ashes (Test *837*).
- First to lead England to 5 wins in an Ashes rubber (*839*).
- First captain to gain 11 victories v Australia (907) – equalling D.G. Bradman's Australian record v England.
- Captained England to 18 wins in 31 Tests, including a record unbeaten 19 home Tests, and Middlesex (1971–82) to 3 Championship titles (plus one shared).
- Amassed record first-class career aggregate for Oxbridge: 4310 runs, avge 38.48.
- Scored 312* on first day for MCC U-25 v North Zone at Peshawar in 1966–67.
- Exceeded 1000 runs in a season 11 times, including 2178 in 1964.

Ref	Series	V	T	Venue	Result	Batting 1st No	R	HO	Batting 2nd No	R	HO	Ct
777/515	1976	WI	1	Nottingham	D	2	0	c	2	17	c	1
778/516			2	Lord's	D	2	40	b	2	13	b	–
788/520	1976–77	I	1	Delhi	W-I & 25	2	5	ro	–	–	–	–
789/521			2	Calcutta	W-10w	3	5	c	–	–	–	2
790/522			3	Madras[1]	W-200	3	59	c	4	29	b	5
791/523			4	Bangalore	L-140	2	4	c	2	4	c	2
792/524			5	Bombay[3]	D	2	91	st	2	18	c	–
803/525	1976–77	A		Melbourne	L-45	2	12	c	2	43	lbw	1
804/526*	1977	A	1	Lord's	D	2	9	c	2	49	c	2
805/527*			2	Manchester	W-9w	2	6	c	2	44	c	1
806/528*			3	Nottingham	W-7w	1	15	c	1	81	b	3
807/529*			4	Leeds	W-I & 85	1	0	c	–	–	–	1
808/530*			5	Oval	D	1	39	c	1	4	c	–
814/531*	1977–78	P	1	Lahore[2]	D	2	23	ro	–	–	–	–
815/532*			2	Hyderabad	D	2	17	c	2	74	c	3
825/537*	1978	P	1	Birmingham	W-I & 57	1	38	ro	–	–	–	2
826/538*			2	Lord's	W-I & 120	1	2	lbw	–	–	–	2
827/539*			3	Leeds	D	1	0	c	–	–	–	2
828/540*	1978	NZ	1	Oval	W-7w	1	2	c	1	11	lbw	2
829/541*			2	Nottingham	W-I & 119	5	50	c	–	–	–	2
830/542*			3	Lord's	W-7w	5	33	c	5	8	*	1
834/543*	1978–79	A	1	Brisbane[2]	W-7w	5	6	c	4	13	c	1
835/544*			2	Perth	W-166	4	17	c	4	0	c	1
836/545*			3	Melbourne	L-103	2	1	lbw	2	0	c	2
837/546*			4	Sydney	W-93	2	17	b	2	53	b	–
838/547*			5	Adelaide	W-205	2	2	c	2	9	lbw	1
839/548*			6	Sydney	W-9w	2	46	c	2	20	*	–
851/549*	1979	I	1	Birmingham	W-I & 83	1	24	c	–	–	–	1
852/550*			2	Lord's	D	1	12	c	–	–	–	2
853/551*			3	Leeds	D	2	15	c	–	–	–	1
854/552*			4	Oval	D	7	34	b	7	11	b	3
868/553*	1979–80	A	1	Perth	L-138	6	64	c	7	11	c	1
870/554*			2	Sydney	L-6w	5	7	c	4	19	c	2
872/555*			3	Melbourne	L-8w	7	60	*	6	10	c	–
876/556*	1979–80	I		Bombay[3]	W-10w	5	5	lbw	–	–	–	1
905/569*	1981	A	3	Leeds	W-18	3	10	c	3	14	c	–
906/570*			4	Birmingham	W-29	2	48	c	2	13	lbw	–
907/571*			5	Manchester	W-103	5	2	lbw	6	3	c	1
908/572*			6	Oval	D	5	0	c	6	51	c	3

Career	M	I	NO	HS	R	Avge	100	50	Ct	St	Balls	R	W	Avge	BB	5w	10w	Rate
Test	39	66	3	91	1442	22.88	–	9	52	–	–	–	–	–	–	–	–	–
F/c	455	768	102	312*	25185	37.81	45	134	418	12	315	192	3	64.00	1-6	–	–	105.00

Mike Brearley directing affairs at Old Trafford in the 1981 series against Australia.

J. M. BREARLEY – TEST BATTING SUMMARY

Series	V	M	I	NO	HS	R	Avge	100	50
1976	WI	2	4	–	40	70	17.50	–	–
1966–77	I	5	8	–	91	215	26.87	–	2
1976–77	A	1	2	–	43	55	27.50	–	–
1977	A	5	9	–	81	247	27.44	–	1
1977–78	P	2	3	–	74	114	38.00	–	1
1978	P	3	3	–	38	40	13.33	–	–
1978	NZ	3	5	1	50	104	26.00	–	1
1978–79	A	6	12	1	53	184	16.72	–	1
1979	I	4	5	–	34	96	19.20	–	–
1979–80	A	3	6	1	64	171	34.20	–	2
1979–80	I	1	1	–	5	5	5.00	–	–
1981	A	4	8	–	51	141	17.62	–	1
	A	19	37	2	81	798	22.80	–	5
	WI	2	4	–	40	70	17.50	–	–
	NZ	3	5	1	50	104	26.00	–	1
	I	10	14	–	91	316	22.57	–	2
	P	5	6	–	74	154	25.66	–	1
Home		21	34	1	81	698	21.15	–	3
Overseas		18	32	2	91	744	24.80	–	6
Totals		39	66	3	91	1442	22.88	–	9

BREARLEY, Walter

Lancashire (1902 to 1911)
London County (1904)

Wisden 1909
Born Bolton, Lancashire 11 Mar 1876
Died Middlesex Hospital, London
13 Jan 1937

NOTABLE FEATS

- Returned the record Lancashire match analysis of 17 for 137, including 4 wickets in 4 balls, v Somerset at Manchester in 1905.
- Took 100 wickets in a season 3 times, including 181 in 1905.

A volatile 15-stone right-arm fast bowler, Walter Brearley derived great pace from a short rolling approach and a massive body swing. He was particularly successful in Roses matches, taking 125 wickets at 16 runs apiece in 14 games. He dismissed Victor Trumper six times in 1905. A fairly hopeless batsman, it was said that whenever he hurried to the crease the groundsman's horse would take up its position between the shafts of the roller. His career was marred by frequent disputes with the Lancashire committee; he refused to play for most of 1906 and all of 1907. He appeared for England in 1912 while playing for Cheshire. Thereafter he coached at Lord's every April until his death.

Walter Brearley

						Batting 1st			Batting 2nd				Bowling 1st			Bowling 2nd		
Ref	**Series**	**V**	**T**	**Venue**	**Result**	**No**	**R**	**HO**	**No**	**R**	**HO**	**Ct**	**Balls**	**R**	**W**	**Balls**	**R**	**W**
86/83	1905	A	4	Manchester	W-I & 80	11	0	c	–	–	–	–	102	72	4	84	54	4
87/84			5	Oval	D	11	11	*	–	–	–	–	187	110	5	66	41	1
103/100	1909	A	3	Leeds	L-126	10	6	b	10	4	*	–	85	42	2	145	36	1
122/113	1912	SA	1	Lord's	W-I & 62	11	0	b	–	–	–	–	–	–	–	36	4	0

Career	M	I	NO	HS	R	Avge	100	50	Ct	St	Balls	R	W	Avge	BB	5w	10w	Rate
Test	4	5	2	11*	21	7.00	–	–	–	–	705	359	17	21.11	5-110	1	–	41.47
F/c	134	185	31	38	907	5.88	–	–	52	–	29530	16305	844	19.31	9-47	93	27	34.98

BRENNAN
Donald Vincent

Yorkshire (1947 to 1953)

TOURS I/SL 1951–52; P 1951–52
Born Eccleshill, Bradford, Yorkshire 10 Feb 1920
Died Ilkley, Yorkshire 9 Jan 1985

After graduating to county cricket via Downside School and the Bradford League, Don Brennan became Yorkshire's regular wicket-keeper for seven seasons. Famed for his unusual white gauntlets and volatile appeals, he was a technician of the highest class, particularly adept at standing up to spin bowling and executing lightning-fast leg-side stumpings. No greater tribute could have been paid to any keeper in 1951 than to be preferred to Godfrey Evans, as Brennan was for his two Test appearances. A dogged defender in a crisis, his only first-class fifty was achieved in India. He was a valuable member of the Yorkshire committee after the demands of his family textile business compelled his early retirement.

Don Brennan watches from behind the stumps as Alec Coxon catches Laurie Fishlock off the bowling of Johnny Wardle during Yorkshire's match against Surrey at The Oval in 1949. Ellis Robinson is at leg slip.

Ref	Series	V	T	Venue	Result	Batting 1st			Batting 2nd			Fielding 1st				Fielding 2nd			
						No	R	HO	No	R	HO	Ct	St	Byes	Balls	Ct	St	Byes	Balls
337/290†	1951	SA	4	Leeds	D	9	16	b	–	–	–	–	–	1	1413	–	–	0	294
338/291†			5	Oval	W-4w	10	0	lbw	–	–	–	–	1	11	639	–	–	11	455

Career	M	I	NO	HS	R	Avge	100	50	Ct	St	Balls	R	W	Avge	BB	5w	10w	Rate
Test	2	2	0	16	16	8.00	–	–	–	1	–	–	–	–	–	–	–	–
F/c	232	258	74	67*	1937	10.52	–	1	318	122	–	–	–	–	–	–	–	–

BRIGGS, John

Lancashire (1879 to 1900)

Wisden 1889
TOURS
A 1884–85, 1886–87, 1887–88, 1891–92, 1894–95, 1897–98; SA 1888–89
Born Sutton in Ashfield, Nottinghamshire 3 Oct 1862
Died Cheadle, Cheshire 11 Jan 1902

Johnny ('Boy') Briggs was first selected for Lancashire chiefly because of his sprightly fielding, and he was played primarily as a fast-scoring batsman during his first six seasons. Not until 1885 did left-arm slow-medium bowling become a dominant feature of his game; from then until the turn of the century he established himself as an outstanding all-rounder making a record six tours of Australia. Just 5ft 5in tall, he bowled tirelessly with an easy action off just two skips and a jump. Besides being able to spin the ball sharply either way, he commanded innumerable variations of flight and had a well-concealed quicker delivery. Extremely popular with the crowds, he was a natural clown with a wonderful sense of humour. Tragedy struck him in 1899 when, on the opening night of Headingley's first-ever Test, he suffered a violent epileptic fit and was admitted to Cheadle Asylum. That marked the end of his Test career, but he recovered to bowl with much of his old skill the following season before another attack led to his return to confinement. There he is said to have engaged upon imaginary bowling stints up and down the ward, proudly announcing his full analysis at the end of each day.

NOTABLE FEATS

- 50 wickets in 16th Test (*32*); 100 wickets (the first bowler to reach this total) in 25th Test (*45*).
- Took 15 for 28 on 26 March 1889 (*32*), the most wickets by a bowler in a single day of Test cricket. That match analysis and his second innings figures of 8 for 11 (the only instance of a bowler taking 8 wickets in a Test innings, all bowled), remain the records for Tests in Cape Town.
- Two hat-tricks: for North v South at Scarborough in 1891 and for England in Test *36*. Also took 3 wickets in 4 balls in Test *32*.
- Exceeded 100 wickets in a season on 12 occasions, 5 times passing 150.
- Took all 10 Worcestershire wickets for 55 at Manchester in 1900.
- Established record for most balls bowled in a county match (630) for Lancashire v Sussex at Manchester in 1897.

						Batting 1st			Batting 2nd				Bowling 1st			Bowling 2nd		
Ref	Series	V	T	Venue	Result	No	R	HO	No	R	HO	Ct	Balls	R	W	Balls	R	W
17/17	1884–85	A	1	Adelaide	W-8w	8	1	c	–	–	–	–	–	–	–	–	–	–
18/18			2	Melbourne	W-10w	7	121	c	–	–	–	1	–	–	–	32	13	0
19/19			3	Sydney	L-6	6	3	c	6	1	b	–	–	–	–	–	–	–
20/20			4	Sydney	L-8w	8	3	c	8	5	ro	–	–	–	–	–	–	–
21/21			5	Melbourne	W-I & 98	8	43	c	–	–	–	2	–	–	–	–	–	–
22/22	1886	A	1	Manchester	W-4w	8	1	c	8	2	*	–	–	–	–	–	–	–
23/23			2	Lord's	W-I & 106	10	0	c	–	–	–	1	136	29	5	153	45	6
24/24			3	Oval	W-I & 217	9	53	c	–	–	–	1	120	28	3	128	30	3
25/25	1886–87	A	1	Sydney	W-13	8	5	c	8	33	b	–	56	25	1	28	7	1
26/26			2	Sydney	W-71	8	17	b	8	16	b	1	80	34	0	88	31	3
27/27	1887–88	A		Sydney	W-126	9	0	b	9	14	c	1	–	–	–	–	–	–
28/28	1888	A	1	Lord's	L-61	10	17	b	8	0	b	–	84	26	3	16	9	1
29/29			2	Oval	W-I & 137	9	0	b	–	–	–	–	148	25	5	24	7	0
30/30			3	Manchester	W-I & 21	9	22	*	–	–	–	–	36	17	1	29	10	2
31/31	1888–89	SA	1	Port Elizabeth	W-8w	7	0	c	–	–	–	1	148	39	4	108	34	2
32/32			2	Cape Town	W-I & 202	3	6	b	–	–	–	–	77	17	7	58	11	8
35/35	1891–92	A	1	Melbourne	L-54	8	41	c	8	4	c	–	18	13	0	126	26	1
36/36			2	Sydney	L-72	9	28	lbw	9	12	c	1	60	24	0	196	69	4
37/37			3	Adelaide	W-I & 230	8	39	b	–	–	–	–	131	49	6	168	87	6
40/40	1893	A	2	Oval	W-I & 43	8	0	b	–	–	–	–	73	34	5	175	114	5
41/41			3	Manchester	D	8	2	b	–	–	–	–	210	81	4	143	64	2
42/42	1894–95	A	1	Sydney	W-10	8	57	b	8	42	b	2	150	96	0	66	25	3
43/43			2	Melbourne	W-94	9	5	c	8	31	lbw	–	83	26	2	72	49	0
44/44			3	Adelaide	L-382	1	12	b	9	0	b	–	48	34	1	114	57	2
45/45			4	Sydney	L-I & 147	3	11	b	8	6	c	1	132	65	4	–	–	–
46/46			5	Melbourne	W-6w	9	0	c	–	–	–	–	142	46	2	96	37	1
51/51	1896	A	2	Manchester	L-3w	9	0	b	9	16	st	–	200	99	2	90	24	1
53/53	1897–98	A	1	Sydney	W-9w	10	1	ro	–	–	–	–	120	42	1	132	86	2
54/54			2	Melbourne	L-I & 55	10	46	*	9	12	c	–	240	96	3	–	–	–
55/55			3	Adelaide	L-I & 13	9	14	c	9	0	*	–	378	128	1	–	–	–
56/56			4	Melbourne	L-8w	9	21	*	1	23	c	–	102	38	1	36	31	0
57/57			5	Sydney	L-6w	9	0	b	9	29	b	–	102	39	1	30	25	0
62/62	1899	A	3	Leeds	D	–	–	–	–	–	–	–	150	53	3	–	–	–

Career	M	I	NO	HS	R	Avge	100	50	Ct	St	Balls	R	W	Avge	BB	5w	10w	Rate
Test	33	50	5	121	815	18.11	1	2	12	–	5332	2094	118	17.74	8-11	9	4	45.18
F/c	535	826	55	186	14092	18.27	10	58	259	–	100119	35430	2221	15.95	10-55	200	52	45.07

Johnny Briggs

J. BRIGGS – TEST BOWLING SUMMARY

Series	V	M	Balls	R	W	Avge	BB	5w	10w	Rate
1884–85	A	5	32	13	0	–	–	–	–	–
1886	A	3	537	132	17	7.76	6-45	2	1	31.58
1886–87	A	2	252	97	5	19.40	3-31	–	–	50.40
1887–88	A	1	–	–	–	–	–	–	–	–
1888	A	3	337	94	12	7.83	5-25	1	–	28.08
1888–89	SA	2	391	101	21	4.80	8-11	2	1	18.61
1891–92	A	3	699	268	17	15.76	6-49	2	1	41.11
1893	A	2	601	293	16	18.31	5-34	2	1	37.56
1894–95	A	5	903	435	15	29.00	4-65	–	–	60.20
1896	A	1	290	123	3	41.00	2-99	–	–	96.66
1987–98	A	5	1140	485	9	53.88	3-96	–	–	126.66
1899	A	1	150	53	3	17.66	3-53	–	–	50.00
	A	31	4941	1993	97	20.54	6-45	7	3	50.93
	SA	2	391	101	21	4.80	8-11	2	1	18.61
Home		10	1915	695	51	13.62	6-45	5	2	37.54
Overseas		23	3417	1399	67	20.88	8-11	4	2	51.00
Totals		33	5332	2094	118	17.74	8-11	9	4	45.18

BROAD
Brian Christopher

Gloucestershire (1979 to 1983)
Nottinghamshire (1984 to date)
Orange Free State (1985–86)

TOURS
A 1986–87, 1987–88; NZ 1987–88;
P 1987–88; Z 1984–85 (Eng Co)
Born Knowle, Bristol 29 Sep 1957

NOTABLE FEATS
- 1000 runs in 15th Test (*1084*) (26 inns).
- Established England records at Perth with his score of 162 and opening stand of 223 with C.W.J. Athey (Test *1059*).
- Became the fourth batsman after J.B. Hobbs, W.R. Hammond and R.A. Woolmer to score hundreds in 3 successive Ashes Tests.

TEST NOTES
- *1085* Bowled in 2nd inns: 0 for 4 (6 balls).

A tall (6ft 4in), left-handed opening batsman, Chris Broad has proved notably more effective overseas than at home, all six of his Test match hundreds being scored outside England. Leaving Gloucestershire after five seasons to advance his Test career prospects, he succeeded within a few weeks of making his debut for Nottinghamshire. He is a strong back-foot player who punishes anything pitched around his legs, favours the straight and off-drive, and has a sound technique against fast bowling. Although highly intelligent and possessing considerable charm, his reaction to being dismissed has frequently been embarrassing, notably his refusal to leave the crease in Lahore and his wicket-demolishing act in the Bicentenary Test.

						Batting 1st			Batting 2nd			
Ref	**Series**	**V**	**T**	**Venue**	**Result**	**No**	**R**	**HO**	**No**	**R**	**HO**	**Ct**
990/602	1984	WI	2	Lord's	L-9w	2	55	c	2	0	c	–
991/603			3	Leeds	L-8w	2	32	c	2	2	c	1
992/604			4	Manchester	L-I & 64	2	42	c	2	21	lbw	–
993/605			5	Oval	L-172	2	4	b	2	39	c	–
994/606	1984	SL		Lord's	D	2	86	c	–	–	–	–
1058/629	1986–87	A	1	Brisbane[2]	W-7w	1	8	c	1	35	*	2
1059/630			2	Perth	D	1	162	c	1	16	lbw	2
1060/631			3	Adelaide	D	1	116	c	1	15	*	1
1061/632			4	Melbourne	W-I & 14	1	112	c	–	–	–	–
1062/633			5	Sydney	L-55	1	6	lbw	1	17	c	–
1076/635	1987	P	2	Lord's	D	1	55	b	–	–	–	–
1077/636			3	Leeds	L-I & 18	1	8	c	1	4	c	–
1078/637			4	Birmingham	D	1	54	c	1	30	c	–
1079/638			5	Oval	D	1	0	c	1	42	c	–
1084/639	1987–88	P	1	Lahore[2]	L-I & 87	2	41	c	2	13	c	1
1085/640			2	Faisalabad	D	2	116	b	2	14	st	–
1086/641			3	Karachi	D	2	7	lbw	2	13	lbw	–
1090/642	1987–88	A		Sydney	D	1	139	b	–	–	–	1
1091/643	1987–88	NZ	1	Christchurch	D	1	114	c	1	20	c	–
1092/644			2	Auckland	D	1	9	c	–	–	–	–
1093/645			3	Wellington	D	1	61	b	–	–	–	–
1098/646	1988	WI	1	Nottingham	D	2	54	b	2	16	c	–
1099/647			2	Lord's	L-134	2	0	lbw	2	1	c	–

Career	M	I	NO	HS	R	Avge	100	50	Ct	St	Balls	R	W	Avge	BB	5w	10w	Rate
Test	23	40	2	162	1579	41.55	6	6	8	–	6	4	–	–	–	–	–	–
F/c	228	400	28	171	13344	35.87	25	74	125	–	1625	1036	16	64.75	2-14	–	–	101.56

Chris Broad during his innings of 162 against Australia at Perth in 1986–87. Tim Zoehrer looks on as Steve Waugh takes evasive action.

B. C. BROAD – TEST BATTING SUMMARY

Series	V	M	I	NO	HS	R	Avge	100	50
1984	WI	4	8	–	55	195	24.37	–	1
1984	SL	1	1	–	86	86	86.00	–	1
1986–87	A	5	9	2	162	487	69.57	3	–
1987	P	4	7	–	55	193	27.57	–	2
1987–88	P	3	6	–	116	204	34.00	1	–
1987–88	A	1	1	–	139	139	139.00	1	–
1987–88	NZ	3	4	–	114	204	51.00	1	1
1988	WI	2	4	–	54	71	17.75	–	1
	A	6	10	2	162	626	78.25	4	–
	WI	6	12	–	55	266	22.16	–	2
	NZ	3	4	–	114	204	51.00	1	1
	P	7	13	–	116	397	30.53	1	2
	SL	1	1	–	86	86	86.00	–	1
Home		11	20	–	86	545	27.25	–	5
Overseas		12	20	2	162	1034	57.44	6	1
Totals		23	40	2	162	1579	41.55	6	6

BROCKWELL William

Surrey (1886 to 1903)
Kimberley (1889 to 1890)
London County (1901 to 1903)

Wisden 1985
TOUR A 1894–95
Born Kingston upon Thames, Surrey 21 Jan 1865
Died Richmond, Surrey 30 Jun 1935

Bill Brockwell was a stylish opening batsman who favoured the back foot. A strong driver on both sides of the wicket, he was also a useful fast-medium right-arm bowler and a specialist second slip. He became a regular member of the powerful Surrey eleven during a period when they won eight titles and shared another. 1894 was 'Brockwell's Year' when, in a difficult, wet season, he headed the national averages and achieved the highest aggregate: 1491 runs at 38.23. Although one of the first English players to coach in South Africa and India and an accomplished writer and photographer, he fell upon hard times and died in abject poverty.

Bill Brockwell

NOTABLE FEATS

- Achieved the 'double' in 1899 and exceeded 1000 runs in a season 6 times.
- Contributed his highest score (225) to a then world record opening stand of 379 with R. Abel for Surrey v Hampshire at The Oval in 1897.
- When Surrey required 346 runs for victory in 170 minutes against Kent at The Oval in 1900, Brockwell (132*) and R. Abel (120*) scored 270 to establish the highest fourth-innings total in Britain without the loss of a wicket.
- Hat-trick for Surrey v Yorkshire at Sheffield in 1900.
- Scored a pre-lunch first-day hundred on 3 occasions for Surrey.

Ref	Series	V	T	Venue	Result	Batting 1st No	R	HO	Batting 2nd No	R	HO	Ct	Bowling 1st Balls	R	W	Bowling 2nd Balls	R	W
41/41	1893	A	3	Manchester	D	7	11	c	–	–	–	1	15	17	0	–	–	–
42/42	1894–95	A	1	Sydney	W-10	5	49	c	5	37	b	1	132	78	1	–	–	–
43/43			2	Melbourne	W-94	5	0	c	5	21	b	1	–	–	–	84	33	3
44/44			3	Adelaide	L-382	3	12	c	6	24	c	1	120	30	1	60	50	0
45/45			4	Sydney	L-I & 147	6	1	c	5	17	c	1	30	25	0	–	–	–
46/46			5	Melbourne	W-6w	2	5	st	2	5	c	–	36	22	0	–	–	–
63/63	1899	A	4	Manchester	D	7	20	c	–	–	–	1	30	18	0	75	36	0

Career	M	I	NO	HS	R	Avge	100	50	Ct	St	Balls	R	W	Avge	BB	5w	10w	Rate
Test	7	12	0	49	202	16.83	–	–	6	–	582	309	5	61.80	3-33	–	–	116.40
F/c	357	539	47	225	13285	27.00	21	53	250	1	28415	13680	553	24.73	8-22	24	1	51.38

BROMLEY-DAVENPORT Hugh Richard OBE

Cambridge University (1892 to 1893)
Middlesex (1896 to 1898)

TOURS
WI 1894–95, 1896–97; SA 1895–96, 1898–99
Born Capesthorne, Cheshire 18 Aug 1870
Died South Kensington, London 23 May 1954

A left-arm fast bowler, useful right-handed lower-order batsman and specialist slip fielder, Hugh Bromley-Davenport was one of the few players of his era to wear glasses on the field. When captain of Eton, *Wisden* had described him as 'the best Public School bowler of 1887', and he went on to gain blues for Cambridge in 1892 and 1893 under the captaincy of F.S. Jackson. After two seasons with his native Cheshire, he appeared spasmodically for Middlesex and gained his Test caps whilst on two tours of South Africa with Lord Hawke. He served as a Lieutenant in the Royal Engineers during the First World War. [*Illus. pp.* 196, 325]

NOTABLE FEATS
- Hat-trick for R.S. Lucas's XI v Demerara at Georgetown in 1894–95.

Ref	Series	V	T	Venue	Result	Batting 1st No	R	HO	Batting 2nd No	R	HO	Ct	Bowling 1st Balls	R	W	Bowling 2nd Balls	R	W
47/47	1895–96	SA	1	Port Elizabeth	W-288	7	26	c	9	7	c	–	60	46	2	35	23	1
48/48			2	Johannesburg[1]	W-I & 197	9	84	c	–	–	–	–	15	13	0	–	–	–
49/49			3	Cape Town	W-I & 33	4	7	b	–	–	–	–	–	–	–	45	16	1
58/58	1898–99	SA	1	Johannesburg[1]	W-32	10	4	c	11	0	b	1	–	–	–	–	–	–

Career	M	I	NO	HS	R	Avge	100	50	Ct	St	Balls	R	W	Avge	BB	5w	10w	Rate
Test	4	6	0	84	128	21.33	–	1	1	–	155	98	4	24.50	2-46	–	–	38.75
F/c	76	119	21	91	1801	18.37	–	11	48	–	6910	3352	187	17.92	7-17	12	1	36.95

BROOKES, Dennis

Northamptonshire (1934 to 1959)

Wisden 1957
TOUR WI 1947–48
Born Kippax, Yorkshire 29 Oct 1915

A stylish and most consistent opening batsman, Dennis Brookes was the backbone of Northamptonshire's batting for 14 seasons after the Second World War. His upright method enabled him to drive freely on both sides of the wicket and he was a masterly exponent of the cut and glance. He was desperately unlucky to be ignored by the selectors after a fractured finger had prematurely ended his only overseas tour. An outstanding cover fielder in his pre-war years, he later specialized in the close positions. A kind and popular man, he was the County's first professional captain and, subsequently, its president and a justice of the peace.

NOTABLE FEATS
- Holds the Northamptonshire first-class records for most appearances (492), most runs (28,980), most hundreds (67), most runs in a season (2198) and most instances of 1000 runs in a season (17, including 2000 on 6 occasions).
- The highest of his 6 double centuries was 257 v Gloucestershire at Bristol in 1949.
- Shared in record 5th-wkt Northamptonshire partnership of 347 with D.W. Barrick v Essex at Northampton in 1952.

Dennis Brookes

						Batting 1st			Batting 2nd			
Ref	Series	V	T	Venue	Result	No	R	HO	No	R	HO	Ct
295/258	1947–48	WI	1	Bridgetown	D	3	10	b	2	7	c	1

Career	M	I	NO	HS	R	Avge	100	50	Ct	St	Balls	R	W	Avge	BB	5w	10w	Rate
Test	1	2	0	10	17	8.50	–	–	1	–	–	–	–	–	–	–	–	–
F/c	525	925	70	257	30874	36.10	71	152	205	–	158	127	3	42.33	1-7	–	–	52.66

BROWN, Alan

Kent (1957 to 1970)

TOURS I/SL 1961–62; P 1961–62
Born Rainworth, Nottinghamshire
17 Oct 1935

Alan Brown

A tall (6ft 2in), well-built right-handed fast-medium bowler with a considerable back-foot drag, Alan Brown had been capable of bursts of devastating speed at the outset of his career. He was a mainstay of the Kent side for more than a decade; a strong, warm-hearted cricketer. A hard-hitting, entertaining batsman, he was also a footballer good enough to appear as centre-forward for Gravesend.

NOTABLE FEATS
- Claimed 116 wickets, avge 19.04, in 1965.
- Took 4 wickets in 5 balls for Kent v Nottinghamshire at Folkestone in 1959.

						Batting 1st			Batting 2nd				Bowling 1st			Bowling 2nd		
Ref	Series	V	T	Venue	Result	No	R	HO	No	R	HO	Ct	Balls	R	W	Balls	R	W
512/374	1961–62	P	1	Lahore[2]	W-5w	11	3	*	–	–	–	–	95	44	0	84	27	3
513/375	1961–62	I	1	Bombay[2]	D	–	–	–	–	–	–	1	114	64	0	30	15	0

Career	M	I	NO	HS	R	Avge	100	50	Ct	St	Balls	R	W	Avge	BB	5w	10w	Rate
Test	2	1	1	3*	3	–	–	–	1	–	323	150	3	50.00	3-27	–	–	107.66
F/c	251	312	87	81	2189	9.72	–	3	104	–	40603	18326	743	24.66	8-47	26	4	54.64

BROWN, David John

Warwickshire (1961 to 1982)

TOURS
A 1965–66; SA 1964–65, 1972–73 (Robins); WI 1967–68; NZ 1965–66; P 1966–67 (MCC U-25), 1968–69, 1970–71 (Int XI); SL 1968–69
Born Walsall, Staffordshire 30 Jan 1942

NOTABLE FEATS
- 50 wickets in 16th Test (*638*).
- Twice took 3 Test wickets in an over (Tests *599* and *628*).

A tall (6ft 4in), cheerful and extremely popular right-handed fast-medium bowler, David Brown's sheer determination made him more successful at Test level than perhaps his natural ability merited. His high action enabled him to extract exceptional bounce and he was at his most effective on hard pitches overseas. Capable of inspired spells on important occasions, he clinched his place on the 1965–66 tour to Australia by bowling Bob Simpson in the first over of each innings for the president of MCC's XI at Lord's. His main asset was the exceptional willpower which enabled him to recover from injuries and loss of form. A straight-bat defence and stubborn temperament developed a batting method based on his considerable reach. From 1980 to 1987 he combined farming with a keen interest in horse-breeding and the duties of Warwickshire's cricket manager.

David Brown bowls Denis Lindsay at The Oval during the final Test against the 1965 South Africans.

						Batting 1st			Batting 2nd				Bowling 1st			Bowling 2nd		
Ref	Series	V	T	Venue	Result	No	R	HO	No	R	HO	Ct	Balls	R	W	Balls	R	W
594/418	1965	SA	1	Lord's	D	9	1	c	9	5	c	1	144	44	3	126	30	3
596/420			3	Oval	D	7	0	c	–	–	–	–	132	63	0	138	63	2
597/421	1965–66	A	1	Brisbane[2]	D	9	3	b	–	–	–	–	168	71	3	–	–	–
599/423			3	Sydney	W-I & 93	7	1	c	–	–	–	–	136	63	5	88	32	1
600/424			4	Adelaide	L-I & 9	10	1	c	10	0	c	–	224	109	1	–	–	–
601/425			5	Melbourne	D	10	12	c	–	–	–	–	248	134	1	–	–	–
602/426	1965–66	NZ	1	Christchurch	D	9	44	b	–	–	–	1	180	80	3	24	6	1
604/428			3	Auckland	D	8	0	b	–	–	–	–	108	32	1	49	8	1
605/429	1966	WI	1	Manchester	L-I & 40	9	14	b	9	10	c	–	168	84	0	–	–	–
619/435	1967	I	2	Lord's	W-I & 124	10	5	c	–	–	–	–	108	61	3	30	10	0
620/436			3	Birmingham	W-132	9	3	ro	9	29	*	–	66	17	3	12	1	0
628/440	1967–68	WI	1	Port-of-Spain	D	9	22	*	–	–	–	–	132	65	2	84	27	3
629/441			2	Kingston	D	9	14	c	9	0	b	–	78	34	1	198	65	2
630/442			3	Bridgetown	D	8	1	b	–	–	–	–	192	66	2	66	61	1
631/443			4	Port-of-Spain	W-7w	9	0	c	–	–	–	–	162	107	3	60	33	0
638/446	1968	A	2	Lord's	D	–	–	–	–	–	–	1	84	42	5	114	40	0
639/447			3	Birmingham	D	9	0	b	–	–	–	–	78	44	1	36	15	0
640/448			4	Leeds	D	10	14	b	–	–	–	–	210	99	2	162	79	0
641/449			5	Oval	W-226	11	2	c	11	1	b	2	132	63	3	48	19	1
647/450	1968–69	P	1	Lahore[2]	D	9	7	b	9	44	*	–	84	43	3	90	47	2
648/451			2	Dacca	D	8	4	c	–	–	–	1	138	51	3	36	18	0
649/452			3	Karachi	D	9	25	*	–	–	–	–	–	–	–	–	–	–
653/453	1969	WI	1	Manchester	W-10w	9	15	b	–	–	–	–	78	39	4	132	59	3
654/454			2	Lord's	D	10	1	c	–	–	–	–	228	99	3	54	25	0
655/455			3	Leeds	W-30	10	12	b	10	34	b	–	45	13	2	126	53	2
656/456	1969	NZ	1	Lord's	W-230	9	11	*	9	7	c	1	72	17	0	30	6	0

Career	M	I	NO	HS	R	Avge	100	50	Ct	St	Balls	R	W	Avge	BB	5w	10w	Rate
Test	26	34	5	44*	342	11.79	–	–	7	–	5098	2237	79	28.31	5-42	2	–	64.53
F/c	390	446	111	79	4110	12.26	–	6	157	–	63339	28961	1165	24.85	8-60	46	5	54.36

D. J. BROWN – TEST BOWLING SUMMARY

Series	V	M	Balls	R	W	Avge	BB	5w	10w	Rate
1965	SA	2	540	200	8	25.00	3-44	–	–	67.50
1965 66	A	4	864	409	11	37.18	5-63	1	–	78.54
1965–66	NZ	2	361	126	6	21.00	3-80	–	–	60.16
1966	WI	1	168	84	0	–	–	–	–	–
1967	I	2	216	89	6	14.83	3-17	–	–	36.00
1967–68	WI	4	972	458	14	32.71	3-27	–	–	69.42
1968	A	4	864	401	12	33.41	5-42	1	–	72.00
1968–69	P	3	348	159	8	19.87	3-43	–	–	43.50
1969	WI	3	663	288	14	20.57	4-39	–	–	47.35
1969	NZ	1	102	23	0	–	–	–	–	–
	A	8	1728	810	23	35.21	5-42	2	–	75.13
	SA	2	540	200	8	25.00	3-44	–	–	67.50
	WI	8	1803	830	28	29.64	4-39	–	–	64.39
	NZ	3	463	149	6	24.83	3-80	–	–	77.16
	I	2	216	89	6	14.83	3-17	–	–	36.00
	P	3	348	159	8	19.87	3-43	–	–	43.50
Home		13	2553	1085	40	27.12	5-42	1	–	63.82
Overseas		13	2545	1152	39	29.53	5-63	1	–	65.25
Totals		26	5098	2237	79	28.31	5-42	2	–	64.53

BROWN
Frederick Richard CBE

Cambridge University (1930 to 1931)
Surrey (1931 to 1948)
Northamptonshire (1949 to 1953)

Wisden 1933
TOURS
A 1932–33, 1950–51; SA 1956–57 (when manager); NZ 1932–33, 1950–51
Born Lima, Peru 16 Dec 1910

Freddie Brown

During a unique career which overcame a 10-year interlude, Freddie Brown undertook virtually every role available to a cricketer. As a strapping youth he had dominated cricket at The Leys School and successively headed the batting and bowling averages in his two seasons as a Cambridge blue. Tall (6ft ½in), ruddy and adorned with a fluttering silk neckerchief, he was a breezy middle-order batsman who drove with immense power and he could bowl either medium-pace off-cutters or brisk leg-breaks and googlies. In his first full season with Surrey he did the 'double' and gained selection for Jardine's 'bodyline' tour of Australia. An amateur, he continued to make spasmodic appearances until, converted into a wartime army officer and captured in North Africa, he spent three years in Italy with his fellow POW, Bill Bowes. A business appointment in Northamptonshire occupied the immediate post-war years until 1949, when he was appointed captain of that county. There his rugged ebullience revitalized a struggling team, achieved another 'double' and regained his Test place. Captain of the 1950–51 MCC tour of Australia, he lost the rubber but had the compensation of inflicting Australia's first post-war defeat in the final Test. Chairman of selectors in 1953, he was persuaded to play in the Lord's Test where he contributed 50 runs and 4 wickets to England's epic rally. After retirement he became an energetic administrator devoted to the development of youth cricket, was manager of two MCC tours (South Africa 1956–57 and Australia/New Zealand 1958–59), and was a member of BBC radio's Test match commentary team. He was president of MCC in 1971–72, chairman of the Cricket Council (1974–79) and successively chairman and president of the NCA.

NOTABLE FEATS

- Achieved the 'double' twice, exceeding 1000 runs in a season 4 times and 100 wickets thrice. Brown and V.W.C. Jupp are alone in doing the 'double' for 2 counties.
- Scored 212 in 200 min (7 sixes) for Surrey v Middlesex at The Oval in 1933, adding 155 for the 8th wkt in 65 min with M.J.C. Allom.
- Shared in record Northamptonshire 8th-wkt stand of 155 with A.E. Nutter v Glamorgan at Northampton in 1952.

Ref	Series	V	T	Venue	Result	Batting 1st No	R	HO	Batting 2nd No	R	HO	Ct	Bowling 1st Balls	R	W	Bowling 2nd Balls	R	W
210/191	1931	NZ	2	Oval	W-I & 26	–	–	–	–	–	–	1	174	52	2	96	38	1
211/192			3	Manchester	D	–	–	–	–	–	–	–	–	–	–	–	–	–
219/193	1932	I		Lord's	W-158	9	1	c	9	29	c	–	150	48	1	84	54	2
225/199	1932–33	NZ	1	Christchurch	D	7	74	c	–	–	–	1	114	34	1	–	–	–
226/200			2	Auckland	D	7	13	c	–	–	–	–	12	19	0	–	–	–
261/230	1937	NZ	2	Manchester	W-130	9	1	b	9	57	b	1	136	81	3	30	14	1
316/274*	1949	NZ	3	Manchester	D	7	22	c	–	–	–	2	108	43	0	126	71	2
317/275*			4	Oval	D	6	21	c	–	–	–	2	30	14	0	60	29	0
326/279*	1950	WI	4	Oval	L-I & 56	7	0	c	7	15	c	–	126	74	1	–	–	–
327/280*	1950–51	A	1	Brisbane[2]	L-70	8	4	c	10	17	c	–	88	63	2	–	–	–
328/281*			2	Melbourne	L-28	7	62	c	8	8	b	–	72	28	1	96	26	4
329/282*			3	Sydney	L-I & 13	6	79	b	6	18	b	–	352	153	4	–	–	–
330/283*			4	Adelaide	L-274	6	16	b	–	–	–	1	24	24	0	24	14	1
331/284*			5	Melbourne	W-8w	6	6	b	–	–	–	3	144	49	5	72	32	1
332/285*	1950–51	NZ	1	Christchurch	D	6	62	c	–	–	–	2	92	34	1	–	–	–
333/286*			2	Wellington	W-6w	6	47	b	6	10	*	2	36	10	1	6	1	0
334/287*	1951	SA	1	Nottingham	L-71	6	29	c	7	7	c	1	204	74	2	–	–	–
335/288*			2	Lord's	W-10w	6	1	b	–	–	–	3	–	–	–	–	–	–
336/289*			3	Manchester	W-9w	6	42	c	–	–	–	1	–	–	–	–	–	–
337/290*			4	Leeds	D	7	2	c	–	–	–	–	228	107	3	66	26	0
338/291*			5	Oval	W-4w	6	1	c	6	40	lbw	1	120	31	2	78	20	0
373/302	1953	A	2	Lord's	D	7	22	c	7	28	c	1	150	53	0	162	82	4

Career	M	I	NO	HS	R	Avge	100	50	Ct	St	Balls	R	W	Avge	BB	5w	10w	Rate
Test	22	30	1	79	734	25.31	–	5	22	–	3260	1398	45	31.06	5-49	1	–	72.44
F/c	355	536	49	212	13325	27.36	22	56	212	–	65967	32007	1221	26.21	8-34	62	11	54.02

BROWN, George

Hampshire (1908 to 1933)

TOURS
SA 1922–23; WI 1910–11, 1931–32 (Tennyson); I/SL 1926–27
Born Cowley, Oxford 6 Oct 1887
Died Winchester, Hampshire 3 Dec 1964

George Brown was an outstanding all-round cricketer in the fullest sense: a dashing left-handed batsman, a medium-pace right-arm bowler, a wicket-keeper good enough to play against Australia and a fearless close fielder, usually at silly point. Not surprisingly he was a dominant force in Hampshire's fortunes between 1909 and 1933. Tall and strongly built, he could temper his natural aggression when the occasion demanded a defensive approach. After Hampshire had been dismissed by Warwickshire for 15 at Edgbaston in 1922 and followed on 208 behind, Brown contributed 172 to a second-innings total of 521 which paved the way for an historic victory. He served for three seasons as a first-class umpire.

NOTABLE FEATS
- Exceeded 1000 runs in a season 11 times, including 2040 in 1926, and scored 3 double centuries.
- Shared in 3 surviving record Hampshire partnerships: 321 (2nd) with E.I.M. Barrett v Glos at Southampton in 1920, 344 (3rd) with C.P. Mead v Yorkshire at Portsmouth in 1927, and 325 (7th) with C.H. Abercrombie v Essex at Leyton in 1913.

George Brown

Ref	Series	V	T	Venue	Result	Batting 1st No	R	HO	Batting 2nd No	R	HO	Fielding 1st Ct	St	Byes	Balls	Fielding 2nd Ct	St	Byes	Balls
142/131†	1921	A	3	Leeds	L-219	7	57	c	1	46	lbw	1	–	16	559	–	–	10	438
143/132†			4	Manchester	D	2	31	c	–	–	–	–	–	22	700	–	–	–	–
144/133†			5	Oval	D	2	32	b	2	84	c	1	2	6	612	–	–	–	–
148/134†	1922–23	SA	1	Johannesburg[1]	L-168	9	22	b	8	1	b	2	–	5	334	–	1	14	747
149/135†			2	Cape Town	W-1w	10	10	*	10	0	ro	1	–	14	336	–	–	15	686
151/137†			4	Johannesburg[1]	D	10	0	b	–	–	–	1	–	11	552	1	–	16	479
152/138†			5	Durban[2]	W-109	10	15	*	1	1	lbw	1	–	14	510	1	–	11	703

Career	M	I	NO	HS	R	Avge	100	50	Ct	St	Balls	R	W	Avge	BB	5w	10w	Rate
Test	7	12	2	84	299	29.90	–	2	9	3	–	–	–	–	–	–	–	–
F/c	612	1012	52	232*	25649	26.71	37	111	568	78	31848	18666	626	29.81	8-55	23	2	50.87

BROWN
John Thomas

Yorkshire (1889 to 1904)

Wisden 1895
TOUR A 1894–95
Born Driffield, Yorkshire 20 Aug 1869
Died Westminster, London 4 Nov 1904

Jack Brown

Jack Brown was a neat, stylish opening batsman, short in stature but powerfully built, who mastered all conditions to become a key player in an exceptionally strong Yorkshire team. He had a full range of strokes and was a brilliant exponent of the late cut. His greatest innings was the breakneck 140 which won the decisive Fifth Test at Melbourne in 1894–95 (see *Notable Feats*). A pleasantly mannered man with a quiet sense of humour, he shared with John Tunnicliffe in 19 three-figure partnerships for Yorkshire's first wicket, most notably their then world record of 554. His slow right-arm leg-spin bowling brought frequent reward and he was a fine fielder. A heavy smoker, he suffered from asthma and a heart condition, the latter bringing about his premature retirement and death at the age of 35.

NOTABLE FEATS

- His 28-min first fifty in Test *46* remains the fastest in Test cricket and his 95-min hundred was a record until 1897–98. His 3rd-wkt stand of 210 with A. Ward set a Test record for any wicket.
- Only batsman to score 2 triple centuries for Yorkshire, contributing 311 and 300 to then world-record opening stands with J. Tunnicliffe: 378 v Sussex at Sheffield in 1897 and 554 (503 on the first day) v Derbyshire at Chesterfield in 1898.
- Exceeded 1000 runs in each of 10 successive seasons (1894–1903).

TEST NOTES

- *51* Kept wicket and caught G.H.S. Trott when A.F.A. Lilley's bowling was required to break a stand.
- *62* Bowled in 2nd inns: 0 for 22 (35 balls).

Ref	Series	V	T	Venue	Result	Batting 1st No	R	HO	Batting 2nd No	R	HO	Ct
42/42	1894–95	A	1	Sydney	W-10	4	22	ro	4	53	c	–
43/43			2	Melbourne	W-94	4	0	c	4	37	c	2
44/44			3	Adelaide	L-382	6	39	*	5	2	b	2
45/45			4	Sydney	L-I & 147	5	20	*	1	0	b	1
46/46			5	Melbourne	W-6w	4	30	b	4	140	c	–
50/50	1896	A	1	Lord's	W-6w	4	9	b	4	36	c	–
51/51			2	Manchester	L-3w	6	22	c	6	19	c	1
62/62	1899	A	3	Leeds	D	1	27	c	1	14	*	1

Career	M	I	NO	HS	R	Avge	100	50	Ct	St	Balls	R	W	Avge	BB	5w	10w	Rate
Test	8	16	3	140	470	36.15	1	1	7	–	35	22	0	–	–	–	–	–
F/c	382	633	47	311	17582	30.46	29	76	229	–	9391	5627	190	29.61	6-52	4	–	49.42

BUCKENHAM
Claude Percival

Essex (1899 to 1914)

TOUR SA 1909–10
Born Herne Hill, Surrey 16 Jan 1876
Died Dundee, Scotland 23 Feb 1937

A tall, sparingly built right-arm bowler with a high action, Claude Buckenham was regarded as one of the deadliest pace bowlers of his time. His figures of 828 first-class wickets for under 23 runs apiece in the period 1905 to 1911 would have been even more impressive but for some desperately poor Essex slip-catching. His ability to hit the ball extremely hard brought him two first-class hundreds. After First World War service in the Royal Garrison Artillery, he became coach at Repton School. [*Illus. p.* 273]

NOTABLE FEATS

- Took 100 wickets in a season 6 times (1906–11).

					Batting 1st			Batting 2nd				Bowling 1st			Bowling 2nd		
Ref	Series	V	T Venue	Result	No	R	HO	No	R	HO	Ct	Balls	R	W	Balls	R	W
106/103	1909–10	SA	1 Johannesburg[1]	L-19	8	0	b	8	1	b	–	114	77	3	234	110	4
107/104			2 Durban[1]	L-95	8	16	b	8	3	c	–	162	51	2	186	94	3
108/105			3 Johannesburg[1]	W-3w	10	1	c	–	–	–	1	186	115	5	138	73	0
109/106			4 Cape Town	L-4w	9	5	b	10	17	c	1	120	61	3	42	12	1

Career	M	I	NO	HS	R	Avge	100	50	Ct	St	Balls	R	W	Avge	BB	5w	10w	Rate
Test	4	7	0	17	43	6.14	–	–	2	–	1182	593	21	28.23	5-115	1	–	56.28
F/c	308	469	79	124	5658	14.50	2	12	172	–	52277	29147	1152	25.30	8-33	85	17	45.37

BUTCHER
Alan Raymond

Surrey (1972 to 1986)
Glamorgan (1987 to date)

TOURS
WI 1982–83 (Int XI);
I 1980–81 (Overseas XI)
Born Croydon, Surrey 7 Jan 1954

Alan Butcher is an accomplished and courageous left-handed opening batsman who moved to Glamorgan after 15 seasons with Surrey. Just 5ft 8½in in height, he favours the back foot but has an attractive repertoire of strokes which have enabled him to exceed 1000 runs in a season nine times. Although a positive, chirpy character, he suffered badly from nerves when batting in the shadow of Boycott during his lone chance at Test level. A handy left-arm purveyor of seam or orthodox spin, he is also a brave close fielder with sharp reflexes. His two younger brothers also played county cricket.

Alan Butcher batting in his only Test, partnered by Geoffrey Boycott.

					Batting 1st			Batting 2nd				Bowling 1st			Bowling 2nd		
Ref	Series	V	T Venue	Result	No	R	HO	No	R	HO	Ct	Balls	R	W	Balls	R	W
854/552	1979	I	4 Oval	D	2	14	c	2	20	c	–	–	–	–	12	9	0

Career	M	I	NO	HS	R	Avge	100	50	Ct	St	Balls	R	W	Avge	BB	5w	10w	Rate
Test	1	2	0	20	34	17.00	–	–	–	–	12	9	0	–	–	–	–	–
F/c	328	557	47	216*	17025	33.38	33	82	150	–	9572	5058	134	37.74	6-48	1	–	71.43

BUTCHER
Roland Orlando

Middlesex (1974 to date)
Barbados (1974–75)
Tasmania (1982–83)

TOURS
WI 1980–81, 1982–83 (Int XI);
P 1981–82 (Int XI); Z 1980–81 (Middx)
Born East Point, St Philip, Barbados
14 Oct 1953

Roland Butcher was the first black West Indian to play for England; he even enjoyed the added delight of making his debut in his native Barbados. Arriving in England at 14, he graduated to the Middlesex staff via Hertfordshire schools cricket. A 35-ball fifty against Australia in a one-day international clinched his place on the 1980–81 Caribbean tour. An attractive and compulsive stroke-maker who intersperses spectacular match-winning hundreds with a surprising number of low scores, he has overcome the effects of an horrific facial injury incurred when he missed an attempted hook at a fast bouncer in 1983. He is an outstanding fielder with a lethal throw, an emergency wicket-keeper, and an occasional right-arm medium-pace seam bowler.

Roland Butcher

Ref	Series	V	T	Venue	Result	Batting 1st No	R	HO	Batting 2nd No	R	HO	Ct
897/564	1980–81	WI	3	Bridgetown	L-298	5	17	c	5	2	lbw	1
898/565			4	St John's	D	5	20	c	–	–	–	2
899/566			5	Kingston	D	6	32	b	6	0	lbw	–

Career	M	I	NO	HS	R	Avge	100	50	Ct	St	Balls	R	W	Avge	BB	5w	10w	Rate
Test	3	5	0	32	71	14.20	–	–	3	–	–	–	–	–	–	–	–	–
F/c	264	404	39	197	11419	31.28	16	64	274	1	295	180	4	45.00	2-37	–	–	73.75

BUTLER
Harold James

Nottinghamshire (1933 to 1954)

TOUR WI 1947–48
Born Clifton, Nottinghamshire
12 Mar 1913

Harold Butler was a tall (6ft 1in), heavily built right-arm fast-medium bowler who gained his chance in the Nottinghamshire team when Harold Larwood returned injured from the 'bodyline' series and eventually succeeded him as Bill Voce's new-ball partner. Despite some Services first-class matches in India, he lost his peak years to the Second World War. After enjoying a belated but successful introduction to Test cricket he was deprived of further opportunities by injuries and increasing weight. A hard-hitting tail-end batsman, he took a mere 30 minutes to compile 62 (out of 68) against Glamorgan at Swansea in 1939. [*Illus. p.* 415]

NOTABLE FEATS
- Took 100 wickets in a season twice.
- Three hat-tricks for Nottinghamshire: v Surrey and Leicestershire in 1937 and v Hampshire in 1939.

Ref	Series	V	T	Venue	Result	Batting 1st No	R	HO	Batting 2nd No	R	HO	Ct	Bowling 1st Balls	R	W	Bowling 2nd Balls	R	W
288/256	1947	SA	4	Leeds	W-10w	–	–	–	–	–	–	–	168	34	4	144	32	3
296/259	1947–48	WI	2	Port-of-Spain	D	11	15	*	11	0	b	1	192	122	3	48	27	2

Career	M	I	NO	HS	R	Avge	100	50	Ct	St	Balls	R	W	Avge	BB	5w	10w	Rate
Test	2	2	1	15*	15	15.00	–	–	1	–	552	215	12	17.91	4-34	–	–	46.00
F/c	319	381	100	62	2962	10.54	–	4	112	–	56935	23276	952	24.44	8-15	46	6	59.80

BUTT, Henry Rigden

Sussex (1890 to 1912)

TOUR SA 1895–96
Born Sands End, Fulham, Middlesex 27 Dec 1865
Died Hastings, Sussex 21 Dec 1928

Short of stature but exceptionally quick-footed, Harry Butt was an underrated wicket-keeper who maintained his exceptional catching ability and reputation for fairness throughout a county career encompassing 23 seasons, during which he established a Sussex record of 1176 dismissals. He was a hard-hitting tail-end batsman who contributed 74* to a Sussex record 10th-wkt stand of 156 with G.R. Cox against Cambridge at Fenner's in 1908. A much-respected first-class umpire from his retirement until his death (1913–28), he stood in six Tests.

TEST NOTES

• *48* C.W. Wright kept wicket after Butt had injured his hand during South Africa's first innings.

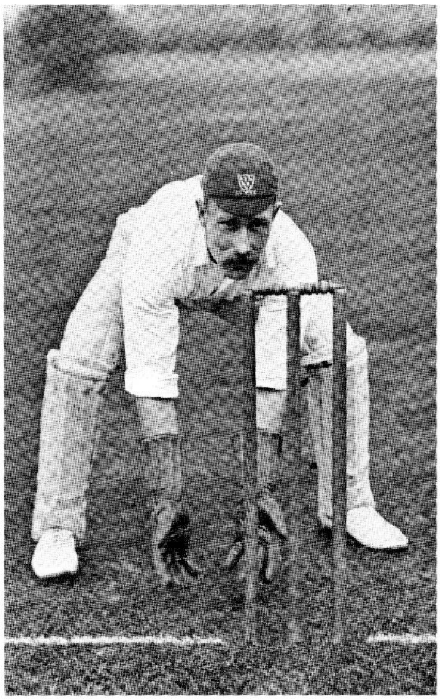

Harry Butt

Ref	Series	V	T	Venue	Result	Batting 1st			Batting 2nd			Fielding 1st				Fielding 2nd			
						No	R	HO	No	R	HO	Ct	St	Byes	Balls	Ct	St	Byes	Balls
47/47 †	1895–96	SA	1	Port Elizabeth	W-288	11	1	c	2	0	b	–	–	2	154	–	–	0	94
48/48 †			2	Johannesburg[1]	W-I & 197	11	8	*	–	–	–	1	–	0	233	–	–	–	–
49/49 †			3	Cape Town	W-I & 33	11	13	c	–	–	–	–	–	5	240	–	1	2	320

Career	M	I	NO	HS	R	Avge	100	50	Ct	St	Balls	R	W	Avge	BB	5w	10w	Rate
Test	3	4	1	13	22	7.33	–	–	1	1	–	–	–	–	–	–	–	–
F/c	550	801	225	96	7391	12.83	–	18	953	275	60	33	0	–	–	–	–	–

CALTHORPE Hon. Frederick Somerset Gough

Sussex (1911 to 1912)
Cambridge University (1912 to 1914, 1919)
Warwickshire (1919 to 1930)

TOURS
A 1922–23; WI 1925–26, 1929–30; NZ 1922–23
Born Kensington, London 27 May 1892
Died Worplesdon, Surrey 19 Nov 1935

The Honourable 'Freddy' Calthorpe was a cavalier all-rounder who captained England in each of his Test matches – the first four ever played by West Indies. A scratch golfer, he was typical of the carefree amateur school of batsmanship which alternates brave sorties down the pitch with vigorous cuts off the back foot. From an eccentric corkscrew approach he swung the new ball late at a brisk medium pace. Via Repton and four seasons at Cambridge divided by wartime RAF service, he progressed to the captaincy of Warwickshire (1920–29), a promotion which he immediately celebrated by achieving his only 'double'. Two years later his share in the spoils of Hampshire's annihilation for 15 was 4 for 4 but he still found himself leading the losing side. It would not have worried him greatly; he enjoyed cricket and life to the full. Although he died before he could inherit the Calthorpe baronetcy, he did manage to start the Folkestone cricket festival and found the Cricketer's Golf Society.

Freddy Calthorpe leads his players on to the field at Bridgetown, Barbados, in the First Test against West Indies in 1929–30: L.E.G. Ames, E.H. Hendren, A. Sandham, W. Rhodes, R.E.S. Wyatt, Hon. F.S.G. Calthorpe, J. O'Connor, W.E. Astill, N.E. Haig, G. Gunn, W. Voce.

						Batting 1st			Batting 2nd				Bowling 1st			Bowling 2nd		
Ref	**Series**	**V**	**T**	**Venue**	**Result**	**No**	**R**	**HO**	**No**	**R**	**HO**	**Ct**	**Balls**	**R**	**W**	**Balls**	**R**	**W**
190/176*	1929–30	WI	1	Bridgetown	D	9	40	b	–	–	–	1	24	14	0	120	38	1
191/177*			2	Port-of-Spain	W-167	9	12	c	9	0	c	1	–	–	–	–	–	–
192/178*			3	Georgetown	L-289	9	15	c	9	49	c	1	36	23	0	–	–	–
193/179*			4	Kingston	D	7	5	c	8	8	st	–	–	–	–	24	16	0

Career	**M**	**I**	**NO**	**HS**	**R**	**Avge**	**100**	**50**	**Ct**	**St**	**Balls**	**R**	**W**	**Avge**	**BB**	**5w**	**10w**	**Rate**
Test	4	7	0	49	129	18.42	–	–	3	–	204	91	1	91.00	1-38	–	–	204.00
F/c	369	576	52	209	12596	24.03	13	55	216	–	50701	23390	782	29.91	6-17	18	–	64.83

CAPEL, David John

Northamptonshire (1981 to date)
Eastern Province
(1985–86 to 1986–87)

TOURS
A 1987–88; NZ 1987–88; P 1987–88
Born Northampton 6 Feb 1963

David Capel

There are few more determined or loyal cricketers than David Capel, the first Northampton-born Northamptonshire player to appear for England. Lean and wiry, he swings the ball at a pace often close to fast-medium and is a talented batsman whose attractive strokeplay is based on a sound defence. He top-scored in his maiden Test innings only to be dropped for the remainder of the series because he failed to take a wicket. Lack of faith in his bowling by successive England captains, a confused selection policy and knee injuries have contributed to a hiatus in his development at international level but he is still young enough to enjoy a full Test career.

Ref	Series	V	T	Venue	Result	Batting 1st No	R	HO	Batting 2nd No	R	HO	Ct	Bowling 1st Balls	R	W	Bowling 2nd Balls	R	W
1077/636	1987	P	3	Leeds	L-I & 18	7	53	c	6	28	c	–	108	64	0	–	–	–
1084/639	1987–88	P	1	Lahore[2]	L-I & 87	6	0	c	7	0	c	–	18	28	0	–	–	–
1085/640			2	Faisalabad	D	7	1	c	7	2	lbw	–	42	23	0	–	–	–
1086/641			3	Karachi	D	6	98	b	6	24	c	–	18	8	1	–	–	–
1090/642	1987–88	A		Sydney	D	6	21	c	–	–	–	–	36	13	2	102	38	1
1091/643	1987–88	NZ	1	Christchurch	D	6	11	c	6	0	c	1	60	32	0	78	16	0
1092/644			2	Auckland	D	6	5	c	–	–	–	2	158	57	2	126	40	1
1093/645			3	Wellington	D	–	–	–	–	–	–	–	234	129	2	–	–	–
1100/648	1988	WI	3	Manchester	L-I & 156	6	1	b	6	0	c	1	72	38	1	–	–	–
1102/650			5	Oval	L-8w	6	16	c	7	12	lbw	–	42	21	0	18	20	0

Career	M	I	NO	HS	R	Avge	100	50	Ct	St	Balls	R	W	Avge	BB	5w	10w	Rate
Test	10	16	–	98	272	17.00	–	2	4	–	1112	527	10	52.70	2-13	–	–	111.20
F/c	167	244	40	134	5736	28.11	4	32	72	–	16507	8872	267	33.22	7-46	9	–	61.82

CARR, Arthur William

Nottinghamshire (1910 to 1934)

Wisden 1923
TOUR SA 1923
Born Mickleham, Surrey 21 May 1893
Died West Witton, Yorkshire 7 Feb 1963

Arthur Carr, flanked by Percy Chapman and Jack Hobbs, leads out England at Leeds against the 1926 Australians. Maurice Tate, George Geary and Frank Woolley are also in view.

TEST NOTES
- 166 J.B. Hobbs deputized as captain on the second and third days after Carr developed tonsillitis.

Arthur Carr was a forthright, vigorous, uncompromising man whose batting and captaincy epitomized his personality. A powerfully built, ferocious straight driver of the fastest bowling, he was a bustling medium-pace bowler and brave close fielder with lightning reflexes. He made his first-class debut before embarking on his final year at Sherborne School where, curiously, he captained every game except cricket. Immediately after wartime service in the Lancers he was appointed captain of Nottinghamshire (1919–34) and in 1929 spurred them to their first title for 22 years. The first Nottinghamshire cricketer to lead England at Trent Bridge, he was an inspiring, if militant, leader and his aggressive exterior concealed a generous personality. Extremely popular with his players, his career was brought to a premature and acrimonious end by his outspoken and unwavering defence of Larwood, Voce and the 'bodyline' bowling tactics which he had helped to evolve. He was an enthusiastic huntsman and steeplechaser.

NOTABLE FEATS
- Exceeded 1000 runs in a season 11 times, including 2000 once.
- Hit a (then) record 48 sixes in first-class matches in 1925.
- Shared 2nd-wkt stand of 333 in just over 3 hours with G.M. Lee v Leicestershire at Nottingham in 1913.

Ref	Series	V	T	Venue	Result	Batting 1st No	R	HO	Batting 2nd No	R	HO	Ct
148/134	1922–23	SA	1	Johannesburg[1]	L-168	4	27	b	3	27	c	–
149/135			2	Cape Town	W-1w	5	42	c	5	6	c	1
150/136			3	Durban[2]	D	5	7	c	3	2	*	–
151/137			4	Johannesburg[1]	D	4	63	lbw	4	6	c	–
152/138			5	Durban[2]	W-109	5	14	lbw	7	5	b	–
163/149*	1926	A	1	Nottingham	D	–	–	–	–	–	–	–
164/150*			2	Lord's	D	–	–	–	–	–	–	1
165/151*			3	Lord's	D	5	13	lbw	–	–	–	–
166/152*			4	Manchester	D	–	–	–	–	–	–	–
184/170*	1929	SA	4	Manchester	W-I & 32	7	10	c	–	–	–	–
185/171*			5	Oval	D	7	15	c	–	–	–	1

Career	M	I	NO	HS	R	Avge	100	50	Ct	St	Balls	R	W	Avge	BB	5w	10w	Rate
Test	11	13	1	63	237	19.75	–	1	3	–	–	–	–	–	–	–	–	–
F/c	468	709	42	206	21051	31.56	45	98	393	1	1816	1150	31	37.09	3-14	–	–	58.58

CARR
Donald Bryce OBE

Derbyshire (1946 to 1963)
Oxford University (1949 to 1951)

Wisden 1960
TOURS
I/SL 1951–52; P 1951–52, 1955–56
Born Wiesbaden, Germany 28 Dec 1926

A talented and highly intelligent all-rounder, Donald Carr was a schoolboy prodigy who made his first-class debut for England in a 'Victory' match against Australian Services at Lord's. He was an enterprising batsman who excelled at pulling, on-driving and cutting, and who later developed a very productive forcing back-foot off-drive. A fascinatingly unorthodox slow left-arm bowler, he turned the ball appreciably, developing his 'Chinamen' and googlies because of A.H. Kardar's presence in the Oxford team as a left-arm leg-spinner. He was a brilliant close fieldsman and an outstanding Derbyshire captain (1955–62). Deputizing as England's leader when Nigel Howard contracted pleurisy, he had the misfortune to become the first England captain to lose to India. The second of three generations of first-class cricketers and a popular administrator, he served as Derbyshire secretary (1959–62), MCC assistant-secretary (1962–74) and TCCB secretary (1973–86) and managed three MCC tours. His exploits as a soccer forward gained him a blue and two Amateur Cup appearances with Pegasus.

NOTABLE FEATS
• Exceeded 1000 runs in a season 11 times, including 2000 once – his 2292 runs in 1959 remains a Derbyshire record.

						Batting 1st			Batting 2nd				Bowling 1st			Bowling 2nd		
Ref	Series	V	T	Venue	Result	No	R	HO	No	R	HO	Ct	Balls	R	W	Balls	R	W
339/292	1951–52	I	1	Delhi	D	4	14	c	5	76	c	–	96	56	0	–	–	–
343/296*			5	Madras[1]	L-I & 8	7	40	st	7	5	c	–	114	84	2	–	–	–

Career	M	I	NO	HS	R	Avge	100	50	Ct	St	Balls	R	W	Avge	BB	5w	10w	Rate
Test	2	4	0	76	135	33.75	–	1	–	–	210	140	2	70.00	2-84	–	–	105.00
F/c	446	745	72	170	19257	38.61	24	100	499	–	20318	11396	328	34.74	7-53	5	–	61.94

RIGHT *Donald Carr (right) leads the MCC 'A' team out against Combined Universities during the 1955–56 tour of Pakistan. With Carr are (left to right) Allan Watkins, Billy Sutcliffe and Jim Parks (obscured).*

FAR RIGHT *Douglas Carr*

CARR, Douglas Ward

Kent (1909 to 1914)

Wisden 1910
Born Cranbrook, Kent 17 Mar 1872
Died Sidmouth, Devon 23 Mar 1950

Douglas Carr's belated and sensational first-class career did not begin until his 38th year. At Oxford his useful right-arm fast-medium bowling had been restricted to minor matches by a knee injury and he remained an unknown club cricketer until his astonishing rise to fame soon after deciding to experiment with leg-breaks and googlies. The 'wrong-un' was then rarely seen at any level of the game and his immediate success in club matches prompted Kent to give him a trial in 1909. He took seven Oxford wickets on his first-class debut, dismissed eight Players on his maiden appearance for the Gentlemen, and was included in England's party for the

Fourth Test against Australia. Omitted because of a slow pitch, he gained his solitary England cap in the final Test and dismissed Syd Gregory, Monty Noble and Warwick Armstrong for 19 runs in his first seven overs. He was then grossly over-bowled but still returned the commendable match analysis of 7 for 282 from 69 overs. He took 60 Championship wickets at 12.16 when Kent won the title in 1910 and 49 at 9.59 in 1912. His meteoric career was ended by the Great War.

					Batting 1st			Batting 2nd				Bowling 1st			Bowling 2nd		
Ref	**Series**	**V**	**T**	**Venue**	**No**	**R**	**HO**	**No**	**R**	**HO**	**Ct**	**Balls**	**R**	**W**	**Balls**	**R**	**W**
105/102	1909	A	5	Oval	D	11	0	b	–	–	–	–	204	146	5	210	136	2

Career	M	I	NO	HS	R	Avge	100	50	Ct	St	Balls	R	W	Avge	BB	5w	10w	Rate
Test	1	1	0	0	0	0.00	–	–	–	–	414	282	7	40.28	5-146	1	–	59.14
F/c	58	68	18	48	447	8.94	–	–	19	–	10699	5585	334	16.72	8-36	31	8	32.03

CARTWRIGHT Thomas William

Warwickshire (1952 to 1969)
Somerset (1970 to 1976)
Glamorgan (1977)

TOUR SA 1964–65
Born Alderman's Green, Coventry, Warwickshire 22 Jul 1935

NOTABLE FEATS

- Achieved the 'double' in 1962, exceeding 1000 runs in a season 3 times and 1000 wickets on 8 occasions.
- Hat-trick for Warwickshire v Somerset at Birmingham in 1969.
- Took 15 for 89 for Warwickshire v Glamorgan at Swansea in 1967.

Tom Cartwright

Tom Cartwright was an outstanding medium-pace seam bowler with a high, flowing action and exceptional control. Late inswing formed the basis of his armoury but he subsequently added a lethal outswinger. A rich assortment of pace variations and cutters made him a daunting prospect on green or crumbling pitches. An effective rather than attractive middle-order batsman, he relied heavily on the sweep. When his benefit gained £3295 from a Rothman's Cavaliers Sunday match in June 1968 the TCCB determined to institute the Sunday League. A few weeks later his withdrawal from MCC's tour to South Africa precipitated the D'Oliveira Affair. In 1970 he moved to Somerset to become coach at Millfield School; his was the first contested registration to be given immediate approval by the TCCB. After a few seasons as cricket manager of Glamorgan, he became a coach to the Welsh CA.

						Batting 1st			Batting 2nd				Bowling 1st			Bowling 2nd		
Ref	**Series**	**V**	**T**	**Venue**	**Result**	**No**	**R**	**HO**	**No**	**R**	**HO**	**Ct**	**Balls**	**R**	**W**	**Balls**	**R**	**W**
564/408	1964	A	4	Manchester	D	9	4	b	–	–	–	–	462	118	2	–	–	–
565/409			5	Oval	D	10	0	c	–	–	–	–	372	110	3	–	–	–
574/413	1964–65	SA	4	Johannesburg[3]	D	9	9	b	8	8	*	2	330	97	1	144	99	1
591/415	1965	NZ	1	Birmingham	W-9w	9	4	b	–	–	–	–	42	14	2	72	12	0
595/419	1965	SA	2	Nottingham	L-94	11	1	*	10	0	lbw	–	189	94	6	–	–	–

Career	M	I	NO	HS	R	Avge	100	50	Ct	St	Balls	R	W	Avge	BB	5w	10w	Rate
Test	5	7	2	9	26	5.20	–	–	2	–	1611	544	15	36.26	6-94	1	–	107.40
F/c	479	737	94	210	13710	21.32	7	67	332	–	84843	29357	1536	19.11	8-39	94	18	55.23

CHAPMAN
Arthur Percy Frank

Cambridge University (1920 to 1922)
Kent (1924 to 1938)

Wisden 1919
TOURS
A 1922–23, 1924–25, 1928–29;
SA 1930–31; WI 1931–32 (Tennyson);
NZ 1922–23
Born The Mount, Reading, Berkshire
3 Sep 1900
Died Alton, Hampshire 16 Sep 1961

No amateur brought a more refreshing outlook to his cricket or had a more intense abhorrence of defensive ploys than Percy Chapman. An exceptionally tall, strong, left-handed, middle-order batsman, he was blessed with that rare gift of natural timing which dismisses the ball with effortless power. He was a punishing but never reckless hitter, a polished, wristy player with a full range of on-side strokes and a majestic off-drive. A cheerful man of great charm he was a captain who commanded easy respect and maximum effort. He was a useful left-handed bowler, who eventually changed from fast-medium to leg-spin, and a superb fielder whose wide arm span and large hands engulfed any offering in the general region of gully. After a remarkable career at Uppingham where he led the 1917 averages with 668 runs at 111.33, he announced his entry into first-class cricket with a century and made his first appearance for England while still representing his native Berkshire. As captain of Kent (1931–36) and England he placed great emphasis on fielding; his 1928–29 team is considered the best English fielding combination to have toured Australia. He led England to an epic Ashes-winning victory at The Oval in 1926.

Percy Chapman batting against Australia at The Oval in his first Test as captain.

NOTABLE FEATS
- Scored 118 for Cambridge U v Essex at Cambridge on debut in 1920.
- Captained England in 17 Tests, winning his first 9 (record) and losing only 2.
- Only batsman to score hundreds at Lord's in a Test against Australia, a Gentlemen v Players fixture, and the University match.
- Shared in record Kent 6th-wkt stand of 284 in 2½ hr with G.B. Legge v Lancashire at Maidstone in 1927, his career-best 260 taking just over 3 hours, including 5 sixes and 32 fours, with his last 50 scored in 15 min. With H.T.W. Hardinge shared record Kent 4th-wkt stand of 297 v Hampshire at Southampton in 1926.

						Batting 1st			Batting 2nd			
Ref	Series	V	T	Venue	Result	No	R	HO	No	R	HO	Ct
153/139	1924	SA	1	Birmingham	W-I & 18	5	8	c	–	–	–	1
154/140			2	Lord's	W-I & 18	–	–	–	–	–	–	–
158/144	1924–25	A	1	Sydney	L-193	7	13	ro	4	44	c	1
159/145			2	Melbourne	L-81	6	28	c	9	4	*	1
160/146			3	Adelaide	L-11	4	26	b	6	58	c	–
161/147			4	Melbourne	W-I & 29	6	12	st	–	–	–	1
163/149	1926	A	1	Nottingham	D	–	–	–	–	–	–	–
164/150			2	Lord's	D	5	50	*	–	–	–	–
165/151			3	Leeds	D	6	15	b	5	42	*	–
167/153*			5	Oval	W-289	5	49	st	5	19	b	–
173/159*	1928	WI	1	Lord's	W-I & 58	6	50	c	–	–	–	1
174/160*			2	Manchester	W-I & 30	6	3	*rh	–	–	–	1
175/161*			3	Oval	W-I & 71	7	5	c	–	–	–	4
176/162*	1928–29	A	1	Brisbane[1]	W-675	7	50	c	7	27	c	4
177/163*			2	Sydney	W-8w	6	20	c	–	–	–	2
178/164*			3	Melbourne	W-3w	4	24	b	6	5	c	–
179/165*			4	Adelaide	W-12	6	39	c	6	0	c	2
194/180*	1930	A	1	Nottingham	W-93	6	52	c	6	29	b	2
195/181*			2	Lord's	L-7w	6	11	c	6	121	c	2
196/182*			3	Leeds	D	8	45	b	–	–	–	2
197/183*			4	Manchester	D	6	1	c	–	–	–	1
204/185*	1930–31	SA	1	Johannesburg[1]	L-28	6	28	c	6	11	c	–
205/186*			2	Cape Town	D	6	0	b	8	4	b	1
206/187*			3	Durban[2]	D	–	–	–	–	–	–	2
207/188*			4	Johannesburg[1]	D	9	5	b	7	3	c	–
208/189*			5	Durban[2]	D	7	24	c	–	–	–	4

TEST NOTES
- *158* Bowled in both inns: 0 for 10 (16 balls) and 0 for 10 (24 balls).
- *174* J.C. White deputized as captain after Chapman pulled a thigh muscle taking a run.

Career	M	I	NO	HS	R	Avge	100	50	Ct	St	Balls	R	W	Avge	BB	5w	10w	Rate
Test	26	36	4	121	925	28.90	1	5	32	–	40	20	0	–	–	–	–	–
F/c	394	554	44	260	16309	31.97	27	75	356	–	1570	921	22	41.86	5-40	1	–	71.36

CHARLWOOD
Henry Rupert James

Sussex (1865 to 1882)

TOUR A 1876–77
Born Horsham, Sussex 19 Dec 1846
Died Scarborough, Yorkshire 6 Jun 1888

Henry Charlwood, who appeared in the first two Test matches ever staged, was a dashing early-order batsman, an occasional lob bowler and an excellent cover-point. For seven seasons he amassed the highest aggregates of runs for his struggling county and was deservedly dubbed the 'Hope of Sussex'. His county career ended prematurely when he moved north, first to Chesterfield and then to Scarborough where he died at the age of 41. [*Illus. p.* 278]

Ref	Series	V	T	Venue	Result	Batting 1st No	R	HO	Batting 2nd No	R	HO	Ct
1/1	1876–77	A	1	Melbourne	L-45	3	36	c	4	13	b	–
2/2			2	Melbourne	W-4w	4	14	c	4	0	b	–

Career	M	I	NO	HS	R	Avge	100	50	Ct	St	Balls	R	W	Avge	BB	5w	10w	Rate
Test	2	4	0	36	63	15.75	–	–	–	–	–	–	–	–	–	–	–	–
F/c	197	350	19	155	7017	21.19	5	33	89	–	128	89	4	22.25	2-12	–	–	32.00

CHATTERTON
William

Derbyshire (1882 to 1902)

TOUR SA 1891–92
Born Thornsett, Derbyshire 27 Dec 1861
Died Flowery Field, Hyde, Cheshire
19 Mar 1913

A dedicated, determined and consistent player, William Chatterton was the leading professional batsman of his time and his efforts were crucial to Derbyshire regaining first-class status in 1894. He was an exceptional fielder and a handy right-arm slow bowler. While Derbyshire were in the wilderness he joined the Lord's staff and appeared in first-class matches for the MCC. He toured South Africa with W.W. Read's team, achieving the highest aggregate (955 runs, avge 41.52) and opening the innings successfully in his only Test match. [*Illus. pp.* 184, 201]

Ref	Series	V	T	Venue	Result	Batting 1st No	R	HO	Batting 2nd No	R	HO	Ct
38/38	1891–92	SA		Cape Town	W-I & 189	1	48	c	–	–	–	–

Career	M	I	NO	HS	R	Avge	100	50	Ct	St	Balls	R	W	Avge	BB	5w	10w	Rate
Test	1	1	0	48	48	48.00	–	–	–	–	–	–	–	–	–	–	–	–
F/c	289	510	39	169	10914	23.17	8	53	239	4	11890	4465	208	21.46	6-24	4	1	57.16

CHILDS, John Henry

Gloucestershire (1975 to 1984)
Essex (1985 to date)

Wisden 1987
Born Lipson, Plymouth, Devon
15 Aug 1951

John Childs is a tall (6ft 0in), patient and determined left-arm orthodox spinner who has justified the adage that slow bowlers mature late. By the time he played in his first Test he was 36 years and 320 days of age and the oldest to make his England debut since Dick Howorth in 1947. After a decade spent largely in David Graveney's shadow at Gloucestershire, this Devonian freelance sign-writer moved to Essex but had a wretched first season. Winter coaching sessions with former England spinners Fred Titmus and Don Wilson produced a longer, faster approach and the quicker trajectory necessary to counteract slow county pitches. The new method brought immediate results, his 85 wickets being a significant contribution towards Essex winning the 1986 Championship. He bowled consistently but without luck on his first Test appearances and his ability to extract bounce would have made him an interesting prospect on the tour of India.

Ref	Series	V	T	Venue	Result	Batting 1st			Batting 2nd			Ct	Bowling 1st			Bowling 2nd		
						No	R	HO	No	R	HO		Balls	R	W	Balls	R	W
1100/648	1988	WI	3	Manchester	L-I & 156	11	2	*	11	0	*	–	240	91	1	–	–	–
1102/650			5	Oval	L-8w	11	0	*	11	0	*	1	36	13	1	240	79	1

Career	M	I	NO	HS	R	Avge	100	50	Ct	St	Balls	R	W	Avge	BB	5w	10w	Rate
Test	2	4	4	2*	2	–	–	–	1	–	516	183	3	61.00	1-13	–	–	172.00
F/c	235	219	105	34*	952	8.35	–	–	80	–	41629	18255	614	29.73	9-56	32	7	67.79

John Childs

The England team which defeated Australia at Lord's in 1884: standing *C.K. Pullin (umpire), E. Peate, A.P. Lucas, Hon. A. Lyttelton, A. Shrewsbury, F.H. Farrands (umpire);* seated *A.G. Steel, Lord Harris (captain), W.G. Grace, W.W. Read, G. Ulyett;* in front *S. Christopherson, R.G. Barlow.*

CHRISTOPHERSON Stanley

Kent (1883 to 1890)

Born Blackheath, Kent 11 Nov 1861
Died St John's Wood, London 6 Apr 1949

A leading fast bowler of the mid-1880s until he suffered severe arm strain, Stanley Christopherson generated considerable pace from a high, fluent action and a fairly substantial run. He had a good control of length and perfected a devastating yorker. Under the captaincy of his father, he and his nine brothers formed a Christopherson XI which played occasional matches in the Blackheath area. War extended his presidency of MCC into the record term of seven years (1939–45) but he survived to succeed (in 1947) the Mackinnon of Mackinnon as the oldest-surviving England cricketer.

Ref	Series	V	T	Venue	Result	Batting 1st			Batting 2nd			Ct	Bowling 1st			Bowling 2nd		
						No	R	HO	No	R	HO		Balls	R	W	Balls	R	W
15/15	1884	A	2	Lord's	W-I & 5	11	17	c	–	–	–	–	104	52	1	32	17	0

Career	M	I	NO	HS	R	Avge	100	50	Ct	St	Balls	R	W	Avge	BB	5w	10w	Rate
Test	1	1	0	17	17	17.00	–	–	–	–	136	69	1	69.00	1-52	–	–	136.00
F/c	66	109	12	47	923	9.51	–	–	41	–	11531	5332	241	22.12	8-41	13	3	47.84

CLARK
Edward Winchester

Northamptonshire (1922 to 1947)

TOURS
WI 1927–28 (Tennyson); I/SL 1933–34
Born Elton, Huntingdonshire 9 Aug 1902
Died West Winch, King's Lynn, Norfolk
28 Apr 1982

'Nobby' Clark was a genuinely fast left-handed bowler with a classic, high, side-on action. He operated most effectively from round the wicket, swinging the ball in to the right-handers and cutting it away viciously towards the slips. A perfectionist, his temperament was extremely suspect and he was easily outraged by dropped catches, loose footholds, tactless criticism or passing gulls. These irritants were compounded by his playing for an abjectly weak side which specialized in dropped catches and by his bowling partner Albert Thomas who delighted in swift maiden overs which allowed scant respite for Clark. A modest batsman and fielder, he twice returned to league cricket after rows with his County. [*Illus. p.* 263]

NOTABLE FEATS
- Dismissed R.H. Catterall with his fourth ball in Test cricket.
- Took 100 wickets in a season twice.
- Hat-trick for Northamptonshire v West Indians at Northampton in 1923.
- Holds Northamptonshire first-class career record for most wickets: 1097.

						Batting 1st			Batting 2nd				Bowling 1st			Bowling 2nd		
Ref	Series	V	T	Venue	Result	No	R	HO	No	R	HO	Ct	Balls	R	W	Balls	R	W
185/171	1929	SA	5	Oval	D	11	7	b	–	–	–	–	216	79	3	–	–	–
228/202	1933	WI	2	Manchester	D	10	0	b	–	–	–	–	240	99	4	90	64	2
229/203			3	Oval	W-I & 17	10	8	*	–	–	–	–	48	16	3	126	54	2
230/204	1933–34	I	1	Bombay[1]	W-9w	11	1	b	–	–	–	–	78	41	1	114	69	3
231/205			2	Calcutta	D	11	10	c	–	–	–	–	156	39	3	117	50	3
232/206			3	Madras[1]	W-202	11	4	*	–	–	–	–	90	37	0	48	27	0
235/209	1934	A	3	Manchester	D	11	2	*	–	–	–	–	240	100	1	24	16	0
237/211			5	Oval	L-562	10	2	*	10	2	*	–	224	110	2	120	98	5

Career	M	I	NO	HS	R	Avge	100	50	Ct	St	Balls	R	W	Avge	BB	5w	10w	Rate
Test	8	9	5	10	36	9.00	–	–	–	–	1931	899	32	28.09	5-98	1	–	60.34
F/c	338	510	195	30	1971	6.25	–	–	104	–	60997	25967	1208	21.49	8-59	63	15	50.49

CLAY, John Charles

Glamorgan (1921 to 1949)
Wales (1923 to 1926)

Born Bonvilston, Glamorgan 18 Mar 1898
Died St Hilary, Cowbridge, Glamorgan
11 Aug 1973

NOTABLE FEATS
- Took 100 wickets in a season 3 times, including Glamorgan record of 176 in 1937 and, when 48, 130 (avge 13.40) in 1946.
- Returned record Glamorgan match analysis of 17 for 212 v Worcestershire at Swansea in 1937.
- Shared record Glamorgan 9th-wkt stand of 203* with J.J. Hills v Worcestershire at Swansea in 1929.

A dedicated and enduring all-rounder, Johnny Clay's first-class career began with Glamorgan's introduction to the County Championship and extended until his 52nd year. An outstanding leg-break bowler at Winchester College, he was persuaded to take up fast bowling during his early days with Glamorgan but converted to off-breaks in his late twenties, spinning the ball sharply from his considerable height (6ft 3in). The epitome of accuracy, he allied a crafty range of variations to a nagging length. In 1948 he contributed match figures of 9 for 79 when Glamorgan clinched their first title with an innings victory against Hampshire. The Welsh County's Founding Father, he was captain (for six seasons in three spells), secretary (1946–55) and president (1960–73), and also served as an England selector (1947–48).

Johnny Clay

Ref	Series	V	T	Venue	Result	Batting 1st No	R	HO	Batting 2nd No	R	HO	Ct	Bowling 1st Balls	R	W	Bowling 2nd Balls	R	W
246/220	1935	SA	5	Oval	D	–	–	–	–	–	–	1	84	30	0	108	45	0

Career	M	I	NO	HS	R	Avge	100	50	Ct	St	Balls	R	W	Avge	BB	5w	10w	Rate
Test	1	–	–	–	–	–	–	–	1	–	192	75	0	–	–	–	–	–
F/c	373	555	90	115*	7186	15.45	2	18	177	–	61587	26028	1317	19.76	9-54	105	28	46.76

CLOSE
Dennis Brian CBE

Yorkshire (1949 to 1970)
Somerset (1971 to 1977)

Wisden 1964
TOURS
A 1950–51; SA 1959–60 (Cwlth), 1972–73 (Int XI), 1973–74 (Robins and Int XI), 1974–75 (Robins); NZ 1950–51; I 1964–65 (Cwlth); P 1955–56
Born Rawdon, Leeds, Yorkshire
24 Feb 1931

Cricketers do not come any more determined or courageous than Brian Close, a 6ft 1in, immensely strong, hard-hitting left-handed batsman and a right-arm utility bowler who changed from seamers to off-spin and back again. An outstanding tactician with a superb cricket brain, he matured after being appointed captain of Yorkshire in 1963. A suicidally courageous fielder, he delighted in placing himself in ultra-aggressive positions. After representing England Schools at cricket and soccer, he celebrated his precocious first appearances for his County and England by becoming, well before his 19th birthday, the youngest to take 100 wickets in his debut season, achieve the 'double' or be capped by Yorkshire. Under his captaincy (1963–70) Yorkshire won their last four Championships and he considerably raised the performances of Somerset during his six seasons at their helm. Recalled in 1976 at the veteran age of 45 to stave off the fiery West Indian pace attack, he defended stoically for 162 grim minutes in his final Test innings, bravely chesting several vicious bouncers. A natural ball player, he played professional soccer for Leeds United, Arsenal and Bradford City before becoming an ambidextrous single-figure handicap golfer. He was an England selector (1979–81), manager and chairman of Yorkshire, and continued making first-class appearances in the Scarborough Festival until he was 55.

NOTABLE FEATS
- At 18 yrs 149 days he remains the youngest to represent England.
- *328* Youngest (19 yrs 301 days) to represent E v A.
- Did the 'double' twice (1949 and 1952). He remains the youngest to achieve this feat and the only player to do so in his first season.
- Exceeded 1000 runs in a season 20 times and 100 wickets twice.
- His career tally of 813 catches is the fifth-highest in first-class cricket.

TEST NOTES
- *547* Deputized for J.M. Parks as wicket-keeper on second morning.

Brian Close

Ref	Series	V	T	Venue	Result	Batting 1st No	R	HO	Batting 2nd No	R	HO	Ct	Bowling 1st Balls	R	W	Bowling 2nd Balls	R	W
316/274	1949	NZ	3	Manchester	D	9	0	c	–	–	–	–	150	39	1	102	46	0
328/281	1950-51	A	2	Melbourne	L-28	6	0	c	7	1	lbw	1	48	20	1	8	8	0
412/326	1955	SA	5	Oval	W-92	2	32	c	2	15	b	–	–	–	–	–	–	–
439/337	1957	WI	1	Birmingham	D	2	15	c	2	42	c	1	–	–	–	12	8	0
440/338			2	Lord's	W-I & 36	7	32	c	–	–	–	1	–	–	–	–	–	–
476/356	1959	I	3	Leeds	W-I & 173	6	27	c	–	–	–	4	30	18	1	66	35	4
510/372	1961	A	4	Manchester	L-54	5	33	lbw	5	8	c	2	–	–	–	48	33	0
543/395	1963	WI	1	Manchester	L-10w	6	30	c	7	32	c	–	60	31	0	–	–	–
544/396			2	Lord's	D	6	9	c	6	70	c	1	54	21	0	–	–	–
545/397			3	Birmingham	W-217	5	55	lbw	4	13	c	–	–	–	–	–	–	–
546/398			4	Leeds	L-221	5	0	b	5	56	c	1	–	–	–	–	–	–

Ref	Series	V	T	Venue	Result	Batting 1st No	R	HO	Batting 2nd No	R	HO	Ct	Bowling 1st Balls	R	W	Bowling 2nd Balls	R	W
547/399			5	Oval	L-8w	5	46	b	5	4	lbw	–	–	–	–	36	36	0
609/433*	1966	WI	5	Oval	W-I & 34	7	4	ro	–	–	–	1	54	21	1	18	7	0
618/434*	1967	I	1	Leeds	W-6w	6	22	*	–	–	–	2	18	0	0	126	48	2
619/435*			2	Lord's	W-I & 124	6	7	c	–	–	–	–	–	–	–	90	28	2
620/436*			3	Birmingham	W-132	6	26	c	6	47	c	–	–	–	–	130	68	4
621/437*	1967	P	1	Lord's	D	6	4	c	6	36	st	3	36	10	0	48	13	0
622/438*			2	Nottingham	W-10w	6	41	c	–	–	–	2	18	12	0	24	11	1
623/439*			3	Oval	W-8w	2	6	c	2	8	b	1	30	15	0	6	4	1
777/515	1976	WI	1	Nottingham	D	4	2	c	4	36	*	2	–	–	–	–	–	–
778/516			2	Lord's	D	4	60	c	5	46	c	1	–	–	–	–	–	–
779/517			3	Manchester	L-425	2	2	lbw	2	20	b	1	–	–	–	–	–	–

Career	M	I	NO	HS	R	Avge	100	50	Ct	St	Balls	R	W	Avge	BB	5w	10w	Rate
Test	22	37	2	70	887	25.34	–	4	24	–	1212	532	18	29.55	4-35	–	–	67.33
F/c	786	1225	173	198	34994	33.26	52	171	813	1	70302	30947	1171	26.42	8-41	43	3	60.03

COLDWELL Leonard John

Worcestershire (1955 to 1969)

TOURS
A 1962–63; WI 1965–66 (Worcs); NZ 1962–63; I 1964–65 (Cwlth); Z 1964–65 (Worcs)
Born Newton Abbot, Devon 10 Jan 1933

Len Coldwell was a 6ft 3in, heavily built, right-arm fast-medium bowler who moved to Worcestershire after two seasons of minor counties apprenticeship with Devon. At New Road he formed an extremely effective new-ball partnership with Jack Flavell which contributed much towards the County's first two Championship titles. Deriving surprising pace from an economical run and a whippy action, he had immense stamina, commanded great accuracy of line and length, and moved his inswinger late.

Len Coldwell

NOTABLE FEATS

- *531* Bowled Imtiaz Ahmed with his fifth ball in Test cricket.
- Took 100 wickets in a season twice, including 152 in 1962.
- Two hat-tricks for Worcestershire: v Leicestershire at Stourbridge in 1957 and v Essex at Brentwood in 1965.

Ref	Series	V	T	Venue	Result	Batting 1st No	R	HO	Batting 2nd No	R	HO	Ct	Bowling 1st Balls	R	W	Bowling 2nd Balls	R	W
531/383	1962	P	2	Lord's	W-9w	11	0	*	–	–	–	–	84	25	3	246	85	6
534/386			5	Oval	W-10w	–	–	–	–	–	–	–	168	53	3	138	60	1
536/388	1962-63	A	2	Melbourne	W-7w	11	1	c	–	–	–	–	136	58	2	200	60	0
537/389			3	Sydney	L-8w	11	2	*	11	0	c	–	120	41	1	–	–	–
540/392	1962-63	NZ	1	Auckland	W-I & 215	–	–	–	–	–	–	1	162	66	1	30	4	1
561/405	1964	A	1	Nottingham	D	10	0	*	10	0	*	–	132	48	3	–	–	–
562/406			2	Lord's	D	11	6	*	–	–	–	–	138	51	1	114	59	0

Career	M	I	NO	HS	R	Avge	100	50	Ct	St	Balls	R	W	Avge	BB	5w	10w	Rate
Test	7	7	5	6*	9	4.50	–	–	1	–	1668	610	22	27.72	6-85	1	–	75.81
F/c	310	347	100	37	1474	5.96	–	–	90	–	56235	22791	1076	21.18	8-38	60	7	52.26

COMPTON
Denis Charles Scott CBE

Middlesex (1936 to 1958)
Holkar (1944–45)
Europeans (1944–45 to 1945–46)

Wisden 1939
TOURS
A 1946–47, 1950–51, 1954–55;
SA 1948–49, 1956–57, 1959–60 (Cwlth);
WI 1953–54, 1963–64 (Cav);
NZ 1946–47, 1950–51
Born Hendon, Middlesex 23 May 1918

Denis Compton (partnered by Willie Watson) lofts a ball from Peter Heine to leg for 2 on the second day of the Fifth Test against South Africa at The Oval, 1955.

TEST NOTES
• *301* Retired hurt when 4* at 33-2 (1st inns); resumed at 119-5.
• *330* Deputized as captain on fifth day after Brown had been injured in car accident.
• *391* Fractured left hand on pickets while fielding.

Denis Compton was an outstanding natural cricketer with a glorious sense of fun and considerable charm. His was a precocious talent: he played in his school 1st XI at ten, joined Middlesex and Arsenal when he left school at 14, and remains the youngest to score 1000 runs in a season or hit a century for England. Calm, confident and resourceful, he was an adaptable player with a large measure of genius and a big-match temperament. His technique was founded on a sound defence and he had a stroke for every ball; a strong on-side player, he was the master and main perpetrator of the sweep. A supreme entertainer, he would often advance down the pitch before the bowler had released the ball and play a totally novel stroke for the sheer hell of it. His major weaknesses were his erratic time-keeping and quirky assessment of what constituted a run; his calling was often a lottery embellished with apologies. His keen sense of fun extended to his unorthodox slow left-arm bowling in which experimental varieties of 'Chinamen' and googlies featured heavily. Before 1949, when surgery to a soccer injury restricted his mobility, he was an outstanding fielder. As vice-captain of the 1950–51 antipodean tour he became the first professional to lead an MCC team in the field; seven years later he turned amateur. A wartime soccer international, he gained League Championship and FA Cup winners' medals with Arsenal. His elder brother Leslie kept wicket for Middlesex and was an Arsenal and England footballer.

NOTABLE FEATS
• 1000 runs in 16th Test (*283*) (26 inns); 2000 runs in 23rd Test (*299*) (37 inns); 3000 runs in 34th Test (*315*) (57 inns); 4000 runs in 56th Test (*383*) (95 inns); 5000 runs in 69th Test (*409*) (113 inns).
• *263* Scored 102 in first Test v A and, at 20 yrs 19 days, remains England's youngest century-maker. His stand of 206 with E. Paynter remains England's 5th-wkt record v A.
• *282* Compton and A.R. Morris each scored hundreds in both innings – unique occurrence in Tests.
• *285* Shared 5th-wkt record E v SA stand of 237 with N.W.D. Yardley.
• *286* Shared (then) world Test record 3rd-wkt stand of 370 with W.J. Edrich. It remains England's highest 3rd-wkt stand in all Tests.
• *388* His 278 in 290 min remains the highest Test score at Trent Bridge and the record in E v P Tests.
• Scored 1004 runs in his debut season, the youngest to achieve this feat.
• Exceeded 1000 runs in a season 14 times (plus 3 overseas), including 2000 on 6 occasions. His first-class aggregates of 3816 runs and 18 hundreds in 1947 remain world records for any season.
• Scored 300* in 181 min for MCC v North-Eastern Transvaal at Benoni in 1948–49; still the fastest 300 in all first-class cricket, his stand of 399 with R.T. Simpson being the 3rd-wkt record in South African first-class cricket.
• His 3rd-wkt stand of 424* with W.J. Edrich v Somerset at Lord's in 1948 remains the Middlesex record for any wicket.
• In all first-class matches at Lord's he scored 16,732 runs (avge 48.08) and 48 hundreds.

						Batting 1st			Batting 2nd				Bowling 1st			Bowling 2nd		
Ref	Series	V	T	Venue	Result	No	R	HO	No	R	HO	Ct	Balls	R	W	Balls	R	W
262/231	1937	NZ	3	Oval	D	4	65	ro	–	–	–	1	–	–	–	36	34	2
263/232	1938	A	1	Nottingham	D	6	102	c	–	–	–	2	–	–	–	–	–	–
264/233			2	Lord's	D	6	6	lbw	7	76	*	1	–	–	–	–	–	–
265/234			4	Leeds	L-5w	6	14	b	6	15	c	–	–	–	–	–	–	–
266/235			5	Oval	W-I & 579	6	1	b	–	–	–	1	–	–	–	–	–	–
272/241	1939	WI	1	Lord's	W-8w	5	120	c	–	–	–	1	–	–	–	24	8	0
273/242			2	Manchester	D	5	4	hw	5	34	*	–	–	–	–	–	–	–
274/243			3	Oval	D	5	21	c	5	10	*	–	40	20	0	–	–	–
276/244	1946	I	1	Lord's	W-10w	3	0	b	–	–	–	–	–	–	–	–	–	–
277/245			2	Manchester	D	3	51	lbw	3	71	*	–	24	18	0	18	5	0
278/246			3	Oval	D	4	24	*	–	–	–	1	30	15	0	–	–	–

						Batting 1st			Batting 2nd				Bowling 1st			Bowling 2nd		
Ref	Series	V	T	Venue	Result	No	R	HO	No	R	HO	Ct	Balls	R	W	Balls	R	W
279/247	1946–47	A	1	Brisbane[2]	L-I & 332	4	17	lbw	4	15	c	–	48	20	0	–	–	–
280/248			2	Sydney	L-I & 33	4	5	c	4	54	c	1	48	38	0	–	–	–
281/249			3	Melbourne	D	4	11	lbw	4	14	ro	1	–	–	–	–	–	–
282/250			4	Adelaide	D	5	147	c	5	103	*	–	24	12	0	–	–	–
283/251			5	Sydney	L-5w	5	17	hw	4	76	c	2	–	–	–	10	8	0
284/252	1946–47	NZ		Christchurch	D	4	38	b	–	–	–	–	–	–	–	–	–	–
285/253	1947	SA	1	Nottingham	D	4	65	c	4	163	c	–	12	6	0	24	14	0
286/254			2	Lord's	W-10w	4	208	c	–	–	–	–	126	32	2	192	46	2
287/255			3	Manchester	W-7w	4	115	c	4	6	hw	1	42	27	0	102	58	1
288/256			4	Leeds	W-10w	4	30	c	–	–	–	1	24	9	0	12	10	0
289/257			5	Oval	D	4	53	c	4	113	c	–	66	31	0	24	30	0
299/262	1948	A	1	Nottingham	L-8w	4	19	b	4	184	hw	–	30	24	0	–	–	–
300/263			2	Lord's	L-409	4	53	c	4	29	c	–	–	–	–	18	11	0
301/264			3	Manchester	D	4	145	*	4	0	c	1	–	–	–	54	18	0
302/265			4	Leeds	L-7w	5	23	c	4	66	c	1	18	15	0	90	82	1
303/266			5	Oval	L-I & 149	4	4	c	4	39	c	–	12	6	0	–	–	–
309/267	1948–49	SA	1	Durban[2]	W-2w	4	72	c	4	28	b	4	16	5	0	128	11	1
310/268			2	Johannesburg[2]	D	4	114	c	–	–	–	–	80	34	1	104	31	0
311/269			3	Cape Town	D	4	1	b	4	51	*	1	202	70	5	24	7	0
312/270			4	Johannesburg[2]	D	4	24	c	3	25	b	1	32	19	0	72	35	0
313/271			5	Port Elizabeth	W-3w	4	49	c	3	42	c	3	56	39	0	72	57	0
314/272	1949	NZ	1	Leeds	D	4	114	st	4	26	c	1	48	23	1	6	5	0
315/273			2	Lord's	D	4	116	c	4	6	b	1	42	33	1	–	–	–
316/274			3	Manchester	D	4	25	b	–	–	–	–	36	28	1	48	28	1
317/275			4	Oval	D	4	13	c	–	–	–	1	12	6	1	6	3	0
326/279	1950	WI	4	Oval	L-I & 56	4	44	ro	4	11	c	–	42	21	0	–	–	–
327/280	1950–51	A	1	Brisbane[2]	L-70	4	3	c	9	0	c	–	–	–	–	–	–	–
329/282			3	Sydney	L-I & 13	4	0	b	4	23	c	–	48	14	0	–	–	–
330/283			4	Adelaide	L-274	4	5	c	4	0	c	1	8	11	0	38	18	1
331/284			5	Melbourne	W-8w	4	11	c	4	11	*	2	–	–	–	–	–	–
332/285	1950–51	NZ	1	Christchurch	D	4	79	b	–	–	–	–	24	21	0	12	10	0
333/286			2	Wellington	W-6w	5	10	b	4	18	b	1	–	–	–	–	–	–
334/287	1951	SA	1	Nottingham	L-71	4	112	c	4	5	lbw	1	12	7	0	–	–	–
335/288			2	Lord's	W-10w	4	79	lbw	–	–	–	1	–	–	–	12	13	0
337/290			4	Leeds	D	4	25	lbw	–	–	–	–	6	4	0	42	16	0
338/291			5	Oval	W-4w	4	73	b	4	18	c	–	6	5	0	–	–	–
351/297	1952	I	1	Leeds	W-7w	4	14	c	4	35	*	1	42	20	0	–	–	–
352/298			2	Lord's	W-8w	4	6	lbw	4	4	*	1	–	–	–	12	10	0
372/301	1953	A	1	Nottingham	D	4	0	c	–	–	–	1	–	–	–	–	–	–
373/302			2	Lord's	D	4	57	c	4	33	lbw	1	–	–	–	18	21	1
374/303			3	Manchester	D	4	45	c	–	–	–	1	–	–	–	–	–	–
375/304			4	Leeds	D	4	0	c	4	61	lbw	–	–	–	–	–	–	–
376/305			5	Oval	W-8w	4	16	c	4	22	*	1	–	–	–	–	–	–
382/306	1953–54	WI	1	Kingston	L-140	4	12	lbw	5	2	b	–	12	5	0	–	–	–
383/307			2	Bridgetown	L-181	4	13	c	4	93	lbw	–	30	29	0	6	13	0
384/308			3	Georgetown	W-9w	4	64	c	–	–	–	1	18	6	0	–	–	–
385/309			4	Port-of-Spain	D	4	133	c	–	–	–	2	52	40	2	42	51	0
386/310			5	Kingston	W-9w	4	31	hw	–	–	–	1	–	–	–	–	–	–
387/311	1954	P	1	Lord's	D	4	0	b	–	–	–	1	–	–	–	78	36	1
388/312			2	Nottingham	W-I & 129	4	278	b	–	–	–	2	–	–	–	–	–	–
389/313			3	Manchester	D	4	93	c	–	–	–	1	–	–	–	–	–	–
390/314			4	Oval	L-24	4	53	c	4	29	c	1	–	–	–	–	–	–
391/315	1954–55	A	1	Brisbane[2]	L-I & 154	11	2	*	10	0	c	–	–	–	–	–	–	–
393/317			3	Melbourne	W-128	5	4	c	5	23	c	–	–	–	–	–	–	–
394/318			4	Adelaide	W-5w	5	44	lbw	5	34	*	–	–	–	–	–	–	–
395/319			5	Sydney	D	5	84	c	–	–	–	–	–	–	–	–	–	–
408/322	1955	SA	1	Nottingham	W-I & 5	4	27	lbw	–	–	–	1	–	–	–	–	–	–
409/323			2	Lord's	W-71	4	20	c	4	69	c	–	–	–	–	–	–	–
410/324			3	Manchester	L-3w	4	158	c	4	71	c	–	–	–	–	–	–	–
411/325			4	Leeds	L-224	5	61	c	5	26	c	–	–	–	–	–	–	–
412/326			5	Oval	W-92	4	30	c	5	30	c	–	–	–	–	–	–	–
429/331	1956	A	5	Oval	D	5	94	c	5	35	*	–	–	–	–	–	–	–
434/332	1956–57	SA	1	Johannesburg[3]	W-131	3	5	c	3	32	c	–	–	–	–	–	–	–

Ref	Series	V	T Venue	Result	Batting 1st No	R	HO	Batting 2nd No	R	HO	Ct	Bowling 1st Balls	R	W	Bowling 2nd Balls	R	W
435/333			2 Cape Town	W-312	3	58	c	3	64	c	–	–	–	–	16	3	0
436/334			3 Durban[2]	D	3	16	b	3	19	c	–	–	–	–	8	5	0
437/335			4 Johannesburg[3]	L-17	5	42	c	6	1	c	–	–	–	–	–	–	–
438/336			5 Port Elizabeth	L-58	3	0	b	6	5	c	–	–	–	–	–	–	–

Career	M	I	NO	HS	R	Avge	100	50	Ct	St	Balls	R	W	Avge	BB	5w	10w	Rate
Test	78	131	15	278	5807	50.06	17	28	49	–	2716	1410	25	56.40	5-70	1	–	108.64
F/c	515	839	88	300	38942	51.85	123	182	416	–	36749	20074	622	32.27	7-36	19	3	59.08

D. C. S. COMPTON – TEST BATTING SUMMARY

Series	V	M	I	NO	HS	R	Avge	100	50
1937	NZ	1	1	–	65	65	65.00	–	1
1938	A	4	6	1	102	214	42.80	1	1
1939	WI	3	5	2	120	189	63.00	1	–
1946	I	3	4	2	71*	146	73.00	–	2
1946–47	A	5	10	1	147	459	51.00	2	2
1946–47	NZ	1	1	–	38	38	38.00	–	–
1947	SA	5	8	–	208	753	94.12	4	2
1948	A	5	10	1	184	562	62.44	2	2
1948–49	SA	5	9	1	114	406	50.75	1	2
1949	NZ	4	6	–	116	300	50.00	2	–
1950	WI	1	2	–	44	55	27.50	–	–
1950–51	A	4	8	1	11*	53	7.57	–	–
1950–51	NZ	2	3	–	79	107	35.66	–	1
1951	SA	4	6	–	112	312	52.00	1	2
1952	I	2	4	2	35*	59	29.50	–	–
1953	A	5	8	1	61	234	33.42	–	2
1953–54	WI	5	7	–	133	348	49.71	1	2

Series	V	M	I	NO	HS	R	Avge	100	50
1954	P	4	5	–	278	453	90.60	1	2
1954–55	A	4	7	2	84	191	38.20	–	1
1955	SA	5	9	–	158	492	54.66	1	3
1956	A	1	2	1	94	129	129.00	–	1
1956–57	SA	5	10	–	64	242	24.20	–	2
	A	28	51	8	184	1842	42.83	5	9
	SA	24	42	1	208	2205	53.78	7	11
	WI	9	14	2	133	592	49.33	2	2
	NZ	8	11	–	116	510	46.36	2	2
	I	5	8	4	71*	205	51.25	–	2
	P	4	5	–	278	453	90.60	1	2
Home		47	76	10	278	3963	60.04	13	18
Overseas		31	55	5	147	1844	36.88	4	10
Totals		78	131	15	278	5807	50.06	17	28

COOK, Cecil

Gloucestershire (1946 to 1964)

Born Tetbury, Gloucestershire
23 Aug 1921

NOTABLE FEATS

- Dismissed J.O. Newton-Thompson of Oxford U with his first ball in first-class cricket (Oxford 19446).
- Took 100 wickets in a season 9 times, including his first season when he became the ninth of 11 bowlers to achieve this feat.

'Sam' Cook was an extremely accurate orthodox slow left-arm bowler whose success in wartime matches for the RAF and Tetbury CC earned him a trial with Gloucestershire. There he impressed Walter Hammond and repaid his confidence by claiming 133 wickets in his first season. A consistent wicket-taker, he was unfortunate to be given only once chance at international level, and that on an unresponsive pitch. He was a first-class umpire (1971–86).

'Sam' Cook

Ref	Series	V	T Venue	Result	Batting 1st No	R	HO	Batting 2nd No	R	HO	Ct	Bowling 1st Balls	R	W	Bowling 2nd Balls	R	W
285/253	1947	SA	1 Nottingham	D	9	0	b	9	4	c	–	126	87	0	54	40	0

Career	M	I	NO	HS	R	Avge	100	50	Ct	St	Balls	R	W	Avge	BB	5w	10w	Rate
Test	1	2	0	4	4	2.00	–	–	–	–	180	127	0	–	–	–	–	–
F/c	506	612	249	35*	1965	5.41	–	–	153	–	106308	36578	1782	20.52	9-42	99	15	59.65

COOK, Geoffrey

Northamptonshire (1971 to date)
Eastern Province
(1978–79 to 1980–81)

TOURS A 1982–83; I/SL 1981–82
Born Middlesbrough, Yorkshire
9 Oct 1951

A consistent opening batsman with a fine array of forcing strokes based on a sound technique, Geoff Cook met with surprisingly little success at Test level. His fielding at short-leg was often worthy of the Brian Close Bravery Award, while his authoritative captaincy of Northamptonshire (1981–88) was rewarded with his election as chairman of the Cricketers' Association by his fellow professionals. He bowled orthodox left-arm spin – very occasionally.

Geoff Cook

NOTABLE FEATS

- Exceeded 1000 runs in a season 11 times.
- Shared in record Northamptonshire 2nd-wkt stand of 344 with R.J. Boyd-Moss v Lancashire at Northampton in 1986.

						Batting 1st			Batting 2nd				Bowling 1st			Bowling 2nd		
Ref	Series	V	T	Venue	Result	No	R	HO	No	R	HO	Ct	Balls	R	W	Balls	R	W
921/579	1981–82	SL		Colombo SO	W-7w	2	11	c	2	0	lbw	3	–	–	–	–	–	
928/580	1982	I	1	Lord's	W-7w	1	4	lbw	1	10	lbw	4	–	–	–	6	4	0
929/581			2	Manchester	D	1	66	b	–	–	–	1	–	–	–	–	–	–
930/582			3	Oval	D	1	50	c	1	8	c	–	–	–	–	–	–	–
938/586	1982–83	A	1	Perth	D	1	1	c	1	7	c	1	24	16	0	–	–	–
941/589			4	Melbourne	W-3	1	10	c	1	26	c	–	–	–	–	–	–	–
942/590			5	Sydney	D	1	8	c	1	2	lbw	–	–	–	–	12	7	0

Career	M	I	NO	HS	R	Avge	100	50	Ct	St	Balls	R	W	Avge	BB	5w	10w	Rate
Test	7	13	0	66	203	15.61	–	2	9	–	42	27	0	–	–	–	–	–
F/c	431	745	61	203	21816	31.89	33	107	410	3	1226	791	15	52.73	3-47	–	–	81.73

COOK Nicholas Grant Billson

Leicestershire (1978 to 1985)
Northamptonshire (1986 to date)

TOURS
NZ 1979–80 (Robins), 1983–84;
P 1983–84; SL 1985–86 (Eng B);
Z 1980–81 (Leics), 1984–85 (Eng Co)
Born Leicester 17 Jun 1956

Six feet tall, Nick Cook is an orthodox left-arm spinner who, called up as a replacement for the injured Phil Edmonds, enjoyed a sensational start to his Test career by taking 32 wickets in his first four matches – one more than the England record set by Tom Richardson. In his very first innings he returned the first five-wicket analysis by an England slow bowler in a home Test for eight years. He made little impression against West Indies in 1984 but was unlucky to be injured soon after regaining favour when Edmonds retired. Unless confronted by extreme pace he is a dogged and determined lower-order batsman.

Nick Cook bowling at Nottingham against New Zealand in 1983.

NOTABLE FEATS

- *978* His match analysis of 11 for 83 remains the record for England in Pakistan.

Ref	Series	V	T	Venue	Result	Batting 1st No	R	HO	Batting 2nd No	R	HO	Ct	Bowling 1st Balls	R	W	Bowling 2nd Balls	R	W
959/593	1983	NZ	3	Lord's	W-127	9	16	b	9	5	c	1	156	35	5	164	90	3
960/594			4	Nottingham	W-165	9	4	c	9	26	c	2	192	63	5	300	87	4
975/595	1983–84	NZ	1	Wellington	D	9	7	c	–	–	–	1	138	43	1	399	153	3
978/598	1983–84	P	1	Karachi	L-3w	9	9	c	9	5	c	–	180	65	6	84	18	5
979/599			2	Faisalabad	D	10	1	*	–	–	–	–	324	133	2	96	38	0
980/600			3	Lahore[2]	D	10	3	c	–	–	–	–	276	117	1	111	73	0
989/601	1984	WI	1	Birmingham	L-I & 180	10	2	c	9	9	ro	–	228	127	1	–	–	–
991/603			3	Leeds	L-8w	10	1	b	8	0	c	–	54	29	1	54	27	2
992/604			4	Manchester	L-I & 64	9	13	b	8	0	c	1	234	114	1	–	–	–
1084/639	1987–88	P	1	Lahore[2]	L-I & 87	11	10	c	11	5	b	–	186	87	3	–	–	–
1085/640			2	Faisalabad	D	6	2	c	–	–	–	–	123	37	2	54	15	1
1086/641			3	Karachi	D	10	2	lbw	10	14	b	–	198	56	1	–	–	–

Career	M	I	NO	HS	R	Avge	100	50	Ct	St	Balls	R	W	Avge	BB	5w	10w	Rate
Test	12	20	1	26	134	7.05	–	–	5	–	3551	1407	47	29.93	6-65	4	1	75.55
F/c	261	267	66	75	2426	12.06	–	4	150	–	50794	19755	687	28.75	7-63	25	3	73.93

COPE
Geoffrey Alan

Yorkshire (1966 to 1980)

TOURS
SA 1975–76 (Robins); NZ 1977–78; I/SL 1976–77; P 1977–78
Born Burmantofts, Leeds, Yorkshire
23 Feb 1947

NOTABLE FEATS

- Hat-trick for Yorkshire v Essex at Colchester in 1970.

Suspicions about the legality of Geoff Cope's bowling action restricted his career as England's prime off-spinner to a single rubber in Pakistan. He came tantalizingly close to a hat-trick in his first Test when, having dismissed Abdul Qadir and Sarfraz Nawaz with successive balls, he had Iqbal Qasim given out caught at slip off his very next delivery – only for the fielder, his captain Mike Brearley, to withdraw the appeal because he was uncertain if the catch had carried. Suspended by the TCCB in 1972 and 1978, he revealed considerable courage and dedication by twice readjusting his arm action and regaining his Yorkshire place. He was a stubborn lower-order batsman and a handy fielder.

Geoff Cope

Ref	Series	V	T	Venue	Result	Batting 1st No	R	HO	Batting 2nd No	R	HO	Ct	Bowling 1st Balls	R	W	Bowling 2nd Balls	R	W
814/531	1977–78	P	1	Lahore[2]	D	9	0	lbw	–	–	–	1	312	102	3	24	7	0
815/532			2	Hyderabad	D	9	22	c	–	–	–	–	112	49	2	192	42	2
816/533			3	Karachi	D	9	18	b	–	–	–	–	224	77	1	–	–	–

Career	M	I	NO	HS	R	Avge	100	50	Ct	St	Balls	R	W	Avge	BB	5w	10w	Rate
Test	3	3	0	22	40	13.33	–	–	1	–	864	277	8	34.62	3-102	–	–	108.00
F/c	246	261	93	78	2383	14.18	–	5	71	–	43448	16948	686	24.70	8-73	35	6	63.33

COPSON
William Henry

Derbyshire (1932 to 1950)

Wisden 1937
TOURS A 1936–37: NZ 1936–37
Born Stonebroom, Derbyshire
27 Apr 1908
Died Clay Cross, Derbyshire
14 Sep 1971

NOTABLE FEATS

- Took the wicket of A. Sandham with his first ball in first-class cricket (The Oval 1932).
- Three hat-tricks for Derbyshire: v Lancashire at Burton upon Trent and v Warwickshire at Derby in 1937, v Oxford U at Oxford in 1939.
- His analysis of 8.2–2–11–8 v Warwickshire at Derby in 1937 included 7 wkts in 23 balls, 6 in 13, 5 in 6 and 4 in 4. He took 4 wkts in 5 balls v Oxford U at Oxford in 1939.
- Took 100 wickets in a season 3 times.

Bill Copson was an auburn-haired, right-arm fast-medium bowler who, after a brief run up, hesitated slightly before releasing the ball. He could conjure deceptive pace from even the most lifeless pitch, swing the ball late either way and produce a lethal break-back. He showed scant interest in cricket until he was 17; then, as a coal miner during the General Strike, he was persuaded by his mates to join impromptu matches on a recreation ground. To his own amazement he found that he could bowl with such pace and accuracy that he soon progressed into Derbyshire League cricket via the Morton Colliery team. Playing for Clay Cross he took all 10 Staveley wickets for 5 runs and not surprisingly attracted the notice of the County. He made a massive contribution to Derbyshire's lone Championship title in 1936 with 160 wickets at 13.34 apiece and some dependable close fielding.

Bill Copson

During a meagre three-match Test career which spanned the Second World War he enjoyed a 9-wicket debut and 3 for 0 finale. Later he umpired first-class matches (1958–67).

						Batting 1st			Batting 2nd				Bowling 1st			Bowling 2nd		
Ref	Series	V	T	Venue	Result	No	R	HO	No	R	HO	Ct	Balls	R	W	Balls	R	W
272/241	1939	WI	1	Lord's	W-8w	–	–	–	–	–	–	1	192	85	5	132	67	4
273/242			2	Manchester	D	–	–	–	–	–	–	–	72	31	2	24	2	1
289/257	1947	SA	5	Oval	D	11	6	b	–	–	–	–	162	46	3	180	66	0

Career	M	I	NO	HS	R	Avge	100	50	Ct	St	Balls	R	W	Avge	BB	5w	10w	Rate
Test	3	1	0	6	6	6.00	–	–	1	–	762	297	15	19.80	5-85	1	–	50.80
F/c	279	359	108	43	1711	6.81	–	–	103	–	50314	20752	1094	18.96	8-11	66	6	45.99

CORNFORD
Walter Latter

Sussex (1921 to 1947)

TOURS A 1929–30; NZ 1929–30
Born Hurst Green, Sussex 25 Dec 1900
Died Elm Grove, Brighton, Sussex
6 Feb 1964

Only fractionally above five feet tall, 'Tich' Cornford was one of the smallest wicket-keepers to play first-class cricket. He had astonishing reflexes and stood up to all types of bowling. Twice in one match he stumped Jack Hobbs on the leg side and he even made stumpings off the fast-medium bowling of Maurice Tate, his closest friend, and Arthur Gilligan. Competition from such contemporaries as Strudwick, Duckworth and Ames restricted his international honours to the first rubber to be staged in New Zealand. He retired in 1939 but made one emergency reappearance in 1947 while coach at Brighton College (1945–62).

'Tich' Cornford

Ref	Series	V	T	Venue	Result	Batting 1st No	R	HO	Batting 2nd No	R	HO	Fielding 1st Ct	St	Byes	Balls	Fielding 2nd Ct	St	Byes	Balls
186/172†	1929–30	NZ	1	Christchurch	W-8w	10	6	c	–	–	–	1	–	7	283	–	1	9	363
187/173†			2	Wellington	D	10	10	c	–	–	–	2	1	17	819	–	–	1	318
188/174†			3	Auckland	D	–	–	–	–	–	–	–	–	0	204	–	–	–	–
189/175†			4	Auckland	D	10	18	c	1	2	b	2	1	31	997	–	–	–	–

Career	M	I	NO	HS	R	Avge	100	50	Ct	St	Balls	R	W	Avge	BB	5w	10w	Rate
Test	4	4	0	18	36	9.00	–	–	5	3	–	–	–	–	–	–	–	–
F/c	496	649	211	82	6554	14.96	–	16	675	342	107	65	0	–	–	–	–	–

COTTAM
Robert Michael Henry

Hampshire (1963 to 1971)
Northamptonshire (1972 to 1976)

TOURS
I 1972–73; P 1968–69, 1970–71 (Cwlth), 1972–73; SL 1968–69, 1972–73
Born Cleethorpes, Lincolnshire
16 Oct 1944

A tall (6ft 3in), right-arm fast-medium bowler, Bob Cottam used his lean body to full effect in a rather slingy action. He was a daunting prospect on responsive pitches when he could extract steep bounce. On moving to Northants he bowled cutters effectively at reduced pace and cultivated a devastating break-back. After a spell as the NCA's chief coach in the West Country he was appointed Warwickshire's cricket manager in 1987.

NOTABLE FEATS
- Took 100 wickets in a season 3 times.
- His innings analysis of 9 for 25 v Lancashire at Manchester in 1965 remains the Hampshire record.

Bob Cottam

Ref	Series	V	T	Venue	Result	Batting 1st No	R	HO	Batting 2nd No	R	HO	Ct	Bowling 1st Balls	R	W	Bowling 2nd Balls	R	W
647/450	1968–69	P	1	Lahore[2]	D	11	4	*	–	–	–	1	134	50	4	78	35	2
648/451			2	Dacca	D	11	4	c	–	–	–	1	163	52	2	180	43	1
703/478	1973–73	I	1	Delhi	W-6w	11	3	c	–	–	–	–	138	66	2	42	18	0
704/479			2	Calcutta	L-28	11	3	lbw	11	13	lbw	–	138	45	3	30	18	0

Career	M	I	NO	HS	R	Avge	100	50	Ct	St	Balls	R	W	Avge	BB	5w	10w	Rate
Test	4	5	1	13	27	6.75	–	–	2	–	903	327	14	23.35	4-50	–	–	64.50
F/c	289	280	97	62*	1278	6.98	–	1	153	–	53053	21125	1010	20.91	9-25	58	6	52.52

COVENTRY
Hon. Charles John

TOUR SA 1888–89
Born Marylebone, London 26 Feb 1867
Died Earl's Croome, Worcestershire
2 Jun 1929

Colonel The Honourable Charles Coventry was an old Etonian who, after appearing with his brother for Worcestershire (then a minor county), toured South Africa with Major Warton's team. A cavalier strokemaker, his entire first-class career was confined to batting at number ten in the first two Tests played in the Union. On a return visit he was reported killed during the Jameson Raid and his funeral service in Worcestershire had almost commenced when news of his survival compelled its hasty conversion to a village green celebration. [*Illus. p.* 51]

Ref	Series	V	T	Venue	Result	Batting 1st No	R	HO	Batting 2nd No	R	HO	Ct
31/31	1888–89	SA	1	Port Elizabeth	W-8W	10	12	c	–	–	–	–
32/32			2	Cape Town	W-I & 202	10	1	*	–	–	–	–

Career	M	I	NO	HS	R	Avge	100	50	Ct	St	Balls	R	W	Avge	BB	5w	10w	Rate
Test	2	2	1	12	13	13.00	–	–	–	–	–	–	–	–	–	–	–	–
F/c	2	2	1	12	13	13.00	–	–	–	–	–	–	–	–	–	–	–	–

COWANS
Norman George

Middlesex (1980 to date)

TOURS

A 1982–83; NZ 1983–84; I 1984–85; P 1983–84; SL 1984–85, 1985–86 (Eng B); Z 1980–81 (Middx)

Born Enfield, St Mary, Jamaica

17 Apr 1961

Norman Cowans, the 500th cricketer and first black Jamaican to represent England in official Test matches, is a tall (6ft 3in), lissom right-handed fast bowler who emigrated to London with his family at the age of seven. Although able to sustain his top pace only for short spells he enjoyed one outstanding performance when England beat Australia by just 3 runs (Test *941*). But he managed only one other 5-wicket return in his next 30 Test innings, injuries contributing to his inability to sustain such early promise.

NOTABLE FEATS

- 50 wickets in 19th Test (*1017*).
- *980* Took 5 wkts in 22 balls, including 3 in his 11th over (2W2W.W).

Norman Cowans

Ref	Series	V	T	Venue	Result	Batting 1st No	R	HO	Batting 2nd No	R	HO	Ct	Bowling 1st Balls	R	W	Bowling 2nd Balls	R	W
938/586	1982–83	A	1	Perth	D	11	4	b	11	36	lbw	1	78	54	0	18	15	0
939/587			2	Brisbane[2]	L-7w	11	10	c	11	5	c	–	36	36	0	54	31	1
941/589			4	Melbourne	W-3	11	3	c	11	10	b	1	96	69	2	156	77	6
942/590			5	Sydney	D	11	0	*	–	–	–	1	126	67	1	78	47	1
957/591	1983	NZ	1	Oval	W-189	11	3	b	–	–	–	–	114	60	1	66	41	0
958/592			2	Leeds	L-5w	11	0	c	11	10	c	–	168	88	3	30	23	0
959/593			3	Lord's	W-127	11	1	*	11	1	c	–	54	30	0	66	36	2
960/594			4	Nottingham	W-165	11	7	c	11	0	b	–	126	74	3	126	95	3
976/596	1983–84	NZ	2	Christchurch	L-I & 132	11	4	c	11	7	c	–	84	52	3	–	–	–
977/597			3	Auckland	D	11	21	c	–	–	–	1	216	98	2	12	4	0
978/598	1983–84	P	1	Karachi	L-3w	11	1	*	11	0	*	2	72	34	0	15	10	0
980/600			3	Lahore[2]	D	11	3	*	9	3	st	–	174	89	2	84	42	5
992/604	1984	WI	4	Manchester	L-I & 64	11	0	b	10	14	b	1	114	76	0	–	–	–
1005/607	1984–85	I	1	Bombay[3]	L-8w	11	0	c	11	0	c	–	168	109	2	30	18	1
1006/608			2	Delhi	W-8w	11	0	*	–	–	–	–	120	70	0	78	43	2
1007/609			3	Calcutta	D	11	1	b	–	–	–	–	246	103	3	24	6	0
1008/610			4	Madras[1]	W-9w	–	–	–	–	–	–	2	77	39	2	90	73	2
1009/611			5	Kanpur	D	11	9	b	–	–	–	–	216	115	2	42	51	0
1017/612	1985	A	1	Leeds	W-5w	11	22	*	–	–	–	–	120	78	1	78	50	1

Career	M	I	NO	HS	R	Avge	100	50	Ct	St	Balls	R	W	Avge	BB	5w	10w	Rate
Test	19	29	7	36	175	7.95	–	–	9	–	3452	2003	51	39.27	6-77	2	–	67.68
F/c	159	158	36	66	1091	8.94	–	1	49	–	21430	11164	475	23.50	6-31	21	1	45.11

N. G. COWANS – TEST BOWLING SUMMARY

Series	V	M	Balls	R	W	Avge	BB	5w	10w	Rate
1982–83	A	4	642	396	11	36.00	6-77	1	–	58.36
1983	NZ	4	750	447	12	37.25	3-74	–	–	62.50
1983–84	NZ	2	312	154	5	30.80	3-52	–	–	62.40
1983–84	P	2	345	175	7	25.00	5-42	1	–	49.28
1984	WI	1	114	76	0	–	–	–	–	–
1984–85	I	5	1091	627	14	44.78	3-103	–	–	77.92
1985	A	1	198	128	2	64.00	1-50	–	–	99.00
	A	5	840	524	13	40.30	6-77	1	–	64.61
	WI	1	114	76	0	–	–	–	–	–
	NZ	6	1062	601	17	35.35	3-52	–	–	62.47
	I	5	1091	627	14	44.78	3-103	–	–	77.92
	P	2	345	175	7	25.00	5-42	1	–	49.28
Home		6	1062	651	14	46.50	3-74	–	–	75.85
Overseas		13	2390	1352	37	36.54	6-77	2	–	64.59
Totals		19	3452	2003	51	39.27	6-77	2	–	67.68

COWDREY Christopher Stuart

Kent (1977 to date)

TOURS
NZ 1979–80 (Robins); I 1984–85;
SL 1977–78 (Robins), 1984–85
Born Farnborough, Kent 20 Oct 1957

The eldest of Colin Cowdrey's three sons, Christopher is an aggressive, predominantly on-side, middle-order batsman, a bustling right-arm medium-pace swing bowler and a quite exceptional fielder. Appointed Kent's captain in 1985 he has proved to be an inspired leader whose enthusiasm and charisma lifted a mediocre Kent team to within one point of the 1988 Championship, an effort which included a notable sequence of six successive victories. Although awarded the England captaincy for the last two Tests against West Indies, a foot injury forced him to withdraw before the second match and he was replaced by Graham Gooch who retained the post for the subsequent Sri Lanka Test and aborted winter tour. His brief elevation completed only the second father/son captaincy double for England after Frank and George Mann.

Chris Cowdrey, during his brief spell as England leader, congratulates Neil Foster on having bowled Viv Richards in the Fourth Test against West Indies at Leeds, 1988.

						Batting 1st			Batting 2nd				Bowling 1st			Bowling 2nd		
Ref	Series	V	T	Venue	Result	No	R	HO	No	R	HO	Ct	Balls	R	W	Balls	R	W
1005/607	1984–85	I	1	Bombay[3]	L-8w	6	13	c	6	14	c	1	30	30	1	–	–	–
1006/608			2	Delhi	W-8w	6	38	c	–	–	–	–	–	–	–	–	–	–
1007/609			3	Calcutta	D	7	27	lbw	–	–	–	1	12	15	0	24	10	0
1008/610			4	Madras[1]	W-9w	8	3	*	–	–	–	2	114	65	2	30	26	0
1009/611			5	Kanpur	D	6	1	c	–	–	–	–	126	103	1	30	39	0
1101/649*	1988	WI	4	Leeds	L-10w	7	0	lbw	6	5	b	–	12	8	0	21	13	0

Career	M	I	NO	HS	R	Avge	100	50	Ct	St	Balls	R	W	Avge	BB	5w	10w	Rate
Test	6	8	1	38	101	14.42	–	–	5	–	399	309	4	77.25	2-65	–	–	99.75
F/c	256	387	57	159	10127	30.68	16	46	259	–	12667	6890	182	37.85	5-46	2	–	69.59

COWDREY
Michael Colin CBE

Kent (1950 to 1976)
Oxford University (1952 to 1954)

Wisden 1956
TOURS
A 1954–55, 1958–59, 1962–63, 1965–66, 1970–71, 1974–75; SA 1956–57; WI 1955–56 (Swanton), 1959–60, 1964–65 (Cav), 1967–68, 1969–70 (Norfolk); NZ 1954–55, 1958–59, 1962–63, 1965–66, 1970–71; I 1961–62 (Int XI), 1963–64, 1964–65 (Cwlth); P 1961–62 (Int XI), 1968–69; SL 1968–69
Born Putumala, Ootacamund, India
24 Dec 1932

Colin Cowdrey in play during his record-breaking partnership with Peter May at Birmingham against the 1957 West Indians.

Colin Cowdrey was a most graceful and prolific batsman of the highest class whose timing was so immaculate that he appeared to caress the ball to the boundary. His initials, bestowed by a cricket-mad father, kindled a life-long enthusiasm and, at seven, his ambition was further fuelled by a letter from Jack Hobbs received when he won a bat for scoring 93 in an inter-school match. At 13 he was picked for the Tonbridge School 1st XI primarily as a right-arm leg-spin bowler; within a few matches he was batting at number three and celebrated being the youngest to appear in a schools match at Lord's by scoring 75 and 44 and taking five wickets. He played for Kent while still at school; even at that early age his batting had a bearing of calm omnipotence and he strongly resembled Wally Hammond in physique, balance, poise and effortless style. In Australia, where the bright light, hard pitches and fast outfields best suited his technique, he played many of his best innings and was a tremendous favourite with the public. He opened for England with some success but was happier a place or two lower. Perhaps because he lacked the killer instinct, or that selfish dedication to records typical of some great batsmen, he converted only three of his 107 hundreds into double centuries. Surprisingly for such a gifted player he was often victim of introspection and qualms about his grip or stance. The selectors allowed him only short bursts of captaincy (27 Tests, 8 wins, 4 defeats) and, although he was vice-captain on four of his Australian tours, he was never entrusted with the role he coveted most. His wrist-spin bowling was seldom required at county level but he became an outstanding slip-catcher and captained Kent benignly from 1957 to 1971. Happily he made a full recovery from the open heart surgery which interrupted his presidency of MCC in the Club's bicenentary year.

NOTABLE FEATS

- 1000 runs in 18th Test (*438*) (31 inns); 2000 runs in 31st Test (*467*) (49 inns); 3000 runs in 47th Test (*494*) (75 inns); 4000 runs in 59th Test (*536*) (97 inns); 5000 runs in 73rd Test (*565*) (120 inns); 6000 runs in 86th Test (*604*) (140 inns); 7000 runs in 100th Test (*639*) (165 inns).
- *393* The 50th England batsman to score 100 v A, he made his runs out of 191 to equal the lowest total in E v A Tests to contain a century and thus share D.G. Bradman's record.
- *439* Shared with P.B.H. May in stand of 411 which remains England's highest for any wicket and the 4th-wkt record in all Test cricket.
- *466* His 100 in 362 min was the slowest in E v A Tests until 1975.
- *508* Set a Test record by winning 9 successive tosses.
- *534* Shared record 2nd-wkt E v P stand of 248 with E.R. Dexter.
- *541* Shared (then) world record 9th-wkt stand of 163* in 161 min with A.C. Smith which remains the England 9th-wkt record in all Tests. First to score 100 v all current opponent countries.
- *602* Became the second non-wicket-keeper after W.R. Hammond to hold 100 catches in Tests.
- *604* His second innings was his 141st in Tests – then a world record.
- *638* Exceeded W.R. Hammond's world record of 110 catches.
- *639* First to play in 100 Test matches. Became second after W.R. Hammond to score 7000 runs in Tests.
- *647* His 22nd and final 100 equalled W.R. Hammond's record for E.
- *674* Exceeded W.R. Hammond's Test record of 7249 runs when 22*.
- *751* Sixth tour of Australia equalled record of J. Briggs.
- *754* Record 42nd appearance in E v A Tests.
- *755* Ended Test career with then world records of 114 matches, 7624 runs, 22 hundreds and 120 catches.
- Exceeded 1000 runs in a season 21 times (plus 6 overseas – English record), including 2000 twice.
- Youngest player to be capped by Kent (18).
- Scored 307 for MCC v S Australia at Adelaide in 1962–63 – highest score by any touring batsman in Australia.
- 16th to score 100 first-class hundreds (1973).

TEST NOTES

- *544* Retired hurt when 19* (2nd inns); resumed at 228–9 with his fractured left-arm in plaster and would have batted left-handed using only his right arm had he been called upon to face the bowling.
- *639* Pulled leg muscle when 58* and batted with a runner, T.W. Graveney deputizing as captain in the field.
- *647* T.W. Graveney deputized as captain throughout the final innings.

Ref	Series	V	T	Venue	Result	Batting 1st No	R	HO	Batting 2nd No	R	HO	Ct	Bowling 1st Balls	R	W	Bowling 2nd Balls	R	W
391/315	1954–55	A	1	Brisbane[2]	L-I & 154	5	40	c	5	10	b	2	–	–	–	–	–	–
392/316			2	Sydney	W-38	5	23	c	5	54	c	1	–	–	–	–	–	–
393/317			3	Melbourne	W-128	4	102	b	4	7	b	1	–	–	–	–	–	–
394/318			4	Adelaide	W-5w	4	79	c	4	4	c	–	–	–	–	–	–	–
395/319			5	Sydney	D	4	0	c	–	–	–	–	–	–	–	–	–	–
401/320	1954–55	NZ	1	Dunedin	W-8w	4	42	lbw	4	0	*	1	–	–	–	–	–	–
402/321			2	Auckland	W-I & 20	4	22	b	–	–	–	–	–	–	–	–	–	–
410/324	1955	SA	3	Manchester	L-3w	5	1	c	5	50	c	–	–	–	–	–	–	–
425/327	1956	A	1	Nottingham	D	2	25	c	2	81	c	–	–	–	–	–	–	–
426/328			2	Lord's	L-185	2	23	c	2	27	lbw	1	–	–	–	–	–	–
427/329			3	Leeds	W-I & 42	2	0	c	–	–	–	–	–	–	–	–	–	–
428/330			4	Manchester	W-I & 170	2	80	c	–	–	–	2	–	–	–	–	–	–
429/331			5	Oval	D	2	0	c	2	8	c	–	–	–	–	–	–	–
434/332	1956–57	SA	1	Johannesburg[3]	W-131	5	59	c	7	6	c	3	–	–	–	–	–	–
435/333			2	Cape Town	W-312	5	101	lbw	5	61	c	2	–	–	–	–	–	–
436/334			3	Durban[2]	D	5	6	lbw	6	24	lbw	2	–	–	–	–	–	–
437/335			4	Johannesburg[3]	L-17	6	8	c	4	55	c	3	–	–	–	–	–	–
438/336			5	Port Elizabeth	L-58	6	3	c	4	8	c	–	–	–	–	–	–	–
439/337	1957	WI	1	Birmingham	D	5	4	c	5	154	c	1	–	–	–	–	–	–
440/338			2	Lord's	W-I & 36	5	152	c	–	–	–	2	–	–	–	–	–	–
441/339			3	Nottingham	D	5	55	ro	–	–	–	–	–	–	–	–	–	–
442/340			4	Leeds	W-I & 5	5	68	c	–	–	–	3	–	–	–	–	–	–
443/341			5	Oval	W-I & 237	5	2	b	–	–	–	2	–	–	–	–	–	–
454/342	1958	NZ	1	Birmingham	W-205	5	81	b	5	70	c	1	–	–	–	–	–	–
455/343			2	Lord's	W-I & 148	5	65	c	–	–	–	2	–	–	–	–	–	–
456/344			3	Leeds	W-I & 71	–	–	–	–	–	–	3	–	–	–	–	–	–
458/346			5	Oval	D	5	25	c	–	–	–	1	–	–	–	–	–	–
464/347	1958–59	A	1	Brisbane[2]	L-8W	5	13	c	6	28	c	1	–	–	–	–	–	–
465/348			2	Melbourne	L-8w	6	44	c	6	12	c	–	–	–	–	–	–	–
466/349			3	Sydney	D	5	34	c	5	100	*	1	–	–	–	–	–	–
467/350			4	Adelaide	L-10w	4	84	b	4	8	b	1	–	–	–	11	9	0
468/351			5	Melbourne	L-9w	4	22	c	4	46	ro	3	–	–	–	–	–	–
472/352	1958–59	NZ	1	Christchurch	W-I & 99	5	15	b	–	–	–	1	–	–	–	–	–	–
473/353			2	Auckland	D	5	5	b	–	–	–	1	–	–	–	–	–	–
474/354	1959	I	1	Nottingham	W-I & 59	3	5	c	–	–	–	1	–	–	–	–	–	–
475/355			2	Lord's	W-8w	3	34	c	3	63	*	–	–	–	–	–	–	–
476/356			3	Leeds	W-I & 173	3	160	c	–	–	–	3	–	–	–	–	–	–
477/357*			4	Manchester	W-171	3	67	c	5	9	c	1	–	–	–	–	–	–
478/358*			5	Oval	W-I & 27	3	6	c	–	–	–	2	–	–	–	–	–	–
487/359	1959–60	WI	1	Bridgetown	D	2	30	c	2	16	*	–	–	–	–	–	–	–
488/360			2	Port-of-Spain	W-256	2	18	b	2	5	c	–	–	–	–	–	–	–
489/361			3	Kingston	D	2	114	c	2	97	c	–	–	–	–	6	4	0
490/362*			4	Georgetown	D	2	65	c	2	27	st	–	–	–	–	–	–	–
491/363*			5	Port-of-Spain	D	2	119	c	2	0	c	1	–	–	–	6	15	0
492/364*	1960	SA	1	Birmingham	W-100	2	3	c	1	0	b	1	–	–	–	–	–	–
493/365*			2	Lord's	W-I & 73	1	4	c	–	–	–	2	–	–	–	–	–	–
494/366*			3	Nottingham	W-8w	2	67	c	2	27	lbw	2	–	–	–	–	–	–
495/367*			4	Manchester	D	4	20	c	2	25	b	–	–	–	–	6	4	0
496/368*			5	Oval	D	2	11	b	2	155	lbw	2	–	–	–	–	–	–
507/369*	1961	A	1	Birmingham	D	4	13	b	4	14	b	–	–	–	–	–	–	–
508/370*			2	Lord's	L-5w	4	16	c	4	7	c	–	–	–	–	–	–	–
509/371			3	Leeds	W-8w	3	93	c	3	22	c	4	–	–	–	–	–	–
511/373			5	Oval	D	3	0	c	5	3	c	–	–	–	–	–	–	–
530/382	1962	P	1	Birmingham	W-I & 24	2	159	c	–	–	–	3	–	–	–	6	1	0
531/383			2	Lord's	W-9w	2	41	c	2	20	c	3	–	–	–	–	–	–
532/384*			3	Leeds	W-I & 117	2	7	c	–	–	–	1	–	–	–	–	–	–
534/386			5	Oval	W-10w	2	182	c	–	–	–	2	–	–	–	–	–	–
535/387	1962–63	A	1	Brisbane[2]	D	4	21	c	4	9	c	–	–	–	–	–	–	–
536/388			2	Melbourne	W-7w	4	113	c	4	58	*	2	–	–	–	–	–	–
537/389			3	Sydney	L-8w	4	85	c	4	8	c	–	–	–	–	–	–	–
538/390			4	Adelaide	D	4	13	c	4	32	ro	3	–	–	–	–	–	–
539/391			5	Sydney	D	2	2	c	5	53	c	–	–	–	–	–	–	–

Ref	Series	V	T	Venue	Result	Batting 1st No	R	HO	Batting 2nd No	R	HO	Ct	Bowling 1st Balls	R	W	Bowling 2nd Balls	R	W
540/392	1962–63	NZ	1	Auckland	W-I& 215	5	86	c	–	–	–	–	–	–	–	–	–	–
541/393			2	Wellington	W-I & 47	8	128	*	–	–	–	1	–	–	–	–	–	–
542/394			3	Christchurch	W-7w	5	43	c	4	35	*	–	–	–	–	–	–	–
543/395	1963	WI	1	Manchester	L-10w	4	4	b	5	12	c	–	–	–	–	–	–	–
544/396			2	Lord's	D	5	4	b	5	19	*	6	–	–	–	–	–	–
555/402	1963–64	I	3	Calcutta	D	4	107	c	4	13	*	3	–	–	–	–	–	–
556/403			4	Delhi	D	6	151	lbw	–	–	–	–	–	–	–	–	–	–
557/404			5	Kanpur	D	6	38	lbw	–	–	–	1	–	–	–	30	34	0
561/405	1964	A	1	Nottingham	D	4	32	b	3	33	b	–	–	–	–	–	–	–
562/406			2	Lord's	D	3	10	c	–	–	–	–	–	–	–	–	–	–
565/409			5	Oval	D	4	20	c	5	93	*	2	–	–	–	–	–	–
591/415	1965	NZ	1	Birmingham	W-9w	5	85	b	–	–	–	–	–	–	–	–	–	–
592/416			2	Lord's	W-7w	4	119	c	5	4	*	–	–	–	–	–	–	–
593/417			3	Leeds	W-I & 187	4	13	b	–	–	–	2	–	–	–	–	–	–
594/418	1965	SA	1	Lord's	D	5	29	b	5	37	lbw	1	–	–	–	–	–	–
595/419			2	Nottingham	L-94	5	105	c	6	20	st	3	–	–	–	–	–	–
596/420			3	Oval	D	4	58	c	5	78	*	1	–	–	–	–	–	–
598/422	1965–66	A	2	Melbourne	D	5	104	c	–	–	–	1	–	–	–	–	–	–
599/423			3	Sydney	W-I & 93	5	0	c	–	–	–	4	–	–	–	–	–	–
600/424			4	Adelaide	L-I & 9	5	38	ro	5	35	c	–	–	–	–	–	–	–
601/425			5	Melbourne	D	5	79	c	5	11	*	–	–	–	–	–	–	–
602/426	1965–66	NZ	1	Christchurch	D	4	0	c	4	21	c	2	–	–	–	–	–	–
603/427			2	Dunedin	D	4	89	*	–	–	–	–	–	–	–	–	–	–
604/428			3	Auckland	D	3	59	ro	3	27	lbw	–	–	–	–	–	–	–
605/429	1966	WI	1	Manchester	L-I & 40	4	12	c	4	69	c	1	–	–	–	–	–	–
606/430*			2	Lord's	D	5	9	c	4	5	c	–	–	–	–	–	–	–
607/431*			3	Nottingham	L-139	5	96	c	5	32	c	2	–	–	–	–	–	–
608/432*			4	Leeds	L-I & 55	5	17	b	5	12	lbw	–	–	–	–	–	–	–
622/438	1967	P	2	Nottingham	W-10w	2	14	c	2	2	*	–	–	–	–	–	–	–
623/439			3	Oval	W-8w	1	16	c	1	9	c	1	–	–	–	–	–	–
628/440*	1967–68	WI	1	Port-of-Spain	D	3	72	c	–	–	–	1	–	–	–	6	1	0
629/441*			2	Kingston	D	3	101	c	3	0	lbw	–	–	–	–	–	–	–
630/442*			3	Bridgetown	D	3	1	c	–	–	–	1	–	–	–	–	–	–
631/443*			4	Port-of-Spain	W-7w	3	148	c	3	71	c	–	–	–	–	–	–	–
632/444*			5	Georgetown	D	3	59	lbw	3	82	lbw	1	–	–	–	–	–	–
637/445*	1968	A	1	Manchester	L-159	3	4	c	3	11	c	1	–	–	–	–	–	–
638/446*			2	Lord's	D	4	45	c	–	–	–	3	–	–	–	–	–	–
639/447*			3	Birmingham	D	3	104	b	–	–	–	–	–	–	–	–	–	–
641/449*			5	Oval	W-226	4	16	lbw	4	35	b	1	–	–	–	–	–	–
647/450*	1968–69	P	1	Lahore[2]	D	3	100	c	3	12	c	–	–	–	–	–	–	–
648/451*			2	Dacca	D	5	7	lbw	–	–	–	–	–	–	–	–	–	–
649/452*			3	Karachi	D	4	14	c	–	–	–	–	–	–	–	–	–	–
674/459	1970–71	A	1	Brisbane[2]	D	5	28	c	–	–	–	2	8	10	0	16	8	0
675/460			2	Perth	D	6	40	c	5	1	c	–	–	–	–	24	18	0
677/462			5	Melbourne	D	4	13	c	–	–	–	1	–	–	–	–	–	–
686/466	1970–71	NZ	2	Auckland	D	3	54	c	6	45	b	–	–	–	–	–	–	–
687/467	1971	P	1	Birmingham	D	3	16	b	3	34	b	1	–	–	–	–	–	–
751/504	1974–75	A	2	Perth	L-9w	3	22	b	2	41	lbw	–	–	–	–	–	–	–
752/505			3	Melbourne	D	3	35	lbw	3	8	c	1	–	–	–	–	–	–
753/506			4	Sydney	L-171	3	22	c	3	1	c	–	–	–	–	–	–	–
754/507			5	Adelaide	L-163	3	26	c	3	3	c	1	–	–	–	–	–	–
755/508			6	Melbourne	W-I & 4	2	7	c	–	–	–	1	–	–	–	–	–	–

Career	M	I	NO	HS	R	Avge	100	50	Ct	St	Balls	R	W	Avge	BB	5w	10w	Rate
Test	114	188	15	182	7624	44.06	22	38	120	–	119	104	0	–	–	–	–	–
F/c	692	1130	134	307	42719	42.89	107	231	638	–	4890	3329	65	51.21	4-22	–	–	75.23

M. C. COWDREY – TEST BATTING SUMMARY

Series	V	M	I	NO	HS	R	Avge	100	50
1954–55	A	5	9	–	102	319	35.44	1	2
1954–55	NZ	2	3	1	42	64	32.00	–	–
1955	SA	1	2	–	50	51	25.50	–	1
1956	A	5	8	–	81	244	30.50	–	2
1956–57	SA	5	10	–	101	331	33.10	1	3
1957	WI	5	6	–	154	435	72.50	2	2
1958	NZ	4	4	–	81	241	60.25	–	3
1958–59	A	5	10	1	100*	391	43.44	1	1
1958–59	NZ	2	2	–	15	20	10.00	–	–
1959	I	5	7	1	160	344	57.33	1	2
1959–60	WI	5	10	1	119	491	54.55	2	2
1960	SA	5	9	–	155	312	34.66	1	1
1961	A	4	8	–	93	168	21.00	–	1
1962	P	4	5	–	182	409	81.80	2	–
1962–63	A	5	10	1	113	394	43.77	1	3
1962–63	NZ	3	4	2	128*	292	146.00	1	1
1963	WI	2	4	1	19*	39	13.00	–	–
1963–64	I	3	4	1	151	309	103.00	2	–
1964	A	3	5	1	93*	188	47.00	–	1
1965	NZ	3	4	1	119	221	73.66	1	1
1965	SA	3	6	1	105	327	65.40	1	2
1965–66	A	4	6	1	104	267	53.40	1	1
1965–66	NZ	3	5	1	89*	196	49.00	–	2
1966	WI	4	8	–	96	252	31.50	–	2
1967	P	2	4	1	16	41	13.66	–	–
1967–68	WI	5	8	–	148	534	66.75	2	4
1968	A	4	6	–	104	215	35.83	1	–
1968–69	P	3	4	–	100	133	33.25	1	–
1970–71	A	3	4	–	40	82	20.50	–	–
1970–71	NZ	1	2	–	54	99	49.50	–	1
1971	P	1	2	–	34	50	25.00	–	–
1974–75	A	5	9	–	41	165	18.33	–	–
	A	43	75	4	113	2433	34.26	5	11
	SA	14	27	1	155	1021	39.26	3	7
	WI	21	36	2	154	1751	51.50	6	10
	NZ	18	24	5	128*	1133	59.63	2	8
	I	8	11	2	160	653	72.55	3	2
	P	10	15	1	182	633	45.21	3	–
Home		55	88	6	182	3537	43.13	9	18
Overseas		59	100	9	151	4087	44.91	13	20
Totals		114	188	15	182	7624	44.06	22	38

COXON, Alexander

Yorkshire (1945 to 1950)

Born Huddersfield, Yorkshire
18 Jan 1916

A fraction under six feet tall, Alec Coxon was a tireless right-arm medium-fast bowler who seamed the ball prodigiously in favourable conditions and an aggressive lower-order batsman. While coaching in South Africa in 1950–51 he surprisingly ended his brief association with Yorkshire and joined Durham. He played centre-forward for Bradford. [*Illus. p.* 61]

NOTABLE FEATS
- Took 100 wickets in a season twice.
- Hat-trick for Yorkshire v Worcestershire at Leeds in 1946.

Ref	Series	V	T	Venue	Result	Batting 1st No	Batting 1st R	Batting 1st HO	Batting 2nd No	Batting 2nd R	Batting 2nd HO	Ct	Bowling 1st Balls	Bowling 1st R	Bowling 1st W	Bowling 2nd Balls	Bowling 2nd R	Bowling 2nd W
300/263	1948	A	2	Lord's	L-409	7	19	c	7	0	lbw	–	210	90	2	168	82	1

Career	M	I	NO	HS	R	Avge	100	50	Ct	St	Balls	R	W	Avge	BB	5w	10w	Rate
Test	1	2	0	19	19	9.50	–	–	–	–	378	172	3	57.33	2-90	–	–	126.00
F/c	146	188	33	83	2817	18.17	–	13	127	–	26513	9893	473	20.91	8-31	24	2	56.05

CRANSTON, James

Gloucestershire (1876 to 1899)

Born King's Norton, Birmingham
9 Jan 1859
Died Bristol 10 Dec 1904

James Cranston was a middle-order batsman who interspersed rigid straight-bat defence with powerful driving. He returned to Bristol in 1889 after a six-year absence, during which he appeared in minor matches for Warwickshire and Worcestershire, to establish himself as the leading left-hander in England. In 1890 he challenged W.G. Grace in both aggregate and average. That August, with Peel, Ulyett and Stoddart unavailable, a desperate Surrey committee recruited him for the Oval Test. There, in a low-scoring game on a rain-ruined pitch, he batted stubbornly against Turner and Ferris and shared in a match-winning stand with Maurice Read. His career was virtually ended by a fit during the following summer, although he did make a four-match reappearance eight seasons later.

James Cranston

Ref	Series	V	T	Venue	Result	Batting 1st No	R	HO	Batting 2nd No	R	HO	Ct
34/34	1890	A	2	Oval	W-2w	5	16	ro	6	15	c	1

Career	M	I	NO	HS	R	Avge	100	50	Ct	St	Balls	R	W	Avge	BB	5w	10w	Rate
Test	1	2	0	16	31	15.50	–	–	1	–	–	–	–	–	–	–	–	–
F/c	118	195	20	152	3450	19.71	5	14	49	–	24	19	0	–	–	–	–	–

CRANSTON Kenneth

Lancashire (1947 to 1948)

TOUR WI 1947–48
Born Aigburth, Liverpool 20 Oct 1917

NOTABLE FEATS

- *288* Ended SA's 2nd inns by taking 4 wickets in an over (W.W.WW).

A gifted all-rounder but a dentist by profession, Ken Cranston allowed himself just two seasons of first-class cricket. Captaining Lancashire in 1947 and 1948, he exceeded 1000 runs and 75 wickets both summers. A forcing middle-order batsman and right-arm medium-fast opening bowler, he made three Test appearances in his first season. When 'Gubby' Allen pulled a calf muscle, while skipping aboard the banana boat on MCC's voyage to the Caribbean, Cranston deputized as captain in the First Test. After his return to full-time dentistry he reappeared in the next two Scarborough Festivals, making his highest score (156*) for MCC against Yorkshire in 1949.

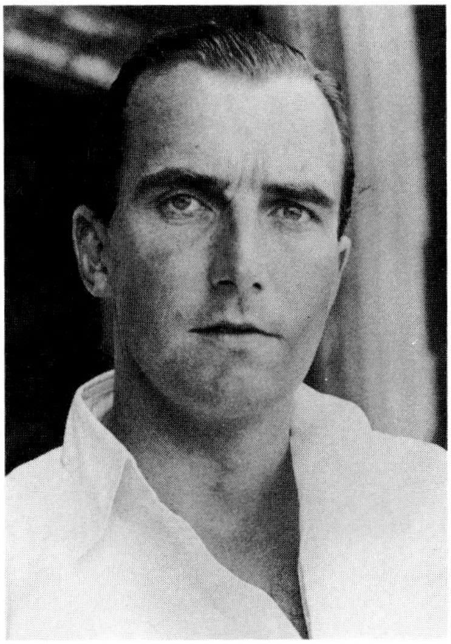

Ken Cranston

Ref	Series	V	T	Venue	Result	Batting 1st No	R	HO	Batting 2nd No	R	HO	Ct	Bowling 1st Balls	R	W	Bowling 2nd Balls	R	W
287/255	1947	SA	3	Manchester	W-7w	7	23	c	–	–	–	–	204	64	2	–	–	–
288/256			4	Leeds	W-10w	7	3	c	–	–	–	1	67	24	1	42	12	4
289/257			5	Oval	D	6	45	st	6	0	c	–	54	25	2	126	61	2
295/258*	1947–48	WI	1	Bridgetown	D	7	2	ro	4	8	lbw	–	90	29	0	78	31	1
296/259			2	Port-of-Spain	D	4	7	c	4	6	c	–	42	29	1	18	18	0
297/260			3	Georgetown	L-7w	6	24	st	6	32	c	–	150	78	4	12	11	0
298/261			4	Kingston	L-10w	5	13	c	5	36	b	–	–	–	–	–	–	–
302/265	1948	A	4	Leeds	L-7w	8	10	b	7	0	c	2	84	51	0	43	28	1

Career	M	I	NO	HS	R	Avge	100	50	Ct	St	Balls	R	W	Avge	BB	5w	10w	Rate
Test	8	14	0	45	209	14.92	–	–	3	–	1010	461	18	25.61	4-12	–	–	56.11
F/c	78	104	15	156*	3099	34.82	3	18	47	–	11642	4985	178	28.00	7-43	10	1	65.40

CRAPP
John Frederick

Gloucestershire (1936 to 1956)

TOURS SA 1948–49; I 1953–54 (Cwlth)
Born St Columb Major, Cornwall
14 Oct 1912
Died Knowle, Bristol 13 Feb 1981

NOTABLE FEATS
- *313* Won match by scoring 10 runs off 3 balls in final over.
- Exceeded 1000 runs 14 times, including 2000 once (2114 in 1949 – the highest aggregate by a Gloucestershire left-hander).

A solidly built, craggy-browed left-hander, Jack Crapp was a sound rather than spectacular early-order batsman, although occasionally he did interrupt his staple grafting to release a burst of latent aggression. He was a fine fielder, especially at slip. The Second World War deprived him of his peak seasons and he was 35 before he made his Test debut and became the first Cornishman to play for England. Gloucestershire's first professional captain (1953–54), he found the responsibility affected his batting – 1954 was the only season he failed to score 1000 runs. A respected and long-serving umpire (1957–78), he stood in four Tests. [*Illus. pp.* 241, 296, 397, 512]

						Batting 1st			Batting 2nd			
Ref	Series	V	T	Venue	Result	No	R	HO	No	R	HO	Ct
301/264	1948	A	3	Manchester	D	5	37	lbw	5	19	*	2
302/265			4	Leeds	L-7w	6	5	b	5	18	b	2
303/266			5	Oval	L-I & 149	5	0	c	5	9	b	2
310/268	1948–49	SA	2	Johannesburg[2]	D	3	56	c	–	–	–	–
311/269			3	Cape Town	D	3	35	c	3	54	c	1
312/270			4	Johannesburg[2]	D	3	51	b	5	5	hw	–
313/271			5	Port Elizabeth	W-3w	3	4	b	6	26	*	–

Career	M	I	NO	HS	R	Avge	100	50	Ct	St	Balls	R	W	Avge	BB	5w	10w	Rate
Test	7	13	2	56	319	29.00	–	3	7	–	–	–	–	–	–	–	–	–
F/c	452	754	80	175	23615	35.03	38	137	385	–	460	306	6	51.00	3-24	–	–	76.66

CRAWFORD
John Neville

Surrey (1904 to 1921)
South Australia
(1909–10 to 1913–14)
Otago (1914–15)
Wellington (1917–18)

Wisden 1907
TOURS
A 1907–08; SA 1905–06;
NZ 1913–14 (Australians)
Born Cane Hill, Surrey 1 Dec 1886
Died Epsom, Surrey 2 May 1963

NOTABLE FEATS
- Exceeded 1000 runs in a season 3 times, 100 wickets twice and achieved the 'double' twice.
- Shared Surrey record 5th-wkt stand of 308 with F.C. Holland v Somerset at The Oval in 1908.
- Scored 354 (14 sixes, 45 fours) in 5½ hr v South Canterbury XV at Temuka, adding 298 in 69 min for 8th wkt with V.T. Trumper and 50 in 9 min with M.A. Noble.

Jack Crawford was a remarkable, bespectacled all-round cricketer: a fearless, hard-hitting middle-order batsman who was a ferocious straight driver of fast bowling and a tireless, accurate, right-arm medium-pace off-break bowler. Cricket was very much in his blood – his father, uncle and two brothers played county cricket – and his prodigious all-round exploits at Repton earned him a debut for Surrey at the age of 17 and with a full school year ahead of him. He met with meteoric success, finishing third in the national averages with 44 wickets at 16.93, including 10 for 78 when he bowled unchanged throughout the match against Gloucestershire. Within a few weeks of leaving Repton he was making his Test debut for 'Plum' Warner's team in South Africa. In 1906 he became the youngest cricketer until Brian Close in 1949 to complete the 'double'. After a mid-season dispute with Surrey's committee in 1909 he became assistant master at St Peter's College, Adelaide and helped South Australia to win the Sheffield Shield twice. Returning to England in 1919 he settled his differences at The Oval and headed the Surrey averages with 417 runs at 83.40.

Jack Crawford

Ref	Series	V	T	Venue	Result	Batting 1st No	R	HO	Batting 2nd No	R	HO	Ct	Bowling 1st Balls	R	W	Bowling 2nd Balls	R	W
88/85	1905–06	SA	1	Johannesburg[1]	L-1w	6	44	c	6	43	b	1	42	14	2	102	49	0
89/86			2	Johannesburg[1]	L-9w	2	23	c	2	6	c	–	66	44	2	12	4	0
90/87			3	Johannesburg[1]	L-243	2	4	b	7	34	c	1	78	51	0	24	17	0
91/88			4	Cape Town	W-4w	7	36	*	2	4	b	1	81	28	1	90	46	1
92/89			5	Cape Town	L-I & 16	1	74	b	1	13	b	3	108	69	3	–	–	–
93/90	1907	SA	1	Lord's	D	8	22	c	–	–	–	–	48	20	0	24	19	0
95/92			3	Oval	D	8	2	c	8	2	c	1	66	33	0	36	14	0
96/93	1907–08	A	1	Sydney	L-2w	8	31	b	8	5	c	1	30	14	0	48	33	2
97/94			2	Melbourne	W-1w	8	16	c	8	10	c	–	174	79	5	198	125	3
98/95			3	Adelaide	L-245	8	62	b	8	7	c	–	84	65	1	275	113	3
99/96			4	Melbourne	L-308	7	1	b	7	0	c	2	143	48	5	150	72	3
100/97			5	Sydney	L-49	6	6	c	10	24	*	3	108	52	3	216	141	5

Career	M	I	NO	HS	R	Avge	100	50	Ct	St	Balls	R	W	Avge	BB	5w	10w	Rate
Test	12	23	2	74	469	22.33	–	2	13	–	2203	1150	39	29.48	5-48	3	–	56.48
F/c	210	325	34	323	9488	32.60	15	41	162	–	35469	16842	815	20.66	8-24	57	12	43.52

CURTIS
Timothy Stephen

Worcestershire (1979 to date)
Cambridge University (1983)

Born Chislehurst, Kent 15 Jan 1960

Tim Curtis is an extremely determined opening batsman with a sound technique. A school master who gained a blue while completing his studies at Cambridge, his two Test caps against the 1988 West Indians were the well-deserved reward for four seasons of consistent performances. A brave hooker, he proved his courage against the tourists' fast bowling when he partnered Graeme Hick in a second-wicket stand of 284 for Worcestershire, helping the Zimbabwean to complete his 1000 runs before June. An agile fielder – he held a breathtaking catch to dismiss Viv Richards at Leeds – he is occasionally allowed to accelerate a declaration with his erratic leg-spin.

Tim Curtis

Ref	Series	V	T	Venue	Result	Batting 1st No	R	HO	Batting 2nd No	R	HO	Ct
1101/649	1988	WI	4	Leeds	L-10w	2	12	lbw	2	12	b	1
1102/650			5	Oval	L-8w	2	30	c	2	15	lbw	1

Career	M	I	NO	HS	R	Avge	100	50	Ct	St	Balls	R	W	Avge	BB	5w	10w	Rate
Test	2	4	0	30	69	17.25	–	–	2	–	–	–	–	–	–	–	–	–
F/c	157	267	36	153	8610	37.27	12	50	83	–	524	362	7	51.71	2-58	–	–	74.85

CUTTELL
Willis Robert

Lancashire (1896 to 1906)

Wisden 1898
TOUR SA 1898–99
Born Sheffield, Yorkshire 13 Sep 1864
Died Nelson, Lancashire 9 Dec 1929

Under A.C. MacLaren's wise captaincy Robert Cuttell developed into a fine all-rounder: a hard-hitting middle-order batsman with a sound defence, a right-arm slow-medium bowler and a superb fielder. He attracted Lancashire's notice as a consistently heavy wicket-taker for Nelson, having failed to impress his native Yorkshire (for whom his father had played). His bowling method combined exceptional control of length with ample spin either way and he specialized in a well-concealed leg-break. After coaching at Rugby School for 20 years he spent two seasons as a first-class umpire. [*Illus. pp.* 196, 315]

NOTABLE FEATS

- First Lancashire player to achieve the 'double' (1898), he scored 1000 runs in a season twice and took 1000 wickets 4 times.

						Batting 1st			Batting 2nd				Bowling 1st			Bowling 2nd		
Ref	Series	V	T	Venue	Result	No	R	HO	No	R	HO	Ct	Balls	R	W	Balls	R	W
58/58	1898–99	SA	1	Johannesburg[1]	W-32	5	19	c	5	21	c	2	85	42	2	160	17	3
59/59			2	Cape Town	W-210	5	7	b	5	18	b	–	40	14	1	–	–	–

Career	M	I	NO	HS	R	Avge	100	50	Ct	St	Balls	R	W	Avge	BB	5w	10w	Rate
Test	2	4	0	21	65	16.25	–	–	2	–	285	73	6	12.16	3-17	–	–	47.50
F/c	227	315	31	137	5938	20.90	5	21	140	–	44411	15519	792	19.59	8-105	50	8	56.07

DAWSON
Edward William

Leicestershire (1922 to 1934)
Cambridge University (1924 to 1927)

TOURS
A 1929–30; SA 1927–28;
WI 1928–29 (Cahn); NZ 1929–30
Born Paddington, London 13 Feb 1904
Died Idmiston, Wiltshire 4 Jun 1979

Through sheer application Eddie Dawson developed into a tenacious opening batsman with the soundest of defensive techniques. The first Etonian to score hundreds against Harrow and Winchester in the same year, he won his blue as a freshman and appeared in four University matches, the last as captain. For Leicestershire he proved to be a most reliable accumulator (exceeding 1000 runs six times), an excellent cover fielder and, until business commitments compelled his retirement, an outstanding captain (1928–29, 1931 and 1933). [*Illus. pp.* 420, 459]

						Batting 1st			Batting 2nd			
Ref	Series	V	T	Venue	Result	No	R	HO	No	R	HO	Ct
172/158	1927–28	SA	5	Durban[2]	L-8w	7	14	lbw	7	9	c	–
186/172	1929–30	NZ	1	Christchurch	W-8w	1	7	c	1	10	lbw	–
187/173			2	Wellington	D	2	44	b	2	7	c	–
188/174			3	Auckland	D	2	23	b	–	–	–	–
189/175			4	Auckland	D	2	55	c	2	6	b	–

Career	M	I	NO	HS	R	Avge	100	50	Ct	St	Balls	R	W	Avge	BB	5w	10w	Rate
Test	5	9	0	55	175	19.44	–	1	–	–	–	–	–	–	–	–	–	–
F/c	282	482	17	146	12598	27.09	14	63	110	–	52	68	0	–	–	–	–	–

DEAN, Harry

Lancashire (1906 to 1921)

Born Burnley, Lancashire 13 Aug 1884
Died Garstang, Lancashire 12 Mar 1957

NOTABLE FEATS

- Took 100 wickets in a season 8 times.
- His match analysis of 17 for 91 (9 for 62 and 8 for 29) at Liverpool in 1913 remains the record for Lancashire, the record for a Roses match and the best by any bowler against Yorkshire.
- Took 9 wickets in an innings on 6 occasions.
- With W. Huddleston bowled unchanged throughout a match for Lancashire on 4 occasions.

Harry Dean was a versatile left-arm bowler and tail-end left-handed batsman. He could swerve the ball deceptively late and vary his pace from fast-medium to slow according to the nature of the pitch. After leaving Lancashire he spent four seasons with Cheshire before becoming coach at Rossall School.

Harry Dean, towards the end of his career, flanked by fellow Lancashire professionals Lawrence Cook (left) and Cecil Parkin.

					Batting 1st			Batting 2nd				Bowling 1st			Bowling 2nd		
Ref	Series	V	T	Venue	Result	No	R	HO	No	R	HO	Ct	Balls	R	W	Balls	R	W
123/114	1912	A	1	Lord's	D	–	–	–	–	–	–	–	174	49	2	–	–	–
124/115		SA	2	Leeds	W-174	11	2	*	11	8	b	1	75	41	3	48	15	2
129/118		A	3	Oval	W-244	11	0	*	11	0	b	1	96	29	0	54	19	4

Career	M	I	NO	HS	R	Avge	100	50	Ct	St	Balls	R	W	Avge	BB	5w	10w	Rate
Test	3	4	2	8	10	5.00	–	–	2	–	447	153	11	13.90	4-19	–	–	40.63
F/c	267	370	122	49*	2559	10.31	–	–	121	–	59221	23606	1301	18.14	9-31	97	24	45.51

DeFREITAS Phillip Anthony Jason

Leicestershire (1985 to 1988)

TOURS
A 1986–87; NZ 1987–88; P 1987–88
Born Scotts Head, Dominica 18 Feb 1966

Potentially a match-winning all-rounder, Phillip DeFreitas has yet to establish himself at Test level. A six foot tall, lissom Dominican who migrated to London at the age of ten, he is a right-arm fast-medium bowler, an aggressive lower-order batsman and a predatory fieldsman with a very powerful and accurate throw. An open-chested action has deprived him of his outswinger and he has yet to become a selective hitter. Although his fiery temperament caused frequent problems at Leicester, his move to Old Trafford should accelerate the maturing process.

Phillip DeFreitas

Ref	Series	V	T	Venue	Result	Batting 1st No	R	HO	Batting 2nd No	R	HO	Ct	Bowling 1st Balls	R	W	Bowling 2nd Balls	R	W
1058/629	1986–87	A	1	Brisbane[2]	W-7w	9	40	c	–	–	–	1	96	32	2	–	–	–
1059/630			2	Perth	D	8	11	lbw	8	15	b	–	144	67	1	182	47	0
1060/631			3	Adelaide	D	9	4	*	–	–	–	–	192	128	1	96	36	1
1061/632			4	Melbourne	W-I & 14	8	7	c	–	–	–	–	66	30	0	72	44	1
1075/634	1987	P	1	Manchester	D	9	11	b	–	–	–	–	72	36	1	–	–	–
1084/639	1987–88	P	1	Lahore[2]	L-I & 87	7	5	lbw	8	15	c	–	174	84	1	–	–	–
1086/641			3	Karachi	D	7	12	b	9	6	lbw	–	143	86	5	–	–	–
1091/643	1987–88	NZ	1	Christchurch	D	9	4	c	9	16	lbw	–	132	39	2	114	26	1
1093/645			3	Wellington	D	–	–	–	–	–	–	1	301	110	1	–	–	–
1098/646	1988	WI	1	Nottingham	D	9	3	b	–	–	–	–	162	93	2	–	–	–
1100/648			3	Manchester	L-I & 156	9	15	c	9	0	c	–	210	81	1	–	–	–
1102/650			5	Oval	L-8w	9	18	c	10	0	c	2	78	33	0	102	46	0

Career	M	I	NO	HS	R	Avge	100	50	Ct	St	Balls	R	W	Avge	BB	5w	10w	Rate
Test	12	17	1	40	182	11.37	–	–	4	–	2338	1080	23	46.95	5-86	1	–	101.65
F/c	85	111	10	113	1964	19.44	2	8	29	–	14856	7211	280	25.75	7-44	17	1	53.05

DENNESS
Michael Henry

Scotland (1959 to 1967)
Kent (1962 to 1976)
Essex (1977 to 1980)

Wisden 1975
TOURS
A 1974–75; SA 1975–76 (Int W); WI 1969–70 (Norfolk), 1973–74; NZ 1974–75; I 1967–68 (Int XI), 1972–73; P 1967–68 (Int XI), 1972–73; SL 1967–68 (Int XI), 1972–73, 1977–78 (Robins)
Born Bellshill, Lanarkshire, Scotland
1 Dec 1940

Mike Denness, watched by Leicestershire's Roger Tolchard.

Mike Denness was a naturally aggressive opening or early-order batsman, an elegant strokemaker with an array of attractive shots. A handsome front-foot driver, he was a particularly fine, quick-footed player of spin. Only exceptionally fast bowling could ruffle his calm and he felt compelled to drop himself for the Fourth Test of 1974–75 after Lillee and Thomson had shredded his confidence. A determined, hard-working cricketer and leader, he was an unselfish team man with an excellent temperament. He was an inspired cover fielder and a very occasional right-arm medium-pace off-break bowler. The first schoolboy to play cricket for Scotland (1959), he was the second Scotsman after Ian Peebles to captain a county (1972–76) and the first to lead England (six wins and five defeats in 19 Tests). Relieved of the Kent leadership, he helped Essex to their first Championship title. At Ayr Academy he had been an outstanding fly-half who would almost certainly have gained a Scotland rugby cap had he not opted for cricket.

Ref	Series	V	T	Venue	Result	Batting 1st No	R	HO	Batting 2nd No	R	HO	Ct
658/458	1969	NZ	3	Oval	W-8w	3	2	c	3	55	*	3
703/478	1972–73	I	1	Delhi	W-6w	4	16	c	4	35	c	–
704/479			2	Calcutta	L-28	4	21	c	4	32	lbw	–
705/480			3	Madras[1]	L-4w	4	17	b	4	76	c	1
706/481			4	Kanpur	D	1	31	c	–	–	–	1
707/482			5	Bombay[2]	D	7	29	c	–	–	–	1
719/483	1972–73	P	1	Lahore[2]	D	1	50	lbw	1	68	c	1
720/484			2	Hyderabad	D	1	8	b	1	0	c	–
721/485			3	Karachi	D	4	47	lbw	–	–	–	3
731/492*	1973–74	WI	1	Port-of-Spain	L-7w	3	9	b	3	44	ro	2
732/493*			2	Kingston	D	5	67	c	5	28	c	2
733/494*			3	Bridgetown	D	1	24	c	1	0	lbw	–
734/495*			4	Georgetown	D	3	42	b	–	–	–	–
735/496*			5	Port of Spain	W-26	3	13	c	3	4	ro	1
739/497*	1974	I	1	Manchester	W-113	4	26	b	5	45	*	–
740/498*			2	Lord's	W-I & 285	4	118	c	–	–	–	2
741/499*			3	Birmingham	W-I & 78	3	100	c	–	–	–	–
742/500*	1974	P	1	Leeds	D	4	9	b	4	44	c	1
743/501*			2	Lord's	D	4	20	b	–	–	–	1
744/502*			3	Oval	D	5	18	c	–	–	–	2

NOTABLE FEATS
- 1000 runs in 17th Test (*741*) (28 inns).
- *741* First England captain since P.B.H. May (1959) to score 100s in successive Test inns.
- *755* Highest score (188) by an England captain in Australia.
- *758* Shared record E v NZ 4th-wkt stand of 266 with K.W.R. Fletcher.
- Exceeded 1000 runs in a season 14 times (plus once on tour).

Ref	Series	V	T	Venue	Result	Batting 1st No	R	HO	Batting 2nd No	R	HO	Ct
750/503*	1974–75	A	1	Brisbane[2]	L-166	4	6	lbw	4	27	c	1
751/504*			2	Perth	L-9w	6	2	c	3	20	c	–
752/505*			3	Melbourne	D	5	8	c	5	2	c	3
754/507*			5	Adelaide	L-163	4	51	c	4	14	c	–
755/508*			6	Melbourne	W-I & 4	4	188	c	–	–	–	2
758/509*	1974–75	NZ	1	Auckland	W-I & 83	4	181	c	–	–	–	–
759/510*			2	Christchurch	D	4	59	*	–	–	–	–
760/511*	1975	A	1	Birmingham	L-I & 85	4	3	c	4	8	b	1

Career	M	I	NO	HS	R	Avge	100	50	Ct	St	Balls	R	W	Avge	BB	5w	10w	Rate
Test	28	45	3	188	1667	39.69	4	7	28	–	–	–	–	–	–	–	–	–
F/c	501	838	65	195	25886	33.48	33	152	411	–	84	62	2	31.00	1-7	–	–	42.00

M. H. DENNESS – TEST BATTING SUMMARY

Series	V	M	I	NO	HS	R	Avge	100	50
1969	NZ	1	2	1	55*	57	57.00	–	1
1972–73	I	5	8	–	76	257	32.12	–	1
1973–73	P	3	5	–	68	173	34.60	–	2
1973–74	WI	5	9	–	67	231	25.66	–	1
1974	I	3	4	1	118	289	96.33	2	–
1974	P	3	4	–	44	91	22.75	–	–
1974–75	A	5	9	–	188	318	35.33	1	1
1974–75	NZ	2	2	1	181	240	240.00	1	1
1975	A	1	2	–	8	11	5.50	–	–

Series	V	M	I	NO	HS	R	Avge	100	50
	A	6	11	–	188	329	29.90	1	1
	WI	5	9	–	67	231	25.66	–	1
	NZ	3	4	2	181	297	148.50	1	2
	I	8	12	1	118	546	49.63	2	1
	P	6	9	–	68	264	29.33	–	2
Home		8	12	2	118	448	44.80	2	1
Overseas		20	33	1	188	1219	38.09	2	6
Totals		28	45	3	188	1667	39.69	4	7

DENTON, David

Yorkshire (1894 to 1920)

Wisden 1906
TOURS SA 1905–06, 1909–10
Born Thornes, Wakefield, Yorkshire
4 Jul 1874
Died Wakefield 16 Feb 1950

NOTABLE FEATS
- *108* His 104 in 100 min was his third 100 in successive first-class inns; in his previous match, v Transvaal, he had become the first to score 100 in each inns of a first-class match in SA.
- Exceeded 1000 runs in a season 21 times, including 2000 on 5 occasions.
- Scored 100 in each inns of a match 3 times.
- Shared (then) Yorkshire 2nd-wkt record stand of 305 with J.W. Rothery v Derbyshire at Chesterfield in 1910.
- His stand of 312 with G.H. Hirst v Hampshire at Southampton in 1914 remains Yorkshire's 4th-wkt record.

Below average height and slightly built, David Denton was a stylish, audacious middle-order batsman who enjoyed a long career either side of the Great War. He was an exciting adventurer who gave many chances and deservedly enjoyed more than his fair share of luck. His strong, flexible wrists enabled him to hit with rare power, even when playing forward defensively. He had a full armoury of strokes, cutting brilliantly on fast pitches and hooking or pulling contemptuously on the slower surfaces. He was a medium-fast right-handed bowler and a superbly fast mover and accomplished catcher in the deep. He became Yorkshire's scorer when poor health accelerated his retirement but surgery eventually enabled him to become a first-class umpire.

David Denton

Ref	Series	V	T	Venue	Result	Batting 1st No	R	HO	Batting 2nd No	R	HO	Ct
85/82	1905	A	3	Leeds	D	4	0	c	4	12	c	–
88/85	1905–06	SA	1	Johannesburg[1]	L-1w	3	0	c	3	34	b	–
89/86			2	Johannesburg[1]	L-9w	3	1	c	3	4	c	2
90/87			3	Johannesburg[1]	L-243	3	4	b	6	61	c	3
91/88			4	Cape Town	W-4w	5	34	c	3	20	b	–
92/89			5	Cape Town	L-I & 16	3	4	b	3	10	b	–
106/103	1909–10	SA	1	Johannesburg[1]	L-19	3	28	c	3	26	c	1
107/104			2	Durban[1]	L-95	3	0	ro	3	6	c	–
108/105			3	Johannesburg[1]	W-3w	3	104	b	3	24	c	–
109/106			4	Cape Town	L-4w	3	0	c	3	10	c	–
110/107			5	Cape Town	W-9w	3	26	c	3	16	*	2

Career	M	I	NO	HS	R	Avge	100	50	Ct	St	Balls	R	W	Avge	BB	5w	10w	Rate
Test	11	22	1	104	424	20.19	1	1	8	–	–	–	–	–	–	–	–	–
F/c	742	1163	70	221	36479	33.37	69	187	396	1	1681	983	34	28.91	5-42	1	–	49.44

DEWES
John Gordon

Cambridge University (1948 to 1950)
Middlesex (1948 to 1956)

TOURS A 1950–51; NZ 1950–51
Born North Latchford, Cheshire
11 Oct 1926

John Dewes was a left-handed opening batsman, a right-arm medium-pace change bowler and an outstanding fielder with a ferocious return. Of average height, his defence was very sound and he used his strong wrists and arms in a full repertoire of strokes. Like Donald Carr he made his first-class debut in a 1945 'Victory' match against Australia at Lord's. His record at Cambridge, where he also won a hockey blue, produced the exceptional aggregate of 3247 runs, average 60.12. His duties as a master, first at Tonbridge School and later at Rugby and Dulwich, restricted his appearances after 1950.

NOTABLE FEATS

- Exceeded 1000 runs in a season 3 times, including 2432 (9 hundreds) in 1950.
- Shared in (then) record English 2nd-wkt stand of 429* with G.H.G. Doggart for Cambridge U v Essex at Fenner's in 1949.
- Contributed 212 to Cambridge U record 1st-wkt stand of 349 with D.S. Sheppard v Sussex at Hove in 1950.
- Shared 1st-wkt stand of 343 with D.S. Sheppard for Cambridge U v West Indians at Fenner's in 1950.

John Dewes (right) and Hubert Doggart after their epic partnership in 1949.

Ref	Series	V	T	Venue	Result	Batting 1st No	R	HO	Batting 2nd No	R	HO	Ct
303/266	1948	A	5	Oval	L-I & 149	2	1	b	2	10	b	–
325/278	1950	WI	3	Nottingham	L-10w	4	0	c	4	67	lbw	–
326/279			4	Oval	L-I & 56	5	17	c	5	3	c	–
327/280	1950–51	A	1	Brisbane[2]	L-70	5	1	c	3	9	b	–
328/281			2	Melbourne	L-28	3	8	c	5	5	c	–

Career	M	I	NO	HS	R	Avge	100	50	Ct	St	Balls	R	W	Avge	BB	5w	10w	Rate
Test	5	10	0	67	121	12.10	–	1	–	–	–	–	–	–	–	–	–	–
F/c	137	229	24	212	8564	41.77	18	45	48	–	114	71	2	35.50	1-0	–	–	57.00

DEXTER
Edward Ralph

Cambridge University (1956 to 1958)
Sussex (1957 to 1968)

Wisden 1961
TOURS
A 1958–59, 1962–63; SA 1962–63 (Cwlth), 1964–65; WI 1959–60, 1963–64 (Cav), 1969–70 (Cav); NZ 1958–59, 1962–63; I/SL 1961–62; P 1961–62
Born Milan, Italy 15 May 1935

Dubbed 'Lord Edward' because of his regal presence, Ted Dexter was a dynamic all-rounder with all the Corinthian attributes. A tall (6ft 1in) dashing figure, he was an imposing striker of the ball with a natural sense of timing. Against Hall and Watson in the Caribbean in 1959–60 he proved himself a most courageous player of the fastest bowling by amassing 526 runs. His 70 in 81 minutes against Hall and Griffith at their peak in 1963 is regarded as one of the most imperious displays of batsmanship against ferocious pace bowling ever seen at Lord's. As a frenetic medium-fast swing bowler of the Keith Miller persuasion, he was prone to inflict sudden bursts of wicket-taking upon an unsuspecting opposition. A somewhat eccentric captain, he was the last man to lead the Gentlemen against the Players (1962), captained Cambridge U (1958) and Sussex (1960–65), and led England in 30 Tests (9 wins, 7 defeats). He was an aggressive cover or close leg-side fielder. A natural games player, he was an outstanding golfer who won the Oxbridge Golfing Society's President's Putter. In 1964 he stood for Parliament as the Conservative candidate for Cardiff SE in opposition to James Callaghan. Tragically for cricket he retired in his prime, qualifying as a pilot known to navigate by motorways but who managed to fly his family to Australia, directing a highly successful PR company, owning racehorses and greyhounds, and becoming a lively TV summarizer. His appointment as England's chairman of selectors brought much-needed zest and original thought to the most testing of tasks.

NOTABLE FEATS

- 1000 runs in 17th Test (*496*) (27 inns); 2000 runs in 30th Test (*519*) (50 inns); 3000 runs in 39th Test (*538*) (64 inns); 4000 runs in 55th Test (*572*) (89 inns). 50 wickets in 39th Test (*538*).
- *519* Batted 495 min for his highest first-class score and England's only 200 in Pakistan.
- *534* Shared record E v P 2nd-wkt stand of 248 with M.C. Cowdrey.
- *539* Completed record aggregate of 481 by an England captain v A.
- *572* Third after M.C. Cowdrey and K.F. Barrington to score 100s v all current opponent countries.
- Exceeded 1000 runs in a season 8 times (plus twice on tour), including 2000 on 3 occasions.

Ted Dexter during his innings of 76 in 84 minutes at Manchester against the 1961 Australians; Richie Benaud at slip and Wally Grout behind the stumps. Despite Dexter's glorious innings, Benaud bowled Australia to victory on the final afternoon with a spell of 5 for 12 in 25 balls.

						Batting 1st			Batting 2nd				Bowling 1st			Bowling 2nd		
Ref	Series	V	T	Venue	Result	No	R	HO	No	R	HO	Ct	Balls	R	W	Balls	R	W
457/345	1958	NZ	4	Manchester	W-I & 13	6	52	lbw	–	–	–	–	30	23	0	–	–	–
466/349	1958–59	A	3	Sydney	D	6	1	lbw	6	11	c	–	–	–	–	–	–	–
468/351			5	Melbourne	L-9w	6	0	c	6	6	c	–	–	–	–	–	–	–
472/352	1958–59	NZ	1	Christchurch	W-I & 99	6	141	b	–	–	–	–	–	–	–	6	3	0
473/353			2	Auckland	D	6	1	c	–	–	–	–	114	23	3	–	–	–
477/357	1959	I	4	Manchester	W-171	6	13	c	3	45	c	–	18	3	0	72	33	1
478/358			5	Oval	W-I & 27	6	0	c	–	–	–	–	96	24	2	42	11	0
487/359	1959–60	WI	1	Bridgetown	D	6	136	*	–	–	–	–	226	85	2	–	–	–
488/360			2	Port-of-Spain	W-256	5	77	c	5	0	b	–	–	–	–	36	7	2
489/361			3	Kingston	D	5	25	c	5	16	b	–	72	38	0	–	–	–
490/362			4	Georgetown	D	5	39	c	3	110	c	1	30	20	0	–	–	–
491/363			5	Port-of-Spain	D	3	76	c	4	47	ro	–	24	20	1	–	–	–
492/364	1960	SA	1	Birmingham	W-100	3	52	b	3	26	b	–	6	4	0	36	4	0
493/365			2	Lord's	W-I & 73	3	56	c	–	–	–	–	–	–	–	24	17	2
494/366			3	Nottingham	W-8w	3	3	b	3	0	c	–	–	–	–	36	12	0
495/367			4	Manchester	D	3	38	b	3	22	c	–	102	41	0	–	–	–
496/368			5	Oval	D	3	28	b	3	16	b	–	180	79	3	2	0	0

						Batting 1st			Batting 2nd				Bowling 1st			Bowling 2nd		
Ref	Series	V	T	Venue	Result	No	R	HO	No	R	HO	Ct	Balls	R	W	Balls	R	W
507/369	1961	A	1	Birmingham	D	3	10	c	3	180	st	1	30	22	0	–	–	–
508/370			2	Lord's	L-5w	3	27	c	3	17	b	–	144	56	3	–	–	–
509/371			3	Leeds	W-8w	5	28	b	–	–	–	1	–	–	–	–	–	–
510/372			4	Manchester	L-54	3	16	c	3	76	c	–	40	16	3	120	61	3
511/373			5	Oval	D	5	24	c	3	0	c	–	144	68	0	–	–	–
512/374*	1961–62	P	1	Lahore[2]	W-5w	5	20	hw	5	66	*	1	42	26	0	42	10	1
513/375*	1961–62	I	1	Bombay[2]	D	5	85	b	5	27	c	–	72	25	1	24	15	0
514/376*			2	Kanpur	D	5	2	c	5	126	*	–	186	84	2	–	–	–
515/377*			3	Delhi	D	5	45	*	–	–	–	–	12	11	0	–	–	–
516/378*			4	Calcutta	L-187	5	57	b	4	62	lbw	–	174	83	0	–	–	–
517/379*			5	Madras[2]	L-128	4	2	b	4	3	c	2	30	22	1	–	–	–
518/380*	1961–62	P	2	Dacca	D	5	12	b	–	–	–	1	168	34	0	30	1	0
519/381*			3	Karachi	D	3	205	c	–	–	–	2	110	48	2	192	86	3
530/382*	1962	P	1	Birmingham	W-I & 24	3	72	c	–	–	–	–	72	23	0	42	16	0
531/383*			2	Lord's	W-9w	3	65	c	3	32	*	1	72	41	1	90	44	0
532/384			3	Leeds	W-I & 117	3	20	b	–	–	–	1	55	10	4	48	24	1
533/385*			4	Nottingham	D	3	85	c	–	–	–	–	–	–	–	42	25	1
534/386*			5	Oval	W-10w	3	172	b	–	–	–	1	–	–	–	36	16	0
535/387*	1962–63	A	1	Brisbane[2]	D	3	70	b	3	99	b	2	80	46	1	128	78	2
536/388*			2	Melbourne	W-7w	3	93	c	3	52	ro	–	48	10	0	72	18	1
537/389*			3	Sydney	L-8w	3	32	c	3	11	c	–	–	–	–	26	27	0
538/390*			4	Adelaide	D	5	61	c	5	10	c	–	184	94	3	136	65	3
539/391*			5	Sydney	D	4	47	c	4	6	st	–	56	24	1	32	11	0
540/392*	1962–63	NZ	1	Auckland	W-I & 215	4	7	c	–	–	–	2	54	20	0	–	–	–
541/393*			2	Wellington	W-I & 47	4	31	c	–	–	–	–	6	2	0	–	–	–
542/394*			3	Christchurch	W-7w	4	46	b	–	–	–	1	54	8	0	60	18	0
543/395*	1963	WI	1	Manchester	L-10w	5	73	c	6	35	c	–	72	16	0	–	–	–
544/396*			2	Lord's	D	3	70	lbw	3	2	b	–	120	41	0	–	–	–
545/397*			3	Birmingham	W-217	3	29	b	5	57	st	–	120	38	4	18	7	1
546/398*			4	Leeds	L-221	3	8	b	3	10	lbw	1	138	68	1	12	15	0
547/399*			5	Oval	L-8w	3	29	c	3	27	c	–	36	8	0	54	34	1
561/405*	1964	A	1	Nottingham	D	3	9	c	1	68	c	–	–	–	–		–	–
562/406*			2	Lord's	D	1	2	b	–	–	–	2	42	16	2	18	5	0
563/407*			3	Leeds	L-7w	3	66	c	5	17	c	–	114	40	0	18	9	0
564/408*			4	Manchester	D	3	174	b	–	–	–	1	24	12	0	–	–	–
565/409*			5	Oval	D	3	23	c	3	25	c	1	78	36	1	–	–	–
571/410	1964–65	SA	1	Durban[2]	W-I & 104	3	28	c	–	–	–	3	–	–	–	–	–	–
572/411			2	Johannesburg[3]	D	3	172	c	–	–	–	1	24	16	0	48	33	1
573/412			3	Cape Town	D	3	61	c	–	–	–	–	12	10	0	102	64	1
574/413			4	Johannesburg[3]	D	3	38	c	3	0	c	–	36	30	0	–	–	–
575/414			5	Port Elizabeth	D	4	40	ro	3	5	*	–	–	–	–	–	–	–
591/415	1965	NZ	1	Birmingham	W-9w	3	57	c	3	0	*	1	–	–	–	30	18	1
592/416			2	Lord's	W-7w	3	62	c	4	80	*	–	48	27	0	–	–	–
640/448	1968	A	4	Leeds	D	3	10	b	3	38	b	1	42	25	0	6	3	0
641/449			5	Oval	W-226	3	21	b	3	28	b	1	–	–	–	–	–	–

Career	M	I	NO	HS	R	Avge	100	50	Ct	St	Balls	R	W	Avge	BB	5w	10w	Rate
Test	62	102	8	205	4502	47.89	9	27	29	–	5317	2306	66	34.93	4-10	–	–	80.56
F/c	327	567	48	205	21150	40.75	51	108	233	–	26219	12539	419	29.92	7-24	9	2	62.57

E. R. DEXTER – TEST SUMMARY

Series	V	M	I	NO	HS	R	Avge	100	50	Balls	R	W	Avge	BB	5w	10w	Rate
1958	NZ	1	1	–	52	52	52.00	–	1	30	23	0	–	–	–	–	–
1958–59	A	2	4	–	11	18	4.50	–	–	–	–	–	–	–	–	–	–
1958–59	NZ	2	2	–	141	142	71.00	1	–	120	26	3	8.66	3-23	–	–	40.00
1959	I	2	3	–	45	58	19.33	–	–	228	71	3	23.66	2-24	–	–	76.00
1959–60	WI	5	9	1	136*	526	65.75	2	2	388	170	5	34.00	2-7	–	–	77.60
1960	SA	5	9	–	56	241	26.77	–	2	386	157	5	31.40	3-79	–	–	77.20
1961	A	5	9	–	180	378	42.00	1	1	478	223	9	24.77	3-16	–	–	53.11

Series	V	M	I	NO	HS	R	Avge	100	50	Balls	R	W	Avge	BB	5w	10w	Rate
1961–62	P	3	4	1	205	303	101.00	1	1	584	205	6	34.16	3-86	–	–	97.33
1961–62	I	5	9	2	126*	409	58.42	1	3	498	240	4	60.00	2-84	–	–	124.50
1962	P	5	6	1	172	446	89.20	1	3	457	199	7	28.42	4-10	–	–	65.28
1962–63	A	5	10	–	99	481	48.10	–	5	762	373	11	33.90	3-65	–	–	69.27
1962–63	NZ	3	3	–	46	84	28.00	–	–	174	48	0	–	–	–	–	–
1963	WI	5	10	–	73	340	34.00	–	3	570	227	7	32.42	4-38	–	–	81.42
1964	A	5	8	–	174	384	48.00	1	2	294	118	3	39.33	2-16	–	–	98.00
1964–65	SA	5	7	1	172	344	57.33	1	1	222	153	2	76.50	1-33	–	–	111.00
1965	NZ	2	4	2	80*	199	99.50	–	3	78	45	1	45.00	1-18	–	–	78.00
1968	A	2	4	–	38	97	24.25	–	–	48	28	0	–	–	–	–	–
	A	19	35	–	180	1358	38.80	2	8	1582	742	23	32.26	3-16	–	–	68.78
	SA	10	16	1	172	585	39.00	1	3	608	310	7	44.28	3-79	–	–	86.85
	WI	10	19	1	136*	866	48.11	2	5	958	397	12	33.08	4-38	–	–	79.83
	NZ	8	10	2	141	477	59.62	1	4	402	142	4	35.50	3-23	–	–	100.50
	I	7	12	2	126*	467	46.70	1	3	726	311	7	44.42	2-24	–	–	103.71
	P	8	10	2	205	749	93.62	2	4	1041	404	13	80.07	4-10	–	–	80.07
Home		32	54	3	180	2195	43.03	3	15	2569	1091	35	73.40	4-10	–	–	73.40
Overseas		30	48	5	205	2307	53.65	6	12	2748	1215	31	88.64	3-23	–	–	88.64
Totals		62	102	8	205	4502	4789	9	27	5317	2306	66	34.93	4-10	–	–	80.56

DILLEY, Graham Roy

Kent (1977 to 1986)
Worcestershire (1987 to date)
Natal (1985–86)

TOURS
A 1979–80, 1986–87; WI 1980–81; NZ 1983–84; I 1981–82; P 1983–84; SL 1981–82
Born Dartford, Kent 18 May 1959

Graham Dilley is a tall (6ft 3in), well-built aggressive fast bowler with a high but slightly open action and an immense delivery stride. Genuinely quick when on song, he has proved depressingly susceptible to a variety of neck, back, knee and leg injuries. He was slow to realize his early promise, taking 23 Tests to return his first five-wicket analysis. He reached peak form in Australia in 1986–87 when, controlling his length and off-stump line superbly, he moved his staple outswinger lethally late. A hard-hitting lower-order left-handed batsman with a good eye and a full pendulum swing, his 56 against the 1981 Australians at Headingley inspired Ian Botham's epic century and England's eventual victory against odds of 500–1. He is a safe catcher in the deep with a strong return.

NOTABLE FEATS

- 50 wickets in 18th Test (*979*); 100 wickets in 31st Test (*1086*).
- Two hat-tricks for Kent: v Surrey at The Oval in 1985 and v Essex at Chelmsford in 1986.

						Batting 1st			Batting 2nd				Bowling 1st			Bowling 2nd		
Ref	Series	V	T	Venue	Result	No	R	HO	No	R	HO	Ct	Balls	R	W	Balls	R	W
868/553	1979–80	A	1	Perth	L-138	9	38	*	9	16	c	–	108	47	2	108	50	1
870/554			2	Sydney	L-6w	9	22	*	10	4	b	1	30	13	0	72	33	0
882/559	1980	WI	3	Manchester	D	10	0	b	–	–	–	–	168	47	3	–	–	–
883/560			4	Oval	D	10	1	b	10	1	c	–	138	57	4	–	–	–
884/561			5	Leeds	D	11	0	b	–	–	–	1	138	79	4	–	–	–
896/563	1980–81	WI	1	Port-of-Spain	L-I & 79	10	0	b	10	1	*	–	168	73	0	–	–	–
897/564			3	Bridgetown	L-298	11	0	c	11	7	*	–	138	51	3	150	111	1
898/565			4	St John's	D	11	2	c	–	–	–	–	150	99	2	–	–	–
899/566			5	Kingston	D	11	1	*	–	–	–	–	172	116	4	–	–	–
903/567	1981	A	1	Nottingham	L-4w	9	34	b	9	13	c	–	120	38	3	67	24	4
904/568			2	Lord's	D	10	7	*	8	27	*	–	180	106	3	47	18	2
905/569			3	Leeds	W-18	9	13	c	9	56	b	1	162	78	2	12	11	0
912/573	1981–82	I	1	Bombay[3]	L-138	8	0	b	8	9	b	–	78	47	4	108	61	1
913/574			2	Bangalore	D	9	52	c	–	–	–	–	144	75	0	–	–	–
916/577			5	Madras[1]	D	7	8	c	–	–	–	–	186	87	1	30	13	0
917/578			6	Kanpur	D	7	1	lbw	–	–	–	1	84	67	1	–	–	–

						Batting 1st			Batting 2nd				Bowling 1st			Bowling 2nd		
Ref	**Series**	**V**	**T**	**Venue**	**Result**	**No**	**R**	**HO**	**No**	**R**	**HO**	**Ct**	**Balls**	**R**	**W**	**Balls**	**R**	**W**
958/592	1983	NZ	2	Leeds	L-5w	8	0	b	8	15	c	1	102	36	0	48	16	0
979/599	1983–84	P	2	Faisalabad	D	9	2	*	–	–	–	–	168	101	3	54	41	2
1046/623	1986	I	1	Lord's	L-5w	10	4	c	10	2	*	1	204	146	4	60	28	2
1047/624			2	Leeds	L-279	10	10	b	11	2	ro	–	146	54	3	102	71	1
1049/626	1986	NZ	1	Lord's	D	9	17	c	–	–	–	–	211	82	4	36	5	1
1051/628			3	Oval	D	–	–	–	–	–	–	–	170	92	4	–	–	–
1058/629	1986/87	A	1	Brisbane[2]	W-7w	11	0	c	–	–	–	1	154	68	5	114	47	1
1059/630			2	Perth	D	–	–	–	–	–	–	–	148	79	4	90	53	1
1060/631			3	Adelaide	D	11	0	b	–	–	–	–	192	111	1	126	38	1
1062/633			5	Sydney	L-55	11	4	*	11	2	*	–	143	67	2	90	48	1
1076/635	1987	P	2	Lord's	D	11	17	b	–	–	–	–	–	–	–	–	–	–
1077/636			3	Leeds	L-I & 18	11	1	*	11	0	b	–	198	89	1	–	–	–
1078/637			4	Birmingham	D	11	2	b	–	–	–	–	210	92	5	108	53	2
1079/638			5	Oval	D	11	0	*	–	–	–	2	285	154	6	–	–	–
1086/641	1987–88	P	3	Karachi	D	11	0	*	11	0	*	–	126	102	1	–	–	–
1090/642	1987–88	A		Sydney	D	11	13	b	–	–	–	–	115	54	3	78	48	0
1091/643	1987–88	NZ	1	Christchurch	D	11	7	*	11	2	c	–	149	38	6	108	32	2
1092/644			2	Auckland	D	11	8	*	–	–	–	–	168	60	5	138	44	2
1093/645			3	Wellington	D	–	–	–	–	–	–	–	66	36	0	–	–	–
1098/646	1988	WI	1	Nottingham	D	11	2	b	–	–	–	1	204	101	1	–	–	–
1099/647			2	Lord's	L-134	11	0	b	11	28	c	–	138	55	5	162	73	4
1100/648			3	Manchester	L-I & 156	10	14	c	10	4	b	–	169	99	4	–	–	–
1101/649			4	Leeds	L-10w	11	8	c	11	2	*	–	120	59	1	24	16	0

Career	**M**	**I**	**NO**	**HS**	**R**	**Avge**	**100**	**50**	**Ct**	**St**	**Balls**	**R**	**W**	**Avge**	**BB**	**5w**	**10w**	**Rate**
Test	39	55	18	56	479	12.94	–	2	10	–	7682	3789	133	28.48	6-38	6	–	57.75
F/c	195	212	71	81	1926	13.65	–	3	68	–	28500	14229	527	27.00	7-63	26	2	54.07

Graham Dilley

G. R. DILLEY – TEST BOWLING SUMMARY

Series	**V**	**M**	**Balls**	**R**	**W**	**Avge**	**BB**	**5w**	**10w**	**Rate**
1979/80	A	2	318	143	3	47.66	2-47	–	–	106.00
1980	WI	3	444	183	11	16.63	4-57	–	–	40.36
1980–81	WI	4	778	450	10	45.00	4-116	–	–	77.80
1981	A	3	588	275	14	19.64	4-24	–	–	42.00
1981–82	I	4	630	350	7	50.00	4-47	–	–	90.00
1983	NZ	1	150	52	0	–	–	–	–	–
1983–84	P	1	222	142	5	28.40	3-101	–	–	44.40
1986	I	2	512	299	10	29.90	4-146	–	–	51.20
1986	NZ	2	417	179	9	19.88	4-82	–	–	46.33
1986–87	A	4	1057	511	16	31.93	5-68	1	–	66.06
1987	P	4	801	388	14	27.71	6-154	2	–	57.21
1987–88	P	1	126	102	1	102.00	1-102	–	–	126.00
1987–88	A	1	193	102	3	34.00	3-54	–	–	64.33
1987–88	NZ	3	629	210	15	14.00	6-38	2	–	41.93
1988	WI	4	817	403	15	26.86	5-55	1	–	54.46
	A	10	2154	1031	36	28.63	5-68	1	–	59.83
	WI	11	2039	1036	36	28.77	5-55	1	–	56.63
	NZ	6	1196	441	24	14.20	6-38	2	–	49.83
	I	6	1442	649	17	38.17	4-47	–	–	84.82
	P	6	1149	632	20	31.60	6-154	2	–	57.45
Home		19	3729	1779	73	24.36	6-154	3	–	51.08
Overseas		20	3953	2010	60	33.50	6-38	3	–	65.38
Totals		39	7682	3789	133	28.48	6-38	6	–	57.75

DIPPER, Alfred Ernest

Gloucestershire (1908 to 1932)

Born Apperley, Gloucestershire
9 Nov 1885
Died Lambeth, London 7 Nov 1945

NOTABLE FEATS
- Exceeded 1000 runs in a season 15 times, including 2000 on 5 occasions.
- Carried his bat through a completed first-class innings 11 times.
- Shared stand of 330 with W.R. Hammond v Lancashire in 1925 which remains the record for the 3rd wkt at Old Trafford.

Making his first-class debut when Gloucestershire, a man short, asked Tewskesbury Cricket Club to provide a batsman, Alf Dipper top-scored with 30* at number nine. From this fortuitous start he gradually developed into a phlegmatic and consistent opening batsman, a dour defender who carried the county's flimsy batting until Walter Hammond descended upon the scene and allowed the luxury of more fluent strokeplay. A conscientious and loyal professional, he was also a useful right-arm slow-medium bowler but his poor fielding limited his international honours to a single Test. After retirement he became a first-class umpire and a celebrated bowls and billiards player.

Alf Dipper

						Batting 1st			Batting 2nd			
Ref	Series	V	T	Venue	Result	No	R	HO	No	R	HO	Ct
141/130	1921	A	2	Lord's	L-8w	2	11	b	2	40	b	–

Career	M	I	NO	HS	R	Avge	100	50	Ct	St	Balls	R	W	Avge	BB	5w	10w	Rate
Test	1	2	0	40	51	25.50	–	–	–	–	–	–	–	–	–	–	–	–
F/c	481	865	69	252*	28075	35.27	53	145	210	–	8968	4903	161	30.45	7-46	5	1	55.70

DOGGART George Hubert Graham

Cambridge University (1948 to 1950)
Sussex (1948 to 1961)

TOUR WI 1955–56 (Swanton)
Born Earl's Court, London 18 Jul 1925

Hubert Doggart was a stylish middle-order batsman, a useful off-spin bowler and a superb slip catcher. At Cambridge (where his father and son also gained blues) he was a prolific and adventurous strokemaker, amassing a record 215* on debut and scoring 1169 runs in his first season. An exceptionally talented ball player, he represented the University at cricket (captain 1950), soccer, squash, rackets and fives. He captained the Rest in the 1950 Test Trial and led Sussex in 1954. His county appearances were restricted by his teaching commitments, first as a master at Winchester College and finally as headmaster of King's School, Bruton. He has been president of MCC (1981–82), the English Schools Cricket Association (ESCA) and the Cricket Society. [*Illus. p.* 104]

NOTABLE FEATS
- Exceeded 1000 runs in a season 4 times, including 2000 once.
- Scored 215* on his first appearance for Cambridge U v Lancashire at Fenner's in 1948 – the highest debut score by a batsman in Britain.
- Contributed a career-best 219* to the (then) record English 2nd-wkt stand of 429* with J.G. Dewes for Cambridge U v Essex at Fenner's in 1949; it remains the CU record for any wicket.

						Batting 1st			Batting 2nd			
Ref	Series	V	T	Venue	Result	No	R	HO	No	R	HO	Ct
323/276	1950	WI	1	Manchester	W-202	4	29	c	3	22	c	2
324/277			2	Lord's	L-326	4	0	lbw	4	25	b	1

Career	M	I	NO	HS	R	Avge	100	50	Ct	St	Balls	R	W	Avge	BB	5w	10w	Rate
Test	2	4	0	29	76	19.00	–	–	3	–	–	–	–	–	–	–	–	–
F/c	210	347	28	219*	10054	31.51	20	50	199	–	4410	2057	60	34.28	4-50	–	–	73.50

D'OLIVEIRA
Basil Lewis OBE

Worcestershire (1964 to 1980)

Wisden 1967
TOURS
A 1970–71; WI 1965–66 (Worcs), 1966–67 (RW), 1967–68; NZ 1970–71; P 1963–64 (Cwlth), 1968–69; SL 1968–69; Z 1961–62 (Cwlth), 1962–63 (Cwlth), 1964–65 (Worcs), 1972–73 (Int W)
Born Signal Hill, Cape Town, South Africa 4 Oct 1931

Basil D'Oliveira's prodigious cricketing talents were nurtured amongst the meagre facilities permitted to Cape Coloureds. On those primitive Cape Town pitches he scored 80 hundreds. His SOS to John Arlott led to a Central Lancashire League engagement with Middleton in 1960 but another five years were to elapse before he qualified for Worcestershire at the advanced age of 33 and contributed six hundreds to their second Championship title. Making his debut at Lord's the following season, he was so proud of his England cap that he claimed to have worn it in bed. 'Dolly' was a natural player; a most effective batsman with a sound defence and immensely strong forearms who, despite the most frugal of back-lifts, hit the ball with astonishing power and perfect timing. He used his feet well, drove fiercely off the back foot and was a magnificent puller and cutter. His right-arm medium-pace swing bowling with its classic action was an effortless masterpiece of deception and proved a frequent breaker of awkward partnerships. A man of rare fighting qualities, he overcame each hurdle in his unprecedented career; he was a natural competitor who reserved his finest performances for crises. His unique background led to the cancellation of England's 1968–69 tour and to South Africa's ultimate banishment from the Test arena. He was appointed Worcestershire's coach when his playing days ended in 1980.

NOTABLE FEATS

- 1000 runs in 17th Test (*647*) (27 inns); 2000 runs in 34th Test (*687*) (53 inns).
- Exceeded 1000 runs in a season 9 times.
- *648* Partnered by last man R.M.H. Cottam for the final 34 runs of his innings, he scored 114* out of 174 on a Dacca pitch totally pitted with holes.

						Batting 1st			Batting 2nd				Bowling 1st			Bowling 2nd		
Ref	Series	V	T	Venue	Result	No	R	HO	No	R	HO	Ct	Balls	R	W	Balls	R	W
606/430	1966	WI	2	Lord's	D	7	27	ro	–	–	–	–	84	24	1	150	46	1
607/431			3	Nottingham	L-139	7	76	b	7	54	lbw	–	180	51	2	204	77	2
608/432			4	Leeds	L-I & 55	6	88	c	3	7	c	–	114	52	0	–	–	–
609/433			5	Oval	W-I & 34	6	4	b	–	–	–	2	126	35	1	102	44	1
618/434	1967	I	1	Leeds	W-6w	5	109	c	4	24	*	2	54	29	1	66	22	0
619/435			2	Lord's	W-I & 124	5	33	c	–	–	–	2	90	38	2	–	–	–
621/437	1967	P	1	Lord's	D	5	59	c	5	81	*	1	90	17	0	–	–	–
622/438			2	Nottingham	W-10w	5	7	ro	–	–	–	–	108	27	1	–	–	–
623/439			3	Oval	W-8w	6	3	c	–	–	–	2	102	41	0	–	–	–
628/440	1967–68	WI	1	Port-of-Spain	D	7	32	b	–	–	–	1	162	49	1	30	21	0
629/441			2	Kingston	D	7	0	st	7	13	*	2	–	–	–	192	51	2
630/442			3	Bridgetown	D	7	51	b	–	–	–	–	114	36	0	24	19	0
631/443			4	Port-of-Spain	W-7w	6	0	b	5	12	*	–	90	62	0	–	–	–
632/444			5	Georgetown	D	6	27	c	6	2	c	–	48	27	0	48	28	0

Ref	Series	V	T	Venue	Result	Batting 1st No	R	HO	Batting 2nd No	R	HO	Ct	Bowling 1st Balls	R	W	Bowling 2nd Balls	R	W
637/445	1968	A	1	Manchester	L-159	7	9	b	7	87	*	1	150	38	1	30	7	1
641/449			5	Oval	W-226	6	158	c	6	9	c	–	24	3	0	30	1	1
647/450	1968–69	P	1	Lahore[2]	D	6	26	c	6	5	c	3	48	28	1	–	–	–
648/451			2	Dacca	D	6	114	*	–	–	–	1	48	15	0	54	12	0
649/452			3	Karachi	D	6	16	c	–	–	–	–	–	–	–	–	–	–
653/453	1969	WI	1	Manchester	W-10w	5	57	c	–	–	–	1	–	–	–	54	29	1
654/454			2	Lord's	D	4	0	c	4	18	c	–	156	46	0	90	45	2
655/455			3	Leeds	W-30	5	48	c	5	39	c	–	90	27	1	60	22	0
656/456	1969	NZ	1	Lord's	W-230	5	37	ro	5	12	c	–	–	–	–	48	6	1
657/457			2	Nottingham	D	5	45	c	–	–	–	1	150	40	1	30	8	0
658/458			3	Oval	W-8w	5	1	c	–	–	–	–	6	4	0	84	19	0
674/459	1970–71	A	1	Brisbane[2]	D	7	57	c	–	–	–	–	128	63	0	56	7	0
675/460			2	Perth	D	7	8	c	6	31	b	1	136	41	1	32	5	0
676/461			4	Sydney	W-299	5	0	c	5	56	c	2	72	20	2	56	16	0
677/462			5	Melbourne	D	5	117	c	–	–	–	–	176	71	1	–	–	–
678/463			6	Adelaide	D	5	47	c	4	5	c	–	–	–	–	120	28	0
679/464			7	Sydney	W-62	5	1	b	5	47	c	1	96	24	0	40	15	2
685/465	1970–71	NZ	1	Christchurch	W-8w	5	100	b	–	–	–	–	24	2	0	–	–	–
686/466			2	Auckland	D	5	58	c	9	5	b	–	–	–	–	–	–	–
687/467	1971	P	1	Birmingham	D	5	73	c	5	22	c	–	228	78	2	–	–	–
688/468			2	Lord's	D	–	–	–	–	–	–	–	60	22	1	–	–	–
689/469			3	Leeds	W-25	5	74	b	5	72	c	2	216	46	3	90	16	2
690/470	1971	I	1	Lord's	D	5	4	c	5	30	b	–	90	20	0	–	–	–
691/471			2	Manchester	D	5	12	c	5	23	*	–	144	40	2	18	1	0
692/472			3	Oval	L-4w	5	2	c	5	17	c	1	42	5	1	54	17	0
698/473	1972	A	1	Manchester	W-89	5	23	b	5	37	c	1	36	13	1	96	23	1
699/474			2	Lord's	L-8w	5	32	lbw	5	3	c	–	102	48	1	48	14	1
700/475			3	Nottingham	D	5	29	lbw	5	50	*	1	108	41	1	42	12	0
701/476			4	Leeds	W-9w	5	12	b	–	–	–	1	12	8	0	–	–	–
702/477			5	Oval	L-5w	5	4	c	5	43	c	–	54	17	0	–	–	–

Career	M	I	NO	HS	R	Avge	100	50	Ct	St	Balls	R	W	Avge	BB	5w	10w	Rate
Test	44	70	8	158	2484	40.06	5	15	29	–	5706	1859	47	39.55	3-46	–	–	121.40
F/c	362	566	88	227	18918	39.57	43	98	211	–	40581	15021	548	27.41	6-29	17	2	74.05

Basil D'Oliveira

B. L. D'OLIVEIRA – TEST BATTING SUMMARY

Series	V	M	I	NO	HS	R	Avge	100	50
1966	WI	4	6	–	88	256	42.66	–	3
1967	I	2	3	1	109	166	83.00	1	–
1967	P	3	4	1	81*	150	50.00	–	2
1967–68	WI	5	8	2	51	137	22.83	–	1
1968	A	2	4	1	158	263	87.66	1	1
1968–69	P	3	4	1	114*	161	53.66	1	–
1969	WI	3	5	–	57	162	32.40	–	1
1969	NZ	3	4	–	45	95	23.75	–	–
1970–71	A	6	10	–	117	369	36.90	1	2
1970–71	NZ	2	3	–	100	163	54.33	1	1
1971	P	3	4	–	74	241	60.25	–	3
1971	I	3	6	1	30	88	17.60	–	–
1972	A	5	9	1	50*	233	29.12	–	1
	A	13	23	2	158	865	41.19	2	4
	WI	12	19	2	88	555	32.64	–	5
	NZ	5	7	–	100	258	36.85	1	1
	I	5	9	2	109	254	36.28	1	–
	P	9	12	2	114*	552	55.20	1	5
Home		28	45	5	158	1654	41.35	2	11
Overseas		16	25	3	117	830	37.72	2	4
Totals		44	70	8	158	2484	40.06	5	15

DOLLERY
Horace Edgar

Warwickshire (1934 to 1955)
Wellington (1950–51)

Wisden 1952
Born Reading, Berkshire 14 Oct 1914
Died Edgbaston, Birmingham
20 Jan 1987

'Tom' Dollery

An attacking but amazingly consistent middle-order batsman, 'Tom' Dollery had reached his peak and just been selected for the 1939–40 tour of India when the War intervened. A prolific batsman during his five seasons at Reading School, he made his first-class debut for the Minor Counties in 1931 whilst playing for Berkshire before qualifying for Warwickshire three years later. He was immensely strong with a complete range of strokes but was a particularly powerful off-side player. Initially a brilliant fielder in the covers, he later became a dependable slip-catcher who even deputized as a wicket-keeper for half of the 1947 season. A popular and astute captain, he became the first professional to lead Warwickshire, sharing the task in 1948 before taking sole charge until his retirement in 1955, and inspired them to their second title in 1951. He was Warwickshire's coach from 1956 to 1969 and an England selector for two seasons (1957–58). Before the War he played soccer for his birthplace.

NOTABLE FEATS
- Exceeded 1000 runs in a season 15 times, including 2000 twice.
- Carried his bat for 104* in Reading School's total of 115 v MCC in 1931 (next highest score was 3).
- In 1951 became the first professional to captain a champion county since A. Shaw of Nottinghamshire in 1886.
- Added 319 for the 4th wkt with R.E.S. Wyatt v Lancashire at Birmingham in 1937 and also shared in 2 Warwickshire record partnerships: 220 (6th wkt) with J. Buckingham v Derbyshire at Derby in 1938, and 250 (7th wkt) with J.S. Ord v Kent at Maidstone in 1953.

						Batting 1st			Batting 2nd			
Ref	Series	V	T	Venue	Result	No	R	HO	No	R	HO	Ct
285/253	1947	SA	1	Nottingham	D	5	9	b	5	17	c	–
300/263	1948	A	2	Lord's	L-409	5	0	b	5	37	b	–
301/264			3	Manchester	D	6	1	b	–	–	–	–
323/276	1950	WI	1	Manchester	W-202	5	8	c	4	0	c	1

Career	M	I	NO	HS	R	Avge	100	50	Ct	St	Balls	R	W	Avge	BB	5w	10w	Rate
Test	4	7	0	37	72	10.28	–	–	1	–	–	–	–	–	–	–	–	–
F/c	436	717	66	212	24413	37.50	50	128	291	13	58	32	0	–	–	–	–	–

DOLPHIN, Arthur

Yorkshire (1905 to 1927)
Patiala (1926–27)

TOURS A 1920–21; I 1926–27
Born Wilsden, Yorkshire 24 Dec 1885
Died Heaton, Bradford, Yorkshire
23 Oct 1942

Arthur Dolphin

Although Arthur Dolphin enjoyed eight Championship successes as Yorkshire's wicket-keeper, his chances of international honours were substantially reduced by his being a contemporary of Herbert Strudwick and 'Tiger' Smith. As a lower-order batsman he frequently defended well in a crisis; in 1919 he contributed 62* to a last-wicket stand of 103 which averted the follow-on against Essex at Leyton. He became a popular and respected umpire who stood in six Tests and remained bare-headed on even the hottest days.

Ref	Series	V	T	Venue	Result	Batting 1st No	R	HO	Batting 2nd No	R	HO	Fielding 1st Ct	St	Byes	Balls	Fielding 2nd Ct	St	Byes	Balls
138/127†	1920–21	A	4	Melbourne	L-8w	9	1	b	9	0	c	1	–	1	673	–	–	5	386

Career	M	I	NO	HS	R	Avge	100	50	Ct	St	Balls	R	W	Avge	BB	5w	10w	Rate
Test	1	2	0	1	1	0.50	–	–	1	–	–	–	–	–	–	–	–	–
F/c	449	465	164	66	3402	11.30	–	7	609	273	66	28	1	28.00	1-18	–	–	66.00

DOUGLAS
John William Henry Tyler

Essex (1901 to 1928)
London County (1903 to 1904)

Wisden 1915
TOURS
A 1911–12, 1920–21, 1924–25;
SA 1913–14; NZ 1906–07
Born Clapton, Middlesex 3 Sep 1882
Died (drowned) near Laeso, Denmark
19 Dec 1930

Johnny Douglas was a remarkable all-rounder with apparently inexhaustible reserves of patience and stamina who dominated Essex cricket for three decades. As a batsman his defensive technique was exceptional but he was usually so intent on protecting his wicket that he carried caution to excess. His cramped style allied to a limited array of strokes often made him tiresome to watch and an Australian barracker suggested that his initials really stood for 'Johnny Won't Hit Today'. As a right-arm fast-medium bowler he maintained pace, line and length for long spells, specializing in late inswingers. He was supremely fit, possessed a 'big match' temperament and never spared himself. Although he made his Essex debut the year he left Felsted School, he took seven seasons to consolidate his county place. This long graduation was partly due to his notable talents as a middleweight boxer (he won the 1905 Amateur Championship and the 1908 Olympic title) and a footballer who gained an England amateur cap. Appointed Essex captain in 1911 (an office he held until his retirement in 1928), he assumed the England mantle a few months later when 'Plum' Warner was taken ill after the opening match of MCC's antipodean tour.

NOTABLE FEATS
- *130* His only 100 for E completed the first instance of both captains scoring hundreds in a Test (H.W. Taylor 109).
- Exceeded 1000 runs in a season 10 times, took 100 wickets 7 times and completed the 'double' on 5 occasions.
- Three hat-tricks: two for Essex at Leyton (v Yorkshire in 1905, when he took 5 for 0 in 8 balls, and v Sussex in 1923, when he took 4 wkts in 6 balls) and one for MCC v NSW at Sydney in 1920–21.
- In 1914 he twice bowled unchanged through both innings: v Surrey at The Oval and v Derbyshire at Derby.
- Shared in 3 Essex record partnerships: 206 for 6th wkt with J. O'Connor in 1923, 261 for 7th wkt with J. Freeman in 1914 and 251 for 9th wkt with S.N. Hare in 1921.

Johnny Douglas and his MCC party about to depart for South Africa, 1913–14: on rail *M.C. Bird, L.H. Tennyson, W. Rhodes;* on haunches *J.B. Hobbs;* standing on deck *M.W. Booth, F.E. Woolley, S.F. Barnes, Douglas (half sitting), unidentified;* standing on windlass *H. Strudwick, J.W. Hearne, A.E. Relf;* in bowler hat *C.P. Mead. E.J. Smith is missing from the group.*

Due largely to the magnificent bowling of Sydney Barnes and Frank Foster England won the rubber 4–1 and regained the Ashes. The Australians were to exact massive retribution on Douglas, comprehensively winning the next seven matches against England under his captaincy, but his full record after 18 Tests in terms of wins and defeats was a commendable 8–8. A born leader, he attained the rank of Lieut-Colonel in the Bedfordshire Regiment during the Great War and developed a rather brusque military manner which concealed a generous nature. He was drowned when returning home from a business trip whilst unsuccessfully attempting to save his father after their steamship (*Oberon*) collided with another (*Arcturus*) in dense fog.

						Batting 1st			Batting 2nd				Bowling 1st			Bowling 2nd		
Ref	Series	V	T	Venue	Result	No	R	HO	No	R	HO	Ct	Balls	R	W	Balls	R	W
116/108*	1911–12	A	1	Sydney	L-146	9	0	c	9	32	b	1	144	62	1	126	50	4
117/109*			2	Melbourne	W-8w	7	9	b	–	–	–	–	90	33	1	60	38	0
118/110*			3	Adelaide	W-7w	7	35	b	–	–	–	–	42	7	1	174	71	2
119/111*			4	Melbourne	W-I & 225	6	0	c	–	–	–	–	–	–	–	107	46	5
120/112*			5	Sydney	W-70	6	18	c	6	8	b	1	42	14	1	54	34	0
129/118	1912	A	3	Oval	W-244	7	18	lbw	7	24	lbw	3	–	–	–	–	–	–
130/119*	1913–14	SA	1	Durban[1]	W-I & 157	6	119	b	–	–	–	–	48	19	2	12	2	0
131/120*			2	Johannesburg[1]	W-I & 12	6	3	c	–	–	–	–	12	11	0	36	27	0
132/121*			3	Johannesburg[1]	W-91	6	30	c	5	77	b	1	42	16	0	82	34	2
133/122*			4	Durban[1]	D	6	0	c	5	7	lbw	1	42	31	0	84	51	1
134/123*			5	Port Elizabeth	W-10w	7	30	c	–	–	–	–	34	14	4	54	34	1
135/124*	1920–21	A	1	Sydney	L-377	6	21	st	6	7	c	–	18	14	0	156	79	2
136/125*			2	Melbourne	L-I & 91	7	15	lbw	7	9	b	–	144	83	2	–	–	–
137/126*			3	Adelaide	L-119	7	60	lbw	7	32	c	1	144	69	2	114	61	0
138/127*			4	Melbourne	L-8w	6	50	c	6	60	st	–	24	17	0	30	13	0
139/128*			5	Sydney	L-9w	7	32	*	7	68	c	–	96	84	2	–	–	–
140/129*	1921	A	1	Nottingham	L-10w	5	11	c	5	13	c	–	78	34	2	–	–	–
141/130*			2	Lord's	L-8w	5	34	b	5	14	b	–	54	53	2	36	23	0
142/131			3	Leeds	L-219	5	75	b	5	8	b	1	120	80	3	66	38	0
143/132			4	Manchester	D	–	–	–	–	–	–	–	30	3	1	–	–	–
144/133			5	Oval	D	10	21	*	–	–	–	–	180	117	3	–	–	–
156/142*	1924	SA	4	Manchester	D	–	–	–	–	–	–	–	48	20	0	–	–	–
159/145	1924–25	A	2	Melbourne	L-81	7	8	c	8	14	b	–	157	95	1	32	9	0

Career	M	I	NO	HS	R	Avge	100	50	Ct	St	Balls	R	W	Avge	BB	5w	10w	Rate
Test	23	35	2	119	962	29.15	1	6	9	–	2812	1486	45	33.02	5-46	1	–	62.48
F/c	651	1035	156	210*	24531	27.90	26	107	364	–	83510	44159	1893	23.32	9-47	113	23	44.11

DOWNTON
Paul Rupert

Kent (1977 to 1979)
Middlesex (1980 to date)

TOURS
WI 1980–81, 1985–86; NZ 1977–78; I/SL 1984–85; P 1977–78; Z 1980–81 (Middx)
Born Farnborough, Kent 4 Apr 1957

The son of a wicket-keeper good enough to deputize for Godfrey Evans in eight matches for Kent in 1948, Paul Downton was immersed in cricket from an early age. He is an all-rounder rather than a specialist: a nimble middle-order batsman who is a fine improviser and judge of a quick single, and an agile and determined wicket-keeper. Having unintentionally acquired some of Alan Knott's mannerisms it was ironic that, after completing his studies at Sevenoaks School and Exeter University, he was eventually compelled to move to Middlesex for regular county cricket. Although he occasionally lost his England place through muffing a vital chance he usually regained it by virtue of his batting ability. During the 1984 series against the the West Indies all-pace attack he survived for more than 16 hours and in the 1987 season he scored an impressive 1120 first-class runs.

Ref	Series	V	T	Venue	Result	Batting 1st No	R	HO	Batting 2nd No	R	HO	Fielding 1st Ct	St	Byes	Balls	Fielding 2nd Ct	St	Byes	Balls
896/563†	1980–81	WI	1	Port-of-Spain	L-I & 79	8	4	b	8	5	c	1	–	0	882	–	–	–	–
898/565†			4	St John's	D	8	13	c	–	–	–	2	–	1	930	–	–	–	–
899/566†			5	Kingston	D	8	0	c	8	26	*	3	–	0	979	–	–	–	–
903/567†	1981	A	1	Nottingham	L-4w	8	8	c	8	3	lbw	1	–	4	521	1	–	1	325
989/601†	1984	WI	1	Birmingham	L-I & 180	9	33	lbw	2	56	c	–	–	6	858	–	–	–	–
990/602†			2	Lord's	L-9w	7	23	*	7	4	lbw	2	–	0	394	–	–	4	397
991/603†			3	Leeds	L-8w	7	17	c	7	27	c	1	–	0	443	–	–	0	195
992/604†			4	Manchester	L-I & 64	7	0	c	3	24	b	3	–	4	963	–	–	–	–
993/605†			5	Oval	L-172	8	16	c	7	10	lbw	1	–	1	420	3	–	0	579
994/606†	1984	SL		Lord's	D	8	10	c	–	–	–	2	–	2	996	1	–	5	480
1005/607†	1984–85	I	1	Bombay[3]	L-8w	8	37	*	7	62	lbw	1	–	4	822	–	1	2	91
1006/608†			2	Delhi	W-8w	7	74	c	–	–	–	3	1	1	752	2	–	6	622
1007/609†			3	Calcutta	D	8	6	*	–	–	–	1	–	0	1200	–	–	0	108
1008/610†			4	Madras[1]	W-9w	9	3	*	–	–	–	3	–	0	407	2	–	1	737
1009/611†			5	Kanpur	D	7	1	b	–	–	–	2	–	9	990	–	–	0	78
1017/612†	1985	A	1	Leeds	W-5w	8	54	c	–	–	–	2	–	0	589	3	–	4	694
1018/613†			2	Lord's	L-4w	7	21	c	9	0	c	1	–	0	748	–	–	0	276
1019/614†			3	Nottingham	D	7	0	c	–	–	–	2	–	6	1208	–	–	–	–
1020/615†			4	Manchester	D	7	23	b	–	–	–	2	1	0	535	–	–	1	840
1021/616†			5	Birmingham	W-I & 118	7	0	*	–	–	–	3	–	0	683	1	–	1	385
1022/617†			6	Oval	W-I & 94	8	16	b	–	–	–	1	–	0	504	4	–	4	279
1038/618†	1985–86	WI	1	Kingston	L-10w	8	2	c	8	3	c	1	–	2	647	–	–	0	6
1039/619†			2	Port-of-Spain	L-7w	8	8	c	8	5	lbw	1	2	0	628	–	–	0	183
1040/620†			3	Bridgetown	L-I & 30	7	11	lbw	8	26	c	1	–	2	757	–	–	–	–
1041/621†			4	Port-of-Spain	L-10w	8	7	c	8	11	*	3	–	0	541	–	–	0	35
1042/622†			5	St John's	L-240	8	5	c	9	13	lbw	–	–	2	807	–	–	4	258
1046/623†	1986	I	1	Lord's	L-5w	8	5	lbw	7	29	c	–	–	0	822	1	–	1	252
1098/646†	1988	WI	1	Nottingham	D	7	16	*	–	–	–	3	–	6	775	–	–	–	–
1099/647†			2	Lord's	L-134	7	11	lbw	7	27	lbw	3	–	0	407	3	–	0	648
1100/648†			3	Manchester	L-I & 156	7	24	c	7	6	c	–	–	0	841	–	–	–	–

Career	M	I	NO	HS	R	Avge	100	50	Ct	St	Balls	R	W	Avge	BB	5w	10w	Rate
Test	30	48	8	74	785	19.62	–	4	70	5	–	–	–	–	–	–	–	–
F/c	270	341	69	126*	6922	25.44	5	38	574	79	48	5	0	–	–	–	–	–

Paul Downton – Neil Foster in background

NOTABLE FEATS

- 50 dismissals in 20th Test (*1021*).

P. R. DOWNTON – TEST SUMMARY

Series	V	M	I	NO	HS	R	Avge	100	50	Ct	St	Byes	Balls
1980–81	WI	3	5	1	26*	48	12.00	–	–	6	–	1	2791
1981	A	1	2	–	8	11	5.50	–	–	2	–	5	846
1984	WI	5	10	1	56	210	23.33	–	1	10	–	15	4249
1984	SL	1	1	–	10	10	10.00	–	–	3	–	7	1476
1984–85	I	5	6	3	74	183	61.00	–	2	14	2	23	5807
1985	A	6	7	1	54	114	19.00	–	1	19	1	16	6741
1985–86	WI	5	10	1	26	91	10.11	–	–	6	2	10	3862
1986	I	1	2	–	29	34	17.00	–	–	1	–	1	1074
1988	WI	3	5	1	27	84	21.00	–	–	9	–	6	2671
	A	7	9	1	54	125	15.62	–	1	21	1	17	7587
	WI	16	30	4	56	433	16.65	–	1	31	2	32	13573
	I	6	8	3	74	217	43.40	–	2	15	2	24	6881
	SL	1	1	–	10	10	10.00	–	–	3	–	7	1476
Home		17	27	3	56	463	19.29	–	2	44	1	50	17057
Overseas		13	21	5	74	322	20.12	–	2	26	4	34	12460
Totals		30	48	8	74	785	19.62	–	4	70	5	84	29517

DRUCE
Norman Frank

Cambridge University (1894 to 1897)
Surrey (1895 to 1897)

Wisden 1898
TOUR A 1897–98
Born Denmark Hill, Surrey 1 Jan 1875
Died Milford on Sea, Hampshire
27 Oct 1954

NOTABLE FEATS

- Contributed 146 to Cambridge U's 507 for 7 v MCC at Lord's in 1896; it remains the world record total by a winning side in the 4th inns of a match and the highest 4th inns total in English first-class cricket.
- His 227* v C.I. Thornton's XI in 1897 was then the record first-class score at Fenner's during a season in which he averaged an unprecedented 66.00 for Cambridge U.

During an extremely brief first-class career Frank Druce established himself as an excitingly stylish and adventurous batsman. He might well have been a prototype for Denis Compton: a brilliantly unorthodox player with a magnificent eye and exceptional powers of timing who specialized in on-side strokes against straight balls. A product of Marlborough College, he gained his blue as a freshman and represented Cambridge in four Varsity matches, the last as captain. After each of his last three unviersity seasons he appeared occasionally for Surrey (12 matches in total) but he virtually ended his career after visiting Australia on A.E. Stoddart's second tour and playing in all five Tests.

Frank Druce

						Batting 1st			Batting 2nd			
Ref	**Series**	**V**	**T**	**Venue**	**Result**	**No**	**R**	**HO**	**No**	**R**	**HO**	**Ct**
53/53	1897–98	A	1	Sydney	W-9w	5	20	c	–	–	–	4
54/54			2	Melbourne	L-I & 55	8	44	lbw	7	15	c	–
55/55			3	Adelaide	L-I & 13	6	24	c	6	27	b	–
56/56			4	Melbourne	L-8w	5	24	lbw	9	16	c	1
57/57			5	Sydney	L-6w	6	64	lbw	6	18	c	–

Career	M	I	NO	HS	R	Avge	100	50	Ct	St	Balls	R	W	Avge	BB	5w	10w	Rate
Test	5	9	0	64	252	28.00	–	1	5	–	–	–	–	–	–	–	–	–
F/c	66	105	8	227*	3416	35.21	9	12	66	–	528	268	8	33.50	1-8	–	–	66.00

DUCAT, Andrew

Surrey (1906 to 1931)

Wisden 1920
TOUR A 1929–30
Born Brixton, Surrey 16 Feb 1886
Died Lord's Cricket Ground,
St John's Wood, London 23 Jul 1942

Andy 'Mac' Ducat was a highly talented forcing batsman and an outstandingly fast and sure-handed outfielder who began his long career in the company of Tom Hayward, Jack Hobbs and Jack Crawford. Although only a little above medium height (5ft 10in), he was powerfully built and kept himself superbly fit. He was a natural timer of the ball, using his immensely strong arms and shoulders to drive and pull with a full pendulum swing of the bat. An excellent cutter and a courageous player of fast bowling, his lone excursion on to the international stage was against the fearsome Australian attack of Gregory and McDonald. The latter dismissed him twice with one ball in his first innings, the express delivery smashing the shoulder off his bat and carrying to slip as the splinter dislodged a bail. Ducat was a double international who played six times for England and captained the FA Cup-winning Aston Villa team in 1929. Quiet and unassuming, he became coach at Eton and a skilful cricket writer. He died of a heart attack while batting at Lord's in a wartime Home Guard match between Surrey and Sussex.

NOTABLE FEATS

- Exceeded 1000 runs in a season 14 times, including 2000 once.
- Scored 306* v Oxford U at The Oval in 1919 (in 280 min and all on the same day), plus 7 double centuries – all for Surrey.
- Shared record Surrey 3rd-wkt stand of 353 with E.G. Hayes v Hampshire at Southampton in 1919, scoring 100 before lunch.
- Shared record Surrey 10th-wkt stand of 173 with A. Sandham v Essex at Leyton in 1921.

Andy Ducat (right) and his Surrey colleague Andy Sandham.

Ref	Series	V	T	Venue	Result	Batting 1st No	R	HO	Batting 2nd No	R	HO	Ct
142/131	1921	A	3	Leeds	L-219	4	3	c	6	2	st	1

Career	M	I	NO	HS	R	Avge	100	50	Ct	St	Balls	R	W	Avge	BB	5w	10w	Rate
Test	1	2	0	3	5	2.50	–	–	1	–	–	–	–	–	–	–	–	–
F/c	429	669	59	306*	23373	38.31	52	109	206	–	1981	903	21	43.00	3-12	–	–	94.33

DUCKWORTH George

Lancashire (1923 to 1938)

Wisden 1929
TOURS
A 1928–29, 1932–33, 1936–37;
SA 1930–31; NZ 1932–33, 1936–37
Born Warrington, Lancashire 9 May 1901
Died Warrington 5 Jan 1966

One of cricket's outstanding and most loved characters, George Duckworth was a wonderfully agile and aggressive wicket-keeper and a gutsy lower-order batsman who revelled in a crisis. A devoted resident of Warrington, he was renowned for a piercing appeal of extraordinary volume for such a tiny man. Although he honed his skills as a keeper against the high pace of Ted McDonald and devious spin of Cecil Parkin, and contributed substantially to Lancashire's five inter-war Championships, he had to compete with Les Ames for a Test place. After his retirement in 1938 (he reappeared in a North v South match in 1947) he enjoyed a season with Cheshire and a brief flirtation with journalism. The War over, he involved himself in hotel management, farming, pigeon breeding, writing, and broadcasting humorous and forthright commentaries on cricket and rugby league. He managed three Commonwealth tours of India, became England's successor to Bill Ferguson as scorer/baggage-master at home and abroad, and gave much wise counsel to young players.

NOTABLE FEATS

- 50 dismissals in 20th Test (*226*).
- Made 107 dismissals (76ct, 31st) in 1928, including a record 97 for Lancashire.
- Made career record 923 dismissals for Lancashire (633ct, 290st).

TEST NOTES

- *205* W.R. Hammond kept on the second day after Duckworth tore a ligament in his hand.

Ref	Series	V	T	Venue	Result	Batting 1st No	R	HO	Batting 2nd No	R	HO	Fielding 1st Ct	St	Byes	Balls	Fielding 2nd Ct	St	Byes	Balls
156/142†	1924	SA	4	Manchester	D	–	–	–	–	–	–	–	–	8	401	–	–	–	–
175/161†	1928	WI	3	Oval	W-I & 71	10	7	*	–	–	–	1	–	2	480	1	–	6	316
176/162†	1928–29	A	1	Brisbane[1]	W-675	11	5	*	–	–	–	–	–	1	304	1	–	0	153
177/163†			2	Sydney	W-8w	10	39	*	3	2	*	1	–	4	650	–	–	5	910
178/164†			3	Melbourne	W-3w	10	3	b	9	0	*	3	–	4	1085	2	1	6	995
179/165†			4	Adelaide	W-12	7	5	c	11	1	lbw	2	–	0	960	1	–	9	911
180/166†			5	Melbourne	L-5w	5	12	c	11	9	lbw	3	–	6	1629	–	–	12	805
181/167†	1929	SA	1	Birmingham	D	11	11	*	–	–	–	–	–	6	1036	–	–	9	358
182/168†			2	Lord's	D	11	8	*	–	–	–	1	1	9	786	–	1	2	306
183/169†			3	Leeds	W-5w	4	21	b	–	–	–	1	1	0	603	1	1	13	667
184/170†			4	Manchester	W-I & 32	–	–	–	–	–	–	1	1	0	453	2	2	13	712
194/180†	1930	A	1	Nottingham	W-93	11	4	lbw	11	14	*	1	1	4	432	1	–	17	836
195/181†			2	Lord's	L-7w	11	18	c	11	0	lbw	–	1	6	1392	1	–	1	170
196/182†			3	Leeds	D	7	33	c	–	–	–	2	–	5	1008	–	–	–	–
197/183†			4	Manchester	D	10	0	*	–	–	–	1	–	23	1003	–	–	–	–
198/184†			5	Oval	L-I & 39	10	3	b	10	15	b	4	–	22	1537	–	–	–	–
204/185†	1930–31	SA	1	Johannesburg[1]	L-28	11	0	*	10	4	lbw	1	–	12	316	2	–	16	572
205/186†			2	Cape Town	D	11	0	lbw	–	–	–	–	–	8	1152	–	–	–	–
206/187†			3	Durban[2]	D	–	–	–	–	–	–	4	–	5	584	1	–	8	420
226/200†	1932–33	NZ	2	Auckland	D	9	6	*	–	–	–	–	1	9	341	–	–	0	51
245/219†	1935	SA	4	Manchester	D	10	2	c	–	–	–	1	–	3	657	–	–	6	498
252/221†	1936	I	1	Lord's	W-9w	9	2	c	–	–	–	–	1	4	331	2	–	4	276
253/222†			2	Manchester	D	10	10	*	–	–	–	2	–	1	409	–	1	9	690
254/223†			3	Oval	W-9w	–	–	–	–	–	–	–	2	8	515	1	–	3	558

Career	M	I	NO	HS	R	Avge	100	50	Ct	St	Balls	R	W	Avge	BB	5w	10w	Rate
Test	24	28	12	39*	234	14.62	–	–	45	15	–	–	–	–	–	–	–	–
F/c	504	545	206	75	4945	14.58	–	6	753	343	68	73	0	–	–	–	–	–

G. DUCKWORTH – TEST SUMMARY

Series	V	M	I	NO	HS	R	Avge	100	50	Ct	St	Byes	Balls
1924	SA	1	–	–	–	–	–	–	–	–	–	8	401
1928	WI	1	1	1	7*	7	–	–	–	2	–	8	796
1928–29	A	5	9	4	39*	76	15.20	–	–	13	1	47	8402
1929	SA	4	3	2	21	40	40.00	–	–	6	7	52	4921
1930	A	5	8	2	33	87	14.50	–	–	10	2	78	6378
1930–31	SA	3	3	1	4	4	2.00	–	–	8	–	49	3044
1932–33	NZ	1	1	1	6*	6	–	–	–	–	1	9	392
1935	SA	1	1	0	2	2	2.00	–	–	1	–	9	1155
1936	I	3	2	1	10*	12	12.00	–	–	5	4	29	2779
	A	10	17	6	39*	163	14.81	–	–	23	3	125	14780
	SA	9	7	3	21	46	11.50	–	–	15	7	118	9521
	WI	1	1	1	7*	7	–	–	–	2	–	8	796
	NZ	1	1	1	6*	6	–	–	–	–	1	9	392
	I	3	2	1	10*	12	12.00	–	–	5	4	29	2779
Home		15	15	6	33	148	16.44	–	–	24	13	184	16430
Overseas		9	13	6	39*	86	12.28	–	–	21	2	105	11838
Totals		24	28	12	39*	234	14.62	–	–	45	15	289	28268

George Duckworth appeals for a catch during the Old Trafford Test against Australia in 1930.

DULEEPSINHJI
Kumar Shri

Sussex (1924 to 1932)
Cambridge University (1925 to 1928)
Hindus (1928–29)

Wisden 1930
TOURS A 1929–30; NZ 1929–30
Born Sarodar, India 13 Jun 1905
Died Bombay, India 5 Dec 1959

Duleep batting against Australia at Old Trafford, 1930. The keeper is Bert Oldfield.

An Indian prince, although he was known throughout the cricketing world as 'Duleep', Ranji's nephew was a supreme batting artist. Even though ill health restricted his first-class career to just eight seasons, he still managed to amass 15,485 runs and 50 hundreds with batting of effortless brilliance. He was a delightfully wristy and quick-footed player; he late cut with the delicate touch of a violinist and was an outstanding player of slow bowling on a wet pitch. At Cheltenham College he had been a considerable all-rounder but afterwards, although he continued to pocket remarkable catches at slip, he rarely bowled his leg-breaks. A friendly and selfless man, he captained Sussex in 1931 and 1932 with great tactical perception before illness compelled his retirement at the tragically early age of 27. After the War and Partition he joined the Indian Foreign Service and became High Commissioner in Australia. A first-class inter-zonal tournament introduced in India two years after his death bears his name.

NOTABLE FEATS

- *195* Emulated his uncle, K.S. Ranjitsinhji, by scoring 100 in his first Test v A.
- Only H. Sutcliffe, E. Paynter and K.F. Barrington have exceeded his Test average of 58.52 for E.
- Exceeded 1000 runs in a season 7 times, including 2000 on 3 occasions.
- His 333 (out of 513 in 330 min) v Northamptonshire at Hove in 1930 remains the highest score for Sussex. Only C.G. Macartney (345) and W.H. Ponsford (352) have scored more runs in a day. During this innings he shared in a Sussex record 6th-wkt stand of 255 with M.W. Tate.
- His 254* v Middlesex at Fenner's in 1927 remains the highest score for Cambridge U.
- Scored 100 in both innings of a first-class match 3 times, including 115 and 246 for Sussex v Kent at Hastings in 1929 and 125 and 103* for the Gentlemen v the Players at Lord's in 1930.
- Hit 12 hundreds in 1931, including 4 in successive innings.

TEST NOTES

- *181* Bowled in 2nd inns: 0 for 7 (6 balls).

						Batting 1st			Batting 2nd			
Ref	Series	V	T	Venue	Result	No	R	HO	No	R	HO	Ct
181/167	1929	SA	1	Birmingham	D	4	12	c	5	1	lbw	–
186/172	1929–30	NZ	1	Christchurch	W-8w	3	49	c	3	33	*	3
187/173			2	Wellington	D	3	40	c	3	56	*	3
188/174			3	Auckland	D	3	117	c	–	–	–	–
189/175			4	Auckland	D	3	63	b	–	–	–	1
195/181	1930	A	2	Lord's	L-7w	4	173	c	4	48	c	–
196/182			3	Leeds	D	4	35	b	4	10	c	–
197/183			4	Manchester	D	4	54	c	–	–	–	2
198/184			5	Oval	L-I & 39	4	50	c	4	46	c	–
209/190	1931	NZ	1	Lord's	D	4	25	c	4	11	c	–
210/191			2	Oval	W-I & 26	3	109	c	–	–	–	1
211/192			3	Manchester	D	3	63	c	–	–	–	–

Career	M	I	NO	HS	R	Avge	100	50	Ct	St	Balls	R	W	Avge	BB	5w	10w	Rate
Test	12	19	2	173	995	58.52	3	5	10	–	6	7	0	–	–	–	–	–
F/c	205	333	23	333	15485	49.95	50	63	256	–	1835	1345	28	48.03	4-49	–	–	65.53

DURSTON
Frederick John

Middlesex (1919 to 1933)

TOUR WI 1928–29 (Cahn)
Born Clophill, Bedfordshire 11 Jul 1893
Died Norwood Green, Southall, Middlesex 8 Apr 1965

Jack Durston was a very large and colourful character; a massively built 6ft 5in right-arm fast bowler who reaped a rich harvest on the hard pitches at Lord's between the Wars. He made his Middlesex debut in 1919 after war-time service in the Royal Engineers and, using a vicious break-back to good effect, he contributed over 100 wickets to the county's 1920 and 1921 Championships. His 11 wickets for Middlesex against Warwick Armstrong's Australians gained him an England cap at Lord's but, although he claimed five victims, he was never selected again. By 1932 his ever-increasing weight (approaching 20 stone) compelled a change to slow off-spin but he still managed to take 102 wickets at 19.55 apiece. He was a hard-hitting lower-order batsman who improved as his career progressed. A keen footballer, he kept goal for Brentford. [*Illus. p.* 297]

NOTABLE FEATS

- Exceeded 100 wickets in a season 6 times.
- Two hat-tricks for Middlesex: v Cambridge U at Fenner's in 1922 and v Oxford U at The Parks in 1923.
- Shared Middlesex record 9th-wkt stand of 160* in 80 min with E.H. Hendren v Essex at Leyton in 1927.

					Batting 1st			Batting 2nd				Bowling 1st			Bowling 2nd		
Ref	**Series**	**V**	**T Venue**	**Result**	**No**	**R**	**HO**	**No**	**R**	**HO**	**Ct**	**Balls**	**R**	**W**	**Balls**	**R**	**W**
141/130	1921	A	2 Lord's	L-8w	11	6	*	11	2	b	–	145	102	4	57	34	1

Career	M	I	NO	HS	R	Avge	100	50	Ct	St	Balls	R	W	Avge	BB	5w	10w	Rate
Test	1	2	1	6*	8	8.00	–	–	–	–	202	136	5	27.20	4-102	–	–	40.40
F/c	386	473	144	92*	3918	11.90	–	6	257	–	72081	29279	1329	22.03	8-27	72	11	54.23

EDMONDS
Philippe Henri

Cambridge University (1971 to 1973)
Middlesex (1971 to 1987)
Eastern Province (1975–76)

TOURS
A 1978–79, 1986–87; SA 1975–76 (Int W); WI 1985–86; NZ 1977–78; I 1984–85; P 1977–78; SL 1984–85
Born Lusaka, Northern Rhodesia 8 Mar 1951

Phil Edmonds never quite fulfilled his cricketing ambitions nor fully developed the abundant all-round talent he first displayed at school in Lusaka and Tunbridge Wells. A tall (6ft 1½in) orthodox slow left-arm spinner with a high, model action, he had a fast bowler's belligerence. His impatience prevented him becoming a consistent batsman although he played a number of outstanding attacking innings and once headed the Middlesex averages. As an aggressive close fielder at short-leg or silly point he was in Brian Close's class and there can be no higher praise. Although he had successfully led Cambridge in his final year, because his abrasive and argumentative nature frequently antagonized both his fellow players and the authorities he was never given the roles he coveted most – the captaincy of Middlesex and England. An articulate and inventive entrepreneur, he now combines some writing and commentating with his many commercial interests. His last two tours were wittily chronicled by his wife, Frances.

NOTABLE FEATS

- 50 wickets in 20th Test (*929*); 100 wickets in 39th Test (*1049*).
- *762* Took 5 for 17 with his first 69 balls in Test cricket.
- *816* His 7 for 66 remains England's best analysis in Pakistan.
- *928* Shared record E v I 7th-wkt stand of 125 with D.W. Randall.
- Hat-trick for Middlesex v Leicestershire at Leicester in 1981.

						Batting 1st			Batting 2nd				Bowling 1st			Bowling 2nd		
Ref	**Series**	**V**	**T**	**Venue**	**Result**	**No**	**R**	**HO**	**No**	**R**	**HO**	**Ct**	**Balls**	**R**	**W**	**Balls**	**R**	**W**
762/513	1975	A	3	Leeds	D	8	13	*	9	8	c	–	120	28	5	102	64	1
763/514			4	Oval	D	8	4	c	9	7	ro	–	228	118	0	37	14	0
815/532	1977–78	P	2	Hyderabad	D	8	4	c	–	–	–	5	192	75	3	180	95	0
816/533			3	Karachi	D	8	6	lbw	–	–	–	–	264	66	7	–	–	–
817/534	1977–78	NZ	1	Wellington	L-72	9	4	lbw	9	11	c	3	24	7	0	8	4	0
818/535			2	Christchurch	W-174	10	50	c	–	–	–	5	272	38	4	48	22	2
819/536			3	Auckland	D	9	8	b	–	–	–	1	80	23	0	360	107	3
825/537	1978	P	1	Birmingham	W-I & 57	9	4	*	–	–	–	–	24	2	0	156	44	4
826/538			2	Lord's	W-I & 120	10	36	*	–	–	–	1	48	6	4	72	21	0
827/539			3	Leeds	D	9	1	*	–	–	–	–	66	22	0	–	–	–
828/540	1978	NZ	1	Oval	W-7w	9	28	lbw	–	–	–	1	102	41	0	205	20	4
829/541			2	Nottingham	W-I & 119	9	6	b	–	–	–	1	94	21	2	199	44	4
830/542			3	Lord's	W-7w	8	5	c	–	–	–	2	72	19	0	–	–	–
834/543	1978–79	A	1	Brisbane[2]	W-7w	9	1	c	–	–	–	1	8	0	0	96	27	0
851/549	1979	I	1	Birmingham	W-I & 83	–	–	–	–	–	–	1	156	60	2	102	37	0
852/550			2	Lord's	D	8	20	c	–	–	–	–	12	1	0	270	62	2
853/551			3	Leeds	D	8	18	ro	–	–	–	–	228	59	1	–	–	–
854/552			4	Oval	D	9	16	c	9	27	*	–	30	17	0	228	87	1
928/580	1982	I	1	Lord's	W-7w	8	64	c	–	–	–	–	12	5	0	90	39	0
929/581			2	Manchester	D	9	12	c	–	–	–	–	222	94	3	–	–	–
930/582			3	Oval	D	8	14	c	–	–	–	1	212	89	3	78	34	0
957/591	1983	NZ	1	Oval	W-189	8	12	c	8	43	*	–	12	19	0	241	101	3
958/592			2	Leeds	L-5w	7	8	c	7	0	c	1	270	101	1	–	–	–
1005/607	1984–85	I	1	Bombay[3]	L-8w	9	48	c	9	8	c	–	198	82	1	48	21	1
1006/608			2	Delhi	W-8w	8	26	c	–	–	–	–	266	83	2	264	60	4
1007/609			3	Calcutta	D	9	8	c	–	–	–	–	282	72	3	24	2	0
1008/610			4	Madras[1]	W-9w	5	36	lbw	–	–	–	–	36	33	0	251	119	2
1009/611			5	Kanpur	D	8	49	lbw	–	–	–	–	288	112	1	–	–	–
1018/613	1985	A	2	Lord's	L-4w	9	21	c	10	1	c	2	154	85	2	96	35	1
1019/614			3	Nottingham	D	10	12	b	–	–	–	–	396	155	2	–	–	–
1020/615			4	Manchester	D	9	1	b	–	–	–	2	91	40	4	324	122	1
1021/616			5	Birmingham	W-I & 118	–	–	–	–	–	–	4	120	47	1	90	13	2
1022/617			6	Oval	W-I & 94	10	12	lbw	–	–	–	–	84	52	2	–	–	–
1038/618	1985–86	WI	1	Kingston	L-10w	10	5	*	10	7	lbw	1	126	53	0	–	–	–
1039/619			2	Port-of-Spain	L-7w	10	3	*	10	13	c	1	180	98	2	75	24	1
1040/620			3	Bridgetown	L-I & 30	9	4	c	6	4	lbw	–	174	85	0	–	–	–
1046/623	1986	I	1	Lord's	L-5w	11	7	*	11	7	c	1	132	41	1	66	51	1
1048/625			3	Birmingham	D	9	18	b	9	10	c	–	144	55	1	168	31	4
1049/626	1986	NZ	1	Lord's	D	7	6	c	7	9	*	2	252	97	4	30	18	0
1050/627			2	Nottingham	L-8w	8	0	c	3	20	lbw	1	168	52	2	24	16	0
1051/628			3	Oval	D	–	–	–	–	–	–	–	132	29	2	–	–	–
1058/629	1986/87	A	1	Brisbane[2]	W-7w	10	9	*	–	–	–	1	72	12	1	144	46	0
1059/630			2	Perth	D	–	–	–	–	–	–	–	126	55	2	162	25	1
1060/631			3	Adelaide	D	10	13	c	–	–	–	1	312	134	2	174	63	1
1061/632			4	Melbourne	W-I & 14	10	19	lbw	–	–	–	–	–	–	–	118	45	3
1062/633			5	Sydney	L-55	9	3	c	9	0	lbw	–	204	79	3	258	79	2
1075/634	1987	P	1	Manchester	D	11	23	*	–	–	–	–	42	2	1	–	–	–
1076/635			2	Lord's	D	10	17	*	–	–	–	–	–	–	–	–	–	–
1077/636			3	Leeds	L-I & 18	10	0	c	10	0	*	1	150	59	1	–	–	–
1078/637			4	Birmingham	D	10	24	*	8	0	ro	2	147	50	1	24	11	1
1079/638			5	Oval	D	10	2	lbw	–	–	–	–	192	97	0	–	–	–

Career	**M**	**I**	**NO**	**HS**	**R**	**Avge**	**100**	**50**	**Ct**	**St**	**Balls**	**R**	**W**	**Avge**	**BB**	**5w**	**10w**	**Rate**
Test	51	65	15	64	975	17.50	–	2	42	–	12028	4273	125	34.18	7-66	2	–	96.22
F/c	390	495	91	142	7651	18.93	3	22	345	–	85799	31933	1242	25.71	8-53	47	9	69.08

Phil Edmonds

P. H. EDMONDS – TEST BOWLING SUMMARY

Series	V	M	Balls	R	W	Avge	BB	5w	10w	Rate
1975	A	2	487	224	6	37.33	5-28	1	–	81.16
1977–78	P	2	636	236	10	23.60	7-66	1	–	63.60
1977–78	NZ	3	792	201	9	22.33	4-38	–	–	88.00
1978	P	3	366	95	8	11.87	4-6	–	–	45.75
1978	NZ	3	672	145	10	14.50	4-20	–	–	67.20
1978–79	A	1	104	27	0	–	–	–	–	–
1979	I	4	1026	323	6	53.83	2-60	–	–	171.00
1982	I	3	614	261	6	43.50	3-89	–	–	102.33
1983	NZ	2	523	221	4	55.25	3-101	–	–	130.75
1984–85	I	5	1657	584	14	41.71	4-60	–	–	118.35
1985	A	5	1355	549	15	36.60	4-40	–	–	90.33
1985–86	WI	3	555	260	3	86.66	2-98	–	–	185.00
1986	I	2	510	178	7	25.42	4-31	–	–	72.85
1986	NZ	3	606	212	8	26.50	4-97	–	–	75.75
1986–87	A	5	1570	538	15	35.86	3-45	–	–	104.66
1987	P	5	555	219	4	54.75	1-2	–	–	138.75
	A	13	3516	1338	36	37.16	5-28	1	–	97.66
	WI	3	555	260	3	86.66	2-98	–	–	185.00
	NZ	11	2593	779	31	25.12	4-20	–	–	83.64
	I	14	3807	1346	33	40.78	4-31	–	–	115.36
	P	10	1557	550	22	25.00	7-66	1	–	70.77
Home		32	6714	2427	74	32.79	5-28	1	–	90.72
Overseas		19	5314	1846	51	36.19	7-66	1	–	104.19
Totals		51	12028	4273	125	34.18	7-66	2	–	96.22

EDRICH
John Hugh MBE

Surrey (1958 to 1978)

Wisden 1966
TOURS
A 1965–66, 1970–71, 1974–75;
SA 1962–63 (Cwlth), 1972–73 (Robins), 1973–74 (Robins); WI 1967–68;
NZ 1965–66, 1970–71, 1974–75;
I 1963–64; P 1968–69; SL 1968–69;
Z 1959–60 (Surrey)
Born Blofield, Norfolk 21 Jun 1937

For more than a decade John Edrich's determined bushy-browed concentration provided a formidable barrier against England's opponent opening attacks. Left-handed and almost oozing application, he was one of the world's most dependable front-line batsmen and as doughty a fighter as the most famous of his four county cricketer cousins, Bill. Although just 5ft 8in tall, he was stockily built with exceptionally strong (and hairy) forearms which enabled him to punch the ball powerfully off his legs and through the covers. Despite limited footwork he was a good player of spin bowling. An assiduous gatherer of runs, he could attack as well as graft but his defence, with head always behind the line of the ball, was the key to his success. His peak season was 1965 during which he slaughtered the New Zealand bowling for a triple century on a seaming green Headingley pitch, many of his record haul of 57 boundaries coming from lofted straight and off-drives. He preferred the perpendicular strokes to the cut or hook and was adept at nudging, pushing and deflecting singles. He became a specialist gully fielder, his natural right-handedness revealing itself in his throwing and very occasional seam bowling. He captained England once when Mike Denness dropped himself during the Lillee and Thomson onslaught, led Surrey from 1973 to 1977 and, following Ken Barrington's sudden death, stood in as an England selector in 1981.

TEST NOTES

- *557* 2nd inns bowling: 0 for 17 (24 balls).
- *603* 2nd inns bowling: 0 for 6 (6 balls).
- *604* Was taken ill with appendicitis after the first day and operated upon before the start of the second.
- *702* Deputized as captain for R. Illingworth from 5.30 on the fourth evening.
- *753* Retired hurt when 0* at 70–2 (2nd inns); resumed at 156–6 with 2 fractured ribs.

NOTABLE FEATS

• 1000 runs in 15th Test (*601*) (22 inns); 2000 runs in 31st Test (*641*) (46 inns); 3000 runs in 43rd Test (*676*) (67 inns); 4000 runs in 61st Test (*740*) (102 inns); 5000 runs in 76th Test (*777*) (124 inns).
• *562* Completed 100 in his first Test v Australia soon after the Queen arrived.
• *593* Scored England's only 300 since 1938, his 310* in 532 min being the highest score for England by a left-hander. It included 5 sixes and 52 fours – the most boundaries in any Test innings. He was on the field throughout the match and his 2nd-wkt stand of 369 in 339 min with K.F. Barrington remains the highest for any wkt in E v NZ Tests.
• *678* Shared century opening stands in both innings with G. Boycott – the third England pair to achieve this feat v Australia.
• *740* His stand of 221 in 226 min with D.L. Amiss was then England's highest for the 2nd wkt v India and remains the record in all Tests at Lord's.
• Exceeded 1000 runs in a season 19 times (plus twice overseas), including 2000 on 6 occasions.
• Scored 9 successive 50s in 1965, the most in England since 1926.
• Scored 100 in both innings of a match for Surrey on 4 occasions.
• Became the 17th batsman (third left-hander after C.P. Mead and F.E. Woolley) to score 100 hundreds when he made 101* for Surrey v Derbyshire at The Oval in 1977.
• Scored the first 50 and won the first match award in a limited-overs international (v A at Melbourne in 1970–71).

John Edrich

						Batting 1st			Batting 2nd			
Ref	**Series**	**V**	**T Venue**		**Result**	**No**	**R**	**HO**	**No**	**R**	**HO**	**Ct**
543/395	1963	WI	1	Manchester	L-10w	2	20	c	2	38	c	1
544/396			2	Lord's	D	2	0	c	2	8	c	1
547/399			5	Oval	L-8w	2	25	c	2	12	c	–
556/403	1963–64	I	4	Delhi	D	2	41	c	–	–	–	–
557/404			5	Kanpur	D	2	35	c	–	–	–	1
562/406	1964	A	2	Lord's	D	2	120	c	–	–	–	–
563/407			3	Leeds	L-7w	2	3	c	2	32	c	–
564/408			4	Manchester	D	2	6	c	–	–	–	1
593/417	1965	NZ	3	Leeds	W-I & 187	2	310	*	–	–	–	–
594/418	1965	SA	1	Lord's	D	3	0	lbw	3	7	*rh	1
597/421	1965–66	A	1	Brisbane[2]	D	3	32	c	3	37	c	–
598/422			2	Melbourne	D	3	109	c	–	–	–	2
599/423			3	Sydney	W-I & 93	3	103	c	–	–	–	–
600/424			4	Adelaide	L-I & 9	3	5	c	3	1	c	1
601/425			5	Melbourne	D	3	85	c	3	3	b	1
602/426	1965–66	NZ	1	Christchurch	D	3	2	c	3	2	lbw	–
603/427			2	Dunedin	D	3	36	c	–	–	–	–
604/428			3	Auckland	D	–	–	–	–	–	–	–
609/433	1966	WI	5	Oval	W-I & 34	3	35	c	–	–	–	1
618/434	1967	I	1	Leeds	W-6w	1	1	c	1	22	c	–
619/435			2	Lord's	W-I & 124	1	12	c	–	–	–	1
628/440	1967–68	WI	1	Port-of-Spain	D	2	25	c	–	–	–	–
629/441			2	Kingston	D	2	96	c	2	6	b	1
630/442			3	Bridgetown	D	1	146	c	–	–	–	–
631/443			4	Port-of-Spain	W-7w	1	32	c	1	29	b	1
632/444			5	Georgetown	D	1	0	c	1	6	c	2
637/445	1968	A	1	Manchester	L-159	1	49	ro	1	38	c	1
638/446			2	Lord's	D	1	7	c	–	–	–	–
639/447			3	Birmingham	D	1	88	c	1	64	c	–
640/448			4	Leeds	D	1	62	c	1	65	c	1
641/449			5	Oval	W-226	1	164	b	1	17	c	–
647/450	1968–69	P	1	Lahore[2]	D	1	54	c	1	8	c	–
648/451			2	Dacca	D	1	24	c	1	12	*	–
649/452			3	Karachi	D	2	32	c	–	–	–	–
653/453	1969	WI	1	Manchester	W-10w	2	58	ro	2	9	*	2
654/454			2	Lord's	D	2	7	c	2	1	c	1
655/455			3	Leeds	W-30	2	79	lbw	2	15	lbw	–
656/456	1969	NZ	1	Lord's	W-230	2	16	c	2	115	c	–
657/457			2	Nottingham	D	2	155	b	–	–	–	–
658/458			3	Oval	W-8w	1	68	b	1	22	c	1
674/459	1970–71	A	1	Brisbane[2]	D	4	79	c	–	–	–	–
675/460			2	Perth	D	3	47	ro	3	115	*	–
676/461			4	Sydney	W-299	3	55	c	3	12	ro	2
677/462			5	Melbourne	D	3	9	c	2	74	*	2
678/463			6	Adelaide	D	2	130	c	2	40	b	1
679/464			7	Sydney	W-62	1	30	c	1	57	c	–
685/465	1970–71	NZ	1	Christchurch	W-8w	2	12	lbw	2	2	c	1
686/466			2	Auckland	D	1	1	c	1	24	c	1
687/467	1971	P	1	Birmingham	D	1	0	c	1	15	c	–
688/468			2	Lord's	D	3	37	c	–	–	–	1
689/469			3	Leeds	W-25	3	2	c	3	33	c	3
690/470	1971	I	1	Lord's	D	3	18	c	3	62	c	1
691/471			2	Manchester	D	3	0	c	3	59	b	1
692/472			3	Oval	L-4w	3	41	c	3	0	b	–
698/473	1972	A	1	Manchester	W-89	2	49	ro	2	26	c	1
699/474			2	Lord's	L-8w	2	10	lbw	2	6	c	–
700/475			3	Nottingham	D	2	37	c	2	15	b	–
701/476			4	Leeds	W-9w	2	45	c	2	4	lbw	–
702/477			5	Oval	L-5w	2	8	lbw	2	18	b	–
739/497	1974	I	1	Manchester	W-113	3	7	b	4	100	*	–
740/498			2	Lord's	W-I & 285	3	96	lbw	–	–	–	–
741/499			3	Birmingham	W-I & 78	–	–	–	–	–	–	1
742/500	1974	P	1	Leeds	D	3	9	c	3	70	c	–

Ref	Series	V	T	Venue	Result	Batting 1st No	R	HO	Batting 2nd No	R	HO	Ct
743/501			2	Lord's	D	3	40	c	–	–	–	–
744/502			3	Oval	D	4	25	c	–	–	–	–
750/503	1974–75	A	1	Brisbane[2]	L-166	3	48	c	3	6	b	–
752/505			3	Melbourne	D	4	49	c	4	4	c	–
753/506*			4	Sydney	L-171	4	50	c	4	33	*	–
755/508			6	Melbourne	W-I & 4	3	70	c	–	–	–	2
758/509	1974–75	NZ	1	Auckland	W-I & 83	3	64	c	–	–	–	2
759/510			2	Christchurch	D	3	11	c	–	–	–	1
760/511	1975	A	1	Birmingham	L-I & 85	1	34	lbw	1	5	c	–
761/512			2	Lord's	D	2	9	lbw	2	175	c	–
762/513			3	Leeds	D	2	62	c	2	35	b	–
763/514			4	Oval	D	2	12	lbw	2	96	b	1
777/515	1976	WI	1	Nottingham	D	1	37	c	1	76	*	1
779/517			3	Manchester	L-425	1	8	c	1	24	b	–

Career	M	I	NO	HS	R	Avge	100	50	Ct	St	Balls	R	W	Avge	BB	5w	10w	Rate
Test	77	127	9	310*	5138	43.54	12	24	43	–	30	23	0	–	–	–	–	–
F/c	564	979	104	310*	39790	45.47	103	188	311	–	91	53	0	–	–	–	–	–

J. H. EDRICH – TEST BATTING SUMMARY

Series	V	M	I	NO	HS	R	Avge	100	50
1963	WI	3	6	–	38	103	17.16	–	–
1963–64	I	2	2	–	41	76	38.00	–	–
1964	A	3	4	–	120	161	40.25	1	–
1965	NZ	1	1	1	310*	310	–	1	–
1965	SA	1	2	1	7*	7	7.00	–	–
1965–66	A	5	8	–	109	375	46.87	2	1
1965–66	NZ	3	3	–	36	40	13.33	–	–
1966	WI	1	1	–	35	35	35.00	–	–
1967	I	2	3	–	22	35	11.66	–	–
1967–68	WI	5	8	–	146	340	42.50	1	1
1968	A	5	9	–	164	554	61.55	1	4
1968–69	P	3	5	1	54	130	32.50	–	1
1969	WI	3	6	1	79	169	31.80	–	2
1969	NZ	3	5	–	155	376	75.20	2	1
1970–71	A	6	11	2	130	648	72.00	2	4
1970–71	NZ	2	4	–	24	39	9.75	–	–
1971	P	3	5	–	37	87	17.40	–	–
1971	I	3	6	–	62	180	30.00	–	2
1972	A	5	10	–	49	218	21.80	–	–
1974	I	3	3	1	100*	203	101.50	1	1
1974	P	3	4	–	70	144	36.00	–	1
1974–75	A	4	7	1	70	260	43.33	–	2
1974–75	NZ	2	2	–	64	75	37.50	–	1
1975	A	4	8	–	175	428	53.50	1	2
1976	WI	2	4	1	76*	145	48.33	–	1
	A	32	57	3	175	2644	48.96	7	13
	SA	1	2	1	7*	7	7.00	–	–
	WI	14	25	2	146	792	34.43	1	4
	NZ	11	15	1	310*	840	60.00	3	2
	I	10	14	1	100*	494	38.00	1	3
	P	9	14	1	70	361	27.76	–	2
Home		45	77	5	310*	3155	43.81	7	14
Overseas		32	50	4	146	1983	43.10	5	10
Totals		77	127	9	310*	5138	43.54	12	24

EDRICH
William John DFC

Middlesex (1937 to 1958)

Wisden 1940
TOURS
A 1946–47, 1954–55; SA 1938–39; NZ 1946–47; I 1937–38 (Tennyson), 1956–57 (Howard)
Born Lingwood, Norfolk 26 Mar 1916
Died Whitehall Court, Chesham, Buckinghamshire 24 Apr 1986

Bill Edrich's aggressive batting with its vast armoury of offensive strokes epitomized the audacious spirit of a man who lived life to the full; utterly fearless, he won the DFC as a daylight RAF bomber pilot and was married five times. Although only 5ft 6in tall, he was a brave and ferocious hooker and puller of short-pitched fast bowling and an exceptionally effective player on poor pitches. Used in short spells during the immediate post-war seasons, his tearaway right-arm bowling with a slinging action off an 11-pace run could be genuinely fast; later he turned to off-spin. He was an outstanding catcher at slip and loved to be involved in the game. Born into a Norfolk cricketing family who ran their own team, he was one of four brothers who progressed to first-class cricket. Although he made an immediate impact at county level, scoring 2154 runs and winning his Middlesex cap in his first season, he had a nightmarish baptism at Test level but, after failing to reach 30 in any of his first 11 innings, he amassed 219 in the time-

Bill Edrich

less Test at Durban. Having begun his career as a professional he adopted amateur status in 1947 and became one of only six cricketers to represent both sides in Gents v Players matches. After sharing the Middlesex captaincy with Denis Compton for two seasons, he was granted sole responsibility (1953–57) and proved an enterprising leader before returning to the minor county scene as captain of Norfolk. A courageous footballer, he appeared briefly at outside right for Norwich City and Tottenham Hotspur.

NOTABLE FEATS

- 1000 runs in 18th Test (*286*) (26 inns); 2000 runs in 29th Test (*317*) (45 inns).
- *271* Shared record E v SA 2nd-wkt stand of 280 with P.A. Gibb.
- *286* Shared record E v SA stand of 370 with D.C.S. Compton which was then the highest for the 3rd wkt in all Test cricket and remains the England record.
- *287* Became the third player after G. Giffen and G.A. Faulkner to score 200 runs and take 8 wickets in a Test.
- Exceeded 1000 runs in a season 15 times, including 2000 on 9 occasions and 3539 (an aggregate exceeded only by D.C.S. Compton) in 1947.
- Scored 9 double centuries, including 8 for Middlesex.
- Carried his bat for 140* out of 303 for Lord Tennyson's XI v Sind at Karachi in 1937–38 on his debut in India.
- Scored 1010 runs before June 1938, the fifth Englishman after W.G. Grace, T.W. Hayward, W.R. Hammond and C. Hallows to achieve this feat. All his runs were scored at Lord's and it remains the only pre-June 1000 to include a duck.
- Shared stand of 424* with D.C.S. Compton for Middlesex v Somerset at Lord's in 1948 which remains the 3rd-wkt record in English first-class cricket and the highest for any wicket at Lord's.

						Batting 1st			Batting 2nd				Bowling 1st			Bowling 2nd		
Ref	**Series**	**V**	**T**	**Venue**	**Result**	**No**	**R**	**HO**	**No**	**R**	**HO**	**Ct**	**Balls**	**R**	**W**	**Balls**	**R**	**W**
263/232	1938	A	1	Nottingham	D	3	5	b	–	–	–	–	–	–	–	78	39	1
264/233			2	Lord's	D	3	0	b	4	10	c	–	24	5	0	32	27	2
265/234			4	Leeds	L-5w	1	12	b	1	28	st	1	18	13	0	–	–	–
266/235			5	Oval	W-I & 579	2	12	lbw	–	–	–	3	60	55	1	–	–	–
267/236	1938–39	SA	1	Johannesburg[1]	D	1	4	c	1	10	c	1	72	44	0	24	7	0
268/237			2	Cape Town	D	6	0	b	–	–	–	1	40	15	0	24	5	0
269/238			3	Durban[2]	W-I & 13	–	–	–	–	–	–	1	32	9	1	56	16	1
270/239			4	Johannesburg[1]	D	7	6	lbw	–	–	–	–	32	11	0	–	–	–
271/240			5	Durban[2]	D	6	1	c	3	219	c	1	72	29	0	48	18	0
278/246	1946	I	3	Oval	D	–	–	–	–	–	–	–	116	68	4	–	–	–
279/247	1946–47	A	1	Brisbane[2]	L-I & 332	3	16	c	3	7	lbw	–	200	107	3	–	–	–
280/248			2	Sydney	L-I & 33	3	71	lbw	3	119	b	–	208	79	3	–	–	–
281/249			3	Melbourne	D	3	89	lbw	3	13	lbw	–	83	50	3	144	86	0
282/250			4	Adelaide	D	3	17	c	3	46	c	–	160	88	0	56	25	0
283/251			5	Sydney	L-5w	3	60	c	3	24	st	1	56	34	0	16	14	0
284/252	1946–47	NZ		Christchurch	D	3	42	c	–	–	–	–	66	35	1	–	–	–
285/253	1947	SA	1	Nottingham	D	3	57	b	3	50	b	–	120	56	1	24	8	0
286/254			2	Lord's	W-10w	3	189	b	–	–	–	4	54	22	0	78	31	3
287/255			3	Manchester	W-7w	3	191	b	3	22	*	–	211	95	4	136	77	4
288/256			4	Leeds	W-10w	3	43	c	–	–	–	1	102	46	3	84	35	1
299/262	1948	A	1	Nottingham	L-8w	3	18	b	3	13	c	1	108	72	0	24	20	0
300/263			2	Lord's	L-409	3	5	b	3	2	c	1	48	43	1	12	11	0
301/264			3	Manchester	D	3	32	c	3	53	ro	–	42	27	1	12	8	0
302/265			4	Leeds	L-7w	3	111	c	3	54	lbw	2	18	19	0	–	–	–
303/266			5	Oval	L-I & 149	3	3	c	3	28	b	1	54	38	1	–	–	–
314/272	1949	NZ	1	Leeds	D	3	36	c	3	70	b	3	54	18	2	12	13	0
315/273			2	Lord's	D	3	9	c	3	31	c	2	24	16	0	–	–	–
316/274			3	Manchester	D	3	78	c	–	–	–	–	24	8	0	30	26	0
317/275			4	Oval	D	3	100	c	–	–	–	4	18	16	0	–	–	–
323/276	1950	WI	1	Manchester	W-202	3	7	c	2	71	c	–	12	4	0	18	10	0
324/277			2	Lord's	L-326	3	8	c	3	8	c	1	96	30	0	78	37	0
374/303	1953	A	3	Manchester	D	2	6	c	–	–	–	2	–	–	–	–	–	–
375/304			4	Leeds	D	2	10	lbw	2	64	c	1	–	–	–	–	–	–
376/305			5	Oval	W-8w	2	21	lbw	2	55	*	3	–	–	–	–	–	–
387/311	1954	P	1	Lord's	D	5	4	b	–	–	–	1	–	–	–	–	–	–

Ref	Series	V	T	Venue	Result	Batting 1st No	R	HO	Batting 2nd No	R	HO	Ct	Bowling 1st Balls	R	W	Bowling 2nd Balls	R	W
391/315	1954–55	A	1	Brisbane[2]	L-I & 154	3	15	c	3	88	b	–	24	28	0	–	–	–
392/316			2	Sydney	W-38	6	10	c	6	29	b	1	–	–	–	–	–	–
393/317			3	Melbourne	W-128	2	4	c	2	13	b	1	–	–	–	–	–	–
394/318			4	Adelaide	W-5w	2	21	b	2	0	b	1	–	–	–	–	–	–

Career	M	I	NO	HS	R	Avge	100	50	Ct	St	Balls	R	W	Avge	BB	5w	10w	Rate
Test	39	63	2	219	2440	40.00	6	13	39	–	3234	1693	41	41.29	4-68	–	–	78.87
F/c	571	964	92	267*	36965	42.39	86	197	529	1	32944	15956	479	33.31	7-48	11	3	68.77

W. J. EDRICH – TEST BATTING SUMMARY

Series	V	M	I	NO	HS	R	Avge	100	50
1938	A	4	6	–	28	67	11.16	–	–
1938–39	SA	5	6	–	219	240	40.00	1	–
1946	I	1	–	–	–	–	–	–	–
1946–47	A	5	10	–	119	462	46.20	1	3
1946–47	NZ	1	1	–	42	42	42.00	–	–
1947	SA	4	6	1	191	552	110.40	2	2
1948	A	5	10	–	111	319	31.90	1	2
1949	NZ	4	6	–	100	324	54.00	1	2
1950	WI	2	4	–	71	94	23.50	–	1
1953	A	3	5	1	64	156	39.00	–	2
1954	P	1	1	–	4	4	4.00	–	–

Series	V	M	I	NO	HS	R	Avge	100	50
1954–55	A	4	8	–	88	180	22.50	–	1
	A	21	39	1	119	1184	31.15	2	8
	SA	9	12	1	219	792	72.00	3	2
	WI	2	4	–	71	94	23.50	–	1
	NZ	5	7	–	100	366	52.28	1	2
	I	1	–	–	–	–	–	–	–
	P	1	1	–	4	4	4.00	–	–
Home		24	38	2	191	1516	42.11	4	9
Overseas		15	25	–	219	924	36.96	2	4
Totals		39	63	2	219	2440	40.00	6	13

ELLIOTT, Harry

Derbyshire (1920 to 1947)

TOURS SA 1927–28; I 1933–34
Born Scarcliffe, Derbyshire 2 Nov 1891
Died Derby 2 Feb 1976

A remarkably consistent wicket-keeper, Harry Elliott's first 426 appearances for Derbyshire were interrupted only by his absence for the 1928 Manchester Test. He was a determined lower-order batsman who relished a defensive role in a crisis. After a single season (1946) as a first-class umpire, he became Derbyshire's coach, reappearing in his 56th year to keep wicket in four matches before resuming his umpiring duties from 1952 until 1960. The uncle of the noted Test umpire and Derbyshire opener C.S. Elliott, it was not until a jubilee reunion of the 1936 Championship-winning side that he revealed he had distorted his true date of birth by four years.

NOTABLE FEATS

- Set Derbyshire match record with 10 dismissals (8ct, 2st) v Lancashire at Manchester in 1935.
- His 90 dismissals (69ct, 21st) in 1935 remains the Derbyshire record.
- Contributed his highest score (94) to a (then) Derbyshire record 3rd-wkt stand of 222 with L.F. Townsend when he also captained the side and did not concede a bye in an innings victory v Leicestershire at Loughborough in 1933.

Derbyshire's Championship winning side of 1936: standing *H. Elliott, L.F. Townsend, W.H. Copson, unidentified, H. Parker (scorer), A.V. Pope, D. Smith, C.S. Elliott;* seated *H. Storer, T.S. Worthington, A.W. Richardson (captain), T.B. Mitchell, A.E. Alderman.*

Ref	Series	V	T	Venue	Result	Batting 1st No	R	HO	Batting 2nd No	R	HO	Fielding 1st Ct	St	Byes	Balls	Fielding 2nd Ct	St	Byes	Balls
172/158 †	1927–28	SA	5	Durban[2]	L-8w	10	1	c	10	3	b	–	–	1	678	–	–	3	141
174/160 †	1928	WI	2	Manchester	W-I & 30	10	6	lbw	–	–	–	–	–	10	634	2	–	1	285
230/204 †	1933–34	I	1	Bombay[1]	W-9w	10	37	*	–	–	–	1	1	2	548	3	–	4	545
232/206 †			3	Madras[1]	W-202	10	14	c	–	–	–	1	–	1	357	1	2	10	416

Career	M	I	NO	HS	R	Avge	100	50	Ct	St	Balls	R	W	Avge	BB	5w	10w	Rate
Test	4	5	1	37*	61	15.25	–	–	8	3	–	–	–	–	–	–	–	–
F/c	532	764	220	94	7580	13.93	–	11	904	302	3	5	0	–	–	–	–	–

ELLISON
Richard Mark

Kent (1981 to date)
Tasmania (1986–87)

Wisden 1986
TOURS WI 1985–86; I/SL 1984–85
Born Willesborough, Ashford, Kent
21 Sep 1959

NOTABLE FEATS

- *1021* Returned match figures of 10 for 104 in his first Test v Australia.
- *1039* Shared England's highest 10th-wkt stand in the West Indies (72 with J.G. Thomas).

Richard Ellison is a tall (6ft 2in), well-built right-arm fast-medium bowler who not only seams the ball off the pitch but can also swing it late in either direction. A left-handed batsman, he intersperses bouts of prodigious hitting with sessions of dogged defence. After completing his studies at Tonbridge School and Exeter University he soon established himself in the Kent team, reaching his peak in 1985 when he headed the national averages with 65 wickets at 17.20. With that summer's Ashes series all square, he was recalled for the last two Tests and inspired innings victories in both matches with some magnificent swing bowling that brought him 17 wickets at 10.88. Pain in the left pelvic area caused him to miss the entire 1987 season but, assisted by an RAF rehabilitation centre, he recovered to spearhead Kent's dramatic challenge for the following season's Championship.

Richard Ellison

Ref	Series	V	T	Venue	Result	Batting 1st No	R	HO	Batting 2nd No	R	HO	Ct	Bowling 1st Balls	R	W	Bowling 2nd Balls	R	W
993/605	1984	WI	5	Oval	L-172	9	20	*	8	13	c	–	108	34	2	156	60	3
994/606	1984	SL		Lord's	D	7	41	c	–	–	–	1	168	70	1	42	36	0
1005/607	1984–85	I	1	Bombay[3]	L-8w	7	1	b	8	0	c	–	108	85	0	–	–	–
1006/608			2	Delhi	W-8w	9	10	b	–	–	–	–	156	66	4	42	20	0
1007/609			3	Calcutta	D	10	1	c	–	–	–	–	318	117	0	6	1	0
1021/616	1985	A	5	Birmingham	W-I & 118	–	–	–	–	–	–	1	191	77	6	54	27	4
1022/617			6	Oval	W-I & 94	9	3	c	–	–	–	–	108	35	2	102	46	5
1038/618	1985–86	WI	1	Kingston	L-10w	9	9	c	9	11	b	–	198	78	5	–	–	–
1039/619			2	Port-of-Spain	L-7w	9	4	lbw	9	36	lbw	–	108	58	0	18	12	0
1042/622			5	St John's	L-240	9	6	c	4	16	lbw	–	147	114	2	24	32	0
1046/623	1986	I	1	Lord's	L-5w	9	12	c	8	19	c	–	174	63	1	36	17	0

Career	M	I	NO	HS	R	Avge	100	50	Ct	St	Balls	R	W	Avge	BB	5w	10w	Rate
Test	11	16	1	41	202	13.46	–	–	2	–	2264	1048	35	29.94	6-77	3	1	64.68
F/c	138	192	45	108	3429	23.32	1	13	52	–	20518	9018	341	26.44	7-75	12	2	60.17

EMBUREY
John Ernest

Middlesex (1973 to date)
Western Province
(1982–83 to 1983–84)

Wisden 1984
TOURS
A 1978–79, 1979–80, 1986–87, 1987–88; SA 1981–82 (SAB); WI 1980–81, 1985–86; NZ 1987–88; I 1979–80, 1981–82; P 1987–88; SL 1977–78 (DHR), 1981–82; Z 1980–81 (Middx)
Born Peckham, London 20 Aug 1952

NOTABLE FEATS

- 50 wickets in 20th Test (*915*); 100 wickets in 38th Test (*1058*).
- 1000 runs and Test 'double' in 46th Test (*1079*) (68 inns).
- *830* Dismisssed B.A. Edgar with his fourth ball in Test cricket.
- *837* By bowling A.G. Hurst he completed the victory which enabled England to retain the Ashes.
- *921* His analysis of 6 for 33, which included a spell of 5 for 5, remains the record for any Test in Sri Lanka.
- 100 wickets in a season once, winning the Swanton Trophy in 1983 for being the first to reach that mark.
- Hit 6 sixes off 7 balls for Western Province v Eastern Province at Cape Town in 1983–84.
- Established a world first-class record by scoring 46 entirely in boundaries (a six and 10 fours) for England XI v Tasmania at Hobart in 1986–87.

Throughout the last decade John Emburey has been England's premier off-spin bowler, despite being banished from Test cricket for three years (32 matches) after touring South Africa with a rebel England team in 1981–82. Tall (6ft 2in) with a high, easy action, he is a miserly bowler who combines probing accuracy with subtle variations of pace, bounce, flight and away drift. Unlike his England predecessors he has been unfortunate in having frequently to adjust his method from the containing accuracy demanded by limited-overs cricket to the attacking approach necessary to win Test matches. Since his successful 1986–87 tour of Australia he has taken only 15 wickets in as many Tests and at a rate of one every 206 balls. Significantly he had to endure 32 instant internationals in 1987, an exercise in futility for a spin bowler similar to Grand Master Karpov practising with only half a set of chessmen. Meanwhile his batting has developed almost to the all-rounder class. Based on stubborn defence, his eccentric but powerful hitting is as devoid of footwork or backlift as a member of Gerard Hoffnung's orchestra of carpet cleaners. He is a specialist close fielder at gully or slip and a tactically shrewd captain who was unlucky to be jettisoned after two defeats at the hands of the 1988 West Indians.

John Emburey

						Batting 1st			Batting 2nd				Bowling 1st			Bowling 2nd		
Ref	Series	V	T	Venue	Result	No	R	HO	No	R	HO	Ct	Balls	R	W	Balls	R	W
830/542	1978	NZ	3	Lord's	W-7w	9	2	b	–	–	–	2	157	39	2	18	1	0
836/545	1978–79	A	3	Melbourne	L-103	9	0	b	9	7	*	1	112	44	0	170	30	3
837/546			4	Sydney	W-93	9	0	c	9	14	c	2	232	57	1	138	46	4
838/547			5	Adelaide	W-205	9	4	b	9	42	b	2	96	13	2	72	16	0
839/548			6	Sydney	W-9w	9	0	b	–	–	–	1	144	48	2	192	52	4
876/556	1979–80	I		Bombay[3]	W-10w	8	8	c	–	–	–	–	–	–	–	–	–	–
882/559	1980	WI	3	Manchester	D	9	3	c	9	28	*	–	63	20	3	–	–	–
883/560			4	Oval	D	9	24	c	5	2	c	–	138	38	2	–	–	–
884/561			5	Leeds	D	9	13	*	–	–	–	2	36	25	1	–	–	–
885/562	1980	A		Lord's	D	9	3	lbw	–	–	–	–	228	104	1	54	35	0
896/563	1980–81	WI	1	Port-of-Spain	L-I & 79	9	17	*	9	1	b	1	312	124	5	–	–	–
897/564			3	Bridgetown	L-298	9	0	c	9	9	b	–	108	45	0	144	57	0
898/565			4	St John's	D	9	10	b	–	–	–	1	210	85	0	–	–	–
899/566			5	Kingston	D	9	1	b	–	–	–	–	336	108	2	–	–	–
904/568	1981	A	2	Lord's	D	7	31	ro	–	–	–	–	150	35	2	126	24	0
906/570			4	Birmingham	W-29	8	3	b	9	37	*	1	161	43	4	132	40	2
907/571			5	Manchester	W-103	9	1	c	9	57	c	–	24	16	1	294	107	2
908/572			6	Oval	D	9	0	lbw	9	5	*	–	138	58	0	138	76	1

Ref	Series	V	T	Venue	Result	Batting 1st No	R	HO	Batting 2nd No	R	HO	Ct	Bowling 1st Balls	R	W	Bowling 2nd Balls	R	W
912/573	1981–82	I	1	Bombay[3]	L-138	7	0	lbw	7	1	c	–	–	–	–	78	35	2
915/576			4	Calcutta	D	9	1	lbw	–	–	–	1	144	44	2	180	62	2
917/578			6	Kanpur	D	9	2	ro	–	–	–	–	192	81	0	–	–	–
921/579	1981–82	SL		Colombo SO	W-7w	8	0	lbw	–	–	–	1	114	55	0	150	33	6
1017/612	1985	A	1	Leeds	W-5w	9	21	b	–	–	–	–	36	23	2	262	82	5
1018/613			2	Lord's	L-4w	8	33	lbw	3	20	b	1	114	57	0	48	24	1
1019/614			3	Nottingham	D	9	16	*	–	–	–	1	330	129	3	–	–	–
1020/615			4	Manchester	D	8	31	*	–	–	–	1	144	41	2	306	99	4
1021/616			5	Birmingham	W-I & 118	–	–	–	–	–	–	–	54	21	0	78	19	1
1022/617			6	Oval	W-I & 94	5	9	c	–	–	–	–	114	48	1	6	1	0
1039/619	1985–86	WI	2	Port-of-Spain	L-7w	7	0	c	7	14	c	–	162	78	5	60	36	2
1040/620			3	Bridgetown	L-I & 30	8	0	c	9	35	*	–	228	96	1	–	–	–
1041/621			4	Port-of-Spain	L-10w	9	8	c	9	0	b	–	162	62	3	–	–	–
1042/622			5	St John's	L-240	10	7	*	10	0	c	–	222	93	2	84	83	1
1046/623	1986	I	1	Lord's	L-5w	7	7	c	9	1	c	1	162	28	1	–	–	–
1047/624			2	Leeds	L-279	8	0	c	9	1	c	2	102	45	1	42	9	0
1048/625			3	Birmingham	D	7	38	c	7	27	*	1	113	40	2	42	19	0
1050/627	1986	NZ	2	Nottingham	L-8w	7	8	c	8	75	c	–	257	87	2	36	15	1
1051/628			3	Oval	D	7	9	*	–	–	–	–	186	39	1	–	–	–
1058/629	1986–87	A	1	Brisbane[2]	W-7w	8	8	c	–	–	–	–	204	66	0	257	80	5
1059/630			2	Perth	D	9	5	*	9	4	*	–	258	110	2	168	41	1
1060/631			3	Adelaide	D	6	49	c	–	–	–	–	276	117	1	132	50	0
1061/632			4	Melbourne	W-I & 14	9	22	c	–	–	–	1	24	16	0	120	43	2
1062/633			5	Sydney	L-55	8	69	b	8	22	b	2	180	62	0	276	78	7
1075/634	1987	P	1	Manchester	D	8	19	c	–	–	–	1	96	28	0	–	–	–
1076/635			2	Lord's	D	8	12	ro	–	–	–	–	–	–	–	–	–	–
1078/637			4	Birmingham	D	8	58	lbw	7	20	ro	2	156	48	0	24	3	0
1079/638			5	Oval	D	7	53	c	–	–	–	–	366	143	0	–	–	–
1084/639	1987–88	P	1	Lahore[2]	L-I & 87	8	0	b	9	38	*	–	288	109	3	–	–	–
1085/640			2	Faisalabad	D	8	15	st	5	10	*	–	126	49	3	12	3	0
1086/641			3	Karachi	D	8	70	c	7	74	*	–	318	90	1	–	–	–
1090/642	1987–88	A		Sydney	D	7	23	st	–	–	–	2	180	57	0	228	98	1
1091/643	1987–88	NZ	1	Christchurch	D	7	42	c	7	19	ro	–	24	2	0	60	16	0
1092/644			2	Auckland	D	7	45	c	–	–	–	–	102	28	1	342	91	1
1093/645			3	Wellington	D	–	–	–	–	–	–	–	275	99	1	–	–	–
1098/646	1988	WI	1	Nottingham	D	8	0	c	–	–	–	–	96	95	2	–	–	–
1099/647*			2	Lord's	L-134	8	7	b	8	30	b	3	36	17	1	90	62	0
1100/648*			3	Manchester	L-I & 156	8	1	c	8	8	c	–	150	54	0	–	–	–
1103/651	1988	SL		Lord's	W-7w	8	0	c	–	–	–	–	12	4	0	108	34	1

Career	M	I	NO	HS	R	Avge	100	50	Ct	St	Balls	R	W	Avge	BB	5w	10w	Rate
Test	57	84	17	75	1409	21.02	–	7	33	–	13315	4763	130	36.63	7-78	6	–	102.42
F/c	353	435	90	133	7874	22.82	3	34	306	–	74897	27551	1092	25.22	7-36	53	8	68.58

J. E. EMBUREY TEST SUMMARY

Season	V	M	I	NO	HS	R	Avge	100	50	Balls	R	W	Avge	BB	5w	10w	Rate
1978	NZ	1	1	–	2	2	2.00	–	–	175	40	2	20.00	2-39	–	–	87.50
1978–79	A	4	7	1	42	67	11.16	–	–	1156	306	16	19.12	4-46	–	–	72.25
1979–80	I	1	1	–	8	8	8.00	–	–	–	–	–	–	–	–	–	–
1980	WI	3	5	2	28*	70	23.33	–	–	237	83	6	13.83	3-20	–	–	39.50
1980	A	1	1	–	3	3	3.00	–	–	282	139	1	139.00	1-104	–	–	282.00
1980–81	WI	4	6	1	17*	38	7.60	–	–	1110	419	7	59.85	5-124	1	–	158.57
1981	A	4	7	2	57	134	26.80	–	1	1163	399	12	33.25	4-43	–	–	96.91
1981–82	I	3	4	–	2	4	1.00	–	–	594	222	6	37.00	2-35	–	–	99.00
1981–82	SL	1	1	–	0	0	0.00	–	–	264	88	6	14.66	6-33	1	–	44.00
1985	A	6	6	2	33	130	32.50	–	–	1492	544	19	28.63	5-82	1	–	78.52
1985–86	WI	4	8	2	35*	64	10.66	–	–	918	448	14	32.00	5-78	1	–	65.57
1986	I	3	6	1	38	74	14.80	–	–	461	141	4	35.25	2-40	–	–	115.25
1986	NZ	2	3	1	75	92	46.00	–	1	479	141	4	35.25	2-87	–	–	119.75
1986–87	A	5	7	2	69	179	33.80	–	1	1895	663	18	36.83	7-78	2	–	105.27
1987	P	4	5	–	58	162	32.40	–	2	642	222	0	–	–	–	–	–

Series	V	M	I	NO	HS	R	Avge	100	50	Balls	R	W	Avge	BB	5w	10w	Rate
1987–88	P	3	6	3	74*	207	69.00	–	2	744	251	7	35.85	3-49	–	–	106.28
1987–88	A	1	1	–	23	23	23.00	–	–	408	155	1	155.00	1-98	–	–	408.00
1987–88	NZ	3	3	–	45	106	35.33	–	–	803	236	3	78.66	1-28	–	–	267.66
1988	WI	3	5	–	30	46	9.20	–	–	372	228	3	76.00	2-95	–	–	124.00
1988	SL	1	1	–	0	0	0.00	–	–	120	38	1	38.00	1-34	–	–	120.00
	A	21	29	7	69	536	24.36	–	2	6396	2206	67	32.92	7-78	3	–	95.46
	WI	14	24	5	35*	218	11.47	–	–	2637	1178	30	39.26	5-78	2	–	87.90
	NZ	6	7	1	75	200	33.33	–	1	1457	417	9	46.33	2-87	–	–	161.88
	I	7	11	1	38	86	8.60	–	–	1055	363	10	36.30	2-35	–	–	105.50
	P	7	11	3	74*	369	46.12	–	4	1386	473	7	67.57	3-49	–	–	198.00
	SL	2	2	–	0	0	0.00	–	–	384	126	7	18.00	6-33	1	–	54.85
Home		28	40	8	75	713	22.28	–	4	5423	1975	52	37.98	5-82	1	–	104.28
Overseas		29	44	9	74*	696	19.88	–	3	7892	2788	78	35.74	7-78	5	–	101.17
Totals		57	84	17	75	1409	21.02	–	7	13315	4763	130	36.63	7-78	6	–	102.42

EMMETT
George Malcolm

Gloucestershire (1936 to 1959)

TOURS
I 1950–51 (Cwlth), 1953–54 (Cwlth); SL 1950–51 (Cwlth)
Born Agra, India 2 Dec 1912
Died Knowle, Bristol 18 Dec 1976

Born and educated in India, George Emmett joined Gloucestershire after a period on the MCC groundstaff and four seasons with Devon. Although only of medium height (5ft 8in) and slight build he was an extremely hard-hitting opening batsman and a bustling right-arm medium-pace change bowler. Wartime service as a sergeant in the Royal Artillery interrupted his prime years but from 1947 until his retirement he provided a dependable and entertaining supply of runs. Although he was an exceptional player of spin bowling, his quick-footed technique on a turning wicket being quite outstanding, unusually for an opener he often proved vulnerable against extreme pace. His only taste of Test cricket caused a major sensation when the 1948 selectors turned to him after deciding to drop Len Hutton for not attempting to dominate the Australian attack. After four years as Gloucestershire's captain (1955–58), he was briefly coach first to the County and then to Cheltenham College before ending his days as general secretary and groundsman at Bristol's Imperial Athletic Club.

NOTABLE FEATS

- Exceeded 1000 runs in a season 13 times (plus once on tour), including 2000 on 3 occasions.
- Carried his bat for 104* in Gloucestershire's total of 156 v Oxford U at The Parks in 1948.
- Made 104 on his debut in India (v Cricket Club of India at Bombay in 1950–51).
- Scored the fastest 100 of 1954 (84 min) for Gloucestershire v Somerset at Taunton.

George Emmett batting at The Oval in 1958; Ken Barrington at slip and Arthur McIntyre behind the stumps.

						Batting 1st			Batting 2nd			
Ref	Series	V	T	Venue	Result	No	R	HO	No	R	HO	Ct
301/264	1948	A	3	Manchester	D	2	10	c	2	0	c	–

Career	M	I	NO	HS	R	Avge	100	50	Ct	St	Balls	R	W	Avge	BB	5w	10w	Rate
Test	1	2	0	10	10	5.00	–	–	–	–	–	–	–	–	–	–	–	–
F/c	509	865	50	188	25602	31.41	37	140	296	–	3964	2641	60	44.01	6-137	2	–	66.06

EMMETT, Thomas

Yorkshire (1866 to 1888)

TOURS A 1876–77, 1878–79, 1881–82
Born Halifax, Yorkshire 3 Sep 1841
Died Leicester 30 Jun 1904

Tom Emmett was one of cricket's earliest left-handed all-rounders, a fiery round-arm fast bowler of the highest class and a handy middle-order batsman. Although 35 when Test cricket began, he played in all but one of the first eight matches, missing his only chance of a home cap when he was not picked for the 1880 Test at The Oval. He captained Yorkshire for five seasons (1878–82) prior to Lord Hawke's long reign and made 22 appearances for the Players against the Gentlemen. After extending his career by slowing his pace and increasing his guile and spin, he became coach at Rugby and influenced the embryo career of 'Plum' Warner. [*Illus. p.* 222]

NOTABLE FEATS

- *3* Became the first England bowler to take 7 wickets in a Test innings.
- Took 100 wickets in a season 4 times.
- Bowled in an unchanged partnership throughout both completed innings of a match on 13 occasions, including 6 with G. Freeman and 5 with A. Hill.

						Batting 1st			Batting 2nd				Bowling 1st			Bowling 2nd		
Ref	Series	V	T	Venue	Result	No	R	HO	No	R	HO	Ct	Balls	R	W	Balls	R	W
1/1	1876–77	A	1	Melbourne	L-45	8	8	b	9	9	b	3	48	13	0	–	–	–
2/2			2	Melbourne	W-4w	7	48	c	6	8	b	1	–	–	–	52	23	0
3/3	1878–79	A		Melbourne	L-10w	8	0	c	9	24	*	–	236	68	7	–	–	–
5/5	1881–82	A	1	Melbourne	D	7	5	b	7	6	b	1	140	61	2	64	19	0
6/6			2	Sydney	L-5w	8	10	b	8	9	c	2	24	24	0	24	17	0
7/7			3	Sydney	L-6w	8	4	b	8	2	b	1	64	37	0	–	–	–
8/8			4	Melbourne	D	8	27	b	–	–	–	1	76	22	0	–	–	–

Career	M	I	NO	HS	R	Avge	100	50	Ct	St	Balls	R	W	Avge	BB	5w	10w	Rate
Test	7	13	1	48	160	13.33	–	–	9	–	728	284	9	31.55	7-68	1	–	80.88
F/c	426	700	90	104	9053	14.84	1	24	276	–	60333	21314	1571	13.56	9-23	121	29	38.40

EVANS, Alfred John

Hampshire (1908 to 1920)
Oxford University (1909 to 1912)
Kent (1921 to 1928)

Born Newtown, Hampshire 1 May 1889
Died Marylebone, London 18 Sep 1960

John Evans was an elegant hard-hitting middle-order batsman and a useful right-arm medium-fast bowler. A talented all-round sportsman at Winchester School, he emulated his father by captining Oxford in his third season and also won blues at racquets and golf. Captured while serving with the Royal Flying Corps during the First World War, he twice escaped, recording his experiences as a POW in one of the first wartime thrillers, *The Escaping Club.* He was chosen for the Lord's Test against Warwick Armstrong's Australians after top-scoring for the MCC against that formidable attack with an unbeaten innings of 69. His father and younger brother also represented Hampshire.

John Evans

						Batting 1st			Batting 2nd			
Ref	Series	V	T	Venue	Result	No	R	HO	No	R	HO	Ct
141/130	1921	A	2	Lord's	L-8w	6	4	b	6	14	lbw	–

Career	M	I	NO	HS	R	Avge	100	50	Ct	St	Balls	R	W	Avge	BB	5w	10w	Rate
Test	1	2	0	14	18	9.00	–	–	–	–	–	–	–	–	–	–	–	–
F/c	90	148	6	143	3499	24.64	6	18	94	–	6085	3062	110	27.83	7-50	4	1	55.31

EVANS
Thomas Godfrey CBE

Kent (1939 to 1967)

Wisden 1951

TOURS

A 1946–47, 1950–51, 1954–55, 1958–59; SA 1948–49, 1956–57, 1959–60 (Cwlth); WI 1947–48, 1953–54, 1963–64 (Cav), 1964–65 (Cav); NZ 1946–47, 1950–51, 1954–55; I 1963–64 (PM XI)

Born Finchley, Middlesex 18 Aug 1920

Godfrey Evans was a brilliant extrovert wicket-keeper, one of the greatest exponents ever seen and an automatic England selection for 13 years. Being a born entertainer he relished the big occasion but managed to combine acrobatic showmanship with glovework of the highest class. A fierce competitor with boundless energy, confidence and enthusiasm, he was magnificent at lifting the flagging spirits of his bowlers and at inspiring his fielders. Of medium height (5ft 8½in) but powerfully built, he was an amazingly agile and swift diver. He would stand up to all but the fastest bowling and often produced catches out of quarter-chances. His hard-hitting quick-footed batting was equally flamboyant but he could defend rigorously in an emergency as when contributing 10* off 98 balls during the stand of 85 in 133 minutes with Denis Compton which enabled England to draw at Adelaide in 1946–47. Five years later he plundered 98 off India's bowling before lunch at Lord's. When he did lose his England place it was not through diminishing form but because of the selectors' need to build a younger side. Although he retired from Kent soon after his last Test in 1959, he was recalled eight years later while Alan Knott was making his England debut and kept with much of his former brilliance. He retained his ebullience long into retirement, keeping in charity matches nearly into his seventies and providing a welcome and cheery presence as a bookmaker's representative ('Godders from Ladders') at England's Test grounds.

Godfrey Evans catches Lindsay Hassett off the bowling of Alec Bedser at The Oval during the finale of the 1953 Test series against Australia. Bill Edrich is at slip.

NOTABLE FEATS

- 50 dismissals in 22nd Test (*310*); 100 dismissals in 42nd Test (*352*); 150 dismissals in 64th Test (*408*); 200 dismissals in 80th Test (*442*).
- 1000 runs in 32nd Test (*328*) (49 inns); 2000 runs in 73rd Test (*435*) (107 inns).
- *280* Celebrated his first Test v Australia by not conceding a bye during a total of 659 off 1384 balls – still the highest Test total without a bye.
- *282* Established a world first-class record by taking 97 min to score his first run in the 2nd inns.
- *352* Became the second wicket-keeper after W.A.S. Oldfield to make 100 dismissals and complete the 1000 runs/100 dismissals double. Scored 98* before lunch on the third day.
- *353* Scored 71 out of 84 in 70 minutes.
- *390* Beat W.A.S. Oldfield's world Test record of 130 dismissals.
- *438* Conceded only 1 bye during 2 inns on a relaid pitch where the ball frequently 'shot'.
- *442* Became the first wicket-keeper to make 200 dismissals and complete the 2000 runs/200 dismissals double.
- Exceeded 1000 runs in a season 4 times.
- Made 9 dismissals (8ct, 1st) for Kent v New Zealanders at Canterbury in 1949.

TEST NOTES

- *410* T.W. Graveney deputized as wicket-keeper throughout the 2nd inns after Evans double-fractured his little finger.
- *467* T.W. Graveney again deputized after the first day when Evans re-fractured his little finger.

						Batting 1st			Batting 2nd			Fielding 1st				Fielding 2nd			
Ref	Series	V	T	Venue	Result	No	R	HO	No	R	HO	Ct	St	Byes	Balls	Ct	St	Byes	Balls
278/246†	1946	I	3	Oval	D	–	–	–	–	–	–	–	–	1	764	–	–	–	–
280/248†	1946–47	A	2	Sydney	L-I & 33	9	5	b	9	9	st	1	–	0	1384	–	–	–	–
281/249†			3	Melbourne	D	8	17	b	9	0	*	2	–	0	779	2	–	14	907
282/250†			4	Adelaide	D	10	0	b	10	10	*	2	–	16	948	–	–	0	352
283/251†			5	Sydney	L-5w	8	29	b	7	20	b	1	–	7	608	1	–	4	418
284/252†	1946–47	NZ		Christchurch	D	7	21	*	–	–	–	2	–	10	616	–	–	–	–
285/253†	1947	SA	1	Nottingham	D	7	2	st	7	74	c	–	1	7	1179	1	–	1	306
286/254†			2	Lord's	W-10w	7	16	b	–	–	–	–	2	0	853	–	–	0	770
287/255†			3	Manchester	W-7w	8	27	b	–	–	–	1	–	3	997	1	–	5	508
288/256†			4	Leeds	W-10w	8	6	*	–	–	–	2	–	0	583	1	–	4	480
289/257†			5	Oval	D	8	45	ro	8	39	*	2	–	3	786	2	1	12	846

Ref	Series	V	T	Venue	Result	Batting 1st No	R	HO	Batting 2nd No	R	HO	Fielding 1st Ct	St	Byes	Balls	Fielding 2nd Ct	St	Byes	Balls
295/258†	1947–48	WI	1	Bridgetown	D	9	26	b	–	–	–	1	–	0	744	2	1	6	636
296/259†			2	Port-of-Spain	D	7	30	c	8	21	st	1	–	2	876	1	–	0	98
297/260†			3	Georgetown	L-7w	9	1	b	7	37	c	–	–	0	634	–	–	0	120
298/261†			4	Kingston	L-10w	8	9	c	8	4	b	–	–	11	880	–	–	0	66
299/262†	1948	A	1	Nottingham	L-8w	8	12	c	8	50	c	2	–	9	1298	–	–	0	171
300/263†			2	Lord's	L-409	8	9	c	8	24	*	1	1	3	777	1	1	22	782
301/264†			3	Manchester	D	8	34	c	–	–	–	2	–	5	558	–	–	0	366
302/265†			4	Leeds	L-7w	9	3	c	8	47	*	–	1	9	818	–	–	6	685
303/266†			5	Oval	L-I & 149	8	1	b	8	8	b	2	1	4	950	–	–	–	–
309/267†	1948–49	SA	1	Durban[2]	W-2w	7	0	c	7	4	b	3	–	3	429	–	–	1	715
310/268†			2	Johannesburg[2]	D	7	18	ro	–	–	–	1	2	4	868	–	–	9	728
311/269†			3	Cape Town	D	7	27	b	–	–	–	–	1	1	954	1	2	0	248
314/272†	1949	NZ	1	Leeds	D	8	27	c	–	–	–	3	–	2	711	–	–	1	294
315/273†			2	Lord's	D	8	5	b	–	–	–	1	–	16	958	–	–	–	–
316/274†			3	Manchester	D	8	12	c	–	–	–	–	1	3	770	–	2	2	660
317/275†			4	Oval	D	7	17	c	–	–	–	3	–	0	673	1	1	10	582
323/276†	1950	WI	1	Manchester	W-202	8	104	c	7	15	c	1	1	0	563	–	2	4	488
324/277†			2	Lord's	L-326	7	8	b	7	2	c	1	2	10	788	1	–	0	1068
325/278†			3	Nottingham	L-10w	7	32	b	7	63	c	–	1	2	1048	–	–	0	219
327/280†	1950–51	A	1	Brisbane[2]	L-70	3	16	c	6	5	c	2	–	5	445	–	–	0	109
328/281†			2	Melbourne	L-28	9	49	c	9	2	b	2	–	4	473	2	–	10	427
329/282†			3	Sydney	L-I & 13	8	23	*	7	14	b	1	–	3	1032	–	–	–	–
330/283†			4	Adelaide	L-274	7	13	c	6	21	c	2	–	2	773	1	–	7	814
331/284†			5	Melbourne	W-8w	7	1	b	–	–	–	1	–	2	552	–	–	2	507
332/285†	1950–51	NZ	1	Christchurch	D	7	19	c	–	–	–	–	1	16	944	2	–	0	78
333/286†			2	Wellington	W-6w	8	13	b	–	–	–	–	–	3	420	–	–	30	434
334/287†	1951	SA	1	Nottingham	L-71	7	5	c	8	0	c	1	–	3	1440	1	1	4	310
335/288†			2	Lord's	W-10w	7	0	c	–	–	–	1	–	0	509	–	–	11	578
336/289†			3	Manchester	W-9w	7	2	c	–	–	–	–	–	0	507	1	–	13	470
351/297†	1952	I	1	Leeds	W-7w	7	66	lbw	–	–	–	2	1	1	759	–	2	0	402
352/298†			2	Lord's	W-8w	7	104	c	–	–	–	–	1	7	567	–	–	29	732
353/299†			3	Manchester	W-I & 207	7	71	c	–	–	–	–	–	0	130	1	–	8	219
354/300†			4	Oval	D	7	1	c	–	–	–	1	–	0	233	–	–	–	–
372/301†	1953	A	1	Nottingham	D	8	8	c	–	–	–	2	–	2	843	–	–	0	236
373/302†			2	Lord's	D	8	0	b	8	11	*	–	1	4	844	1	–	8	797
374/303†			3	Manchester	D	9	44	*	–	–	–	2	1	6	699	1	2	0	108
375/304†			4	Leeds	D	8	25	lbw	8	1	c	1	–	4	497	–	1	3	198
376/305†			5	Oval	W-8w	7	28	ro	–	–	–	4	–	4	489	–	–	11	305
382/306†	1953–54	WI	1	Kingston	L-140	7	10	c	7	0	b	–	–	9	934	1	–	10	402
383/307†			2	Bridgetown	L-181	8	10	b	8	5	b	1	1	0	751	–	–	4	576
384/308†			3	Georgetown	W-9w	8	19	lbw	–	–	–	1	–	8	635	1	–	2	705
386/310†			5	Kingston	W-9w	7	28	c	–	–	–	1	–	0	364	–	–	4	1020
387/311†	1954	P	1	Lord's	D	7	25	b	–	–	–	–	1	4	503	–	–	0	314
388/312†			2	Nottingham	W-I & 129	7	4	b	–	–	–	1	–	9	390	2	–	4	676
389/313†			3	Manchester	D	7	31	c	–	–	–	–	–	4	341	–	–	2	90
390/314†			4	Oval	L-24	6	0	c	5	3	b	3	–	0	310	–	–	3	552
392/316†	1954–55	A	2	Sydney	W-38	8	3	c	8	4	c	1	–	5	444	2	–	0	428
393/317†			3	Melbourne	W-128	7	20	lbw	7	22	c	2	–	7	501	3	–	1	251
394/318†			4	Adelaide	W-5w	7	37	c	7	6	*	2	–	3	793	1	–	4	346
395/319†			5	Sydney	D	7	10	c	–	–	–	1	–	10	484	1	–	0	230
401/320†	1954–55	NZ	1	Dunedin	W-8w	7	0	b	–	–	–	1	1	5	488	–	–	7	339
402/321†			2	Auckland	W-I & 20	7	0	c	–	–	–	2	–	3	532	–	–	0	162
408/322†	1955	SA	1	Nottingham	W-I & 5	7	12	c	–	–	–	1	–	1	684	1	–	8	579
409/323†			2	Lord's	W-71	7	20	c	7	14	c	3	1	6	612	3	–	11	346
410/324†			3	Manchester	L-3w	8	0	c	11	36	c	1	–	15	1170	–	–	–	–
425/327†	1956	A	1	Nottingham	D	7	0	c	5	8	*	–	–	0	499	–	–	10	516
426/328†			2	Lord's	L-185	7	0	st	7	20	c	2	1	0	877	4	–	2	557
427/329†			3	Leeds	W-I & 42	9	40	b	–	–	–	1	–	4	427	–	–	7	597
428/330†			4	Manchester	W-I & 170	8	47	st	–	–	–	–	1	0	244	–	–	12	902
429/331†			5	Oval	D	8	0	lbw	–		–	–	–	6	552	–	–	1	229
434/332†	1956–57	SA	1	Johannesburg[3]	W-131	7	20	c	8	30	c	1	1	1	713	2	–	2	268
435/333†			2	Cape Town	W-312	7	62	c	6	1	c	4	–	1	798	1	–	0	401
436/334†			3	Durban[2]	D	7	0	st	7	10	c	1	1	0	770	–	–	5	464

Ref	Series	V	T	Venue	Result	Batting 1st No	R	HO	Batting 2nd No	R	HO	Fielding 1st Ct	St	Byes	Balls	Fielding 2nd Ct	St	Byes	Balls
437/335†			4	Johannesburg[3]	L-17	7	7	c	8	8	b	2	–	0	814	1	–	4	480
438/336†			5	Port Elizabeth	L-58	7	5	b	7	21	c	3	–	0	696	3	–	1	647
439/337†	1957	WI	1	Birmingham	D	8	14	b	6	29	*	1	–	1	1150	–	–	7	360
440/338†			2	Lord's	W-I & 36	8	82	b	–	–	–	1	–	2	309	3	–	4	577
441/339†			3	Nottingham	D	7	26	*	–	–	–	3	–	5	964	4	–	2	890
442/340†			4	Leeds	W-I & 5	7	10	b	–	–	–	–	–	0	513	1	–	0	218
443/341†			5	Oval	W-I & 237	7	40	c	–	–	–	–	–	0	340	1	1	4	246
454/342†	1958	NZ	1	Birmingham	W-205	7	2	c	7	0	c	2	–	0	417	–	–	0	465
455/343†			2	Lord's	W-I & 148	7	11	c	–	–	–	–	–	0	195	–	–	0	303
456/344†			3	Leeds	W-I & 71	–	–	–	–	–	–	1	–	0	359	–	–	6	608
457/345†			4	Manchester	W-I & 13	7	3	c	–	–	–	2	–	4	773	1	–	5	312
458/346†			5	Oval	D	7	12	c	–	–	–	–	–	0	450	1	–	2	330
464/347†	1958–59	A	1	Brisbane[2]	L-8w	7	4	c	7	4	lbw	2	–	4	577	–	–	2	415
465/348†			2	Melbourne	L-8w	7	4	c	7	11	ro	2	–	0	802	–	1	0	137
467/350†			4	Adelaide	L-10w	10	4	c	11	0	c	1	–	2	769	–	–	–	–
474/354†	1959	I	1	Nottingham	W-I & 59	7	73	c	–	–	–	1	–	5	617	–	–	0	585
475/355†			2	Lord's	W-8w	7	0	b	–	–	–	1	–	0	466	1	1	0	475

Career	M	I	NO	HS	R	Avge	100	50	Ct	St	Balls	R	W	Avge	BB	5w	10w	Rate
Test	91	133	14	104	2439	20.49	2	8	173	46	–	–	–	–	–	–	–	–
F/c	465	753	52	144	14882	21.22	7	59	816	250	283	245	2	122.50	2-50	–	–	141.50

T. G. EVANS – TEST SUMMARY

Series	V	M	I	NO	HS	R	Avge	100	50	Ct	St	Byes	Balls
1946	I	1	–	–	–	–	–	–	–	–	–	1	764
1946–47	A	4	8	2	29	90	15.00	–	–	9	–	41	5396
1946–47	NZ	1	1	1	21*	21	–	–	–	2	–	10	616
1947	SA	5	7	2	74	209	41.80	–	1	10	4	35	7308
1947–48	WI	4	7	–	37	128	18.28	–	–	6	1	19	4054
1948	A	5	9	2	50	188	26.85	–	1	8	4	58	6405
1948–49	SA	3	4	–	27	49	12.25	–	–	5	5	18	3942
1949	NZ	4	4	–	27	61	15.25	–	–	8	4	34	4648
1950	WI	3	6	–	104	224	37.33	1	1	3	6	16	4174
1950–51	A	5	9	1	49	144	18.00	–	–	11	–	35	5132
1950–51	NZ	2	2	–	19	32	16.00	–	–	2	1	49	1876
1951	SA	3	4	–	5	7	1.75	–	–	4	1	31	3814
1952	I	4	4	–	104	242	60.50	1	2	4	4	45	3042
1953	A	5	7	2	44	117	23.40	–	–	11	5	42	5016
1953–54	WI	4	6	–	28	72	12.00	–	–	5	1	37	5387
1954	P	4	5	–	31	63	12.60	–	–	6	1	26	3176
1954–55	A	4	7	1	37	102	17.00	–	–	13	–	30	3477
1954–55	NZ	2	2	–	0	0	0.00	–	–	3	1	15	1521
1955	SA	3	5	–	36	82	16.40	–	–	9	1	41	3391
1956	A	5	7	1	47	115	19.16	–	–	7	2	42	5400
1956–57	SA	5	10	–	62	164	16.40	–	1	18	2	14	6051
1957	WI	5	6	2	82	201	50.25	–	1	14	1	25	5567
1958	NZ	5	5	–	12	28	5.60	–	–	7	–	17	4212
1958–59	A	3	6	–	11	27	4.50	–	–	5	1	8	2700
1959	I	2	2	–	73	73	36.50	–	1	3	1	5	2143
	A	31	53	9	50	783	17.79	–	1	64	12	256	33526
	SA	19	30	2	74	511	18.25	–	2	46	13	139	24506
	WI	16	25	2	104	625	27.17	1	2	28	9	97	19182
	NZ	14	14	1	27	142	10.92	–	–	22	6	125	12873
	I	7	6	–	104	315	52.50	1	3	7	5	51	5949
	P	4	5	–	31	63	12.60	–	–	6	1	26	3176
Home		54	71	9	104	1610	25.96	2	7	94	34	418	59060
Overseas		37	62	5	62	829	14.54	–	1	79	12	276	40152
Totals		91	133	14	104	2439	20.49	2	8	173	46	694	99212

FAGG, Arthur Edward

Kent (1932 to 1957)

TOUR A 1936–37
Born Chartham, Kent 18 Jun 1915
Died Tunbridge Wells, Kent 13 Sep 1977

A consistent scorer for Kent, Arthur Fagg was a very dependable opening batsman whose opportunities at Test level were considerably reduced by illness and the Second World War. He had scarcely recovered from the bout of rheumatic fever that prematurely ended his only tour and caused his absence throughout the 1937 season when hostilities deprived him of his prime years. An attractive strokemaker, he was a particularly adept hooker of fast bowling. Originally a wicket-keeper, he was a capable slip-catcher and a very occasional right-arm medium-pace change bowler. From 1959 until his death he umpired county cricket and stood in 18 Tests. At the Edgbaston Test of 1973 he refused to take the field for the first over of the third day because of dissent shown by Kanhai, the West Indies captain, when he did not uphold an appeal against Boycott for a catch at the wicket on the previous afternoon. [*Illus. p.* 167]

NOTABLE FEATS

- Exceeded 1000 runs in a season 13 times, including 2000 on 5 occasions. In July 1938 he scored 1016 runs (avge 72.57).
- Only batsman to score double centuries in both innings of a first-class match: 244 (300 min) and 202* (170 min) for Kent v Essex at Colchester in 1938. His match aggregate of 446 is the highest ever scored in England and has been exceeded only by Hanif Mohammad and D.G. Bradman. In the 2nd inns he shared a Kent record 1st-wkt stand of 283 with P.R. Sunnucks.
- Scored 5 fifties in successive first-class innings between 1939 and 1946: 138 (1939), 131 (1945), 86, 75 and 109 (1946).

						Batting 1st			Batting 2nd			
Ref	Series	V	T	Venue	Result	No	R	HO	No	R	HO	Ct
253/222	1936	I	2	Manchester	D	2	39	lbw	–	–	–	–
254/223			3	Oval	W-9w	2	8	c	2	22	c	2
255/224	1936–37	A	1	Brisbane[2]	W-322	3	4	c	3	27	st	2
256/225			2	Sydney	W-I & 22	1	11	c	–	–	–	–
273/242	1939	WI	2	Manchester	D	2	7	b	2	32	b	1

Career	M	I	NO	HS	R	Avge	100	50	Ct	St	Balls	R	W	Avge	BB	5w	10w	Rate
Test	5	8	0	39	150	18.75	–	–	5	–	–	–	–	–	–	–	–	–
F/c	435	803	46	269*	27291	36.05	58	128	425	7	72	47	0	–	–	–	–	–

FAIRBROTHER Neil Harvey

Lancashire (1982 to date)

TOURS
NZ 1987–88; P 1987–88;
WI 1987–88 (Lancs)
Born Warrington, Lancashire 9 Sep 1963

Whether it has happened by accident or design, it is appropriate that Neil Fairbrother should have developed into a nimble-footed left-handed middle-order batsman and an outstandingly agile cover fielder like the Australian Test cricketer whose names he was given. Despite an unlucky and traumatic start to his Test career, he has scored so consistently and stylishly for Lancashire that many observers are convinced that he has the ability to establish himself at international level.

Neil Fairbrother

TEST NOTES

- *1092* 2nd inns bowling: 0 to 9 (12 balls).

NOTABLE FEATS

- Has exceeded 1000 runs in each of the last 5 seasons (1984–88).

Ref	Series	V	T	Venue	Result	Batting 1st No	R	HO	Batting 2nd No	R	HO	Ct
1075/634	1987	P	1	Manchester	D	4	0	lbw	–	–	–	1
1086/641	1987–88	P	3	Karachi	D	5	3	c	5	1	c	–
1092/644	1987–88	NZ	2	Auckland	D	5	1	c	–	–	–	–
1093/645			3	Wellington	D	–	–	–	–	–	–	2

Career	M	I	NO	HS	R	Avge	100	50	Ct	St	Balls	R	W	Avge	BB	5w	10w	Rate
Test	4	4	0	3	5	1.25	–	–	3	–	12	9	0	–	–	–	–	–
F/c	140	220	30	164*	7028	36.98	13	43	83	–	542	323	4	80.75	2-91	–	–	135.50

FANE
Frederick Luther

Essex (1895 to 1922)
Oxford University (1896 to 1898)
London County (1901)

TOURS
A 1902–03, 1907–08; SA 1905–06, 1909–10; WI 1901–02; NZ 1902–03; Z 1909–10 (Leveson Gower)
Born Curragh Camp, Ireland
27 Apr 1875
Died Kelvedon Hatch, Brentwood, Essex 27 Nov 1960

Freddie Fane was a stylish opening batsman who, having learned his cricket on plumb pitches at Charterhouse, had a predominantly front-foot technique. He gained blues in his last two years at Oxford before serving Essex for two decades interrupted by the Great War. Although he headed the England averages with 342 runs at 38.00 against googly bowlers on South African matting in 1905–06, he was never selected for a home Test. When A.O. Jones was taken ill in Australia, as tour vice-captain he became the first Essex player to lead his country. He later deputized for Leveson Gower in similar circumstances in South Africa despite not enjoying captaincy – he led Essex for only three seasons (1904–06) during his long career. Confusion with his cousin Francis L. Fane resulted in his reading his own obituary in *Wisden* six years prematurely. Curiously his father had also seen his own notices. [*Illus. pp.* 141, 268, 273]

Ref	Series	V	T	Venue	Result	Batting 1st No	R	HO	Batting 2nd No	R	HO	Ct
88/85	1905–06	SA	1	Johannesburg[1]	L-1w	2	1	c	2	3	b	1
89/86			2	Johannesburg[1]	L-9w	4	8	c	4	65	b	–
90/87			3	Johannesburg[1]	L-243	4	143	c	5	7	c	1
91/88			4	Cape Town	W-4w	4	9	b	4	66	*	–
92/89			5	Cape Town	L-I & 16	4	30	b	4	10	b	–
96/93*	1907–08	A	1	Sydney	L-2w	1	2	c	1	33	c	–
97/94*			2	Melbourne	W-1w	1	13	b	1	50	b	1
98/95*			3	Adelaide	L-245	2	48	ro	2	0	b	–
100/97			5	Sydney	L-49	2	0	b	2	46	b	–
106/103	1909–10	SA	1	Johannesburg[1]	L-19	4	23	c	4	0	lbw	–
107/104			2	Durban[1]	L-95	4	6	c	4	6	c	1
108/105			3	Johannesburg[1]	W-3w	2	39	c	6	17	b	–
109/106			4	Cape Town	L-4w	4	14	c	5	37	c	1
110/107			5	Cape Town	W-9w	4	6	b	–	–	–	1

Career	M	I	NO	HS	R	Avge	100	50	Ct	St	Balls	R	W	Avge	BB	5w	10w	Rate
Test	14	27	1	143	682	26.23	1	3	6	–	–	–	–	–	–	–	–	–
F/c	418	723	44	217	18567	27.34	25	83	194	–	56	49	2	24.50	2-17	–	–	28.00

FARNES, Kenneth

Essex (1930 to 1939)
Cambridge University (1931 to 1933)

Wisden 1939
TOURS
A 1936–37; SA 1938–39; WI 1934–35; NZ 1936–37
Born Leytonstone, Essex 8 Jul 1911
Died Chipping Warden, Oxfordshire 20 Oct 1941

NOTABLE FEATS

- 50 wickets in 13th Test (*269*).
- *233* Became the third England bowler after F. Martin and T. Richardson to take 10 wickets in his first Test v Australia.
- *259* Took 6 for 96 in total of 604 in perfect batting conditions.
- *264* Deprived of a hat-trick by a dropped slip catch.
- Took 100 wickets in a season twice.
- Hat-trick for Essex v Nottinghamshire at Clacton in 1939.
- Contributed 97* to Essex 10th-wkt stand of 149 with T.H. Wade v Somerset at Taunton in 1936.

Ken Farnes was one of the fastest bowlers of all time and the leading amateur opening bowler of the 1930s. A 6ft 5in tall powerfully built right-handed giant, he gained his prodigious pace from a run of just 11 strides. His high delivery arm and excellent wrist action enabled him to extract vast bounce and late movement. He arrived in the Essex side via Romford's Royal Liberty School and Cambridge, where he had gained a blue in each of his three years. Although his appearances were greatly restricted by his teaching engagement at Worksop College, for three seasons he formed a devastating partnership with H.D. Read which was the fastest in England. His Test selection came soon after he had ravaged the powerful Yorkshire batting with an 11-wicket analysis and he celebrated his debut with five Australian wickets in each innings. His 8 for 43 in the 1938 Gents v Players match was the reward for some of the fastest bowling ever seen at Lord's. He was a capable close fielder who seldom took his batting seriously. His early death whilst on flying training as a wartime RAF pilot officer was a particularly tragic loss for English cricket.

Ken Farnes, Hedley Verity and Les Ames follow their captain Walter Hammond on to the field at Nottingham after England's declaration at 658 for 8 during the First Test against the 1938 Australians.

						Batting 1st			Batting 2nd				Bowling 1st			Bowling 2nd		
Ref	Series	V	T	Venue	Result	No	R	HO	No	R	HO	Ct	Balls	R	W	Balls	R	W
233/207	1934	A	1	Nottingham	L-238	10	1	b	10	0	c	–	242	102	5	150	77	5
234/208			2	Lord's	W-I & 38	10	1	b	–	–	–	–	72	43	0	24	6	0
238/212	1934–35	WI	1	Bridgetown	W-4w	–	–	–	1	5	c	–	90	40	4	54	23	1
241/215			4	Kingston	L-I & 161	10	5	b	9	0	c	–	144	72	1	–	–	–
258/227	1936–37	A	4	Adelaide	L-148	11	0	*	11	7	*	–	166	71	3	192	89	2
259/228			5	Melbourne	L-I & 200	11	0	*	11	0	c	1	229	96	6	–	–	–
263/232	1938	A	1	Nottingham	D	–	–	–	–	–	–	–	222	106	4	144	78	0
264/233			2	Lord's	D	11	5	*	–	–	–	–	258	135	3	78	51	0
265/234			4	Leeds	L-5w	10	2	c	10	7	b	–	156	77	4	69	17	1
266/235			5	Oval	W-I & 579	–	–	–	–	–	–	–	78	54	1	73	63	4
267/236	1938–39	SA	1	Johannesburg[1]	D	10	0	b	–	–	–	–	184	87	1	56	17	0
268/237			2	Cape Town	D	10	1	*	–	–	–	–	104	37	0	64	23	1
269/238			3	Durban[2]	W-I & 13	–	–	–	–	–	–	–	104	29	4	226	80	3
270/239			4	Johannesburg[1]	D	9	4	c	–	–	–	–	208	64	2	–	–	–
271/240			5	Durban[2]	D	10	20	b	–	–	–	–	368	108	1	177	74	4

Career	M	I	NO	HS	R	Avge	100	50	Ct	St	Balls	R	W	Avge	BB	5w	10w	Rate
Test	15	17	5	20	58	4.83	–	–	1	–	3932	1719	60	28.65	6-96	3	1	65.53
F/c	168	201	59	97*	1182	8.32	–	2	84	–	28391	14804	690	21.45	8-38	44	8	41.14

K. FARNES – TEST BOWLING SUMMARY

Series	V	M	Balls	R	W	Avge	BB	5w	10w	Rate
1934	A	2	488	228	10	22.80	5-77	2	1	48.80
1934–35	WI	2	288	135	6	22.50	4-40	–	–	48.00
1936–37	A	2	587	256	11	23.27	6-96	1	–	53.56
1938	A	4	1078	581	17	34.17	4-63	–	–	63.41
1938–39	SA	5	1491	519	16	32.43	4-29	–	–	93.18
	A	8	2153	1065	38	28.02	6-96	3	1	56.65
	SA	5	1491	519	16	32.43	4-29	–	–	93.18
	WI	2	288	135	6	22.50	4-40	–	–	48.00
Home		6	1566	809	27	29.96	5-77	2	1	58.00
Overseas		9	2366	910	33	27.57	6-96	1	–	71.69
Totals		15	3932	1719	60	28.65	6-96	3	1	65.53

FARRIMOND William

Lancashire (1924 to 1945)

TOURS SA 1930–31; WI 1934–35
Born Daisy Hill, Lancashire 23 May 1903
Died Westhoughton, Bolton, Lancashire 15 Nov 1979

Although an excellent wicket-keeper and sound batsman Bill Farrimond spent most of his career in the shadow of his Lancashire colleague George Duckworth. No two keepers could have been more dissimilar: while Duckworth was an extrovert showman with a ferocious appeal, his understudy was quiet and unobtrusive – and a better batsman. An immensely reliable technician, he was exceptionally good on the legside. His four excursions into the Test arena occurred when either Duckworth or Ames was injured and while he was not even a regular member of the County team. He was a most loyal servant of Lancashire, declining several offers to qualify for other counties whilst enjoying only two full seasons of Championship cricket (1938–39). [*Illus. pp.* 490, 510]

NOTABLE FEATS

• Made 7 dismissals in an inns (6ct, 1st) for Lancashire v Kent at Manchester in 1930 to equal the English first-class record which stood until 1985 and set the current Lancashire record.

					Batting 1st			Batting 2nd			Fielding 1st				Fielding 2nd			
Ref	Series	V	T Venue	Result	No	R	HO	No	R	HO	Ct	St	Byes	Balls	Ct	St	Byes	Balls
207/188†	1930–31	SA	4 Johannesburg[1]	D	7	28	c	–	–	–	–	–	6	827	–	–	6	576
208/189†			5 Durban[2]	D	6	35	c	3	9	c	1	–	0	784	–	2	8	492
239/213†	1934–35	WI	2 Port-of-Spain	L-217	10	16	c	1	2	c	1	–	2	570	1	–	3	618
243/217†	1935	SA	2 Lord's	L-157	8	13	b	8	13	b	1	–	1	549	1	–	3	730

Career	M	I	NO	HS	R	Avge	100	50	Ct	St	Balls	R	W	Avge	BB	5w	10w	Rate
Test	4	7	0	35	116	16.57	–	–	5	2	–	–	–	–	–	–	–	–
F/c	153	168	45	174	2908	23.64	1	16	255	77	18	16	0	–	–	–	–	–

FENDER
Percy George Herbert

Sussex (1910 to 1913)
Surrey (1914 to 1935)

Wisden 1915
TOURS
A 1920–21; SA 1922–23;
WI 1926–27 (Tennyson)
Born Balham, Surrey 22 Aug 1892
Died Exeter, Devon 15 Jun 1985

Percy Fender was a fine all-round cricketer and a quite exceptional captain. A tall, bespectacled extrovert, he dominated Surrey cricket for more than a decade after the Great War as a forceful, strong-wristed middle-order batsman, canny right-arm medium-pace leg-break bowler, and breathtaking slip fielder. But it was as an inspired captain (1921–31) who skilfully manipulated a moderate attack on shirt-front wickets that he made his lasting impression. He made his debut for Sussex while still at St Paul's School but achieved little before moving to his native Surrey. Thereafter he was seldom far from centre stage, a brilliant showman and, with his elongated features and sweater, a cartoonist's delight. His 35-minute century at Northampton will remain one of the classic cricketing feats. Curiously he was never offered the captaincy of England or selected for an entire home series. He covered several MCC tours for newspapers and had five books published. Until he sustained serious injury he kept goal for the Casuals, Corinthians and Fulham. He remained involved in his wine business well into old age. Although blind, he was the oldest player to attend the 1977 Centenary Test in Melbourne and became the oldest living Test cricketer.

NOTABLE FEATS

- Exceeded 1000 runs in a season 9 times, took 100 wickets 7 times and did the 'double' on 6 occasions.
- Scored the fastest first-class 100 in 35 min (since equalled in farcical circumstances) for Surrey v Northamptonshire at Northampton in 1920. His 6th-wkt partnership with H.A. Peach of 171* in 42 min (244 runs/hr) was the fastest on record lasting over 30 min.
- First to complete 'treble' of 1000 runs, 100 wickets and 50 catches in a first-class season (1921).
- Two hat-tricks for Surrey at The Oval: v Somerset in 1914 and v Gloucestershire in 1924.
- Took 7 wickets in 19 balls for Surrey v Middlesex at Lord's in 1927 (spell included 4 in 5, 5 in 7 and 6 in 12).
- Scored 6 runs off one ball (all run) for Surrey v Warwickshire at The Oval in 1914.

Percy Fender

						Batting 1st			Batting 2nd				Bowling 1st			Bowling 2nd		
Ref	Series	V	T	Venue	Result	No	R	HO	No	R	HO	Ct	Balls	R	W	Balls	R	W
137/126	1920–21	A	3	Adelaide	L-119	8	2	b	8	42	c	1	72	52	1	132	105	1
138/127			4	Melbourne	L-8w	8	3	c	7	59	c	–	192	122	5	80	39	0
139/128			5	Sydney	L-9w	8	2	c	9	40	c	2	120	90	5	6	2	0
143/132	1921	A	4	Manchester	D	6	44	*	–	–	–	–	90	30	2	–	–	–
144/133			5	Oval	D	8	0	c	3	6	c	–	114	82	0	–	–	–
148/134	1922–23	SA	1	Johannesburg[1]	L-168	6	0	c	7	9	ro	3	42	17	1	72	64	0
149/135			2	Cape Town	W-1w	7	3	c	6	2	c	2	84	29	4	120	52	1
150/136			3	Durban[2]	D	6	60	c	–	–	–	–	174	72	1	–	–	–
151/137			4	Johannesburg[1]	D	6	44	c	6	9	b	1	120	78	2	102	60	0
152/138			5	Durban[2]	W-109	6	1	b	8	0	b	3	66	25	1	66	21	0
153/139	1924	SA	1	Birmingham	W-I & 18	6	36	c	–	–	–	–	–	–	–	102	56	0
154/140			2	Lord's	W-I & 18	–	–	–	–	–	–	1	54	45	1	84	25	1
181/167	1929	SA	1	Birmingham	D	7	6	c	4	12	c	1	192	64	2	94	55	1

Career	M	I	NO	HS	R	Avge	100	50	Ct	St	Balls	R	W	Avge	BB	5w	10w	Rate
Test	13	21	1	60	380	19.00	–	2	14	–	2178	1185	29	40.86	5-90	2	–	75.10
F/c	557	783	69	185	19034	26.65	21	102	600	–	95456	47458	1894	25.05	8-24	100	16	50.39

FERRIS, John James

NSW (1886–87 to 1897–98)
Gloucestershire (1892 to 1895)
South Australia (1895–96)
Australia (1886–87 to 1890)

Wisden 1889
TOURS
SA 1891–92; Australia to E 1888, 1890
Born Sydney, Australia 21 May 1867
Died Addington, Johannesburg, South Africa 17 Nov 1900

A left-hander, 'J.J.' Ferris was one of five cricketers who have played for both England and Australia. As a bowler he could vary his pace from medium to slow and maintain an accurate length and line. He formed a devastatingly successful Australian opening partnership with C.T.B. Turner, the pair operating unchanged to celebrate their joint Test debuts by dismissing England for 45. A tail-end batsman for most of his career, he was promoted in the order by Gloucestershire and responded by compiling 1056 runs in 1893. Having settled in England he joined W.W. Read's team to South Africa and claimed the astonishing haul of 235 wickets in all matches. Playing in that mission's lone Test, he celebrated his only appearance for England with a match analysis of 13 for 91. He died of enteric fever while serving with the Imperial Light Horse in the Boer War. [*Illus. p.* 201].

NOTABLE FEATS

- *25* Bowled unchanged with C.T.B. Turner to dismiss England for 45 – still their lowest total in all Test cricket.
- Took 100 wickets on each of his tours of England: 199 in 1888 and 186 in 1890.
- Bowled unchanged throughout both innings with C.T.B. Turner for the Australians v Middlesex at Lord's and v an England XI at Stoke-on-Trent in 1888.
- Twice carried his bat through a completed innings in 1892: for Gentlemen v Players at Scarborough and for Gloucestershire v Sussex at Bristol.

						Batting 1st			Batting 2nd				Bowling 1st			Bowling 2nd		
Ref	Series	V	T	Venue	Result	No	R	HO	No	R	HO	Ct	Balls	R	W	Balls	R	W
For Australia																		
25/25	1886–87	E	1	Sydney	L-13	11	1	c	11	0	*	–	71	27	4	244	76	5
26/26			2	Sydney	L-71	10	1	b	10	2	ro	1	180	71	5	240	69	4
27/27	1887–88	E		Sydney	L-126	11	0	c	11	5	c	–	188	60	4	64	43	2
28/28	1888	E	1	Lord's	W-61	11	14	c	9	20	*	1	84	19	3	92	26	5
29/29			2	Oval	L-I & 137	11	13	*	6	16	ro	–	142	73	1	–	–	–
30/30			3	Manchester	L-I & 21	11	0	*	10	3	c	–	160	49	2	–	–	–
33/31	1890	E	1	Lord's	L-7w	9	8	b	8	8	lbw	2	200	55	2	125	42	2
34/32			2	Oval	L-2w	8	6	c	3	1	b	–	125	25	4	115	49	5
For England																		
38/38	1891–92	SA		Cape Town	W-I & 189	9	16	ro	–	–	–	–	147	54	6	125	37	7

Career	M	I	NO	HS	R	Avge	100	50	Ct	Balls	R	W	Avge	BB	5w	10w	Rate
Test (E)	1	1	0	16	16	16.00	–	–	–	272	91	13	7.00	7-37	2	1	20.92
Test (A)	8	16	4	20*	98	8.16	–	–	4	2030	684	48	14.25	5-26	4	–	42.29
Test Combined	9	17	4	20*	114	8.76	–	–	4	2302	775	61	12.70	7-37	6	–	137.73
F/c	198	328	56	106	4264	15.67	1	15	90	38396	14260	812	17.54	8-41	63	11	47.28

FIELDER, Arthur

Kent (1900 to 1914)

Wisden 1907
TOURS A 1903–04, 1907–08
Born Plaxtol, Tonbridge, Kent 19 Jul 1877
Died Lambeth, London 30 Aug 1949

Arthur Fielder was an exceptionally strong right-arm fast bowler who spearheaded the Kent attack from the turn of the century up to the Great War. His immense stamina enabled him to maintain his pace for extremely long spells without obvious signs of weariness. In modern terms, his method of attack was to explore the 'corridor of uncertainty' outside the off stump with late outswingers and break-backs. He was fortunate in having a top-class wicket-keeper and slip cordon which allowed few offerings to escape, a combination which made a major contribution to Kent's first four Championships (1906–09–10–13). Although very much a tail-end batsman, he shared in a (then) world record last-wicket partnership and featured in an epic one-wicket victory against Australia.

NOTABLE FEATS

- *97* Shared match-winning 10th-wkt stand of 39* with S.F. Barnes.
- Exceeded 100 wickets in a season 5 times.
- Took 10 for 90 for Players v Gentlemen in 1906 – the only instance of this feat in matches between these sides at Lord's.
- Scored 112* for Kent v Worcestershire at Stourbridge in 1909 – the first instance in England of a number 11 making 100 – and shared in a 10th-wkt stand of 235 with F.E. Woolley which remains the English first-class record.

The MCC team to Australia, 1907–08: standing *R.A. Young, E.G. Hayes, A. Fielder, C. Blythe, J. Humphries, J.B. Hobbs;* seated *J.N. Crawford, L.C. Braund, A.O. Jones (capt), F.L. Fane, K.L. Hutchings, W. Rhodes;* in front *S.F. Barnes, J. Hardstaff sr, Col P. Trevor (manager), G. Gunn.*

					Batting 1st			Batting 2nd				Bowling 1st			Bowling 2nd		
Ref	Series	V	T	Venue	Result	No	R	HO	No	R	HO	Ct	Balls	R	W	Balls	R	W
79/76	1903–04	A	2	Melbourne	W-185	11	1	b	10	4	c	2	–	–	–	–	–	–
80/77			3	Adelaide	L-216	11	6	b	11	14	*	–	42	33	0	150	51	1
96/93	1907–08	A	1	Sydney	L-2w	11	1	*	11	6	lbw	–	182	82	6	165	88	3
97/94			2	Melbourne	W-1w	11	6	*	11	18	*	–	167	77	2	162	74	1
98/95			3	Adelaide	L-245	11	0	*	11	1	c	–	167	80	4	138	81	1
99/96			4	Melbourne	L-308	11	1	st	11	20	b	2	132	54	4	186	91	4

Career	M	I	NO	HS	R	Avge	100	50	Ct	St	Balls	R	W	Avge	BB	5w	10w	Rate
Test	6	12	5	20	78	11.14	–	–	4	–	1491	711	26	27.34	6-82	1	–	57.34
F/c	287	380	175	112*	2320	11.31	1	2	119	–	51791	26852	1277	21.02	10-90	97	28	40.69

FISHLOCK
Laurence Barnard

Surrey (1931 to 1952)

Wisden 1947
TOURS
A 1936–37, 1946–47;
I/SL 1950–51 (Cwlth)
Born Battersea, London 2 Jan 1907
Died London 26 Jun 1986

An attacking left-handed opening batsman, Laurie Fishlock was one of many cricketers whose careers were crucially interrupted by the Second World War. He also had the gross misfortune to sustain hand fractures during each of his antipodean tours. A mainstay of the Surrey side he played very straight, could drive off either foot and, like most left-handers, was very strong off his legs. Of medium height (5ft 9in) and stockily built, he remained a superb outfielder to the end of his career and occasionally bowled slow left-arm spin. Gaining a regular place in the Surrey team four seasons after his debut, he had to wait another three years before he was promoted to open. He was Surrey's first left-handed batsman of any stature since the 1870s and his maiden hundred in 1935 was the first by a left-hander for them in Championship matches. Although 39 when county cricket restarted in 1946, he continued to score consistently until his retirement after Surrey had gained the first of their seven successive titles. A fine outside-left, he gained an England amateur football cap before turning professional and appearing for Crystal Palace, Millwall, Aldershot, Southampton and Gillingham. He became a much respected coach at St Dunstan's College, Catford.

NOTABLE FEATS

- Exceeded 1000 runs in a season 12 times (plus once on tour), including 2000 on 6 occasions.
- Scored 100 in each inns of a first-class match 4 times (all for Surrey).
- Scored 3 hundreds in successive innings for Surrey in 1937.
- Carried his bat for 81* in Surrey's total of 141 v Australians at The Oval in 1948.

Laurie Fishlock

						Batting 1st			Batting 2nd			
Ref	Series	V	T	Venue	Result	No	R	HO	No	R	HO	Ct
253/222	1936	I	2	Manchester	D	5	6	b	–	–	–	–
254/223			3	Oval	W-9w	6	19	*	–	–	–	–
278/246	1946	I	3	Oval	D	3	8	c	–	–	–	–
283/251	1946–47	A	5	Sydney	L-5w	4	14	b	1	0	lbw	1

Career	M	I	NO	HS	R	Avge	100	50	Ct	St	Balls	R	W	Avge	BB	5w	10w	Rate
Test	4	5	1	19*	47	11.75	–	–	1	–	–	–	–	–	–	–	–	–
F/c	417	699	54	253	25376	39.34	56	135	216	–	859	504	11	45.81	4-62	–	–	78.09

FLAVELL John Alfred

Worcestershire (1949 to 1967)

Wisden 1965
TOURS
WI 1965–66 (Worcs);
Z 1964–65 (Worcs)
Born Wall Heath, Staffordshire
15 May 1929

NOTABLE FEATS

- Took 100 wickets in a season 8 times.
- Three hat-tricks for Worcestershire: v Kent at Kidderminster 1951, v Cambridge U at Fenner's 1953, and v Lancashire (all lbw) at Manchester 1963.

Jack Flavell was a russet-haired right-arm fast bowler who contributed over 100 wickets to each of Worcestershire's first two Championships but achieved little during his few excursions into Test cricket. A little above average height (5ft 10½in), muscular and determined, he was initially one of the quickest bowlers on the county scene. His control was rather erratic until he sacrificed a little pace and became far more effective. Immense stamina and a wholehearted approach enabled him to overcome several injuries, his unstinting efforts producing some dramatic bursts of wicket-taking, notably three hat-tricks and a trio of nine-wicket analyses. He was a left-handed tail-end batsman of no great ambition.

Jack Flavell

						Batting 1st			Batting 2nd				Bowling 1st			Bowling 2nd		
Ref	Series	V	T	Venue	Result	No	R	HO	No	R	HO	Ct	Balls	R	W	Balls	R	W
510/372	1961	A	4	Manchester	L-54	11	0	*	11	0	*	–	132	61	1	178	65	2
511/373			5	Oval	D	11	14	c	–	–	–	–	186	105	2	–	–	–
561/405	1964	A	1	Nottingham	D	–	–	–	9	7	c	–	96	28	1	26	11	1
563/407			3	Leeds	L-7w	11	5	c	11	5	c	–	174	97	0	–	–	–

Career	M	I	NO	HS	R	Avge	100	50	Ct	St	Balls	R	W	Avge	BB	5w	10w	Rate
Test	4	6	2	14	31	7.75	–	–	–	–	792	367	7	52.42	2-65	–	–	113.14
F/c	401	453	141	54	2032	6.51	–	1	128	–	72676	32847	1529	21.48	9-30	86	15	47.53

FLETCHER
Keith William Robert
OBE

Essex (1962 to 1988)

Wisden 1974
TOURS
A 1970–71, 1974–75, 1976–77; WI 1964–65 (Cav), 1973–74; NZ 1970–71, 1974–75; I 1967–68 (Int XI), 1972–73, 1976–77, 1981–82; P 1966–67 (MCC U-25), 1967–68 (Int XI), 1968–69, 1972–73; SL 1967–68 (Int XI), 1968–69, 1969–70, 1972–73, 1976–77, 1981–82
Born Worcester 20 May 1944

For 27 seasons Keith Fletcher was a vital member of an ever-improving Essex team. An exciting and talented middle-order batsman, he developed into a highly astute captain. Dubbed 'The Gnome' because he appeared smaller than he claimed (5ft 9in), he was a fleet-footed player of spin and could hit the ball with amazing power off either foot. Although he possessed a complete repertoire of strokes and was capable of taking an attack apart, he inexplicably allowed himself to be tied down by ordinary bowling on occasions. His sound technique and inexhaustible patience eventually stood him in good stead in a struggling England batting line-up; after waiting 20 matches for his first hundred he added six more in his next 25. He captained Essex (1974–85, 1988) with quiet efficiency and great tactical acumen, leading them to their first flurry of titles (three Championships and five one-day trophies). Recalled to captain England in India and Sri Lanka in 1981–82, he was then summarily and inexcusably dismissed. He was a fine all-purpose fielder and an occasional leg-break bowler whose control was erratic but who could turn the ball considerably.

NOTABLE FEATS

- 1000 runs in 23rd Test (*721*) (38 inns); 2000 runs in 35th Test (*740*) (59 inns); 3000 runs in 54th Test (*913*) (88 inns).
- *705* Shared record E v I 9th-wkt stand of 83 with N. Gifford.
- *707* Shared stand of 254 with A.W. Greig which remains England's highest for the 5th wkt in all Tests.
- *723* His 178 in 379 min averted England's first defeat by NZ.
- *744* His 100 in 458 min remains the slowest in English first-class cricket.
- *758* Shared record E v NZ 4th-wkt stand of 266 with M.H. Denness.
- *917* Only England captain to win the toss 5 times in a 6-Test series. First England captain to insert opposition in India.
- Exceeded 1000 runs in a season 20 times.
- Holds Essex first-class career records for most runs (29,434) and most catches in the field (519).

Keith Fletcher during his match-saving 178 at Lord's against the 1973 New Zealanders; Ken Wadsworth behind the stumps.

						Batting 1st			Batting 2nd				Bowling 1st			Bowling 2nd		
Ref	Series	V	T	Venue	Result	No	R	HO	No	R	HO	Ct	Balls	R	W	Balls	R	W
640/448	1968	A	4	Leeds	D	6	0	c	6	23	*	–	–	–	–	–	–	–
647/450	1968–69	P	1	Lahore[2]	D	5	20	c	5	83	b	2	–	–	–	48	31	0
648/451			2	Dacca	D	4	16	c	–	–	–	–	–	–	–	–	–	–
649/452			3	Karachi	D	5	38	b	–	–	–	–	–	–	–	–	–	–
656/456	1969	NZ	1	Lord's	W-230	4	9	b	4	7	b	1	–	–	–	–	–	–
657/457			2	Nottingham	D	4	31	b	–	–	–	1	18	14	0	–	–	–
674/459	1970–71	A	1	Brisbane[2]	D	6	34	c	–	–	–	–	–	–	–	72	48	1
675/460			2	Perth	D	5	22	b	4	0	lbw	–	8	4	0	32	18	0
676/461			4	Sydney	W-299	4	23	c	4	8	c	2	–	–	–	8	6	0
678/463			6	Adelaide	D	3	80	b	3	5	b	–	–	–	–	32	16	0
679/464			7	Sydney	W-62	3	33	c	3	20	c	1	–	–	–	8	9	0
685/465	1970–71	NZ	1	Christchurch	W-8w	3	4	b	3	2	c	3	–	–	–	–	–	–
691/471	1971	I	2	Manchester	D	4	1	lbw	4	28	*	–	–	–	–	–	–	–
692/472			3	Oval	L-4w	4	1	c	4	0	c	1	–	–	–	–	–	–
701/476	1972	A	4	Leeds	W-9w	4	5	lbw	–	–	–	–	–	–	–	–	–	–
703/478	1972–73	I	1	Delhi	W-6w	3	2	b	3	0	c	1	–	–	–	–	–	–
704/479			2	Calcutta	L-28	3	16	c	3	5	lbw	3	–	–	–	–	–	–
705/480			3	Madras[1]	L-4w	5	97	*	5	21	c	–	–	–	–	–	–	–
706/481			4	Kanpur	D	5	58	c	–	–	–	1	–	–	–	–	–	–
707/482			5	Bombay[2]	D	5	113	lbw	–	–	–	1	–	–	–	–	–	–
719/483	1972–73	P	1	Lahore[2]	D	5	55	c	5	12	c	–	–	–	–	–	–	–
720/484			2	Hyderabad	D	3	78	c	3	21	c	1	18	22	0	–	–	–
721/485			3	Karachi	D	3	54	c	3	1	*	1	–	–	–	–	–	–

Ref	Series	V	T	Venue	Result	Batting 1st			Batting 2nd			Ct	Bowling 1st			Bowling 2nd		
						No	R	HO	No	R	HO		Balls	R	W	Balls	R	W
722/486	1973	NZ	1	Nottingham	W-38	5	17	lbw	5	8	b	–	–	–	–	–	–	–
723/487			2	Lord's	D	4	25	c	4	178	c	1	–	–	–	–	–	–
724/488			3	Leeds	W-I & 1	4	81	c	–	–	–	1	–	–	–	–	–	–
725/489	1973	WI	1	Oval	L-158	5	11	c	5	5	c	–	–	–	–	–	–	–
726/490			2	Birmingham	D	7	52	c	4	44	*	–	–	–	–	–	–	–
727/491			3	Lord's	L-I & 226	5	68	c	6	86	*	–	–	–	–	–	–	–
731/492	1973–74	WI	1	Port-of-Spain	L-7w	5	4	b	5	0	c	1	–	–	–	5	5	0
733/494			3	Bridgetown	D	5	37	c	5	129	*	1	–	–	–	–	–	–
734/495			4	Georgetown	D	4	41	c	–	–	–	–	–	–	–	–	–	–
735/496			5	Port-of-Spain	W-26	4	6	c	4	45	b	4	–	–	–	–	–	–
739/497	1974	I	1	Manchester	W-113	5	123	*	–	–	–	–	–	–	–	–	–	–
740/498			2	Lord's	W-I & 285	5	15	c	–	–	–	1	–	–	–	–	–	–
741/499			3	Birmingham	W-I & 78	4	51	*	–	–	–	–	–	–	–	–	–	–
742/500	1974	P	1	Leeds	D	5	11	lbw	5	67	*	2	–	–	–	–	–	–
743/501			2	Lord's	D	5	8	lbw	–	–	–	–	–	–	–	–	–	–
744/502			3	Oval	D	6	122	ro	–	–	–	–	–	–	–	–	–	–
750/503	1974–75	A	1	Brisbane[2]	L-166	5	17	b	5	19	c	2	–	–	–	–	–	–
751/504			2	Perth	L-9w	5	4	c	5	0	c	1	–	–	–	–	–	–
753/506			4	Sydney	L-171	5	24	c	5	11	c	–	–	–	–	–	–	–
754/507			5	Adelaide	L-163	5	40	c	5	63	lbw	–	–	–	–	–	–	–
755/508			6	Melbourne	W-I & 4	5	146	c	–	–	–	–	–	–	–	–	–	–
758/509	1974–75	NZ	1	Auckland	W-I & 83	5	216	c	–	–	–	5	–	–	–	–	–	–
759/510			2	Christchurch	D	–	–	–	–	–	–	–	–	–	–	–	–	–
760/511	1975	A	1	Birmingham	L-I & 85	3	6	c	3	51	c	2	–	–	–	–	–	–
762/513			3	Leeds	D	5	8	c	4	14	c	–	–	–	–	–	–	–
788/520	1976–77	I	1	Delhi	W-I & 25	5	8	b	–	–	–	1	–	–	–	–	–	–
791/523			4	Bangalore	L-140	3	10	c	3	1	c	1	–	–	–	–	–	–
792/524			5	Bombay[3]	D	4	14	c	4	58	*	2	–	–	–	–	–	–
803/525	1976–77	A		Melbourne	L-45	6	4	c	5	1	c	2	–	–	–	–	–	–
912/573*	1981–82	I	1	Bombay[3]	L-138	5	15	lbw	5	3	lbw	1	–	–	–	–	–	–
913/574*			2	Bangalore	D	6	25	c	5	12	*	1	–	–	–	–	–	–
914/575*			3	Delhi	D	5	51	b	–	–	–	1	–	–	–	–	–	–
915/576*			4	Calcutta	D	5	69	lbw	6	60	*	1	–	–	–	18	6	1
916/577*			5	Madras[1]	D	3	3	b	–	–	–	–	–	–	–	6	9	0
917/578*			6	Kanpur	D	3	14	b	–	–	–	1	12	5	0	–	–	–
921/579*	1981–82	SL		Colombo SO	W-7w	5	45	c	5	0	*	3	–	–	–	–	–	–

Career	M	I	NO	HS	R	Avge	100	50	Ct	St	Balls	R	W	Avge	BB	5w	10w	Rate
Test	59	96	14	216	3272	39.90	7	19	54	–	285	193	2	96.50	1-6	–	–	142.50
F/c	730	1167	170	228*	37665	37.77	63	222	644	–	2980	2296	51	45.01	5-41	1	–	58.43

K. W. R. FLETCHER – TEST BATTING SUMMARY

Series	V	M	I	NO	HS	R	Avge	100	50
1968	A	1	2	1	23*	23	23.00	–	–
1968–69	P	3	4	–	83	157	39.25	–	1
1969	NZ	2	3	–	31	47	15.66	–	–
1970–71	A	5	9	–	80	225	25.00	–	1
1970–71	NZ	1	2	–	4	6	3.00	–	–
1971	I	2	4	1	28*	30	10.00	–	–
1972	A	1	1	–	5	5	5.00	–	–
1972–73	I	5	8	1	113	312	44.57	1	2
1972–73	P	3	6	1	78	221	44.20	–	3
1973	NZ	3	5	–	178	309	61.80	1	1
1973	WI	3	6	2	86*	266	66.50	–	3
1973–74	WI	4	7	1	129*	262	43.66	1	–
1974	I	3	3	2	123*	189	189.00	1	1
1974	P	3	4	1	122	208	69.33	1	1
1974–75	A	5	9	–	146	324	36.00	1	1
1974–75	NZ	2	1	–	216	216	216.00	1	–

Series	V	M	I	NO	HS	R	Avge	100	50
1975	A	2	4	–	51	79	19.75	–	1
1976–77	I	3	5	1	58*	91	22.75	–	1
1976–77	A	1	2	–	4	5	2.50	–	–
1981–82	I	6	9	2	69	252	36.00	–	3
1981–82	SL	1	2	1	45	45	45.00	–	–
	A	15	27	1	146	661	25.42	1	3
	WI	7	13	3	129*	528	52.80	1	3
	NZ	8	11	–	216	578	52.54	2	1
	I	19	29	7	123*	874	39.72	2	7
	P	9	14	2	122	586	48.83	1	5
	SL	1	2	1	45	45	45.00	–	–
Home		20	32	7	178	1156	46.24	3	7
Overseas		39	64	7	216	2116	37.12	4	12
Totals		59	96	14	216	3272	39.90	7	19

FLOWERS, Wilfred

Nottinghamshire (1877 to 1896)

TOURS A 1884–85, 1886–87
Born Calverton, Nottinghamshire
7 Dec 1856
Died Carlton, Nottingham 1 Nov 1926

Wilfred Flowers was a popular right-handed all-rounder who served Notts for 20 seasons whilst also being engaged on the MCC staff (1878–99). Stockily built and of medium height (5ft 9in), he was the first professional to do the 'double' (1883). A middle-order batsman with a sound defence and a resounding off-drive, he bowled off-breaks with pin-point accuracy and deceptive flight. He umpired first-class matches (1907–12) until his sight began to fail. Formerly a framework knitter, he died suddenly whilst working as a lacehand.

Wilfred Flowers

NOTABLE FEATS

- Exceeded 100 runs in a season twice and took 100 wickets twice, completing the 'double' in 1883.
- Two hat-tricks: for Nottinghamshire v Kent at Maidstone in 1888 and for MCC v Oxford U at The Parks in 1892.
- Scored 122 and took 14 for 80 for MCC v Cambridge U at Lord's in 1884 in a 12-a-side match.
- Scored 107 for Nottinghamshire v Sussex at Nottingham in 1896 in his final first-class innings.

					Batting 1st			Batting 2nd				Bowling 1st			Bowling 2nd		
Ref	Series	V	T	Venue	Result	No	R	HO	No	R	HO	Ct	Balls	R	W	Balls	R	W
17/17	1884–85	A	1	Adelaide	W-8w	6	15	lbw	2	7	c	–	40	27	0	64	27	0
18/18			2	Melbourne	W-10w	5	5	c	–	–	–	1	116	46	2	44	11	0
19/19			3	Sydney	L-6	7	24	c	7	56	c	–	184	46	5	80	19	0
20/20			4	Sydney	L-8w	7	14	b	7	7	c	–	56	27	1	15	3	0
21/21			5	Melbourne	W-I & 98	7	16	b	–	–	–	–	36	9	0	84	34	3
25/25	1886–87	A	1	Sydney	W-13	10	2	b	10	14	c	–	–	–	–	–	–	–
26/26			2	Sydney	W-71	9	37	c	9	18	b	1	32	9	2	52	17	0
39/39	1893	A	1	Lord's	D	7	35	b	6	4	b	–	55	21	1	–	–	–

Career	M	I	NO	HS	R	Avge	100	50	Ct	St	Balls	R	W	Avge	BB	5w	10w	Rate
Test	8	14	0	56	254	18.14	–	1	2	–	858	296	14	21.14	5-46	1	–	61.28
F/c	442	696	54	173	12891	20.07	9	56	222	–	56875	18887	1188	15.89	8-22	73	15	47.87

FORD Francis Gilbertson Justice

Middlesex (1886 to 1899)
Cambridge University (1887 to 1890)

TOUR A 1894–95
Born Paddington, London 14 Dec 1866
Died Burwash, Sussex 7 Feb 1940

Francis Ford was the youngest of seven brothers, all Reptonians, three of whom represented Cambridge and Middlesex. A left-handed middle-order batsman, slow left-arm bowler and slip fielder, he gained his blue as a freshman; captain in his penultimate (third) year, he led his side to victory by an innings. Tall (6ft 2½in) and extremely lean, he straight-drove exceptionally hard, using his reach to turn good length balls into half volleys. He was a stylish back-foot player of short-pitched bowling, especially adept at cutting, and played several notable innings on treacherous pitches. His accurate bowling, delivered with a classic high action, caused ample problems with its spin and drift. Poor health compelled his early retirement. He won a soccer blue as a goalkeeper. [*Illus. p.* 292]

NOTABLE FEATS

- Exceeded 1000 runs in a season twice.
- Contributed his career-best score of 191 to Cambridge U's 703 for 9 dec v Sussex at Hove in 1890, still the highest second innings total in English first-class cricket.
- Scored 100 in 55 min for Middlesex v Philadelphians at Lord's in 1897.

Ref	Series	V	T	Venue	Result	Batting 1st No	R	HO	Batting 2nd No	R	HO	Ct	Bowling 1st Balls	R	W	Bowling 2nd Balls	R	W
42/42	1894–95	A	1	Sydney	W-10	7	30	st	7	48	c	2	66	47	1	–	–	–
43/43			2	Melbourne	W-94	7	9	c	7	24	c	1	–	–	–	36	7	0
44/44			3	Adelaide	L-382	8	21	c	8	14	c	1	48	19	0	36	33	0
45/45			4	Sydney	L-I & 147	7	0	c	7	11	c	–	12	14	0	–	–	–
46/46			5	Melbourne	W-6w	8	11	c	–	–	–	1	12	9	0	–	–	–

Career	M	I	NO	HS	R	Avge	100	50	Ct	St	Balls	R	W	Avge	BB	5w	10w	Rate
Test	5	9	0	48	168	18.66	–	–	5	–	210	129	1	129.00	1-47	–	–	210.00
F/c	168	289	17	191	7359	27.05	14	30	131	–	10223	4757	200	23.78	7-65	8	1	51.11

FOSTER
Frank Rowbotham

Warwickshire (1908 to 1914)

Wisden 1912
TOUR A 1911–12
Born Deritend, Birmingham 31 Jan 1889
Died Northampton 3 May 1958

The highlight of Frank Foster's spectacular but tragically brief career came in 1911 when, at the age of 22, he led Warwickshire to their first Championship and did the 'double'. It was an astonishing achievement, particularly because, prior to the opening match which Surrey won by an innings, he had reacted to a broken engagement by retiring from the game. He led the County up to the Great War, during which a motorcycle accident left him with a disabled foot. Tall (6ft), he was a daring and uninhibited right-handed middle-order batsman, a supple and fast-scoring natural hitter. His left-arm fast-medium inswing bowling from an eight-pace run was delivered with a high effortless action and seemed to gather pace off the pitch. One of the earliest bowlers to employ 'leg theory' tactics, he could also cause his late inswingers to break towards the slips. His new-ball partnership with Sydney Barnes in Australia in 1911–12 was probably the greatest in England's history. Unrelated to the Worcestershire Fosters, his younger brother (A.W.) also played for Warwickshire.

NOTABLE FEATS

- *120* Completed an Ashes-winning series with 32 wickets at 21.62, sharing 66 wickets with S.F. Barnes.
- Exceeded 1000 runs in a season twice, took 100 wickets 4 times and completed the 'double' twice.
- His 305* in 260 min on the 2nd day v Worcestershire at Dudley in 1914 remains the highest score for Warwickshire.
- Reached 50 in 15 min for Warwickshire v Middlesex at Birmingham in 1914.
- Took 9-118 and scored 105 for Warwickshire v Yorkshire at Birmingham in 1911.

Members of the 1911–12 MCC team to Australia, including Frank Foster whose 226 runs and 32 wickets made a notable all-round contribution to the 4–1 victory in the Tests: standing S.P. Kinneir, E.J. Smith, F.E. Woolley, S.F. Barnes, J. Iremonger, R.C. Campbell (not a member of the team), J. Vine, H. Strudwick; seated W. Rhodes, J.W.H.T. Douglas (captain after Warner fell ill), P.F. Warner (captain), F.R. Foster, T. Pawley (manager), J.B. Hobbs, G. Gunn; in front *J.W. Hearne, J.W. Hitch;* inset *C.P. Mead.*

						Batting 1st			Batting 2nd				Bowling 1st			Bowling 2nd		
Ref	**Series**	**V**	**T**	**Venue**	**Result**	**No**	**R**	**HO**	**No**	**R**	**HO**	**Ct**	**Balls**	**R**	**W**	**Balls**	**R**	**W**
116/108	1911–12	A	1	Sydney	L-146	7	56	b	6	21	c	1	174	105	2	189	92	5
117/109			2	Melbourne	W-8w	6	9	c	–	–	–	–	96	52	1	228	91	6
118/110			3	Adelaide	W-7w	6	71	b	–	–	–	–	156	36	5	294	103	1
119/111			4	Melbourne	W-I & 225	5	50	c	–	–	–	1	132	77	4	114	38	3
120/112			5	Sydney	W-70	5	15	st	5	4	b	–	96	55	1	181	43	4
122/113	1912	SA	1	Lord's	W-I & 62	8	11	lbw	–	–	–	2	79	16	5	162	54	3
123/114		A	1	Lord's	D	7	20	c	–	–	–	1	216	42	2	–	–	–
124/115		SA	2	Leeds	W-174	8	30	c	8	0	b	2	96	29	0	138	51	2
126/116		A	2	Manchester	D	7	13	c	–	–	–	–	6	3	0	–	–	–
128/117		SA	3	Oval	W-10w	8	8	st	–	–	–	3	36	15	0	42	19	1
129/118		A	3	Oval	W-244	8	19	b	8	3	*	1	12	5	0	–	–	–

Career	M	I	NO	HS	R	Avge	100	50	Ct	St	Balls	R	W	Avge	BB	5w	10w	Rate
Test	11	15	1	71	330	23.57	–	3	11	–	2447	926	45	20.57	6-91	4	–	54.37
F/c	159	263	17	305*	6548	26.61	7	35	121	–	33296	14879	717	20.75	9-118	53	8	46.43

FOSTER, Neil Alan

Essex (1980 to date)

Wisden 1988
TOURS
A 1986–87, 1987–88; WI 1985–86; NZ 1983–84, 1987–88; I/SL 1984–85; P 1983–84, 1987–88
Born Colchester, Essex 6 May 1962

A right-arm fast-medium bowler and the spearhead of the current Essex attack, Neil Foster has spent most of his brief career overcoming crippling injuries. Spinal problems afflicting him as a teenager required the temporary insertion of a metal support, and recurring knee injuries demanded further surgery in 1988. Tall (6ft 3in) and slender, he has a high, model action which enables him to extract awkward bounce. He is very accurate and can move the ball either way off the seam. His remarkable 11-wicket haul against India at Madras was a match-winning performance achieved in unhelpful conditions against a strong batting side. An improving batsman who excels at lofted straight hitting and has a textbook cover-drive, he has the makings of an all-rounder.

						Batting 1st			Batting 2nd				Bowling 1st			Bowling 2nd		
Ref	**Series**	**V**	**T**	**Venue**	**Result**	**No**	**R**	**HO**	**No**	**R**	**HO**	**Ct**	**Balls**	**R**	**W**	**Balls**	**R**	**W**
959/593	1983	NZ	3	Lord's	W-127	8	10	c	8	3	c	1	96	40	0	72	35	1
975/595	1983–84	NZ	1	Wellington	D	10	10	c	–	–	–	1	144	60	1	222	91	2
977/597			3	Auckland	D	9	18	*	–	–	–	–	180	78	1	–	–	–
979/599	1983–84	P	2	Faisalabad	D	–	–	–	–	–	–	1	180	109	1	30	10	1
980/600			3	Lahore[2]	D	9	6	lbw	8	0	lbw	–	192	67	5	90	44	0
990/602	1984	WI	2	Lord's	L-9w	10	6	c	10	9	*	–	36	13	0	72	69	0
1008/610	1984–85	I	4	Madras[1]	W-9w	6	5	b	–	–	–	–	138	104	6	168	59	5
1009/611			5	Kanpur	D	9	8	c	–	–	–	–	216	123	3	–	–	–
1018/613	1985	A	2	Lord's	L-4w	10	3	c	11	0	c	–	138	83	1	–	–	–
1040/620	1985–86	WI	3	Bridgetown	L-I & 30	10	0	lbw	10	0	c	–	114	76	3	–	–	–
1041/621			4	Port-of-Spain	L-10w	10	0	c	10	14	b	–	144	68	2	17	15	0
1042/622			5	St John's	L-240	11	10	c	11	0	*	–	168	86	2	60	40	0
1048/625	1986	I	3	Birmingham	D	8	17	b	8	0	ro	–	246	93	3	132	48	1
1049/626	1986	NZ	1	Lord's	D	10	8	b	–	–	–	–	150	56	0	18	13	1
1075/634	1987	P	1	Manchester	D	10	8	b	–	–	–	–	90	34	1	–	–	–
1076/635			2	Lord's	D	9	21	b	–	–	–	–	–	–	–	–	–	–
1077/636			3	Leeds	L-I & 18	9	9	c	9	22	b	–	278	107	8	–	–	–
1078/637			4	Birmingham	D	9	29	ro	–	–	–	1	222	107	2	162	59	4
1079/638			5	Oval	D	9	4	c	–	–	–	–	72	32	0	–	–	–
1084/639	1987–88	P	1	Lahore[2]	L-I & 87	9	39	lbw	10	1	c	–	138	58	2	–	–	–
1085/640			2	Faisalabad	D	9	0	c	6	0	c	–	108	42	4	18	4	0
1090/642	1987/88	A		Sydney	D	9	19	c	–	–	–	1	114	27	2	90	27	0
1101/649	1988	WI	4	Leeds	L-10w	10	8	*	10	0	c	1	194	98	3	42	36	0
1102/650			5	Oval	L-8w	10	7	c	5	34	c	–	96	64	5	108	52	1
1103/651	1988	SL		Lord's	W-7w	10	14	*	–	–	–	–	126	51	3	198	98	2

Career	M	I	NO	HS	R	Avge	100	50	Ct	St	Balls	R	W	Avge	BB	5w	10w	Rate
Test	25	37	5	39	342	10.68	–	–	6	–	5079	2376	76	31.26	8-107	5	1	66.82
F/c	146	175	40	74*	2415	17.88	–	5	64	–	28256	13940	578	24.11	8-107	34	6	48.88

Neil Foster

N. A. FOSTER – TEST BOWLING SUMMARY

Series	V	M	Balls	R	W	Avge	BB	5w	10w	Rate
1983	NZ	1	168	75	1	75.00	1-35	–	–	168.00
1983–84	NZ	2	546	229	4	57.25	2-91	–	–	136.50
1983–84	P	2	492	230	7	32.85	5-67	1	–	70.28
1984	WI	1	108	82	0	–	–	–	–	–
1984–85	I	2	522	286	14	20.42	6-104	2	1	37.28
1985	A	1	138	83	1	83.00	1-83	–	–	138.00
1985–86	WI	3	503	285	7	40.71	3-76	–	–	71.85
1986	I	1	378	141	4	35.25	3-93	–	–	94.50
1986	NZ	1	168	69	1	69.00	1-13	–	–	168.00
1987	P	5	824	339	15	22.60	8-107	1	–	54.93
1987–88	P	2	264	104	6	17.33	4-42	–	–	44.00
1987–88	A	1	204	54	2	27.00	2-27	–	–	102.00
1988	WI	2	440	250	9	27.77	5-64	1	–	48.88
1988	SL	1	324	149	5	29.80	3-51	–	–	64.80
	A	2	342	137	3	45.66	2-27	–	–	114.00
	WI	6	1051	617	16	38.56	5-64	1	–	65.68
	NZ	4	882	373	6	62.16	2-91	–	–	147.00
	I	3	900	427	18	23.72	6-104	2	1	50.00
	P	9	1580	673	28	24.03	8-107	2	–	56.42
	SL	1	324	149	5	29.80	3-51	–	–	64.80
Home		13	2548	1188	36	33.00	8-107	2	–	70.77
Overseas		12	2531	1188	40	29.70	6-104	3	1	63.27
Totals		25	5079	2376	76	31.26	8-107	5	1	66.82

NOTABLE FEATS

- 50 wickets in 18th Test (*1078*).
- Took 100 wickets in a season once (105 in 1986).

FOSTER
Reginald Erskine

Oxford University (1897 to 1900)
Worcestershire (1899 to 1912)

Wisden 1901
TOUR A 1903–04
Born Malvern, Worcestershire
16 Apr 1878
Died Kensington, London 13 May 1914

The third and most talented of seven sons of a clergyman who each graced the Malvern and Worcestershire elevens, 'Tip' Foster was a brilliant middle-order batsman, an occasional right-arm fast bowler and an outstanding slip-catcher. Tall and lithe, he was a fast-moving, dynamic and elegant batsman who adopted a square-on stance without decreasing the range and power of his off-side strokes; he was a magnificent cover-driver and also excelled at the late cut. After dominating the Malvern XI, he won his blue as an Oxford freshman and, in 1900, set Oxbridge records for the most runs and hundreds while leading the side to victory in five matches out of nine. Within a fortnight of making the record score in Varsity matches he became the first to score a century in each innings of a Gentlemen v Players contest. He captained Worcestershire in 1901, his only season of regular county cricket, and scored 2128 runs at 50.66. His career was severely restricted by his business interests – he had to decline the captaincy of MCC's 1907–08 tour of Australia – and terminated by diabetes which caused his premature death a few weeks before the Great War. A superb footballer, he played in two Varsity matches and captained England.

'Tip' Foster

NOTABLE FEATS

- *78* His 287 in 419 min was the record Test score until 1929–30 when A. Sandham scored 325. It remains the highest by a player in his first Test, the highest for England in Australia and the record for any Test at Sydney. He was the first to share in 3 hundred partnerships in the same Test innings, and his 10th-wkt stand of 130 in 60 min with W. Rhodes is still the record in E v A Tests. His 214 runs in a day remains England's best v A and the record for either country in Australia. L.G. Rowe (for WI in 1971–72) is the only other batsman to exceed 300 runs in his first Test.
- Exceeded 1000 runs in a season 3 times including 2000 once.
- Scored 930 runs (avge 77.50) with 5 hundreds, including 3 in consecutive innings, for Oxford U in 1900 (both then Oxbridge records), including the then record University match score of 171.
- Scored 100 in each innings of a match 3 times and was the first to do so in a Gentlemen v Players match: 102* and 136 (on debut for the Gentlemen) at Lord's in 1900.
- Scored 100 before lunch on 6 occasions in first-class matches.
- Only man to captain England at both cricket and association football.

TEST NOTES

- *79* Retired hurt with a severe chill after the first day at 221-2.

						Batting 1st			Batting 2nd			
Ref	**Series**	**V**	**T**	**Venue**	**Result**	**No**	**R**	**HO**	**No**	**R**	**HO**	**Ct**
78/75	1903–04	A	1	Sydney	W-5w	5	287	c	4	19	st	2
79/76			2	Melbourne	W-185	4	49	*ri	–	–	–	–
80/77			3	Adelaide	L-216	4	21	c	5	16	b	–
81/78			4	Sydney	W-157	4	19	c	1	27	c	3
82/79			5	Melbourne	L-218	6	18	b	2	30	c	3
93/90*	1907	SA	1	Lord's	D	4	8	st	–	–	–	1
94/91*			2	Leeds	W-53	4	0	b	4	22	lbw	2
95/92*			3	Oval	D	4	51	lbw	4	35	c	2

Career	M	I	NO	HS	R	Avge	100	50	Ct	St	Balls	R	W	Avge	BB	5w	10w	Rate
Test	8	14	1	287	602	46.30	1	1	13	–	–	–	–	–	–	–	–	–
F/c	139	234	17	287	9076	41.82	22	41	179	–	1816	1153	25	46.12	3-54	–	–	72.64

FOTHERGILL Arnold James

Somerset (1882 to 1884)

TOUR SA 1888–89
Born Newcastle upon Tyne, Northumberland 26 Aug 1854
Died Newcastle upon Tyne 1 Aug 1932

Arnold Fothergill was a left-arm medium-fast bowler and a hard-hitting left-handed tail-end batsman who appeared in Somerset's earliest first-class matches. Touring South Africa with Major Warton's team, he ended his career with some useful all-round performances in the first Test matches staged in the Union. A member of the Lord's staff, he made half his first-class appearances for the MCC and also represented his native Northumberland. [*Illus. p.* 51].

						Batting 1st			Batting 2nd				Bowling 1st			Bowling 2nd		
Ref	**Series**	**V**	**T**	**Venue**	**Result**	**No**	**R**	**HO**	**No**	**R**	**HO**	**Ct**	**Balls**	**R**	**W**	**Balls**	**R**	**W**
31/31	1888–89	SA	1	Port Elizabeth	W-8w	11	32	c	–	–	–	–	96	15	1	73	19	4
32/32			2	Cape Town	W-I & 202	11	1	b	–	–	–	–	96	26	2	56	30	1

Career	M	I	NO	HS	R	Avge	100	50	Ct	St	Balls	R	W	Avge	BB	5w	10w	Rate
Test	2	2	0	32	33	16.50	–	–	–	–	321	90	8	11.25	4-19	–	–	40.12
F/c	40	69	9	74	843	14.05	–	1	15	–	5423	2164	119	18.18	6-43	6	1	45.57

FOWLER, Graeme

Lancashire (1979 to date)

TOURS
A 1982–83; WI 1982–83 (Int XI), 1987–88 (Lancs); NZ 1983–84; I/SL 1984–85; P 1983–84
Born Accrington, Lancashire
20 Apr 1957

A dashing left-handed opening batsman, Graeme Fowler's meteoric excursion into Test cricket coincided exactly with the period of Graham Gooch's ban for touring South Africa; few players can have been dropped after scoring 201 and 69 in their last two Tests. Of medium height (5ft 9½in) and slightly built, he is nimble-footed, fast-moving, and strikes the ball hard. A strong off-side repertoire makes for attractive watching although he has always lived dangerously outside his off stump. He is the only batsman to score hundreds in both innings of a first-class match with the aid of a runner (126 and 128* for Lancashire v Warwickshire at Southport in 1982); when he completed his second century his runner waved his bat to acknowledge the crowd's applause and had his hand shaken by a fielder. A handy emergency wicket-keeper and an athletic outfielder, his medium-pace right-arm bowling is not taken seriously.

NOTABLE FEATS

- 1000 runs in 19th Test (*1007*) (34 inns).
- *957* Shared E v NZ 1st-wkt record stand of 223 with C.J. Tavaré – first instance since 1960 of England openers both scoring 100s in the same inns.
- *1008* First instance of 2 double hundreds in an England innings (M.W. Gatting 207).
- Exceeded 1000 runs in a season 7 times.
- Scored 100 in 46 min (in farcical circumstances against non-bowlers) for Lancs v Leics at Manchester in 1983 – including 10 consecutive scoring strokes for six (first-class world record). His 1st-wkt stand of 201 in 43 min with S.J. O'Shaughnessy is the fastest on record lasting over 30 min (280 runs/hr).

TEST NOTES

- *979* Bowled in 2nd inns: 0 for 3 (6 balls).
- *993* Retired hurt when 12* at 21-1 (1st inns); resumed at 83-5.
- *994* Bowled in 2nd inns: 0 for 8 (6 balls).
- *1007* Bowled in 2nd inns: 0 for 0 (6 balls).

						Batting 1st			Batting 2nd			
Ref	Series	V	T	Venue	Result	No	R	HO	No	R	HO	Ct
933/585	1982	P	3	Leeds	W-3w	2	9	b	2	86	c	1
939/587	1982–83	A	2	Brisbane[2]	L-7w	2	7	c	2	83	c	–
940/588			3	Adelaide	L-8w	2	11	c	2	37	c	–
941/589			4	Melbourne	W-3	2	4	c	2	65	b	1
957/591	1983	NZ	1	Oval	W-189	1	1	lbw	1	105	ro	–
958/592			2	Leeds	L-5w	1	9	c	1	19	c	–
976/596	1983–84	NZ	2	Christchurch	L-I & 132	1	4	b	1	10	c	–
977/597			3	Auckland	D	1	0	c	–	–	–	–
979/599	1983–84	P	2	Faisalabad	D	6	57	c	–	–	–	–
980/600			3	Lahore[2]	D	6	58	c	1	19	c	1
989/601	1984	WI	1	Birmingham	L-I & 180	1	0	c	1	7	lbw	–
990/602			2	Lord's	L-9w	1	106	c	1	11	lbw	1
991/603			3	Leeds	L-8w	1	10	lbw	1	50	c	1
992/604			4	Manchester	L-I & 64	1	38	b	1	0	b	–
993/605			5	Oval	L-172	1	31	c	1	7	c	1
994/606	1984	SL		Lord's	D	1	25	c	–	–	–	2
1005/607	1984–85	I	1	Bombay[3]	L-8w	1	28	c	1	55	lbw	–
1006/608			2	Delhi	W-8w	1	5	c	1	29	c	1
1007/609			3	Calcutta	D	1	49	c	–	–	–	1
1008/610			4	Madras[1]	W-9w	1	201	c	1	2	c	–
1009/611			5	Kanpur	D	1	69	c	–	–	–	–

Graeme Fowler at Lord's in 1984.

G. FOWLER – TEST BATTING SUMMARY

Series	V	M	I	NO	HS	R	Avge	100	50
1982	P	1	2	–	86	95	47.50	–	1
1982–83	A	3	6	–	83	207	34.50	–	2
1983	NZ	2	4	–	105	134	33.50	1	–
1983–84	NZ	2	3	–	10	14	4.66	–	–
1983–84	P	2	3	–	58	134	44.66	–	2
1984	WI	5	10	–	106	260	26.00	1	1
1984	SL	1	1	–	25	25	25.00	–	–
1984–85	I	5	8	–	201	438	54.75	1	2
	A	3	6	–	83	207	34.50	–	2
	WI	5	10	–	106	260	26.00	1	1
	NZ	4	7	–	105	148	21.14	1	–
	I	5	8	–	201	438	54.75	1	2
	P	3	5	–	86	229	45.80	–	3
	SL	1	1	–	25	25	25.00	–	–
Home		9	17	–	106	514	30.23	2	2
Overseas		12	20	–	201	793	39.65	1	6
Totals		21	37	–	201	1307	35.32	3	8

Career	M	I	NO	HS	R	Avge	100	50	Ct	St	Balls	R	W	Avge	BB	5w	10w	Rate
Test	21	37	0	201	1307	35.32	3	8	10	–	18	11	0	–	–	–	–	–
F/c	201	337	17	226	11843	37.00	27	60	103	5	232	171	7	24.42	2-34	–	–	33.14

FREEMAN
Alfred Percy

Kent (1914 to 1936)

Wisden 1923
TOURS
A 1922–23, 1924–25, 1928–29;
SA 1927–28; NZ 1922–23
Born Lewisham, Kent 17 May 1888
Died Bearsted, Kent 28 Jan 1965

'Tich' Freeman; Jack Hobbs as umpire

TEST NOTES

• *171* Kept wicket on third day after R.T. Stanyforth was injured.

'Tich' Freeman was 26 when he claimed the first of his 3776 first-class wickets, a total exceeded only by Wilfred Rhodes. One of the finest right-arm leg-break, top-spin and googly bowlers of all time, he was just 5ft 2in high but, although he had correspondingly tiny hands, his wide-fingered grip was strong enough to turn his leg-break sharply. His well-flighted and concealed offerings were delivered with extraordinary accuracy maintained throughout long spells from a five-pace approach. A length bowler, he relied on his opponents' impatience and many of his dismissals were stumped by Les Ames. The only bowler to take 300 wickets in a season (304 in 1928), he exceeded 200 in each of the next seven summers to complete the incredible tally of 2090 wickets in eight seasons. Despite his phenomenally consistent success at county level he achieved only modest returns in Test matches and appeared in just 12 of the 100 matches played by England during his career. After delivering more than 150,000 balls, he was entitled to name his retirement home 'Dunbowlin'.

NOTABLE FEATS

• 50 wickets in 10th Test (*183*).
• *183* Celebrated his recall with 7 wickets in the post-lunch session.
• Exceeded 100 wickets in a season 17 times. His seasons wicket totals of 150 (14 times), 200 (8 times), 250 (6 times) and 300 (once) are all first-class records. He was the last bowler to take 250 wickets in a season (298 in 1933). Holds record for the earliest date to take 200 wickets: 27 July 1928.
• Holds Championship career records for most wickets (3151) and most instances of 10 or more wickets in a match (123); his 252 wickets (1933) remains the record.
• Holds Kent career records for most wickets (3340) and most instances of 100 wickets in a season (17).
• Took 15 or more wickets in a first-class match 9 times (world record), all for Kent. He remains alone in taking 17 wickets in a first-class match twice: 17 for 67 v Sussex at Hove in 1922 and 17 for 92 v Warwickshire at Folkestone in 1932.
• Took all 10 wickets on 3 occasions (world first-class record), all for Kent: v Lancs at Maidstone in 1929, v Essex at Southend in 1930, and v Lancs at Manchester in 1931.
• Three hat-tricks: for Kent v Middlesex at Canterbury in 1920 and v Surrey at Blackheath in 1934; and for MCC v South Australia at Adelaide in 1922–23.
• Holds first-class records for most runs conceded (5489 in 1928) and most balls bowled (12,234 in 1933) in a season.
• Conceded the most runs in a first-class match in England: 331 from 68 overs (6 for 199 and 2 for 132) for Kent v MCC at Folkestone in 1934.

						Batting 1st			Batting 2nd				Bowling 1st			Bowling 2nd		
Ref	Series	V	T	Venue	Result	No	R	HO	No	R	HO	Ct	Balls	R	W	Balls	R	W
158/144	1924–25	A	1	Sydney	L-193	10	0	b	10	50	*	1	392	124	2	296	134	3
160/146			3	Adelaide	L-11	11	6	*	10	24	c	–	144	107	1	136	94	2
169/155	1927–28	SA	2	Cape Town	W-87	11	7	st	11	0	*	–	174	58	4	132	66	3
170/156			3	Durban[2]	D	11	3	b	–	–	–	–	99	44	1	198	122	3
171/157			4	Johannesburg[1]	L-4w	11	9	*	11	4	lbw	–	18	18	1	78	34	1
172/158			5	Durban[2]	L-8w	11	0	*	11	1	c	1	96	57	1	–	–	–
173/159	1928	WI	1	Lord's	W-I & 58	11	1	b	–	–	–	–	111	40	2	127	37	4
174/160			2	Manchester	W-I & 30	11	0	lbw	–	–	–	–	202	54	5	108	39	5
175/161			3	Oval	W-I & 71	11	19	c	–	–	–	1	162	85	2	130	47	4
183/169	1929	SA	3	Leeds	W-5w	11	15	b	–	–	–	–	195	115	7	210	92	3
184/170			4	Manchester	W-I & 32	–	–	–	–	–	–	–	192	71	7	238	100	5
185/171			5	Oval	D	10	15	c	–	–	–	1	294	169	0	–	–	–

Career	M	I	NO	HS	R	Avge	100	50	Ct	St	Balls	R	W	Avge	BB	5w	10w	Rate
Test	12	16	5	50*	154	14.00	–	1	4	–	3732	1707	66	25.86	7-71	5	3	56.54
F/c	592	716	194	66	4961	9.50	–	4	238	1	154414	69577	3776	18.42	10-53	386	140	40.89

A. P. FREEMAN – TEST BOWLING SUMMARY

Series	V	M	Balls	R	W	Avge	BB	5w	10w	Rate
1924–25	A	2	968	459	8	57.37	3-134	–	–	121.00
1927–28	SA	4	795	399	14	28.50	4-58	–	–	56.78
1928	WI	3	840	302	22	13.72	5-39	2	1	38.18
1929	SA	3	1129	547	22	24.86	7-71	3	2	51.31
	A	2	968	459	8	57.37	3-134	–	–	121.00
	SA	7	1924	946	36	26.27	7-71	3	2	53.44
	WI	3	840	302	22	13.72	5-39	2	1	38.18
Home		6	1969	849	44	19.29	7-71	5	3	44.75
Overseas		6	1763	858	22	39.00	4-58	–	–	80.13
Totals		12	3732	1707	66	25.86	7-71	5	3	56.55

FRENCH
Bruce Nicholas

Nottinghamshire (1976 to date)

TOURS
A 1986–87, 1987–88; WI 1985–86;
NZ 1987–88; I/SL 1984–85; P 1987–88
Born Warsop, Nottinghamshire
13 Aug 1959

A diminutive (5ft 6in) wicket-keeper, Bruce French is an undemonstrative, highly skilled technican who made a precocious entry into first-class cricket having been well schooled alongside his father and four brothers in the Welbeck Colliery team. His England baptism came a full decade later after two tours as understudy to Paul Downton. Apart from the 1986–87 series in Australia, he held his Test place for two years until overdue surgery to a finger caused him to miss most of the 1988 season. An ever-growing list of bizarre injuries includes being bitten by a dog while on a training run. On the 1987–88 Pakistan tour he was hit on the head during practice by a ball returned by a spectator. As he walked across hospital grounds to have his gashed eyebrow stitched he was knocked down but not seriously damaged by an erratically driven car. He then completed a notable hat-trick by smashing his head on an overhead light as he rose from the stitching operation. His tendency towards disaster has not afflicted his mountaineering.

						Batting 1st			Batting 2nd			Fielding 1st				Fielding 2nd			
Ref	Series	V	T	Venue	Result	No	R	HO	No	R	HO	Ct	St	Byes	Balls	Ct	St	Byes	Balls
1047/624†	1986	I	2	Leeds	L-279	9	8	b	10	5	c	2	–	0	626	1	–	4	459
1048/625†			3	Birmingham	D	10	8	b	10	1	c	3	–	3	839	3	–	1	468
1049/626†	1986	NZ	1	Lord's	D	8	0	*rh	–	–	–	–	–	0	1	–	–	0	90
1050/627†			2	Nottingham	L-8w	10	21	c	10	12	*	1	–	0	1019	–	–	0	144
1051/628†			3	Oval	D	–	–	–	–	–	–	2	–	1	770	–	–	0	6
1075/634†	1987	P	1	Manchester	D	5	59	c	–	–	–	2	–	9	384	–	–	–	–
1076/635†			2	Lord's	D	6	42	b	–	–	–	–	–	–	–	–	–	–	–
1078/637†			4	Birmingham	D	6	0	b	9	1	*	1	–	4	1041	–	–	0	441
1079/638†			5	Oval	D	8	1	c	–	–	–	1	–	2	1323	–	–	–	–
1084/639†	1987–88	P	1	Lahore[2]	L-I & 87	10	38	*	6	9	lbw	–	1	18	804	–	–	–	–
1085/640†			2	Faisalabad	D	10	2	st	–	–	–	3	–	0	507	–	–	4	144
1086/641†			3	Karachi	D	9	31	c	8	0	lbw	4	–	0	803	–	–	–	–
1090/642†	1987–88	A		Sydney	D	8	47	st	–	–	–	4	–	0	577	–	–	3	810
1091/643†	1987–88	NZ	1	Christchurch	D	8	7	c	8	3	c	4	–	2	491	1	–	6	462
1092/644†			2	Auckland	D	8	13	c	–	–	–	4	–	1	806	2	–	8	1014
1093/645†			3	Wellington	D	–	–	–	–	–	–	–	–	0	1182	–	–	–	–

Career	M	I	NO	HS	R	Avge	100	50	Ct	St	Balls	R	W	Avge	BB	5w	10w	Rate
Test	16	21	4	59	308	18.11	–	1	38	1	–	–	–	–	–	–	–	–
F/c	259	334	65	98	5023	18.67	–	18	598	61	6	22	0	–	–	–	–	–

NOTABLE FEATS

- Youngest cricketer to represent Nottinghamshire (16 years 287 days on debut).
- Made 87 dismissals (76ct, 11st) for Nottinghamshire in 1984, including 10 (7ct, 3st) v Oxford U at The Parks (both County records).
- Six dismissals in an innings on 3 occasions (equalling Nottinghamshire record).

TEST NOTES

- *1049* Retired hurt when at 259-6. In NZ's 1st inns the wicket-keeping duties were shared by C.W.J. Athey (overs 1-2), R.W. Taylor (overs 3-76), R.J. Parks (overs 77-140) and French (final ball only).

Watched by an admiring Mike Gatting, Bruce French makes a low catch in front of John Emburey to dismiss New Zealander John Wright off Graham Dilley during the Auckland Test, 1987–88.

FRY
Charles Burgess

Oxford University (1892 to 1895)
Sussex (1894 to 1908)
London County (1900 to 1902)
Hampshire (1909 to 1921)
Europeans (1921–22)

Wisden 1895
TOUR SA 1895–96
Born West Croydon, Surrey 25 Apr 1872
Died Hampstead, Middlesex 7 Sep 1956

Charles Fry was an exceptionally talented all-round athlete and a brilliant scholar and conversationalist who, in modern terms, would have more than matched the combined attributes of Daley Thompson and Mike Brearley. After captaining Repton, he gained blues at cricket, soccer and athletics, only narrowly missing a fourth at rugby because of injury. As a fleet-footed full-back he played soccer for England against Ireland in 1901 and for Southampton in the 1902 FA Cup Final; in addition to being an outstanding sprinter, he shared the world long jump record of 23ft 5in for 21 years; and he gained first-class honours in Classical Moderations. Beyond all those varied triumphs he is best remembered for his batting performances. His technique was based on determination, concentration and a flawless defence; it was evolved from a detailed analysis of the game's mechanics. A ferocious straight driver, he favoured the back foot and was particularly strong on the leg side. Until he was called for throwing in 1898, he was a useful right-arm fast-medium bowler. His other commitments restricted his appearances abroad and he declined two tours of Australia. He led Sussex for five seasons (1904–08), one jointly, and was England's undefeated captain during the 1912 Triangular Tournament. After the 1908 season he transferred to Hampshire to direct the Hamble-based training ship *Mercury* and, with his wife and on an entirely voluntary basis, instil his young charges with a classical sense of values. He edited his own monthly magazine, wrote a definitive analysis of batsmanship and several other books including an autobiography, reported and broadcast cricket until his death, stood as a Liberal candidate for Parliament three times, represented India at the League of Nations and declined the throne of Albania.

NOTABLE FEATS

- 1000 runs in 20th Test (*105*) (33 inns).
- His 94 first-class hundreds included 16 double centuries (then a record).
- Exceeded 1000 runs in a season 12 times, including 2000 or more on 6 occasions. Scored 3147 runs (avge 78.67) in 1901, including 13 hundreds (the record until 1925) and 1000 runs in a month twice: 1130 in June and 1116 in August.
- Headed the first-class batting averages 6 times between 1901 and 1912.
- Scored 6 hundreds in consecutive first-class innings in 1901 to set world record subsequently equalled: 106, 209, 149, 105 and 140 for Sussex, 105 for Rest of England.
- His 232* at Lord's in 1903 remained the highest score for the Gentlemen v the Players and the record for either side in 137 matches at Lord's. His 3rd-wkt stand of 309* with A.C. MacLaren was the highest partnership for any wicket in this fixture.
- Scored 100 in each innings of a match 5 times.
- Twice scored 8 fifties in consecutive innings.
- Carried his bat through a completed innings on 3 occasions.
- Hat-trick for Oxford U v MCC at Lord's in 1894.

TEST NOTES

- *64* Bowled in 2nd inns: 0 for 3 (10 balls).

C.B. Fry

Ref	Series	V	T	Venue	Result	Batting 1st No	R	HO	Batting 2nd No	R	HO	Ct
47/47	1895–96	SA	1	Port Elizabeth	W-288	4	43	b	5	15	c	–
48/48			2	Johannesburg[1]	W-I & 197	4	64	c	–	–	–	1
60/60	1899	A	1	Nottingham	D	2	50	b	2	9	c	1
61/61			2	Lord's	L-10w	2	13	c	2	4	b	1
62/62			3	Leeds	D	6	38	b	–	–	–	2
63/63			4	Manchester	D	2	9	b	2	4	c	–
64/64			5	Oval	D	4	60	c	–	–	–	1
70/70	1902	A	1	Birmingham	D	2	0	c	–	–	–	2
71/71			2	Lord's	D	2	0	c	–	–	–	–
72/72			3	Sheffield	L-143	5	1	st	5	4	lbw	–
84/81	1905	A	2	Lord's	D	4	73	c	4	36	*	1
85/82			3	Leeds	D	2	32	c	2	30	c	–
86/83			4	Manchester	W-I & 80	4	17	b	–	–	–	2
87/84			5	Oval	D	4	144	b	5	16	c	1
93/90	1907	SA	1	Lord's	D	1	33	b	–	–	–	1
94/91			2	Leeds	W-53	2	2	b	2	54	lbw	1
95/92			3	Oval	D	2	129	c	2	3	b	–
101/98	1909	A	1	Birmingham	W-10w	4	0	b	2	35	*	–
103/100			3	Leeds	L-126	1	1	lbw	1	7	b	1
105/102			5	Oval	D	4	62	ro	4	35	*	–
122/113*	1912	SA	1	Lord's	W-I & 62	4	29	b	–	–	–	–
123/114*		A	1	Lord's	D	4	42	ro	–	–	–	–
124/115*		SA	2	Leeds	W-174	4	10	lbw	4	7	c	–
126/116*		A	2	Manchester	D	4	19	c	–	–	–	–
128/117*		SA	3	Oval	W-10w	4	9	c	–	–	–	–
129/118*		A	3	Oval	W-244	4	5	c	4	79	c	2

Career	M	I	NO	HS	R	Avge	100	50	Ct	St	Balls	R	W	Avge	BB	5w	10w	Rate
Test	26	41	3	144	1223	32.18	2	7	17	–	10	3	0	–	–	–	–	–
F/c	394	658	43	258*	30886	50.22	94	124	240	–	9036	4872	166	29.34	6-78	9	2	54.43

C. B. FRY – TEST BATTING SUMMARY

Series	V	M	I	NO	HS	R	Avge	100	50
1895–96	SA	2	3	–	64	122	40.66	–	1
1899	A	5	8	–	60	187	23.37	–	2
1902	A	3	4	–	4	5	1.25	–	–
1905	A	4	7	1	144	348	58.00	1	1
1907	SA	3	5	–	129	221	44.20	1	1
1909	A	3	6	2	62	140	35.00	–	1
1912	SA	3	4	–	29	55	13.75	–	–

Series	V	M	I	NO	HS	R	Avge	100	50
1912	A	3	4	–	79	145	36.25	–	1
	A	18	29	3	144	825	31.73	1	5
	SA	8	12	–	129	398	33.16	1	2
Home		24	38	3	144	1101	31.45	2	6
Overseas		2	3	–	64	122	40.66	–	1
Totals		26	41	3	144	1223	32.18	2	7

GATTING
Michael William OBE

Middlesex (1975 to date)

Wisden 1984

TOURS

A 1986–87, 1987–88; WI 1980–81, 1985–86; NZ 1977–78, 1983–84, 1987–88; I/SL 1981–82, 1984–85; P 1977–78, 1983–84, 1987–88; Z 1980–81 (Mddx)

Born Kingsbury, Middlesex 6 Jun 1957

Mike Gatting is a bold, exciting and pugnacious batsman whose approach has changed little from his teenage club cricket days with Brondesbury. A capacious cheese and Branston addict who appears lower than his measured height of 5ft 10in, his march to the crease and threatening block-bashing ritual whilst awaiting the ball promises mayhem on a massive scale. He will intersperse a wide range of brutal drives and pulls with delicate dabs and cuts; occasionally that forbidden reverse sweep will be saucily revealed. Spin bowlers are given a clear message that they should not be bowling and no batsman since Denis Compton has ventured further down the pitch to molest their trifles. Although a consistent plunderer of county attacks, he took an unconscionably long time to establish an England place before his long-awaited first Test hundred (in his 54th innings) unblocked a reservoir that yielded over 1000 runs in the next nine months. Even when his features were rearranged by a Malcolm Marshall special his cheery con-

fidence survived undented. Although Middlesex captain since 1983 he never sought the England throne and, even after retaining the Ashes in 1986–87, remained less than happy in the role. A straightforward Londoner, he found the intrigue and chicanery of Pakistan's cricket totally unacceptable and the hideous Shakoor Rana incident ensued. Having survived that ignominy and a series of monumental tedium in New Zealand, it was ironic that he should be removed from office for a bit of nocturnal dalliance with a barmaid in the heart of England. He is certain to return and wreak his vengeance.

NOTABLE FEATS

- 1000 runs in 28th Test (*979*) (48 inns); 2000 runs in 39th Test (*1020*) (68 inns); 3000 runs in 52nd Test (*1061*) (90 inns).
- *1008* First instance of 2 double hundreds in an England innings (G. Fowler 201).
- *1061* Became the third England captain to retain the Ashes in Australia.
- Exceeded 1000 runs in a season 12 times (plus once on tour), including 2000 once.
- Headed first-class batting averages with 2257 runs, avge 68.39, in 1984.

Mike Gatting

						Batting 1st			Batting 2nd				Bowling 1st			Bowling 2nd		
Ref	**Series**	**V**	**T**	**Venue**	**Result**	**No**	**R**	**HO**	**No**	**R**	**HO**	**Ct**	**Balls**	**R**	**W**	**Balls**	**R**	**W**
816/533	1977–78	P	3	Karachi	D	5	5	lbw	5	6	lbw	2	–	–	–	–	–	–
819/536	1977–78	NZ	3	Auckland	D	5	0	b	–	–	–	1	–	–	–	8	1	0
881/558	1980	WI	2	Lord's	D	5	18	b	–	–	–	–	–	–	–	–	–	–
882/559			3	Manchester	D	5	33	c	5	56	c	–	–	–	–	–	–	–
883/560			4	Oval	D	5	48	b	6	15	c	1	–	–	–	–	–	–
884/561			5	Leeds	D	5	1	c	4	1	lbw	–	–	–	–	–	–	–
885/562	1980	A		Lord's	D	5	12	lbw	5	51	*	1	–	–	–	–	–	–
897/564	1980–81	WI	3	Bridgetown	L-298	3	2	c	3	0	b	1	–	–	–	–	–	–
903/567	1981	A	1	Nottingham	L-4w	5	52	lbw	5	15	lbw	1	–	–	–	–	–	–
904/568			2	Lord's	D	5	59	lbw	5	16	c	1	–	–	–	–	–	–
905/569			3	Leeds	W-18	5	15	lbw	5	1	lbw	2	–	–	–	–	–	–
906/570			4	Birmingham	W-29	5	21	c	5	39	b	1	–	–	–	–	–	–
907/571			5	Manchester	W-103	6	32	c	5	11	lbw	1	–	–	–	18	13	0
908/572			6	Oval	D	4	53	c	4	56	c	2	–	–	–	–	–	–
913/574	1981–82	I	2	Bangalore	D	8	29	lbw	–	–	–	–	–	–	–	–	–	–
914/575			3	Delhi	D	7	5	b	–	–	–	–	–	–	–	–	–	–
915/576			4	Calcutta	D	8	0	c	7	2	*	–	–	–	–	–	–	–
916/577			5	Madras[1]	D	6	0	c	–	–	–	–	–	–	–	6	4	0
917/578			6	Kanpur	D	6	32	c	–	–	–	–	–	–	–	–	–	–
931/583	1982	P	1	Birmingham	W-113	6	17	b	5	5	c	–	–	–	–	–	–	–
932/584			2	Lord's	L-10w	6	32	*	6	7	c	1	–	–	–	–	–	–
933/585			3	Leeds	W-3w	3	25	lbw	3	25	lbw	2	48	17	0	12	4	0
959/593	1983	NZ	3	Lord's	W-127	5	81	c	5	15	b	1	–	–	–	–	–	–
960/594			4	Nottingham	W-165	5	14	lbw	5	11	c	3	30	8	0	12	5	0
975/595	1983–84	NZ	1	Wellington	D	5	19	lbw	–	–	–	2	–	–	–	48	14	1
976/596			2	Christchurch	L-I & 132	7	19	*	5	0	c	–	12	14	0	–	–	–
978/598	1983–84	P	1	Karachi	L-3w	2	26	b	2	4	lbw	–	–	–	–	–	–	–
979/599			2	Faisalabad	D	2	75	c	–	–	–	2	18	17	1	12	18	0
980/600			3	Lahore[2]	D	2	0	lbw	3	53	ro	4	–	–	–	–	–	–
990/602	1984	WI	2	Lord's	L-9w	5	1	lbw	5	29	lbw	2	–	–	–	–	–	–
1005/607	1984–85	I	1	Bombay[3]	L-8w	3	15	c	3	136	c	–	42	20	0	–	–	–
1006/608			2	Delhi	W-8w	3	26	b	3	30	*	1	12	5	0	6	3	0
1007/609			3	Calcutta	D	5	48	b	–	–	–	1	12	1	0	–	–	–
1008/610			4	Madras[1]	W-9w	3	207	c	3	10	*	2	–	–	–	–	–	–
1009/611			5	Kanpur	D	3	62	c	3	41	*	–	–	–	–	6	7	0
1017/612	1985	A	1	Leeds	W-5w	4	53	c	4	12	c	–	–	–	–	–	–	–
1018/613			2	Lord's	L-4w	4	14	lbw	6	75	*	–	–	–	–	–	–	–
1019/614			3	Nottingham	D	4	74	ro	4	35	*	–	6	2	0	–	–	–
1020/615			4	Manchester	D	4	160	c	–	–	–	–	–	–	–	24	14	0
1021/616			5	Birmingham	W-I & 118	4	100	*	–	–	–	–	–	–	–	–	–	–
1022/617			6	Oval	W-I & 94	4	4	c	–	–	–	–	–	–	–	–	–	–

Ref	Series	V	T	Venue	Result	Batting 1st No	R	HO	Batting 2nd No	R	HO	Ct	Bowling 1st Balls	R	W	Bowling 2nd Balls	R	W
1042/622	1985–86	WI	5	St John's	L-240	6	15	c	7	1	b	2	–	–	–	–	–	–
1046/623	1986	I	1	Lord's	L-5w	4	0	b	4	40	b	1	–	–	–	–	–	–
1047/624*			2	Leeds	L-279	5	13	c	5	31	*	2	–	–	–	–	–	–
1048/625*			3	Birmingham	D	5	183	*	5	26	lbw	–	–	–	–	12	10	0
1049/626*	1986	NZ	1	Lord's	D	5	2	b	5	26	c	2	–	–	–	–	–	–
1050/627*			2	Nottingham	L-8w	5	17	b	6	4	c	–	–	–	–	–	–	–
1051/628*			3	Oval	D	5	121	b	–	–	–	–	–	–	–	–	–	–
1058/629*	1986–87	A	1	Brisbane[2]	W-7w	3	61	b	3	12	c	1	6	2	0	12	2	0
1059/630*			2	Perth	D	4	14	c	3	70	b	–	–	–	–	30	3	0
1060/631*			3	Adelaide	D	3	100	c	3	0	b	–	54	22	0	12	4	0
1061/632*			4	Melbourne	W-I & 14	3	40	c	–	–	–	2	6	4	0	–	–	–
1062/633*			5	Sydney	L-55	3	0	lbw	5	96	c	2	6	2	0	12	0	0
1075/634*	1987	P	1	Manchester	D	3	42	b	–	–	–	–	–	–	–	–	–	–
1076/635*			2	Lord's	D	5	43	ro	–	–	–	–	–	–	–	–	–	–
1077/636*			3	Leeds	L-I & 18	5	8	lbw	5	9	c	1	54	16	0	–	–	–
1078/637*			4	Birmingham	D	5	124	c	5	8	ro	1	18	6	0	–	–	–
1079/638*			5	Oval	D	5	61	c	5	150	*	–	60	18	0	–	–	–
1084/639*	1987–88	P	1	Lahore[2]	L-I & 87	4	0	lbw	4	23	lbw	–	–	–	–	–	–	–
1085/640*			2	Faisalabad	D	4	79	b	4	8	c	–	–	–	–	–	–	–
1086/641*			3	Karachi	D	4	18	b	4	0	lbw	1	–	–	–	–	–	–
1090/642*	1987–88	A		Sydney	D	4	13	c	–	–	–	–	–	–	–	–	–	–
1091/643*	1987–88	NZ	1	Christchurch	D	4	8	c	4	23	b	–	–	–	–	–	–	–
1092/644*			2	Auckland	D	4	42	c	–	–	–	–	–	–	–	102	40	1
1093/645*			3	Wellington	D	4	33	*	–	–	–	–	36	21	1	–	–	–
1098/646*	1988	WI	1	Nottingham	D	3	5	c	3	29	b	1	–	–	–	–	–	–
1100/648			3	Manchester	L-I & 156	3	0	lbw	3	4	c	–	–	–	–	–	–	–

Career	M	I	NO	HS	R	Avge	100	50	Ct	St	Balls	R	W	Avge	BB	5w	10w	Rate
Test	67	115	14	207	3848	38.09	9	18	51	–	752	317	4	79.25	1-14	–	–	188.00
F/c	341	526	76	258	21060	46.80	50	109	295	–	8411	4026	145	27.76	5-34	2	–	58.00

M. W. GATTING – TEST BATTING SUMMARY

Series	V	M	I	NO	HS	R	Avge	100	50
1977–78	P	1	2	–	6	11	5.50	–	–
1977–78	NZ	1	1	–	0	0	0.00	–	–
1980	WI	4	7	–	56	172	24.57	–	1
1980	A	1	2	1	51*	63	63.00	–	1
1980–81	WI	1	2	–	2	2	1.00	–	–
1981	A	6	12	–	59	370	30.83	–	4
1981–82	I	5	6	1	32	68	11.60	–	–
1982	P	3	6	1	32*	111	22.20	–	–
1983	NZ	2	4	–	81	121	30.25	–	1
1983–84	NZ	2	3	1	19*	38	19.00	–	–
1983–84	P	3	5	–	75	158	31.60	–	2
1984	WI	1	2	–	29	30	15.00	–	–
1984–85	I	5	9	3	207	575	95.83	2	1
1985	A	6	9	3	160	527	87.83	2	3
1985–86	WI	1	2	–	15	16	8.00	–	–
1986	I	3	6	2	183*	293	73.25	1	–

Series	V	M	I	NO	HS	R	Avge	100	50
1986	NZ	3	5	–	121	170	34.00	1	–
1986–87	A	5	9	–	100	393	43.66	1	3
1987	P	5	8	1	150*	445	63.57	2	1
1987–88	P	3	6	–	79	128	21.33	–	1
1987–88	A	1	1	–	13	13	13.00	–	–
1987–88	NZ	3	4	1	42	106	35.33	–	–
1988	WI	2	4	–	29	38	9.50	–	–
	A	19	33	4	160	1366	47.10	3	11
	WI	9	17	–	56	258	15.17	–	1
	NZ	11	17	2	121	435	29.00	1	1
	I	13	21	6	207	936	62.40	3	1
	P	15	27	2	150*	853	34.12	2	4
Home		36	60	8	183*	2340	45.00	6	11
Overseas		31	50	6	207	1508	34.27	3	7
Totals		67	115	14	207	3848	38.09	9	18

GAY, Leslie Hewitt

Cambridge University (1891 to 1893)
Somerset (1894)
Hampshire (1900)

TOUR A 1894–95
Born Brighton, Sussex 24 Mar 1871
Died Salcombe Regis, Devon 1 Nov 1949

Leslie Gay

A wicket-keeper and tail-end batsman, Leslie Gay gained a blue in his second year at Cambridge before enjoying a brief but varied county career which comprised four matches for Somerset followed six years later by nine appearances for Hampshire. Touring Australia with Stoddart's team, he made his only Test appearance in the opening match. Although he shared a ninth-wicket partnership of 73 with Johnny Briggs, he missed four catches plus a run out and was replaced by Hylton Philipson for the remainder of the rubber. A soccer blue and double international, he had kept goal for England in three matches the previous winter.

					Batting 1st			Batting 2nd			Fielding 1st				Fielding 2nd			
Ref	Series	V	T Venue	Result	No	R	HO	No	R	HO	Ct	St	Byes	Balls	Ct	St	Byes	Balls
42/42†	1894–95	A	1 Sydney	W-10	10	33	c	10	4	b	1	–	8	1035	2	1	2	408

Career	M	I	NO	HS	R	Avge	100	50	Ct	St	Balls	R	W	Avge	BB	5w	10w	Rate
Test	1	2	0	33	37	18.50	–	–	3	1	–	–	–	–	–	–	–	–
F/c	46	80	15	60*	1005	15.46	–	2	69	20	–	–	–	–	–	–	–	–

GEARY, George

Leicestershire (1912 to 1938)

Wisden 1927
TOURS
A 1928–29; SA 1924–25 (Joel), 1927–28; WI 1931–32 (Tennyson); I/SL 1926–27
Born Barwell, Leicestershire 9 Jul 1893
Died Leicester 6 Mar 1981

George Geary (right) and George Macaulay after their match-saving stand at Headingley against the 1926 Australians.

Self taught, George Geary was one of Leicestershire's most dependable and long-serving professionals. Large, strong and good-humoured he thrived on hard work, bowling right-arm fast-medium with a high, easy action off an economical run. He swung a new ball late, varied his stock off-breaks with seamers and leg-cutters and could maintain a high degree of accuracy throughout long spells. By changing to slow spin if conditions warranted, he proved just as effective on hard pitches overseas and was particularly dangerous on the Johannesburg matting where he claimed 12 wickets in 1927–28. His lower-order batting was based on a resolute and sound technique and produced some valuable innings, including three hundreds in his final season at the age of 45. With his vast hands and long reach he held some miraculous catches at slip, including two decisive blinders off Larwood in the final Ashes Test of 1926. As a popular, skilful and greatly respected coach at Charterhouse School he fired a young Peter May with the enthusiasm and ambition to become a first-class cricketer.

NOTABLE FEATS

- *165* Shared a match-saving 9th-wkt stand of 108 with G.G. Macaulay.
- *180* Bowled 81 overs (486 balls), then the longest innings spell in Test cricket.
- Took 100 wickets in a season 11 times.
- His innings (10 for 18) and match (16 for 96) analyses v Glamorgan at Pontypridd in 1929 remain Leicestershire records. Only H. Verity (10 for 10 in 1932) has taken all 10 first-class wickets more cheaply.
- Hat-trick for Leicestershire v Gloucestershire at Bristol in 1922 when he bowled unchanged throughout both innings with W.E. Astill.

Ref	Series	V	T	Venue	Result	Batting 1st			Batting 2nd			Ct	Bowling 1st			Bowling 2nd		
						No	R	HO	No	R	HO		Balls	R	W	Balls	R	W
156/142	1924	SA	4	Manchester	D	–	–	–	–	–	–	–	66	21	0	–	–	–
165/151	1926	A	3	Leeds	D	9	35	*	–	–	–	1	246	130	2	–	–	–
167/153			5	Oval	W-289	8	9	ro	8	1	c	3	162	43	0	39	15	1
168/154	1927–28	SA	1	Johannesburg[1]	W-10w	10	3	lbw	–	–	–	1	165	70	7	162	60	5
169/155			2	Cape Town	W-87	9	0	lbw	9	1	b	1	138	50	0	–	–	–
177/163	1928/29	A	2	Sydney	W-8w	8	66	lbw	1	8	b	–	108	35	5	190	55	2
178/164			3	Melbourne	W-3w	8	1	lbw	8	4	*	–	191	83	3	180	94	2
179/165			4	Adelaide	W-12	9	3	ro	8	6	c	1	72	32	0	96	42	1
180/166			5	Melbourne	L-5w	9	4	b	9	3	b	2	486	105	5	120	31	1
184/170	1929	SA	4	Manchester	W-I & 32	8	31	*	–	–	–	2	135	18	2	222	50	2
185/171			5	Oval	D	9	12	*	–	–	–	–	294	121	3	–	–	–
196/182	1930	A	3	Leeds	D	6	0	ro	–	–	–	–	210	95	1	–	–	–
233/207	1934	A	1	Nottingham	L-238	8	53	st	8	0	c	–	258	101	3	138	46	1
234/208			2	Lord's	W-I & 38	8	9	c	–	–	–	2	132	56	0	–	–	–

Career	M	I	NO	HS	R	Avge	100	50	Ct	St	Balls	R	W	Avge	BB	5w	10w	Rate
Test	14	20	4	66	249	15.56	–	2	13	–	3810	1353	46	29.41	7-70	4	1	82.82
F/c	549	820	138	122	13504	19.80	8	54	451	–	116287	41339	2063	20.03	10-18	125	30	56.36

GIBB, Paul Antony

Scotland (1934 to 1938)
Cambridge University (1935 to 1938)
Yorkshire (1935 to 1946)
Essex (1951 to 1956)

TOURS
A 1946–47; SA 1938–39;
WI 1935–36 (Yorks);
I 1937–38 (Tennyson), 1953–54 (Cwlth)
Born Brandsby, Yorkshire 11 Jul 1913
Died Guildford, Surrey 7 Dec 1977

Paul Gibb behind the stumps; Colin McCool out lbw to Doug Wright for 95 during the Brisbane Test, 1946–47.

Paul Gibb was one of the most versatile of Test cricketers. Educated at St Edward's School, Oxford, he gained a blue as a Cambridge freshman and averaged 54 in his four Varsity matches. After playing 36 times for Yorkshire as an amateur and captaining their pre-War Jamaican tour, he dropped out of first-class cricket on his return from Australia in 1947. When he reappeared for Essex in 1951 he became the first cricket blue ever to turn professional and was compelled to suspend his MCC membership. A specialist batsman during his first year at Cambridge, he kept wicket when S.C. Griffith was injured the following season and was preferred to him in his third year. Favouring the back foot, he was a resolute workman-like batsman with a massive defence and immense powers of concentration and patience. His keeping seldom aspired beyond being serviceable. Of medium height (5ft 8in) and slight build, he was as keen a trencherman as cricket has ever produced, his speed into the dining room and capacity for consuming spare meals, left-overs and ice cream being quite prodigious. Bald and bespectacled, he travelled the circuit by caravan during his career as a first-class umpire (1957–66). Invited to the Melbourne Centenary Test in 1977 he appeared wearing a wig and contact lenses and initially went unrecognized by his former colleagues. At the time of his death he was a bus driver in Guildford.

NOTABLE FEATS

- *267* Scored 93 and 106 in his first Test, sharing 2nd-wkt stands of 184 and 168 with E. Paynter.
- *271* Shared record E v SA 2nd-wkt stand of 280 with W.J. Edrich, his 120 in 451 min including only 2 boundaries.
- Exceeded 1000 runs in a season 5 times.
- First amateur to score 100 on Yorkshire debut: 157* v Nottinghamshire at Sheffield in 1935.
- Carried his bat for 80* for Cambridge U (163) v Australians at Fenner's in 1938.
- Shared in record Essex stand for any wkt: 343 with R. Horsfall v Kent at Blackheath in 1951.

TEST NOTES

- Would have made his debut in abandoned 1938 Test v Australia at Manchester.

Ref	Series	V	T	Venue	Result	Batting 1st			Batting 2nd			Fielding 1st				Fielding 2nd			
						No	R	HO	No	R	HO	Ct	St	Byes	Balls	Ct	St	Byes	Balls
267/236	1938–39	SA	1	Johannesburg[1]	D	2	93	c	2	106	c	–	–	–	–	–	–	–	–
268/237			2	Cape Town	D	2	58	c	–	–	–	–	–	–	–	–	–	–	–
269/238			3	Durban[2]	W-I & 13	2	38	c	–	–	–	–	–	–	–	–	–	–	–
270/239			4	Johannesburg[1]	D	2	9	c	2	45	c	–	–	–	–	–	–	–	–
271/240			5	Durban[2]	D	2	4	c	2	120	b	–	–	–	–	–	–	–	–
276/244†	1946	I	1	Lord's	W-10w	6	60	c	–	–	–	1	1	10	457	–	–	10	487
277/245†			2	Manchester	D	6	24	b	6	0	c	–	–	10	492	1	–	5	366
279/247†	1946–47	A	1	Brisbane[2]	L-I & 332	8	13	b	8	11	lbw	1	–	5	1270	–	–	–	–

Career	M	I	NO	HS	R	Avge	100	50	Ct	St	Balls	R	W	Avge	BB	5w	10w	Rate
Test	8	13	0	120	581	44.69	2	3	3	1	–	–	–	–	–	–	–	–
F/c	287	479	33	204	12520	28.07	19	51	425	123	269	161	5	32.20	2-40	–	–	53.80

GIFFORD
Norman MBE

Worcestershire (1960 to 1982)
Warwickshire (1983 to 1988)

Wisden 1975
TOURS
A 1971–72 (RW); I 1972–73; P 1961–62 (Int XI), 1970–71 (Cwlth), 1972–73; SL 1985–86 (Eng B); Z 1961–62 (Int XI), 1964–65 (Worcs), 1972–73 (Int W)
Born Ulverston, Lancashire 30 Mar 1940

NOTABLE FEATS

- *705* Shared record E v I 9th-wkt stand of 83 with K.W.R. Fletcher.
- *722* Shared record E v NZ 10th-wkt stand of 59 with A.P.E. Knott.
- Took 100 wickets in a season 4 times.
- Hat-trick for Worcestershire v Derbyshire at Chesterfield in 1965.
- Won the first match award in a Lord's cup final (1963).

TEST NOTES

- *691* Fractured his thumb fielding and was unable to bowl in the match.
- *706* Fractured his left little finger fielding before lunch on the first day and took no further part in the match.

Norman Gifford, who retired in 1988 after three decades of service to county cricket, was a very fine left-arm spinner, a determined left-handed tail-end batsman, and a shrewd captain with a dry wit. His bowling, usually delivered from wide of the stumps with a flat trajectory, was never easy to hit. He was extremely accurate but turned the ball more than most and could cause havoc on a responsive surface. On flat dry pitches overseas he was sometimes preferred to Derek Underwood and there could be no higher praise. He was a batsman who could defend tenaciously in a crisis and a handy fielder at gully. Worcestershire won their third Championship during his ten years as captain (1971–80). After combining his final year at Worcester with the duties of an England selector, he celebrated a new start with Warwickshire by taking over a hundred wickets in his first season and accepting the captaincy when Bob Willis retired (1985–87). He was a conscientious and cheerful assistant manager on three England tours (1982–85) and his pipe-smoking, rubicund presence as coach to Sussex should soon reap rewards.

Norman Gifford

Ref	Series	V	T	Venue	Result	Batting 1st			Batting 2nd			Ct	Bowling 1st			Bowling 2nd		
						No	R	HO	No	R	HO		Balls	R	W	Balls	R	W
562/406	1964	A	2	Lord's	D	10	5	c	–	–	–	–	72	14	2	102	17	1
563/407			3	Leeds	L-7w	10	1	*	7	1	b	1	204	62	2	120	47	0
688/468	1971	P	2	Lord's	D	–	–	–	–	–	–	1	72	13	1	–	–	–
689/469			3	Leeds	W-25	11	3	*	11	2	*	–	322	69	3	204	51	2

						Batting 1st			Batting 2nd				Bowling 1st			Bowling 2nd		
Ref	Series	V	T	Venue	Result	No	R	HO	No	R	HO	Ct	Balls	R	W	Balls	R	W
690/470	1971	I	1	Lord's	D	10	17	b	10	7	*	1	273	84	4	114	43	4
691/471			2	Manchester	D	10	8	c	–	–	–	–	–	–	–	–	–	–
698/473	1972	A	1	Manchester	W-89	10	15	ro	10	0	c	–	–	–	–	18	29	0
699/474			2	Lord's	L-8w	10	3	c	10	16	*	1	66	20	0	–	–	–
700/475			3	Nottingham	D	6	16	c	–	–	–	1	30	18	1	90	49	0
705/480	1972-73	I	3	Madras[1]	L-4w	10	19	lbw	10	3	*	1	204	64	3	47	22	0
706/481			4	Kanpur	D	–	–	–	–	–	–	–	48	17	0	–	–	–
720/484	1972-73	P	2	Hyderabad	D	9	24	b	–	–	–	1	312	111	3	–	–	–
721/485			3	Karachi	D	11	4	*	–	–	–	1	276	88	2	174	55	5
722/486	1973	NZ	1	Nottingham	W-38	11	25	*	–	–	–	–	–	–	–	102	35	0
723/487			2	Lord's	D	11	8	c	11	2	*	–	234	107	0	–	–	–

Career	M	I	NO	HS	R	Avge	100	50	Ct	St	Balls	R	W	Avge	BB	5w	10w	Rate
Test	15	20	9	25*	179	16.27	–	–	8	–	3084	1026	33	31.09	5-55	1	–	93.45
F/c	710	805	264	89	7047	13.02	–	3	319	–	128386	48731	2068	23.56	8-28	93	14	62.08

GILLIGAN
Arthur Edward Robert

Cambridge University (1919 to 1920)
Surrey (1919)
Sussex (1920 to 1932)

Wisden 1924
TOURS
A 1924–25; SA 1922–23; I/SL 1926–27
Born Denmark Hill, Surrey 23 Dec 1894
Died Mare Hill, Pulborough, Sussex
5 Sep 1976

At his peak Arthur Gilligan was a genuinely fast bowler, a dashing late-order batsman, a superb mid-off fielder and an inspiring, popular and aggressive captain. He moved to Sussex after captaining Dulwich College, playing three matches for his native Surrey, and gaining blues in both his years at Cambridge. At Hove he was involved for the rest of his days as captain (1922–29), chairman, president and patron. Under his influence a fairly ordinary side gained confidence and huge support by its magnificent fielding and attractive cricket. He was an attacking bowler with a low action who preferred to aim on or just outside the off stump and seldom bowled short. In 1924 he took 74 wickets before July and within a period of 11 days his lethal bowling partnership with Maurice Tate accounted for three strong batting sides: Surrey for 53, Middlesex for 41 and South Africa for 30 (the latter on Gilligan's debut as England captain). A fortnight later he was struck over the heart by a lifting ball and thereafter had to assume the role of a change bowler. An audacious fast-scoring batsman, he loved to set about fast bowling. He led England to their first victory against Australia after the Great War, captained the first touring team to play first-class matches in Ceylon, served as MCC president (1967–68), wrote several well-researched cricket books and won respect as a radio commentator. A prominent golfer, he was president of the English Golf Union, Sussex GU and County Cricketers' Golfing Society.

NOTABLE FEATS

- *152* Shared record E v SA 10th-wkt stand of 92 with C.A.G. Russell.
- *153* Took 6 for 7 as South Africa were dismissed for 30 in 48 min off 75 balls; it remains the only Test innings in which no batsman reached double figures.
- Exceeded 1000 runs in a season twice, took 100 wickets 3 times and achieved the 'double' once.
- Hat-trick for Sussex v Surrey at The Oval in 1923.
- Scored 101 (his maiden century) at number 11 for Cambridge U v Sussex at Hove in 1919, sharing record CU 10th-wkt stand of 177 with J.H. Naumann.
- Shared record Cambridge U 8th-wkt stand of 145 with H. Ashton v Free Foresters at Fenner's in 1920.

						Batting 1st			Batting 2nd				Bowling 1st			Bowling 2nd		
Ref	Series	V	T	Venue	Result	No	R	HO	No	R	HO	Ct	Balls	R	W	Balls	R	W
148/134	1922–23	SA	1	Johannesburg[1]	L-168	11	18	b	11	7	b	1	42	23	0	120	69	3
152/138			5	Durban[2]	W-109	11	4	c	11	39	*	–	138	35	3	216	78	3
153/139*	1924	SA	1	Birmingham	W-I & 18	9	13	b	–	–	–	–	39	7	6	168	83	5
154/140*			2	Lord's	W-I & 18	–	–	–	–	–	–	1	186	70	3	144	54	2
155/141*			3	Leeds	W-9w	8	28	c	–	–	–	–	60	27	1	108	37	0
157/143*			5	Oval	D	8	36	c	–	–	–	–	96	44	0	–	–	–
158/144*	1924–25	A	1	Sydney	L-193	9	1	b	9	1	b	–	184	92	1	216	114	2
159/145*			2	Melbourne	L-81	10	17	*	10	0	c	1	208	114	3	88	40	0
160/146*			3	Adelaide	L-11	10	9	c	9	31	c	–	63	17	1	–	–	–
161/147*			4	Melbourne	W-I & 29	9	0	c	–	–	–	–	48	24	0	56	26	1
162/148*			5	Sydney	L-307	10	5	st	10	0	*	–	104	46	1	120	46	1

Career	M	I	NO	HS	R	Avge	100	50	Ct	St	Balls	R	W	Avge	BB	5w	10w	Rate
Test	11	16	3	39*	209	16.07	–	–	3	–	2404	1046	36	29.05	6-7	2	1	66.77
F/c	337	510	55	144	9140	20.08	12	26	180	–	47734	20141	868	23.20	8-25	42	4	54.99

Arthur Gilligan's 1924–25 MCC team to Australia: standing *H. Howell, R.K. Tyldesley, A.P.F. Chapman, F.C. Toone (manager), M.W. Tate, W.W. Whysall, J.L. Bryan;* seated *F.E. Woolley, J.W. Hearne, J.W.H.T. Douglas, A.E.R. Gilligan, J.B. Hobbs, E.H. Hendren, H. Strudwick;* in front *R. Kilner, A.P. Freeman, H. Sutcliffe, A. Sandham*

Harold Gilligan

GILLIGAN
Alfred Herbert Harold

Sussex (1919 to 1931)

TOURS
A 1929–30; SA 1924–25 (Joel); NZ 1929–30
Born Denmark Hill, Surrey 29 Jun 1896
Died Shamley Green, Surrey 5 May 1978

Harold Gilligan was a stylish but impetuous opening or middle-order batsman who captained England shrewdly in New Zealand's first official rubber – his only four Tests. A handy leg-spinner and exceptional cover-point, he often led Sussex in the absence of his elder brother (A.E.R.) and was the official captain in 1930. As a First World War Royal Naval Air Service pilot he had flown the first aircraft over the German fleet at Kiel, only to spend 72 hours in the North Sea when engine trouble occurred. Honorary treasurer and later vice-president of Surrey, his daughter Virginia married Peter May.

NOTABLE FEATS

- Exceeded 1000 runs in a season 3 times. His 1186 runs in 1923 were obtained from a record 70 innings and at the lowest average (17.70) by any batsman scoring 1000 runs.

Ref	Series	V	T	Venue	Result	Batting 1st No	R	HO	Batting 2nd No	R	HO	Ct
186/172*	1929–30	NZ	1	Christchurch	W-8w	2	10	c	2	4	b	–
187/173*			2	Wellington	D	8	32	b	–	–	–	–
188/174*			3	Auckland	D	–	–	–	–	–	–	–
189/175*			4	Auckland	D	8	25	b	–	–	–	–

Career	M	I	NO	HS	R	Avge	100	50	Ct	St	Balls	R	W	Avge	BB	5w	10w	Rate
Test	4	4	0	32	71	17.75	–	–	–	–	–	–	–	–	–	–	–	–
F/c	321	525	31	143	8873	17.96	1	44	123	–	7127	3872	115	33.66	4-13	–	–	61.97

GIMBLETT, Harold

Somerset (1935 to 1954)

Wisden 1953
TOUR I/SL 1950–51 (Cwlth)
Born Bicknoller, Somerset 19 Oct 1914
Died Verwood, Dorset 30 Mar 1978

Harold Gimblett

Harold Gimblett was a cavalier opening batsman whose sensational baptism in county cricket was straight out of the *Boys' Own Paper.* Given a month's trial by Somerset, he was discarded before that period had elapsed only to be recalled in an emergency because of his energetic fielding and medium-pace bowling. Going in to face England fast bowler Morris Nichols with the score 107 for 6, he earned a reassessment by hitting 123 in 80 minutes. Although it was the first of 49 centuries for Somerset and he maintained a career average of 36, he gained only three Test caps, all before the War. Powerfully built, he was a prolific cutter, puller and cover-driver and a magnificent hooker. A lively outfielder with a strong throw, he held some marvellous catches in the covers. He died by his own hand.

NOTABLE FEATS

- *252* His 67* in 100 min contained 11 fours, including 4 off successive balls from Mahomed Nissar, and was the highest score of the match.
- Exceeded 1000 runs in a season 12 times (Somerset record), plus once on tour, including 2000 twice. His career totals of 21,142 runs and 49 hundreds remain Somerset records. He hit 265 sixes in county cricket.
- Scored 123 out of 175 in 80 min on his first-class debut for Somerset v Essex at Frome in 1935, reaching 50 in 28 min and 100 in 63 min to win the Lawrence Trophy for the fastest 100 of the season.
- His 310 v Sussex at Eastbourne in 1948 remained the record Somerset score until 1985.

Ref	Series	V	T	Venue	Result	Batting 1st No	R	HO	Batting 2nd No	R	HO	Ct
252/221	1936	I	1	Lord's	W-9w	2	11	c	2	67	*	–
253/222			2	Manchester	D	1	9	b	–	–	–	–
272/241	1939	WI	1	Lord's	W-8w	2	22	b	2	20	b	1

Career	M	I	NO	HS	R	Avge	100	50	Ct	St	Balls	R	W	Avge	BB	5w	10w	Rate
Test	3	5	1	67*	129	32.25	–	1	1	–	–	–	–	–	–	–	–	–
F/c	368	673	37	310	23007	36.17	50	122	247	1	3955	2124	41	51.80	4-10	–	–	96.46

GLADWIN, Clifford

Derbyshire (1939 to 1958)

TOUR SA 1948–49
Born Doe Lea, Derbyshire 3 Apr 1916
Died Chesterfield, Derbyshire
10 Apr 1988

NOTABLE FEATS

- Took 100 wickets in a season 12 times (Derbyshire record), missing the 'double' by 86 runs in 1949.
- Two hat-tricks: for MCC v N.E. Transvaal at Benoni in 1948–49 (when he took 4 wickets in 5 balls) and for Derbyshire v New Zealanders at Derby in 1958.

A tall (6ft 2¾in), strong, right-arm fast-medium bowler, Cliff Gladwin was exceptionally accurate, interspersing late inswingers with occasional leg-cutters and changing to slower off-spin when conditions warranted. He established his county place with 109 wickets at 18.36 in his first full season (1946) and, with Les Jackson, from 1947 to 1958 formed the most destructive attack in Derbyshire's history. An aggressive and unsophisticated tail-end batsman, his moment of glory came at Durban (Test *309*) when England needed 8 runs to win off the final 8-ball over from Lindsay Tuckett. All four results were possible before the sixth ball when his ninth-wicket partner, Alec Bedser, brought the scores level. Gladwin missed the next ball. He also missed the last which bounced off his thigh for a scampered leg-bye. It seems odd that Gladwin and not Bedser, who masterminded the run, should have received most of the credit for the only last-ball victory in Test cricket.

Cliff Gladwin

						Batting 1st			Batting 2nd				Bowling 1st			Bowling 2nd		
Ref	Series	V	T	Venue	Result	No	R	HO	No	R	HO	Ct	Balls	R	W	Balls	R	W
287/255	1947	SA	3	Manchester	W-7w	9	16	b	–	–	–	–	300	58	2	96	28	1
289/257			5	Oval	D	9	51	*	–	–	–	1	96	39	0	96	33	0
309/267	1948–49	SA	1	Durban[2]	W-2w	10	0	*	10	7	*	–	96	21	3	56	15	0
310/268			2	Johannesburg[2]	D	10	23	lbw	–	–	–	–	160	29	1	128	37	0
311/269			3	Cape Town	D	10	17	*	–	–	–	–	240	51	1	80	27	0
312/270			4	Johannesburg[2]	D	9	19	b	8	7	*	–	192	43	2	128	39	1
313/271			5	Port Elizabeth	W-3w	9	10	c	7	15	c	1	245	70	3	48	14	0
315/273	1949	NZ	2	Lord's	D	9	5	ro	–	–	–	–	168	67	1	–	–	–

Career	M	I	NO	HS	R	Avge	100	50	Ct	St	Balls	R	W	Avge	BB	5w	10w	Rate
Test	8	11	5	51*	170	28.33	–	1	2	–	2129	571	15	38.06	3-21	–	–	141.93
F/c	374	510	148	124*	6283	17.35	1	15	134	–	81201	30265	1653	18.30	9-41	101	18	49.12

GODDARD Thomas William John

Gloucestershire (1922 to 1952)

Wisden 1938
TOURS SA 1930–31, 1938–39
Born Gloucester 1 Oct 1900
Died Gloucester 22 May 1966

A large (6ft 3in) raw-boned man with huge hands, Tom Goddard took more wickets than any other off-spinner after spending six summers with Gloucestershire as an unsuccessful right-arm fast bowler. Having devoted 1928 to learning to bowl medium-pace off-spin on the MCC staff at Lord's, he returned to Bristol to take 184 wickets the following season and form a redoubtable partnership with Charlie Parker. Usually bowling round the wicket, he turned the ball so sharply as to be at times unplayable. Extracting steep bounce from his high action, he made the ball fizz off the pitch, had magnificent control of flight and length and gained many wickets caught at slip from his angled top-spinner. In 1947, at the age of 46, he took no fewer than 238 wickets and, when Mortimore and Wells were absent on national service in 1952, he emerged from retirement to take 45 wickets in 13 matches.

NOTABLE FEATS

- *267* Achieved hat-trick in dismissing A.D. Nourse, N. Gordon and W.W. Wade.
- Took 100 wickets in a season 16 times (Gloucestershire record), including 200 on 4 occasions. Holds Gloucestershire record with 222 wickets in 1937 and 1947. Headed national bowling averages in 1947 and 1949.
- Took all 10 Worcestershire wickets for 113 runs at Cheltenham in 1937 and on 8 other occasions took 9 wickets in an innings for Gloucestershire.
- Equalled world record by taking 17 wickets in one day for Gloucestershire v Kent at Bristol in 1939 to complete sequence of 30 wickets in 4 inns. Took 15 or more wickets in a match 7 times.
- Six hat-tricks (only D.V.P. Wright has taken more): 4 for Gloucestershire (v Sussex at Eastbourne in 1924, v Glamorgan at Swansea in 1930 and 1947, v Somerset at Bristol in 1947); for MCC v Rhodesia at Salisbury in 1938–39; and for England (above). Twice took 5 wickets in 7 balls.

Tom Goddard bowling at The Oval in 1934.

						Batting 1st			Batting 2nd				Bowling 1st			Bowling 2nd		
Ref	Series	V	T	Venue	Result	No	R	HO	No	R	HO	Ct	Balls	R	W	Balls	R	W
197/183	1930	A	4	Manchester	D	–	–	–	–	–	–	–	193	49	2	–	–	–
261/230	1937	NZ	2	Manchester	W-130	11	4	*	11	1	*	–	108	48	0	88	29	6
262/231			3	Oval	D	–	–	–	–	–	–	–	60	25	0	108	41	2
267/236	1938–39	SA	1	Johannesburg[1]	D	11	0	*	–	–	–	1	216	54	3	88	31	0
268/237			2	Cape Town	D	–	–	–	–	–	–	–	304	64	3	88	68	1
270/239			4	Johannesburg[1]	D	10	8	c	–	–	–	–	144	65	1	–	–	–
273/242	1939	WI	2	Manchester	D	–	–	–	–	–	–	1	32	43	2	38	15	1
274/243			3	Oval	D	10	0	b	–	–	–	1	96	56	1	–	–	–

Career	M	I	NO	HS	R	Avge	100	50	Ct	St	Balls	R	W	Avge	BB	5w	10w	Rate
Test	8	5	3	8	13	6.50	–	–	3	–	1563	588	22	26.72	6-29	1	–	71.04
F/c	593	775	217	71	5234	9.37	–	4	313	–	142232	59116	2979	19.84	10-113	251	86	47.74

GOOCH
Graham Alan

Essex (1973 to date)
Western Province
(1982–83 to 1983–84)

Wisden 1980
TOURS
A 1978–79, 1979–80; SA 1981–82 (SAB); WI 1980–81, 1985–86; I 1979–80, 1981–82; P 1987–88; SL 1981–82
Born Leytonstone, Essex 23 Jul 1953

Graham Gooch is a tall (6ft), powerfully built opener who is particularly strong off his back foot. England's most consistent batsman of the 1980s, he is an ideal example of the modern technique with his upright stance and heavy (3lb) bat held aloft as the bowler approaches. Application, a sound defence and the ability to bludgeon the ball with awesome ferocity make him a daunting prospect to bowl at. His aggregate of 459 against the formidable West Indies pace attack in 1988 confirmed his world class. He bowls right-arm medium-pace outswing and is a splendid mimic of famous contemporary bowling actions. Although he has a long throw he usually fields at slip. His international career started disastrously with a 'pair' and he had completed 1000 runs in Tests before he at last made his first hundred in his 36th innings. Ironically, no sooner had he established his place than he was banned from Test cricket for three years for leading a rebel tour of South Africa. In 1986 he took over the Essex captaincy after a long apprenticeship under Keith Fletcher but resigned after two seasons when

Graham Gooch

the responsibility coincided with a loss of batting form. Appointed England's fourth captain against West Indies in 1988 when Chris Cowdrey withdrew because of injury, he retained the post against Sri Lanka and successfully ended England's record run of 18 matches without a win. But his appointment as captain for the 1988–89 tour of India (after he had withdrawn from a playing contract with Western Province) precipitated the cancellation of that mission when the Indian government refused to issue entry visas to Gooch and seven other 'black-listed' members of his team.

NOTABLE FEATS

- 1000 runs in 21st Test (*880*) (34 inns); 2000 runs in 35th Test (*907*) (63 inns); 3000 runs in 48th Test (*1022*) (84 inns); 4000 runs in 63rd Test (*1098*) (112 inns).
- *1022* Scored his first 100 v A in his 40th inns and shared 2nd-wkt stand of 351 in 337 min with D.I. Gower – England's second-highest partnership for any wicket v A.
- *1049* His 183 off 368 balls is the highest score for E v NZ at Lord's.
- Exceeded 1000 runs in a season 12 times (plus once on tour), including 2000 on 3 occasions.
- Shared Essex record 2nd-wkt stand of 321 with K.S. McEwan v Northamptonshire at Ilford in 1978.
- Established Essex first-class record of 2559 runs in 1984.
- Scored 100 before lunch for Essex 4 times.
- Played in 2 first-class matches on 30 August 1988, fielding for Essex v Surrey at The Oval after batting for England v Sri Lanka at Lord's.
- Holds record for highest scores in the Benson and Hedges Cup (198*) and Sunday League (176) limited-overs competitions.

TEST NOTES

- *915* Imitating D.R. Doshi he bowled slow left-arm spin in the closing stages.
- *916* Kept wicket for the final 12 overs.

						Batting 1st			Batting 2nd				Bowling 1st			Bowling 2nd		
Ref	Series	V	T	Venue	Result	No	R	HO	No	R	HO	Ct	Balls	R	W	Balls	R	W
760/511	1975	A	1	Birmingham	L-I & 85	5	0	c	5	0	c	1	–	–	–	–	–	–
761/512			2	Lord's	D	5	6	c	5	31	b	1	–	–	–	–	–	–
826/538	1978	P	2	Lord's	W-I & 120	2	54	lbw	–	–	–	1	–	–	–	–	–	–
827/539			3	Leeds	D	2	20	lbw	–	–	–	1	–	–	–	–	–	–
828/540	1978	NZ	1	Oval	W-7w	2	0	lbw	2	91	*	–	–	–	–	–	–	–
829/541			2	Nottingham	W-I & 119	1	55	c	–	–	–	1	–	–	–	–	–	–
830/542			3	Lord's	W-7w	1	2	c	1	42	*	–	60	29	0	–	–	–
834/543	1978/79	A	1	Brisbane[2]	W-7w	2	2	c	2	2	c	1	8	1	0	–	–	–
835/544			2	Perth	W-166	2	1	c	2	43	lbw	3	–	–	–	–	–	–
836/545			3	Melbourne	L-103	4	25	c	4	40	lbw	–	–	–	–	–	–	–
837/546			4	Sydney	W-93	4	18	c	4	22	c	2	40	14	0	–	–	–
838/547			5	Adelaide	W-205	4	1	c	4	18	b	–	–	–	–	–	–	–
839/548			6	Sydney	W-9w	4	74	st	–	–	–	3	–	–	–	–	–	–
851/549	1979	I	1	Birmingham	W-I & 83	4	83	c	–	–	–	4	–	–	–	36	8	0
852/550			2	Lord's	D	3	10	b	–	–	–	–	60	16	1	12	8	0
853/551			3	Leeds	D	3	4	c	–	–	–	1	18	2	0	–	–	–
854/552			4	Oval	D	3	79	c	3	31	lbw	1	12	6	0	12	9	0
870/554	1979–80	A	2	Sydney	L-6w	1	18	b	1	4	c	1	66	16	2	48	20	0
872/555			3	Melbourne	L-8w	1	99	ro	1	51	b	–	–	–	–	–	–	–
876/556	1979–80	I		Bombay[3]	W-10w	1	8	c	1	49	*	1	24	3	0	–	–	–
880/557	1980	WI	1	Nottingham	L-2w	1	17	c	1	27	ro	–	42	11	1	12	2	0
881/558			2	Lord's	D	1	123	lbw	1	47	b	2	42	26	0	–	–	–
882/559			3	Manchester	D	1	2	lbw	1	26	c	2	–	–	–	–	–	–
883/560			4	Oval	D	1	83	lbw	1	0	lbw	1	6	2	0	–	–	–
884/561			5	Leeds	D	1	14	c	1	55	lbw	–	48	18	2	–	–	–
885/562	1980	A		Lord's	D	1	8	c	1	16	lbw	–	48	16	0	–	–	–
896/563	1980–81	WI	1	Port-of-Spain	L-I & 79	1	41	b	1	5	lbw	–	12	3	0	–	–	–
897/564			3	Bridgetown	L-298	1	26	b	1	116	c	2	12	13	0	–	–	–
898/565			4	St John's	D	1	33	ro	1	83	c	–	12	0	0	–	–	–
899/566			5	Kingston	D	1	153	c	1	3	c	1	48	20	0	–	–	–

Ref	Series	V	T	Venue	Result	Batting 1st No	R	HO	Batting 2nd No	R	HO	Ct	Bowling 1st Balls	R	W	Bowling 2nd Balls	R	W
903/567	1981	A	1	Nottingham	L-4w	1	10	c	1	6	c	–	–	–	–	–	–	–
904/568			2	Lord's	D	1	44	c	1	20	lbw	–	60	28	0	–	–	–
905/569			3	Leeds	W-18	1	2	lbw	1	0	c	–	–	–	–	–	–	–
906/570			4	Birmingham	W-29	4	21	c	4	21	b	–	–	–	–	–	–	–
907/571			5	Manchester	W-103	1	10	lbw	1	5	b	1	–	–	–	–	–	–
912/573	1981–82	I	1	Bombay[3]	L-138	1	2	b	1	1	c	–	–	–	–	–	–	–
913/574			2	Bangalore	D	1	58	c	1	40	lbw	1	–	–	–	–	–	–
914/575			3	Delhi	D	1	71	c	1	20	*	1	49	12	2	–	–	–
915/576			4	Calcutta	D	1	47	c	1	63	b	2	36	10	0	12	4	0
916/577			5	Madras[1]	D	1	127	c	–	–	–	–	54	27	0	48	24	0
917/578			6	Kanpur	D	1	58	b	–	–	–	–	–	–	–	–	–	–
921/579	1981–82	SL		Colombo SO	W-7w	1	22	lbw	1	31	b	1	–	–	–	–	–	–
1017/612	1985	A	1	Leeds	W-5w	1	5	lbw	1	28	lbw	1	126	57	2	54	21	0
1018/613			2	Lord's	L-4w	1	30	lbw	1	17	c	1	18	11	0	–	–	–
1019/614			3	Nottingham	D	1	70	c	1	48	c	1	50	13	0	–	–	–
1020/615			4	Manchester	D	1	74	lbw	–	–	–	–	–	–	–	–	–	–
1021/616			5	Birmingham	W-I & 118	1	19	c	–	–	–	–	–	–	–	–	–	–
1022/617			6	Oval	W-I & 94	1	196	c	–	–	–	1	–	–	–	–	–	–
1038/618	1985–86	WI	1	Kingston	L-10w	1	51	c	1	0	b	1	12	6	0	–	–	–
1039/619			2	Port-of-Spain	L-7w	1	2	c	1	43	lbw	3	–	–	–	–	–	–
1040/620			3	Bridgetown	L-I & 30	1	53	c	1	11	b	1	–	–	–	–	–	–
1041/621			4	Port-of-Spain	L-10w	1	14	c	1	0	c	–	–	–	–	–	–	–
1042/622			5	St John's	L-240	1	51	lbw	1	51	lbw	1	30	21	1	–	–	–
1046/623	1986	I	1	Lord's	L-5w	1	114	b	1	8	lbw	1	–	–	–	–	–	–
1047/624			2	Leeds	L-279	1	8	c	1	5	c	2	36	19	1	42	12	0
1048/625			3	Birmingham	D	1	0	c	1	40	lbw	2	–	–	–	–	–	–
1049/626	1986	NZ	1	Lord's	D	1	18	c	1	183	c	2	78	23	1	–	–	–
1050/627			2	Nottingham	L-8w	1	18	lbw	1	17	c	1	12	0	0	–	–	–
1051/628			3	Oval	D	1	32	c	–	–	–	3	24	15	0	–	–	–
1084/639	1987–88	P	1	Lahore[2]	L-I & 87	1	12	b	1	15	c	1	–	–	–	–	–	–
1085/640			2	Faisalabad	D	1	28	c	1	65	lbw	2	–	–	–	12	4	0
1086/641			3	Karachi	D	1	12	c	1	93	b	–	–	–	–	–	–	–
1098/646	1988	WI	1	Nottingham	D	1	73	b	1	146	c	2	–	–	–	–	–	–
1099/647			2	Lord's	L-134	1	44	b	1	16	lbw	1	–	–	–	–	–	–
1100/648			3	Manchester	L-I & 156	1	27	c	1	1	lbw	–	–	–	–	–	–	–
1101/649			4	Leeds	L-10w	1	9	c	1	50	c	1	–	–	–	–	–	–
1102/650*			5	Oval	L-8w	1	9	c	1	84	c	2	–	–	–	–	–	–
1103/651*	1988	SL		Lord's	W-7w	1	75	lbw	1	36	c	3	–	–	–	–	–	–

Career	M	I	NO	HS	R	Avge	100	50	Ct	St	Balls	R	W	Avge	BB	5w	10w	Rate
Test	68	123	4	196	4541	38.15	8	27	69	–	1431	550	13	42.30	2-12	–	–	110.07
F/c	389	660	52	275	26745	43.98	66	137	380	–	15507	6868	210	32.70	7-14	3	–	73.84

G. A. GOOCH – TEST BATTING SUMMARY

Series	V	M	I	NO	HS	R	Avge	100	50
1975	A	2	4	–	31	37	9.25	–	–
1978	P	2	2	–	54	74	37.00	–	1
1978	NZ	3	5	2	91*	190	63.33	–	2
1978–79	A	6	11	–	74	246	22.36	–	1
1979	I	4	5	–	83	207	41.40	–	2
1979–80	A	2	4	–	99	172	43.00	–	2
1979–80	I	1	2	1	49*	57	57.00	–	–
1980	WI	5	10	–	123	394	39.40	1	2
1980	A	1	2	–	16	24	12.00	–	–
1980–81	WI	4	8	–	153	460	57.50	2	1
1981	A	5	10	–	44	139	13.90	–	–
1981–82	I	6	10	1	127	487	54.11	1	4
1981–82	SL	1	2	–	31	53	26.50	–	–
1985	A	6	9	–	196	487	54.11	1	2
1985–86	WI	5	10	–	53	276	27.60	–	4
1986	I	3	6	–	114	175	29.16	1	–

Series	V	M	I	NO	HS	R	Avge	100	50
1986	NZ	3	5	–	183	268	53.60	1	–
1987–88	P	3	6	–	93	225	37.50	–	2
1988	WI	5	10	–	146	459	45.90	1	3
1988	SL	1	2	–	75	111	55.50	–	1
	A	22	40	–	196	1105	27.62	1	5
	WI	19	38	–	153	1589	41.81	4	10
	NZ	6	10	2	183	458	57.25	1	2
	I	14	23	2	127	926	44.09	2	6
	P	5	8	–	93	299	37.37	–	3
	SL	2	4	–	75	164	41.00	–	1
Home		40	70	2	196	2565	37.72	5	13
Overseas		28	53	2	153	1976	38.74	3	14
Totals		68	123	4	196	4541	38.15	8	27

GOVER
Alfred Richard

Surrey (1928 to 1947)

Wisden 1937
TOUR I 1937–38 (Tennyson)
Born Epsom, Surrey 29 Feb 1908

Born on a leap day, Alf Gover was a tall (6ft 2½in) right-arm fast bowler who spearheaded Surrey's attack with considerable success on plumb batting pitches throughout the 1930s. In 1936 he became the only fast bowler since Tom Richardson in 1897 to take 200 wickets in a season and he repeated the feat the following summer. At the end of a frenetic arm-pumping approach, his high delivery and powerful body action often produced awkward bounce as he interwove his late outswingers with deadly break-backs. Although his batting seldom progressed beyond a series (usually brief) of pastoral heaves, he became a much respected all-round cricket coach and proprietor of a famous South London indoor cricket school. Even in his late seventies he would don his whites and advise some of the world's outstanding future players; Viv Richards and Andy Roberts were sent to him as soon as they arrived in England. In his youth he was a fine amateur soccer goalkeeper.

NOTABLE FEATS

- Took 100 wickets in a season 8 times, including 200 twice.
- Hat-trick and 4 wickets in 4 balls for Surrey v Worcestershire at Worcester in 1935.

The tall Alf Gover makes his England debut along with Arthur Fagg and Laurie Fishlock against India at Old Trafford, 1936: standing H. Gimblett, A.E. Fagg, J. Hardstaff jr, A.R. Gover, T.S. Worthington, L.B. Fishlock; seated H. Verity, R.W.V. Robins, G.O.B. Allen (captain), W.R. Hammond, G. Duckworth.

Ref	Series	V	T	Venue	Result	Batting 1st No	R	HO	Batting 2nd No	R	HO	Ct	Bowling 1st Balls	R	W	Bowling 2nd Balls	R	W
253/222	1936	I	2	Manchester	D	–	–	–	–	–	–	–	90	39	0	120	61	0
260/229	1937	NZ	1	Lord's	D	11	2	*	–	–	–	–	132	49	2	108	27	1
262/231			3	Oval	D	–	–	–	–	–	–	1	168	85	3	72	42	1
278/236	1946	I	3	Oval	D	–	–	–	–	–	–	–	126	56	1	–	–	–

Career	M	I	NO	HS	R	Avge	100	50	Ct	St	Balls	R	W	Avge	BB	5w	10w	Rate
Test	4	1	1	2*	2	–	–	–	1	–	816	359	8	44.87	3-85	–	–	102.00
F/c	362	414	167	41*	2312	9.36	–	–	171	–	77269	36753	1555	23.63	8-34	95	17	49.69

GOWER
David Ivon

Leicestershire (1975 to date)

Wisden 1979
TOURS
A 1978–79, 1979–80, 1982–83, 1986–87;
WI 1980–81, 1985–86; NZ 1983–84;
I 1979–80, 1981–82, 1984–85;
P 1983–84; SL 1977–78 (Robins),
1981–82, 1984–85
Born Tunbridge Wells, Kent 1 Apr 1957

From the moment that he pulled his very first ball to the boundary David Gower has brought a new excitement to Test cricket. No contemporary player can match the elegance of his driving or the deftness of his cutting; he has the felicitous touch and timing of a violinist and few bats have sounded sweeter. Tall (6ft), lean and left-handed, he caresses the ball gracefully with a full arc of the bat and has a complete range of attacking strokes. With a player of Gower's class the quality of his runs is more important than their quantity. It is therefore surprising to find that he has reached 7000 in Test cricket without ever having totalled 2000 in a first-class season, a revelation that confirms his big-match temperament and his difficulty in motivating his talents on the humdrum county circuit. He probably reached his peak against the 1985 Australians when he scored 732 runs (avge 82.33) and led England's successful Ashes campaign. His final captaincy record of 5 wins and 14 defeats in 26 Tests does him less than justice, as did the unceremonious manner of his sacking. In 1984–85 he skippered with shrewd control in India but his record was slightly deflated by ten successive losses to the mighty West Indians. Virtually an automatic England selection since his debut, it was no surprise when he gained his 100th cap. The fact that he was the youngest by four years to reach that landmark and that it had taken him only 10 years 50 days, three and and half years less than his four predecessors, confirmed the proliferation of Test cricket and the continuous pressure imposed on modern players. Formerly a fleet-footed cover, he has fielded close to the bat since problems with his right shoulder crippled his throwing powers; with luck it will also prevent him bowling any more failed off-breaks.

David Gower, watched by Tim Zoehrer, during his century against Australia in the Perth Test, 1986–87.

					Batting 1st			Batting 2nd			
Ref	Series	V	T Venue	Result	No	R	HO	No	R	HO	Ct
825/537	1978	P	1 Birmingham	W-I & 57	4	58	c	–	–	–	–
826/538			2 Lord's	W-I & 120	4	56	b	–	–	–	–
827/539			3 Leeds	D	4	39	lbw	–	–	–	–

NOTABLE FEATS

• 1000 runs in 13th Test (*851*) (20 inns); 2000 runs in 30th Test (*906*) (51 inns); 3000 runs in 46th Test (*939*) (78 inns); 4000 runs in 58th Test (*979*) (100 inns); 5000 runs in 7 yrs 62 days – fastest for E – 74th Test (*1020*) (127 inns); 6000 runs in 85th Test (*1050*) (147 inns); 7000 runs in 100th Test (*1101*) (172 inns).
• *979* First England captain to score a Test 100 since A.W. Greig in 1976–77. Shared record E v P 7th-wkt stand of 167 with V.J. Marks.
• *1019* His 166 is the highest score by an England captain at Nottingham.
• *1021* His 215 is the highest score v A at Birmingham and the second-highest by an England captain v A anywhere. Shared 2nd-wkt stand of 331 with R.T. Robinson.
• *1022* Completed 2000 runs v A and shared 2nd-wkt stand of 351 with G.A. Gooch – England's second-highest for any wicket v A.
• *1059* His stand of 207 with C.J. Richards is an England 6th-wkt record in Australia.
• *1101* Completed 7000 runs in his 100th Test and extended his world record sequence of Test innings without a 'duck' to 99.
• Exceeded 1000 runs in a season 8 times.
• Shared with J.C. Balderstone record Leicestershire 2nd-wkt stand of 289* v Essex at Leicester in 1981.
• His 158 v NZ at Brisbane in 1982–83 remains England's highest score in limited-overs internationals.

TEST NOTES

• *916* Bowled in 2nd inns: 0 for 1 (6 balls).
• *917* Bowled in 1st inns: 1 fopr 1 (6 balls).
• *1007* Bowled in 1st inns: 0 for 13 (18 balls).
• *1049* Bowled in 2nd inns: 0 for 1 (6 balls).
• *1050* Bowled in 2nd inns: 0 for 4 (0 balls – Gower became the first England bowler to be no-balled for throwing in a Test in England).

						Batting 1st			Batting 2nd			
Ref	Series	V	T	Venue	Result	No	R	HO	No	R	HO	Ct
828/540	1978	NZ	1	Oval	W-7w	4	111	ro	4	11	c	–
829/541			2	Nottingham	W-I & 119	4	46	c	–	–	–	–
830/542			3	Lord's	W-7w	4	71	c	4	46	c	–
834/543	1978–79	A	1	Brisbane[2]	W-7w	6	44	c	5	48	*	–
835/544			2	Perth	W-166	5	102	b	5	12	c	–
836/545			3	Melbourne	L-103	5	29	lbw	5	49	lbw	1
837/546			4	Sydney	W-93	5	7	c	5	34	c	–
838/547			5	Adelaide	W-205	5	9	lbw	5	21	lbw	2
839/548			6	Sydney	W-9w	5	65	c	–	–	–	1
851/549	1979	I	1	Birmingham	W-I & 83	5	200	*	–	–	–	–
852/550			2	Lord's	D	4	82	b	–	–	–	1
853/551			3	Leeds	D	4	0	lbw	–	–	–	–
854/552			4	Oval	D	4	0	lbw	4	7	c	1
868/553	1979–80	A	1	Perth	L-138	4	17	c	4	23	c	1
870/554			2	Sydney	L-6w	6	3	b	7	98	*	1
872/555			3	Melbourne	L-8w	4	0	lbw	4	11	b	1
876/556	1979–80	I		Bombay[3]	W-10w	4	16	lbw	–	–	–	–
880/557	1980	WI	1	Nottingham	L-2w	5	20	c	5	1	lbw	1
885/562	1980	A		Lord's	D	4	45	b	4	35	b	–
896/563	1980–81	WI	1	Port-of-Spain	L-I & 79	4	48	lbw	4	27	c	1
897/564			3	Bridgetown	L-298	4	17	c	4	54	b	–
898/565			4	St John's	D	4	32	c	4	22	c	1
899/566			5	Kingston	D	4	22	b	4	154	*	–
903/567	1981	A	1	Nottingham	L-4w	4	26	c	4	28	c	1
904/568			2	Lord's	D	4	27	c	4	89	c	1
905/569			3	Leeds	W-18	4	24	c	4	9	c	–
906/570			4	Birmingham	W-29	3	0	c	3	23	c	–
907/571			5	Manchester	W-103	4	23	c	4	1	c	1
912/573	1981–82	I	1	Bombay[3]	L-138	4	5	ro	4	20	lbw	–
913/574			2	Bangalore	D	4	82	lbw	4	34	*	–
914/575			3	Delhi	D	4	0	lbw	–	–	–	–
915/576			4	Calcutta	D	4	11	c	4	74	ro	–
916/577			5	Madras[1]	D	4	64	lbw	–	–	–	–
917/578			6	Kanpur	D	4	85	lbw	–	–	–	1
921/579	1981–82	SL		Colombo SO	W-7w	4	89	c	4	42	*	4
928/580	1982	I	1	Lord's	W-7w	4	37	c	5	14	*	1
929/581			2	Manchester	D	4	9	c	–	–	–	–
930/582			3	Oval	D	4	47	c	4	45	c	1
931/583	1982	P	1	Birmingham	W-113	4	74	c	4	13	c	1
932/584*			2	Lord's	L-10w	4	29	c	4	0	c	–
933/585			3	Leeds	W-3w	5	74	c	5	7	c	1
938/586	1982–83	A	1	Perth	D	3	72	c	3	28	lbw	–
939/587			2	Brisbane[2]	L-7w	3	18	c	3	34	c	–
940/588			3	Adelaide	L-8w	3	60	c	3	114	b	2
941/589			4	Melbourne	W-3	4	18	c	4	3	c	–
942/590			5	Sydney	D	3	70	c	4	24	c	2
957/591	1983	NZ	1	Oval	W-189	3	11	b	3	25	c	2
958/592			2	Leeds	L-5w	3	9	c	3	112	*	1
959/593			3	Lord's	W-127	3	108	lbw	3	34	c	1
960/594			4	Nottingham	W-165	3	72	b	3	33	c	2
975/595	1983–84	NZ	1	Wellington	D	3	33	c	–	–	–	2
976/596			2	Christchurch	L-I & 132	3	2	lbw	3	8	c	–
977/597			3	Auckland	D	3	26	b	–	–	–	–
978/598	1983–84	P	1	Karachi	L-3w	3	58	lbw	3	57	c	–
979/599*			2	Faisalabad	D	5	152	st	–	–	–	–
980/600*			3	Lahore[2]	D	3	9	c	4	173	*	3
989/601*	1984	WI	1	Birmingham	L-I & 180	4	10	c	4	12	c	1
990/602*			2	Lord's	L-9w	3	3	lbw	3	21	c	–
991/603*			3	Leeds	L-8w	4	2	lbw	4	43	c	1
992/604*			4	Manchester	L-I & 64	4	4	c	4	57	*	–
993/605*			5	Oval	L-172	5	12	c	4	7	lbw	1
994/606*	1984	SL		Lord's	D	4	55	c	–	–	–	1
1005/607*	1984–85	I	1	Bombay[3]	L-8W	4	13	b	4	2	c	2

Ref	Series	V	T	Venue	Result	Batting 1st No	R	HO	Batting 2nd No	R	HO	Ct
1006/608*			2	Delhi	W-8w	5	5	lbw	–	–	–	1
1007/609*			3	Calcutta	D	3	19	c	–	–	–	1
1008/610*			4	Madras[1]	W-9w	7	18	b	–	–	–	1
1009/611*			5	Kanpur	D	5	78	lbw	1	32	*	1
1017/612*	1985	A	1	Leeds	W-5w	3	17	c	3	5	c	1
1018/613*			2	Lord's	L-4w	3	86	c	5	22	c	–
1019/614*			3	Nottingham	D	3	166	c	3	17	c	–
1020/615*			4	Manchester	D	3	47	c	–	–	–	1
1021/616*			5	Birmingham	W-I & 118	3	215	c	–	–	–	3
1022/617*			6	Oval	W-I & 94	3	157	c	–	–	–	1
1038/618*	1985–86	WI	1	Kingston	L-10w	3	16	lbw	3	9	c	–
1039/619*			2	Port-of-Spain	L-7w	3	66	lbw	3	47	b	1
1040/620*			3	Bridgetown	L-I & 30	3	66	c	3	23	c	1
1041/621*			4	Port-of-Spain	L-10w	3	10	c	3	22	lbw	–
1042/622*			5	St John's	L-240	4	90	c	5	21	c	1
1046/623*	1986	I	1	Lord's	L-5w	3	18	c	3	8	lbw	–
1048/625			3	Birmingham	D	4	49	lbw	4	26	c	2
1049/626	1986	NZ	1	Lord's	D	4	62	c	4	3	b	3
1050/627			2	Nottingham	L-8w	4	71	lbw	5	26	c	–
1051/628			3	Oval	D	3	131	b	–	–	–	–
1058/629	1986–87	A	1	Brisbane[2]	W-7w	5	51	c	5	15	*	–
1059/630			2	Perth	D	5	136	c	5	48	c	–
1060/631			3	Adelaide	D	5	38	lbw	–	–	–	–
1061/632			4	Melbourne	W-I & 14	5	7	c	–	–	–	1
1062/633			5	Sydney	L-55	5	72	c	3	37	c	–
1075/634	1987	P	1	Manchester	D	6	22	c	–	–	–	–
1076/635			2	Lord's	D	4	8	c	–	–	–	–
1077/636			3	Leeds	L-I & 18	4	10	b	4	55	b	1
1078/637			4	Birmingham	D	4	61	c	3	18	b	–
1079/638			5	Oval	D	4	28	b	4	34	c	1
1098/646	1988	WI	1	Nottingham	D	4	18	c	4	88	*	–
1099/647			2	Lord's	L-134	4	46	c	4	1	c	1
1100/648			3	Manchester	L-I & 156	4	9	c	4	34	c	–
1101/649			4	Leeds	L-10w	4	13	c	4	2	c	1

Career	M	I	NO	HS	R	Avge	100	50	Ct	St	Balls	R	W	Avge	BB	5w	10w	Rate
Test	100	172	13	215	7000	44.02	14	35	68	–	36	20	1	20.00	1-1	–	–	36.00
F/c	341	546	50	215	19889	40.09	40	105	209	1	259	223	4	55.75	3-47	–	–	64.75

D. I. GOWER – TEST BATTING SUMMARY

Series	V	M	I	NO	HS	R	Avge	100	50
1978	P	3	3	–	58	153	51.00	–	2
1978	NZ	3	5	–	111	285	57.00	1	1
1978–79	A	6	11	1	102	420	42.00	1	1
1979	I	4	5	1	200*	289	72.25	1	1
1979–80	A	3	6	1	98*	152	30.40	–	1
1979–80	I	1	1	–	16	16	16.00	–	–
1980	WI	1	2	–	20	21	10.50	–	–
1980	A	1	2	–	45	80	40.00	–	–
1980–81	WI	4	8	1	154*	376	53.71	1	1
1981	A	5	10	–	89	250	25.00	–	1
1981–82	I	6	9	1	85	375	46.87	–	4
1981–82	SL	1	2	1	89	131	131.00	–	1
1982	I	3	5	1	47	152	38.00	–	–
1982	P	3	6	–	74	197	32.83	–	2
1982–83	A	5	10	–	114	441	44.10	1	3
1983	NZ	4	8	1	112*	404	57.71	2	1
1983–84	NZ	3	4	–	33	69	17.25	–	–
1983–84	P	3	5	1	173*	449	112.25	2	2
1984	WI	5	10	1	57*	171	19.00	–	1

Series	V	M	I	NO	HS	R	Avge	100	50
1984	SL	1	1	–	55	55	55.00	–	1
1984–85	I	5	7	1	78	167	27.83	–	1
1985	A	6	9	–	215	732	81.33	3	1
1985–86	WI	5	10	–	90	370	37.00	–	3
1986	I	2	4	–	49	101	25.25	–	–
1986	NZ	3	5	–	131	293	58.60	1	2
1986–87	A	5	8	1	136	404	57.71	1	2
1987	P	5	8	–	61	236	29.50	–	2
1988	WI	4	8	1	88*	211	30.14	–	1
	A	31	56	3	215	2479	46.77	6	9
	WI	19	38	3	154*	1149	32.82	1	6
	NZ	13	22	1	131	1051	50.04	4	4
	I	21	31	4	200*	1100	40.74	1	6
	P	14	22	1	173*	1035	49.28	2	8
	SL	2	3	1	89	186	93.00	–	2
Home		53	91	5	215	3630	42.20	8	16
Overseas		47	81	8	173*	3370	46.16	6	19
Totals		100	172	13	215	7000	44.02	14	35

GRACE, Edward Mills

Gloucestershire (1870 to 1895)

Born Downend, Bristol 28 Nov 1841
Died Thornbury, Gloucestershire
20 May 1911

During a career lasting more than three decades, Dr Edward Grace was second only to his younger brother, W.G., as the most remarkable all-round match-winner of his day. Primarily an unorthodox attacking batsman with a marvellous eye, he was an exceptionally fast scorer in his younger days and one of the first major cricketers to employ the pull. In 1863 he exceeded 3000 runs in all matches. Originally a fast round-arm bowler, he reverted to old-fashioned lobs with devastating success in club matches for Thornbury. He was a magnificent field at the key position of point. Known as 'The Coroner' (he was coroner for West Gloucestershire), he toured Australia with George Parr's 1863–64 team (not first-class) and was secretary of Gloucestershire from the Club's inception (1871) until 1909.

NOTABLE FEATS

- Carried his bat for 192* out of 344 and took 10 for 69 (15 for 146 in a 12-a-side match) for Gentlemen of MCC v Gentlemen of Kent at Canterbury in 1862.
- Played in 2 first-class Canterbury Festival matches on the same day (9 Aug 1865): The South v The North and Gentlemen of MCC v Gentlemen of Kent.

Ref	Series	V	T	Venue	Result	Batting 1st No	R	HO	Batting 2nd No	R	HO	Ct
4/4	1880	A		Oval	W-5w	1	36	c	6	0	b	1

Career	M	I	NO	HS	R	Avge	100	50	Ct	St	Balls	R	W	Avge	BB	5w	10w	Rate
Test	1	2	0	36	36	18.00	–	–	1	–	–	–	–	–	–	–	–	–
F/c	314	555	18	192*	10025	18.66	5	44	369	1	13441	6213	305	20.37	10-69	17	2	44.06

The Gloucestershire side of 1877, dominated by the Grace brothers: E.M. is seated at the end of the bench next to W.G., and G.F. is at the back sporting the white cap. Billy Midwinter, the only cricketer to have played for and against Australia, is the gentleman in pads.

GRACE George Frederick

Gloucestershire (1870 to 1880)

Born Downend, Bristol 13 Dec 1850
Died Basingstoke, Hampshire
22 Sep 1880

Fred Grace was a tall, well-built, dashing middle-order batsman, a right-handed round-arm fast bowler and a fine athletic fielder. The fifth and youngest of the famous brethren, he remains the second-youngest English first-class cricketer, having made his debut for the Gentlemen of England against Oxford University in 1866 at the age of 15 years 159 days. He toured Australia with W.G.'s team in 1873–74 (not first-class) and, together with W.G. and E.M., he appeared in the inaugural Test in England. Although he bagged a 'pair' and did not bowl, he held a magnificent running catch off such a towering hit by George Bonnor that the batsmen almost completed their third run. Two weeks later, on his way to a match at Winchester, he died of congestion of the lungs following a severe cold.

Ref	Series	V	T	Venue	Result	Batting 1st No	R	HO	Batting 2nd No	R	HO	Ct
4/4	1880	A		Oval	W-5w	9	0	c	2	0	b	2

Career	M	I	NO	HS	R	Avge	100	50	Ct	St	Balls	R	W	Avge	BB	5w	10w	Rate
Test	1	2	0	0	0	0.00	–	–	2	–	–	–	–	–	–	–	–	–
F/c	195	316	40	189*	6910	25.03	8	32	170	3	18740	6599	329	20.05	8-43	17	5	56.96

GRACE
William Gilbert

Gloucestershire (1870 to 1899)
London County (1900 to 1904)

Wisden 1896
TOUR A 1891–92
Born Downend, Bristol 18 Jul 1848
Died Mottingham, Kent 23 Oct 1915

W.G. Grace

The fourth of five sons of a Gloucestershire doctor, W.G. Grace is indisputably the most famous of all cricketers and the game's greatest single influence. His striking appearance, formidable personality, legendary gamesmanship, prodigious all-round feats and remarkably long career combined to make him one of the most dominant national figures of the latter half of the Victorian era. Tall, strong, heavily bearded from youth and later very heavily built, his early interest in cricket had been inspired by his mother, the former Martha Pocock and the first female to gain admission to *Wisden*'s sacred Births and Deaths. He was a model for any opening batsman: a notable player of fast bowling, equally proficient off front foot or back, an exceptional judge of length and a master of every stroke. Although his technique was orthodox, his approach to batting introduced a new range of aggression and he developed many of the front-foot shots. As a glance at his *Notable Feats* will confirm, he created or broke virtually every major batting record and did so in an age of uncovered and frequently hazardous pitches. His supremacy was total; when he amassed the unprecedented aggregate of 2739 runs in 1871 he averaged 78 while his nearest rival, the admirable Richard Daft, managed only 34. Five years later he made 400* against 22 of Grimsby with the equivalent of two teams in the field. His right-handed round-arm bowling was originally medium in pace but from about 1872 he relied on a slower style with cunning variations of break, flight and angle. As a teenager he had been a superb outfielder and a fine all-round athlete; in 1866 he had won the 440 yards hurdles at the first National Olympian Association meeting at Crystal Palace after scoring 244* for England against Surrey at The Oval on the two previous days. Together with his family he played a major role in founding Gloucestershire CCC and was captain for the first 29 years of their history (1871–99) before moving to London as manager of the London County Club. While there he developed his interest in bowls and, in 1903, helped form the English Bowling Association. Known in his later years as 'The Doctor' (he was a qualified surgeon), he celebrated his 58th birthday and last appearance in a Gentlemen v Players match by scoring 74. Another eight years passed before he played his final innings of all (69* for Eltham against Grove Park) just ten days before the outbreak of the First World War. According to one opposing wicket-keeper he seldom washed behind his ears.

NOTABLE FEATS

- 1000 runs in 19th Test (*50*) (29 inns).
- *4* With E.M. and G.F. Grace provided the first instance of three brothers playing in the same Test. Scored England's first Test century on his debut and remains the only Englishman to score 100 v A in England in his first Test. With A.P. Lucas shared in Test cricket's first century partnership – 120 for the 2nd wkt.
- *16* Only player to hold a catch off his first ball as a wicket-keeper in Test cricket when he deputized for A. Lyttelton who was bowling.

NOTABLE FEATS *cont.*

- *24* Made 170 out of 216 in 270 min to reclaim record England score he had lost to A. Shrewsbury in the previous match. Shared stand of 170 with W.H. Scotton which remained Test 1st-wkt record until 1899.
- *60* Ended his England career aged 50 yrs 320 days and remains oldest Test captain.
- Exceeded 1000 runs in a season 28 times (a record equalled by F.E. Woolley), including 2000 on 5 occasions. First batsman to score 2000 runs (1871).
- Took 100 wickets in a season 10 times.
- First to achieve the 'double' of 1000 runs and 100 wickets in a first-class season (1874). He repeated this performance in each of the next 4 seasons but not until 1882 was it emulated. Did the 'double' 8 times, including first instance of 2000 runs and 100 wickets in 1876.
- In 1895, at the age of 46 yrs 10 mths, he achieved the first instance of 1000 runs in May alone.
- First batsman to score 100 first-class hundreds. His record of 126 centuries (including 10 doubles and 3 triples) stood until 1925. Scored 100 in each innings of a match 3 times and on 5 occasions scored hundreds in 3 successive innings.
- First batsman to score 10 first-class hundreds in a season (1871).
- First batsman to score 100 before lunch on the first day of an 'important match': 116* for MCC v Kent at Canterbury in 1869. Repeated the feat 6 times, including twice in successive innings, and achieved it 3 times on other days.
- His 344 for MCC v Kent at Canterbury in 1876 was the first triple century, remained the highest first-class score until 1895, and is still the record for MCC anywhere. It contained the first instance of 50 fours (51). Ten days later he made 318* v Yorkshire at Cheltenham – still Gloucestershire's highest score.
- Carried his bat through a completed innings on 17 occasions (world record equalled by C.J.B. Wood for Leicestershire).
- Scored 126 out of 159 for United South v United North at Hull in 1876, still the highest proportion of a first-class total (79.2%) by an Englishman and the world record until 1943–44.
- Took 13 for 84 on debut – Gents of South v Players of South at The Oval in 1865.
- Took 15 wickets in a match 5 times; his 17 for 89 for Gloucestershire v Nottinghamshire at Cheltenham in 1877 included a spell of 7 wickets in 17 balls.
- Scored 104 and took all 10 for 49 for MCC v Oxford U at Oxford in 1886.
- Achieved the match 'double' of 100 runs and 10 wickets on 15 occasions (6 more than any other cricketer), including the only 3 instances in Gentleman v Players matches, a fixture in which he made the record total of 85 appearances.
- He made 26 hundreds in minor matches for London County between the age of 51 and 60. In all cricket he is estimated as scoring 80,000 runs and taking 7000 wickets.

						Batting 1st			Batting 2nd				Bowling 1st			Bowling 2nd		
Ref	Series	V	T	Venue	Result	No	R	HO	No	R	HO	Ct	Balls	R	W	Balls	R	W
4/4	1880	A		Oval	W-5w	2	152	b	7	9	*	1	5	2	1	112	66	2
9/9	1882	A		Oval	L-7	2	4	b	1	32	c	4	–	–	–	–	–	–
14/14	1884	A	1	Manchester	D	1	8	c	1	31	b	2	44	2	1	–	–	–
15/15			2	Lord's	W-I & 5	1	14	c	–	–	–	2	28	13	1	–	–	–
16/16			3	Oval	D	1	19	ro	–	–	–	1	96	23	1	–	–	–
22/22	1886	A	1	Manchester	W-4w	2	8	c	2	4	c	2	36	21	1	4	1	0
23/23			2	Lord's	W-I & 106	1	18	c	–	–	–	2	–	–	–	–	–	–
24/24			3	Oval	W-I & 217	1	170	c	–	–	–	4	–	–	–	–	–	–
28/28	1888	A	1	Lord's	L-61	1	10	c	1	24	c	3	–	–	–	–	–	–
29/29*			2	Oval	W-I & 137	1	1	c	–	–	–	1	–	–	–	–	–	–
30/30*			3	Manchester	W-I & 21	1	38	c	–	–	–	4	–	–	–	–	–	–
33/33*	1890	A	1	Lord's	W-7w	1	0	c	1	75	*	1	–	–	–	70	12	2
34/34*			2	Oval	W-2w	2	0	c	2	16	c	–	–	–	–	–	–	–
35/35*	1891–92	A	1	Melbourne	L-54	1	50	b	1	25	c	2	–	–	–	–	–	–
36/36*			2	Sydney	L-72	2	26	b	2	5	c	5	–	–	–	96	34	0
37/37*			3	Adelaide	W-I & 230	1	58	b	–	–	–	2	–	–	–	–	–	–
40/40*	1893	A	2	Oval	W-I & 43	1	68	c	–	–	–	1	–	–	–	–	–	–
41/41*			3	Manchester	D	2	40	b	2	45	c	1	–	–	–	–	–	–
50/50*	1896	A	1	Lord's	W-6w	1	66	c	1	7	c	–	–	–	–	30	14	0
51/51*			2	Manchester	L-3w	2	2	st	2	11	c	–	35	11	0	–	–	–
52/52*			3	Oval	W-66	1	24	c	1	9	b	–	–	–	–	–	–	–
60/60*	1899	A	1	Nottingham	D	1	28	c	1	1	b	1	100	31	0	10	6	0

Career	M	I	NO	HS	R	Avge	100	50	Ct	St	Balls	R	W	Avge	BB	5w	10w	Rate
Test	22	36	2	170	1098	32.29	2	5	39	–	666	236	9	26.22	2-12	–	–	74.00
F/c	879	1493	105	344	54896	39.55	126	249	887	5	126030	51545	2864+12	17.99	10-49	247	66	44.00

W. G. GRACE – TEST BATTING SUMMARY

Series	V	M	I	NO	HS	R	Avge	100	50
1880	A	1	2	1	152	161	161.00	1	–
1882	A	1	2	–	32	36	18.00	–	–
1884	A	3	4	–	31	72	18.00	–	–
1886	A	3	4	–	170	200	50.00	1	–
1888	A	3	4	–	38	73	18.25	–	–
1890	A	2	4	1	75*	91	30.33	–	1
1891–92	A	3	5	–	58	164	32.80	–	2
1893	A	2	3	–	68	153	51.00	–	1
1896	A	3	6	–	66	119	19.83	–	1
1899	A	1	2	–	28	29	14.50	–	–
Home		19	31	2	170	934	32.20	2	3
Overseas		3	5	–	58	164	32.80	–	2
Totals		22	36	2	170	1098	32.29	2	5

GRAVENEY
Thomas William OBE

Gloucestershire (1948 to 1960)
Worcestershire (1961 to 1970)
Queensland (1969–70 to 1971–72)

Wisden 1953
TOURS
A 1954–55, 1958–59, 1962–63;
SA 1959–60 (Cwlth), 1960–61 (Cav);
WI 1953–54, 1955–56 (Swanton),
1956–57 (Norfolk), 1963–64 (Cav),
1966–67 (RW), 1967–68;
NZ 1954–55, 1958–59, 1961–62 (Int XI);
I 1951–52, 1956–57 (Howard),
1961–62 (Int XI); P 1951–52,
1961–62 (Int XI), 1963–64 (Cwlth),
1968–69; SL 1951–52, 1968–69;
Z 1961–62 (Int XI), 1964–65 (Worcs)
Born Riding Mill, Northumberland
16 Jun 1927

Tom Graveney was an elegant batting artist, a supremely graceful stylist whose cover-driving evoked memories of his Gloucestershire forebear Wally Hammond. Essentially a front-foot player, he used his height (6ft 1in) and reach to maximum effect and seldom went on to his back foot even to hook. His positioning of head, feet and hands were models for any aspiring batsman, as was his masterly technique against spin. He was also a very reliable close catcher, usually at slip, and a handy right-arm leg-spin bowler. Although he was a talented and consistent strokemaker who overcame all the many and varied peculiarities of county pitches, he took some time to establish his England place and remove doubts about his ability under pressure and against the fastest bowling. It was only after leaving Bristol because of a captaincy dispute that he reached his peak at the highest level. Recalled to the Test arena in 1966 on his 39th birthday, he celebrated with a magnificent 96 against the fiery pace of Hall and Griffith. He proceeded to enjoy a remarkable Indian summer, remaining an automatic selection for three years until he was suspended for playing in a Sunday benefit match during what transpired to be his final Test. In 1964 and 1965 he had made vast contributions to Worcestershire's first Championships and he skippered them enthusiastically for three summers (1968–70) before taking up a coaching engagement in Brisbane. The first of three Graveneys to captain Gloucestershire (1959–60), he was succeeded by his brother Ken (1963–64) and nephew David (1982–88). He remains a highly talented golfer and respected television summarizer.

NOTABLE FEATS

- 1000 runs in 19th Test (*386*) (30 inns); 2000 runs in 37th Test (*443*) (59 inns); 3000 runs in 53rd Test (*536*) (81 inns); 4000 runs in 65th Test (*623*) (101 inns).
- *340* His 175 in 495 min was England's highest score in India until 1976–77.
- *395* Became the 100th player to score a century in E v A Tests.
- *441* Shared record E v WI 2nd-wkt stand of 266 with P.E. Richardson.
- *531* Shared record E v P 9th-wkt stand of 76 with F.S. Trueman.
- *606* Shared record E v WI 5th-wkt stand of 130* with C. Milburn.
- *607* Scored his third 100 in consecutive Tests at Nottingham.
- *609* Shared record E v WI 8th-wkt stand of 217 in 235 min with J.T. Murray.
- *621* Shared record E v P 3rd-wkt stand of 201 in 223 min with K.F. Barrington.
- Exceeded 1000 runs in a season 20 times (plus twice on tour), including 2000 runs on 7 occasions.

Tom Graveney

NOTABLE FEATS *cont.*

- In 1964 he became the 15th batsman to score 100 first-class hundreds, his final tally of 122 including 7 double centuries.
- Only player to score 10,000 runs for 2 counties and first with an entirely post-war career to score either 30,000 runs or 100 hundreds.
- Scored 100 in each innings of a match on 4 occasions.
- His 4th-wkt stand of 402 with W. Watson for MCC v British Guiana at Georgetown in 1953–54 remains the record for any wicket by an English touring team.
- Scored 200 of Gloucestershire's 298 v Glamorgan at Newport in 1956 – lowest completed total to include a 200.
- Shared record Gloucestershire 2nd-wkt stand of 256 with C.T.M. Pugh v Derbyshire at Chesterfield in 1960.
- Shared record Worcestershire 3rd-wkt stand of 314 with M.J. Horton v Somerset at Worcester in 1962.

TEST NOTES

- *410* Deputized for T.G. Evans as wicket-keeper throughout 2nd inns.
- *467* Deputized for T.G. Evans as wicket-keeper after first day.
- *639* Deputized as captain when M.C. Cowdrey was unable to field.
- *647* Deputized for M.C. Cowdrey as captain throughout the final innings.

						Batting 1st			Batting 2nd				Bowling 1st			Bowling 2nd		
Ref	**Series**	**V**	**T**	**Venue**	**Result**	**No**	**R**	**HO**	**No**	**R**	**HO**	**Ct**	**Balls**	**R**	**W**	**Balls**	**R**	**W**
336/289	1951	SA	3	Manchester	W-9w	4	15	b	–	–	–	–	–	–	–	–	–	–
340/293	1951–52	I	2	Bombay[2]	D	3	175	c	3	25	*	–	–	–	–	–	–	–
341/294			3	Calcutta	D	3	24	c	3	21	c	–	–	–	–	6	9	0
342/295			4	Kanpur	W-8w	3	6	b	3	48	*	1	–	–	–	–	–	–
343/296			5	Madras[1]	L-I & 8	3	39	st	3	25	c	–	–	–	–	–	–	–
351/297	1952	I	1	Leeds	W-7w	5	71	b	5	20	*	–	–	–	–	–	–	–
352/298			2	Lord's	W-8w	5	73	c	–	–	–	–	–	–	–	–	–	–
353/299			3	Manchester	W-I & 207	5	14	lbw	–	–	–	2	–	–	–	–	–	–
354/300			4	Oval	D	5	13	c	–	–	–	–	–	–	–	–	–	–
372/301	1953	A	1	Nottingham	D	5	22	c	–	–	–	2	–	–	–	–	–	–
373/302			2	Lord's	D	3	78	b	3	2	c	1	–	–	–	–	–	–
374/303			3	Manchester	D	3	5	c	–	–	–	–	–	–	–	–	–	–
375/304			4	Leeds	D	3	55	c	3	3	b	1	–	–	–	–	–	–
376/305			5	Oval	W-8w	5	4	c	–	–	–	–	–	–	–	–	–	–
382/306	1953–54	WI	1	Kingston	L-140	5	16	lbw	4	34	c	2	–	–	–	–	–	–
383/307			2	Bridgetown	L-181	5	15	c	5	64	*	1	–	–	–	–	–	–
384/308			3	Georgetown	W-9w	5	0	b	1	33	*	2	–	–	–	–	–	–
385/309			4	Port-of-Spain	D	6	92	c	5	0	*	1	18	26	0	30	33	0
386/310			5	Kingston	W-9w	6	11	lbw	1	0	b	2	–	–	–	–	–	–
388/312	1954	P	2	Nottingham	W-I & 129	5	84	c	–	–	–	1	–	–	–	–	–	–
389/313			3	Manchester	D	5	65	st	–	–	–	1	–	–	–	–	–	–
390/314			4	Oval	L-24	5	1	c	6	0	lbw	1	–	–	–	–	–	–
392/316	1954–55	A	2	Sydney	W-38	4	21	c	4	0	c	2	–	–	–	–	–	–
395/319			5	Sydney	D	2	111	c	–	–	–	2	–	–	–	48	34	1
401/320	1954–55	NZ	1	Dunedin	W-8w	2	41	b	2	32	*	–	–	–	–	–	–	–
402/321			2	Auckland	W-I & 20	2	13	c	–	–	–	2	–	–	–	–	–	–
408/322	1955	SA	1	Nottingham	W-I & 5	2	42	c	–	–	–	3	–	–	–	–	–	–
409/323			2	Lord's	W-71	2	15	c	2	60	c	2	–	–	–	–	–	–
410/324			3	Manchester	L-3w	2	0	c	2	1	b	2	–	–	–	–	–	–
411/325			4	Leeds	L-224	6	10	lbw	1	36	c	–	–	–	–	–	–	–
412/326			5	Oval	W-92	6	13	c	3	42	b	2	–	–	–	–	–	–
425/327	1956	A	1	Nottingham	D	3	8	c	4	10	*	–	–	–	–	36	6	0
426/328			2	Lord's	L-185	3	5	b	3	18	c	1	–	–	–	–	–	–
440/338	1957	WI	2	Lord's	W-I & 36	3	0	lbw	–	–	–	1	–	–	–	–	–	–
441/339			3	Nottingham	D	3	258	b	3	28	*	–	–	–	–	30	14	0
442/340			4	Leeds	W-I & 5	3	22	b	–	–	–	–	–	–	–	–	–	–
443/341			5	Oval	W-I & 237	3	164	b	–	–	–	–	–	–	–	–	–	–
454/342	1958	NZ	1	Birmingham	W-205	3	7	c	3	19	c	1	–	–	–	–	–	–
455/343			2	Lord's	W-I & 148	3	37	c	–	–	–	1	–	–	–	–	–	–
456/344			3	Leeds	W-I & 71	3	31	c	–	–	–	–	–	–	–	–	–	–
457/345			4	Manchester	W-I & 13	3	25	c	–	–	–	–	–	–	–	–	–	–
464/347	1958–59	A	1	Brisbane[2]	L-8w	3	19	c	4	36	ro	2	–	–	–	–	–	–

Ref	Series	V	T	Venue	Result	Batting 1st No	R	HO	Batting 2nd No	R	HO	Ct	Bowling 1st Balls	R	W	Bowling 2nd Balls	R	W
465/348			2	Melbourne	L-8w	4	0	lbw	4	3	c	1	–	–	–	–	–	–
466/349			3	Sydney	D	3	33	c	3	22	lbw	1	–	–	–	–	–	–
467/350			4	Adelaide	L-10w	5	41	c	5	53	*	–	–	–	–	–	–	–
468/351			5	Melbourne	L-9w	5	19	c	5	54	c	1	–	–	–	–	–	–
472/352	1958–59	NZ	1	Christchurch	W-I & 99	3	42	lbw	–	–	–	1	–	–	–	–	–	–
473/353			2	Auckland	D	3	46	b	–	–	–	1	–	–	–	–	–	–
530/382	1962	P	1	Birmingham	W-I & 24	4	97	c	–	–	–	3	–	–	–	–	–	–
531/383			2	Lord's	W-9w	4	153	b	–	–	–	3	–	–	–	–	–	–
532/384			3	Leeds	W-I & 117	4	37	c	–	–	–	1	–	–	–	–	–	–
533/385			4	Nottingham	D	4	114	c	–	–	–	1	–	–	–	–	–	–
536/388	1962–63	A	2	Melbourne	W-7w	6	41	ro	–	–	–	1	24	10	0	–	–	–
538/390			4	Adelaide	D	6	22	c	6	36	*	2	–	–	–	–	–	–
539/391			5	Sydney	D	5	14	c	6	3	c	3	–	–	–	32	24	0
606/430	1966	WI	2	Lord's	D	3	96	c	6	30	*	–	–	–	–	–	–	–
607/431			3	Nottingham	L-139	4	109	c	4	32	c	1	–	–	–	–	–	–
608/432			4	Leeds	L-I & 55	4	8	b	4	19	b	1	–	–	–	–	–	–
609/433			5	Oval	W-I & 34	4	165	ro	–	–	–	3	–	–	–	–	–	–
618/434	1967	I	1	Leeds	W-6w	4	59	c	3	14	b	–	–	–	–	–	–	–
619/435			2	Lord's	W-I & 124	4	151	st	–	–	–	1	–	–	–	–	–	–
620/436			3	Birmingham	W-132	4	10	c	4	17	c	1	–	–	–	–	–	–
621/437	1967	P	1	Lord's	D	4	81	b	4	30	c	1	–	–	–	–	–	–
622/438			2	Nottingham	W-10w	4	28	c	–	–	–	–	–	–	–	–	–	–
623/439			3	Oval	W-8w	4	77	c	–	–	–	–	–	–	–	–	–	–
628/440	1967–68	WI	1	Port-of-Spain	D	5	118	b	–	–	–	4	–	–	–	–	–	–
629/441			2	Kingston	D	5	30	b	5	21	c	1	–	–	–	–	–	–
630/442			3	Bridgetown	D	5	55	c	–	–	–	2	–	–	–	–	–	–
631/443			4	Port-of-Spain	W-7w	5	8	c	4	2	b	1	–	–	–	–	–	–
632/444			5	Georgetown	D	4	27	c	4	0	c	1	–	–	–	–	–	–
637/445	1968	A	1	Manchester	L-159	4	2	c	4	33	c	1	–	–	–	–	–	–
638/446			2	Lord's	D	6	14	c	–	–	–	1	–	–	–	–	–	–
639/447			3	Birmingham	D	5	96	b	3	39	*	–	–	–	–	–	–	–
640/448*			4	Leeds	D	4	37	c	4	41	c	2	–	–	–	–	–	–
641/449			5	Oval	W-226	5	63	c	5	12	ro	–	–	–	–	–	–	–
647/450	1968–69	P	1	Lahore[2]	D	4	13	c	4	12	ro	–	–	–	–	36	11	0
648/451			2	Dacca	D	3	46	b	–	–	–	–	–	–	–	–	–	–
649/452			3	Karachi	D	3	105	c	–	–	–	–	–	–	–	–	–	–
653/453	1969	WI	1	Manchester	W-10w	4	75	b	–	–	–	1	–	–	–	–	–	–

Career	M	I	NO	HS	R	Avge	100	50	Ct	St	Balls	R	W	Avge	BB	5w	10w	Rate
Test	79	123	13	258	4882	44.38	11	20	80	–	260	167	1	167.00	1-34	–	–	260.00
F/c	732	1223	159	258	47793	44.91	122	232	550	1	5473	3037	80	37.96	5-28	1	–	68.41

T. W. GRAVENEY – TEST BATTING SUMMARY

Series	V	M	I	NO	HS	R	Avge	100	50
1951	SA	1	1	–	15	15	15.00	–	–
1951–52	I	4	8	2	175	363	60.50	1	–
1952	I	4	5	1	73	191	47.75	–	2
1953	A	5	7	–	78	169	24.14	–	2
1953–54	WI	5	10	3	92	265	37.85	–	2
1954	P	3	4	–	84	150	37.80	–	2
1954–55	A	2	3	–	111	132	44.00	1	–
1954–55	NZ	2	3	1	41	86	43.00	–	–
1955	SA	5	9	–	60	219	24.33	–	1
1956	A	2	4	1	18	41	13.66	–	–
1957	WI	4	5	1	258	472	118.00	2	–
1958	NZ	4	5	–	37	119	23.80	–	–
1958–59	A	5	10	1	54	280	31.11	–	2
1958–59	NZ	2	2	–	46	88	44.00	–	–
1962	P	4	4	–	153	401	100.25	2	1
1962–63	A	3	5	1	41	116	29.00	–	–
1966	WI	4	7	1	165	459	76.50	2	1
1967	I	3	5	–	151	251	50.20	1	1
1967	P	3	4	–	81	216	54.00	–	2
1967–68	WI	5	8	–	118	261	32.62	1	1
1968	A	5	9	1	96	337	42.12	–	2
1968–69	P	3	4	–	105	176	44.00	1	–
1969	WI	1	1	–	75	75	75.00	–	1
	A	22	38	4	111	1075	31.61	1	6
	SA	6	10	–	60	234	23.40	–	1
	WI	19	31	5	258	1532	58.92	5	5
	NZ	8	10	1	46	293	32.55	–	–
	I	11	18	3	175	805	53.66	2	3
	P	13	16	–	153	943	58.93	3	5
Home		48	70	5	258	3115	47.92	7	15
Overseas		31	53	8	175	1767	39.26	4	5
Totals		79	123	13	258	4882	44.38	11	20

GREENHOUGH Thomas

Lancashire (1951 to 1966)

TOURS
WI 1956–57 (Norfolk), 1959–60
Born Cronkey Shaw, Rochdale, Lancashire 9 Nov 1931

One of the last members of a doomed breed, Tommy Greenhough was a very talented right-arm leg-break and googly bowler. Cradling the ball during a long, prancing run, he could spin it sharply and took 100 wickets in a season twice. He was a fairly inept tail-end batsman who once surprised himself (and Gloucestershire's bowlers) by scoring 76*. Slightly accident prone, he was susceptible to hand injuries and once fractured both ankles when he fell off a ladder.

Tommy Greenhough

						Batting 1st			Batting 2nd				Bowling 1st			Bowling 2nd		
Ref	Series	V	T	Venue	Result	No	R	HO	No	R	HO	Ct	Balls	R	W	Balls	R	W
474/354	1959	I	1	Nottingham	W-I & 59	10	0	c	–	–	–	–	156	58	1	138	48	2
475/355			2	Lord's	W-8w	11	0	*	–	–	–	–	96	35	5	109	31	2
478/358			5	Oval	W-I & 27	11	2	c	–	–	–	1	174	36	2	162	47	2
496/368	1960	SA	5	Oval	D	11	2	b	–	–	–	–	264	99	2	30	3	0

Career	M	I	NO	HS	R	Avge	100	50	Ct	St	Balls	R	W	Avge	BB	5w	10w	Rate
Test	4	4	1	2	4	1.33	–	–	1	–	1129	357	16	22.31	5-35	1	–	70.56
F/c	255	313	85	76*	1913	8.39	–	1	84	–	42176	16802	751	22.37	7-56	34	5	56.15

GREENWOOD Andrew

Yorkshire (1869 to 1880)

TOUR A 1876–77
Born Cowmes Lepton, Huddersfield, Yorkshire 20 Aug 1847
Died Huddersfield 12 Feb 1889

Andrew Greenwood was a small, gutsy Yorkshire batsman who played in cricket's first two Test matches. He had previously toured Australia with W.G. Grace's team (not first-class). Quick-footed and determined, he was a sound technician equally at home opening or in the middle order. He carried his bat for 78* out of 151 against Gloucestershire at Clifton in 1874. An outstanding fielder in the deep, he was a nephew of Luke Greenwood, the former Yorkshire batsman who umpired Spofforth's famous 1882 Test match which resulted in the birth of the Ashes. [*Illus. p.* 278]

						Batting 1st			Batting 2nd			
Ref	Series	V	T	Venue	Result	No	R	HO	No	R	HO	Ct
1/1	1876–77	A	1	Melbourne	L-45	5	1	c	2	5	c	1
2/2			2	Melbourne	W-4w	3	49	b	3	22	b	1

Career	M	I	NO	HS	R	Avge	100	50	Ct	St	Balls	R	W	Avge	BB	5w	10w	Rate
Test	2	4	0	49	77	19.25	–	–	2	–	–	–	–	–	–	–	–	–
F/c	141	249	14	111	4307	18.32	1	18	70	–	16	9	0	–	–	–	–	–

GREIG
Anthony William

Border (1965–66 to 1969–70)
Sussex (1966 to 1978)
Eastern Province
(1970–71 to 1971–72)

Wisden 1975
TOURS
A 1971–72 (RW), 1974–75, 1976–77;
SA 1974–75 (Robins); WI 1969–70
(Norfolk), 1973–74; NZ 1974–75;
I 1967–68 (Int XI), 1972–73, 1976–77;
P 1967–68 (Int XI), 1972–73;
SL 1967–68 (Int XI), 1972–73, 1976–77
Born Queenstown, South Africa
6 Oct 1946

At 6ft 7½in the tallest cricketer to represent England, Tony Greig had established himself as the country's leading all-rounder by the time he defected to World Series cricket. A desperately keen and ruthless competitor who flourished in adversity, he was a handsome front-foot strokeplayer, an ever-improving right-arm medium-fast swing bowler who developed slow-medium off-spin for responsive conditions, and a brilliant slip-catcher. Born of a Scottish RAF pilot and a South African mother, he was educated in Queenstown and learned his cricket there. He launched his dramatic career by scoring a magnificent 156 for Sussex in his very first Championship match and made his England debut in the unofficial 1970 Rest of the World series. Two summers later, a brace of fifties and five wickets against Australia proclaimed a Test career comprising an unbroken sequence of 58 matches. Well before it was terminated by his clandestine recruiting activities for Kerry Packer's cricketing circus, he had become the first to complete the 'double' of 3000 runs and 100 wickets for England. Using his immense reach to full advantage, he delighted in straight- and off-driving the ball vast distances and could hit it equally hard off the back foot. His 110 against the awesome speed of Lillee and Thomson on a Brisbane mud heap (Test *750*) confirmed his abundant courage. It was Greig who, in India in 1972–73, devised the now universally popular bail-high backlift to counteract the steepling bounce of leg-spinner Chandrasekhar. His bowling role was normally that of third or fourth seamer but he turned to high-bouncing off-breaks with record-breaking rewards in the Caribbean. Although he won only three and lost five of his 14 Tests, he was a brave, popular and belligerent leader; his tour of India was an outstandingly triumphant mission in every respect. His captaincy of Sussex (1973–77) was less successful. He emigrated to Sydney in 1978 to combine a highly lucrative career as chairman of an insurance company with television comments and presentation. Only after his playing career had ended was it revealed that he was an epileptic.

NOTABLE FEATS

- 1000 runs in 14th Test (*722*) (24 inns); 2000 runs in 31st Test (*750*) (48 inns); 3000 runs in 49th Test (*789*) (78 inns).
- 50 wickets in 22nd Test (*733*); 100 wickets and Test 'double' in 37th Test (*758*).
- *703* Shared 5th-wkt stand of 101* with A.R. Lewis which, on Christmas Day, secured England's first victory in India since 1951–52 and their first ever at Delhi.
- *707* Shared stand of 254 with K.W.R. Fletcher which remains England's 5th-wkt record in all Tests.
- *733* First to score 100 and take 5 wickets in an innings of the same Test for England. Shared record E v WI 6th-wkt stand of 163 with A.P.E. Knott.
- *735* His innings and match analysis remain E v WI records; his match figures are a record for Trinidad Tests.
- *750* Scored England's first 100 at Brisbane since 1936–37.
- *758* Emulated W. Rhodes and T.E. Bailey by scoring 2000 runs and taking 100 wickets for England.
- *789* First to score 3000 runs and take 100 wickets for England.
- Exceeded 1000 runs in a season 7 times (plus once on tour).
- Hat-trick for E. Province v Natal at Port Elizabeth in 1971–72.

Opposing captains Tony Greig and Greg Chappell and wicket-keeper Alan Knott look on as Kerry O'Keeffe is caught Brearley bowled Underwood 0 during the 1976–77 Centenary Test at Melbourne.

Ref	Series	V	T	Venue	Result	Batting 1st			Batting 2nd			Ct	Bowling 1st			Bowling 2nd		
						No	R	HO	No	R	HO		Balls	R	W	Balls	R	W
698/473	1972	A	1	Manchester	W-89	6	57	lbw	6	62	b	2	42	21	1	116	53	4
699/474			2	Lord's	L-8w	6	54	c	6	3	c	2	174	74	1	18	17	0
700/475			3	Nottingham	D	7	7	c	6	36	*	1	232	88	2	72	46	0
701/476			4	Leeds	W-9w	6	24	c	–	–	–	1	60	25	0	–	–	–
702/477			5	Oval	L-5w	6	16	c	6	29	c	2	108	25	0	153	49	2
703/478	1972–73	I	1	Delhi	W-6w	6	68	*	6	40	*	5	138	32	2	36	16	0
704/479			2	Calcutta	L-28	6	29	c	6	67	lbw	–	54	13	1	119	24	5
705/480			3	Madras[1]	L-4w	6	17	lbw	6	5	c	2	72	35	0	–	–	–
706/481			4	Kanpur	D	6	8	c	–	–	–	2	174	40	1	60	6	1
707/482			5	Bombay[2]	D	6	148	lbw	–	–	–	–	132	62	0	78	19	1
719/483	1972–73	P	1	Lahore[2]	D	6	41	c	6	72	c	2	176	86	4	36	28	2
720/484			2	Hyderabad	D	6	36	b	6	64	c	–	78	39	0	–	–	–
721/485			3	Karachi	D	7	48	b	–	–	–	1	120	76	0	60	26	0
722/486	1973	NZ	1	Nottingham	W-38	6	2	c	6	139	lbw	–	64	33	4	271	101	3
723/487			2	Lord's	D	5	63	c	5	12	c	1	–	–	–	–	–	–
724/488			3	Leeds	W-I & 1	5	0	c	–	–	–	–	78	29	1	36	22	0
725/489	1973	WI	1	Oval	L-158	6	38	c	6	0	c	1	183	81	2	48	22	0
726/490			2	Birmingham	D	5	27	c	–	–	–	2	156	84	0	46	35	2
727/491			3	Lord's	L-I & 226	6	44	c	7	13	lbw	2	198	180	3	–	–	–
731/492	1973–74	WI	1	Port-of-Spain	L-7w	6	37	c	6	20	b	1	102	60	0	12	4	0
732/493			2	Kingston	D	6	45	c	6	14	b	1	294	102	3	–	–	–
733/494			3	Bridgetown	D	6	148	c	6	25	c	2	276	164	6	–	–	–
734/495			4	Georgetown	D	5	121	b	–	–	–	1	144	57	2	–	–	–
735/496			5	Port-of-Spain	W-26	5	19	lbw	6	1	c	2	217	86	8	198	70	5
739/497	1974	I	1	Manchester	W-113	7	53	c	–	–	–	–	30	18	0	151	35	3
740/498			2	Lord's	W-I & 285	6	106	c	–	–	–	–	126	63	1	–	–	–
741/499			3	Birmingham	W-I & 78	–	–	–	–	–	–	2	18	11	0	96	49	2
742/500	1974	P	1	Leeds	D	6	37	c	6	12	c	6	66	14	1	54	23	1
743/501			2	Lord's	D	6	9	ro	–	–	–	4	53	23	3	114	55	1
744/502			3	Oval	D	7	32	b	–	–	–	1	150	92	2	42	15	0
750/503	1974/75	A	1	Brisbane[2]	L-166	6	110	c	6	2	b	1	128	70	1	104	60	0
751/504			2	Perth	L-9w	4	23	c	4	32	c	1	72	69	1	–	–	–
752/505			3	Melbourne	D	6	28	ro	6	60	c	1	192	63	2	144	56	4
753/506			4	Sydney	L-171	6	9	c	6	54	st	2	183	104	4	96	64	0
754/507			5	Adelaide	L-163	6	19	c	6	20	lbw	4	80	63	0	16	9	0
755/508			6	Melbourne	W-I & 4	6	89	c	–	–	–	3	71	35	1	255	88	4
758/509	1974–75	NZ	1	Auckland	W-I & 83	6	51	b	–	–	–	–	208	98	5	120	51	5
759/510			2	Christchurch	D	–	–	–	–	–	–	1	72	27	2	–	–	–
760/511	1975	A	1	Birmingham	L-I & 85	6	8	c	6	7	c	–	90	43	1	–	–	–
761/512*			2	Lord's	D	6	96	c	6	41	c	1	90	47	1	156	82	2
762/513*			3	Leeds	D	6	51	ro	5	49	c	1	18	14	0	54	20	0
763/514*			4	Oval	D	6	17	c	6	15	c	2	144	107	3	30	9	1
777/515*	1976	WI	1	Nottingham	D	6	0	b	–	–	–	1	162	82	1	6	16	0
778/516*			2	Lord's	D	6	6	c	7	20	c	1	–	–	–	84	42	2
779/517*			3	Manchester	L-425	7	9	b	6	3	b	2	48	24	0	12	8	0
780/518*			4	Leeds	L-55	6	116	c	6	76	*	2	60	57	0	–	–	–
781/519*			5	Oval	L-231	6	12	b	6	1	b	–	204	96	2	12	11	0
788/520*	1976/77	I	1	Delhi	W-I & 25	6	25	lbw	–	–	–	1	–	–	–	240	84	2
789/521*			2	Calcutta	W-10w	6	103	lbw	–	–	–	2	–	–	–	60	27	2
790/522*			3	Madras[1]	W-200	6	54	c	6	41	lbw	–	24	4	0	–	–	–
791/523*			4	Bangalore	L-140	6	2	c	6	31	st	1	108	44	2	138	74	0
792/524*			5	Bombay[3]	D	5	76	b	5	10	c	1	132	64	3	84	39	1
803/525*	1976–77	A		Melbourne	L-45	7	18	b	6	41	c	4	–	–	–	112	66	2
804/526	1977	A	1	Lord's	D	5	5	b	4	91	c	–	–	–	–	–	–	–
805/527			2	Manchester	W-9w	5	76	c	–	–	–	3	78	37	1	72	19	1
806/528			3	Nottingham	W-7w	5	11	b	4	0	b	3	90	35	1	54	24	1
807/529			4	Leeds	W-I & 85	5	43	b	–	–	–	3	–	–	–	120	64	2
808/530			5	Oval	D	5	0	c	–	–	–	–	48	17	1	–	–	–

Career	M	I	NO	HS	R	Avge	100	50	Ct	St	Balls	R	W	Avge	BB	5w	10w	Rate
Test	58	93	4	148	3599	40.43	8	20	87	–	9802	4541	141	32.20	8-86	6	2	69.51
F/c	350	579	45	226	16660	31.19	26	96	345	–	52407	24702	856	28.85	8-25	33	8	61.22

A. W. GREIG – TEST SUMMARY

Series	V	M	I	NO	HS	R	Avge	100	50	Balls	R	W	Avge	BB	5w	10w	Rate
1972	A	5	9	1	62	288	36.00	–	3	975	398	10	39.80	4-53	–	–	97.30
1972–73	I	5	8	2	148	382	63.66	1	2	863	247	11	22.45	5-24	1	–	56.86
1972–73	P	3	5	–	72	261	52.20	–	2	470	255	6	42.50	4-86	–	–	78.33
1973	NZ	3	5	–	139	216	43.20	1	1	449	185	8	23.12	4-33	–	–	56.12
1973	WI	3	5	–	44	122	24.40	–	–	631	402	7	57.42	3-180	–	–	90.14
1973–74	WI	5	9	–	148	430	47.77	2	–	1243	543	24	22.62	8-86	3	1	51.79
1974	I	3	2	–	106	159	79.50	1	1	421	176	6	29.33	3-35	–	–	70.16
1974	P	3	4	–	37	90	22.50	–	–	479	222	8	27.75	3-23	–	–	59.87
1974–75	A	6	11	–	110	446	40.54	1	3	1341	681	17	40.05	4-56	–	–	78.88
1974–75	NZ	2	1	–	51	51	51.00	–	1	400	176	12	14.66	5-51	2	1	33.33
1975	A	4	8	–	96	284	35.50	–	2	582	322	8	40.25	3-107	–	–	72.75
1976	WI	5	9	1	116	243	30.37	1	1	588	336	5	67.20	2-42	–	–	117.60
1976–77	I	5	8	–	103	342	42.75	1	2	786	336	10	33.60	3-64	–	–	78.60
1976–77	A	1	2	–	41	59	29.50	–	–	112	66	2	33.00	2-66	–	–	56.00
1977	A	5	7	–	91	226	32.28	–	2	462	196	7	28.00	2-64	–	–	66.00
	A	21	37	1	110	1303	36.19	1	10	3472	1663	44	37.79	4-53	–	–	78.90
	WI	13	23	1	148	795	36.13	3	1	2462	1281	36	35.58	8-86	3	1	68.38
	NZ	5	6	–	139	267	44.50	1	2	849	361	20	18.05	5-51	2	1	42.45
	I	13	18	2	148	883	55.18	3	5	2070	759	27	28.11	5-24	1	–	76.66
	P	6	9	–	72	351	39.00	–	2	949	477	14	34.07	4-86	–	–	67.78
Home		31	49	2	139	1628	34.63	3	10	4587	2237	59	37.91	4-33	–	–	77.74
Overseas		27	44	2	148	1971	46.92	5	10	5215	2304	82	28.09	8-86	6	2	63.59
Totals		58	93	4	148	3599	40.43	8	20	9802	4541	141	32.20	8-86	6	2	69.51

GREIG
Ian Alexander

Border (1974–75 to 1979–80)
Griqualand West (1975–76)
Cambridge University (1977 to 1979)
Sussex (1980 to 1985)
Surrey (1987 to date)

Born Queenstown, South Africa
8 Dec 1955

Ian Greig is a determined all-rounder who read Law at Cambridge after four matches for Border and a solitary appearance during national service for Griqualand West. A tall (5ft 11½in) right-arm medium-pace bowler, his high action produces bounce and nip off the pitch; he can swing the ball late and seam it either way. He is an assertive middle-order batsman and a safe slip-catcher. At Cambridge he ended an impressive season of captaincy by inspiring an innings victory against Oxford. Striking all-round figures for Sussex in 1981 (911 runs at 30.36 and 76 wickets at 19.32, including the match 'double' of a century and ten wickets against Hampshire) earned him two Test caps against Pakistan the following summer. Appropriately he celebrated the ninth instance of brothers representing England by returning an identical analysis to that achieved by his elder brother Tony on his debut: 4 for 53. His career appeared closed after the 1985 season when he was released by Sussex for reasons of financial expediency and settled in Brisbane. But two years later Surrey perceptively tempted him back to county cricket by appointing him captain and he swiftly instilled a new confidence at The Oval. He gained two rugby blues at Cambridge.

Ian Greig

Ref	Series	V	T Venue	Result	Batting 1st No	R	HO	Batting 2nd No	R	HO	Ct	Bowling 1st Balls	R	W	Bowling 2nd Balls	R	W
931/583	1982	P	1 Birmingham	W-113	8	14	c	8	7	b	–	86	53	4	24	19	0
932/584			2 Lord's	L-10w	8	3	lbw	8	2	lbw	–	78	42	0	–	–	–

Career	M	I	NO	HS	R	Avge	100	50	Ct	St	Balls	R	W	Avge	BB	5w	10w	Rate
Test	2	4	0	14	26	6.50	–	–	–	–	188	114	4	28.50	4-53	–	–	47.00
F/c	187	245	30	147*	5419	25.20	5	24	122	–	21629	11143	385	28.94	7-43	10	2	57.67

GRIEVE
Basil Arthur Firebrace

TOUR SA 1888–89
Born Kilburn, Middlesex 28 May 1864
Died Eastbourne, Sussex 19 Nov 1917

Basil Grieve's appearances during Major Warton's tour in the first two Tests staged on South African soil comprise his entire first-class career. Watched by 16,000 spectators at Lord's in 1883, he had opened the bowling against Eton in his final year at Harrow and taken 4 for 61 from 29 four-ball overs. He joined MCC two years later and became a wine merchant. It is assumed that he was a right-handed medium-pace bowler and lower-order batsman. His death during the First World War was from natural causes. [*Illus. p.* 51]

Ref	Series	V	T Venue	Result	Batting 1st No	R	HO	Batting 2nd No	R	HO	Ct
31/31	1888–89	SA	1 Port Elizabeth	W-8w	9	14	*	4	12	*	–
32/32			2 Cape Town	W-I & 202	8	14	c	–	–	–	–

Career	M	I	NO	HS	R	Avge	100	50	Ct	St	Balls	R	W	Avge	BB	5w	10w	Rate
Test	2	3	2	14*	40	40.00	–	–	–	–	–	–	–	–	–	–	–	–
F/c	2	3	2	14*	40	40.00	–	–	–	–	–	–	–	–	–	–	–	–

GRIFFITH
Stewart Cathie CBE, DFC

Cambridge University (1934 to 1936)
Surrey (1934)
Sussex (1937 to 1954)

TOURS
A 1935–36; SA 1948–49; WI 1947–48; NZ 1935–36
Born Wandsworth, Surrey 16 Jun 1914

A devoted and able administrator, 'Billy' Griffith was MCC assistant-secretary (1952–62) during some of cricket's more turbulent years. An exceptional fielder who took to wicket-keeping in his penultimate summer at Dulwich College, he gained a blue in his second year at Cambridge and toured Australasia before taking his finals. Qualifying for Sussex after a single appearance for his native Surrey, he was selected for the aborted 1939–40 tour of India and, after wartime service as an Airborne Division glider pilot, during which he reached the rank of Lieutenant-Colonel and won the DFC at Arnhem, he kept wicket in all five 'Victory' Tests against Australia. Although only slightly built and of average height (5ft 9in), he was a resolute lower-order batsman who could hit powerfully – as he proved during his epic 354-minute innings of 140 when pressed into service as an opener in Test *296*. Neat, safe and unobtrusive, he was preferred to Godfrey Evans for two Tests in South Africa. He served Sussex as captain (1946), secretary (1946–50) and president 1976; was president of MCC (1979–80); and prepared the 1980 code of The Laws of Cricket. His son Mike captained Sussex and remains the only man to play first-class cricket and international hockey at Lord's. [*Illus pp.* 241, 415, 512]

NOTABLE FEATS

- *296* Remains the only England player to score his maiden first-class hundred in his first Test, his 140 being the highest score of that tour.

NOTABLE FEATS *cont.*

- Held 6 catches in an innings for England v Australian Services at Manchester in 1945.
- Kept throughout two innings over 500 at Hove without conceding a bye: on his Sussex debut v New Zealanders (546) in 1937 and v South Africans (555-6d) in 1947.

					Batting 1st			Batting 2nd			Fielding 1st				Fielding 2nd			
Ref	Series	V	T	Venue	Result	No	R	HO	No	R	HO	Ct	St	Byes	Balls	Ct	St	Byes	Balls
296/259	1947–48	WI	2	Port-of-Spain	D	2	140	lbw	2	4	c	–	–	–	–	–	–	–	–
312/270 †	1948–49	SA	4	Johannesburg[2]	D	10	8	c	–	–	–	3	–	4	680	–	–	7	520
313/271 †			5	Port Elizabeth	W-3w	10	5	c	8	0	b	1	–	2	1151	1	–	6	464

Career	M	I	NO	HS	R	Avge	100	50	Ct	St	Balls	R	W	Avge	BB	5w	10w	Rate
Test	3	5	0	140	157	31.40	1	–	5	–	–	–	–	–	–	–	–	–
F/c	215	336	41	140	4846	16.42	3	15	328	80	18	23	0	–	–	–	–	–

GUNN, George

Nottinghamshire (1902 to 1932)

Wisden 1914

TOURS

A 1907–08, 1911–12; WI 1929–30

Born Hucknall Torkard, Nottinghamshire 13 Jun 1879

Died Tylers Green, Cuckfield, Sussex 29 Jun 1958

George Gunn was an audacious batting genius, a slim little improvizer with amazing reflexes who compensated for his lack of height by advancing down the wicket to bowlers even of such speed as Gregory and McDonald. A nephew of William and the younger brother of John, he was a quizzically humorous but moody character who would for no apparent reason sometimes steadfastly block indifferent bowling or rampage to a fast hundred against a top-class attack. He defended his eccentricity by claiming that he 'always batted according'! Convalescing in Australia after a lung disorder he was recruited into England's team when the captain, A.O. Jones, fell ill and responded by top-scoring in both innings with 119 and 74. His spasmodic Test career included a 17-year hiatus, an average of 46.83 in Australia and only one appearance in England. An occasional right-arm bowler, he was a prolific slip-catcher. He celebrated his 50th birthday by scoring 164* against Worcestershire, once scored 777* in a single-wicket match and batted in the Trent Bridge nets with a walking stick when he was well into his seventies.

NOTABLE FEATS

- 1000 runs in 15th Test (*193*) (28 inns).
- *96* Became the fifth batsman to score 100 on debut for England.
- *190* Was recalled at the age of 50 after a record interval of 17 yrs 316 days and ended his final series as Test cricket's fourth-oldest player (50 yrs 303 days).
- Exceeded 1000 runs in a season 20 times, including 12 in succession.
- Scored 100 in each innings of a Nottinghamshire match on 3 occasions, the last when he was 48, and carried his bat through a completed innings 8 times.
- Headed the national batting averages in 1919 (1451 runs at 63.08).
- Shared 40 century 1st-wkt partnerships for Nottinghamshire with W.W. Whysall.
- Shared with A. Sandham a then record West Indian 1st-wkt stand of 322 for MCC v Jamaica at Kingston in 1929–30.
- When 52 he achieved with G.V. Gunn the only instance of a father and son each scoring hundreds in the same first-class innings: 183 and 100* respectively for Nottinghamshire v Warwickshire at Birmingham in 1931.
- His career aggregates of 583 matches and 31,592 runs remain Nottinghamshire records.

TEST NOTES

- *190* Bowled in 2nd inns: 0 for 8 (12 balls).

Brothers George (left) and John Gunn going out to bat for Nottinghamshire.

Ref	Series	V	T	Venue	Result	Batting 1st No	R	HO	Batting 2nd No	R	HO	Ct
96/93	1907–08	A	1	Sydney	L-2w	3	119	c	3	74	c	1
97/94			2	Melbourne	W-1w	3	15	lbw	3	0	lbw	–
98/95			3	Adelaide	L-245	3	65	b	3	11	c	2
99/96			4	Melbourne	L-308	2	13	c	2	43	b	1
100/97			5	Sydney	L-49	3	122	*	3	0	b	3
102/99	1909	A	2	Lord's	L-9w	4	1	lbw	4	0	b	–
116/108	1911–12	A	1	Sydney	L-146	3	4	b	3	62	c	1
117/109			2	Melbourne	W-8w	4	10	lbw	3	43	c	2
118/110			3	Adelaide	W-7w	3	29	c	3	45	c	1
119/111			4	Melbourne	W-I & 225	3	75	c	–	–	–	1
120/112			5	Sydney	W-70	3	52	st	3	61	b	1
190/176	1929–30	WI	1	Bridgetown	D	1	35	lbw	1	29	b	–
191/177			2	Port-of-Spain	W-167	1	1	ro	1	23	c	1
192/178			3	Georgetown	L-289	1	11	hw	1	45	c	–
193/179			4	Kingston	D	1	85	st	1	47	ro	1

Career	M	I	NO	HS	R	Avge	100	50	Ct	St	Balls	R	W	Avge	BB	5w	10w	Rate
Test	15	29	1	122*	1120	40.00	2	7	15	–	12	8	0	–	–	–	–	–
F/c	643	1061	82	220	35208	35.96	62	194	473	–	4223	2355	66	35.68	5-50	1	–	63.98

G. GUNN – TEST BATTING SUMMARY

Series	V	M	I	NO	HS	R	Avge	100	50
1907–08	A	5	10	1	122*	462	51.33	2	2
1909	A	1	2	–	1	1	0.50	–	–
1911–12	A	5	9	–	75	381	42.33	–	4
1929–30	WI	4	8	–	85	276	34.50	–	1

Series	V	M	I	NO	HS	R	Avge	100	50
	A	11	21	1	122*	844	42.20	2	6
	WI	4	8	–	85	276	34.50	–	1
Home		1	2	–	1	1	0.50	–	–
Overseas		14	27	1	122*	1119	43.03	2	7
Totals		15	29	1	122*	1120	40.00	2	7

GUNN
John Richmond

Nottinghamshire (1896 to 1925)
London County (1904)

Wisden 1904
TOUR A 1901–02
Born Hucknall Torkard,
Nottinghamshire 19 Jul 1876
Died Basford, Nottingham 21 Aug 1963

A 5ft 8in left-handed all-rounder, John Gunn was a nephew of William and the elder brother of George. Originally a defensive batsman, his range of strokes blossomed with experience but he never overcame a weakness against fast bowling. Although he began his county career as a medium-pace bowler, he cut his pace to slow-medium in 1903 to increase his accuracy of length and took 423 wickets in the next four seasons. He then further reduced his pace and for the remainder of his career bowled very slowly, deceptively varying his flight and turn from a negligible run. His anticipation at cover-point remained outstanding throughout his long career. He became Sir Julien Cahn's head groundsman at Stanford Hall.

NOTABLE FEATS

- Exceeded 1000 runs in a season 11 times, took 100 wickets on 5 occasions and achieved the 'double' 4 times (in successive years).
- Achieved unique Nottinghamshire career 'double' of 20,000 runs and 1000 wickets.
- Amassed then record Nottinghamshire score of 294 in 265 min v Leicestershire at Nottingham in 1903, sharing a then world first-class record 3rd-wkt stand of 369 with W. Gunn. The total of 739 for 7 dec and first day score of 484 for 2 remain Nottinghamshire records.
- His stand of 361 with A.O. Jones v Essex at Leyton in 1905 remains the Nottinghamshire 4th-wkt record.
- Two hat-tricks for Nottinghamshire: v Middlesex at Lord's in 1899 and v Derbyshire at Chesterfield in 1904.
- Twice achieved the match 'double' of 100 runs and 10 wickets.
- Took 28 Championship wickets in a single week in August 1903.

Ref	Series	V	T	Venue	Result	Batting 1st No	R	HO	Batting 2nd No	R	HO	Ct	Bowling 1st Balls	R	W	Bowling 2nd Balls	R	W
65/65	1901–02	A	1	Sydney	W-I & 124	9	21	c	–	–	–	–	30	27	0	–	–	–
66/66			2	Melbourne	L-229	6	0	st	9	2	c	–	–	–	–	36	13	0
67/67			3	Adelaide	L-4w	9	24	b	9	5	lbw	1	252	76	5	228	88	3
68/68			4	Sydney	L-7w	10	0	*	10	13	*	–	96	48	1	51	17	2
69/69			5	Melbourne	L-32	10	8	b	10	4	c	2	102	38	4	168	53	2
83/80	1905	A	1	Nottingham	W-213	7	8	b	–	–	–	–	36	27	1	–	–	–

Career	M	I	NO	HS	R	Avge	100	50	Ct	St	Balls	R	W	Avge	BB	5w	10w	Rate
Test	6	10	2	24	85	10.62	–	–	3	–	999	387	18	21.50	5-76	1	–	55.50
F/c	535	845	105	294	24557	33.18	40	129	248	–	70043	30463	1242	24.52	8-65	82	17	56.39

GUNN, William

Nottinghamshire (1880 to 1904)

Wisden 1890
TOUR A 1886–87
Born St Anne's, Nottingham 4 Dec 1858
Died Nottingham 29 Jan 1921

NOTABLE FEATS

- *26* Deputized as umpire on the final morning when J.S. Swift was absent.
- *41* His 250-min century was the first in a Test at Old Trafford.
- *60* The only Nottinghamshire player to appear in the first Test staged at Trent Bridge.
- Exceeded 1000 runs in a season 12 times, including 2000 once.
- Made 8 double centuries, his 228 for the Players at Lord's in 1890 being the then highest score against an Australian team in England.
- Shared in 26 century partnerships with A. Shrewsbury, 2 of them surviving Nottinghamshire records (and former world records) and both v Sussex: 398 (2nd wkt) at Nottingham in 1890 and 266 (5th wkt) at Hove in 1884.
- His 3rd-wkt stand of 369 with J.R. Gunn v Leicestershire at Nottingham in 1903 was then a world first-class record and remains the Nottinghamshire record for that wicket.

Billy Gunn was a tall (6ft 2½in), graceful, patient batsman of the classical school, a strong-wristed stylist who used his long reach to hit with a full arc of the bat. He seldom skied the ball and excelled at the cover-drive. Together with Arthur Shrewsbury he pioneered the technique of pad play as a form of defence against off-break and inswing bowling. The uncle of John and George, his ability to run 100 yards inside 11 seconds and judge steepling catches made him an outstanding deep fielder. As a useful right-handed change bowler he converted from slow round-arm to lobs late in his career. He was a double international, gaining two England soccer caps as an outside left during his career with Notts County, the club of which he was later a director. In 1885 he co-founded the famous bat-making firm of Gunn and Moore.

The Players of 1894, led by William Gunn: standing *W. Chatterton, W.H. Lockwood, J.T. Hearne, W. Flowers, W. Hearn (umpire);* seated *E. Wainwright, A. Ward, W. Gunn, F. Martin, W. Brockwell;* in front *J. Briggs, W. Storer.*

Ref	Series	V	T Venue	Result	Batting 1st No	R	HO	Batting 2nd No	R	HO	Ct
25/25	1886–87	A	1 Sydney	W-13	6	0	b	6	4	b	1
26/26			2 Sydney	W-71	4	9	b	5	10	c	3
28/28	1888	A	1 Lord's	L-61	9	2	c	7	8	b	1
30/30			3 Manchester	W-I & 21	7	15	lbw	–	–	–	–
33/33	1890	A	1 Lord's	W-7w	3	14	ro	3	34	c	–
34/34			2 Oval	W-2w	3	32	b	3	1	st	–
39/39	1893	A	1 Lord's	D	3	2	c	3	77	c	–
40/40			2 Oval	W-I & 43	4	16	b	–	–	–	–
41/41			3 Manchester	D	4	102	*	4	11	b	–
50/50	1896	A	1 Lord's	W-6w	5	25	c	6	13	*	–
60/60	1899	A	1 Nottingham	D	4	14	b	4	3	b	–

Career	M	I	NO	HS	R	Avge	100	50	Ct	St	Balls	R	W	Avge	BB	5w	10w	Rate
Test	11	20	2	102*	392	21.77	1	1	5	–	–	–	–	–	–	–	–	–
F/c	521	850	72	273	25691	33.02	48	117	333	1	3540	1800	76	23.68	6-48	2	1	46.57

HAIG, Nigel Esmé MC

Middlesex (1912 to 1934)

TOUR WI 1929–30
Born Kensington, London 12 Dec 1887
Died Eastbourne, Sussex 27 Oct 1966

Although he failed to find a place in the XI at Eton, Nigel Haig became an outstanding all-rounder who made a massive contribution to Middlesex cricket between the Wars. A nephew of Lord Harris, he was a right-arm medium-fast swing bowler, a hard-hitting middle-order batsman and an agile fielder. Lean and wiry, he had immense stamina and could maintain nagging accuracy for long spells. His unorthodox batting was vulnerable to fast bowling but he could strike the ball with surprising power and twice scored a hundred before lunch. Middlesex won successive Championships during his career, the second (1921) coinciding with the first of his three 'doubles', and he was captain for the last six full summers of his career (1929–34), the last two jointly. An erudite man, he was also a fine all-round games player who excelled at real tennis and played golf, racquets, squash and lawn tennis impressively. He won the MC during First World War service with the Royal Field Artillery. [*Illus. pp.* 74, 297]

NOTABLE FEATS

- Exceeded 1000 runs in a season 6 times, took 100 wickets 5 times and achieved the 'double' on 3 occasions.
- Contributed to the first instance of the first 4 batsmen in the order each scoring hundreds: P.F. Warner, H.W. Lee, J.W. Hearne and Haig (131) for Middlesex v Sussex at Lord's in 1920.
- Shared record 9th-wkt Gentlemen v Players stand of 193 with G.O.B. Allen at The Oval in 1925.

Ref	Series	V	T Venue	Result	Batting 1st No	R	HO	Batting 2nd No	R	HO	Ct	Bowling 1st Balls	R	W	Bowling 2nd Balls	R	W
141/130	1921	A	2 Lord's	L-8w	8	3	c	8	0	b	–	120	61	2	18	27	0
190/176	1929–30	WI	1 Bridgetown	D	7	47	c	–	–	–	1	60	27	0	120	40	1
191/177			2 Port-of-Spain	W-167	7	5	c	7	5	c	–	48	33	1	126	33	2
192/178			3 Georgetown	L-289	7	4	b	7	0	b	1	138	61	1	60	44	2
193/179			4 Kingston	D	8	28	c	6	34	c	2	180	73	3	156	49	1

Career	M	I	NO	HS	R	Avge	100	50	Ct	St	Balls	R	W	Avge	BB	5w	10w	Rate
Test	5	9	0	47	126	14.00	–	–	4	–	1026	448	13	34.46	3-73	–	–	78.92
F/c	513	779	51	131	15220	20.90	12	61	221	–	78288	30698	1117	27.48	7-33	47	2	70.08

HAIGH, Schofield

Yorkshire (1895 to 1913)

Wisden 1901
TOURS SA 1898–99, 1905–06
Born Berry Brow, Huddersfield, Yorkshire 19 Mar 1871
Died Taylor Hill, Huddersfield, 27 Feb 1921

Schofield Haigh

Schofield Haigh was a right-arm bowler who could vary his pace from medium to almost fast while still turning his off-break sharply. On helpful pitches he could be virtually unplayable and his partnership with Hirst and Rhodes produced the formidable attack which brought Lord Hawke's famous side four Championships in five seasons (1898–1902) and eight titles during Haigh's career. He was a keen fielder and a determined but underrated lower- or middle-order batsman who rattled up a hundred before lunch against Nottinghamshire in 1901. A humorous, friendly man, his premature death after seven popular years as coach at Winchester College was much mourned.

NOTABLE FEATS

- *59* Bowled unchanged through 2nd inns with A.E. Trott, taking 6 for 11 as South Africa were dismissed for 35 in the space of 114 balls.
- Took 100 wickets in a season 11 times, heading the national bowling averages on 5 occasions and being leading wicket-taker 3 times. He exceeded 1000 runs once, completing the 'double' in 1904.
- Five hat-tricks: for Lord Hawke's XI v Cape Colony at Cape Town in 1898–99, for MCC v Army (4 wickets in 4 balls) at Pretoria in 1905–06, and 3 for Yorkshire (v Derbyshire at Bradford in 1897, v Somerset at Sheffield in 1902, and v Lancashire at Manchester in 1909).
- Bowled unchanged through both completed innings of a match on 4 occasions – 3 with W. Rhodes and one with G.H. Hirst.
- Bowled 8 batsmen in an innings for Lord Hawke's XI v Cape Colony at Cape Town in 1898–99.
- Shared record Yorkshire 9th-wkt stand of 192 with G.H. Hirst v Surrey at Bradford in 1898.

						Batting 1st			Batting 2nd				Bowling 1st			Bowling 2nd		
Ref	Series	V	T	Venue	Result	No	R	HO	No	R	HO	Ct	Balls	R	W	Balls	R	W
58/58	1898–99	SA	1	Johannesburg[1]	W-32	11	2	*	7	1	c	–	150	101	3	60	20	2
59/59			2	Cape Town	W-210	7	0	c	7	25	c	2	135	88	3	59	11	6
84/81	1905	A	2	Lord's	D	10	14	b	–	–	–	1	72	40	2	–	–	–
85/82			3	Leeds	D	9	11	c	–	–	–	–	66	19	1	84	36	1
88/85	1905–06	SA	1	Johannesburg[1]	L-1w	8	23	b	8	0	lbw	1	–	–	–	6	9	0
89/86			2	Johannesburg[1]	L-9w	8	3	c	10	0	*	–	116	64	4	–	–	–
90/87			3	Johannesburg[1]	L-243	9	0	c	4	16	c	2	90	50	0	144	72	1
91/88			4	Cape Town	W-4w	10	0	c	–	–	–	2	114	38	1	12	12	0
92/89			5	Cape Town	L-I & 16	10	1	c	10	2	c	–	36	18	0	–	–	–
102/99	1909	A	2	Lord's	L-9w	11	1	*	11	5	ro	–	114	41	0	–	–	–
126/116	1912	A	2	Manchester	D	9	9	c	–	–	–	–	36	3	0	–	–	–

Career	M	I	NO	HS	R	Avge	100	50	Ct	St	Balls	R	W	Avge	BB	5w	10w	Rate
Test	11	18	3	25	113	7.53	–	–	8	–	1294	622	24	25.91	6-11	1	–	53.91
F/c	561	747	119	159	11713	18.65	4	47	299	–	78819	32091	2012	15.94	9-25	135	30	39.17

HALLOWS, Charles

Lancashire (1914 to 1932)

Wisden 1928
Born Little Lever, Lancashire 4 Apr 1895
Died Bolton, Lancashire 10 Nov 1972

Charlie Hallows learned his cricket in the yard of his father's stone-mason's works and made his first-class debut immediately before his wartime service in the King's Liverpools. He survived to become a stylish left-handed opening batsman of astonishing consistency, an occasional slow left-arm bowler, and a very fast outfielder. Although he was a member of the mighty Lancashire side which won the Championship three years in succession (1926–28) and maintained a career average of over 40, his misfortune in being a contemporary of Hobbs, Holmes, Sandham and Sutcliffe condemned him to just two Test appearances and not a single tour. Tall

Charlie Hallows (left) and Harry Makepeace

and slim, he was a most attractive and elegant strokemaker who blended well with the dour defence of his partner, Harry Makepeace. After five years as head coach at Worcester he returned to his native Old Trafford to enjoy similar duties until his 75th year.

NOTABLE FEATS

- Exceeded 1000 runs in a season 11 times, including 2000 on 3 occasions, and headed the national averages in 1927.
- The last of 3 batsmen to score 1000 runs in May alone (1928) – his average of 125.00 is the highest for such an instance.
- His total of 11 hundreds in 1928 remains the Lancashire record.
- Scored 5 hundreds in 6 successive innings during 1927 and 1928.
- Carried his bat through a completed Lancashire innings on 6 occasions.
- First to hold professional league engagements in England, Ireland, Scotland and Wales.

						Batting 1st			Batting 2nd			
Ref	Series	V	T	Venue	Result	No	R	HO	No	R	HO	Ct
143/132	1921	A	4	Manchester	D	–	–	–	1	16	*	–
173/159	1928	WI	1	Lord's	W-I & 58	2	26	c	–	–	–	–

Career	M	I	NO	HS	R	Avge	100	50	Ct	St	Balls	R	W	Avge	BB	5w	10w	Rate
Test	2	2	1	26	42	42.00	–	–	–	–	–	–	–	–	–	–	–	–
F/c	383	586	66	233*	20926	40.24	55	94	140	–	1632	784	19	41.26	3-28	–	–	85.89

HAMMOND Walter Reginald

Gloucestershire (1920 to 1951)
South African Air Force (1942–43)

Wisden 1928
TOURS
A 1928–29, 1932–33, 1936–37, 1946–47;
SA 1927–28, 1930–31, 1938–39;
WI 1925–26, 1934–35;
NZ 1932–33, 1946–47
Born Buckland, Dover, Kent 19 Jun 1903
Died Durban, South Africa 1 Jul 1965

Wally Hammond was a supreme all-round cricketer: he was the outstanding English batsman of the inter-war years and headed the national batting averages for eight successive summers (1933–46); his intelligent right-arm medium-fast outswing bowling was nippily effective, especially with the new ball; and his remarkably consistent catching at slip was frequently quite brilliant. The Dover-born son of a soldier, he cut his cricketing teeth in China and against a wicket chalked on a gun shed in Malta. An innings of 365* in a house match at Cirencester Grammar School confirmed his prowess and he was just 17 when he made his Gloucestershire debut as an amateur. Kent's immediate attempt to reclaim him resulted in a compulsory two-year hiatus for qualification but allowed a soccer interlude with Bristol Rovers. In 1923 he launched his professional career with scores of 110 and 92 against Surrey and soon established himself as an audacious but polished hitter, an implusive hooker of the fastest bowling and a ferocious driver. Test cricket and possibly the influence of Douglas Jardine curbed his flamboyance and he matured into a more orthodox, composed and disciplined batsman with a classical off-drive, who operated mainly off the back foot but seldom hooked. A glance at his *Notable Feats* confirms his application, concentration and immense appetite for large scores. Tall (6ft) and powerfully built, he was an imposing, superbly balanced athlete; a majestic champion noted for the coloured handkerchief adorning his trousers pocket. Returning to amateur status in 1938, he achieved a unique double by captaining both sides to victory in successive years – the Players in 1937 and the Gentlemen in 1938. He led Gloucestershire for two seasons either side of the Second World War and during his 20-match reign as England captain (four wins, three defeats) enjoyed the luxury of declaring against Australia with the scoreboard boasting a total of 903. His final total of 7249 runs remained the world Test record until 1970 when Colin Cowdrey overhauled it. Although favoured by the recent proliferation of Test cricket, no England player has exceeded his total of 22 hundreds. Only two batsmen have surpassed his tally of 167 first-class hundreds and only three fielders his bag of 819 catches. Having emigrated to South Africa, he was coach and groundsman at Natal University at the time of his death.

NOTABLE FEATS

• 1000 runs in 12th Test (*179*) (18 inns); 2000 runs in 23rd Test (*204*) (39 inns); 3000 runs in 36th Test (*224*) (61 inns); 4000 runs in 47th Test (*238*) (76 inns); 5000 runs in 59th Test (*256*) (97 inns); first to score 6000 runs – in 70th Test (*267*) (114 inns); first to score 7000 runs – in 80th Test (*278*) (131 inns – record). 50 wickets in 34th Test (*222*). First fielder to hold 100 catches – in 76th Test (*273*).

• *178* First to score double centuries in successive Test innings.

• *179* Fourth to score 100 in each innings of a Test and second (after H. Sutcliffe in 1924–25) to score 4 hundreds in a rubber. Shared record E v A 3rd-wkt stand of 262 with D.R. Jardine.

• *180* His series aggregate of 905 runs has been exceeded only by D.G. Bradman's 974 in 1930.

• *196* Completed 1000 runs v A in 14 innings (8 Tests).

• *225* Shared record E v NZ 5th-wkt stand of 242 runs in 144 min with L.E.G. Ames.

• *226* His 336* in 318 min completed a unique 700 runs in 4 Test innings and remained the highest score in Tests until 1938 and included the fastest Test triple century (288 min). It included 10 sixes (Test record), 3 off successive balls from J. Newman. His average of 563.00 is the highest for any rubber.

• *254* Shared record E v I 4th-wkt stand of 266 with T.S. Worthington.

• *260* Shared record E v NZ 3rd-wkt stand of 245 with J. Hardstaff jr and passed record Test aggregate of 5410 by J.B. Hobbs.

• *264* His 240 remains the highest score v A at Lord's and the record for an England captain v A. Shared record E v A 4th-wkt stand of 222 with E. Paynter.

• *268* Shared record E v SA 4th-wkt stand of 197 with L.E.G. Ames.

• *270* Won toss for eighth successive time.

• *274* Shared record E v WI 3rd-wkt stand of 264 with L. Hutton.

• Exceeded 1000 runs in a season 17 times (plus 5 on tour), including 3000 on 3 occasions and 2000 on 9 others.

• Holds record for most runs in May (1042 in 1927 when he emulated W.G. Grace's feat) and August (1281 in 1936). Also scored 1060 runs in August 1933.

• Scored 31,165 runs in the 1930s – the record for one decade.

• Achieved the quickest 100 hundreds in first-class cricket, only 12 years elapsing between his first century and his 100th.

• Scored 36 double centuries (second only to D.G. Bradman's 37) including 3 instances of 2 in successive innings. Only Englishman to make 4 triple centuries. Holds Championship records for most 100s in a season (13 in 1938) and most 200s in a career (22).

• Holds Gloucestershire records for most runs in a season (2860 in 1933) and most runs (33,664) and hundreds (113) in a career.

• Scored 100 in each innings 7 times (record until 1982–83).

• Twice scored 4 hundreds in successive innings – in 1936–37 and in 1945 and 1946 when he made 6 hundreds in 7 innings. Scored 9 50s in consecutive innings in 1932–33 and 1933.

• Scored 100 before lunch on 6 occasions.

• Completed 3000 runs on 20 August 1937 to equal T.W. Hayward's 1906 record for fastest 3000 in a season.

• His 1553 runs in 1928–29 remains the record for any tourist in Australia.

• Shared in 3 record Gloucestershire partnerships: 336 (3rd wkt) with B.H. Lyon v Leicestershire at Leicester in 1933, 321 (4th wkt) with W.L. Neale v Leicestershire at Gloucester in 1937, and 239 (8th wkt) with A.E. Wilson v Lancashire at Bristol in 1938.

• Took 15 for 128 (9 for 23 and 6 for 105) for Gloucestershire v Worcestershire at Cheltenham in 1928.

• His 10 catches in the match for Gloucestershire v Surrey at Cheltenham in 1928 (he also scored 139 and 143) and 78 catches for that season remain the records for non-wicket-keepers.

• During the 1928 Cheltenham Week he scored 362 runs, took 16 wickets and held 11 catches.

TEST NOTES

• *205* Deputised for G. Duckworth as wicket-keeper on second day.

Wally Hammond

Ref	Series	V	T	Venue	Result	Batting 1st			Batting 2nd			Ct	Bowling 1st			Bowling 2nd		
						No	R	HO	No	R	HO		Balls	R	W	Balls	R	W
168/154	1927–28	SA	1	Johannesburg[1]	W-10w	4	51	c	–	–	–	–	48	21	0	128	36	5
169/155			2	Cape Town	W-87	4	43	lbw	4	14	c	3	102	53	3	180	50	2
170/156			3	Durban[2]	D	4	90	b	4	1	*	1	96	54	0	96	37	0
171/157			4	Johannesburg[1]	L-4w	4	28	c	4	25	lbw	1	132	62	3	54	20	1
172/158			5	Durban[2]	L-8w	4	66	c	4	3	c	1	72	41	0	60	25	1
173/159	1928	WI	1	Lord's	W-I & 58	4	45	b	–	–	–	2	–	–	–	90	20	1
174/160			2	Manchester	W-I & 30	4	63	c	–	–	–	3	36	16	0	36	23	1
175/161			3	Oval	W-I & 71	4	3	c	–	–	–	4	48	40	1	24	4	0
176/162	1928–29	A	1	Brisbane[1]	W-675	4	44	c	4	28	c	–	90	38	0	6	2	0
177/163			2	Sydney	W-8w	3	251	b	–	–	–	–	30	18	0	54	43	0
178/164			3	Melbourne	W-3w	3	200	c	4	32	ro	–	48	19	1	96	30	0
179/165			4	Adelaide	W-12	3	119	*	3	177	c	1	54	32	0	84	21	0
180/166			5	Melbourne	L-5w	3	38	c	4	16	c	–	96	31	1	156	53	3
181/167	1929	SA	1	Birmingham	D	3	18	b	3	138	*	–	132	25	0	18	19	0
182/168			2	Lord's	D	3	8	c	5	5	b	–	48	19	1	–	–	–
183/169			3	Leeds	W-5w	3	65	c	3	0	c	2	48	13	0	42	19	0
185/171			5	Oval	D	3	17	st	3	101	*	–	–	–	–	–	–	–
194/180	1930	A	1	Nottingham	W-93	3	8	lbw	3	4	lbw	4	–	–	–	174	74	0
195/181			2	Lord's	L-7w	3	38	b	3	32	c	1	210	82	1	26	6	0
196/182			3	Leeds	D	3	113	c	3	35	c	–	102	46	1	–	–	–
197/183			4	Manchester	D	3	3	b	–	–	–	–	126	24	2	–	–	–
198/184			5	Oval	L-I & 39	5	13	b	5	60	c	–	252	70	1	–	–	–
204/185	1930–31	SA	1	Johannesburg[1]	L-28	3	49	lbw	3	63	st	2	–	–	–	150	63	4
205/186			2	Cape Town	D	2	57	c	2	65	c	–	60	27	0	–	–	–
206/187			3	Durban[2]	D	2	136	*	–	–	–	1	–	–	–	66	9	2
207/188			4	Johannesburg[1]	D	3	75	c	3	15	c	4	168	50	1	66	27	0
208/189			5	Durban[2]	D	2	29	c	2	28	c	2	114	36	2	30	28	0
209/190	1931	NZ	1	Lord's	D	3	7	b	3	46	ro	3	63	8	1	126	50	1
210/191			2	Oval	W-I & 26	4	100	*	–	–	–	2	6	10	0	–	–	–
211/192			3	Manchester	D	4	16	c	–	–	–	–	–	–	–	–	–	–
219/193	1932	I		Lord's	W-158	4	35	b	4	12	b	2	24	15	0	33	9	3
220/194	1932–33	A	1	Sydney	W-10w	3	112	c	–	–	–	1	86	34	1	90	37	2
221/195			2	Melbourne	L-111	3	8	b	4	23	c	1	60	21	0	65	21	3
222/196			3	Adelaide	W-338	3	2	c	5	85	b	–	106	30	1	54	27	0
223/197			4	Brisbane[2]	W-6w	3	20	b	4	14	c	3	138	61	2	60	18	0
224/198			5	Sydney	W-8w	3	101	lbw	4	75	*	1	48	32	0	18	10	0
225/199	1932–33	NZ	1	Christchurch	D	3	227	b	–	–	–	2	–	–	–	12	2	0
226/200			2	Auckland	D	3	336	*	–	–	–	–	18	11	0	12	6	0
227/201	1933	WI	1	Lord's	W-I & 27	3	29	c	–	–	–	1	–	–	–	–	–	–
228/202			2	Manchester	D	3	34	c	–	–	–	3	30	27	0	–	–	–
229/203			3	Oval	W-I & 17	3	11	c	–	–	–	–	–	–	–	–	–	–
233/207	1934	A	1	Nottingham	L-238	3	25	c	3	16	st	5	78	29	0	72	25	1
234/208			2	Lord's	W-I & 38	3	2	c	–	–	–	3	24	6	0	78	38	1
235/209			3	Manchester	D	4	4	b	–	–	–	1	171	111	3	12	2	0
236/210			4	Leeds	D	3	37	b	3	20	ro	–	174	82	0	–	–	–
237/211			5	Oval	L-562	4	15	c	4	43	c	3	72	53	0	42	18	0
238/212	1934–35	WI	1	Bridgetown	W-4w	3	43	c	6	29	*	1	–	–	–	6	1	0
239/213			2	Port-of-Spain	L-217	3	1	c	5	9	b	2	84	28	0	60	17	0
240/214			3	Georgetown	D	5	47	ro	4	1	b	1	–	–	–	–	–	–
241/215			4	Kingston	L-I & 161	3	11	c	3	34	b	–	–	–	–	–	–	–
242/216	1935	SA	1	Nottingham	D	3	28	lbw	–	–	–	1	–	–	–	–	–	–
243/217			2	Lord's	L-157	4	27	b	4	27	c	2	33	8	2	88	26	1
244/218			3	Leeds	D	4	63	lbw	4	87	*	3	72	13	1	42	10	1
245/219			4	Manchester	D	4	29	b	4	63	*	–	102	49	1	30	15	0
246/220			5	Oval	D	4	65	st	–	–	–	1	54	25	0	–	–	–
253/222	1936	I	2	Manchester	D	3	167	b	–	–	–	1	54	34	0	72	19	1
254/223			3	Oval	W-9w	3	217	b	3	5	*	1	48	17	0	42	24	0
255/224	1936–37	A	1	Brisbane[2]	W-322	4	0	c	4	25	hw	2	32	12	0	–	–	–
256/225			2	Sydney	W-I & 22	3	231	*	–	–	–	–	32	6	0	127	29	3
257/226			3	Melbourne	L-365	3	32	c	3	51	b	–	43	16	2	176	89	0
258/227			4	Adelaide	L-148	3	20	c	4	39	b	3	48	30	2	122	57	5
259/228			5	Melbourne	L-I & 200	4	14	c	4	56	c	–	128	62	0	–	–	–
260/229	1937	NZ	1	Lord's	D	4	140	c	–	–	–	1	36	12	0	–	–	–

Ref	Series	V	T	Venue	Result	Batting 1st No	R	HO	Batting 2nd No	R	HO	Ct	Bowling 1st Balls	R	W	Bowling 2nd Balls	R	W
261/230			2	Manchester	W-130	4	33	b	4	0	c	–	90	27	1	36	18	0
262/231			3	Oval	D	6	31	c	–	–	–	–	42	25	1	66	19	2
263/232*	1938	A	1	Nottingham	D	4	26	b	–	–	–	3	114	44	0	72	15	0
264/233*			2	Lord's	D	4	240	b	6	2	c	2	–	–	–	–	–	–
265/234*			4	Leeds	L-5w	4	76	b	4	0	c	2	–	–	–	–	–	–
266/235*			5	Oval	W-I & 579	4	59	lbw	–	–	–	1	12	8	0	–	–	–
267/236*	1938–39	SA	1	Johannesburg[1]	D	4	24	lbw	4	58	lbw	–	80	27	0	48	13	1
268/237*			2	Cape Town	D	4	181	b	–	–	–	–	–	–	–	72	25	0
269/238*			3	Durban[2]	W-I & 13	4	120	c	–	–	–	5	16	2	0	24	11	1
270/239*			4	Johannesburg[1]	D	4	1	c	4	61	*	–	56	19	1	–	–	–
271/240*			5	Durban[2]	D	4	24	st	4	140	st	1	112	34	0	72	30	0
272/241*	1939	WI	1	Lord's	W-8w	4	14	c	4	30	*	1	–	–	–	–	–	–
273/242*			2	Manchester	D	4	22	st	4	32	b	3	–	–	–	–	–	–
274/243*			3	Oval	D	4	43	c	4	138	b	1	–	–	–	–	–	–
276/244*	1946	I	1	Lord's	W-10w	4	33	b	–	–	–	2	–	–	–	–	–	–
277/245*			2	Manchester	D	4	69	b	4	8	c	–	6	3	0	–	–	–
278/246*			3	Oval	D	5	9	*	–	–	–	–	–	–	–	–	–	–
279/247*	1946–47	A	1	Brisbane[2]	L-I & 332	5	32	lbw	5	23	b	1	–	–	–	–	–	–
280/248*			2	Sydney	L-I & 33	5	1	c	5	37	c	1	–	–	–	–	–	–
281/249*			3	Melbourne	D	5	9	c	5	26	b	3	–	–	–	–	–	–
282/250*			4	Adelaide	D	4	18	b	4	22	c	1	–	–	–	–	–	–
284/252*	1946–47	NZ		Christchurch	D	5	79	c	–	–	–	1	–	–	–	–	–	–

Career	M	I	NO	HS	R	Avge	100	50	Ct	St	Balls	R	W	Avge	BB	5w	10w	Rate
Test	85	140	16	336*	7249	58.45	22	24	110	–	7969	3138	83	37.80	5-36	2	–	96.01
F/c	634	1005	104	336*	50551	56.10	167	184	819	3	51456	22389	732	30.58	9-23	22	3	70.29

W. R. HAMMOND – TEST SUMMARY

Series	V	M	I	NO	HS	R	Avge	100	50	Balls	R	W	Avge	BB	5w	10w	Rate
1927–28	SA	5	9	1	90	321	40.12	–	3	968	399	15	26.60	5-36	1	–	64.53
1928	WI	3	3	–	63	111	37.00	–	1	234	103	3	34.33	1-20	–	–	78.00
1928–29	A	5	9	1	251	905	113.12	4	–	714	287	5	57.40	3-53	–	–	142.80
1929	SA	4	8	2	138*	352	58.66	2	1	288	95	1	95.00	1-19	–	–	288.00
1930	A	5	9	–	113	306	34.00	1	1	890	302	5	60.40	2-24	–	–	178.00
1930–31	SA	5	9	1	136*	517	64.62	1	4	654	240	9	26.66	4-63	–	–	72.66
1931	NZ	3	4	1	100*	169	56.33	1	–	195	68	2	34.00	1-8	–	–	97.50
1932	I	1	2	–	35	47	23.50	–	–	57	24	3	8.00	3-9	–	–	19.00
1932–33	A	5	9	1	112	440	55.00	2	2	725	291	9	32.33	3-21	–	–	80.55
1932–33	NZ	2	2	1	336*	563	563.00	2	–	42	19	0	–	–	–	–	–
1933	WI	3	3	–	34	74	24.66	–	–	30	27	0	–	–	–	–	–
1934	A	5	8	–	43	162	20.25	–	–	723	364	5	72.80	3-111	–	–	144.60
1934–35	WI	4	8	1	47	175	25.00	–	–	150	46	0	–	–	–	–	–
1935	SA	5	8	2	87*	389	64.83	–	4	421	146	6	24.33	2-8	–	–	70.16
1936	I	2	3	1	217	389	194.50	2	–	216	94	1	94.00	1-19	–	–	216.00
1936–37	A	5	9	1	231*	468	58.50	1	2	708	301	12	25.08	5-57	1	–	59.00
1937	NZ	3	4	–	140	204	51.00	1	–	270	101	4	25.25	2-19	–	–	67.50
1938	A	4	6	–	240	403	67.16	1	2	198	67	0	–	–	–	–	–
1938–39	SA	5	8	1	181	609	87.00	3	2	480	161	3	53.66	1-11	–	–	160.00
1939	WI	3	6	1	138	279	55.80	1	–	–	–	–	–	–	–	–	–
1946	I	3	4	1	69	119	39.66	–	1	6	3	0	–	–	–	–	–
1946–47	A	4	8	–	37	168	21.00	–	–	–	–	–	–	–	–	–	–
1946–47	NZ	1	1	–	79	79	79.00	–	1	–	–	–	–	–	–	–	–
	A	33	58	3	251	2852	51.85	9	7	3958	1612	36	44.77	5-57	1	–	109.94
	SA	24	42	7	181	2188	62.51	6	14	2811	1041	34	30.61	5-36	1	–	82.67
	WI	13	20	2	138	639	35.50	1	1	414	176	3	58.66	1-20	–	–	138.00
	NZ	9	11	2	336*	1015	112.77	4	1	507	188	6	31.33	2-19	–	–	84.50
	I	6	9	2	217	555	79.28	2	1	279	121	4	30.25	3-9	–	–	69.75
Home		44	68	8	240	3004	50.06	9	10	3528	1394	30	46.46	3-9	–	–	117.60
Overseas		41	72	8	336*	4245	66.32	13	14	4441	1744	53	32.90	5-36	2	–	83.79
Totals		85	140	16	336*	7249	58.45	22	24	7969	3138	83	37.80	5-36	2	–	96.01

HAMPSHIRE
John Harry

Yorkshire (1961 to 1981)
Tasmania (1967–68 to 1978–79)
Derbyshire (1982 to 1984)

TOURS
A 1970–71; SA 1972–73 (Robins), 1974–75 (Robins); WI 1964–65 (Cav); NZ 1970–71; P 1967–68 (Cwlth); SL 1969–70; Z 1980–81 (Leics XI)
Born Thurnscoe, Yorkshire 10 Feb 1941

Tall (6ft) and strongly built, John Hampshire was an attractive middle-order batsman, a superb close fielder and, in his early days, an effective leg-spin bowler. A courageous player who hit the ball with tremendous power off the front foot, he began his Test career with a unique century at Lord's, only to be dropped after the very next match. His spasmodic international appearances mirrored his erratic county form and he failed to realize his true potential. An almost exact contemporary of Geoffrey Boycott, he exceeded his colleague's natural talent but lacked his exceptional application and concentration. His thorough knowledge of the game served Tasmanian cricket well and he was an enthusiastic captain of an unspectacular Yorkshire team (1979–80) before escaping their internal bickering and ending his career quietly with Derbyshire. He toured Zimbabwe with a Leicestershire XI as an unregistered guest player. A first-class umpire since 1985, he was appointed to the Test match panel in 1989. His father and younger brother made fleeting appearances for Yorkshire.

John Hampshire

NOTABLE FEATS
- *654* Became the only England player to score 100 at Lord's on debut in Tests.
- Exceeded 1000 runs in a season 15 times.

						Batting 1st			Batting 2nd			
Ref	Series	V	T	Venue	Result	No	R	HO	No	R	HO	Ct
654/454	1969	WI	2	Lord's	D	6	107	lbw	6	5	ro	3
655/455			3	Leeds	W-30	4	1	c	4	22	lbw	1
678/463	1970–71	A	6	Adelaide	D	6	55	c	5	3	lbw	–
679/464			7	Sydney	W-62	4	10	c	4	24	c	2
685/465	1970–71	NZ	1	Christchurch	W-8w	4	40	c	4	51	*	–
686/466			2	Auckland	D	4	9	c	4	0	c	1
702/477	1972	A	5	Oval	L-5w	4	42	c	4	20	c	1
762/513	1975	A	3	Leeds	D	4	14	lbw	7	0	c	1

Career	M	I	NO	HS	R	Avge	100	50	Ct	St	Balls	R	W	Avge	BB	5w	10w	Rate
Test	8	16	1	107	403	26.86	1	2	9	–	–	–	–	–	–	–	–	–
F/c	577	924	112	183*	28059	34.55	43	156	446	–	2539	1637	30	54.56	7-52	2	–	84.63

HARDINGE
Harold Thomas William

Kent (1902 to 1933)

Wisden 1915
Born Greenwich, Kent 25 Feb 1886
Died Cambridge, Kent 8 May 1965

'Wally' Hardinge was a stylish and consistent opening batsman, a useful slow left-arm bowler and an exceptionally fast fielder. His long and distinguished career began at the age of 16, encompassed Kent's first four Championships and was almost evenly divided by the Great War. A prolific county opener during an era that saw the prime of such players as Hobbs and Sutcliffe, he was destined to play only once for England and was never invited on tour. A double international, he played soccer for Newcastle United, Sheffield United and Arsenal and was capped at centre-forward for England against Scotland in 1910. He coached Leicestershire before joining the staff of John Wisden and Co.

Wally Hardinge

NOTABLE FEATS

• Exceeded 1000 runs in a season 18 times, including 2000 on 5 occasions.
• Scored 5 hundreds in 6 innings for Kent in 1913 and made 100 in each innings of a match on 4 occasions.
• Carried his bat for 113* out of the Rest's 220 v an England XI at Lord's in 1911 (his first representative match) and repeated the feat on 10 other occasions for Kent.
• Shared Kent record 4th-wkt stand of 297 with A.P.F. Chapman v Hampshire at Southampton in 1926.
• Took 6 for 9 for Kent v Warwickshire at Tunbridge Wells in 1929.

						Batting 1st			Batting 2nd			
Ref	Series	V	T	Venue	Result	No	R	HO	No	R	HO	Ct
142/131	1921	A	3	Leeds	L-219	2	25	lbw	2	5	c	–

Career	M	I	NO	HS	R	Avge	100	50	Ct	St	Balls	R	W	Avge	BB	5w	10w	Rate
Test	1	2	0	25	30	15.00	–	–	–	–	–	–	–	–	–	–	–	–
F/c	623	1021	103	263*	33519	36.51	75	158	297	–	24481	9825	371	26.48	7-64	8	1	65.98

HARDSTAFF Joseph Sr

Nottinghamshire (1902 to 1924)

TOUR A 1907–08
Born Kirkby in Ashfield, Nottinghamshire 9 Nov 1882
Died Nuncargate, Nottinghamshire 2 Apr 1947

Joe Hardstaff senior was an attractive middle-order batsman and a mainstay of the Nottinghamshire team for two decades on either side of the Great War. Although only 5ft 6in tall, he was stockily built and commanded a full range of powerful strokes based on a sound defence. He was a brilliant outfielder, as befits an occasional Nottingham Forest footballer, and a frenetic right-arm fast-medium change bowler. In 1907 he helped Notts win their first title since the Championship was officially constituted and his innings of 124* and 48 against the touring South Africans gained him a place on the 1907–08 tour of Australia. There he amassed a record aggregate for an antipodean season, a feat which earned him an illuminated address when he returned home to Kirkby in Ashfield. A first-class umpire from 1927 until his death, he stood in 21 Tests, including the four-match 1929–30 series in the Caribbean, before his international career was curtailed by his son's inclusion in the England team. [*Illus. p.* 141]

NOTABLE FEATS

• Exceeded 1000 runs in a season 7 times, plus once on tour. His aggregate of 1360, avge 52.30, in 1907–08 was then a record for an Australian season.
• Scored 124* before lunch on the second day for Nottinghamshire v South Africans at Nottingham in 1907.

						Batting 1st			Batting 2nd			
Ref	Series	V	T	Venue	Result	No	R	HO	No	R	HO	Ct
96/93	1907–08	A	1	Sydney	L-2w	6	12	b	5	63	b	–
97/94			2	Melbourne	W-1w	6	12	b	6	19	c	–
98/95			3	Adelaide	L-245	6	61	b	6	72	c	–
99/96			4	Melbourne	L-308	3	8	c	3	39	c	1
100/97			5	Sydney	L-49	5	17	c	5	8	b	–

Career	M	I	NO	HS	R	Avge	100	50	Ct	St	Balls	R	W	Avge	BB	5w	10w	Rate
Test	5	10	0	72	311	31.10	–	3	1	–	–	–	–	–	–	–	–	–
F/c	377	620	73	213*	17146	31.34	26	94	187	2	3587	2244	58	38.68	5-133	1	–	61.84

HARDSTAFF Joseph Jr

Nottinghamshire (1930 to 1955)
Services in India
(1943–44 to 1944–45)
Europeans (1944–45)
Auckland (1948–49 to 1949–50)

Wisden 1938
TOURS
A 1935–36, 1936–37, 1946–47;
WI 1947–48; NZ 1935–36, 1936–37,
1938–39 (Cahn), 1946–47;
I 1937–38 (Tennyson)
Born Nuncargate, Nottinghamshire
3 Jul 1911

Joe Hardstaff jr

Young Joe Hardstaff was an extremely elegant middle-order batsman, a right-arm medium-pace change bowler and a magnificent outfielder. The son of a famous Notts batsman and Test umpire, he was a tall (5ft 11in) strong-wristed, nimble-footed strokemaker and one of the most graceful batting artists of the 1930s. He had reached his peak and was an automatic selection for England when the Second World War began. Without that hiatus he would undoubtedly have taken his tally of first-class hundreds well into three figures and doubled his Test output. Afterwards he was 35 and gave only glimpses of his past glory. It is astonishing 40 years on to discover that his Plunket Shield appearances for Auckland during post-war winter coaching engagements provoked considerable discussion about infringement of his county qualification. His own son, also confusingly named Joseph, became a senior RAF officer and played in two first-class matches.

NOTABLE FEATS

- 1000 runs in 16th Test (*274*) (25 inns).
- *260* Shared record E v NZ 3rd-wkt stand of 245 in 210 min with W.R. Hammond.
- *266* Contributed 169* in 326 min towards the record Test total of 903 for 7 dec and shared a record E v A 6th-wkt stand of 215 with L. Hutton.
- *276* His 205* in 315 min remains the highest score v India at Lord's.
- Exceeded 1000 runs in a season 13 times (plus once on tour), including 2000 on 4 occasions. Headed the national averages in 1949 with 2251 runs at 72.61. Scored 1150 runs in August 1937.
- His 83 first-class hundreds included a record 65 for Nottinghamshire. He scored 10 double centuries.
- Won the 1937 Lawrence Trophy for scoring 100 in 51 min for Nottinghamshire v Kent at Canterbury.

Ref	Series	V	T	Venue	Result	Batting 1st No	R	HO	Batting 2nd No	R	HO	Ct
244/218	1935	SA	3	Leeds	D	6	10	c	6	0	b	–
252/221	1936	I	1	Lord's	W-9w	6	2	b	–	–	–	1
253/222			2	Manchester	D	6	94	c	–	–	–	1
255/224	1936–37	A	1	Brisbane[2]	W-322	7	43	c	8	20	st	1
256/225			2	Sydney	W-I & 22	7	26	b	–	–	–	–
257/226			3	Melbourne	L-365	8	3	b	6	17	c	1
258/227			4	Adelaide	L-148	7	20	c	3	43	b	–
259/228			5	Melbourne	L-I & 200	3	83	c	3	1	b	–
260/229	1937	NZ	1	Lord's	D	3	114	c	3	64	c	–
261/230			2	Manchester	W-130	3	58	st	3	11	c	–
262/231			3	Oval	D	5	103	b	–	–	–	–
265/234	1938	A	4	Leeds	L-5w	3	4	ro	3	11	b	–
266/235			5	Oval	W-I & 579	7	169	*	–	–	–	1
272/241	1939	WI	1	Lord's	W-8w	6	3	*	–	–	–	1
273/242			2	Manchester	D	6	76	c	6	1	c	1
274/243			3	Oval	D	6	94	b	–	–	–	–
276/244	1946	I	1	Lord's	W-10w	5	205	*	–	–	–	–
277/245			2	Manchester	D	5	5	c	5	0	b	–
282/250	1946–47	A	4	Adelaide	D	6	67	b	6	9	b	–
295/258	1947–48	WI	1	Bridgetown	D	4	98	b	5	0	c	–
297/260			3	Georgetown	L-7w	4	3	b	4	63	c	1
298/261			4	Kingston	L-10w	4	9	c	4	64	b	1
299/262	1948	A	1	Nottingham	L-8w	5	0	c	5	43	c	–

Career	M	I	NO	HS	R	Avge	100	50	Ct	St	Balls	R	W	Avge	BB	5w	10w	Rate
Test	23	38	3	205*	1636	46.74	4	10	9	–	–	–	–	–	–	–	–	–
F/c	517	812	94	266	31847	44.35	83	166	123	–	3894	2141	36	59.47	4-43	–	–	108.16

J. HARDSTAFF Jr – TEST BATTING SUMMARY

Series	V	M	I	NO	HS	R	Avge	100	50
1935	SA	1	2	–	10	10	5.00	–	–
1936	I	2	2	–	94	96	48.00	–	1
1936–37	A	5	9	–	83	256	28.44	–	1
1937	NZ	3	5	–	114	350	70.00	2	2
1938	A	2	3	1	169*	184	92.00	1	–
1939	WI	3	4	1	94	174	58.00	–	2
1946	I	2	3	1	205*	210	105.00	1	–
1946–47	A	1	2	–	67	76	38.00	–	1
1947–48	WI	3	6	–	98	237	39.50	–	3
1948	A	1	2	–	43	43	21.50	–	–

Series	V	M	I	NO	HS	R	Avge	100	50
	A	9	16	1	169*	559	37.26	1	2
	SA	1	2	–	10	10	5.00	–	–
	WI	6	10	1	98	411	45.66	–	5
	NZ	3	5	–	114	350	70.00	2	2
	I	4	5	1	205*	306	76.50	1	1
Home		14	21	3	205*	1067	59.27	4	5
Overseas		9	17	–	98	569	33.47	–	5
Totals		23	38	3	205*	1636	46.74	4	10

HARRIS, 4th Lord
GCSI, GCIE, CB
(Sir George Robert Canning Harris)

Kent (1870 to 1911)
Oxford University (1871 to 1874)

TOUR A 1878–79
Born St Anne's, Trinidad 3 Feb 1851
Succeeded to title 1872
Died Belmont, Faversham, Kent
24 Mar 1932

With the notable exception of W.G. Grace, the most influential and devoted figure in the universal development of cricket was the Fourth Lord Harris. Although he was a considerable cricketer, it was his formidable personality and administrative ability which exerted such a tremendous effect. Educated at Eton and Oxford (where he gained blues in three of his four years), he was a punishing middle-order batsman who loved to attack quick bowling, a useful right-handed fast round-arm change bowler, and an outstanding fielder. He served Kent cricket for half a century, reviving the Club's fortunes during his years as captain (1875–89), secretary (1875–80), and president (1895). As committee member, trustee, treasurer or president from 1916 until his death, he was MCC's fount of all knowledge in matters financial and cricket. He proved a staunch supporter of the professionals and, as when stamping out the throwing epidemic of the 1880s, a fearless upholder of the game's Laws. Although his playing career was hampered by political offices – he held two posts in Salisbury's administration and was Governor of Bombay (1890–95) – he enjoyed the longest of all county careers (41 years), led teams to North Africa and Australia, and captained England in each of his four Tests, including the first ever staged at home. He was 79 when he played his final match at Eton.

NOTABLE FEATS

- *16* First Test captain to bowl his entire XI in an innings (declarations were not permitted until 1889).
- Remains the oldest man to play first-class cricket in Britain – he was 60 yrs 151 days at the end of his final appearance for Kent (v All India at Catford in 1911).

TEST NOTES

- *3* Bowled in 1st inns: 0 for 14 (12 balls)
- *16* Bowled in 1st inns: 0 for 15 (20 balls)

Lord Harris

						Batting 1st			Batting 2nd			
Ref	Series	V	T	Venue	Result	No	R	HO	No	R	HO	Ct
3/3*	1878–79	A		Melbourne	L-10w	5	33	b	5	36	c	–
4/4*	1880	A		Oval	W-5w	5	52	c	–	–	–	1
15/15*	1884	A	2	Lord's	W-I & 5	6	4	b	–	–	–	–
16/16*			3	Oval	D	8	14	lbw	4	6	*	1

Career	M	I	NO	HS	R	Avge	100	50	Ct	St	Balls	R	W	Avge	BB	5w	10w	Rate
Test	4	6	1	52	145	29.00	–	1	2	–	32	29	0	–	–	–	–	–
F/c	224	395	23	176	9990	26.85	11	55	190	–	3446	1758	70+5	25.11	5-57	1	–	49.22

HARTLEY
John Cabourn

Oxford University (1895 to 1897)
Sussex (1895 to 1898)

TOURS
A 1922–23; SA 1905–06; NZ 1922–23
Born Lincoln 15 Nov 1874
Died Woodhall Spa, Lincolnshire
8 Mar 1963

John Hartley

Colonel John Hartley was a right-arm slow-medium leg-break bowler and a modest lower-order batsman who learned his cricket at Tonbridge. Strongly built and a little over medium height, he toured America with Frank Mitchell's team before going up to Oxford and celebrating the first of his two blues (1896) by contributing 11 wickets (including eight on the first day) to a notable victory in the Varsity match. His Test record was less impressive than his service in the Boer and Great Wars when he survived being twice wounded to be mentioned in dispatches four times.

						Batting 1st			Batting 2nd				Bowling 1st			Bowling 2nd		
Ref	Series	V	T	Venue	Result	No	R	HO	No	R	HO	Ct	Balls	R	W	Balls	R	W
90/87	1905–06	SA	3	Johannesburg[1]	L-243	8	0	b	2	9	c	2	114	62	1	42	31	0
92/89			5	Cape Town	L-I & 16	8	6	ro	9	0	c	–	36	22	0	–	–	–

Career	M	I	NO	HS	R	Avge	100	50	Ct	St	Balls	R	W	Avge	BB	5w	10w	Rate
Test	2	4	0	9	15	3.75	–	–	2	–	192	115	1	115.00	1-62	–	–	192.00
F/c	83	126	19	84*	1366	12.76	–	2	52	–	10244	5626	221	25.45	8-161	12	4	46.35

HAWKE, 7th Lord
(Hon. Martin Bladen)

Yorkshire (1881 to 1911)
Cambridge University (1882 to 1885)

Wisden 1909
TOURS
A 1887–88; SA 1895–96, 1898–99;
WI 1896–97; I 1892–93
Born Willingham Rectory, Gainsborough,
Lincolnshire 16 Aug 1860
Succeeded to title 1887
Died West End, Edinburgh, Scotland
10 Oct 1938

Besides controlling the affairs of Yorkshire for more than half a century, Lord Hawke played a foremost part in the modernization of first-class cricket and in promoting the game overseas. A tall, robust middle-order batsman with a full armoury of punishing off-side strokes and a fast, safe outfielder, he learned his cricket at Eton and gained three blues during his four years at Cambridge. By a vast distance he was the longest-serving Yorkshire captain (1883–1910), bringing tact and sound judgment to the role and gaining the County's first eight official titles, before reigning as president for the last 40 years of his life. He devoted considerable energy to his MCC committee work, serving as president (1914–19), trustee, treasurer (1932–38) and selector (1899–1909 and 1933) – an appointment he instituted. By introducing a winter pay scheme and investing a proportion of benefit income, he did much to improve the welfare of Yorkshire's professionals. He also instilled a strict discipline concerning alcohol and remedied a sadly lacking pride in their appearance. A keen upholder of the game's traditions, his personally conducted overseas tours fostered much enthusiasm; his portrait still abounds in cricket pavilions throughout America, Canada, the Argentine, South Africa, West Indies, Australia, New Zealand and India.

NOTABLE FEATS

- Contributed 166 to Yorkshire's 887 in 10 hr 50 min v Warwickshire at Birmingham in 1896; the highest and longest innings in County cricket, it was the first first-class match to include hundreds by 4 batsmen. His stand of 292 with R. Peel remains the 8th-wkt record for first-class matches in Britain.

Lord Hawke's 1898–99 team to South Africa: standing *G.A. Lohmann (manager), W.R. Cuttell, F. Mitchell, F.W. Milligan, A.G. Archer, A.A. White (umpire);* seated *S. Haigh, H.R. Bromley-Davenport, Lord Hawke (captain), A.E. Trott, J.H. Board;* in front *J.T. Tyldesley, C.E.M. Wilson, P.F. Warner.*

Ref	Series	V	T	Venue	Result	Batting 1st			Batting 2nd			Ct
						No	R	HO	No	R	HO	
47/47	1895–96	SA	1	Port Elizabeth	W-288	8	0	b	10	30	c	–
48/48*			2	Johannesburg[1]	W-I & 197	7	4	lbw	–	–	–	1
49/49*			3	Cape Town	W-I & 33	9	12	*	–	–	–	2
58/58*	1898–99	SA	1	Johannesburg[1]	W-32	8	0	c	9	5	b	–
59/59*			2	Cape Town	W-210	11	1	b	11	3	c	–

Career	M	I	NO	HS	R	Avge	100	50	Ct	St	Balls	R	W	Avge	BB	5w	10w	Rate
Test	5	8	1	30	55	7.85	–	–	3	–	–	–	–	–	–	–	–	–
F/c	630	931	105	166	16685	20.19	13	67	209	–	20	16	0	–	–	–	–	–

HAYES
Ernest George MBE

Surrey (1896 to 1919)
London County (1903)
Leicestershire (1926)

Wisden 1907
TOURS
A 1907–08; SA 1905–06; WI 1904–05
Born Peckham, Surrey 6 Nov 1876
Died West Dulwich, Surrey 2 Dec 1953

Ernie Hayes was an attractive middle-order batsman, a handy right-arm leg-break bowler and an outstanding slip fielder. A powerful driver and puller, he scored consistently against county bowling but failed abysmally in his spasmodic and brief international career. His marvellous catching off the express bowling of Tom Richardson and Bill Lockwood contributed to two of Surrey's early titles but also caused contractures in his right hand. His career was virtually ended by the Great War, in which he was commissioned with the Sportsman's Battalion, was wounded and won the MBE. He reappeared as an amateur in 1919 before becoming head coach to Leicestershire (1923–28) and playing for them (at the age of 50) when he headed their batting averages after being run out for 99 in his first innings. He returned to The Oval as coach (1929–34) before ending his working days as a licensee in West Norwood. [*Illus. p.* 141]

NOTABLE FEATS

- Exceeded 1000 runs in a season 16 times, including 2000 twice.
- Contributed 276 (the highest of his 4 double centuries) to the record Surrey 2nd-wkt stand of 371 with J.B. Hobbs v Hampshire at The Oval in 1909.

NOTABLE FEATS *cont.*

• Shared record Surrey 3rd-wkt stand of 353 with A. Ducat v Hampshire at Southampton in 1919. Both batsmen scored 100s before lunch, one of 8 such instances by Hayes.

					Batting 1st			Batting 2nd				Bowling 1st			Bowling 2nd		
Ref	Series	V	T Venue	Result	No	R	HO	No	R	HO	Ct	Balls	R	W	Balls	R	W
88/85	1905–06	SA	1 Johannesburg[1]	L-1w	5	20	c	5	3	c	–	–	–	–	54	28	1
90/87			3 Johannesburg[1]	L-243	6	35	c	9	11	*	–	–	–	–	–	–	–
91/88			4 Cape Town	W-4w	9	0	lbw	7	0	b	1	–	–	–	–	–	–
105/102	1909	A	5 Oval	D	7	4	lbw	3	9	c	–	24	10	0	12	14	0
128/117	1912	SA	3 Oval	W-10w	5	4	b	–	–	–	1	–	–	–	–	–	–

Career	M	I	NO	HS	R	Avge	100	50	Ct	St	Balls	R	W	Avge	BB	5w	10w	Rate
Test	5	9	1	35	86	10.75	–	–	2	–	90	52	1	52.00	1-28	–	–	90.00
F/c	560	896	48	276	27318	32.21	48	142	609	2	27022	13754	515	26.70	8-22	12	2	52.46

HAYES, Frank Charles

Lancashire (1970 to 1984)

TOURS

SA 1972–73 (Robins), 1974–75 (Robins), 1975–76 (Robins); WI 1973–74; I 1980–81 (Overseas XI); P 1981–82 (Int XI); Z 1975–76 (Int XI)

Born Preston, Lancashire 6 Dec 1946

Frank Hayes, watched by his captain Tony Greig, hooks West Indian Andy Roberts to the boundary during the Old Trafford Test, 1976.

Frank Hayes was a stylish middle-order batsman and a superb fielder, particularly at cover. He completed his science degree at Sheffield University before celebrating his arrival on the county scene with scores of 94 and 99 in his first two matches. He confirmed his reputation as an attractive and punishing player, notably strong off the back foot, with a memorable innings in the 1973 Test trial. When he began his Test career with an exhilarating century he was hailed as a new master batsman. Sadly it was not to be; he failed to reach 30 in any of his remaining 15 innings – all against the West Indies – frequently falling victim to severe nerves or an ill-judged hook. Lancashire remained entrenched in the lower half of the table during his three seasons of captaincy (1978–80) and, although he maintained a healthy batting average, he was forced to retire when, after fracturing his ankle while batting, he was found to be suffering from a brittle bone condition.

NOTABLE FEATS

• *725* Scored 106* on Test debut (2nd inns).
• Exceeded 1000 runs in a season 6 times.
• Scored 34 (646666) off an over from M.A. Nash for Lancashire v Glamorgan at Swansea in 1977 – second-highest total from a 6-ball over without no-balls.

					Batting 1st			Batting 2nd			
Ref	Series	V	T Venue	Result	No	R	HO	No	R	HO	Ct
725/489	1973	WI	1 Oval	L-158	4	16	c	4	106	*	1
726/490			2 Birmingham	D	4	29	c	3	0	lbw	1
727/491			3 Lord's	L-I & 226	4	8	c	5	0	c	–
731/492	1973–74	WI	1 Port-of-Spain	L-7w	4	12	c	4	8	b	2
732/493			2 Kingston	D	4	10	c	4	0	ro	–
734/495			4 Georgetown	D	6	6	c	–	–	–	–
735/496			5 Port-of-Spain	W-26	6	24	c	7	0	lbw	–
779/517	1976	WI	3 Manchester	L-425	6	0	c	5	18	c	1
780/518			4 Leeds	L-55	3	7	c	3	0	c	2

Career	M	I	NO	HS	R	Avge	100	50	Ct	St	Balls	R	W	Avge	BB	5w	10w	Rate
Test	9	17	1	106*	244	15.25	1	–	7	–	–	–	–	–	–	–	–	–
F/c	272	421	58	187	13018	35.86	23	67	176	–	50	15	0	–	–	–	–	–

HAYWARD
Thomas Walter

Surrey (1893 to 1914)

Wisden 1895
TOURS
A 1897–98, 1901–02, 1903–04;
SA 1895–96
Born Cambridge 29 Mar 1871
Died Cambridge 19 Jul 1939

Tom Hayward at The Oval in 1898 after his triple century against Lancashire.

Tom Hayward was a remarkably prolific batsman who scored consistently throughout the two decades preceding the First World War. Promoted to open around 1900, he formed a formidable partnership first with Bobby Abel and then with Jack Hobbs, a fellow Cambridgeshire man and his illustrious ally in 40 century stands, four of them in a single week. Hayward's father and grandfather both played for Surrey and his uncle Thomas had been the leading professional batsman of the 1860s. Calm, watchful and upright at the crease, he was a precise placer of singles and a handsome off-side player who favoured the drive and cut. Tallish and well-built, his technique was to play very straight and this enabled him to overcome the erratic bounce of poor pitches. Until he gave up bowling in 1904, his brisk, awkwardly bouncing right-arm off-breaks had been effective enough to achieve the 'double'. An automatic England selection for ten years, he enjoyed three successful tours of Australia. By a quirky twist of fate it was at his beloved Oval in 1907, during his last Test appearance there, that he was out to the very first ball of the match – a fate suffered by no other England batsman in a home Test before or since.

NOTABLE FEATS

- 1000 runs in 16th Test (65) (25 inns).
- 64 His stand of 185 with F.S. Jackson was then England's highest for any wicket in England and the record opening partnership by either side in E v A Tests.
- Exceeded 1000 runs in a season 20 times in succession (1895–1914), including 3000 twice and 2000 on 8 other occasions. His record of 3518 runs in 1906 survived until 1947.
- Took 100 wickets in a season once, completing the 'double' in 1897.
- Second batsman after W.G. Grace (and first professional) to score 100 first-class hundreds.
- Scored 315* for Surrey v Lancashire at The Oval in 1898 – then the sixth-highest first-class score. His 7 double centuries included 203 for Players v Gentlemen at The Oval in 1904.
- Holds Surrey records for most runs (3246) and hundreds (13) in a season (latter equalled by J.B. Hobbs).
- Scored 1074 runs before June 1900.
- In 1906 set records for earliest dates to complete 2000 (5 July) and 3000 runs (20 August – equalled by W.R. Hammond).
- Only batsman to score hundreds in each innings of successive first-class matches in Britain: within 6 days during away matches for Surrey in 1906 – 144* and 100 v Nottinghamshire and 143 and 125 v Leicestershire. This sequence was included in the first instance of 9 consecutive first-class fifties.
- Carried his bat through a completed innings on 8 occasions.
- Scored 100 before lunch 5 times.
- Shared in Surrey's record partnership for any wicket: 448 for the 4th-wkt with R. Abel v Yorkshire at The Oval in 1899.
- Shared record Surrey 8th-wkt stand of 204 with L.C. Braund v Lancashire at The Oval in 1898.
- Shared 40 Surrey 1st-wkt stands of 100 or more with J.B. Hobbs, their highest being 352 v Warwickshire at The Oval in 1909.
- Two hat-tricks for Surrey in 1899: v Gloucestershire at The Oval and v Derbyshire at Chesterfield.
- With T. Richardson bowled unchanged throughout both Leicestershire innings for Surrey at Leicester in 1897.

						Batting 1st			Batting 2nd				Bowling 1st			Bowling 2nd		
Ref	Series	V	T	Venue	Result	No	R	HO	No	R	HO	Ct	Balls	R	W	Balls	R	W
47/47	1895–96	SA	1	Port Elizabeth	W-288	3	30	c	4	6	c	2	15	7	1	10	0	1
48/48			2	Johannesburg[1]	W-I & 197	3	122	c	–	–	–	–	–	–	–	20	21	0
49/49			3	Cape Town	W-I & 33	3	31	b	–	–	–	2	–	–	–	–	–	–
50/50	1896	A	1	Lord's	W-6w	7	12	*	3	13	b	1	–	–	–	55	44	0
52/52			3	Oval	W-66	6	0	b	6	13	c	1	10	17	0	–	–	–
53/53	1897–98	A	1	Sydney	W-9w	3	72	c	–	–	–	1	18	11	0	30	16	0
54/54			2	Melbourne	L-I & 55	5	23	c	4	33	c	–	54	23	1	–	–	–
55/55			3	Adelaide	L-I & 13	5	70	b	4	1	c	–	48	36	0	–	–	–
56/56			4	Melbourne	L-8w	4	22	c	5	25	c	1	60	24	0	60	24	2
57/57			5	Sydney	L-6w	4	47	b	4	43	c	–	24	12	0	18	18	1
60/60	1899	A	1	Nottingham	D	6	0	ro	6	28	b	2	15	14	0	30	16	0
61/61			2	Lord's	L-10w	6	1	b	1	77	c	1	30	25	0	–	–	–
62/62			3	Leeds	D	7	40	*	–	–	–	–	–	–	–	50	45	2
63/63			4	Manchester	D	6	130	c	–	–	–	–	–	–	–	15	10	0
64/64			5	Oval	D	2	137	c	–	–	–	1	–	–	–	55	38	1

Ref	Series	V	T	Venue	Result	Batting 1st No	R	HO	Batting 2nd No	R	HO	Ct	Bowling 1st Balls	R	W	Bowling 2nd Balls	R	W
65/65	1901–02	A	1	Sydney	W-I & 124	2	69	c	–	–	–	–	–	–	–	–	–	–
66/66			2	Melbourne	L-229	2	0	c	2	12	st	1	–	–	–	–	–	–
67/67			3	Adelaide	L-4w	2	90	ro	2	47	b	1	–	–	–	42	28	0
68/68			4	Sydney	L-7w	2	41	b	2	12	b	–	–	–	–	–	–	–
69/69			5	Melbourne	L-32	5	19	c	2	15	c	–	96	22	4	132	63	1
74/74	1902	A	5	Oval	W-1w	4	0	b	4	7	c	–	–	–	–	–	–	–
78/75	1903–04	A	1	Sydney	W-5w	1	15	b	1	91	st	–	–	–	–	–	–	–
79/76			2	Melbourne	W-185	2	58	c	2	0	c	1	–	–	–	–	–	–
80/77			3	Adelaide	L-216	2	20	b	2	67	lbw	–	–	–	–	–	–	–
81/78			4	Sydney	W-157	2	18	c	2	52	lbw	–	–	–	–	–	–	–
82/79			5	Melbourne	L-218	1	0	b	–	–	–	–	–	–	–	–	–	–
83/80	1905	A	1	Nottingham	W-213	1	5	b	1	47	c	1	–	–	–	–	–	–
84/81			2	Lord's	D	2	16	lbw	2	8	c	–	–	–	–	–	–	–
85/82			3	Leeds	D	1	26	b	1	60	b	2	–	–	–	–	–	–
86/83			4	Manchester	W-I & 80	2	82	c	–	–	–	–	–	–	–	–	–	–
87/84			5	Oval	D	2	59	hw	2	2	lbw	–	–	–	–	–	–	–
93/90	1907	SA	1	Lord's	D	2	21	st	–	–	–	–	–	–	–	–	–	–
94/91			2	Leeds	W-53	1	24	st	1	15	st	1	–	–	–	–	–	–
95/92			3	Oval	D	1	0	lbw	1	3	c	–	–	–	–	–	–	–
102/99	1909	A	2	Lord's	L-9w	1	16	st	1	6	ro	–	–	–	–	–	–	–

Career	M	I	NO	HS	R	Avge	100	50	Ct	St	Balls	R	W	Avge	BB	5w	10w	Rate
Test	35	60	2	137	1999	34.46	3	12	19	–	887	514	14	36.71	4-22	–	–	63.35
F/c	712	1138	96	315*	43551	41.79	104	218	492	–	20927	11042	481	22.95	8-89	18	2	43.50

T. W. HAYWARD – TEST BATTING SUMMARY

Series	V	M	I	NO	HS	R	Avge	100	50
1895–96	SA	3	4	–	122	189	47.25	1	–
1896	A	2	4	1	13	38	12.66	–	–
1897–98	A	5	9	–	72	336	37.33	–	2
1899	A	5	7	1	137	413	68.83	2	1
1901–02	A	5	9	–	90	305	33.88	–	2
1902	A	1	2	–	7	7	3.50	–	–
1903–04	A	5	9	–	91	321	35.66	–	4
1905	A	5	9	–	82	305	33.88	–	3
1907	SA	3	5	–	24	63	12.60	–	–
1909	A	1	2	–	16	22	11.00	–	–
	A	29	51	2	137	1747	35.65	2	12
	SA	6	9	–	122	252	28.00	1	–
Home		17	29	2	137	848	31.40	2	4
Overseas		18	31	–	122	1151	37.12	1	8
Totals		35	60	2	137	1999	34.46	3	12

HEARNE, Alec

Kent (1884 to 1906)

Wisden 1894
TOUR SA 1891–92
Born Ealing, Middlesex 22 Jul 1863
Died Beckenham, Kent 16 May 1952

Alec Hearne, younger brother of George and Frank, began his Kent career as a brisk right-arm leg-spin bowler and a safe slip. Elbow trouble eventually persuaded him to switch to off-breaks but not before he had improved his batting to such a remarkable extent that within five seasons he had established himself as a genuine all-rounder. As a defensive opening or middle-order batsman, he was neat, consistent and extremely obdurate, strong off the back foot and adept at cutting and hooking. A quiet, modest man with a shrewd cricket brain, he was coach at Kent's Tonbridge nursery before serving as the County's scorer from 1925 until the Second World War.
[*Illus. p.* 201]

NOTABLE FEATS

- *38* The Hearnes provided the second instance of 3 brothers playing in the same Test: A. and G.G. for England and F. for South Africa.
- Exceeded 1000 runs in a season 4 times.
- Carried his bat through a completed Kent innings 6 times.
- Shared record Kent 3rd-wkt stand of 321* with J.R. Mason v Nottinghamshire at Nottingham in 1899.
- Two hat-tricks: for MCC v Yorkshire at Lord's in 1888 and for Kent v Gloucestershire at Clifton in 1900.
- Bowled unchanged in partnership with C. Blythe throughout both completed innings for Kent v Surrey at The Oval in 1903.

Ref	Series	V	T	Venue	Result	Batting 1st No	R	HO	Batting 2nd No	R	HO	Ct
38/38	1891–92	SA		Cape Town	W-I & 189	2	9	lbw	–	–	–	1

Career	M	I	NO	HS	R	Avge	100	50	Ct	St	Balls	R	W	Avge	BB	5w	10w	Rate
Test	1	1	0	9	9	9.00	–	–	1	–	–	–	–	–	–	–	–	–
F/c	488	833	78	194	16346	21.65	15	71	404	–	61070	23120	1160	19.93	8-15	52	9	52.64

HEARNE, Frank

Kent (1879 to 1889)
Western Province
(1889–90 to 1903–04)
South Africa (1891–92 to 1895–96)

TOUR SA 1888–89
Born Ealing, Middlesex 23 Nov 1858
Died Cape Town, South Africa
14 Jul 1949

Frank Hearne, middle brother of George and Alec, was a steady opening batsman, a right-handed round-arm bowler who could maintain a rapid pace for short spells, and a sure-handed cover-point. Just 5ft 5in high, he was a fine off-side player with a good defence. Ill-health compelled him to abandon county cricket and he settled in Cape Town and opened a sports outfitters after Major Warton's tour ended in 1889. An invitation to play for Western Province led to the start of his second international career. He revisited England in 1894 with the first Springbok team to tour anywhere (whose fixtures were not even deemed first-class) and holds the unique record of playing in the first six Tests to feature South Africa. His son, G.A.L. Hearne, visited with the 1924 South Africans. [*Illus. p.* 51]

NOTABLE FEATS

- *38* First cricketer to represent both England and South Africa in Tests. The Hearnes provided the second instance of 3 brothers playing in the same Test: A. and G.G. for England and F. for South Africa.

Ref	Series	V	T	Venue	Result	Batting 1st No	R	HO	Batting 2nd No	R	HO	Ct	Bowling 1st Balls	R	W	Bowling 2nd Balls	R	W
For England																		
31/31	1888–89	SA	1	Port Elizabeth	W-8w	4	27	c	–	–	–	1	–	–	–	–	–	–
32/32			2	Cape Town	W-I & 202	5	20	b	–	–	–	–	–	–	–	–	–	–
For South Africa																		
38/3	1891–92	E		Cape Town	L-I & 189	2	24	b	2	23	b	–	62	40	2	–	–	–
47/4	1895–96	E	1	Port Elizabeth	L-288	2	23	c	2	5	b	–	–	–	–	–	–	–
48/5			2	Johannesburg[1]	L-I & 197	4	0	c	4	16	c	1	–	–	–	–	–	–
49/6			3	Cape Town	L-I & 33	2	0	c	2	30	c	1	–	–	–	–	–	–

Career	M	I	NO	HS	R	Avge	100	50	Ct	Balls	R	W	Avge	BB	5w	10w	Rate
Test (E)	2	2	0	27	47	23.50	–	–	1	–	–	–	–	–	–	–	–
Test (SA)	4	8	0	30	121	15.12	–	–	2	62	40	2	20.00	2-40	–	–	31.00
Combined	6	10	0	30	168	16.80	–	–	3	62	40	2	20.00	2-40	–	–	31.00
F/c	161	285	20	144	4760	17.96	4	21	111	2904	1346	58	23.20	5-45	2	–	50.06

HEARNE George Gibbons

Kent (1875 to 1895)

TOUR SA 1891–92
Born Ealing, Middlesex 7 Jul 1856
Died Denmark Hill, Surrey 13 Feb 1932

George Hearne, elder brother of Frank and Alec, was a useful left-handed all-rounder whose career with Kent spanned 21 summers. Known as 'G.G.', he was primarily a round-arm medium-fast bowler who ran the ball away towards the slips. He developed into a correct and watchful middle-order batsman whose massive defence enabled him to survive skilfully on hazardous pitches. He was an alert fielder at point or mid-wicket. [*Illus. p.* 201]

NOTABLE FEATS

- *38* The Hearnes provided the second instance of 3 brothers playing in the same Test: A. and G.G. for England and F. for South Africa.
- Exceeded 1000 runs in a season once and took 100 wickets twice.
- Hat-trick for Kent v Lancashire at Manchester in 1875.

Ref	Series	V	T	Venue	Result	Batting 1st No	R	HO	Batting 2nd No	R	HO	Ct
38/38	1891/92	SA		Cape Town	W-I & 189	4	0	c	–	–	–	–

Career	M	I	NO	HS	R	Avge	100	50	Ct	St	Balls	R	W	Avge	BB	5w	10w	Rate
Test	1	1	0	0	0	0.00	–	–	–	–	–	–	–	–	–	–	–	–
F/c	328	571	56	126	9020	17.51	5	39	214	–	32574	11506	685	16.79	8-21	40	12	47.55

HEARNE
John Thomas

Middlesex (1888 to 1923)

Wisden 1892
TOURS A 1897–98; SA 1891–92
Born Chalfont St Giles, Buckinghamshire 3 May 1867
Died Chalfont St Giles, 17 Apr 1944

NOTABLE FEATS
- *62* Achieved the only hat-trick against Australia in England during the 2nd inns when he dismissed C. Hill, S.E. Gregory and M.A. Noble for 'ducks'.
- Took 100 wickets in a season 15 times, including 200 on 3 occasions. His total of 257 wickets in 1896 (from 10,016 balls) has been exceeded by only 4 bowlers. Headed the national bowling averages 4 times: 1896, 1898, 1904 and 1910.
- Took his 100th wicket of 1896 on 12 June – the earliest date this target has been reached (equalled by C.W.L. Parker in 1931).
- Took 9 wickets in an innings 8 times – 5 for MCC and 3 for Middlesex.
- Took 15 wickets in a match 4 times, equalling G. Burton's Middlesex record by taking 16 for 114 (v Lancashire at Manchester in 1898).
- Three hat-tricks for Middlesex (plus Test *62* above): v Kent at Tonbridge in 1896, v Essex at Lord's in 1902 (4 wickets in 5 balls) and v Warwickshire at Lord's in 1912.
- Bowled in an unchanged partnership throughout both completed innings of a match on 7 occasions.
- Twice bowled 8 Lancashire batsmen in an innings for Middlesex: at Lord's in 1891 and at Manchester in 1900.

Jack Hearne was an outstanding right-arm bowler of lively medium pace whose career aggregate of 3061 wickets has been exceeded only by the three spinners, Rhodes, Freeman and Parker. Tallish (5ft 10½in), he had a fairly long rhythmic run-up and a classic, high side-on delivery action. Exceptionally accurate, he varied his pace craftily and interspersed faster outswingers with sharp off-breaks. Quiet and dignified, he thrived on hard work, bowling over 10,000 balls in 1896, and was the stock bowler not only for Middlesex but also from 1891 to 1924 for the MCC. Summoned to Lord's by telegram for his first Championship match after qualifying by residence, he was relieved to find Middlesex batting when his arrival almost coincided with lunch. He took six Nottinghamshire wickets in his first innings and remained in the Middlesex team from 1890 until the Great War effectively ended his career. A handy lower-order batsman in an emergency and a dependable catcher at slip, he became a much-respected coach; many of his later years being spent with Oxford in The Parks and for six winters he was employed by the Maharaja of Patiala in India. A cousin of the Kent Hearnes (George, Frank and Alec) and also, distantly, of J.W. Hearne ('Young Jack'), he was one of the first professionals to be elected to the Middlesex committee.

The 1891–92 English team in South Africa, featuring three of the five Hearnes who played for England: standing *J. Leaney (umpire), E.J. Leaney, F. Martin, G.W. Ayres, A.D. Pougher, W. Chatterton, E. Ash (manager);* seated *H. Wood, G.G. Hearne, J.T. Hearne, W.W. Read (captain), J.J. Ferris, W.L. Murdoch;* in front *W. Brockwell, G. Brann, V.A. Barton, A. Hearne.*

						Batting 1st			Batting 2nd				Bowling 1st			Bowling 2nd		
Ref	**Series**	**V**	**T**	**Venue**	**Result**	**No**	**R**	**HO**	**No**	**R**	**HO**	**Ct**	**Balls**	**R**	**W**	**Balls**	**R**	**W**
38/38	1891–92	SA		Cape Town	W-I & 189	10	40	c	–	–	–	1	40	12	1	–	–	–
50/50	1896	A	1	Lord's	W-6w	10	11	c	–	–	–	–	–	–	–	180	76	5
51/51			2	Manchester	L-3w	10	18	c	10	9	c	–	140	53	0	120	22	0
52/52			3	Oval	W-66	10	8	b	10	1	b	–	131	41	6	65	19	4
53/53	1897–98	A	1	Sydney	W-9w	9	17	c	–	–	–	–	121	42	5	228	99	4
54/54			2	Melbourne	L-I & 55	9	1	b	10	0	c	–	216	94	1	–	–	–
55/55			3	Adelaide	L-I & 13	10	0	b	10	4	c	–	265	94	2	–	–	–
56/56			4	Melbourne	L-8w	10	0	c	10	4	*	2	214	98	6	42	19	0
57/57			5	Sydney	L-6w	10	2	*	10	3	*	–	126	40	1	90	52	1
60/60	1899	A	1	Nottingham	D	11	4	*	–	–	–	–	295	71	4	145	70	1
62/62			3	Leeds	D	9	3	b	–	–	–	–	115	69	1	158	50	4
63/63			4	Manchester	D	10	1	c	–	–	–	1	50	7	0	235	54	3

Career	**M**	**I**	**NO**	**HS**	**R**	**Avge**	**100**	**50**	**Ct**	**St**	**Balls**	**R**	**W**	**Avge**	**BB**	**5w**	**10w**	**Rate**
Test	12	18	4	40	126	9.00	–	–	4	–	2976	1082	49	22.08	6-41	4	1	60.73
F/c	639	919	318	71	7205	11.98	–	8	426	–	144532	54352	3061	17.75	9-32	255	66	47.21

HEARNE John William

Middlesex (1909 to 1936)

Wisden 1912
TOURS
A 1911–12, 1920–21, 1924–25;
SA 1913–14; WI 1910–11
Born Hillingdon, Middlesex 11 Feb 1891
Died West Drayton, Middlesex
14 Sep 1965

'Young Jack' Hearne

'Young Jack' Hearne, a distant couson of 'J.T.', joined the Lord's staff as a 15-year-old match-card boy and developed into an outstanding all-rounder. Slim and of medium height, he was an elegant middle-order batsman and a high-class right-arm leg-break and googly bowler. His patient straight-batted defence stood him in good stead on spiteful pitches and he was a master at placing the ball between fielders, particularly on the leg-side. His partnerships with 'Patsy' Hendren were as famous between the Wars as those involving their Middlesex successors, Compton and Edrich, two decades later. Before ill-health and frequent accidents encouraged a more cautious approach he was a dashing strokemaker; on the 1920–21 tour of Australia he was taken ill after the first day of the Second Test and took no further part in the mission. He would have easily exceeded 100 first-class hundreds but for the onset of the Great War just when he was at his peak. His bowling derived maximum effect from the minimum of effort, a cleverly disguised but frequently erratic assortment of wrist-spin and off-breaks being propelled from an extremely abbreviated run-up. So sharply spun were his leg-breaks that on a responsive pitch he would employ two slips and a gully. A career record of 1839 wickets at just over 24 runs apiece is a remarkable return for such a bowler, let alone a front-line batsman. In his later years he ran his sports shop in Ealing and coached at indoor cricket schools.

NOTABLE FEATS

- *117* Youngest to score 100 for England (20 yrs 324 days) until 1938 (D.C.S. Compton) and remains the second-youngest.
- Exceeded 1000 runs in a season 19 times, including 2000 on 4 occasions. Headed the national batting averages in 1914. Took 100 wickets 5 times. Exceeded 2000 runs on 3 of the 5 occasions he achieved the 'double'.
- The last of his 11 double centuries, all scored for Middlesex, was his highest: 285* v Essex at Leyton in 1929.
- Scored 100 before lunch 3 times.
- Shared record Middlesex 2nd-wkt stand of 380 with F.A. Tarrant v Lancashire at Lord's in 1914.
- Shared record Middlesex 4th-wkt stand of 325 with E.H. Hendren v Hampshire at Lord's in 1919.
- Twice took 9 wickets in an innings (for Middlesex).
- Two hat-tricks for Middlesex v Essex: at Lord's in 1911 and at Leyton in 1922.
- Achieved the match 'double' 6 times – all for Middlesex.

Ref	Series	V	T	Venue	Result	Batting 1st No	R	HO	Batting 2nd No	R	HO	Ct	Bowling 1st Balls	R	W	Bowling 2nd Balls	R	W
116/108	1911–12	A	1	Sydney	L-146	6	76	c	7	43	b	1	60	44	1	78	51	0
117/109			2	Melbourne	W-8w	3	114	c	4	12	*	–	6	8	0	6	5	0
118/110			3	Adelaide	W-7w	4	12	c	4	2	c	–	12	6	0	60	61	0
119/111			4	Melbourne	W-I & 225	4	0	c	–	–	–	3	6	4	0	18	17	0
120/112			5	Sydney	W-70	4	4	c	4	18	b	–	–	–	–	–	–	–
123/114	1912	A	1	Lord's	D	8	21	*	–	–	–	–	72	31	0	–	–	–
124/115		SA	2	Leeds	W-174	5	45	b	5	35	b	–	–	–	–	12	5	1
126/116		A	2	Manchester	D	5	9	b	–	–	–	–	–	–	–	–	–	–
128/117		SA	3	Oval	W-10w	7	20	lbw	2	5	*	2	–	–	–	–	–	–
129/118		A	3	Oval	W-244	6	1	c	6	14	c	–	–	–	–	–	–	–
132/121	1913–14	SA	3	Johannesburg[1]	W-91	3	27	c	4	0	lbw	2	96	49	5	84	58	1
133/122			4	Durban[1]	D	3	2	c	3	8	*	–	–	–	–	66	46	0
134/123			5	Port Elizabeth	W-10w	4	32	c	–	–	–	1	54	34	1	72	30	0
135/124	1902–21	A	1	Sydney	L-377	3	14	c	3	57	b	–	204	77	3	252	124	1
136/125			2	Melbourne	L-I & 91	–	–	–	–	–	–	1	84	38	0	–	–	–
142/131	1921	A	3	Leeds	L-219	3	7	b	3	27	c	1	30	21	0	–	–	–
154/140	1924	SA	2	Lord's	W-I & 18	–	–	–	–	–	–	–	108	35	1	114	35	1
155/141			3	Leeds	W-9w	3	20	lbw	3	23	*	–	–	–	–	114	54	1
157/143			5	Oval	D	3	35	c	–	–	–	–	138	90	3	–	–	–
158/144	1924–25	A	1	Sydney	L-193	3	7	c	3	0	b	–	97	28	1	200	88	0
159/145			2	Melbourne	L-81	4	9	b	4	23	lbw	1	104	69	0	232	84	4
161/147			4	Melbourne	W-I & 29	3	44	c	–	–	–	1	155	77	3	160	76	1
162/148			5	Sydney	L-307	6	16	lbw	6	24	lbw	–	56	33	0	176	84	2
163/149	1926	A	1	Nottingham	D	–	–	–	–	–	–	–	–	–	–	–	–	–

Career	M	I	NO	HS	R	Avge	100	50	Ct	St	Balls	R	W	Avge	BB	5w	10w	Rate
Test	24	36	5	114	806	26.00	1	2	13	–	2926	1462	30	48.73	5-49	1	–	97.53
F/c	647	1025	116	285*	37252	40.98	96	157	348	–	93573	44926	1839	24.42	9-61	107	23	50.88

HEMMINGS
Edward Ernest

Warwickshire (1966 to 1978)
Nottinghamshire (1979 to date)

TOURS
A 1982–83; SA 1974–75 (Robins);
WI 1982–83 (Int XI); P 1981–82 (Int XI)
Born Leamington Spa, Warwickshire
20 Feb 1949

Eddie Hemmings

After an unhappy apprenticeship with Warwickshire, Eddie Hemmings found a new lease of life when he moved to Trent Bridge at the age of 30. Within three summers he had contributed a 90-wicket yield to Nottinghamshire's first Championship for 52 years and gained an England cap. Somewhat cuddly and looking less than his declared height (5ft 10in), he is a right-arm off-spin bowler (originally a medium-pace seamer), a spirited tail-end batsman, a determined but not excessively mobile fielder and a zany humorist. He has an easy action, can turn the ball sharply on responsive pitches and, as he courageously proved when bowling Viv Richards in the 1987 World Cup, he is not afraid to give the ball some air.

NOTABLE FEATS

- *931* Dismissed Javed Miandad with his fourth ball in Test cricket.
- *942* His 95 in 226 min was the fifth-highest score by a 'night-watchman' in Tests.
- Two hat-tricks: for Warwickshire v Worcestershire at Birmingham in 1977 and for Nottinghamshire v Northamptonshire at Nottingham in 1984.
- Only bowler to take all 10 wickets in a first-class match in the West Indies. His 10 for 175 for International XI v West Indies Invitation XI at Kingston in 1982–83 is the most expensive 10-wicket analysis in all first-class cricket and the Invitation team's total of 419 is the highest in which any bowler has taken all 10 wickets.

						Batting 1st			Batting 2nd				Bowling 1st			Bowling 2nd		
Ref	Series	V	T	Venue	Result	No	R	HO	No	R	HO	Ct	Balls	R	W	Balls	R	W
931/583	1982	P	1	Birmingham	W-113	9	2	lbw	9	19	c	2	144	56	2	60	27	1
932/584			2	Lord's	L-10w	9	6	b	9	14	c	–	120	53	0	13	13	0
939/587	1982–83	A	2	Brisbane[2]	L-7w	9	15	*	9	18	b	1	201	81	0	174	43	2
940/588			3	Adelaide	L-8w	10	0	b	10	0	c	1	288	96	1	24	5	0
942/590			5	Sydney	D	9	29	c	3	95	c	–	162	68	3	282	116	3
1085/640	1987–88	P	2	Faisalabad	D	11	1	*	–	–	–	–	108	35	1	42	16	0
1090/642	1987–88	A		Sydney	D	10	8	*	–	–	–	–	132	53	3	312	107	0
1093/645	1987–88	NZ	3	Wellington	D	–	–	–	–	–	–	–	270	107	0	–	–	–

Career	M	I	NO	HS	R	Avge	100	50	Ct	St	Balls	R	W	Avge	BB	5w	10w	Rate
Test	8	12	3	95	207	23.00	–	1	4	–	2332	876	16	54.75	3-53	–	–	145.75
F/c	413	537	124	127*	8152	19.73	1	22	178	–	78856	34882	1201	29.04	10-175	59	14	65.65

HENDREN
Elias Henry

Middlesex (1907 to 1937)

Wisden 1920
TOURS
A 1920–21, 1924–25, 1928–29; SA 1930–31; WI 1929–30, 1934–35
Born Turnham Green, Middlesex 5 Feb 1889
Died Tooting Bec, Surrey 4 Oct 1962

Quite apart from his prolific feats with the bat, 'Patsy' Hendren was one of cricket's happiest personalities. He was much loved by crowds because of the fun he communicated through his brilliant batting, his spontaneous clowning on the field or just by laughing as he signed his autograph with those two special dots under the last 'n'. When, at the age of 47, he celebrated his final appearance for Middlesex by scoring 100 against Surrey, the Lord's crowd stopped play for five minutes by singing 'For he's a jolly good fellow'. A cockney with Irish forbears, he was short and sturdily built, immensely strong, especially in the arms and wrists, and not always orthodox. Extremely nimble-footed, he was a superb player of spin, a ferocious driver, a deft cutter and, against short-pitched fast bowling, one of the finest hookers of all time, moving inside the line and playing the stroke square rather than fine. His crouching, resolute stance, well-organized defence and full array of strokes made him the most feared middle-order batsman for a decade after the Great War. An engineering apprentice who played for Turnham Green, he joined the Lord's staff in 1905 as a right-arm slow bowler but he was only 17 when he made his Middlesex debut as a batsman and terrier-like outfielder. He met with outstanding success on all his MCC tours, exceeding 1000 runs on each of his three visits to Australia and breaking all records on his expedition to the Caribbean where the adoring crowds named hundreds of children after him. In his younger days he was a notable soccer wing forward who played for Brentford, QPR, Manchester City and Coventry, as well as appearing in a 1919 'Victory' international against Wales. His later years were spent in coaching, first at Harrow School and later with Sussex at Hove. He served on the Middlesex committee and was their scorer for nine seasons (1952–60). When he left the stage he had amassed the third-highest tally of first-class runs and only Jack Hobbs had scored more centuries. No cricketer had won more friends.

'Patsy' Hendren acknowledging the cheers of the crowd at Old Trafford after his 132 against Australia in the 1934 Test.

NOTABLE FEATS

• 1000 runs in 16th Test (*161*) (24 inns); 2000 runs in 34th Test (*191*) (53 inns); 3000 runs in 43rd Test (*208*) (69 inns).
• *164* Scored the only 100 by a Middlesex player v A at Lord's. At 37 he was the youngest of the 4 century-makers in the match.
• *176* Shared record E v A 8th-wkt stand of 124 with H. Larwood.
• *191* Scored first double century in E v WI Tests.
• *235* At 45 yrs 151 days he became the second-oldest batsman after J.B. Hobbs to score a Test century.
• Exceeded 1000 runs in a season 21 times (plus 4 times on tour), including 3000 on 3 occasions and 2000 on 12 others. Headed national first-class batting averages 3 times (1920–22–23).
• Scored 1000 runs in a month 3 times: June 1925, August 1933 and August 1936.
• Only J.B. Hobbs and F.E. Woolley have exceeded his total of 57,611 runs and only Hobbs his total of 170 hundreds.
• Scored 22 double centuries (only D.G. Bradman and W.R. Hammond made more) including one triple century: 301* for Middlesex v Worcestershire at Dudley in 1933.
• His aggregate of 1765 runs (avge 135.76) in 1929–30 remains the record for a West Indies season and included the record sequence by an English batsman of 630 (205*, 254* and 171) before being dismissed. His total of 4 double centuries (2 in successive innings twice) was equalled by G.M. Turner in 1971–72.
• Scored 100 in each innings of a match on 4 occasions. Made hundreds in 3 consecutive innings 4 times and, in 1933, scored 5 hundreds in 6 innings.
• Holds Middlesex career records for most runs (40,302), most hundreds (119), most instances of 1000 runs in a season (20), and most catches in the field (562).
• Holds Middlesex record for most runs in a season: 2669 in 1923.
• Shared in 3 record Middlesex stands: 4th-wkt of 325 with J.W. Hearne v Hampshire at Lord's in 1919; 7th-wkt of 271* with F.T. Mann v Nottinghamshire at Nottingham in 1925; and 9th-wkt of 160* with F.J. Durston v Essex at Leyton in 1927.

						Batting 1st			Batting 2nd			
Ref	Series	V	T	Venue	Result	No	R	HO	No	R	HO	Ct
135/124	1920–21	A	1	Sydney	L-377	4	28	c	4	56	b	1
136/125			2	Melbourne	L-I & 91	4	67	c	4	1	c	–
137/126			3	Adelaide	L-119	4	36	c	4	51	b	1
138/127			4	Melbourne	L-8w	4	30	c	4	32	b	–
139/128			5	Sydney	L-9w	4	5	c	6	13	st	1
140/129	1921	A	1	Nottingham	L-10w	4	0	b	4	7	b	–
141/130			2	Lord's	L-8w	4	0	b	4	10	c	–
153/139	1924	SA	1	Birmingham	W-I & 18	4	74	c	–	–	–	1
154/140			2	Lord's	W-I & 18	4	50	*	–	–	–	–
155/141			3	Leeds	W-9w	5	132	c	–	–	–	1
156/142			4	Manchester	D	–	–	–	–	–	–	–
157/143			5	Oval	D	6	142	c	–	–	–	–
158/144	1924–25	A	1	Sydney	L-193	5	74	*	5	9	c	2
159/145			2	Melbourne	L-81	5	32	c	6	18	b	–
160/146			3	Adelaide	L-11	8	92	c	4	4	lbw	2
161/147			4	Melbourne	W-I & 29	5	65	b	–	–	–	1
162/148			5	Sydney	L-307	5	10	c	5	10	c	–
163/149	1926	A	1	Nottingham	D	–	–	–	–	–	–	–
164/150			2	Lord's	D	4	127	*	–	–	–	–
165/151			3	Leeds	D	4	0	c	4	4	*	1
166/152			4	Manchester	D	5	32	*	–	–	–	1
167/153			5	Oval	W-289	4	8	b	4	15	c	–
175/161	1928	WI	3	Oval	W-I & 71	6	14	c	–	–	–	1
176/162	1928–29	A	1	Brisbane[1]	W-675	6	169	c	6	45	c	–
177/163			2	Sydney	W-8w	5	74	c	–	–	–	1
178/164			3	Melbourne	W-3w	5	19	c	5	45	b	1
179/165			4	Adelaide	W-12	5	13	b	5	11	c	1
180/166			5	Melbourne	L-5w	6	95	c	6	1	b	–
181/167	1929	SA	1	Birmingham	D	5	70	b	6	8	*	–
182/168			2	Lord's	D	5	43	b	4	11	b	2
183/169			3	Leeds	W-5w	6	0	c	5	5	c	–
184/170			4	Manchester	W-I & 32	5	12	b	–	–	–	–

TEST NOTES

• *160* Bowled in 1st inns: 1 for 27 (41 balls).
• *235* Bowled in 2nd inns: 0 for 4 (6 balls).

						Batting 1st			Batting 2nd			
Ref	**Series**	**V**	**T**	**Venue**	**Result**	**No**	**R**	**HO**	**No**	**R**	**HO**	**Ct**
190/176	1929–30	WI	1	Bridgetown	D	4	80	c	4	36	*	2
191/177			2	Port-of-Spain	W-167	4	77	b	4	205	*	2
192/178			3	Georgetown	L-289	4	56	b	4	123	lbw	1
193/179			4	Kingston	D	4	61	c	4	55	b	1
194/180	1930	A	1	Nottingham	W-93	5	5	b	5	72	c	–
195/181			2	Lord's	L-7w	5	48	c	5	9	c	–
204/185	1930–31	SA	1	Johannesburg[1]	L-28	4	8	c	4	3	c	1
205/186			2	Cape Town	D	4	93	b	4	86	b	–
206/187			3	Durban[2]	D	–	–	–	–	–	–	–
207/188			4	Johannesburg[1]	D	4	64	c	4	45	c	2
208/189			5	Durban[2]	D	4	30	c	–	–	–	–
233/207	1934	A	1	Nottingham	L-238	6	79	b	5	3	c	–
234/208			2	Lord's	W-I & 38	4	13	c	–	–	–	2
235/209			3	Manchester	D	5	132	c	–	–	–	1
236/210			4	Leeds	D	4	29	b	4	42	lbw	–
238/212	1934–35	WI	1	Bridgetown	W-4w	4	3	c	4	20	b	1
239/213			2	Port-of-Spain	L-217	6	41	c	6	11	ro	2
240/214			3	Georgetown	D	6	38	c	6	38	*	–
241/215			4	Kingston	L-I & 161	7	40	c	4	11	c	–

Career	M	I	NO	HS	R	Avge	100	50	Ct	St	Balls	R	W	Avge	BB	5w	10w	Rate
Test	51	83	9	205*	3525	47.63	7	21	33	–	47	31	1	31.00	1-27	–	–	47.00
F/c	833	1300	166	301*	57611	50.80	170	272	754	–	4830	2574	47	54.76	5-43	1	–	102.76

E. H. HENDREN – TEST BATTING SUMMARY

Series	V	M	I	NO	HS	R	Avge	100	50
1920–21	A	5	10	–	67	329	32.90	–	3
1921	A	2	4	–	10	17	4.25	–	–
1924	SA	5	4	1	142	398	132.66	2	2
1924–25	A	5	9	1	92	314	39.25	–	3
1926	A	5	6	3	127*	186	62.00	1	–
1928	WI	1	1	–	14	14	14.00	–	–
1928–29	A	5	9	–	169	472	52.44	1	2
1929	SA	4	7	1	70	149	24.83	–	1
1929–30	WI	4	8	2	205*	683	113.83	2	5
1930	A	2	4	–	72	134	33.50	–	1
1930–31	SA	5	7	–	93	329	47.00	–	3
1934	A	4	6	–	132	298	49.66	1	1
1934–35	WI	4	8	1	41	202	28.85	–	–
	A	28	48	4	169	1750	39.77	3	10
	SA	14	18	2	142	876	54.75	2	6
	WI	9	17	3	205*	899	64.21	2	5
Home		23	32	5	142	1196	44.29	4	5
Overseas		28	51	4	205*	2329	49.55	3	16
Totals		51	83	9	205*	3525	47.63	7	21

HENDRICK Michael

Derbyshire (1969 to 1981)
Nottinghamshire (1982 to 1984)

Wisden 1978
TOURS
A 1974–75, 1978–79, 1979–80;
SA 1975–76 (Robins), 1981–82 (SAB);
WI 1973–74; NZ 1974–75, 1977–78;
P 1977–78
Born Darley Dale, Derbyshire
22 Oct 1948

As a right-arm fast-medium seam bowler, Mike Hendrick was a most worthy successor to such Derbyshire stalwarts as Gladwin and Jackson. Tall (6ft 3in) and strongly built with a high, lively action, he could maintain exceptional accuracy for long spells and extract awkward bounce. His staple delivery left the right-handers either in the air or off the pitch but he commanded a fine break-back. Although he often beat the bat he failed to take five wickets in any of his 54 Test innings, possibly because either he pitched a shade too short or he aimed fractionally too wide of the off stump. In limited-overs games he was far more effective and frequently a match-winner. Laconically witty, he was an outstanding fielder close to the wicket, usually at slip, but his batting ambitions seemed to expire after his first boundary. At The Oval in 1977 his frequent mid-pitch collisions with his batting partner, Willis, brought the Australian fielders to their knees. A torn hamstring ended his first tour of Australia and persistent shoulder and knee injuries eventually enforced his retirement and curtailed his aspirations to become a first-class umpire.

Ref	Series	V	T	Venue	Result	Batting 1st No	R	HO	Batting 2nd No	R	HO	Ct	Bowling 1st Balls	R	W	Bowling 2nd Balls	R	W
739/497	1974	I	1	Manchester	W-113	–	–	–	–	–	–	3	120	57	3	102	39	1
740/498			2	Lord's	W-I & 285	11	1	*	–	–	–	1	108	46	3	6	2	0
741/499			3	Birmingham	W-I & 78	–	–	–	–	–	–	–	86	28	4	88	43	3
742/500	1974	P	1	Leeds	D	11	1	*	–	–	–	–	156	91	2	108	39	3
743/501			2	Lord's	D	11	6	c	–	–	–	2	54	36	1	90	29	0
750/503	1974–75	A	1	Brisbane[2]	L-166	11	4	c	11	0	b	–	152	64	2	104	47	0
752/505			3	Melbourne	D	11	8	*	11	0	*	–	22	8	0	–	–	–
759/510	1974–75	NZ	2	Christchurch	D	–	–	–	–	–	–	2	160	89	2	–	–	–
777/515	1976	WI	1	Nottingham	D	11	5	c	–	–	–	3	144	59	1	42	22	0
779/517			3	Manchester	L-425	11	0	b	11	0	*	–	84	48	2	144	63	1
806/528	1977	A	3	Nottingham	W-7w	10	1	b	–	–	–	4	128	46	2	192	56	2
807/529			4	Leeds	W-I & 85	10	4	c	–	–	–	1	93	41	4	137	54	4
808/530			5	Oval	D	10	15	b	–	–	–	–	222	93	2	–	–	–
817/534	1977–78	NZ	1	Wellington	L-72	10	0	lbw	10	0	c	–	136	46	0	80	16	2
829/541	1978	NZ	2	Nottingham	W-I & 119	10	7	c	–	–	–	1	90	18	1	120	30	1
830/542			3	Lord's	W-7w	10	12	b	–	–	–	2	168	39	1	–	–	–
835/544	1978–79	A	2	Perth	W-166	11	7	*	11	1	b	–	112	39	2	64	11	2
836/545			3	Melbourne	L-103	11	6	*	11	0	b	2	184	50	3	112	25	1
837/546			4	Sydney	W-93	11	10	b	11	7	c	1	192	50	2	80	17	2
838/547			5	Adelaide	W-205	11	0	*	11	3	*	–	152	45	2	112	19	3
839/548			6	Sydney	W-9w	11	0	c	–	–	–	–	96	21	1	56	22	1
851/549	1979	I	1	Birmingham	W-I & 83	–	–	–	–	–	–	1	145	36	2	124	45	4
852/550			2	Lord's	D	–	–	–	–	–	–	–	90	15	2	150	56	0
853/551			3	Leeds	D	11	0	c	–	–	–	–	84	13	1	–	–	–
854/552			4	Oval	D	11	0	c	–	–	–	1	135	38	3	48	15	0
880/557	1980	WI	1	Nottingham	L-2w	11	7	*	11	2	*	1	114	69	1	84	40	1
881/558			2	Lord's	D	11	10	*	–	–	–	–	66	32	0	–	–	–
885/562	1980	A		Lord's	D	11	5	c	–	–	–	–	180	67	1	90	53	0
903/567	1981	A	1	Nottingham	L-4w	11	6	*	11	0	*	–	120	43	2	120	33	0
908/572			6	Oval	D	11	0	*	–	–	–	–	186	63	0	176	82	4

Career	M	I	NO	HS	R	Avge	100	50	Ct	St	Balls	R	W	Avge	BB	5w	10w	Rate
Test	30	35	15	15	128	6.40	–	–	25	–	6208	2248	87	25.83	4-28	–	–	71.35
F/c	267	267	109	46	1601	10.13	–	–	176	–	42371	15785	770	20.50	8-45	30	3	55.02

NOTABLE FEATS

- 50 wickets in 17th Test (*835*).
- *739* Dismissed E.D. Solkar with his third ball in Test cricket.
- Hat-trick for Derbyshire v West Indians at Chesterfield in 1980.

Mike Hendrick

M. HENDRICK – TEST BOWLING SUMMARY

Series	V	M	Balls	R	W	Avge	BB	5w	10w	Rate
1974	I	3	510	215	14	15.35	4-28	–	–	36.42
1974	P	2	408	195	6	32.50	3-39	–	–	68.00
1974–75	A	2	278	119	2	59.50	2-64	–	–	140.50
1974–75	NZ	1	160	89	2	44.50	2-89	–	–	80.00
1976	WI	2	414	192	4	48.00	2-48	–	–	103.50
1977	A	3	772	290	14	20.71	4-41	–	–	55.14
1977–78	NZ	1	216	62	2	31.00	2-16	–	–	108.00
1978	NZ	2	378	87	3	29.00	1-18	–	–	126.00
1978–79	A	5	1160	299	19	15.73	3-19	–	–	61.05
1979	I	4	776	218	12	18.16	4-45	–	–	64.66
1980	WI	2	264	141	2	70.50	1-40	–	–	132.00
1980	A	1	270	120	1	120.00	1-67	–	–	270.00
1981	A	2	602	221	6	36.83	4-82	–	–	100.33
	A	13	3082	1049	42	24.97	4-41	–	–	73.38
	WI	4	678	333	6	55.50	2-48	–	–	113.00
	NZ	4	754	238	7	33.00	2-16	–	–	107.71
	I	7	1286	433	26	16.65	4-28	–	–	49.46
	P	2	408	195	6	32.50	3-39	–	–	68.00
Home		21	4394	1679	62	27.08	4-28	–	–	70.87
Overseas		9	1814	569	25	22.76	3-19	–	–	72.56
Totals		30	6208	2248	87	25.83	4-28	–	–	71.35

HESELTINE Christopher OBE

Hampshire (1895 to 1904)

TOURS
SA 1895–96; WI 1896–97; I 1892–93
Born Knightsbridge, London 26 Nov 1869
Died Walhampton, Lymington, Hampshire 13 Jun 1944

Christopher Heseltine

Christopher Heseltine was a right-arm fast bowler who made three overseas tours with sides organized and captained by Lord Hawke. He developed late, failing to make the eleven at Eton or to play first-class cricket at Cambridge (where he gained a soccer blue in 1891–92). A tall man with a high action, he was capable of short, fiery spells before tiring and dismissed the great Bobby Abel for three successive 'ducks'. He first appeared for Hampshire when they were second-class and was their president from 1936 until his death. He played first-class cricket for the MCC from 1892 to 1914 and was a committee member for several years. Lt-Col Heseltine served in the Boer War with the Imperial Yeomanry and in the Great War with the Royal Fusiliers when he was twice mentioned in dispatches.

						Batting 1st			Batting 2nd				Bowling 1st			Bowling 2nd		
Ref	Series	V	T	Venue	Result	No	R	HO	No	R	HO	Ct	Balls	R	W	Balls	R	W
48/48	1895–96	SA	2	Johannesburg[1]	W-I & 197	10	0	lbw	–	–	–	2	45	29	0	82	38	5
49/49			3	Cape Town	W-I & 33	8	18	c	–	–	–	1	30	17	0	–	–	–

Career	M	I	NO	HS	R	Avge	100	50	Ct	St	Balls	R	W	Avge	BB	5w	10w	Rate
Test	2	2	0	18	18	9.00	–	–	3	–	157	84	5	16.80	5-38	1	–	31.40
F/c	79	121	8	77	1390	12.30	–	3	54	–	8212	4171	170	24.53	7-106	7	–	48.30

HIGGS, Kenneth

Lancashire (1958 to 1969)
Leicestershire (1972 to 1986)

Wisden 1968
TOURS
A 1965–66; WI 1967–68; NZ 1965–66
Born Sandyford, Staffordshire 14 Jan 1937

Ken Higgs was a tall (6ft), robust right-arm fast-medium bowler who gave yeoman service to Lancashire and England. He generated violent momentum from a compact, bustling approach and hit the pitch so forcefully that he would jar batsmen's hands more painfully than bowlers who were quicker through the air. He celebrated his first appearance for England with 8 wickets in England's final match against South Africa and was the only player to appear in all five Tests against the 1966 West Indians. A resolute left-handed lower-order batsman, his simple technique based on pushing forward with a straight bat was rewarded with shares in two record last-wicket partnerships. Tempted out of early retirement he produced some fine performances at medium pace for Leicestershire whom he captained in 1979. Now their coach, he reappeared in an emergency in 1986 and gave his students an object lesson by taking 5 for 22 against Yorkshire. He played soccer at half-back for Port Vale.

						Batting 1st			Batting 2nd				Bowling 1st			Bowling 2nd		
Ref	**Series**	**V**	**T**	**Venue**	**Result**	**No**	**R**	**HO**	**No**	**R**	**HO**	**Ct**	**Balls**	**R**	**W**	**Balls**	**R**	**W**
596/420	1965	SA	3	Oval	D	10	2	b	–	–	–	–	144	47	4	247	96	4
597/421	1965–66	A	1	Brisbane[2]	D	10	4	lbw	–	–	–	–	240	102	2	–	–	–
602/426	1965–66	NZ	1	Christchurch	D	10	8	*	–	–	–	1	180	51	3	54	5	4
603/427			2	Dunedin	D	10	0	*	–	–	–	1	120	29	3	78	12	2
604/428			3	Auckland	D	9	0	c	–	–	–	–	168	33	2	168	27	3
605/429	1966	WI	1	Manchester	L-I & 40	10	1	c	10	5	st	–	186	94	3	–	–	–
606/430			2	Lord's	D	10	13	c	–	–	–	–	198	91	6	204	82	2
607/431			3	Nottingham	L-139	9	5	c	9	4	c	–	154	71	4	228	109	3
608/432			4	Leeds	L-I & 55	9	49	c	9	7	c	–	258	94	4	–	–	–
609/433			5	Oval	W-I & 34	10	63	c	–	–	–	1	102	52	1	90	18	1
618/434	1967	I	1	Leeds	W-6w	–	–	–	–	–	–	–	84	19	0	144	71	1
621/437	1967	P	1	Lord's	D	9	14	lbw	9	1	c	–	234	81	3	36	6	0
622/438			2	Nottingham	W-10w	10	0	*	–	–	–	–	114	35	4	36	8	2
623/439			3	Oval	W-8w	10	7	b	–	–	–	–	174	61	3	120	58	5
637/445	1968	A	1	Manchester	L-159	10	2	lbw	10	0	c	1	213	80	2	138	41	0

Career	M	I	NO	HS	R	Avge	100	50	Ct	St	Balls	R	W	Avge	BB	5w	10w	Rate
Test	15	19	3	63	185	11.56	–	1	4	–	4112	1473	71	20.74	6-91	2	–	57.9
F/c	511	530	207	98	3648	11.29	–	3	311	–	89436	36267	1536	23.61	7-19	50	5	58.22

Ken Higgs

K. HIGGS – TEST BOWLING SUMMARY

Series	V	M	Balls	R	W	Avge	BB	5w	10w	Rate
1965	SA	1	391	143	8	17.87	4-47	–	–	48.87
1965–66	A	1	240	102	2	51.00	2-102	–	–	120.00
1965–66	NZ	3	768	157	17	9.23	4-5	–	–	45.17
1966	WI	5	1420	611	24	25.45	6-91	1	–	59.16
1967	I	1	228	90	1	90.00	1-71	–	–	228.00
1967	P	3	714	249	17	14.64	5-58	1	–	42.00
1968	A	1	351	121	2	60.50	2-80	–	–	175.50
	A	2	591	223	4	55.75	2-80	–	–	147.75
	SA	1	391	143	8	17.87	4-47	–	–	48.87
	WI	5	1420	611	24	25.45	6-91	1	–	59.16
	NZ	3	768	157	17	9.23	4-5	–	–	45.17
	I	1	228	90	1	90.00	1-71	–	–	228.00
	P	3	714	249	17	14.64	5-58	1	–	42.00
Home		11	3104	1214	52	23.34	6-91	2	–	59.69
Overseas		4	1008	259	19	13.63	4-5	–	–	53.05
Totals		15	4112	1473	71	20.74	6-91	2	–	57.91

NOTABLE FEATS

- 50 wickets in 10th Test (*609*).
- *609* Shared record E v WI 10th-wkt stand of 128 in 140 min with J.A. Snow at The Oval in 1966, both batsmen scoring their maiden first-class fifties. It remains the highest 10th-wkt stand for England at home.
- Took 100 wickets in a season 5 times.
- Three hat-tricks: for Lancashire v Essex at Blackpool in 1960 and v Yorkshire at Leeds in 1968; and for Leicestershire v Hampshire at Leicester in 1977.
- Shared record Leicestershire 10th-wkt stand of 228 with R. Illingworth v Northamptonshire at Leicester in 1977.
- Only bowler to take a hat-trick in a Lord's final (for Leicestershire v Surrey in the 1974 Benson and Hedges Cup).

HILL, Allen

Yorkshire (1871 to 1882)

TOUR A 1876–77
Born Kirkheaton, Yorkshire 14 Nov 1843
Died Leyland, Lancashire 29 Aug 1910

Allen Hill was a notable right-handed fast bowler who derived great pace from a relatively brief run and could break the ball sharply from the off. Although he began his first-class career after over-arm bowling had been legalized, he retained the old round-arm method with the hand barely above the shoulder at the moment of delivery. In his first season for Yorkshire he bowled six Surrey batsmen in each innings and, in a North v South match at Tunbridge Wells in 1875 he dismissed W.G. Grace and H.R.J. Charlwood with his first two balls and G.F. Grace with his fourth. Playing in the first matches against Australia on level terms he took the first wicket and held the first catch in Test history. A kind, gentle and highly popular man, he umpired Test *33* and ended his working days in Lancashire. [*Illus. p.* 278]

NOTABLE FEATS

- *1* Took the first wicket to fall in Test cricket when he bowled N. Thompson and held the first catch when he dismissed T.P. Horan.
- Took 100 wickets in a season 3 times.
- Three hat-tricks: for Yorkshire v United South at Bradford in 1874 and v Surrey at The Oval in 1880; for Players v Gentlemen at Lord's in 1874.
- Bowled in an unchanged partnership throughout both completed innings of a match on 9 occasions, including 5 with T. Emmett.

						Batting 1st			Batting 2nd				Bowling 1st			Bowling 2nd		
Ref	Series	V	T	Venue	Result	No	R	HO	No	R	HO	Ct	Balls	R	W	Balls	R	W
1/1	1876–77	A	1	Melbourne	L-45	9	35	*	1	0	c	1	92	42	1	56	18	1
2/2			2	Melbourne	W-4w	8	49	ro	7	17	*	–	108	27	4	84	43	1

Career	M	I	NO	HS	R	Avge	100	50	Ct	St	Balls	R	W	Avge	BB	5w	10w	Rate
Test	2	4	2	49	101	50.50	–	–	1	–	340	130	7	18.57	4-27	–	–	48.57
F/c	193	312	35	49	2478	8.94	–	–	142	–	30024	10686	745+5	14.34	8-48	57	10	40.30

HILL Arthur James Ledger

Cambridge University (1890 to 1893)
Hampshire (1895 to 1921)

TOURS SA 1895–96; I 1892–93
Born Bassett, Hampshire 26 Jul 1871
Died Sparsholt, Hampshire 6 Sep 1950

Arthur Hill

Arthur Hill's final Test appearance in 1896 was the last for England by a Hampshire-born Hampshire cricketer. A banker by profession, he was a tall, elegant batsman, a capable right-arm fast-medium bowler who achieved two hat-tricks in minor matches before he changed to lobs, and a reliable catcher at slip. After three years in the Marlborough eleven, he appeared for Wiltshire and gained blues in each of his four seasons at Cambridge. He became president of Hampshire in 1929, nine years after appearing in the same County team as his son, Anthony. A remarkably talented all-round sportsman, he captained Hampshire at rugby and hockey and was accomplished at boxing, racquets, hunting and fishing.

Ref	Series	V	T	Venue	Result	Batting 1st No	R	HO	Batting 2nd No	R	HO	Ct	Bowling 1st Balls	R	W	Bowling 2nd Balls	R	W
47/47	1895–96	SA	1	Port Elizabeth	W-288	5	25	ro	7	37	b	–	–	–	–	–	–	–
48/48			2	Johannesburg[1]	W-I & 197	5	65	b	–	–	–	1	–	–	–	–	–	–
49/49			3	Cape Town	W-I & 33	2	124	c	–	–	–	–	–	–	–	40	8	4

Career	M	I	NO	HS	R	Avge	100	50	Ct	St	Balls	R	W	Avge	BB	5w	10w	Rate
Test	3	4	0	124	251	62.75	1	1	1	–	40	8	4	2.00	4-8	–	–	10.00
F/c	221	396	26	199	10353	27.98	19	44	143	–	16927	8537	305	27.99	7-36	4	1	55.49

HILTON
Malcolm Jameson

Lancashire (1946 to 1961)

Wisden 1957
TOURS I/SL 1951–52; P 1951–52
Born Chadderton, Lancashire
2 Aug 1928

Malcolm Hilton was a tallish (5ft 10in) left-handed slow bowler who spun his leg-breaks viciously on a responsive surface but seldom gave the ball enough air. Although his first ten wickets in first-class cricket were remarkably those of Test cricketers, including Don Bradman twice at Old Trafford in 1948, he took four years to claim a regular place in the Lancashire team. His outstanding fielding, either as a close catcher or fast and accurate deep retriever, made him a frequent choice as England's twelfth man. An enthusiastic lower-order batsman with a flamboyant off-drive, he scored an undefeated century at Northampton in 1955.

NOTABLE FEATS

- *342* Took the first 5 wickets to fall in the second innings.
- Took 100 wickets in a season 4 times, including 158 (avge 13.96) in 1956.
- Bowled 68 balls before conceding a run for Lancashire v Sussex at Horsham in 1948.
- Took 103 wickets (avge 10.89) for Lancashire 2nd XI in 1949.

Malcolm Hilton

Ref	Series	V	T	Venue	Result	Batting 1st No	R	HO	Batting 2nd No	R	HO	Ct	Bowling 1st Balls	R	W	Bowling 2nd Balls	R	W
326/279	1950	WI	4	Oval	L-I & 56	10	3	b	10	0	c	–	246	91	0	–	–	–
337/290	1951	SA	4	Leeds	D	11	9	*	–	–	–	1	369	176	3	60	17	0
342/295	1951–52	I	4	Kanpur	W-8w	6	10	st	–	–	–	–	137	32	4	192	61	5
343/296			5	Madras[1]	L-I & 8	8	0	st	8	15	st	–	240	100	2	–	–	–

Career	M	I	NO	HS	R	Avge	100	50	Ct	St	Balls	R	W	Avge	BB	5w	10w	Rate
Test	4	6	1	15	37	7.40	–	–	1	–	1244	477	14	34.07	5-61	1	–	88.85
F/c	270	324	42	100*	3416	12.11	1	6	202	–	55375	19542	1006	19.42	8-19	51	8	55.04

HIRST
George Herbert

Yorkshire (1891 to 1929)
Europeans (1921–22)

Wisden 1901
TOURS A 1897–98, 1903–04
Born Kirkheaton, Yorkshire 7 Sep 1871
Died Egerton, Huddersfield, Yorkshire
10 May 1954

The spectacular statistics of George Hirst's career will ensure his place in perpetuity amongst cricket's greatest all-rounders; his 11 consecutive 'doubles', his incredible output of 2385 runs and 208 wickets in 1906, and even his record Yorkshire score of 341 are achievements that are unlikely ever to be equalled. Only his illustrious friend from Kirkheaton, Wilfred Rhodes, achieved the 'double' more times. A blunt, loyal, tenacious Yorkshireman, he was one of the game's outstanding personalities. Short and sturdy, his broad dialect and humour were as memorable as his many magnificent performances. He was an aggressive quick-footed middle-order batsman who saw the ball very early and was a master of the pull and hook. Originally a good but straightforward left-arm medium-fast seam bowler whose energetic run and easy action extracted surprising nip off the pitch, he attained greatness in 1901 when he introduced the art of late inswing. When he allied this vast, late movement with inverse break off the pitch, he had discovered a potent menace which few batsmen could handle. The following summer he and Rhodes trundled out Australia for 36 (Test *70*) and won the final Test (*74*) with a last-ditch stand of 15 prefaced by Hirst's alleged (but disclaimed) command, 'We'll get 'em by singles, Wilfred'. In addition to his ability with bat and.ball, Hirst was also a remarkable fielder, usually at mid-off where many of his 602 catches came from thundering drives. Considering his wonderful contributions to Yorkshire's ten Championships during his full-time career (1891–1921), his record in Tests is surprisingly modest. Although he continued to play for Yorkshire until 1929, he made few appearances after starting his 18-year engagement with Eton College. There his kindness and patience won him the devoted respect of many fine cricketers who gained immeasurably from his advice.

						Batting 1st			Batting 2nd				Bowling 1st			Bowling 2nd		
Ref	Series	V	T	Venue	Result	No	R	HO	No	R	HO	Ct	Balls	R	W	Balls	R	W
53/53	1897–98	A	1	Sydney	W-9w	6	62	b	–	–	–	–	168	57	0	78	49	0
54/54			2	Melbourne	L-I & 55	7	0	b	6	3	lbw	2	150	89	1	–	–	–
55/55			3	Adelaide	L-I & 13	7	85	c	7	6	lbw	–	132	62	1	–	–	–
57/57			5	Sydney	L-6w	7	44	b	7	7	c	1	24	14	0	42	33	0
60/60	1899	A	1	Nottingham	D	9	6	b	–	–	–	1	120	42	1	55	20	0
70/70	1902	A	1	Birmingham	D	7	48	c	–	–	–	–	66	15	3	54	10	0
71/71			2	Lord's	D	–	–	–	–	–	–	–	–	–	–	–	–	–
72/72			3	Sheffield	L-143	8	8	c	9	0	b	2	90	59	0	60	40	0
74/74			5	Oval	W-1w	8	43	c	8	58	*	–	174	77	5	30	7	1
78/75	1903–04	A	1	Sydney	W-5w	7	0	b	6	60	*	–	144	47	2	174	79	0
79/76			2	Melbourne	W-185	7	7	c	5	4	c	2	48	33	1	88	38	2
80/77			3	Adelaide	L-216	6	58	c	7	44	b	1	90	58	2	78	36	1
81/78			4	Sydney	W-157	7	25	b	7	18	c	–	78	36	0	77	32	2
82/79			5	Melbourne	L-218	7	0	c	6	1	c	1	114	44	0	101	48	5
85/82	1905	A	3	Leeds	D	6	35	c	6	40	*	2	42	37	1	60	26	1
86/83			4	Manchester	W-I & 80	7	25	c	–	–	–	–	12	12	0	42	19	0
87/84			5	Oval	D	7	5	c	–	–	–	1	138	86	3	54	32	1
93/90	1907	SA	1	Lord's	D	6	7	b	–	–	–	–	108	35	1	96	26	1
94/91			2	Leeds	W-53	6	17	c	6	2	b	2	54	22	1	54	21	1
95/92			3	Oval	D	6	4	c	7	16	hw	1	132	39	3	78	42	3
101/98	1909	A	1	Birmingham	W-10w	6	15	lbw	–	–	–	2	138	28	4	143	58	5
102/99			2	Lord's	L-9w	7	31	b	7	1	b	–	161	83	3	48	28	0
103/100			3	Leeds	L-126	7	4	b	8	0	b	–	156	65	2	102	39	1
104/101			4	Manchester	D	9	1	c	–	–	–	–	42	15	0	72	32	1

Career	M	I	NO	HS	R	Avge	100	50	Ct	St	Balls	R	W	Avge	BB	5w	10w	Rate
Test	24	38	3	85	790	22.57	–	5	18	–	3967	1770	59	30.00	5-48	3	–	67.23
F/c	825	1215	151	341	36323	34.13	60	201	602	–	123192	51282	2739	18.72	9-23	184	40	44.97

NOTABLE FEATS

- 50 wickets in 21st Test (*101*).
- *74* Shared the last 15 runs in a match-winning 10th-wkt partnership with W. Rhodes.
- *101* Shared all 20 Australian wickets with fellow left-arm bowler C. Blythe (11 for 102).
- Exceeded 1000 runs in a season 19 times, including 2000 on 3 occasions. Took 100 wickets 15 times, including 200 once.
- Achieved the 'double' 14 times, including a record 11 seasons in succession (1903–13). Only player to achieve the double 'double' of 2000 runs and 200 wickets (1906). On 2 other occasions (1904 and 1905) he scored 2000 runs and took 100 wickets. On 28 June 1906 he completed the earliest and fastest 'double' after just 16 matches; also recorded the second-earliest (12 July 1901).
- In Championship matches alone he did the 'double' a record 8 times, his feat of scoring 27,318 runs and taking 2096 wickets between 1891 and 1921 being matched only by W. Rhodes.
- His 341 v Leicestershire at Leicester in 1905 remains Yorkshire's highest score. Made 3 double centuries – all for Yorkshire.
- Scored 3 hundreds in consecutive innings in 1899.
- Scored 100 before lunch on 5 occasions.
- Took 9 wickets in an innings 4 times (all for Yorkshire), best analysis: 9 for 23 (8 bowled) v Lancashire at Leeds in 1910. Took 15 wickets in a match once: 15 for 63 for Yorkshire v Leicestershire at Hull in 1907.
- Two hat-tricks for Yorkshire v Leicestershire: at Leicester in 1895 and at Hull in 1907.
- Bowled in an unchanged partnership throughout both completed innings of a match on 4 occasions, including 3 with W. Rhodes.
- Took 5 for 9 v Australians (23 all out) for Yorkshire at Leeds in 1902.
- Only player to score 100 in each innings and take 5 wickets twice in the same first-class match: 111 and 117*, 6 for 70 and 5 for 45 for Yorkshire v Somerset at Bath in 1906. Achieved the match 'double' of 100 runs and 10 wickets on 3 other occasions.

George Hirst (centre) and Wilfred Rhodes at Lord's about 1926 with their blazered captain A.W. Lupton.

G. H. HIRST – TEST BOWLING SUMMARY

Series	V	M	Balls	R	W	Avge	BB	5w	10w	Rate
1897–98	A	4	594	304	2	152.00	1-62	–	–	297.00
1899	A	1	175	62	1	62.00	1-42	–	–	175.00
1902	A	4	474	208	9	23.11	5-77	1	–	52.66
1903–04	A	5	992	451	15	30.06	5-48	1	–	66.13
1905	A	3	348	212	6	35.33	3-86	–	–	58.00
1907	SA	3	522	185	10	18.50	3-39	–	–	52.20
1909	A	4	862	348	16	21.75	5-58	1	–	53.87
	A	21	3445	1585	49	32.34	5-48	3	–	70.30
	SA	3	522	185	10	18.50	3-39	–	–	52.22
Home		15	2381	1015	42	24.16	5-58	2	–	56.69
Overseas		9	1586	755	17	44.41	5-48	1	–	93.29
Totals		24	3967	1770	59	30.00	5-48	3	–	67.23

HITCH
John William

Surrey (1907 to 1925)

Wisden 1914
TOURS A 1911–12, 1920–21
Born Radcliffe, Lancashire 7 May 1886
Died Rumney, Cardiff 7 Jul 1965

Bill Hitch was a firm believer in brighter cricket and few have played with such consistent energy and enthusiasm. Known as 'Billitch' by his adoring fans at The Oval, he was a bustling right-arm fast bowler, a vast-hitting tail-end batsman and a brilliant short-leg fielder. He played his early cricket in Cambridgeshire and joined Surrey after being recommended by Tom Hayward. Although his unrhythmic run-up included two or three hops, he was capable of blistering speed, broke stumps on several occasions and once sent a bail over 55 yards. A spectacularly brutal hitter, he frequently struck balls right out of The Oval. He was renowned for his suicidally close fielding long before the days of helmets and other protection. Oddly, he achieved little in Test cricket or on tour. Leaving Surrey he took 289 wickets in four seasons of Lancashire League cricket with Todmorden before becoming a first-class umpire and standing in four Tests, three of them in India in 1933–34. He finally settled in South Wales and was coach to Glamorgan. [*Illus. pp.* 146, 383]

NOTABLE FEATS
- *144* Scored 50 in 35 min – second-fastest 50 in E v A Tests.
- Took 100 wickets in a season 7 times, including 174 in 1913, and scored 1061 runs in 1921.
- Two hat-tricks for Surrey at The Oval: v Cambridge U in 1911 (4 wickets in 5 balls) and v Warwickshire in 1914.

						Batting 1st			Batting 2nd				Bowling 1st			Bowling 2nd		
Ref	Series	V	T	Venue	Result	No	R	HO	No	R	HO	Ct	Balls	R	W	Balls	R	W
117/109	1911–12	A	2	Melbourne	W-8w	11	0	*	–	–	–	–	42	37	1	30	21	0
118/110			3	Adelaide	W-7w	11	0	c	–	–	–	1	12	2	1	66	69	1
120/112			5	Sydney	W-70	11	4	c	11	4	c	1	54	31	2	36	23	0
126/116	1912	A	2	Manchester	D	11	4	b	–	–	–	–	–	–	–	–	–	–
128/117		SA	3	Oval	W-10w	11	0	*	–	–	–	2	–	–	–	–	–	–
135/124	1920–21	A	1	Sydney	L-377	8	3	c	8	19	c	–	60	37	0	48	40	0
144/133	1921	S	5	Oval	D	9	18	b	4	51	*	–	114	65	2	–	–	–

Career	M	I	NO	HS	R	Avge	100	50	Ct	St	Balls	R	W	Avge	BB	5w	10w	Rate
Test	7	10	3	51*	103	14.71	–	1	4	–	462	325	7	46.42	2-31	–	–	66.00
F/c	350	480	51	107	7643	17.81	3	32	230	–	56917	29915	1387	21.56	8-38	101	24	41.03

HOBBS
Sir John Berry

Surrey (1905 to 1934)

Wisden 1909
TOURS
A 1907–08, 1911–12, 1920–21, 1924–25, 1928–29; SA 1909–10, 1913–14
Born Barnwell, Cambridge 16 Dec 1882
Knighted for services to cricket 1953
Died Hove, Sussex 21 Dec 1963

Jack Hobbs was arguably the most accomplished batsman of all time. Certainly he was the most skilful on all surfaces and in all conditions; he fully justified the epithet of 'The Master' bestowed upon him by his admiring friends. Serenely calm and classically effortless, he scored more runs and hundreds in first-class cricket than any other man. Incredibly 98 of those centuries were amassed after his 40th birthday. Born in Cambridge the eldest of 12 children of the groundsman and umpire at Jesus College, he developed his immaculate technique during primitive games against the college servants and received no formal coaching. He followed his boyhood hero Tom Hayward to Surrey where, compelled to qualify by two years' residence, he eventually made his debut at the advanced age of 22. His first three-figure score included 137 before lunch and was compiled against Essex, the very county that had spurned first option on his services. That sensational performance, in his first Championship match, immediately

Jack Hobbs

won him his Surrey cap. His method, based on perfect sight, a supreme judgement of length, strong and flexible wrists, and an innate ability always to be in the right position, was deceptively straightforward, graceful and correct. A spring-heeled front-foot aggressor before his First World War service as an air mechanic in the Royal Flying Corps, he developed into a predominantly back-foot player. His long career at The Oval spanned 30 seasons and then, as an honorary life member, he served on the Surrey committee from 1934 until his death. He played against two other cricketing giants: W.G. Grace captained the opposition on his first appearance for Surrey in 1905 and, in his final Test in 1930, he fielded against Donald Bradman's 232. When, in his last season and 52nd year, George Duckworth asked him to play in his benefit match at Old Trafford, he scored the only century against that summer's county champions. Curiously only five of his 15 Test hundreds were scored in England and just one of them was made on his beloved ground at Kennington. Slim, agile and of medium height, his speed and accuracy at cover-point were quite remarkable and, in his younger days, he was a right-arm medium-pace swing bowler sufficiently menacing to open England's attack in three Tests on the 1909–10 tour of South Africa. A man of the highest integrity and great humility, he had a marvellous sense of humour and was an incorrigible leg-puller. In Queen Elizabeth's Coronation Year he became the first professional to be knighted for his services to cricket. The Master's Club, a select band of his most devoted admirers instituted by John Arlott, still celebrates Sir Jack's birthday with an annual lunch in The Oval's committee room.

NOTABLE FEATS

- 1000 runs in 13th Test (*116*) (24 inns); 2000 runs in 23rd Test (*129*) (41 inns); 3000 runs in 35th Test (*153*) (60 inns); first to score 4000 runs – in 45th Test (*164*) (75 inns); first to score 5000 runs – in 55th Test (*180*) (90 inns).
- *118* His 187 remains England's highest score at Adelaide.
- *119* Shared record E v A 1st-wkt stand of 323 in 268 min with W. Rhodes.
- *153* Shared the first of 15 three-figure partnerships with H. Sutcliffe at the first attempt.
- *154* Contributed 211 (then the highest Test innings in England) to the world-record 503 runs added by England on the second day when he took his score from 12* to 114* before lunch. His stand of 268 with H. Sutcliffe remains the 1st-wkt record for all Lord's Tests.
- *158* His first opening stands against Australia with H. Sutcliffe realised 157 and 110.
- *159* Became the first to score 2000 runs for E v A. With H. Sutcliffe achieved the first instance of a batting partnership enduring throughout a full day's Test match play; they remain the only England pair to achieve this feat. Their stand of 283 in 289 min remains the longest for the 1st wkt in this series.
- *165* Broke C. Hill's record aggregate of 2660 runs in E v A Tests.
- *180* At 46 yrs 82 days became the oldest batsman to score a hundred in Test cricket. His tally of 12 hundreds remains the E v A record.
- His aggregate of 3636 runs v A remains the England record against another country.
- Exceeded 1000 runs in each of his 24 seasons (plus twice on tour), including 2000 on a record 17 occasions and 3000 once (3024 in 1925). His 1317 runs in 1905 was then the highest aggregate by a batsman in his first season. Scored 1112 runs in June 1925.
- Scored a record 61,237 runs in first-class matches, including the record total of 197 hundreds. His 100th century was scored v Somerset at Bath in 1923. He equalled and passed the previous record of 126 first-class hundreds by W.G. Grace when he scored 101 and 101* v Somerset at Taunton on 16–17 August 1925.
- Holds Surrey records for most appearances (598), most runs (43,554), most hundreds (144) and most times 1000 runs in a season (24). His 16 hundreds (including a record-equalling 13 for Surrey and 5 in 6 innings) in 1925 survived as the first-class record until 1947.
- His highest score of 316* for Surrey v Middlesex in 1926 remains the record for first-class matches at Lord's. Made 15 other double centuries.
- Shared in 166 three-figure 1st-wkt partnerships in first-class cricket, including 66 with A. Sandham, 40 (including 4 in a week) with T.W. Hayward and 26 (15 in Tests) with H. Sutcliffe.
- Shared in 2 record Surrey stands, both at The Oval: 428 (1st-wkt) with A. Sandham v Oxford U in 1926 and 371 with E.G. Hayes v Hampshire in 1909 when Surrey scored 645 for 4 in 320 min – the Championship record for one day.
- Scored 100 in each innings of a match 6 times – all for Surrey.
- Twice scored 4 hundreds in consecutive innings (1920 and 1925) and on 3 other occasions scored 3 in successive innings.
- Carried his bat through a completed innings on 7 occasions.
- Scored 100 before lunch on 20 occasions, including a record 13 on the first day.
- Headed the national batting averages 4 times in 5 seasons (1925–29).
- Achieved unique treble in 1919 by scoring hundreds for Players v Gentlemen in all 3 matches (at Lord's, The Oval and Scarborough). His total of 16 hundreds is the record for this fixture.
- His 266* at Scarborough in 1925 is the highest score in Gentlemen v Players matches and his tallies of 49 appearances and 22 matches as captain are records for the Players.

Ref	Series	V	T	Venue	Result	Batting 1st			Batting 2nd			Ct	Bowling 1st			Bowling 2nd		
						No	R	HO	No	R	HO		Balls	R	W	Balls	R	W
97/94	1907–08	A	2	Melbourne	W-1w	2	83	b	2	28	b	–	–	–	–	–	–	–
98/95			3	Adelaide	L-245	1	26	c	1	23	*	–	–	–	–	–	–	–
99/96			4	Melbourne	L-308	1	57	b	1	0	c	–	–	–	–	–	–	–
100/97			5	Sydney	L-49	1	72	b	1	13	c	1	–	–	–	42	13	0
101/98	1909	A	1	Birmingham	W-10w	2	0	lbw	1	62	*	1	–	–	–	–	–	–
102/99			2	Lord's	L-9w	2	19	c	2	9	c	–	–	–	–	–	–	–
103/100			3	Leeds	L-126	2	12	b	2	30	b	–	–	–	–	–	–	–
106/103	1909–10	SA	1	Johannesburg[1]	L-19	1	89	c	1	35	b	–	36	20	0	36	16	0
107/104			2	Durban[1]	L-95	1	53	b	1	70	c	1	30	5	0	12	5	0
108/105			3	Johannesburg[1]	W-3w	7	11	b	5	93	*	–	–	–	–	–	–	–
109/106			4	Cape Town	L-4w	1	1	c	1	0	c	–	–	–	–	–	–	–
110/107			5	Cape Town	W-9w	1	187	hw	–	–	–	–	24	11	0	48	19	1
116/108	1911–12	S	1	Sydney	L-146	1	63	c	1	22	c	1	–	–	–	–	–	–
117/109			2	Melbourne	W-8w	2	6	b	2	126	*	2	–	–	–	–	–	–
118/110			3	Adelaide	W-7w	1	187	c	1	3	lbw	1	–	–	–	–	–	–
119/111			4	Melbourne	W-I & 225	1	178	c	–	–	–	–	–	–	–	–	–	–
120/112			5	Sydney	W-70	1	32	c	1	45	c	–	–	–	–	–	–	–
122/113	1912	SA	1	Lord's	W-I & 62	1	4	b	–	–	–	–	–	–	–	66	36	0
123/114		A	1	Lord's	D	1	107	b	–	–	–	–	–	–	–	–	–	–
124/115		SA	2	Leeds	W-174	1	27	c	1	55	c	1	–	–	–	–	–	–
126/116		A	2	Manchester	D	1	19	b	–	–	–	–	–	–	–	–	–	–
128/117		SA	3	Oval	W-10w	1	68	c	1	9	*	–	–	–	–	–	–	–
129/118		A	3	Oval	W-244	1	66	c	1	32	c	–	–	–	–	–	–	–
130/119	1913–14	SA	1	Durban[1]	W-I & 157	1	82	b	–	–	–	1	–	–	–	–	–	–
131/120			2	Johannesburg[1]	W-I & 12	3	23	lbw	–	–	–	–	–	–	–	–	–	–
132/121			3	Johannesburg[1]	W-91	1	92	c	1	41	c	–	–	–	–	–	–	–
133/122			4	Durban[1]	D	1	64	c	1	97	b	–	–	–	–	–	–	–
134/123			5	Port Elizabeth	W-10w	1	33	c	1	11	*	–	–	–	–	–	–	–
135/124	1920–21	A	1	Sydney	L-377	2	49	b	2	59	lbw	1	–	–	–	–	–	–
136/125			2	Melbourne	L-I & 91	1	122	c	1	20	b	–	–	–	–	–	–	–
137/126			3	Adelaide	L-119	1	18	c	1	123	b	–	–	–	–	42	16	0
138/127			4	Melbourne	L-8w	1	27	c	1	13	lbw	–	–	–	–	–	–	–
139/128			5	Sydney	L-9w	1	40	lbw	5	34	c	1	–	–	–	–	–	–
142/131	1921	A	3	Leeds	L-219	–	–	–	–	–	–	–	–	–	–	–	–	–
153/139	1924	SA	1	Birmingham	W-I & 18	1	76	lbw	–	–	–	2	–	–	–	–	–	–
154/140			2	Lord's	W-I & 18	1	211	c	–	–	–	1	–	–	–	–	–	–
155/141			3	Leeds	W-9w	1	31	c	1	7	b	–	–	–	–	–	–	–
157/143			5	Oval	D	1	30	c	–	–	–	–	–	–	–	–	–	–
158/144	1924–25	A	1	Sydney	L-193	1	115	c	1	57	c	–	16	13	0	–	–	–
159/145			2	Melbourne	L-81	1	154	b	1	22	lbw	–	–	–	–	–	–	–
160/146			3	Adelaide	L-11	5	119	c	1	27	c	–	24	11	0	–	–	–
161/147			4	Melbourne	W-I & 29	1	66	st	–	–	–	–	–	–	–	–	–	–
162/148			5	Sydney	L-307	1	0	c	1	13	st	–	–	–	–	–	–	–
163/149	1926	A	1	Nottingham	D	1	19	*	–	–	–	–	–	–	–	–	–	–
164/150			2	Lord's	D	1	119	c	–	–	–	–	–	–	–	–	–	–
165/151			3	Leeds	D	1	49	c	1	88	b	–	–	–	–	–	–	–
166/152			4	Manchester	D	1	74	c	–	–	–	–	–	–	–	–	–	–
167/153			5	Oval	W-289	1	37	b	1	100	b	–	–	–	–	–	–	–
174/160	1928	WI	2	Manchester	W-I & 30	1	53	c	–	–	–	–	–	–	–	–	–	–
175/161			3	Oval	W-I & 71	1	159	c	–	–	–	–	–	–	–	–	–	–
176/162	1928–29	A	1	Brisbane[1]	W-675	1	49	ro	1	11	lbw	–	–	–	–	–	–	–
177/163			2	Sydney	W-8w	1	40	c	–	–	–	–	–	–	–	–	–	–
178/164			3	Melbourne	W-3w	1	20	c	1	49	lbw	–	–	–	–	–	–	–
179/165			4	Adelaide	W-12	1	74	c	1	1	c	–	–	–	–	–	–	–
180/166			5	Melbourne	L-5w	1	142	lbw	1	65	c	–	–	–	–	–	–	–
185/171	1929	SA	5	Oval	D	1	10	c	1	52	c	–	–	–	–	–	–	–
194/180	1930	A	1	Nottingham	W-93	1	78	c	1	74	st	1	–	–	–	–	–	–
195/181			2	Lord's	L-7w	1	1	c	1	19	b	1	–	–	–	–	–	–
196/182			3	Leeds	D	1	29	c	1	13	ro	1	–	–	–	–	–	–
197/183			4	Manchester	D	1	31	c	–	–	–	–	–	–	–	–	–	–
198/184			5	Oval	L-I & 39	1	47	c	1	9	b	–	–	–	–	–	–	–

Career	M	I	NO	HS	R	Avge	100	50	Ct	St	Balls	R	W	Avge	BB	5w	10w	Rate
Test	61	102	7	211	5410	56.94	15	28	17	–	376	165	1	165.00	1-19	–	–	376.00
F/c	826	1315	106	316*	61237	50.65	197	270	334	–	5199	2676	107	25.00	7-56	3	–	48.58

J. B. HOBBS – TEST BATTING SUMMARY

Series	V	M	I	NO	HS	R	Avge	100	50
1907–08	A	4	8	1	83	302	43.14	–	3
1909	A	3	6	1	62*	132	26.40	–	1
1909–10	SA	5	9	1	187	539	67.37	1	4
1911–12	A	5	9	1	187	662	82.75	3	1
1912	SA	3	5	1	68	163	40.75	–	2
1912	A	3	4	–	107	224	56.00	1	1
1913–14	SA	5	8	1	97	443	63.28	–	4
1920–21	A	5	10	–	123	505	50.50	2	1
1921	A	1	–	–	–	–	–	–	–
1924	SA	4	5	–	211	355	71.00	1	1
1924–25	A	5	9	–	154	573	63.66	3	2
1926	A	5	7	1	119	486	81.00	2	2
1928	WI	2	2	–	153	212	106.00	1	1
1928–29	A	5	9	–	142	451	50.11	1	2
1929	SA	1	2	–	52	62	31.00	–	1
1930	A	5	9	–	78	301	33.44	–	2
	A	41	71	4	187	3636	54.26	12	15
	SA	18	29	3	211	1562	60.07	2	12
	WI	2	2	–	153	212	106.00	1	1
Home		27	40	3	211	1935	52.29	5	11
Overseas		34	62	4	187	3475	59.91	10	17
Totals		61	102	7	211	5410	56.94	15	28

TEST NOTES

- *142* Contracted appendicitis on the first afternoon and played no further cricket that season.
- *166* Deputised as captain on the second and third days when A.W. Carr developed tonsillitis – the first professional to lead England since A. Shrewsbury in 1886–87.

HOBBS
Robin Nicholas Stuart

Essex (1961 to 1975)
Glamorgan (1979 to 1981)

TOURS
SA 1964–65, 1972–73 (Robins);
WI 1963–64 (Cav), 1967–68, 1969–70 (Norfolk);
P 1966–67 (MCC U-25), 1968–69, 1970–71 (Cwlth), 1973–74 (RW)
Born Chippenham, Wiltshire
8 May 1942

NOTABLE FEATS

- 100 wickets in a season twice.
- Scored 100 in 44 min for Essex v Australians at Chelmsford in 1975 – the fastest 100 for Essex and the fastest conceded by any touring team.

Robin Hobbs was the last specialist right-arm leg-break and googly bowler to appear for England. Although not a big spinner of the ball, he was exceptionally accurate for his style and he varied his flight and pace skilfully. As a dashing lower-order basman, he made compulsive viewing. Splendidly unconventional, his sharp reflexes and quick eye produced some spectacularly improbable hits; he possessed a quite remarkable ability to cut half-volleys and yorkers. His aggressive fielding at cover made him a popular choice for twelfth man duties, especially on tour. He retired prematurely to pursue a career in commerce and play for Suffolk but, in 1979, he was persuaded to reappear as the first of a disastrous sequence of six Glamorgan captains in seven seasons. Quick-witted, enthusiastic and convivial, he was an excellent tourist.

Robin Hobbs

Ref	Series	V	T	Venue	Result	Batting 1st No	R	HO	Batting 2nd No	R	HO	Ct	Bowling 1st Balls	R	W	Bowling 2nd Balls	R	W
618/434	1967	I	1	Leeds	W-6w	–	–	–	–	–	–	1	134	45	3	272	100	1
619/435			2	Lord's	W-I & 124	9	7	b	–	–	–	–	–	–	–	36	16	0
620/436			3	Birmingham	W-132	11	15	*	11	2	c	3	39	25	3	192	73	2
621/437	1967	P	1	Lord's	D	11	1	*	11	1	*	1	210	46	1	96	28	0
628/440	1967–68	WI	1	Port-of-Spain	D	10	2	c	–	–	–	1	90	34	1	78	44	1
649/452	1968–69	P	3	Karachi	D	–	–	–	–	–	–	–	–	–	–	–	–	–
689/469	1971	P	3	Leeds	W-25	9	6	c	9	0	b	2	120	48	0	24	22	0

Career	M	I	NO	HS	R	Avge	100	50	Ct	St	Balls	R	W	Avge	BB	5w	10w	Rate
Test	7	8	3	15*	34	6.80	–	–	8	–	1291	481	12	40.08	3-25	–	–	107.58
F/c	440	546	138	100	4940	12.10	2	2	295	–	62555	29776	1099	27.09	8-63	50	8	56.91

HOLLIES
William Eric

Warwickshire (1932 to 1957)

Wisden 1955
TOURS
A 1950–51; WI 1934–35; NZ 1950–51
Born Old Hill, Staffordshire 5 Jun 1912
Died Chinley, Derbyshire 16 Apr 1981

NOTABLE FEATS
- *303* Bowled D.G. Bradman second ball for 0 in his final Test innings leaving the Australian captain 4 runs short of 7000 and a career average of 100.
- Took 100 wickets in a season 14 times, including a record 180 for Warwickshire in 1946.
- His career total of 2201 wickets remains the Warwickshire record.
- Took all 10 Nottinghamshire wickets for 49 runs in 1946 (7 bowled, 3 lbw) and twice took 9 wickets in an innings, all 3 feats occuring at Birmingham.

Eric Hollies was a right-arm leg-break and googly bowler whose prime years were lost to the Second World War. Sturdily built and just 5ft 7½in tall, he was not a vast spinner of the ball but his brisk pace and exceptional accuracy made him invaluable as a stock bowler. Ever cheerful, his brief run and fluent action enabled him to undertake a heavy workload. He relied mainly on his leg-break and top-spinner but will always be remembered for the perfect googly with which he ended Bradman's Test career. In 1951 his bowling was a decisive factor in Warwickshire's first Championship for 40 years. He captained the county in 1956 and took 132 wickets at 18.94 in his final season. Immensely popular, with a deep Black Country accent, he made a few appearances for his native Staffordshire before returning to the Birmingham League where he continued to take wickets well into his sixties.

Eric Hollies bowling against Australia at The Oval, 1948.

Ref	Series	V	T	Venue	Result	Batting 1st No	R	HO	Batting 2nd No	R	HO	Ct	Bowling 1st Balls	R	W	Bowling 2nd Balls	R	W
238/212	1934–35	WI	1	Bridgetown	W-4w	–	–	–	–	–	–	–	96	36	2	–	–	–
240/214			3	Georgetown	D	11	1	*	–	–	–	–	156	50	7	30	17	0
241/215			4	Kingston	L-I & 161	11	1	*	10	6	b	–	276	114	1	–	–	–
285/253	1947	SA	1	Nottingham	D	11	0	*	10	18	*	–	332	123	5	54	33	0
286/254			2	Lord's	W-10w	–	–	–	–	–	–	–	168	52	2	120	32	0
287/255			3	Manchester	W-7w	11	5	c	–	–	–	1	138	42	1	84	49	1
303/266	1948	A	5	Oval	L-I & 149	11	0	*	11	0	c	–	336	131	5	–	–	–
314/272	1949	NZ	1	Leeds	D	11	0	*	–	–	–	–	150	57	0	66	33	0
315/273			2	Lord's	D	–	–	–	–	–	–	–	348	133	5	–	–	–
316/274			3	Manchester	D	10	0	c	–	–	–	–	108	29	0	156	52	2
317/275			4	Oval	D	10	1	*	–	–	–	–	120	51	1	102	30	2
323/276	1950	WI	1	Manchester	W-202	10	0	c	10	3	c	–	198	70	3	212	63	5
325/278			3	Nottingham	L-10w	11	2	*	11	0	lbw	1	262	134	2	42	1	0

Career	M	I	NO	HS	R	Avge	100	50	Ct	St	Balls	R	W	Avge	BB	5w	10w	Rate
Test	13	15	8	18*	37	5.28	–	–	2	–	3554	1332	44	30.27	7-50	5	–	80.77
F/c	515	616	282	47	1673	5.00	–	–	179	–	132369	48656	2323	20.94	10-49	182	40	56.98

HOLMES
Errol Reginald Thorold

Surrey (1924 to 1955)
Oxford University (1925 to 1927)

Wisden 1936
TOURS
A 1935–36;
WI 1926–27 (Tennyson), 1934–35;
NZ 1935–36
Born Calcutta, India 21 Aug 1905
Died Marylebone, London 16 Aug 1960

NOTABLE FEATS

- Exceeded 1000 runs in a season 6 times.
- Scored 2 double centuries, his 236 for Oxford U v Free Foresters at Oxford in 1927 including 4 sixes off consecutive balls.
- Shared record Surrey 9th-wkt stand of 168 with E.W.J. Brooks v Hampshire at The Oval in 1936.

Errol Holmes was a carefree, hard-hitting middle-order batsman and a tearaway right-arm medium-fast bowler who enjoyed an outstanding all-round career at Malvern College. His approach to batting typified his enjoyment of cricket. Tall, well-built and strong-wristed, he was a fine, attacking front-foot player whose hallmark was the cover drive. He made his debut for Surrey before going up to Oxford where he captained both cricket and soccer. Because of business commitments he played little cricket during the next six seasons but returned to captain Surrey when Jardine relinquished the leadership. His return in Jack Hobbs's last season heralded a new era in which his cavalier spirit vitalised the team's approach in all areas. Vice-captain of the 1934–35 West Indies tour and captain of the goodwill mission to the antipodes the following winter, he was chosen as 'Gubby' Allen's deputy for the 1936–37 tour of Australia but declined through business pressures. He retired in 1938 after four seasons of Surrey captaincy but was persuaded to return for a further two-year term in 1947. He served on the MCC and Surrey committees, entitled his autobiography *Flannelled Foolishness* and died after a heart attack shortly before his 55th birthday.

Errol Holmes

						Batting 1st			Batting 2nd				Bowling 1st			Bowling 2nd		
Ref	Series	V	T	Venue	Result	No	R	HO	No	R	HO	Ct	Balls	R	W	Balls	R	W
238/212	1934–35	WI	1	Bridgetown	W-4w	8	0	c	3	6	c	1	–	–	–	–	–	–
239/213			2	Port-of-Spain	L-217	8	85	*	11	0	*	2	18	10	1	–	–	–
240/214			3	Georgetown	D	10	2	b	–	–	–	–	–	–	–	18	16	1
241/215			4	Kingston	L-I & 161	5	0	b	6	3	lbw	–	48	40	0	–	–	–
243/217	1935	SA	2	Lord's	L-157	6	10	c	6	8	b	1	–	–	–	24	10	0

Career	M	I	NO	HS	R	Avge	100	50	Ct	St	Balls	R	W	Avge	BB	5w	10w	Rate
Test	5	9	2	85*	114	16.28	–	1	4	–	108	76	2	38.00	1-10	–	–	54.00
F/c	301	465	51	236	13598	32.84	24	67	192	–	18297	9530	283	33.67	6-16	4	–	64.65

HOLMES, Percy

Yorkshire (1913 to 1933)

Wisden 1920
TOURS
SA 1924–25 (Joel), 1927–28; WI 1925–26
Born Oakes, Huddersfield, Yorkshire
25 Nov 1886
Died Marsh, Huddersfield 3 Sep 1971

Percy Holmes (left) and Herbert Sutcliffe at Leyton, 1932.

Percy Holmes was an amazingly consistent Yorkshire opening batsman and an outstanding slip fielder whose early career was lost to the Great War. Afterwards he began his long and famous association with Herbert Sutcliffe which culminated in their world-record partnership of 555 at Leyton when Holmes was in his 45th year and afflicted with lumbago. Jaunty and stockily built, he was a deft-footed, attacking, versatile player with a marvellous technique. He was an artist who loved to improvise and communicate his obvious enjoyment of batting. Particularly strong at hooking and late-cutting, he commanded a complete range of strokes. In his only Test against Australia (*140*) he top-scored after surviving for 90 minutes against the ferocious pace of Gregory and McDonald. Desperately unlucky to be a contemporary of Jack Hobbs, he was fortunately a cheerful, humorous man.

NOTABLE FEATS

- Exceeded 1000 runs in a season 14 times (1919–32 inclusive) plus once on tour, including 2000 on 7 occasions. Scored 1021 runs in June 1925.
- Scored two triple centuries and 10 other double centuries; his 302* for Yorkshire at Portsmouth in 1920 remains the record score v Hampshire and his 315* v Middlesex in 1925 broke the record for Lord's set by W. Ward in 1820.
- Shared 69 century 1st-wkt stands with H. Sutcliffe, including 18 over 250 – notably the English record of 555 in 445 min v Essex at Leyton in 1932.
- His stand of 327 with W.E. Astill for MCC v Jamaica at Kingston in 1925–26 remains the 5th-wkt record in the West Indies.
- Carried his bat through a completed innings for Yorkshire 3 times.
- First batsman to score a hundred in each innings of a Roses match: 126 and 111* at Manchester in 1920.

						Batting 1st			Batting 2nd			
Ref	Series	V	T	Venue	Result	No	R	HO	No	R	HO	Ct
140/129	1921	A	1	Nottingham	L-10w	2	30	b	2	8	c	–
168/154	1927–28	SA	1	Johannesburg[1]	W-10w	1	0	lbw	1	15	*	–
169/155			2	Cape Town	W-87	1	9	b	1	88	c	1
170/156			3	Durban[2]	D	1	70	c	1	56	c	–
171/157			4	Johannesburg[1]	L-4w	1	1	b	1	63	b	–
172/158			5	Durban[2]	L-8w	1	0	c	1	0	lbw	2
219/193	1932	I		Lord's	W-158	1	6	b	1	11	b	–

Career	M	I	NO	HS	R	Avge	100	50	Ct	St	Balls	R	W	Avge	BB	5w	10w	Rate
Test	7	14	1	88	357	27.46	–	4	3	–	–	–	–	–	–	–	–	–
F/c	555	810	84	315*	30573	42.11	67	141	342	–	252	185	2	92.50	1-5	–	–	126.00

HONE, Leland

MCC (1878 to 1880)

TOUR A 1878–79
Born Dublin, Ireland 30 Jan 1853
Died St Stephen's Green, Dublin
31 Dec 1896

Although educated at Rugby School, Leland Hone belonged to a celebrated Irish cricketing family. A middle-order batsman and occasional keeper, he was selected for Lord Harris's tour of Australia a few weeks after making his first-class debut for the MCC. When the team was found to lack a wicket-keeper he was pressed into service and made his only Test appearance, thus becoming the first man to represent England without playing for a first-class county. His nephew, W.P. Hone, captained Ireland and wrote the standard history of the game there. [*Illus. p.* 222]

						Batting 1st			Batting 2nd			Fielding 1st				Fielding 2nd			
Ref	Series	V	T	Venue	Result	No	R	HO	No	R	HO	Ct	St	Byes	Balls	Ct	St	Byes	Balls
3/3†	1878–79	A		Melbourne	L-10w	10	7	c	10	6	b	2	–	19	639	–	–	0	12

Career	M	I	NO	HS	R	Avge	100	50	Ct	St	Balls	R	W	Avge	BB	5w	10w	Rate
Test	1	2	0	7	13	6.50	–	–	2	–	–	–	–	–	–	–	–	–
F/c	8	13	1	27	85	7.08	–	–	10	2	–	–	–	–	–	–	–	–

HOPWOOD John Leonard

Lancashire (1923 to 1939)

Born Newton Hyde, Cheshire 30 Oct 1903
Died Denton, Lancashire 15 Jun 1985

Len Hopwood

After taking almost a decade to establish himself in the strong Lancashire side which won five titles in nine years, Len Hopwood became an extremely useful but mainly defensive all-rounder. His stubborn right-handed batting with its minimal backlift was tailor-made for the role of a grafting opener. Although he could be devastating on a helpful pitch, his flat, accurate left-arm bowling, delivered at just under medium pace, often from over the wicket and supported by six leg-side fielders, was usually employed as a brake. He made his Lancashire debut on the same day as George Duckworth but dropped out after three seasons and spent the next two summers with Cheshire and Wallasey. Returning in 1928 he gradually honed his skills in both departments to such an extent that in 1934, when Lancashire won their last Championship, he completed his first 'double' and gained two England caps against Australia. In 1982 he became the first professional to be elected president of Lancashire.

NOTABLE FEATS

- Exceeded 1000 runs in a season 8 times and took 100 wickets twice, completing the 'double' in 1934 and 1935.
- Scored 220 for Lancashire v Gloucestershire at Bristol in 1934.
- Carried his bat through a completed Lancashire innings twice.
- Took 9 for 33 v Leicestershire at Manchester in 1933 (when he achieved the match 'double') and 9 for 69 (15 for 112 in the match) v Worcestershire at Blackpool in 1934.

					Batting 1st			Batting 2nd				Bowling 1st			Bowling 2nd		
Ref	Series	V	T	Venue	Result	No	R	HO	No	R	HO	Ct	Balls	R	W	Balls	R	W
235/209	1934	A	3	Manchester	D	8	2	b	–	–	–	–	228	46	0	54	16	0
236/210			4	Leeds	D	8	8	lbw	8	2	*	–	180	93	0	–	–	–

Career	M	I	NO	HS	R	Avge	100	50	Ct	St	Balls	R	W	Avge	BB	5w	10w	Rate
Test	2	3	1	8	12	6.00	–	–	–	–	462	155	0	–	–	–	–	–
F/c	400	575	55	220	15548	29.90	27	70	198	–	43391	15110	673	22.45	9-33	35	6	64.67

HORNBY Albert Neilson

Lancashire (1867 to 1899)

TOUR A 1878–79
Born Blackburn, Lancashire 10 Feb 1847
Died Nantwich, Cheshire 17 Dec 1925

'Monkey' Hornby was a punishing front-foot batsman noted for his dashing strokeplay and swift but impulsive running between the wickets. His long association with Lancashire and his famous opening partnerships with the stonewalling R.G. Barlow prompted Francis Thompson's verse, 'O my Hornby and my Barlow long ago'. He was also a magnificent fielder at cover-point and he could bowl with either arm, a talent which must have caused great confusion. He made his first appearance at Lord's (for Harrow against Eton) 13 days before W.G. Grace and when he weighed under six stone. Although he was to make a major contribution as a batsman – he was Lancashire's sole century maker between 1870 and 1881 – his captaincy (1880–93 and 1897–8) was equally valuable. As a leader he extracted maximum effort by being enthusiastic, genial, courageous and firm. It was the diminutive but belligerent Hornby who 'arrested' Lord Harris's assailant at Sydney in 1879. A double international, he gained nine rugby caps and is

NOTABLE FEATS

- Exceeded 1000 runs in a season twice.
- Set a world record by scoring 10 runs off a ball from J. Street of Surrey for Lancashire at The Oval in 1873.
- Carried his bat through a completed innings twice.

one of only two men to have captained England at both sports. In addition to the Lancashire presidency and service on MCC committees, he devoted much of his later life to hunting. His son (A.H.) captained Lancashire from 1908 until the Great War.

Members of Lord Harris's touring party to Australia, 1878–79: standing *R.D.Walker, F.Penn, Lord Harris, L. Hone, F.A. MacKinnon;* seated *A.P. Lucas, S.S. Schultz, Mrs Hornby, Lady Harris, H.C. Maul, C.A. Absolom;* in front *A.N. Hornby, Miss Ingram, V.P.F.A. Royle, A.J. Webbe.*

						Batting 1st			Batting 2nd				Bowling 1st			Bowling 2nd		
Ref	Series	V	T	Venue	Result	No	R	HO	No	R	HO	Ct	Balls	R	W	Balls	R	W
3/3	1878–79	A		Melbourne	L-10w	4	2	b	4	4	b	–	28	0	1	–	–	–
9/9*	1882	A		Oval	L-7	10	2	b	2	9	b	–	–	–	–	–	–	–
14/14*	1884	A	1	Manchester	D	2	0	st	9	4	st	–	–	–	–	–	–	–

Career	M	I	NO	HS	R	Avge	100	50	Ct	St	Balls	R	W	Avge	BB	5w	10w	Rate
Test	3	6	0	9	21	3.50	–	–	–	–	28	0	1	0.00	1-0	–	–	28.00
F/c	437	710	41	188	16109	24.07	16	75	313	3	593	258	11	23.45	4-40	–	–	53.90

HORTON
Martin John

Worcestershire (1952 to 1966)
Northern Districts
(1967–68 to 1970–71)

TOURS
WI 1965–66 (Worcs);
Z 1964–65 (Worcs)
Born Worcester 21 Apr 1934

Martin Horton was a strongly built all-rounder of medium height (5ft 9in) who played a substantial role in Worcestershire's first two Championships. As a solid and reliable opening batsman with a meagre backlift, he relished the cut and played the stroke exceptionally well. His handy off-break bowling enabled him to complete the 'double' twice and dismiss nine South Africans at New Road in 1955. He left Worcestershire in 1967 to become New Zealand's national coach, his 17-year tenure coinciding with a major upsurge in that country's performances.

Martin Horton

NOTABLE FEATS

- Exceeded 1000 runs in a season 11 times (including 2468 in 1959), and took 100 wickets twice, completing the 'double' in 1955 and 1961.
- Contributed career-best score of 233 to Worcestershire record 3rd-wkt stand of 314 with T.W. Graveney v Somerset at Worcester in 1962. His other double century was 212 v Essex at Leyton in 1959.
- Took 9 for 56 for Worcestershire v South Africans at Worcester in 1955.
- Hat-trick for Worcestershire v Somerset at Bath in 1956.

					Batting 1st			Batting 2nd				Bowling 1st			Bowling 2nd		
Ref	Series	V	T	Venue	Result	No	R	HO	No	R	HO	Ct	Balls	R	W	Balls	R	W
474/354	1959	I	1	Nottingham	W-I & 59	6	58	c	–	–	–	1	30	15	0	114	20	0
475/355			2	Lord's	W-8w	6	2	b	–	–	–	1	94	24	2	–	–	–

Career	M	I	NO	HS	R	Avge	100	50	Ct	St	Balls	R	W	Avge	BB	5w	10w	Rate
Test	2	2	0	58	60	30.00	–	1	2	–	238	59	2	29.50	2-24	–	–	119.00
F/c	410	724	49	233	19945	29.54	23	112	166	–	54352	22226	825	26.94	9-56	40	7	65.88

HOWARD Nigel David

Lancashire (1946 to 1953)

TOUR I/P 1951–52
Born Gee Cross, Hyde, Cheshire 18 May 1925
Died Douglas, Isle of Man 31 May 1979

Nigel Howard was a stylish batsman with a full array of strokes and a superb fielder. After his wartime education at Rossall School and Manchester University, he became Cyril Washbrook's opening partner before being appointed Lancashire's youngest captain in 1949. Although he led the county to a shared Championship the following season and captained MCC and England with great enthusiasm and tact on the Indian subcontinent, he was compelled to retire after the 1953 season to devote his energies to the family textile business. A fine all-round sportsman he represented Cheshire at hockey and golf. His father (who was the County secretary and a manager of MCC tours) and younger brother also appeared for Lancashire.

Nigel Howard and his fellow MCC cricketers on the 1951–52 tour of India, Pakistan and Ceylon: back row *R.T. Spooner, M.J. Hilton, C.J. Poole, F. Ridgway, E. Leadbeater;* middle row *D. Kenyon, J.B. Statham, R. Tattersall, T.W. Graveney, D. Shackleton, F.A. Lowson;* seated *J.D.B. Robertson, D.V. Brennan, D.B. Carr, N.D. Howard (captain), C.G. Howard (manager), A.J. Watkins.*

Ref	Series	V	T	Venue	Result	Batting 1st No	R	HO	Batting 2nd No	R	HO	Ct
339/292*	1951–52	I	1	Delhi	D	7	13	st	7	9	lbw	–
340/293*			2	Bombay[2]	D	7	20	c	–	–	–	3
341/294*			3	Calcutta	D	7	23	c	7	20	*	1
342/295*			4	Kanpur	W-8w	8	1	b	–	–	–	–

Career	M	I	NO	HS	R	Avge	100	50	Ct	St	Balls	R	W	Avge	BB	5w	10w	Rate
Test	4	6	1	23	86	17.20	–	–	4	–	–	–	–	–	–	–	–	–
F/c	198	279	30	145	6152	24.70	3	36	153	–	90	52	1	52.00	1-14	–	–	90.00

HOWELL, Henry

Warwickshire (1913 to 1928)

TOURS A 1920–21, 1924–25
Born Ladywood, Birmingham
29 Nov 1890
Died Selly Oak, Birmingham 9 Jul 1932

Although Harry Howell's peak seasons as a right-arm fast bowler were lost to the Great War, he still gave devoted and often spectacular service to Warwickshire as a major strike force throughout the 1920s. His pace, derived from a lengthy approach and rhythmic action, was distinctly sharp and he obeyed the vital maxim of aiming at the stumps. His introduction to Test cricket in Australia would have been more successful if he had been given slip fielders who could catch. He played soccer for several clubs including Wolverhampton Wanderers and his younger brother also played cricket for Warwickshire. [*Illus. pp.* 161, 183]

NOTABLE FEATS

- Took 100 wickets in a season 6 times, twice exceeding 150.
- Bowled 8 Northamptonshire batsmen in an innings for Warwickshire at Northampton in 1922.
- Took 6 for 7 in 29 balls when Hampshire were dismissed for 15 at Birmingham in 1922 (they recovered to win by 155 runs).
- Took all 10 Yorkshire wickets for 51 runs at Birmingham in 1923.

Ref	Series	V	T	Venue	Result	Batting 1st No	R	HO	Batting 2nd No	R	HO	Ct	Bowling 1st Balls	R	W	Bowling 2nd Balls	R	W
136/125	1920–21	A	2	Melbourne	L-I & 91	10	5	st	10	0	*	–	222	142	3	–	–	–
137/126			3	Adelaide	L-119	11	2	c	11	4	*	–	156	89	0	204	115	4
138/127			4	Melbourne	L-8w	11	0	*	11	0	*	–	102	86	0	60	36	0
140/129	1921	A	1	Nottingham	L-10w	10	0	*	10	4	*	–	54	22	0	–	–	–
157/143	1924	SA	5	Oval	D	–	–	–	–	–	–	–	120	69	0	–	–	–

Career	M	I	NO	HS	R	Avge	100	50	Ct	St	Balls	R	W	Avge	BB	5w	10w	Rate
Test	5	8	6	5	15	7.50	–	–	–	–	918	559	7	79.85	4-115	–	–	131.14
F/c	227	326	111	36	1679	7.80	–	–	67	–	43112	20700	975	21.23	10-51	75	18	44.21

HOWORTH, Richard

Worcestershire (1933 to 1951)
Europeans (1944–45)

TOUR WI 1947–48
Born Bacup, Lancashire 26 Apr 1909
Died Worcester 2 Apr 1980

Dick Howorth, who gave such splendid service to Worcestershire, was yet another cricketer whose prime years were lost to war. A shrewd, determined and versatile left-handed all-rounder, he was a forcing middle-order batsman who was happy to open, an extremely accurate slow leg-break bowler who could bowl seamers, and a reliable catcher at gully who could field in the deep. When he eventually forced the selectors' hand in 1947 by the sheer weight of his runs (1510) and wickets (164), he was in his 39th year. He celebrated the big event with a match haul of 68 runs for once out, six wickets, including one with his very first ball, and two good catches. Although he returned a six-wicket analysis against the powerful West

Indies batting on the subsequent Caribbean tour, he was never selected again. He became disenchanted with the first-class game and retired after a season in which he headed the County's averages with 118 wickets at 17.97. Afterwards he played in the Birmingham League, served on the Worcestershire committee and bought a newsagent's shop within sight of the cathedral and county ground.

NOTABLE FEATS

- *289* Dismissed D.V. Dyer with his first ball in Test cricket – the last England bowler to achieve this feat.
- Exceeded 1000 runs in a season 4 times, took 100 wickets on 9 occasions and completed the 'double' 3 times (missing a fourth by 3 runs).
- Shared record Worcestershire 7th-wkt stand of 197 with H.H.I. Gibbons v Surrey at The Oval in 1938.
- Hat-trick for Worcestershire v Warwickshire at Birmingham in 1950.

Dick Howorth

						Batting 1st			Batting 2nd				Bowling 1st			Bowling 2nd		
Ref	Series	V	T	Venue	Result	No	R	HO	No	R	HO	Ct	Balls	R	W	Balls	R	W
289/257	1947	SA	5	Oval	D	7	23	c	7	45	*	2	234	64	3	222	85	3
295/258	1947–48	WI	1	Bridgetown	D	8	14	c	3	16	b	–	180	68	1	246	124	6
296/259			2	Port-of-Spain	D	6	14	b	7	14	b	–	192	76	2	6	2	0
297/260			3	Georgetown	L-7w	7	4	c	9	2	lbw	–	138	58	0	54	25	1
298/261			4	Kingston	L-10w	9	12	*	9	1	st	–	240	106	3	24	27	0

Career	M	I	NO	HS	R	Avge	100	50	Ct	St	Balls	R	W	Avge	BB	5w	10w	Rate
Test	5	10	2	45*	145	18.12	–	–	2	–	1536	635	19	33.42	6-124	1	–	80.84
F/c	372	611	56	114	11479	20.68	4	52	197	–	71812	29425	1345	21.87	7-18	74	7	53.39

HUMPHRIES Joseph

Derbyshire (1899 to 1914)

TOUR A 1907–08
Born Stonebroom, Derbyshire
19 May 1876
Died Chesterfield, Derbyshire
7 May 1946

Joe Humphries was a notable member of Derbyshire's impressive heritage of wicket-keepers. Beginning as understudy to Bill Storer, he followed his senior's tactic of courageously standing up to the fastest bowlers. Eventually his consistent glovework and dogged batting were rewarded with a tour to Australia. There he shared his Test debut with Jack Hobbs and, in the final innings, made a vital contribution to England's single-wicket victory by adding 34 for the ninth wicket with S.F. Barnes. The Great War ended his career and, although he was recalled for a benefit match in 1920, rain prevented a ball from being bowled. [*Illus. p.* 141]

						Batting 1st			Batting 2nd			Fielding 1st				Fielding 2nd			
Ref	Series	V	T	Venue	Result	No	R	HO	No	R	HO	Ct	St	Byes	Balls	Ct	St	Byes	Balls
97/94†	1907–08	A	2	Melbourne	W-1w	10	6	b	10	16	lbw	1	–	0	605	1	–	12	730
98/95†			3	Adelaide	L-245	10	7	ro	10	1	b	2	–	3	569	–	–	20	1007
99/96†			4	Melbourne	L-308	10	3	*	10	11	c	–	–	1	515	3	–	7	744

Career	M	I	NO	HS	R	Avge	100	50	Ct	St	Balls	R	W	Avge	BB	5w	10w	Rate
Test	3	6	1	16	44	8.80	–	–	7	–	–	–	–	–	–	–	–	–
F/c	302	514	129	68	5464	14.19	–	11	564	110	61	43	3	14.33	1-5	–	–	20.33

HUNTER, Joseph

Yorkshire (1878 to 1888)

TOUR A 1884–85
Born Scarborough, Yorkshire
3 Aug 1855
Died Rotherham, Yorkshire 4 Jan 1891

Joe Hunter was a handy county wicket-keeper who played in all five Tests on Shaw and Shrewsbury's second visit to Australia. When ill health compelled his premature retirement he was succeeded in the Yorkshire team by his younger brother David. He continued to make occasional appearances for his native Scarborough during the two summers before his tragically early death at the age of 35. [*Illus. p.* 392]

NOTABLE FEATS

- Held 6 catches in an innings (9 in match) for Yorkshire v Gloucestershire at Gloucester in 1887.

					Batting 1st			Batting 2nd			Fielding 1st				Fielding 2nd			
Ref	Series	V	T Venue	Result	No	R	HO	No	R	HO	Ct	St	Byes	Balls	Ct	St	Byes	Balls
17/17†	1884–85	A	1 Adelaide	W-8w	11	1	ro	–	–	–	2	–	7	597	–	1	7	465
18/18†			2 Melbourne	W-10w	11	39	*	–	–	–	–	–	3	1097	2	–	0	459
19/19†			3 Sydney	L-6	11	13	b	11	5	*	2	2	3	670	–	–	1	628
20/20†			4 Sydney	L-8w	11	13	b	11	4	b	–	–	5	679	–	–	0	95
21/21†			5 Melbourne	W-I & 98	11	18	b	–	–	–	2	–	5	424	–	–	5	409

Career	M	I	NO	HS	R	Avge	100	50	Ct	St	Balls	R	W	Avge	BB	5w	10w	Rate
Test	5	7	2	39*	93	18.60	–	–	8	3	–	–	–	–	–	–	–	–
F/c	162	240	71	60*	1330	7.86	–	2	234	122	–	–	–	–	–	–	–	–

HUTCHINGS Kenneth Lotherington

Kent (1902 to 1912)

Wisden 1907
TOUR A 1907–08
Born Southborough, Kent 7 Dec 1882
Died Ginchy, France 3 Sep 1916

After five outstanding seasons in the Tonbridge School XI, Kenneth Hutchings began his Kent career with great expectations. Only in 1906, when he scored 1454 runs, averaged 60.58 and contributed most to Kent's first Championship, did he really fulfil them. As a batsman he was a daring extrovert who relied on fitness, footwork and a keen eye. He would get on to the front foot to attack whenever possible and then drive with ferocious power. The back foot was reserved almost entirely for defence. When on song he could dispatch perfect length balls at will. Even George Hirst, fearless at mid-off, would retreat before his onslaught. He was a useful right-arm fast bowler and a brilliant fielder. Whilst serving as a Lieutenant with the King's Liverpool Regiment he was struck by a shell and killed instantaneously. His two elder brothers also appeared for Kent. [*Illus. p.* 141]

NOTABLE FEATS

- *97* Reached his 100 in 128 min, the second 50 taking 43 min.
- Exceeded 1000 runs in a season 6 times.
- Scored 100 in 50 min for Kent v Gloucestershire at Catford in 1909.
- Twice scored 100 before lunch for Kent.

					Batting 1st			Batting 2nd				Bowling 1st			Bowling 2nd		
Ref	Series	V	T Venue	Result	No	R	HO	No	R	HO	Ct	Balls	R	W	Balls	R	W
96/93	1907–08	A	1 Sydney	L-2w	4	42	c	4	17	c	1	–	–	–	–	–	–
97/94			2 Melbourne	W-1w	4	126	b	4	39	c	2	–	–	–	–	–	–
98/95			3 Adelaide	L-245	4	23	c	4	0	b	4	12	5	1	42	34	0
99/96			4 Melbourne	L-308	4	8	b	4	3	b	–	–	–	–	12	24	0
100/97			5 Sydney	L-49	4	13	ro	4	2	b	1	–	–	–	–	–	–
104/101	1909	A	4 Manchester	D	6	9	b	–	–	–	1	–	–	–	–	–	–
105/102			5 Oval	D	8	59	c	–	–	–	–	–	–	–	24	18	0

Career	M	I	NO	HS	R	Avge	100	50	Ct	St	Balls	R	W	Avge	BB	5w	10w	Rate
Test	7	12	0	126	341	28.41	1	1	9	–	90	81	1	81.00	1-5	–	–	90.00
F/c	207	311	12	176	10054	33.62	22	56	179	–	1439	938	24	39.08	4-15	–	–	59.95

HUTTON Sir Leonard

Yorkshire (1934 to 1955)

Wisden 1938
TOURS
A 1946–47, 1950–51, 1954–55;
SA 1938–39, 1948–49;
WI 1935–36 (Yorks), 1947–48, 1953–54;
NZ 1950–51, 1954–55
Born Fulneck, Pudsey, Yorkshire
23 Jun 1916
Knighted for services to cricket 1956

Len Hutton

Len Hutton remains pre-eminent amongst all post-war England batsmen as the supreme technician on all types of pitch and he was undoubtedly one of the most complete opening batsmen of all time. His innings of 62* on a Brisbane 'sticky' in 1950–51 was one of the most remarkable in Test cricket. Few have matched him for style, balance, correctness of technique or stroke production. He was also a competent right-arm leg-break bowler and a good fielder anywhere, especially at slip or leg-slip. A little over average height (5ft 10½in) and slightly built, he had been heralded in Yorkshire as a potentially great player long before his marathon innings of 364. By the time Hitler's activities brought a six-year hiatus to first-class cricket, Hutton had established himself as a master batsman. The return of peace found him with his left arm shortened from a compound fracture sustained during an accident in an Army gymnasium. From 1948 his methods were also hampered by the responsibility of shielding an uncertain England batting line-up. Occasionally there were displays of his superb strokeplay such as during his memorable and chanceless 145 against the 1953 Australians at Lord's. In 1952 he became the first professional to be appointed captain of England since Arthur Shrewsbury in 1886–87. He enjoyed captaincy and proved to be a canny and effective leader who relished a dour battle, especially against 'the old enemy'. Although sometimes criticised for being too defensive, England drew only eight Tests under his command, winning 11 and losing four. He was even accused of being too reckless after his disastrous decision to put Australia in at Brisbane in 1954–55 (the first such gamble by an England captain in Australia since 1911–12) had resulted in Australia amassing 601 and winning by an innings. His crafty manipulation of the over rate and careful handling of Tyson and Statham enabled him to recover the series and hold the Ashes reclaimed so dramatically in Coronation Year. Surprisingly he was the first England captain to regain the urn and lead a successful campaign in its defence. He ended his Test career on a high note, being top scorer in his final innings and then orchestrating New Zealand's dismissal for the lowest total in Test history (26). Back trouble and general weariness prompted his retirement later that year when he was only 39. In 1956 he became the second professional after Jack Hobbs to be knighted for his services to cricket. Moving to Surrey he concentrated on a successful business career and remained largely aloof from the first-class scene for two decades until he returned briefly as a Test selector (1975–76). His profound comments and humorous asides have entertained readers of *The Observer* for many summers.

NOTABLE FEATS

- 1000 runs in 11th Test (*272*) (16 inns); 2000 runs in 25th Test (*288*) (42 inns); 3000 runs in 35th Test (*311*) (61 inns); 4000 runs in 44th Test (*326*) (77 inns); 5000 runs in 55th Test (*337*) (98 inns); 6000 runs in 66th Test (*382*) (124 inns).
- *263* Scored 100 in his first Test v Australia.
- *266* His score (364) and batting time (13hr 17min – the longest innings in English first-class cricket) remain England records and were world Test records until 1958. It remains the highest score at The Oval and by a No. 1 batsman in Tests. His 2nd-wkt stand of 382 with M. Leyland is the England record for the 2nd wkt in all Tests and the highest for any wicket v Australia. Also shared record E v A 6th-wkt stand of 216 with J. Hardstaff jr – unique instance of a batsman sharing in two stands of 200 in the same Test innings. 770 runs were scored during his innings (Test record) which was England's 100th century v A and contained 35 fours. England's total of 903 for 7 dec remains the Test record.
- *272* Added 248 for the 4th wkt with D.C.S. Compton in 140 min.
- *274* Shared (then) world-record 3rd-wkt stand of 264 with W.R. Hammond which remains the record for E v WI. Hutton's last 8 Tests had brought him 1109 runs.
- *303* Last out in the 1st inns, he was on the field for all but the final 57 min of the match.
- *310* Shared (then) world-record 1st-wkt stand of 359 in 310 min with C. Washbrook on the opening day of Test cricket at Ellis Park. It remains England's highest opening stand in all Tests.
- *326* Scored England's first 200 in a home Test v WI and remains alone in carrying his bat for E v WI; his 202* (in 470 min) is the highest score by an England batsman achieving this feat.
- *330* Only England batsman to carry his

NOTABLE FEATS *cont.*

bat throughout a complete Test innings twice and second after R. Abel (1891–92) to do so for any country v Australia.

• *336* Missed becoming the first to score his 100th first-class hundred in a Test match by just 2 runs.

• *338* Only batsman to be out 'obstructing the field' in Test cricket.

• *376* Became the first captain to win a rubber after losing the toss in all 5 Tests.

• *386* Scored the first 200 by an England captain in a Test overseas.

• Exceeded 1000 runs in a season 12 times (plus 5 times on tour), including 3429 (fourth-highest seasonal aggregate) in 1949 and 2000 on 8 other occasions.

• One of only 4 batsmen to score 1000 runs in a month twice in the same season: 1294 (June – the record for one batsman in a month) and 1050 (August) in 1949. Headed the national batting averages in 1953.

• Scored 100 first-class centuries in 619 innings, then (1951) the fewest to reach this mark by an Englishman.

• Scored 11 double centuries, including one triple century (364 above).

• Scored 100 in each innings of match 3 times (all for Yorkshire). On 3 occasions scored hundreds in 3 consecutive innings and once scored 7 successive fifties.

• Carried his bat through a completed innings of a first-class match 4 times.

• Contributed 149 to a 1st-wkt stand of 263 in 156 min with W.J. Edrich which formed the base of MCC's total of 676 v Griqualand West at Kimberley in 1938–39; it remains the highest first-class total in South Africa.

• First professional to be elected to honorary membership of the MCC before his career had ended.

TEST NOTES

• *283* Retired ill – hospitalised with tonsillitis.

• *323* Retired hurt at 22–0 (1st inns); resumed at 249-6 and batted virtually one-handed.

						Batting 1st			Batting 2nd				Bowling 1st			Bowling 2nd		
Ref	Series	V	T	Venue	Result	No	R	HO	No	R	HO	Ct	Balls	R	W	Balls	R	W
260/229	1937	NZ	1	Lord's	D	2	0	b	2	1	c	–	12	4	0	–	–	–
261/230			2	Manchester	W-130	2	100	c	2	14	c	–	–	–	–	–	–	–
262/231			3	Oval	D	2	12	c	–	–	–	2	12	7	0	16	4	1
263/232	1938	A	1	Nottingham	D	2	100	lbw	–	–	–	–	–	–	–	–	–	–
264/233			2	Lord's	D	2	4	c	2	5	c	1	–	–	–	–	–	–
266/235			5	Oval	W-I & 579	1	364	c	–	–	–	–	–	–	–	–	–	–
268/237	1938–39	SA	2	Cape Town	D	1	17	b	–	–	–	–	–	–	–	–	–	–
269/238			3	Durban[2]	W-I & 13	1	31	lbw	–	–	–	1	–	–	–	–	–	–
270/239			4	Johannesburg[1]	D	1	92	b	1	32	c	1	–	–	–	–	–	–
271/240			5	Durban[2]	D	1	38	ro	1	55	b	1	–	–	–	8	10	0
272/241	1939	WI	1	Lord's	W-8w	1	196	c	1	16	b	2	–	–	–	–	–	–
273/242			2	Manchester	D	1	13	c	1	17	c	1	–	–	–	–	–	–
274/243			3	Oval	D	1	73	c	1	165	*	–	56	45	1	–	–	–
276/244	1946	I	1	Lord's	W-10w	1	7	c	1	22	*	–	–	–	–	–	–	–
277/245			2	Manchester	D	1	67	c	1	2	c	–	–	–	–	–	–	–
278/246			3	Oval	D	1	25	lbw	–	–	–	–	–	–	–	–	–	–
279/247	1946–47	A	1	Brisbane[2]	L-I & 332	1	7	b	1	0	c	–	–	–	–	–	–	–
280/248			2	Sydney	L-I & 33	1	39	c	1	37	hw	–	–	–	–	–	–	–
281/249			3	Melbourne	D	1	2	c	1	40	c	1	–	–	–	24	28	0
282/250			4	Adelaide	D	1	94	lbw	1	76	b	–	–	–	–	–	–	–
283/251			5	Sydney	L-5w	1	122	*ri	–	–	–	–	–	–	–	–	–	–
285/253	1947	SA	1	Nottingham	D	1	17	lbw	1	9	b	1	–	–	–	12	15	0
286/254			2	Lord's	W-10w	1	18	b	1	13	*	–	–	–	–	–	–	–
287/255			3	Manchester	W-7w	1	12	c	1	24	c	3	–	–	–	–	–	–
288/256			4	Leeds	W-10w	1	100	ro	1	32	*	–	–	–	–	–	–	–
289/257			5	Oval	D	1	83	b	1	36	c	1	–	–	–	12	14	0
297/260	1947–48	WI	3	Georgetown	L-7w	1	31	c	1	24	b	–	–	–	–	–	–	–
298/261			4	Kingston	L-10w	1	56	b	1	60	c	3	–	–	–	–	–	–
299/262	1948	A	1	Nottingham	L-8w	1	3	b	1	74	b	2	–	–	–	–	–	–
300/263			2	Lord's	L-409	1	20	b	1	13	c	3	–	–	–	–	–	–
302/265			4	Leeds	L-7w	1	81	b	1	57	c	–	–	–	–	24	30	0
303/266			5	Oval	L-I & 149	1	30	c	1	64	c	–	–	–	–	–	–	–
309/267	1948–49	SA	1	Durban[2]	W-2w	1	83	c	1	5	c	–	–	–	–	–	–	–
310/268			2	Johannesburg[2]	D	1	158	c	–	–	–	1	–	–	–	–	–	–
311/269			3	Cape Town	D	1	41	ro	1	87	b	1	–	–	–	–	–	–
312/270			4	Johannesburg[2]	D	1	2	b	1	123	b	–	–	–	–	–	–	–
313/271			5	Port Elizabeth	W-3w	1	46	c	1	32	st	–	–	–	–	–	–	–
314/272	1949	NZ	1	Leeds	D	1	101	c	1	0	c	–	–	–	–	18	23	0
315/273			2	Lord's	D	1	23	b	1	66	c	1	–	–	–	–	–	–
316/274			3	Manchester	D	1	73	st	–	–	–	–	–	–	–	6	0	0
317/275			4	Oval	D	1	206	c	–	–	–	1	–	–	–	–	–	–
323/276	1950	WI	1	Manchester	W-202	1	39	b	8	45	c	–	–	–	–	–	–	–
324/277			2	Lord's	L-326	1	35	st	1	10	b	1	–	–	–	–	–	–
326/279			4	Oval	L-I & 56	1	202	*	1	2	c	1	–	–	–	–	–	–

Ref	Series	V	T	Venue	Result	Batting 1st No	R	HO	Batting 2nd No	R	HO	Ct	Bowling 1st Balls	R	W	Bowling 2nd Balls	R	W
327/280	1950–51	A	1	Brisbane[2]	L-70	6	8	*	8	62	*	2	–	–	–	–	–	–
328/281			2	Melbourne	L-28	4	12	c	4	40	c	2	–	–	–	–	–	–
329/282			3	Sydney	L-I & 13	1	62	lbw	1	9	c	–	–	–	–	–	–	–
330/283			4	Adelaide	L-274	1	156	*	1	45	c	2	–	–	–	–	–	–
331/284			5	Melbourne	W-8w	1	79	b	1	60	*	3	–	–	–	–	–	–
332/285	1950–51	NZ	1	Christchurch	D	1	28	b	–	–	–	–	–	–	–	18	7	0
333/286			2	Wellington	W-6w	1	57	c	1	29	c	–	–	–	–	–	–	–
334/287	1951	SA	1	Nottingham	L-71	1	63	c	1	11	c	1	–	–	–	–	–	–
335/288			2	Lord's	W-10w	1	12	lbw	1	12	*	2	–	–	–	–	–	–
336/289			3	Manchester	W-9w	1	27	c	1	98	*	2	–	–	–	–	–	–
337/290			4	Leeds	D	1	100	b	–	–	–	–	–	–	–	–	–	–
338/291			5	Oval	W-4w	1	28	lbw	1	27	obs	3	–	–	–	–	–	–
351/297*	1952	I	1	Leeds	W-7w	1	10	c	1	10	b	–	–	–	–	–	–	–
352/298*			2	Lord's	W-8w	1	150	c	1	39	*	1	–	–	–	–	–	–
353/299*			3	Manchester	W-I & 207	1	104	c	–	–	–	1	–	–	–	–	–	–
354/300*			4	Oval	D	1	86	c	–	–	–	1	–	–	–	–	–	–
372/301*	1953	A	1	Nottingham	D	1	43	c	1	60	*	1	–	–	–	–	–	–
373/302*			2	Lord's	D	1	145	c	1	5	c	–	–	–	–	–	–	–
374/303*			3	Manchester	D	1	66	lbw	–	–	–	1	–	–	–	–	–	–
375/304*			4	Leeds	D	1	0	b	1	25	c	1	–	–	–	–	–	–
376/305*			5	Oval	W-8w	1	82	b	1	17	ro	1	–	–	–	–	–	–
382/306*	1953–54	WI	1	Kingston	L-140	2	24	b	2	56	lbw	–	–	–	–	–	–	–
383/307*			2	Bridgetown	L-181	1	72	c	1	77	c	1	–	–	–	–	–	–
384/308*			3	Georgetown	W-9w	2	169	c	–	–	–	–	–	–	–	–	–	–
385/309*			4	Port-of-Spain	D	1	44	c	4	30	*	–	–	–	–	36	43	0
386/310*			5	Kingston	W-9w	1	205	c	–	–	–	–	–	–	–	–	–	–
387/311*	1954	P	1	Lord's	D	1	0	b	–	–	–	–	–	–	–	–	–	–
390/314*			4	Oval	L-24	1	14	c	1	5	c	–	–	–	–	–	–	–
391/315*	1954–55	A	1	Brisbane[2]	L-I & 154	1	4	c	1	13	lbw	–	–	–	–	–	–	–
392/316*			2	Sydney	W-38	1	30	c	1	28	c	2	–	–	–	–	–	–
393/317*			3	Melbourne	W-128	1	12	c	1	42	lbw	–	–	–	–	–	–	–
394/318*			4	Adelaide	W-5w	1	80	c	1	5	c	–	–	–	–	–	–	–
395/319*			5	Sydney	D	1	6	c	–	–	–	–	–	–	–	6	2	1
401/320*	1954–55	NZ	1	Dunedin	W-8w	1	11	c	1	3	c	–	–	–	–	–	–	–
402/321*			2	Auckland	W-I & 20	5	53	b	–	–	–	1	–	–	–	–	–	–

Career	M	I	NO	HS	R	Avge	100	50	Ct	St	Balls	R	W	Avge	BB	5w	10w	Rate
Test	79	138	15	364	6971	56.67	19	33	57	–	260	232	3	77.33	1-2	–	–	86.66
F/c	513	814	91	364	40140	55.51	129	177	400	–	9774	5106	173	29.51	6-76	4	1	56.49

L. HUTTON – TEST BATTING SUMMARY

Series	V	M	I	NO	HS	R	Avge	100	50
1937	NZ	3	5	–	100	127	25.40	1	–
1938	A	3	4	–	364	473	118.25	2	–
1938–39	SA	4	6	–	92	265	44.16	–	2
1939	WI	3	6	1	196	480	96.00	2	1
1946	I	3	5	1	67	123	30.75	–	1
1946–47	A	5	9	1	122*	417	52.12	1	2
1947	SA	5	10	2	100	344	43.00	1	1
1947–48	WI	2	4	–	60	171	42.75	–	2
1948	A	4	8	–	81	342	42.75	–	4
1948–49	SA	5	9	–	158	577	64.11	2	2
1949	NZ	4	6	–	206	469	78.16	2	2
1950	WI	3	6	1	202*	333	66.60	1	–
1950–51	A	5	10	4	156*	533	88.83	1	4
1950–51	NZ	2	3	–	57	114	38.00	–	1
1951	SA	5	9	2	100	378	54.00	1	2
1952	I	4	6	1	150	399	79.80	2	1
1953	A	5	9	1	145	443	55.37	1	3
1953–54	WI	5	8	1	205	677	96.71	2	3
1954	P	2	3	–	14	19	6.33	–	–
1954–55	A	5	9	–	80	220	24.44	–	1
1954–55	NZ	2	3	–	53	67	22.33	–	1
	A	27	49	6	364	2428	56.46	5	14
	SA	19	34	4	158	1564	52.13	4	7
	WI	13	24	3	205	1661	79.09	5	6
	NZ	11	17	–	206	777	45.70	3	4
	I	7	11	2	150	522	58.00	2	2
	P	2	3	–	14	19	6.33	–	–
Home		44	77	9	364	3930	57.79	13	15
Overseas		35	61	6	205	3041	55.29	6	18
Totals		79	138	15	364	6971	56.67	19	33

HUTTON
Richard Anthony

Yorkshire (1962 to 1974)
Cambridge University (1962 to 1964)
Transvaal (1975–76)

TOURS
A 1971–72 (RW); WI 1963–64 (Swanton);
P 1966–67 (MCC U-25)
Born Pudsey, Yorkshire 6 Sep 1942

NOTABLE FEATS

- *692* Shared stand of 103 in 66 min with A.P.E. Knott which was the 7th-wkt E v I record until 1982.
- Exceeded 1000 runs in a season twice.
- Hat-trick for MCC U-25 v North Zone at Peshawar in 1966–67.

Although compelled to live in the shadow of his father, Richard Hutton was his own man and totally dissimilar to Sir Leonard as a cricketer. He arrived at Yorkshire dressing room after an outstanding career at Repton School and Cambridge (where he gained blues in each of his three years). An aggressive all-rounder with a well-honed but frequently sarcastic wit, he proved a worthy match for even the more militant campaigners in the Yorkshire dressing room. Tall (6ft 4½in) and strongly built, he was an efficient batsman, equally at home as an opener or in the middle order; he used his exceptional reach to advantage and was a powerful driver. With a high, smooth action his right-arm fast-medium bowling extracted awkward bounce and he was an accomplished seamer and cutter of the new ball. He was a reliable slip, a position from where he was able to launch his barbed comments with most telling effect. A devoted critic of Boycott's selfish behaviour as a captain, he eventually exchanged the internal strife of his native county for a career in accountancy and banking.

Richard Hutton

						Batting 1st			Batting 2nd				Bowling 1st			Bowling 2nd		
Ref	Series	V	T	Venue	Result	No	R	HO	No	R	HO	Ct	Balls	R	W	Balls	R	W
688/468	1971	P	2	Lord's	D	–	–	–	2	58	*	1	96	36	2	–	–	–
689/469			3	Leeds	W-25	8	28	c	8	4	c	3	246	72	3	36	18	0
690/470	1971	I	1	Lord's	D	8	20	b	8	0	b	2	144	38	2	18	12	0
691/471			2	Manchester	D	8	15	c	–	–	–	1	84	35	1	42	16	1
692/472			3	Oval	L-4w	8	81	b	8	13	*	2	72	30	0	–	–	–

Career	M	I	NO	HS	R	Avge	100	50	Ct	St	Balls	R	W	Avge	BB	5w	10w	Rate
Test	5	8	2	81	219	36.50	–	2	9	–	738	257	9	28.55	3-72	–	–	82.00
F/c	281	410	58	189	7561	21.48	5	29	216	–	34225	15008	625	24.01	8-50	21	3	54.76

IDDON, John

Lancashire (1924 to 1945)

TOURS
WI 1928–29 (Cahn), 1934–35
Born Mawdesley, Lancashire 8 Jan 1902
Died Madeley, Staffordshire
17 Apr 1946

The son of a professional at the Lancaster club, John Iddon honed his all-round skills for the Leyland Motors team as a forceful, hard-driving, middle-order batsman, a left-arm leg-break bowler especially dangerous on a wearing pitch, and a fine all-purpose fielder. His successful elevation to county cricket contributed to five Lancashire Championships. He also played soccer for Bolton Wanderers. A technical representative to a firm of brake-lining experts in Manchester, he was killed in a car accident while returning home from a business visit to the Rolls-Royce works. [*Illus. p.* 510]

NOTABLE FEATS

- Exceeded 1000 runs in a season 13 times, including 2381 in 1934.
- Scored 5 double centuries, all for Lancashire.
- Shared Lancashire record 6th-wkt stand of 278 with H.R.W. Butterworth v Sussex at Manchester in 1932.
- Took 9 for 42 for Lancashire v Yorkshire at Sheffield in 1937.

Ref	Series	V	T	Venue	Result	Batting 1st No	R	HO	Batting 2nd No	R	HO	Ct	Bowling 1st Balls	R	W	Bowling 2nd Balls	R	W
238/212	1934–35	WI	1	Bridgetown	W-4w	7	14	*	–	–	–	–	–	–	–	–	–	–
239/213			2	Port-of-Spain	L-217	7	73	c	10	0	c	–	–	–	–	–	–	–
240/214			3	Georgetown	D	9	0	lbw	–	–	–	–	–	–	–	–	–	–
241/215			4	Kingston	L-I & 161	8	54	lbw	1	0	lbw	–	42	24	0	–	–	–
242/216	1935	SA	1	Nottingham	D	7	29	c	–	–	–	–	24	3	0	–	–	–

Career	M	I	NO	HS	R	Avge	100	50	Ct	St	Balls	R	W	Avge	BB	5w	10w	Rate
Test	5	7	1	73	170	28.33	–	2	–	–	66	27	0	–	–	–	–	–
F/c	504	712	95	222	22681	36.76	46	112	217	–	38689	14823	551	26.90	9-42	14	2	70.21

IKIN, John Thomas

Lancashire (1939 to 1957)

TOURS
A 1946–47; WI 1947–48; NZ 1946–47; I/SL 1950–51 (Cwlth)
Born Bignall End, Staffordshire
7 Mar 1918
Died Bignall End 15 Sep 1984

Jack Ikin

Jack Ikin was a sound left-handed opening or middle-order batsman and an inspired close fielder at slip or short leg. It was this adaptability which made him such a frequent choice for England when his output of just three fifties in 31 innings scarcely justified such confidence. He even appeared for England before he had been awarded his Lancashire cap. Slightly built and of medium height (5ft 9in), he was a determined and courageous player who never gave his wicket away without a fight. There have been few braver displays than his second innings vigil in Test 336 when he with-stood a cruel onslaught from Cuan McCarthy on a lively pitch in poor light to partner Hutton towards an England victory. When, some 25 years later, Hutton was reminded of the occasion and Ikin's contribution was described as 'a great innings', Sir Leonard shook his head gravely and said: 'No. It wasn't a great knock. He was down the wrong end!' Ikin was an accurate right-arm leg-break and googly bowler who produced several fine perform-ances at county level. He played for Staffordshire before and after leaving Lancashire, captaining his native county from 1958 to 1968. A calm, affable and generous man, he was a popular assistant manager in Australia and New Zealand on the 1965–66 tour and contributed much as a coach, first at Denstone College and subsequently at schools throughout the North and Midlands.

NOTABLE FEATS

- Exceeded 1000 runs in a season 10 times (plus once on tour).
- Carried his bat through a completed Lancashire innings twice.
- Hat-trick for Lancashire v Somerset at Taunton in 1949.
- Achieved the match 'double' for Lancashire v Nottinghamshire at Manchester in 1947.
- Held 5 catches in an innings for MCC v Auckland in 1946–47 to equal the New Zealand record. Held 55 catches in 1946.

Ref	Series	V	T	Venue	Result	Batting 1st No	R	HO	Batting 2nd No	R	HO	Ct	Bowling 1st Balls	R	W	Bowling 2nd Balls	R	W
276/244	1946	I	1	Lord's	W-10w	7	16	c	–	–	–	2	–	–	–	60	43	1
277/245			2	Manchester	D	7	2	c	7	29	*	3	12	11	0	–	–	–
279/247	1946–47	A	1	Brisbane[2]	L-I & 332	6	0	c	6	32	b	–	16	24	0	–	–	–
280/248			2	Sydney	L-133	6	60	c	6	17	b	1	24	15	0	–	–	–
281/249			3	Melbourne	D	6	48	c	6	5	c	–	–	–	–	–	–	–
282/250			4	Adelaide	D	7	21	c	7	1	lbw	–	16	9	0	–	–	–
283/251			5	Sydney	L-5w	7	0	b	5	0	st	3	–	–	–	–	–	–
284/252	1946–47	NZ		Christchurch	D	6	45	c	–	–	–	–	–	–	–	–	–	–
295/258	1947–48	WI	1	Bridgetown	D	5	3	c	–	–	–	4	96	38	1	72	48	0
296/259			2	Port-of-Spain	D	3	21	b	3	19	lbw	1	120	60	0	–	–	–
297/260			3	Georgetown	L-7w	5	7	c	8	24	ro	–	30	22	0	–	–	–
298/261			4	Kingston	L-10w	7	5	ro	7	3	c	–	114	69	1	12	15	0

Ref	Series	V	T	Venue	Result	Batting 1st No	R	HO	Batting 2nd No	R	HO	Ct	Bowling 1st Balls	R	W	Bowling 2nd Balls	R	W
334/287	1951	SA	1	Nottingham	L-71	2	1	c	2	33	b	3	–	–	–	–	–	–
335/288			2	Lord's	W-10w	2	51	b	2	4	*	4	–	–	–	–	–	–
336/289			3	Manchester	W-9w	2	22	c	2	38	b	5	–	–	–	–	–	–
353/299	1952	I	3	Manchester	W-I & 207	3	29	c	–	–	–	3	–	–	–	–	–	–
354/300			4	Oval	D	3	53	c	–	–	–	1	–	–	–	–	–	–
412/326	1955	SA	5	Oval	W-92	1	17	c	1	0	c	1	–	–	–	–	–	–

Career	M	I	NO	HS	R	Avge	100	50	Ct	St	Balls	R	W	Avge	BB	5w	10w	Rate
Test	18	31	2	60	606	20.89	–	3	31	–	572	354	3	118.00	1-38	–	–	190.66
F/c	365	554	66	192	17968	36.81	27	108	419	–	22654	10262	339	30.27	6-21	11	1	66.82

ILLINGWORTH Raymond CBE

Yorkshire (1951 to 1983)
Leicestershire (1969 to 1978)

Wisden 1960

TOURS

A 1962–63, 1970–71; SA 1960–61 (Cav); WI 1959–60; NZ 1962–63, 1970–71

Born Pudsey, Yorkshire 8 Jun 1932

Ray Illingworth

Ray Illingworth crowded three separate playing careers into a span of 33 summers. Joining Yorkshire as a medium-pace swing bowler, he served them loyally for 18 seasons (1951–68) as a sound middle-order batsman, meanly accurate off-spinner and aggressive gully fielder. Tall (5ft 11½in), strong, determined and militantly professional, he was the vital member of a team which ended Surrey's domination and gained Yorkshire its last seven Championships. Then, following a dispute over his contract, he moved to Leicestershire as captain. Within a few weeks Colin Cowdrey had torn an Achilles tendon and he found himself captain of England. Although his tenure was originally meant to be temporary, he revealed such admirable leadership qualities and sound tactical skills that he held the post for 31 Tests. His tally of 12 wins and five defeats included a sequence of 19 matches before his first defeat and under his careful direction the Ashes were regained and successfully defended. Importantly, his new responsibility lifted his own game at the highest level; having achieved little of note in 30 Tests spread over 13 rubbers before his appointment, he now bowled shrewdly at decisive moments and embarked on a succession of telling innings based on rugged defence and bold front-foot strokes. By the time he retired from the county scene in his 47th year he had led Leicestershire for ten seasons (1969–78) and gained them their first-ever trophies: the 1975 Championship and four one-day titles. Yorkshire, who had achieved little except internal mayhem since his departure, immediately recruited him as cricket manager (1979–84). When the petals fell off the white rose during the 1982 season, he was persuaded to step into the breach, becoming at the age of 50 Yorkshire's oldest appointed captain. In 1986 a fourth career chapter offered itself in the form of the England team managership but 'Illy' wanted more power than the TCCB was inclined to bestow, a decision welcomed by those who enjoy his pithy comments as a TV pundit.

NOTABLE FEATS

- 1000 runs in 41st Test (*678*) (57 inns). 50 wickets in 26th Test (*620*); 100 wickets and the Test 'double' in 47th Test (*689*).
- *691* Shared record E v I 8th-wkt stand of 168 with P. Lever.
- Exceeded 1000 runs in a season 8 times, took 100 wickets on 10 occasions and completed the 'double' 6 times.
- Shared record Leicestershire 10th-wkt stand of 228 with K. Higgs v Northamptonshire at Leicester in 1977.
- Took 9 for 42 for Yorkshire v Worcestershire at Worcester in 1957 and achieved match figures of 15 for 123 for Yorkshire v Glamorgan at Swansea in 1960.
- Hat-trick for Leicestershire v Surrey at The Oval in 1975.
- Acheived match 'double' (135 runs and 14 for 101) for Yorkshire v Kent at Dover in 1964.

						Batting 1st			Batting 2nd				Bowling 1st			Bowling 2nd		
Ref	Series	V	T	Venue	Result	No	R	HO	No	R	HO	Ct	Balls	R	W	Balls	R	W
457/345	1958	NZ	4	Manchester	W-I & 13	8	3	*	–	–	–	–	168	39	1	102	20	2
477/357	1959	I	4	Manchester	W-171	7	21	c	7	47	*	3	96	16	2	234	63	1
478/358			5	Oval	W-I & 27	7	50	c	–	–	–	2	6	2	0	174	43	1
487/359	1959–60	WI	1	Bridgetown	D	7	5	b	–	–	–	–	282	106	0	–	–	–
488/360			2	Port-of-Spain	W-256	7	10	b	7	41	*	–	42	8	0	168	38	0
489/361			3	Kingston	D	7	17	c	7	6	b	1	180	46	2	78	35	0
490/362			4	Georgetown	D	7	4	b	6	9	c	–	258	72	0	–	–	–
491/363			5	Port-of-Spain	D	8	0	c	–	–	–	–	72	25	0	96	53	2
492/364	1960	SA	1	Birmingham	W-100	7	1	b	6	16	c	–	102	15	3	144	57	3
493/365			2	Lord's	W-I & 73	8	0	*	–	–	–	–	–	–	–	6	0	0
494/366			3	Nottingham	W-8w	7	37	c	–	–	–	1	–	–	–	114	33	0
495/367			4	Manchester	D	8	22	*	4	5	c	–	66	35	0	30	6	0
507/369	1961	A	1	Birmingham	D	7	15	c	–	–	–	2	264	110	2	–	–	–
508/370			2	Lord's	L-5w	7	13	b	7	0	c	3	69	16	1	–	–	–
534/386	1962	P	5	Oval	W-10w	7	2	*	–	–	–	–	78	27	0	126	54	1
538/390	1962–63	A	4	Adelaide	D	8	12	c	–	–	–	–	160	85	1	40	23	0
539/391			5	Sydney	D	6	27	c	2	18	c	–	40	15	0	80	8	0
540/392	1962–63	NZ	1	Auckland	W-I & 215	2	20	c	–	–	–	2	6	5	0	108	34	4
541/393			2	Wellington	W-I & 47	2	46	c	–	–	–	2	–	–	–	162	34	1
542/394			3	Christchurch	W-7w	2	2	c	–	–	–	–	–	–	–	–	–	–
593/417	1965	NZ	3	Leeds	W-I & 187	–	–	–	–	–	–	–	168	42	4	42	28	0
607/431	1966	WI	3	Nottingham	L-139	8	0	c	8	4	c	1	48	21	0	150	82	0
609/433			5	Oval	W-I & 34	8	3	c	–	–	–	1	90	40	2	90	22	2
618/434	1967	I	1	Leeds	W-6w	–	–	–	6	12	*	1	132	31	3	348	100	4
619/435			2	Lord's	W-I & 124	8	4	lbw	–	–	–	1	12	0	1	135	29	6
620/436			3	Birmingham	W-132	8	2	c	8	10	c	–	42	14	2	258	92	4
621/437	1967	P	1	Lord's	D	8	4	b	8	9	c	–	186	48	2	90	10	1
639/447	1968	A	3	Birmingham	D	8	27	lbw	–	–	–	1	132	37	3	32	4	0
640/448			4	Leeds	D	8	6	c	–	–	–	–	174	47	1	306	87	6
641/449			5	Oval	W-226	8	8	lbw	8	10	b	–	288	87	2	168	29	1
653/453*	1969	WI	1	Manchester	W-10w	7	21	c	–	–	–	2	36	23	0	180	52	1
654/454*			2	Lord's	D	8	113	c	7	9	*	2	96	39	0	162	66	3
655/455*			3	Leeds	W-30	7	1	b	7	19	c	–	–	–	–	84	38	1
656/456*	1969	NZ	1	Lord's	W-230	7	53	c	7	0	c	2	132	37	4	108	24	0
657/457*			2	Nottingham	D	7	33	lbw	–	–	–	–	72	15	2	12	3	1
658/458*			3	Oval	W-8w	7	4	c	–	–	–	1	195	55	3	90	20	0
674/459*	1970–71	A	1	Brisbane[2]	D	8	8	c	–	–	–	1	88	47	0	144	19	1
675/460*			2	Perth	D	8	34	b	7	29	c	2	104	43	1	32	12	0
676/461*			4	Sydney	W-299	6	25	b	6	53	st	–	112	59	1	72	9	0
677/462*			5	Melbourne	D	6	41	c	–	–	–	–	104	59	2	–	–	–
678/463*			6	Adelaide	D	7	24	b	6	48	*	1	40	14	1	112	32	0
679/464*			7	Sydney	W-62	6	42	b	6	29	lbw	–	88	16	1	160	39	3
685/465*	1970–71	NZ	1	Christchurch	W-8w	6	36	b	–	–	–	2	48	12	0	136	45	0
686/466*			2	Auckland	D	6	0	c	4	22	c	–	144	45	0	–	–	–
687/467*	1971	P	1	Birmingham	D	6	1	b	6	1	c	–	156	72	3	–	–	–
688/468*			2	Lord's	D	–	–	–	–	–	–	–	42	1	0	–	–	–
689/469*			3	Leeds	W-25	7	20	b	7	45	c	–	168	31	0	156	58	3
690/470*	1971	I	1	Lord's	D	7	33	c	7	20	c	3	150	43	0	96	33	2
691/471*			2	Manchester	D	7	107	c	–	–	–	–	42	16	0	–	–	–
692/472*			3	Oval	L-4w	7	11	b	7	4	c	1	207	70	5	216	40	0
698/473*	1972	A	1	Manchester	W-89	8	26	*	8	14	c	1	–	–	–	–	–	–
699/474*			2	Lord's	L-8w	8	30	lbw	8	12	c	1	42	13	1	–	–	–
700/475*			3	Nottingham	D	9	24	*	–	–	–	–	–	–	–	90	41	1
701/476*			4	Leeds	W-9w	8	57	lbw	–	–	–	4	126	32	2	115	32	2
702/477*			5	Oval	L-5w	7	0	c	7	31	lbw	–	102	53	1	53	26	0
722/486*	1973	NZ	1	Nottingham	W-38	7	8	b	7	3	c	1	–	–	–	126	31	0
723/487*			2	Lord's	D	6	3	c	6	22	c	–	234	87	0	–	–	–
724/488*			3	Leeds	W-I & 1	6	65	lbw	–	–	–	–	36	20	0	12	1	0
725/489*	1973	WI	1	Oval	L-158	7	27	lbw	8	40	b	–	90	43	0	144	50	3
726/490*			2	Birmingham	D	8	27	lbw	–	–	–	–	192	37	1	156	67	1
727/491*			3	Lord's	L-I & 226	7	0	c	8	13	c	–	190	114	1	–	–	–

Career	M	I	NO	HS	R	Avge	100	50	Ct	St	Balls	R	W	Avge	BB	5w	10w	Rate
Test	61	90	11	113	1836	23.24	2	5	45	–	11934	3807	122	31.20	6-29	3	–	97.81
F/c	787	1073	213	162	24134	28.06	22	105	446	–	117866	42023	2072	20.28	9-42	104	11	56.88

R. ILLINGWORTH – TEST SUMMARY

Series	V	M	I	NO	HS	R	Avge	100	50	Balls	R	W	Avge	BB	5w	10w	Rate
1958	NZ	1	1	1	3*	3	–	–	–	270	59	3	19.66	2-20	–	–	90.00
1959	I	2	3	1	50	118	59.00	–	1	510	124	4	31.00	2-16	–	–	127.50
1959–60	WI	5	8	1	41*	92	13.14	–	–	1176	383	4	95.75	2-46	–	–	294.00
1960	SA	4	6	2	37	81	20.25	–	–	462	146	6	24.33	3-15	–	–	77.00
1961	A	2	3	–	15	28	9.33	–	–	333	126	3	42.00	2-110	–	–	111.00
1962	P	1	1	1	2*	2	–	–	–	204	81	1	81.00	1-54	–	–	204.00
1962–63	A	2	3	–	27	57	19.00	–	–	320	131	1	131.00	1-85	–	–	320.00
1962–63	NZ	3	3	–	46	68	22.66	–	–	276	73	5	14.60	4.34	–	–	55.20
1965	NZ	1	–	–	–	–	–	–	–	210	70	4	17.50	4-42	–	–	52.50
1966	WI	2	3	–	4	7	2.33	–	–	378	165	4	41.25	2-22	–	–	94.50
1967	I	3	4	1	12*	28	9.33	–	–	927	266	20	13.30	6-29	1	–	46.35
1967	P	1	2	–	9	13	6.50	–	–	276	58	3	19.33	2-48	–	–	92.00
1968	A	3	4	–	27	51	12.75	–	–	1100	291	13	22.38	6-87	1	–	84.61
1969	WI	3	5	1	113	163	40.75	1	–	558	218	5	43.60	3-66	–	–	111.60
1969	NZ	3	4	–	53	90	22.50	–	1	609	154	10	15.40	4-37	–	–	60.90
1970–71	A	6	10	1	53	333	37.00	–	1	1056	349	10	34.90	3-39	–	–	105.60
1970–71	NZ	2	3	–	36	58	19.33	–	–	328	102	0	–	–	–	–	–
1971	P	3	4	–	45	67	16.75	–	–	522	162	6	27.00	3-58	–	–	87.00
1971	I	3	5	–	107	175	35.00	1	–	711	202	7	28.85	5-70	1	–	101.57
1972	A	5	8	2	57	194	32.33	–	1	528	197	7	28.14	2-32	–	–	75.42
1973	NZ	3	5	–	65	101	20.20	–	1	408	139	0	–	–	–	–	–
1973	WI	3	5	–	40	107	21.40	–	–	772	311	6	51.83	3-50	–	–	128.66
	A	18	28	3	57	663	25.52	–	2	3337	1094	34	32.17	6-87	1	–	98.14
	SA	4	6	2	37	81	20.25	–	–	462	146	6	24.33	3-15	–	–	77.00
	WI	13	21	2	113	369	19.42	1	–	2884	1077	19	56.68	3-50	–	–	151.78
	NZ	13	16	1	65	320	21.33	–	2	2101	597	22	27.13	4-34	–	–	95.50
	I	8	12	2	107	321	32.10	1	1	2148	592	31	19.09	6-29	2	–	69.29
	P	5	7	1	45	82	13.66	–	–	1002	301	10	30.10	3-58	–	–	100.20
Home		43	63	9	113	1228	22.74	2	4	8778	2769	102	27.14	6-29	3	–	86.05
Overseas		18	27	2	53	608	24.32	–	1	3156	1038	20	51.90	4-34	–	–	157.80
Totals		61	90	11	113	1836	23.24	2	5	11934	3807	122	31.20	6-29	3	–	97.81

TEST NOTES

• *702* J.H. Edrich deputised as captain from 5.20 on the fourth evening when Illingworth damaged his ankle in the bowlers' rough.

INSOLE
Douglas John CBE

Cambridge University (1947 to 1949)
Essex (1947 to 1963)

Wisden 1956
TOUR SA 1956–57
Born Clapton, Middlesex 18 Apr 1926

Doug Insole was a rugged, unorthodox but extremely consistent, prolific and resolute early-order batsman who was unlucky not to find greater favour with the selectors. When he did appear throughout a complete series he produced his best form and headed the England averages. Of medium height (5ft 9½in) and stockily built, he was also a handy right-arm medium-pace change bowler and a daring all-purpose fielder who could keep wicket in an emergency. At Cambridge he was a blue in each of his three years and captain in his last. He led Essex (1950–60), improving their performances with much good humour and tactical skill. Despite his demanding schedule as executive of a construction company, he has been a tireless and tactful administrator since his playing career. His many roles have included Test selector and chairman, TCCB chairman and manager of

Doug Insole

two tours to Australia. He was one of England's two negotiators at the 1989 ICC special meeting which agreed a ban on players visiting South Africa. A soccer blue, he captained Cambridge and appeared for Corinthian Casuals in the 1955–56 FA Amateur Cup Final.

NOTABLE FEATS

- Exceeded 1000 runs in a season 13 times, including 2000 on 3 occasions.
- Scored 1237 runs in the season of his first-class debut (1947).
- His 9 hundreds in 1955 equalled the Essex record set in 1934 by J. O'Connor.
- Held 5 catches in an innings for Essex v Lancashire at Blackpool in 1958.

						Batting 1st			Batting 2nd			
Ref	Series	V	T	Venue	Result	No	R	HO	No	R	HO	Ct
325/278	1950	WI	3	Nottingham	L-10w	6	21	lbw	6	0	st	1
411/325	1955	SA	4	Leeds	L-224	7	3	lbw	4	47	c	–
427/329	1956	A	3	Leeds	W-I & 42	7	5	c	–	–	–	–
434/332	1956–57	SA	1	Johannesburg[3]	W-131	6	1	c	5	29	c	4
435/333			2	Cape Town	W-312	6	29	c	7	3	*	–
436/334			3	Durban[2]	D	6	13	b	4	110	*	1
437/335			4	Johannesburg[3]	L-17	3	47	ro	3	68	c	2
438/336			5	Port Elizabeth	L-58	5	4	lbw	5	8	c	–
439/337	1957	WI	1	Birmingham	D	3	20	b	3	0	b	–

Career	M	I	NO	HS	R	Avge	100	50	Ct	St	Balls	R	W	Avge	BB	5w	10w	Rate
Test	9	17	2	110*	408	27.20	1	1	8	–	–	–	–	–	–	–	–	–
F/c	450	743	72	219*	25241	37.61	54	126	366	6	9068	4680	138	33.91	5-22	1	–	65.71

JACKMAN Robin David

Surrey (1966 to 1982)
Western Province (1971–72)
Rhodesia (1972–73 to 1979–80)

Wisden 1981
TOURS
A 1982–83; SA 1972–73 (Robins); WI 1980–81
Born Simla, India 13 Aug 1945

NOTABLE FEATS

- *897* Dismissed C.G. Greenidge with his fifth ball in Test cricket.
- Took 121 wickets (avge 15.40) in 1980 (leading bowler).
- Three hat-tricks: two for Surrey – v Kent at Canterbury in 1971 and v Yorkshire at Leeds in 1973; and one for Western Province v Natal at Pietermaritzburg in 1971–72.

As a right-arm fast-medium bowler Robin Jackman came into the 'terrier' category: he was lively, moved about a lot and was constantly barking the most piercing appeals. Just a touch above medium height (5ft 9½in) and far from robust in build, his main assets were his stamina, dogged determination, accuracy and the ability to move the ball away late. He reserved some of his more dramatic bursts of wicket-taking for Yorkshire and frequently dismissed high-class players. He arrived at The Oval as a batsman but long spells of labour with the ball condemned him to a life in the lower-order and only occasionally did he reveal some spirited but often impromptu strokes and a sound defence. He was an energetic and aggressive fielder. At the age of 35 he was summoned to the Caribbean as a substitute for a damaged Bob Willis. His South African connections offended the Forbes Burnham administration to such an extent

Robin Jackman

that his visa was revoked soon after his arrival in Guyana, thus prompting the Cricket Council to cancel the Georgetown Test. Alan Gibson's 'Shoreditch Sparrow' now combines the management of Western Province with coaching and broadcasting, returning to England each summer for a brief interlude as a chirpy radio and TV pundit.

Ref	Series	V	T	Venue	Result	Batting 1st No	R	HO	Batting 2nd No	R	HO	Ct	Bowling 1st Balls	R	W	Bowling 2nd Balls	R	W
897/564	1980–81	WI	3	Bridgetown	L-298	10	7	c	10	7	b	–	132	65	3	150	76	2
899/566			5	Kingston	D	10	0	c	–	–	–	–	158	57	1	–	–	–
932/584	1982	P	2	Lord's	L-10w	11	0	lbw	11	17	c	–	216	110	4	24	22	0
933/585			3	Leeds	W-3w	10	11	c	–	–	–	–	222	74	3	168	41	1

Career	M	I	NO	HS	R	Avge	100	50	Ct	St	Balls	R	W	Avge	BB	5w	10w	Rate
Test	4	6	0	17	42	7.00	–	–	–	–	1070	445	14	31.78	4-110	–	–	76.42
F/c	399	478	157	92*	5681	17.69	–	7	177	–	68263	31978	1402	22.80	8-40	67	8	48.68

JACKSON
Rt Hon. Sir Francis Stanley GCSI, GCIE

Cambridge University (1890 to 1893)
Yorkshire (1890 to 1907)

Wisden 1894
TOUR I 1892–93
Born Chapel Allerton, Yorkshire
21 Nov 1870
Died Knightsbridge, London 9 May 1947

F.S. Jackson

F.S. (later Sir Stanley) Jackson epitomised cricket's 'Golden Age' of the Edwardian era. Tall and impressive, he was a stylish middle-order batsman who combined natural timing with a keen appetite for driving and cutting, a right-arm brisk-medium bowler who mixed off-breaks with subtle changes of pace, and an athletic cover fielder. Captain of cricket at Harrow where Winston Churchill was his fag, 'Jacker' also led Cambridge astutely in the final half of his four-blue residence. At Yorkshire he played all his cricket under the command of Lord Hawke, being destined like Len Hutton after him to skipper his country but never his county. Business duties prevented his touring Australia and permitted just one uninterrupted summer at home. During it he revealed his considerable all-round talents by scoring 1566 runs and taking 104 wickets. The pinnacle of a Test career confined exclusively to playing against Australia in England was reached in 1905 ('Jackson's Year') when he totally dominated a series in which he won every toss, headed both the batting and bowling averages and retained the Ashes. Curiously, Joe Darling, his rival captain in that rubber, was born on exactly the same day. It was the season in which he also took 8 for 13 in a Roses match. His devotion to cricket led to a keen involvement in administration for the last 40 years of his life, his various roles including the presidencies of MCC and Yorkshire and chairman of selectors. In between he found a few moments to serve in the Boer War, and be MP for the Howdenshire division of Yorkshire (1915–26), financial secretary to the War Office and chairman of the Unionist party. As Governor of Bengal he narrowly escaped assassination.

NOTABLE FEATS

- 1000 runs in 16th Test (*83*) (26 inns).
- *40* His 100 took 135 min and was the first in a Test in England to be completed with a hit over the boundary (then worth only 4 runs).
- *64* His stand of 185 with T.W. Hayward was then England's highest for any wicket in England and the record opening partnership by either side in E v A Tests.
- *83* Dismissed M.A. Noble, C. Hill and J. Darling in one over (W.1W.W).
- *85* Batted 268 min for 144* – the first 100 in a Leeds Test.
- *86* First to score 5 Test hundreds in England and remains the only batsman to score 5 hundreds v Australia in England.
- *87* First captain to win every toss in a 5-match rubber.
- Exceeded 1000 runs in a season 10 times and took 100 wickets once (1898) to complete the 'double'.
- Contributed 117 to Yorkshire's 887 in 10hr 50min v Warwickshire at Birmingham in 1896; the highest and longest innings in county cricket, it was the first first-class match to include hundreds by 4 batsmen.
- Took 4 wickets in 5 balls for Yorkshire v Australians at Leeds in 1902.
- Bowled unchanged throughout both innings with S.M.J. Woods for Gentlemen v Players at Lord's in 1894.

						Batting 1st			Batting 2nd				Bowling 1st			Bowling 2nd		
Ref	Series	V	T	Venue	Result	No	R	HO	No	R	HO	Ct	Balls	R	W	Balls	R	W
39/39	1893	A	1	Lord's	D	4	91	c	4	5	c	–	25	10	0	–	–	–
40/40			2	Oval	W-I & 43	7	103	ro	–	–	–	2	–	–	–	55	33	0
50/50	1896	A	1	Lord's	W-6w	6	44	c	–	–	–	1	–	–	–	55	28	0
51/51			2	Manchester	L-3w	5	18	ro	5	1	c	2	80	34	0	–	–	–
52/52			3	Oval	W-66	2	45	c	2	2	b	1	–	–	–	–	–	–
60/60	1899	A	1	Nottingham	D	3	8	c	3	0	b	–	55	27	0	130	57	3
61/61			2	Lord's	L-10w	5	73	b	5	37	c	–	90	31	0	–	–	–
62/62			3	Leeds	D	5	9	b	–	–	–	–	25	18	0	55	13	1
63/63			4	Manchester	D	5	44	c	5	14	*	–	18	9	1	90	36	0
64/64			5	Oval	D	1	118	b	–	–	–	–	70	39	0	65	54	0
70/70	1902	A	1	Birmingham	D	4	53	b	–	–	–	1	–	–	–	24	7	0
71/71			2	Lord's	D	4	55	*	–	–	–	–	–	–	–	–	–	–
72/72			3	Sheffield	L-143	4	3	c	6	14	b	1	31	11	1	102	60	3
73/73			4	Manchester	L-3	6	128	c	6	7	c	–	66	58	0	–	–	–
74/74			5	Oval	W-1w	5	2	c	5	49	c	1	120	66	2	24	7	0
83/80*	1905	A	1	Nottingham	W-213	5	0	b	5	82	*	1	89	52	5	30	6	0
84/81*			2	Lord's	D	5	29	c	5	0	b	–	90	50	4	–	–	–
85/82*			3	Leeds	D	5	144	*	5	17	c	–	24	10	1	48	10	0
86/83*			4	Manchester	W-I & 80	5	113	c	–	–	–	–	42	26	2	30	20	0
87/84*			5	Oval	D	5	76	c	6	31	b	–	54	27	1	–	–	–

Career	M	I	NO	HS	R	Avge	100	50	Ct	St	Balls	R	W	Avge	BB	5w	10w	Rate
Test	20	33	4	144*	1415	48.79	5	6	10	–	1587	799	24	33.29	5-52	1	–	66.12
F/c	309	505	35	160	15901	33.83	31	76	195	–	54624	15767	774	20.37	8-54	42	6	70.57

F. S. JACKSON – TEST BATTING SUMMARY

Series	V	M	I	NO	HS	R	Avge	100	50
1893	A	2	3	–	103	199	66.33	1	1
1896	A	3	5	–	45	110	22.00	–	–
1899	A	5	8	1	118	303	43.28	1	1
1902	A	5	8	1	128	311	44.42	1	2
1905	A	5	9	2	144*	492	70.28	2	2
Totals		20	33	4	144*	1415	48.79	5	6

JACKSON
Herbert Leslie

Derbyshire (1947 to 1963)

Wisden 1959
TOUR I 1950–51 (Cwlth)
Born Whitwell, Derbyshire 5 Apr 1921

NOTABLE FEATS

• Took 100 wickets in a season 10 times, including 143 at 10.99 in 1958 – the lowest average for 100 wkts or more since 1894 – and 160 in 1960. Headed the national averages in 1953 and 1958.
• Holds the Derbyshire record for most wickets in a career (1670).
• Took 9 for 17 v Cambridge U at Fenner's in 1959 and 9 for 60 v Lancashire at Manchester in 1952, both for Derbyshire.

Les Jackson

• Two hat-tricks for Derbyshire v Worcestershire: at Kidderminster in 1958 and at Derby in 1960.

Les Jackson was a tall (6ft), strong right-arm fast-medium bowler with a slinging action. Hostile and meanly accurate, he gained exceptional seam movement, particularly from Derbyshire's well-grassed pitches. From 1947 to 1958 he formed with Cliff Gladwin the most feared attack in Derbyshire's history. After Gladwin's retirement he continued to bear a vast workload, his mining stamina enabling him to maintain his form and fitness into his early forties. During a period when England's new-ball bowling resources virtually began and ended with Alec Bedser, it is astonishing that Jackson was chosen for only two Test matches and those almost 12 years apart. His only tour ended in severe illness after just two matches.

						Batting 1st			Batting 2nd				Bowling 1st			Bowling 2nd		
Ref	Series	V	T	Venue	Result	No	R	HO	No	R	HO	Ct	Balls	R	W	Balls	R	W
316/274	1949	NZ	3	Manchester	D	11	7	*	–	–	–	–	162	47	2	72	25	1
509/371	1961	A	3	Leeds	W-8w	11	8	ro	–	–	–	1	186	57	2	78	26	2

Career	M	I	NO	HS	R	Avge	100	50	Ct	St	Balls	R	W	Avge	BB	5w	10w	Rate
Test	2	2	1	8	15	15.00	–	–	1	–	498	155	7	22.14	2-26	–	–	71.14
F/c	418	489	153	39*	2083	6.19	–	–	136	–	83212	30101	1733	17.36	9-17	115	20	48.01

JAMESON
John Alexander

Warwickshire (1960 to 1976)

TOURS
WI 1973–74; Z 1972–73 (Int XI)
Born Byculla, Bombay, India 30 Jun 1941

John Jameson was a tall (6ft), robust, excitingly aggressive opening batsman who struck the ball cleanly and with great gusto. Medium pacers were his special prey and he would drive and pull them mercilessly. He was also a useful right-arm change bowler whose brisk off-breaks once produced a hat-trick, a capable emergency wicket-keeper and a sound fielder, initially at cover-point and later in the slip cordon. Quiet and unassuming off the field, he changed character completely when he picked up his bat and sighted a shiny new ball. From his early days at Taunton School he always sought to dominate the bowling and he gave many a Warwickshire innings a rousing start, none more so than during his world-record partnership with Rohan Kanhai. When his dashing approach eventually found favour with the selectors his prospects were not improved by his being run out in three of his first four innings, including England's only instance of twice in the same Test. It was splendidly typical of his style that his first ball in Test cricket in the Caribbean should be mis-hooked for six over the slips. He retired early to take a coaching engagement at his old school before becoming, successively, a first-class umpire (1984–87), senior coach to Sussex (1988) and MCC assistant secretary (1989).

NOTABLE FEATS

- Exceeded 1000 runs in a season 11 times.
- Contributed his highest score (240*) to world record 2nd-wkt stand of 465* with R.B. Kanhai for Warwickshire v Gloucestershire at Birmingham in 1974. It is the 10th-highest partnership in all first-class cricket and the highest unbroken stand in Britain.
- Scored hundreds in 3 consecutive innings in 1974.
- Scored 100 before lunch on 3 occasions, including his final first-class innings (v Glamorgan at Birmingham in 1976).
- Hat-trick for Warwickshire v Gloucestershire at Birmingham in 1965.
- Held 5 catches in an innings for Warwickshire v Indians at Birmingham in 1971.

John Jameson

						Batting 1st			Batting 2nd				Bowling 1st			Bowling 2nd		
Ref	Series	V	T	Venue	Result	No	R	HO	No	R	HO	Ct	Balls	R	W	Balls	R	W
691/471	1971	I	2	Manchester	D	2	15	c	2	28	ro	–	–	–	–	–	–	–
692/472			3	Oval	L-4w	2	82	ro	2	16	ro	–	–	–	–	–	–	–
732/493	1973–74	WI	2	KIngston	D	3	23	st	3	38	c	–	42	17	1	–	–	–
733/494			3	Bridgetown	D	3	3	c	3	9	lbw	–	–	–	–	–	–	–

Career	M	I	NO	HS	R	Avge	100	50	Ct	St	Balls	R	W	Avge	BB	5w	10w	Rate
Test	4	8	0	82	214	26.75	–	1	–	–	42	17	1	17.00	1-17	–	–	42.00
F/c	361	611	43	240*	18941	33.34	33	88	255	1	7275	3782	89	42.49	4-22	–	–	81.74

JARDINE
Douglas Robert

Oxford University (1920 to 1923)
Surrey (1921 to 1933)

Wisden 1928
TOURS
A 1928–29, 1932–33; NZ 1932–33; I/SL 1933–34
Born Malabar Hill, Bombay, India 23 Oct 1900
Died Montreux, Switzerland 18 Jun 1958

Douglas Jardine

Douglas Jardine was the most controversial captain in Test match history but many of his contemporaries assessed him as England's greatest leader. A man of formidable and resolute character, his single-minded dedication to reducing Bradman's run-making to normal proportions by devising and directing contentious fast leg-theory or 'bodyline' tactics produced the most turbulent Test series in history. His strategy provoked an exchange of cables between the Australian Board and MCC, then the governing body of English cricket, that threatened to end the tour and sever relations between the two bodies. An uneasy peace resulted, Bradman – career Test average 99.94 – was confined to 396 runs at 56.57, England regained the Ashes and 'bodyline' was eventually banned. England lost only once and won nine times during Jardine's 15-match reign. To his players he was a fair man with admirable self discipline who inspired great loyalty; the proudest possession in Harold Larwood's collection was a silver ashtray inscribed: 'To Harold for the Ashes 1932–33. From a grateful skipper'. Jardine developed his cricket at Winchester under the expert guidance of Rockley Wilson, the former Yorkshire captain, before gaining three blues at Oxford (a knee injury deprived him of a fourth). Tall (6ft), angular and austere, he was of Scottish descent; his father, an Oxford captain, played six matches for Middlesex before returning to India and becoming advocate-general of Bombay. Usually sporting the colourful Oxford Harlequin cap, he was a dominant figure at the crease; a determined and stylish batsman of immense courage who was strong off the back foot and favoured the on-side. When the West Indian fast bowlers Constantine and Martindale gave him a violent dose of his own medicine soon after the 'bodyline' series, he countered with a brave and skilful century. He was a handy leg-break bowler and reliable fielder. Although still in his prime as a batsman and despite having captained Surrey astutely for two seasons, he decided to retire after leading the first Test-playing tour of India. He stayed on to enjoy some big-game hunting of a different type before writing four cricket books. Fifteen years and one world war later he made his farewell appearance – for an England XI against Glamorgan. He died at the age of 57 after contracting tick fever in Southern Rhodesia. It was Jardine who dubbed Jack Hobbs 'The Master'.

						Batting 1st			Batting 2nd			
Ref	Series	V	T	Venue	Result	No	R	HO	No	R	HO	Ct
173/159	1928	WI	1	Lord's	W-I & 58	5	22	lbw	–	–	–	2
174/160			2	Manchester	W-I & 30	5	83	ro	–	–	–	1
176/162	1928–29	A	1	Brisbane[1]	W-675	5	35	c	5	65	*	1
177/163			2	Sydney	W-8w	4	28	ro	–	–	–	–
178/164			3	Melbourne	W-3w	6	62	c	3	33	b	3
179/165			4	Adelaide	W-12	4	1	lbw	4	98	c	–
180/166			5	Melbourne	L-5w	2	19	c	2	0	c	–
209/190*	1931	NZ	1	Lord's	D	5	38	c	7	0	*	1
210/191*			2	Oval	W-I & 26	6	7	*	–	–	–	1
211/192*			3	Manchester	D	5	28	*	–	–	–	–
219/193*	1932	I		Lord's	W-158	5	79	c	5	85	*	2
220/194*	1932–33	A	1	Sydney	W-10w	6	27	c	–	–	–	–
221/195*			2	Melbourne	L-111	6	1	c	5	0	c	1
222/196*			3	Adelaide	W-338	2	3	b	2	56	lbw	2
223/197*			4	Brisbane[2]	W-6w	1	46	c	1	24	lbw	3
224/198*			5	Sydney	W-8w	1	18	c	1	24	c	3
225/199*	1932–33	NZ	1	Christchurch	D	5	45	c	–	–	–	–
227/201*	1933	WI	1	Lord's	W-I & 27	5	21	c	–	–	–	–
228/202*			2	Manchester	D	5	127	c	–	–	–	–
230/204*	1933–34	I	1	Bombay[1]	W-9w	5	60	b	–	–	–	1
231/205*			2	Calcutta	D	5	61	c	–	–	–	5
232/206*			3	Madras[1]	W-202	5	65	c	7	35	*	–

NOTABLE FEATS

- 1000 runs in 19th Test (*228*) (29 inns).
- *179* Shared record E v A 3rd-wkt stand of 262 with W.R. Hammond.
- Exceeded 1000 runs in a season 8 times (plus once on tour).
- Achieved seventh-highest batting average by anyone scoring 1000 runs in a season: 1002 runs at 91.09 in 1927.
- Twice scored hundreds in 3 consecutive innings (1927 and 1928–29).

TEST NOTES

- *178* Bowled in 2nd inns: 0 for 10 (6 balls).

Career	M	I	NO	HS	R	Avge	100	50	Ct	St	Balls	R	W	Avge	BB	5w	10w	Rate
Test	22	33	6	127	1296	48.00	1	10	26	–	6	10	0	–	–	–	–	–
F/c	262	378	61	214	14848	46.83	35	72	188	–	2582	1493	48	31.10	6-28	1	–	53.79

D. R. JARDINE – TEST BATTING SUMMARY

Series	V	M	I	NO	HS	R	Avge	100	50
1928	WI	2	2	–	83	105	52.50	–	1
1928–29	A	5	9	1	98	341	42.62	–	3
1931	NZ	3	4	3	38	73	73.00	–	–
1932	I	1	2	1	85*	164	164.00	–	2
1932–33	A	5	9	–	56	199	22.11	–	1
1932–33	NZ	1	1	–	45	45	45.00	–	–
1933	WI	2	2	–	127	148	74.00	1	–
1933–34	I	3	4	1	65	221	73.66	–	3

Series	V	M	I	NO	HS	R	Avge	100	50
	A	10	18	1	98	540	31.76	–	4
	WI	4	4	–	127	253	63.25	1	1
	NZ	4	5	3	45	118	59.00	–	–
	I	4	6	2	85*	385	96.25	–	5
Home		8	10	4	127	490	81.66	1	3
Overseas		14	23	2	98	806	38.38	–	7
Totals		22	33	6	127	1296	48.00	1	10

JARVIS
Paul William

Yorkshire (1981 to date)

TOURS
WI 1986–87 (Yorks); NZ 1987–88; P 1987–88
Born Redcar, Yorkshire 29 Jun 1965

Paul Jarvis is an intelligent and determined right-arm fast-medium bowler whose career has been hampered by a series of breakdowns and maladies ranging from severe back strain to blood poisoning. Of medium height (5ft 10in) and wirily built, he lacks the robust physique of a fast bowler and has at times been grossly overworked in a Yorkshire team desperately short of class bowling. His accuracy and ability to swing the ball away from the right-handers enabled him to make an impressive start at Test level before his back demanded another rest. An enthusiastic tail-end batsman with a repertoire of handsome off-side strokes, he is also a keen and athletic fielder.

NOTABLE FEATS

- Youngest player to represent Yorkshire (16 years 75 days).
- Hat-trick for Yorkshire v Derbyshire at Chesterfield in 1985.

Paul Jarvis

Ref	Series	V	T	Venue	Result	Batting 1st No	Batting 1st R	Batting 1st HO	Batting 2nd No	Batting 2nd R	Batting 2nd HO	Ct	Bowling 1st Balls	Bowling 1st R	Bowling 1st W	Bowling 2nd Balls	Bowling 2nd R	Bowling 2nd W
1091/643	1987–88	NZ	1	Christchurch	D	10	14	c	10	10	*	–	126	43	2	102	30	1
1092/644			2	Auckland	D	9	10	c	–	–	–	–	198	74	2	162	54	1
1098/646	1988	WI	1	Nottingham	D	10	6	b	–	–	–	–	109	63	2	–	–	–
1099/647			2	Lord's	L-134	10	7	c	10	29	*	–	78	47	0	156	107	4

Career	M	I	NO	HS	R	Avge	100	50	Ct	St	Balls	R	W	Avge	BB	5w	10w	Rate
Test	4	6	2	29*	76	19.00	–	–	–	–	931	418	12	34.83	4.107	–	–	77.58
F/c	88	98	34	47	923	14.42	–	–	30	–	14243	7611	283	26.89	7-55	14	3	50.32

JENKINS
Roland Oliver

Worcestershire (1938 to 1958)

Wisden 1950
TOUR SA 1948–49
Born Rainbow Hill, Worcester
24 Nov 1918

Few professional cricketers have derived greater pleasure from their work than 'Roly' Jenkins; he retained his boyish enthusiasm throughout a long career which was denied its early years by the Second World War. Ever cheerful and exuberant, he would gleefully celebrate each of his wickets with a jubilant skip and a clap. He was a valuable all-rounder who combined aggressive batting based on a sound defence with skilful right-arm leg-break and googly bowling. Of medium height (5ft 10in) and sturdily built, his becapped jaunty run-up resembled a nautical roll. Although he was expensive at times, he generally compensated by taking wickets quickly – there was always plenty of action and entertainment when he had the ball. Still a frequent and popular visitor to the Worcester ground, he looks as energetic as when he was fielding with such brilliance at cover-point and considerably younger than his three score years and ten.

MCC to South Africa, 1948–49: L. Hutton, F.G. Mann (captain), C.H. Palmer (manager), D.C.S. Compton, R.T. Simpson, C. Washbrook, J.F. Crapp, T.G. Evans, D.V.P. Wright, S.C. Griffith, C. Gladwin, J.A. Young, M.F. Tremlett, R.O. Jenkins, A.J. Watkins, W. Ferguson (scorer and baggage master), A.V. Bedser.

NOTABLE FEATS

- *309* Dismissed E.A.B. Rowan with his third ball in Test cricket.
- Exceeded 1000 runs in a season 4 times, took 100 wickets 5 times (including 183 in 1949) and achieved the 'double' twice.
- Took 15 for 122 for Worcestershire v Sussex at Dudley in 1953.
- Three hat-tricks for Worcestershire v Surrey: at The Oval in 1948 and one in each innings at Worcester in 1949. He is the fourth and last bowler to take 2 hat-tricks in the same match in Britain.

					Batting 1st			Batting 2nd				Bowling 1st			Bowling 2nd		
Ref	Series	V	T Venue	Result	No	R	HO	No	R	HO	Ct	Balls	R	W	Balls	R	W
309/267	1948-49	SA	1 Durban[2]	W-2w	8	5	c	8	22	c	–	112	50	1	179	64	3
310/268			2 Johannesburg[2]	D	8	4	c	–	–	–	–	172	88	3	152	54	0
311/269			3 Cape Town	D	8	1	c	–	–	–	–	88	46	1	72	48	4
312/270			4 Johannesburg[2]	D	7	25	lbw	–	–	–	–	64	39	1	72	26	0
313/271			5 Port Elizabeth	W-3w	7	29	lbw	–	–	–	1	120	53	3	32	27	0
324/277	1950	WI	2 Lord's	L-326	8	4	c	8	4	b	1	212	116	5	354	174	4
325/278			3 Nottingham	L-10w	9	39	b	9	6	*	1	78	73	1	66	46	0
351/297	1952	I	1 Leeds	W-7w	8	38	c	–	–	–	1	162	78	1	78	50	4
352/298			2 Lord's	W-8w	8	21	st	–	–	–	–	45	26	1	60	40	0

Career	M	I	NO	HS	R	Avge	100	50	Ct	St	Balls	R	W	Avge	BB	5w	10w	Rate
Test	9	12	1	39	198	18.00	–	–	4	–	2118	1098	32	34.31	5-116	1	–	66.18
F/c	386	573	120	109	10073	22.23	1	40	213	–	59581	30945	1309	23.64	8-62	92	20	45.51

JESSOP
Gilbert Laird

Gloucestershire (1894 to 1914)
Cambridge University (1896 to 1899)
London County (1900 to 1903)

Wisden 1898
TOUR A 1901–02
Born Cheltenham, Gloucestershire
19 May 1874
Died Fordington, Dorset 11 May 1955

Gilbert Jessop

Gilbert Jessop was undoubtedly the most devastating hitter and consistently fast scorer that cricket has produced. Although only a modest 5ft 7in in height, he was lynx eyed, long armed, immensely strong and exceptionally nimble footed. Dubbed 'The Croucher' because of his unusually low stance, he would run out of his crease to unleash vast pulls and drives against even the swiftest bowling and he was also a very powerful cutter. His range of hitting has never been equalled and very few batsmen have struck the ball more ferociously. His daring method of attacking from the start of his innings changed the course of many matches. He was also an exhilarating fielder, with a wickedly fast and accurate throw, who made fine extra-cover his specialist position. A right-arm fast bowler, he opened England's attack in his first Test and twice took 100 wickets in a season. Cheltenham born and bred, he had two summers in the Gloucestershire team before going up to Cambridge and gaining a blue in each of his four years. He captained his county for 13 seasons from 1900. His most famous innings was his onslaught against Australia at The Oval in 1902 (Test *74*). Set 263 to win against bowling of the highest class, England were 48 for 5 on a rain-damaged pitch when Jessop began his innings. He scored 22 off his first 12 balls, survived two chances and was 29* at lunch after 20 minutes. He reached his 50 in 43 minutes and completed England's fastest-ever century out of 135 in 75 mintues off the same number of balls. England went on to gain an epic one-wicket victory with Hirst and Rhodes scrambling the last 15 runs. Before 1907 only hits out of the ground scored six runs and most of Jessop's fastest innings were handicapped by his being credited with only four runs for strokes which cleared the playing area but not the ground's perimeter. Although he was invalided out of the Manchester Regiment after serving as a captain in the Great War, he lived until a few days short of his 81st birthday. A friendly and modest man, he made his mark at hockey, soccer, rugby, golf and billiards and ran 100 yards in 10.2 seconds.

NOTABLE FEATS

• *74* Scored 100 in 75 min off 75 balls; then the fastest 100 in Test cricket it remains the quickest for England by both measures.
• *93* Shared 6th-wkt stand of 145 in 75 min with L.C. Braund.
• Exceeded 1000 runs in a season 14 times, including 2000 twice.
• Took 100 wickets twice, completing the 'double' on each occasion – notably

NOTABLE FEATS *cont.*

2210 runs and 104 wickets in 1900, a feat achieved by only 13 players.
• Scored 5 double centuries, including 4 in 140 min or less.
• Scored 200 in 120 min for Gloucestershire v Sussex at Hove in 1903 – the fastest first-class 200 until 1984–85.
• Scored the fastest 150 in all first-class cricket in 63 min for the Gentlemen of the South v Players of the South at Hastings in 1907; his 191 out of 234 in 90 min included a 42-min century.
• Completed 14 centuries in an hour or less, his fastest being 40 min for Gloucestershire v Yorkshire at Harrogate in 1897.
• Scored 100 before lunch on 14 occasions, including the only instance of this feat being achieved twice in the same match (on the second and third days) for Gloucestershire v Yorkshire at Bradford in 1900. Added 164 runs before lunch on the second day for Gloucestershire v Somerset at Bristol in 1905 – the fourth-highest pre-lunch score in Britain.
• Twice scored 50 in 15 min for Gloucestershire: v Somerset at Bristol in 1904 and v Hampshire at Cheltenham in 1907.
• Scored 100 in each innings of a Gloucestershire match on 4 occasions.
• Shared record Gloucestershire 6th-wkt stand of 320 with J.H. Board v Sussex at Hove in 1903.

TEST NOTES

• *103* Strained his back on the first day and was unable to bat.

						Batting 1st			Batting 2nd				Bowling 1st			Bowling 2nd		
Ref	Series	V	T	Venue	Result	No	R	HO	No	R	HO	Ct	Balls	R	W	Balls	R	W
61/61	1899	A	2	Lord's	L-10w	8	51	c	8	4	c	–	186	105	3	30	19	0
65/65	1901–02	A	1	Sydney	W-I & 124	5	24	b	–	–	–	2	6	4	0	–	–	–
66/66			2	Melbourne	L-229	5	27	st	5	32	c	–	–	–	–	6	9	0

Ref	Series	V	T	Venue	Result	Batting 1st No	R	HO	Batting 2nd No	R	HO	Ct	Bowling 1st Balls	R	W	Bowling 2nd Balls	R	W
67/67			3	Adelaide	L-4w	4	1	c	5	16	b	–	42	19	0	148	41	2
68/68			4	Sydney	L-7w	5	0	c	5	15	b	–	156	68	4	42	23	0
69/69			5	Melbourne	L-32	2	35	c	4	16	c	–	6	13	0	–	–	–
70/70	1902	A	1	Birmingham	D	8	6	c	–	–	–	2	–	–	–	–	–	–
71/71			2	Lord's	D	–	–	–	–	–	–	–	–	–	–	–	–	–
72/72			3	Sheffield	L-143	9	12	c	1	55	lbw	–	–	–	–	24	15	0
74/74			5	Oval	W-1w	7	13	b	7	104	c	–	36	11	0	–	–	–
83/80	1905	A	1	Nottingham	W-213	8	0	b	–	–	–	1	42	18	1	6	1	0
93/90	1907	SA	1	Lord's	D	7	93	c	–	–	–	1	12	8	0	–	–	–
94/91			2	Leeds	W-53	7	0	c	7	10	c	–	–	–	–	–	–	–
95/92			3	Oval	D	7	2	c	6	11	st	2	–	–	–	–	–	–
101/98	1909	A	1	Birmingham	W-10w	7	22	b	–	–	–	2	–	–	–	–	–	–
103/100			3	Leeds	L-126	–	–	–	–	–	–	–	–	–	–	–	–	–
122/113	1912	SA	1	Lord's	W-I & 62	7	3	b	–	–	–	1	–	–	–	–	–	–
124/115			2	Leeds	W-174	7	16	b	7	1	b	–	–	–	–	–	–	–

Career	M	I	NO	HS	R	Avge	100	50	Ct	St	Balls	R	W	Avge	BB	5w	10w	Rate
Test	18	26	0	104	569	21.88	1	3	11	–	742	354	10	35.40	4-68	–	–	74.20
F/c	493	855	37	286	26698	32.63	53	127	463	–	42390	19904	873	22.79	8-29	41	4	48.55

JONES, Arthur Owen

Cambridge University (1892 to 1893)
Nottinghamshire (1892 to 1914)
London County (1901)

Wisden 1900
TOURS A 1901–02, 1907–08
Born Shelton, Nottinghamshire
16 Aug 1872
Died Dunstable, Bedfordshire
21 Dec 1914

Arthur Jones was probably the most outstanding all-round fielder that the game has ever seen. Infallible in his specialist role at slip, he introduced the gully position and was superb in the deep. His left-handed catching of Monty Noble at short-leg from a full-blooded hit (Test *101*) was a supreme piece of anticipation. It was primarily as a fielder that he won his blue at Cambridge after captaining Bedford Modern School in his last three years and playing one season for Bedfordshire. As an aggressive batsman he was too rash for Test cricket but enjoyed much success for Nottinghamshire, sharing in 24 three-figure opening partnerships with James Iremonger. Despite his awkward splay-footed, bent-kneed stance, he was a graceful strokemaker, especially powerful on the off-side. His leg-spin bowling also proved effective in county cricket and his inspired and enthusiastic captaincy (1900–14) brought the 1907 Championship to Trent Bridge. It also earned him the leadership of that winter's MCC tour to Australia but he missed the first three Tests through illness. Just over medium height (5ft 10½in) and a little under 12 stone, he was an outstanding rugby three-quarter and captain for Leicester and subsequently became a notable referee. His health never recovered after a bitter afternoon at Old Trafford produced a severe chill and he died of tuberculosis in his 43rd year.

NOTABLE FEATS

- Exceeded 1000 runs in a season 9 times, including 2292 in 1901.
- Scored 4 double centuries, all for Nottinghamshire; his 296 at Nottingham in 1903 was then the County record and remains the highest by any batsman against Gloucestershire.
- Twice scored 100 before lunch.
- Shared in two record Nottinghamshire stands: 392 (1st wkt) with A. Shrewsbury v Gloucestershire at Bristol in 1899 (then the second-highest stand in all first-class cricket) and 361 (4th wkt) with J.R. Gunn v Essex at Leyton in 1905.
- Holds Nottinghamshire record for most catches by a non-wicket-keeper (466).
- Held 5 catches in an innings for Nottinghamshire v Sussex at Hove in 1907 and 7 in the match v Gloucestershire at Nottingham in 1908.

Arthur Jones

Ref	Series	V	T	Venue	Result	Batting 1st No	R	HO	Batting 2nd No	R	HO	Ct	Bowling 1st Balls	R	W	Bowling 2nd Balls	R	W
64/64	1899	A	5	Oval	D	9	31	b	–	–	–	2	150	73	3	60	43	0
65/65	1901-02	A	1	Sydney	W-I & 124	6	9	c	–	–	–	1	–	–	–	–	–	–
66/66			2	Melbourne	L-229	8	0	c	8	6	c	2	–	–	–	6	2	0
67/67			3	Adelaide	L-4w	8	5	ro	8	11	c	–	–	–	–	–	–	–
68/68			4	Sydney	L-7w	9	15	c	9	6	c	1	–	–	–	–	–	–
69/69			5	Melbourne	L-32	9	10	c	9	28	c	2	–	–	–	–	–	–
83/80	1905	A	1	Nottingham	W-213	2	4	b	4	30	b	2	–	–	–	–	–	–
84/81			2	Lord's	D	6	1	b	6	5	c	1	–	–	–	–	–	–
99/96*	1907-08	A	4	Melbourne	L-308	8	3	b	8	31	c	2	–	–	–	–	–	–
100/97*			5	Sydney	L-49	10	0	b	9	34	b	1	–	–	–	–	–	–
101/98	1909	A	1	Birmingham	W-10w	5	28	c	–	–	–	1	–	–	–	–	–	–
102/99			2	Lord's	L-9w	8	8	b	6	26	lbw	–	12	15	0	–	–	–

Career	M	I	NO	HS	R	Avge	100	50	Ct	St	Balls	R	W	Avge	BB	5w	10w	Rate
Test	12	21	0	34	291	13.85	–	–	15	–	228	133	3	44.33	3-73	–	–	76.00
F/c	472	774	47	296	22935	31.54	34	117	577	2	18122	10929	333	32.81	8-71	8	1	54.42

JONES
Ivor Jeffrey

Glamorgan (1960 to 1968)

TOURS
A 1965–66; WI 1967–68; NZ 1965–66; I 1963–64
Born Dafen, Carmarthenshire
10 Dec 1941

NOTABLE FEATS

- *600* Only Glamorgan bowler to take 5 or more wickets in a Test innings for England.
- Took 100 wickets (average 19.49) in 1967.
- Took 8 for 11 for Glamorgan v Leicestershire at Leicester in 1965.
- Hat-trick for Glamorgan v Yorkshire at Harrogate in 1962.

Jeff Jones was a tall (6ft 1in) and strongly built left-arm fast-medium bowler with an easy approach and high rhythmic action. Away from the moribund surfaces of Wales he produced some sustained spells of hostile and accurate bowling at high pace. Although his batting ability can be realistically assessed by a career average which was extended to 3.97 only with the assistance of 84 'not outs', by surviving a whole over from Lance Gibbs in his final Test (*632*) he did enable England to salvage a draw and win the series. Affable and immensely popular, he was compelled to retire at the tender age of 26 after tearing ligaments in his left elbow.

Jeff Jones

Ref	Series	V	T	Venue	Result	Batting 1st No	R	HO	Batting 2nd No	R	HO	Ct	Bowling 1st Balls	R	W	Bowling 2nd Balls	R	W
554/401	1963-64	I	2	Bombay[2]	D	10	5	ro	–	–	–	–	78	48	0	66	31	0
598/422	1965-66	A	2	Melbourne	D	11	1	b	–	–	–	–	192	92	3	160	92	1
599/423			3	Sydney	W-I & 93	11	16	b	–	–	–	–	160	51	2	56	35	0
600/424			4	Adelaide	L-I & 9	11	0	*	11	8	c	–	232	118	6	–	–	–
601/425			5	Melbourne	D	11	4	*	–	–	–	–	232	145	3	–	–	–
602/426	1965-66	NZ	1	Christchurch	D	11	0	b	–	–	–	–	172	71	4	42	13	0
603/427			2	Dunedin	D	–	–	–	–	–	–	–	156	46	3	90	32	2
604/428			3	Auckland	D	10	0	b	–	–	–	1	126	52	2	150	28	3
605/429	1966	WI	1	Manchester	L-I & 40	11	0	*	11	0	*	–	168	100	0	–	–	–
606/430			2	Lord's	D	11	0	*	–	–	–	–	126	64	1	150	95	0

Ref	Series	V	T	Venue	Result	Batting 1st No	R	HO	Batting 2nd No	R	HO	Ct	Bowling 1st Balls	R	W	Bowling 2nd Balls	R	W
628/440	1967–68	WI	1	Port-of-Spain	D	11	2	c	–	–	–	–	114	63	3	90	32	1
629/441			2	Kingston	D	11	0	*	–	–	–	–	85	39	2	180	90	3
630/442			3	Bridgetown	D	11	1	*	–	–	–	1	127	56	1	66	53	0
631/443			4	Port-of-Spain	W-7w	11	1	b	–	–	–	1	174	108	2	66	20	0
632/444			5	Georgetown	D	11	0	*	11	0	*	1	186	114	1	102	81	1

Career	M	I	NO	HS	R	Avge	100	50	Ct	St	Balls	R	W	Avge	BB	5w	10w	Rate
Test	15	17	9	16	38	4.75	–	–	4	–	3546	1769	44	40.20	6-118	1	–	80.59
F/c	198	213	84	21	513	3.97	–	–	46	–	30798	13278	511	25.98	8-11	18	–	60.27

JUPP, Henry

Surrey (1862 to 1881)

TOUR A 1876–77
Born Dorking, Surrey 19 Nov 1841
Died Bermondsey, London 8 Apr 1889

W.G. Grace and Harry Jupp

Harry Jupp was Surrey's first outstanding opening batsman. A short, strong, rugged, earthy character, he was one of the most prolific scorers of his era. His method was founded on such an exceptional defensive technique that he was dubbed 'Young Stonewall'. Usually posted to the deep because of his powerful throw, he could also bowl swiftly with a right-handed round-arm action and keep wicket in an emergency. He played in the first two Test matches, faced the first ball bowled to an England batsman and scored his country's first 50.

NOTABLE FEATS

- *1* Top-scored with 63 in England's first Test innings.
- Exceeded 1000 runs in a season 6 times.
- Carried his bat through an innings 12 times, a tally exceeded only by W.G. Grace, C.J.B. Wood and L. Hall. First to achieve this feat in both innings of a match – Surrey v Yorkshire at The Oval in 1874. On 2 other occasions he carried his bat through the first innings and was last out in the second.

TEST NOTES

- *2* Kept wicket in place of J. Selby from lunch on the first day.

Ref	Series	V	T	Venue	Result	Batting 1st No	R	HO	Batting 2nd No	R	HO	Ct
1/1	1876–77	A	1	Melbourne	L-45	1	63	lbw	3	4	lbw	–
2/2			2	Melbourne	W-4w	1	0	b	1	1	b	2

Career	M	I	NO	HS	R	Avge	100	50	Ct	St	Balls	R	W	Avge	BB	5w	10w	Rate
Test	2	4	0	63	68	17.00	–	1	2	–	–	–	–	–	–	–	–	–
F/c	378	692	48	165	15319	23.78	12	73	229	19	635	316	7	45.14	3-75	–	–	90.71

JUPP
Vallance William Crisp

Sussex (1909 to 1922)
Northamptonshire (1923 to 1938)

Wisden 1928
TOUR SA 1922–23
Born Burgess Hill, Sussex 27 Mar 1891
Died Spratton, Northamptonshire
9 Jul 1960

Vallance Jupp

Vallance Jupp was an amazingly consistent all-rounder whose record of ten 'doubles' has been surpassed only by Rhodes and Hirst. Shortish, and prematurely bald, he was powerfully built with long arms. He varied his batting style according to the situation; he was equally adept at vigilant defence as at employing his favourite drives in bursts of explosive strokeplay. He had attracted the notice of Sussex by acquiring a three-figure average as captain of St John's School in Burgess Hill and established his county place as a professional before his progress was interrupted by the Great War. He served first with the Royal Engineers in France, Salonika and Palestine and then with the RAF. After that varied interlude his career underwent extraordinary metamorphosis: he turned amateur and changed his bowling style from right-arm brisk-medium to off-spin. This he bowled from a jaunty, nautical approach and could achieve considerable turn. When not employed as a bowler he would expend his vast supply of energy in the covers. In 1921 he accepted the secretaryship of Northamptonshire and had to refuse an invitation to tour Australia; he subsequently became captain (1927–31). 'Juppy' collapsed and died in his garden beside the picturesque village of Spratton in his 70th year.

NOTABLE FEATS

- Exceeded 1000 runs in a season 13 times, including 2169 in 1921, and took 100 wickets in a season 10 times, including 166 in 1928, achieving the 'double' 10 times (twice with Sussex and 8 times with Northamptonshire) – the record for an amateur. F.R. Brown is the only other player to do the 'double' for 2 counties. One of only 13 players to score 2000 runs and take 100 wickets in a season (1921). Completed the 'double' on 17 July 1928 – the fourth-fastest.
- His analysis of 10 for 127 v Kent at Tunbridge Wells in 1932 remains the record for Northamptonshire.
- Took 15 for 52 (including 7 in 25 balls) for Northamptonshire v Glamorgan at Swansea in 1925.
- Five hat-tricks (only 3 bowlers have taken more): 3 for Sussex (v Surrey at Hove in 1911 and v Essex at Leyton in 1919 and at Colchester in 1921) and 2 for Northamptonshire (v Glamorgan at Swansea in 1925 and v Gloucestershire at Bristol in 1931).
- Took 5 wickets in 9 balls for Northamptonshire v Worcestershire at Dudley in 1928.
- Scored 102 and took a hat-trick for Sussex v Essex at Colchester in 1921 – the fourth of only 8 such instances in first-class cricket.
- Achieved the match 'double' 3 times.

						Batting 1st			Batting 2nd				Bowling 1st			Bowling 2nd		
Ref	Series	V	T	Venue	Result	No	R	HO	No	R	HO	Ct	Balls	R	W	Balls	R	W
140/129	1921	A	1	Nottingham	L-10w	7	8	c	7	15	c	1	30	14	1	19	13	0
142/131			3	Leeds	L-219	6	14	c	7	28	c	1	108	70	2	78	45	2
148/134	1922–23	SA	1	Johannesburg[1]	L-168	7	1	c	9	33	st	–	126	59	4	186	87	3
149/135			2	Cape Town	W-1w	8	12	c	8	38	st	1	54	18	2	66	23	0
150/136			3	Durban[2]	D	8	16	st	–	–	–	1	136	70	2	–	–	–
151/137			4	Johannesburg[1]	D	8	7	c	7	10	*	–	90	36	3	72	39	0
173/159	1928	WI	1	Lord's	W-I & 58	7	14	b	–	–	–	–	138	37	4	90	66	3
174/160			2	Manchester	W-I & 30	8	12	c	–	–	–	1	108	39	2	–	–	–

Career	M	I	NO	HS	R	Avge	100	50	Ct	St	Balls	R	W	Avge	BB	5w	10w	Rate
Test	8	13	1	38	208	17.33	–	–	5	–	1301	616	28	22.00	4-37	–	–	46.46
F/c	529	876	84	217*	23296	29.41	30	120	222	–	72413	38166	1658	23.01	10-127	111	18	43.67

KEETON
William Walter

Nottinghamshire (1926 to 1952)

Wisden 1940
Born Shirebrook, Derbyshire
30 Apr 1905
Died Forest Town, Nottinghamshire
10 Oct 1980

Walter Keeton was a very good county opening batsman in an era of plenty and, although he made a magnificent contribution to Nottinghamshire cricket, he failed to impress in his two isolated Test matches. He was a strong on-side player with a sound defence who mastered that most difficult of strokes, the on-drive, to perfection. His annual scoring was exceptionally consistent and he was a most stylish and attractive batsman to watch; nimble feet and strong wrists enabled him to cover-drive and cut handsomely. Many cricket quizzes have featured the venue of his record Nottinghamshire score of 312* in seven and three-quarter hours against Middlesex; the match was played at The Oval because Eton were playing Harrow at Lord's – an interesting precedence. His form was unimpaired after six years of war (he shared an opening stand of 318 with Reg Simpson in 1949) but Hutton and Washbrook were then established as England's openers. A fast and agile deep fielder, he enjoyed a successful soccer career at inside right for Sunderland and Nottingham Forest. A sports shop and work for the National Coal Board occupied his later years.

NOTABLE FEATS

- Exceeded 1000 runs in a season 12 times, including 2000 on 6 occasions. Scored 1102 runs in August 1933.
- His 312* v Middlesex at The Oval in 1939 remains the record score and sole triple century for Nottinghamshire. Scored 6 other double centuries – all for Nottinghamshire.
- Shared 45 century 1st-wkt stands with C.B. Harris, including 5 over 200.
- Twice scored 3 hundreds in consecutive innings (1933 and 1949).

Len Hutton (left) and Walter Keeton opening for England in 1939.

						Batting 1st			Batting 2nd			
Ref	Series	V	T	Venue	Result	No	R	HO	No	R	HO	Ct
236/210	1934	A	4	Leeds	D	2	25	c	2	12	b	–
274/243	1939	WI	3	Oval	D	2	0	b	2	20	b	–

Career	M	I	NO	HS	R	Avge	100	50	Ct	St	Balls	R	W	Avge	BB	5w	10w	Rate
Test	2	4	0	25	57	14.25	–	–	–	–	–	–	–	–	–	–	–	–
F/c	397	657	43	312*	24276	39.53	54	118	76	–	164	103	2	51.50	2-16	–	–	82.00

KENNEDY
Alexander Stuart

Hampshire (1907 to 1936)

Wisden 1933
TOURS SA 1922–23, 1924–25 (Joel)
Born Edinburgh, Scotland 24 Jan 1891
Died Hythe, Southampton 15 Nov 1959

The sturdily built Alec Kennedy was Hampshire's most prolific and consistent all-rounder. Between 1909 and 1930 his partnership with Jack Newman formed the backbone of the County's attack and a formidable duo they were. A right-arm medium-pace inswing bowler with a high action and longish approach, he had exceptional stamina and determination. His impeccable accuracy allied to his ability to spin the ball from leg and vary his pace subtly made him a most awkward adversary. As a resolute batsman with a sound defence, he appeared at every position in the order and once carried his bat for 152 out of 344. During his earliest years his family had migrated to Southampton and he made his first-class debut at the age of 16. In retirement he continued to coach, first at Cheltenham College and then, from 1947 to 1954, in South Africa.

NOTABLE FEATS

- Exceeded 1000 runs in a season 5 times and took 1000 wickets 15 times, including 200 once and over 150 on 5 other occasions.
- Completed the 'double' 5 times, notably 1129 runs and 205 wickets in 1922; A.E. Trott and M.W. Tate are the only other players to score 1000 runs and take 200 wickets in a season.
- Holds the Hampshire record for most wickets in a season: 190 in 1922.
- His analysis of 10 for 37 for the Players at The Oval in 1927 was the record for either side in Gentlemen v Players matches. Twice took 9 wickets in an innings for Hampshire, notably 9 for 33 v Lancashire at Liverpool in 1920.
- Took 15 for 116 for Hampshire v Somerset at Bath in 1922.
- His analysis of 7 for 8 for Hampshire v Warwickshire at Portsmouth in 1927 included 6 wickets in 14 balls.
- Three hat-tricks (Hampshire record): v Gloucestershire at Southampton twice (1920 and 1924) and v Somerset at Bournemouth in 1920.
- Bowled in an unchanged partnership throughout both completed innings of a match on 3 occasions, 2 of them with J.A. Newman.

Alec Kennedy (left) *and Jack Newman.*

						Batting 1st			Batting 2nd				Bowling 1st			Bowling 2nd		
Ref	Series	V	T	Venue	Result	No	R	HO	No	R	HO	Ct	Balls	R	W	Balls	R	W
148/134	1922–23	SA	1	Johannesburg[1]	L-168	10	41	*	5	0	c	3	124	37	4	249	132	4
149/135			2	Cape Town	W-1w	9	2	c	9	11	*	–	108	24	1	212	58	4
150/136			3	Durban[2]	D	9	8	c	–	–	–	1	234	88	5	–	–	–
151/137			4	Johannesburg[1]	D	9	16	c	–	–	–	1	144	68	3	167	70	3
152/138			5	Durban[2]	W-109	8	14	c	2	1	c	–	150	46	2	295	76	5

Career	M	I	NO	HS	R	Avge	100	50	Ct	St	Balls	R	W	Avge	BB	5w	10w	Rate
Test	5	8	2	41*	93	15.50	–	–	5	–	1683	599	31	19.32	5-76	2	–	54.29
F/c	677	1025	130	163*	16586	18.53	10	64	530	–	150256	61034	2874	21.23	10-37	225	45	52.28

KENYON
Donald MBE

Worcestershire (1946 to 1967)

Wisden 1963

TOURS

WI 1965–66 (Worcs); I/SL 1951–52; P 1951–52; Z 1964–65 (Worcs)

Born Wordsley, Staffordshire
15 May 1924

NOTABLE FEATS

- Exceeded 1000 runs in a season 19 times, including 2000 on 7 occasions.
- Holds the Worcestershire career records for most appearances (589), most runs (34,490) and most instances of 1000 runs in a season (19).
- Scored 7 double centuries, all for Worcestershire.

Although Don Kenyon was 22 by the time post-war cricket started, he became the heaviest and most consistent scorer in Worcestershire's history. As a bonus to his sound and polished batting, his shrewd captaincy (1959–67) produced the County's first two Championships. Such is the gulf between county and Test cricket that even such a successful opener as Kenyon found little joy on his missions for England, his 15 innings producing just one 50 and 11 single-figure dismissals. A little above medium height (5ft 10in) and snugly built, he was an occasional right-arm medium-pace change bowler and an excellent fielder. A popular figure with a dry sense of humour, he became a Test selector (1965–72) and was president when Worcestershire won the Championship in 1988.

Don Kenyon

Ref	Series	V	T	Venue	Result	Batting 1st No	R	HO	Batting 2nd No	R	HO	Ct
339/292	1951–52	I	1	Delhi	D	3	35	b	3	6	c	–
340/293			2	Bombay[2]	D	5	21	lbw	2	2	lbw	1
341/294			3	Calcutta	D	5	3	c	5	0	b	–
372/301	1953	A	1	Nottingham	D	2	8	c	2	16	c	1
373/302			2	Lord's	D	2	3	c	2	2	c	–
408/322	1955	SA	1	Nottingham	W-I & 5	1	87	lbw	–	–	–	–
409/323			2	Lord's	W-71	1	1	b	1	2	lbw	2
410/324			3	Manchester	L-3w	1	5	c	1	1	c	1

Career	M	I	NO	HS	R	Avge	100	50	Ct	St	Balls	R	W	Avge	BB	5w	10w	Rate
Test	8	15	0	87	192	12.80	–	1	5	–	–	–	–	–	–	–	–	–
F/c	643	1159	59	259	37002	33.63	74	180	327	–	206	187	1	187.00	1-8	–	–	206.00

KILLICK
Rev. Edgar Thomas

Middlesex (1926 to 1939)
Cambridge University (1927 to 1930)

Born Fulham, Middlesex 9 May 1907
Died Northampton 18 May 1953

Tom Killick was an exceptionally capable and stylish opening batsman who would almost certainly have become an established Test cricketer had he not decided to be a clergyman. A graceful front-foot off-side player, he was an outstanding fielder in the deep. He made his first-class debut for Middlesex while still at St Paul's School, captained the Public Schools against the 1926 Australians and gained blues in his last three years at Cambridge where he scored two double centuries. Afterwards he became chaplain at Harrow School and his duties allowed scant opportunity for cricket; he would have been an automatic selection for the 1932–33 tour of Australia had he been available. During the Second World War he was senior padre of the RAF West Africa Command. Afterwards he appeared for the Free Foresters when he was vicar of Bishop's Stortford and died while batting for St Albans against Coventry in a diocesan clergy match shortly after his 46th birthday.

NOTABLE FEATS

- Exceeded 1000 runs in a season twice.
- Scored 2 double centuries for Cambridge and one for Middlesex (206 v Warwickshire at Lord's when his opening stand with G.T.S. Stevens produced 277 runs) in the only Championship match he appeared in during 1931.
- Scored 100 in 60 min and before lunch for Cambridge U v Glamorgan at Fenner's in 1929.

Tom Killick

Ref	Series	V	T	Venue	Result	Batting 1st No	R	HO	Batting 2nd No	R	HO	Ct
181/167	1929	SA	1	Birmingham	D	2	31	c	2	23	b	–
182/168			2	Lord's	D	2	3	b	2	24	c	2

Career	M	I	NO	HS	R	Avge	100	50	Ct	St	Balls	R	W	Avge	BB	5w	10w	Rate
Test	2	4	0	31	81	20.25	–	–	2	–	–	–	–	–	–	–	–	–
F/c	92	153	11	206	5730	40.35	15	26	50	–	293	229	3	76.33	1-20	–	–	97.66

KILNER, Roy

Yorkshire (1911 to 1927)

Wisden 1924
TOURS A 1924–25; WI 1925–26
Born Low Valley, Wombwell, Yorkshire
17 Oct 1890
Died Kendray, Barnsley, Yorkshire
5 Apr 1928

Before the Great War, Roy Kilner's role in the Yorkshire XI was confined to batting but afterwards the absence of Booth, Drake and Hirst led to him becoming one of the country's leading left-arm leg-spin bowlers and developing into a genuine all-rounder. The elder brother of Norman (Yorkshire and Warwickshire), he was an aggressive left-handed batsman whose favourite strokes were the off-drive and the pull. Although he could play defensively when the situation demanded it was very much against his nature. He was far more patient as a bowler, nagging away with relentless accuracy and little variations of pace and angle. He contributed to six Yorkshire Championships. A generous, modest character he particularly enjoyed the serious warfare of Roses matches: 'What we want is no umpires and fair cheating all round!' He contracted enteric fever on his way home from a coaching engagement in India and died at the age of 37. [*Illus. pp.* 16, 161, 336]

NOTABLE FEATS

• Exceeded 1000 runs in a season 10 times, took 100 wickets 5 times and completed the 'double' on 4 occasions.

						Batting 1st			Batting 2nd				Bowling 1st			Bowling 2nd		
Ref	Series	V	T	Venue	Result	No	R	HO	No	R	HO	Ct	Balls	R	W	Balls	R	W
153/139	1924	SA	1	Birmingham	W-I & 18	7	59	c	–	–	–	1	–	–	–	132	40	0
156/142			4	Manchester	D	–	–	–	–	–	–	–	72	19	0	–	–	–
160/146	1924–25	A	3	Adelaide	L-11	9	6	lbw	7	24	c	1	448	127	4	177	51	4
161/147			4	Melbourne	W-I & 29	8	74	lbw	–	–	–	1	104	29	3	128	41	2
162/148			5	Sydney	L-307	8	24	st	8	1	c	–	304	97	4	272	54	0
163/149	1926	A	1	Nottingham	D	–	–	–	–	–	–	–	–	–	–	–	–	–
164/150			2	Lord's	D	–	–	–	–	–	–	1	209	70	4	132	49	0
165/151			3	Leeds	D	7	36	c	–	–	–	–	222	106	2	–	–	–
166/152			4	Manchester	D	7	9	*	–	–	–	2	168	51	1	–	–	–

Career	M	I	NO	HS	R	Avge	100	50	Ct	St	Balls	R	W	Avge	BB	5w	10w	Rate
Test	9	8	1	74	233	33.28	–	2	6	–	2368	734	24	30.58	4-51	–	–	98.66
F/c	413	540	55	206*	14419	29.72	17	81	264	–	58113	18321	991	18.48	8-26	47	10	58.64

KING, John Herbert

Leicestershire (1895 to 1925)

Born Lutterworth, Leicestershire
16 Apr 1871
Died Denbigh, Denbighshire
18 Nov 1946

John King was an accomplished left-handed all-rounder who gave long and distinguished service to Leicestershire before becoming a first-class umpire. He was an exceptional player of fast bowling, particularly adept at cutting and driving, and a reliable slip fielder. As a leg-spin bowler he varied his pace from slow to medium, maintained an accurate length and was a canny exponent of flight. He was the last batsman to be given out 'hit the ball twice' in England: playing against Surrey at The Oval in 1906, he 'ran' after defending his wicket by hitting the ball a second time. When he eventually made his only Test appearance at the advanced age of 38, he celebrated by being top scorer in his first innings with 60. A curious piece of team selection condemned him to opening the bowling, his figures not being helped by having Ransford and Trumper dropped in the same over. [*Illus. p.* 252]

NOTABLE FEATS

• Exceeded 1000 runs in a season 14 times and took 100 wickets twice, completing the 'double' once (1912).

• Scored the second of his double centuries (205 v Hampshire at Leicester in 1923) at the age of 52.

• Twice scored 100 in each innings of a match, notably and uniquely 104 and 109* for Players v Gentlemen at Lord's in 1904.

• Two hat-tricks for Leicestershire: v Sussex at Hove in 1903 and v Somerset at Weston in 1920.

• Took 8 for 17 (including 7 for 0 in 20 balls) for Leicestershire v Yorkshire at Leicester in 1911.

Ref	Series	V	T	Venue	Result	Batting 1st No	R	HO	Batting 2nd No	R	HO	Ct	Bowling 1st Balls	R	W	Bowling 2nd Balls	R	W
102/99	1909	A	2	Lord's	L-9w	5	60	c	5	4	b	–	162	99	1	–	–	–

Career	M	I	NO	HS	R	Avge	100	50	Ct	St	Balls	R	W	Avge	BB	5w	10w	Rate
Test	1	2	0	60	64	32.00	–	1	–	–	162	99	1	99.00	1-99	–	–	162.00
F/c	552	988	69	227*	25122	27.33	34	130	340	–	70084	30312	1204	25.17	8-17	69	11	58.20

KINNEIR
Septimus Paul

Warwickshire (1898 to 1914)

Wisden 1912
TOUR A 1911–12
Born Corsham, Wiltshire 13 May 1871
Died Birmingham 16 Oct 1928

Paul Kinneir was a most reliable left-handed opening batsman who forfeited his chance of forming a regular partnership with Jack Hobbs because of his indifferent fielding. He saw England off to reasonable starts in both innings of his only Test and had contributed the largest aggregate to Warwickshire's first Championship success the previous summer. After a lengthy baptism with his native Wiltshire he began his first-class career at the advanced age of 27 (a fact he disguised by two years). A graceful and orthodox batsman, he was a sound player of fast bowling and would occasionally discard his normally patient method to indulge in abandoned strokeplay in which the cut and off-drive featured heavily. Until the First World War ended his career he remained a most consistent scorer and a handy left-arm leg-break change bowler. [*Illus. p.* 146]

NOTABLE FEATS

- Exceeded 1000 runs in a season 8 times.
- Contributed 215* to record Warwickshire 3rd-wkt stand of 327 with W.G. Quaife v Lancashire at Birmingham in 1901. His other double century, 268* v Hampshire at Birmingham in 1911, was then the record score for Warwickshire.
- Carried his bat through a completed Warwickshire innings on 3 occasions, including both innings of the match v Leicestershire at Leicester in 1907 (a feat achieved by only 3 other batsmen in all first-class matches).

Ref	Series	V	T	Venue	Result	Batting 1st No	R	HO	Batting 2nd No	R	HO	Ct
116/108	1911–12	A	1	Sydney	L-146	2	22	b	2	30	c	–

Career	M	I	NO	HS	R	Avge	100	50	Ct	St	Balls	R	W	Avge	BB	5w	10w	Rate
Test	1	2	0	30	52	26.00	–	–	–	–	–	–	–	–	–	–	–	–
F/c	312	525	47	268*	15641	32.72	26	83	181	–	3714	1492	48	31.08	3-13	–	–	77.37

KNIGHT
Albert Ernest

Leicestershire (1895 to 1912)
London County (1903 to 1904)

Wisden 1904
TOUR A 1903–04
Born Leicester 8 Oct 1872
Died Edmonton, Middlesex 25 Apr 1946

Albert Knight was a careful middle-order batsman and an aggressive cover-point. He became a sound and consistent player through sheer application and concentration. Risky leg-side strokes like the pull and hook had no place in an orthodox but limited repertoire dominated by the off-drive and square cut. After an outstanding season in 1903, including a century for Players against Gentlemen at Lord's, he was selected for that winter's tour of Australia. There he met with little success apart from his tenacious and vital contribution to England's victory in the Fourth Test which clinched the Ashes. He was a keen student of the game and his ambitiously entitled *The Complete Cricketer* was published in 1906. A Methodist lay preacher who prayed before and sometimes during each innings, he became coach first to Highgate School and then to Dublin's Belvedere College.

NOTABLE FEATS

• *81* Batted 260 min for the highest innings of the match.
• Exceeded 1000 runs in a season 10 times.
• Scored 2 double centuries for Leicestershire.
• Carried his bat through a completed Leicestershire innings on 5 occasions.

The Leicestershire side of 1903 which included Albert Knight (standing, wearing a boater) and John King (next to Knight, in a cap).

Ref	Series	V	T	Venue	Result	Batting 1st No	R	HO	Batting 2nd No	R	HO	Ct
79/76	1903–04	A	2	Melbourne	W-185	6	2	b	7	0	lbw	–
81/78			4	Sydney	W-157	5	70	*	5	9	c	–
82/79			5	Melbourne	L-218	9	0	b	4	0	c	1

Career	M	I	NO	HS	R	Avge	100	50	Ct	St	Balls	R	W	Avge	BB	5w	10w	Rate
Test	3	6	1	70*	81	16.20	–	1	1	–	–	–	–	–	–	–	–	–
F/c	391	702	40	229*	19357	29.24	34	91	132	–	156	117	4	29.25	2-34	–	–	39.00

KNIGHT
Barry Rolfe

Essex (1955 to 1966)
Leicestershire (1967 to 1969)

TOURS
A 1962–63, 1965–66; WI 1964–65 (Cav); NZ 1962–63, 1965–66; I 1961–62, 1963–64, 1964–65 (Cwlth); P 1961–62; SL 1961–62
Born Chesterfield, Derbyshire
18 Feb 1938

Barry Knight was a highly talented and athletic all-rounder who made a massive contribution to Essex cricket before a dispute led to his departure to Leicester. An instinctive cricketer, he could adapt his game to any given situation but by nature was flamboyant and aggressive. His middle-order batting featured many stylish strokes and he clinched one Test victory (*542*) by hitting successive balls for 6, 4 and 4. The 1968 Australians will recall his incisive right-arm fast-medium bowling and how its late movement claimed three vital wickets as they collapsed to 78 all out (Test *638*). Tallish (5ft 10½in) but slimly built, he had immense stamina and was an exceptional fielder. Independent and by nature a gambler, he allowed his energies little respite off the field. He emigrated to Sydney after the 1969 season and established a thriving indoor cricket school.

NOTABLE FEATS

• 50 wickets in 22nd Test (*606*).
• *540* Shared stand of 240 with P.H. Parfitt which remains England's 6th-wkt record in all Tests.
• *638* Took his 1000th first-class wicket when he dismissed A.P. Sheahan.
• Exceeded 1000 runs in a season 5 times, took 100 wickets 5 times and completed the 'double' in 4 successive seasons (1962–65) including the eighth-fastest on 25 July 1963.
• Scored 84 out of 88 in boundaries for Essex v Warwickshire at Birmingham in 1962.
• Contributed his highest score of 165 (including 100 before lunch) to record-equalling Essex 6th-wkt stand of 206 with R.A.G. Luckin v Middlesex at Brentwood in 1962.

Ref	Series	V	T	Venue	Result	Batting 1st No	R	HO	Batting 2nd No	R	HO	Ct	Bowling 1st Balls	R	W	Bowling 2nd Balls	R	W
514/376	1961–62	I	2	Kanpur	D	8	12	c	–	–	–	1	216	80	2	–	–	–
515/377			3	Delhi	D	–	–	–	–	–	–	–	147	72	2	–	–	–
516/378			4	Calcutta	L-187	7	12	st	7	39	*	–	108	61	0	42	18	2
517/379			5	Madras[2]	L-128	7	19	c	7	33	c	–	84	62	2	24	12	0
518/380	1961–62	P	2	Dacca	D	8	10	b	–	–	–	1	174	52	1	84	19	0
519/381			3	Karachi	D	7	6	c	–	–	–	–	114	66	4	102	43	1
533/385	1962	P	4	Nottingham	D	6	14	c	–	–	–	–	102	38	4	126	48	0
534/386			5	Oval	W-10w	6	3	b	–	–	'	1	54	11	1	66	33	1
535/387	1962–63	A	1	Brisbane[2]	D	9	0	c	8	4	*	1	141	65	3	112	63	0
540/392	1962–63	NZ	1	Auckland	W-I & 215	7	125	b	–	–	–	–	64	23	2	60	13	0
541/393			2	Wellington	W-I & 47	6	31	c	–	–	–	1	126	32	3	24	7	1
542/394			3	Christchurch	W-7w	7	32	b	5	20	*	1	138	39	2	60	38	1
553/400	1963–64	I	1	Madras[2]	D	6	6	b	4	7	c	–	162	73	1	42	22	0
554/401			2	Bombay[2]	D	4	12	b	–	–	–	1	120	53	2	78	28	2
555/402			3	Calcutta	D	8	13	c	–	–	–	–	80	39	1	24	33	0
556/403			4	Delhi	D	8	21	c	–	–	–	–	66	46	0	48	47	0
557/404			5	Kanpur	D	4	127	c	–	–	–	–	6	4	0	12	12	0
598/422	1965–66	A	2	Melbourne	D	8	1	c	–	–	–	–	213	84	4	168	61	2
601/425			5	Melbourne	D	9	13	c	–	–	–	–	290	105	2	–	–	–
603/427	1965–66	NZ	2	Dunedin	D	8	12	c	–	–	–	2	192	41	2	18	3	0
604/428			3	Auckland	D	6	25	c	6	13	*	1	96	40	0	108	21	1
606/430	1966	WI	2	Lord's	D	8	6	b	–	–	–	1	126	63	2	180	106	2
638/446	1968	A	2	Lord's	D	7	27	*	–	–	–	1	64	16	3	96	35	0
639/447			3	Birmingham	D	6	6	c	4	1	b	–	84	34	1	–	–	–
653/453	1969	WI	1	Manchester	W-10w	8	31	lbw	–	–	–	–	12	11	0	72	15	2
654/454			2	Lord's	D	9	0	lbw	9	1	*	–	228	65	1	167	78	2
655/455			3	Leeds	W-30	8	7	c	8	27	c	–	132	63	4	110	47	2
656/456	1969	NZ	1	Lord's	W-230	8	29	c	8	49	b	–	60	20	0	18	5	0
657/457			2	Nottingham	D	8	18	*	–	–	–	2	113	44	2	24	14	0

Career	M	I	NO	HS	R	Avge	100	50	Ct	St	Balls	R	W	Avge	BB	5w	10w	Rate
Test	29	38	7	127	812	26.19	2	–	14	–	5377	2223	70	31.75	4-38	–	–	76.81
F/c	379	602	83	165	13336	25.69	12	66	263	–	57813	26205	1089	24.06	8-69	45	8	53.08

Barry Knight

B. R. KNIGHT – TEST BOWLING SUMMARY

Series	V	M	Balls	R	W	Avge	BB	5w	10w	Rate
1961–62	I	4	621	305	8	38.12	2-28	–	–	77.62
1961–62	P	2	474	180	6	30.00	4-66	–	–	79.00
1962	P	2	348	130	6	21.66	4-38	–	–	58.00
1962–63	A	1	253	128	3	42.66	3-65	–	–	84.33
1962–63	NZ	3	472	152	9	16.88	3-32	–	–	52.44
1963–64	I	5	638	357	6	59.50	2-28	–	–	106.33
1965–66	A	2	671	250	8	31.25	4-84	–	–	83.87
1965–66	NZ	2	414	105	3	35.00	2-41	–	–	138.00
1966	WI	1	306	169	4	42.25	2-63	–	–	76.50
1968	A	2	244	85	4	21.25	3-16	–	–	61.00
1969	WI	3	721	279	11	25.36	4-63	–	–	65.54
1969	NZ	2	215	83	2	29.00	2-44	–	–	107.50
	A	5	1168	463	15	30.86	4-84	–	–	77.86
	WI	4	1027	448	15	29.86	4-63	–	–	68.46
	NZ	7	1101	340	14	24.28	3-32	–	–	78.64
	I	9	1259	662	14	47.28	2-18	–	–	89.92
	P	4	822	310	12	25.83	4-38	–	–	68.50
Home		10	1834	746	27	27.62	4-38	–	–	67.92
Overseas		19	3543	1477	43	34.34	4-66	–	–	82.39
Totals		29	5377	2223	70	31.75	4-38	–	–	76.81

KNIGHT
Donald John

Surrey (1911 to 1937)
Oxford University (1914 and 1919)

Wisden 1915
Born Sutton, Surrey 12 May 1894
Died Marylebone, London 5 Jan 1960

Donald Knight was a brilliant schoolboy cricketer who made his first 50 for Surrey before his final year at Malvern; he had appeared for the County 2nd XI at the age of 15. His university studies were divided by the Great War but he gained blues in both his years at Oxford, playing a vital role in their 1919 victory. That summer he amassed nine centuries including one on his first appearance for the Gentlemen at Lord's; replacing Sandham as partner to Hobbs, he headed the Surrey batting averages. He was an exceptionally graceful and beautifully balanced batsman in the classic tradition. A brave close fielder, he suffered a terrible blow on the head at short-leg in 1920. He recovered to play in the opening Tests against Armstrong's mighty side and was England's highest scorer at Trent Bridge. He retired from regular county cricket after that season to concentrate on his life as a master at Westminster School. A modest and generous man he was persuaded to return for a dozen matches in 1937 when, aged 43, he scored a century against Hampshire.

NOTABLE FEATS

- Exceeded 1000 runs in a season twice.
- Scored 2860 runs (avge 46.88) in 5 seasons for Malvern College.
- Scored 3 consecutive hundreds for Surrey in 1919, including 114 and 101 v Yorkshire at The Oval.

Donald Knight

						Batting 1st			Batting 2nd			
Ref	Series	V	T	Venue	Result	No	R	HO	No	R	HO	Ct
140/129	1921	A	1	Nottingham	L-10w	1	8	c	1	38	ro	1
141/130			2	Lord's	L-8w	1	7	c	1	1	c	–

Career	M	I	NO	HS	R	Avge	100	50	Ct	St	Balls	R	W	Avge	BB	5w	10w	Rate
Test	2	4	0	38	54	13.50	–	–	1	–	–	–	–	–	–	–	–	–
F/c	139	215	13	156*	6231	30.84	13	30	74	–	52	25	3	8.33	2-0	–	–	17.33

KNOTT
Alan Philip Eric

Kent (1964 to 1985)
Tasmania (1969–70)

Wisden 1970
TOURS
A 1970–71, 1974–75, 1976–77;
SA 1981–82 (SAB); WI 1964–65 (Cav), 1967–68, 1973–74; NZ 1970–71, 1974–75; I 1972–73, 1976–77;
P 1966–67 (MCC U-25), 1968–69, 1972–73; SL 1968–69, 1972–73, 1976–77
Born Belvedere, Kent 9 Apr 1946

Nimble-footed and quick-witted with lightning reflexes, Alan Knott was a beautifully balanced wicket-keeper – one of the greatest ever seen – and a supremely gifted middle-order batsman. He worked hard on his agility and his on-field calisthenics became a familiar sight during his long international career. An automatic selection after replacing Jim Parks on the 1967–68 West Indies tour, he went on to make a record 65 consecutive appearances for England before opting to join the World Series circus. His later decision to join the rebel tour of South Africa resulted in a three-year ban and effectively ended his Test career. Of average height (5ft 8in) and lightly built, his remarkable powers of concentration and dedication to fitness and practice enabled him to be as impressive at the close of a hot, frustrating day as at the start. His anticipation of Derek Underwood's varied pace and movement on difficult pitches was unbelievable. Highly superstitious and fanatical about his health, he would completely change his clothing and shower during every interval and seemed to exist entirely on fresh fruit and milk. Originally an inveterate cap wearer, he adopted a floppy hat after injuring his neck in a crash on the racing circuit at Brands Hatch because its more uplifted rim allowed him to see the ball without bending his neck uncomfortably. His proficiency in front of the stumps made him one of Test cricket's great all-rounders and he could have held his place on batting alone. His hundred against Lillee and Thomson in Adelaide (Test *754*) was a testament to his incredible powers of improvisation. His fast footwork and canny positioning enabled him to play every stroke and he was especially adept at sweeping and cutting. Again, concentration was the key to his success – plus his exceptional judgment of line and length. He had to wait two years for his maiden Test hundred after a frenzied, banner-bearing Karachi horde had stormed on to the outfield and caused a Test to be abandoned when his score was 96. Curiously he had been taken on to the Kent staff as an outstanding schoolboy batsman eager to bowl off-breaks.

NOTABLE FEATS

- 1000 runs in 25th Test (*686*) (37 inns); 2000 runs in 43rd Test (*720*) (66 inns); 3000 runs in 66th Test (*754*) (102 inns); first wicket-keeper to score 4000 runs (unique 'double' of 4000 runs and 200 dismissals) in 87th Test (*806*) (135 inns).
- 50 dismissals in 16th Test (*656*); 100 dismissals and fastest wicket-keepers' 'double' for England in 30th Test (*691*); 150 dismissals in 47th Test (*724*); 200 dismissals (second after T.G. Evans) in 66th Test (*754*); first to make 250 dismissals – in 88th Test (*807*).
- *679* His total of 24 dismissals remains the England record for any series.
- *686* Dismissed 4 runs short of becoming the first wicket-keeper to score 100 in each innings of a Test. Shared record E v NZ 7th-wkt stand of 149 with P. Lever.
- *687* Shared (then) record E v P 7th-wkt stand of 159 with P. Lever.
- *692* Shared (then) record E v I 7th-wkt stand of 103 in 66 min with R.A. Hutton.
- *722* Shared record E v NZ 10th-wkt stand of 59 with N. Gifford.
- *733* Shared record E v WI 6th-wkt stand of 163 with A.W. Greig.
- *739* Made 5 dismissals in an innings – his only instance.
- *750* Set world Test record of 174 catches (beating T.G. Evans).
- *754* His 100 was the second by a wicket-keeper in E v A Tests and the first since 1934 (L.E.G. Ames).
- *777* First to hold 200 catches in Tests.
- *781* Set world record of 220 dismissals in his 78th Test (beating T.G. Evans's total from 91 Tests).
- *803* Set E v A record of 85 dismissals.
- *806* His 135 is the highest score by any wicket-keeper in E v A Tests. Shared record-equalling E v A 6th-wkt stand of 215 with G. Boycott.
- *907* First to make 100 dismissals v Australia.
- *908* Second after R.W. Marsh to hold 250 catches in Tests.
- Only R.W. Marsh has exceeded his total of 269 Test dismissals or his 95 appearances as a wicket-keeper.
- Exceeded 1000 runs in a season twice and made 98 dismissals in 1967.
- His career total of 1344 dismissals is the fourth-highest in first-class cricket. He is one of only 12 (3 for Kent) to achieve the career 'double' of 10,000 runs and 1000 dismissals.
- Made 6 dismissals in an innings 7 times (6 for Kent) and 9 in a match once (Kent v Leicestershire at Maidstone in 1977).
- Scored 127* and 118* for Kent v Surrey at Maidstone in 1972.

TEST NOTES

- *707* Deputised as captain when A.R. Lewis and M.H. Denness were off the field on the fourth evening.

						Batting 1st			Batting 2nd			Fielding 1st				Fielding 2nd			
Ref	Series	V	T	Venue	Result	No	R	HO	No	R	HO	Ct	St	Byes	Balls	Ct	St	Byes	Balls
622/438 †	1967	P	2	Nottingham	W-10w	8	0	c	–	–	–	3	–	0	414	4	–	0	384
623/439 †			3	Oval	W-8w	8	28	c	–	–	–	2	–	5	612	3	1	1	607
631/443 †	1967–68	WI	4	Port-of-Spain	W-7w	7	69	*	–	–	–	1	–	0	798	–	–	1	180
632/444 †			5	Georgetown	D	7	7	lbw	7	73	*	2	–	0	904	1	–	1	398
637/445 †	1968	A	1	Manchester	L-159	8	5	c	8	4	lbw	2	–	0	783	1	–	2	528
638/446 †			2	Lord's	D	8	33	ro	–	–	–	2	–	0	202	–	–	0	402
639/447 †			3	Birmingham	D	7	4	b	5	4	*	–	–	1	546	–	–	0	170
640/448 †			4	Leeds	D	7	4	lbw	–	–	–	1	–	0	802	1	3	13	925
641/449 †			5	Oval	W-226	7	28	c	7	34	ro	3	1	4	981	1	–	0	501
647/450 †	1968–69	P	1	Lahore[2]	D	7	52	lbw	7	30	b	2	–	8	422	–	–	3	474
648/451 †			2	Dacca	D	7	2	c	–	–	–	3	–	4	661	1	–	0	606
649/452 †			3	Karachi	D	7	96	*	–	–	–	–	–	–	–	–	–	–	–
653/453 †	1969	WI	1	Manchester	W-10w	6	0	c	–	–	–	–	1	0	288	1	–	4	687
654/454 †			2	Lord's	D	7	53	b	8	11	b	2	–	5	948	1	–	4	605
655/455 †			3	Leeds	W-30	6	44	c	6	31	c	2	–	0	387	4	–	0	638
656/456 †	1969	NZ	1	Lord's	W-230	6	8	c	6	10	lbw	1	–	4	525	3	–	5	455
657/457 †			2	Nottingham	D	6	15	c	–	–	–	2	–	1	767	–	–	0	138
658/548 †			3	Oval	W-8w	6	21	c	–	–	–	–	1	0	495	3	1	3	699

Ref	Series	V	T	Venue	Result	Batting 1st			Batting 2nd			Fielding 1st				Fielding 2nd			
						No	R	HO	No	R	HO	Ct	St	Byes	Balls	Ct	St	Byes	Balls
674/459†	1970–71	A	1	Brisbane[2]	D	3	73	c	–	–	–	3	–	7	923	1	1	4	749
675/460†			2	Perth	D	4	24	c	8	30	*	3	–	5	917	–	–	4	256
676/461†			4	Sydney	W-299	7	6	st	7	21	*	–	–	0	614	3	–	2	453
677/462†			5	Melbourne	D	7	19	lbw	–	–	–	–	–	10	1024	2	–	8	368
678/463†			6	Adelaide	D	4	7	c	–	–	–	4	–	0	609	1	–	2	920
679/464†			7	Sydney	W-62	7	27	c	7	15	b	3	1	0	670	1	1	2	498
686/466†	1970–71	NZ	2	Auckland	D	7	101	b	5	96	b	–	–	7	848	–	–	0	128
687/467†	1971	P	1	Birmingham	D	7	116	b	7	4	*	–	–	6	1170	–	–	–	–
688/468†			2	Lord's	D	–	–	–	–	–	–	4	–	5	436	–	–	–	–
689/469†			3	Leeds	W-25	6	10	b	6	7	c	4	–	6	1258	2	1	17	531
690/470†	1971	I	1	Lord's	D	6	67	c	6	24	c	2	–	7	993	1	1	0	300
691/471†			2	Manchester	D	6	41	b	–	–	–	4	–	1	558	1	–	0	162
692/472†			3	Oval	L-4w	6	90	c	6	1	c	–	–	6	705	2	–	6	606
698/473†	1972	A	1	Manchester	W-89	7	18	c	7	1	c	2	–	1	348	2	–	0	512
699/474†			2	Lord's	L-8w	7	43	c	7	12	c	2	–	0	733	1	–	0	161
700/475†			3	Nottingham	D	8	0	c	–	–	–	3	–	4	712	–	–	0	552
701/476†			4	Leeds	W-9w	7	0	st	–	–	–	2	–	0	521	3	–	0	337
702/477†			5	Oval	L-5w	8	92	c	8	63	b	1	–	0	911	1	–	0	554
703/478†	1972–73	I	1	Delhi	W-6w	7	4	c	–	–	–	2	–	0	508	1	1	8	592
704/479†			2	Calcutta	L-28	7	35	st	7	2	c	1	–	0	586	2	–	8	407
705/480†			3	Madras[1]	L-4w	3	10	c	3	13	c	1	–	6	811	1	–	0	203
706/481†			4	Kanpur	D	3	40	c	–	–	–	1	–	1	1002	–	–	5	504
707/482†			5	Bombay[2]	D	3	56	lbw	3	8	b	–	–	4	830	2	–	0	576
719/483†	1972–73	P	1	Lahore[2]	D	7	29	c	7	34	c	–	–	1	950	–	–	0	228
720/484†			2	Hyderabad	D	7	71	c	7	63	*	2	–	14	1152	–	–	–	–
721/485†			3	Karachi	D	8	2	b	–	–	–	–	–	4	924	2	–	0	435
722/486†	1973	NZ	1	Nottingham	W-38	8	49	b	8	2	c	4	–	8	250	1	–	0	1129
723/487†			2	Lord's	D	7	0	b	7	0	c	3	–	0	1229	–	–	–	–
724/488†			3	Leeds	W-I & 1	7	21	c	–	–	–	2	–	5	592	2	–	1	423
725/489†	1973	WI	1	Oval	L-158	8	4	*	9	5	lbw	1	–	1	870	2	–	2	523
726/490†			2	Birmingham	D	6	0	b	–	–	–	–	–	0	897	4	–	0	622
727/491†			3	Lord's	L-I & 226	8	21	c	3	5	c	–	–	1	1012	–	–	–	–
731/492†	1973–74	WI	1	Port-of-Spain	L-7w	7	7	b	7	21	c	3	–	3	736	–	–	0	227
732/493†			2	Kingston	D	7	39	c	8	6	ro	–	–	16	1176	–	–	–	–
733/494†			3	Bridgetown	D	7	87	b	7	67	lbw	–	–	3	924	–	–	–	–
734/495†			4	Georgetown	D	7	61	c	–	–	–	–	–	6	521	–	–	–	–
735/496†			5	Port-of-Spain	W-26	7	33	*	8	44	lbw	1	–	11	703	–	–	9	531
739/497†	1974	I	1	Manchester	W-113	8	0	lbw	–	–	–	2	–	3	504	4	1	1	511
740/498†			2	Lord's	W-I & 285	7	26	c	–	–	–	2	–	4	611	3	–	0	102
741/499†			3	Birmingham	W-I & 78	–	–	–	–	–	–	3	–	1	356	1	–	0	406
742/500†	1974	P	1	Leeds	D	7	35	c	7	5	c	3	–	0	611	2	–	0	409
743/501†			2	Lord's	D	7	83	c	–	–	–	–	–	0	269	–	–	0	587
744/502†			3	Oval	D	8	9	b	–	–	–	1	–	6	992	1	–	5	180
750/503†	1974–75	A	1	Brisbane[2]	L-166	7	12	c	7	19	b	2	–	0	741	2	–	1	680
751/504†			2	Perth	L-9w	7	51	c	6	18	c	3	1	7	870	–	–	0	31
752/505†			3	Melbourne	D	7	52	b	7	4	c	3	–	2	741	1	–	6	640
753/506†			4	Sydney	L-171	7	82	b	7	10	b	2	–	0	791	–	–	0	515
754/507†			5	Adelaide	L-163	7	5	c	7	106	*	1	–	4	546	2	–	0	528
755/508†			6	Melbourne	W-I & 4	7	5	c	–	–	–	3	–	2	295	3	–	9	855
758/509†	1974–75	NZ	1	Auckland	W-I & 83	7	29	*	–	–	–	2	–	5	712	1	–	0	461
759/510†			2	Christchurch	D	–	–	–	–	–	–	–	–	3	717	–	–	–	–
760/511†	1975	A	1	Birmingham	L-I & 85	7	14	b	7	38	c	2	–	1	726	–	–	–	–
761/512†			2	Lord's	D	7	69	lbw	7	22	*	1	–	0	466	–	–	4	654
762/513†			3	Leeds	D	7	14	lbw	8	31	c	–	–	0	461	–	–	4	438
763/514†			4	Oval	D	7	9	lbw	7	64	c	1	–	0	1086	–	–	0	103
777/515†	1976	WI	1	Nottingham	D	7	9	c	–	–	–	2	–	0	921	–	–	0	216
778/516†			2	Lord's	D	7	17	b	8	4	lbw	1	–	2	304	–	–	3	519
779/517†			3	Manchester	L-425	8	1	c	7	14	c	–	–	0	420	–	–	5	684
780/518†			4	Leeds	L-55	7	116	c	8	2	c	1	–	1	532	–	–	4	309
781/519†			5	Oval	L-231	8	50	b	7	57	b	1	1	1	1097	–	–	4	192
788/520†	1976–77	I	1	Delhi	W-I & 25	7	75	st	–	–	–	1	–	0	311	2	–	3	664
789/521†			2	Calcutta	W-10w	7	2	c	–	–	–	1	–	0	450	2	–	2	425
790/522†			3	Madras[1]	W-200	7	45	c	7	11	c	1	–	0	443	1	–	5	233

Ref	Series	V	T	Venue	Result	Batting 1st No	R	HO	Batting 2nd No	R	HO	Fielding 1st Ct	St	Byes	Balls	Fielding 2nd Ct	St	Byes	Balls
791/523†			4	Bangalore	L-140	7	29	b	7	81	*	3	–	8	510	1	–	1	546
792/524†			5	Bombay[3]	D	6	24	b	6	1	b	1	1	0	634	–	1	4	424
803/525†	1976–77	A		Melbourne	L-45	8	15	lbw	7	42	lbw	1	–	4	350	3	–	0	774
804/526†	1977	A	1	Lord's	D	7	8	c	6	8	c	2	–	0	685	–	–	0	234
805/527†			2	Manchester	W-9w	6	39	c	–	–	–	4	–	0	656	–	–	0	491
806/528†			3	Nottingham	W-7w	7	135	c	3	2	c	1	–	4	494	–	–	1	762
807/529†			4	Leeds	W-I & 85	7	57	lbw	–	–	–	2	–	0	189	2	–	1	539
808/530†			5	Oval	D	7	6	c	–	–	–	1	–	1	789	–	–	–	–
880/557†	1980	WI	1	Nottingham	L-2w	8	6	lbw	8	7	lbw	3	–	1	547	3	–	0	412
881/558†			2	Lord's	D	9	9	c	–	–	–	1	–	1	884	–	–	–	–
882/559†			3	Manchester	D	8	2	ro	8	6	c	3	–	2	435	–	–	–	–
883/560†			4	Oval	D	7	3	c	9	3	lbw	1	–	0	572	–	–	–	–
907/571†	1981	A	5	Manchester	W-103	8	13	c	8	59	c	2	–	0	182	3	–	0	815
908/572†			6	Oval	D	8	36	b	8	70	*	–	–	4	792	1	–	1	626

Career	M	I	NO	HS	R	Avge	100	50	Ct	St	Balls	R	W	Avge	BB	5w	10w	Rate
Test	95	149	15	135	4389	32.75	5	30	250	19	–	–	–	–	–	–	–	–
F/c	511	745	134	156	18105	29.63	17	97	1211	133	104	87	2	43.50	1-5	–	–	52.00

Alan Knott

A. P. E. KNOTT – TEST SUMMARY

Series	V	M	I	NO	HS	R	Avge	100	50	Ct	St	Byes	Balls
1967	P	2	2	–	28	28	14.00	–	–	12	1	6	2017
1967–68	WI	2	3	2	73*	149	149.00	–	2	4	–	2	2280
1968	A	5	8	1	34	116	16.57	–	–	11	4	20	5840
1968–69	P	3	4	1	96*	180	60.00	–	2	6	–	15	2163
1969	WI	3	5	–	53	139	27.80	–	1	10	1	13	3553
1969	NZ	3	4	–	21	54	13.50	–	–	9	2	13	3079
1970–71	A	6	9	2	73	222	31.71	–	1	21	3	44	8001
1970–71	NZ	1	2	–	101	197	98.50	1	1	–	–	7	976
1971	P	3	4	1	116	137	45.66	1	–	10	1	34	3395
1971	I	3	5	–	90	223	44.60	–	2	10	1	20	3324
1972	A	5	8	–	92	229	28.37	–	2	17	–	5	5341
1972–73	I	5	8	–	56	168	21.00	–	1	11	1	32	6019
1972–73	P	3	5	1	71	199	49.75	–	2	4	–	19	3689
1973	NZ	3	5	–	49	72	14.40	–	–	12	–	14	3623
1973	WI	3	5	1	21	35	8.75	–	–	7	–	4	3924
1973–74	WI	5	9	1	87	365	45.62	–	3	4	–	48	4818
1974	I	3	2	–	26	26	13.00	–	–	15	1	9	2490
1974	P	3	4	–	83	132	33.00	–	1	7	–	11	3048
1974–75	A	6	11	1	106*	364	36.40	1	3	22	1	31	7233
1974–75	NZ	2	1	1	29*	29	–	–	–	3	–	8	1890
1975	A	4	8	1	69	261	37.28	–	2	4	–	9	3934
1976	WI	5	9	–	116	270	30.00	1	2	5	1	20	5194
1976–77	I	5	8	1	81*	268	38.28	–	2	13	2	23	4640
1976–77	A	1	2	–	42	57	28.50	–	–	4	–	4	1124
1977	A	5	7	–	135	255	36.42	1	1	12	–	7	4839
1980	WI	4	7	–	9	36	5.14	–	–	11	–	4	2850
1981	A	2	4	1	70*	178	59.33	–	2	6	–	5	2415
	A	34	57	6	135	1682	32.98	2	11	97	8	125	38727
	WI	22	38	4	116	994	29.23	1	8	41	2	91	22619
	NZ	9	12	1	101	352	32.00	1	1	24	2	42	9568
	I	16	23	1	90	685	31.13	–	5	49	5	84	16473
	P	14	19	3	116	676	42.25	1	5	39	2	85	14312
Home		56	87	5	135	2191	26.71	3	13	158	12	194	58866
Overseas		39	62	10	106*	2198	42.26	2	17	92	7	233	42833
Totals		95	149	15	135	4389	32.75	5	30	250	19	427	101699

KNOX
Neville Alexander

Surrey (1904 to 1910)

Wisden 1907
Born Clapham, Surrey 10 Oct 1884
Died Surbiton, Surrey 3 Mar 1935

Neville Knox

Neville Knox was rated by Jack Hobbs as 'the best fast bowler I ever saw'. Well over six feet tall, loose-limbed and with a long run angled in from deep mid-off, he bowled right-handed and very fast, breaking the ball in from the off and making good length deliveries rear awkwardly. After impressing at Dulwich College at both cricket and rugby he appeared twice for Surrey in 1904. The following year his haul of 129 wickets enabled Surrey to rise from 11th to fourth in the Championship. In 1906 he took 144 wickets at only 19.63 apiece, including 12 for 183 (seven clean bowled) in the Gentlemen's victory at Lord's. His meteoric career was cut tragically short by an acute form of shin soreness which rendered him lame after bowling. He joined the RAOC in 1915 and, remaining in the Army after the War, attained the rank of major.

						Batting 1st			Batting 2nd				Bowling 1st			Bowling 2nd		
Ref	Series	V	T	Venue	Result	No	R	HO	No	R	HO	Ct	Balls	R	W	Balls	R	W
94/91	1907	SA	2	Leeds	W-53	11	8	c	11	5	ro	–	18	13	1	–	–	–
95/92			3	Oval	D	11	8	*	11	3	b	–	60	39	2	48	53	0

Career	M	I	NO	HS	R	Avge	100	50	Ct	St	Balls	R	W	Avge	BB	5w	10w	Rate
Test	2	4	1	8*	24	8.00	–	–	–	–	126	105	3	35.00	2-39	–	–	42.00
F/c	88	129	40	45*	905	10.16	–	–	32	–	14624	8860	411	21.55	8-48	38	9	35.58

LAKER, James Charles

Surrey (1946 to 1959)
Essex (1962 to 1964)
Auckland (1951–52)

Wisden 1952
TOURS
A 1958–59; SA 1956–57; WI 1947–48, 1953–54, 1963–64 (Cav), 1964–65 (Cav); NZ 1958–59; I 1950–51 (Cwlth)
Born Frizinghall, Bradford, Yorkshire 9 Feb 1922
Died Putney, London 23 Apr 1986

Jim Laker became the most accomplished off-spin bowler since the Second World War and, in his heyday, was probably the best of all time. Tall (6ft) and strongly built, he gave an impression of detached boredom as he sauntered back to his mark, often gazing heavenwards as if he were wondering if he had left the gas on. As he turned and began his measured approach his mood changed dramatically and few slow bowlers have managed to convey such intimidation. Jaw firmly set and left leg braced, he would windmill his arm in a classic high action and often the ball would hum its menace as it flew down the pitch. Exceptionally accurate and highly intelligent, he was a master of flight and angle variations and, as his frequently blistered and arthritic spinning finger would testify, he could turn the ball prodigiously. He was a capable batsman despite an idiosyncratic backlift which involved the bat being swung full circle starting in the direction of the bowler. His close fielding, usually in the gully, was very reliable. At school and in the Bradford league he had been a batsman and fast bowler

NOTABLE FEATS

- 50 wickets in 12th Test (*351*); 100 wickets in 27th Test (*427*); 150 wickets in 36th Test (*441*).
- *295* Took 7 for 103 in his first Test innings, including 6 for 25 on the second morning.
- *428* 'Laker's match' in which he set 4 world records: most wickets (19) in any first-class match; best innings (10 for 53) and match analysis (19 for 90) in Test cricket; first bowler to dismiss all 11 batsmen during a Test; and only bowler to take all 10 wickets in a season twice (*see below*). He ended the 1st inns with a 22-ball spell of 7 for 8.
- *429* Set current E v A series record of 46 wickets (avge 9.60); it also remains the record for any series in England.
- Took 100 wickets in a season 11 times (166 in 1950).
- Took 10 for 88 for Surrey v Australians at The Oval on 16 May 1956 during 46 overs bowled in 4¼ hours interrupted only by the lunch and tea intervals. Also 10 for 53 (*above*).
- Took 8 for 2 for England v The Rest (all out 27) at Bradford in the 1950 Test trial – statistically the most remarkable analysis in English first-class cricket.
- Took 15 for 97 for Surrey v MCC at Lord's in 1954.
- Four hat-tricks: three for Surrey – v Gloucestershire at Gloucester in 1951, v Warwickshire at The Oval in 1953 and v Cambridge U at Guildford in 1953; and one for P.F. Warner's XI v South of England at Hastings in 1947.

who had begun to experiment with off-spin. During wartime service with the RAOC in the Middle East he was able to develop his new style against some notable players in Cairo and Alexandria. Afterwards he had begun to resume his banking career when a chance billeting in Catford resulted in a trial at The Oval. There his bowling, usually in harness with the left-arm leg-spin of Tony Lock, was a key factor in Surrey's record run of seven Championship titles (1952–58). Although he was England's most successful bowler on his first tour, he took heavy punishment at the hands of the 1948 Australians and failed to command a regular place until his historic summer of 1956. Then, as a mature campaigner in his prime, he totally demoralised the Australians taking 19 wickets at Old Trafford and a record 46 in the series. No other bowler has exceeded 17 wickets in any first-class match and, astonishingly, although he frequently switched ends with the hapless Lock (1 for 106), all 19 wickets were taken from the Stretford End. Delayed by interruptions from rain, England began the final 115-minute session needing four wickets to retain the Ashes. Laker completed the task with 33 minutes to spare; heavy rain the following day washed out the entire first-class programme. An earlier all-ten that summer had led to Surrey's defeat of an Australian team totally baffled by off-spin. He retired after the 1959 season and wrote a controversial book (*Over to Me*) which resulted in his MCC and Surrey privileges being withdrawn for a time. Through Trevor Bailey's persuasion he returned to play in 30 matches for Essex as an amateur. The well-grassed Essex wickets must have come as a shock after the dustbowls at Kennington; asked to give his opinion of the Romford pitch before the start of one match he shambled back after ten minutes and reported to his captain: 'I'm sorry, Trevor, I couldn't find it!' For his last two decades he once again became a popular household name as a TV commentator and analyst renowned for his laconic asides and silent 'Gs' (battin', bowlin' and fieldin').

TEST NOTES

- *385* Retired hurt after being struck in the right eye by a bouncer from F.M. King at 515–8 (1st inns).

Ref	Series	V	T	Venue	Result	Batting 1st			Batting 2nd				Bowling 1st			Bowling 2nd		
						No	R	HO	No	R	HO	Ct	Balls	R	W	Balls	R	W
295/258	1947–48	WI	1	Bridgetown	D	10	2	c	–	–	–	–	222	103	7	180	95	2
296/259			2	Port-of-Spain	D	9	55	c	5	24	c	–	216	108	2	–	–	–
297/260			3	Georgetown	L-7w	8	10	c	10	6	c	–	216	94	2	54	34	2
298/261			4	Kingston	L-10w	10	6	c	10	6	*	1	220	103	3	12	11	0
299/262	1948	A	1	Nottingham	L-8w	9	63	c	9	4	b	–	330	138	4	–	–	–
300/263			2	Lord's	L-409	9	28	c	9	0	b	–	42	17	0	188	111	2
302/265			4	Leeds	L-7w	10	4	c	10	15	*	–	180	113	3	192	93	0
317/275	1949	NZ	4	Oval	D	8	0	c	–	–	–	–	18	11	0	174	78	4
323/276	1950	WI	1	Manchester	W-202	9	4	b	9	40	c	–	102	43	0	84	43	1
336/289	1951	SA	3	Manchester	W-9w	8	27	c	–	–	–	–	162	47	1	114	42	3
338/291			5	Oval	W-4w	7	6	b	7	13	*	1	222	64	4	168	55	6
351/297	1952	I	1	Leeds	W-7w	9	15	b	–	–	–	1	135	39	4	78	17	0
352/298			2	Lord's	W-8w	9	23	*	–	–	–	1	72	21	0	234	102	4
353/299			3	Manchester	W-I & 207	8	0	c	–	–	–	1	12	7	0	–	–	–
354/300			4	Oval	D	8	6	*	–	–	–	–	12	3	0	–	–	–
374/303	1953	A	3	Manchester	D	10	5	lbw	–	–	–	–	102	42	1	54	11	2
375/304			4	Leeds	D	9	10	c	9	48	c	–	54	33	0	12	17	1
376/305			5	Oval	W-8w	8	1	c	–	–	–	–	30	34	1	101	75	4
383/307	1953–54	WI	2	Bridgetown	L-181	9	1	c	9	0	lbw	–	181	81	4	180	62	0
384/308			3	Georgetown	W-9w	9	27	b	–	–	–	–	126	32	2	216	56	2
385/309			4	Port-of-Spain	D	8	7	*rh	–	–	–	1	300	154	2	–	–	–
386/310			5	Kingston	W-9w	10	9	b	–	–	–	2	24	13	0	300	71	4

						Batting 1st			Batting 2nd				Bowling 1st			Bowling 2nd		
Ref	**Series**	**V**	**T**	**Venue**	**Result**	**No**	**R**	**HO**	**No**	**R**	**HO**	**Ct**	**Balls**	**R**	**W**	**Balls**	**R**	**W**
387/311	1954	P	1	Lord's	D	9	13	*	–	–	–	–	132	17	1	62	22	1
412/326	1955	SA	5	Oval	W-92	9	2	c	9	12	b	–	138	28	2	226	56	5
425/327	1956	A	1	Nottingham	D	8	9	*	–	–	–	–	175	58	4	180	29	2
426/328			2	Lord's	L-185	8	12	b	8	4	c	–	175	47	3	42	17	0
427/329			3	Leeds	W-I & 42	10	5	b	–	–	–	–	174	58	5	249	55	6
428/330			4	Manchester	W-I & 170	9	3	ro	–	–	–	–	100	37	9	308	53	10
429/331			5	Oval	D	9	4	c	–	–	–	–	192	80	4	108	8	3
434/332	1956–57	SA	1	Johannesburg[3]	W-131	10	0	c	10	3	*	–	168	33	1	16	5	1
435/333			2	Cape Town	W-312	9	0	b	–	–	–	–	224	65	1	113	7	2
436/334			3	Durban[2]	D	9	0	*	9	6	c	1	96	47	0	144	29	2
437/335			4	Johannesburg[3]	L-17	9	17	lbw	9	5	c	–	120	49	1	56	26	1
438/336			5	Port Elizabeth	L-58	10	6	b	10	3	*	–	112	37	1	112	26	1
439/337	1957	WI	1	Birmingham	D	9	7	b	–	–	–	–	324	119	4	144	13	2
441/339			3	Nottingham	D	–	–	–	–	–	–	1	372	101	3	258	98	1
442/340			4	Leeds	W-I & 5	9	1	c	–	–	–	–	102	24	2	38	16	1
443/341			5	Oval	W-I & 237	10	10	*	–	–	–	–	138	39	3	102	38	2
454/342	1958	NZ	1	Birmingham	W-205	10	11	*	–	–	–	1	30	9	1	54	14	1
455/343			2	Lord's	W-I & 148	10	1	c	–	–	–	1	72	13	4	78	24	1
456/344			3	Leeds	W-I & 71	–	–	–	–	–	–	–	132	17	5	216	27	3
458/346			5	Oval	D	9	15	c	–	–	–	–	84	44	1	120	25	1
464/347	1958–59	A	1	Brisbane[2]	L-8w	9	13	c	9	15	c	–	81	15	2	136	39	1
465/348			2	Melbourne	L-8w	9	22	*	9	3	c	–	96	47	0	32	7	1
466/349			3	Sydney	D	10	2	c	–	–	–	–	368	107	5	64	10	2
468/351			5	Melbourne	L-9w	11	2	c	11	5	*	–	245	93	4	–	–	–

Career	**M**	**I**	**NO**	**HS**	**R**	**Avge**	**100**	**50**	**Ct**	**St**	**Balls**	**R**	**W**	**Avge**	**BB**	**5w**	**10w**	**Rate**
Test	46	63	15	63	676	14.08	–	2	12	–	12027	4101	193	21.24	10-53	9	3	62.31
F/c	450	548	108	113	7304	16.60	2	18	270	–	101974	35791	1944	18.41	10-53	127	32	52.45

J. C. LAKER – TEST BOWLING SUMMARY

Series	**V**	**M**	**Balls**	**R**	**W**	**Avge**	**BB**	**5w**	**10w**	**Rate**
1947–48	WI	4	1120	548	18	30.44	7-103	1	–	62.22
1948	A	3	932	472	9	52.44	4-138	–	–	103.55
1949	NZ	1	192	89	4	22.25	4-78	–	–	48.00
1950	WI	1	186	86	1	86.00	1-43	–	–	186.00
1951	SA	2	666	208	14	14.85	6-55	1	1	47.57
1952	I	4	543	189	8	23.62	4-39	–	–	67.87
1953	A	3	353	212	9	23.55	4-75	–	–	35.30
1953–54	WI	4	1327	469	14	33.50	4-71	–	–	94.78
1954	P	1	194	39	2	19.50	1-17	–	–	97.00
1955	SA	1	364	84	7	12.00	5-56	1	–	52.00
1956	A	5	1703	442	46	9.60	10-53	4	2	37.02
1956–57	SA	5	1161	324	11	29.45	2-7	–	–	105.54
1957	WI	4	1478	448	18	24.88	4-119	–	–	82.11
1958	NZ	4	786	173	17	10.17	5-17	1	–	46.23
1958–59	A	4	1022	318	15	21.20	5-107	1	–	68.13
	A	15	4010	1444	79	18.27	10-53	5	2	50.75
	SA	8	2191	616	32	19.25	6-55	2	1	68.46
	WI	13	4111	1551	51	30.41	7-103	1	–	80.60
	NZ	5	978	262	21	12.47	5-17	1	–	46.57
	I	4	543	189	8	23.62	4-39	–	–	67.87
	P	1	194	39	2	19.50	1-17	–	–	97.00
Home		29	7397	2442	135	18.08	10-53	7	3	54.79
Overseas		17	4630	1659	58	28.60	7-103	2	–	79.82
Totals		46	12027	4101	193	21.24	10-53	9	3	62.31

Jim Laker at Old Trafford, 1956.

LAMB, Allan Joseph

Western Province
(1972–73 to 1981–82)
Northamptonshire (1978 to date)
Orange Free State (1987–88)

Wisden 1981
TOURS
A 1982–83, 1986–87; WI 1985–86;
NZ 1983–84; I/SL 1984–85; P 1983–84
Born Langebaanweg, Cape Province,
South Africa 20 Jun 1954

Allan Lamb

Born of English parents in a country banished from the cricketing map, Allan Lamb made his England debut almost immediately after becoming qualified by residence in 1982. His selection would not have required too long a conference; he is a class batsman with all the strokes and a sound defence who averaged in excess of 60 for his adopted Northamptonshire in each of the two previous summers. Compact (5ft 8in), determined and tough, he remained an automatic choice for 45 Test matches. An outstanding player of fast bowling he took three hundreds off the mighty West Indian pace machine in 1984. Four years later at Lord's he scored another against their successors and then astounded everyone at Headingley by hobbling out to bat after tearing a calf muscle. Last seen on crutches, he defied the pace attack for 87 minutes, batting on one leg and hitting three boundaries. The West Indies bowlers showed him no mercy and, despite the pain-killing injection administered just before his journey to the middle, even the nuggety 'Lamby' frequently winced in agony. Curiously for one brought up on South African pitches, all his eight Test hundreds have been scored in England. A veteran of 80 one-day internationals, he is an outstanding exponent of that game where his powers of improvisation, allied to his fast aggressive outfielding, assume great value. After playing a major part in England's reaching the 1987 World Cup final, he was astonishingly omitted from the serious part of the team's convoluted winter. Returning to the Union he promptly hit a career-best 294 against a strong Eastern Province side, his 394-minute marathon winning 50,000 rand for being the highest score in the history of the Currie Cup, another 50,000 rand for sharing a record partnership of 355, and a further 15,000 rand for scoring 150 off fewer then 300 balls and 200 in under 400 balls. It was a fairly strong message to the selectors. County captaincy should provide some worthy challenges for this gritty and humorous emigrant but hopefully he will be persuaded to keep his right-arm medium-pace bowling securely under wraps.

						Batting 1st			Batting 2nd			
Ref	Series	V	T	Venue	Result	No	R	HO	No	R	HO	Ct
928/580	1982	I	1	Lord's	W-7w	3	9	lbw	4	37	*	–
929/581			2	Manchester	D	3	9	c	–	–	–	–
930/582			3	Oval	D	3	107	ro	3	45	b	–
931/583	1982	P	1	Birmingham	W-113	3	6	c	3	5	lbw	–
932/584			2	Lord's	L-10w	3	33	c	3	0	lbw	1
933/585			3	Leeds	W-3w	4	0	c	4	4	lbw	–
938/586	1982–83	A	1	Perth	D	4	46	c	4	56	c	2
939/587			2	Brisbane[2]	L-7w	4	72	c	4	12	c	1
940/588			3	Adelaide	L-8w	4	82	c	4	8	c	–
941/589			4	Melbourne	W-3	5	83	c	5	26	c	1
942/590			5	Sydney	D	4	0	b	5	29	c	1
957/591	1983	NZ	1	Oval	W-189	4	24	b	4	102	*	2
958/592			2	Leeds	L-5w	4	58	c	4	28	b	1
959/593			3	Lord's	W-127	4	17	c	4	4	c	6
960/594			4	Nottingham	W-165	4	22	c	4	137	*	1
975/595	1983–84	NZ	1	Wellington	D	4	13	c	–	–	–	1
976/596			2	Christchurch	L-I & 132	4	11	c	4	9	c	–
977/597			3	Auckland	D	4	49	lbw	–	–	–	–
978/598	1983–84	P	1	Karachi	L-3w	4	4	c	4	20	c	2
979/599			2	Faisalabad	D	4	19	c	–	–	–	2
980/600			3	Lahore[2]	D	4	29	c	5	6	c	–
989/601	1984	WI	1	Birmingham	L-I & 180	5	15	c	5	13	c	1
990/602			2	Lord's	L-9w	4	23	lbw	4	110	c	–
991/603			3	Leeds	L-8w	5	100	b	5	3	lbw	–
992/604			4	Manchester	L-I & 64	5	100	*	5	9	b	–
993/605			5	Oval	L-172	6	12	lbw	5	1	c	2

NOTABLE FEATS

• 1000 runs in 15th Test (*960*) (29 inns); 2000 runs in 33rd Test (*1017*) (58 inns).
• *959* Equalled England fielding records by holding 4 catches in an innings and 6 in the match.
• *990* Batted on all 5 days.
• *992* First to score hundreds in 3 successive Tests within a series for England since K.F. Barrington in 1967.
• *994* Equalled record of 4 Test hundreds in an English season shared by H. Sutcliffe (1929), D.G. Bradman (1930) and D.C.S. Compton (1947).
• Exceeded 1000 runs in a season 8 times, including 2049 in 1981.
• Contributed his highest score of 294 to South African record 5th-wkt stand of 355 with J.J. Strydom for Orange Free State v Eastern Province at Bloemfontein in 1987–88 (record score for OFS).
• Hit 30 (644664) off an over from A.I. Kallicharran for Northamptonshire v Warwickshire at Birmingham in 1982.

						Batting 1st			Batting 2nd			
Ref	Series	V	T	Venue	Result	No	R	HO	No	R	HO	Ct
994/606	1984	SL		Lord's	D	5	107	c	–	–	–	1
1005/607	1984–85	I	1	Bombay[3]	L-8w	5	9	c	5	1	st	3
1006/608			2	Delhi	W-8w	4	52	c	4	37	*	3
1007/609			3	Calcutta	D	6	67	c	–	–	–	–
1008/610			4	Madras[1]	W-9w	4	62	b	–	–	–	3
1009/611			5	Kanpur	D	4	13	c	–	–	–	–
1017/612	1985	A	1	Leeds	W-5w	5	38	b	5	31	*	2
1018/613			2	Lord's	L-4w	5	47	c	7	9	c	3
1019/614			3	Nottingham	D	5	17	lbw	–	–	–	–
1020/615			4	Manchester	D	5	67	ro	–	–	–	1
1021/616			5	Birmingham	W-I & 118	5	46	c	–	–	–	1
1022/617			6	Oval	W-I & 94	6	1	c	–	–	–	–
1038/618	1985–86	WI	1	Kingston	L-10w	5	49	b	5	13	c	–
1039/619			2	Port-of-Spain	L-7w	5	62	c	5	40	lbw	2
1040/620			3	Bridgetown	L-I & 30	5	5	c	5	6	c	–
1041/621			4	Port-of-Spain	L-10w	5	36	b	5	11	b	–
1042/622			5	St John's	L-240	5	1	c	6	1	b	1
1046/623	1986	I	1	Lord's	L-5w	5	6	c	5	39	c	2
1047/624			2	Leeds	L-279	4	10	c	4	10	c	–
1051/628	1986	NZ	3	Oval	D	4	0	b	–	–	–	–
1058/629	1986–87	A	1	Brisbane[2]	W-7w	4	40	lbw	4	9	lbw	1
1059/630			2	Perth	D	3	0	c	4	2	lbw	1
1060/631			3	Adelaide	D	4	14	c	4	9	*	1
1061/632			4	Melbourne	W-I & 14	4	43	c	–	–	–	–
1062/633			5	Sydney	L-55	4	24	c	4	3	c	3
1098/646	1988	WI	1	Nottingham	D	5	0	lbw	5	6	*	–
1099/647			2	Lord's	L-134	5	10	lbw	5	113	ro	–
1100/648			3	Manchester	L-I & 156	5	33	c	5	9	c	–
1101/649			4	Leeds	L-10w	5	64	*rh	8	19	c	–
1103/651	1988	SL		Lord's	W-7w	5	63	b	4	8	c	1

TEST NOTES

• *938* Bowled in 2nd inns: 0 for 0 (6 balls).
• *994* Bowled in 2nd inns: 0 for 6 (6 balls).
• *1007* Bowled in 2nd inns: 1 for 6 (6 balls).
• *1020* Bowled in 2nd inns: 0 for 10 (6 balls).
• *1038* Bowled in 2nd inns: 0 for 1 (1 no-ball).
• *1059* Bowled in 2nd inns: 0 for 0 (6 nballs).

Career	M	I	NO	HS	R	Avge	100	50	Ct	St	Balls	R	W	Avge	BB	5w	10w	Rate
Test	56	98	9	137*	2969	33.35	8	12	53	–	30	23	1	23.00	1-6	–	–	30.00
F/c	327	548	87	294	21756	47.19	55	119	245	–	277	164	6	27.33	1-1	–	–	46.16

A. J. LAMB – TEST BATTING SUMMARY

Series	V	M	I	NO	HS	R	Avge	100	50
1982	I	3	5	1	107	207	51.75	1	–
1982	P	3	6	–	33	48	8.00	–	–
1982–83	A	5	10	–	83	414	41.40	–	4
1983	NZ	4	8	2	137*	392	65.33	2	1
1983–84	NZ	3	4	–	49	82	20.50	–	–
1983–84	P	3	5	–	29	78	15.60	–	–
1984	WI	5	10	1	110	386	42.88	3	–
1984	SL	1	1	–	107	107	107.00	1	–
1984–85	I	5	7	1	67	241	40.16	–	3
1985	A	6	8	1	67	256	36.57	–	1
1985–86	WI	5	10	–	62	224	22.40	–	1
1986	I	2	4	–	39	65	16.25	–	–
1986	NZ	1	1	–	0	0	0.00	–	–

Series	V	M	I	NO	HS	R	Avge	100	50
1986–87	A	5	9	1	43	144	18.00	–	–
1988	WI	4	8	2	113	254	42.33	1	1
1988	SL	1	2	–	63	71	35.50	–	1
	A	16	27	2	83	814	32.56	–	5
	WI	14	28	3	113	864	34.56	4	2
	NZ	8	13	2	137*	474	43.09	2	1
	I	10	16	2	107	513	36.64	1	3
	P	6	11	–	33	126	11.45	–	–
	SL	2	3	–	107	178	59.33	1	1
Home		30	53	7	137*	1786	38.82	8	4
Overseas		26	45	2	83	1183	27.51	–	8
Totals		56	98	9	137*	2969	33.35	8	12

LANGRIDGE, James

Sussex (1924 to 1953)
Auckland (1927–28)

Wisden 1932
TOURS
A 1935–36, 1946–47; NZ 1935–36;
I/SL 1933–34, 1937–38 (Tennyson)
Born Chailey, Sussex 10 Jul 1906
Died Brighton, Sussex 10 Sep 1966

Jim Langridge, elder brother of John and father of Richard, devoted his life to Sussex cricket. He was a tallish (5ft 10½in), skilful and very consistent left-handed all-rounder: a patient middle-order batsman, an exceptionally accurate left-arm slow bowler who was hard to attack, and a very reliable fielder. Originally a specialist batsman, his bowling talents bore little fruit until 1929. Then only the presence of Hedley Verity kept him out of the England team. After wartime duties with the National Fire Service, he found himself in Australia at the age of 40 as Verity's replacement. Practising before making his first appearance against Australia he tore a groin muscle and closed his Test career. He continued to render Sussex magnificent service, becoming only the second professional in modern times after Tom Dollery to be appointed captain (1950–52). In retirement he became their coach (1953–59) and subsequently a minor counties umpire (1960–65).

NOTABLE FEATS

- *228* Took 7 for 56 in his second Test innings and completed the 'double' for that season's first-class matches.
- Exceeded 1000 runs in a season 20 times, including 2082 in 1937, and took 1000 wickets 6 times, completing the 'double' on 6 occasions. One of only 13 players to score 2000 runs and take 100 wickets in a season (1937).
- Holds Sussex records for most appearances (622) and most instances of 1000 runs in a season (20).
- Shared record Sussex 4th-wkt stand of 326* with G. Cox v Yorkshire at Leeds in 1949.
- Took 9 for 34 for Sussex v Yorkshire at Sheffield in 1934.
- Took 7 for 8 for Sussex v Gloucestershire at Cheltenham in 1932.
- Hat-trick for Sussex v Derbyshire at Derby in 1939.
- Took 4 wickets in 5 balls for Sussex v Somerset at Weston in 1948.
- Achieved match 'double' (116 runs and 11 wickets) for Sussex v Glamorgan at Swansea in 1929.

MCC in India, 1933–34: standing *A.H. Bakewell, L.F. Townsend, E.W. Clark, Major E. Ricketts (manager), C.J. Barnett, A. Mitchell, J. Langridge, R.J. Gregory;* seated *M.S. Nichols, H. Elliott, C.F. Walters, D.R. Jardine (captain), B.H. Valentine, C.S. Marriott, H. Verity;* in front *J.H. Human, W.H.V. Levett.*

					Batting 1st			Batting 2nd				Bowling 1st			Bowling 2nd		
Ref	Series	V	T	Venue	Result	No	R	HO	No	R	HO	Ct	Balls	R	W	Balls	R	W
228/202	1933	WI	2	Manchester	D	7	9	c	–	–	–	2	54	23	0	102	56	7
229/203			3	Oval	W-I & 17	6	22	c	–	–	–	1	–	–	–	42	23	0
230/204	1933–34	I	1	Bombay[1]	W-9w	4	31	lbw	–	–	–	–	102	42	3	96	32	1
231/205			2	Calcutta	D	4	70	c	–	–	–	–	102	27	0	60	19	0
232/206			3	Madras[1]	W-202	4	1	lbw	6	46	c	–	36	9	1	144	63	5
243/217	1935	SA	2	Lord's	L-157	7	27	c	7	17	lbw	1	78	27	2	60	19	0
252/221	1936	I	1	Lord's	W-9w	7	19	c	–	–	–	2	24	9	0	–	–	–
278/246	1946	I	3	Oval	D	–	–	–	–	–	–	–	174	64	0	–	–	–

Career	M	I	NO	HS	R	Avge	100	50	Ct	St	Balls	R	W	Avge	BB	5w	10w	Rate
Test	8	9	0	70	242	26.88	–	1	6	–	1074	413	19	21.73	7-56	2	–	56.52
F/c	695	1058	157	167	31716	35.20	42	181	384	–	89833	34524	1530	22.56	9-34	91	14	58.71

LARKINS, Wayne

Northamptonshire (1972 to date)
Eastern Province
(1982–83 to 1983–84)

TOURS
A 1979–80; SA 1981–82 (SAB);
I 1979–80, 1980–81 (Overseas XI)
Born Roxton, Bedfordshire 22 Nov 1953

Wayne Larkins

Wayne Larkins is an aggressive opening batsman who, on his day, can take apart any attack and give the innings an impressive and rousing start. He is a natural timer of the ball and has a fine array of attractive high-class strokes. Tallish (5ft 11in) and of average build, he took several seasons to establish his place in the Northamptonshire side. Then everything fell into place and his consistently high scoring earned him a tour of Australia. A long Test career seemed assured but, despite several useful starts, the large innings necessary to cement his England place continued to prove elusive. Surprisingly omitted from the 1981–82 tour of India, he gained himself a three-year ban from Test cricket for joining a mercenary expedition to South Africa. Recalled in 1986 when his first-class average for the season was in single figures, he managed to fracture his thumb before testing one of the more bizarre of selectorial hunches. He is a handy right-arm medium-pace swing bowler and a daringly athletic fielder.

NOTABLE FEATS
- Exceeded 1000 runs in a season 10 times.
- Two double centuries for Northamptonshire, both in 1983.
- Shared (then) record Northamptonshire 2nd-wkt stand of 322 with R.G. Williams v Leicestershire at Leicester in 1980.

						Batting 1st			Batting 2nd			
Ref	Series	V	T	Venue	Result	No	R	HO	No	R	HO	Ct
872/555	1979–80	A	3	Melbourne	L-8w	3	25	c	3	3	lbw	1
876/556	1979–80	I		Bombay[3]	W-10w	3	0	lbw	–	–	–	–
882/559	1980	WI	3	Manchester	D	4	11	lbw	4	33	c	1
883/560			4	Oval	D	4	7	lbw	4	0	b	–
884/561			5	Leeds	D	4	9	b	3	30	lbw	1
908/572	1981	A	6	Oval	D	2	34	c	2	24	c	–

Career	M	I	NO	HS	R	Avge	100	50	Ct	St	Balls	R	W	Avge	BB	5w	10w	Rate
Test	6	11	0	34	176	16.00	–	–	3	–	–	–	–	–	–	–	–	–
F/c	352	607	37	252	19266	33.80	42	76	201	–	3271	1760	42	41.90	5-59	1	–	77.88

LARTER John David Frederick

Northamptonshire (1960 to 1969)

TOURS
A 1962–63, 1965–66;
SA 1961–62 (Int XI); NZ 1960–61, 1962–63, 1965–66; I 1963–64;
P 1961–62 (Int XI); Z 1961–62 (Int XI)
Born Inverness, Scotland 24 Apr 1940

David Larter was an exceptionally tall (6ft 7in) right-arm fast-medium bowler who learned his craft at Framlingham College. Bounding over his 20-yard approach in just ten giraffe-like strides, he varied his pace, was fairly accurate and extracted an awkward degree of bounce. Fast bowling imposed too great a burden on his elongated frame and an assortment of strain-related injuries curtailed and finally ended his career. He was one of only six Scottish-born cricketers to represent England.

NOTABLE FEATS
- *534* Took 5 wickets in his first Test innings and 9 in his first match.
- Took 100 wickets in a season twice.

David Larter

Ref	Series	V	T	Venue	Result	Batting 1st No	R	HO	Batting 2nd No	R	HO	Ct	Bowling 1st Balls	R	W	Bowling 2nd Balls	R	W
534/386	1962	P	5	Oval	W-10w	–	–	–	–	–	–	–	150	57	5	127	88	4
540/392	1962–63	NZ	1	Auckland	W-I & 215	–	–	–	–	–	–	–	156	51	3	85	26	4
541/393			2	Wellington	W-I & 47	–	–	–	–	–	–	2	84	52	0	42	18	0
542/394			3	Christchurch	W-7w	11	2	b	–	–	–	–	126	59	0	138	32	3
553/400	1963–64	I	1	Madras[2]	D	11	2	*	–	–	–	–	114	62	0	66	33	0
554/401			2	Bombay[2]	D	9	0	c	–	–	–	1	63	35	2	30	13	0
555/402			3	Calcutta	D	11	0	c	–	–	–	1	108	61	1	48	27	2
593/417	1965	NZ	3	Leeds	W-I & 187	–	–	–	–	–	–	–	169	66	4	132	54	2
594/418	1965	SA	1	Lord's	D	11	0	*	–	–	–	–	156	47	0	102	67	1
595/419			2	Nottingham	L-94	10	2	b	11	10	c	1	102	25	1	174	68	5

Career	M	I	NO	HS	R	Avge	100	50	Ct	St	Balls	R	W	Avge	BB	5w	10w	Rate
Test	10	7	2	10	16	3.20	–	–	5	–	2172	941	37	25.43	5-57	2	–	58.70
F/c	182	162	57	51*	639	6.08	–	1	56	–	31395	13013	666	19.53	8-28	27	5	47.13

LARWOOD, Harold

Nottinghamshire (1924 to 1938)
Europeans (1936–37)

Wisden 1927
TOURS A 1928–29, 1932–33
Born Nuncargate, Nottinghamshire
14 Nov 1904

Harold Larwood was the most feared and accurate fast bowler of all time. Although barely of medium height (5ft 8in), he was immensely strong and fit – a legacy from his early days as a miner. During a run-up of 18 paces he would gradually and rhythmically accelerate until he arrived at the crease at top speed, perfectly poised to launch into that superb action in which his right arm described a full arc and frequently scraped the ground as he followed through. His long arms enabled him to extract bounce from barely short of a length. A fiercely determined competitor, he would maintain his speed for long spells and in great heat; his best England analysis (6 for 32 in Test *176*) was returned in ideal batting conditions at Brisbane during a match in which he also contributed 107 runs with the bat. Often he would ignore the pain of damaged muscles and, in his final Test, he scored 98 runs after bowling over 32 overs with a splintered bone in his foot. A hard-hitting batsman with a good eye, he took great delight in scoring straight boundaries. He was at the height of his powers when he paid his second visit to Australia under the captaincy of Douglas Jardine. Without Larwood's exceptional pace and precision Jardine would have been unable to launch his ruthless 'bodyline' campaign on Bradman. The plan proved outstandingly successful: 'The Don' – career Test average 99.94 – was confined to 396 runs at 56.57, four times falling victim to Larwood. Back in

Bill Woodfull on the receiving end of a Larwood bouncer during the Brisbane Test, 1932–33.

England after the tour Larwood was told to apologise to the MCC for his bowling. As he had only been obeying Jardine's instructions, he not surprisingly refused. From that moment he was ignored by England's selectors and, disillusioned, he soon retired from Nottinghamshire. In 1950 he sold his confectionery shop in Blackpool and, accompanied by his wife and five daughters, sailed for Australia on the *Orontes*, the very ship that had carried the MCC team there in 1932. A quietly proud man, he has found much happiness in Australia where his family has grown to include 13 grandchildren and four great-grandchildren. Although virtually blind, he can easily find his way around the house he moved into soon after his arrival. His proudest possession is a silver ashtray presented to him by Jardine and inscribed: 'To Harold for the Ashes 1932–33. From a grateful skipper.' Sadly all honours lists have passed him by.

NOTABLE FEATS

- 50 wickets in 17th Test (*220*).
- *176* Shared record E v A 8th-wkt stand of 124 with E.H. Hendren.
- *224* His 98 in 135 min was the highest score by a 'night-watchman' in Tests until 1962.
- Took 100 wickets in a season 8 times (162 in 1932).
- Headed national bowling averages 5 times: 1927–28–31–32–36.
- Took 9 for 41 for Nottinghamshire v Kent at Nottingham in 1931.
- Two hat-tricks for Nottinghamshire: v Cambridge U at Fenner's in 1926 and v Glamorgan at Nottingham in 1931.
- Bowled unchanged for Nottinghamshire throughout both Leicestershire innings in partnership with W. Voce at Nottingham in 1932.

H. LARWOOD – TEST BOWLING SUMMARY

Series	V	M	Balls	R	W	Avge	BB	5w	10w	Rate
1926	A	2	570	252	9	28.00	3-34	–	–	63.33
1928	WI	2	300	114	6	19.00	3-41	–	–	50.00
1928–29	A	5	1555	724	18	40.22	6-32	1	–	86.38
1929	SA	3	616	186	8	23.25	5-57	1	–	77.00
1930	A	3	606	292	4	73.00	1-9	–	–	151.50
1931	NZ	1	–	–	–	–	–	–	–	–
1932–33	A	5	1322	644	33	19.51	5-28	2	1	40.06
	A	15	4053	1912	64	29.87	6-32	3	1	63.32
	SA	3	616	186	8	23.25	5-57	1	–	77.00
	WI	2	300	114	6	19.00	3-41	–	–	50.00
	NZ	1	–	–	–	–	–	–	–	–
Home		11	2092	844	27	31.25	5-57	1	–	77.48
Overseas		10	2877	1368	51	26.82	6-32	3	1	56.41
Totals		21	4969	2212	78	28.35	6-32	4	1	63.70

						Batting 1st			Batting 2nd				Bowling 1st			Bowling 2nd		
Ref	Series	V	T	Venue	Result	No	R	HO	No	R	HO	Ct	Balls	R	W	Balls	R	W
164/150	1926	A	2	Lord's	D	–	–	–	–	–	–	–	192	99	2	90	37	1
167/153			5	Oval	W-289	10	0	c	10	5	b	1	204	82	3	84	34	3
173/159	1928	WI	1	Lord's	W-I & 58	10	17	*	–	–	–	1	90	27	1	–	–	–
175/161			3	Oval	W-I & 71	9	32	c	–	–	–	2	126	46	2	84	41	3
176/162	1928–29	A	1	Brisbane[1]	W-675	9	70	lbw	9	37	c	4	88	32	6	42	30	2
177/163			2	Sydney	W-8w	7	43	c	–	–	–	–	158	77	3	210	105	1
178/164			3	Melbourne	W-3w	7	0	c	–	–	–	–	222	127	3	96	37	1
179/165			4	Adelaide	W-12	8	3	b	7	5	lbw	2	222	92	1	120	60	0
180/166			5	Melbourne	L-5w	8	4	b	3	11	b	–	204	83	1	193	81	0
181/167	1929	SA	1	Birmingham	D	9	6	lbw	–	–	–	–	256	57	5	66	12	0
182/168			2	Lord's	D	9	35	b	9	9	b	–	120	65	1	72	17	1
183/169			3	Leeds	W-5w	10	0	c	–	–	–	–	102	35	1	–	–	–
194/180	1930	A	1	Nottingham	W-93	7	18	b	9	7	b	–	90	12	1	30	9	1
196/182			3	Leeds	D	10	10	*	–	–	–	2	198	139	1	–	–	–
198/184			5	Oval	L-I & 39	9	19	lbw	9	9	c	1	288	132	1	–	–	–
211/192	1931	NZ	3	Manchester	D	–	–	–	–	–	–	–	–	–	–	–	–	–
220/194	1932–33	A	1	Sydney	W-10w	10	0	lbw	–	–	–	–	186	96	5	108	28	5
221/195			2	Melbourne	L-111	9	9	b	9	4	c	–	123	52	2	90	50	2
222/196			3	Adelaide	W-338	11	3	*	9	8	c	–	150	55	3	114	71	4
223/197			4	Brisbane[2]	W-6w	9	23	b	–	–	–	1	186	101	4	105	49	3
224/198			5	Sydney	W-8w	4	98	c	–	–	–	1	194	98	4	66	44	1

Career	M	I	NO	HS	R	Avge	100	50	Ct	St	Balls	R	W	Avge	BB	5w	10w	Rate
Test	21	28	3	98	485	19.40	–	2	15	–	4969	2212	78	28.35	6-32	4	1	63.70
F/c	361	438	72	102*	7290	19.91	3	23	234	–	58092	24994	1427	17.51	9-41	98	20	40.70

LAWRENCE David Valentine

Gloucestershire (1981 to date)

TOURS
SL 1985–86 (Eng B), 1986–87 (Glos)
Born Gloucester 28 Jan 1964

David Lawrence was the first English-born black cricketer to represent a first-class county or his country. Dubbed 'Syd' after the late band leader (who was an enthusiastic and highly individual slow bowler), he is probably also the first England cricketer to cite break-dancing as his main recreation. Tall (6ft 2in) and massively-built, he is a dedicated boxer, weight trainer and general fitness fanatic. He conveys the supreme enthusiasm of a Tony Lock: after charging in for 25 overs on a hot day he will still chase hits to the boundary and throw his vast frame around in the field. His vigorous right-arm fast bowling terrorised the Sri Lankan batsmen on his first morning as a Test cricketer and he was desperately unlucky to collect only three wickets in the match – and even more unfortunate that his first major tour was cancelled when his was the one visa unlikely to be challenged. His batting is spectacular but mostly ineffective. Lawrence and his great friend 'Jack' Russell were the first Gloucestershire-born players from that county to represent England since David Allen in 1966.

'Syd' Lawrence

						Batting 1st			Batting 2nd				Bowling 1st			Bowling 2nd		
Ref	Series	V	T	Venue	Result	No	R	HO	No	R	HO	Ct	Balls	R	W	Balls	R	W
1103/651	1988	SL		Lord's	W-7w	11	4	c	–	–	–	–	90	37	1	126	74	2

Career	M	I	NO	HS	R	Avge	100	50	Ct	St	Balls	R	W	Avge	BB	5w	10w	Rate
Test	1	1	–	4	4	4.00	–	–	–	–	216	111	3	37.00	2-74	–	–	72.00
F/c	123	136	26	65*	1040	9.45	–	1	26	–	17726	11007	331	33.25	7-47	14	–	53.55

LEADBEATER, Edric

Yorkshire (1949 to 1956)
Warwickshire (1957 to 1958)

TOUR I/SL 1951–52
Born Lockwood, Huddersfield, Yorkshire
15 Aug 1927

'Eddie' Leadbeater was a perky little (5ft 6in) right-arm leg-break bowler – the last such specialist to appear regularly for Yorkshire. He was very accurate for his type but tended to vary his wares with the occasional top-spinner rather than the more dramatic googly. He was an aggressive and courageous fielder and a very capable lower-order batsman. Flown to India as a replacement for A.E.G. Rhodes, he played in two Tests but, despite 81 appearances for Yorkshire and 27 for Warwickshire, he was never awarded a county 1st XI cap. [*Illus. p.* 223]

						Batting 1st			Batting 2nd				Bowling 1st			Bowling 2nd		
Ref	Series	V	T	Venue	Result	No	R	HO	No	R	HO	Ct	Balls	R	W	Balls	R	W
340/293	1951–52	I	2	Bombay[2]	D	8	2	lbw	–	–	–	1	66	38	1	85	62	0
341/294			3	Calcutta	D	9	38	ro	–	–	–	2	90	64	1	48	54	0

Career	M	I	NO	HS	R	Avge	100	50	Ct	St	Balls	R	W	Avge	BB	5w	10w	Rate
Test	2	2	0	38	40	20.00	–	–	3	–	289	218	2	109.00	1-38	–	–	144.50
F/c	118	138	36	116	1548	15.17	1	3	74	–	16509	7947	289	27.49	8-83	11	2	57.12

LEE, Henry William

Middlesex (1911 to 1934)
Cooch Behar's XI (1917–18)
England (in India) (1918–19)

TOUR SA 1930–31
Born Marylebone, London 26 Oct 1890
Died Westminster, London 21 Apr 1981

NOTABLE FEATS

- Exceeded 1000 runs in a season 13 times.
- Scored 4 double centuries, twice scored hundreds in both innings of a match and twice carried his bat through a completed innings – all for Middlesex.
- Achieved the match 'double' (119 runs and 11 wickets) for Middlesex v Sussex at Lord's in 1920.

Harry Lee survived being reported killed in action in the Great War and lived to celebrate his 90th birthday. His career as a Middlesex all-rounder was equally resilient. Invalided home in 1916 with one leg shorter than its neighbour as a result of a compound fracture of the thigh, he was told he would never play again. By the time county cricket resumed he had spent more than a year playing in India and had recovered so remarkably that few guessed he had been wounded. A patient opening batsman with a cramped stance and strong right hand, he was a versatile bowler who could offer brisk off-spin and away-floaters but who frequently took the new ball. He made vital all-round contributions to the Middlesex Championship successes of 1920 and 1921. His winters were spent coaching in South Africa and it was while he was there in 1930–31 that he was recruited to open England's innings when Andy Sandham was injured in a car crash. His two younger brothers, Frank and Jack, transferred from Middlesex to Somerset, a move which led to one of cricket's prize dismissals at Lord's in 1933: H.W. Lee, c F.S. Lee b J.W. Lee 82. [*Illus. p.* 297]

Ref	Series	V	T	Venue	Result	Batting 1st			Batting 2nd			Ct
						No	R	HO	No	R	HO	
207/188	1930–31	SA	4	Johannesburg[1]	D	2	18	lbw	2	1	c	–

Career	M	I	NO	HS	R	Avge	100	50	Ct	St	Balls	R	W	Avge	BB	5w	10w	Rate
Test	1	2	0	18	19	9.50	–	–	–	–	–	–	–	–	–	–	–	–
F/c	435	720	49	243*	20007	29.81	37	80	179	–	26353	12100	390	31.02	8-39	12	3	67.57

LEES, Walter Scott

Surrey (1896 to 1911)
London County (1903)

Wisden 1906
TOUR SA 1905–06
Born Sowerby Bridge, Yorkshire
25 Dec 1875
Died West Hartlepool, Co. Durham
10 Sep 1924

Walter Lees was an extremely accurate right-arm fast-medium bowler who was at his most effective on hard pitches from which he could extract pace and bounce. He was at his peak between 1903 and 1910, taking 1031 wickets during those eight summers, form which brought him a place on MCC's first official tour of South Africa. Although the Springboks gained their first Test victories in this series which was played entirely on matting, Lees enjoyed consistent success taking 26 wickets at low cost. He was an adventurous lower-order batsman with an excellent eye and a good range of bold, attacking strokes. His early death was from double pneumonia.

MCC to South Africa, 1905–06: standing C. Blythe, D. Denton, A.E. Relf, W.S. Lees, J.H. Board; seated J.N. Crawford, F.L. Fane, P.F. Warner (captain), S. Haigh, L.J. Moon, Captain E.G. Wynyard.

NOTABLE FEATS

• Took 100 wickets in a season 7 times, including 193 (avge 18.01) in 1905.
• Took 9 for 81 for Surrey v Sussex at Eastbourne in 1905.
• Twice took 5 for 7 for Surrey in 1904, one instance including the dismissals of W.G. Grace, W.L. Murdoch and A.C. MacLaren.
• Scored 100 in 60 min for Surrey v Hampshire at Aldershot in 1905.
• Hat-trick for Surrey v Hampshire at Southampton in 1897.
• Bowled unchanged for Surrey throughout both Lancashire innings in partnership with T. Rushby at Manchester in 1908.

						Batting 1st			Batting 2nd				Bowling 1st			Bowling 2nd		
Ref	Series	V	T	Venue	Result	No	R	HO	No	R	HO	Ct	Balls	R	W	Balls	R	W
88/85	1905–06	SA	1	Johannesburg[1]	L-1w	10	11	st	10	1	*	1	139	34	5	198	74	3
89/86			2	Johannesburg[1]	L-9w	10	25	*	8	4	b	–	156	47	1	24	16	1
90/87			3	Johannesburg[1]	L-243	10	6	c	10	3	c	1	189	78	6	156	85	3
91/88			4	Cape Town	W-4w	11	5	c	–	–	–	–	162	42	1	84	27	4
92/89			5	Cape Town	L-I & 16	9	9	*	8	2	b	–	148	64	2	–	–	–

Career	M	I	NO	HS	R	Avge	100	50	Ct	St	Balls	R	W	Avge	BB	5w	10w	Rate
Test	5	9	3	25*	66	11.00	–	–	2	–	1256	467	26	17.96	6-78	2	–	48.30
F/c	364	522	76	137	7642	17.13	2	17	125	–	69778	30008	1402	21.40	9-81	97	20	49.77

LEGGE Geoffrey Bevington

Kent (1924 to 1931)
Oxord University (1925 to 1926)

TOURS A 1929–30; SA 1927–28; NZ 1929–30
Born Bromley, Kent 26 Jan 1903
Died Brampford Speke, Devon 21 Nov 1940

NOTABLE FEATS

• *189* His 196 in 280 min with 23 fours was the record score in E v NZ Tests until 1932–33 and the highest of his first-class career.
• Shared record Kent 6th-wkt stand of 284 in 2½ hr with A.P.F. Chapman v Lancashire at Maidstone in 1927.

True to the tradition of Malvern College where he was captain, Geoffrey Legge was a stylish batsman, particularly strong at off-driving and cutting. A useful right-arm slow bowler and remarkably prehensile catcher at slip, he made his debut for Kent before going up to Oxford and heading the averages in successive years, the second of which he captained. Afterwards he quickly established himself in the Kent side. Taking over the captaincy, he led them to second place in his first year (1928) but business pressures compelled his resignation after three seasons and he retired the following summer. As a lieutenant in the RNVR he was killed while flying with the Fleet Air Arm during the Second World War.

Geoffrey Legge

						Batting 1st			Batting 2nd				Bowling 1st			Bowling 2nd		
Ref	Series	V	T	Venue	Result	No	R	HO	No	R	HO	Ct	Balls	R	W	Balls	R	W
168/154	1927–28	SA	1	Johannesburg[1]	W-10w	7	0	c	–	–	–	–	–	–	–	–	–	–
186/172	1929–30	NZ	1	Christchurch	W-8w	5	36	b	–	–	–	1	–	–	–	–	–	–
187/173			2	Wellington	D	5	39	c	5	9	c	–	–	–	–	–	–	–
188/174			3	Auckland	D	5	19	*	–	–	–	–	30	34	0	–	–	–
189/175			4	Auckland	D	5	196	c	4	0	b	–	–	–	–	–	–	–

Career	M	I	NO	HS	R	Avge	100	50	Ct	St	Balls	R	W	Avge	BB	5w	10w	Rate
Test	5	7	1	196	299	49.83	1	–	1	–	30	34	0	–	–	–	–	–
F/c	147	210	11	196	4955	24.89	7	16	121	–	179	181	8	22.62	3-23	–	–	22.37

LESLIE Charles Frederick Henry

Oxford University (1881 to 1883)
Middlesex (1881 to 1886)

TOUR A 1882–83
Born Westminster, London 8 Dec 1861
Died Westminster 12 Feb 1921

Charles Leslie was an outstanding all-rounder at Rugby School where he captained cricket in his last three years. As a hard-hitting middle-order batsman with a solid defence he was probably the best public schoolboy of his era; he was also a useful right-arm fast bowler and an athletic cover-point. Although he won blues in each of his three seasons at Oxford, he was never able to recapture his wonderful form as a freshman when he averaged 57. In Australia with Ivo Bligh's team he achieved his best first-class bowling analysis in his first Test and scored 54 in his second. His only other tour success was an innings of 144 against New South Wales and he played little first-class cricket after his return. He also appeared for Shropshire and represented Oxford at soccer and racquets. [*Illus. p.* 42]

NOTABLE FEATS

- Scored 111* for Oxford U v MCC at Oxford on his first-class debut in 1881.

Ref	Series	V	T	Venue	Result	Batting 1st No	R	HO	Batting 2nd No	R	HO	Ct	Bowling 1st Balls	R	W	Bowling 2nd Balls	R	W
10/10	1882–83	A	1	Melbourne	L-9w	3	4	c	7	4	b	–	44	31	3	–	–	–
11/11			2	Melbourne	W-I & 27	3	54	ro	–	–	–	–	–	–	–	–	–	–
12/12			3	Sydney	W-69	3	0	b	1	8	b	–	–	–	–	–	–	–
13/13			4	Sydney	L-4w	3	17	c	3	19	b	1	20	11	1	32	2	0

Career	M	I	NO	HS	R	Avge	100	50	Ct	St	Balls	R	W	Avge	BB	5w	10w	Rate
Test	4	7	0	54	106	15.14	–	1	1	–	96	44	4	11.00	3-31	–	–	24.00
F/c	48	86	5	144	1860	22.96	4	10	18	–	332	165	8	20.62	3-31	–	–	41.50

LEVER, John Kenneth

Essex (1967 to date)
Natal (1982–83 to 1984–85)

Wisden 1979
TOURS
A 1976–77, 1978–79, 1979–80;
SA 1972–73 (Robins), 1973–74 (Robins), 1981–82 (SAB); NZ 1977–78; I 1976–77, 1979–80, 1980–81 (Overseas XI), 1981–82; P 1977–78; SL 1976–77, 1977–78 (Robins), 1981–82
Born Stepney, London 24 Feb 1949

John ('JK') Lever is a highly talented left-arm fast-medium swing bowler who celebrated his long overdue Test selection with the best bowling performance achieved by any England player on his first appearance. Tall (6ft 0½in) and wirily built, he has fulfilled an enormous workload during more than two decades with Essex – a tribute to his immense stamina and dedication to physical fitness. He is the complete professional and it is significant that his career has coincided with the only trophies in the County's history: four Championships and five limited-overs titles. His well-honed rhythmic approach and ideal body action enable him to swing the ball late and his pinpoint accuracy have made him exceptionally economical in limited-overs games. His right-handed lower-order batting has often produced vital runs and he is a high-class outfielder. There have been few more popular cricketers or more dedicated team-men; he was a model tourist.

NOTABLE FEATS

- 50 wickets in 15th Test (*852*).
- *788* Only A.L. Valentine, R.A.L. Massie and N.D. Hirwani have improved upon his analysis of 7 for 46 in their first Test innings; he was the sixth England bowler to take 10 wickets on debut and the first also to score a fifty.
- Took 100 wickets in a season 4 times.

Ref	Series	V	T	Venue	Result	Batting 1st No	R	HO	Batting 2nd No	R	HO	Ct	Bowling 1st Balls	R	W	Bowling 2nd Balls	R	W
788/520	1976–77	I	1	Delhi	W-I & 25	9	53	c	–	–	–	1	138	46	7	82	24	3
789/521			2	Calcutta	W-10w	9	2	c	–	–	–	2	132	57	2	18	12	0
790/522			3	Madras[1]	W-200	8	23	c	3	2	c	–	119	59	5	41	18	2
791/523			4	Bangalore	L-140	9	20	*	9	11	c	–	102	48	1	54	28	1
792/524			5	Bombay[3]	D	8	7	c	8	4	c	2	106	42	3	106	46	2
803/525	1976–77	A		Melbourne	L-45	10	11	c	9	4	lbw	–	96	36	2	168	95	2
804/526	1977	A	1	Lord's	D	9	8	b	9	3	c	1	114	61	1	30	4	0

Ref	Series	V	T	Venue	Result	Batting 1st No	R	HO	Batting 2nd No	R	HO	Ct	Bowling 1st Balls	R	W	Bowling 2nd Balls	R	W
805/527			2	Manchester	W-9w	9	10	b	–	–	–	1	150	60	3	24	11	0
808/530			5	Oval	D	8	3	lbw	–	–	–	–	132	61	1	–	–	–
814/531	1977–78	P	1	Lahore[2]	D	10	0	c	–	–	–	1	128	47	2	24	13	1
815/532			2	Hyderabad	D	10	4	b	3	0	*	–	134	41	1	160	62	0
816/533			3	Karachi	D	10	33	*	–	–	–	–	96	32	0	–	–	–
819/536	1977–78	NZ	3	Auckland	D	10	1	c	–	–	–	–	272	96	3	136	59	2
835/544	1978–79	A	2	Perth	W-166	9	14	c	8	10	c	–	56	20	1	65	28	4
852/550	1979	I	2	Lord's	D	10	6	*	–	–	–	–	59	29	1	144	69	1
872/555	1979–80	A	3	Melbourne	L-8w	10	22	b	10	12	c	1	318	111	4	46	18	0
876/556	1979–80	I		Bombay[3]	W-10w	9	21	b	–	–	–	1	138	82	1	121	65	3
880/557	1980	WI	1	Nottingham	L-2w	9	15	c	9	4	c	1	120	76	1	48	25	0
913/574	1981–82	I	2	Bangalore	D	5	1	lbw	–	–	–	–	216	100	5	–	–	–
914/575			3	Delhi	D	9	2	b	–	–	–	–	222	104	2	–	–	–
1047/624	1986	I	2	Leeds	L-279	11	0	*	7	0	c	–	180	102	2	138	64	4

Career	M	I	NO	HS	R	Avge	100	50	Ct	St	Balls	R	W	Avge	BB	5w	10w	Rate
Test	21	31	5	53	306	11.76	–	1	11	–	4433	1951	73	26.72	7-46	3	1	60.72
F/c	520	531	192	91	3622	10.68	–	3	184	–	89716	41016	1696	24.18	8-37	84	12	52.89

John Lever

J. K. LEVER – TEST BOWLING SUMMARY

Series	V	M	Balls	R	W	Avge	BB	5w	10w	Rate
1976–77	I	5	898	380	26	14.61	7-46	2	1	34.53
1976–77	A	1	264	131	4	32.75	2-36	–	–	66.00
1977	A	3	450	197	5	39.40	3-60	–	–	90.00
1977–78	P	3	542	195	4	48.75	2-47	–	–	135.50
1977–78	NZ	1	408	155	5	31.00	3-96	–	–	81.60
1978–79	A	1	121	48	5	9.60	4-28	–	–	24.20
1979	I	1	203	98	2	49.00	1-29	–	–	101.50
1979–80	A	1	364	129	4	32.25	4-111	–	–	91.00
1979–80	I	1	259	147	4	36.75	3-65	–	–	64.75
1980	WI	1	168	101	1	101.00	1-76	–	–	168.00
1981–82	I	2	438	204	7	29.14	5-100	1	–	62.57
1986	I	1	318	1666	6	27.66	4-64	–	–	53.00
	A	6	1199	505	18	28.05	4-28	–	–	66.61
	WI	1	168	101	1	101.00	1-76	–	–	168.00
	NZ	1	408	155	5	31.00	3-96	–	–	81.60
	I	10	2116	995	45	22.11	7-46	3	1	47.02
	P	3	542	195	4	48.75	2-47	–	–	135.50
Home		6	1139	562	14	40.14	4-64	–	–	81.35
Overseas		15	3294	1389	59	23.54	7-46	3	1	55.83
Totals		21	4433	1951	73	26.72	7-46	3	1	60.72

LEVER, Peter

Lancashire (1960 to 1976)
Tasmania (1971–72)

TOURS
A 1970–71, 1974–75; NZ 1970–71, 1974–75
Born Todmorden, Yorkshire
17 Sep 1940

Peter Lever was a tall (6ft) determined, strong right-arm fast-medium bowler and a fine competitive successor to Brian Statham and Ken Higgs. Despite an overlong run and not over-attractive action he maintained good control and moved the ball away late. Originally considered as an all-rounder, he remained an above-average tail-end batsman and he was a swift outfielder with a powerful throw. He enjoyed a highly successful dress rehearsal for his official England career when he took 7 for 83 against the powerful Rest of the World side on his unofficial debut in 1970. He will not want to be reminded of the bouncer he bowled at Auckland in 1974–75 which Ewen Chatfield deflected into his left temple. The tail-ender collapsed unconscious with a hairline skull fracture and his heart stopped beating for several seconds; only heart massage and mouth-to-mouth resus-

Peter Lever

citation by MCC's physiotherapist, Bernard Thomas, saved his life. Back problems compelled Lever's retirement but he contributed another decade of dedicated service at Old Trafford as Lancashire's coach.

NOTABLE FEATS

- *686* Shared record E v NZ 7th-wkt stand of 149 with A.P.E. Knott.
- *687* Shared (then) record E v P 7th-wkt stand of 159 with A.P.E. Knott.
- *689* Completed victory with a spell of 3 wickets in 4 balls.
- *691* His 88* in 227 min remained his highest first-class score; shared in record E v I 8th-wkt stand of 168 with R. Illingworth.
- *755* His best Test analysis included a spell of 4 wickets for 5 runs.
- Hat-trick for Lancashire v Nottinghamshire at Manchester in 1969.

						Batting 1st			Batting 2nd				Bowling 1st			Bowling 2nd		
Ref	Series	V	T	Venue	Result	No	R	HO	No	R	HO	Ct	Balls	R	W	Balls	R	W
675/460	1970–71	A	2	Perth	D	11	2	b	–	–	–	2	168	78	1	40	10	1
676/461			4	Sydney	W-299	9	36	c	–	–	–	1	70	31	2	88	24	1
677/462			5	Melbourne	D	9	19	ro	–	–	–	1	200	79	0	96	53	0
678/463			6	Adelaide	D	9	5	b	–	–	–	1	137	49	4	136	49	0
679/464			7	Sydney	W-62	9	4	c	9	17	c	–	118	43	3	96	23	1
685/465	1970–71	NZ	1	Christchurch	W-8w	9	4	b	–	–	–	–	40	1	0	120	30	1
686/466			2	Auckland	D	8	64	c	7	0	lbw	–	152	43	0	16	6	0
687/467	1971	P	1	Birmingham	D	8	47	c	–	–	–	2	228	126	1	–	–	–
688/468			2	Lord's	D	–	–	–	–	–	–	–	96	38	2	–	–	–
689/469			3	Leeds	W-25	10	19	c	10	8	b	–	186	65	1	21	10	3
691/471	1971	I	2	Manchester	D	9	88	*	–	–	–	–	156	70	5	42	14	0
700/475	1972	A	3	Nottingham	D	11	9	c	–	–	–	–	156	61	1	114	76	0
750/503	1974–75	A	1	Brisbane[2]	L-166	8	4	c	8	14	c	2	128	53	0	144	58	0
755/508			6	Melbourne	W-I & 4	11	6	*	–	–	–	–	88	38	6	128	65	3
758/509	1974–75	NZ	1	Auckland	W-I & 83	–	–	–	–	–	–	–	160	75	0	93	37	2
759/510			2	Christchurch	D	–	–	–	–	–	–	1	144	66	1	–	–	–
761/512	1975	A	2	Lord's	D	11	4	lbw	–	–	–	1	90	83	2	120	55	0

Career	M	I	NO	HS	R	Avge	100	50	Ct	St	Balls	R	W	Avge	BB	5w	10w	Rate
Test	17	18	2	88*	350	21.87	–	2	11	–	3571	1509	41	36.80	6-38	2	–	87.09
F/c	301	314	66	88*	3534	14.25	–	11	106	–	45997	20377	796	25.59	7-70	28	2	57.78

LEVESON GOWER
Sir Henry Dudley Gresham

Oxford University (1893 to 1896)
Surrey (1895 to 1920)

TOURS
SA 1905–06, 1909–10; WI 1896–97;
Z 1909–10 (own team)
Born Titsey, Surrey 8 May 1873
Knighted for services to cricket 1953
Died Kensington, London 1 Feb 1954

Seventh in a batting order of a dozen brothers, Henry Leveson Gower (pronounced 'Loosen Gore') was an important influence in English cricket for almost six decades. Dubbed 'Shrimp' because of his tiny physique, he was a middle-order batsman, a right-arm slow-medium outswing and leg-break bowler and a spirited fielder at cover. Strong-wristed cutting was a major feature of his energetic batting. He captained Winchester College, led Oxford to a dramatic victory in the last of his four seasons as a blue, skippered Surrey for three highly successful summers (1908–10) and commanded England in his only three Tests. Always affable but determined, he was an enthusiastic organiser of private tours and, from 1899 until 1950, selected the teams for the Scarborough Festival. A noted administrator, he was knighted in 1953 for his services to cricket which also included committee work for MCC and Surrey (where he was president for ten years) and two spells as chairman of selectors.

England to South Africa, 1909–10: standing *G.J. Thompson, W. Rhodes, F.E. Woolley, J.B. Hobbs, H. Strudwick;* seated *G.H.T. Simpson-Hayward, Captain E.G. Wynyard, H.D.G. Leveson Gower (captain), D. Denton, C.P. Buckenham, M.C. Bird;* in front *N.C. Tufnell, F.L. Fane, C. Blythe.*

						Batting 1st			Batting 2nd			
Ref	Series	V	T	Venue	Result	No	R	HO	No	R	HO	Ct
106/103*	1909–10	SA	1	Johannesburg[1]	L-19	9	17	c	9	31	b	1
107/104*			2	Durban[1]	L-95	9	6	*	9	23	b	–
108/105*			3	Johannesburg[1]	W-3w	6	6	lbw	9	12	*	–

Career	M	I	NO	HS	R	Avge	100	50	Ct	St	Balls	R	W	Avge	BB	5w	10w	Rate
Test	3	6	2	31	95	23.75	–	–	1	–	–	–	–	–	–	–	–	–
F/c	277	400	78	155	7638	23.72	4	42	103	–	2261	1378	46	29.95	6-49	3	–	49.15

LEVETT
William Howard Vincent

Kent (1930 to 1947)

TOUR I/SL 1933–34
Born Goudhurst, Kent 25 Jan 1908

'Hopper' Levett was an outstanding wicket-keeper even in his Brighton College days when he was selected for the Public Schools against the 1926 Australians. He began his career for Kent as deputy to Leslie Ames but frequently played alongside him to allow the England all-rounder to concentrate his energies on batting. His appearances for the Gentlemen at Lord's broke the exclusivity of Oxbridge keepers. An enterprising batsman with a sound defence, especially against fast bowling, he once scored 66 as an opener during the Folkestone Festival and was sometimes played for his batting and fielding alone. He made his solitary appearance for England in the first Test staged at Eden Gardens. An inveterate and entertaining chatterer, he has lived to be a fit and cheery octogenarian despite, or he would argue because of, a full and often rumbustious life. [*Illus pp.* 263, 385]

NOTABLE FEATS

- Dismissed 9 batsmen in a match for Kent on 3 occasions and 6 in an innings twice.

						Batting 1st			Batting 2nd			Fielding 1st				Fielding 2nd			
Ref	Series	V	T	Venue	Result	No	R	HO	No	R	HO	Ct	St	Byes	Balls	Ct	St	Byes	Balls
231/205†	1933–34	I	2	Calcutta	D	7	5	lbw	4	2	*	–	–	5	646	3	–	10	543

Career	M	I	NO	HS	R	Avge	100	50	Ct	St	Balls	R	W	Avge	BB	5w	10w	Rate
Test	1	2	1	5	7	7.00	–	–	3	–	–	–	–	–	–	–	–	–
F/c	175	264	58	76	2524	12.25	–	2	283	195	3	6	0	–	–	–	–	–

LEWIS
Anthony Robert

Glamorgan (1955 to 1974)
Cambridge University (1960 to 1962)

TOURS
WI 1969–70 (Glam); I 1972–73;
P 1967–68 (Cwlth), 1972–73;
SL 1969–70, 1972–73
Born Uplands, Swansea, Glamorgan
6 Jul 1938

Tony Lewis

An elegant and high-quality batsman, Tony Lewis proved to be a persuasive leader and sound tactician during his temporary reign as England's captain. He made his first appearances for Glamorgan while still at Neath Grammar School where cricket had to compete with his role as a violinist in the Welsh Youth Orchestra. Then came national service and Cambridge where, as a freshman, he won a rugby blue at full-back before a knee injury ended that career. During his days at Fenner's – he was a light blue in each of his three seasons and captain in his last – he looked an outstanding batting prospect; a forceful driver and cutter, he was equally adept at all the on-side strokes. He found it hard to maintain such consistency on the less perfect surfaces around the county circuit and, apart from a sniff of the Test scene as 12th man in 1966, he was passed by. With Don Shepherd as his trusty confidant, he captained Glamorgan with easy assurance (1967–72) and was rewarded with the County's second Championship despite occasionally airing his leg-spin bowling. Having also led a successful MCC tour of Asia, he was an obvious deputy when Ray Illingworth made himself unavailable for the 1972–73 tour of India, Sri Lanka and Pakistan. He had always been impressive against spin and he immediately established his confidence at Test level with an innings of great character which helped win his first match. A century followed and he retained his place but under Illingworth's restored captaincy the following summer. Sadly his knee protested too strongly and he retired at the end of the next season to concentrate on the broadcasting and writing career which had already begun to flourish. Those talents have happily kept him within the first-class game as cricket correspondent of the *Sunday Telegraph*, as a radio and TV commentator and presenter, and as author of *Double Century*, an outstanding bicentenary history of MCC.

NOTABLE FEATS

- *703* Captaining in his first Test he shared a 5th-wkt stand of 101* with A.W. Greig which, soon after Christmas Day lunch, achieved England's first victory in Delhi and their first in India since 1951–52.
- Exceeded 1000 runs in a season 11 times, including 2000 twice; his aggregate of 1365 in 1962 is the second-highest in a season for Cambridge U.
- Scored 233 for Glamorgan v Kent at Gravesend in 1966.
- Shared (then) record Glamorgan 2nd-wkt stand of 238 with A. Jones v Sussex at Hastings in 1962.

TEST NOTES

- *707* A.P.E. Knott deputised as captain when Lewis and vice-captain M.H. Denness were off the field on the fourth evening.

						Batting 1st			Batting 2nd			
Ref	Series	V	T	Venue	Result	No	R	HO	No	R	HO	Ct
703/478*	1972–73	I	1	Delhi	W-6w	5	0	lbw	5	70	*	–
704/479*			2	Calcutta	L-28	5	4	lbw	5	3	c	–
705/480*			3	Madras	L-4w	7	4	c	7	11	c	–
706/481*			4	Kanpur	D	4	125	b	–	–	–	–
707/482*			5	Bombay[2]	D	1	0	b	4	17	*	–
719/483*	1972–73	P	1	Lahore[2]	D	4	29	b	4	74	b	–
720/484*			2	Hyderabad	D	4	7	c	4	21	c	–
721/485*			3	Karachi	D	5	88	c	–	–	–	–
722/486	1973	NZ	1	Nottingham	W-38	4	2	c	4	2	c	–

Career	M	I	NO	HS	R	Avge	100	50	Ct	St	Balls	R	W	Avge	BB	5w	10w	Rate
Test	9	16	2	125	457	32.64	1	3	–	–	–	–	–	–	–	–	–	–
F/c	409	708	76	223	20495	32.42	30	113	193	–	521	432	6	72.00	3-18	–	–	86.83

LEYLAND, Morris

Yorkshire (1920 to 1947)
Patiala (1926–27)

Wisden 1929
TOURS
A 1928–29, 1932–33, 1936–37; SA 1930–31; WI 1934–35, 1935–36 (Yorks); I 1926–27
Born New Park, Harrogate, Yorkshire 20 Jul 1900
Died Scotton Banks, Harrogate 1 Jan 1967

Maurice Leyland

A cheerful and pugnacious Yorkshireman, 'Maurice' Leyland was an outstanding left-handed middle-order batsman between the two World Wars. Robustly built, he was a powerful strokeplayer with a high grip and a splay-footed stance; at the Scarborough Festival in 1928 he hit Wilfred Rhodes for three sixes and a four in one over. He relished a scrap and was the ideal man for a crisis. Unbelievably consistent, he scored over 1000 runs in each of 17 successive seasons and achieved a Test match output which was second only to those of Hammond and Sutcliffe amongst his contemporaries. He averaged over 40 on each of his three tours of Australia and was described by writers there as the 'English Clem Hill'. The son of a former league professional who became groundsman at Headingley, he graduated to the Yorkshire team via the Lancashire league, wartime Army service and three seasons as professional to Harrogate. He had to wait eight years for his Test cap but then remained an automatic choice for a similar period, a sequence ended prematurely by war when he was 39. His unorthodox left-arm slow bowling baffled many accomplished batsmen with its 'Chinamen' (left-handed off-breaks) and googlies, and he was a quite outstanding outfielder. After the Hitler War he played a full season, helping Yorkshire to the 12th Championship of his career, before becoming their devoted, good humoured and much loved coach (1951–63).

NOTABLE FEATS

- 1000 runs in 18th Test (*222*) (27 inns); 2000 runs in 33rd Test (*246*) (53 inns).
- *180* Scored 137 in his first innings v Australia.
- *255* Scored England's only 100 at 'The Gabba' until 1974–75.
- *266* Contributed 187 in 381 min to record Test total of 903 for 7 dec, sharing in England's highest stand v Australia (all wkts) and record 2nd-wkt stand in all Tests: 382 with L. Hutton. First to score hundreds in his first and last innings v Australia.
- Exceeded 1000 runs in a season 17 times (1923–39 consecutively), including 2000 on 3 occasions. Scored 1013 in August 1932.
- Five double centuries (all for Yorkshire), notably 263 v Essex at Hull in 1936.
- Scored hundreds in 3 successive innings for Yorkshire in 1934.
- Shared in 3 Yorkshire partnership records: 346 (2nd wkt) with W. Barber v Middlesex at Sheffield in 1932; 323* (3rd wkt) with H. Sutcliffe v Glamorgan at Huddersfield in 1928; and 276 (6th wkt) with E. Robinson v Glamorgan at Swansea in 1926.
- Hat-trick for Yorkshire v Surrey at Sheffield in 1935.

						Batting 1st			Batting 2nd				Bowling 1st			Bowling 2nd		
Ref	Series	V	T	Venue	Result	No	R	HO	No	R	HO	Ct	Balls	R	W	Balls	R	W
175/161	1928	WI	3	Oval	W-I & 71	5	0	b	–	–	–	–	18	6	1	–	–	–
180/166	1928–29	A	5	Melbourne	L-5w	7	137	c	7	53	*	–	18	11	0	–	–	–
181/167	1929	SA	1	Birmingham	D	6	3	c	–	–	–	–	–	–	–	–	–	–
182/168			2	Lord's	D	6	73	b	3	102	c	1	30	9	0	–	–	–
183/169			3	Leeds	W-5w	7	45	c	6	0	b	1	–	–	–	18	19	0
184/170			4	Manchester	W-I & 32	6	55	c	–	–	–	1	–	–	–	–	–	–
185/171			5	Oval	D	6	16	b	–	–	–	–	54	25	0	–	–	–
196/182	1930	A	3	Leeds	D	5	44	b	5	1	*	–	66	44	0	–	–	–
197/183			4	Manchester	D	5	35	b	–	–	–	–	48	17	0	–	–	–
198/184			5	Oval	L-I & 39	6	3	b	6	20	b	–	96	34	0	–	–	–
204/185	1930–31	SA	1	Johannesburg[1]	L-28	2	29	c	2	15	c	–	–	–	–	–	–	–
205/186			2	Cape Town	D	3	52	b	3	28	c	–	180	91	3	–	–	–
206/187			3	Durban[2]	D	3	31	*	–	–	–	–	–	–	–	54	32	0
207/188			4	Johannesburg[1]	D	5	91	lbw	5	46	c	–	–	–	–	24	11	0
208/189			5	Durban[2]	D	3	8	lbw	–	–	–	–	–	–	–	–	–	–
220/194	1932–33	A	1	Sydney	W-10w	5	0	c	–	–	–	1	–	–	–	–	–	–
221/195			2	Melbourne	L-111	5	22	b	2	19	b	–	–	–	–	–	–	–
222/196			3	Adelaide	W-338	5	83	b	6	42	c	1	–	–	–	–	–	–
223/197			4	Brisbane[2]	W-6w	5	12	c	3	86	c	–	–	–	–	–	–	–
224/198			5	Sydney	W-8w	5	42	ro	3	0	b	–	–	–	–	–	–	–

Ref	Series	V	T	Venue	Result	Batting 1st No	R	HO	Batting 2nd No	R	HO	Ct	Bowling 1st Balls	R	W	Bowling 2nd Balls	R	W
227/201	1933	WI	1	Lord's	W-I & 27	4	1	c	–	–	–	–	–	–	–	–	–	–
233/207	1934	A	1	Nottingham	L-238	5	6	c	6	18	c	1	6	5	0	–	–	–
234/208			2	Lord's	W-I & 38	6	109	b	–	–	–	–	24	10	0	–	–	–
235/209			3	Manchester	D	6	153	c	–	–	–	–	–	–	–	–	–	–
236/210			4	Leeds	D	6	16	lbw	6	49	*	–	30	20	0	–	–	–
237/211			5	Oval	L-562	6	110	b	5	17	c	–	18	20	0	–	–	–
238/212	1934–35	WI	1	Bridgetown	W-4w	2	3	c	5	2	c	2	–	–	–	–	–	–
239/213			2	Port-of-Spain	L-217	5	0	lbw	9	18	lbw	–	54	31	0	78	41	1
240/214			3	Georgetown	D	7	13	c	7	0	b	–	12	12	0	–	–	–
242/216	1935	SA	1	Nottingham	D	5	69	c	–	–	–	–	42	18	0	–	–	–
243/217			2	Lord's	L-157	3	18	b	3	4	b	–	–	–	–	–	–	–
245/219			4	Manchester	D	6	53	c	5	37	c	–	–	–	–	72	28	0
246/220			5	Oval	D	5	161	st	–	–	–	–	–	–	–	42	15	0
252/221	1936	I	1	Lord's	W-9w	4	60	lbw	–	–	–	1	–	–	–	–	–	–
254/223			3	Oval	W-9w	4	26	b	–	–	–	–	12	5	0	18	19	0
255/224	1936–37	A	1	Brisbane[2]	W-322	5	126	b	5	33	c	2	–	–	–	–	–	–
256/225			2	Sydney	W-I & 22	4	42	lbw	–	–	–	–	–	–	–	–	–	–
257/226			3	Melbourne	L-365	4	17	c	4	111	*	–	–	–	–	–	–	–
258/227			4	Adelaide	L-148	4	45	c	5	32	c	1	–	–	–	16	6	0
259/228			5	Melbourne	L-I & 200	5	7	b	5	28	c	–	24	26	0	–	–	–
266/235	1938	A	5	Oval	W-I & 579	3	187	ro	–	–	–	1	19	11	1	30	19	0

Career	M	I	NO	HS	R	Avge	100	50	Ct	St	Balls	R	W	Avge	BB	5w	10w	Rate
Test	41	65	5	187	2764	46.06	9	10	13	–	1103	585	6	97.50	3-91	–	–	183.63
F/c	686	932	101	263	33660	40.50	80	154	246	–	29012	13659	466	29.31	8-63	11	1	62.25

M. LEYLAND – TEST BATTING SUMMARY

Series	V	M	I	NO	HS	R	Avge	100	50
1928	WI	1	1	–	0	0	0.00	–	–
1928–29	A	1	2	1	137	190	190.00	1	1
1929	SA	5	7	–	102	294	42.00	1	2
1930	A	3	5	1	44	103	25.75	–	–
1930–31	SA	5	8	1	91	300	42.85	–	2
1932–33	A	5	9	–	86	306	34.00	–	2
1933	WI	1	1	–	1	1	1.00	–	–
1934	A	5	8	1	153	478	68.28	3	–
1934–35	WI	3	6	–	18	36	6.00	–	–
1935	SA	4	6	–	161	342	57.00	1	2
1936	I	2	2	–	60	86	43.00	–	1

Series	V	M	I	NO	HS	R	Avge	100	50
1936–37	A	5	9	1	126	441	55.12	2	–
1938	A	1	1	–	187	187	187.00	1	–
	A	20	34	4	187	1705	56.83	7	3
	SA	14	21	1	161	936	46.80	2	6
	WI	5	8	–	18	37	4.62	–	–
	I	2	2	–	60	86	43.00	–	1
Home		22	31	2	187	1491	51.41	6	5
Overseas		19	34	3	137	1273	41.06	3	5
Totals		41	65	5	187	2764	46.06	9	10

LILLEY
Arthur Frederick Augustus

Warwickshire (1894 to 1911)
London County (1900 to 1901)

Wisden 1897
TOURS A 1901–02, 1903–04
Born Holloway Head, Birmingham 28 Nov 1866
Died Brislington, Bristol 17 Nov 1929

'Dick' Lilley's quiet reliability as an outstanding wicket-keeper was in direct contrast to his flamboyant forcing methods as a valuable middle-order batsman. He began his 23-year association with Warwickshire before they had attained major county status and even in those early days was rated as a high-class technician with a fine cricket brain. For 13 years he remained an automatic choice for England. At the end of his long career his hands showed hardly a trace of the burden they had borne, a testament to his remarkable timing in days when protective gloves were somewhat primitive. He settled in Bristol after retiring and helped re-establish Gloucestershire's cricket after the Great War.

NOTABLE FEATS

- 50 dismissals in 18th Test (*78*).
- Exceeded 1000 runs 3 times.
- Dismissed 6 Worcs batsmen in an inns for Warwicks at Birmingham in 1906.

TEST NOTES

- *51* Bowled leg spin in 1st inns: 1 for 23 (25 balls) – J.T. Brown deputised.
- *87* A.O. Jones (substitute) kept wicket in 1st inns; R.H. Spooner in 2nd inns.

Ref	Series	V	T	Venue	Result	Batting 1st No	R	HO	Batting 2nd No	R	HO	Fielding 1st Ct	St	Byes	Balls	Fielding 2nd Ct	St	Byes	Balls
50/50†	1896	A	1	Lord's	W-6w	8	0	b	–	–	–	2	–	1	113	2	–	7	665
51/51†			2	Manchester	L-3w	8	65	*	8	19	c	2	–	6	850	3	–	0	423
52/52†			3	Oval	W-66	9	2	c	9	6	c	–	–	8	266	–	–	2	130
61/61†	1899	A	2	Lord's	L-10w	9	19	*	9	12	b	4	–	0	851	–	–	0	50
62/62†			3	Leeds	D	8	55	c	–	–	–	2	1	2	386	2	–	17	428
63/63†			4	Manchester	D	8	58	lbw	–	–	–	2	–	14	413	1	–	14	905
64/64†			5	Oval	D	10	37	b	–	–	–	1	–	5	718	1	–	7	500
65/65†	1901–02	A	1	Sydney	W-I & 124	7	84	c	–	–	–	–	1	1	433	3	1	5	346
66/66†			2	Melbourne	L-229	7	6	c	6	0	c	2	1	6	193	1	–	7	938
67/67†			3	Adelaide	L-4w	5	10	lbw	7	21	b	–	–	2	678	–	–	9	814
68/68†			4	Sydney	L-7w	8	40	c	8	0	c	2	–	7	834	1	–	0	219
69/69†			5	Melbourne	L-32	7	41	c	7	9	c	1	–	7	318	1	–	3	535
70/70†	1902	A	1	Birmingham	D	6	2	c	–	–	–	2	1	3	138	–	–	0	168
71/71†			2	Lord's	D	–	–	–	–	–	–	–	–	–	–	–	–	–	–
72/72†			3	Sheffield	L-143	6	8	b	7	9	b	1	–	3	397	1	–	0	433
73/73†			4	Manchester	L-3	8	7	b	8	4	c	3	–	5	457	1	–	1	286
74/74†			5	Oval	W-1w	10	0	c	10	16	c	2	–	5	743	1	–	7	360
78/75†	1903–04	A	1	Sydney	W-5w	9	4	c	–	–	–	2	–	0	710	2	1	10	872
79/76†			2	Melbourne	W-185	9	4	c	8	0	st	–	1	0	182	1	–	0	184
80/77†			3	Adelaide	L-216	10	28	ro	8	0	c	1	1	7	697	–	1	8	689
81/78†			4	Sydney	W-157	10	24	c	10	6	b	1	–	1	315	1	3	10	401
82/79†			5	Melbourne	L-218	11	6	*	9	0	lbw	–	1	4	491	–	1	1	263
83/80†	1905	A	1	Nottingham	W-213	9	37	c	–	–	–	1	1	16	383	–	2	4	436
84/81†			2	Lord's	D	9	0	lbw	–	–	–	1	–	3	301	–	–	–	–
85/82†			3	Leeds	D	8	11	b	–	–	–	2	–	4	320	–	1	11	546
86/83†			4	Manchester	W-I & 80	10	28	lbw	–	–	–	–	–	9	275	–	–	4	315
87/84†			5	Oval	D	10	17	b	–	–	–	–	–	–	–	–	–	–	–
93/90†	1907	SA	1	Lord's	D	10	48	c	–	–	–	2	–	9	390	–	–	15	348
94/91†			2	Leeds	W-53	9	3	c	9	0	lbw	2	2	3	191	–	–	3	268
95/92†			3	Oval	D	9	42	b	9	9	*	1	1	3	381	–	–	5	243
101/98†	1909	A	1	Birmingham	W-10w	9	0	c	–	–	–	–	–	0	276	1	–	7	317
102/99†			2	Lord's	L-9w	10	47	c	9	25	*	3	–	16	719	1	–	4	94
103/100†			3	Leeds	L-126	8	4	*	7	2	lbw	2	–	0	439	2	–	15	577
104/101†			4	Manchester	D	8	26	*	–	–	–	–	–	6	327	–	–	9	507
105/102†			5	Oval	D	9	2	*	–	–	–	–	–	1	537	–	1	4	600

Career	M	I	NO	HS	R	Avge	100	50	Ct	St	Balls	R	W	Avge	BB	5w	10w	Rate
Test	35	52	8	84	903	20.52	–	4	70	22	25	23	1	23.00	1-23	–	–	25.00
F/c	416	639	46	171	15597	26.30	16	77	717	194	2324	1485	41	36.21	6-46	1	–	56.68

'Dick' Lilley

A. F. A. LILLEY – TEST SUMMARY

Series	V	M	I	NO	HS	R	Avge	100	50	Ct	St	Byes	Balls
1896	A	3	5	1	65*	92	23.00	–	1	9	–	24	2447
1899	A	4	5	1	58	181	45.25	–	2	13	1	59	4251
1901–02	A	5	9	–	84	211	23.44	–	1	11	3	47	5308
1902	A	5	7	–	16	46	6.57	–	–	11	1	24	2982
1903–04	A	5	9	1	28	72	9.00	–	–	8	9	41	4804
1905	A	5	5	–	37	93	18.60	–	–	4	4	51	2576
1907	SA	3	5	1	48	102	25.50	–	–	5	3	38	1821
1909	A	5	7	4	47	106	35.33	–	–	9	1	62	4393
	A	32	47	7	84	801	20.02	–	4	65	19	308	26761
	SA	3	5	1	48	102	25.50	–	–	5	3	38	1821
Home		25	34	7	65*	620	22.96	–	3	51	10	258	18470
Overseas		10	18	1	84	283	16.64	–	1	19	12	88	10112
Totals		35	52	8	84	903	20.52	–	4	70	22	346	28582

LILLYWHITE James Jr

Sussex (1862 to 1883)

TOUR A 1876–77
Born Westhampnett, Sussex 23 Feb 1842
Died Westerton, Sussex 25 Oct 1929

NOTABLE FEATS

- Took 100 wickets in a season once (110, avge 13.34, in 1873).
- His innings (9 for 29) and match (14 for 57) analyses for Sussex v MCC at Lord's in 1862 remain the best recorded by a bowler making his first-class debut in Britain; he bowled unchanged throughout both innings with H. Stubberfield.
- Took 10 for 129 for South v North at Canterbury in 1872 and 9 for 73 for Sussex v Kent at Folkestone in 1863.
- Bowled in an unchanged partnership throughout both completed innings on 13 occasions, including 6 with J. Southerton and 6 (3 in successive matches) with R. Fillery.
- Bowled 8 MCC batsmen in taking 8 for 55 for Sussex at Hove in 1867.

James Lillywhite captained England in the first two Test matches and outlived his entire team by seven years. Cousin of James senior and John, and nephew of William (the 'Nonpareil'), he was an exceptionally consistent left-arm slow-medium bowler with a high delivery and an energetic left-handed lower-order batsman. Launching his career with a sensational 14-wicket haul, he went on to enjoy an unbroken sequence of appearances for Sussex which endured for 20 seasons (1862–81). A few weeks before he became England's first Test captain, leading England in the first encounters with an Australian team on even terms, his pioneering team of professionals had challenged 22 of Goulburn. During the match play was disrupted for several minutes when the field was invaded by six hares and two young kangaroos. He visited Australia on five other tours, the first with W.G. Grace and the rest in business association with Shaw and Shrewsbury. He appeared in no other first-class matches there but gave notable service as a manager, umpire and wise counsellor.

England's pioneer Test cricketers prior to their departure for Australia, 1876–77: standing *H. Jupp, T. Emmett, A. Hobgen (who financed the tour), A. Hill, T. Armitage;* seated *E. Pooley, J. Southerton, J. Lillywhite jr (captain), A. Shaw, G. Ulyett, A. Greenwood;* in front *H.R.J. Charlwood, J. Selby.*

					Batting 1st			Batting 2nd				Bowling 1st			Bowling 2nd		
Ref	Series	V	T	Venue	Result	No	R	HO	No	R	HO	Ct	Balls	R	W	Balls	R	W
1/1*	1876–77	A	1	Melbourne	L-45	10	10	c	10	4	b	–	56	19	1	4	1	1
2/2*			2	Melbourne	W-4w	10	2	*	–	–	–	1	116	36	2	164	70	4

Career	M	I	NO	HS	R	Avge	100	50	Ct	St	Balls	R	W	Avge	BB	5w	10w	Rate
Test	2	3	1	10	16	8.00	–	–	1	–	340	126	8	15.75	4-70	–	–	42.50
F/c	256	445	59	126*	5523	14.30	2	12	109	–	57072	18436	1210	15.23	10-129	96	22	47.16

LLOYD, David

Lancashire (1965 to 1983)

TOURS
A 1974–75; SA 1975–76 (Robins)
Born Accrington, Lancashire
18 Mar 1947

David Lloyd

David Lloyd was a competent left-handed opening or middle-order batsman with a sound technique and a range of attractive strokes, especially off the front foot. Although he had an admirable temperament and used his feet well against the spinners (as evidenced by his double century against India), he had his Test career and confidence wrecked by the ferocious pace and steep bounce of Lillee and Thomson. He was a handy left-arm slow bowler and a brave and athletic short-leg. Dubbed 'Bumble' because of his incessant talking, he captained Lancashire with chirpy assurance for five seasons (1973–77). After spending 1987 on the first-class umpires list, he was appointed TCCB development officer for 'Kwik' cricket from its inception. He has combined his task of promoting this plastic-packaged edition of the game around the schools with some highly entertaining performances on the public speaking circuit.

NOTABLE FEATS

- *741* His 214* in 448 min off 396 balls remained the highest score of his first-class career; he was on the field throughout the match.
- Exceeded 1000 runs in a season 11 times.

TEST NOTES

- *740* Bowled in 1st inns: 0 for 4 (12 balls).
- *744* Bowled in 1st inns: 0 for 13 (12 balls).
- *751* Retired hurt when 17* at 52–0 (2nd inns); resumed at 106–2.

						Batting 1st			Batting 2nd			
Ref	**Series**	**V**	**T**	**Venue**	**Result**	**No**	**R**	**HO**	**No**	**R**	**HO**	**Ct**
740/498	1974	I	2	Lord's	W-I & 285	2	46	c	–	–	–	–
741/499			3	Birmingham	W-I & 78	2	214	*	–	–	–	1
742/500	1974	P	1	Leeds	D	2	48	c	2	9	c	1
743/501			2	Lord's	D	2	23	c	2	12	*	3
744/502			3	Oval	D	2	4	c	–	–	–	–
751/504	1974–75	A	2	Perth	L-9w	1	49	c	1	35	c	2
752/505			3	Melbourne	D	2	14	c	2	44	c	2
753/506			4	Sydney	L-171	2	19	c	2	26	c	2
754/507			5	Adelaide	L-163	2	4	c	2	5	c	–

Career	M	I	NO	HS	R	Avge	100	50	Ct	St	Balls	R	W	Avge	BB	5w	10w	Rate
Test	9	15	2	214*	552	42.46	1	–	11	–	24	17	0	–	–	–	–	–
F/c	407	652	74	214*	19269	33.33	38	93	334	–	15577	7172	237	30.26	7-38	5	1	65.72

LLOYD
Timothy Andrew

Warwickshire (1977 to date)
Orange Free State
(1978–79 to 1979–80)

TOUR Z 1984–85 (Eng Co)
Born Oswestry, Shropshire 5 Nov 1956

Andy Lloyd was the first Shropshire-born cricketer to play in a home Test (Shrewsbury-born Billy Newham having appeared at Sydney in 1887–88). Tragically his career was only 33 minutes old when, batting on his county ground, he was struck on the temple of his helmet by a fast, sharply lifting ball from Malcolm Marshall. Hospitalised for several days because of blurred vision, he played no further cricket that year. Just over medium height (5ft 10in) and elegantly built, he has recovered his full sight and has continued to develop as a confident left-handed opening bat with an attractive range of strokes. He celebrated his return to the Warwickshire side after that injury with an innings of 160. His appointment as Warwickshire captain in 1988 produced a nine-place improvement in the Championship but led to a slight over-use of his very moderate right-arm medium-pace cum slow off-spin bowling – as figures of 2 for 208 off 31 overs confirm.

NOTABLE FEATS
- Exceeded 1000 runs in a season 7 times.
- Scored 208* for Warwickshire v Gloucestershire at Birmingham in 1983.

Ref	Series	V	T	Venue	Result	Batting 1st No	R	HO	Batting 2nd No	R	HO	Ct
989/601	1984	WI	1	Birmingham	L-I & 180	2	10	*rh	–	–	–	–

Career	M	I	NO	HS	R	Avge	100	50	Ct	St	Balls	R	W	Avge	BB	5w	10w	Rate
Test	1	1	1	10*	10	–	–	–	–	–	–	–	–	–	–	–	–	–
F/c	230	411	38	208*	13396	35.91	25	65	116	–	1584	1189	15	79.26	3-62	–	–	105.60

▲

Andy Lloyd

Peter Loader

▼

LOADER, Peter James

Surrey (1951 to 1963)
Western Australia (1963–64)

Wisden 1958
TOURS
A 1954–55, 1958–59; SA 1956–57;
I 1953–54 (Cwlth); Z 1959–60 (Surrey), 1962–63 (Cwlth)
Born Wallington, Surrey 25 Oct 1929

Peter Loader was a tall (6ft) aggressive, sinewy right-arm fast bowler. Throughout their halcyon years (1952–58) he was a member of that famous Surrey quartet of demolition experts: Alec Bedser, Laker, Lock and Loader. His long prancing run was a prelude to a high, vigorous action which swung the new ball late; he commanded a wicked bouncer and was a master of deceptive pace variations. Despite his hat-trick against the 1957 West Indians (the first in post-war Test cricket and the last for England), his Test career was restricted by competition from Trueman, Statham and Tyson. Emigrating to Perth after retiring from The Oval, he founded a highly successful transport business and became an erudite and lucid broadcaster.

NOTABLE FEATS
- *442* Dismissed J.D.C. Goddard, S. Ramadhin and R. Gilchrist to complete the first hat-trick for England in a home Test since 1899.
- Took 100 wickets in a season 7 times.
- Twice took 9 wickets for Surrey: 9 for 28 v Kent at Blackheath in 1953 and 9 for 17 v Warwickshire at The Oval in 1958.
- Two hat-tricks: for Surrey v Leicestershire at The Oval in 1963 and for England (*above*).

Ref	Series	V	T	Venue	Result	Batting 1st			Batting 2nd			Ct	Bowling 1st			Bowling 2nd		
						No	R	HO	No	R	HO		Balls	R	W	Balls	R	W
390/314	1954	P	4	Oval	L-24	11	8	*	9	5	c	–	108	35	3	96	26	0
411/325	1955	SA	4	Leeds	L-224	11	0	*	11	0	*	–	114	52	4	174	67	0
435/333	1956–57	SA	2	Cape Town	W-312	10	10	c	–	–	–	–	168	33	2	56	11	0
436/334			3	Durban[2]	D	10	1	c	10	3	lbw	–	200	79	2	64	21	1
437/335			4	Johannesburg[3]	L-17	10	13	c	10	7	c	–	184	78	1	104	33	0
438/336			5	Port Elizabeth	L-58	11	0	*	11	0	c	–	160	35	3	32	1	0
442/340	1957	WI	4	Leeds	W-I & 5	11	1	c	–	–	–	1	123	36	6	84	50	3
443/341			5	Oval	W-I & 237	11	0	lbw	–	–	–	–	42	12	1	18	2	0
454/342	1958	NZ	1	Birmingham	W-205	11	17	b	–	–	–	–	129	37	1	138	40	3
455/343			2	Lord's	W-I & 148	11	4	c	–	–	–	1	24	6	0	54	7	2
456/344			3	Leeds	W-I & 71	–	–	–	–	–	–	–	30	10	0	78	14	0
464/347	1958–59	A	1	Brisbane[2]	L-8w	11	6	*	11	0	*	–	152	56	4	72	27	0
465/348			2	Melbourne	L-8w	11	1	b	11	0	b	–	218	97	3	40	13	0

Career	M	I	NO	HS	R	Avge	100	50	Ct	St	Balls	R	W	Avge	BB	5w	10w	Rate
Test	13	19	6	17	76	5.84	–	–	2	–	2662	878	39	22.51	6-36	1	–	68.25
F/c	371	382	110	81	2314	8.50	–	2	120	–	62544	25260	1326	19.04	9-17	70	13	47.16

LOCK
Graham Anthony Richard

Surrey (1946 to 1963)
Leicestershire (1965 to 1967)
Western Australia
(1962–63 to 1970–71)

Wisden 1954
TOURS
A 1958–59; SA 1956–57; WI 1953–54, 1967–68; NZ 1958–59; I/SL 1961–62; P 1955–56, 1961–62; Z 1959–60 (Surrey)
Born Limpsfield, Surrey 5 Jul 1929

NOTABLE FEATS

- 50 wickets in 14th Test (*427*); 100 wickets in 24th Test (*457*); 150 wickets in 40th Test (*518*).
- *443* (Then) record E v WI match analysis of 11 for 48.
- *456* (Then) record E v NZ match analysis of 11 for 65.
- *458* Record E v NZ aggregate of 34 wickets (avge 7.47).
- *632* Contributed his highest first-class score (89) to record E v WI 9th-wkt stand of 109 with P.I. Pocock.
- Took 100 wickets in a season 14 times, including 200 twice – his 212 wickets at 12.02 apiece in 1957 being the last such instance. *(cont.)*

Tony Lock was a remarkable left-arm leg-spin bowler, an extremely useful lower-order batsman who could block or tackle as the situation demanded, and a world-class close fielder whose brilliant catching at backward short-leg or off his own bowling has seldom been approached. He was a unique cricketer who enjoyed great success with his two counties, with his adopted state and for England. Tall (6ft) and youthfully exuberant, he had the temperament of a fast bowler. One glance as he ran in to bowl, pate shimmering, shirt billowing around a girth which became increasingly ample as the seasons passed, wrist cocked menacingly, was sufficient to identify a dynamic hypo-energetic arch-competitor. Originally his was a slow orthodox action but he changed it during the winter of 1951–52 into one that allowed him to spin the ball at a brisk pace approaching medium to counteract the slow turning pitches then prevalent. The effects of this metamorphosis were dramatic and immediate: he became a deadly and often unplayable bowler, was selected for his first Tests and set Surrey on their relentlessly triumphant run. His faster ball with its low trajectory (fashioned at a Croydon indoor net with a squat roof) was so rapid that when Doug Insole was castled by it he asked the umpire if he had been run out rather than bowled. It caused him to be called for 'throwing' in four first-class matches and one Test (*382*) in the period 1952 to 1960. After seeing film of his action he decided to revert to his original slow style and concentrate on flight and length. It was a remarkable transition for a mature and key Test bowler to embark upon and a great credit to him. He succeeded and was free from criticism during the last decade of his career. Omitted from Dexter's tour Down Under, he went there in another capacity – as professional to Western Australia. He spent nine seasons with them, all but the first as their captain, and led them to the Sheffield Shield title in 1967–68. Few bowlers have achieved any success after either changing their action or emigrating; for Lock to do both was quite extraordinary. He decided to settle in Perth after retiring from Surrey in 1963; that he was induced back to county cricket after only one summer is an indication of the notable persuasive powers of Leicestershire's secretary, Mike Turner. Appointed captain in his second season, 'Beau' Lock raised the game

NOTABLE FEATS *cont.*

- Took all 10 for 54 for Surrey v Kent at Blackheath in 1956, his analysis of 16 for 83 in that match remaining the Surrey record. Two years later he returned match figures of 15 for 182 in the identical fixture.
- Four hat-tricks: for Surrey v Somerset at Weston in 1955; two for MCC in Bahawalpur and Multan in 1955–56; and for Leicestershire v Hampshire at Portsmouth in 1967 (the first first-class hat-trick in England to be completed on a Sunday).
- Held 8 catches in match for Surrey v Warwickshire at The Oval in 1957.
- Only F.E. Woolley and W.G. Grace have exceeded his first-class career total of 830 catches in the field; he held 64 in 1957.
- His career aggregate of 10,342 runs in first-class matches is the highest not to include a century and his average of 15.88 is the lowest by any batsman scoring 10,000 runs.

impressively and was the first county leader to hug and kiss his successful bowlers. In his final year (1967) they reached an uncharted area of the table: equal second. By now he was the outstanding slow bowler in Australia and had just led his team to the Sheffield Shield. He can have entertained no possible thoughts of an England recall in his 39th year and yet, when Titmus was separated from four of his toes in a boating accident, he found himself winging across the world to play in the Caribbean for the first time in 14 years. It was inevitable that, after helping Cowdrey's side to victory in Trinidad, he should contribute the highest score of his career to the draw which gained them the rubber.

Tony Lock bowling to Keith Miller on the penultimate and decisive afternoon of the Oval Test when he and Laker spun out the 1953 Australians. Arthur Morris is the non-striker; Peter May is at mid-on.

						Batting 1st			Batting 2nd				Bowling 1st			Bowling 2nd		
Ref	Series	V	T	Venue	Result	No	R	HO	No	R	HO	Ct	Balls	R	W	Balls	R	W
353/299	1952	I	3	Manchester	W-I & 207	10	1	*	–	–	–	2	–	–	–	57	36	4
354/300			4	Oval	D	–	–	–	–	–	–	1	36	1	0	–	–	–
375/304	1953	A	4	Leeds	D	10	9	b	10	8	c	3	138	53	1	48	48	1
376/305			5	Oval	W-8w	9	4	c	–	–	–	–	54	19	1	126	45	5
382/306	1953–54	WI	1	Kingston	L-140	8	4	b	8	0	b	–	246	76	3	84	36	2
383/307			2	Bridgetown	L-181	10	0	*	10	0	b	–	246	116	1	198	100	0
384/308			3	Georgetown	W-9w	10	13	b	–	–	–	1	167	60	2	150	41	1
385/309			4	Port-of-Spain	D	9	10	lbw	–	–	–	–	378	178	2	60	40	1
386/310			5	Kingston	W-9w	9	4	b	–	–	–	3	90	31	1	162	40	1
410/324	1955	SA	3	Manchester	L-3w	9	19	*	6	17	c	–	384	121	2	42	23	1
411/325			4	Leeds	L-224	4	17	lbw	9	7	c	1	36	20	1	252	88	1
412/326			5	Oval	W-92	10	18	c	10	1	lbw	1	132	39	4	198	62	4
425/327	1956	A	1	Nottingham	D	9	0	lbw	–	–	–	3	216	61	3	132	23	1
427/329			3	Leeds	W-I & 42	6	21	c	–	–	–	1	163	41	4	240	40	3
428/330			4	Manchester	W-I & 170	10	25	*	–	–	–	3	84	37	1	330	69	0
429/331			5	Oval	D	6	0	c	–	–	–	3	150	49	2	109	17	1
438/336	1956–57	SA	5	Port Elizabeth	L-58	8	14	b	8	12	c	–	88	21	1	120	17	1
439/337	1957	WI	1	Birmingham	D	7	0	b	–	–	–	2	208	55	0	162	31	3
442/340			4	Leeds	W-I & 5	8	20	b	–	–	–	1	84	23	0	6	6	1
443/341			5	Oval	W-I & 237	8	17	c	–	–	–	1	130	28	5	96	20	6
454/342	1958	NZ	1	Birmingham	W-205	8	4	lbw	–	–	–	–	12	0	0	51	25	3
455/343			2	Lord's	W-I & 148	8	23	*	–	–	–	2	69	17	5	75	12	4
456/344			3	Leeds	W-I & 71	–	–	–	–	–	–	–	109	14	4	212	51	7
457/345			4	Manchester	W-I & 13	9	7	lbw	–	–	–	1	198	61	1	144	35	7
458/346			5	Oval	D	8	25	c	–	–	–	3	78	19	2	108	20	1

Ref	Series	V	T	Venue	Result	Batting 1st No	R	HO	Batting 2nd No	R	HO	Ct	Bowling 1st Balls	R	W	Bowling 2nd Balls	R	W
464/347	1958–59	A	1	Brisbane[2]	L-8w	8	5	c	8	1	b	–	80	17	0	119	37	1
465/348			2	Melbourne	L-8w	8	5	st	8	6	c	–	136	54	0	25	11	0
466/349			3	Sydney	D	8	21	lbw	9	11	*	1	346	130	4	88	23	0
467/350			4	Adelaide	L-10w	8	2	c	8	9	b	–	200	96	0	16	8	0
472/352	1958–59	NZ	1	Christchurch	W-I & 99	10	15	b	–	–	–	4	156	31	5	170	53	6
473/353			2	Auckland	D	–	–	–	–	–	–	–	123	29	2	–	–	–
508/370	1961	A	2	Lord's	L-5w	9	5	c	9	1	b	–	156	48	0	–	–	–
509/371			3	Leeds	W-8w	9	30	lbw	–	–	–	1	174	68	2	60	32	0
511/373			5	Oval	D	8	3	c	8	0	c	–	252	102	1	–	–	–
513/375	1961–62	I	1	Bombay[2]	D	9	23	b	7	22	*	1	270	74	4	96	33	1
514/376			2	Kanpur	D	10	49	c	–	–	–	1	264	93	3	–	–	–
515/377			3	Delhi	D	–	–	–	–	–	–	–	240	83	1	–	–	–
516/378			4	Calcutta	L-187	10	2	*	10	1	ro	2	216	63	2	276	111	4
517/379			5	Madras[2]	L-128	10	0	c	10	11	c	2	240	106	1	237	65	6
518/380	1961–62	P	2	Dacca	D	11	4	c	–	–	–	2	438	155	4	252	70	4
519/381			3	Karachi	D	10	0	*	–	–	–	2	84	25	1	222	86	1
530/382	1962	P	1	Birmingham	W-I & 24	–	–	–	–	–	–	1	114	37	2	216	80	3
531/383			2	Lord's	W-9w	9	7	c	–	–	–	–	–	–	–	84	78	0
533/385			4	Nottingham	D	–	–	–	–	–	–	1	84	19	0	90	27	1
545/397	1963	WI	3	Birmingham	W-217	10	1	b	10	56	b	2	12	5	0	–	–	–
546/398			4	Leeds	L-221	10	53	b	10	1	c	2	172	54	3	43	54	1
547/399			5	Oval	L-8w	9	4	hw	9	0	b	3	174	65	1	150	52	1
631/443	1967–68	WI	4	Port-of-Spain	W-7w	10	3	lbw	–	–	–	1	192	129	1	–	–	–
632/444			5	Georgetown	D	9	89	b	9	2	c	1	168	61	2	54	22	1

Career	M	I	NO	HS	R	Avge	100	50	Ct	St	Balls	R	W	Avge	BB	5w	10w	Rate
Test	49	63	9	89	742	13.74	–	3	59	–	13147	4451	174	25.58	7-35	9	3	75.55
F/c	654	812	161	89	10342	15.88	–	27	830	–	151051	54709	2844	19.23	10-54	196	50	53.11

TEST NOTES

• *382* Called once in the second innings, he was the second bowler after E. Jones (1897–98) to be no-balled for throwing in a Test match.

G. A. R. LOCK – TEST BOWLING SUMMARY

Series	V	M	Balls	R	W	Avge	BB	5w	10w	Rate
1952	I	2	93	37	4	9.25	4-36	–	–	23.25
1953	A	2	366	165	8	20.62	5-45	1	–	45.75
1953–54	WI	5	1781	718	14	51.28	3-76	–	–	127.21
1955	SA	3	1044	353	13	27.15	4-39	–	–	80.30
1956	A	4	1424	337	15	22.46	4-41	–	–	94.93
1956–57	SA	1	208	38	2	19.00	1-17	–	–	104.00
1957	WI	3	686	163	15	10.86	6-20	2	1	45.73
1958	NZ	5	1056	254	34	7.47	7-35	3	1	31.05
1958–59	A	4	1010	376	5	75.20	4-130	–	–	202.00
1958–59	NZ	2	449	113	13	8.69	6-53	2	1	34.53
1961	A	3	642	250	3	83.33	2-68	–	–	214.00
1961–62	I	5	1839	628	22	28.54	6-65	1	–	83.59
1961–62	P	2	996	336	10	33.60	4-70	–	–	99.60
1962	P	3	588	241	6	40.16	3-80	–	–	98.00
1963	WI	3	551	230	6	38.33	3-54	–	–	91.83
1967–68	WI	2	414	212	4	53.00	2-61	–	–	103.50
	A	13	3442	1128	31	36.38	5-45	1	–	111.03
	SA	4	1252	391	15	26.06	4-39	–	–	83.46
	WI	13	3432	1323	39	33.92	6-20	2	1	88.00
	NZ	7	1505	367	47	7.80	7-35	5	2	32.02
	I	7	1932	665	26	25.57	6-65	1	–	74.30
	P	5	1584	577	16	36.06	4-70	–	–	99.00
Home		28	6450	2030	104	19.51	7-35	6	2	62.01
Overseas		21	6697	2421	70	34.58	6-53	3	1	95.67
Totals		49	13147	4451	174	25.58	7-35	9	3	75.55

LOCKWOOD
William Henry

Nottinghamshire (1886 to 1887)
Surrey (1889 to 1904)

Wisden 1899
TOUR A 1894–95
Born Old Radford, Nottinghamshire
25 Mar 1868
Died Old Radford 26 Apr 1932

Bill Lockwood was a high-class right-arm fast bowler who, for almost his entire career with Surrey, formed a lethal opening partnership with Tom Richardson. If the latter was the quicker of the pair, Lockwood's subtle variations of pace made him equally dangerous; his splendidly disguised slower ball required no perceptible change of action. With his moderate run-up, classic high action, nip off the pitch and sharp break-backs, he was capable of devastating bursts of wicket-taking. He was one of the most effective fast bowlers of his era; he took eight or more wickets in an innings for Surrey on 13 occasions and contributed to a spate of six Championships in ten seasons. His first-class batting record with 15 centuries and an average of almost 22 certainly entitled him to be classed as an all-rounder and, without his enormous workload as a bowler, he had the talent to be a frontline batsman. Curiously, he had a poor tour of Australia during an extremely hot summer and lost form during the next three seasons to such an extent that Surrey dropped him. A winter spent on improving his fitness worked wonders and he made a miraculous return to peak performance in 1898. A close encounter with a shark and a double domestic tragedy had led to over-indulgence in the falling over water; cricket has known no more courageous episode of drying out. After seven more seasons with Surrey he returned to his native Nottinghamshire (he had achieved little for them in five matches before moving south) where he continued to play club cricket into his fifties.

NOTABLE FEATS

- *70* Shared record E v A (in England) 10th-wkt stand of 81* with W. Rhodes.
- Exceeded 1000 runs in a season twice and took 100 wickets 7 times, completing the 'double' in 1899 and 1900.
- Took 9 wickets in an innings for Surrey on 3 occasions. His best match analysis was 15 for 184 for Surrey v Gloucestershire at Cheltenham in 1899.
- Three hat-tricks for Surrey: v Cambridge U at Fenner's in 1893, v Derbyshire at The Oval in 1901 and v Yorkshire at Sheffield in 1903.
- Achieved the match 'double' (100 runs and 12 wickets) for Surrey v Lancashire at The Oval in 1902.

TEST NOTES

- *45* Unable to bat because his hand had been badly gashed by an exploding soda water bottle.

Bill Lockwood

						Batting 1st			Batting 2nd				Bowling 1st			Bowling 2nd		
Ref	Series	V	T	Venue	Result	No	R	HO	No	R	HO	Ct	Balls	R	W	Balls	R	W
39/39	1893	A	1	Lord's	D	9	22	b	7	0	b	–	225	101	6	–	–	–
40/40			2	Oval	W-I & 43	9	10	c	–	–	–	1	95	37	4	145	96	4
42/42	1894–95	A	1	Sydney	W-10	9	18	c	9	29	b	–	18	1	0	96	40	0
43/43			2	Melbourne	W-94	8	3	*	9	33	*	–	30	17	1	150	60	0
44/44			3	Adelaide	L-382	9	0	c	10	1	c	2	48	33	1	90	71	1
45/45			4	Sydney	L-I & 147	–	–	–	–	–	–	–	50	22	1	–	–	–
46/46			5	Melbourne	W-6w	7	5	c	–	–	–	1	162	72	1	96	24	0
64/64	1899	A	5	Oval	D	8	24	b	–	–	–	–	203	71	7	75	33	0
70/70	1902	A	1	Birmingham	D	10	52	*	–	–	–	–	–	–	–	–	–	–
71/71			2	Lord's	D	–	–	–	–	–	–	–	–	–	–	–	–	–
73/73			4	Manchester	L-3	9	7	ro	9	0	b	–	121	48	6	102	28	5
74/74			5	Oval	W-1w	9	25	c	9	2	lbw	–	144	85	1	120	45	5

Career	M	I	NO	HS	R	Avge	100	50	Ct	St	Balls	R	W	Avge	BB	5w	10w	Rate
Test	12	16	3	52*	231	17.76	–	1	4	–	1970	884	43	20.55	7-71	5	1	45.81
F/c	362	531	45	165	10673	21.96	15	48	140	–	52140	25247	1376	18.34	9-59	121	29	37.89

LOHMANN
George Alfred

Surrey (1884 to 1896)
Western Province
(1894–95 to 1896–97)

Wisden 1889
TOURS
A 1886–87, 1887–88, 1891–92;
SA 1895–96
Born Kensington, London 2 Jun 1865
Died Worcester, Cape Province, South Africa 1 Dec 1901

George Lohmann

On statistics alone George Lohmann has the strongest claim to be considered the greatest Test match bowler of all time. As his *Notable Feats* show, he was the most economical and penetrative bowler in the history of Test cricket. At county level he was the key factor in Surrey's success when they won the title five times out of six after it had been officially constituted from 1890. In South Africa he was outrageously successful and he took 63 wickets at 11.98 during his 1887–88 tour of Australia. His quick-footed forcing batsmanship and quite exceptional catching at slip elevated him to all-rounder status but it was his bowling which made the greatest impact. His greatest contemporaries rated him the finest and most hostile of his type in their memory. Operating at a brisk-medium with an occasional deceptive variation of pace, angle and flight, he proved the master of all atmospheric conditions and pitches – especially the jute mats of South Africa. He could break the ball in either direction from an impeccable length and, despite constant experiments with grip and wrist action, that accuracy never wavered. A tall, handsome, confident man with a robust physique, he gave unstinting effort to every aspect of his cricket and undertook a colossal workload. It may well have been because of this enormous drain on his energy that he contracted tuberculosis in 1892. With the help of winters in South Africa he extended his Surrey career until 1896 and, after emigrating to the Union, he returned to England as manager of the 1901 Springbok team. Later that year he died when in only his 37th year.

NOTABLE FEATS

• 50 wickets in 10th Test (*33*); 100 wickets in 16th Test (*48*) – fastest in terms of fewest matches played and balls bowled (3421) and the cheapest (fewest runs conceded – 1066).
• Lowest career average by any bowler taking 25 or more Test wickets (10.75) and highest wicket-taking rate (1 every 34 balls).
• *26* First bowler to take 8 wickets in a Test innings; his 8 for 35 remains the E v A record in Australia and the record for all Tests at Sydney.
• *47* His innings (8 for 7 – then the Test record) and match (15 for 45) analyses remain the record for all Tests at Port Elizabeth. He ended the match with a hat-trick, dismissing F.J. Cook, J. Middleton and J.T. Willoughby.
• *48* First bowler to take 9 wickets in a Test innings; his 9 for 28 remains the record for E v SA and for Tests at Johannesburg, and the second-best analysis in all Tests after J.C. Laker's 10 for 53. His 35 wickets at 5.80 remains the lowest average by any bowler taking 25 or more wickets in a series.
(cont.)

						Batting 1st			Batting 2nd				Bowling 1st			Bowling 2nd		
Ref	Series	V	T	Venue	Result	No	R	HO	No	R	HO	Ct	Balls	R	W	Balls	R	W
22/22	1886	A	1	Manchester	W-4w	9	32	b	–	–	–	3	92	41	1	20	14	0
23/23			2	Lord's	W-I & 106	11	7	*	–	–	–	1	28	21	0	56	11	0
24/24			3	Oval	W-I & 217	11	7	b	–	–	–	1	122	36	7	148	68	5
25/25	1886–87	A	1	Sydney	W-13	9	17	c	7	3	lbw	–	84	30	3	96	20	3
26/26			2	Sydney	W-71	6	2	b	6	6	b	–	100	35	8	160	52	2
27/27	1887–88	A		Sydney	W-126	8	12	c	7	0	c	–	76	17	5	128	35	4
28/28	1888	A	1	Lord's	L-61	4	2	lbw	10	0	st	4	80	28	2	56	33	4
29/29			2	Oval	W-I & 137	10	62	*	–	–	–	3	119	21	1	24	11	0
30/30			3	Manchester	W-I & 21	10	0	ro	–	–	–	1	68	31	1	32	20	3
33/33	1890	A	1	Lord's	W-7w	9	19	c	–	–	–	1	105	43	0	145	28	3
34/34			2	Oval	W-2w	8	3	c	7	2	c	2	162	34	3	105	32	3
35/35	1891–92	A	1	Melbourne	L-54	7	3	lbw	7	0	c	3	168	40	0	234	53	2
36/36			2	Sydney	L-72	7	10	b	7	15	c	1	260	58	8	306	84	2
37/37			3	Adelaide	W-I & 230	7	0	lbw	–	–	–	1	126	46	3	36	8	1
47/47	1895–96	SA	1	Port Elizabeth	W-288	2	0	c	6	0	b	1	79	38	7	49	7	8
48/48			2	Johannesburg[1]	W-I & 197	2	2	c	–	–	–	3	72	28	9	85	43	3
49/49			3	Cape Town	W-I & 33	7	8	b	–	–	–	2	120	42	7	115	45	1
50/50	1896	A	1	Lord's	W-6w	9	1	c	–	–	–	1	55	13	3	110	39	0

Career	M	I	NO	HS	R	Avge	100	50	Ct	St	Balls	R	W	Avge	BB	5w	10w	Rate
Test	18	26	2	62*	213	8.87	–	1	28	–	3821	1205	112	10.75	9-28	9	5	34.11
F/c	293	427	39	115	7247	18.67	3	29	337	–	71724	25295	1841	13.73	9-28	176	57	38.95

NOTABLE FEATS *cont.*

- Took 100 wickets in a season 8 times, including 200 in 3 consecutive seasons (1888–90).
- Took 9 for 67 (15 for 98 in match) for Surrey v Sussex at Hove in 1889.
- Took 4 wickets in 5 balls for Surrey v Lancashire at Manchester in 1888.
- Bowled in an unchanged partnership throughout both completed innings of a match on 6 occasions, including the last instance in first-class cricket in Australia (with J. Briggs for A. Shrewsbury's XI v Australian XI at Sydney in 1887–88).

G. A. LOHMANN – TEST BOWLING SUMMARY

Series	V	M	Balls	R	W	Avge	BB	5w	10w	Rate
1886	A	3	466	191	13	14.69	7-36	2	1	35.84
1886–87	A	2	440	137	16	8.56	8-35	1	1	27.50
1887–88	A	1	204	52	9	5.77	5-17	1	–	22.66
1888	A	3	379	144	11	13.09	4-33	–	–	34.45
1890	A	2	517	137	9	15.22	3-28	–	–	57.44
1891–92	A	3	1130	289	16	18.06	8-58	1	1	70.62
1895–96	SA	3	520	203	35	5.80	9-28	4	2	14.85
1896	A	1	165	52	3	17.33	3-13	–	–	55.00
	A	15	3301	1002	77	13.01	8-58	5	3	42.87
	SA	3	520	203	35	5.80	9-28	4	2	14.85
Home		9	1527	524	36	14.55	7-36	2	1	42.41
Overseas		9	2294	681	76	8.96	9-28	7	4	30.18
Totals		18	3821	1205	112	10.75	9-28	9	5	34.11

LOWSON
Frank Anderson

Yorkshire (1949 to 1958)

TOURS I/SL 1951–52; P 1951–52
Born Bradford, Yorkshire 1 Jul 1925
Died Pool-in-Wharfedale, Yorkshire 8 Sep 1984

Len Hutton (left) and Frank Lowson going out to bat against Surrey at The Oval, 1955.

A product of the Yorkshire league, Frank Lowson was a patient opening batsman who modelled his very correct method on that of Len Hutton, his partner throughout most of his career. He launched into the county scene with such a sequence of impressive scores that, within a few weeks of his debut in 1949, he had scored 64 in a Test trial; he went on to win his cap and achieve an aggregate for a first season which has been exceeded only by Herbert Sutcliffe. A little above medium height (5ft 10½in) and trimly built, he was a strong on-side player, especially adept at dealing with inswing and off-spin, but he could cut and cover-drive handsomely. By dint of dedicated effort he became a reliable catcher in the leg-trap. After scoring 58 in his first Test innings he was selected for that winter's mission to India but had a disappointing series despite amassing over 1000 runs on the tour. He was out of form when he was recalled in an emergency three years later and a double failure marked the end of his international career. In 1951 surgery on varicose veins had interrupted his summer. Further leg trouble six years afterwards ended his season in mid-June and, following a run of low scores the next summer, he was dropped and not re-engaged. After just ten seasons and at the age of 33 he turned his attention successfully to insurance.

NOTABLE FEATS

- Exceeded 1000 runs in a season 8 times, including 2152 in 1950, plus once on tour.
- Scored 1799 runs in 1949 – second-highest total for a debut season.
- Scored 259* for Yorkshire v Worcestershire at Worcester in 1953.

						Batting 1st			Batting 2nd			
Ref	Series	V	T	Venue	Result	No	R	HO	No	R	HO	Ct
337/290	1951	SA	4	Leeds	D	2	58	c	–	–	–	1
338/291			5	Oval	W-4w	2	0	c	2	37	c	1
339/292	1951–52	I	1	Delhi	D	2	4	lbw	2	68	c	–
340/293			2	Bombay[2]	D	1	5	c	1	22	c	–
342/295			4	Kanpur	W-8w	1	26	hw	1	12	c	2
343/296			5	Madras[1]	L-I & 8	1	1	b	1	7	c	–
411/325	1955	SA	4	Leeds	L-224	2	5	lbw	2	0	b	1

Career	M	I	NO	HS	R	Avge	100	50	Ct	St	Balls	R	W	Avge	BB	5w	10w	Rate
Test	7	13	0	68	245	18.84	–	2	5	–	–	–	–	–	–	–	–	–
F/c	277	449	37	259*	15321	37.18	31	72	190	–	30	31	0	–	–	–	–	–

LUCAS, Alfred Perry

Surrey (1874 to 1882)
Cambridge University (1875 to 1878)
Middlesex (1883 to 1888)
Essex (1894 to 1907)

TOUR A 1878–79
Born Westminster, London 20 Feb 1857
Died Great Waltham, Essex 12 Oct 1923

Although 'Bunny' Lucas was predominantly an ultra-defensive opening batsman, his was such a classic technique and he was so positive in his play off either foot that he was seldom boring. H.H. Stephenson's star pupil at Uppingham School, he gained blues in each of his four years at Cambridge before assisting three counties during a first-class career lasting 33 years. His appearances were limited by other commitments but he captained Essex for three seasons (1892–94) before they were admitted to the Championship. During his prime he was an automatic selection for the Gentlemen and scored 107 in the Lord's fixture of 1882. A right-handed slow round-arm change bowler, he found himself as the main support for the professionals Emmett and Ulyett on Lord Harris's tour of Australia. [*Illus. pp.* 80, 222]

NOTABLE FEATS

- 4 With W.G. Grace shared Test cricket's first century partnership – 120 for the 2nd wkt.
- Carried his bat through a completed innings on 3 occasions – for Surrey, MCC and Gentlemen.

Ref	Series	V	T	Venue	Result	Batting 1st No	R	HO	Batting 2nd No	R	HO	Ct	Bowling 1st Balls	R	W	Bowling 2nd Balls	R	W
3/3	1878–79	A		Melbourne	L-10w	2	6	b	2	13	c	–	72	31	0	–	–	–
4/4	1880	A		Oval	W-5w	3	55	b	3	2	c	1	–	–	–	48	23	0
9/9	1882	A		Oval	L-7	4	9	c	5	5	b	–	–	–	–	–	–	–
14/14	1884	A	1	Manchester	D	6	15	*	2	24	b	–	–	–	–	–	–	–
15/15			2	Lord's	W-I & 5	2	28	c	–	–	–	–	–	–	–	–	–	–

Career	M	I	NO	HS	R	Avge	100	50	Ct	St	Balls	R	W	Avge	BB	5w	10w	Rate
Test	5	9	1	55	157	19.62	–	1	1	–	120	54	0	–	–	–	–	–
F/c	256	435	46	145	10263	26.38	8	50	152	–	7824	2849	155	18.38	6-10	4	–	50.47

LUCKHURST Brian William

Kent (1958 to 1985)

Wisden 1971
TOURS
A 1970–71, 1974–75; WI 1969–70 (Cav); NZ 1970–71; P 1967–68 (Cwlth)
Born Sittingbourne, Kent 5 Feb 1939

Brian Luckhurst was a most dependable and effective opening batsman who bridged the gulf between county and Test cricket with consummate ease. A consistent scorer for Kent, he was 31 when given an international dress rehearsal against the powerful Rest of the World side in 1970. His 113* at Trent Bridge saw England to their only victory of that unofficial rubber. Of medium height (5ft 9½in) and build, he was a courageous player who always sold his wicket dearly and twice in his opening series in Australia scored hundreds despite severely damaging his hand early in the innings. A strong right hand made him a predominantly on-side player but he was a highly efficient cutter especially square. An occasional left-arm slow bowler, he was an exceptional and athletic all-purpose fielder. He retired after the 1976 season and subsequently became first manager and then cricket administrator of Kent, reappearing for them in an emergency against the 1985 Australians.

						Batting 1st			Batting 2nd				Bowling 1st			Bowling 2nd		
Ref	Series	V	T	Venue	Result	No	R	HO	No	R	HO	Ct	Balls	R	W	Balls	R	W
674/459	1970–71	A	1	Brisbane[2]	D	2	74	ro	2	20	*	1	–	–	–	–	–	–
675/460			2	Perth	D	2	131	b	2	19	c	1	–	–	–	–	–	–
676/461			4	Sydney	W-299	2	38	lbw	2	5	c	1	–	–	–	–	–	–
677/462			5	Melbourne	D	2	109	b	–	–	–	2	–	–	–	–	–	–
679/464			7	Sydney	W-62	2	0	c	2	59	c	–	–	–	–	–	–	–
685/465	1970–71	NZ	1	Christchurch	W-8w	1	10	c	1	29	*	2	–	–	–	–	–	–
686/466			2	Auckland	D	2	14	c	2	15	c	–	–	–	–	16	6	0
687/467	1971	P	1	Birmingham	D	2	35	c	2	108	*	1	–	–	–	–	–	–
688/468			2	Lord's	D	2	46	c	1	53	*	–	–	–	–	–	–	–
689/469			3	Leeds	W-25	2	0	c	2	0	c	1	–	–	–	–	–	–
690/470	1971	I	1	Lord's	D	2	30	c	2	1	b	1	–	–	–	–	–	–
691/471			2	Manchester	D	1	78	c	1	101	st	–	–	–	–	–	–	–
692/472			3	Oval	L-4w	1	1	c	1	33	c	–	–	–	–	12	9	1
698/473	1972	A	1	Manchester	W-89	3	14	b	3	0	c	1	–	–	–	–	–	–
699/474			2	Lord's	L-8w	3	1	b	3	4	c	1	–	–	–	5	5	0
700/475			3	Nottingham	D	1	23	lbw	1	96	c	1	–	–	–	–	–	–
701/476			4	Leeds	W-9w	1	18	c	1	12	*	–	–	–	–	–	–	–
726/490	1973	WI	2	Birmingham	D	3	12	lbw	1	42	c	1	–	–	–	24	12	0
727/491			3	Lord's	L-I & 226	3	1	c	4	12	c	–	–	–	–	–	–	–
750/503	1974–75	A	1	Brisbane[2]	L-166	2	1	c	2	3	c	–	–	–	–	–	–	–
751/504			2	Perth	L-9w	2	27	c	7	23	c	–	–	–	–	–	–	–

Career	M	I	NO	HS	R	Avge	100	50	Ct	St	Balls	R	W	Avge	BB	5w	10w	Rate
Test	21	41	5	131	1298	36.05	4	5	14	–	57	32	1	32.00	1-9	–	–	57.00
F/c	389	662	77	215	22303	38.12	48	115	391	–	5642	2744	64	42.87	4-32	–	–	88.15

Brian Luckhurst pulls Asif Iqbal to the boundary for his century in the First Test against Pakistan, 1971.

B. W. LUCKHURST – TEST BATTING SUMMARY

Series	V	M	I	NO	HS	R	Avge	100	50
1970–71	A	5	9	1	131	455	56.87	2	2
1970–71	NZ	2	4	1	29*	68	22.66	–	–
1971	P	3	6	2	108*	242	60.50	1	1
1971	I	3	6	–	101	244	40.66	1	1
1972	A	4	8	1	96	168	24.00	–	1
1973	WI	2	4	–	42	67	16.75	–	–
1974–75	A	2	4	–	27	54	13.50	–	–
	A	11	21	2	131	677	35.63	2	3
	WI	2	4	–	42	67	16.75	–	–
	NZ	2	4	1	29*	68	22.66	–	–
	I	3	6	–	101	244	40.66	1	1
	P	3	6	2	108*	242	60.50	1	1
Home		12	24	3	108*	721	34.33	2	3
Overseas		9	17	2	131	577	38.46	2	2
Totals		21	41	5	131	1298	36.05	4	5

NOTABLE FEATS

- 1000 runs in 13th Test (*692*) (25 inns).
- *675* Scored 131 in his second Test despite a damaged thumb.
- *677* Scored 109 despite fracturing his left little finger early in the innings.
- *688* Shared in 1st-wkt stands of 124 and 117* with G. Boycott and R.A. Hutton respectively.
- Exceeded 1000 runs in a season 14 times.
- Two double centuries for Kent.
- Carried his bat through a completed Kent innings twice.

LYTTELTON
Rt Hon. Alfred KC

Cambridge University (1876 to 1879)
Middlesex (1877 to 1887)

Born London 7 Feb 1857
Died Marylebone, London 5 Jul 1913

One of eight sons of the 4th Lord Lyttelton, six of whom played at first-class level, Alfred was a cavalier front-foot batsman in the classic straight-bat tradition and the outstanding amateur wicket-keeper of his generation. He was the first England keeper to stand up close to the stumps without the traditional long-stop. An occasional right-handed lob bowler, he is celebrated for taking four Test wickets while still wearing his pads. He captained Eton and, during the last of his four summers as a blue, Cambridge. At the age of 28 he abandoned first-class cricket in favour of his work at the Bar. Tall, handsome, affable and unselfish, he was an exceptionally gifted sportsman. The leading amateur tennis player of his day, he represented Cambridge at real tennis, racquets and athletics; a double international, he also played soccer for England in 1877 after appearing for Old Etonians in the previous year's FA Cup Final. He found time to sit on MCC's committee for ten years and be their president in 1898, this despite the demands of a political career which included serving as an MP from 1895 until his death following a brief illness after surgery. [*Illus. p.* 80]

NOTABLE FEATS
- *16* His analysis of 4 for 19 (off 48 balls in 1st inns) remains the best in Test cricket by a player who began the innings as a wicket-keeper.

						Batting 1st			Batting 2nd			Fielding 1st				Fielding 2nd			
Ref	Series	V	T	Venue	Result	No	R	HO	No	R	HO	Ct	St	Byes	Balls	Ct	St	Byes	Balls
4/4†	1880	A		Oval	W-5w	8	11	*	1	13	b	–	–	9	301	–	–	7	711
9/9†	1882	A		Oval	L-7	5	2	c	6	12	b	–	–	1	320	1	–	6	252
15/15†	1884	A	2	Lord's	W-I & 5	9	31	b	–	–	–	–	–	5	422	–	–	1	377
16/16†			3	Oval	D	9	8	b	2	17	b	1	–	7	1244	–	–	–	–

Career	M	I	NO	HS	R	Avge	100	50	Ct	St	Balls	R	W	Avge	BB	5w	10w	Rate
Test	4	7	1	31	94	15.66	–	–	2	–	48	19	4	4.75	4-19	–	–	12.00
F/c	101	171	12	181	4429	27.85	7	20	134	70	316	172	4	43.00	4-19	–	–	79.00

MACAULAY
George Gibson

Yorkshire (1920 to 1935)

Wisden 1924
TOUR SA 1922–23
Born Thirsk, Yorkshire 7 Dec 1897
Died Sullom Voe, Shetland Islands 13 Dec 1940

George Macaulay was a 23-year-old right-arm fast bowler when he began his celebrated Yorkshire career with a few appearances in 1920. By the following season Hirst and Rhodes had persuaded him to reduce his pace to around medium and concentrate on length, swing and spin. So responsive was their pupil that he gave up his banking career and took 101 wickets that summer, including an inspired spell of 6 for 3 against Derbyshire. Mixing late swing with sharp off-breaks, he was quite unplayable at times. Exceptionally accurate and radiating confidence, he would open the attack off a short, bustling run before switching to his vast off-breaks, usually from around the wicket. Not far short of being a genuine all-rounder, he was a determined and capable lower-order batsman and a superb catcher in the close positions. It was no coincidence that during his 15 complete seasons Yorkshire won the Championship eight times. He was still at the peak of his form when an injury to his spinning finger from an attempted return catch compelled his retirement to league cricket. In the First World War he served in the Royal Field Artillery; he died on active service in the Second soon after being commissioned as an RAF Pilot Officer. [*Illus. p.* 157]

NOTABLE FEATS
- *149* Fourth bowler (third for England) to take a wicket (G.A.L. Hearne) with his first ball in Test cricket. Made winning hit in the fourth of only six Tests to be decided by a one-wicket margin.
- *165* Shared a match-saving 9th-wkt stand of 108 with G. Geary.
- Took 100 wickets in a season 10 times, including 211 in 1925.
- Four hat-tricks (Yorkshire record equalled by F.S. Trueman): v Warwickshire at Birmingham in 1923, v Leicestershire at Hull in 1930, v Glamorgan at Cardiff in 1933 and v Lancashire (4 wickets in 5 balls) at Manchester in 1933.
- Bowled in an unchanged partnership with E. Robinson throughout both completed Worcestershire innings for Yorkshire at Leeds in 1927.

Ref	Series	V	T Venue	Result	Batting 1st No	R	HO	Batting 2nd No	R	HO	Ct	Bowling 1st Balls	R	W	Bowling 2nd Balls	R	W
149/135	1922–23	SA	2 Cape Town	W-1w	11	19	b	11	1	*	2	78	19	2	222	64	5
150/136			3 Durban[2]	D	9	3	*	2	2	c	–	174	55	1	–	–	–
151/137			4 Johannesburg[1]	D	11	1	*	–	–	–	1	162	80	2	102	27	1
152/138			5 Durban[2]	W-109	9	0	lbw	10	1	b	2	120	42	3	108	39	2
155/141	1924	SA	3 Leeds	W-9w	11	0	*	–	–	–	–	69	23	1	162	60	1
165/151	1926	A	3 Leeds	D	10	76	c	–	–	–	–	192	123	1	–	–	–
227/201	1933	WI	1 Lord's	W-I & 27	11	9	b	–	–	–	–	108	25	1	120	57	4
228/202			2 Manchester	D	–	–	–	–	–	–	–	84	48	0	–	–	–

Career	M	I	NO	HS	R	Avge	100	50	Ct	St	Balls	R	W	Avge	BB	5w	10w	Rate
Test	8	10	4	76	112	18.66	–	1	5	–	1701	662	24	27.58	5-64	1	–	70.87
F/c	468	460	125	125*	6056	18.07	3	20	373	–	90102	32440	1837	17.65	8-21	126	31	49.04

MacBRYAN John Crawford William

Somerset (1911 to 1931)
Cambridge University (1919 to 1920)

Wisden 1925
TOUR SA 1924–25 (Joel)
Born Box, Wiltshire 22 Jul 1892
Died London 14 Jul 1983

NOTABLE FEATS
- Exceeded 1000 runs in a season 4 times.
- Shared record Somerset 2nd-wkt stand of 290 with M.D. Lyon v Derbyshire at Buxton in 1924.

Despite his short, sturdy figure, Jack MacBryan was a neat and elegant batsman. His predominantly back-foot technique allowed scope for the cut and hook. Strong off his legs, he was a sound player against spin on responsive pitches. After captaining Exeter School he joined the Army and was a cadet at Sandhurst when he made his debut for Somerset at the end of the 1911 season. Wounded in his right arm and captured at Le Cateau, he was imprisoned for virtually the entire First World War but found ample cricket in Holland during the latter months. Afterwards he won a blue in his second year at Cambridge and headed Somerset's batting averages for six seasons out of eight. After convincing innings in successive Test trials he was eventually selected for the Fourth Test of 1924. There he fell victim to Manchester's notorious climate and the grand total of 165 minutes play possible in that contest encompassed his entire Test career. He remains the only Test cricketer who did not bat, bowl or dismiss anyone in the field. At least he had the compensation of becoming England's oldest surviving cricketer before dying eight days short of his 91st birthday. [*Illus. p.* 446]

Ref	Series	V	T Venue	Result	Batting 1st No	R	HO	Batting 2nd No	R	HO	Ct
156/142	1924	SA	4 Manchester	D	–	–	–	–	–	–	–

Career	M	I	NO	HS	R	Avge	100	50	Ct	St	Balls	R	W	Avge	BB	5w	10w	Rate
Test	1	–	–	–	–	–	–	–	–	–	–	–	–	–	–	–	–	–
F/c	206	362	12	164	10322	29.49	18	48	128	–	66	61	0	–	–	–	–	–

McCONNON James Edward

Glamorgan (1950 to 1961)

TOURS A 1954–55; I 1953–54 (Cwlth)
Born Burnopfield, Co. Durham
21 Jun 1922

Jim McConnon was a tall (6ft 2in) lean, right-arm off-break bowler, a tail-end batsman who produced some valuable innings for Glamorgan and a superb fielder at gully. His high action and long fingers were ideal for his craft but he sometimes struggled with his temperament and needed encouragement and careful handling. He visited India with a Commonwealth side in 1953–54 but was most surprisingly preferred to Laker on Hutton's tour of Australia the following winter. Injuries compelled his premature return from both expeditions. After his career with Glamorgan he spent three seasons with Cheshire (1962–64) before becoming coach at Stonyhurst School. He played soccer for Aston Villa. [*Illus. p.* 11]

NOTABLE FEATS
- *389* Began his brief Test career with a spell of 3 for 12 in 6 overs and by holding 4 outstanding catches.
- Took 100 wickets in a season 3 times.
- Hat-trick for Glamorgan v South Africans at Swansea in 1951.

Ref	Series	V	T	Venue	Result	Batting 1st			Batting 2nd			Ct	Bowling 1st			Bowling 2nd		
						No	R	HO	No	R	HO		Balls	R	W	Balls	R	W
389/313	1954	P	3	Manchester	D	10	5	*	–	–	–	4	78	19	3	–	–	–
390/314			4	Oval	L-24	9	11	c	10	2	ro	–	54	35	0	84	20	1

Career	M	I	NO	HS	R	Avge	100	50	Ct	St	Balls	R	W	Avge	BB	5w	10w	Rate
Test	2	3	1	11	18	9.00	–	–	4	–	216	74	4	18.50	3-19	–	–	54.00
F/c	256	366	42	95	4661	14.38	–	13	151	–	37449	16285	819	19.88	8-36	49	12	45.72

McGAHEY Charles Percy

Essex (1894 to 1921)
London County (1901 to 1904)

Wisden 1902
TOUR A 1901–02
Born Hackney, Middlesex 12 Feb 1871
Died Whipps Cross, Essex 10 Jan 1935

NOTABLE FEATS
- Exceeded 1000 runs in a season 10 times.
- Three double centuries for Essex, notably 277 v Derbyshire at Leyton in 1905.
- Shared in then world record 3rd-wkt stand of 323 with P.A. Perrin for Essex v Kent at Leyton in 1900.
- Two match 'doubles' for Essex: 157 runs and 12 wickets v Gloucestershire at Clifton in 1901; 103 runs and 10 wickets v Nottinghamshire at Leyton in 1906.

Charlie McGahey was a tall (6ft 2in) aggressive middle-order batsman who served Essex as player, captain, assistant secretary and scorer for more than four decades. He was a self-taught natural hitter who developed by sheer application into a consistent county batsman. A powerful front-foot player, he was a mighty driver on either side of the wicket, hitting the ball with great ferocity. He drove very straight and his partners had always to be on the alert, especially after one had his arm fractured by a direct hit. In 1908 he struck a ball right over the Leyton pavilion and into the street. He met with frequent success as a slow right-arm leg-break bowler and was a capable fielder either deep or at slip. His long partnerships with the similarly built Percy Perrin caused the veteran Essex scorer Joe Armour such problems that he dubbed them the 'Essex Twins' and asked one to wear a scarf. After enjoying his best season in 1901, he toured Australia with Archie MacLaren's team but met with little success. A cheery man with a dry wit, his eagerness to help younger players made him a popular captain (1907–10). During his five seasons as scorer (1930–34) he recorded Yorkshire's historic opening partnership and was involved in the 'recount' which arrived at the accepted 555. His 'double' of club captain and scorer may well be unique. A strong soccer full-back, his clubs included Tottenham Hotspur, Arsenal and Sheffield United. He died of septicaemia after a Christmas Day fall on a slippery pavement grazed his finger.

England in Australia, 1901–02: standing *J.T. Tyldesley, L.C. Braund, H. Garnett, Major Wardill (Sec. Melbourne CC), C. Robson, S.F. Barnes, C. Blythe, J.R. Gunn, W.G. Quaife;* seated *G.L. Jessop, T.W. Hayward, A.C. MacLaren (captain), A.O. Jones, C.P. McGahey, A.F.A. Lilley.*

Ref	Series	V	T	Venue	Result	Batting 1st No	R	HO	Batting 2nd No	R	HO	Ct
68/68	1901–02	A	4	Sydney	L-7w	7	18	b	7	13	c	–
69/69			5	Melbourne	L-32	8	0	b	8	7	c	1

Career	M	I	NO	HS	R	Avge	100	50	Ct	St	Balls	R	W	Avge	BB	5w	10w	Rate
Test	2	4	0	18	38	9.50	–	–	1	–	–	–	–	–	–	–	–	–
F/c	437	751	65	277	20723	30.20	31	106	151	–	19486	10300	330	31.21	7-27	12	3	59.04

MacGREGOR Gregor

Cambridge University (1888 to 1891)
Middlesex (1892 to 1907)
Scotland (1905)

Wisden 1891
TOUR A 1891–92
Born Merchiston, Edinburgh, Scotland 31 Aug 1869
Died Marylebone, London 20 Aug 1919

Gregor MacGregor was renowned as a brilliant wicket-keeper of extraordinary dexterity at the precocious age of 18 when he went up to Cambridge after his apprenticeship at Uppingham. Even Alfred Lyttelton's staunchest admirers had to concede that 'Mac' was a superior stumper because he took the ball closer to the wicket. He formed a famous partnership with Sammy Woods throughout his four years at Fenner's and, following the fashion of that era, stood up unflinchingly to the fastest amateur bowler in the country. His incredible reflexes enabled him to take even the most wayward of deliveries from Woods and contributed much to Light Blue victories in his last three seasons, the final one under his captaincy. Playing against Australia at Lord's while still an undergraduate he allowed no byes in either innings. He captained Middlesex with quiet authority (1899–1907), leading them to the 1903 Championship, and later became their treasurer. He won two blues and 13 Scottish caps as a rugby full-back or centre.

NOTABLE FEATS
- 33 Kept in the first Test in which no byes were conceded.
- Contributed 131 to the highest second innings total in Britain: 703 for 9 dec by Cambridge U v Sussex at Hove in 1890.

TEST NOTES
- 37 H. Philipson kept wicket.

Cambridge players C.P. Foley (left), F.G.J. Ford and G. MacGregor – centurions in the historic match against Sussex in 1890.

Ref	Series	V	T	Venue	Result	Batting 1st No	R	HO	Batting 2nd No	R	HO	Fielding 1st Ct	St	Byes	Balls	Fielding 2nd Ct	St	Byes	Balls
33/33†	1890	A	1	Lord's	W-7w	10	0	b	–	–	–	–	2	0	430	1	–	0	702
34/34†			2	Oval	W-2w	9	1	c	9	2	*	2	–	0	327	–	–	7	302
35/35†	1891–92	A	1	Melbourne	L-54	10	9	*	9	16	c	1	–	5	907	1	–	0	1151
36/36†			2	Sydney	L-72	8	3	lbw	8	12	c	1	–	6	566	–	–	6	1318
37/37			3	Adelaide	W-I & 230	10	31	ro	–	–	–	–	–	–	–	–	–	–	–
39/39†	1893	A	1	Lord's	D	10	5	*	–	–	–	3	–	15	571	–	–	–	–
40/40†			2	Oval	W-I & 43	10	5	lbw	–	–	–	3	–	5	186	–	–	18	490
41/41†			3	Manchester	D	9	12	st	–	–	–	2	–	5	484	–	1	4	478

Career	M	I	NO	HS	R	Avge	100	50	Ct	St	Balls	R	W	Avge	BB	5w	10w	Rate
Test	8	11	3	31	96	12.00	–	–	14	3	–	–	–	–	–	–	–	–
F/c	265	412	58	141	6381	18.02	3	20	411	148	–	–	–	–	–	–	–	–

McINTYRE Arthur John William

Surrey (1938 to 1963)

Wisden 1958
TOURS
A 1950–51; NZ 1950–51;
Z 1959–60 (Surrey)
Born Kensington, London 14 May 1918

Arriving at The Oval as a leg-break bowler, Arthur McIntyre was called up to keep wicket in an emergency. So successfully did he adopt this role that in his first full season (1947) he made 95 dismissals. Short (5ft 6in), nimble-footed, assured and consistent, he played a major part in Surrey's continuous triumphs of the 1950s. His anticipation and speed of reaction when standing up to the late movement of Alec Bedser or the viperish spin of Laker and Lock were almost uncanny. Bedser rated him at least equal to even the great Godfrey Evans in his ability to make stumpings off him and only the Kent player's presence separated 'Mac' from a long Test career. He had to be content with twice deputising when Evans was injured and once being played for his sound but entertaining batting – when, with England in some disarray, he contrived to run himself out attempting a fourth run. For 21 seasons he was Surrey's coach (1958–78). [*Illus. pp.* 130, 336]

NOTABLE FEATS
- Exceeded 1000 runs in a season 3 times.

TEST NOTES
- 327 T.G. Evans kept wicket.

					Batting 1st			Batting 2nd			Fielding 1st				Fielding 2nd			
Ref	Series	V	T Venue	Result	No	R	HO	No	R	HO	Ct	St	Byes	Balls	Ct	St	Byes	Balls
326/279†	1950	WI	4 Oval	L-I & 56	8	4	c	8	0	c	3	–	5	1166	–	–	–	–
327/280	1950–51	A	1 Brisbane²	L-70	7	1	b	7	7	ro	1	–	–	–	–	–	–	–
411/325†	1955	SA	4 Leeds	L-224	8	3	lbw	7	4	c	2	–	0	422	2	–	8	1253

Career	M	I	NO	HS	R	Avge	100	50	Ct	St	Balls	R	W	Avge	BB	5w	10w	Rate
Test	3	6	0	7	19	3.16	–	–	8	–	–	–	–	–	–	–	–	–
F/c	390	567	79	143*	11145	22.83	7	51	639	156	287	180	4	45.00	1-10	–	–	71.75

MacKINNON Francis Alexander (The 35th MacKinnon of MacKinnon)

Cambridge University (1870)
Kent (1875 to 1885)

TOUR A 1878–79
Born Kensington, London 9 Apr 1848
Died Forres, Morayshire, Scotland 27 Feb 1947

Although Francis MacKinnon's skill as a steady opening batsman failed to impress the selectors at Harrow, he won his blue at Cambridge and played in the famous match that ended in a 2-run victory thanks to Cobden's timely hat-trick. He carried his bat against Yorkshire in 1881 but the most successful of his ten seasons with Kent came three years later. Then he scored hundreds against Hampshire and Yorkshire as well as contributing to the only defeat of the touring Australians. He retired after the next season and was Kent's president in 1889, four years before he became the 35th chief of the MacKinnon clan. He survived to the remarkable age of 98 years and 234 days; at the time of his death he was the oldest Harrovian, the oldest blue and the senior MCC member. He remains the longest-lived Test cricketer. Interviewed at Canterbury by Jim Swanton shortly before the 1946–47 tour of Australia he had clear memories of the Melbourne ground where he had played his only Test some 68 years previously. The bat he used in that match is on show in the museum at Forres. [*Illus. p.* 222]

					Batting 1st			Batting 2nd			
Ref	Series	V	T Venue	Result	No	R	HO	No	R	HO	Ct
3/3	1878–79	A	Melbourne	L-10w	7	0	b	7	5	b	–

Career	M	I	NO	HS	R	Avge	100	50	Ct	St	Balls	R	W	Avge	BB	5w	10w	Rate
Test	1	2	0	5	5	2.50	–	–	–	–	–	–	–	–	–	–	–	–
F/c	88	163	16	115	2318	15.76	2	7	38	–	–	–	–	–	–	–	–	–

MacLAREN
Archibald Campbell

Lancashire (1890 to 1914)

Wisden 1895
TOURS
A 1894–95, 1897–98, 1901–02, 1922–23;
NZ 1922–23
Born Whalley Range, Manchester
1 Dec 1871
Died Warfield Park, Bracknell, Berkshire
17 Nov 1944

Archie MacLaren

NOTABLE FEATS

- 1000 runs in 17th Test (*64*) (31 inns).
- *53* Scored 109 in his first Test as captain.
- *55* First England batsman to score 2 hundreds in the same rubber.
- *65* First to score 4 hundreds in Test cricket. Not until 1958–59 (P.B.H. May) did another England captain score a Test hundred in Australia.
- *71* Surpassed S.E. Gregory's record aggregate of 1366 for E v A Tests.
- *83* First Test century at Trent Bridge; first to score 5 Test hundreds.
- Exceeded 1000 runs in a season 8 times (plus once on tour).
- Scored 108 on first-class debut – for Lancashire v Sussex at Hove in 1890.
- Scored 424 in 470 min for Lancashire v Somerset at Taunton in 1895 – comprising a six, 62 fours, 11 threes, 37 twos and 63 singles it remains the highest

Archie MacLaren was one brilliant schoolboy cricketer who managed to fulfil his early promise and become an outstanding international player. Picked for Lancashire only a month after captaining Harrow, he celebrated the occasion with a century in his very first innings. That memorable display launched a county career spanning 25 seasons up to the First World War which was to include an innings of 424 that has so far survived for 93 years as the highest first-class score ever made in England. Tall, majestic and powerfully built, he had an exaggeratedly high backlift and a wide range of classic strokes in which the off- and straight-drive featured prominently. A lumbago sufferer, he loved the heat of Australia and averaged over 50 there, seven of his 12 first-class hundreds coming at Sydney. In addition to his aggressive opening batting, he was an occasional right-arm fast bowler and a good catcher at slip. As captain he was an awesome authoritative figure with trenchant if inflexible views and an exceptional tactical appreciation of the game. His two spells in charge of Lancashire (1894–96 and 1899–1907) brought the Championship to Old Trafford in 1904 but his record for England was less impressive: 11 defeats and four wins in 22 matches, all against Australia and involving five rubbers, all of which were lost. Even so, he could be an inspired tactician and he often blamed his fellow selectors for giving him inadequate players. It was MacLaren who plucked Sydney Barnes from the obscurity of league cricket for the 1901–02 tour of Australia, and when, in his 50th year, he vowed to find a team of amateurs to beat Warwick Armstrong's all-conquering Australians, he duly inflicted the tourists' first defeat in an epic encounter at Eastbourne. The reverse of the coin shows some erratic thinking, notably at Manchester in 1902 when he sent Fred Tate, a specialist slip, to deep square leg where he dropped the catch that cost England the Ashes. At The Oval seven years later when Australia were 9 for 1, he replaced a rampant Barnes with John Sharp (career record: 3 wickets in three Tests) and then grossly over-bowled the 37-year-old debutant googly specialist Douglas Carr for an hour and a half. His batting skills survived into his 52nd year when he scored 200* for his MCC team against a full New Zealand XI at Wellington in his final first-class match. He did gain the dubious honour of being the first batsman to be dismissed by the opening ball of a Test match, falling to Arthur Coningham in Test *43*.

						Batting 1st			Batting 2nd			
Ref	Series	V	T	Venue	Result	No	R	HO	No	R	HO	Ct
42/42	1894–95	A	1	Sydney	W-10	1	4	c	1	20	b	1
43/43			2	Melbourne	W-94	1	0	c	1	15	b	–
44/44			3	Adelaide	L-382	2	25	b	2	35	c	–
45/45			4	Sydney	L-I & 147	1	1	st	4	0	c	–
46/46			5	Melbourne	W-6w	5	120	hw	5	20	*	1
51/51	1896	A	2	Manchester	L-3w	7	0	c	7	15	c	–
52/52			3	Oval	W-66	5	20	b	5	6	b	2
53/53*	1897–98	A	1	Sydney	W-9w	2	109	c	2	50	*	–
54/54*			2	Melbourne	L-I & 55	1	35	c	1	38	c	–
55/55			3	Adelaide	L-I & 13	1	14	b	1	124	c	–
56/56			4	Melbourne	L-8w	1	8	b	3	45	c	–
57/57*			5	Sydney	L-6w	1	65	b	1	0	b	1
61/61*	1899	A	2	Lord's	L-10w	1	4	b	6	88	*	–
62/62*			3	Leeds	D	2	9	c	–	–	–	1
63/63*			4	Manchester	D	4	8	b	4	6	c	1
64/64*			5	Oval	D	5	49	b	–	–	–	–
65/65*	1901–02	A	1	Sydney	W-I & 124	1	116	lbw	–	–	–	1
66/66*			2	Melbourne	L-229	1	13	c	1	1	c	2
67/67*			3	Adelaide	L-4w	1	67	ro	1	44	b	1

NOTABLE FEATS *cont.*

first-class score in Britain and was the world record until 1922–23. Only P.A. Perrin (68) and Hanif Mohammad (64) have hit more boundaries in a first-class innings. His score is the seventh-highest match aggregate in first-class cricket. Scored 5 other double centuries (3 for Lancashire).

- Shared in two record Lancashire stands: 368 (1st wkt) with R.H. Spooner v Gloucestershire at Liverpool in 1903; and 324 (4th wkt) with J.T. Tyldesley v Nottinghamshire at Nottingham in 1904.
- Shared in the highest stand by either side in Gentlemen v Players matches: 309* with C.B. Fry (3rd wkt) at Lord's in 1903.
- Twice scored 3 100s in successive inns – for Lancs in 1895 and for A.E. Stoddart's XI and England in 1897–98.
- Scored 100 before lunch on 7 occasions.

						Batting 1st			Batting 2nd			
Ref	Series	V	T	Venue	Result	No	R	HO	No	R	HO	Ct
68/68*			4	Sydney	L-7w	1	92	c	1	5	c	2
69/69*			5	Melbourne	L-32	1	25	c	1	49	ro	2
70/70*	1902	A	1	Birmingham	D	1	9	ro	–	–	–	–
71/71*			2	Lord's	D	1	47	*	–	–	–	–
72/72*			3	Sheffield	L-143	1	31	b	4	63	c	1
73/73*			4	Manchester	L-3	4	1	b	2	35	c	1
74/74*			5	Oval	W-1w	1	10	c	1	2	b	3
83/80	1905	A	1	Nottingham	W-213	4	2	c	2	140	c	–
84/81			2	Lord's	D	1	56	b	1	79	b	–
86/83			4	Manchester	W-I & 80	1	14	c	–	–	–	1
87/84			5	Oval	D	1	6	c	3	6	c	1
101/98*	1909	A	1	Birmingham	W-10w	1	5	b	–	–	–	2
102/99*			2	Lord's	L-9w	6	7	c	8	24	b	1
103/100*			3	Leeds	L-126	5	17	b	5	1	c	1
104/101*			4	Manchester	D	7	16	lbw	–	–	–	2
105/102*			5	Oval	D	2	15	lbw	–	–	–	1

Career	M	I	NO	HS	R	Avge	100	50	Ct	St	Balls	R	W	Avge	BB	5w	10w	Rate
Test	35	61	4	140	1931	33.87	5	8	29	–	–	–	–	–	–	–	–	–
F/c	423	701	52	424	22141	34.11	47	95	451	–	321	267	1	267.00	1-44	–	–	321.00

A. C. MacLAREN – TEST BATTING SUMMARY

Series	V	M	I	NO	HS	R	Avge	100	50
1894–95	A	5	10	1	120	240	26.66	1	–
1896	A	2	4	–	20	41	10.25	–	–
1897–98	A	5	10	1	109	488	54.22	2	2
1899	A	4	6	1	88	164	32.80	–	1
1901–02	A	5	9	–	116	412	45.77	1	2
1902	A	5	8	1	63	198	28.28	–	1

Series	V	M	I	NO	HS	R	Avge	100	50
1905	A	4	7	–	140	303	43.28	1	2
1909	A	5	7	–	24	85	12.14	–	–
Home		20	32	2	140	791	26.36	1	4
Overseas		15	29	2	120	1140	42.22	4	4
Totals		35	61	4	140	1931	33.87	5	8

McMASTER
Joseph Emile Patrick

TOUR SA 1888–89
Born Gilford, Co. Down, Ireland
16 Mar 1861
Died London 7 Jun 1929

Joseph McMaster holds an extraordinary Test record: his entire first-class career lasted less than two days and remains the shortest of any England cricketer. He shares with Charles Coventry and Basil Grieve the curious distinction of having played no first-class cricket apart from appearing for Major Warton's team against the South Africans in matches subsequently accepted as the Union's first official Tests. Less fortunate than his fellow novices, McMaster, an Irish batsman in his 29th year, appeared in only half the series and failed to score a run. [*Illus. p.* 51]

						Batting 1st			Batting 2nd			
Ref	Series	V	T	Venue	Result	No	R	HO	No	R	HO	Ct
32/32	1888–89	SA	2	Cape Town	W-I & 202	9	0	c	–	–	–	–

Career	M	I	NO	HS	R	Avge	100	50	Ct	St	Balls	R	W	Avge	BB	5w	10w	Rate
Test	1	1	0	0	0	0.00	–	–	–	–	–	–	–	–	–	–	–	–
F/c	1	1	0	0	0	0.00	–	–	–	–	–	–	–	–	–	–	–	–

MAKEPEACE
Joseph William Henry

Lancashire (1906 to 1930)

TOUR A 1920–21
Born Middlesbrough, Yorkshire
22 Aug 1881
Died Spital, Bebington, Cheshire
19 Dec 1952

A Yorkshireman, Harry Makepeace was an obdurate opening batsman who gave Lancashire devoted service for 46 years. Relying heavily on an almost impregnable defence, his technique against spin was immaculate. A thoughtful and patient player, he nudged, tickled, pushed and squeezed his runs in numerous large partnerships first with A.H. Hornby and later, when the Championship went to Old Trafford four times in five years, with Charlie Hallows. He was also a handy right-arm leg-break bowler and a superb cover-point. Given a belated taste of international cricket in his 40th year, he gratefully seized his chance and played a succession of impressive innings in a losing series against one of Australia's most powerful attacks. He was chief coach to Lancashire from 1932 until 1951. A double-international, his career as a right-half included four caps for England and an FA Cup-winner's medal with Everton. [*Illus. pp.* 187, 383]

NOTABLE FEATS
- *138* At 39 yrs 173 days, he remains the oldest player to score a maiden Test hundred.
- Exceeded 1000 runs in a season 13 times, including 2000 twice.
- Two double centuries for Lancashire – both in 1923.
- Carried his bat through a completed Lancashire innings on 4 occasions.

						Batting 1st			Batting 2nd			
Ref	Series	V	T	Venue	Result	No	R	HO	No	R	HO	Ct
136/125	1920–21	A	2	Melbourne	L-I & 91	3	4	lbw	3	4	c	–
137/126			3	Adelaide	L-119	3	60	c	3	30	c	–
138/127			4	Melbourne	L-8w	3	117	c	3	54	lbw	–
139/128			5	Sydney	L-9w	3	3	c	3	7	c	–

Career	M	I	NO	HS	R	Avge	100	50	Ct	St	Balls	R	W	Avge	BB	5w	10w	Rate
Test	4	8	0	117	279	34.87	1	2	–	–	–	–	–	–	–	–	–	–
F/c	499	778	66	203	25799	36.23	43	140	194	–	4043	1971	42	46.92	4-33	–	–	96.26

MANN
Francis George CBE

Middlesex (1937 to 1954)
Cambridge University (1938 to 1939)

TOUR SA 1948–49
Born Byfleet, Surrey 6 Sep 1917

George Mann captained Eton and gained blues in the last two pre-war years at Cambridge. Of medium height (5ft 10in) and build, he was a middle-order batsman who liked to play his strokes, particularly those on the leg-side. A powerful driver, his hurricane display in Test *314* included a vast straight hit which landed on the Leeds rugby ground via the main stand's roof. He was capable of sterling defence and his 136* at Port Elizabeth was a major innings which converted the threat of defeat into an eventual victory and enabled his team to return undefeated after 23 matches. There has been no more popular England captain; he possessed that rare gift of leadership which moulds players into contented and successful teams. He would have taken the 1950–51 side to Australia but for the claims of the family brewery which allowed him to lead Middlesex for just two summers (1948–49). Like his father, Frank, he was captain on each of his Test appearances. Until 1988 the Mann family provided the only instance of successive generations skippering England. He proved an equally accomplished and esteemed TCCB chairman during some of cricket's more contentious years (1978–83) and was a worthy president of MCC in 1984–85.

NOTABLE FEATS
- *314* Scored 49* in 24 min, missing the chance of the fastest Test 50 by declaring.
- Exceeded 1000 runs in a season 3 times.

TEST NOTES
- *315* Created Test history by declaring on the first day – later found to be invalid as the experimental law allowing declarations on the first day of a 3-day match did not apply to this rubber.

George Mann (left) *and Jack Crapp on the 1948–49 tour of South Africa.*

Ref	Series	V	T	Venue	Result	Batting 1st No	Batting 1st R	Batting 1st HO	Batting 2nd No	Batting 2nd R	Batting 2nd HO	Ct
309/267*	1948–49	SA	1	Durban[2]	W-2w	6	19	c	3	13	c	2
310/268*			2	Johannesburg[2]	D	6	7	c	–	–	–	–
311/269*			3	Cape Town	D	6	44	c	–	–	–	1
312/270*			4	Johannesburg[2]	D	6	17	c	4	16	lbw	–
313/271*			5	Port Elizabeth	W-3w	6	136	*	4	2	c	–
314/272*	1949	NZ	1	Leeds	D	6	38	c	6	49	*	–
315/273*			2	Lord's	D	6	18	b	6	17	c	–

Career	M	I	NO	HS	R	Avge	100	50	Ct	St	Balls	R	W	Avge	BB	5w	10w	Rate
Test	7	12	2	136*	376	37.60	1	–	3	–	–	–	–	–	–	–	–	–
F/c	166	262	17	136*	6350	25.91	7	32	72	–	414	389	3	129.66	2-16	–	–	138.00

MANN
Francis Thomas

Cambridge University (1909 to 1911)
Middlesex (1909 to 1931)

TOUR SA 1922–23
Born Winchmore Hill, Middlesex
3 Mar 1888
Died Milton Lilbourne, Wiltshire
6 Oct 1964

NOTABLE FEATS

- Exceeded 1000 runs in a season 3 times.
- Shared record Middlesex 7th-wkt stand of 271* with E.H. Hendren v Nottinghamshire at Nottingham in 1925; the Middlesex winning total of 502 for 6 remains the highest in the fourth innings of any Championship match.
- Scored 50 in 14 min with 13 scoring strokes for Middlesex v Nottinghamshire at Lord's in 1921 – then the fastest in English first-class cricket.

Frank Mann learned his cricket at Malvern but achieved little of note during his three years as a Cambridge blue. It was with Middlesex that he developed into one of the lustiest hitters of all time. A burly figure, he achieved several sensational bursts of savagery, notably his four mighty blows on to the roof of the Lord's pavilion off Yorkshire's bowling and, at Hove in 1920, his three sixes off successive balls from the redoubtable Maurice Tate. A year later came his epic onslaught against Nottinghamshire which had the scorers writing with both hands in an attempt to record his 53 in 19 minutes. A very occasional right-arm slow bowler, he was a very good fielder, usually at mid-off. He led Middlesex for eight summers (1921–28), winning a famous Championship at his first attempt, and under his captaincy MCC in South Africa won 14 times and lost only once in 22 matches. Like his elder son who emulated his role for Middlesex and England, he was extremely popular. During the First World War he was wounded three times and gained a similar number of mentions in dispatches. He was a Test selector in 1930 and president of Middlesex.

Frank Mann's Middlesex side of 1926: standing *H.W. Lee, J.W. Hearne, F.J. Durston, A.R. Tanner, H.R. Murrell, E.H. Hendren;* seated *Hon. C.N. Bruce, N.E. Haig, F.T. Mann (captain), G.T.S. Stevens, G.O.B. Allen.*

Ref	Series	V	T	Venue	Result	Batting 1st No	R	HO	Batting 2nd No	R	HO	Ct
148/134*	1922–23	SA	1	Johannesburg[1]	L-168	2	4	c	6	28	*	1
149/135*			2	Cape Town	W-1w	6	4	lbw	7	45	c	1
150/136*			3	Durban[2]	D	7	84	c	–	–	–	–
151/137*			4	Johannesburg[1]	D	7	34	c	7	59	c	1
152/138*			5	Durban[2]	W-109	7	8	b	9	15	lbw	1

Career	M	I	NO	HS	R	Avge	100	50	Ct	St	Balls	R	W	Avge	BB	5w	10w	Rate
Test	5	9	1	84	281	35.12	–	2	4	–	–	–	–	–	–	–	–	–
F/c	398	612	47	194	13235	23.42	9	68	174	–	236	249	3	83.00	1-7	–	–	78.66

MARKS, Victor James

Oxford University (1975 to 1978)
Somerset (1975 to date)
Western Australia (1986–87)

TOURS
A 1982–83; NZ 1983–84; I/SL 1984–85; P 1983–84
Born Middle Chinnock, Somerset
25 Jun 1955

NOTABLE FEATS

- *979* Shared record E v P 7th-wkt stand of 167 with D.I. Gower.
- 1000 runs in a season twice, finishing 14 wickets short of the 'double' in 1984.
- Took 8 for 17 for Somerset v Lancashire at Bath in 1985.
- His 5 for 20 v NZ at Wellington in 1983–84 remains England's best analysis in limited-overs internationals.

Despite a modest self-effacing manner, Vic Marks is an extremely dedicated and determined all-rounder. A competent middle-order batsman with an excellent temperament, his last three scores in Test cricket were 83, 74 and 55. Although shorter (5ft 9in) than some of the great off-spin bowlers, he now rivals Emburey and Hemmings for the England berth. He flights the ball more than either and is a keen fielder. Captain of Oxford in the last two of his four summers as a blue, he led Somerset with quiet authority after replacing Peter Roebuck mid-way through the 1988 season. Such is his perception and wit as a writer and broadcaster that he may soon lose the incentive to continue as a player.

Vic Marks

Ref	Series	V	T	Venue	Result	Batting 1st No	R	HO	Batting 2nd No	R	HO	Ct	Bowling 1st Balls	R	W	Bowling 2nd Balls	R	W
933/585	1982	P	3	Leeds	W-3w	8	7	b	8	12	*	–	30	23	0	12	8	1
957/591	1983	NZ	1	Oval	W-189	7	4	c	7	2	c	–	–	–	–	258	78	3
977/597	1983–84	NZ	3	Auckland	D	8	6	c	–	–	–	–	242	115	3	–	–	–
978/598	1983–84	P	1	Karachi	L-3w	7	5	c	7	1	b	–	78	40	0	72	23	1
979/599			2	Faisalabad	D	8	83	b	–	–	–	–	162	59	1	48	26	1
980/600			3	Lahore[2]	D	7	74	c	7	55	c	–	120	59	1	60	53	0

Career	M	I	NO	HS	R	Avge	100	50	Ct	St	Balls	R	W	Avge	BB	5w	10w	Rate
Test	6	10	1	83	249	27.66	–	3	–	–	1082	484	11	44.00	3-78	–	–	98.36
F/c	322	468	78	134	11597	29.73	5	69	136	–	58247	26339	812	32.43	8-17	39	5	71.73

MARRIOTT Charles Stowell

Lancashire (1919 to 1921)
Cambridge University (1920 to 1921)
Kent (1924 to 1937)

TOURS SA 1924–25 (Joel); I/SL 1933–34
Born Heaton Moor, Lancashire 14 Sep 1895
Died Dollis Hill, Middlesex 13 Oct 1966

'Father' Marriott

Charles 'Father' Marriott enjoyed a unique career. After learning the art of right-arm leg-break and googly bowling at St Columba's School in Dublin, he made his debut for Lancashire before claiming 14 wickets in his two Varsity matches for Cambridge. Throughout the inter-war period, and despite his Kent appearances being limited to holidays from his duties as master-in-charge of cricket at Dulwich College, he remained the best of his type in England. Astonishingly he was selected for only one Test match despite an outstanding performance which scuppered the West Indies by an innings in two days and ten minutes. Over six feet tall and with a goose-stepping run starting at mid-off, he had a high supple action with his delivery arm starting its swing behind his back. Even on good pitches his ability to turn the ball sharply and indulge in crafty variations of flight, pace and angle caused grave problems; on helpful surfaces he gave no hope of survival. As a cricketer his qualities began and ended with his bowling. He was a quite appalling fielder and his career aggregate of wickets always comfortably exceeded his meagre tally of runs. One wonders how he fared during the Second World War as a Home Guard anti-aircraft gunner.

NOTABLE FEATS
- *229* Only F. Martin (12 for 102) has surpassed his 11 for 96 on Test debut for England.
- Hat-trick for MCC v Madras at Madras in 1933–34.

						Batting 1st			Batting 2nd				Bowling 1st			Bowling 2nd		
Ref	Series	V	T	Venue	Result	No	R	HO	No	R	HO	Ct	Balls	R	W	Balls	R	W
229/203	1933	WI	3	Oval	W-I & 17	11	0	b	–	–	–	1	71	37	5	176	59	6

Career	M	I	NO	HS	R	Avge	100	50	Ct	St	Balls	R	W	Avge	BB	5w	10w	Rate
Test	1	1	0	0	0	0.00	–	–	1	–	247	96	11	8.72	6-59	2	1	22.45
F/c	159	178	48	21	574	4.41	–	–	47	–	37215	14304	711	20.11	8-98	48	10	52.34

MARTIN, Frederick

Kent (1885 to 1899)

Wisden 1892
TOUR SA 1891–92
Born Dartford, Kent 12 Oct 1861
Died Dartford 13 Dec 1921

For three seasons (1889–91) Fred Martin was one of the most dangerous left-arm bowlers in county cricket. He operated at almost medium-pace with a smooth, high action, maintaining an extremely accurate length and spinning the ball appreciably. When the selectors found their first-choice left-arm spinners Peel and Briggs unavailable, they turned to 'Nutty' Martin. He responded with a deadly display of bowling on a rain-affected pitch, claimed an England record that has survived for almost a century and won a famous victory. Although as a member of the MCC staff he was often in the selectors' sight, he was not given another match against Australia. He was a moderate left-handed tail-end batsman. [*Illus. pp.* 184, 201]

NOTABLE FEATS
- *34* First bowler to take 12 wickets in his first Test; his analysis remains the England record on debut.
- Took 100 wickets in a season 6 times, notably 190 (avge 13.05) in 1890.
- Four wickets in 4 balls for MCC v Derbyshire at Lord's in 1895 and a hat-trick for Kent v Surrey at The Oval in 1890.
- Bowled in an unchanged partnership throughout both completed innings of a match on 5 occasions, including 3 with W. Wright.

Ref	Series	V	T	Venue	Result	Batting 1st No	R	HO	Batting 2nd No	R	HO	Ct	Bowling 1st Balls	R	W	Bowling 2nd Balls	R	W
34/34	1890	A	2	Oval	W-2w	11	1	c	–	–	–	–	135	50	6	152	52	6
38/38	1891–92	SA		Cape Town	W-I & 189	11	13	c	–	–	–	2	–	–	–	123	39	2

Career	M	I	NO	HS	R	Avge	100	50	Ct	St	Balls	R	W	Avge	BB	5w	10w	Rate
Test	2	2	0	13	14	7.00	–	–	2	–	210	141	14	10.07	6-50	2	1	29.28
F/c	317	492	118	90	4545	12.15	–	8	120	–	67754	22901	1317	17.38	8-45	95	23	51.44

MARTIN
John William

Kent (1939 to 1953)

Born Catford, Kent 16 Feb 1917
Died Woolwich, London 4 Jan 1987

Jack Martin was a tall (6ft 1½in), deep-chested right-arm fast bowler and a determined lower-order batsman. Exceptional strength and a high smooth action enabled him to generate considerable pace from a modest run-up. His kindly attention to a ten-year-old autograph hunter meeting an England sweater for the first time belied a military bearing enhanced by a trim moustache and centrally parted sleek hair. He played most of his cricket for Catford Wanderers, appearing for Kent during his holidays from the Legal and General Assurance Society whose Woolwich office he later managed. A post-war dearth of fast bowlers led to his appearance against the 1947 Springboks when, on an unresponsive Trent Bridge featherbed, he bowled his heart out and shared in a match-saving tenth-wicket stand of 51 with that unlikely batting partner, Eric Hollies. A few years before his death he met the similarly named Australian Test spin bowler at a Primary Club match north of Sydney.

Jack Martin

Ref	Series	V	T	Venue	Result	Batting 1st No	R	HO	Batting 2nd No	R	HO	Ct	Bowling 1st Balls	R	W	Bowling 2nd Balls	R	W
285/253	1947	SA	1	Nottingham	D	10	0	c	11	26	b	–	216	111	1	54	18	0

Career	M	I	NO	HS	R	Avge	100	50	Ct	St	Balls	R	W	Avge	BB	5w	10w	Rate
Test	1	2	0	26	26	13.00	–	–	–	–	270	129	1	129.00	1-111	–	–	270.00
F/c	44	69	15	40	623	11.53	–	–	32	–	9608	3888	162	24.00	7-53	8	1	59.32

MASON
John Richard

Kent (1893 to 1914)

Wisden 1898
TOUR A 1897–98
Born Blackheath, Kent 26 Mar 1874
Died Cooden, Sussex 15 Oct 1958

Jack Mason was one of Kent's finest all-rounders: a stylish middle-order batsman, a skilful right-arm fast-medium bowler and an accomplished slip. Just a few weeks after achieving the last of a series of remarkable all-round feats for Winchester College, he featured in Kent's defeat of the 1893 Australians. Very tall, he made full use of his height in a classic front-foot, straight-bat technique and was particularly adept at cutting and driving. His value as a bowler was almost as great, his late outswing being the product of a high, smooth action. In view of his first-class record it is astonishing that, apart from being included in the 14 assembled for the Birmingham Test of 1902, he was never selected for a home Test. He captained Kent (1898–1902) with distinction and good humour until the claims of his work as a solicitor compelled his resignation. After 1906 he hardly played at all.

NOTABLE FEATS

- Exceeded 1000 runs in a season 8 times and took 100 wickets once, completing the 'double' in 1901.
- Shared record Kent 3rd-wkt stand of 321* with A. Hearne v Nottinghamshire at Nottingham in 1899.
- Twice scored hundreds for Kent in 3 consecutive innings (1904 and 1909).
- Bowled in an unchanged partnership with C. Blythe throughout both completed Somerset innings for Kent at Taunton in 1901.
- Achieved the match 'double' for Kent 5 times.

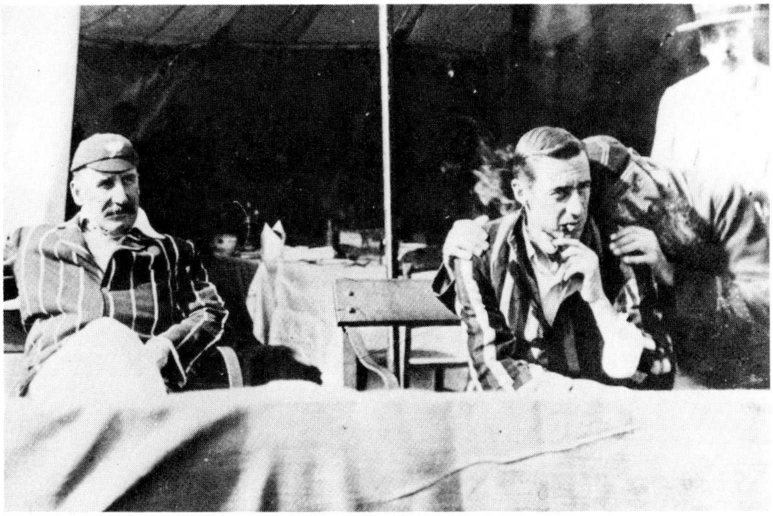

Lord Hawke (left), *Jack Mason and W.G. Grace at the Hastings Festival, 1901.*

					Batting 1st			Batting 2nd				Bowling 1st			Bowling 2nd		
Ref	Series	V	T Venue	Result	No	R	HO	No	R	HO	Ct	Balls	R	W	Balls	R	W
53/53	1897–98	A	1 Sydney	W-9w	1	6	b	1	32	b	1	12	8	1	12	10	0
54/54			2 Melbourne	L-I & 55	2	3	b	2	3	b	–	66	33	1	–	–	–
55/55			3 Adelaide	L-I & 13	2	11	b	2	0	c	–	66	41	0	–	–	–
56/56			4 Melbourne	L-8w	7	30	b	8	26	b	1	–	–	–	24	10	0
57/57			5 Sydney	L-6w	8	7	c	8	11	b	1	78	20	0	66	27	0

Career	M	I	NO	HS	R	Avge	100	50	Ct	St	Balls	R	W	Avge	BB	5w	10w	Rate
Test	5	10	0	32	129	12.90	–	–	3	–	324	149	2	74.50	1-8	–	–	162.00
F/c	339	557	36	183	17337	33.27	34	86	390	–	41813	18989	848	22.39	8-29	35	9	49.30

MATTHEWS Austin David George

Northamptonshire (1927 to 1936)
Glamorgan (1937 to 1947)

Born Penarth, Glamorgan 3 May 1904
Died Penrhyn Bay, Denbighshire 29 July 1977

Austin Matthews was a tall, accurate right-arm fast-medium bowler, a hard-hitting late-order batsman and a safe slip. After achieving little during his ten seasons with a weak Northamptonshire team, he took up a coaching engagement at Stowe School in 1937 and joined Glamorgan. The change brought dramatic results and sudden fame. Within three weeks of his first appearance for the Welsh county, he had taken 14 wickets against Sussex on a good batting pitch at Hastings and won a Test cap against New Zealand. He continued to take wickets economically for Glamorgan, returning for two post-war seasons as an amateur while he also fulfilled the role of assistant secretary. His forthright views on coaching were imparted to Cambridge University players from 1930 until 1950, duties he combined with those at Stowe. An exceptional all-round sportsman, he was a Welsh table tennis international and a rugby trialist. [*Illus. p.* 376]

					Batting 1st			Batting 2nd				Bowling 1st			Bowling 2nd		
Ref	Series	V	T Venue	Result	No	R	HO	No	R	HO	Ct	Balls	R	W	Balls	R	W
262/231	1937	NZ	3 Oval	D	9	2	*	–	–	–	1	132	52	1	48	13	1

Career	M	I	NO	HS	R	Avge	100	50	Ct	St	Balls	R	W	Avge	BB	5w	10w	Rate
Test	1	1	1	2*	2	–	–	–	1	–	180	65	2	32.50	1-13	–	–	90.00
F/c	281	447	70	116	5919	15.70	2	14	124	–	47914	19099	816	23.40	7-57	45	6	58.71

MAY
Peter Barker Howard CBE

Surrey (1950 to 1963)
Cambridge University (1950 to 1952)

Wisden 1952
TOURS
A 1954–55, 1958–59; SA 1956–57; WI 1953–54, 1959–60; NZ 1954–55, 1958–59
Born Reading, Berkshire 31 Dec 1929

Peter May in action against Derbyshire in 1952.

Peter May was the outstanding English batsman of the last 40 years and, for the latter half of the 1950s, he was the best in the world. Tall (6ft 1in) with wide shoulders and a fine physique, he combined the elegant classical strokeplay of the old-fashioned amateur with a hard streak of professional competitiveness. He played very straight, had the gift of timing, hit even his defensive strokes hard and rarely lofted the ball. His footwork and forward defensive technique were an object lesson. Apart from the hook he had every stroke and was murderously strong off his legs, with the on-drive his speciality. When May arrived at Charterhouse, coach George Geary quickly assessed his potential and, putting him in the 1st XI at 14, was rewarded by a series of innings which headed the averages. He played for Berkshire at 16 and, during national service in the Royal Navy (where, rather oddly, he never aspired beyond the rank of writer), he made his first-class debut for the Combined Services. Afterwards he gained a blue in each of his three summers at Cambridge but was elected captain of soccer and not cricket. A year after his Surrey debut he celebrated his England cap with a century in his first innings. It was the start of an illustrious international career which included the longest reign by an England captain, 35 of his 41 matches being an unbroken sequence, and the most wins. His regular appearances for Surrey coincided with all but the first two months of their seven consecutive titles, the last two during his captaincy (1957–62). He rarely experienced a run of poor form but in South Africa in 1956–57 he suffered the worst series of his career after beginning the tour with four hundreds, the last a double. The highlight of his career was his contribution of 285* to the match-saving record partnership of 411 with Colin Cowdrey which destroyed Ramadhin. English cricket could ill afford his retirement from the Test match scene at the age of 31, a decision brought about by a combination of pressures. The son-in-law of the late A.H.H. Gilligan, he has served on numerous MCC, TCCB and Surrey committees, was an England selector for two terms (1965–68 and 1982–88), the second as chairman, and was president of MCC in 1980–81.

						Batting 1st			Batting 2nd			
Ref	Series	V	T	Venue	Result	No	R	HO	No	R	HO	Ct
337/290	1951	SA	4	Leeds	D	3	138	b	–	–	–	–
338/291			5	Oval	W-4w	3	33	b	3	0	c	1
351/297	1952	I	1	Leeds	W-7w	3	16	b	3	4	c	1
352/298			2	Lord's	W-8w	3	74	c	3	26	c	–
353/299			3	Manchester	W-I & 207	4	69	c	–	–	–	1
354/300			4	Oval	D	4	17	c	–	–	–	1
372/301	1953	A	1	Nottingham	D	6	9	c	–	–	–	–
376/305			5	Oval	W-8w	3	39	c	3	37	c	–
382/306	1953–54	WI	1	Kingston	L-140	3	31	c	3	69	c	–
383/307			2	Bridgetown	L-181	3	7	c	3	62	c	–
384/308			3	Georgetown	W-9w	3	12	lbw	2	12	b	–
385/309			4	Port-of-Spain	D	3	135	c	3	16	c	–
386/310			5	Kingston	W-9w	3	30	c	3	40	*	–
387/311	1954	P	1	Lord's	D	3	27	b	–	–	–	–
388/312			2	Nottingham	W-I & 129	3	0	b	–	–	–	1
389/313			3	Manchester	D	3	14	c	–	–	–	–
390/314			4	Oval	L-24	3	26	c	3	53	c	2
391/315	1954–55	A	1	Brisbane[2]	L-I & 154	4	1	b	4	44	lbw	1
392/316			2	Sydney	W-38	3	5	c	3	104	b	–
393/317			3	Melbourne	W-128	3	0	c	3	91	b	–
394/318			4	Adelaide	W-5w	3	1	c	3	26	c	4
395/319			5	Sydney	D	3	79	c	–	–	–	1
401/320	1954–55	NZ	1	Dunedin	W-8w	3	10	b	3	13	b	–
402/321			2	Auckland	W-I & 20	3	48	b	–	–	–	1
408/322*	1955	SA	1	Nottingham	W-I & 5	3	83	c	–	–	–	3
409/323*			2	Lord's	W-71	3	0	c	3	112	hw	–

NOTABLE FEATS

- 1000 runs in 18th Test (*391*) (29 inns); 2000 runs in 29th Test (*412*) (48 inns); 3000 runs in 42nd Test (*441*) (69 inns); 4000 runs in 56th Test (*473*) (89 inns).
- *337* Seventh England batsman to score 100 in his first Test innings and only instance v SA in England.
- *427* First to score 5 consecutive fifties for E v A.
- *439* His career-best 285* remains the highest score by an England captain and the record Test score at Edgbaston. His stand of 411 with M.C. Cowdrey remains England's highest for any wicket and the Test record for the 4th wkt.
- *465* First 100 by an England captain in Australia since 1901–02.
- *476* Equalled F.E. Woolley's England record of 52 successive appearances.
- Holds England captaincy records for most Tests (41) and most wins (21).
- Exceeded 1000 runs in a season 11 times (plus 3 times on tour), including 2000 on 5 occasions. Leading batsman 1951–55–57–58.
- Scored 5 double centuries, including 2 for Surrey in 1954.
- Scored hundreds in his first 4 first-class innings in SA in 1956–57.
- Twice scored hundreds in 3 consecutive innings (1952 and 1958).
- Scored 100 in each innings of a match on 3 occasions – once for Surrey and twice for MCC.
- Scored 165 for Surrey v New Zealanders at The Oval in 1958 when the next highest innings was 25.

						Batting 1st			Batting 2nd			
Ref	Series	V	T	Venue	Result	No	R	HO	No	R	HO	Ct
410/324*			3	Manchester	L-3w	3	34	c	3	117	b	1
411/325*			4	Leeds	L-224	3	47	b	3	97	lbw	2
412/326*			5	Oval	W-92	3	3	c	4	89	*	1
425/327*	1956	A	1	Nottingham	D	4	73	c	–	–	–	–
426/328*			2	Lord's	L-185	4	63	b	5	53	c	–
427/329*			3	Leeds	W-I & 42	4	101	c	–	–	–	–
428/330*			4	Manchester	W-I & 170	4	43	c	–	–	–	–
429/331*			5	Oval	D	4	83	*	4	37	*	3
434/332*	1956–57	SA	1	Johannesburg[3]	W-131	4	6	c	6	14	c	–
435/333*			2	Cape Town	W-312	4	8	c	4	15	c	2
436/334*			3	Durban[2]	D	4	2	c	5	2	lbw	–
437/335*			4	Johannesburg[3]	L-17	4	61	b	5	0	c	–
438/336*			5	Port Elizabeth	L-58	4	24	c	3	21	lbw	–
439/337*	1957	WI	1	Birmingham	D	4	30	c	4	285	*	1
440/338*			2	Lord's	W-I & 36	4	0	c	–	–	–	2
441/339*			3	Nottingham	D	4	104	lbw	–	–	–	1
442/340*			4	Leeds	W-I & 5	4	69	c	–	–	–	–
443/341*			5	Oval	W-I & 237	4	1	c	–	–	–	1
454/342*	1958	NZ	1	Birmingham	W-205	4	84	c	4	11	c	–
455/343*			2	Lord's	W-I & 148	4	19	c	–	–	–	3
456/344*			3	Leeds	W-I & 71	4	113	*	–	–	–	1
457/345*			4	Manchester	W-I & 13	4	101	c	–	–	–	–
458/346*			5	Oval	D	4	9	c	–	–	–	–
464/347*	1958–59	A	1	Brisbane[2]	L-8w	4	26	c	5	4	lbw	–
465/348*			2	Melbourne	L-8w	5	113	b	5	17	c	1
466/349*			3	Sydney	D	4	42	c	4	92	b	–
467/350*			4	Adelaide	L-10w	3	37	b	3	59	lbw	–
468/351*			5	Melbourne	L-9w	3	11	c	3	4	c	–
472/352*	1958–59	NZ	1	Christchurch	W-I & 99	4	71	c	–	–	–	1
473/353*			2	Auckland	D	4	124	*	–	–	–	–
474/354*	1959	I	1	Nottingham	W-I & 59	4	106	c	–	–	–	2
475/355*			2	Lord's	W-8w	4	9	b	4	33	*	2
476/356*			3	Leeds	W-I & 173	4	2	b	–	–	–	1
487/359*	1959–60	WI	1	Bridgetown	D	4	1	c	–	–	–	–
488/360*			2	Port-of-Spain	W-256	4	0	c	4	28	c	–
489/361*			3	Kingston	D	4	9	c	4	45	b	–
508/370	1961	A	2	Lord's	L-5w	5	17	c	5	22	c	–
509/371*			3	Leeds	W-8w	4	26	c	4	8	*	–
510/372*			4	Manchester	L-54	4	95	c	4	0	b	–
511/373*			5	Oval	D	4	71	c	4	33	c	–

Career	M	I	NO	HS	R	Avge	100	50	Ct	St	Balls	R	W	Avge	BB	5w	10w	Rate
Test	66	106	9	285*	4537	46.77	13	22	42	–	–	–	–	–	–	–	–	–
F/c	388	618	77	285*	27592	51.00	85	126	282	–	102	49	0	–	–	–	–	–

P. B. H. MAY – TEST BATTING SUMMARY

Series	V	M	I	NO	HS	R	Avge	100	50
1951	SA	2	3	–	138	171	57.00	1	–
1952	I	4	6	–	74	206	34.33	–	2
1953	A	2	3	–	39	85	28.33	–	–
1953–54	WI	5	10	1	135	414	46.00	1	2
1954	P	4	5	–	53	120	24.00	–	1
1954–55	A	5	9	–	104	351	39.00	1	2
1954–55	NZ	2	3	–	48	71	23.66	–	–
1955	SA	5	9	1	117	582	97.00	2	3
1956	A	5	7	2	101	453	90.60	1	4
1956–57	SA	5	10	–	61	153	15.30	–	1
1957	WI	5	6	1	285*	489	97.80	2	1
1958	NZ	5	6	1	113*	337	67.40	2	1
1958–59	A	5	10	–	113	405	40.50	1	2
1958–59	NZ	2	2	1	124*	195	195.00	1	1
1959	I	3	4	1	106	150	50.00	1	–
1959–60	WI	3	5	–	45	83	16.60	–	–
1961	A	4	8	1	95	272	38.85	–	2
	A	21	37	3	113	1566	46.05	3	10
	SA	12	22	1	138	906	43.14	3	4
	WI	13	21	2	285*	986	51.89	3	3
	NZ	9	11	2	124*	603	67.00	3	2
	I	7	10	1	106	356	39.55	1	2
	P	4	5	–	53	120	24.00	–	1
Home		39	57	7	285*	2865	57.30	9	14
Overseas		27	49	2	135	1672	35.57	4	8
Totals		66	106	9	285*	4537	46.77	13	22

MAYNARD Matthew Peter

Glamorgan (1985 to date)

Born Oldham, Lancashire 21 Mar 1966

Matthew Maynard

Matthew Maynard is an exceptionally talented and exciting middle-order batsman with a smack of Greg Chappell's elegance, build and dismissive authority and he bowls similar medium-paced swing. His upright stance, balanced footwork, cover-driving and straight hitting are from Malvern's classical school of batting but he was educated, probably uniquely for an England Test cricketer, in Anglesey. In 1988 he played many outstanding innings for a struggling Glamorgan; suitable preparation, thought the selectors, for England's final encounter with the 1988 West Indians. The baptism was ill-timed and no one appeared to have reminded him that he was playing in a five-day match. Looking frenetically nervous during a maiden innings lasting only six balls, he managed only narrowly to avoid being decapitated by a Marshall bouncer, survive a close run-out appeal and be dropped at short-leg. He briefly raised our hopes with a sumptuous cover-drive before finally perishing to an attempted slash at a bouncer well outside his off stump. He had the compensation of winning the Cricket Writers' Club 'Cricketer of the Year' award and there can be little doubt that a major international career lies ahead.

NOTABLE FEATS

- Exceeded 1000 runs in a season 3 times.
- Scored 102 out of 117 in 87 min for Glamorgan on his first-class debut v Yorkshire at Swansea in 1985, reaching his 100 with 3 sixes off successive balls from P. Carrick.

						Batting 1st			Batting 2nd			
Ref	Series	V	T	Venue	Result	No	R	HO	No	R	HO	Ct
1102/650	1988	WI	5	Oval	L-8w	5	3	c	6	10	c	–

Career	M	I	NO	HS	R	Avge	100	50	Ct	St	Balls	R	W	Avge	BB	5w	10w	Rate
Test	1	2	–	10	13	6.50	–	–	–	–	–	–	–	–	–	–	–	–
F/c	75	124	15	160	4311	39.55	8	30	66	–	295	161	4	40.25	3-21	–	–	73.75

MEAD, Charles Philip

Hampshire (1905 to 1936)

Wisden 1912
TOURS
A 1911–12, 1928–29; SA 1913–14, 1922–23; WI 1927–28 (Tennyson)
Born Battersea, London 9 Mar 1887
Died Boscombe, Hampshire 26 Mar 1958

Philip Mead was a highly professional left-handed middle-order batsman with a formidable defence. He was a superb technician; an exceptionally sound and effective player who, in a career spanning 31 years, amassed a first-class aggregate of 55,061 runs which has been exceeded only by Hobbs, Woolley and Hendren. His tally of 153 hundreds has been shaded only by Hobbs, Hendren and Hammond. Despite this extremely impressive log, his lack of mobility and endeavour in the field barred him from automatic selection at Test level. He played only twice for England at home and his two tours of Australia were separated by such a lengthy interval that on his later visit he was frequently mistaken for his own son. If Essex kicked themselves for missing out on Jack Hobbs, Surrey must have inflicted similar self-abuse over Mead. At his Battersea school he was principally a left-arm medium-pace bowler and Surrey engaged him for two summers as a ground-boy before discharging him. Soon afterwards they changed their mind but it was too late; two days after leaving The Oval Mead had accepted an invitation to qualify for Hampshire. Tall and heavily built, his method was deceptively ponderous with a full repertoire of safe, orthodox strokes which, although lacking in excitement, kept the board moving at a healthy rate. He was a master at memorising field settings and placing the ball for an easy single. His technique against all bowling in all conditions was flawless and his judgment of what to leave alone, especially late

NOTABLE FEATS

- 1000 runs in 15th Test (*151*) (21 inns).
- *144* Scored 109 (19* to 128*) in 147 min before lunch on the second day. His 182* was the E v A highest score in England until 1938.
- *150* Scored first 100 in Tests at Kingsmead.

outswingers, was quite uncanny. He was a man of superstition and ritual who, despite his large total of centuries, experienced desperate attacks of nervousness in the nineties. Before settling into his rather cramped stance he would undergo a lengthy routine involving looking around the field, tugging his cap and shuffling his feet. So much physical and nervous energy was expended in batting that it was hardly surprising that he opted for a quiet graze in the outfield and could seldom be persuaded to bowl his left-arm spin. It says something for his appetite for runs that when his long career with Hampshire was over, he played minor county cricket for Suffolk until the War, averaging 71 in his final season at the age of 52. A keen footballer in his youth he had been good enough to keep goal for Southampton. Although he was blind for the final decade of his life he continued to attend and enjoy Hampshire's matches.

NOTABLE FEATS *cont.*

- Exceeded 1000 runs in a season 27 times, including 3000 twice (3179 in 1921 and 3027 in 1928) and 2000 on a further 9 occasions. Scored 1014 runs in his first full season (1906) having played 1 match in 1905. Scored 1159 runs in June 1921 and 1070 runs in July 1923. Leading batsman 1913 and 1921.
- Holds Hampshire career records for most appearances (700), most runs (48,892), most hundreds (138), most instances of 1000 in a season (27) and most catches in the field (629); also the most runs and most hundreds in a season (2854 runs and 12 hundreds in 1928).
- Scored 13 double centuries (11 for Hampshire), notably 280* v Nottinghamshire at Southampton in 1921.
- Shared record Hampshire 3rd-wkt stand of 344 with G. Brown v Yorkshire at Portsmouth in 1927.
- Four times scored hundreds for Hampshire in 3 consecutive innings: 1921–22–23–33.
- Scored 100 in each innings of a match for Hampshire on 3 occasions.
- Scored 100 before lunch on 4 occasions.
- Carried his bat through a completed Hampshire innings on 3 occasions.
- Held 5 catches in an innings for Hampshire v Middlesex at Portsmouth in 1912.

						Batting 1st			Batting 2nd			
Ref	Series	V	T	Venue	Result	No	R	HO	No	R	HO	Ct
116/108	1911–12	A	1	Sydney	L-146	5	0	c	4	25	ro	–
117/109			2	Melbourne	W-8w	5	11	c	–	–	–	1
118/110			3	Adelaide	W-7w	5	46	c	5	2	*	1
119/111			4	Melbourne	W-I & 225	8	21	b	–	–	–	1
130/119	1913–14	SA	1	Durban[1]	W-I & 157	5	41	c	–	–	–	–
131/120			2	Johannesburg[1]	W-I & 12	4	102	c	–	–	–	–
132/121			3	Johannesburg[1]	W-91	4	0	b	3	86	c	–
133/122			4	Durban[1]	D	4	31	c	4	1	c	–
134/123			5	Port Elizabeth	W-10w	5	117	c	–	–	–	–
143/132	1921	A	4	Manchester	D	4	47	c	–	–	–	–
144/133			5	Oval	D	5	182	*	–	–	–	–
148/134	1922–23	SA	1	Johannesburg[1]	L-168	5	1	b	2	49	b	–
149/135			2	Cape Town	W-1w	4	21	c	4	31	lbw	–
150/136			3	Durban[2]	D	4	181	c	–	–	–	–
151/137			4	Johannesburg[1]	D	5	38	b	5	0	c	–
152/138			5	Durban[2]	W-109	4	66	lbw	5	5	c	1
176/162	1928–29	A	1	Brisbane[1]	W-675	3	8	lbw	3	73	lbw	–

Career	M	I	NO	HS	R	Avge	100	50	Ct	St	Balls	R	W	Avge	BB	5w	10w	Rate
Test	17	26	2	182*	1185	49.37	4	3	4	–	–	–	–	–	–	–	–	–
F/c	814	1340	185	280*	55061	47.67	153	258	671	–	18516	9613	277	34.70	7-18	5	–	66.84

C. P. MEAD – TEST BATTING SUMMARY

Series	V	M	I	NO	HS	R	Avge	100	50
1911–12	A	4	6	1	46	105	21.00	–	–
1913–14	SA	5	7	–	117	378	54.00	2	1
1921	A	2	2	1	182*	229	229.00	1	–
1922–23	SA	5	9	–	181	392	43.55	1	1
1928–29	A	1	2	–	73	81	40.50	–	1
	A	7	10	2	182*	415	51.87	1	1
	SA	10	16	–	181	770	48.12	3	2
Home		2	2	1	182*	229	229.00	1	–
Overseas		15	24	1	181	956	41.56	3	3
Totals		17	26	2	182*	1185	49.37	4	3

Lionel Tennyson (left) and Philip Mead about to open for Hampshire.

MEAD, Walter

Essex (1894 to 1913)
London County (1904)

Wisden 1904
Born Clapton, Middlesex 1 Apr 1868
Died Chipping Ongar, Essex
18 Mar 1954

Walter Mead was an outstanding right-arm slow-medium bowler who, apart from two summers when a dispute over winter pay prompted him to take his talents to London County, was the mainstay of the Essex attack during their first two decades in the Championship. He imparted great spin from an effortless action, relying mainly on off-breaks but reaping a rich haul with occasional leg-spin. His ability to turn the ball on even the most unresponsive of surfaces, allied to his consistent control of length, made him a very valuable bowler. Before Essex had been accorded first-class status he took 17 wickets against the 1893 Australians. The Roald Dahl of tail-end batsman, he was a master of the unexpected; he stunned everyone with an innings of 119 against Leicestershire at Leyton in 1902 and nine years previously had scored 66* at Sheffield when the rest of the side failed to pass 20. He was on the MCC staff from 1891 until 1918. [*Illus. p.* 452]

NOTABLE FEATS

- Took 100 wickets in a season 10 times. Leading bowler 1903.
- Took 9 wickets in an innings 3 times, all for Essex – notably 9 for 40 v Hampshire at Southampton in 1900.
- Holds Essex record for best match analysis: 17 for 119 v Hampshire at Southampton in 1895. Also took 15 for 115 v Leicestershire at Leyton in 1903.
- Bowled in an unchanged partnership throughout both completed innings of a match twice (1906 and 1907).

					Batting 1st			Batting 2nd				Bowling 1st			Bowling 2nd		
Ref	Series	V	T	Venue	Result	No	R	HO	No	R	HO	Ct	Balls	R	W	Balls	R	W
61/61	1899	A	2	Lord's	L-10w	10	7	b	11	0	lbw	1	265	91	1	–	–	–

Career	M	I	NO	HS	R	Avge	100	50	Ct	St	Balls	R	W	Avge	BB	5w	10w	Rate
Test	1	2	0	7	7	3.50	–	–	1	–	265	91	1	91.00	1-91	–	–	265.00
F/c	429	618	148	119	4991	10.61	1	5	194	–	89756	36388	1916	18.99	9-40	152	39	46.84

MIDWINTER William Evans

Victoria (1874–75 to 1886–87)
Gloucestershire (1877 to 1882)
Australia (1876–77 to 1886–87)

TOURS
A 1881–82; Australia to E 1878, 1884
Born St Briavels, Gloucestershire
19 Jun 1851
Died Yarra Bend, Kew, Melbourne,
Australia 3 Dec 1890

Billy Midwinter holds the unique record of having played for both sides in Tests between England and Australia. A hard-hitting but reliable middle-order batsman, a right-arm medium-pace bowler and a safe fielder in the deep, he was the first of cricket's international commuters. Leaving his native Gloucestershire, he emigrated to Melbourne where he became a professional and played a major part in Australia's victory in the first-ever Test. He went back with the English team to play for Gloucestershire and returned to Melbourne in the autumn to continue his career with Victoria. The following year found him back in England with the 1878 Australians until, midway through the tour, W.G. Grace paid a visit to the tourists' dressing room at Lord's and recaptured him for Gloucestershire with whom he spent the rest of the summer. As a regular Gloucestershire player he returned to Australia in 1881–82 with Alfred Shaw's tour and played for England in all four Tests. After a final summer at Bristol he returned to the antipodes for phase three of his extraordinary Test career. This involved appearing for Australia in two more home series and making another tour of England, this time uninterrupted. He was also a notable billiards player. The tragic deaths of his wife and two children deranged him and he died a few months after being admitted to Kew Asylum. [*Illus. p.* 171]

NOTABLE FEATS

- *1* First bowler to take 5 wickets in a Test innings.
- *5* Made his debut for England and remains the only cricketer to play for both sides in E v A Tests or to have played for and against Australia.

Ref	Series	V	T	Venue	Result	Batting 1st			Batting 2nd			Ct	Bowling 1st			Bowling 2nd		
						No	R	HO	No	R	HO		Balls	R	W	Balls	R	W
For Australia																		
1/1	1876–77	E	1	Melbourne	W-45	6	5	c	6	17	c	1	216	78	5	76	23	1
2/2			2	Melbourne	L-4w	6	31	c	6	12	c	–	84	30	1	53	25	1
For England																		
5/5	1881–82	A	1	Melbourne	D	6	36	b	6	4	c	–	156	50	2	–	–	–
6/6			2	Sydney	L-5w	6	4	c	6	8	b	–	136	43	1	72	23	1
7/7			3	Sydney	L-6w	6	12	b	6	10	b	3	248	75	2	–	–	–
8/8			4	Melbourne	D	6	21	c	–	–	–	2	164	81	4	–	–	–
For Australia																		
13/13	1882–83	E	4	Sydney	W-4w	6	10	b	8	8	*	–	188	50	2	92	21	2
14/14	1884	E	1	Manchester	D	5	37	c	–	–	–	1	–	–	–	–	–	–
15/15			2	Lord's	L-I & 5	5	3	b	7	6	b	–	52	29	0	–	–	–
16/16			3	Oval	D	7	30	c	–	–	–	1	124	41	1	12	15	0
25/25	1886–87	E	1	Sydney	L-13	8	0	c	8	10	lbw	2	–	–	–	16	10	0
26/26			2	Sydney	L-71	6	1	b	7	4	c	–	12	2	0	24	9	1

Career	M	I	NO	HS	R	Avge	100	50	Ct	Balls	R	W	Avge	BB	5w	10w	Rate
Test (A)	8	14	1	37	174	13.38	–	–	5	949	333	14	23.78	5-78	1	–	67.78
Test (E)	4	7	0	36	95	13.57	–	–	5	776	272	10	27.20	4-81	–	–	77.60
Combined	12	21	1	37	269	13.45	–	–	10	1725	605	24	25.20	5-78	1	–	71.87
F/c	160	264	27	137*	4534	19.13	3	12	122	23292	7298	419	17.41	7-27	27	3	55.58

MILBURN, Colin

Northamptonshire (1960 to 1974)
Western Australia
(1966–67 to 1968–69)

Wisden 1967
TOURS WI 1967–68; P 1968–69
Born Burnopfield, Co. Durham
23 Oct 1941

Colin Milburn

Even 20 years on, any mention of Colin Milburn recalls the chilling shock caused by news of the loss of his left eye in a car accident on 23 May 1969 when he was at the peak of his very considerable powers. English cricket, then in such desperate poverty that it introduced the mass importation of overseas players and the Sunday 40-over knock-about, could ill afford to lose its most entertaining character. His colossal dimensions of 5ft 10½in and 18 stone (when trimmed down to fighting weight) concealed a fine cricket brain commanding fast reflexes, abundant courage and a wide repertoire of bold orthodox strokes. He was as proficient off the back foot, hooking or indulging in his favourite square-drive, as the front. Although his technique at first glance smacked of the simple block or tackle method, closer examination revealed a more complex strategy and a straight-batted discipline to his legside hitting forward of square. With such a crowd-pulling and exceptionally attacking batsman at their disposal it is a terrible indictment of the selectors that he was chosen for only nine of the 24 Tests that England played from his debut to his last appearance. Even that finale was unscheduled. After a triumphant season for Western Australia, he was summoned to riot-torn Pakistan as an emergency re-enforcement to a beleaguered England team on an ill-conceived mission replacing the cancelled tour of South Africa; his 139 in totally alien conditions was an astonishing piece of batting. He was a handy right-arm medium-pace change bowler but fielding presented its problems and he had to be employed either as a quick-thinking short-leg or as an effective barrier who could cover first, second and third slip simultaneously. Although he reappeared for Northamptonshire in 1973 and 1974, he was forced to accept the inevitable after scoring only one 50 in 35 attempts. Returning to his native Durham, for whom he had scored a century in his only outing prior to joining Northamptonshire, he continued to turn out for the Lord's Taverners until 1987. A lively and idiosyncratic cricket broadcaster, he aptly entitled his autobiography *Largely Cricket.*

NOTABLE FEATS

- *606* Shared record E v WI 5th-wkt stand of 130* with T.W. Graveney.
- *649* Reached 100 off 163 balls in his first innings in Pakistan.
- Exceeded 1000 runs in a season 6 times (plus once overseas).
- Scored 2 double centuries: 243 for Western Australia v Queensland at Brisbane in 1968–69 – out to the first post-tea ball on the first day having added 181 in the 2-hour second session – and 203 for Northamptonshire v Essex at Clacton in 1966.
- Reached 50 with 13 scoring strokes for Northamptonshire v Middlesex at Peterborough in 1963.

Ref	Series	V	T	Venue	Result	Batting 1st No	R	HO	Batting 2nd No	R	HO	Ct
605/429	1966	WI	1	Manchester	L-I & 40	1	0	ro	1	94	b	–
606/430			2	Lord's	D	2	6	lbw	2	126	*	2
607/431			3	Nottingham	L-139	2	7	c	2	12	c	–
608/432			4	Leeds	L-I & 55	3	29	*	7	42	b	–
620/436	1967	I	3	Birmingham	W-132	2	40	c	2	15	b	2
621/437	1967	P	1	Lord's	D	1	3	c	1	32	c	1
638/446	1968	A	2	Lord's	D	3	83	c	–	–	–	–
641/449			5	Oval	W-226	2	8	b	2	18	c	2
649/452	1968–69	P	3	Karachi	D	1	139	c	–	–	–	–

- Scored 100 before lunch for Northamptonshire on 4 occasions.
- Holds Northamptonshire record for most catches taken in the field in a season: 43 in 1964.

Career	M	I	NO	HS	R	Avge	100	50	Ct	St	Balls	R	W	Avge	BB	5w	10w	Rate
Test	9	16	2	139	654	46.71	2	2	7	–	–	–	–	–	–	–	–	–
F/c	255	435	34	243	13262	33.07	23	75	224	–	7033	3171	99	32.03	6-59	1	–	71.04

MILLER Audley Montague

MCC (1896 to 1903)

TOUR SA 1895–96
Born Brentry, Westbury-on-Trym, Gloucestershire 19 Oct 1869
Died Clifton, Bristol 26 Jun 1959

Audley Miller made his first-class debut in the First Test of Lord Hawke's first tour of South Africa. Although he scored 24 runs as a tail-ender without being dismissed, it was his only appearance; he umpired the remaining two Tests. An Old Etonian, he was a middle-order batsman and a right-arm medium-fast bowler. Subsequently he played first-class and minor out-cricket for MCC. For 25 years he was captain and honorary secretary of Wiltshire. [*Illus. p.* 325]

Ref	Series	V	T	Venue	Result	Batting 1st No	R	HO	Batting 2nd No	R	HO	Ct
47/47	1895–96	SA	1	Port Elizabeth	W-288	10	4	*	11	20	*	–

Career	M	I	NO	HS	R	Avge	100	50	Ct	St	Balls	R	W	Avge	BB	5w	10w	Rate
Test	1	2	2	20*	24	–	–	–	–	–	–	–	–	–	–	–	–	–
F/c	5	9	2	36	105	15.00	–	–	–	–	70	49	1	49.00	1-1	–	–	70.00

MILLER, Geoffrey

Derbyshire (1973 to 1986)
Essex (1987 to date)
Natal (1983–84)

TOURS
A 1976–77, 1978–79, 1979–80, 1982–83; WI 1980–81; NZ 1977–78; I/SL 1976–77; P 1977–78
Born Chesterfield, Derbyshire 8 Sep 1952

Geoff ('Dusty') Miller is a tall (6ft 1in) all-rounder whose talents would have borne far heavier fruit had he possessed a killer instinct. The Packer revolution provided him with the opportunity to enjoy a prolonged Test career but, apart from his outstanding all-round series against a mediocre and abysmally captained Australian side in 1978–79, his performances were inconsistent. A correct batsman with a good defence off either foot, he looked as confident as anyone against a rampant Lillee at Perth in 1976–77 and should have played in the Melbourne Centenary Test. He had the ability to make big scores and it was incomprehensible that it took him 380 attempts spread over 12 summers and six winter tours to score his maiden first-class hundred. His off-spin bowling has a nice loop and he is adept at drifting the ball in helpful breezes. An excellent all-round fielder, he has become a safe catcher at slip. His brief tenure as Derbyshire's captain

(1979–81) affected his form and it was after he had returned to the ranks that he enjoyed his best all-round season, ending 1984 just 67 runs and 13 wickets short of the elusive 'double'. Highly intelligent, witty and affable, he is easily the best calligrapher amongst post-war Test cricketers.

NOTABLE FEATS

- 1000 runs and 50 wickets in 28th Test (*938*) (38 inns).

TEST NOTES

- *896* Deputised as captain when I.T. Botham went off for repairs to a damaged finger on the second day.

Geoff Miller

						Batting 1st			Batting 2nd				Bowling 1st			Bowling 2nd		
Ref	Series	V	T	Venue	Result	No	R	HO	No	R	HO	Ct	Balls	R	W	Balls	R	W
781/519	1976	WI	5	Oval	L-231	9	36	c	8	24	b	–	162	106	1	–	–	–
805/527	1977	A	2	Manchester	W-9w	7	6	c	–	–	–	–	60	18	2	54	24	1
806/528			3	Nottingham	W-7w	6	13	c	–	–	–	–	–	–	–	30	5	0
814/531	1977–78	P	1	Lahore[2]	D	6	98	*	–	–	–	1	296	102	3	80	24	0
815/532			2	Hyderabad	D	6	5	c	–	–	–	1	72	57	0	16	8	0
816/533			3	Karachi	D	6	11	c	6	3	c	–	112	71	1	–	–	–
817/534	1977–78	NZ	1	Wellington	L-72	3	24	b	3	4	c	–	–	–	–	–	–	–
818/535			2	Christchurch	W-174	5	89	c	–	–	–	2	–	–	–	–	–	–
819/536			3	Auckland	D	8	15	lbw	–	–	–	1	8	0	0	240	99	3
825/537	1978	P	1	Birmingham	W-I & 57	6	48	c	–	–	–	1	–	–	–	72	19	2
826/538			2	Lord's	W-I & 120	6	0	c	–	–	–	–	–	–	–	54	9	0
827/539			3	Leeds	D	6	18	*	–	–	–	–	54	22	0	–	–	–
828/540	1978	NZ	1	Oval	W-7w	6	0	lbw	–	–	–	1	150	31	2	204	35	2
829/541			2	Nottingham	W-I & 119	7	4	c	–	–	–	–	36	14	0	36	10	0
834/543	1978–79	A	1	Brisbane[2]	W-7w	8	27	lbw	–	–	–	–	–	–	–	272	52	2
835/544			2	Perth	W-166	7	40	b	7	25	c	–	128	31	1	56	21	3
836/545			3	Melbourne	L-103	7	7	b	7	1	c	–	152	35	3	112	39	2
837/546			4	Sydney	W-93	7	4	c	7	17	lbw	–	104	37	1	160	38	3
838/547			5	Adelaide	W-205	7	31	lbw	7	64	c	–	–	–	–	144	36	2
839/548			6	Sydney	W-9w	7	18	lbw	–	–	–	1	72	13	1	217	44	5
851/549	1979	I	1	Birmingham	W-I & 83	7	63	*	–	–	–	–	66	18	0	54	27	0
852/550			2	Lord's	D	7	62	st	–	–	–	1	–	–	–	102	37	0
853/551			3	Leeds	D	7	27	c	–	–	–	–	192	52	2	–	–	–
868/553	1979–80	A	1	Perth	L-138	5	25	c	5	8	c	1	66	30	0	60	36	0
896/563	1980–81	WI	1	Port-of-Spain	L-I & 79	5	3	c	5	8	c	1	108	42	1	–	–	–
929/581	1982	I	2	Manchester	D	7	98	c	–	–	–	–	96	51	1	–	–	–
931/583	1982	P	1	Birmingham	W-113	7	47	b	7	5	b	1	12	1	0	46	26	2
938/586	1982–83	A	1	Perth	D	7	30	c	8	0	c	–	198	70	4	24	8	0
939/587			2	Brisbane[2]	L-7w	7	0	c	7	60	c	–	117	35	1	18	10	0
940/588			3	Adelaide	L-8w	7	7	c	7	17	lbw	–	84	33	0	–	–	–
941/589			4	Melbourne	W-3	7	10	c	7	14	lbw	1	90	44	3	96	30	1
942/590			5	Sydney	D	7	34	lbw	8	21	*	2	102	34	1	297	133	3
989/601	1984	WI	1	Birmingham	L-I & 180	7	22	c	7	11	c	1	90	83	1	–	–	–
990/602			2	Lord's	L-9w	8	0	ro	8	9	b	1	12	14	0	66	45	0

Career	M	I	NO	HS	R	Avge	100	50	Ct	St	Balls	R	W	Avge	BB	5w	10w	Rate
Test	34	51	4	98*	1213	25.80	–	7	17	–	5149	1859	60	30.98	5-44	1	–	85.81
F/c	359	520	83	130	11448	26.19	2	69	295	–	55785	23082	843	27.38	8-70	38	7	66.17

G. MILLER – TEST SUMMARY

Series	V	M	I	NO	HS	R	Avge	100	50	Balls	R	W	Avge	BB	5w	10w	Rate
1976	WI	1	2	–	36	60	30.00	–	–	162	106	1	106.00	1-106	–	–	162.00
1977	A	2	2	–	13	19	9.50	–	–	144	47	3	15.66	2-18	–	–	48.00
1977–78	P	3	4	1	98*	117	39.00	–	1	576	262	4	65.50	3-102	–	–	144.00
1977–78	NZ	3	4	–	89	132	33.00	–	1	248	99	3	33.00	3-99	–	–	82.66
1978	P	3	3	1	48	66	33.00	–	–	180	50	2	25.00	2-19	–	–	90.00
1978	NZ	2	2	–	4	4	2.00	–	–	426	90	4	22.50	2-31	–	–	106.50
1978–79	A	6	10	–	64	234	23.40	–	1	1417	346	23	15.04	5-44	1	–	61.60
1979	I	3	3	1	63*	152	76.00	–	2	414	134	2	67.00	2-52	–	–	207.00
1979–80	A	1	2	–	25	33	16.50	–	–	126	66	0	–	–	–	–	–
1980–81	WI	1	2	–	8	11	5.50	–	–	108	42	1	42.00	1-42	–	–	108.00
1982	I	1	1	–	98	98	98.00	–	1	96	51	1	51.00	1-51	–	–	96.00
1982	P	1	2	–	47	52	26.00	–	–	58	27	2	13.50	2-26	–	–	29.00
1982–83	A	5	10	1	60	193	21.44	–	1	1026	397	13	30.53	4-70	–	–	78.92
1984	WI	2	4	–	22	42	10.50	–	–	168	142	1	142.00	1-83	–	–	168.00
	A	14	24	1	64	479	20.82	–	2	2713	856	39	21.94	5-44	1	–	69.56
	WI	4	8	–	36	113	14.12	–	–	438	290	3	96.66	1-42	–	–	146.00
	NZ	5	6	–	89	136	22.66	–	1	674	189	7	27.00	3-99	–	–	96.28
	I	4	4	1	98	250	83.33	–	3	510	185	3	61.66	2-52	–	–	170.00
	P	7	9	2	98*	235	33.57	–	1	814	339	8	42.37	3-102	–	–	101.75
Home		15	19	2	98	493	29.00	–	3	1648	647	16	40.43	2-18	–	–	103.00
Overseas		19	32	2	98*	720	24.00	–	4	3501	1212	44	27.54	5-44	1	–	79.56
Totals		34	51	4	98*	1213	25.80	–	7	5149	1859	60	30.98	5-44	1	–	85.81

MILLIGAN Frank William

Yorkshire (1894 to 1898)

TOUR SA 1898–99
Born Aldershot, Hampshire 19 Mar 1870
Died Ramatlabama, Bechuanaland
31 May 1900

A dashing Old Etonian all-rounder, Frank Milligan was a hard-hitting middle-order batsman, a right-arm fast bowler and a fine fielder. One of the few Yorkshire cricketers to have been born outside the county, he also appeared for Staffordshire. Soon after achieving his career-best bowling analysis of 7 for 61 for Gentlemen v Players at Scarborough in 1898, he visited South Africa with Lord Hawke's second tour and played in both Tests. Within a year he had been killed in the Boer War while serving as a lieutenant with Colonel Plumer's troops during an attempted relief of Mafeking. [*Illus. p.* 196]

						Batting 1st			Batting 2nd				Bowling 1st			Bowling 2nd		
Ref	Series	V	T	Venue	Result	No	R	HO	No	R	HO	Ct	Balls	R	W	Balls	R	W
58/58	1898–99	SA	1	Johannesburg[1]	W-32	7	11	c	8	8	st	–	35	29	0	–	–	–
59/59			2	Cape Town	W-210	8	1	b	8	38	b	1	10	0	0	–	–	–

Career	M	I	NO	HS	R	Avge	100	50	Ct	St	Balls	R	W	Avge	BB	5w	10w	Rate
Test	2	4	0	38	58	14.50	–	–	1	–	45	29	0	–	–	–	–	–
F/c	94	133	10	74	2226	18.09	–	10	52	–	6545	3324	142	23.40	7-61	6	2	46.09

MILLMAN, Geoffrey

Nottinghamshire (1957 to 1965)

TOURS I 1961–62; P 1961–62
Born Bedford 2 Oct 1934

NOTABLE FEATS

- Exceeded 1000 runs in a season twice.
- Made 6 dismissals in an innings v Northamptonshire at Nottingham in 1959 (equalling Notts record).
- Made 9 dismissals for Nottinghamshire in match with Warwickshire at Nottingham in 1964.
- Made the first catch in limited-overs county cricket (1962).

Geoff Millman was a highly skilled wicket-keeper and a determined but rather limited lower-order batsman who was sometimes pressed into service as an opener. After establishing his place in Bedfordshire's team, he was called up for two years' national service and made his first-class debut for the Combined Services. The following season he began his nine-season career with Nottinghamshire. Some impressive displays on the arduous tour of the subcontinent ensured that he retained his England place for the opening matches of the following summer's series. John Murray and Jim Parks blocked further national honours and, after a spell as Nottinghamshire's captain (1963–65), he returned to his native county and concentrated on business.

Geoff Millman

						Batting 1st			Batting 2nd			Fielding 1st				Fielding 2nd			
Ref	Series	V	T	Venue	Result	No	R	HO	No	R	HO	Ct	St	Byes	Balls	Ct	St	Byes	Balls
516/378†	1961–62	I	4	Calcutta	L-187	9	0	c	9	4	b	1	–	2	936	2	2	0	608
517/379†			5	Madras[2]	L-128	9	32	*	9	14	c	1	–	4	867	2	–	6	567
518/380†	1961–62	P	2	Dacca	D	10	3	*	–	–	–	–	–	4	1155	–	–	5	805
519/318†			3	Karachi	D	9	0	c	–	–	–	2	–	2	570	1	–	8	1002
530/382†	1962	P	1	Birmingham	W-I & 24	–	–	–	–	–	–	1	–	8	606	1	–	1	738
531/383†			2	Lord's	W-9w	8	7	c	–	–	–	1	–	1	262	1	–	6	717

Career	M	I	NO	HS	R	Avge	100	50	Ct	St	Balls	R	W	Avge	BB	5w	10w	Rate
Test	6	7	2	32*	60	12.00	–	–	13	2	–	–	–	–	–	–	–	–
F/c	282	471	59	131*	7771	18.86	3	25	559	97	39	32	0	–	–	–	–	–

MILTON Clement Arthur

Gloucestershire (1948 to 1974)

Wisden 1959
TOUR A 1958–59
Born Bedminster, Bristol 10 Mar 1928

Arthur Milton was the last man to play cricket and soccer for England. He made his one appearance as an international footballer against Austria at Wembley in 1951–52 after producing consistently brilliant performances in his first dozen games as an outside-right for Arsenal; after that one indifferent match his whole game fell away and he was transferred to third division Bristol City. Of average height (5ft 9½in) and trimly built, he was a naturally athletic ball player but lacked the competitive streak necessary for success at the highest level; he resigned the Gloucestershire captaincy after just one season (1968) because he did not enjoy the responsibility. As a batsman he was determined and stylish, very strong off the back foot and particularly adept at pulling and cutting, always dependable in a crisis and an uncanny judge of the stolen single. Quick reflexes allowed him to play the ball late and his technique was equally successful against pace or spin. He was a right-arm medium-pace change bowler who could bowl outswing and, with his express reactions, he was a quite outstanding close fielder, usually at slip or short-leg. This last attribute once earned him the England twelfth man slot in 1953 but another five years passed before he made his

Arthur Milton

first appearance. Although he scored an undefeated century on debut, only one of his subsequent eight innings was over 17. He continued to be a constant source of runs and catches for Gloucestershire, eventually retiring in his 47th year after 27 summers. Afterwards he became a postman and retained his keen interest in greyhound racing and golf.

NOTABLE FEATS

• *456* First Gloucestershire player since W.G. Grace (1880) to score 100 for England on debut. First England player to be on the field throughout a Test match and is alone in achieving this feat in his first Test.
• Exceeded 1000 runs in a season 16 times, including 2089 in 1967.
• Carried his bat through a Gloucestershire innings 3 times and twice scored hundreds in each innings of a match.
• Holds Gloucestershire career record for most catches by a non-wicket-keeper (719). His aggregate of 758 catches in all first-class cricket is the eighth-highest.
• Held 63 catches in the Field in 1956.
• Equalled world first-class record by holding 7 catches in a day for Gloucestershire v Sussex at Hove in 1952 (held 8 in match).
• Held 5 catches in an innings for Gloucestershire v Pakistanis at Cheltenham in 1954.

TEST NOTES

• *458* Bowled in 2nd inns: 0 for 12 (24 balls).

						Batting 1st			Batting 2nd			
Ref	Series	V	T	Venue	Result	No	R	HO	No	R	HO	Ct
456/344	1958	NZ	3	Leeds	W-I & 71	2	104	*	–	–	–	2
458/346			5	Oval	D	2	36	lbw	–	–	–	2
464/347	1958–59	A	1	Brisbane[2]	L-8w	2	5	b	2	17	c	1
466/349			3	Sydney	D	2	8	c	2	8	c	–
474/354	1959	I	1	Nottingham	W-I & 59	1	9	b	–	–	–	–
475/355			2	Lord's	W-8w	1	14	c	1	3	c	–

Career	M	I	NO	HS	R	Avge	100	50	Ct	St	Balls	R	W	Avge	BB	5w	10w	Rate
Test	6	9	1	104*	204	25.50	1	–	5	–	24	12	0	–	–	–	–	–
F/c	620	1078	125	170	32150	33.73	56	160	758	–	8416	3630	79	45.94	5-64	1	–	106.53

MITCHELL, Arthur

Yorkshire (1922 to 1945)

TOURS
WI 1935–36 (Yorks); I/SL 1933–34
Born Baildon, Yorkshire 13 Sep 1902
Died Bradford, Yorkshire 25 Dec 1976

NOTABLE FEATS

• Exceeded 1000 runs in a season 10 times, including 2300 in 1933.
• Scored hundreds in 4 successive innings for Yorkshire and H.D.G. Leveson Gower's XI in 1933.

TEST NOTES

• *244* Bowled in 2nd inns: 0 for 4 (6 balls).

Arthur Mitchell was a steady and very determined batsman whose long playing career with Yorkshire was virtually terminated by the Second World War. Afterwards he became a dedicated and greatly respected coach (1945–70). He was a highly effective player with a formidable defensive technique and a keen appetite for a crisis. If he was often content to accumulate with on-side strokes, he could suddenly change mood and indulge in a spasm of off-drives and cuts. Such an innings was the century he scored at Lord's in 1934 on his only appearance for the Players; after taking 125 minutes for his 50, he added another 70 in an hour. Although he made his debut in 1922, so strong was the Yorkshire batting that he did not command a regular place for another six seasons; in 1930 he was one of five batsmen who averaged over 50. After Percy Holmes retired in 1933 he was promoted to open and enjoyed his most prolific season. It ended with a purple patch of four successive hundreds in which he scored 508 for once out. He met with only moderate success in the first three Tests staged in India but, called from his garden when Leyland was stricken with lumbago a year later, he scored 58 and 72. In his early Bradford league days he had been a very limited fielder but by sheer determination and hard work he became one of the best close catchers in the world. He was also one of the most talkative, his constant chatter earning him the nickname 'Ticker'. [*Illus. pp.* 263, 498]

Ref	Series	V	T	Venue	Result	Batting 1st No	R	HO	Batting 2nd No	R	HO	Ct
230/204	1933–34	I	1	Bombay[1]	W-9w	1	5	b	1	9	lbw	2
231/205			2	Calcutta	D	2	47	c	–	–	–	–
232/206			3	Madras[1]	W-202	3	25	lbw	8	28	c	3
244/218	1935	SA	3	Leeds	D	5	58	c	1	72	c	1
246/220			5	Oval	D	2	40	b	–	–	–	1
252/221	1936	I	1	Lord's	W-9w	1	14	b	1	0	c	2

Career	M	I	NO	HS	R	Avge	100	50	Ct	St	Balls	R	W	Avge	BB	5w	10w	Rate
Test	6	10	0	72	298	29.80	–	2	9	–	6	4	0	–	–	–	–	–
F/c	426	593	72	189	19523	37.47	44	98	438	–	523	327	7	46.71	3-49	–	–	74.71

MITCHELL, Frank

Cambridge University (1894 to 1897)
Yorkshire (1894 to 1904)
London County (1901)
Transvaal (1902–03 to 1903–04)
South Africa (1912)

Wisden 1902
TOURS
SA 1898–99; South Africa to E 1904, 1912
Born Market Weighton, Yorkshire
13 Aug 1872
Died Blackheath, Kent 11 Oct 1935

NOTABLE FEATS

- Exceeded 1000 runs in a season twice.
- Contributed his highest score (194) to a Yorkshire 5th-wkt stand of 329 with E. Wainwright v Leicestershire at Leicester in 1899.

An outstanding all-round sportsman, Frank Mitchell was a unique double international who gained six caps as an England rugby forward as well as representing both England and South Africa at cricket. After captaining St Peter's School, York, he played soccer for Sussex as a goalkeeper during his two years as a master at Brighton. At Cambridge he gained blues for cricket, rugby and putting the weight; he captained both rugby and cricket, creating history and a change in the laws in the latter role when he ordered his fast bowler to give away extras to avoid making Oxford follow on. He made his Yorkshire debut after the first of his four summers as a blue. When Lord Hawke introduced him to South Africa in 1898–99, he played so impressively that he was given a regular place in the County side the following summer. Although no great stylist, he was a highly effective and aggressive middle-order batsman who adapted to all types of pitch. He favoured the off-side strokes, was a very strong driver and could also be used as a right-arm medium-pace change bowler. In between scoring over 1000 runs in each of his only two full seasons of county cricket, he fought in the Boer War with the Yorkshire Dragoons. Returning to the Union as secretary to Sir Abe Bailey, he played for the Transvaal and captained the 1904 and 1912 South African tours to England. As a Lieut-Colonel in the Great War he was mentioned in dispatches and embarked on the prolific career as a journalist which later encompassed cricket and rugby. [*Illus. p.* 196]

Ref	Series	V	T	Venue	Result	Batting 1st No	R	HO	Batting 2nd No	R	HO	Ct
For England												
58/58	1898–99	SA	1	Johannesburg[1]	W-32	1	28	b	1	1	lbw	1
59/59			2	Cape Town	W-210	1	18	c	1	41	lbw	1
For South Africa												
121/30*	1912	A	1	Manchester	L-I & 88	7	11	b	7	0	b	–
122/31*		E	1	Lord's	L-I & 62	7	1	c	7	1	b	–
125/33*		A	2	Lord's	L-10w	8	12	b	8	3	b	–

Career	M	I	NO	HS	R	Avge	100	50	Ct/St	Balls	R	W	Avge	BB	5w	10w	Rate
Test (E)	2	4	0	41	88	22.00	–	–	2/–	–	–	–	–	–	–	–	–
Test (SA)	3	6	0	12	28	4.66	–	–	–/–	–	–	–	–	–	–	–	–
Combined	5	10	0	41	116	11.60	–	–	2/–	–	–	–	–	–	–	–	–
F/c	198	304	19	194	9117	31.98	17	38	146/2	1596	828	35	23.65	5-57	1	–	45.60

MITCHELL Thomas Bignall

Derbyshire (1928 to 1939)

TOURS A 1932–33; NZ 1932–33
Born Creswell, Derbyshire 4 Sep 1902

Tommy Mitchell was one of cricket's great characters, a naturally funny man whose antics and remarks frequently reduced his fellow players to helpless laughter. A bespectacled coal-miner, he was given a trial by Derbyshire after some impressive performances as a right-arm leg-break and googly bowler with Creswell Colliery in the Bassetlaw league. After a shaky start, he became a consistent wicket-taker, spinning the ball sharply on any surface, occasionally offering a straightforward off-break and subtly varying the flight and angle of his delivery. He was in devastating form in Australia with Jardine's tour but played in only the vital Brisbane Test when he dismissed Woodfull twice. In 1936 he played a vital part in gaining Derbyshire's only Championship title. [*Illus. p.* 126]

NOTABLE FEATS

- Took 100 wickets in a season 10 times; his Derbyshire total of 168 in 1935 remains the County record.
- Took all 10 for 64 for Derbyshire v Leicestershire at Leicester in 1935.
- Took 8 wickets in 36 balls v Worcestershire at Stourbridge and 6 in 13 balls v Middlesex at Derby, both for Derbyshire in 1934.

						Batting 1st			Batting 2nd				Bowling 1st			Bowling 2nd		
Ref	Series	V	T	Venue	Result	No	R	HO	No	R	HO	Ct	Balls	R	W	Balls	R	W
223/197	1932–33	A	4	Brisbane[2]	W-6w	11	0	lbw	–	–	–	1	96	49	2	30	11	1
226/200	1932–33	NZ	2	Auckland	D	–	–	–	–	–	–	–	108	49	1	–	–	–
233/207	1934	A	1	Nottingham	L-238	11	1	*	11	4	lbw	–	126	62	1	78	46	0
236/210			4	Leeds	D	10	9	st	–	–	–	–	138	117	0	–	–	–
243/217	1935	SA	2	Lord's	L-157	11	5	*	11	1	st	–	120	71	1	198	93	2

Career	M	I	NO	HS	R	Avge	100	50	Ct	St	Balls	R	W	Avge	BB	5w	10w	Rate
Test	5	6	2	9	20	5.00	–	–	1	–	894	498	8	62.25	2-49	–	–	111.75
F/c	328	412	107	57	2431	7.97	–	1	132	–	62880	30543	1483	20.59	10-64	118	30	42.40

MITCHELL-INNES Norman Stewart

Somerset (1931 to 1949)
Oxford University (1934 to 1937)
Scotland (1937)

TOURS A 1935–36; NZ 1935–36
Born Calcutta, India 7 Sep 1914

NOTABLE FEATS

- Exceeded 1000 runs in a season 3 times.
- Holds Oxford U record for most runs in a career (3319).
- Scored 207 for Oxford U v H.D.G. Leveson Gower XI at Reigate in 1936.

Norman Mitchell-Innes played for Somerset as a right-arm fast-medium bowler when he was still a schoolboy at Sedbergh. Such was the improvement in his batting that it prompted the selectors to choose him as a specialist in that role for his only Test match and while he was a second-year undergraduate at Brasenose College. Confident and stylish, he scored more runs for Oxford than any batsman before or since, captaining the University in the third of those four highly prolific summers. After going down he appeared for Scotland before joining the Sudan civil service. These varied diversions, allied to his constant battles with a chronic asthmatic allergy, meant that, although his career with Somerset spanned 13 seasons, it comprised only 69 matches. He was their joint captain in 1948.

Norman Mitchell-Innes

Ref	Series	V	T	Venue	Result	Batting 1st			Batting 2nd			Ct
						No	R	HO	No	R	HO	
242/216	1935	SA	1	Nottingham	D	4	5	lbw	–	–	–	–

Career	M	I	NO	HS	R	Avge	100	50	Ct	St	Balls	R	W	Avge	BB	5w	10w	Rate
Test	1	1	0	5	5	5.00	–	–	–	–	–	–	–	–	–	–	–	–
F/c	132	239	18	207	6944	31.42	13	32	152	–	4902	2846	82	34.70	4-65	–	–	59.78

MOLD, Arthur Webb

Lancashire (1889 to 1901)

Wisden 1892
Born Middleton Cheney, Northamptonshire 27 May 1863
Died Middleton Cheney 29 Apr 1921

Arthur Mold was a devastating fast bowler whose action was considered to be suspect even while he was playing for his native Northamptonshire. After qualifying for Lancashire he enjoyed the spoils of 11 prolific summers before he was actually no-balled for the first time. Jim Phillips was the umpire involved in that match against Nottinghamshire at Trent Bridge in 1900 and, after the county captains had condemned his action by 11 votes to one, it was Phillips who ended his career by calling him 16 times in 10 overs when Somerset visited Old Trafford the following season.

The Lancashire side of 1901: standing *Lunt (scorer), A.W. Mold, J. Sharp, W.R. Cuttell, S. Webb, J.J. Broughton, W.J. Hibbert;* seated *A. Ward, H.G. Garnett, A.C. MacLaren (captain), A. Priestley, J. Hallows;* in front *J.T. Tyldesley, C. Smith.*

NOTABLE FEATS

- Took 100 wickets in a season 9 times, including 200 twice.
- Second bowler to take 100 wickets in his debut season in first-class cricket: 102 in 1889.
- Took 9 wickets in an innings 4 times, notably 9 for 29 for Lancashire v Kent at Tonbridge in 1892.
- Took 16 for 111 in match for Lancashire v Kent at Manchester in 1895 and took 15 wickets on 3 other occasions for Lancashire.
- Two hat-tricks for Lancashire: v Somerset at Manchester in 1894 (within spell of 7 for 0 in 20 balls) and v Nottinghamshire (4 wickets in 4 balls) at Nottingham in 1895.
- Bowled in an unchanged partnership for Lancashire throughout both completed innings of a match on 7 occasions, including 5 with J. Briggs.
- Bowled 8 Sussex batsmen in taking 8 for 49 for Lancashire at Hove in 1893.
- Sent a bail 63yd 6in in bowling G.A. Lohmann of Surrey at The Oval in 1896.
- Contributed his highest first-class score of 57 to Lancashire's 10th-wkt stand of 111 with A. Ward v Leicestershire at Manchester in 1895.

Ref	Series	V	T	Venue	Result	Batting 1st			Batting 2nd			Ct	Bowling 1st			Bowling 2nd		
						No	R	HO	No	R	HO		Balls	R	W	Balls	R	W
39/39	1893	A	1	Lord's	D	11	0	b	–	–	–	–	101	44	3	–	–	–
40/40			2	Oval	W-I & 43	11	0	*	–	–	–	–	20	12	0	115	73	1
41/41			3	Manchester	D	11	0	b	–	–	–	1	140	48	1	115	57	2

Career	M	I	NO	HS	R	Avge	100	50	Ct	St	Balls	R	W	Avge	BB	5w	10w	Rate
Test	3	3	1	0*	0	0.00	–	–	1	–	491	234	7	33.42	3-44	–	–	70.14
F/c	287	389	130	57	1850	7.14	–	2	111	–	62224	26010	1673	15.54	9-29	152	56	37.19

MOON, Leonard James

Cambridge University (1897 to 1900)
Middlesex (1899 to 1909)

TOUR SA 1905–06
Born Kensington, London 9 Feb 1878
Died near Karasouli, Salonica, Greece 23 Nov 1916

Leonard Moon was a lively and aggressive opening batsman who specialised in the cut and could keep wicket. After three productive years of batting for Westminster School, he gained blues in his last two years at Cambridge and scored 138 against the 1899 Australians. During 63 appearances for Middlesex he twice shared opening partnerships in excess of 200 with Sir Pelham Warner. A notable footballer, he gained a soccer blue and played for the Corinthians. As a 2nd Lieutenant with the Devon Regiment, he died of wounds during the First World War. [*Illus. p.* 268]

TEST NOTES

• *90* Moon kept wicket only in this Test.

						Batting 1st			Batting 2nd			Fielding 1st				Fielding 2nd			
Ref	Series	V	T	Venue	Result	No	R	HO	No	R	HO	Ct	St	Byes	Balls	Ct	St	Byes	Balls
89/86	1905–06	SA	2	Johannesburg[1]	L-9w	5	30	lbw	5	0	c	–	–	–	–	–	–	–	–
90/87 †			3	Johannesburg[1]	L-243	5	36	b	8	15	b	1	–	10	711	–	–	9	606
91/88			4	Cape Town	W-4w	8	33	b	5	28	lbw	1	–	–	–	–	–	–	–
92/89			5	Cape Town	L-I & 16	5	7	lbw	2	33	lbw	2	–	–	–	–	–	–	–

Career	M	I	NO	HS	R	Avge	100	50	Ct	St	Balls	R	W	Avge	BB	5w	10w	Rate
Test	4	8	0	36	182	22.75	–	–	4	–	–	–	–	–	–	–	–	–
F/c	96	163	8	162	4166	26.87	7	8	72	13	96	55	1	55.00	1-5	–	–	96.00

MORLEY, Frederick

Nottinghamshire (1872 to 1883)

TOUR A 1882–83
Born Sutton in Ashfield, Nottinghamshire 16 Dec 1850
Died Sutton in Ashfield 28 Sep 1884

Fred Morley was an exceptionally accurate left-arm bowler who, at his peak, was rated the finest fast bowler in England. Although he was lacking in height (5ft 8½in), he swung the ball and maintained an immaculate length and line. Highlights of a string of sensational performances were 13 wickets when Oxford were routed twice in a day, his eight wickets in the first Test played in England and an astonishing haul of 100 wickets at 3.54 on Richard Daft's tour of Canada and the United States in 1879. The summit of his ambitions as a left-handed tail-ender was to hold up his end for a few overs and, although he had an accurate throw, his fielding was poor. A polite and unassuming man, he was injured during the voyage with Bligh's team when their ship was in collision with another as it left Colombo. After he had played in discomfort for several weeks in Australia it was discovered that he had fractured a rib. He never fully recovered and died of congestion and dropsy the year after the team returned. [*Illus. p.* 42]

NOTABLE FEATS

• *4* First to take 5 wickets in a Test innings in England.
• Took 100 wickets in a season 7 times, notably in 1878 when he became the first to achieve this feat for Nottinghamshire and, in all matches, achieved his best aggregate: 197 (avge 12.16).
• Achieved world record match analysis (in terms of fewest runs per wicket): 13 wickets for 14 runs for MCC v Oxford University at Cowley Marsh, Oxford, in 1877. His first innings analysis of 7 for 6 contributed to Oxford's dismissal for the lowest innings total in all first-class cricket (12 – since equalled).
• Took 15 for 35 in match for Nottinghamshire v Kent at Town Malling in 1878 on a pitch described as 'rough'.
• Bowled in an unchanged partnership with A. Shaw throughout both completed innings of a match on 8 occasions, including 4 in 1878.

Ref	Series	V	T	Venue	Result	Batting 1st No	R	HO	Batting 2nd No	R	HO	Ct	Bowling 1st Balls	R	W	Bowling 2nd Balls	R	W
4/4	1880	A		Oval	W-5w	11	2	ro	–	–	–	2	128	56	5	244	90	3
11/11	1882–83	A	2	Melbourne	W-I & 27	11	0	*	–	–	–	2	92	13	0	8	7	0
12/12			3	Sydney	W-69	11	2	*	11	0	b	–	136	47	4	140	34	2
13/13			4	Sydney	L-4w	11	0	b	11	2	c	–	176	45	2	48	4	0

Career	M	I	NO	HS	R	Avge	100	50	Ct	St	Balls	R	W	Avge	BB	5w	10w	Rate
Test	4	6	2	2*	6	1.50	–	–	4	–	972	296	16	18.50	5-56	1	–	60.75
F/c	232	355	95	31	1404	5.40	–	–	107	–	80076	17103	1273 +1	13.43	8-26	119	36	62.90

MORTIMORE
John Brian

Gloucestershire (1950 to 1975)

TOURS
A 1958–59; NZ 1958–59; I 1963–64, 1964–65 (Cwlth)
Born Southmead, Bristol 14 May 1933

NOTABLE FEATS

- Exceeded 1000 runs in a season 5 times and took 100 wickets 3 times (completing the 'double' on each occasion).
- Took 4 wickets in 5 balls for Gloucestershire v Lancashire at Cheltenham in 1962.

In a career spanning 26 summers, John Mortimore was a worthy member of Gloucestershire's impressive line of notable spinners. For most of that period he bowled in partnership with his fellow right-arm off-break bowler, David Allen, their two differing styles of attack complementing one another admirably. If Allen was the bigger finger spinner, Mortimore's exceptional accuracy enabled him to plan the batsman's downfall over a planned and sometimes lengthy sequence of deliveries. His immaculate control enabled him to nag away on unresponsive pitches, compelling the batsman to take risks if he wanted to score. He turned the ball enough to beat the bat, had a well-hidden away-drifter and could be quite devastating on a turning wicket. Tall (6ft) and slim, he was undemonstrative and always neatly attired. A very effective lower-order batsman with a high backlift and good defence, he was essentially a front-foot player and a fine driver. He captained Gloucestershire for three seasons (1965–67).

John Mortimore

Ref	Series	V	T	Venue	Result	Batting 1st No	R	HO	Batting 2nd No	R	HO	Ct	Bowling 1st Balls	R	W	Bowling 2nd Balls	R	W
468/351	1958–59	A	5	Melbourne	L-9w	8	44	*	8	11	b	–	88	41	1	–	–	–
472/352	1958–59	NZ	1	Christchurch	W-I & 99	7	11	c	–	–	–	–	132	40	1	126	27	1
473/353			2	Auckland	D	7	9	b	–	–	–	–	24	24	0	–	–	–
476/356	1959	I	3	Leeds	W-I & 173	7	7	b	–	–	–	–	48	24	0	112	36	3
477/357			4	Manchester	W-171	8	29	c	9	7	c	–	78	46	0	96	29	1
553/400	1963–64	I	1	Madras[2]	D	9	0	c	5	73	*	–	228	110	0	90	41	2
556/403			4	Delhi	D	9	21	c	–	–	–	2	228	74	3	192	52	0
557/404			5	Kanpur	D	8	19	b	–	–	–	1	288	39	1	138	28	0
564/408	1964	A	4	Manchester	D	8	12	c	–	–	–	–	294	122	0	–	–	–

Career	M	I	NO	HS	R	Avge	100	50	Ct	St	Balls	R	W	Avge	BB	5w	10w	Rate
Test	9	12	2	73*	243	24.30	–	1	3	–	2162	733	13	56.38	3-36	–	–	166.30
F/c	640	989	122	149	15891	18.32	4	65	348	–	113592	41904	1807	23.18	8-59	75	8	62.86

MOSS, Alan Edward

Middlesex (1950 to 1963)

TOURS
SA 1960–61 (Cwlth); WI 1953–54, 1956–57 (Norfolk)
Born Tottenham, Middlesex 14 Nov 1930

NOTABLE FEATS

- Took 100 wickets in a season 5 times.
- Hat-trick for Middlesex v Gloucestershire at Lord's in 1956.

Alan Moss was a tall, strong, right-arm fast-medium bowler who opened the Middlesex attack, often in partnership with John Warr, throughout the 1950s. Such was his enthusiasm that, during his national service, he managed to arrange his RAF duties so that he was available for half of the county programme. Hard-working, determined and capable of long spells, he steadily improved his control of line and movement. His action in profile was quite distinctive as he arched back like a bow immediately before delivery. He was a useful tail-end batsman who used his reach effectively to defend stubbornly or drive over the top. After his playing days were over he ran a printing business.

Alan Moss

						Batting 1st			Batting 2nd				Bowling 1st			Bowling 2nd		
Ref	Series	V	T	Venue	Result	No	R	HO	No	R	HO	Ct	Balls	R	W	Balls	R	W
382/306	1953–54	WI	1	Kingston	L-140	11	0	b	11	16	ro	–	156	84	1	60	30	1
425/327	1956	A	1	Nottingham	D	–	–	–	–	–	–	–	24	1	0	–	–	–
474/354	1959	I	1	Nottingham	W-I & 59	11	11	c	–	–	–	–	144	33	2	72	13	0
475/355			2	Lord's	W-8w	10	26	b	–	–	–	–	84	31	0	138	30	2
476/356			3	Leeds	W-I & 173	–	–	–	–	–	–	1	132	30	2	36	10	1
487/359	1959–60	WI	1	Bridgetown	D	11	4	b	–	–	–	–	282	116	0	–	–	–
491/363			5	Port-of-Spain	D	11	1	b	–	–	–	–	204	94	2	24	16	1
493/365	1960	SA	2	Lord's	W-I & 73	–	–	–	–	–	–	–	63	35	4	84	41	1
494/366			3	Nottingham	W-8w	11	3	*	–	–	–	–	60	26	1	94	36	3

Career	M	I	NO	HS	R	Avge	100	50	Ct	St	Balls	R	W	Avge	BB	5w	10w	Rate
Test	9	7	1	26	61	10.16	–	–	1	–	1657	626	21	29.80	4-35	–	–	78.90
F/c	382	410	171	40	1671	6.99	–	–	143	–	63523	27035	1301	20.78	8-31	65	13	48.82

MOXON Martyn Douglas

Yorkshire (1981 to date)
Griqualand West (1982–83 to 1983–84)

TOURS
A 1987–88; WI 1986–87 (Yorks); NZ 1987–88; I 1984–85; SL 1984–85, 1985–86 (Eng B)
Born Barnsley, Yorkshire 4 May 1960

Martyn Moxon is a tall (6ft), well-built opening batsman and a right-arm medium-pace change bowler. He has a sound technique and limitless patience – attributes strengthened by watching Boycott at close quarters in his early days. Like his mentor he has exchanged his spectacles for contact lenses. After a sensational start to his career when he became the first Yorkshire batsman to score hundreds in each of his first two Championship matches, he went on to celebrate his first Roses match with an innings of 153. He made a sound 74 in his first Test innings before losing the selectors' confidence by falling to Richard Hadlee's bowling four times in succession. As Gooch's deputy he played two innings of great tenacity to head England's averages for the 1987–88 series in New Zealand and was unlucky to be denied his maiden Test hundred twice in successive innings. At Auckland he was out after being kept on 99 for 18 agonising minutes and when a well-timed sweep for three runs off Bracewell early in his innings

Martyn Moxon

had been signalled as leg-byes by umpire McHarg; the bowler subsequently admitted that the ball came off Moxon's bat. Having become the ninth England player (and fourth Yorkshireman) to perish on 99, he was then left 81* when rain washed out the last two days of the Wellington Test.

NOTABLE FEATS

- Exceeded 1000 runs in a season 4 times.
- Scored 116 on first-class debut for Yorkshire v Essex at Leeds in 1981 and, in his next match, 111 v Derbyshire at Sheffield.

TEST NOTES

- *1079* Bowled in 1st inns: 0 for 27 (36 balls).
- *1092* Bowled in 2nd inns: 0 for 3 (12 balls).

						Batting 1st			Batting 2nd			
Ref	Series	V	T	Venue	Result	No	R	HO	No	R	HO	Ct
1049/626	1986	NZ	1	Lord's	D	2	74	lbw	2	5	lbw	–
1050/627			2	Nottingham	L-8w	2	9	b	2	23	c	1
1079/638	1987	P	5	Oval	D	2	8	c	2	15	c	3
1090/642	1987–88	A		Sydney	D	2	40	b	–	–	–	1
1091/643	1987–88	NZ	1	Christchurch	D	2	1	c	2	27	c	2
1092/644			2	Auckland	D	2	99	c	–	–	–	2
1093/645			3	Wellington	D	2	81	*	–	–	–	–
1099/647	1988	WI	2	Lord's	L-134	3	26	c	3	14	ro	1
1100/648			3	Manchester	L-I & 156	2	0	b	2	15	c	–

Career	M	I	NO	HS	R	Avge	100	50	Ct	St	Balls	R	W	Avge	BB	5w	10w	Rate
Test	9	15	1	99	437	31.21	–	3	10	–	48	30	0	–	–	–	–	–
F/c	155	262	18	191	9373	38.41	21	49	124	–	1900	1100	18	61.11	3-26	–	–	105.55

MURDOCH William Lloyd

New South Wales (1875–76 to 1893–94)
Sussex (1893 to 1899)
London County (1901 to 1904)
Australia (1876–77 to 1890)

TOURS
SA 1891–92;
Australia to E 1878, 1880, 1884, 1890
Born Sandhurst, Victoria, Australia 18 Oct 1854
Died Yarra Park, East Melbourne, Australia 18 Feb 1911

Billy Murdoch has many claims to fame in addition to being the outstanding Australian batsman of his era: he was the first Test captain to score a century; he captained Australia in the first Test staged in England; he made a world record Test score and a record first-class score in Australia; and he is the only Australian captain to lead his country on four tours of England, to play for England, or to captain an English county. A stylish front-foot batsman, he favoured the off-side with the drive and cut his most productive strokes. Nimble footwork enabled him to compensate for limited reach. On good surfaces he was the complete master and his orthodox straight-bat method enabled him to score 140 for the Gentlemen when in his 50th year. In his youth he was a first-rate wicket-keeper and it was because he was not selected for the inaugural Test in 1876–77 that Spofforth refused to play. After his marriage in 1884–85 he retired from major cricket until he led the 1890 Australian tour to England. He then captained Sussex (1893–99), played for London County with his great friend W.G. Grace until the club was dissolved, and made his lone appearance for England during W.W. Read's tour of South Africa. He suffered a stroke during the lunch interval of the second day of the Fourth Test between Australia and the 1910–11 South Africans at the MCG and died a few hours later. [*Illus. p.* 201]

NOTABLE FEATS

- *4* First Test captain to score 100; it was his maiden first-class 100 and his first match as Australia's captain.
- *15* First substitute fielder to hold a catch in Test cricket, a feat he achieved while fielding for the opposition.

(*cont.*)

TEST NOTES

- *6* Stumped W. Bates in 1st inns. J.M. Blackham deputised as wicket-keeper for part of the 2nd inns.
- *13* Batted 70 min before scoring his first run.
- *38* Kept wicket in the 2nd inns and stumped C.S. Wimble.

NOTABLE FEATS *cont.*

- *16* Scored the first 200 in Test cricket, his 211 taking 485 min; it was the highest Test innings until 1903–04. Shared 3rd-wkt stand of 207 with H.J.H. Scott – then the world Test record for any wicket.
- Exceeded 1000 runs 3 times during tours of England.
- Scored 321 for NSW v Victoria at Sydney in 1881–82 (the record score in Australia until 1900–01) and 4 other double centuries, his highest score in England being 286* for Australians v Sussex at Hove in 1882.

Ref	Series	V	T	Venue	Result	Batting 1st No	R	HO	Batting 2nd No	R	HO	Ct
For Australia												
2/2	1876–77	E	2	Melbourne	L-4w	8	3	ro	5	8	c	1
3/3	1878–79	E		Melbourne	W-10w	2	4	c	2	4	*	–
4/4*	1880	E		Oval	L-5w	2	0	c	3	153	*	–
5/5*	1881–82	E	1	Melbourne	D	3	39	b	4	22	*	–
6/6* †			2	Sydney	W-5w	4	10	c	3	49	c	1
7/7*			3	Sydney	W-6w	3	6	c	3	4	c	–
8/8*			4	Melbourne	D	1	85	b	–	–	–	1
9/9*	1882	E		Oval	W-7	3	13	b	4	29	ro	1
10/10*	1882–83	E	1	Melbourne	W-9w	3	48	b	3	33	*	–
11/11*			2	Melbourne	L-I & 27	3	19	*	1	17	b	–
12/12*			3	Sydney	L-69	3	19	lbw	3	0	c	2
13/13*			4	Sydney	W-4w	3	0	b	2	17	c	4
14/14*	1884	E	1	Manchester	D	3	28	c	–	–	–	–
15/15*			2	Lord's	L-I & 5	3	10	lbw	3	17	c	–
16/16*			3	Oval	D	3	211	c	–	–	–	1
17/17*	1884–85	E	1	Adelaide	L-8w	3	5	c	3	7	b	–
33/33*	1890	E	1	Lord's	L-7w	3	9	c	5	19	b	–
34/34*			2	Oval	L-2w	3	2	b	5	6	b	2
For England												
38/38	1891–92	SA		Cape Town	W-I & 189	3	12	c	–	–	–	–

Career	M	I	NO	HS	R	Avge	100	50	Ct/St	Balls	R	W	Avge	BB	5w	10w	Rate
Test (A)	18	33	5	211	896	32.00	2	1	13/1	–	–	–	–	–	–	–	–
Test (E)	1	1	0	12	12	12.00	–	–	–/1	–	–	–	–	–	–	–	–
Combined	19	34	5	211	908	31.31	2	1	13/2	–	–	–	–	–	–	–	–
F/c	391	679	48	321	16953	26.86	19	85	218/25	764	430	10	43.00	2-11	–	–	76.40

MURRAY
John Thomas MBE

Middlesex (1952 to 1975)

Wisden 1967

TOURS

A 1962–63, 1965–66; SA 1964–65, 1972–73 (Robins), 1973–74 (Robins); WI 1963–64 (Cav), 1966–67 (RW), 1969–70 (Cav); NZ 1960–61, 1962–63, 1965–66; I 1961–62; P 1961–62, 1963–64 (Cwlth), 1967–68 (Cwlth), 1968–69, 1970–71 (Cwlth); SL 1968–69

Born North Kensington, London
1 Apr 1935

John Murray defied the dual handicaps imposed by his date of birth and given names to become one of the best post-war batsmen wicket-keepers. Athletically built, of medium height (5ft 9in) and a perfectionist, he was a high-class technician whose excellent positioning and balance enabled him to become equally proficient at taking both pace and spin. He was extremely agile and missed very little within remote diving range when standing back. Always immaculately attired and capped, he was a most elegant and correct lower-order batsman whose stylish front-foot strokeplay led to him frequently being confused with Tom Graveney during their long partnership at The Oval in 1966. A few weeks later another century, the product of a most courageous display against formidable fast bowling, enabled the Rest of the World to defeat a very strong Barbados team. After a brilliant start to his Test career against the 1961 Australians he was beset first by injuries and later by a selectorial policy of strengthening the England batting with the inclusion of Jim Parks. When not adding to the tally of dismissals which became the wicket-keeping first-class record, 'JT' liked to adopt the role of right-arm medium-pace swing bowler. For two seasons he was an England selector (1977–78).

John Murray at full stretch during the 1961 Oval Test against Australia.

NOTABLE FEATS

• 50 dismissals in 19th Test (*619*).
• *510* Equalled E v A record of 7 catches in a match.
• *511* Set (then) England record with 18 dismissals in a home series.
• *609* Shared record E v WI 8th-wkt stand of 217 in 235 min with T.W. Graveney.
• *619* Equalled (then) Test record of 6 catches in an innings.
• *620* Shared (then) record E v I 10th-wkt stand of 57 with R.N.S. Hobbs.
• Exceeded 1000 runs in a season 6 times and made 100 dismissals in a season twice (1957 and 1960) – only L.E.G. Ames has reached the 100-mark more often.
• Second after L.E.G. Ames to complete the wicket-keepers' 'double' with 1025 runs and 104 dismissals in 1957.
• Set world record for most dismisssals in a first-class career, his final total of 1527 surviving until surpassed by R.W. Taylor in 1982–83.
• Holds Middlesex records for most first-class dismissals in a career (1223), in a season (99) and in a match (equalled record with 9 v Hampshire at Lord's in 1965).

TEST NOTES

• *537* P.H. Parfitt deputised as wicket-keeper after Murray injured his shoulder catching W.M. Lawry early in the 1st inns. Defending one-handed, he spent 74 min before scoring and survived 100 min for 3*.
• *575* J.M. Parks kept wicket.
• *603* W.E. Russell deputised as wicket-keeper after tea on the last day.

						Batting 1st			Batting 2nd			Fielding 1st				Fielding 2nd			
Ref	Series	V	T	Venue	Result	No	R	HO	No	R	HO	Ct	St	Byes	Balls	Ct	St	Byes	Balls
507/369†	1961	A	1	Birmingham	D	8	16	c	–	–	–	1	–	8	917	–	–	–	–
508/370†			2	Lord's	L-5w	8	18	lbw	8	25	c	2	–	1	837	2	–	0	125
509/371†			3	Leeds	W-8w	7	6	b	–	–	–	1	1	7	660	2	–	0	317
510/372†			4	Manchester	L-54	7	24	c	7	4	c	3	–	4	382	4	–	6	1030
511/373†			5	Oval	D	7	27	c	7	40	c	2	–	10	995	–	–	–	–
512/374†	1961–62	P	1	Lahore[2]	W-5w	8	4	b	–	–	–	3	–	4	857	2	–	9	455
513/375†	1961–62	I	1	Bombay[2]	D	7	8	c	6	2	b	–	–	33	1008	–	–	4	438
514/376†			2	Kanpur	D	7	2	b	7	9	*	–	1	2	1188	–	–	–	–
515/377†			3	Delhi	D	–	–	–	–	–	–	–	–	2	1065	–	–	–	–
532/384†	1962	P	3	Leeds	W-I & 117	8	29	c	–	–	–	1	–	8	391	1	–	0	448
533/385†			4	Nottingham	D	–	–	–	–	–	–	4	–	2	517	1	–	0	606
534/386†			5	Oval	W-10w	–	–	–	2	14	*	3	–	0	582	–	–	4	667
537/389†	1962–63	A	3	Sydney	L-8w	8	0	lbw	8	3	*	1	–	10	808	–	–	–	–
540/392†	1962–63	NZ	1	Auckland	W-I & 215	9	9	*	–	–	–	2	–	5	664	–	–	2	319
575/414	1964–65	SA	5	Port Elizabeth	D	2	4	lbw	2	8	*	–	–	–	–	–	–	–	–
603/427†	1965–66	NZ	2	Dunedin	D	7	50	c	–	–	–	4	–	4	634	–	–	10	492
609/433†	1966	WI	5	Oval	W-I & 34	9	112	lbw	–	–	–	1	–	1	587	2	–	1	511
618/434†	1967	I	1	Leeds	W-6w	–	–	–	5	4	c	1	–	0	524	1	–	10	1256
619/435†			2	Lord's	W-I & 124	7	7	lbw	–	–	–	6	–	2	334	–	–	11	339
620/436†			3	Birmingham	W-132	7	77	c	7	4	b	–	1	4	219	1	–	5	676
621/437†	1967	P	1	Lord's	D	7	0	b	7	0	c	1	–	1	1093	–	–	1	372

Career	M	I	NO	HS	R	Avge	100	50	Ct	St	Balls	R	W	Avge	BB	5w	10w	Rate
Test	21	28	5	112	506	22.00	1	2	52	3	–	–	–	–	–	–	–	–
F/c	635	936	136	142	18872	23.59	16	84	1270	257	341	243	6	40.50	2-10	–	–	56.83

J. T. MURRAY – TEST SUMMARY

Series	V	M	I	NO	HS	R	Avge	100	50	Ct	St	Byes	Balls
1961	A	5	8	–	40	160	20.00	–	–	17	1	36	5263
1961–62	P	1	1	–	4	4	4.00	–	–	5	–	13	1312
1961–62	I	3	4	1	9*	21	7.00	–	–	–	1	41	3699
1962	P	3	2	1	29	43	43.00	–	–	10	–	14	3211
1962–63	A	1	2	1	3*	3	3.00	–	–	1	–	10	808
1962–63	NZ	1	1	1	9*	9	–	–	–	2	–	7	983
1964–65	SA	1	2	1	8*	12	12.00	–	–	–	–	–	–
1965–66	NZ	1	1	–	50	50	50.00	–	1	4	–	14	1126
1966	WI	1	1	–	112	112	112.00	1	–	3	–	2	1098
1967	I	3	4	–	77	92	23.00	–	1	9	1	32	3348
1967	P	1	2	–	0	0	0.00	–	–	1	–	2	1465
	A	6	10	1	40	163	18.11	–	–	18	1	46	6071
	SA	1	2	1	8*	12	12.00	–	–	–	–	–	–
	WI	1	1	–	112	112	112.00	1	–	3	–	2	1098
	NZ	2	2	1	50	59	59.00	–	1	6	–	21	2109
	I	6	8	1	77	113	16.14	–	1	9	2	73	7047
	P	5	5	1	29	47	11.75	–	–	16	–	29	5988
Home		13	17	1	112	407	25.43	1	1	40	2	86	14385
Overseas		8	11	4	50	99	14.14	–	1	12	1	85	7928
Totals		21	28	5	112	506	22.00	1	2	52	3	171	22313

NEWHAM, William

Sussex (1881 to 1905)

TOUR A 1887–88
Born Shrewsbury, Shropshire
12 Dec 1860
Died Portslade, Brighton, Sussex
26 Jun 1944

NOTABLE FEATS

- Exceeded 1000 runs in a season 4 times.
- Scored 201* for Sussex v Somerset at Hove in 1896.
- Shared record English 7th-wkt stand of 344 with K.S. Ranjitsinhji for Sussex v Essex at Leyton in 1902.
- Carried his bat for 110* through a completed Sussex innings of 174 against Lancashire's A.W. Mold and J. Briggs at Manchester in 1894.

From 1881 until his death in 1944, a remarkable span of 63 years, Billy Newham served Sussex as a player, captain (1889 and 1891), secretary (1889–1907) and assistant-secretary. An entertaining fast-scoring middle-order batsman, he learned his cricket at Ardingly College and remained there as a master until 1887. Strongly built and of medium height, he was an exceptional player of fast bowling and especially adept at leg-side forces off the back foot. He was also a proficient cutter and drove powerfully on either side of the wicket. The only Shropshire-born cricketer to represent England before 1984, he played soccer for the Corinthians.

Billy Newham

Ref	Series	V	T	Venue	Result	Batting 1st No	R	HO	Batting 2nd No	R	HO	Ct
27/27	1887–88	A		Sydney	W-126	7	9	c	8	17	lbw	–

Career	M	I	NO	HS	R	Avge	100	50	Ct	St	Balls	R	W	Avge	BB	5w	10w	Rate
Test	1	2	0	17	26	13.00	–	–	–	–	–	–	–	–	–	–	–	–
F/c	368	643	43	201*	14657	24.42	19	74	183	–	1127	615	10	61.50	3-57	–	–	112.70

NEWPORT
Philip John

Worcestershire (1982 to date)
Boland (1987–88)

Born High Wycombe, Buckinghamshire 11 Oct 1962

NOTABLE FEATS

- Shared record Worcestershire 7th-wkt stand of 205 with G.A. Hick v Yorkshire at Worcester in 1988.

Philip Newport is a tall (6ft 3in), slim, right-arm fast-medium bowler and improving lower-order batsman whose all-round contributions of 85 wickets and 421 runs played a major part in Worcestershire's winning the 1988 Championship. Graduating from Buckinghamshire (1981–82), he made steady progress without giving too strong a hint of international potential until 1987. Then the arrival of Ian Botham inspired grander ambitions and no cricketer has worked harder at his technique and fitness. He credits Botham for the motivation and self-confidence which led to his ousting Richard Ellison as the best of our medium-fast bowlers who can swing the ball late. He took full advantage of a gentle England baptism against Sri Lanka and was awarded the Cornhill match award. The planned tour of India would have provided a perfect opportunity for consolidating his Test place.

Philip Newport

Ref	Series	V	T	Venue	Result	Batting 1st No	R	HO	Batting 2nd No	R	HO	Ct	Bowling 1st Balls	R	W	Bowling 2nd Balls	R	W
1103/651	1988	SL		Lord's	W-7w	9	26	c	–	–	–	–	126	77	3	159	87	4

Career	M	I	NO	HS	R	Avge	100	50	Ct	St	Balls	R	W	Avge	BB	5w	10w	Rate
Test	1	1	0	26	26	26.00	–	–	–	–	285	164	7	23.42	4-87	–	–	40.71
F/c	112	124	41	86	2173	26.18	–	6	35	–	15377	8536	319	26.75	8-52	16	2	48.20

NICHOLS
Morris Stanley

Essex (1924 to 1939)

Wisden 1934

TOURS

A 1929–30; WI 1928–29 (Cahn), 1931–32 (Tennyson); NZ 1929–30; I/SL 1933–34

Born Stondon Massey, Essex 6 Oct 1900
Died Newark, Nottinghamshire 26 Jan 1961

Percy Perrin deserves most credit for converting Stan Nichols from a specialist left-handed middle-order batsman into one of the best all-rounders of the 1930s. Noting his height and powerful physique, Perrin encouraged his development as an exceptionally accurate right-arm fast bowler with abundant stamina. So responsive was his pupil that he achieved the 'double' nine times, an output exceeded only by Rhodes, Hirst, Jupp and Astill. The Hitler war terminated a run of five successive 'doubles', deprived him of a second tour of India and ended his first-class career. Afterwards he played as a professional in the Birmingham league. He kept goal for Queen's Park Rangers.

Stan Nichols

NOTABLE FEATS

- Exceeded 1000 runs in a season 9 times and took 100 wickets 11 times, the latter being the Essex record. He completed the 'double' 8 times, including 5 seasons in succession (1935–39).
- Scored 205 for Essex v Hampshire at Southend in 1936.
- Took 9 wickets in an inns 4 times for Essex, notably 9 for 32 v Notts at Nottingham in 1936. His best match analysis was 15 for 165 for Essex v Gloucestershire at Gloucester in 1938 (he also scored 159).
- Hat-trick for Essex v Yorkshire at Leeds in 1931.
- Achieved the match 'double' for Essex 3 times, notably at Gloucester in 1938 (above).
- Held 5 catches in an innings for Essex v Sussex at Hove in 1926.

						Batting 1st			Batting 2nd				Bowling 1st			Bowling 2nd		
Ref	Series	V	T	Venue	Result	No	R	HO	No	R	HO	Ct	Balls	R	W	Balls	R	W
186/172	1929–30	NZ	1	Christchurch	W-8w	6	21	c	–	–	–	2	102	28	4	87	23	2
187/173			2	Wellington	D	6	78	*	6	3	*	–	120	66	0	54	22	1
188/174			3	Auckland	D	6	1	*	–	–	–	–	30	18	0	–	–	–
189/175			4	Auckland	D	6	75	b	3	7	*	–	114	45	1	–	–	–
197/183	1930	A	4	Manchester	D	8	7	*	–	–	–	–	126	33	2	–	–	–
229/203	1933	WI	3	Oval	W-I & 17	9	49	b	–	–	–	–	60	36	1	84	51	2
230/204	1933–34	I	1	Bombay[1]	W-9w	8	2	ro	–	–	–	3	140	53	3	143	55	5
231/205			2	Calcutta	D	8	13	lbw	–	–	–	3	168	78	3	120	48	1
232/206			3	Madras[1]	W-202	7	1	b	5	8	c	2	72	30	1	36	23	0
242/216	1935	SA	1	Nottingham	D	8	13	*	–	–	–	1	143	35	6	30	14	1
243/217			2	Lord's	L-157	9	10	c	9	7	*	–	126	47	2	108	64	1
244/218			3	Leeds	D	8	4	lbw	8	2	b	–	130	58	3	132	65	0
246/220			5	Oval	D	7	30	c	–	–	–	–	138	79	0	30	20	0
274/243	1939	WI	3	Oval	D	7	24	ro	–	–	–	–	272	161	2	–	–	–

Career	M	I	NO	HS	R	Avge	100	50	Ct	St	Balls	R	W	Avge	BB	5w	10w	Rate
Test	14	19	7	78*	355	29.58	–	2	11	–	2565	1152	41	28.09	6-35	2	–	62.56
F/c	483	756	85	205	17827	26.56	20	91	326	–	83746	39666	1833	21.63	9-32	118	23	45.68

OAKMAN
Alan Stanley Myles

Sussex (1947 to 1968)

TOURS
SA 1956–57; WI 1955–56 (Swanton)
Born Hastings, Sussex 20 Apr 1930

NOTABLE FEATS

- Exceeded 1000 runs in a season 9 times, including 2000 twice.
- Scored 229* for Sussex v Nottinghamshire at Worksop in 1961.
- Hat-trick for Sussex v Somerset at Hove in 1952.
- Twice held 5 catches in an innings for Sussex: v Glamorgan at Worthing in 1958 (7 in match) and v Lancashire at Hastings in 1961. He held 57 catches in 1958.

Alan Oakman was a fine all-round cricketer whose two-match Test career coincided with a brace of England wins by innings margins, his finale being 'Laker's Match' in which he caught five of the off-spinner's 19 wickets. At 6ft 6in he was one of the tallest England Test cricketers and probably the only one to have done his national service in the Grenadier Guards. As a calm front-foot batsman, he was in his element on hard pitches where he could employ his vast reach to drive. He was an effective right-arm off-break bowler, taking 99 wickets in 1954, and an outstanding catcher at slip or in the leg trap. His exceptional span proved a big advantage in the close fielding positions, as it did in his goalkeeping days with Hastings United. After retiring from Sussex he became a first-class umpire (1969) before joining Warwickshire, first as senior coach (1970–87) and currently as assistant-secretary. When Arthur Fagg, protesting about the dissent shown by the visiting captain, refused to umpire the first over of the third day's play in the 1973 West Indies Test at Edgbaston, Oakman deputised.

Alan Oakman

Ref	Series	V	T Venue	Result	Batting 1st No	R	HO	Batting 2nd No	R	HO	Ct	Bowling 1st Balls	R	W	Bowling 2nd Balls	R	W
427/329	1956	A	3 Leeds	W-I & 42	3	4	b	–	–	–	2	–	–	–	–	–	–
428/330			4 Manchester	W-I & 170	7	10	c	–	–	–	5	–	–	–	48	21	0

Career	M	I	NO	HS	R	Avge	100	50	Ct	St	Balls	R	W	Avge	BB	5w	10w	Rate
Test	2	2	0	10	14	7.00	–	–	7	–	48	21	0	–	–	–	–	–
F/c	538	912	79	229*	21800	26.17	22	101	594	–	48481	20343	736	27.63	7-39	31	2	65.87

O'BRIEN
Sir Timothy Carew (3rd Baronet)

Middlesex (1881 to 1898)
Oxford University (1884 to 1885)
Ireland (1902 to 1907)

TOURS A 1887–88; SA 1895–96
Born Dublin, Ireland 5 Nov 1861
Died Ramsey, Isle of Man 9 Dec 1948

Although very much an Irishman, Timmy O'Brien learned his cricket at Downside School and in London where his performances for the Kensington Park Club earned him a trial with Middlesex. He achieved little success until he decided to go up to Oxford with the sole ambition of furthering his cricket career by gaining a blue. Having soon made certain of that honour by scoring a match-winning 92 against the 1884 Australians, he suffered the ignominy of being bowled for nought in each innings of his first Varsity match. A second major contribution to another defeat of the tourists (for MCC) gained him his first England cap that same summer. A tall, powerfully built Irishman who sired 10 children, his approach to batting was founded on immense confidence and his exceptional ability as a full-blooded hitter. High on the list of his many remarkable and supremely entertaining innings was the epic hundred at Lord's in 1889 which snatched a sensational win against Yorkshire, his last 83 runs coming in 35 minutes. Aged 52 in his final first-class match he scored 90 and 111 for Lionel Robinson's XI against Oxford at Attleborough. He lived to be 87 and was the oldest England cricketer to have played in a home Test against Australia.

Lord Hawke's team in South Africa, 1895–96: standing E.J. Tyler, Sir T.C. O'Brien, A.M. Miller, T.W. Hayward, G.A. Lohmann; seated C.B. Fry, Hon. J.D. Logan, Lord Hawke (captain), C.W. Wright, C. Heseltine, A.J.L. Hill; in front S.M.J. Woods, H.R. Bromley-Davenport, H.R. Butt.

NOTABLE FEATS

- Exceeded 1000 runs in a season 3 times.
- Scored 202 for Middlesex v Sussex at Hove in 1895.
- Shared record Middlesex 5th-wkt stand of 338 in 200 min with R.S. Lucas v Sussex at Hove in 1895.

Ref	Series	V	T Venue	Result	Batting 1st No	R	HO	Batting 2nd No	R	HO	Ct
14/14	1884	A	1 Manchester	D	8	0	b	8	20	c	–
28/28	1888	A	1 Lord's	L-61	6	0	b	5	4	b	1
47/47*	1895–96	SA	1 Port Elizabeth	W-288	1	17	c	3	16	b	2
48/48			2 Johannesburg[1]	W-I & 197	1	0	b	–	–	–	1
49/49			3 Cape Town	W-I & 33	6	2	c	–	–	–	–

Career	M	I	NO	HS	R	Avge	100	50	Ct	St	Balls	R	W	Avge	BB	5w	10w	Rate
Test	5	8	0	20	59	7.37	–	–	4	–	–	–	–	–	–	–	–	–
F/c	266	452	30	202	11397	27.00	15	58	173	2	484	340	4	85.00	1-10	–	–	121.00

O'CONNOR, Jack

Essex (1921 to 1939)

TOURS
WI 1926–27 (Tennyson), 1928–29 (Cahn), 1929–30
Born Cambridge 6 Nov 1897
Died Buckhurst Hill, Essex 22 Feb 1977

Small, nimble-footed and from cricketing stock, Jack O'Connor was a very effective middle-order county batsman. Although he was an outstanding player of spin bowling and a fine driver and hooker, his open dislike of fast bowling rendered him prone to bouts of failure. His many successes, including 72 hundreds and a career average approaching 35, were ample compensation. He was also an unusual right-arm slow bowler whose repertoire included both off-spin and leg-breaks. The Second World War ended his Essex career but he coached first at Eton and later at Chigwell and, for two seasons (1946–47) appeared for Buckinghamshire. [*Illus. p.* 74]

NOTABLE FEATS

- Exceeded 1000 runs in a season 16 times, including 2000 on 4 occasions.
- Scored 2 double centuries for Essex, notably 248 v Surrey at Brentwood in 1934.
- Holds Essex records for most hundreds in a season (9 in 1934 – since equalled) and in a career (71).
- Shared in 3 record Essex partnerships: 333 (3rd wkt – since beaten) with R.M. Taylor v Northamptonshire at Colchester in 1937; 287 (5th wkt) with C.T. Ashton at Brentwood in 1934; and 206 with J.W.H.T. Douglas v Gloucestershire at Cheltenham.
- Hat-trick for Essex v Worcestershire at Worcester in 1925.

						Batting 1st			Batting 2nd				Bowling 1st			Bowling 2nd		
Ref	Series	V	T	Venue	Result	No	R	HO	No	R	HO	Ct	Balls	R	W	Balls	R	W
182/168	1929	SA	2	Lord's	D	4	0	b	6	11	c	–	–	–	–	–	–	–
190/176	1929–30	WI	1	Bridgetown	D	5	37	c	–	–	–	2	60	31	1	–	–	–
191/177			2	Port-of-Spain	W-167	5	30	c	3	21	c	–	–	–	–	24	9	0
193/179			4	Kingston	D	6	51	c	3	3	c	–	12	0	0	66	32	0

Career	M	I	NO	HS	R	Avge	100	50	Ct	St	Balls	R	W	Avge	BB	5w	10w	Rate
Test	4	7	0	51	153	21.85	–	1	2	–	162	72	1	72.00	1-31	–	–	162.00
F/c	540	903	79	248	28764	34.90	72	129	226	1	39784	18325	557	32.89	7-52	18	2	71.42

OLD Christopher Middleton

Yorkshire (1966 to 1982)
Northern Transvaal (1981–82 to 1982–83)
Warwickshire (1983 to 1985)

Wisden 1979
TOURS
A 1974–75, 1976–77, 1978–79; SA 1981–82 (SAB); WI 1969–70 (Norfolk), 1973–74, 1980–81; NZ 1974–75, 1977–78; I/SL 1972–73, 1976–77; P 1972–73, 1977–78; Z 1975–76 (Int W)
Born Middlesbrough, Yorkshire 22 Dec 1948

Chris Old began his career as a hard-hitting left-handed batsman who could bowl but he ended up succeeding Fred Trueman as Yorkshire's premier new-ball strike force. Tall (6ft 3in), he bowled right-arm fast-medium outswingers and break-backs using his height, a rhythmic approach and a classic side-on action to extract awkward bounce from the deadest pitches. When he was not bedevilled by injuries (he underwent major surgery to his knees in 1970 and 1971) his determination and stamina enabled him to bowl long spells upwind and in hot, steamy climates. His control of length and line was usually outstanding, as when he conceded only 41 runs during 41.4 overs against Pakistan at Leeds in 1978. At county level and against anything less than fast-medium he was a confident and belligerent striker whose driving was high class. But his back-foot defence was awkward and he never learned to cope with bouncers. He was an enthusiastic all-purpose fielder and a very safe catcher. Appointed captain of Yorkshire in 1981 at the height of their internal torment, he was summarily dismissed midway through the following season and made an acrimonious departure for Edgbaston. There his brief stay was plagued by an infinite variety of strains and maladies which led to Graham Gooch enlivening the dreary final stages of a Test match with a wicked impersonation of 'Chilly' which involved a dramatic clutching of the back as he was halfway through his run-up. An elder brother, Alan, also played cricket for Warwickshire and Durham as well as appearing at fly-half for England.

						Batting 1st			Batting 2nd				Bowling 1st			Bowling 2nd		
Ref	Series	V	T	Venue	Result	No	R	HO	No	R	HO	Ct	Balls	R	W	Balls	R	W
704/479	1972–73	I	2	Calcutta	L-28	8	33	*	8	17	*	1	156	72	2	126	43	4
705/480			3	Madras[1]	L-4w	8	4	c	8	9	c	1	120	51	0	54	19	2
706/481			4	Kanpur	D	8	4	lbw	–	–	–	2	144	69	4	66	28	0
707/482			5	Bombay[2]	D	9	28	c	–	–	–	1	128	78	3	18	11	0
719/483	1972–73	P	1	Lahore[2]	D	8	0	b	8	17	*	–	162	98	0	–	–	–
723/487	1973	NZ	2	Lord's	D	8	7	b	8	7	c	–	251	113	5	–	–	–
724/488			3	Leeds	W-I & 1	8	34	lbw	–	–	–	–	120	71	4	84	41	2
726/490	1973	WI	2	Birmingham	D	9	0	ro	–	–	–	–	180	86	3	84	65	1
731/492	1973–74	WI	1	Port-of-Spain	L-7w	8	11	c	8	3	c	–	124	89	3	18	18	0
732/493			2	Kingston	D	8	2	c	9	19	b	–	138	72	2	–	–	–
733/494			3	Bridgetown	D	8	1	c	8	0	b	–	168	102	0	–	–	–
734/495			4	Georgetown	D	9	14	c	–	–	–	–	78	32	0	–	–	–
739/497	1974	I	1	Manchester	W-113	9	12	c	–	–	–	–	96	46	1	96	20	4
740/498			2	Lord's	W-I & 285	8	3	b	–	–	–	–	126	67	4	48	21	5
741/499			3	Birmingham	W-I & 78	–	–	–	–	–	–	1	78	43	1	90	52	3
742/500	1974	P	1	Leeds	D	8	0	c	8	10	*	–	126	65	3	102	54	3
743/501			2	Lord's	D	8	41	c	–	–	–	1	30	17	0	84	39	0
744/502			3	Oval	D	9	65	lbw	–	–	–	1	177	143	0	12	6	1
751/504	1974–75	A	2	Perth	L-9w	9	7	c	9	43	c	–	182	85	3	–	–	–
755/508			6	Melbourne	W-I & 4	8	0	b	–	–	–	–	88	50	3	144	75	0
758/509	1974–75	NZ	1	Auckland	W-I & 83	8	9	*	–	–	–	1	56	17	1	–	–	–
760/511	1975	A	1	Birmingham	L-I & 85	9	13	c	8	7	c	1	198	111	2	–	–	–
762/513			3	Leeds	D	9	5	b	6	10	st	1	66	30	1	102	61	1
763/514			4	Oval	D	9	25	*	8	0	c	2	168	74	3	12	7	0
777/515	1976	WI	1	Nottingham	D	8	33	b	–	–	–	1	207	80	3	60	64	1
778/516			2	Lord's	D	8	19	b	9	13	ro	1	60	58	1	84	46	1
788/520	1976–77	I	1	Delhi	W-I & 25	8	15	c	–	–	–	–	77	28	2	24	6	0
789/521			2	Calcutta	W-10w	8	52	c	–	–	–	1	120	37	2	72	38	3
790/522			3	Madras[1]	W-200	9	2	c	8	4	c	2	78	19	2	30	11	0
791/523			4	Bangalore	L-140	8	9	lbw	8	13	lbw	1	72	43	0	60	19	1
803/525	1976–77	A		Melbourne	L-45	9	3	c	8	2	c	–	96	39	3	222	104	4
804/526	1977	A	1	Lord's	D	8	9	c	8	0	c	1	210	70	2	84	46	2
805/527			2	Manchester	W-9w	8	37	c	–	–	–	1	120	57	1	48	26	0
814/531	1977–78	P	1	Lahore[2]	D	7	2	c	–	–	–	–	168	63	1	32	18	0
817/534	1977–78	NZ	1	Wellington	L-72	8	10	b	8	9	lbw	–	240	54	6	72	32	1
818/535			2	Christchurch	W-174	9	8	b	5	1	b	–	112	55	0	56	9	1
825/537	1978	P	1	Birmingham	W-I & 57	8	5	c	–	–	–	1	136	50	7	150	38	1
826/538			2	Lord's	W-I & 120	9	0	c	–	–	–	–	60	26	1	90	36	0
827/539			3	Leeds	D	–	–	–	–	–	–	–	250	41	4	–	–	–
828/540	1978	NZ	1	Oval	W-7w	10	16	c	–	–	–	–	120	43	1	30	13	0
834/543	1978–79	A	1	Brisbane[2]	W-7w	10	29	*	–	–	–	–	79	24	2	136	60	2
884/561	1980	WI	5	Leeds	D	10	6	c	–	–	–	–	173	64	2	–	–	–
885/562	1980	A		Lord's	D	10	24	*	–	–	–	–	210	91	3	120	47	3
896/563	1980–81	WI	1	Port-of-Spain	L-I & 79	11	1	b	11	0	c	–	96	49	1	–	–	–
905/569	1981	A	3	Leeds	W-18	10	0	c	10	29	b	–	258	91	0	54	21	1
906/570			4	Birmingham	W-29	10	11	*	8	23	c	–	126	44	3	66	19	1

Career	M	I	NO	HS	R	Avge	100	50	Ct	St	Balls	R	W	Avge	BB	5w	10w	Rate
Test	46	66	9	65	845	14.82	–	2	22	–	8858	4020	143	28.11	7-50	4	–	61.94
F/c	379	463	91	116	7756	20.84	6	27	214	–	57822	25127	1070	23.48	7-20	39	2	54.03

Chris Old

C. M. OLD – TEST BOWLING SUMMARY

Series	V	M	Balls	R	W	Avge	BB	5w	10w	Rate
1972–73	I	4	812	371	15	24.73	4-43	–	–	54.13
1972–73	P	1	162	98	0	–	–	–	–	–
1973	NZ	2	455	225	11	20.45	5-113	1	–	41.36
1973	WI	1	264	151	4	37.75	3-86	–	–	66.00
1973–74	WI	4	526	313	5	62.60	3-89	–	–	105.20
1974	I	3	534	249	18	13.83	5-21	1	–	29.66
1974	P	3	531	324	7	46.28	3-54	–	–	75.85
1974–75	A	2	414	210	6	35.00	3-50	–	–	69.00
1974–75	NZ	1	56	17	1	17.00	1-17	–	–	56.00
1975	A	3	546	283	7	40.42	3-74	–	–	78.00
1976	WI	2	411	248	6	41.33	3-80	–	–	68.50
1976–77	I	4	533	201	10	20.10	3-38	–	–	53.30
1976–77	A	1	318	143	7	20.42	4-104	–	–	45.42
1977	A	2	462	199	5	39.80	2-46	–	–	92.40
1977–78	P	1	200	81	1	81.00	1-63	–	–	200.00
1977–78	NZ	2	480	150	8	18.75	6-54	1	–	60.00
1978	P	3	686	191	13	14.69	7-50	1	–	52.76
1978	NZ	1	150	56	1	56.00	1-43	–	–	150.00
1978–79	A	1	215	84	4	21.00	2-24	–	–	53.75
1980	WI	1	173	64	2	32.00	2-64	–	–	86.50
1980	A	1	330	138	6	23.00	3-47	–	–	55.00
1980–81	WI	1	96	49	1	49.00	1-49	–	–	96.00
1981	A	2	504	175	5	35.00	3-44	–	–	100.80
	A	12	2789	1232	40	3080	4-104	–	–	69.72
	WI	9	1470	825	18	45.83	3-80	–	–	81.66
	NZ	6	1141	448	21	21.33	6-54	2	–	54.33
	I	11	1879	821	43	19.09	5-21	1	–	43.69
	P	8	1579	694	21	33.04	7-50	1	–	75.19
Home		24	5046	2303	85	27.09	7-50	3	–	59.36
Overseas		22	3812	1717	58	29.60	6-54	1	–	65.72
Totals		46	8858	4020	143	28.11	7-50	4	–	61.94

NOTABLE FEATS

- 50 wickets in 15th Test (*741*); 100 wickets in 32nd Test (*804*).
- *825* Took 4 wickets in 5 balls in his 19th over (.WW no-ball WW1) to emulate the feat of M.J.C. Allom.
- Scored 100 in 37 min for Yorkshire v Warwickshire at Birmingham in 1977 (third-fastest in first-class cricket). It came off 72 balls, some bowled by occasional bowlers; his second 50 took 9 min. His full innings of 107 took 41 min.

OLDFIELD, Norman

Lancashire (1935 to 1939)
Northamptonshire (1948 to 1954)

TOURS
NZ 1938–39 (Cahn); I/SL 1949–50 (Cwlth); P 1949–50 (Cwlth)
Born Dukinfield, Cheshire 5 May 1911

'Buddy' Oldfield was a stylish opening batsman on the threshold of a long Test career when the Second World War arrived. An amazingly consistent and entertaining strokemaker, he made 1000 runs in his first season and continued in the same groove throughout his career with Lancashire. A little under average height, he was a quick-footed versatile player with a very sound defence. After two post-war summers in the league he moved to Northampton and set a new County record in 1949. Little escaped his alert fielding at gully. He became a first-class umpire (1954–65) and stood in two Test matches.

'Buddy' Oldfield

NOTABLE FEATS

- Exceeded 1000 runs in a season 11 times, including 2192 in 1949 (the Northamptonshire record until D. Brookes exceeded it by 6 runs in 1952).
- Scored 1066 runs in his debut season (1935).
- Shared Northamptonshire record 1st-wkt stand of 361 with V. Broderick v Scotland at Peterborough in 1953.
- Shared Lancashire record 3rd-wkt stand of 306 with E. Paynter v Hampshire at Southampton in 1938.

						Batting 1st			Batting 2nd			
Ref	Series	V	T	Venue	Result	No	R	HO	No	R	HO	Ct
274/243	1939	WI	3	Oval	D	3	80	c	3	19	c	–

Career	M	I	NO	HS	R	Avge	100	50	Ct	St	Balls	R	W	Avge	BB	5w	10w	Rate
Test	1	2	0	80	99	49.50	–	1	–	–	–	–	–	–	–	–	–	–
F/c	332	521	51	168	17811	37.89	38	100	96	–	190	121	2	60.50	1-0	–	–	95.00

PADGETT
Douglas Ernest Vernon

Yorkshire (1951 to 1971)

TOUR NZ 1960–61
Born Dirk Hall, Bradford, Yorkshire
20 Jul 1934

Rosy-faced and determined, Doug Padgett was a neat, orthodox batsman of average height (5ft 9in), equally at home opening or in the middle-order. Light footwork, good balance and a sound defensive technique made him a proficient player in all conditions and ideally suited to the coaching role he has fulfilled since his retirement. The youngest player to represent Yorkshire until 1981 when Paul Jarvis made his first appearance, he was a handy right-arm medium-pace change bowler and a sure catcher.

The Yorkshire side of 1962: standing *J.H. Hampshire, W.B. Stott, K. Taylor, D. Wilson, M. Ryan, D.E.V. Padgett, P.J. Sharpe;* seated *R. Illingworth, D.B. Close, J.V. Wilson (captain), F.S. Trueman, J.G. Binks.*

NOTABLE FEATS

- Exceeded 1000 runs in a season 12 times, including 2181 in 1959.

TEST NOTES

- *495* Bowled in 2nd inns: 0 for 8 (12 balls).

Ref	Series	V	T	Venue	Result	Batting 1st No	R	HO	Batting 2nd No	R	HO	Ct
495/367	1960	SA	4	Manchester	D	6	5	c	5	2	c	–
496/368			5	Oval	D	6	13	c	7	31	ro	–

Career	M	I	NO	HS	R	Avge	100	50	Ct	St	Balls	R	W	Avge	BB	5w	10w	Rate
Test	2	4	0	31	51	12.75	–	–	–	–	12	8	0	–	–	–	–	–
F/c	506	806	67	161*	21124	28.58	32	97	261	–	586	216	6	36.00	1-2	–	–	97.66

PAINE
George Alfred Edward

Middlesex (1926)
Warwickshire (1929 to 1947)

Wisden 1935
TOUR WI 1934–35
Born Paddington, London 11 Jun 1908
Died Solihull, Warwickshire 30 Mar 1978

After assisting Paddington's Droop Street School to win its league and cup in 1922, George Paine emulated his father and grandfather by joining the Lord's staff. He made five appearances for Middlesex in 1926, his eight wickets against Warwickshire prompting Sydney Santall to invite him to join the staff at Edgbaston. By 1934 he was heading the national first-class averages. Over 6ft tall, he was a left-arm leg-break bowler who used his height in a classic action. Although slower than Verity he was more defensive and spun the ball less. Highly professional, he used to practise assiduously by sticking white tape on the ball to show how much spin he was imparting. He became an effective lower-order batsman and a safe-handed slip but, from 1935, he began to be plagued with rheumatism. Three years later he forsook his county career (turning out in 1947 in an emergency) for league cricket. For many years he was coach and groundsman to Solihull School; later he became an expert on artificial pitches. He took many of the photographs adorning the facilities at Edgbaston. [*Illus. p.* 510]

NOTABLE FEATS

- Took 100 wickets in a season 5 times and was the leading bowler in 1934 with 156 wickets at 17.07.
- Two hat-tricks for Warwickshire: v Middlesex at Lord's in 1932 and v Glamorgan at Cardiff in 1933.

Ref	Series	V	T	Venue	Result	Batting 1st No	R	HO	Batting 2nd No	R	HO	Ct	Bowling 1st Balls	R	W	Bowling 2nd Balls	R	W
238/212	1934–35	WI	1	Bridgetown	W-4w	–	–	–	7	2	c	4	54	14	3	6	0	0
239/213			2	Port-of-Spain	L-217	11	4	lbw	3	14	lbw	–	156	85	2	252	109	3
240/214			3	Georgetown	D	4	49	st	3	18	c	1	198	63	2	42	28	2
241/215			4	Kingston	L-I & 161	4	0	lbw	7	10	*	–	336	168	5	–	–	–

Career	M	I	NO	HS	R	Avge	100	50	Ct	St	Balls	R	W	Avge	BB	5w	10w	Rate
Test	4	7	1	49	97	16.16	–	–	5	–	1044	467	17	27.47	5-168	1	–	61.41
F/c	258	349	62	79	3430	11.95	–	7	160	–	59044	23334	1021	22.85	8-43	74	13	57.82

PALAIRET Lionel Charles Hamilton

Oxford University (1890 to 1893)
Somerset (1891 to 1909)

Wisden 1893
Born Grange-over-Sands, Lancashire 27 May 1870
Died Exmouth, Devon 27 Mar 1933

Renowned as the most graceful strokemaker of his time, Lionel Palairet was also one of the most effective of opening batsmen. Tall, his upright and effortless style was the product of Repton School and Oxford; in each establishment he captained the last two of his four years in the team. He combined a sound defence with a full range of classic strokes and was a particularly handsome off-driver and cutter; at Taunton his drives into the churchyard and River Tone are well recorded. A fast and entertaining scorer, his world record opening partnership of 346 with the left-handed Herbert Hewett took only 3½ hours. 'Stork' was also an excellent fielder and a right-arm medium-pace bowler who, as a ten-year-old in a school match, took 7 wickets with successive balls; he could also bowl accurate underarm lobs. His international appearances coincided with two of the most dramatic Test match finishes in history. He captained Somerset in 1906 and was their president in 1929. An all-round sportsman, he gained a blue in the three-mile event and played soccer for the Corinthians.

NOTABLE FEATS

- Exceeded 1000 runs in a season 7 times.
- Scored 2 double centuries for Somerset, notably 292 v Hampshire at Southampton in 1896.
- Shared Somerset record 1st-wkt stand of 346 with H.T. Hewett v Yorkshire at Taunton in 1892 (highest Somerset partnership for any wicket and then the record for all first-class cricket).
- Carried his bat through a Somerset innings on 4 occasions.
- Scored 100 before lunch on 6 occasions; all 5 of his hundreds in 1901 were scored in the first session.

L.C.H. Palairet and H.T. Hewett after their record opening stand for Somerset against Yorkshire at Taunton, 1892.

Ref	Series	V	T	Venue	Result	Batting 1st No	R	HO	Batting 2nd No	R	HO	Ct
73/73	1902	A	4	Manchester	L-3	1	6	c	1	17	b	2
74/74			5	Oval	W-1w	2	20	b	2	6	b	–

Career	M	I	NO	HS	R	Avge	100	50	Ct	St	Balls	R	W	Avge	BB	5w	10w	Rate
Test	2	4	0	20	49	12.25	–	–	2	–	–	–	–	–	–	–	–	–
F/c	267	488	19	292	15777	33.63	27	83	248	15	8811	4849	143	33.90	6-84	2	–	61.61

PALMER
Charles Henry CBE

Worcestershire (1938 to 1949)
Leicestershire (1950 to 1959)
Europeans (1945–46)

Wisden 1954
TOURS SA 1948–49; WI 1953–54
Born Old Hill, Staffordshire
15 May 1919

NOTABLE FEATS

- Exceeded 1000 runs in a season 8 times, including 2071 in 1952.
- Scored 201 for Leicestershire v Northamptonshire at Northampton in 1953.
- Took 8 for 7 in 14 overs for Leicestershire v Surrey at Leicester in 1955; he took all 8 wickets (7 bowled) before conceding a run.

A trimly-built and bespectacled all-rounder of modest height (5ft 7½in), Charles Palmer began his 50-year association with first-class cricket at Worcester. His post-war appearances were curtailed by his duties at Bromsgrove School but, in 1950, he abandoned teaching and transferred to Leicestershire for an eight-season term (1950–57) as captain and secretary. It was a most successful move; 17th when he took over, Leicestershire rallied to an all-time high of third in 1953. Two hundreds for the Gentlemen at Lord's eventually earned him a place as player-manager on Hutton's tour of the West Indies and a Test cap at Bridgetown. An entertaining middle-order batsman whose timing enabled him to drive with surprising power, he was also a right-arm medium-pace swing bowler of exceptional accuracy who would occasionally revert to very slow donkey-dropping off-breaks.

Charles Palmer

His 8 for 0 in 1955 was one of the most remarkable spells in history. Since serving as chairman of Leicestershire, he has been president of MCC (1978–79) and chairman of the TCCB (1983–85); in 1986 his committee produced the Palmer Report.

					Batting 1st			Batting 2nd				Bowling 1st			Bowling 2nd		
Ref	Series	V	T	Venue	No	R	HO	No	R	HO	Ct	Balls	R	W	Balls	R	W
383/307	1953–54	WI	2	Bridgetown	6	22	c	6	0	c	–	–	–	–	30	15	0

Result: L-181

Career	M	I	NO	HS	R	Avge	100	50	Ct	St	Balls	R	W	Avge	BB	5w	10w	Rate
Test	1	2	0	22	22	11.00	–	–	–	–	30	15	0	–	–	–	–	–
F/c	336	588	38	201	17458	31.74	33	98	147	–	26621	9183	365	25.15	8-7	5	–	72.93

PALMER
Kenneth Ernest

Somerset (1955 to 1969)

TOURS
SA 1964–65; WI 1963–64 (Cav);
P 1963–64 (Cwlth)
Born Winchester, Hampshire
22 Apr 1937

Ken Palmer

Ken Palmer's Test career owed everything to his being in the right place at the right time; namely, coaching in South Africa when the MCC team touring there urgently required a replacement new-ball bowler for the final Test. Strongly built, a little above medium height (5ft 10½in), determined and hard-working, he was an effective middle-order batsman and a right-arm fast-medium bowler. Appointed to the first-class list in 1972, he is a much-respected umpire who has officiated in 17 Tests since 1978. His brother (another first-class umpire) and son also played for Somerset.

NOTABLE FEATS

- Exceeded 1000 runs in a season once and took 100 wickets 4 times, completing the 'double' in 1961.
- Contributed 125* to record Somerset 6th-wkt stand of 265 with W.E. Alley v Northamptonshire at Northampton in 1961.
- Took 9 for 57 for Somerset v Nottinghamshire at Nottingham in 1963.

						Batting 1st			Batting 2nd				Bowling 1st			Bowling 2nd		
Ref	Series	V	T	Venue	Result	No	R	HO	No	R	HO	Ct	Balls	R	W	Balls	R	W
575/414	1964–65	SA	5	Port Elizabeth	D	11	10	lbw	–	–	–	–	210	113	1	168	76	0

Career	M	I	NO	HS	R	Avge	100	50	Ct	St	Balls	R	W	Avge	BB	5w	10w	Rate
Test	1	1	0	10	10	10.00	–	–	–	–	378	189	1	189.00	1-113	–	–	378.00
F/c	314	481	105	125*	7771	20.66	2	27	156	–	44254	18485	866	21.34	9-57	46	5	51.10

PARFITT
Peter Howard

Middlesex (1956 to 1972)

Wisden 1963
TOURS
A 1962–63, 1965–66; SA 1964–65; NZ 1962–63, 1965–66; I/SL 1961–62, 1963–64; P 1961–62
Born Billingford, North Elmham, Norfolk 8 Dec 1936

Peter Parfitt

Joining Middlesex after a minor counties baptism with Norfolk, Peter Parfitt was chosen to play against Yorkshire. As he walked past the bowler, a certain Fred Trueman, to take guard at the Nursery End, he heard himself addressed. 'Good morning,' said FS affably, 'I hear you can hook!' A strongly built left-handed middle-order batsman of medium height (5ft 9in), he survived that encounter to enjoy a long and prosperous county career. His fortunes at Test level fluctuated from brilliant to mundane, possibly because he always seemed much happier on the front foot. Had he been three inches taller that technique would have been far more effective. He averaged 92 against Pakistan's bowlers and would have challenged most of Bradman's records if they had been England's sole opponents. An occasional right-arm off-break bowler, a fine all-purpose fielder and an occasional wicket-keeper, he captained Middlesex for 2½ seasons (1968–70). His youthful footballing skills earned him appearances for Norwich City. A confident chatty character, 'Parf' acquired the most extraordinary hybrid accent which was part Norfolk, part Old Kent Road and part Sloane Ranger. After a decade of owning a successful independent pub on the Yorkshire moors, he is heavily involved in event hospitality and has become a popular and convivial feature at major sporting occasions.

NOTABLE FEATS

- 1000 runs in 17th Test (*557*) (22 inns).
- *530* Shared record E v P 6th-wkt stand of 153* with D.A. Allen.
- *532* Shared record E v P 8th-wkt stand of 99 with D.A. Allen.
- *533* His third 100 in successive innings within a week against the tourists and his sixth in 7 innings against Pakistan bowling.
- *540* Shared record England 6th-wkt stand (all Tests) of 240 with B.R. Knight.
- Exceeded 1000 runs in a season 14 times (plus once on tour), including 2000 on 3 occasions.
- Scored 200* for Middlesex v Nottinghamshire at Nottingham in 1964.
- Scored 100 in each innings for Middlesex twice and, in 1962, scored 7 fifties in consecutive innings.
- Holds Middlesex record for most catches by a non-wicket-keeper in a season (46 twice – 1960 and 1966).
- Held 5 catches in an innings for MCC v SA Universities at Pietermaritzburg in 1964–65.

TEST NOTES

- *537* Deputised as wicket-keeper after J.T. Murray was injured catching W.M. Lawry in the early overs of the 1st inns.
- *563* Retired hurt after his first ball at 13–1 (2nd inns); resumed at 192–7.

Ref	Series	V	T	Venue	Result	Batting 1st No	R	HO	Batting 2nd No	R	HO	Ct	Bowling 1st Balls	R	W	Bowling 2nd Balls	R	W
516/378	1961–62	I	4	Calcutta	L-187	4	21	c	6	46	lbw	4	–	–	–	–	–	–
517/379			5	Madras[2]	L-128	6	25	c	6	33	c	3	66	22	1	66	24	1
518/380	1961–62	P	2	Dacca	D	7	9	c	–	–	–	1	–	–	–	48	14	0
519/381			3	Karachi	D	5	111	c	–	–	–	2	–	–	–	18	4	0
530/382	1962	P	1	Birmingham	W-I & 24	6	101	*	–	–	–	2	12	2	0	–	–	–
531/383			2	Lord's	W-9w	7	16	b	–	–	–	–	–	–	–	–	–	–
532/384			3	Leeds	W-I & 117	6	119	c	–	–	–	–	–	–	–	–	–	–
533/385			4	Nottingham	D	5	101	*	–	–	–	–	–	–	–	6	5	0
534/386			5	Oval	W-10w	5	3	c	–	–	–	3	–	–	–	–	–	–
535/387	1962–63	A	1	Brisbane[2]	D	7	80	c	6	4	c	–	–	–	–	–	–	–
537/389			3	Sydney	L-8w	6	0	c	6	28	c	–	–	–	–	–	–	–
540/392	1962–63	NZ	1	Auckland	W-I & 215	6	131	*	–	–	–	–	–	–	–	–	–	–
541/393			2	Wellington	W-I & 47	5	0	c	–	–	–	1	–	–	–	–	–	–
542/394			3	Christchurch	W-7w	6	4	lbw	3	31	c	5	–	–	–	–	–	–
555/402	1963–64	I	3	Calcutta	D	6	4	c	–	–	–	1	–	–	–	204	71	2
556/403			4	Delhi	D	5	67	c	–	–	–	–	30	7	0	114	81	1
557/404			5	Kanpur	D	5	121	lbw	–	–	–	–	180	61	1	162	68	1
562/406	1964	A	2	Lord's	D	5	20	lbw	–	–	–	4	–	–	–	–	–	–
563/407			3	Leeds	L-7w	5	32	b	3	6	c	1	–	–	–	–	–	–
564/408			4	Manchester	D	5	12	c	–	–	–	–	–	–	–	–	–	–
565/409			5	Oval	D	6	3	b	–	–	–	2	–	–	–	–	–	–
571/410	1964–65	SA	1	Durban[2]	W-I & 104	5	0	c	–	–	–	–	–	–	–	12	6	0
572/411			2	Johannesburg[3]	D	5	52	c	–	–	–	–	24	6	0	–	–	–
573/412			3	Cape Town	D	5	44	b	–	–	–	1	48	28	0	114	74	1
574/413			4	Johannesburg[3]	D	5	122	*	5	22	c	–	–	–	–	–	–	–
575/414			5	Port Elizabeth	D	8	0	lbw	–	–	–	2	–	–	–	–	–	–
592/416	1965	NZ	2	Lord's	W-7w	5	11	c	–	–	–	1	–	–	–	36	25	1
593/417			3	Leeds	W-I & 187	5	32	b	–	–	–	–	–	–	–	–	–	–
595/419	1965	SA	2	Nottingham	L-94	6	18	c	7	86	b	2	–	–	–	–	–	–
596/420			3	Oval	D	5	24	c	3	46	lbw	–	–	–	–	–	–	–
602/426	1965–66	NZ	1	Christchurch	D	6	54	c	6	46	*	–	18	14	0	36	5	2
603/427			2	Dunedin	D	6	4	c	–	–	–	2	–	–	–	102	30	1
604/428			3	Auckland	D	1	3	b	1	30	b	–	12	9	0	–	–	–
654/454	1969	WI	2	Lord's	D	3	4	c	3	39	c	–	6	8	0	–	–	–
700/475	1972	A	3	Nottingham	D	3	0	b	3	46	b	4	–	–	–	–	–	–
701/476			4	Leeds	W-9w	3	2	c	3	0	*	1	–	–	–	–	–	–
702/477			5	Oval	L-5w	3	51	b	3	18	b	–	–	–	–	12	10	0

Career	M	I	NO	HS	R	Avge	100	50	Ct	St	Balls	R	W	Avge	BB	5w	10w	Rate
Test	37	52	6	131*	1882	40.91	7	6	42	–	1326	574	12	47.83	2-5	–	–	110.50
F/c	498	845	104	200*	26924	36.33	58	144	564	–	18373	8401	277	30.32	6-45	5	–	66.32

P. H. PARFITT – TEST BATTING SUMMARY

Series	V	M	I	NO	HS	R	Avge	100	50
1961–62	I	2	4	–	46	125	31.25	–	–
1961–62	P	2	2	–	111	120	60.00	1	–
1962	P	5	5	2	119	340	113.33	3	–
1962–63	A	2	4	–	80	112	28.00	–	1
1962–63	NZ	3	4	1	131*	166	55.33	1	–
1963–64	I	3	3	–	121	192	64.00	1	1
1964	A	4	5	–	32	73	14.60	–	–
1964–65	SA	5	6	1	122*	240	48.00	1	1
1965	NZ	2	2	–	32	43	21.50	–	–
1965	SA	2	4	–	86	174	43.50	–	1
1965–66	NZ	3	5	1	54	137	34.25	–	1
1969	WI	1	2	–	39	43	21.50	–	–
1972	A	3	6	1	51	117	23.40	–	1
	A	9	15	1	80	302	21.57	–	2
	SA	7	10	1	122*	414	46.00	1	2
	WI	1	2	–	39	43	21.50	–	–
	NZ	8	11	2	131*	346	38.44	1	1
	I	5	7	–	121	317	45.28	1	1
	P	7	7	2	119	460	92.00	4	–
Home		17	24	3	119	790	37.61	3	2
Overseas		20	28	3	131*	1092	43.68	4	4
Totals		37	52	6	131*	1882	40.91	7	6

PARKER
Charles Warrington Leonard

Gloucestershire (1903 to 1935)

Wisden 1923
TOUR SA 1924–25 (Joel)
Born Prestbury, Gloucestershire
14 Oct 1882
Died Cranleigh, Surrey 11 Jul 1959

Charlie Parker

From the distance of more than half a century it is quite incomprehensible that a bowler with Charlie Parker's prolific wicket-taking record as a left-arm leg-spinner should have been selected for just one Test match. Only Rhodes and Freeman have exceeded his total of 3278 first-class wickets and no bowler has taken at least nine wickets in an innings more times. Introduced to the County by W.G. Grace, he made little impression before the Great War. Then his bowling reached a new dimension of accuracy, flight and venom. He became the epitome of Gloucestershire cricket, wheeling away with his high action at slow-medium pace on an immaculate length. With Goddard to provide complementary off-spin and Wally Hammond to catch even the half chances, it was a world-class combination – as the 1930 Australians discovered when, needing only 118 to win, they were held to a tie (Parker 7 for 54 in the final innings). On a pitch giving the slightest assistance he could be quite deadly. He was also a useful right-handed batsman who made over 500 runs in 1921. When he retired in his 53rd year, he had taken 100 wickets for the 16th successive season (1920–35). He then umpired for two summers before moving to Surrey, becoming coach to Cranleigh School and devoting more time to his other devotion – golf.

NOTABLE FEATS

- Took 100 wickets in a season 16 times, including 200 on 5 occasions, and in 1931 (during his 11th match) he equalled the earliest date to take 100 wickets (12 June).
- Holds Gloucestershire career records for most appearances (602), most wickets (3170), most instances of 100 wickets in a season (16) and most hat-tricks (6); and also their record match analysis: 17 for 56 (9 for 44 and 8 for 12) v Essex at Gloucester in 1925.
- Holds world record for most first-class wickets in 3 consecutive innings: 26 (9, 8, 9) in 1925.
- Took 15 or more wickets in a match 7 times, a tally exceeded only by A.P. Freeman. His 16 for 109 at Cheltenham in 1930 remains the best analysis against Middlesex.
- Took all 10 for 79 for Gloucestershire v Somerset at Bristol in 1929 and took 9 wickets in an innings on 8 other occasions – all for Gloucestershire. Bowled 8 batsmen in taking 9 for 87 v Derbyshire at Gloucester in 1922.
- Hit the stumps with 5 consecutive balls (unique first-class feat) in his benefit match v Yorkshire at Bristol in 1922 but the second was a no-ball. Also took 4 in 5 v Warwickshire at Bristol in 1920 to become the first to achieve this feat twice.
- Six hat-tricks (UK record equalled by D.V.P. Wright) for Gloucestershire, including a record 3 in the same season (1924) and 2 in the same match (v Middlesex at Bristol in 1924).
- Achieved the most expensive innings analysis in Championship matches: 6 for 231 in 63 overs v Somerset at Bristol in 1923.
- Bowled in an unchanged partnership with P.T. Mills throughout both completed Worcestershire innings at Gloucester in 1922.
- Twice bowled over 10,000 balls in a season (1926–27).

						Batting 1st			Batting 2nd				Bowling 1st			Bowling 2nd		
Ref	Series	V	T	Venue	Result	No	R	HO	No	R	HO	Ct	Balls	R	W	Balls	R	W
143/132	1921	A	4	Manchester	D	–	–	–	3	3	*	–	168	32	2	–	–	–

Career	M	I	NO	HS	R	Avge	100	50	Ct	St	Balls	R	W	Avge	BB	5w	10w	Rate
Test	1	1	1	3*	3	–	–	–	–	–	168	32	2	16.00	2-32	–	–	84.00
F/c	635	954	195	82	7951	10.47	–	10	248	–	157059	63817	3278	19.46	10-79	277	91	47.91

PARKER
Paul William Giles

Cambridge University (1976 to 1978)
Sussex (1976 to date)

Born Bulawayo, Southern Rhodesia
15 Jan 1956

Paul Parker

Paul Parker made an extraordinary entry into first-class cricket, his first ten scores as a Cambridge freshman being 0, 16, 8, 8, 2, 215, 0, 0, 40 and 148. To follow a scintillating double century by being dismissed for a 'pair' by Underwood must have provided an early and harsh object lesson in the fickleness of fortune and the hazards of his future career; certainly the sequence typifies the inconsistent scores which have prevented him from adding to his solitary England cap. Athletically built and a little above average height (5ft 10in), he is a very correct middle-order batsman with a pleasing style and a healthy appetite for sixes. Quick-footed against spin, he is also an extremely fast runner between the wickets. Although his right-arm change bowling (medium-pace or leg-spin) is seldom revealed nowadays, he deserves to be classed as an all-rounder because of his quite magnificent fielding in the covers and, on the evidence of his first season as captain of Sussex (1988), his above-average potential as a leader and tactician. The son of sports journalist John Parker, his dramatic start at Fenner's guaranteed him a blue in each of his three seasons at Cambridge but he unluckily missed a similar honour for rugby because of injury.

NOTABLE FEATS

- Exceeded 1000 runs in a season 8 times, including 1115 in his debut season (1976).
- Scored 215 for Cambridge U v Essex at Fenner's in 1976 in the sixth first-class innings of his career; it remains the highest innings for Cambridge since 1952.
- Hit 32 runs (466646) off one over from A.I. Kallicharran for Sussex v Warwickshire at Birmingham in 1982.

						Batting 1st			Batting 2nd			
Ref	Series	V	T	Venue	Result	No	R	HO	No	R	HO	Ct
908/572	1981	A	6	Oval	D	6	0	c	5	13	c	–

Career	M	I	NO	HS	R	Avge	100	50	Ct	St	Balls	R	W	Avge	BB	5w	10w	Rate
Test	1	2	0	13	13	6.50	–	–	–	–	–	–	–	–	–	–	–	–
F/c	285	486	68	215	14588	34.89	36	64	199	–	863	582	11	52.90	2-21	–	–	78.45

PARKHOUSE
William Gilbert Anthony

Glamorgan (1948 to 1964)

TOURS A 1950–51; NZ 1950–51
Born Swansea, Glamorgan 12 Oct 1925

Having learned his cricket at Wycliffe College, Gilbert Parkhouse honed his skills as a stylish opening batsman in wartime matches but Army duties afterwards delayed his first-class debut until 1948. Then the impact of his 1204 runs and exceptional catching close to the wicket played no small part in Glamorgan's first Championship. Impressive displays in his first two Tests guaranteed a place on Freddie Brown's antipodean tour but then the bubble burst. Illness and scant opportunities on that mission resulted in modest returns and caused the selectors to avert their eyes for the next eight summers. Even two good scores when he was recalled against the 1959 Indians could not prevent his file being closed permanently. Trimly built and a shade above medium height (5ft 10in), his speed and mobility as a fielder were also seen to advantage when he played rugby for Swansea. He coached Worcestershire in 1966 before accepting a similar appointment at Melville College, Edinburgh.

NOTABLE FEATS

- *476* Shared (then) record E v I 1st-wkt record of 146 with G. Pullar.
- Exceeded 1000 runs in a season 15 times, including 2243 in 1959 and 1204 in his debut season (1948).
- Scored 201 for Glamorgan v Kent at Swansea in 1956.
- Scored hundreds in 3 successive innings for Glamorgan in 1950.

BELOW LEFT *Gilbert Parkhouse; Arthur McIntyre keeping wicket.*

BELOW RIGHT *England taking the field against the Rest during the 1924 Test trial at Trent Bridge: R. Kilner, H. Sutcliffe, G.E.C. Wood, J.W. Hearne, J.B. Hobbs, A.E.R. Gilligan (captain), C.H. Parkin, P.G.H. Fender, M.W. Tate, E.H. Hendren, F.E. Woolley.*

						Batting 1st			Batting 2nd			
Ref	Series	V	T	Venue	Result	No	R	HO	No	R	HO	Ct
324/277	1950	WI	2	Lord's	L-326	5	0	b	5	48	c	–
325/278			3	Nottingham	L-10w	3	13	c	3	69	lbw	–
328/281	1950–51	A	2	Melbourne	L-28	5	9	c	6	28	lbw	1
329/282			3	Sydney	L-I & 13	5	25	c	5	15	ro	–
333/286	1950–51	NZ	2	Wellington	W-6w	3	2	b	3	20	c	1
476/356	1959	I	3	Leeds	W-I & 173	1	78	c	–	–	–	1
477/357			4	Manchester	W-171	1	17	c	1	49	c	–

Career	M	I	NO	HS	R	Avge	100	50	Ct	St	Balls	R	W	Avge	BB	5w	10w	Rate
Test	7	13	0	78	373	28.69	–	2	3	–	–	–	–	–	–	–	–	–
F/c	455	791	49	201	23508	31.68	32	129	324	–	229	125	2	62.50	1-4	–	–	114.50

PARKIN, Cecil Harry

Yorkshire (1906)
Lancashire (1914 to 1926)

Wisden 1924
TOUR A 1920–21
Born Eaglescliffe, Co. Durham
18 Feb 1886
Died Cheetham Hill, Manchester
15 Jun 1943

NOTABLE FEATS

- Took 100 wickets in a season 4 times, including 200 twice.
- Took 9 for 32 for Lancashire v Leicestershire at Ashby-de-la-Zouch in 1924 and 9 for 85 for Players v Gentlemen at The Oval in 1920. His best match analysis was 15 for 95 v Glamorgan at Blackpool in 1923.
- Bowled in an unchanged partnership with R.K. Tyldesley throughout both completed Warwickshire innings at Manchester in 1924.

Conjurer, juggler and comedian, Cecil Parkin was one of cricket's great eccentrics. When not entertaining the crowd or his fellow players with his humour and clowning, he found time to bamboozle batsmen with a highly unusual repertoire of right-arm spin. Trimly built and of average height, he was constantly experimenting. His basic delivery was the off-break, a ball which he bowled with every conceivable variation of flight, speed and angle. Intermingled were leg-breaks, high-flighted slower balls, quicker balls and top-spinners. If this unique armoury gave batsmen's minds little respite, it caused equal problems of field-setting for his captain. 'Ciss' played his early cricket on Tees-side while learning to be a pattern-maker. After taking 106 wickets in 16 matches as professional for Ossett, he made just one appearance for Yorkshire before they discovered that he had been born 20 yards outside the county border. Eight years of league and minor county cricket passed before, on the eve of the Great War, he celebrated his Lancashire debut with 14 Leicestershire wickets. It was not until 1921, after he had headed England's bowling honours in a disastrous series in Australia, that he played county cricket fulltime. Having been on the losing side in his first seven Tests, it was ironic that, immediately after his first taste of victory, his England career should end because he criticised his captain in a national newspaper. Two years later, a colourful disagreement with the Lancashire committee terminated his brief but highly productive first-class career and he returned to league cricket and his business in Blackpool.

Ref	Series	V	T	Venue	Result	Batting 1st No	R	HO	Batting 2nd No	R	HO	Ct	Bowling 1st Balls	R	W	Bowling 2nd Balls	R	W
135/124	1920–21	A	1	Sydney	L-377	10	4	*	10	4	b	–	161	58	1	213	102	3
136/125			2	Melbourne	L-I & 91	8	4	c	8	9	c	–	162	116	2	–	–	–
137/126			3	Adelaide	L-119	9	12	st	10	17	st	–	120	60	5	240	109	2
138/127			4	Melbourne	L-8w	10	10	ro	10	4	c	–	132	64	1	72	46	1
139/128			5	Sydney	L-9w	10	9	c	10	36	c	–	114	83	1	54	32	0
141/130	1921	A	2	Lord's	L-8w	9	0	b	9	11	c	2	120	72	2	54	31	1
142/131			3	Leeds	L-219	10	5	*	10	4	b	1	121	106	4	120	91	1
143/132			4	Manchester	D	–	–	–	2	23	c	–	178	38	5	–	–	–
144/133			5	Oval	D	–	–	–	–	–	–	–	138	82	3	–	–	–
153/139	1924	SA	1	Birmingham	W-I & 218	11	8	*	–	–	–	–	–	–	–	96	38	0

Career	M	I	NO	HS	R	Avge	100	50	Ct	St	Balls	R	W	Avge	BB	5w	10w	Rate
Test	10	16	3	36	160	12.30	–	–	3	–	2095	1128	32	35.25	5-38	2	–	65.46
F/c	197	239	33	57	2425	11.77	–	4	126	–	42080	18434	1048	17.58	9-32	93	27	40.15

PARKS, James Horace

Sussex (1924 to 1939)
Canterbury (1946–47)

Wisden 1938
TOURS
A 1935–36; NZ 1935–36; I 1937–38 (Tennyson)
Born Haywards Heath, Sussex 12 May 1903
Died Cuckfield, Sussex 21 Nov 1980

Jim Parks sr

Jim Parks senior was a fine county all-rounder, highly dependable and loyal but without that spark of genius which separates the highest class of cricketer. For one season, 1937, it appeared that he had moved into that loftier circle when, with an output of 3000 runs and a bag of 100 wickets, he achieved a 'double' which even a player combining the talents of Graeme Hick and Malcolm Marshall would fine hard to emulate. Stockily built, he was a sound and courageous batsman who excelled at the cut, a right-arm slow-medium inswing bowler and an outstanding close fielder. In those roles he performed yeoman service for Sussex until the War ended his career at the age of 36. Afterwards he played Lancashire league cricket before becoming coach first to Nottinghamshire (1953–57) and later at Hove. His younger brother, son and grandson have ensured that, 1977–79 apart, at least one Parks has been playing county cricket every summer since 1924.

NOTABLE FEATS

- Exceeded 1000 runs in a season 12 times, his only instance of 2000 or more being 3003 in 1937 when, with 101 wickets, he achieved a unique 'double'.
- Took 100 wickets in a season twice, completing the 'double' both times.
- Shared (then) Sussex record 1st-wkt stand of 368 with E.H. Bowley v Gloucestershire at Hove in 1929.
- Shared Sussex record 5th-wkt stand of 297 with H.W. Parks v Hampshire at Portsmouth in 1937.
- Carried his bat through a completed Sussex innings twice.

Ref	Series	V	T	Venue	Result	Batting 1st No	R	HO	Batting 2nd No	R	HO	Ct	Bowling 1st Balls	R	W	Bowling 2nd Balls	R	W
260/229	1937	NZ	1	Lord's	D	1	22	b	1	7	b	–	66	26	2	60	10	1

Career	M	I	NO	HS	R	Avge	100	50	Ct	St	Balls	R	W	Avge	BB	5w	10w	Rate
Test	1	2	0	22	29	14.50	–	–	–	–	126	36	3	12.00	2-26	–	–	42.00
F/c	468	758	63	197	21369	30.74	41	94	325	–	60819	22789	852	26.74	7-17	24	1	71.38

PARKS, James Michael

Sussex (1949 to 1972)
Somerset (1973 to 1976)

Wisden 1968
TOURS
A 1965–66; SA 1956–57, 1964–65; WI 1959–60, 1967–68; NZ 1960–61, 1965–66; I 1963–64; P 1955–56; Z 1972–73 (Int W)
Born Haywards Heath, Sussex
21 Oct 1931

Young Jim Parks (son of J.H.) had been an exceptionally gifted batsman and an outstanding cover-point for ten seasons, two overseas tours and one Test match before Sussex converted him into their regular wicket-keeper midway through the summer of 1958. So swiftly did he adapt to his new role that the following season he made 93 dismissals and scored 2313 runs. A little over average height (5ft 10½in) and comfortably built, he was an entertainingly free-flowing strokemaker who developed a very open stance in his later years. His superbly quick footwork and ability to hit over an inner ring of fielders with great precision made him the scourge of slow bowlers. His wicket-keeping began when he donned the gloves in an emergency. He was always adequate and when standing back, as he was required to do most of the time, he missed very little and was often brilliant; standing up, he improved steadily and was more efficient than he sometimes appeared to the distant onlooker. Like Ken Barrington, he was introduced too early to Test cricket and had to wait nearly six years for a second chance. Then, as with Ken Palmer, it was a case of being at hand on a coaching engagement when the touring England team needed a replacement for the final match. Literally seizing his chance with both hands, he kept wicket well and scored a match-saving century. That performance heralded the dawn of a long Test career in which his batting probably suffered as a result of his duties behind the stumps and his promising leg-spin bowling was seldom revealed. Appointed captain of Sussex in 1967, he resigned halfway through the following season when the added responsibility affected his form and health. After a short but successful interlude with Somerset and a convivial career representing a brewery, he returned to Hove in 1988 as marketing manager and immediately transformed the secretary's office into a hospitality suite.

TEST NOTES

- *389* A.J.W. McIntyre kept wicket.
- *547* D.B. Close deputised as wicket-keeper on the second morning.
- *554/5* J.G. Binks kept wicket.
- *557* Bowled in 2nd inns: 1 for 43 (36 balls).
- *598* K.F. Barrington deputised as wicket-keeper on the fourth day from the start of the innings until tea.
- *602* Bowled in 2nd inns: 0 for 8 (18 balls).

NOTABLE FEATS

- 1000 runs in 22nd Test (*571*) (34 inns).
- 50 dismissals in 24th Test (*573*); 100 dismissals and wicket-keepers' 'double' in 41st Test (*606*).
- *491* Shared record England 7th-wkt stand (all Tests) of 197 with M.J.K. Smith.
- *571* Shared record E v SA 6th-wkt stand of 206* with K.F. Barrington.
- *630* Became second England keeper after T.G. Evans to hold 100 catches in Tests (excluding 2 held in the field).
- Exceeded 1000 runs in a season 20 times, including 2000 on 3 occasions.
- Scored 205* for Sussex v Somerset at Hove in 1955.
- Equalled Sussex record with 6 dismissals in an innings v Worcestershire at Dudley in 1959.

						Batting 1st			Batting 2nd			Fielding 1st				Fielding 2nd			
Ref	Series	V	T	Venue	Result	No	R	HO	No	R	HO	Ct	St	Byes	Balls	Ct	St	Byes	Balls
389/313	1954	P	3	Manchester	D	6	15	b	–	–	–	–	–	–	–	1	–	–	–
491/363†	1959–60	WI	5	Port-of-Spain	D	7	43	c	8	101	*	–	1	6	717	1	1	0	312
492/364†	1960	SA	1	Birmingham	W-100	6	35	c	5	4	b	1	–	2	497	1	–	7	504
493/365†			2	Lord's	W-I & 73	6	3	c	–	–	–	3	–	0	261	3	–	0	342
494/366†			3	Nottingham	W-8w	6	16	ro	–	–	–	1	–	4	171	4	–	0	568
495/367†			4	Manchester	D	7	36	lbw	6	20	c	2	–	1	539	–	–	3	156
496/368†			5	Oval	D	7	23	c	5	17	c	–	–	6	1027	1	–	0	176
544/396†	1963	WI	2	Lord's	D	7	35	b	7	17	lbw	–	–	10	800	3	–	5	588
545/397†			3	Birmingham	W-217	7	12	c	7	5	c	–	–	0	414	3	–	0	207
546/398†			4	Leeds	L-221	7	22	c	7	57	lbw	2	–	4	988	1	–	0	403
547/399†			5	Oval	L-8w	7	19	c	7	23	lbw	1	–	0	625	–	–	4	570
553/400†	1963–64	I	1	Madras[2]	D	7	27	b	3	30	c	1	–	1	972	2	1	0	522
554/401			2	Bombay[2]	D	3	1	ro	5	40	*	–	–	–	–	–	–	–	–
555/402			3	Calcutta	D	5	30	lbw	–	–	–	–	–	–	–	1	–	–	–
556/403†			4	Delhi	D	7	32	c	–	–	–	1	–	0	888	–	1	5	990
557/404†			5	Kanpur	D	7	51	*	–	–	–	2	–	5	1093	–	–	5	798

Ref	Series	V	T	Venue	Result	Batting 1st No	R	HO	Batting 2nd No	R	HO	Fielding 1st Ct	St	Byes	Balls	Fielding 2nd Ct	St	Byes	Balls
561/405†	1964	A	1	Nottingham	D	7	15	c	5	19	c	2	–	0	461	1	–	0	56
562/406†			2	Lord's	D	7	12	c	–	–	–	–	–	8	504	–	–	8	444
563/407†			3	Leeds	L-7w	7	68	c	6	23	c	1	1	1	951	–	–	1	342
564/408†			4	Manchester	D	6	60	c	–	–	–	1	–	1	1535	–	–	0	12
565/409†			5	Oval	D	7	10	c	–	–	–	–	–	4	1065	–	–	–	–
571/410†	1965–65	SA	1	Durban[2]	W-I & 104	7	108	*	–	–	–	–	–	4	449	1	–	9	737
572/411†			2	Johannesburg[3]	D	7	26	lbw	–	–	–	–	–	0	959	1	–	4	840
573/412†			3	Cape Town	D	7	59	c	–	–	–	2	–	5	1076	2	–	1	715
574/413†			4	Johannesburg[3]	D	7	0	c	7	10	c	2	–	0	876	–	–	0	528
575/414†			5	Port Elizabeth	D	9	35	c	–	–	–	–	–	10	1135	–	–	1	360
591/415†	1965	NZ	1	Birmingham	W-9w	7	34	c	–	–	–	1	–	1	378	1	1	17	1054
592/416†			2	Lord's	W-7w	7	2	b	–	–	–	2	–	3	449	3	–	8	894
593/417†			3	Leeds	W-I & 187	–	–	–	–	–	–	3	–	5	529	–	–	0	504
594/418†	1965	SA	1	Lord's	D	7	32	ro	7	7	c	–	1	0	717	2	–	4	660
595/419†			2	Nottingham	L-94	8	6	c	9	44	*	2	1	0	609	–	–	4	664
596/420†			3	Oval	D	8	42	c	–	–	–	–	–	0	578	–	–	1	799
597/421†	1965–66	A	1	Brisbane[2]	D	6	52	c	–	–	–	2	–	0	1096	–	–	–	–
598/422†			2	Melbourne	D	7	71	c	–	–	–	2	–	2	861	–	1	1	1032
599/423†			3	Sydney	W-I & 93	8	13	c	–	–	–	3	2	7	673	–	–	3	483
600/424†			4	Adelaide	L-I & 9	7	49	c	7	16	ro	4	–	4	1008	–	–	–	–
601/425†			5	Melbourne	D	7	89	ro	–	–	–	1	–	6	1234	–	–	–	–
602/426†	1965–66	NZ	1	Christchurch	D	7	30	c	7	4	*	5	–	7	862	3	–	2	288
604/428†			3	Auckland	D	5	38	lbw	5	45	*	1	–	1	797	2	–	2	616
605/429†	1966	WI	1	Manchester	L-I & 40	6	43	c	6	11	c	1	–	8	919	–	–	–	–
606/430†			2	Lord's	D	6	91	lbw	5	0	b	3	–	2	564	2	–	0	798
607/431†			3	Nottingham	L-139	6	11	c	6	7	c	2	–	3	544	–	–	0	1068
608/432†			4	Leeds	L-I & 55	7	2	lbw	6	16	c	1	–	1	984	–	–	–	–
628/440†	1967–68	WI	1	Port-of-Spain	D	6	42	lbw	–	–	–	1	–	4	810	–	–	0	540
629/441†			2	Kingston	D	6	3	c	6	3	lbw	3	–	12	289	2	–	33	810
630/442†			3	Bridgetown	D	6	0	lbw	–	–	–	2	–	1	859	1	–	8	318

Career	M	I	NO	HS	R	Avge	100	50	Ct	St	Balls	R	W	Avge	BB	5w	10w	Rate
Test	46	68	7	108*	1962	32.16	2	9	103	11	54	51	1	51.00	1-43	–	–	54.00
F/c	739	1227	172	205*	36673	34.76	51	213	1088	93	3837	2235	51	43.82	3-23	–	–	75.23

Jim Parks jr, watched by wicket-keeper John Waite, hits Tayfield for six during the Fourth Test against South Africa, 1960.

J. M. PARKS – TEST SUMMARY

Series	V	M	I	NO	HS	R	Avge	100	50	Ct	St	Byes	Balls
1954	P	1	1	–	15	15	15.00	–	–	1	–	–	–
1959–60	WI	1	2	1	101*	144	144.00	1	–	1	2	6	1029
1960	SA	5	8	–	36	154	19.25	–	–	16	–	23	4241
1963	WI	4	8	–	57	190	23.75	–	1	10	–	23	4595
1963–64	I	5	7	2	51*	211	42.20	–	1	7	2	16	5263
1964	A	5	7	–	68	207	29.57	–	2	5	1	23	5370
1964–65	SA	5	6	1	108*	238	47.60	1	1	8	–	34	7675
1965	NZ	3	2	–	34	36	18.00	–	–	10	1	34	3808
1965	SA	3	5	1	44*	131	32.75	–	–	4	2	9	4027
1965–66	A	5	6	–	89	290	48.33	–	3	12	3	23	6387
1965–66	NZ	2	4	2	45*	117	58.50	–	–	11	–	12	2563
1966	WI	4	8	–	91	181	22.62	–	1	9	–	14	4877
1967–68	WI	3	4	–	42	48	12.00	–	–	9	–	58	3626
	A	10	13	–	89	497	38.23	–	5	17	4	46	11757
	SA	13	19	2	108*	523	30.76	1	1	28	2	66	15943
	WI	12	22	1	101*	563	26.80	1	2	29	2	101	14127
	NZ	5	6	2	45*	153	38.25	–	–	21	1	46	6371
	I	5	7	2	51*	211	42.20	–	1	7	2	16	5263
	P	1	1	–	15	15	15.00	–	–	1	–	–	–
Home		25	39	1	91	914	24.05	–	4	55	4	126	26918
Overseas		21	29	6	108*	1048	45.56	2	5	48	7	149	26543
Totals		46	68	7	108*	1962	32.16	2	9	103	11	275	53461

PATAUDI
Nawab of, Sr
(Iftikhar Ali Khan)

Oxford University (1928 to 1931)
Patiala (1931–32)
Worcestershire (1932 to 1938)
Western Indian States (1943–44)
Southern Punjab (1945–46)
India (1946)

Wisden 1932
TOURS A 1932–33; India to E 1946
Born Pataudi, India 16 Mar 1910
Died New Delhi, India 5 Jan 1952

The Nawab of Pataudi sr (left) and 'Gubby' Allen going out to bat against Australia during the First Test at Sydney, 1932–33.

The only cricketer to play Tests for both England and India, the senior Nawab of Pataudi was a tall (6ft) supple, stylish middle-order batsman who came to England via Chief's College in Lahore when he was 16. After coaching from Frank Woolley he went up to Oxford, failed to gain a blue in his first year and achieved little in his second until the Varsity match when he turned the tide with match-saving innings of 106 and 84. In his final year, he scored four successive hundreds on Oxford's tour before crowning his summer with a record 238* at Lord's. 'Pat' had vowed to beat Alan Ratcliffe's 201 made the previous day and after he had completed his task he collapsed from nervous and physical pressure. He also gained blues for hockey and billiards. Quick of foot and eye, he had a superb array of strokes and only ill health separated him from a long and illustrious career. After 1934 his appearances for Worcestershire became increasingly rare and his return as captain of the 1946 Indians caused much surprise. After that tour he virtually retired from cricket but had planned to return for some matches at Worcester in 1952. A few weeks after MCC had approved the renewal of his registration and when still only 41, he suffered a fatal heart attack while playing polo. He died on the 11th birthday of his son who was destined also to captain India, score a hundred for Oxford in his first Varsity match and enter *Wisden*'s hall of fame.

NOTABLE FEATS

- *220* Emulated his fellow Indian princes 'Ranji' and 'Duleep' by scoring 100 in his first Test against Australia.
- Exceeded 1000 runs in a season twice.
- His 238* for Oxford U v Cambridge U at Lord's in 1931 remains the highest score by either side in the University match. Scored 4 double centuries for Worcestershire, including 3 in 1933.
- Shared (then) record Worcestershire 2nd-wkt stand of 274 with H.H.I. Gibbons at Worcester twice: v Kent in 1933 and v Glamorgan in 1934.
- Scored 5 hundreds in 6 innings for Oxford U in 1931, including 4 in succession.

						Batting 1st			Batting 2nd			
Ref	Series	V	T	Venue	Result	No	R	HO	No	R	HO	Ct
For England												
220/194	1932–33	A	1	Sydney	W-10w	4	102	b	–	–	–	–
221/195			2	Melbourne	L-111	4	15	b	3	5	c	–
233/207	1934	A	1	Nottingham	L-238	4	12	c	4	10	c	–
For India												
276/8*	1946	E	1	Lord's	L-10w	6	9	c	6	22	b	–
277/9*			2	Manchester	D	7	11	b	3	4	b	–
278/10*			3	Oval	D	3	9	b	–	–	–	–

Career	M	I	NO	HS	R	Avge	100	50	Ct	Balls	R	W	Avge	BB	5w	10w	Rate
Test (E)	3	5	0	102	144	28.80	1	–	–	–	–	–	–	–	–	–	–
Test (I)	3	5	0	22	55	11.00	–	–	–	–	–	–	–	–	–	–	–
Combined	6	10	0	102	199	19.90	1	–	–	–	–	–	–	–	–	–	–
F/c	127	204	24	238*	8750	48.61	29	34	58	756	529	15	35.26	6-111	1	–	50.40

PAYNTER, Edward

Lancashire (1926 to 1945)

Wisden 1938
TOURS
A 1932–33; SA 1938–39; NZ 1932–33; I 1950–51 (Cwlth)
Born Oswaldtwistle, Lancashire 5 Nov 1901
Died Keighley, Yorkshire 5 Feb 1979

Eddie Paynter was a great-hearted left-handed batsman who earned a special niche in cricket history for his courageous innings at Brisbane on Jardine's tour. With England in some disarray and although suffering from acute tonsillitis, he left a nursing home sick bed, refused a runner and battled almost four hours for an epic 83; afterwards he insisted on fielding for a session and later struck the match-winning six which regained the Ashes. Despite usually beginning his innings in a crisis, he averaged an incredible 84.42 for his seven Tests against Australia and his overall Test average was almost 60. Small, wiry and extremely quick-footed, he was an aggressive batsman and an exceptionally fine player of spin. He would cut and hook short-pitched fast bowling and was a powerful driver. The loss of the top joints of the first two fingers on his right hand soon after leaving school did nothing to impair his brilliant work in the covers or, occasionally, behind the stumps; he was also a handy right-arm medium-pace change bowler. His relatively brief career as a Lancashire player was delayed until he was nearly 25, did not assume a regular footing until five years later and was terminated in its prime by the Second World War. When peace was restored he was 45 and he decided to play Saturday league cricket rather than return to the county circuit. He bade a spectacular farewell in a 1947 Festival, sneaked in a final first-class appearance when he was scoring for the Commonwealth team in India and became a first-class umpire the following summer (1951).

Eddie Paynter during his heroic innings at Brisbane, 1932–33.

						Batting 1st			Batting 2nd			
Ref	Series	V	T	Venue	Result	No	R	HO	No	R	HO	Ct
211/192	1931	NZ	3	Manchester	D	2	3	c	–	–	–	–
219/193	1932	I		Lord's	W-158	6	14	lbw	6	54	b	–
222/196	1932–33	A	3	Adelaide	W-338	7	77	c	10	1	*	–
223/197			4	Brisbane[2]	W-6w	8	83	c	6	14	*	–
224/198			5	Sydney	W-8w	8	9	b	–	–	–	–
225/199	1932–33	NZ	1	Christchurch	D	2	0	b	–	–	–	–
226/200			2	Auckland	D	4	36	b	–	–	–	–
260/229	1937	NZ	1	Lord's	D	5	74	c	–	–	–	1
261/230			2	Manchester	W-130	5	33	lbw	5	7	c	–
263/232	1938	A	1	Nottingham	D	5	216	*	–	–	–	2
264/233			2	Lord's	D	5	99	lbw	5	43	ro	1
265/234			4	Leeds	L-5w	5	28	st	5	21	*	–
266/235			5	Oval	W-I & 579	5	0	lbw	–	–	–	–
267/236	1938–39	SA	1	Johannesburg[1]	D	3	117	b	3	100	c	–
268/237			2	Cape Town	D	3	1	lbw	–	–	–	1
269/238			3	Durban[2]	W-I & 13	3	243	c	–	–	–	–
270/239			4	Johannesburg[1]	D	3	40	c	3	15	c	–
271/240			5	Durban[2]	D	3	62	lbw	5	75	c	2
272/241	1939	WI	1	Lord's	W-8w	3	34	c	3	32	*	–
273/242			2	Manchester	D	3	9	c	3	0	c	–

NOTABLE FEATS

- 1000 runs in 14th Test (*236*) (21 inns).
- *263* Shared record E v A 5th-wkt stand of 206 in 138 min with D.C.S. Compton. His 216* was then the record E v A score in England.
- *264* Shared record E v A 4th-wkt stand of 222 in 182 min with W.R. Hammond.
- *267* Became the fifth batsman to score 100 in each innings for England.
- *269* First to score 200 v A and SA; his 243 is the record score in E v SA Tests. Shared 3rd-wkt stand of 242 in under 2 hours with W.R. Hammond, the second 100 taking 52 min.
- Exceeded 1000 runs in a season 9 times (plus once on tour), including 2000 on 4 occasions – notably 2904 in 1937.
- Scored 322 for Lancashire v Sussex at Hove in 1937. His score was made out of 546 in 300 min and is the sixth-highest on the first day of any first-class match. He scored 6 other double centuries.
- Shared Lancashire record 3rd-wkt stand of 306 with N. Oldfield v Hampshire at Southampton in 1938.
- Contributed 158 (including 9 sixes) to the record total in South African first-class cricket: 676 by MCC v Griqualand West at Kimberley in 1938–39.
- Scored hundreds in 3 successive innings for Lancashire in 1936.
- Scored 154, 73 and 127 (in 85 min) in his final first-class innings in England – during the 1947 Harrogate Festival.

TEST NOTES

- *264* Deputised for L.E.G. Ames as wicket-keeper and caught B.A. Barnett.

Career	M	I	NO	HS	R	Avge	100	50	Ct	St	Balls	R	W	Avge	BB	5w	10w	Rate
Test	20	31	5	243	1540	59.23	4	7	7	–	–	–	–	–	–	–	–	–
F/c	352	533	58	322	20075	42.26	45	95	160	–	3101	1371	30	45.70	3-13	–	–	103.36

E. PAYNTER – TEST BATTING SUMMARY

Series	V	M	I	NO	HS	R	Avge	100	50
1931	NZ	1	1	–	3	3	3.00	–	–
1932	I	1	2	–	54	68	34.00	–	1
1932–33	A	3	5	2	83	184	61.33	–	2
1932–33	NZ	2	2	–	36	36	18.00	–	–
1937	NZ	2	3	–	74	114	38.00	–	1
1938	A	4	6	2	216*	407	101.75	1	1
1938–39	SA	5	8	–	243	653	81.62	3	2
1939	WI	2	4	1	34	75	25.00	–	–

Series	V	M	I	NO	HS	R	Avge	100	50
	A	7	11	4	216*	591	84.42	1	3
	SA	5	8	–	243	653	81.62	3	2
	WI	2	4	1	34	75	25.00	–	–
	NZ	5	6	–	74	153	25.50	–	1
	I	1	2	–	54	68	34.00	–	1
Home		10	16	3	216*	667	51.30	1	3
Overseas		10	15	2	243	873	67.15	3	4
Totals		20	31	5	243	1540	59.23	4	7

PEATE, Edmund

Yorkshire (1879 to 1887)

TOUR A 1881–82
Born Holbeck, Leeds, Yorkshire
2 Mar 1855
Died Newlay, Leeds 11 Mar 1900

Ted Peate's cricket career, like his life, was brilliant, incident packed and brief. A left-handed leg-break bowler with an easy delivery, he was extremely accurate without being a sharp spinner of the ball. Effective on most pitches, he could be unplayable on wet ones. For a few seasons he was the best slow bowler in England, probably in the world. As England's main hope of victory in the dramatic 1882 Test, he opened the bowling and claimed 8 wickets as Australia were dismissed for 63 and 122; even that fine performance could not prevent the tourists' 7-run victory or the Ashes from being conceived. Dismissed from Yorkshire during Lord Hawke's purge of the more wayward of his flock and despite putting on considerable weight, Peate continued to be very successful in Leeds club cricket. In poor health for some time, he died of pneumonia a few days after his 45th birthday. [*Illus. p.* 80]

NOTABLE FEATS

- Took 100 wickets in a season 6 times, including 214 in 1882.
- Two hat-tricks for Yorkshire: v Kent at Sheffield in 1882 and v Gloucestershire at Moreton-in-Marsh in 1884.
- Bowled in an unchanged partnership throughout both completed innings of a match on 4 occasions.

						Batting 1st			Batting 2nd				Bowling 1st			Bowling 2nd		
Ref	Series	V	T	Venue	Result	No	R	HO	No	R	HO	Ct	Balls	R	W	Balls	R	W
5/5	1881–82	A	1	Melbourne	D	11	4	*	11	2	ro	–	236	64	1	44	22	0
6/6			2	Sydney	L-5w	11	1	*	11	1	*	–	208	53	1	80	22	0
7/7			3	Sydney	L-6w	11	11	*	11	8	*	–	180	43	5	100	14	3
8/8			4	Melbourne	D	11	13	c	–	–	–	–	80	38	1	–	–	–
9/9	1882	A		Oval	L-7	11	0	c	11	2	b	–	152	31	4	84	40	4
14/14	1884	A	1	Manchester	D	11	2	b	11	8	*	–	196	62	3	–	–	–
15/15			2	Lord's	W-I & 5	10	8	*	–	–	–	1	160	85	6	64	34	0
16/16			3	Oval	D	11	4	*	–	–	–	1	252	99	2	–	–	–
22/22	1886	A	1	Manchester	W-4w	10	6	st	–	–	–	–	76	30	0	184	45	1

Career	M	I	NO	HS	R	Avge	100	50	Ct	St	Balls	R	W	Avge	BB	5w	10w	Rate
Test	9	14	8	13	70	11.66	–	–	2	–	2096	682	31	22.00	6-85	2	–	67.61
F/c	209	312	88	95	2384	10.64	–	3	132	–	45916	14515	1076	13.48	8-5	94	27	42.67

PEEBLES
Ian Alexander Ross

Middlesex (1928 to 1948)
Oxford University (1930)
Scotland (1937)

Wisden 1931
TOURS
SA 1927–28, 1930–31;
I 1937–38 (Tennyson)
Born Aberdeen, Scotland 20 Jan 1908
Died Speen, Buckinghamshire
27 Feb 1980

Ian Peebles

The only cricketer to make his first-class debut in the Gentlemen v Players fixture, Ian Peebles was a 19-year-old playing for Chiswick Park when he celebrated his new status at The Oval in 1927 by clean bowling Andrew Sandham to claim the first wicket of the match. He went on to play Test cricket for England before appearing for a county. A right-arm leg-break and googly bowler, he learned his skills at Glasgow Academy and, as a 13-year-old, was discovered by George Geary when Leicestershire visited Scotland and advised to try his luck in London. When he did, Aubrey Faulkner rewarded him with the secretaryship of his world famous cricket school and 'Plum' Warner gave him a similar post on MCC's tour of South Africa. By the time he began his 20-year association with Middlesex, he had played in four Tests and become a mature craftsman. Tall, with an easy run-up and a high flowing action, he cultivated deceptive flight and a well-disguised googly. Soon after taking 13 Cambridge wickets in his only Varsity match, he bemused, confounded and dismissed Bradman in the 1930 Old Trafford Test. His Oxford career ended when he accepted another MCC tour of the Union. In 1933 he toured North America with Sir Julien Cahn's team and took 70 wickets at 6 runs apiece. The strain of incessant bowling, particularly in the indoor nets where he attempted to relieve the problem by bowling left-handed, had taken heavy toll of his shoulder; his leg-break suffered and he was forced to rely more on the googly. Although his appearances for Middlesex became increasingly intermittent, he returned in 1939 as captain and led them to their customary second place. Severe damage to his right eye during a wartime air-raid virtually ended his career but happily he found time, despite his involvement in the wine trade, to reveal his talents as a witty and erudite cricket writer.

NOTABLE FEATS

- *207* Ended 1st inns with a spell of 5 for 18 in 9.5 overs, including 3 wickets with his last 5 balls.
- Took 100 wickets in a season 3 times.
- Only O.S. Wheatley and A.G. Steel (Cambridge U) have exceeded his total in an Oxbridge season of 70 first-class wickets for Oxford U in 1930.
- Hat-trick for Middlesex v Gloucestershire at Lord's in 1932.

						Batting 1st			Batting 2nd				Bowling 1st			Bowling 2nd		
Ref	Series	V	T	Venue	Result	No	R	HO	No	R	HO	Ct	Balls	R	W	Balls	R	W
168/154	1927–28	SA	1	Johannesburg[1]	W-10w	11	2	*	–	–	–	–	72	22	0	42	25	0
169/155			2	Cape Town	W-87	10	3	*	10	6	c	–	84	27	0	73	26	1
170/156			3	Durban[2]	D	10	18	*	–	–	–	–	96	69	3	66	29	1
171/157			4	Johannesburg[1]	L-4w	8	26	c	8	7	lbw	–	72	48	0	–	–	–
197/183	1930	A	4	Manchester	D	9	6	c	–	–	–	–	330	150	3	–	–	–
198/184			5	Oval	L-I & 39	11	3	*	11	0	*	–	426	204	6	–	–	–
204/185	1930–31	SA	1	Johannesburg[1]	L-28	9	0	b	11	13	*	–	84	43	4	42	41	0
205/186			2	Cape Town	D	10	7	*	7	0	b	1	168	95	0	–	–	–
207/188			4	Johannesburg[1]	D	8	3	c	10	2	c	–	233	63	6	162	86	1
208/189			5	Durban[2]	D	11	2	*	–	–	–	1	166	67	4	150	71	3
209/190	1931	NZ	1	Lord's	D	8	0	st	–	–	–	1	156	77	5	256	150	4
210/191			2	Oval	W-I & 26	–	–	–	–	–	–	2	72	35	0	132	63	4
211/192			3	Manchester	D	–	–	–	–	–	–	–	–	–	–	–	–	–

Career	M	I	NO	HS	R	Avge	100	50	Ct	St	Balls	R	W	Avge	BB	5w	10w	Rate
Test	13	17	8	26	98	10.88	–	–	5	–	2882	1391	45	30.91	6-63	3	–	64.04
F/c	251	330	101	58	2213	9.66	–	2	172	–	42849	19738	923	21.38	8-24	62	15	46.42

PEEL, Robert

Yorkshire (1882 to 1897)

Wisden 1889
TOURS
A 1884–85, 1887–88, 1891–92, 1894–95
Born Churwell, Yorkshire 12 Feb 1857
Died Morley, Yorkshire 12 Aug 1941

A remarkable all-round cricketer, Bobby Peel succeeded Peate and preceded Rhodes and Verity in Yorkshire's extraordinary lineage of world-class left-arm slow bowlers. In his early years he could only hold his place in the team through his magnificent fielding in the covers and his forceful left-handed batting. When Peate was dismissed, the small and sturdily built Peel was an ample replacement. From an easy round-arm action he imparted sharp spin at a pace approaching medium and maintained excellent control, supreme accuracy of length being the basis of his method. On a 'sticky' wicket he was nigh on unplayable – as the Australians (needing 64 to win with 8 wickets in hand) discovered at Sydney in 1894–95 (Test 42). Despite his many fine batting performances, he was the only player to be dismissed for a 'pair' in successive Test matches until Pat Pocock emulated his misfortune in 1984. He was at his peak and by some distance the best bowler of his type in England when his county career came to an abrupt end. A spectacularly inebriated interlude on the field at Bramall Lane left Lord Hawke with no option but dismissal.

NOTABLE FEATS

- 50 wickets in 9th Test (*30*); 100 wickets in 20th Test (*52*) – all v Australia.
- Exceeded 1000 runs in a season once and took 100 wickets 8 times, completing the 'double' in 1896.
- Contributed 210* to Yorkshire's 887 in 10 hr 50 min v Warwickshire at Birmingham in 1896; the highest and longest innings in county cricket, it was the first first-class match to include hundreds by 4 batsmen. His stand of 292 with Lord Hawke remains the 8th-wkt record for first-class matches in Britain.
- Took 9 for 22 (15 for 50 in the match) for Yorkshire v Somerset at Leeds in 1895.
- Hat-trick for Yorkshire v Kent at Halifax in 1897.
- Bowled in an unchanged partnership with E. Wainwright throughout both completed Sussex innings at Dewsbury in 1894.

Bobby Peel

					Batting 1st			Batting 2nd				Bowling 1st			Bowling 2nd		
Ref	Series	V	T	Venue	Result	No	R	HO	No	R	HO	Ct	Balls	R	W	Balls	R	W
17/17	1884–85	A	1	Adelaide	W-8w	10	4	b	–	–	–	1	164	68	3	161	51	5
18/18			2	Melbourne	W-10w	10	5	b	–	–	–	–	409	78	3	176	45	3
19/19			3	Sydney	L-6	10	8	*	10	3	c	2	128	51	0	80	24	1
20/20			4	Sydney	L-8w	10	17	*	10	0	c	–	124	53	1	36	16	1
21/21			5	Melbourne	W-I & 98	10	0	b	–	–	–	3	164	28	3	120	37	1
27/27	1887–88	A		Sydney	W-126	6	3	hw	6	9	st	–	75	18	5	132	40	5
28/28	1888	A	1	Lord's	L-61	7	8	ro	5	4	b	–	84	36	4	42	14	4
29/29			2	Oval	W-I & 137	8	25	b	–	–	–	–	32	14	1	114	49	4
30/30			3	Manchester	W-I & 21	8	11	lbw	–	–	–	–	106	31	7	64	37	4
33/33	1890	A	1	Lord's	W-7w	7	16	c	–	–	–	–	120	28	3	215	59	3
35/35	1891–92	A	1	Melbourne	L-54	6	19	b	6	6	b	1	258	54	3	101	25	2
36/36			2	Sydney	L-72	6	20	c	6	6	st	–	–	–	–	210	49	1
37/37			3	Adelaide	W-I & 230	6	83	c	–	–	–	3	–	–	–	–	–	–
39/39	1893	A	1	Lord's	D	6	12	c	9	0	*	1	110	36	0	–	–	–
42/42	1894–95	A	1	Sydney	W-10	6	4	c	6	17	b	2	318	140	2	180	67	6
43/43			2	Melbourne	W-94	6	6	c	6	53	st	–	84	21	1	241	77	4
44/44			3	Adelaide	L-382	7	0	b	7	0	c	2	96	43	0	204	96	4
45/45			4	Sydney	L-I & 147	8	0	st	6	0	st	–	144	74	3	–	–	–
46/46			5	Melbourne	W-6w	6	73	c	6	15	*	2	288	114	4	276	89	3
52/52	1896	A	3	Oval	W-66	8	0	b	8	0	b	–	100	30	2	60	23	6

Career	M	I	NO	HS	R	Avge	100	50	Ct	St	Balls	R	W	Avge	BB	5w	10w	Rate
Test	20	33	4	83	427	14.72	–	3	17	–	5216	1715	102	16.81	7-31	6	2	51.13
F/c	433	689	66	210*	12135	19.47	7	48	214	–	87711	28442	1753	16.22	9-22	121	33	50.03

R. PEEL – TEST BOWLING SUMMARY

Series	V	M	Balls	R	W	Avge	BB	5w	10w	Rate
1884–85	A	5	1562	451	21	21.47	5-51	1	–	74.38
1887–88	A	1	207	58	10	5.80	5-18	2	1	20.70
1888	A	3	442	181	24	7.54	7-31	1	1	18.41
1890	A	1	335	87	6	14.50	3-28	–	–	55.83
1891–92	A	3	569	128	6	21.33	3-54	–	–	94.83
1893	A	1	110	36	0	–	–	–	–	–
1894–95	A	5	1831	721	27	26.70	6-67	1	–	67.81
1896	A	1	160	53	8	6.62	6-23	1	–	20.00
Home		6	1047	357	38	9.39	7-31	2	1	27.55
Overseas		14	4169	1358	64	21.21	6-67	4	1	65.14
Totals		20	5216	1715	102	16.81	7-31	6	2	51.13

PENN, Frank

Kent (1875 to 1881)

TOUR A 1878–79
Born Lewisham, Kent 7 Mar 1851
Died Bifrons, Patrixbourne, Kent 26 Dec 1916

Frank Penn hit the winning boundary against Australia at The Oval in 1880 to end the first Test match played in England. The following year, when he was at his peak, a heart disorder prevented him from running and he was compelled to give up the game. He had been in the top flight of batsmen; a fine attacking middle-order player with a sound defence. He played his many strokes with great authority and was an extremely powerful leg-side hitter, particularly square. A magnificent fielder in the deep, he was an occasional right-handed round-arm slow bowler. Two years after progressing straight from club cricket into the first-class game he had become an automatic choice for the Gentlemen. He did much to help Lord Harris re-establish Kent cricket; in 1905 he was president of the club for which his two brothers and son also appeared. [*Illus. p.* 222]

						Batting 1st			Batting 2nd				Bowling 1st			Bowling 2nd		
Ref	Series	V	T	Venue	Result	No	R	HO	No	R	HO	Ct	Balls	R	W	Balls	R	W
4/4	1880	A		Oval	W-5w	6	23	b	4	27	*	–	–	–	–	12	2	0

Career	M	I	NO	HS	R	Avge	100	50	Ct	St	Balls	R	W	Avge	BB	5w	10w	Rate
Test	1	2	1	27*	50	50.00	–	–	–	–	12	2	0	–	–	–	–	–
F/c	98	172	14	160	4291	27.15	6	17	49	–	898	370	10	37.00	3-36	–	–	89.80

PERKS Reginald Thomas David

Worcestershire (1930 to 1955)

TOUR SA 1938–39
Born Hereford 4 Oct 1911
Died Worcester 22 Nov 1977

Reg Perks played his earliest cricket for Herefordshire before enjoying two teenage summers of minor counties cricket with Monmouthshire (1928–29). By the time he had qualified for Worcestershire and claimed Jack Hobbs as his first wicket, he was a confident right-arm fast-medium bowler and a bold, hard-hitting left-handed lower-order batsman. Tall, broad-shouldered, aggressive but always cheerful, he had a long approach, a high but slightly chest-on action and a distinctive follow-through; extremely accurate, he always attacked the stumps. Basically an inswing bowler, he could also move the ball away and break it in either direction off the pitch. Despite the loss of six peak summers to the Second World War, he took 100 wickets in a season 16 times, a tally exceeded only by Rhodes, Shackleton and Freeman. Having taken five wickets in the first innings of each of his only two Tests, it is fair to assume that war denied him a signifi-

Reg Perks

cant international career. In his final season (1955) Worcestershire appointed him as their first professional captain. A close friend of John Arlott, he was a popular and genial visitor to the Worcester commentary box.

NOTABLE FEATS

- Took 100 wickets in a season 16 times, notably 159 in 1939.
- Holds Worcestershire career records for most wickets (2143) and most instances of 100 in a season (15).
- Twice took 9 wickets in an innings for Worcestershire: 9 for 40 v Glamorgan at Stourbridge in 1939 and 9 for 42 v Gloucestershire at Cheltenham in 1946. His best match analysis was 15 for 106 v Essex at Worcester in 1937.
- Two hat-tricks for Worcestershire: v Kent at Stourbridge in 1931 and v Warwickshire at Birmingham in 1933.
- Hit 3 sixes off successive balls on 3 occasions, the bowlers being A.P. Freeman (1936), W. Murray-Wood (1936) and J.M. Sims (1948).

						Batting 1st			Batting 2nd				Bowling 1st			Bowling 2nd		
Ref	Series	V	T	Venue	Result	No	R	HO	No	R	HO	Ct	Balls	R	W	Balls	R	W
271/240	1938–39	SA	5	Durban²	D	11	2	*	–	–	–	–	328	100	5	256	99	1
274/243	1939	WI	3	Oval	D	11	1	*	–	–	–	1	245	156	5	–	–	–

Career	M	I	NO	HS	R	Avge	100	50	Ct	St	Balls	R	W	Avge	BB	5w	10w	Rate
Test	2	2	2	2*	3	–	–	–	1	–	829	355	11	32.27	5-100	2	–	75.36
F/c	595	884	150	75	8956	12.20	–	14	240	–	115719	53770	2233	24.07	9-40	143	24	51.82

PHILIPSON, Hylton

Oxford University (1887 to 1889)
Middlesex (1895 to 1898)

TOURS A 1891–92, 1894–95
Born Tynemouth, Northumberland 8 Jun 1866
Died Westminster, London 4 Dec 1935

Known as 'Punch', Hylton Philipson was an outstanding wicket-keeper batsman and a very fine all-round Etonian sportsman. At Oxford he was a blue in each of his three years and captain in his last; he also gained blues at racquets, tennis and soccer. He was in the top flight of keepers, standing up to most bowling and taking the ball with stylish timing. His batting fell away after Oxford but he had a good defence and plenty of front-foot strokes. A contemporary of Gregor MacGregor, he made only ten appearances for Middlesex. He later played for Northumberland. [*Illus. p.* 36]

NOTABLE FEATS

- Contributed 150 to a record Oxford U 7th-wkt stand of 340 with K.J. Key v Middlesex at Chiswick Park in 1887; it remains the highest Oxford partnership for any wicket. His stand of 160 with A.C.M. Croome v MCC at Lord's in 1889 remains the Oxford 8th-wkt record.

						Batting 1st			Batting 2nd			Fielding 1st				Fielding 2nd			
Ref	Series	V	T	Venue	Result	No	R	HO	No	R	HO	Ct	St	Byes	Balls	Ct	St	Byes	Balls
37/37†	1891–92	A	3	Adelaide	W-I & 230	9	1	c	–	–	–	–	–	5	257	–	1	3	408
43/43†	1894–95	A	2	Melbourne	W-94	10	1	c	10	30	b	2	–	0	335	–	–	5	823
44/44†			3	Adelaide	L-382	10	7	c	4	1	b	1	–	2	486	1	–	7	692
45/45†			4	Sydney	L-I & 147	9	4	c	9	9	c	1	2	3	500	–	–	–	–
46/46†			5	Melbourne	W-6w	10	10	*	–	–	–	2	–	3	892	1	–	5	740

Career	M	I	NO	HS	R	Avge	100	50	Ct	St	Balls	R	W	Avge	BB	5w	10w	Rate
Test	5	8	1	30	63	9.00	–	–	8	3	–	–	–	–	–	–	–	–
F/c	85	139	27	150	1951	17.41	2	7	103	47	–	–	–	–	–	–	–	–

PIGOTT
Anthony Charles Shackleton

Sussex (1978 to date)
Wellington (1982–83 to 1983–84)

TOURS NZ 1979–80 (Robins), 1983–84
Born Fulham, London 4 June 1958

NOTABLE FEATS

- *976* Took the wicket of B.A. Edgar with his seventh ball in Tests.
- Hat-trick for Sussex v Surrey at Hove in 1978 (his first first-class wickets).

Tony Pigott (right) receiving encouragement from Bob Taylor during his surprise appearance for England in New Zealand, 1983–84.

Like Ken Palmer in South Africa, Tony Pigott became a Test cricketer by virtue of being in the right place at the right time; when England, with Foster and Dilley injured, were seeking a replacement bowler for the Christchurch Test, he happened to be in New Zealand on an engagement with Wellington. He was also engaged to be married and had to postpone the ceremony in order to take part in a disastrous match which England lost in under 12 hours of actual play. A tall (6ft 1in) Harrovian, he is a determined right-arm fast-medium bowler and a hard-hitting lower-order batsman. Capable of bursts of dramatic hostility, his early performances for Sussex excited hopes of a new John Snow but persistent back injuries have hampered his progress.

						Batting 1st			Batting 2nd				Bowling 1st			Bowling 2nd		
Ref	Series	V	T	Venue	Result	No	R	HO	No	R	HO	Ct	Balls	R	W	Balls	R	W
976/596	1983–84	NZ	2	Christchurch	L-I & 132	9	4	lbw	9	8	*	–	102	75	2	–	–	–

Career	M	I	NO	HS	R	Avge	100	50	Ct	St	Balls	R	W	Avge	BB	5w	10w	Rate
Test	1	2	1	8*	12	12.00	–	–	–	–	102	75	2	37.50	2-75	–	–	51.00
F/c	156	185	41	104*	2934	20.37	1	11	74	–	21319	11880	417	28.48	7-74	18	1	51.12

PILLING, Richard

Lancashire (1877 to 1889)

Wisden 1891
TOURS A 1881–82, 1887–88
Born Bedford 5 Jul 1855
Died Old Trafford, Manchester 28 Mar 1891

Richard Pilling, 'the Prince of Wicket-Keepers', richly deserved that tag; he was considered to be the outstanding professional wicket-keeper of his era. Even when at the height of his powers, that exceptional amateur stumper, Gregor MacGregor, had to concede pride of place to Pilling. He took all types of bowling with casual elegance and minimal fuss. His dexterity and courage in standing up to the stumps to take a bowler of the high pace (and dubious action) of Lancashire's John Crossland was remarkable. Marvellously agile and quite brilliant on the leg-side, he rarely missed a stumping. He was at his peak and only 34 when inflammation of the lungs, contracted after playing soccer in 1889–90, compelled his retirement. Although Lancashire paid for him to convalesce in Australia during the following winter, he died six days after returning home.

Dick Pilling

NOTABLE FEATS

- Shared record Lancashire 10th-wkt stand of 173 with J. Briggs v Surrey at Liverpool in 1885.

Ref	Series	V	T	Venue	Result	Batting 1st No	R	HO	Batting 2nd No	R	HO	Fielding 1st Ct	St	Byes	Balls	Fielding 2nd Ct	St	Byes	Balls
5/5†	1881–82	A	1	Melbourne	D	10	5	c	10	3	b	1	2	4	948	–	–	9	220
6/6†			2	Sydney	L-5w	10	3	b	10	9	b	–	–	1	778	–	–	3	432
7/7†			3	Sydney	L-6w	10	12	b	10	23	b	2	–	6	688	1	–	2	179
8/8†			4	Melbourne	D	10	6	*	–	–	–	1	–	2	653	–	–	–	–
14/14†	1884	A	1	Manchester	D	10	0	c	10	3	b	1	–	0	520	–	–	–	–
22/22†	1886	A	1	Manchester	W-4w	11	2	c	–	–	–	1	–	0	549	1	–	3	473
27/27†	1887–88	A		Sydney	W-126	11	3	ro	11	5	b	1	1	6	151	1	–	2	278
30/30†	1888	A	3	Manchester	W-I & 21	11	17	c	–	–	–	–	1	2	210	–	–	2	125

Career	M	I	NO	HS	R	Avge	100	50	Ct	St	Balls	R	W	Avge	BB	5w	10w	Rate
Test	8	13	1	23	91	7.58	–	–	10	4	–	–	–	–	–	–	–	–
F/c	250	372	111	78	2572	9.85	–	2	461	206	–	–	–	–	–	–	–	–

PLACE, Winston

Lancashire (1937 to 1955)

TOURS
WI 1947–48; I/SL 1949–50 (Cwlth); P 1949–50 (Cwlth)
Born Rawtenstall, Lancashire 7 Dec 1914

Winston Place overcame the loss of six vital summers to the Second World War to emerge from the conflict as the ideal opening partner for Cyril Washbrook. Tallish (5ft 11in) and trimly built, he was a steady, reliable batsman with a sound technique who played the turning ball as well as he handled the new one. He combined application with a good sense of stroke selection and could offer the bonus of being a very safe fielder. His magnificent form of 1947 earned him a berth on the MCC tour of the Caribbean, where, after failing in his first five attempts for England, he scored a century in the final innings of the series. Surprisingly, he was ignored while all manner of desperate experiments were tried against the all-conquering 1948 Australians and he was never selected again. He became a first-class umpire in 1957. [*Illus. p.* 415]

NOTABLE FEATS

- Exceeded 1000 runs in a season 8 times, including 2501 in 1947.
- Scored 3 double centuries for Lancashire, notably 266* v Oxford U at The Parks in 1947.
- Scored hundreds in 3 consecutive innings for Lancashire in 1947.
- Shared 1st-wkt stand of 350* with C. Washbrook for Lancashire v Sussex at Manchester in 1947.

Ref	Series	V	T	Venue	Result	Batting 1st No	R	HO	Batting 2nd No	R	HO	Ct
295/258	1947–48	WI	1	Bridgetown	D	2	12	c	6	1	*	–
297/260			3	Georgetown	L-7w	3	1	c	3	15	b	–
298/261			4	Kingston	L-10w	3	8	st	3	107	st	–

Career	M	I	NO	HS	R	Avge	100	50	Ct	St	Balls	R	W	Avge	BB	5w	10w	Rate
Test	3	6	1	107	144	28.80	1	–	–	–	–	–	–	–	–	–	–	–
F/c	324	487	49	266*	15609	35.63	36	71	190	–	66	42	1	42.00	1-2	–	–	66.00

POCOCK, Patrick Ian

Surrey (1964 to 1986)
Northern Transvaal (1971–72)

TOURS
WI 1967–68, 1973–74; I 1972–73, 1984–85; P 1966–67 (MCC U-25), 1968–69, 1970–71 (RW), 1972–73; SL 1968–69, 1969–70, 1972–73, 1984–85
Born Bangor, Caernarvonshire
24 Sep 1946

There have been few more wholehearted, entertaining or friendly cricketers than 'Percy' Pocock. Tall (6ft 1in), thoughtful and talkative, he was an aggressive off-break bowler with a deceptive dipping flight. A frequently blistered spinning finger confirmed that he gave the ball a considerable tweak. Rather than adopt the metronome method of some off-spinners, he was always eager to experiment with changes of grip, angle, pace and flight. If he sometimes overdid that aspect of his bowling, he was more likely to take wickets quickly than his rivals – as Sussex discovered when he inflicted upon them one of the most dramatic spells of wicket-taking in first-class cricket with a world record 7 wickets in 11 balls, including 5 in one over. The boating disaster which separated Fred Titmus from four of his toes accelerated his promotion to the Test match scene. 'Percy's' first response was to consult a *Wisden* to see how many English off-spinners had taken 100 Test wickets. He came through that baptism with great credit in all departments and a few weeks later took 6 for 79 against Australia. It remained his best Test analysis but astonishingly it proved to be his only appearance in Ashes Tests. Grotesquely treated by the selectors, it was also the only home match in his first 15 games at this level. Recalled in 1984 after missing 86 Tests – only Les Jackson (96) has endured a longer wait – he emulated Bobby Peel in 1894–95 by bagging 'pairs' in successive England Tests. The selection of Chris Cowdrey that winter enabled him to become only the second England player after Wilfred Rhodes (who appeared with Fred and Maurice Tate) to play alongside two generations of a family. He was a popular and conscientious Surrey captain in his final season (1986).

NOTABLE FEATS

- 50 wickets in 18th Test (*992*).
- *632* Shared record E v WI 9th-wkt stand of 109 with G.A.R. Lock. Took 82 min to score first run – then the second-longest time on 0 in all first-class cricket.
- Took 112 wickets in 1967.
- Set world records for Surrey v Sussex at Eastbourne in 1972 by taking 6 wickets in 9 balls and 7 in 11 (including 4 in 4 and 5 in 6). Took 5 wickets in his final over – world record for any over in first-class cricket. Also took a hat-trick v Worcestershire at Guildford in 1971.
- Took 9 for 57 for Surrey v Glamorgan at Cardiff in 1979.

					Batting 1st			Batting 2nd				Bowling 1st			Bowling 2nd		
Ref	Series	V	T	Venue	No	R	HO	No	R	HO	Ct	Balls	R	W	Balls	R	W
630/442	1967–68	WI	3	Bridgetown	D	10	6	b	–	–	–	1	168	55	1	78	78	1
632/444			5	Georgetown	D	10	13	c	10	0	c	–	228	78	1	102	66	2
637/445	1968	A	1	Manchester	L-159	11	6	c	11	10	lbw	2	150	77	0	198	79	6
647/450	1968–69	P	1	Lahore[2]	D	10	12	b	10	1	b	3	60	39	1	96	41	0
703/478	1972–73	I	1	Delhi	W-6w	9	0	lbw	–	–	–	1	36	13	0	198	72	3
704/479			2	Calcutta	L-28	9	3	b	9	5	c	–	114	26	0	48	19	0
705/480			3	Madras[1]	L-4w	11	2	lbw	11	0	c	–	276	114	4	78	28	4
707/482			5	Bombay[2]	D	11	0	*	–	–	–	–	150	63	1	162	75	2
719/483	1972–73	P	1	Lahore[2]	D	11	5	c	–	–	–	1	144	73	0	90	42	1
720?484			2	Hyderabad	D	11	33	b	–	–	–	1	312	169	5	–	–	–
721/485			3	Karachi	D	6	4	c	–	–	–	1	228	93	2	–	–	–
731/492	1973–74	WI	1	Port-of-Spain	L-7w	9	2	b	9	0	c	–	258	110	5	96	49	1
732/493			2	Kingston	D	10	23	c	10	4	c	–	342	152	0	–	–	–
733/494			3	Bridgetown	D	10	18	c	–	–	–	–	168	93	0	–	–	–
735/496			5	Port-of-Spain	W-26	10	0	c	5	5	c	3	186	86	2	150	60	1
778/516	1976	WI	2	Lord's	D	11	0	*	3	3	c	–	18	13	0	162	52	1
779/517			3	Manchester	L-425	4	7	c	10	3	c	–	24	10	1	162	98	2
992/604	1984	WI	4	Manchester	L-I & 64	10	0	b	9	0	c	–	273	121	4	–	–	–
993/605			5	Oval	L-172	3	0	c	10	0	c	–	–	–	–	48	24	0
994/606	1984	SL		Lord's	D	10	2	c	–	–	–	–	246	75	2	174	78	1
1005/607	1984–85	I	1	Bombay[3]	L-8w	10	8	c	10	22	*	–	276	133	3	13	10	0
1006/608			2	Delhi	W-8w	10	0	b	–	–	–	2	198	70	3	232	93	4
1007/609			3	Calcutta	D	4	5	c	–	–	–	–	312	108	1	12	4	0
1008/610			4	Madras[1]	W-9w	–	–	–	–	–	–	–	42	28	0	198	130	1
1009/611			5	Kanpur	D	10	4	*	–	–	–	–	144	79	1	–	–	–

Career	M	I	NO	HS	R	Avge	100	50	Ct	St	Balls	R	W	Avge	BB	5w	10w	Rate
Test	25	37	4	33	206	6.24	–	–	15	–	6650	2976	67	44.41	6-79	3	–	99.25
F/c	554	585	156	75*	4867	11.34	–	3	186	–	100414	42648	1607	26.53	9-57	60	7	62.48

P. I. POCOCK – TEST BOWLING SUMMARY

Series	V	M	Balls	R	W	Avge	BB	5w	10w	Rate
1967–68	WI	2	576	277	5	55.40	2-66	–	–	115.20
1968	A	1	348	156	6	26.00	6-79	1	–	58.00
1968–69	P	1	156	80	1	80.00	1-39	–	–	156.00
1972–73	I	4	1062	410	14	29.28	4-28	–	–	75.85
1972–73	P	3	774	377	8	47.12	5-169	1	–	96.75
1973–74	WI	4	1200	550	9	61.11	5-110	1	–	133.33
1976	WI	2	366	173	4	43.25	2-98	–	–	91.50
1984	WI	2	321	145	4	36.25	4-121	–	–	80.25
1984	SL	1	420	153	3	51.00	2-75	–	–	140.00
1984–85	I	5	1427	655	13	50.38	4-93	–	–	109.76
	A	1	348	156	6	26.00	6.79	1	–	58.00
	WI	10	2463	1145	22	52.04	5-110	1	–	111.95
	I	9	2489	1065	27	39.44	4-28	–	–	92.18
	P	4	930	457	9	50.77	5-169	1	–	103.33
	SL	1	420	153	3	51.00	2-75	–	–	140.00
Home		6	1455	627	17	36.88	6-79	1	–	85.58
Overseas		19	5195	2349	50	46.98	5-110	2	–	103.90
Totals		25	6650	2976	67	44.41	6-79	3	–	99.25

Pat Pocock

POLLARD, Richard

Lancashire (1933 to 1950)

TOURS A 1946–47; NZ 1946–47
Born Westhoughton, Lancashire
19 Jun 1912
Died Westhoughton 16 Dec 1985

Dick Pollard was a tremendous trier who overcame his heavy flat-footed build to produce some fine performances as a right-arm fast-medium bowler. Tallish (5ft 11in), he had immense stamina and was extremely accurate with the skill to swing the ball late and break it off the pitch. He was just about at his peak when war was declared, having taken 149 wickets in 1938. After Army service, he returned with all his former determination and enthusiasm to paddle down that long run and celebrate his first England cap with a five-wicket analysis. He earned national acclaim for dismissing Bradman three times in first-class matches, including twice in successive Tests. Very much a tail-end batsman, he was capable of some mighty blows, as Sid Barnes would no doubt have confirmed having been stretchered away from short-leg after intercepting a full-blooded pull with his ribs (Test *301*). He reserved his lighter touch for his accomplished renderings on the piano. [*Illus. p.* 414]

NOTABLE FEATS

- *277* Took 4 for 7 in 5 overs as India collapsed from 124–0 to 170 all out.
- Took 100 wickets in a season 7 times.
- Two hat-tricks for Lancashire: v Glamorgan at Preston in 1939 and v Warwickshire at Blackpool in 1947.

						Batting 1st			Batting 2nd				Bowling 1st			Bowling 2nd		
Ref	Series	V	T	Venue	Result	No	R	HO	No	R	HO	Ct	Balls	R	W	Balls	R	W
277/245	1946	I	2	Manchester	D	9	10	*	–	–	–	2	162	24	5	150	63	2
284/252	1946–47	NZ		Christchurch	D	–	–	–	–	–	–	–	178	73	3	–	–	–
301/264	1948	A	3	Manchester	D	10	3	b	–	–	–	–	192	53	3	60	6	0
302/265			4	Leeds	L-7w	11	0	*	–	–	–	1	228	104	2	132	55	0

Career	M	I	NO	HS	R	Avge	100	50	Ct	St	Balls	R	W	Avge	BB	5w	10w	Rate
Test	4	3	2	10*	13	13.00	–	–	3	–	1102	378	15	25.20	5-24	1	–	73.46
F/c	298	328	63	63	3522	13.29	–	7	225	–	62328	25314	1122	22.56	8-33	60	10	55.55

POOLE, Cyril John

Nottinghamshire (1948 to 1962)

TOUR I/SL 1951–52
Born Forest Town, Mansfield, Nottinghamshire 13 Mar 1921

NOTABLE FEATS

- Exceeded 1000 runs in a season 12 times, notably 1860 in 1961.
- Scored 2 double centuries for Nottinghamshire, notably 222* v Indians at Nottingham in 1952.
- Scored 100 in 60 min for Nottinghamshire v Leicestershire at Nottingham in 1949, adding 251 in 91 min for the 2nd wkt with R.T. Simpson and finishing with 154* in 97 min.

Although he batted impressively in wartime matches, Cyril Poole had to wait until 1948 and the comparatively advanced age of 27 before he made his first-class debut for Nottinghamshire. A lively, chirpy character of middle height (5ft 9in) and wiry build, he was a fine aggressive left-handed middle-order batsman. A brilliant strokemaker with a sound defence, his exceptionally quick footwork enabled him to play spin bowling with ease, field with speed and agility in the deep and become a nimble footballer for Gillingham and Mansfield Town. His versatility even extended to left-arm medium-pace change bowling and emergency wicket-keeping. When Jack Ikin was forced to withdraw from MCC's first post-war tour of India, Poole was an obvious replacement and he responded by scoring two fifties in his first Test. In his later years he ran a pub beside the A1. [*Illus. p.* 223]

TEST NOTES

- *341* Bowled in 2nd inns: 0 for 9 (30 balls).

						Batting 1st			Batting 2nd			
Ref	Series	V	T	Venue	Result	No	R	HO	No	R	HO	Ct
341/294	1951–52	I	3	Calcutta	D	6	55	c	6	69	*	–
342/295			4	Kanpur	W-8w	7	19	b	–	–	–	1
343/296			5	Madras[1]	L-I & 8	6	15	b	6	3	c	–

Career	M	I	NO	HS	R	Avge	100	50	Ct	St	Balls	R	W	Avge	BB	5w	10w	Rate
Test	3	5	1	69*	161	40.25	–	2	1	–	30	9	0	–	–	–	–	–
F/c	383	637	42	222*	19364	32.54	24	127	224	5	550	347	4	86.75	1-8	–	–	137.50

POPE, George Henry

Derbyshire (1933 to 1948)

TOURS
I 1937–38 (Tennyson), 1949–50 (Cwlth); P 1949–50 (Cwlth); SL 1949–50 (Cwlth)
Born Tibshelf, Derbyshire 27 Jun 1911

NOTABLE FEATS

- Exceeded 1000 runs in a season 4 times and took 100 wickets 3 times, completing the 'double' twice.
- Contributed 207* to a record Derbyshire 7th-wkt stand of 241* with A.E.G. Rhodes v Hampshire at Portsmouth in 1948.
- Hat-trick for Derbyshire v Nottinghamshire at Ilkeston in 1947.

Tall (6ft 3in) and gangling, George Pope was the middle of three brothers who became Derbyshire professionals. He was a strong right-arm medium-fast bowler specialising in late inswing and a very capable hard-hitting but disciplined middle-order batsman. Having been selected for the cancelled 1939–40 tour of India, he managed to retain his fine all-round form in wartime games and afterwards appeared for England in all three 'Victory' matches. His Test chance came against the 1947 Springboks and although he managed only one wicket on a slow Lord's pitch it was one more than Alec Bedser took. The following autumn, after completing the 'double' for the second time, his wife's ill health compelled his retirement. Much later he returned to the scene as a first-class umpire (1966–74). It was in this role that he subsequently accompanied a private cricket tour of France and Germany. While sharing a Paris hotel room with him, this chronicler, seeking a nocturnal glass of water in an unlit bathroom, had an alarming introduction to the Pope dentures.

George Pope

Ref	Series	V	T Venue	Result	Batting 1st No	R	HO	Batting 2nd No	R	HO	Ct	Bowling 1st Balls	R	W	Bowling 2nd Balls	R	W
286/254	1947	SA	2 Lord's	W-10w	8	8	*	–	–	–	–	116	49	1	102	36	0

Career	M	I	NO	HS	R	Avge	100	50	Ct	St	Balls	R	W	Avge	BB	5w	10w	Rate
Test	1	1	1	8*	8	–	–	–	–	–	218	85	1	85.00	1-49	–	–	218.00
F/c	205	312	44	207*	7518	28.05	8	43	157	–	30781	13488	677	19.92	8-38	40	7	45.46

POUGHER
Arthur Dick

Leicestershire (1894 to 1901)

TOURS A 1887–88; SA 1891–92
Born Leicester 19 Apr 1865
Died Aylestone Park, Leicester 20 May 1926

Dick Pougher contributed many outstanding all-round performances to Leicestershire's earliest matches as a first-class county and was a member of the MCC playing staff for 23 seasons (1887–1909). A tall, loose-limbed right-arm fast-medium bowler, he had a high action and combined deadly break-backs with clever variations of pace, his slower ball usually drifting from leg. His sensational spell of bowling against the 1896 Australians caused them to be dismissed for the lowest total recorded by any touring team (18); they had already attained that figure when he was given the ball. Even that performance was insufficient to earn him a Test against the Old Enemy. He was a well-organised middle-order batsman and a capable fielder. After his playing days were over, he kept in touch with the game as landlord of the Old Cricket Ground Hotel at Aylestone Park. [*Illus. p.* 201]

NOTABLE FEATS

- Took 112 wickets in 1895 and scored 1121 runs in 1896.
- Achieved the match 'double' (scoring 5 and 109* and taking 6 for 29 and 8 for 60) in his initial first-class match for Leicestershire (v Essex at Leyton in 1894).
- Took 9 for 34 for an England XI v Surrey at The Oval in 1895.
- Took 5 for 0 in 15 balls for MCC v Australians (18 all out) at Lord's in 1896.
- Hat-trick for MCC v Cambridge U at Lord's in 1887.
- Twice bowled in an unchanged partnership with J.T. Hearne throughout both completed innings of a match.

Ref	Series	V	T Venue	Result	Batting 1st No	R	HO	Batting 2nd No	R	HO	Ct	Bowling 1st Balls	R	W	Bowling 2nd Balls	R	W
38/38	1891–92	SA	Cape Town	W-I & 189	7	17	b	–	–	–	2	105	26	3	–	–	–

Career	M	I	NO	HS	R	Avge	100	50	Ct	St	Balls	R	W	Avge	BB	5w	10w	Rate
Test	1	1	0	17	17	17.00	–	–	2	–	105	26	3	8.66	3-26	–	–	35.00
F/c	164	275	30	114	4555	18.59	5	13	98	–	25581	10179	535	19.02	9-34	31	7	48.37

PRICE
John Sidney Ernest

Middlesex (1961 to 1975)

TOURS SA 1964–65; I 1963–64
Born Harrow, Middlesex 22 Jul 1937

Tall (6ft 1in), sturdy and unflappable, John 'Sport' Price was a right-arm fast bowler with an idiosyncratic round-the-corner run of some length. To reduce the return journeys to his distant bowling mark in the intense heat of India, he adapted the theorem of Pythagoras so that he walked back along the shorter hypotenuse and ran in round the other two sides. It was an ingenious method which he retained for the rest of his career, leaving a trail of footprints like giant hockey sticks around the major grounds. His high, powerful body action generated great pace, swung the ball away and produced the occasional break-back. Had he applied himself more to his left-handed batting, he had the reach and range of strokes to have

approached all-round status. He made a stylish 53* against the 1969 West Indians and, opening the Lord's Taverners innings against Corfu, scored an epic hundred. A safe catcher in the deep, few have matched the power and speed of his flat returns from the boundary. His career was greatly restricted by injuries, mostly to his back, but some 13 years after his final match a congenital heart disorder was discovered which had astonishingly withstood his prolonged exertions as a fast bowler.

NOTABLE FEATS

• *688* Dismissed Wasim Bari and Asif Masood with successive balls but was denied a chance of the hat-trick when Pervez Sajjad was declared 'absent ill'.

John Price

						Batting 1st			Batting 2nd				Bowling 1st			Bowling 2nd		
Ref	Series	V	T	Venue	Result	No	R	HO	No	R	HO	Ct	Balls	R	W	Balls	R	W
554/401	1963–64	I	2	Bombay[2]	D	8	32	b	–	–	–	1	114	66	3	102	47	2
555/402			3	Calcutta	D	10	1	*	–	–	–	1	138	73	5	42	31	0
556/403			4	Delhi	D	11	0	b	–	–	–	–	138	71	1	54	36	1
557/404			5	Kanpur	D	–	–	–	–	–	–	–	97	32	2	60	27	0
564/408	1964	A	4	Manchester	D	10	1	b	–	–	–	2	270	183	3	–	–	–
565/409			5	Oval	D	11	0	*	–	–	–	–	126	67	1	–	–	–
571/410	1964–65	SA	1	Durban[2]	W-I & 104	–	–	–	–	–	–	1	36	19	1	54	7	1
572/411			2	Johannesburg[3]	D	11	0	b	–	–	–	1	192	66	2	90	49	0
573/412			3	Cape Town	D	11	0	*	–	–	–	–	204	133	0	66	19	1
574/413			4	Johannesburg[3]	D	11	0	c	–	–	–	–	102	68	2	84	56	1
688/468	1971	P	2	Lord's	D	–	–	–	–	–	–	–	70	29	3	–	–	–
690/470	1971	I	1	Lord's	D	11	5	*	11	0	c	1	150	46	2	24	26	1
691/471			2	Manchester	D	11	0	ro	–	–	–	–	132	44	2	60	30	2
692/472			3	Oval	L-4w	11	1	*	11	3	lbw	–	90	51	1	30	10	0
699/474	1972	A	2	Lord's	L-8w	11	4	*	11	19	c	–	157	87	2	42	28	1

Career	M	I	NO	HS	R	Avge	100	50	Ct	St	Balls	R	W	Avge	BB	5w	10w	Rate
Test	15	15	6	32	66	7.33	–	–	7	–	2724	1401	40	35.02	5-73	1	–	68.10
F/c	279	223	91	53*	1108	8.39	–	1	103	–	42295	19221	817	23.52	8-48	26	4	51.76

PRICE
Wilfred Frederick Frank

Middlesex (1926 to 1947)

TOUR WI 1929–30
Born Westminster, London 25 Apr 1902
Died Hendon, Middlesex 13 Jan 1969

A highly skilled wicket-keeper, especially strong on the leg-side, Fred Price was unlucky to be a contemporary of Les Ames. In 1937 he set a world record by holding seven catches in an innings. His batting developed to such an extent that he frequently went in first for Middlesex and, in 1934, scored 92 and 107 against Kent. As a first-class umpire (1949–67) he was quite fearless and caused a sensation by being the first to call Tony Lock for throwing. He stood in eight Tests.

NOTABLE FEATS

• Scored 1298 runs in 1934.
• Shared 5th-wkt stand of 332 with E.H. Hendren for Middlesex v Worcestershire at Dudley in 1933.
• Held 7 catches in an innings for Middlesex v Yorkshire at Lord's in 1937 – then the world first-class record and still the record for Middlesex. Made 6 dismissals in an inns on 2 other occasions.

Fred Price behind the stumps for Middlesex in 1939; Bill Edrich at slip.

Ref	Series	V	T Venue	Result	Batting 1st No	Batting 1st R	Batting 1st HO	Batting 2nd No	Batting 2nd R	Batting 2nd HO	Fielding 1st Ct	Fielding 1st St	Fielding 1st Byes	Fielding 1st Balls	Fielding 2nd Ct	Fielding 2nd St	Fielding 2nd Byes	Fielding 2nd Balls
265/234 †	1938	A	4 Leeds	L-5w	7	0	c	7	6	lbw	2	–	2	592	–	–	4	195

Career	M	I	NO	HS	R	Avge	100	50	Ct	St	Balls	R	W	Avge	BB	5w	10w	Rate
Test	1	2	0	6	6	3.00	–	–	2	–	–	–	–	–	–	–	–	–
F/c	402	590	97	111	9035	18.32	3	35	666	321	–	–	–	–	–	–	–	–

PRIDEAUX
Roger Malcolm

Cambridge University (1958 to 1960)
Kent (1960 to 1961)
Northamptonshire (1962 to 1970)
Sussex (1971 to 1973)
Orange Free State
(1971–72 to 1974–75)

TOURS
NZ 1960–61; P 1967–68 (Cwlth), 1968–69; SL 1968–69
Born Chelsea, London 13 Jul 1939

An authoritative batsman with a fluent style, Roger Prideaux combined the soundest of defences with a fine range of attractive strokes. Although probably best suited to opening the innings, he proved during his three-year stay with Sussex that he was just as effective batting a place lower. Tall (6ft 2in) and broad-shouldered, he had an upright method and was happier operating off his front foot. After an impressive career at Tonbridge, he gained blues in each of his three years at Cambridge and, in his final summer, amassed the second-highest aggregate then achieved at either place. He was captain for his last four seasons at Northampton (1967–70). It was Prideaux who set in motion the extraordinary chain of events which led to the 'D'Oliveira Affair'; when he withdrew from the team for the final Test of 1968, he enabled the selectors to recall the Worcestershire all-rounder. A right-arm medium-pace change bowler, he is unique in limiting his Test match output to two maiden overs.

NOTABLE FEATS

- Exceeded 1000 runs in a season 13 times, notably 1993 in 1968.
- His aggregate of 1311 runs for Cambridge in 1960 was then the second-highest in a season for either university.
- Scored 202* for Northamptonshire v Oxford U at Oxford in 1963.
- Scored 100 in 52 min for North v South at Blackpool in 1961.
- Scored hundreds in 3 consecutive innings for Northamptonshire in 1966 and made 100 in each innings of a match twice.

TEST NOTES

- *647* Bowled in 2nd inns: 0 for 0 (12 balls).

Roger Prideaux

Ref	Series	V	T Venue	Result	Batting 1st No	Batting 1st R	Batting 1st HO	Batting 2nd No	Batting 2nd R	Batting 2nd HO	Ct
640/448	1968	A	4 Leeds	D	2	64	c	2	2	b	–
647/450	1968–69	P	1 Lahore[2]	D	2	9	c	2	5	b	–
648/451			2 Dacca	D	2	4	c	2	18	*	–

Career	M	I	NO	HS	R	Avge	100	50	Ct	St	Balls	R	W	Avge	BB	5w	10w	Rate
Test	3	6	1	64	102	20.40	–	1	–	–	12	0	0	–	–	–	–	–
F/c	446	808	75	202*	25136	34.29	41	130	303	–	333	176	3	58.66	2-13	–	–	111.00

PRINGLE
Derek Raymond

Essex (1978 to date)
Cambridge University (1979 to 1982)

TOURS A 1982–83; SL 1985–86 (Eng B)
Born Nairobi, Kenya 18 Sep 1958

Very tall (6ft 4½in) and comfortably built, Derek Pringle is a highly intelligent all-round cricketer who is still sufficiently young to improve even further. So impressive was his form for Felsted School and Cambridge that he was selected for England during the last of his four summers at Fenner's; in order to appear in his second Test match, he had to forfeit the honour of captaining the Light Blues at Lord's and allow them to win without him. The son of Don Pringle, tragically killed in a car accident soon after representing East Africa in the first World Cup, he has matured rapidly under Keith Fletcher's influence at Essex. His bowling – right-arm medium-fast with a high, classic action to extract awkward bounce – has gained considerable control and he has learned to adapt his pace and length to the demands of different pitches. His 5-wicket analysis against West Indies at Leeds in 1988 was the just reward for a thoroughly professional effort. His batting has not developed so significantly. A hard-hitting and somewhat flamboyant strokemaker in his Cambridge days, he has become more restricted and introvert. His determination and natural ability should improve his technique against spin and redress the balance between defence and attack. He has the flair and tactical acumen to be a notable captain.

Derek Pringle

TEST NOTES

• *1102* Deputised for G.A. Gooch as captain after 1 over of the 2nd inns.

						Batting 1st			Batting 2nd				Bowling 1st			Bowling 2nd		
Ref	Series	V	T	Venue	Result	No	R	HO	No	R	HO	Ct	Balls	R	W	Balls	R	W
928/580	1982	I	1	Lord's	W-7w	7	7	c	–	–	–	–	54	16	2	114	58	2
929/581			2	Manchester	D	8	23	st	–	–	–	–	90	33	1	–	–	–
930/582			3	Oval	D	7	9	st	–	–	–	–	168	80	0	66	32	2
932/584	1982	P	2	Lord's	L-10w	7	5	c	7	14	c	–	156	62	0	–	–	–
938/586	1982–83	A	1	Perth	D	8	0	b	9	47	*	–	60	37	0	12	3	0
940/588			3	Adelaide	L-8w	9	1	*	8	9	c	–	198	97	2	11	11	0
941/589			4	Melbourne	W-3	8	9	c	8	42	c	–	90	40	1	72	26	1
989/601	1984	WI	1	Birmingham	L-I & 180	8	4	c	8	46	*	1	186	108	5	–	–	–
990/602			2	Lord's	L-9w	9	2	lbw	9	8	lbw	1	66	54	0	48	44	0
991/603			3	Leeds	L-8w	8	19	c	9	2	lbw	1	78	26	0	51	25	0
1046/623	1986	I	1	Lord's	L-5w	6	63	b	6	6	c	1	150	58	3	90	30	1
1047/624			2	Leeds	L-279	7	8	c	8	8	lbw	1	162	47	3	135	73	4
1048/625			3	Birmingham	D	6	44	c	6	7	c	2	126	61	2	96	33	0
1050/627	1986	NZ	2	Nottingham	L-8w	6	21	c	7	9	c	–	120	58	0	12	16	0
1098/646	1988	WI	1	Nottingham	D	6	39	b	–	–	–	–	204	82	1	–	–	–
1099/647			2	Lord's	L-134	6	1	c	6	0	lbw	–	42	20	0	126	60	2
1101/649			4	Leeds	L-10w	9	0	c	9	3	b	–	162	95	5	–	–	–
1102/650			5	Oval	L-8w	8	1	c	9	8	b	–	102	45	3	78	24	0
1103/651	1988	SL		Lord's	W-7w	7	14	c	–	–	–	–	41	17	2	66	30	1

Career	M	I	NO	HS	R	Avge	100	50	Ct	St	Balls	R	W	Avge	BB	5w	10w	Rate
Test	19	33	3	63	479	15.96	–	1	7	–	3232	1501	43	34.90	5-95	2	–	75.16
F/c	203	299	55	128	6556	26.86	8	32	111	–	29633	13438	493	27.25	7-32	16	1	60.10

PULLAR, Geoffrey

Lancashire (1954 to 1968)
Gloucestershire (1969 to 1970)

Wisden 1960
TOURS A 1962–63; SA 1960–61 (Cav); WI 1959–60; NZ 1962–63; I/SL 1961–62; P 1961–62
Born Swinton, Lancashire 1 Aug 1935

Originally a middle-order batsman, Geoff Pullar was selected for England as an opener because of his unruffled temperament, very sound defensive technique and left-handedness. The experiment was an instant success; he scored 75 and 131 in his first two outings, formed a calm and lucrative partnership in the Caribbean with another reluctant opener, Colin Cowdrey, and remained an automatic selection for almost four years. Tall (6ft 1½in), reliable and consistent, his ability to relax and fall asleep instantly and anywhere earned him the unoriginal nickname of 'Noddy'. He joined Lancashire as an amateur but turned professional in 1956. With his extra height and reach, he could afford to employ a predominantly front-foot technique and no one played the West Indian pace battery with more ease and assurance. He missed little on the leg-side and was an adept placer of singles. Injuries and loss of form in Australia eventually ended his Test career. He returned to the middle-order and, after another five summers at Old Trafford, enjoyed a brief postscript with Gloucestershire before the discomfort of an arthritic knee persuaded him to remuster as the owner of a fish and chip shop.

NOTABLE FEATS

- 1000 runs in 13th Test (*508*) (24 inns).
- *476* Shared (then) record E v I 1st-wkt stand of 146 with W.G.A. Parkhouse.
- *477* First Lancashire player to score a Test 100 at Old Trafford.
- *491* Took wicket of F.M.M. Worrell with his sixth ball in Tests (right-arm leg-spin).
- *496* Shared 1st-wkt stand of 290 with M.C. Cowdrey.
- *513* Shared (then) record E v I 1st-wkt stand of 159 in 170 min with P.E. Richardson.
- *515* Shared (then) record E v I 2nd-wkt stand of 164 with K.F. Barrington.
- *518* Shared record E v P 1st-wkt stand of 198 with R.W. Barber; his 165 is the highest score in any Test at Dacca.
- Exceeded 1000 runs in a season 9 times (plus once on tour), including 2000 twice, notably 2647 in 1959.
- First Lancastrian to score 5 hundreds v Yorkshire (including 3 in 1959).
- Scored 7 consecutive first-class fifties in 1959.

Geoff Pullar

TEST NOTES

- *491* Bowled in 2nd inns; 1 for 1 (6 balls).
- *492* Fractured bone in left wrist (1st inns); played 1 ball single-handed in 2nd inns.
- *495* Bowled in 2nd inns: 0 for 6 (6 balls).
- *518* Bowled in 2nd inns: 0 for 30 (54 balls).

						Batting 1st			Batting 2nd			
Ref	Series	V	T	Venue	Result	No	R	HO	No	R	HO	Ct
476/356	1959	I	3	Leeds	W-I & 173	2	75	c	–	–	–	–
477/357			4	Manchester	W-171	2	131	c	2	14	c	–
478/358			5	Oval	W-I & 27	1	22	c	–	–	–	–
487/359	1959–60	WI	1	Bridgetown	D	1	65	ro	1	46	*	–
488/360			2	Port-of-Spain	W-256	1	17	c	1	28	c	–
489/361			3	Kingston	D	1	19	c	1	66	lbw	–
490/362			4	Georgetown	D	1	33	c	1	47	lbw	–
491/363			5	Port-of-Spain	D	1	10	c	1	54	c	–
492/364	1960	SA	1	Birmingham	W-100	1	37	c	11	1	*	–
495/367			4	Manchester	D	1	12	b	1	9	c	–
496/368			5	Oval	D	1	59	c	1	175	st	–
507/369	1961	A	1	Birmingham	D	1	17	b	1	28	c	–
508/370			2	Lord's	L-5w	1	11	b	1	42	c	–
509/371			3	Leeds	W-8w	1	53	b	1	26	*	–
510/372			4	Manchester	L-54	1	63	b	1	26	c	–
511/373			5	Oval	D	1	8	b	1	13	c	–
512/374	1961–62	P	1	Lahore[2]	W-5w	2	0	c	2	0	b	1
513/375	1961–62	I	1	Bombay[2]	D	2	83	st	–	–	–	–
514/376			2	Kanpur	D	2	46	c	2	119	c	–
515/377			3	Delhi	D	2	89	c	–	–	–	1
518/380	1961–62	P	2	Dacca	D	1	165	c	1	8	*	–
519/381			3	Karachi	D	2	60	c	–	–	–	–
530/382	1962	P	1	Birmingham	W-I & 24	1	22	b	–	–	–	–
533/385			4	Nottingham	D	1	5	lbw	–	–	–	–
535/387	1962–63	A	1	Brisbane[2]	D	1	33	c	1	56	c	–
536/388			2	Melbourne	W-7w	2	11	b	2	5	c	–
537/389			3	Sydney	L-8w	1	53	c	1	0	b	–
538/390			4	Adelaide	D	1	9	b	1	3	c	–

Career	M	I	NO	HS	R	Avge	100	50	Ct	St	Balls	R	W	Avge	BB	5w	10w	Rate
Test	28	49	4	175	1974	43.86	4	12	2	–	66	37	1	37.00	1-1	–	–	66.00
F/c	400	672	63	175	21528	35.34	41	111	125	–	665	387	10	38.70	3-91	–	–	66.50

G. PULLAR – TEST BATTING SUMMARY

Series	V	M	I	NO	HS	R	Avge	100	50
1959	I	3	4	–	131	242	60.50	1	1
1959–60	WI	5	10	1	66	385	42.77	–	3
1960	SA	3	6	1	175	293	58.60	1	1
1961	A	5	10	1	63	287	31.88	–	2
1961–62	P	3	5	1	165	233	58.25	1	1
1961–62	I	3	4	–	119	337	84.25	1	2
1962	P	2	2	–	22	27	13.50	–	–
1962–63	A	4	8	–	56	170	21.25	–	2

Series	V	M	I	NO	HS	R	Avge	100	50
	A	9	18	1	63	457	26.88	–	4
	SA	3	6	1	175	293	58.60	1	1
	WI	5	10	1	66	385	42.77	–	3
	I	6	8	–	131	579	72.37	2	3
	P	5	7	1	165	260	43.33	1	1
Home		13	22	2	175	849	42.45	2	4
Overseas		15	27	2	165	1125	45.00	2	8
Totals		28	49	4	175	1974	43.86	4	12

QUAIFE
William George

Warwickshire (1894 to 1928)
London County (1900 to 1903)
Griqualand West (1912–13)

Wisden 1902
TOUR A 1901–02
Born Newhaven, Sussex 17 Mar 1872
Died Edgbaston, Birmingham 13 Oct 1951

Willie Quaife

TEST NOTES

• 63 Bowled in 2nd inns: 0 for 6 (15 balls).

Willie Quaife was one of the smallest cricketers to represent England but his exact height is unknown. Even his own son, Bernard, who played for Warwickshire alongside his father, was uncertain and could only narrow it down to 'between 5ft 2in and 5ft 5in'. Known as 'the other W.G.', he overcame his slight stature to become the most durable of all the County's representatives, enjoying a career spanning 35 years, and was the first Warwickshire player to receive two benefits. He was a sound, defensive but stylish and perfectly balanced middle-order batsman, who combined model footwork with a straight-batted technique. He was also an outstanding fielder at cover-point and a right-arm leg-break bowler who overcame considerable doubts about his early action to claim nearly 1000 first-class wickets. At the age of 56 and playing his only innings of the season, he batted with all his old skill for more than four hours to crown his final appearance for Warwickshire with a century. In retirement he became a cricket bat manufacturer and, having shared in Warwickshire's first Championship, lived to see Tom Dollery's team win its successor 40 years on.

NOTABLE FEATS

- Exceeded 1000 runs in a season 24 times, including 2060 in 1905.
- Holds Warwickshire record for most first-class appearances (665).
- Scored 4 double centuries for Warwickshire, notably 255* v Surrey at The Oval in 1905.
- Shared in 2 record Warwickshire partnerships: 327 (3rd wkt) with S.P. Kinneir v Lancashire at Birmingham in 1901; 268 (5th wkt) with W. Quaife v Essex at Leyton in 1900.
- Scored hundreds in 3 consecutive innings twice (1901 and 1913).
- Completed match 'double' (104* and 12 wickets) for Warwickshire v Worcestershire at Birmingham in 1901.
- Scored 115 in 260 min v Derbyshire at Birmingham in 1928 in his final innings for Warwickshire.

						Batting 1st			Batting 2nd			
Ref	Series	V	T	Venue	Result	No	R	HO	No	R	HO	Ct
62/62	1899	A	3	Leeds	D	4	20	b	2	1	*	–
63/63			4	Manchester	D	1	8	c	1	15	c	–
65/65	1901–02	A	1	Sydney	W-I & 124	4	21	b	–	–	–	2
66/66			2	Melbourne	L-229	4	0	b	4	25	b	1
67/67			3	Adelaide	L-4w	6	68	c	4	44	lbw	–
68/68			4	Sydney	L-7w	4	4	c	4	15	lbw	–
69/69			5	Melbourne	L-32	3	3	c	3	4	lbw	1

Career	M	I	NO	HS	R	Avge	100	50	Ct	St	Balls	R	W	Avge	BB	5w	10w	Rate
Test	7	13	1	68	228	19.00	–	1	4	–	15	6	0	–	–	–	–	–
F/c	719	1203	185	255*	36012	35.37	72	163	354	1	52080	25443	931	27.32	7-76	32	2	55.93

RADFORD
Neal Victor

Transvaal (1978–79 to 1987–88)
Lancashire (1980 to 1984)
Worcestershire (1985 to date)

Wisden 1986
TOUR NZ 1987–88
Born Luanshya, Northern Rhodesia
7 Jun 1957

NOTABLE FEATS

- Took 101 first-class wickets in 1985 and 109 in 1987.

Neal Radford is another example of a seam bowler who, after being outstandingly successful at county level, has been unable to make any impression against top-class batsmen on the superior pitches found in Test cricket. Born in what is now Zambia and educated in Johannesburg, he arrived at Worcester after five seasons of injuries and lost opportunities with Lancashire. The change brought an instant reward with 101 wickets in his first season. During his first three summers at New Road his bustling right-arm fast-medium bowling claimed 285 Championship wickets; a prodigious output and the reward for sustained hostility, stamina and attention to fitness. With his similar terrier-like qualities and bustling, mincing run-up, he is reminiscent of Robin Jackman. His batting is equally flamboyant and determined and he is a tigerish fielder and safe catcher. If he could have added two inches to his 5ft 11in, he could well have become an established international bowler.

Neal Radford

						Batting 1st			Batting 2nd				Bowling 1st			Bowling 2nd		
Ref	Series	V	T	Venue	Result	No	R	HO	No	R	HO	Ct	Balls	R	W	Balls	R	W
1048/625	1986	I	3	Birmingham	D	11	0	c	11	1	c	–	210	131	2	18	17	0
1049/626	1986	NZ	1	Lord's	D	11	12	*	–	–	–	–	150	71	1	–	–	–
1092/644	1987–88	NZ	2	Auckland	D	10	8	b	–	–	–	–	180	79	0	120	53	1

Career	M	I	NO	HS	R	Avge	100	50	Ct	St	Balls	R	W	Avge	BB	5w	10w	Rate
Test	3	4	1	12*	21	7.00	–	–	–	–	678	351	4	87.75	2-131	–	–	169.50
F/c	181	183	46	76*	2269	16.56	–	4	93	–	32401	16924	667	25.37	9-70	34	6	48.57

RADLEY
Clive Thornton

Middlesex (1964 to 1987)

Wisden 1979
TOURS
A 1978–79; SA 1972–73 (Robins), 1974–75 (Robins); NZ 1977–78; Z 1980–81 (Middx)
Born Hertford 13 May 1944

Clive Radley proved that phenomenal application, determination and commonsense can overcome any shortfall in natural talent, style or grace. Just 5ft 8in tall and far from robust, he was an uncomplicated accumulator; a gutsy player with a fine temperament. He had an uncanny knack of pushing the ball into untenanted parts of the field and was one of the sharpest – and noisiest – runners of stolen singles. Hertford-born but Norwich-schooled, he followed the Norfolk–Middlesex connection of Bill Edrich and Peter Parfitt. A keen competitor, he soon became an accomplished and consistent grafter. His technique, based on a sound defence, was elementary: get in line, watch the ball and play within your limitations. Nearly 34 when he was promoted to Test cricket, his county methods produced an England average of 48 and a vigil approaching 11 hours in only his second match. His unorthodox style and skill as an improviser put fielding sides under

Clive Radley

special pressure in the limited-overs game and he played a major part in the five 'instant' trophies won by Middlesex in just ten seasons (1977–86). It was no coincidence that in virtually the same period they won the Championship five times and shared it once. He was a safe and agile close fielder and he acquired an impressive career bowling average with some judiciously timed spells of optimistic right-arm leg-spin.

NOTABLE FEATS

- *819* His 158 in 648 min was then the longest innings in NZ. His 150 in 594 was then the slowest in first-class matches and his 100 (487 min) the fourth-slowest.
- Exceeded 1000 runs in a season 16 times.
- Scored 200 for Middlesex v Northamptonshire at Uxbridge in 1985.
- Shared record Middlesex 6th-wkt stand of 227 with F.J. Titmus v South Africans at Lord's in 1965.

						Batting 1st			Batting 2nd			
Ref	Series	V	T	Venue	Result	No	R	HO	No	R	HO	Ct
818/535	1977–78	NZ	2	Christchurch	W-174	6	15	c	–	–	–	–
819/536			3	Auckland	D	3	158	c	–	–	–	–
825/537	1978	P	1	Birmingham	W-I & 157	3	106	lbw	–	–	–	1
826/538			2	Lord's	W-I & 120	3	8	c	–	–	–	1
827/539			3	Leeds	D	3	7	b	–	–	–	–
828/540	1978	NZ	1	Oval	W-7w	3	49	ro	3	2	lbw	1
829/541			2	Nottingham	W-I & 119	3	59	lbw	–	–	–	–
830/542			3	Lord's	W-7w	3	77	c	3	0	b	1

Career	M	I	NO	HS	R	Avge	100	50	Ct	St	Balls	R	W	Avge	BB	5w	10w	Rate
Test	8	10	0	158	481	48.10	2	2	4	–	–	–	–	–	–	–	–	–
F/c	559	880	134	200	26441	35.44	46	139	517	–	278	160	8	20.00	2-38	–	–	34.75

RANDALL
Derek William

Nottinghamshire (1972 to date)

Wisden 1980
TOURS
A 1976–77, 1978–79, 1979–80, 1982–83;
SA 1975–76 (Robins);
NZ 1977–78, 1983–84;
I 1976–77; P 1977–78, 1983–84;
SL 1976–77, 1985–86 (Eng B)
Born Retford, Nottinghamshire
24 Feb 1951

The name of Derek Randall would have to feature on any list of the most idiosyncratic batsmen of all time. Throughout his innings he would fidget, fiddle and scratch – if he ever adopted a patron saint it would have to be St Vitus; unlike the greatest players, he was constantly on the move, shuffling across his stumps as the bowler ran in. He antagonised the opposition, especially the Australians, by incessantly talking to himself: 'Come on, Rags. Get behind the ball. Don't take chances. Get forward. You idiot, Rags. Come on, England.' He was especially adept at goading bowlers; without really trying he had Dennis Lillee beside himself with rage. Smallish (5ft 8½in) and slim but with relatively enormous feet (size 11), he was highly nervous and quick-moving. Like Denis Compton, he delighted in the outrageous, would suddenly produce an absolutely impudent stroke and, given the identical ball twice in succession, would respond with two entirely different reactions. Beneath the clowning was a shrewd cricket brain, a marvellous eye and a gift of improvisation which made him such a wonderfully exciting player to watch. Exceptionally fast in the field – he was dubbed 'Arkle' after the celebrated racehorse – he covered amazing areas of ground and would usually go in to bat with 20 runs already to his credit. His right-arm medium-pace change bowling was equally eccentric. A reporter arriving at his house one snowy January was surprised to find Randall casually dressed but wearing a new pair of batting pads. 'Just breaking them in for the new season,' explained Arkle. 'Come and meet the missus.' She was sitting in an armchair knitting – and wearing another pair of new pads.

Derek Randall pulls Lillee for four during his memorable innings in the Centenary Test at Melbourne, 1976–77.

NOTABLE FEATS

- 1000 runs in 21st Test (*838*) (36 inns); 2000 runs in 40th Test (*960*) (67 inns).
- *803* His 172 in 446 min off 353 balls was the second-highest score by a debutant in E v A Tests.
- *837* His 100 in 406 min (353 balls) remains the slowest in E v A Tests.
- *928* Shared record E v I 7th-wkt stand of 125 with P.H. Edmonds.
- *939* Completed 1000 runs v Australia.
- Exceeded 1000 runs in a season 11 times, including 2151 in 1985.
- Scored 3 double centuries for Nottinghamshire, notably 237 v Derbyshire at Nottingham in 1988.
- Scored 209 and 146 v Middlesex at Nottingham in 1979.

TEST NOTES

- *814* Bowled in 2nd inns: 0 for 2 (8 balls).
- *818* Run out while backing up by the bowler (E.J. Chatfield).
- *819* Bowled in 2nd inns: 0 for 1 (8 balls).

						Batting 1st			Batting 2nd			
Ref	Series	V	T	Venue	Result	No	R	HO	No	R	HO	Ct
789/521	1976–77	I	2	Calcutta	W-10w	4	37	lbw	–	–	–	–
790/522			3	Madras[1]	W-200	4	2	ro	5	0	c	1
791/523			4	Bangalore	L-140	4	10	c	4	0	c	2
792/524			5	Bombay[3]	D	3	22	c	3	15	c	–
803/525	1976–77	A		Melbourne	L-45	4	4	c	3	174	c	–
804/526	1977	A	1	Lord's	D	4	53	c	7	0	c	–
805/527			2	Manchester	W-9w	4	79	lbw	–	–	–	2
806/528			3	Nottingham	W-7w	4	13	ro	5	19	*	1
807/529			4	Leeds	W-I & 85	4	20	lbw	–	–	–	1
808/530			5	Oval	D	4	3	c	4	20	*	–
814/531	1977–78	P	1	Lahore[2]	D	4	19	c	–	–	–	–
815/532			2	Hyderabad	D	4	7	c	–	–	–	–
816/533			3	Karachi	D	3	23	lbw	3	55	b	–
817/534	1977–78	NZ	1	Wellington	L-72	5	4	c	4	9	lbw	–
818/535			2	Christchurch	W-174	3	0	c	3	13	ro	–
819/536			3	Auckland	D	2	30	lbw	–	–	–	2
834/543	1978–79	A	1	Brisbane[2]	W-7w	3	75	c	3	74	*	–
835/544			2	Perth	W-166	3	0	c	3	45	c	–
836/545			3	Melbourne	L-103	3	13	lbw	3	2	lbw	3
837/546			4	Sydney	W-93	3	0	c	3	150	lbw	–
838/547			5	Adelaide	W-205	3	4	c	3	15	c	1
839/548			6	Sydney	W-9w	3	7	lbw	3	0	*	–
851/549	1979	I	1	Birmingham	W-I & 83	3	15	c	–	–	–	2
852/550			2	Lord's	D	5	57	ro	–	–	–	2
853/551			3	Leeds	D	5	11	b	–	–	–	–
868/553	1979/80	A	1	Perth	L-138	1	0	c	1	1	lbw	1
870/554			2	Sydney	L-6w	3	0	c	6	25	c	–
928/580	1982	I	1	Lord's	W-7w	6	126	c	–	–	–	–
929/581			2	Manchester	D	6	0	c	–	–	–	1
930/582			3	Oval	D	6	95	st	–	–	–	–
931/583	1982	P	1	Birmingham	W-113	1	17	b	1	105	b	1
932/584			2	Lord's	L-10w	1	29	b	1	9	b	–
933/585			3	Leeds	W-3w	7	8	ro	7	0	lbw	2
938/586	1982–83	A	1	Perth	D	6	78	c	6	115	b	–
939/587			2	Brisbane[2]	L-7w	6	37	c	5	4	c	1
940/588			3	Adelaide	L-8w	6	0	b	6	17	c	1
942/590			5	Sydney	D	5	70	b	6	44	b	1

Ref	Series	V	T	Venue	Result	Batting 1st No	R	HO	Batting 2nd No	R	HO	Ct
957/591	1983	NZ	1	Oval	W-189	6	75	*	6	3	c	1
958/592			2	Leeds	L-5w	6	4	c	6	16	c	2
960/594			4	Nottingham	W-165	7	83	c	7	13	b	–
975/595	1983–84	NZ	1	Wellington	D	7	164	c	–	–	–	–
976/596			2	Christchurch	L-I & 132	5	0	c	7	25	c	1
977/597			3	Auckland	D	5	104	c	–	–	–	1
978/598	1983–84	P	1	Karachi	L-3w	5	8	b	5	16	b	–
979/599			2	Faisalabad	D	3	65	b	–	–	–	–
980/600			3	Lahore[2]	D	5	14	c	6	0	c	–
989/601	1984	WI	1	Birmingham	L-I & 180	3	0	b	3	1	c	1

Career	M	I	NO	HS	R	Avge	100	50	Ct	St	Balls	R	W	Avge	BB	5w	10w	Rate
Test	47	79	5	174	2470	33.37	7	12	31	–	16	3	0	–	–	–	–	–
F/c	402	683	62	237	23255	37.44	41	136	301	–	451	383	12	31.91	3-15	–	–	37.58

D. W. RANDALL – TEST BATTING SUMMARY

Series	V	M	I	NO	HS	R	Avge	100	50
1976–77	I	4	7	–	37	86	12.28	–	–
1976–77	A	1	2	–	174	178	89.00	1	–
1977	A	5	8	2	79	207	34.50	–	2
1977–78	P	3	4	–	55	104	26.00	–	1
1977–78	NZ	3	5	–	30	56	11.20	–	–
1978–79	A	6	12	2	150*	385	38.50	1	2
1979	I	3	3	–	57	83	27.66	–	1
1979–80	A	2	4	–	25	26	6.50	–	–
1982	I	3	3	–	126	221	73.66	1	1
1982	P	3	6	–	105	168	28.00	1	–
1982–83	A	4	8	–	115	365	45.62	1	2
1983	NZ	3	6	1	83	194	38.80	–	2
1983–84	NZ	3	4	–	164	293	73.25	2	–
1983–84	P	3	5	–	65	103	20.60	–	1
1984	WI	1	2	–	1	1	0.50	–	–
	A	18	34	4	174	1161	38.70	3	6
	WI	1	2	–	1	1	0.50	–	–
	NZ	9	15	1	164	543	38.78	2	2
	I	10	13	–	126	390	30.00	1	2
	P	9	15	–	105	375	25.00	1	2
Home		18	28	3	126	874	34.96	2	6
Overseas		29	51	2	174	1596	32.57	5	6
Totals		47	79	5	174	2470	33.37	7	12

RANJITSINHJI Kumar Shri (later HH Shri Sir Ranjitsinhji Vibhaji, Jam Sahib of Nawanagar)

Cambridge University (1893 to 1894)
Sussex (1895 to 1920)
London County (1901 to 1904)

Wisden 1897
TOUR A 1897–98
Born Sarodar, India 10 Sep 1872
Inherited title in 1907
Died Jamnagar, India 2 Apr 1933

Prince Ranjitsinhji ('Kumar Shri' signifies 'Prince') must rank with the finest batsmen of all time. Apart from his prodigious feat in achieving the highest first-class career average (56.37) of any England-based batsman scoring 10,000 runs, he added new dimensions to the art of batting. Completely unorthodox and with exceptionally fast reactions, 'Ranji' was the first to employ the back stroke as a basis of defence and he played the late-cut and leg-glance later and with more exquisite timing than anyone before or since. He would also dart down the pitch and drive with great power and had a vast range of wristy, graceful strokes at his command. His placement and improvisation enabled him to score very quickly; he is alone in scoring a century in each innings on the same day and once went in to lunch after scoring 180 in the session. His great reserves of energy enabled him to register his highest score (285*) after spending the entire night fishing. He played no organised cricket before going up to Cambridge (where he was known as 'Smith') and he failed to gain a blue until his final year. He was a right-arm slow bowler and a fine fielder at slip. After captaining Sussex for five summers (1899–1903) he played only one more complete season before returning to India. In 1907 he inherited the title of Maharaja Jam Sahib of Nawanagar and became increasingly involved in that State's administration. He also served as chancellor of the Indian Council of

'Ranji'

Princes and as a delegate to the League of Nations. After returning for a few matches in 1908 and 1912, he lost an eye in a shooting accident. Undeterred, in 1920 he returned to play three final matches as research for a chapter on the art of batting with one eye; captaining Sussex against Yorkshire at Leeds he helped save the match by surviving for 40 minutes against Wilfred Rhodes (8 for 39). In 1934 the Ranji Trophy was instituted to commemorate his death and, from 1946–47, it replaced the Bombay Pentangular Tournament as India's premier championship.

NOTABLE FEATS

- *51* First Indian to play Test cricket; emulated W.G. Grace in scoring 100 on debut for England. First to score 100 before lunch in a Test – added 113 (41* to 154*) in 130 min on third day; still most pre-lunch runs in an E v A Test.
- *53* Emulated H. Graham by scoring 100 in his first Test in Australia having also done so in England. His 175 was then the highest score for England in Australia.
- Exceeded 1000 runs in a season 11 times (plus once on tour), including the first instance of 3000 in a season (3159 in 1899), 3065 in 1900 and over 2000 runs on 3 other occasions (his 2780 in 1896 surpassed W.G. Grace's record).
- In 1899 he scored 1037 runs in June and 1011 runs in August – first to achieve that feat twice in the same season; he also scored 1059 in July 1900.
- Statistically he was the leading batsman in 1896, 1900 and 1904.
- Scored 14 double centuries for Sussex, notably 285* v Somerset at Taunton in 1901.
- Only batsman to score 2 first-class hundreds on the same day: 100 and 125* on 22 Aug 1896 for Sussex v Yorkshire at Hove (began the day with his first innings overnight score 0*).
- Scored hundreds in each innings of a match for Sussex twice (1896 and 1900) and in the same seasons scored hundreds in 3 consecutive innings.
- Holds English first-class record for most runs scored in a pre-lunch session: 180 for Sussex v Surrey at Hastings in 1902 (took his overnight score from 54* to 234* in 150 min on second day). Scored 10 pre-lunch first-class hundreds.
- Shared record English 7th-wkt stand of 344 with W. Newham for Sussex v Essex at Leyton in 1902 and record Sussex 3rd-wkt stand of 298 with E.H. Killick v Lancashire at Hove in 1901.
- Scored 77* and 150 on his Sussex debut, v MCC at Lord's in 1895.

						Batting 1st			Batting 2nd				Bowling 1st			Bowling 2nd		
Ref	**Series**	**V**	**T**	**Venue**	**Result**	**No**	**R**	**HO**	**No**	**R**	**HO**	**Ct**	**Balls**	**R**	**W**	**Balls**	**R**	**W**
51/51	1896	A	2	Manchester	L-3w	3	62	c	3	154	*	2	–	–	–	–	–	–
52/52			3	Oval	W-66	3	8	b	3	11	st	–	–	–	–	–	–	–
53/53	1897–98	A	1	Sydney	W-9w	7	175	c	3	8	*	–	–	–	–	–	–	–
54/54			2	Melbourne	L-I & 55	4	71	b	3	27	b	1	–	–	–	–	–	–
55/55			3	Adelaide	L-I & 13	3	6	c	3	77	c	–	–	–	–	–	–	–
56/56			4	Melbourne	L-8w	3	24	c	4	55	b	–	–	–	–	22	9	0
57/57			5	Sydney	L-6w	3	2	c	3	12	lbw	2	–	–	–	–	–	–
60/60	1899	A	1	Nottingham	D	5	42	b	5	93	*	2	–	–	–	–	–	–
61/61			2	Lord's	L-10w	3	8	c	3	0	c	1	10	6	0	–	–	–
62/62			3	Leeds	D	3	11	c	–	–	–	3	–	–	–	–	–	–
63/63			4	Manchester	D	3	21	c	3	49	*	2	5	1	0	60	23	1
64/64			5	Oval	D	3	54	c	–	–	–	–	–	–	–	–	–	–
70/70	1902	A	1	Birmingham	D	3	13	b	–	–	–	–	–	–	–	–	–	–
71/71			2	Lord's	D	3	0	b	–	–	–	–	–	–	–	–	–	–
73/73			4	Manchester	L-3	5	2	lbw	4	4	lbw	–	–	–	–	–	–	–

Career	**M**	**I**	**NO**	**HS**	**R**	**Avge**	**100**	**50**	**Ct**	**St**	**Balls**	**R**	**W**	**Avge**	**BB**	**5w**	**10w**	**Rate**
Test	15	26	4	175	989	44.95	2	6	13	–	97	39	1	39.00	1-23	–	–	97.00
F/c	307	500	62	285*	24692	56.37	72	109	233	–	8056	4601	133	34.59	6-53	4	–	60.57

READ Holcombe Douglas

Surrey (1933)
Essex (1933 to 1935)

TOURS A 1935–36; NZ 1935–36
Born Woodford Green, Essex
28 Jan 1910

NOTABLE FEATS

- Hat-trick for Essex v Gloucestershire at Bristol in 1935.

'Hopper' Read was a tearaway right-arm fast bowler whose career in Test and county cricket involved a mere three summers. Operating from a lengthy run he achieved awesome pace but his control of length and direction was distinctly haphazard. In June 1933 he played for Surrey against both Cambridge and Oxford before making a wicketless Championship debut for Essex less than a month later. His next appearance was the following season when he took 55 Championship wickets to finish second to Ken Farnes in the Essex averages. His final summer produced 97 first-class wickets, including the spectacular 6 for 11 which dismissed Yorkshire (that season's champions) for 31 before 12.30pm on the first day. It must have contributed to his selection for England, when he bowled whole-heartedly to take six wickets on a very flat pitch, and for the MCC's 'goodwill' mission to the antipodes. That tour marked the end of his representative career although his final first-class match (for MCC) was not until 1948.

'Hopper' Read

					Batting 1st			Batting 2nd				Bowling 1st			Bowling 2nd		
Ref	Series	V	T Venue	Result	No	R	HO	No	R	HO	Ct	Balls	R	W	Balls	R	W
246/220	1935	SA	5 Oval	D	–	–	–	–	–	–	–	210	136	4	60	64	2

Career	M	I	NO	HS	R	Avge	100	50	Ct	St	Balls	R	W	Avge	BB	5w	10w	Rate
Test	1	–	–	–	–	–	–	–	–	–	270	200	6	33.33	4-136	–	–	45.00
F/c	54	70	27	25*	158	3.67	–	–	21	–	8382	5023	219	22.93	7-35	13	2	38.27

READ, John Maurice

Surrey (1880 to 1895)

Wisden 1890
TOURS
A 1884–85, 1886–87, 1887–88, 1891–92;
SA 1888–89
Born Thames Ditton, Surrey 9 Feb 1859
Died Winchester, Hampshire 17 Feb 1929

NOTABLE FEATS

- Exceeded 1000 runs in a season 3 times.
- Contributed 186* to a 4th-wkt partnership of 241 with R. Abel v Australians at The Oval in 1886.

For 16 summers until he retired to take up an appointment on the Tichborne estate, Maurice Read was an integral part of the Surrey team which won five Championships in six years. For almost a decade he was an automatic choice for England, making four tours of Australia and playing in the earliest Test matches in South Africa. A nephew of H.H. Stephenson, he was an entertaining and aggressive strokemaker who, despite being unorthodox, managed to score consistently. He hit the ball hard, even in defence, and was a strong cutter and off-driver. Before the arrival of Lohmann he was a stopgap right-arm fast-medium bowler and his fielding in the deep, usually at third man, was remarkably swift and accurate. Immensely popular with everyone from his fellow players to the watching public, his fine example considerably raised the status of the professional cricketer; he was the forerunner of a new order which was far more civilised and better turned out than its predecessors. He spent his latter playing days massacring visiting bowlers at Tichborne Park; it was a poor year if he did not average over 100 and his best scores included four double centuries.

Maurice Read

Ref	Series	V	T	Venue	Result	Batting 1st No	R	HO	Batting 2nd No	R	HO	Ct
9/9	1882	A		Oval	L-7	7	19	*	8	0	b	1
17/17	1884-85	A	1	Adelaide	W-8w	7	14	c	–	–	–	1
18/18			2	Melbourne	W-10w	6	3	b	–	–	–	1
19/19			3	Sydney	L-6	8	4	c	8	56	b	1
20/20			4	Sydney	L-8w	6	47	b	6	6	c	1
21/21			5	Melbourne	W-I & 98	3	13	b	–	–	–	–
25/25	1886-87	A	1	Sydney	W-13	5	5	c	5	0	b	1
26/26			2	Sydney	W-71	3	11	b	4	2	st	–
27/27	1887-88	A		Sydney	W-126	5	0	c	5	39	c	–
31/31	1888-89	SA	1	Port Elizabeth	W-8w	3	1	c	3	3	b	–
32/32			2	Cape Town	W-I & 202	4	12	c	–	–	–	–
33/33	1890	A	1	Lord's	W-7w	5	34	b	5	2	*	–
34/34			2	Oval	W-2w	6	19	c	5	35	c	–
35/35	1891-92	A	1	Melbourne	L-54	5	38	c	4	11	b	1
36/36			2	Sydney	L-72	5	3	c	5	22	c	1
37/37			3	Adelaide	W-I & 230	4	57	c	–	–	–	–
39/39	1893	A	1	Lord's	D	5	6	b	5	1	c	–

Career	M	I	NO	HS	R	Avge	100	50	Ct	St	Balls	R	W	Avge	BB	5w	10w	Rate
Test	17	29	2	57	463	17.14	–	2	8	–	–	–	–	–	–	–	–	–
F/c	380	611	43	186*	14010	24.66	11	70	215	–	3912	1807	73	24.75	6-41	1	–	53.58

READ, Walter William

Surrey (1873 to 1897)

Wisden 1893
TOURS A 1882–83, 1887–88; SA 1891–92
Born Reigate, Surrey 23 Nov 1855
Died Addiscombe, Surrey 6 Jan 1907

Walter Read did much to re-establish Surrey cricket in the early 1880s. His natural belligerency communicated itself in his batting which revolved around thunderous off-drives; when Lord Harris demoted him to number ten at The Oval in 1884, he responded with the highest innings ever made from that position. Originally a right-handed round-arm fast-medium bowler, he subsequently switched to slow lobs. He fielded aggressively at point. Although England won both Tests under his captaincy, he was never given the command of Surrey.

NOTABLE FEATS

- *16* His match-saving 117 remains the highest score by a No. 10 in Test cricket. Scored 100 in 113 min with 36 scoring strokes. Shared record E v A 9th-wkt stand of 151 with W.H. Scotton.
- Exceeded 1000 runs in a season 9 times.
- Scored 338 in 390 min for Surrey v Oxford U at The Oval in 1888.
- First to score double centuries in successive innings – for Surrey in 1887: 247 v Lancashire at Manchester and 244* v Cambridge U at The Oval.
- Carried his bat through a completed innings twice.
- Scored 4 hundreds in successive innings v Derbyshire (1885–87).
- Hat-trick for the Gentlemen v M. Sherwin's XI at Scarborough in 1891.

Walter Read

Ref	Series	V	T	Venue	Result	Batting 1st No	R	HO	Batting 2nd No	R	HO	Ct
10/10	1882–83	A	1	Melbourne	L-9w	6	19	b	6	29	b	–
11/11			2	Melbourne	W-I & 27	5	75	c	–	–	–	1
12/12			3	Sydney	W-69	5	66	c	5	21	b	–
13/13			4	Sydney	L-4w	5	11	c	5	7	b	–
15/15	1884	A	2	Lord's	W-I & 5	8	12	b	–	–	–	–
16/16			3	Oval	D	10	117	b	–	–	–	2
22/22	1886	A	1	Manchester	W-4w	4	51	c	4	9	c	–
23/23			2	Lord's	W-I & 106	4	22	c	–	–	–	–
24/24			3	Oval	W-I & 217	4	94	c	–	–	–	3
27/27*	1887–88	A		Sydney	W-126	4	10	b	4	8	b	2

TEST NOTES

- *10* Bowled in 1st inns: 0 for 27 (32 balls).
- *16* Bowled in 1st inns: 0 for 36 (28 balls). Deputised as wicket-keeper during A. Lyttelton's first bowling spell on the first evening.

						Batting 1st			Batting 2nd			
Ref	Series	V	T	Venue	Result	No	R	HO	No	R	HO	Ct
28/28	1888	A	1	Lord's	L-61	5	4	st	4	3	b	–
29/29			2	Oval	W-I & 137	4	18	b	–	–	–	1
30/30			3	Manchester	W-I & 21	4	19	b	–	–	–	2
33/33	1890	A	1	Lord's	W-7w	4	1	c	4	13	b	–
34/34			2	Oval	W-2w	4	1	b	4	6	b	1
38/38*	1891–92	SA		Cape Town	W-I & 189	6	40	b	–	–	–	–
40/40	1893	A	2	Oval	W-I & 43	6	52	b	–	–	–	2
41/41			3	Manchester	D	6	12	b	6	0	*	2

Career	M	I	NO	HS	R	Avge	100	50	Ct	St	Balls	R	W	Avge	BB	5w	10w	Rate
Test	18	27	1	117	720	27.69	1	5	16	–	60	63	0	–	–	–	–	–
F/c	467	749	52	338	22349	32.06	38	112	381	20	5539	3483	108	32.25	6-24	1	–	51.28

RELF, Albert Edward

Sussex (1900 to 1921)
London County (1904)
Auckland (1907–08 to 1909–10)

Wisden 1914
TOURS
A 1903–04; SA 1905–06, 1913–14; WI 1912–13
Born Burwash, Sussex 26 Jun 1874
Died Wellington College, Crowthorne, Berkshire 26 Mar 1937

NOTABLE FEATS

- Exceeded 1000 runs in a season 11 times, and took 100 wickets 11 times, completing the 'double' on 8 occasions.
- Second batsman to score 1000 runs in his debut season (1059 in 1900).
- Took 9 for 95 for Sussex v Warwickshire at Hove in 1910.
- Hat-trick for Sussex v Worcestershire at Hove in 1902.
- Achieved the match 'double' twice.

The eldest of three brothers to represent Sussex, Albert Relf was an extremely effective cricketer in all three departments. Although he was nearly 26 when, after appearing for Norfolk and Berkshire, he returned to his native county and began his first-class career, he was still a most effective player 21 years later. Only Rhodes, Hirst, Jupp and Astill achieved the 'double' more often. His main strength was as a right-arm medium-pace off break bowler. Operating off a brief run with a fluent action, he was quite tireless and could maintain an accurate length for long spells. He turned the ball sharply at that brisk pace and was a fairly lethal proposition if the pitch helped him. He was also an outstanding slip where he held most of his impressive career tally of 537 catches. It was as a batsman that he made his initial impression, scoring over 1000 runs in his first season; no great stylist, his defence looked especially awkward. After the First World War he became coach at Wellington College and was available only in the school holidays. It was there that he shot himself in a fit of depression attributed to his wife's serious illness. Ironically she recovered and inherited a handsome estate.

Albert Relf

						Batting 1st			Batting 2nd				Bowling 1st			Bowling 2nd		
Ref	Series	V	T	Venue	Result	No	R	HO	No	R	HO	Ct	Balls	R	W	Balls	R	W
78/75	1903–04	A	1	Sydney	W-5w	10	31	c	–	–	–	3	36	27	0	78	35	0
79/76			2	Melbourne	W-185	10	3	*	9	10	*	2	12	12	1	6	5	0
88/85	1905–06	SA	1	Johannesburg[1]	L-1w	7	8	b	7	17	c	2	–	–	–	131	47	2
89/86			2	Johannesburg[1]	L-9w	7	24	c	7	37	c	–	108	36	1	–	–	–
90/87			3	Johannesburg[1]	L-243	7	33	c	3	18	c	1	84	47	1	54	37	0
91/88			4	Cape Town	W-4w	2	28	lbw	6	18	b	–	36	17	1	–	–	–
92/89			5	Cape Town	L-I & 16	6	25	c	5	21	b	1	126	40	3	–	–	–
102/99	1909	A	2	Lord's	L-9w	9	17	c	10	3	b	–	270	85	5	46	9	1

Ref	Series	V	T Venue	Result	Batting 1st No	R	HO	Batting 2nd No	R	HO	Ct	Bowling 1st Balls	R	W	Bowling 2nd Balls	R	W
130/119	1913–14	SA	1 Durban[1]	W-I & 157	3	1	c	–	–	–	2	30	9	0	98	31	3
131/120			2 Johannesburg[1]	W-I & 12	2	63	b	–	–	–	1	84	34	0	54	19	1
132/121			3 Johannesburg[1]	W-91	8	0	lbw	8	25	b	1	84	24	1	174	40	2
133/122			4 Durban[1]	D	9	11	b	–	–	–	–	48	15	0	–	–	–
134/123			5 Port Elizabeth	W-10w	11	23	*	–	–	–	1	66	26	1	139	29	2

Career	M	I	NO	HS	R	Avge	100	50	Ct	St	Balls	R	W	Avge	BB	5w	10w	Rate
Test	13	21	3	63	416	23.11	–	1	14	–	1764	624	25	24.96	5-85	1	–	70.56
F/c	565	900	70	189*	22238	26.79	26	112	537	–	108193	39724	1897	20.94	9-95	114	23	57.03

RHODES
Harold James

Derbyshire (1953 to 1975)

TOURS

SA 1959–60 (Cwlth); WI 1960–61 (Swanton); NZ 1961–62 (Int XI); I 1961–62 (Int XI), 1967–68 (Int XI); P 1961–62 (Int XI), 1967–68 (Int XI); SL 1967–68 (Int XI); Z 1961–62 (Int XI)

Born Hadfield, Glossop, Derbyshire 22 Jul 1936

NOTABLE FEATS

- *476* Dismissed Pankaj Roy and C.G. Borde with his 4th and 12th balls in Test cricket.
- Took 100 wickets in a season 3 times, notably 119 at only 11.04 apiece in 1965 when he headed the national averages.
- Hat-trick for Derbyshire v Oxford U at Buxton in 1961.

Tall (6ft 2in), slim and loose-limbed, Harold Rhodes joined Derbyshire as a right-arm off-spinner and experimented with leg-breaks before eventually embarking upon his highly controversial career as a fast bowler. In 1959 he made a dramatic entry into Test cricket, when, replacing the injured Brian Statham, he took two wickets in his first two overs. But his lively, whippy arm action was already causing suspicion during the witch-hunt for 'chuckers' that followed MCC's 1958–59 tour of Australia. In 1960 he was called six times in one innings by Paul Gibb and again by the same umpire the following year. In 1965, Syd Buller no-balled him for the same offence. An MCC subcommittee ruled that his action was generally fair, but they were undecided about whether his over-extended right elbow joint constituted an illegal delivery; this unusual condition allowed his forearm to bend back beyond the normal 180 degrees. It was Buller who requested that he be taken off during a match in 1966 but, in December 1968, his action was officially pronounced as fair by the TCCB. Despite that ruling, Rhodes retired from first-class cricket in 1969 to combine a league engagement with some limited-overs games for Nottinghamshire. He returned for a final appearance against Oxford in 1975. Throughout this saga, his father, the former Derbyshire all-rounder A.E.G. Rhodes, was a first-class umpire.

Harold Rhodes

Ref	Series	V	T Venue	Result	Batting 1st No	R	HO	Batting 2nd No	R	HO	Ct	Bowling 1st Balls	R	W	Bowling 2nd Balls	R	W
476/356	1959	I	3 Leeds	W-I & 173	–	–	–	–	–	–	–	113	50	4	60	35	0
477/357			4 Manchester	W-171	11	0	*	–	–	–	–	108	72	3	168	87	2

Career	M	I	NO	HS	R	Avge	100	50	Ct	St	Balls	R	W	Avge	BB	5w	10w	Rate
Test	2	1	1	0*	0	–	–	–	–	–	449	244	9	27.11	4-50	–	–	49.88
F/c	322	399	143	48	2427	9.48	–	–	86	–	55536	21145	1073	19.70	7-38	42	4	51.75

RHODES, Wilfred

Yorkshire (1898 to 1930)
Europeans (1921–22)
Patiala (1926–27)

Wisden 1899
TOURS
A 1903–04, 1907–08, 1911–12, 1920–21; SA 1909–10, 1913–14; WI 1929–30
Born Kirkheaton, Yorkshire 29 Oct 1877
Died Branksome Park, Dorset 8 Jul 1973

Wilfred Rhodes

Wilfred Rhodes was the most remarkable all-round cricketer in history. Seizing his chance at the age of 20 to be Yorkshire's slow left-arm bowler when Bobby Peel's career was abruptly terminated, he took 154 wickets in his first summer and went on to become the only bowler to reach the 4000 mark. Beginning as a tail-ender, he developed into one of the leading batsmen of his era and stands 16th in the table of most prolific scorers. After exactly half of his 58 Tests he had batted in all 11 positions for England; as last man he had helped George Hirst 'get 'em by singles' and, as an opener, he had partnered Jack Hobbs in England's highest stand for any wicket in Australia. As a sideline he held 764 catches, the seventh-highest total by a non-wicket-keeper. He was also the most durable Test cricketer, enjoying the longest international career of all time and being the oldest to appear at that level. He made his debut at Trent Bridge in W.G. Grace's final Test in 1899 and played his final match in 1930 at the end of the first Test rubber in the Caribbean. Four years earlier he had been recalled at the age of 48 to play a vital role in that historic win at The Oval which regained the Ashes. Rhodes was the first England cricketer to complete the Test 'double' and the first from any country to extend it to 2000 runs and 100 wickets. He also played in the most first-class, county and Championship matches. His bowling was relentlessly accurate, with subtle variations of flight, angle, pace and spin, all from a brief approach and easy rhythmic action which he could maintain for hours without tiring. That same precision and thought went into his batting which was based on a tenacious defence and careful placements. His was the tough, dour, pragmatic approach that has come to typify the Yorkshire spirit. There has been no more dedicated player and 12 Championships during his 29 summers stand as a fitting tribute to a contribution that will never be approached. He coached at Harrow School until his sight began to fade. Even after it deserted him completely in 1952, he remained a frequent visitor to matches and became an uncannily accurate judge of a batsman's timing from the sound of the ball being hit.

NOTABLE FEATS

- 1000 runs in 32nd Test (*116*) (54 inns); 2000 runs in 48th Test (*135*) (79 inns).
- 50 wickets in 10th Test (*79*); 100 wickets and first 'double' for England in 44th Test (*131*).
- *70* His innings analysis of 7 for 17 remains the record for all Tests at Edgbaston.
- *74* Scored the last 15 runs in a match-winning 10th-wkt partnership with G.H. Hirst.
- *78* Shared record E v A 10th-wkt stand of 130 in 66 min with R.E. Foster.
- *79* First to take 15 wickets in E v A Tests; his match analysis of 15 for 124 remains the record for all Tests at Melbourne.
- *119* Shared record E v A 1st-wkt stand of 323 in 268 min with J.B. Hobbs.
- *135* First to score 2000 runs and take 100 wickets in Test cricket.
- *137* Third bowler to take 100 wickets v Australia.
- *167* Set (then) record of 109 wickets v Australia.
- *193* Ended the world's longest Test career (31 yrs 315 days) as the oldest Test cricketer (52 yrs 165 days).
- Holds world record for most appearances in first-class cricket (1107) and also played in most Championship matches (763).
- Exceeded 1000 runs in a season 20 times (plus once on tour), including 2000 twice.
- Took 100 wickets in a season 23 times (record), including 200 in 3 successive years, notably 261 in 1900.
- His total of 4187 wickets is the first-class record and the only instance of 4000.
- Took 154 wickets in 1898 to finish second in national averages (14.60) in his first season (most wickets in debut season).
- Was statistically (100 wickets at lowest cost) the leading bowler of the first-class season 8 times: 1900–01, 1919–23 and 1926.
- He completed the 'double' 16 times (record), twice scoring 2000 runs and taking 100 wickets.
- Holds Yorkshire career records for most appearances (881), most wickets (3608) and most instances of 100 wickets in a season (22). His total of 240 wickets in 1900 is also a Yorkshire record.
- Scored 3 double centuries, notably 267* for Yorkshire v Leicestershire at Leeds in 1921.
- Scored hundreds in 3 consecutive innings in Australia in 1911–12.
- Carried his bat through a completed innings on 3 occasions.
- Shared record Yorkshire 7th-wkt stand of 254 with D.C.F. Burton v Hampshire at Dewsbury in 1919.
- Took 15 for 56 in Yorkshire's match v Essex at Leyton in 1899.

(continued overleaf)

Ref	Series	V	T	Venue	Result	Batting 1st No	R	HO	Batting 2nd No	R	HO	Ct	Bowling 1st Balls	R	W	Bowling 2nd Balls	R	W
60/60	1899	A	1	Nottingham	D	10	6	c	–	–	–	–	177	58	4	100	60	3
61/61			2	Lord's	L-10w	11	2	b	10	2	c	–	195	108	3	25	9	0
64/64			5	Oval	D	11	8	*	–	–	–	1	125	79	0	110	27	3
70/70	1902	A	1	Birmingham	D	11	38	*	–	–	–	–	66	17	7	60	9	1
71/71			2	Lord's	D	–	–	–	–	–	–	–	–	–	–	–	–	–
72/72			3	Sheffield	L-143	10	7	*	10	7	*	1	78	33	1	103	63	5
73/73			4	Manchester	L-3	10	5	c	10	4	*	2	150	104	4	88	26	3
74/74			5	Oval	W-1w	11	0	*	11	6	*	1	168	46	0	132	38	1
78/75	1903–04	A	1	Sydney	W-5w	11	40	*	–	–	–	–	104	41	2	242	94	5
79/76			2	Melbourne	W-185	8	2	lbw	6	9	lbw	3	92	56	7	90	68	8
80/77			3	Adelaide	L-216	8	9	c	10	8	ro	1	84	45	1	126	46	1
81/78			4	Sydney	W-157	11	10	st	11	29	c	–	66	33	4	66	12	0
82/79			5	Melbourne	L-218	2	3	c	8	16	*	1	72	41	1	90	52	2
83/80	1905	A	1	Nottingham	W-213	10	29	c	7	39	*	–	108	37	1	180	58	1
84/81			2	Lord's	D	8	15	b	–	–	–	–	97	70	3	–	–	–
86/83			4	Manchester	W-I & 80	9	27	*	–	–	–	5	35	25	2	69	36	3
87/84			5	Oval	D	9	36	b	–	–	–	1	126	59	0	48	29	0
96/93	1970–08	A	1	Sydney	L-2w	7	1	ro	2	29	c	–	30	13	1	42	13	0
97/94			2	Melbourne	W-1w	7	32	b	7	15	ro	–	66	37	1	96	38	0
98/95			3	Adelaide	L-245	7	38	c	7	9	c	1	90	35	0	162	81	0
99/96			4	Melbourne	L-308	6	0	c	6	2	c	–	30	21	0	144	66	1
100/97			5	Sydney	L-49	8	10	c	7	69	b	–	60	15	0	226	102	4
101/98	1909	A	1	Birmingham	W-10w	8	15	*	–	–	–	2	–	–	–	6	8	0
103/100			3	Leeds	L-126	6	12	c	6	16	c	1	48	38	4	114	44	2
104/101			4	Manchester	D	5	5	c	5	0	*	–	–	–	–	150	83	5
105/102			5	Oval	D	3	66	c	2	54	st	3	72	34	0	84	35	0
106/103	1909–10	SA	1	Johannesburg[1]	L-19	2	66	b	2	2	c	2	54	34	1	54	25	0
107/104			2	Durban[1]	L-95	2	44	c	2	17	c	2	30	11	0	114	43	0
108/105			3	Johannesburg[1]	W-3w	1	14	c	4	1	c	2	6	4	1	24	6	0
109/106			4	Cape Town	L-4w	2	0	c	2	5	b	2	–	–	–	18	2	0
110/107			5	Cape Town	W-9w	2	77	b	2	0	*	2	–	–	–	42	22	0
116/108	1911–12	A	1	Sydney	L-146	4	41	c	5	0	c	1	48	26	0	18	4	0
117/109			2	Melbourne	W-8w	1	61	c	1	28	c	–	–	–	–	18	3	0
118/110			3	Adelaide	W-7w	2	59	b	2	57	*	1	–	–	–	6	6	0
119/111			4	Melbourne	W-I & 225	2	179	c	–	–	–	2	12	1	0	–	–	–
120/112			5	Sydney	W-70	2	8	b	2	30	lbw	1	–	–	–	12	17	0
122/113	1912	SA	1	Lord's	W-I & 62	2	36	b	–	–	–	–	–	–	–	–	–	–
123/114		A	1	Lord's	D	2	59	b	–	–	–	–	116	59	3	–	–	–
124/115		SA	2	Leeds	W-174	2	7	c	2	10	b	–	–	–	–	24	14	0
126/116		A	2	Manchester	D	2	92	b	–	–	–	–	–	–	–	–	–	–
128/117		SA	3	Oval	W-10w	2	0	b	–	–	–	1	–	–	–	–	–	–
129/118		A	3	Oval	W-244	2	49	b	2	4	b	2	–	–	–	12	1	0
130/119	1913–14	SA	1	Durban[1]	W-I & 157	2	18	c	–	–	–	1	42	26	0	–	–	–
131/120			2	Johannesburg[1]	W-I & 12	1	152	c	–	–	–	3	78	23	1	54	20	0
132/121			3	Johannesburg[1]	W-91	2	35	lbw	2	0	c	2	23	9	1	36	17	0
133/122			4	Durban[1]	D	2	22	lbw	2	35	lbw	2	84	33	3	156	53	1
134/123			5	Port Elizabeth	W-10w	2	27	b	2	0	*	2	–	–	–	60	14	0
135/124	1920–21	A	1	Sydney	L-377	7	3	c	7	45	c	–	–	–	–	132	67	0
136/125			2	Melbourne	L-I & 91	2	7	b	2	28	c	1	51	26	1	–	–	–
137/126			3	Adelaide	L-119	2	16	ro	2	4	lbw	1	30	23	0	155	61	3
138/127			4	Melbourne	L-8w	2	11	c	2	73	c	2	–	–	–	60	25	0
139/128			5	Sydney	L-9w	2	26	c	2	25	ro	–	42	23	0	44	20	0
140/129	1921	A	1	Nottingham	L-10w	8	19	c	8	10	c	2	78	33	2	–	–	–
167/153	1926	A	5	Oval	W-289	7	28	c	7	14	lbw	–	150	35	2	120	44	4
190/176	1929–30	WI	1	Bridgetown	D	10	14	*	–	–	–	2	163	44	0	306	110	3
191/177			2	Port-of-Spain	W-167	10	2	lbw	10	6	*	–	120	40	1	132	31	0
192/178			3	Georgetown	L-289	10	0	b	10	10	*	1	240	96	2	306	93	2
193/179			4	Kingston	D	10	8	*	10	11	*	–	125	17	1	144	22	1

Career	M	I	NO	HS	R	Avge	100	50	Ct	St	Balls	R	W	Avge	BB	5w	10w	Rate
Test	58	98	21	179	2325	30.19	2	11	60	–	8231	3425	127	26.96	8-68	6	1	64.81
F/c	1107	1528	237	267*	39802	30.83	58	196	764	–	184142	69993	4187	16.71	9-24	287	68	43.97

W. RHODES - TEST SUMMARY

Series	V	M	I	NO	HS	R	Avge	100	50	Balls	R	W	Avge	BB	5w	10w	Rate
1899	A	3	4	1	8*	18	6.00	–	–	732	341	13	26.23	4-58	–	–	56.30
1902	A	5	7	6	38*	67	67.00	–	–	845	336	22	15.27	7-17	2	–	38.40
1903–04	A	5	9	2	40*	126	18.00	–	–	1032	488	31	15.74	8-68	3	1	33.29
1905	A	4	5	2	39*	146	48.66	–	–	663	314	10	31.40	3-36	–	–	66.30
1907–08	A	5	10	–	69	205	20.50	–	1	946	421	7	60.14	4-102	–	–	135.14
1909	A	4	7	2	66	168	33.60	–	2	474	242	11	22.00	5-83	1	–	43.09
1909–10	SA	5	10	1	77	226	25.11	–	2	342	147	2	73.50	1-4	–	–	171.00
1911–12	A	5	9	1	179	463	57.87	1	3	114	57	0	–	–	–	–	–
1912	SA	3	4	–	36	53	13.25	–	–	24	14	0	–	–	–	–	–
1912	A	3	4	–	92	204	51.00	–	2	128	60	3	20.00	3-59	–	–	42.66
1913–14	SA	5	8	1	152	289	41.28	1	–	533	195	6	32.50	3-33	–	–	88.83
1920–21	A	5	10	–	73	238	23.80	–	1	514	245	4	61.25	3-61	–	–	128.50
1921	A	1	2	–	19	29	14.50	–	–	78	33	2	16.50	2-33	–	–	39.00
1926	A	1	2	–	28	42	21.00	–	–	270	79	6	13.16	4-44	–	–	45.00
1929–30	WI	4	7	5	14*	51	25.50	–	–	1536	453	10	45.30	3-110	–	–	153.60
	A	41	69	14	179	1706	31.01	1	9	5796	2616	109	24.00	8-68	6	1	53.17
	SA	13	22	2	152	568	28.40	1	2	899	356	8	44.50	3-33	–	–	112.37
	WI	4	7	5	14*	51	25.50	–	–	1536	453	10	45.30	3-110	–	–	153.60
Home		24	35	11	92	727	30.29	–	4	3214	1419	67	21.17	7-17	3	–	47.97
Overseas		34	63	10	179	1598	30.15	2	7	5017	2006	60	33.43	8-68	3	1	83.61
Totals		58	98	21	179	2325	30.19	2	11	8231	3425	127	26.96	8-68	6	1	64.81

NOTABLE FEATS *cont.*

- Took 9 for 24 (including 7 in 24 balls) for C.I. Thornton's XI v Australians at Scarborough in 1899. Twice took 9 wickets v Essex at Leyton: 9 for 28 in 1899 and 9 for 39 in 1929.
- Took 5 for 6 when MCC dismissed Victoria for 15 (lowest total in Australian first-class cricket) at Melbourne in 1903–04.
- Two hat-tricks for Yorkshire: v Kent at Canterbury in 1901 and v Derbyshire at Derby in 1920.
- Took 7 wickets in 28 balls for Yorkshire v Essex at Leyton in 1929.
- Bowled in an unchanged partnership throughout both completed innings of a match on 6 occasions – 3 with S. Haigh and 3 with G.H. Hirst.
- Achieved the match 'double' (183 runs and 12 wickets) for Europeans v Parsees at Bombay in 1921–22.
- He took a wicket with his final ball in first-class cricket.

RICHARDS
Clifton James

Surrey (1976 to 1988)
Orange Free State (1983–84)

TOURS
A 1986–87; WI 1982–83 (Int XI); NZ 1979–80 (Robins), 1987–88; I/SL 1981–82
Born Penzance, Cornwall 10 Aug 1958

The second Cornishman after Jack Crapp to play Test cricket for England, 'Jack' Richards was a worthy member of Surrey's succession of high-class wicket-keepers. Tallish (5ft 11in), lively and neat, he always wore his collar raised and his shirt buttoned at the neck and cuffs. At his peak he was almost in the Knott and Taylor class, alert, agile and with that easy timing as he 'rode' with the ball. His nimble footwork made him an above-average middle-order batsman and his gifts for improvisation and hitting on the 'up' were ideally suited to the limited-overs game. Occasionally he would produce an innings of sustained brilliance as at Perth in his second Test match. Highly strung and ambitious, he eventually proved a disruptive influence at The Oval and his career came to a sad and contentious conclusion after a record-breaking benefit.

'Jack' Richards

NOTABLE FEATS

- *1059* Shared record E in A 6th-wkt stand of 207 with D.I. Gower.
- Scored 1006 runs in 1986.
- Contributed 172* to record Surrey 7th-wkt stand of 262 with K.T. Medlycott v Kent at The Oval in 1987.
- Made 10 dismissals in the match for Surrey v Sussex at Guildford in 1987.

Ref	Series	V	T	Venue	Result	Batting 1st No	R	HO	Batting 2nd No	R	HO	Fielding 1st Ct	St	Byes	Balls	Fielding 2nd Ct	St	Byes	Balls
1058/629†	1986–87	A	1	Brisbane[2]	W-7w	7	0	b	–	–	–	3	–	2	628	–	1	5	701
1059/630†			2	Perth	D	7	133	c	7	15	c	1	–	9	808	–	–	9	582
1060/631†			3	Adelaide	D	8	29	c	–	–	–	2	–	0	1026	–	–	4	540
1061/632†			4	Melbourne	W-I & 14	7	3	c	–	–	–	5	–	1	328	–	–	0	442
1062/633†			5	Sydney	L-55	7	46	c	7	38	b	3	–	12	869	1	–	5	702
1077/636†	1987	P	3	Leeds	L-I & 18	8	6	lbw	7	2	c	2	–	5	788	–	–	–	–
1101/649†	1988	WI	4	Leeds	L-10w	8	2	b	7	8	b	1	–	0	488	–	–	0	87
1102/650†			5	Oval	L-8w	7	0	c	8	3	c	1	–	0	354	1	–	2	546

Career	M	I	NO	HS	R	Avge	100	50	Ct	St	Balls	R	W	Avge	BB	5w	10w	Rate
Test	8	13	–	133	285	21.92	1	–	20	1	–	–	–	–	–	–	–	–
F/c	286	371	87	172*	8012	28.21	8	37	604	72	282	224	5	44.80	2-42	–	–	56.40

RICHARDSON
Derek Walter

Worcestershire (1952 to 1967)

TOURS
WI 1965–66 (Worcs); Z 1964–65 (Worcs)
Born Hereford 3 Nov 1934

NOTABLE FEATS

- Exceeded 1000 runs in a season 9 times.
- Holds Worcestershire records for most catches by a non-wicket-keeper in a career (412) and in a season (65 in 1961).

'Dick' Richardson was a fluent left-handed middle-order batsman and a brilliant close fielder; his left-arm medium-pace bowling was seldom employed. At 5ft 10½in he was taller than his elder and more famous brother and, with his far higher backlift, his strokeplay was much freer. He joined Worcestershire as an amateur after leaving Hereford Cathedral School but turned professional in 1956. His solitary Test cap was sufficient to provide the first instance of brothers appearing together for England since 1891–92. There has been none since.

'Dick' Richardson

Ref	Series	V	T	Venue	Result	Batting 1st No	R	HO	Batting 2nd No	R	HO	Ct
441/339	1957	WI	3	Nottingham	D	6	33	b	–	–	–	1

Career	M	I	NO	HS	R	Avge	100	50	Ct	St	Balls	R	W	Avge	BB	5w	10w	Rate
Test	1	1	0	33	33	33.00	–	–	1	–	–	–	–	–	–	–	–	–
F/c	383	660	65	169	16303	27.40	16	89	422	–	588	354	8	44.25	2-11	–	–	73.50

RICHARDSON
Peter Edward

Worcestershire (1949 to 1958)
Kent (1959 to 1965)

Wisden 1957
TOURS
A 1958–59; SA 1956–57; WI 1963–64 (Cav), 1964–65 (Cav); NZ 1958–59; I 1961–62, 1964–65 (Cwlth); P 1955–56, 1961–62, 1963–64 (Cwlth); SL 1961–62
Born Hereford 4 Jul 1931

Peter Richardson in the Manchester Test of 1958. He was later stumped by New Zealand captain John Reid who was deputising for the injured Petrie.

Peter Richardson's batting technique reflected his temperament and was completely different from that of his younger brother, 'Dick'. Shorter (5ft 9in), he employed a minimal backlift and was an accomplished manipulator of the nudge, push and steer. He founded his innings on patience, resolute defence and stolen singles, only occasionally breaking free of his shackles to lever the ball away with those immensely strong arms. At cover-point he was always alert and threatening. Like his nearest brother, he joined Worcestershire as an amateur straight from Hereford Cathedral School and subsequently turned professional (1959). He met with immediate success when introduced to Test cricket and remained an automatic choice for three years until he failed along with several others on England's disastrous 1958–59 tour of Australia. That loss of form coincided with the end of his career at Worcester where he had just completed a spell as captain (1956–58) and joint-secretary (1956–57). After a fallow season qualifying for Kent, he quickly adapted to his new surroundings and developed a more fluent style. Besides adding to his idiosyncratic range of left-handed strokes, he found time and inspiration to pen more letters from fictitious colonels to a certain august cricket correspondent.

NOTABLE FEATS

- 1000 runs in 13th Test (*441*) (22 inns); 2000 runs in 32nd Test (*518*) (53 inns).
- *425* Scored 81 and 73 on debut.
- *441* Shared record E v WI 2nd-wkt stand of 266 with T.W. Graveney.

D.W. Richardson's only Test match provided the last instance of brothers appearing in the same Test for England (first instance since 1891–92).

- *513* Shared (then) record E v I 1st-wkt stand of 159 in 170 min with G. Pullar.
- Exceeded 1000 runs in a season 11 times (plus once on tour), including 2000 on 4 occasions – notably 2294 in 1953 (his second full season).
- Scored hundreds in 3 consecutive innings in 1956.
- Carried his bat through a completed innings twice.
- Scored 100 before lunch on 4 occasions.
- Last of only 6 cricketers to appear for both sides in Gentlemen (1955–58) v Players (1959) matches.

						Batting 1st			Batting 2nd				Bowling 1st			Bowling 2nd		
Ref	Series	V	T	Venue	Result	No	R	HO	No	R	HO	Ct	Balls	R	W	Balls	R	W
425/327	1956	A	1	Nottingham	D	1	81	c	1	73	c	–	–	–	–	–	–	–
426/328			2	Lord's	L-185	1	9	c	1	21	c	–	–	–	–	–	–	–
427/329			3	Leeds	W-I & 42	1	5	c	–	–	–	1	–	–	–	–	–	–
428/330			4	Manchester	W-I & 170	1	104	c	–	–	–	–	–	–	–	–	–	
429/331			5	Oval	D	1	37	c	1	34	c	–	–	–	–	–	–	–
434/332	1956–57	SA	1	Johannesburg[3]	W-131	1	117	lbw	1	10	lbw	–	–	–	–	–	–	–
435/333			2	Cape Town	W-312	1	45	lbw	1	44	c	–	–	–	–	–	–	–
436/334			3	Durban[2]	D	1	68	lbw	1	32	b	–	–	–	–	–	–	–
437/335			4	Johannesburg[3]	L-17	1	11	c	1	39	b	–	–	–	–	–	–	–
438/336			5	Port Elizabeth	L-58	1	0	lbw	1	3	b	–	–	–	–	–	–	–
439/337	1957	WI	1	Birmingham	D	1	47	c	1	34	c	–	–	–	–	–	–	–
440/338			2	Lord's	W-I & 36	1	76	b	–	–	–	–	–	–	–	–	–	–
441/339			3	Nottingham	D	1	126	c	1	11	c	–	–	–	–	–	–	–
442/340			4	Leeds	W-I & 5	1	10	c	–	–	–	–	–	–	–	–	–	–
443/341			5	Oval	W-I & 237	1	107	b	–	–	–	–	–	–	–	–	–	–
454/342	1958	NZ	1	Birmingham	W-205	1	4	lbw	1	100	c	–	–	–	–	–	–	–
455/343			2	Lord's	W-I & 148	1	36	c	–	–	–	–	–	–	–	–	–	–
457/345			4	Manchester	W-I & 13	1	74	st	–	–	–	–	–	–	–	–	–	–
458/346			5	Oval	D	1	28	b	–	–	–	–	–	–	–	–	–	–
464/347	1958–59	A	1	Brisbane[2]	L-8w	1	11	c	1	8	c	–	–	–	–	–	–	–
465/348			2	Melbourne	L-8w	1	3	c	1	2	c	–	–	–	–	–	–	–
467/350			4	Adelaide	L-10w	1	4	lbw	1	43	lbw	–	–	–	–	–	–	–
468/351			5	Melbourne	L-9w	1	68	c	1	23	lbw	–	–	–	–	–	–	–

Ref	Series	V	T	Venue	Result	Batting 1st			Batting 2nd			Ct	Bowling 1st			Bowling 2nd		
						No	R	HO	No	R	HO		Balls	R	W	Balls	R	W
472/352	1958–59	NZ	1	Christchurch	W-I & 99	1	8	c	–	–	–	–	–	–	–	–	–	–
473/353			2	Auckland	D	1	67	c	–	–	–	–	–	–	–	–	–	–
512/374	1962–62	P	1	Lahore[2]	W-5w	1	4	c	1	48	c	–	–	–	–	–	–	–
513/375	1961–62	I	1	Bombay[2]	D	1	71	c	1	43	c	2	–	–	–	36	10	2
514/376			2	Kanpur	D	1	22	c	1	48	c	1	–	–	–	–	–	–
515/377			3	Delhi	D	1	1	lbw	–	–	–	1	–	–	–	–	–	–
516/378			4	Calcutta	L-187	1	62	c	1	42	b	–	–	–	–	–	–	–
517/379			5	Madras[2]	L-128	1	13	c	1	2	c	–	–	–	–	–	–	–
518/380	1961–62	P	2	Dacca	D	6	19	c	2	21	*	1	–	–	–	72	28	1
519/381			3	Karachi	D	1	26	c	–	–	–	–	–	–	–	12	10	0
545/397	1963	WI	3	Birmingham	W-217	1	2	b	1	14	c	–	–	–	–	–	–	–

Career	M	I	NO	HS	R	Avge	100	50	Ct	St	Balls	R	W	Avge	BB	5w	10w	Rate
Test	34	56	1	126	2061	37.47	5	9	6	–	120	48	3	16.00	2-10	–	–	40.00
F/c	454	794	41	185	26055	34.60	44	140	220	–	763	499	11	45.36	2-10	–	–	69.36

P. E. RICHARDSON – TEST BATTING SUMMARY

Series	V	M	I	NO	HS	R	Avge	100	50
1956	A	5	8	–	104	364	45.50	1	2
1956–57	SA	5	10	–	117	369	36.90	1	1
1957	WI	5	7	–	126	411	58.71	2	1
1958	NZ	4	5	–	100	242	48.40	1	1
1958–59	A	4	8	–	68	162	20.25	–	1
1958–59	NZ	2	2	–	67	75	37.50	–	1
1961–62	P	3	5	1	48	118	29.50	–	–
1961–62	I	5	9	–	71	304	33.77	–	2
1963	WI	1	2	–	14	16	8.00	–	–

Series	V	M	I	NO	HS	R	Avge	100	50
	A	9	16	–	104	526	32.87	1	3
	SA	5	10	–	117	369	36.90	1	1
	WI	6	9	–	126	427	47.44	2	1
	NZ	6	7	–	100	317	45.28	1	2
	I	5	9	–	71	304	33.77	–	2
	P	3	5	1	48	118	29.50	–	–
Home		15	22	–	126	1033	46.95	4	4
Overseas		19	34	1	117	1028	31.15	1	5
Totals		34	56	1	126	2061	37.47	5	9

RICHARDSON
Thomas

Surrey (1892 to 1904)
London County (1904)
Somerset (1905)

Wisden 1897
TOURS A 1894–95, 1897–98
Born Byfleet, Surrey 11 Aug 1870
Died St Jean D'Arvey, Savoie, France
2 Jul 1912

Any bowler who can take 1005 first-class wickets in just four summers has to be a bit special; when those figures were achieved by a genuinely fast bowler playing half his matches on the heavily rolled shirt-front pitches at The Oval and with only one ball available for even the longest innings, their perpetrator, Tom Richardson, must be rated as one of the greatest of his type. Tall, strongly built and of gypsy stock, he was a right-arm fast bowler with a long, smoothly accelerating run and a high, leaping, side-on delivery. Extremely accurate, he had the stamina and willpower to maintain his high pace for long periods and a body action which enabled him consistently to break the ball back sharply. His output each summer was extraordinary for a fast bowler. He thrived on hard sun-baked surfaces and was far less effective on wet ones when the footholds were less firm; if the pitch was dry on top and damp underneath his vicious break-back made him virtually unplayable. He remains the only genuinely fast bowler to have taken 250 wickets in a season and 'Tich' Freeman is alone in surpassing his incredible 1895 haul of 290 wickets. Not surprisingly, that was one of four seasons during his career in which Surrey won the Championship. His Test match performances and striking rate were equally remarkable. He cared little for batting and preferred to save his valuable energy for the more serious business of bowling. After his second arduous tour of Australia a combination of his massive workload, rheumatism and increasing weight began to take its toll. When Surrey failed to renew terms after 1904, he moved to Bath and turned out once for Somerset before spending his few years of retirement as a publican. He died in his 42nd year, probably from a cerebral thrombosis, while holidaying among the French mountains.

Ref	Series	V	T	Venue	Result	Batting 1st No	R	HO	Batting 2nd No	R	HO	Ct	Bowling 1st Balls	R	W	Bowling 2nd Balls	R	W
41/41	1893	A	3	Manchester	D	10	16	b	–	–	–	–	119	49	5	220	107	5
42/42	1894–95	A	1	Sydney	W-10	11	0	*	11	12	*	–	333	181	5	66	27	1
43/43			2	Melbourne	W-94	11	0	c	11	11	c	–	138	57	5	240	100	2
44/44			3	Adelaide	L-382	11	0	c	11	12	c	–	126	75	5	188	89	3
45/45			4	Sydney	L-I & 147	10	2	c	10	10	*	1	132	78	2	–	–	–
46/46			5	Melbourne	W-6w	11	11	lbw	–	–	–	–	252	138	3	272	104	6
50/50	1896	A	1	Lord's	W-6w	11	6	c	–	–	–	–	58	39	6	235	134	5
51/51			2	Manchester	L-3w	11	2	ro	11	1	c	1	340	168	7	213	76	6
52/52			3	Oval	W-66	11	1	*	11	10	*	1	25	22	0	5	0	0
53/53	1897–98	A	1	Sydney	W-9w	11	24	*	–	–	–	1	162	71	3	246	121	2
54/54			2	Melbourne	L-I & 55	11	3	b	11	2	*	1	288	114	1	–	–	–
55/55			3	Adelaide	L-I & 13	11	25	*	11	0	c	–	336	164	4	–	–	–
56/56			4	Melbourne	L-8w	11	20	b	11	2	c	–	156	102	2	–	–	–
57/57			5	Sydney	L-6w	11	1	b	11	6	b	–	217	94	8	130	110	2

Career	M	I	NO	HS	R	Avge	100	50	Ct	St	Balls	R	W	Avge	BB	5w	10w	Rate
Test	14	24	8	25*	177	11.06	–	–	5	–	4497	2220	88	25.22	8-94	11	4	51.10
F/c	358	479	124	69	3424	9.64	–	2	126	–	78992	38794	2104	18.43	10-45	200	72	37.54

Tom Richardson

T. RICHARDSON – TEST BOWLING SUMMARY

Series	V	M	Balls	R	W	Avge	BB	5w	10w	Rate
1893	A	1	339	156	10	15.60	5-49	2	1	33.90
1894–95	A	5	1747	849	32	26.53	6-104	4	–	54.59
1896	A	3	876	439	24	18.29	7-168	4	2	36.50
1897–98	A	5	1535	776	22	35.27	8-94	1	1	69.77
Home		4	1215	595	34	17.50	7-168	6	3	35.73
Overseas		10	3282	1625	54	30.09	8-94	5	1	60.77
Totals		14	4497	2220	88	25.22	8-94	11	4	51.10

NOTABLE FEATS

- 50 wickets in 7th Test (*50*).
- Took 100 wickets in a season 10 times, including 200 in 3 successive years, notably 290 in 1895 (the record until 1928 and still the third-highest total) and 273 in 1897.
- Was statistically (100 wickets at lowest cost) the leading bowler of the first-class season twice: 1894 and 1897.
- Took all 10 for 45 (including 8 bowled) for Surrey v Essex at The Oval in 1894 and took 9 wickets in an innings on 3 other occasions.
- Took 15 wickets in a match for Surrey on 5 occasions, the most economical being 15 for 83 v Warwickshire at The Oval in 1898.
- His Championship record of taking 10 or more wickets 15 times in a season (1895) has been equalled (A.P. Freeman) but never beaten.
- Holds Surrey career records for most wickets (1775) and most instances of 100 wickets in a season (10); also most wickets in a season (252 in 1895).
- Four hat-tricks (Surrey record): 3 at The Oval – v Gloucestershire (1893), Leicestershire (1896) and Warwickshire (1989) – and v Sussex at Hove in 1898.
- Bowled in an unchanged partnership throughout both completed innings of a match for Surrey on 3 occasions.

RICHMOND Thomas Leonard

Nottinghamshire (1912 to 1928)

Born Radcliffe on Trent, Nottinghamshire 23 Jun 1890
Died Saxondale, Nottinghamshire 29 Dec 1957

'Tich' Richmond was a diminutive (under 5ft 7in) right-arm slow bowler who became increasingly rotund. For a few seasons after the Great War he was sufficiently talented to challenge his Kent counterpart, 'Tich' Freeman, as the best leg-break and googly bowler in England. He was extremely accurate for a bowler of his type and, given any help in the pitch, could be virtually unplayable. His skills fell away sharply after 1926, mainly because of his added girth. Apart from once startling everyone, including himself, by scoring 70 in an hour, his batting record was distinctly modest. He was something of a passenger in the field.

'Tich' Richmond

NOTABLE FEATS

- Took 100 wickets in a season 7 times, notably 169 (avge 13.48) in 1922 which survived as the Nottinghamshire record until 1954.
- Twice took 9 wickets in an innings for Nottinghamshire at Trent Bridge: 9 for 21 v Hampshire in 1922 and 9 for 55 v Northamptonshire in 1925.
- Took 14 wickets in a day (7 for 30 and 7 for 53) for Nottinghamshire v Gloucestershire at Cheltenham in 1925.
- Hat-trick for Nottinghamshire v Lancashire at Nottingham in 1926.
- Contributed 70 to Nottinghamshire's 10th-wkt stand of 140 with S.J. Staples v Derbyshire at Worksop in 1922.

						Batting 1st			Batting 2nd				Bowling 1st			Bowling 2nd		
Ref	Series	V	T	Venue	Result	No	R	HO	No	R	HO	Ct	Balls	R	W	Balls	R	W
140/129	1921	A	1	Nottingham	L-10w	1	4	c	1	2	b	–	96	69	2	18	17	0

Career	M	I	NO	HS	R	Avge	100	50	Ct	St	Balls	R	W	Avge	BB	5w	10w	Rate
Test	1	2	0	4	6	3.00	–	–	–	–	114	86	2	43.00	2-69	–	–	57.00
F/c	252	281	116	70	1644	9.96	–	2	39	–	48048	24959	1176	21.22	9-21	90	19	40.85

RIDGWAY, Frederick

Kent (1946 to 1961)

TOURS
I/SL 1950–51 (Cwlth), 1951–52;
P 1951–52
Born Stockport, Cheshire 10 Aug 1923

A hostile right-arm fast-medium bowler, Fred Ridgway moved the ball either way. Just medium height (5ft 9in), he often surprised batsmen with his fast skidding deliveries but otherwise compensated for his lack of inches with determination and effort. On his day he could be distinctly sharp. He was a good fielder close to the wicket and enjoyed several successful days as a totally aggressive batsman. Although he played in the 1949 Test trial and was twelfth man for England at Lord's in 1951, his Test appearances were restricted to a complete series in India. He played some Kent league soccer for Ramsgate. [*Illus. p.* 223]

NOTABLE FEATS

- Took 105 wickets in 1949.
- Took 4 wickets in 4 balls for Kent v Derbyshire at Folkestone in 1951 and a hat-trick v Oxford U at Oxford in 1958.
- Shared record Kent 9th-wkt stand of 161 with B.R. Edrich v Sussex at Tunbridge Wells in 1949.

Ref	Series	V	T	Venue	Result	Batting 1st No	R	HO	Batting 2nd No	R	HO	Ct	Bowling 1st Balls	R	W	Bowling 2nd Balls	R	W
339/292	1951-52	I	1	Delhi	D	11	15	b	–	–	–	–	120	55	0	–	–	–
340/293			2	Bombay[2]	D	11	5	c	–	–	–	–	192	137	0	96	33	2
341/294			3	Calcutta	D	10	24	st	–	–	–	–	229	83	4	12	8	0
342/295			4	Kanpur	W-8w	10	5	b	–	–	–	3	42	16	0	–	–	–
343/296			5	Madras[1]	L-I & 8	10	0	lbw	10	0	b	–	102	47	1	–	–	–

Career	M	I	NO	HS	R	Avge	100	50	Ct	St	Balls	R	W	Avge	BB	5w	10w	Rate
Test	5	6	0	24	49	8.16	–	–	3	–	793	379	7	54.14	4-83	–	–	113.28
F/c	341	486	115	94	4081	11.00	–	9	234	–	56677	25381	1069	23.74	8-39	41	6	53.01

ROBERTSON
John David Benbow

Middlesex (1937 to 1959)

Wisden 1948
TOURS
WI 1947–48; I/SL 1951–52; P 1951–52
Born Chiswick, Middlesex 22 Feb 1917

Jack Robertson

Jack Robertson was one of the most composed and stylishly correct of opening batsmen; he was also one of the most selfless. Tallish (5ft 11in) and elegant, he was a handsomely balanced player and a supremely gifted timer who constantly reminded Middlesex followers of J.W. Hearne. An outstanding player of the new ball, he also had a marvellous technique against spin; he always knew where his off stump was and became a master of the wristy late cut. In 1947 his opening partnerships with Sid Brown were invaluable in paving the way for the famous onslaughts by Compton and Edrich. Before beginning his career at Lord's, he was coached by Jack Durston at the Acton Cricket School and used to open Turnham Green's batting with his father. Although he was 22 when the Hitler War began, he seemed unaffected by the long break and proceeded to score more than 2000 runs in each of his next seven seasons. His meagre ration of 11 Test matches was packed into that period, only two of them at home. He headed England's batting averages in the Caribbean and, replacing the injured Washbrook at Lord's in 1949, discovered that even a score of 121 was insufficient to retain his place. He loved to tell the tale about the aftermath of his scoring 331 in a day at Worcester. After he had changed he was surprised to discover that one of his car tyres had a puncture; he was even more surprised when none of the home bowlers would help him with the repairs. A handy off-break bowler, he was a capable fielder anywhere. One of the most evocative of wartime cricket photographs appeared in the 1945 *Wisden* and shows Jack Robertson (Army) and the RAF fielders lying prone on the turf at Lord's. They were taking 'evasive action' against an approaching flying bomb. Robertson duly celebrated the passing of danger by hitting a six. As Middlesex coach from 1960, he spent much of his spare time lecturing and guiding young cricketers and continued to open the Lord's Taverners batting until well into his sixties.

NOTABLE FEATS

- Exceeded 1000 runs in a season 14 times (plus once on tour), including 2000 on 9 occasions, notably 2917 in 1951.
- Made Middlesex record score of 331* in 390 min v Worcestershire at Worcester in 1949; it also remains the highest score v Worcestershire, the highest score at Worcester and the fourth-highest score in a single day. He made 3 other double centuries, all for Middlesex.
- Scored 12 hundreds in 1947.
- Twice scored hundreds in 3 consecutive innings for Middlesex (1947 and 1954).
- Scored 100 before lunch on 3 occasions.
- Shared (then) record Middlesex 1st-wkt stand of 310 with S.M. Brown v Nottinghamshire at Lord's in 1947.
- Scored 9 runs off 1 ball from H.S. Squires for MCC v Surrey at Lord's in 1948.

						Batting 1st			Batting 2nd				Bowling 1st			Bowling 2nd		
Ref	Series	V	T	Venue	Result	No	R	HO	No	R	HO	Ct	Balls	R	W	Balls	R	W
289/257	1947	SA	5	Oval	D	3	4	c	3	30	b	–	–	–	–	–	–	–
295/258	1947–48	WI	1	Bridgetown	D	1	80	lbw	1	51	*	2	–	–	–	–	–	–
296/259			2	Port-of-Spain	D	1	2	ro	1	133	c	1	–	–	–	–	–	–
297/260			3	Georgetown	L-7w	2	23	c	2	9	lbw	–	–	–	–	–	–	–
298/261			4	Kingston	L-10w	2	64	lbw	2	28	b	–	–	–	–	–	–	–
315/273	1949	NZ	2	Lord's	D	2	26	c	2	121	c	1	–	–	–	–	–	–
339/292	1951–52	I	1	Delhi	D	1	50	lbw	1	22	c	–	30	12	0	–	–	–
340/293			2	Bombay[2]	D	2	44	c	–	–	–	1	6	1	0	–	–	–
341/294			3	Calcutta	D	1	13	c	1	22	st	1	–	–	–	30	10	0
342/295			4	Kanpur	W-8w	4	21	lbw	4	5	*	–	–	–	–	42	17	2
343/296			5	Madras[1]	L-I & 8	4	77	c	4	56	lbw	–	30	18	0	–	–	–

Career	M	I	NO	HS	R	Avge	100	50	Ct	St	Balls	R	W	Avge	BB	5w	10w	Rate
Test	11	21	2	133	881	46.36	2	6	6	–	138	58	2	29.00	2-17	–	–	69.00
F/c	509	897	46	331*	31914	37.50	67	161	350	–	5685	2536	73	34.73	4-37	–	–	77.87

ROBINS
Robert Walter Vivian

Middlesex (1925 to 1951)
Cambridge University (1926 to 1928)

Wisden 1930
TOUR A 1936–37
Born Stafford 3 Jun 1906
Died Marylebone, London 12 Dec 1968

As a batsman, bowler, fielder, captain, manager, selector or administrator, Walter Robins was quick-witted and fast-moving; no man has exerted more energy or enthusiasm in everything he attempted. Known as 'Cock' Robins because of his small stature and bouncy, chirpy manner, he was an outstanding all-rounder at Highgate School and appeared for Middlesex during his final term there before gaining blues in each of his three years at Cambridge; in his final Varsity match he scored a century and took 8 wickets. A fast-scoring, nimble-footed batsman with an exceptionally high backlift, he was also an adventurous right-arm leg-break and googly bowler who spun the ball considerably but often pitched erratically, and a brilliant fielder in the covers. When his business commitments permitted, he was a most dynamic captain who made things happen. He led Middlesex in three spells (1935–38, 1946–47 and 1950), winning the Championship in 1947. He also captained MCC to Canada in 1951, managed the 1959–60 tour of the West Indies and served two terms as a Test selector (1946–48 and 1962–64), the latter one as chairman. As an inside-left he gained a soccer blue and represented Nottingham Forest.

England v New Zealand at The Oval, 1937: standing *C. Washbrook, L. Hutton, A.D.G. Matthews, A.R. Gover, J. Hardstaff jr, D.C.S. Compton;* seated *T.W.J. Goddard, L.E.G. Ames, R.W.V. Robins (captain), W.R. Hammond, C.J. Barnett.*

Ref	Series	V	T	Venue	Result	Batting 1st No	R	HO	Batting 2nd No	R	HO	Ct	Bowling 1st Balls	R	W	Bowling 2nd Balls	R	W
182/168	1929	SA	2	Lord's	D	8	4	c	8	0	c	–	144	47	2	114	32	3
194/180	1930	A	1	Nottingham	W-93	8	50	*	8	4	b	1	102	51	4	104	81	3
195/181			2	Lord's	L-7w	9	5	c	9	11	*	–	252	172	1	54	34	2
209/190	1931	NZ	1	Lord's	D	10	12	c	–	–	–	–	78	38	3	222	126	2
219/193	1932	I		Lord's	W-158	8	21	c	8	30	c	3	102	39	2	84	57	1
227/201	1933	WI	1	Lord's	W-I & 27	9	8	b	–	–	–	–	71	32	6	72	36	1
228/202			2	Manchester	D	8	55	st	–	–	–	1	172	111	3	67	41	1
242/216	1935	SA	1	Nottingham	D	–	–	–	–	–	–	1	114	65	1	–	–	–
245/219			4	Manchester	D	7	108	b	6	14	c	–	60	34	1	114	31	2
246/220			5	Oval	D	8	10	*	–	–	–	1	132	73	3	102	61	2
252/221	1936	I	1	Lord's	W-9w	10	0	c	–	–	–	1	78	50	3	30	17	1
253/222			2	Manchester	D	8	76	c	–	–	–	1	55	34	2	174	103	3
255/224	1936–37	A	1	Brisbane[2]	W-322	8	38	c	9	0	c	–	136	48	0	–	–	–
256/225			2	Sydney	W-I & 22	–	–	–	–	–	–	–	8	5	0	56	26	0
257/226			3	Melbourne	L-365	7	0	c	8	61	b	1	56	31	2	88	46	0
258/227			4	Adelaide	L-148	9	10	c	9	4	b	–	56	26	1	48	38	1
260/229*	1937	NZ	1	Lord's	D	8	18	c	6	38	*	1	126	58	3	96	51	1
261/230*			2	Manchester	W-130	8	14	b	7	12	c	–	–	–	–	–	–	–
262/231*			3	Oval	D	8	9	c	–	–	–	1	85	40	4	66	24	0

Career	M	I	NO	HS	R	Avge	100	50	Ct	St	Balls	R	W	Avge	BB	5w	10w	Rate
Test	19	27	4	108	612	26.60	1	4	12	–	3318	1758	64	27.46	6-32	1	–	51.84
F/c	379	565	39	140	13884	26.39	11	73	221	–	37221	22580	969	23.30	8-69	54	4	38.41

R. W. V. ROBINS – TEST BOWLING SUMMARY

Series	V	M	Balls	R	W	Avge	BB	5w	10w	Rate
1929	SA	1	258	79	5	15.80	3-32	–	–	51.60
1930	A	2	512	338	10	33.80	4-51	–	–	51.20
1931	NZ	1	300	164	5	32.80	3-38	–	–	60.00
1932	I	1	186	96	3	32.00	2-39	–	–	62.00
1933	WI	2	382	220	11	20.00	6-32	1	–	34.63
1935	SA	3	522	264	9	29.33	3-73	–	–	58.00
1936	I	2	337	204	9	22.66	3-50	–	–	37.44
1936–37	A	4	448	220	4	55.00	2-31	–	–	112.00
1937	NZ	3	373	173	8	21.62	4-40	–	–	46.62
	A	6	960	558	14	39.85	4-51	–	–	68.57
	SA	4	780	343	14	24.50	3-32	–	–	55.71
	WI	2	382	220	11	20.00	6-32	1	–	34.72
	NZ	4	673	337	13	25.92	4-40	–	–	51.76
	I	3	523	300	12	25.00	3-50	–	–	43.58
Home		15	2870	1538	60	25.63	6-32	1	–	47.83
Overseas		4	448	220	4	55.00	2-31	–	–	112.00
Totals		19	3318	1758	64	27.46	6-32	1	–	51.84

NOTABLE FEATS

- 50 wickets in 12th Test (*253*).
- *245* Scored 108 in 130 min.
- *262* Ended NZ's 1st inns with 7-ball spell of 3 for 1.
- Exceeded 1000 runs in a season 4 times and took 100 wickets once (162), completing the 'double' in 1929 (his first full season with Middlesex). Took 99 wickets in 1937.
- Took 9 for 69 for Middlesex v Gloucestershire at Lord's in 1929.
- Two hat-tricks for Middlesex at Lord's: v Leicestershire in 1929 and v Somerset in 1937.

ROBINSON
Robert Timothy

Nottinghamshire (1978 to date)

Wisden 1986
TOURS
A 1987–88; NZ 1987–88; WI 1985–86; I/SL 1984–85; P 1987–88
Born Sutton in Ashfield, Nottinghamshire 21 Nov 1958

Tim Robinson during his innings of 160 against India at Delhi, 1984–85.

NOTABLE FEATS

• 1000 runs in 15th Test (*1042*) (25 inns).
• *1017* Only R.E. Foster (287) has made a higher score in his first Test v Australia.
• *1019* His 77* is the highest score by a Nottinghamshire player v Australia at Trent Bridge.
• *1021* Shared 2nd-wkt stand of 331 with D.I. Gower.
• Exceeded 1000 runs in a season 6 times, including 2032 in 1984.
• Scored 207 for Nottinghamshire v Warwickshire at Nottingham in 1983.

Until the relentless West Indies pace attack ruthlessly exposed weaknesses in his technique and temperament, Tim Robinson seemed to have established a lengthy tenure as an England opening batsman. Tall (6ft) and trimly built, he has a neat, calm method and plays very straight. Although he is by nature patient and watchful, he has a pleasant habit of despatching off-line balls to the boundary and is quite capable of taking an attack apart with a fine repertoire of strokes – as he revealed during his match-winning 166 against Northern Districts on England's 1987–88 tour of New Zealand. He showed exceptional application and concentration when he batted nearly ten hours in the heat of India in only his second Test match. Like Ken Barrington he goes in to bat expecting to set out his stall for the day – a bed and breakfast job. His appetite for the long innings is shown by the fact that the lowest of his four Test hundreds is 148. Although born in Nottinghamshire, he was educated in Bedfordshire and played his early cricket with Dunstable Town before going up to Sheffield University. He came successfully through a difficult first summer as captain of Nottinghamshire and should have many significant years of cricket ahead.

						Batting 1st			Batting 2nd			
Ref	Series	V	T	Venue	Result	No	R	HO	No	R	HO	Ct
1005/607	1984–85	I	1	Bombay[3]	L-8w	2	22	c	2	1	lbw	–
1006/608			2	Delhi	W-8w	2	160	c	2	18	ro	–
1007/609			3	Calcutta	D	2	36	b	–	–	–	–
1008/610			4	Madras[1]	W-9w	2	74	c	2	21	*	–
1009/611			5	Kanpur	D	2	96	lbw	2	16	*rh	–
1017/612	1985	A	1	Leeds	W-5w	2	175	c	2	21	b	1
1018/613			2	Lord's	L-4w	2	6	lbw	2	12	b	–
1019/614			3	Nottingham	D	2	38	c	2	77	*	1
1020/615			4	Manchester	D	2	10	c	–	–	–	–
1021/616			5	Birmingham	W-I & 118	2	148	b	–	–	–	2
1022/617			6	Oval	W-I & 94	2	3	b	–	–	–	1
1038/618	1985–86	WI	1	Kingston	L-10w	2	6	c	2	0	b	–
1040/620			3	Bridgetown	L-I & 30	2	3	c	2	43	b	–
1041/621			4	Port-of-Spain	L-10w	2	0	c	2	5	b	–
1042/622			5	St John's	L-240	3	12	b	3	3	ro	1
1046/623	1986	I	1	Lord's	L-5w	2	35	c	2	11	c	–
1075/634	1987	P	1	Manchester	D	2	166	c	–	–	–	–
1076/635			2	Lord's	D	2	7	c	–	–	–	–
1077/636			3	Leeds	L-I & 18	2	0	lbw	2	2	c	–
1078/637			4	Birmingham	D	2	80	c	2	4	c	–
1079/638			5	Oval	D	3	30	b	3	10	c	–
1084/639	1987–88	P	1	Lahore[2]	L-I & 87	3	6	c	3	1	lbw	–
1085/640			2	Faisalabad	D	5	2	c	8	7	*	1
1090/642	1987–88	A		Sydney	D	3	43	c	–	–	–	–
1091/643	1987–88	NZ	1	Christchurch	D	3	70	c	3	2	c	–
1092/644			2	Auckland	D	3	54	c	–	–	–	–
1093/645			3	Wellington	D	3	0	c	–	–	–	–
1103/651	1988	SL		Lord's	W-7w	2	19	c	2	34	*	–

TEST NOTES

• *1007* Bowled right-arm medium-pace in 2nd inns: 0 for 0 (6 balls).
• *1009* Retired hurt with dust under his contact lenses.

Career	M	I	NO	HS	R	Avge	100	50	Ct	St	Balls	R	W	Avge	BB	5w	10w	Rate
Test	28	47	5	175	1589	37.83	4	6	7	–	6	0	0	–	–	–	–	–
F/c	221	379	46	207	13548	40.68	31	66	122	–	150	165	2	82.50	1-22	–	–	75.00

R. T. ROBINSON – TEST BATTING SUMMARY

Series	V	M	I	NO	HS	R	Avge	100	50
1984–85	I	5	9	2	160	444	63.42	1	2
1985	A	6	9	1	175	490	61.25	2	1
1985–86	WI	4	8	–	43	72	9.00	–	–
1986	I	1	2	–	35	46	23.00	–	–
1987	P	5	8	–	166	299	37.37	1	1
1987–88	P	2	4	1	7*	16	5.33	–	–
1987–88	A	1	1	–	43	43	43.00	–	–
1987–88	NZ	3	4	–	70	126	31.50	–	2
1988	SL	1	2	1	34*	53	53.00	–	–

Series	V	M	I	NO	HS	R	Avge	100	50
	A	7	10	1	175	533	59.22	2	1
	WI	4	8	–	43	72	9.00	–	–
	NZ	3	4	–	70	126	31.50	–	2
	I	6	11	2	160	490	54.44	1	2
	P	7	12	1	166	315	28.63	1	1
	SL	1	2	1	34*	53	53.00	–	–
Home		13	21	2	175	888	46.73	3	2
Overseas		15	26	3	160	701	30.47	1	4
Totals		28	47	5	175	1589	37.83	4	6

ROOPE
Graham Richard James

Surrey (1964 to 1982)
Griqualand West (1973–74)

TOURS

SA 1973–74 (Robins/Int XI), 1974–75 (Int XI); NZ 1977–78; I 1972–73; P 1972–73, 1977–78; SL 1969–70, 1972–73; Z 1975–76 (Int XI)

Born Fareham, Hampshire 12 Jul 1946

NOTABLE FEATS

- Exceeded 1000 runs in a season 8 times.
- Held 59 catches in 1971.
- Held 5 catches in an innings for Surrey v Cambridge U at Fenner's in 1980.

In 1978, just when Graham Roope appeared to have established his England place with a run of useful innings, he was summarily discarded and we shall now never know if he could have become a consistent performer as a Test match batsman. There was never any doubt of his international rating as a close fielder. He was quite outstanding at slip, as befits a Corinthian Casuals goalkeeper, and became one of only 11 fielders with entirely post-war careers to hold 600 first-class catches. He was a tall (6ft 1in), correct and stylish strokemaker; his deftness of touch, particularly when playing off his legs, suggested a very light bat. Always an impressive driver, he learned to tighten his defensive technique. His right-arm medium-pace inswing bowling could have elevated him to true all-rounder status had he been given more opportunities and he was an extremely competent emergency wicket-keeper. Educated at Bradfield College, he represented Berkshire in 1963 and returned to their fold after his Surrey days were over.

Graham Roope

					Batting 1st			Batting 2nd				Bowling 1st			Bowling 2nd		
Ref	Series	V	T Venue	Result	No	R	HO	No	R	HO	Ct	Balls	R	W	Balls	R	W
706/481	1972–73	I	4 Kanpur	D	2	11	c	–	–	–	1	–	–	–	30	14	0
707/482			5 Bombay[2]	D	2	10	c	2	26	*	2	–	–	–	–	–	–
719/483	1972–73	P	1 Lahore[2]	D	3	15	c	3	0	st	3	–	–	–	–	–	–
720/484			2 Hyderabad	D	5	27	st	5	18	b	2	–	–	–	–	–	–
722/486	1973	NZ	1 Nottingham	W-38	3	28	lbw	3	2	c	4	–	–	–	54	17	0
723/487			2 Lord's	D	3	56	lbw	3	51	c	–	36	15	0	–	–	–
724/488			3 Leeds	W-I & 1	3	18	c	–	–	–	3	–	–	–	–	–	–
725/489	1973	WI	1 Oval	L-158	3	9	b	3	31	c	2	36	26	0	–	–	–
763/514	1975	A	4 Oval	D	4	0	c	4	77	b	1	–	–	–	–	–	–
807/529	1977	A	4 Leeds	W-I & 85	6	34	c	–	–	–	–	–	–	–	–	–	–
808/530			5 Oval	D	6	38	b	–	–	–	–	–	–	–	–	–	–
814/531	1977/78	P	1 Lahore[2]	D	5	19	b	–	–	–	–	–	–	–	–	–	–
815/532			2 Hyderabad	D	5	1	c	–	–	–	1	–	–	–	8	2	0
816/533			3 Karachi	D	4	56	lbw	4	33	*	2	–	–	–	–	–	–

Ref	Series	V	T Venue	Result	Batting 1st No	R	HO	Batting 2nd No	R	HO	Ct	Bowling 1st Balls	R	W	Bowling 2nd Balls	R	W
817/534	1977–78	NZ	1 Wellington	L-72	6	37	c	5	0	c	3	–	–	–	–	–	–
818/535			2 Christchurch	W-174	4	50	c	6	9	*	2	–	–	–	–	–	–
819/536			3 Auckland	D	4	68	c	–	–	–	3	–	–	–	8	2	0
825/537	1978	P	1 Birmingham	W-I & 57	5	32	b	–	–	–	3	–	–	–	–	–	–
826/538			2 Lord's	W-I & 120	5	69	c	–	–	–	3	–	–	–	–	–	–
827/539			3 Leeds	D	5	11	c	–	–	–	–	–	–	–	–	–	–
828/540	1978	NZ	1 Oval	W-7w	5	14	b	5	10	*	–	–	–	–	–	–	–

Career	M	I	NO	HS	R	Avge	100	50	Ct	St	Balls	R	W	Avge	BB	5w	10w	Rate
Test	21	32	4	77	860	30.71	–	7	35	–	172	76	0	–	–	–	–	–
F/c	403	647	129	171	19116	36.90	26	107	602	2	17501	8404	225	37.35	5-14	4	–	77.78

ROOT
Charles Frederick

Derbyshire (1910 to 1920)
Worcestershire (1921 to 1932)

TOUR WI 1925–26
Born Somercotes, Derbyshire
16 Apr 1890
Died Wolverhampton, Staffordshire
20 Jan 1954

Fred Root was one of the leading exponents of 'leg-theory' bowling and delighted in swerving his late inswingers at the batsman's legs with a five-man leg trap ready to pounce. A tall, powerfully built right-arm fast-medium bowler, he had immense stamina and thrived on hard work. His batting style came under the heading of 'block and tackle': a combination of rugged defence and massive lofted drives. Brought up at Leicester where his father was the County's groundsman, he played for the Club and Ground and made such an impression against Derbyshire that he was invited to assist his native county. During the First World War he served with the Notts and Derbyshire Regiment as a dispatch rider, was shot in the chest but recovered after spending two years in hospital. Afterwards he accepted a business engagement in Dudley, qualified for Worcestershire and led their attack for 11 full seasons. Before completely turning his attentions to cricket writing, he helped Todmorden win the Lancashire league and coached Leicestershire. [*Illus. p.* 16]

NOTABLE FEATS

- Took 100 wickets in a season 9 times, including 219 in 1925, and scored 1044 runs in 1928 to complete the 'double'.
- Holds Worcestershire records for most wickets in a season (207 in 1925) and best innings analysis (9 for 23 v Lancashire at Worcester in 1931). He took 9 wickets on 2 earlier occasions for the County.
- Took 5 wickets in 9 balls for Worcestershire v Gloucestershire at Cheltenham in 1924.

Ref	Series	V	T Venue	Result	Batting 1st No	R	HO	Batting 2nd No	R	HO	Ct	Bowling 1st Balls	R	W	Bowling 2nd Balls	R	W
163/149	1926	A	1 Nottingham	D	–	–	–	–	–	–	–	–	–	–	–	–	–
164/150			2 Lord's	D	–	–	–	–	–	–	1	216	70	2	114	40	2
166/152			4 Manchester	D	–	–	–	–	–	–	–	312	84	4	–	–	–

Career	M	I	NO	HS	R	Avge	100	50	Ct	St	Balls	R	W	Avge	BB	5w	10w	Rate
Test	3	–	–	–	–	–	–	–	1	–	642	194	8	24.25	4-84	–	–	80.25
F/c	365	586	51	107	7911	14.78	1	23	243	–	80614	31933	1512	21.11	9-23	125	33	53.31

ROSE, Brian Charles

Somerset (1969 to 1987)

Wisden 1980
TOURS
WI 1980–81; NZ 1977–78; P 1977–78
Born Dartford, Kent 4 Jun 1950

Brian Rose

During just six seasons of skilled and enthusiastic captaincy (1978–83), Brian Rose led Somerset to the first five titles in the Club's history, winning four Lord's cup finals and the Sunday league. Tall (6ft 1½in), slim and rather languid, he was a left-handed opening batsman who favoured the front foot, drove handsomely and cut with great gusto. He was an outstanding fielder and a useful but seldom employed left-arm medium-pace change bowler. Just when he appeared to have established his Test place with a series of confident innings against the 1980 West Indians, he developed an eye defect which prompted his return from the Caribbean and signalled the end of his international career. Although spectacles solved that problem, he was then plagued with back trouble and gradually disappeared from the first-class game via teaching and a spell as Somerset's cricket development officer. He caused a sensation when he exploited a loophole in the rules of the 1979 Benson and Hedges Cup by declaring after one over to take advantage of the scoring rate in a zonal match. Somerset were suspended from that season's competition and a clause banning declarations was quickly inserted in the rules of all instant cricket.

NOTABLE FEATS

- Exceeded 1000 runs in a season 8 times.
- Scored 205 for Somerset v Northamptonshire at Weston-super-Mare in 1977.

TEST NOTES

- *817* Retired hurt when 4* at 14–2 (2nd inns); resumed at 63–9.
- *884* Batted 145 min with G.A. Gooch as his runner (2nd inns).

						Batting 1st			Batting 2nd			
Ref	Series	V	T	Venue	Result	No	R	HO	No	R	HO	Ct
814/531	1977–78	P	1	Lahore[2]	D	3	1	lbw	–	–	–	1
815/532			2	Hyderabad	D	3	27	b	–	–	–	–
816/533			3	Karachi	D	2	10	c	2	18	c	–
817/534	1977–78	NZ	1	Wellington	L-72	1	21	c	1	5	*	1
818/535			2	Christchurch	W-174	1	11	c	1	7	c	–
882/559	1980	WI	3	Manchester	D	3	70	b	3	32	c	–
883/560			4	Oval	D	3	50	b	3	41	lbw	2
884/561			5	Leeds	D	3	7	b	5	43	*	–
896/563	1980–81	WI	1	Port-of-Spain	L-I & 79	3	10	c	3	5	c	–

Career	M	I	NO	HS	R	Avge	100	50	Ct	St	Balls	R	W	Avge	BB	5w	10w	Rate
Test	9	16	2	70	358	25.57	–	2	4	–	–	–	–	–	–	–	–	–
F/c	270	448	50	205	13236	33.25	25	53	124	–	445	289	8	36.12	3-9	–	–	55.62

ROYLE Rev. Vernon Peter Fanshawe Archer

Lancashire (1873 to 1891)
Oxford University (1875 to 1876)

TOUR A 1878–79
Born Brooklands, Cheshire 29 Jan 1854
Died Stanmore Park, Middlesex
21 May 1929

Of medium height (5ft 9in) and strongly built, Vernon Royle was a stylish batsman who got in line and drove powerfully. Having developed his game at Rossall School, he appeared for Lancashire before gaining blues in successive years at Oxford. It was his superb fielding at cover-point in his second Varsity match that made him famous. Fast moving, ambidextrous and with a lethally accurate throw, he prevented scores of runs in county cricket once his reputation spread. His fielding won great praise during his tour of Australia with Lord Harris's team and he held four catches in the second innings of their final match against Victoria. Although Lancashire seldom had need of his right-handed round-arm slow bowling, it had captured four important Cambridge wickets in Oxford's 6-run victory of 1875. He gave up regular county cricket when he became a master at Elstree School (1879–99) and it was during his years there that he was ordained. At the time of his death he was headmaster of Stanmore Park Preparatory School in Middlesex and president of Lancashire CCC. [*Illus. p.* 222]

Ref	Series	V	T	Venue	Result	Batting 1st No	R	HO	Batting 2nd No	R	HO	Ct	Bowling 1st Balls	R	W	Bowling 2nd Balls	R	W
3/3	1878–79	A		Melbourne	L-10w	6	3	b	6	18	c	2	16	6	0	–	–	–

Career	M	I	NO	HS	R	Avge	100	50	Ct	St	Balls	R	W	Avge	BB	5w	10w	Rate
Test	1	2	0	18	21	10.50	–	–	2	–	16	6	0	–	–	–	–	–
F/c	102	165	15	81	2322	15.48	–	9	69	–	783	376	15	25.06	4-51	–	–	52.20

RUMSEY
Frederick Edward

Worcestershire (1960 to 1962)
Somerset (1963 to 1968)
Derbyshire (1970)

Born Stepney, London 4 Dec 1935

Very tall (6ft 4in) and massively built, Fred Rumsey was a left-arm fast-medium bowler who operated from a very long run. He achieved little during his three seasons with Worcestershire but his arrival at Taunton coincided with advice that he should release the ball a little later in his delivery stride. This elementary message produced such dramatic and immediate results that during that first summer he contributed 99 wickets to Somerset's third place in the Championship. The following year found him in England colours against Australia. He changed course again in 1969 and joined Derbyshire as cricket's first public relation's officer. His playing activities were confined to limited-overs games but he did appear in one Championship match – against Somerset in 1970. An enthusiastic but not very agile fielder with a strong throw, he would have enjoyed the prospect of bowling against his own (right-handed) batting. It was not surprising that a cricketer who had represented three different counties should eventually become a successful travel agent specialising in cricket tours to the Caribbean.

Fred Rumsey

NOTABLE FEATS

- Took 100 wickets in a season 3 times.

Ref	Series	V	T	Venue	Result	Batting 1st No	R	HO	Batting 2nd No	R	HO	Ct	Bowling 1st Balls	R	W	Bowling 2nd Balls	R	W
564/408	1964	A	4	Manchester	D	11	3	*	–	–	–	–	215	99	2	–	–	–
591/415	1965	NZ	1	Birmingham	W-9w	11	21	*	–	–	–	–	54	22	0	102	32	0
592/416			2	Lord's	W-7w	10	3	b	–	–	–	–	78	25	4	156	42	1
593/417			3	Leeds	W-I & 187	–	–	–	–	–	–	–	144	59	1	90	49	3
594/418	1965	SA	1	Lord's	D	10	3	b	10	0	*	–	180	84	3	126	49	3

Career	M	I	NO	HS	R	Avge	100	50	Ct	St	Balls	R	W	Avge	BB	5w	10w	Rate
Test	5	5	3	21*	30	15.00	–	–	–	–	1145	461	17	27.11	4-25	–	–	67.35
F/c	180	204	84	45	1015	8.45	–	–	92	–	28876	11773	580	20.29	8-26	30	5	49.78

RUSSELL
Charles Albert George
(also known as
Albert Charles Russell)

Essex (1908 to 1930)

Wisden 1923
TOURS
A 1920–21; SA 1922–23, 1924–25 (Joel)
Born Leyton, Essex 7 Oct 1887
Died Whipps Cross, Essex 23 Mar 1961

The son of an Essex wicket-keeper, 'Jack' Russell was born near the Leyton ground where he was destined almost 34 years later to play his highest innings. During a career with Essex which spanned 22 years and the Great War, he established himself as a most dependable opening batsman, a very capable right-arm slow-medium change bowler and an outstanding catcher at slip. Although no stylist, he was extremely effective and produced at least 1000 runs every season from the War until his retirement. Apart from the occasional off-drive he was very much an on-side player; at Old Trafford in 1921 he scored 81 of his 101 runs on the leg-side. His feat in becoming the first England batsman to score a century in each innings of a Test was commemorated by the planting of a tree at the Kingsmead ground. The achievement was one of the more remarkable in Test history. Taken ill before that final match started and with the series level, he left his sick bed before the start of each innings, a most courageous and match-winning effort. Ironically, with Hobbs and Sutcliffe available for England's next series 16 months later, it proved to be his final Test, his last three international scores being 96, 140 and 111.

MCC to Australia, 1920–21: standing *A. Dolphin, J.W. Hitch, C.H. Parkin, F.C. Toone (manager), F.E. Woolley, C.A.G. Russell, A. Waddington;* seated *H. Strudwick, W. Rhodes, E.R. Wilson, J.W.H.T. Douglas (captain), P.G.H. Fender, J.B. Hobbs;* in front *H. Howell, E.H. Hendren, J.W. Hearne, J.W.H. Makepeace.*

NOTABLE FEATS

- *152* First to score 100 in each innings of a Test for England. Shared record E v SA 10th-wkt stand of 92 with A.E.R. Gilligan.
- Exceeded 1000 runs in a season 13 times, including 2000 on 5 occasions, notably 2575 in 1922.
- Scored 273 for Essex v Northamptonshire at Leyton in 1921 and 201 for MCC v South Australia at Adelaide in 1920–21.
- Scored 100 in each innings of a match for Essex twice (1922 and 1928).

						Batting 1st			Batting 2nd			
Ref	Series	V	T	Venue	Result	No	R	HO	No	R	HO	Ct
135/124	1920–21	A	1	Sydney	L-377	1	0	b	1	5	c	1
136/125			2	Melbourne	L-I & 91	5	0	c	5	5	c	1
137/126			3	Adelaide	L-119	6	135	*	6	59	b	–
139/128			5	Sydney	L-9w	6	19	c	8	35	c	–
143/132	1921	A	4	Manchester	D	1	101	b	–	–	–	1
144/133			5	Oval	D	1	13	c	1	102	*	–
149/135	1922–23	SA	2	Cape Town	W-1w	1	39	c	1	8	lbw	–
150/136			3	Durban[2]	D	1	34	c	–	–	–	–
151/137			4	Johannesburg[1]	D	1	8	b	1	96	c	4
152/138			5	Durban[2]	W-109	1	140	c	6	111	c	1

Career	M	I	NO	HS	R	Avge	100	50	Ct	St	Balls	R	W	Avge	BB	5w	10w	Rate
Test	10	18	2	140	910	56.87	5	2	8	–	–	–	–	–	–	–	–	–
F/c	437	717	59	273	27358	41.57	71	135	314	–	19805	7637	283	26.98	5-25	5	–	69.98

RUSSELL
Robert Charles

Gloucestershire (1981 to date)

TOURS P 1987–88; SL 1986–87 (Glos)
Born Stroud, Gloucestershire
15 Aug 1963

NOTABLE FEATS

- *1103* His 94 was his highest score in first-class cricket and the sixth-highest by a night-watchman in Test cricket.
- Held 3 catches off successive balls for Gloucestershire v Surrey at The Oval in 1986 (the first off C.A. Walsh, followed by two off D.V. Lawrence) to equal the world first-class record set by G.O. Dawkes in 1958.

The most incomprehensible of numerous quirky decisions by the England selectors in 1988 was their refusal to pick the outstanding wicket-keeper in English first-class cricket until the sixth Test of a disastrous summer. Ask any player, umpire or professional cricket watcher and their unanimous opinion would have confirmed that Gloucestershire's 'Jack' Russell was so far above the rest technically that he should have been an automatic selection since the start of the 1987 season. If the selectors had qualms about his ability as a left-handed batsman, he removed them by making his highest first-class score (94) in his first Test innings – having entered the match with a season's average standing at 31.65. A 5ft 8½in high sprite with lightning reactions and a lightness of touch, he is as accomplished standing up to spinners as he is diving to hold snicks off the fast men. Most keepers are superstitious and Russell's talisman is his special sun hat, an item so jealously protected that it accompanies him to bed. His artistry extends to sketching and a book of his skilful and varied draughtsmanship was published soon after his England baptism.

'Jack' Russell

Ref	Series	V	T	Venue	Result	Batting 1st			Batting 2nd			Fielding 1st				Fielding 2nd			
						No	R	HO	No	R	HO	Ct	St	Byes	Balls	Ct	St	Byes	Balls
1103/651	1988	SL		Lord's	W-7w	3	94	c	–	–	–	2	–	1	395	1	–	0	657

Career	M	I	NO	HS	R	Avge	100	50	Ct	St	Balls	R	W	Avge	BB	5w	10w	Rate
Test	1	1	–	94	94	94.00	–	1	3	–	–	–	–	–	–	–	–	–
F/c	152	197	48	94	3663	24.58	–	16	310	62	13	19	0	–	–	–	–	–

RUSSELL
William Eric

Middlesex (1956 to 1972)

TOURS
A 1965–66; NZ 1960–61, 1965–66;
I 1961–62; P 1961–62
Born Dumbarton, Scotland 3 Jul 1936

Eric Russell was an extremely elegant opening batsman; modest and composed, he combined dependable run-making with an attractive spectacle. Besides being a confident driver off either foot, he was possibly the last major batsman to indulge in those innovations of 'Ranji', the late-cut and the leg-glance. Tall (6ft) and slim, he had the slightly rounded shoulders of a clerk and always wore his sleeves neatly rolled at half-mast to protect his elbows. His nickname of 'Legs' was a tribute to his tendency towards bandiness. He was a useful right-arm medium-pace change bowler and a capable fielder. His opportunities at Test level were not improved by the contemporary presence of Geoffrey Boycott and John Edrich, nor by his being doubly injured in Australia immediately after scoring 42, 93, 0*, 110 and 45*. He spent two seasons with Berkshire after leaving Middlesex.

Eric Russell

NOTABLE FEATS

- Exceeded 1000 runs in a season 13 times, including 2000 on 3 occasions, notably 2342 in 1964.

TEST NOTES

- *512* Bowled in 1st inns: 0 for 25 (114 balls).
- *516* Bowled in 1st inns: 0 for 19 (30 balls).
- *597* Split webbing of right hand fielding (began Test with a fractured thumb).
- *603* Deputised for J.T. Murray as wicket-keeper after tea on the last day – he had last kept in 1959.

						Batting 1st			Batting 2nd			
Ref	Series	V	T	Venue	Result	No	R	HO	No	R	HO	Ct
512/374	1961–62	P	1	Lahore[2]	W-5w	6	34	b	6	0	b	–
516/378	1961–62	I	4	Calcutta	L-187	2	10	b	2	9	b	–
596/420	1965	SA	3	Oval	D	2	0	lbw	2	70	c	–
597/421	1965–66	A	1	Brisbane[2]	D	11	0	*	–	–	–	–
602/426	1965–66	NZ	1	Christchurch	D	2	30	b	2	25	b	1
603/427			2	Dunedin	D	2	11	b	–	–	–	–
604/428			3	Auckland	D	2	56	lbw	2	1	c	2
605/429	1966	WI	1	Manchester	L-I & 40	2	26	c	2	20	b	1
607/431			3	Nottingham	L-139	3	4	b	3	11	c	–
621/437	1967	P	1	Lord's	D	2	43	b	2	12	b	–

Career	M	I	NO	HS	R	Avge	100	50	Ct	St	Balls	R	W	Avge	BB	5w	10w	Rate
Test	10	18	1	70	362	21.29	–	2	4	–	144	44	0	–	–	–	–	–
F/c	448	796	64	193	25525	34.87	41	134	304	–	1938	993	22	45.13	3-20	–	–	88.09

SANDHAM, Andrew

Surrey (1911 to 1937)

Wisden 1923
TOURS
A 1924–25; SA 1922–23, 1930–31; WI 1928–29 (Cahn), 1929–30; I/SL 1926–27
Born Streatham, Surrey 6 Jul 1890
Died Westminster, London 20 Apr 1982

Sandham batting; Levett keeping wicket.

After serving Surrey for a period of 60 years which spanned two world wars, Andy Sandham returned to The Oval during the summer following his retirement to see his friends and watch some cricket. The steward in charge of the Hobbs Gates did not recognise him and would not let him in. He had much the same trouble with England's selectors; despite being a sound and successful opening partner to Jack Hobbs for 15 seasons, he had to give way to Herbert Sutcliffe when Test teams were formed and the Surrey pair never opened for their country. His 14 international appearances stretched over ten years and included only three home matches. In four Tests he had to bat out of position and in one he did not bat at all. His career had developed slowly and he did not command a regular place until 1919 when he proved to be the ideal partner for 'The Master'. A quiet, selfless but humorous man, he was content to stay in faithful support while Hobbs took the plaudits and as big a share of the bowling as he wanted. When, having equalled W.G. Grace's tally of hundreds in his first innings at Taunton in 1925, Hobbs had an opportunity of claiming the record outright in the second innings, Sandham ensured he received the strike and dismissed any thoughts of a century for himself. A small, neat man, he was extremely nimble on his feet and very strong off his legs. He was a fine player of fast bowling, excelling in the hook, pull and cut. His outstanding fielding in the deep included a powerful low throw which comfortably travelled even the full playing area of The Oval in use in those days. He scored Test cricket's first triple century in his last match for England and a century on his final appearance for Surrey. Then he got down to the serious business of being Surrey's coach (1946–58) and scorer (1959–70).

NOTABLE FEATS

- *193* The first 300 in Test cricket, his 325 in 10 hrs was the record score for only 3 months but it remains the highest by a No. 2 batsman in Tests. His match aggregate of 375 was the Test record until 1973–74.
- Exceeded 1000 runs in a season 18 times (plus twice on tour), including 2000 on 8 occasions, notably 2565 in 1929. Leading batsman of 1924.
- Apart from his 325 for England (above), he scored 10 double centuries for Surrey, notably 292* v Northamptonshire at The Oval in 1921 and 219 at The Oval in 1934 which remains the highest score for any county v the Australians.
- Shared 63 century 1st-wkt stands with J.B. Hobbs, including the Surrey record of 428 v Oxford U at Oxford in 1926.
- Shared in 2 other record Surrey stands: 298 (6th wkt) with H.S. Harrison v Sussex at The Oval in 1913 and 173 (10th wkt) with A. Ducat v Essex at Leyton in 1921.
- His 2nd-wkt stand of 344 with R.J. Gregory at The Oval in 1937 remains the highest for any wicket v Glamorgan.
- Carried his bat through a completed innings on 7 occasions.
- Scored 100 before lunch on the first day twice.
- Scored 102 v Sussex at Hove in 1937 in his final first-class match in England.

						Batting 1st			Batting 2nd			
Ref	Series	V	T	Venue	Result	No	R	HO	No	R	HO	Ct
144/133	1921	A	5	Oval	D	6	21	b	–	–	–	–
148/134	1922–23	SA	1	Johannesburg[1]	L-168	1	26	b	1	25	lbw	–
149/135			2	Cape Town	W-1w	2	19	c	2	17	lbw	–
150/136			3	Durban[2]	D	2	0	c	–	–	–	–
151/137			4	Johannesburg[1]	D	2	6	c	2	58	lbw	–
152/138			5	Durban[2]	W-109	2	1	c	4	40	b	–
156/142	1924	SA	4	Manchester	D	–	–	–	–	–	–	–
157/143			5	Oval	D	5	46	c	–	–	–	1
158/144	1924–25	A	1	Sydney	L-193	6	7	b	7	2	c	–
162/148			5	Sydney	L-307	3	4	ro	3	15	lbw	–
190/176	1929–30	WI	1	Bridgetown	D	2	152	lbw	2	51	b	1
191/177			2	Port-of-Spain	W-167	2	0	b	2	5	b	1
192/178			3	Georgetown	L-289	2	9	c	2	0	c	–
193/179			4	Kingston	D	2	325	b	7	50	lbw	1

Career	M	I	NO	HS	R	Avge	100	50	Ct	St	Balls	R	W	Avge	BB	5w	10w	Rate
Test	14	23	0	325	879	38.21	2	3	4	–	–	–	–	–	–	–	–	–
F/c	643	1000	79	325	41284	44.82	107	165	158	–	1008	560	18	31.11	3-27	–	–	56.00

SCHULTZ
Sandford Spence

(later changed name to Storey)

Cambridge University (1876 to 1877)
Lancashire (1877 to 1882)

TOUR A 1878–79
Born Birkenhead, Cheshire 29 Aug 1857
Died South Kensington, London 18 Dec 1937

Sandford Schultz was a right-handed round-arm fast-medium bowler, a useful lower-order batsman and an agile slip fielder. After leaving Uppingham, he gained a blue in his second year at Cambridge, appeared for Lancashire nine times in six summers and toured Australia under Lord Harris. Apart from appearances for Huntingdonshire, Lincolnshire and a final first-class match in 1885 for C.I. Thornton's XI, he confined himself to club cricket. There his exploits included a 9-wicket analysis and an innings of 286. He may well be the only man to be dismissed first ball twice in the same first-class innings. Playing for the Gentlemen of England against Oxford at the Christ Church ground in June 1881, he was one of three men dismissed before an injury caused the game to be restarted on the New Ground in the Parks. When German popularity was on the wane in Britain he changed his name to Storey. [*Illus. p.* 222]

						Batting 1st			Batting 2nd				Bowling 1st			Bowling 2nd		
Ref	Series	V	T	Venue	Result	No	R	HO	No	R	HO	Ct	Balls	R	W	Balls	R	W
3/3	1878–79	A		Melbourne	L-10w	11	0	*	11	20	c	–	27	16	1	8	10	0

Career	M	I	NO	HS	R	Avge	100	50	Ct	St	Balls	R	W	Avge	BB	5w	10w	Rate
Test	1	2	1	20	20	20.00	–	–	–	–	35	26	1	26.00	1-16	–	–	35.00
F/c	42	70	9	90	1046	17.14	–	5	29	–	2272	1143	28	40.82	4-37	–	–	81.14

SCOTTON William Henry

Nottinghamshire (1875 to 1890)

TOURS A 1881–82, 1884–85, 1886–87
Born Nottingham 15 Jan 1856
Died St John's Wood, London 9 Jul 1893

William Scotton

William Scotton is remembered for his impregnable straight-batted defence and can most sympathetically be described as an ultra-cautious left-handed opening batsman. He was a blocker supreme and twice in first-class matches he batted an hour without scoring. In terms of runs accumulated he was the most successful left-hander in England for the three seasons 1884–86. Of medium height (5ft 10in), he was a left-arm fast-medium change bowler and an accomplished outfielder. Playing for the Smokers against the Non-Smokers at East Melbourne in 1886–87 he blocked the final ball of a drawn match and picked it up as a souvenir – only to become the first batsman to be given out 'handled the ball' in a first-class match in Australia. He played soccer for Notts County, was a licensee and was on the MCC staff at Lord's when he killed himself while depressed over losing his place in the Nottinghamshire team.

NOTABLE FEATS

- *16* Batted 340 min for 90 and shared record E v A 9th-wkt stand of 151 with W.W. Read.
- *24* Shared stand of 170 with W.G. Grace which remained the Test 1st-wkt record until 1899; his 34 took 225 min and included a runless interlude of 67 min.
- Carried his bat through a completed innings on 4 occasions.

TEST NOTES

- *16* Bowled in 1st inns: 0 for 20 (20 balls).

						Batting 1st			Batting 2nd			
Ref	Series	V	T	Venue	Result	No	R	HO	No	R	HO	Ct
5/5	1881–82	A	1	Melbourne	D	8	21	ro	8	50	*	–
6/6			2	Sydney	L-5w	7	30	b	7	12	lbw	–
7/7			3	Sydney	L-6w	7	18	c	7	1	b	–
8/8			4	Melbourne	D	7	26	st	–		–	1
16/16	1884	A	3	Oval	D	2	90	c	–	–	–	–
17/17	1884–85	A	1	Adelaide	W-8w	1	82	st	1	2	c	–
18/18			2	Melbourne	W-10w	2	13	b	2	7	*	–
19/19			3	Sydney	L-6	1	22	c	1	2	b	1
20/20			4	Sydney	L-8w	3	4	c	3	0	c	–
21/21			5	Melbourne	W-I & 98	1	27	b	–	–	–	–
22/22	1886	A	1	Manchester	W-4w	1	21	c	1	20	b	2
23/23			2	Lord's	W-I & 106	2	19	b	–	–	–	–
24/24			3	Oval	W-I & 217	2	34	b	–	–	–	–
25/25	1886–87	A	1	Sydney	W-13	7	1	c	9	6	c	–
26/26			2	Sydney	W-71	7	0	b	7	2	b	–

Career	M	I	NO	HS	R	Avge	100	50	Ct	St	Balls	R	W	Avge	BB	5w	10w	Rate
Test	15	25	2	90	510	22.17	–	3	4	–	20	20	0	–	–	–	–	–
F/c	237	377	33	134	6527	18.97	4	23	123	–	765	410	8	51.25	1-7	–	–	95.62

SELBY, John

Nottinghamshire (1870 to 1887)

TOURS A 1876–77, 1881–82
Born Nottingham 1 Jul 1849
Died Nottingham 11 Mar 1894

John Selby was an all-round athlete who combined his work as a professional cricketer with bouts of professional sprinting. Running as 'Bendigo's Novice' (the name of the prize-fighter who was his patron) he excelled at the 120 yards distance. Although he was lacking in height (5ft 6in), he was a fine player of fast bowling with a sound defence and full range of crisp attacking strokes. He enjoyed an outstanding season in 1878, heading the national averages with 938 runs at 31.26. According to one match report he must have been a powerful striker of the ball, one straight drive at Prince's going 'all along the ground past the chestnut trees for 5'. A very occasional right-arm medium-pace change bowler, he could keep wicket in an emergency and had to fulfil this role during the first two Test matches after Pooley had been confiscated by the New Zealand authorities for suspected

TEST NOTES

• 2 H. Jupp deputised as wicket-keeper after lunch on the first day.

gambling irregularities. Selby was involved in a number of scandals and failed financial manoeuvres. Shortly before suffering a stroke a few months before his death, he had been acquitted of a criminal charge. [*Illus. p.* 278]

NOTABLE FEATS

• *5* Shared 2nd-wkt stand of 137 with G. Ulyett which was then the Test record for any wicket.

						Batting 1st			Batting 2nd			Fielding 1st				Fielding 2nd			
Ref	Series	V	T	Venue	Result	No	R	HO	No	R	HO	Ct	St	Byes	Balls	Ct	St	Byes	Balls
1/1†	1876–77	A	1	Melbourne	L-45	2	7	c	5	38	c	–	–	4	679	1	–	5	272
2/2†			2	Melbourne	W-4w	5	7	b	2	2	b	–	–	–	–	–	–	–	–
5/5	1881–82	A	1	Melbourne	D	3	55	ro	3	70	c	–	–	–	–	–	–	–	–
6/6			2	Sydney	L-5w	3	6	c	3	2	c	–	–	–	–	–	–	–	–
7/7			3	Sydney	L-6w	3	13	c	3	1	b	–	–	–	–	–	–	–	–
8/8			4	Melbourne	D	3	7	b	3	48	*	–	–	–	–	–	–	–	–

Career	M	I	NO	HS	R	Avge	100	50	Ct	St	Balls	R	W	Avge	BB	5w	10w	Rate
Test	6	12	1	70	256	23.27	–	2	1	–	–	–	–	–	–	–	–	–
F/c	222	355	25	128*	6215	18.83	4	27	128	4	436	188	5	37.60	2-27	–	–	87.20

SELVEY
Michael Walter William

Surrey (1968 to 1971)
Cambridge University (1971)
Middlesex (1972 to 1982)
Orange Free State (1973–74)
Glamorgan (1983 to 1984)

TOURS
A 1976–77; I 1976–77; P 1981–82 (Int XI); Z 1980–81 (Middx)
Born Chiswick, Middlesex 25 Apr 1948

Mike Selvey's early career as a right-arm fast-medium bowler gave little hint of his dramatic entry into Test cricket. Not until he joined Middlesex at the age of 24, via Battersea Grammar School, Beddington CC, Surrey and the universities of Manchester and Cambridge (where he gained a blue in his only year), did he graduate as a first-class cricketer. Tall (6ft 2in) and strongly built, he swung the ball late either way at an uncomfortable pace and kept a full length. His high action frequently produced alarming bounce. He was unlucky for his peak summers to coincide with those of a wealth of similar talent but a bizarre assortment of injuries to England's established attack resulted in a late call-up against the powerful West Indies batting in 1976. Undeterred by the enormity of his task, he calmly removed Fredericks, Richards and Kallicharran with his first 20 balls. A pluperfect wicket at The Oval and John Lever's incredible form in India prevented an extended international career but at least he had one magnificent session to savour. After scoring just one run and enduring a runless sequence of nine successive innings within his first 15 matches for Middlesex, he decided there was scope for improvement in his batting technique. Four half-centuries and a career average of 12 represent massive progress. When a persistent knee injury ended his career he was in his second season as Glamorgan's captain. The shrewd cricket brain in evidence during that challenging period has found a worthy platform in his role as cricket correspondent of *The Guardian*.

NOTABLE FEATS

• *779* Dismissed R.C. Fredericks with his sixth ball in Test cricket and took 3 for 6 in his first 20 balls.
• Took 101 wickets in 1978.

Mike Selvey

Ref	Series	V	T	Venue	Result	Batting 1st No	R	HO	Batting 2nd No	R	HO	Ct	Bowling 1st Balls	R	W	Bowling 2nd Balls	R	W
779/517	1976	WI	3	Manchester	L-425	10	2	*	9	4	c	–	102	41	4	156	111	2
781/519			5	Oval	L-231	10	0	b	10	4	*	1	90	67	0	54	44	0
792/524	1976–77	I	5	Bombay[3]	D	10	5	*	–	–	–	–	90	80	0	–	–	–

Career	M	I	NO	HS	R	Avge	100	50	Ct	St	Balls	R	W	Avge	BB	5w	10w	Rate
Test	3	5	3	5*	15	7.50	–	–	1	–	492	343	6	57.16	4-41	–	–	82.00
F/c	278	278	88	67	2405	12.65	–	4	79	–	45516	20582	772	26.66	7-20	38	4	58.95

SHACKLETON Derek

Hampshire (1948 to 1969)

Wisden 1959
TOURS
I/SL 1950–51 (Cwlth), 1951–52; P 1951–52
Born Todmorden, Yorkshire
12 Aug 1924

If ever one bowler epitomised accuracy it was Derek Shackleton. A little over average height (5ft 10½in) and carrying no surplus weight, he bowled day in and day out for Hampshire for 22 summers to produce the eighth-highest aggregate of first-class wickets. Originally right-arm fast-medium, he gradually slowed to medium without any diminution of effect. Such was his precision that batsmen counted themselves extremely fortunate if his total of half-volleys and long-hops in a season entered double figures. His high easy action scarcely tired him and allowed him to swing the ball either way and deceptively late. Only Wilfred Rhodes (23) took 100 wickets in a season more often and no one approaches 'Shack's' record of 20 instances in successive years. Such was his skill and accuracy that, unlike most bowlers, his career average decreased as the years progressed. His astonishing consistency became even more remarkable when he revealed after his retirement that he was blind in one eye. In his younger days his stylish batting had taken him to the fringe of a 'double' and powerful throwing had been a feature of his fielding. When he at last decided to allow Hampshire's opponent batsmen some reprieve, he combined coaching at Canford School (1969–78) with appearances for Dorset (1971–74) before becoming a first-class umpire (1979–81). His son played for Gloucestershire.

NOTABLE FEATS

- *544* Ended the WI 1st inns by taking 3 wickets in 4 balls.
- Took 100 wickets in a season 20 times consecutively (1949–68) – record. In Championship matches alone he took 100 wickets a record 18 times.
- Holds Hampshire career records for most wickets (2669) and most instances of 100 wickets in a season (19).
- Took 9 wickets for Hampshire on 4 occasions, notably 9 for 30 v Warwickshire at Portsmouth in 1960.
- Took 8 for 4 in 11.1 overs for Hampshire v Somerset at Weston-super-Mare in 1955.
- Took 5 wickets in 9 balls for Hampshire v Leicestershire at Leicester in 1950.
- Twice bowled in an unchanged partnership throughout both completed innings of a Hampshire match: with V.H.D. Cannings v Kent at Southampton in 1952 and with M. Heath v Derbyshire at Burton upon Trent in 1958.

Derek Shackleton

Ref	Series	V	T	Venue	Result	Batting 1st No	R	HO	Batting 2nd No	R	HO	Ct	Bowling 1st Balls	R	W	Bowling 2nd Balls	R	W
325/278	1950	WI	3	Nottingham	L-10w	8	42	b	8	1	c	–	258	128	1	36	7	0
338/291	1951	SA	5	Oval	W-4w	8	14	c	8	5	*	–	90	20	1	60	19	0
339/292	1951–52	I	1	Delhi	D	8	10	st	8	21	*	–	174	76	1	–	–	–
544/396	1963	WI	2	Lord's	D	11	8	b	11	4	ro	–	302	93	3	204	72	4
545/397			3	Birmingham	W-217	11	6	*	–	–	–	–	126	60	1	102	37	2
546/398			4	Leeds	L-221	11	1	*	11	1	*	1	252	88	1	156	63	3
547/399			5	Oval	L-8w	11	0	*	11	0	*	–	126	37	1	192	68	0

Career	M	I	NO	HS	R	Avge	100	50	Ct	St	Balls	R	W	Avge	BB	5w	10w	Rate
Test	7	13	7	42	113	18.83	–	–	1	–	2078	768	18	42.66	4-72	–	–	115.44
F/c	647	852	197	87*	9574	14.61	–	20	221	–	158856	53303	2857	18.65	9-30	194	38	55.60

SHARP, John

Lancashire (1899 to 1925)

Born Hereford 15 Feb 1878
Died Wavertree, Liverpool, Lancashire
28 Jan 1938

The first Test cricketer to be born in Hereford, John Sharp was a short, sturdily built all-rounder who batted right-handed, bowled left-arm medium-fast and fielded brilliantly at cover-point. In 1904 he helped Lancashire win the Championship without losing a match. A powerful striker of the ball, he was a proficient cutter, puller and off-driver. His bowling relied on break-backs and awkward bounce. He was a superb cover-point. After 15 seasons as a professional, he became an amateur after the Great War and captained Lancashire in his last three summers (1923–25). A Test selector in 1924, he also appeared for Herefordshire and was a double international, playing soccer (outside-right) for Aston Villa, Everton and England. [*Illus. p.* 315]

NOTABLE FEATS

- Exceeded 1000 runs in a season 10 times, including 2099 in 1911.
- Took 112 wickets in 1910.
- Scored 211 for Lancashire v Leicestershire at Manchester in 1912.
- Shared record Lancashire 7th-wkt stand of 245 with A.H. Hornby v Leicestershire at Manchester in 1912.
- Took 9 for 77 for Lancashire v Worcestershire at Worcester in 1901.
- Bowled in an unchanged partnership with S. Webb throughout both completed Kent innings for Lancashire at Manchester in 1901.

Ref	Series	V	T	Venue	Result	Batting 1st No	R	HO	Batting 2nd No	R	HO	Ct	Bowling 1st Balls	R	W	Bowling 2nd Balls	R	W
103/100	1909	A	3	Leeds	L-126	4	61	st	4	11	b	1	–	–	–	6	7	0
104/101			4	Manchester	D	4	3	b	4	8	*	–	–	–	–	6	3	0
105/102			5	Oval	D	5	105	c	5	0	*	–	99	67	3	72	34	0

Career	M	I	NO	HS	R	Avge	100	50	Ct	St	Balls	R	W	Avge	BB	5w	10w	Rate
Test	3	6	2	105	188	47.00	1	1	1	–	183	111	3	37.00	3-67	–	–	61.00
F/c	534	805	75	211	22715	31.11	38	117	236	–	22126	12088	441	27.41	9-77	18	3	50.17

SHARPE John William

Surrey (1889 to 1893)
Nottinghamshire (1894)

Wisden 1892
TOUR A 1891–92
Born Ruddington, Nottinghamshire
9 Dec 1866
Died Ruddington 19 Jun 1936

As a right-arm fast-medium bowler who commanded a vast break-back and a lethal yorker, John Sharpe enjoyed two seasons of exhilarating success. During them he took 247 wickets and Surrey won the Championship both times. In the second of those seasons, 1891, he finished third in the national averages. Touring Australia with Lord Sheffield's team that winter, he took six wickets in the First Test but was asked to bowl 105 six-ball overs in the match, a phenomenal workload for a fast bowler in Australian heat. Afterwards his wonderful form vanished as quickly as it had appeared. He was slightly built – just 5ft 7in high and barely 11 stone – and, trying to bowl too fast, he burnt himself out. The accuracy of his bowling in that period is the more remarkable because he had lost an eye in his youth. A determined batsman, he featured in several large tenth-wicket stands and was an enthusiastic fielder with a powerful throw. During his next two summers at The Oval he totalled only 39 wickets and was not re-engaged. He tried his hand with his native Nottinghamshire but fared no better and his meteoric career ended. He returned to his birthplace and resumed his work as a framework knitter, dying of cancer in his 70th year. [*Illus. p.* 36]

NOTABLE FEATS

- Took 100 wickets in a season twice.
- Returned the remarkable analysis of 21.1–18–5–5 on his first-class debut for Surrey v Oxford U at Oxford in 1889.
- Took 9 for 47 for Surrey v Middlesex at The Oval in 1891.
- Twice bowled in an unchanged partnership with G.A. Lohmann throughout both completed innings of a match for Surrey.

Ref	Series	V	T	Venue	Result	Batting 1st No	R	HO	Batting 2nd No	R	HO	Ct	Bowling 1st Balls	R	W	Bowling 2nd Balls	R	W
34/34	1890	A	2	Oval	W-2w	10	5	*	10	2	*	1	30	8	1	45	10	1
35/35	1891–92	A	1	Melbourne	L-54	11	2	c	11	5	*	–	306	84	6	324	81	2
36/36			2	Sydney	L-72	11	26	c	11	4	*	1	60	31	0	210	91	1

Career	M	I	NO	HS	R	Avge	100	50	Ct	St	Balls	R	W	Avge	BB	5w	10w	Rate
Test	3	6	4	26	44	22.00	–	–	2	–	975	305	11	27.72	6-84	1	–	88.63
F/c	82	116	39	36	657	8.53	–	–	48	–	14855	5430	338	16.06	9-47	22	7	43.94

SHARPE, Philip John

Yorkshire (1958 to 1974)
Derbyshire (1975 to 1976)

Wisden 1963
TOURS
SA 1962–63 (Cav); WI 1969–70 (Cav/Norfolk); I 1963–64
Born Shipley, Yorkshire 27 Dec 1936

NOTABLE FEATS

- Exceeded 1000 runs in a season 12 times, including 2252 in 1962.
- Scored 3 double centuries, one each for Minor Counties, Yorkshire and Derbyshire.
- His 71 first-class catches in 1962 (including a record-equalling 70 for Yorkshire) is the fourth-highest total by a fielder.

Despite his entertaining and, on firm pitches, effective strokeplay as a very positive opening batsman, Philip Sharpe will be best remembered for his quite brilliant fielding. Short (5ft 7in) and chunky, with a very low centre of gravity, he was one of the greatest slip fielders of all time, capable of making difficult catches look simple and miraculously clinging on to the fiercest of cuts. He often casually appeared to clasp the ball after it had passed him before impishly hiding it in the pocket of his capacious flannels. In 1963 he was brought into the England side against Frank Worrell's powerful team chiefly for his slip fielding and it was a distinct bonus when he headed the series averages with 267 runs at 53.40 from just three Tests. When, after 19 summers, he left the fast lanes of Yorkshire and Derbyshire for the pastures of Norfolk (1977–81) and the conundrums of Test selection (1983–88), he had notched up the ninth-highest total of catches by a fielder with an entirely post-war career. When, in his early days with Yorkshire, lack of concentration and application had led to some poor trots with the bat, his outstanding fielding kept him in the side – except in 1959 when he ended the season deputising for their sick scorer. An occasional purveyor of high-flighted off-breaks, he was justly proud of his prize analysis of 1 for 1. He played hockey for Yorkshire and has sung in many amateur operatic productions.

Philip Sharpe pulls off a spectacular catch to dismiss Carew off the bowling of D'Oliveira during the Old Trafford Test against West Indies, 1969.

Ref	Series	V	T	Venue	Result	Batting 1st No	R	HO	Batting 2nd No	R	HO	Ct
545/397	1963	WI	3	Birmingham	W-217	6	23	c	6	85	*	2
546/398			4	Leeds	L-221	6	0	c	6	13	c	2
547/399			5	Oval	L-8w	6	63	c	6	83	c	–
553/400	1963–64	I	1	Madras[2]	D	3	27	lbw	7	31	*	–
561/405	1964	A	1	Nottingham	D	6	35	*	6	1	c	–
562/406			2	Lord's	D	6	35	lbw	–	–	–	–
653/453	1969	WI	1	Manchester	W-10w	3	2	b	–	–	–	2
654/454			2	Lord's	D	5	11	b	5	86	c	3
655/455			3	Leeds	W-30	3	6	c	3	15	lbw	3
656/456	1969	NZ	1	Lord's	W-230	3	20	c	3	46	c	2
657/457			2	Nottingham	D	3	111	c	–	–	–	1
658/458			3	Oval	W-8w	4	48	lbw	4	45	*	2

Career	M	I	NO	HS	R	Avge	100	50	Ct	St	Balls	R	W	Avge	BB	5w	10w	Rate
Test	12	21	4	111	786	46.23	1	4	17	–	–	–	–	–	–	–	–	–
F/c	493	811	78	228	22530	30.73	29	111	617	–	302	197	3	65.66	1-1	–	–	100.66

SHAW, Alfred

Nottinghamshire (1864 to 1897)
Sussex (1894 to 1895)

TOURS A 1876–77, 1881–82
Born Burton Joyce, Nottinghamshire
29 Aug 1842
Died Gedling, Nottinghamshire
16 Jan 1907

NOTABLE FEATS

- Took 100 wickets in a season 9 times, including 201 in 1878. His average of 8.54 runs per wicket in 1880 is the lowest recorded by a bowler taking 100 wickets.
- Took all 10 for 73 for MCC v North at Lord's in 1874.
- Took 7 for 7 in 41.2 4-ball overs for Nottinghamshire v MCC at Lord's in 1875.
- Three hat-tricks for Nottinghamshire: v Derbyshire at Derby in 1875 and in each innings v Gloucestershire at Nottingham in 1884. This first instance of two hat-tricks in the same first-class match was accompanied by his taking another 3 in 4 balls, a combination of feats that remains unequalled.
- Holds record for most balls bowled in a Championship match: 501 for Sussex v Nottinghamshire at Nottingham in 1895.
- Bowled in an unchanged partnership throughout both completed innings of a match on 12 occasions, including a record 8 occasions with F. Morley.
- Holds record for most successive maiden 4-ball overs: 23 for North v South at Nottingham in 1876.
- In all matches on Richard Daft's 1879 tour of North America he took 178 wickets at 2.70 runs apiece.

Alfred Shaw bowled the first ball in Test cricket and achieved England's first five-wicket analysis. Short (5ft 6½in) and increasingly stocky, he was a right-arm medium-pace bowler (who later reduced his speed to slow-medium) and the unrivalled master of precision bowling. By adhering to an exact line and length he became the most economical bowler of his generation and achieved the remarkable feat of bowling more overs than he conceded runs. In his later and slower mode he spun the ball sharply. Originally his batting was good enough for him to be considered an all-rounder but he abandoned interest in it once he had established himself as the country's leading bowler. One of the prime movers behind the strike of Nottinghamshire professionals against the committee in 1881, he was eventually appointed captain (1883–86) because of his influence over the other professionals and his fine tactical brain. When Nottinghamshire decided to retire him at the age of 45, he concentrated on his employment with Lord Sheffield which involved managing Sheffield Park Cricket Ground and coaching young Sussex cricketers. Six years later he returned to county cricket in Sussex colours and headed their bowling averages. Shrewd but honest, he was the joint promoter of four tours of Australia and once played cricket by the midnight sun on the Spitzbergen ice fiord. A keen shot, he had a narrow escape on Boxing Day 1876 when his powder flask exploded in the pocket of his shooting jacket. A partner in the sports goods firm of Shaw and Shrewsbury, he was also a first-class umpire (1898–1905).

Alfred Shaw's team to Australia, 1884–85: standing *R. Peel, W. Barnes, J. Hunter, W. Attewell, J. Lillywhite jr (umpire), J.M. Read, anon, anon, W. Bates;* seated *A. Shrewsbury (captain), A. Shaw (manager), W.H. Scotton;* in front *W. Flowers, G. Ulyett, J. Briggs.*

						Batting 1st			Batting 2nd				Bowling 1st			Bowling 2nd		
Ref	Series	V	T	Venue	Result	No	R	HO	No	R	HO	Ct	Balls	R	W	Balls	R	W
1/1	1876–77	A	1	Melbourne	L-45	7	10	b	7	2	st	–	223	51	3	136	38	5
2/2			2	Melbourne	W-4w	2	1	st	8	0	*	1	168	30	0	128	27	0
4/4	1880	A		Oval	W-5w	10	0	b	–	–	–	2	52	21	1	132	42	1
5/5*	1881–82	A	1	Melbourne	D	9	5	c	9	40	c	–	80	21	0	–	–	–
6/6*			2	Sydney	L-5w	9	11	c	9	30	b	1	–	–	–	84	12	1
7/7*			3	Sydney	L-6w	9	3	b	9	6	b	–	32	14	0	–	–	–
8/8*			4	Melbourne	D	9	3	c	–	–	–	–	64	29	1	–	–	–

Career	M	I	NO	HS	R	Avge	100	50	Ct	St	Balls	R	W	Avge	BB	5w	10w	Rate
Test	7	12	1	40	111	10.09	–	–	4	–	1099	285	12	23.75	5-38	1	–	91.58
F/c	404	630	101	88	6585	12.44	–	12	368	–	101774	24580	2027+1	12.12	10-73	177	44	50.20

SHEPPARD
Rt Rev. David Stuart

Sussex (1947 to 1962)
Cambridge University (1950 to 1952)

Wisden 1953
TOURS
A 1950–51, 1962–63;
NZ 1950–51, 1962–63
Born Reigate, Surrey 6 Mar 1929
Ordained 1955

David Sheppard

David Sheppard, Bishop of Liverpool since 1975, remains the only ordained minister to play Test cricket; other Test cricketers have been ordained after their careers were over. Tall (6ft), he was a stylish opening batsman with immense powers of concentration. He made his Sussex debut during his school holidays from Sherborne and was an accomplished player, especially strong on the off-side, by the time he began his record-breaking exploits at Cambridge. There he was a blue all three summers and captain in his last. The following season he led Sussex from 13th to 2nd – equalling their most successful performance since the Championship was officially constituted in 1890. That triumph marked his final season of regular first-class cricket. Thereafter he made come-backs, several of them dramatic, as in 1954 when he deputised as England's captain when Hutton was unwell and in 1962–63 when he took a winter sabbatical from his post as warden of the Mayflower Family Centre to make his second tour of the antipodes. A very occasional left-arm leg-break bowler, he was a superb close field in his early days. Ordained in September 1955, he was a Suffragan Bishop of Woolwich (1969–75) before moving to Liverpool.

NOTABLE FEATS

- 1000 runs in 18th Test (*538*) (27 inns).
- Exceeded 1000 runs in a season 6 times (plus once on tour), including 2000 on 3 occasions, notably 2270 in 1953. Leading batsman of 1952.
- Holds Oxbridge records for most runs (1581 in 1952) and most hundreds (7 in 1952) in a season. His 14 hundreds constitute the career record for either university and his career aggregate of 3445 runs is second only to that of J.M. Brearley.
- Scored 3 double centuries, notably 239* for Cambridge U v Worcestershire at Worcester in 1952.
- In 1950 he shared with J.G. Dewes in Cambridge U 1st-wkt stands of 349 v Sussex at Hove and 343 v West Indians at Fenner's.

						Batting 1st			Batting 2nd			
Ref	Series	V	T	Venue	Result	No	R	HO	No	R	HO	Ct
326/279	1950	WI	4	Oval	L-I & 56	3	11	b	3	29	c	–
330/283	1950–51	A	4	Adelaide	L-274	5	9	b	5	41	lbw	–
331/284			5	Melbourne	W-8w	5	1	c	–	–	–	–
333/286	1950–51	NZ	2	Wellington	W-6w	4	3	b	5	4	*	1
353/299	1952	I	3	Manchester	W-I & 207	2	34	lbw	–	–	–	1
354/300			4	Oval	D	2	119	lbw	–	–	–	–
388/312*	1954	P	2	Nottingham	W-I & 129	1	37	c	–	–	–	2
389/313*			3	Manchester	D	1	13	b	–	–	–	2
428/330	1956	A	4	Manchester	W-I & 170	3	113	b	–	–	–	–
429/331			5	Oval	D	3	24	c	3	62	c	–
442/340	1957	WI	4	Leeds	W-I & 5	6	68	c	–	–	–	1
443/341			5	Oval	W-I & 237	2	40	c	–	–	–	1
533/385	1962	P	4	Nottingham	D	2	83	c	–	–	–	–
534/386			5	Oval	W-10w	1	57	c	1	9	*	–
535/387	1962–63	A	1	Brisbane[2]	D	2	31	c	2	53	c	1
536/388			2	Melbourne	W-7w	1	0	lbw	1	113	ro	–
537/389			3	Sydney	L-8w	2	3	c	2	12	c	–
538/390			4	Adelaide	D	2	30	st	2	1	c	1
539/391			5	Sydney	D	1	19	c	1	68	c	–
540/392	1962–63	NZ	1	Auckland	W-I & 215	1	12	c	–	–	–	1
541/393			2	Wellington	W-I & 47	1	0	c	–	–	–	1
542/394			3	Christchurch	W-7w	1	42	b	2	31	b	–

Career	M	I	NO	HS	R	Avge	100	50	Ct	St	Balls	R	W	Avge	BB	5w	10w	Rate
Test	22	33	2	119	1172	37.80	3	6	12	–	–	–	–	–	–	–	–	–
F/c	230	395	31	239*	15838	43.51	45	75	195	–	120	88	2	44.00	1-5	–	–	60.00

D. S. SHEPPARD – TEST BATTING SUMMARY

Series	V	M	I	NO	HS	R	Avge	100	50
1950	WI	1	2	–	29	40	20.00	–	–
1950–51	A	2	3	–	41	51	17.00	–	–
1950–51	NZ	1	2	1	4*	7	7.00	–	–
1952	I	2	2	–	119	153	76.50	1	–
1954	P	2	2	–	37	50	25.00	–	–
1956	A	2	3	–	113	199	66.33	1	1
1957	WI	2	2	–	68	108	54.00	–	1
1962	P	2	3	1	83	149	74.50	–	2
1962–63	A	5	10	–	113	330	33.00	1	2
1962–63	NZ	3	4	–	42	85	21.25	–	–

Series	V	M	I	NO	HS	R	Avge	100	50
	A	9	16	–	113	580	36.25	2	3
	WI	3	4	–	68	148	37.00	–	1
	NZ	4	6	1	42	92	18.40	–	–
	I	2	2	–	119	153	76.50	1	–
	P	4	5	1	83	199	49.75	–	2
Home		11	14	1	119	699	53.76	2	4
Overseas		11	19	1	113	473	26.27	1	2
Totals		22	33	2	119	1172	37.80	3	6

SHERWIN, Mordecai

Nottinghamshire (1876 to 1896)

Wisden 1891
TOUR A 1886–87
Born Kimberley, Nottinghamshire
26 Feb 1851
Died Nottingham 3 Jul 1910

Although, at nearly 17 stone, he was probably the heaviest Test wicket-keeper of all time, Mordecai Sherwin was extremely agile, strong and energetic. He stood up to the fastest bowling, rarely missed anything and his timing was so accurate that his large hands remained virtually unscathed even after 14 seasons (1880–93) as Nottinghamshire's regular stumper. In the mid-1880s he was rated as the best professional keeper in England and became an automatic selection for the Players. Just medium height (5ft 9½in), he was a very cheery and popular character who enjoyed his tail-end efforts with the bat and had one match-winning fling as a right-arm fast bowler. He was on the Lord's staff for 25 years (1877–1902) and captained Nottinghamshire for two seasons (1887–88). As a first-class umpire (1896–1901) he stood in the Headingley Test of 1899. In his younger days he had been a lively showman as goalkeeper for Notts County. He was also the convivial licensee of a succession of Nottinghamshire pubs.

Mordecai Sherwin

Ref	Series	V	T	Venue	Result	Batting 1st No	R	HO	Batting 2nd No	R	HO	Fielding 1st Ct	St	Byes	Balls	Fielding 2nd Ct	St	Byes	Balls
25/25†	1886–87	A	1	Sydney	W-13	11	0	*	11	21	*	1	–	1	453	–	–	12	428
26/26†			2	Sydney	W-71	11	4	*	11	5	b	–	–	5	212	2	2	9	440
28/28†	1888	A	1	Lord's	L-61	11	0	*	11	0	c	1	–	5	286	1	–	3	118

Career	M	I	NO	HS	R	Avge	100	50	Ct	St	Balls	R	W	Avge	BB	5w	10w	Rate
Test	3	6	4	21*	30	15.00	–	–	5	2	–	–	–	–	–	–	–	–
F/c	328	454	147	37	2332	7.59	–	–	611	225	270	108	8	13.50	2-7	–	–	33.75

SHREWSBURY Arthur

Nottinghamshire (1875 to 1902)

Wisden 1890
TOURS
A 1881–82, 1884–85, 1886–87, 1887–88
Born New Lenton, Nottinghamshire
11 Apr 1856
Died Gedling, Nottinghamshire
19 May 1903

Arthur Shrewsbury

For most of the last 20 years of the nineteenth century, Arthur Shrewsbury was unchallenged as the leading professional batsman in England. His greatest accolade came from W.G. himself; when asked which contemporary batsman he rated highest he would reply: 'Give me Arthur'. A master batsman against the turning ball, he evolved his own style of backplay which made maximum use of the batting crease; he would watch the ball right on to the bat and play it as late as possible. He was a most graceful stylist and a supreme judge of length. Of average height (5ft 8in) and comfortably built, he was seldom without a cap or a bowler hat; quiet and retiring, he was by nature an extremely patient perfectionist. England's last professional captain before Hutton was appointed in 1952, he led England to victory in five of his seven attempts. He remained an outstanding fielder throughout his long career, initially in the deep but at point from 1883. The joint-sponsor of several tours of Australia, he shot himself when he was convinced that he had an incurable illness which would prevent him from playing further first-class cricket.

NOTABLE FEATS

- 1000 runs in 21st Test (*39*) (36 inns).
- *21* First England captain to score a Test hundred.
- *23* His 164 in 410 min on a difficult pitch was the England record for one match; shared (then) record England 5th-wkt stand of 161 with W. Barnes.
- *39* First to score 1000 runs in Tests (and E v A Tests); first to score 3 hundreds for England.
- Exceeded 1000 runs in a season 13 times, notably 1653 at the then record average of 78.71 in 1887.
- Headed first-class batting averages in 1886–87–90–91–92 and 1902.
- Scored 10 double centuries (7 for Nottinghamshire and 3 in Australia).
- Shared (then) world record 1st-wkt stand of 398 with W. Gunn for Nottinghamshire v Sussex at Nottingham in 1890 which survived for 44 years; it remains the Nottinghamshire record for any wicket.
- Shared 2 other record Nottinghamshire stands: 391 (1st wkt) with A.O. Jones v Gloucestershire at Bristol in 1899 and 266 (5th wkt) with W. Gunn v Sussex at Hove in 1884.
- Carried his bat through a completed innings on 8 occasions.

						Batting 1st			Batting 2nd			
Ref	Series	V	T	Venue	Result	No	R	HO	No	R	HO	Ct
5/5	1881–82	A	1	Melbourne	D	5	11	c	5	16	b	–
6/6			2	Sydney	L-5w	5	7	b	5	22	c	3
7/7			3	Sydney	L-6w	5	82	c	5	47	c	–
8/8			4	Melbourne	D	5	1	lbw	–	–	–	1
14/14	1884	A	1	Manchester	D	4	43	b	4	25	b	1
15/15			2	Lord's	W-I & 5	3	27	st	–	–	–	2
16/16			3	Oval	D	4	10	c	3	37	c	–
17/17*	1884–85	A	1	Adelaide	W-8w	2	0	b	3	26	*	3
18/18*			2	Melbourne	W-10w	1	72	c	1	0	*	1
19/19*			3	Sydney	L-6	2	18	c	2	24	b	1
20/20*			4	Sydney	L-8w	2	40	b	2	16	c	1
21/21*			5	Melbourne	W-I & 98	5	105	*	–	–	–	–
22/22	1886	A	1	Manchester	W-4w	3	31	b	3	4	c	1
23/23			2	Lord's	W-I & 106	3	164	c	–	–	–	1
24/24			3	Oval	W-I & 217	3	44	c	–	–	–	2
25/25*	1886–87	A	1	Sydney	W-13	2	2	c	2	29	b	3
26/26*			2	Sydney	W-71	1	9	b	1	6	b	–
27/27	1887–88	A		Sydney	W-126	2	44	c	2	1	b	6
33/33	1890	A	1	Lord's	W-7w	2	4	b	2	13	lbw	–
34/34			2	Oval	W-2w	1	4	c	1	9	lbw	–
39/39	1893	A	1	Lord's	D	1	106	c	1	81	b	1
40/40			2	Oval	W-I & 43	3	66	c	–	–	–	1
41/41			3	Manchester	D	3	12	c	3	19	*	1

TEST NOTES

- *16* Bowled in 1st inns: 0 for 2 (12 balls).

Career	M	I	NO	HS	R	Avge	100	50	Ct	St	Balls	R	W	Avge	BB	5w	10w	Rate
Test	23	40	4	164	1277	35.47	3	4	29	–	12	2	0	–	–	–	–	–
F/c	498	813	90	267	26505	36.65	59	114	377	–	16	2	0	–	–	–	–	–

A. SHREWSBURY – TEST BATTING SUMMARY

Series	V	M	I	NO	HS	R	Avge	100	50
1881–82	A	4	7	–	82	186	26.57	–	1
1884	A	3	5	–	43	142	28.40	–	–
1884–85	A	5	9	3	105*	301	50.16	1	1
1886	A	3	4	–	164	243	60.75	1	–
1886–87	A	2	4	–	29	46	11.50	–	–
1887–88	A	1	2	–	44	45	22.50	–	–
1890	A	2	4	–	13	30	7.50	–	–
1893	A	3	5	1	106	284	71.00	1	2
Home		11	18	1	164	699	41.11	2	2
Overseas		12	22	3	105*	578	30.42	1	2
Totals		23	40	4	164	1277	35.47	3	4

SHUTER, John

Kent (1874)
Surrey (1877 to 1909)

Born Thornton Heath, Surrey
9 Feb 1855
Died Blackheath, Kent 5 Jul 1920

Although only 5ft 6in high, John Shuter was an extremely graceful batsman and an outstanding Surrey captain. After skippering Winchester College in his last summer, he appeared in one Championship match for Kent before lack of opportunities prompted a return to his native county. He was a stylish player with a range of handsome off-side strokes which he played with surprising power in view of his size. He was a fine fielder, a most unselfish team man and an exceptionally successful leader. He captained Surrey for 14 seasons (1880–93) and, making maximum use of the talents of such notable players as George Lohmann and Walter Read, won the first three official Championships (1890–92). Business commitments forced his retirement and it is on record that as a testimonial he received a grand piano and a pair of pistols. It is not revealed if the second item was related to his proficiency with the first. He returned to The Oval after the First World War as secretary but died before he had completed a year in office.

John Shuter

Ref	Series	V	T	Venue	Result	Batting 1st			Batting 2nd			Ct
						No	R	HO	No	R	HO	
29/29	1888	A	2	Oval	W-I & 137	2	28	b	–	–	–	–

Career	M	I	NO	HS	R	Avge	100	50	Ct	St	Balls	R	W	Avge	BB	5w	10w	Rate
Test	1	1	0	28	28	28.00	–	–	–	–	–	–	–	–	–	–	–	–
F/c	306	503	23	135	10206	21.26	8	49	157	–	44	49	0	–	–	–	–	–

SHUTTLEWORTH Kenneth

Lancashire (1964 to 1975)
Leicestershire (1977 to 1980)

TOURS
A 1970–71; NZ 1970–71;
P 1967–68 (Cwlth)
Born St Helens, Lancashire 13 Nov 1944

Tall (6ft 3in) and rangy, Ken Shuttleworth was an above-average right-arm fast bowler who never realised the rich promise of his early seasons with Lancashire. First sight of his long run evoked memories of Brian Statham and his magnificent side-on action with its long delivery stride was very reminiscent of Fred Trueman; somewhow the end product seldom matched the presentation. When not plagued by an endless assortment of injuries he enjoyed spells of destruction and made one telling contribution to the regaining of the Ashes on Ray Illingworth's tour. He also had some rewarding days as a flamboyant and hard-hitting tail-end batsman before transferring via Leicestershire to league cricket in Staffordshire.

NOTABLE FEATS

- Hat-trick for Leicestershire v Surrey at The Oval in 1977.

Ken Shuttleworth; Jack Crapp is the umpire.

Ref	Series	V	T	Venue	Result	Batting 1st No	Batting 1st R	Batting 1st HO	Batting 2nd No	Batting 2nd R	Batting 2nd HO	Ct	Bowling 1st Balls	Bowling 1st R	Bowling 1st W	Bowling 2nd Balls	Bowling 2nd R	Bowling 2nd W
674/459	1970–71	A	1	Brisbane[2]	D	11	7	c	–	–	–	1	216	81	0	141	47	5
675/460			2	Perth	D	10	2	b	–	–	–	–	224	105	2	24	9	0
685/465	1970–71	NZ	1	Christchurch	W-8w	10	5	b	–	–	–	–	64	14	3	96	27	2
686/466			2	Auckland	D	9	0	c	8	11	c	–	136	49	0	32	12	0
687/467	1971	P	1	Birmingham	D	9	21	c	–	–	–	–	138	83	0	–	–	–

Career	M	I	NO	HS	R	Avge	100	50	Ct	St	Balls	R	W	Avge	BB	5w	10w	Rate
Test	5	6	0	21	46	7.66	–	–	1	–	1071	427	12	35.58	5-47	1	–	89.25
F/c	239	241	85	71	2589	16.59	–	3	128	–	34144	15270	623	24.51	7-41	21	1	54.80

SIDEBOTTOM Arnold

Yorkshire (1973 to date)
Orange Free State
(1981–82 to 1983–84)

TOUR WI 1986–87 (Yorks)
Born Shawlands, Barnsley, Yorkshire
1 Apr 1954

Tall (6ft 1in), lean and sandy-haired, Arnie Sidebottom is an all-round sportsman who fell just short of international class as a cricketer and footballer. His soccer skills reached their peak in the strong Manchester United team before he was transferred to Huddersfield and then Halifax. As a talented all-round Yorkshire cricketer, his right-arm medium-fast swing bowling and capable lower-order batting had brought him close to Test selection when, having just headed the Orange Free State bowling averages, he was persuaded to join the rebel England tour of South Africa. Although he played in no first-class matches on that expedition, he was still banned from Test cricket for three of his most potentially effective summers. When an injury to Neil Foster at last gave him a chance at the highest level, he was unlucky to be hampered by a damaged toe and an unresponsive pitch.

Arnie Sidebottom

Ref	Series	V	T Venue	Result	Batting 1st No	R	HO	Batting 2nd No	R	HO	Ct	Bowling 1st Balls	R	W	Bowling 2nd Balls	R	W
1019/614	1985	A	3 Nottingham	D	8	2	c	–	–	–	–	112	65	1	–	–	–

Career	M	I	NO	HS	R	Avge	100	50	Ct	St	Balls	R	W	Avge	BB	5w	10w	Rate
Test	1	1	0	2	2	2.00	–	–	–	–	112	65	1	65.00	1-65	–	–	112.00
F/c	205	234	56	124	4042	22.70	1	18	51	–	26776	12752	523	24.38	8-72	18	2	51.19

SIMPSON
Reginald Thomas

Sind (1944–45 to 1945–46)
Europeans (1944–45 to 1945–46)
Nottinghamshire (1946 to 1963)

Wisden 1950
TOURS
A 1950–51, 1954–55; SA 1948–49;
NZ 1950–51, 1954–55;
I 1953–54 (Cwlth), 1956–57 (Howard)
Born Sherwood Rise, Nottingham
27 Feb 1920

Reg Simpson steps out to on-drive Iverson after reaching his century against Australia during the Melbourne Test, 1950–51.

Reg Simpson was an outstanding player of fast bowling. Against the bouncer he would seldom chance the hook but would simply sway inside the line of the ball and allow it to pass behind him before giving the bowler a disdainful look to persuade him not to waste his energy. Perhaps such tactics would compel a drastic review of the current West Indies fast bowling methods. A tall (6ft), slim opening batsman, he played his early cricket for Nottingham High School before making his first-class debut in India during wartime service with the RAF. This fortunate dress rehearsal provided a vital confidence booster for the start of his long county career with Nottinghamshire. Capped in his first summer, he began his ten-season reign of enterprising captaincy in 1951. He was an extremely graceful player who timed the ball easily, played a full range of elegant strokes and was particularly strong off the back foot. His magnificent innings of 156* (Test *331*) enabled England to gain their first post-war victory against Australia. A handy off-spin bowler, he was a superb fielder, usually in the covers. He has been a member of the Nottinghamshire committee since his retirement and is a former managing director of Gunn and Moore.

NOTABLE FEATS

- 1000 runs in 17th Test (*351*) (30 inns).
- *316* Scored 103 in his first home Test, his last 53 runs taking 28 min.
- *325* Shared record E v WI 1st-wkt stand of 212 with C. Washbrook.
- *331* Completed 100 on his 31st birthday and scored 64 out of 10th-wkt stand of 74 in 55 min with R. Tattersall.
- *334/388* He remains the only Nottinghamshire player to score a century for England at Trent Bridge.
- Exceeded 1000 runs in a season 13 times (plus once on tour), including 2000 on 5 occasions, notably 2576 in 1950. Leading batsman of 1950 and 1962.
- Scored 259 for MCC v NSW at Sydney in 1950–51 and 9 other double centuries for Nottinghamshire.
- Scored hundreds in 3 consecutive innings for Nottinghamshire in 1959. Scored 7 consecutive fifties in 1949.
- Carried his bat through a completed innings twice.
- Shared 3rd-wkt stand of 399 in 181 min with D.C.S. Compton for MCC v NE Transvaal at Venoni in 1948–49; it remains the 3rd-wkt record in South African first-class cricket.
- Scored 100 before lunch on the first day on 3 occasions.

TEST NOTES

- *375* Retired hurt (1st inns); resumed at 149–8.

Ref	Series	V	T Venue	Result	Batting 1st No	R	HO	Batting 2nd No	R	HO	Ct	Bowling 1st Balls	R	W	Bowling 2nd Balls	R	W
309/267	1948–49	SA	1 Durban[2]	W-2w	3	5	c	6	0	c	–	–	–	–	–	–	–
316/274	1949	NZ	3 Manchester	D	5	103	c	–	–	–	–	–	–	–	12	9	0
317/275			4 Oval	D	2	68	c	–	–	–	–	–	–	–	–	–	–
323/276	1950	WI	1 Manchester	W-202	2	27	c	1	0	c	–	–	–	–	–	–	–
325/278			3 Nottingham	L-10w	1	4	c	1	94	ro	–	–	–	–	9	9	0
326/279			4 Oval	L-I & 56	2	30	c	2	16	b	–	–	–	–	–	–	–

Ref	Series	V	T	Venue	Result	Batting 1st No	R	HO	Batting 2nd No	R	HO	Ct	Bowling 1st Balls	R	W	Bowling 2nd Balls	R	W
327/280	1950–51	A	1	Brisbane[2]	L-70	1	12	b	1	0	b	4	–	–	–	–	–	–
328/281			2	Melbourne	L-28	1	4	c	1	23	b	–	–	–	–	–	–	–
329/282			3	Sydney	L-I & 13	3	49	c	3	0	c	–	–	–	–	–	–	–
330/283			4	Adelaide	L-274	3	29	b	3	61	c	–	–	–	–	–	–	–
331/284			5	Melbourne	W-8w	3	156	*	3	15	ro	–	–	–	–	–	–	–
332/285	1950–51	NZ	1	Christchurch	D	3	81	c	–	–	–	–	–	–	–	24	4	2
333/286			2	Wellington	W-6w	2	6	b	2	5	b	–	–	–	–	–	–	–
334/287	1951	SA	1	Nottingham	L-71	3	137	c	3	7	c	–	–	–	–	–	–	–
335/288			2	Lord's	W-10w	3	26	lbw	–	–	–	–	–	–	–	–	–	–
336/289			3	Manchester	W-9w	3	11	st	3	4	*	–	–	–	–	–	–	–
351/297	1952	I	1	Leeds	W-7w	2	23	c	2	51	c	–	–	–	–	–	–	–
352/298			2	Lord's	W-8w	2	53	b	2	2	ro	–	–	–	–	–	–	–
372/301	1953	A	1	Nottingham	D	3	0	lbw	3	28	*	1	–	–	–	–	–	–
374/303			3	Manchester	D	7	31	c	–	–	–	–	–	–	–	–	–	–
375/304			4	Leeds	D	6	15	c	6	0	c	–	–	–	–	–	–	–
387/311	1954	P	1	Lord's	D	2	40	lbw	–	–	–	–	–	–	–	–	–	–
388/312			2	Nottingham	W-I & 129	2	101	b	–	–	–	–	–	–	–	–	–	–
390/314			4	Oval	L-24	2	2	c	2	27	c	–	–	–	–	–	–	–
391/315	1954–55	A	1	Brisbane[2]	L-I & 154	2	2	b	2	9	ro	–	–	–	–	–	–	–
401/320	1954–55	NZ	1	Dunedin	W-8w	5	21	b	–	–	–	–	–	–	–	–	–	–
402/321			2	Auckland	W-I & 20	1	23	c	–	–	–	–	–	–	–	–	–	–

Career	M	I	NO	HS	R	Avge	100	50	Ct	St	Balls	R	W	Avge	BB	5w	10w	Rate
Test	27	45	3	156*	1401	33.35	4	6	5	–	45	22	2	11.00	2-4	–	–	22.50
F/c	495	852	55	259	30546	38.32	64	158	193	–	4660	2227	59	37.74	3-22	–	–	78.98

R. T. SIMPSON – TEST BATTING SUMMARY

Series	V	M	I	NO	HS	R	Avge	100	50
1948–49	SA	1	2	–	5	5	2.50	–	–
1949	NZ	2	2	–	103	171	85.50	1	1
1950	WI	3	6	–	94	171	28.50	–	1
1950–51	A	5	10	1	156*	349	38.77	1	1
1950–51	NZ	2	3	–	81	92	30.66	–	1
1951	SA	3	5	1	137	185	46.25	1	–
1952	I	2	4	–	53	129	32.25	–	2
1953	A	3	5	1	31	74	18.50	–	–
1954	P	3	4	–	101	170	42.50	1	–
1954–55	A	1	2	–	9	11	5.50	–	–
1954–55	NZ	2	2	–	23	44	22.00	–	–

Series	V	M	I	NO	HS	R	Avge	100	50
	A	9	17	2	156*	434	28.93	1	1
	SA	4	7	1	137	190	31.66	1	–
	WI	3	6	–	94	171	28.50	–	1
	NZ	6	7	–	103	307	43.85	1	2
	I	2	4	–	53	129	32.25	–	2
	P	3	4	–	101	170	42.50	1	–
Home		16	26	2	137	900	37.50	3	4
Overseas		11	19	1	156*	501	27.83	1	2
Totals		27	45	3	156*	1401	33.35	4	6

SIMPSON-HAYWARD George Hayward Thomas

Cambridge University (1895 to 1897)
Worcestershire (1899 to 1914)

TOURS

SA 1909–10; WI 1904–05; NZ 1906–07; I 1902–03 (Oxford Authentics)

Born Stoneleigh, Kenilworth, Warwickshire 7 Jun 1875

Died Icomb, Gloucestershire 2 Oct 1936

George Simpson-Hayward was the last specialist lob bowler to appear regularly in first-class cricket. He was also one of the most unusual in that he bowled off-breaks – a ball spun underarm with the natural right-handed wrist action would normally turn from leg to off. Instead of flighting the ball, he bowled it briskly along a low trajectory and thrived on the matting pitches of South Africa which responded eagerly to his exceptionally strong spin. A capable forcing batsman in the Malvern tradition, he failed to gain a cricket blue at Cambridge but had the compensation of making three appearances against Oxford as a soccer full-back. Originally plain Simpson he became hyphenated and extended after leaving university. [*Illus. p.* 273]

NOTABLE FEATS

- *106* Bowled J.W. Zulch with his fifth ball in Test cricket.

Ref	Series	V	T	Venue	Result	Batting 1st No	R	HO	Batting 2nd No	R	HO	Ct	Bowling 1st Balls	R	W	Bowling 2nd Balls	R	W
106/103	1909–10	SA	1	Johannesburg[1]	L-19	10	29	*	10	14	c	–	96	43	6	144	59	2
107/104			2	Durban[1]	L-95	10	0	c	10	16	lbw	–	143	42	4	138	66	3
108/105			3	Johannesburg[1]	W-3w	9	5	c	–	–	–	–	84	46	1	132	69	5
109/106			4	Cape Town	L-4w	8	13	b	9	9	c	–	54	33	1	30	12	0
110/107			5	Cape Town	W-9w	8	19	c	–	–	–	1	29	15	1	48	35	0

Career	M	I	NO	HS	R	Avge	100	50	Ct	St	Balls	R	W	Avge	BB	5w	10w	Rate
Test	5	8	1	29*	105	15.00	–	–	1	–	898	420	23	18.26	6-43	2	–	39.04
F/c	199	324	26	130	5548	18.61	3	9	133	–	20062	10709	500	21.41	7-54	31	1	40.12

SIMS, James Morton

Middlesex (1929 to 1952)

TOURS
A 1935–36, 1936–37;
NZ 1935–36, 1936–37
Born Leyton, Essex 13 May 1903
Died Canterbury, Kent 27 Apr 1973

NOTABLE FEATS

- Took 100 wickets in a season 8 times.
- Took all 10 for 90 for East v West at Kingston upon Thames in 1948 and 9 for 92 for Middlesex v Lancashire at Manchester in 1934.
- Hat-trick for Middlesex v South Africans at Lord's in 1947.

One of cricket's greatest raconteurs and characters, Jim Sims was also an extremely capable right-arm leg-break and googly bowler. He began his long, war-interrupted career as a batsman who frequently opened the innings but, when peace was restored, he specialised as a bowler. Tall and lean, he had a well-concealed googly and a laconic wit. Famous for his dead-pan asides delivered from the side of his mouth and behind his hand, he was an inveterate leg-puller and an inexhaustible source of cricketing anecdotes, many featuring his old friend, 'Patsy' Hendren. He had intended retiring at the end of the 1948 season, but stayed on for another four summers after taking all ten wickets in a Kingston Festival match. When he finally left the Middlesex dressing room in his 50th year, he coached the 2nd XI before becoming scorer. He died in his hotel on the eve of a pre-season friendly match against Kent.

Jim Sims

Ref	Series	V	T	Venue	Result	Batting 1st No	R	HO	Batting 2nd No	R	HO	Ct	Bowling 1st Balls	R	W	Bowling 2nd Balls	R	W
244/218	1935	SA	3	Leeds	D	9	12	b	–	–	–	–	54	20	0	162	48	1
254/223	1936	I	3	Oval	W-9w	9	1	lbw	–	–	–	1	113	73	5	150	95	2
256/225	1936–37	A	2	Sydney	W-I & 22	–	–	–	–	–	–	3	16	20	0	136	80	1
257/226			3	Melbourne	L-365	5	3	c	10	0	lbw	2	72	35	0	184	109	2

Career	M	I	NO	HS	R	Avge	100	50	Ct	St	Balls	R	W	Avge	BB	5w	10w	Rate
Test	4	4	0	12	16	4.00	–	–	6	–	887	480	11	43.63	5-73	1	–	80.63
F/c	462	635	116	123	8983	17.30	4	21	253	–	76912	39401	1581	24.92	10-90	98	21	48.64

SINFIELD
Reginald Albert

Gloucestershire (1924 to 1939)

Born Beamington, Stevenage, Hertfordshire 24 Dec 1900
Died Ham Green, Bristol 17 Mar 1988

NOTABLE FEATS

- Exceeded 1000 runs in a season 10 times, took 100 wickets 4 times and completed the 'double' twice (1934 and 1937).
- Scored 209* for Gloucestershire v Glamorgan at Cardiff in 1935.
- Carried his bat through a completed Gloucestershire innings on 5 occasions.
- Took 9 for 111 for Gloucestershire v Middlesex at Lord's in 1936.

Reg Sinfield was a determined batsman who often opened the Gloucestershire innings and an extremely versatile right-arm slow-medium bowler. He appeared for his native Hertfordshire and made his first-class debut for MCC before beginning his all-round service as one of Gloucestershire's most loyal professionals. As a batsman he had immense powers of concentration, sound footwork and an appetite for the on-side. He always wore his cap while bowling what was basically off-spin with astute variations of flight, angle and pace. Like his great friend, Charlie Parker, he played in only one Test; his first international wicket was that of Bradman. An honest, good-natured Tommy Trinder lookalike, he was a dedicated church warden and sidesman at Tickenham parish church and an enthusiastic gardener. He lived into his 88th year and was the oldest surviving England Test cricketer.

Reg Sinfield

For more than 40 years he had coached first at Clifton College and then Colston's School, the latter engagement bringing him into contact with the teenaged Chris Broad.

						Batting 1st			Batting 2nd				Bowling 1st			Bowling 2nd		
Ref	Series	V	T	Venue	Result	No	R	HO	No	R	HO	Ct	Balls	R	W	Balls	R	W
263/232	1938	A	1	Nottingham	D	9	6	lbw	–	–	–	–	168	51	1	210	72	1

Career	M	I	NO	HS	R	Avge	100	50	Ct	St	Balls	R	W	Avge	BB	5w	10w	Rate
Test	1	1	0	6	6	6.00	–	–	–	–	378	123	2	61.50	1-51	–	–	189.00
F/c	430	696	86	209*	15674	25.69	16	62	178	–	74619	28734	1173	24.49	9-111	66	9	63.61

SLACK
Wilfred Norris

Middlesex (1977 to 1988)
Windward Islands
(1981–82 to 1982–83)

TOURS
A 1986–87; WI 1985–86;
P 1981–82 (Int XI); SL 1985–86 (Eng B);
Z 1980–81 (Middx)

Born Troumaca, St Vincent, Windward Islands 12 Dec 1954
Died Banjul, The Gambia 15 Jan 1989

The saddest moment in England's muddled and tourless winter of 1988–89 was when the news arrived of Wilf Slack's death from a heart attack while batting on a private tour of The Gambia. A most likeable and dedicated cricketer, he was always eager to help junior players; his many friends were left to realise how much he had meant to them and to Middlesex. A left-handed opener, he was primarily a front-foot player but his ability to ride back with the ball made him a sound negotiator of fast bowling. His best performances for Middlesex were achieved in partnership with Graham Barlow; naturally self-effacing, Slack needed a partner to dominate him. Tallish (5ft 11in) and trim, he was a handy right-arm medium-pace change bowler and an agile fielder whose quick reactions usually landed him at short leg. He migrated with his parents to High Wycombe when he was 11, playing his early cricket for the town club. It was when he represented Buckinghamshire in 1976 that he was spotted by Don Bennett, the eagle-eyed Middlesex coach. One of the fittest county players, he suffered three

Wilf Slack

mysterious black-outs during the summer of 1988, two at the wicket and one fielding. Extensive tests failed to identify the cause and he was passed fit to continue with the job he loved most – batting.

NOTABLE FEATS

- Exceeded 1000 runs in a season 8 times, notably 1900 in 1985.
- Scored 3 double centuries for Middlesex, notably 248* v Worcestershire at Lord's in 1981.
- Shared record Middx 1st-wkt stand of 367* with G.D. Barlow v Kent at Lord's in 1981.

Ref	Series	V	T	Venue	Result	Batting 1st No	R	HO	Batting 2nd No	R	HO	Ct
1039/619	1985–86	WI	2	Port-of-Spain	L-7w	2	2	c	2	0	ro	–
1042/622			5	St John's	L-240	2	52	c	2	8	b	1
1047/624	1986	I	2	Leeds	L-279	2	0	b	2	19	c	2

Career	M	I	NO	HS	R	Avge	100	50	Ct	St	Balls	R	W	Avge	BB	5w	10w	Rate
Test	3	6	0	52	81	13.50	–	1	3	–	–	–	–	–	–	–	–	–
F/c	237	398	40	248*	13950	38.96	25	75	174	–	1519	688	21	32.76	3-17	–	–	72.33

SMAILES
Thomas Francis

Yorkshire (1932 to 1948)

TOUR WI 1935–36 (Yorks)
Born Ripley, Yorkshire 27 Mar 1910
Died Harrogate, Yorkshire 1 Dec 1970

Frank Smailes was a very fine right-arm medium-pace bowler and an aggressive left-handed lower-order batsman. Tall (6ft), he learned the basics of his swing bowling at Pocklington School before playing a key role in a Yorkshire career reduced to 11 summers by the Second World War. His high action, late movement and exceptional command of length brought rich dividends and played a vital part in the winning of seven Championships in that short period. He also had the ability to switch to off-spin if conditions favoured it. Included in England's 13 for the abandoned Old Trafford Test of 1938, he had to wait until after wartime service as a captain in the Royal Artillery before his chance came again. [*Illus. p.* 498]

NOTABLE FEATS

- Took 100 wickets in a season 4 times and scored 1002 runs in 1938 when he completed the 'double'.
- Took all 10 for 47 for Yorkshire v Derbyshire at Sheffield in 1939; it remains the record analysis v Derbyshire.

Ref	Series	V	T	Venue	Result	Batting 1st No	R	HO	Batting 2nd No	R	HO	Ct	Bowling 1st Balls	R	W	Bowling 2nd Balls	R	W
276/244	1946	I	1	Lord's	W-10w	8	25	c	–	–	–	–	30	18	0	90	44	3

Career	M	I	NO	HS	R	Avge	100	50	Ct	St	Balls	R	W	Avge	BB	5w	10w	Rate
Test	1	1	0	25	25	25.00	–	–	–	–	120	62	3	20.66	3-44	–	–	40.00
F/c	269	349	43	117	5892	19.25	3	24	154	–	41008	17114	822	20.81	10-47	41	6	49.88

SMALL
Gladstone Cleophas

Warwickshire (1980 to date)
South Australia (1985–86)

TOURS
A 1986–87; NZ 1979–80 (Robins);
P 1981–82 (Int XI)
Born St George, Barbados 18 Oct 1961

Since he shortened his extravagant run-up in 1985, Gladstone Small's bowling career has made a rapacious advance. Before that transition he was too erratic and prone to over-stepping to be serious considered as a Test prospect. A little above average height (5ft 11in), with a lean and hunched physique, he is a right-arm fast-medium bowler who moves the ball late at a deceptively rapid pace. His redesigned approach produced a dramatic increase in sustained accuracy and was rewarded with five-wicket analyses in each of his first two Tests against Australia. Arriving from Barbados as a 15-year-old, he completed his studies in Birmingham before joining Warwickshire as a batsman. His obvious ability with the ball necessitated a major reclassification. Early in the 1988 season he had established himself as the most effective new-ball bowler in England but another spate of injuries halted his progress. His batting has also made a major advance and his 1988 tally of 554 runs with an average of 25 holds promise of all-rounder status. Extremely popular and friendly, he responds happily to being addressed as 'Gladys'.

Gladstone Small

						Batting 1st			Batting 2nd				Bowling 1st			Bowling 2nd		
Ref	Series	V	T	Venue	Result	No	R	HO	No	R	HO	Ct	Balls	R	W	Balls	R	W
1050/627	1986	NZ	2	Nottingham	L-8w	11	2	*	11	12	lbw	–	228	88	3	48	10	1
1051/628			3	Oval	D	–	–	–	–	–	–	–	108	36	0	–	–	–
1061/632	1986–87	A	4	Melbourne	W-I & 14	11	21	*	–	–	–	1	136	48	5	90	40	2
1062/633			5	Sydney	L-55	10	14	b	10	0	c	–	198	75	5	48	17	0
1099/647	1988	WI	2	Lord's	L-134	9	5	*	9	7	c	–	113	64	4	114	76	0

Career	M	I	NO	HS	R	Avge	100	50	Ct	St	Balls	R	W	Avge	BB	5w	10w	Rate
Test	5	7	3	21*	61	15.25	–	–	1	–	1083	454	20	22.70	5-48	2	–	54.15
F/c	188	240	57	70	2731	14.92	–	4	53	–	29560	15139	546	27.72	7-15	24	2	54.13

SMITH
Alan Christopher

Warwickshire (1958 to 1974)
Oxford University (1958 to 1960)

TOURS
A 1962–63; WI 1960–61 (Swanton);
NZ 1962–63, 1974–75
(when asst-manager)
Born Hall Green, Birmingham
25 Oct 1936

Alan ('AC') Smith was an exceptionally versatile and effective all-round cricketer who has become one of the game's senior administrators. Tallish (5ft 11½in) and trim, he began his serious cricket at King Edward's School at Edgbaston before going up to Oxford. There he was a blue in each of his three summers and captain in his last two. Within the next three years he had completed a seven-match Test career at the expense of John Murray. He was a useful middle-order batsman who could defend stubbornly, an effective but not particularly stylish wicket-keeper capable of inspired performances, and a right-arm medium-fast swing bowler whose idiosyncratic whippy action culminated in a hop and the ball being released off the wrong foot. He captained Warwickshire enterprisingly for seven seasons (1968–74) and was secretary for 11 years (1976–86) during which he also served two terms as a Test selector (1969–73 and 1982–86) and managed four MCC or England tours. During this period he became renowned for his ultra-careful statements; 'No comment – but don't quote me,' indicated one of his more forthcoming moods. He handled the Jackman affair with great efficiency and sensitivity. A soccer blue and former director of Aston Villa, he was appointed the TCCB's first chief executive in 1987.

NOTABLE FEATS

- *541* Shared (then) world record 9th-wkt stand of 163* with M.C. Cowdrey – it remains the England record.
- Scored 1201 runs in 1962 and made 82 dismissals.
- Hat-trick for Warwickshire v Essex at Clacton in 1965 after keeping wicket earlier in the innings – unique achievement in English first-class cricket.
- Held 6 catches in an innings for Warwickshire v Derbyshire at Derby in 1970.

					Batting 1st			Batting 2nd			Fielding 1st				Fielding 2nd			
Ref	Series	V	T Venue	Result	No	R	HO	No	R	HO	Ct	St	Byes	Balls	Ct	St	Byes	Balls
535/387†	1962–63	A	1 Brisbane[2]	D	6	21	c	–	–	–	2	–	5	853	1	–	4	696
536/388†			2 Melbourne	W-7w	8	6	*	–	–	–	2	–	2	736	1	–	4	768
538/390†			4 Adelaide	D	9	13	c	–	–	–	2	–	0	825	3	–	1	723
539/391†			5 Sydney	D	9	6	b	9	1	c	1	–	6	1050	1	–	4	576
541/393†	1962–63	NZ	2 Wellington	W-I & 47	10	69	*	–	–	–	3	–	13	459	–	–	13	588
542/394†			3 Christchurch	W-7w	10	2	*	–	–	–	2	–	1	710	2	–	0	502

Career	M	I	NO	HS	R	Avge	100	50	Ct	St	Balls	R	W	Avge	BB	5w	10w	Rate
Test	6	7	3	69*	118	29.50	–	1	20	–	–	–	–	–	–	–	–	–
F/c	428	612	85	145	11027	20.92	3	38	715	61	7158	3074	131	23.46	5-32	2	–	54.64

LEFT *Alan Smith*
RIGHT *Aubrey Smith*

SMITH
Sir Charles Aubrey

Cambridge University (1882 to 1885)
Sussex (1882 to 1896)
Transvaal (1889–90)

TOURS A 1887–88; SA 1888–89
Born City of London 21 Jul 1863
Knighted for services to Anglo-American amity 1944
Died Beverly Hills, California, USA 20 Dec 1948

Aubrey Smith captained Major Warton's pioneer team to victory in South Africa's inaugural first-class match. Subsequently elevated to Test status, it enabled him to become the only player to captain England on his sole appearance in Test cricket. The son of a doctor, he learned his right-arm fast-medium bowling at Charterhouse before gaining blues in each of his four summers at Cambridge. He captained Sussex for two seasons (1887–88) and skippered both his overseas tours. Tall (6ft 2½in), broad-shouldered and imposing, he derived awkward lift and off-spin from a high action and was very accurate. He was dubbed 'Round-the-Corner' Smith because of his unusual bowling run-up which, like that of John Price, started from deep mid-off. When he bowled round the wicket his approach was concealed from the batsman by the umpire until he emerged disconcertingly just a moment before releasing the ball. He was an aggressive front-foot batsman and a safe catcher at slip. After missing the Second Test against South Africa because of a fever, he remained in the Union and formed a stock-broking firm with Monty Bowden. He contracted typhoid fever, pleurisy and pneumonia but survived to read his own obituary in the *Graaf-Reinet Advertiser* before leading Transvaal to victory against Kimberley in the inaugural Currie Cup match. Returning to England he became more involved with amateur dramatics and began his first professional stage engagement in August 1892. Not until he was 63 did he move to Hollywood, launch his third career as a film actor, galvanise Californian cricket and help found the Hollywood Cricket Club. Another 18 years passed before the Grand Old Man of Hollywood was knighted 'for services to Anglo-American amity' just four years before his death.

Ref	Series	V	T	Venue	Result	Batting 1st No	Batting 1st R	Batting 1st HO	Batting 2nd No	Batting 2nd R	Batting 2nd HO	Ct	Bowling 1st Balls	Bowling 1st R	Bowling 1st W	Bowling 2nd Balls	Bowling 2nd R	Bowling 2nd W
31/31*	1888–89	SA	1	Port Elizabeth	W-8w	8	3	c	–	–	–	–	54	19	5	100	42	2

Career	M	I	NO	HS	R	Avge	100	50	Ct	St	Balls	R	W	Avge	BB	5w	10w	Rate
Test	1	1	0	3	3	3.00	–	–	–	–	154	61	7	8.71	5-19	1	–	22.00
F/c	143	247	28	85	2986	13.63	–	10	97	–	17962	7728	346	22.33	7-16	19	1	51.91

SMITH
Cedric Ivan James

Middlesex (1934 to 1939)

Wisden 1935
TOUR WI 1934–35
Born Corsham, Wiltshire 25 Aug 1906
Died Mellor, Lancashire 9 Feb 1979

'Big Jim' Smith was an extremely tall (6ft 4in) and immensely strong right-arm fast bowler who attacked the stumps and had inexhaustible stamina. Devastating as his bowling could be, and he finished sixth in the national averages with 172 wickets at 18.88 in his first season with Middlesex, it is as one of the biggest hitters of all time that he is renowned. He was a prodigious smiter who struck a great number of sixes in first-class cricket; at Lord's his hits frequently peppered the area between the Old Tavern and 'Q' Stand and sometimes carried into St John's Wood Road. His method owed little to technique and a great deal to the bowler trying to hit his stumps. He simply planted his large left boot well down the pitch and swung his bat in a full arc with as much strength as he could muster. If he connected the ball would disappear along a flat trajectory for a vast distance. His 11-minute fifty at Bristol was the fastest genuine first-class fifty; it was made against normal bowling as opposed to the 8-minute farce by Clive Inman against non-bowlers feeding him quick runs for a declaration. He was nearly 28 when he made his debut for Middlesex after eight seasons of combining his duties on the MCC staff with appearances for his native Wiltshire; four years earlier he had made his first-class debut for the Minor Counties. [*Illus. p.* 510]

NOTABLE FEATS

- *240* Promoted after the openers had scored 38 in 90 min, he hit 3 sixes and scored 25 in 10 min.
- Took 100 wickets in a season 4 times, notably 172 in 1934.
- Holds Middlesex record for the fastest 50: 11 min v Gloucestershire at Bristol in 1938; it remains the second-fastest in all first-class cricket. He also shared the third-best time with 50 in 14 min v Kent at Maidstone in 1935. He reached both fifties in only 12 scoring strokes.
- Scored 101* in 81 min for Middlesex v Kent at Canterbury in 1939, contributing 98 to a 10th-wkt stand of 116 with I.A.R. Peebles.
- Holds world record (since equalled) for minor cricket with 9 sixes off successive balls for a Middlesex XI v Harrow and District at Harrow in 1935.
- Hat-trick for Middlesex v Lancashire at Manchester in 1939.

Ref	Series	V	T	Venue	Result	Batting 1st No	R	HO	Batting 2nd No	R	HO	Ct	Bowling 1st Balls	R	W	Bowling 2nd Balls	R	W
238/212	1934–35	WI	1	Bridgetown	W-4w	6	0	c	2	0	c	–	42	8	0	48	16	5
239/213			2	Port-of-Spain	L-217	9	8	b	4	3	ro	–	156	100	4	180	73	2
240/214			3	Georgetown	D	3	25	c	5	4	b	–	132	37	0	24	13	0
241/215			4	Kingston	L-I & 161	9	10	b	8	4	b	–	132	83	0	–	–	–
261/230	1937	NZ	2	Manchester	W-130	10	21	c	10	27	c	1	132	29	2	84	34	2

Career	M	I	NO	HS	R	Avge	100	50	Ct	St	Balls	R	W	Avge	BB	5w	10w	Rate
Test	5	10	0	27	102	10.20	–	–	1	–	930	393	15	26.20	5-16	1	–	62.00
F/c	208	304	31	101*	4007	14.67	1	15	99	–	43047	16271	845	19.25	8-102	47	8	50.94

SMITH
Christopher Lyall

Natal (1977–78 to 1982–83)
Glamorgan (1979)
Hampshire (1980 to date)

Wisden 1984
TOURS
NZ 1983–84; P 1983–84;
SL 1985–86 (Eng B)
Born Durban, South Africa 15 Oct 1958

Although Chris Smith is not as naturally talented as his younger brother Robin, he has overcome this shortfall by sheer determination and hard work. His grandfather, Vernon Shearer, had represented Edinburgh University at three sports before emigrating to South Africa, playing for Natal and becoming mayor of Durban. 'Kippy' Smith's earliest ambitions revolved around playing cricket in England. His chance came after only three seasons in the Natal team when Hampshire needed a replacement opening batsman while Greenidge was on duty with the West Indies. He seized it to score three hundreds in his first six Championship matches. Although Greenidge's return blocked his opportunities during the next two summers, he celebrated becoming qualified for England in May 1983 by scoring 1000 runs before July. His long-awaited Test baptism, reserved for the historic setting of Lord's, produced the traumatic experience of a first-ball dismissal by Richard Hadlee. He overcame that horrific start with a 204-minute vigil in the second innings and played well on England's subsequent combined tour of New Zealand and Pakistan. Although he has appeared only once in England colours since, he has continued to be a consistent and resolute competitor for Hampshire. About average height (5ft 10in) and stockily built, he is a tempting and very slow off-break bowler.

Chris Smith

NOTABLE FEATS
- Exceeded 1000 runs in a season three times.
- Contributed 186* to a 4th-wkt partnership of 241 with R. Abel v Australians at The Oval in 1886.

Ref	Series	V	T	Venue	Result	Batting 1st No	R	HO	Batting 2nd No	R	HO	Ct	Bowling 1st Balls	R	W	Bowling 2nd Balls	R	W
959/593	1983	NZ	3	Lord's	W-127	2	0	lbw	2	43	c	–	–	–	–	–	–	–
960/594			4	Nottingham	W-165	2	31	c	2	4	c	2	–	–	–	72	31	2
975/595	1983–84	NZ	1	Wellington	D	2	27	c	2	30	*	–	–	–	–	18	6	0
977/597			3	Auckland	D	2	91	c	–	–	–	–	–	–	–	–	–	–
978/598	1983–84	P	1	Karachi	L-3w	1	28	c	1	5	lbw	1	–	–	–	–	–	–
979/599			2	Faisalabad	D	1	66	b	–	–	–	–	–	–	–	–	–	–
980/600			3	Lahore[2]	D	1	18	c	2	15	ro	2	6	2	1	6	0	0
1047/624	1986	I	2	Leeds	L-279	3	6	b	3	28	c	–	–	–	–	–	–	–

Career	M	I	NO	HS	R	Avge	100	50	Ct	St	Balls	R	W	Avge	BB	5w	10w	Rate
Test	8	14	1	91	392	30.15	–	2	5	–	102	39	3	13.00	2-31	–	–	34.00
F/c	212	368	46	217	13359	41.48	35	63	138	–	3965	2453	43	57.04	5-69	1	–	92.20

SMITH, Denis

Derbyshire (1927 to 1952)

Wisden 1936
TOURS A 1935–36; NZ 1935–36
Born Somercotes, Derbyshire
24 Jan 1907
Died Derby 12 Sep 1979

Denis Smith was a left-handed batsman, a right-arm medium-pace change bowler and a specialist slip fielder who served Derbyshire loyally for 44 years. He spent most of his batting career as a very reliable opener and in that guise made his two appearances for England against the 1935 South Africans. Tall and elegant, he was an entertaining and attractive strokemaker, although a more ponderous mover than Frank Woolley whose style he tried to emulate; like most left-handers he was exceptionally strong off his legs. By 1934 he had changed from a cautious player into an extremely fast scorer and two years later he contributed 1256 runs to Derbyshire's lone Championship. During the War he took up wicket-keeping in league matches and afterwards appeared for Derbyshire in this role until George Dawkes arrived from Leicestershire. He then spent 21 seasons as the County coach (1951–71). [*Illus. p.* 126]

NOTABLE FEATS

- Exceeded 1000 runs in a season 12 times, including 2175 in 1935.
- Holds Derbyshire career records for most runs (20,516), most hundreds (30) and most instances of 1000 runs in a season (12).
- Scored 2 double centuries for Derbyshire.
- Carried his bat through a completed innings twice.
- Shared record Derbyshire 4th-wkt stand of 328 with P. Vaulkhard v Nottinghamshire at Nottingham in 1946.

						Batting 1st			Batting 2nd			
Ref	Series	V	T	Venue	Result	No	R	HO	No	R	HO	Ct
244/218	1935	SA	3	Leeds	D	2	36	c	2	57	b	1
245/219			4	Manchester	D	1	35	c	1	0	lbw	–

Career	M	I	NO	HS	R	Avge	100	50	Ct	St	Balls	R	W	Avge	BB	5w	10w	Rate
Test	2	4	0	57	128	32.00	–	1	1	–	–	–	–	–	–	–	–	–
F/c	443	753	63	225	21843	31.65	32	116	381	5	1516	734	20	36.70	5-37	1	–	75.80

SMITH, David Mark

Surrey
(1973 to 1983 and 1987 to 1988)
Worcestershire (1984 to 1986)

TOUR WI 1985–86
Born Balham, London 9 Jan 1956

A very tall (6ft 4in) left-handed opening batsman, David Smith is one of the most capable and courageous negotiators of fast bowling. When he gave a timely demonstration of that almost unique ability in 1985 by taming a rampant Malcolm Marshall with innings of 112 and 87 for Worcestershire against Hampshire at Portsmouth, he virtually booked his place on England's imminent tour of the Caribbean. Given just one match as practice before being asked to make his debut on an atrocious Sabina Park pitch as replacement for the injured Gatting, it was no great surprise when he failed. Recalled for the Fourth Test, he gave two impressive displays but his recurring back trouble forced him to miss the final Test on Antigua's excel-

David M. Smith

lent batting surface. That back injury had ended the career as a right-arm medium-pace bowler which had first attracted Surrey's interest. Although he swung the ball sharply, his awkward wrong-footed action probably caused the back trouble which compelled the development of his batting. His back, together with other injuries and an unpredictable and fiery temperament, prompted Surrey to dispense with his services on three occasions. Twice they relented and reinstated him. Sandwiched in between his fragmented career at Kennington was a successful interlude at Worcester but he terminated that relationship in order to advance his painting and decorating business in London. It will be interesting to see how he fares with Sussex.

NOTABLE FEATS

- Exceeded 1000 runs in a season 4 times.

Ref	Series	V	T Venue	Result	Batting 1st No	R	HO	Batting 2nd No	R	HO	Ct
1038/618	1985–86	WI	1 Kingston	L-10w	4	1	c	7	0	c	–
1041/621			4 Port-of-Spain	L-10w	4	47	c	4	32	lbw	–

Career	M	I	NO	HS	R	Avge	100	50	Ct	St	Balls	R	W	Avge	BB	5w	10w	Rate
Test	2	4	0	47	80	20.00	–	–	–	–	–	–	–	–	–	–	–	–
F/c	230	357	71	189*	10165	35.54	19	48	142	–	2736	1520	30	50.66	3-40	–	–	91.20

SMITH, David Robert

Gloucestershire (1956 to 1970)

TOURS
NZ 1960–61; I 1961–62; P 1961–62
Born Fishponds, Bristol 5 Oct 1934

NOTABLE FEATS

- Took 100 wickets in a season 5 times.

David Smith was a little dynamo of a bowler and the nearest thing to perpetual motion when given the ball. Of medium height (5ft 10in) and with a strong back and shoulders, he bowled right-arm medium-pace but was capable of producing the occasional delivery which was distinctly rapid. He swung the ball either way, was extremely accurate and, being a willing work-horse, was usually over-bowled. A reliable fielder and spirited tail-ender, he liked to be involved in the game. In his early years he played outside-right for Bristol City and Millwall.

David R. Smith

Ref	Series	V	T Venue	Result	Batting 1st No	R	HO	Batting 2nd No	R	HO	Ct	Bowling 1st Balls	R	W	Bowling 2nd Balls	R	W
513/375	1961–62	I	1 Bombay[2]	D	–	–	–	–	–	–	–	186	54	1	42	18	1
514/376			2 Kanpur	D	11	0	lbw	–	–	–	–	264	111	0	–	–	–
515/377			3 Delhi	D	–	–	–	–	–	–	1	180	66	1	–	–	–
516/378			4 Calcutta	L-187	11	0	b	11	2	c	1	186	60	2	18	15	0
517/379			5 Madras[2]	L-128	11	34	b	11	2	*	–	54	20	0	42	15	1

Career	M	I	NO	HS	R	Avge	100	50	Ct	St	Balls	R	W	Avge	BB	5w	10w	Rate
Test	5	5	1	34	38	9.50	–	–	2	–	972	359	6	59.83	2-60	–	–	162.00
F/c	386	520	116	74	4970	12.30	–	6	292	–	72496	29654	1250	23.72	7-20	51	6	57.99

SMITH, Donald Victor

Sussex (1946 to 1962)

TOUR WI 1956–57 (Norfolk)
Born Broadwater, Sussex 14 Jun 1923

NOTABLE FEATS

- Exceeded 1000 runs in a season 8 times, including 2088 in 1957.
- Scored 206* for Sussex v Nottinghamshire at Nottingham in 1950.
- Hit 9 sixes in his 166 for Sussex v Gloucestershire at Hove in 1957.
- Two hat-tricks: for MCC v Oxford U at Lord's in 1956 and Sussex v Cambridge U at Fenner's in 1958.

A sound left-handed opening batsman and left-arm medium-pace bowler, Don Smith's career with Sussex spanned 17 seasons but he took several summers to secure his place. Tallish (5ft 11in), genial and quietly spoken, he was capable of sudden bursts of dramatic strokeplay. Originally a left-arm spinner, he found he could swing the ball dramatically from his crescent-shaped approach. He spent more than two decades as coach and groundsman at Lancing College (1963–86) before suddenly leaving home, starting a new life in Australia and then accepting the post of national coach in Sri Lanka.

Don Smith

Ref	Series	V	T	Venue	Result	Batting 1st No	Batting 1st R	Batting 1st HO	Batting 2nd No	Batting 2nd R	Batting 2nd HO	Ct	Bowling 1st Balls	Bowling 1st R	Bowling 1st W	Bowling 2nd Balls	Bowling 2nd R	Bowling 2nd W
440/338	1957	WI	2	Lord's	W-I & 36	2	8	lbw	–	–	–	–	–	–	–	–	–	–
441/339			3	Nottingham	D	2	1	c	2	16	*	–	72	38	0	72	23	0
442/340			4	Leeds	W-I & 5	2	0	b	–	–	–	–	102	24	0	24	12	1

Career	M	I	NO	HS	R	Avge	100	50	Ct	St	Balls	R	W	Avge	BB	5w	10w	Rate
Test	3	4	1	16*	25	8.33	–	–	–	–	270	97	1	97.00	1-12	–	–	270.00
F/c	377	625	66	206*	16960	30.33	19	88	234	–	22233	9670	340	28.44	7-40	6	1	65.39

SMITH, Ernest James

Warwickshire (1904 to 1930)

TOURS
A 1911–12; SA 1913–14; WI 1925–26
Born Birmingham 6 Feb 1886
Died Northfield, Birmingham
31 Aug 1979

NOTABLE FEATS

- Exceeded 1000 runs in a season 6 times.
- Set a world record which survived until 1985 when he made 7 dismissals in an innings for Warwickshire v Derbyshire at Birmingham in 1926; it remains the Warwickshire record.
- Holds Warwickshire career record for most wicket-keeping dismissals (800).

Jim ('Tiger') Smith became a cricketer by accident. When he was working in the Bournville chocolate factory he was persuaded to keep wicket for their team, enjoyed it and, despite losing the tips of two fingers in a works mishap, offered his services to Warwickshire and began an association which endured for 75 years. From 1904 until 1910 he was fortunate to be apprenticed to 'Dick' Lilley, then England's wicket-keeper. His first full season coincided with the County's first Championship, and some impressive performances, particularly when standing up to the sharp swing and break of F.R. Foster's left-arm pace bowling, earned him selection for that winter's tour of Australia. Because he was more familiar with his County captain's signals to the keeper, 'Tiger' replaced Strudwick for the last four Tests. Although tall and robust, he was marvellously agile and very skilled on the leg-side. He became an effective attacking batsman with a solid defence and played many fine innings for Warwickshire. He spent the Great War with the St John Ambulance Brigade and the Second as an air-raid warden. For nine seasons (1931–39) he was a first-class umpire and stood in 9 Tests. He spent the first 25 post-war summers as Warwickshire's coach and thereafter was a constant visitor to Edgbaston where he would hold court in the players' dining room with its end-on view of play. The oldest living Test cricketer, he had played with and against W.G. Grace and was the last survivor of pre-1914 Tests.

						Batting 1st			Batting 2nd			Fielding 1st				Fielding 2nd			
Ref	Series	V	T	Venue	Result	No	R	HO	No	R	HO	Ct	St	Byes	Balls	Ct	St	Byes	Balls
117/109†	1911–12	A	2	Melbourne	W-8w	9	5	b	–	–	–	3	–	5	373	1	–	14	553
118/110†			3	Adelaide	W-7w	9	22	c	–	–	–	1	1	3	360	1	–	26	922
119/111†			4	Melbourne	W-I & 225	10	7	c	–	–	–	–	–	1	391	1	–	9	371
120/112†			5	Sydney	W-70	9	0	b	9	13	b	1	–	14	318	1	–	22	613
122/113†	1912	SA	1	Lord's	W-I & 62	9	2	b	–	–	–	–	–	12	157	1	–	17	492
123/114†		A	1	Lord's	D	9	14	*	–	–	–	2	–	17	764	–	–	–	–
124/115†		SA	2	Leeds	W-174	9	13	ro	9	11	c	1	–	4	339	1	1	5	350
126/116†		A	2	Manchester	D	8	4	c	–	–	–	–	–	2	78	–	–	–	–
128/117†		SA	3	Oval	W-10w	9	9	b	–	–	–	–	–	8	255	1	1	18	196
129/118†		A	3	Oval	W-244	9	4	b	9	0	b	1	–	12	320	–	–	1	136
131/120	1913–14	SA	2	Johannesburg[1]	W-I & 12	9	9	lbw	–	–	–	1	–	–	–	–	–	–	–

Career	M	I	NO	HS	R	Avge	100	50	Ct	St	Balls	R	W	Avge	BB	5w	10w	Rate
Test	11	14	1	22	113	8.69	–	–	17	3	–	–	–	–	–	–	–	–
F/c	496	814	55	177	16997	22.39	20	63	722	156	167	102	2	51.00	1-0	–	–	83.50

TEST NOTES

- *128* R.H. Spooner deputised as wicket-keeper for most of the first session.
- *131* H. Strudwick kept wicket.

'Tiger' Smith

The Gloucestershire side of 1923: standing *B.S. Bloodworth, W.R. Hammond, T.W.J. Goddard, J. Bessant, C.W.L. Parker, W.L. Neale;* seated *H. Smith, E.G. Dennett, P.F.C. Williams (captain), B.H. Lyon, A.E. Dipper.*

SMITH, Harry

Gloucestershire (1912 to 1935)

Born Gloucester 21 May 1891
Died Downend, Bristol 12 Nov 1937

Harry Smith began his cricketing life as a batsman and slow bowler. Playing for Bristol Colts against Gloucestershire in 1911, he was asked to keep wicket in an emergency. His performance was so impressive that he was offered a trial and taken on as deputy to Jack Board. After the Great War he was picked solely as a batsman for three summers before becoming the regular keeper for 11 seasons. Illness effectively ended his career in 1932 but he recovered to play in his final 15 Championship matches in 1935. During four consecutive innings in 1927 he conceded just one bye while 1374 runs were scored. He appeared for Bolton Wanderers in his youth and became a licensee at Downend after he retired.

NOTABLE FEATS

- Exceeded 1000 runs in a season 5 times.
- Set Gloucestershire record (since equalled) with 6 dismissals in an innings v Sussex at Bristol in 1923.

Ref	Series	V	T Venue	Result	Batting 1st No	R	HO	Batting 2nd No	R	HO	Fielding 1st Ct	St	Byes	Balls	Fielding 2nd Ct	St	Byes	Balls
173/159†	1928	WI	1 Lord's	W-I & 58	9	7	b	–	–	–	1	–	13	501	–	–	10	439

Career	M	I	NO	HS	R	Avge	100	50	Ct	St	Balls	R	W	Avge	BB	5w	10w	Rate
Test	1	1	0	7	7	7.00	–	–	1	–	–	–	–	–	–	–	–	–
F/c	402	656	56	149	13413	22.35	10	75	457	266	18	7	0	–	–	–	–	–

SMITH
Michael John Knight
OBE

Leicestershire (1951 to 1955)
Oxford University (1954 to 1956)
Warwickshire (1956 to 1975)

Wisden 1960
TOURS
A 1965–66; SA 1960–61 (Cav), 1964–65; WI 1959–60; NZ 1965–66; I 1961–62, 1963–64; P 1961–62; SL 1961–62
Born Westcotes, Leicester 30 Jun 1933

Mike Smith

One of the most prolific scorers in post-war cricket, Mike ('MJK') Smith was a tall (6ft 1in), athletic middle-order batsman, a superb short-leg fielder and an enormously popular touring captain. His class was soon apparent and some exceptional performances at Stamford earned him his Leicestershire debut during the school holidays. After national service he launched into a brilliant career at Oxford. A blue all three years and captain in his last, he set new records for aggregate and hundreds in Varsity matches before transferring to Warwickshire and taking on the captaincy for 11 summers (1957–67). For six consecutive seasons he exceeded 2000 runs, including the third-fastest 3000. During this same period he played his first 22 Tests but without approaching his consistency of performance at county level. His first 35 innings for England included nine scores over 50 and as many ducks. Thereafter he was stuck with the label of being a poor starter, especially against pace, an impression accentuated by the fact that he wore spectacles. Closer examination might have introduced the nerve factor because that same group of high scores included 98, 96, 99 and 99. Once set he was extremely hard to contain; few players have become so adept at working the ball on the leg-side, at finding the gaps or chipping over the infield. His quiet but firm manner and dry humour earned him the tag 'unflappable' but concealed a strong-willed determination. No one who toured with him has anything but praise for his astute, fair and kindly leadership. He won five and lost only three of his 25 matches as captain. His well-concealed bowling was usually described as right-arm slow-medium. He was England's last cricketing double international; as a rugby fly-half he gained two blues and represented England against Wales in 1956.

NOTABLE FEATS

- 1000 runs in 20th Test (*517*) (32 inns); 2000 runs in 44th Test (*602*) (67 inns).
- *478* Shared record E v I 3rd-wkt stand of 169 with R. Subba Row.
- *491* Shared record England 7th-wkt stand (all Tests) of 197 with J.M. Parks.
- Exceeded 1000 runs in a season 19 times (plus once on tour), including 2000 in 6 consecutive years (1957–62), notably 3245 in 1959 when he completed 3000 on the third-earliest date of 21 Aug (one day after shared record). Leading batsman of 1959 and 1963.
- Scored 1540 runs in his first full season (1954) after appearing in 3 matches in 1951.
- Scored record July aggregate of 1209 in 1959.
- Holds Warwickshire records for most runs (2417 in 1959); and for most catches by a fielder in a career (422), in a season (52 in 1961) and in an innings (6 v Leicestershire at Hinckley in 1962).
- Only batsman to score hundreds in 3 Varsity matches: 201* in 1954, 105 in 1955 and 117 in 1956. Holds record aggregate for 3 Varsity matches: 477 runs.
- Scored 2 other double centuries: for Warwickshire v Worcestershire at Birmingham in 1959 and 204 for Cavaliers v Natal at Durban in 1960–61.

Ref	Series	V	T	Venue	Result	Batting 1st No	R	HO	Batting 2nd No	R	HO	Ct	Bowling 1st Balls	R	W	Bowling 2nd Balls	R	W
454/342	1958	NZ	1	Birmingham	W-205	2	0	lbw	2	7	c	1	–	–	–	–	–	–
455/343			2	Lord's	W-I & 148	2	47	c	–	–	–	–	–	–	–	–	–	–
456/344			3	Leeds	W-I & 71	1	3	c	–	–	–	2	–	–	–	–	–	–
477/357	1959	I	4	Manchester	W-171	4	100	c	4	9	c	1	–	–	–	–	–	–
478/358			5	Oval	W-I & 27	4	98	b	–	–	–	–	–	–	–	–	–	–
487/359	1959–60	WI	1	Bridgetown	D	5	39	c	–	–	–	1	–	–	–	–	–	–
488/360			2	Port-of-Spain	W-256	6	108	c	6	12	lbw	1	–	–	–	–	–	–
489/361			3	Kingston	D	6	0	b	6	10	lbw	1	–	–	–	–	–	–
490/362			4	Georgetown	D	6	0	b	5	23	c	–	–	–	–	–	–	–
491/363			5	Port-of-Spain	D	6	20	b	7	96	c	–	–	–	–	6	15	0
492/364	1960	SA	1	Birmingham	W-100	5	54	c	4	28	c	1	–	–	–	–	–	–
493/365			2	Lord's	W-I & 73	5	99	c	–	–	–	1	–	–	–	–	–	–
494/366			3	Nottingham	W-8w	5	0	lbw	–	–	–	–	–	–	–	–	–	–
496/368			5	Oval	D	5	0	b	6	11	c	2	–	–	–	–	–	–
507/369	1961	A	1	Birmingham	D	6	0	c	6	1	*	–	–	–	–	–	–	–
512/374	1961–62	P	1	Lahore[2]	W-5w	4	99	ro	4	34	c	2	–	–	–	–	–	–
513/375	1961–62	I	1	Bombay[2]	D	4	36	c	4	0	b	–	–	–	–	48	10	1
514/376			2	Kanpur	D	4	0	c	4	0	lbw	–	–	–	–	–	–	–
515/377			3	Delhi	D	4	2	b	–	–	–	–	–	–	–	–	–	–
517/379			5	Madras[2]	L-128	5	73	c	5	15	c	1	–	–	–	–	–	–
518/380	1961–62	P	2	Dacca	D	4	10	lbw	–	–	–	1	–	–	–	–	–	–
519/381			3	Karachi	D	4	56	c	–	–	–	1	–	–	–	–	–	–
553/400*	1963–64	I	1	Madras[2]	D	2	3	c	2	57	c	1	–	–	–	–	–	–
554/401*			2	Bombay[2]	D	2	46	c	4	31	*	1	–	–	–	–	–	–
555/402*			3	Calcutta	D	3	19	c	3	75	*	1	–	–	–	–	–	–
556/403*			4	Delhi	D	3	37	c	–	–	–	1	–	–	–	78	52	0
557/404*			5	Kanpur	D	3	38	c	–	–	–	–	–	–	–	–	–	–
571/410*	1964–65	SA	1	Durban[2]	W-I & 104	6	35	c	–	–	–	4	–	–	–	–	–	–
572/411*			2	Johannesburg[3]	D	6	25	c	–	–	–	4	–	–	–	–	–	–
573/412*			3	Cape Town	D	6	121	c	–	–	–	2	–	–	–	66	43	0
574/413*			4	Johannesburg[3]	D	6	42	c	6	8	b	–	–	–	–	–	–	–
575/414*			5	Port Elizabeth	D	7	26	c	–	–	–	–	–	–	–	–	–	–
591/415*	1965	NZ	1	Birmingham	W-9w	6	0	lbw	–	–	–	1	–	–	–	–	–	–
592/416*			2	Lord's	W-7w	6	44	c	–	–	–	1	–	–	–	–	–	–
593/417*			3	Leeds	W-I & 187	6	2	*	–	–	–	1	–	–	–	–	–	–
594/418*	1965	SA	1	Lord's	D	6	26	c	6	13	c	–	–	–	–	–	–	–
595/419*			2	Nottingham	L-94	7	32	b	8	24	lbw	–	–	–	–	–	–	–
596/420*			3	Oval	D	6	7	lbw	6	10	*	2	–	–	–	–	–	–
597/421*	1965–66	A	1	Brisbane[2]	D	5	16	b	5	10	*	–	–	–	–	–	–	–
598/422*			2	Melbourne	D	6	41	c	–	–	–	1	–	–	–	16	8	0
599/423*			3	Sydney	W-I & 93	6	6	c	–	–	–	3	–	–	–	–	–	–
600/424*			4	Adelaide	L-I & 9	6	29	b	6	5	c	–	–	–	–	–	–	–
601/425*			5	Melbourne	D	6	0	c	–	–	–	–	–	–	–	–	–	–
602/426*	1965–66	NZ	1	Christchurch	D	5	54	c	5	87	c	3	–	–	–	–	–	–
603/427*			2	Dunedin	D	5	20	c	–	–	–	2	–	–	–	–	–	–
604/428*			3	Auckland	D	4	18	b	4	30	lbw	3	–	–	–	–	–	–
605/429*	1966	WI	1	Manchester	L-I & 40	5	5	c	5	6	b	2	–	–	–	–	–	–
698/473	1972	A	1	Manchester	W-89	4	10	lbw	4	34	c	1	–	–	–	–	–	–
699/474			2	Lord's	L-8w	4	34	b	4	30	c	2	–	–	–	–	–	–
700/475			3	Nottingham	D	4	17	b	4	15	lbw	1	–	–	–	–	–	–

Career	M	I	NO	HS	R	Avge	100	50	Ct	St	Balls	R	W	Avge	BB	5w	10w	Rate
Test	50	78	6	121	2278	31.63	3	11	53	–	214	128	1	128.00	1-10	–	–	214.00
F/c	637	1091	139	204	39832	41.84	69	241	593	–	487	305	5	61.00	1-0	–	–	97.40

M. J. K. SMITH – TEST BATTING SUMMARY

Series	V	M	I	NO	HS	R	Avge	100	50
1958	NZ	3	4	–	47	57	14.25	–	–
1959	I	2	3	–	100	207	69.00	1	1
1959–60	WI	5	9	–	108	308	34.22	1	1
1960	SA	4	6	–	99	192	32.00	–	2
1961	A	1	2	1	1*	1	1.00	–	–
1961–62	P	3	4	–	99	199	49.75	–	2
1961–62	I	4	7	–	73	126	18.00	–	1
1963–64	I	5	8	2	75*	306	51.00	–	2
1964–65	SA	5	6	–	121	257	42.83	1	–
1965	NZ	3	3	1	44	46	23.00	–	–
1965	SA	3	6	1	32	112	22.40	–	–
1965–66	A	5	7	1	41	107	17.83	–	–
1965–66	NZ	3	5	–	87	209	41.80	–	2
1966	WI	1	2	–	6	11	5.50	–	–
1972	A	3	6	–	34	140	23.33	–	–

Series	V	M	I	NO	HS	R	Avge	100	50
	A	9	15	2	41	248	19.07	–	–
	SA	12	18	1	121	561	33.00	1	2
	WI	6	11	–	108	319	29.00	1	1
	NZ	9	12	1	87	312	28.36	–	2
	I	11	18	2	100	639	39.93	1	4
	P	3	4	–	99	199	49.75	–	2
Home		20	32	3	100	766	26.41	1	3
Overseas		30	46	3	121	1512	35.16	2	8
Totals		50	78	6	121	2278	31.63	3	11

SMITH, Robin Arnold

Natal (1980–81 to 1984–85)
Hampshire (1982 to date)

Born Durban, South Africa
13 Sep 1963

Robin Smith

Robin Smith's resolute batting in the last two Tests against the 1988 West Indians provided a much-needed source of cheer for English cricket followers in a season of national despair. There had been many flattering reports of Chris Smith's highly talented younger brother even before he began his career with Hampshire in 1982. But his progress had been erratic to such a degree that serious doubts had formed concerning his temperament, particularly when subjected to the severe pressure of a Test match. One innings shortly before his selection removed all doubts. Played in the quarter-final of the Benson and Hedges Cup on a hazardous pitch at Worcester, his 87 out of 170 for 7 was a masterly display of courage, tenacity, technical maturity and improvisation against an attack including Dilley, Radford and Newport. A little over medium height (5ft 11in) and strongly built, he is a powerful and clean striker of the ball. He plays right forward in defence, times his leg-side strokes well and square-cuts anything short with the force of a lumberjack. A competent fielder and an entertaining but very occasional right-arm leg-spinner, he was unlucky to miss his first overseas tour when the Indian expedition was sabotaged.

NOTABLE FEATS

- Exceeded 1000 runs in a season 3 times.
- Scored 209* for Hampshire v Essex at Southend in 1987.

						Batting 1st			Batting 2nd			
Ref	Series	V	T	Venue	Result	No	R	HO	No	R	HO	Ct
1101/649	1988	WI	4	Leeds	L-10w	6	38	c	5	11	lbw	1
1102/650			5	Oval	L-8w	4	57	c	4	0	lbw	–
1103/651	1988	SL		Lord's	W-7w	6	31	b	5	8	*	1

Career	M	I	NO	HS	R	Avge	100	50	Ct	St	Balls	R	W	Avge	BB	5w	10w	Rate
Test	3	6	1	57	145	29.00	–	–	2	–	–	–	–	–	–	–	–	–
F/c	135	228	42	209*	7333	39.42	15	35	87	–	602	443	9	49.22	2-11	–	–	66.88

SMITH
Thomas Peter Bromly

Essex (1929 to 1951)

Wisden 1947
TOURS
A 1946–47; NZ 1938–39 (Cahn), 1946–47; I 1937–38 (Tennyson)
Born Ipswich, Suffolk 30 Oct 1908
Died Hyeres, France 4 Aug 1967

Peter Smith was an extremely skilful and accurate right-arm leg-break and googly bowler and an aggressive lower-order batsman. Just above average height (5ft 10½in) and very trim, he began his Essex career as a medium-pacer. The Second World War arrived and robbed him of a tour of India when he was on the threshold of his prime bowling years. He played some cricket against top class opposition at Alexandria during his Army service in the Middle East and quickly recovered his form afterwards. His first England cap came 13 years after he had reported to the same ground as the very disappointed victim of a hoax telegram. He will always be remembered for his record-breaking display of controlled hitting as a No. 11 at Chesterfield. Commencing his innings when Essex were still 24 behind the Derbyshire first innings total of 223, his 163 included 3 sixes and 22 fours and led to his side's 5-wicket victory. A cousin of Raymond Smith, an Essex contemporary, he died from a brain haemorrhage following a fall whilst on holiday in France.

NOTABLE FEATS

- Took 100 wickets in a season 6 times, notably 172 in 1947 when he also scored 1065 runs (his only 1000) to complete the 'double'.
- Holds Essex records for most wickets in season (172 in 1947) and most in a career (1610).
- Scored 163 (world record score by a No. 11), sharing in record Essex 10th-wkt stand of 218 with F.H. Vigar v Derbyshire at Chesterfield in 1947.
- Took 16 for 215 (9 for 77 and 7 for 138) for Essex v Middlesex at Colchester in 1947.
- Took 9 wickets in an innings on 2 other occasions for Essex and once on tour: his analysis of 9 for 121 for MCC v NSW at Sydney in 1946–47 remains the record for a touring English bowler in Australia.
- Completed another match 'double' (102 runs and 10 wickets) for Essex v Middlesex at Chelmsford in 1938.
- Took 3 wickets in 4 balls on 3 occasions but failed to take a hat-trick.

MCC to Australia, 1946–47: back row *J. Langridge, D.C.S. Compton, T.G. Evans, L. Hutton;* middle row *D.V.P. Wright, C. Washbrook, J.T. Ikin, A.V. Bedser, R. Pollard, T.P.B. Smith, Major R. Howard (manager);* front row *W. Voce, P.A. Gibb, N.W.D. Yardley, W.R. Hammond (captain), W.J. Edrich, L.B. Fishlock, J. Hardstaff jr.*

Ref	Series	V	T	Venue	Result	Batting 1st No	R	HO	Batting 2nd No	R	HO	Ct	Bowling 1st Balls	R	W	Bowling 2nd Balls	R	W
278/246	1946	I	3	Oval	D	–	–	–	–	–	–	–	126	58	1	–	–	–
280/248	1946–47	A	2	Sydney	L-I & 33	8	4	lbw	8	2	c	–	296	172	2	–	–	–
283/251			5	Sydney	L-5w	9	2	b	8	24	c	1	64	38	0	16	8	0
284/252	1946–47	NZ		Christchurch	D	8	1	c	–	–	–	–	36	43	0	–	–	–

Career	M	I	NO	HS	R	Avge	100	50	Ct	St	Balls	R	W	Avge	BB	5w	10w	Rate
Test	4	5	0	24	33	6.60	–	–	1	–	538	319	3	106.33	2-172	–	–	179.33
F/c	465	690	123	163	10142	17.88	8	32	346	–	94925	45059	1697	26.55	9-77	120	28	55.93

SMITHSON Gerald Arthur

Yorkshire (1946 to 1950)
Leicestershire (1951 to 1956)

TOUR WI 1947–48
Born Spofforth, Yorkshire 1 Nov 1926
Died Abingdon, Berkshire 6 Sep 1970

Gerald Smithson's selection for MCC's 1947–48 tour of the West indies led to a question being asked in the House of Commons. At the time he was a 'Bevin Boy' conscripted to the coal mines and only after his case had been discussed in Parliament was he granted permission to join the tour. A left-handed middle-order batsman of just over average height (5ft 10½in), he was a forcing strokemaker and a fine outfielder. A severe arm injury sustained on that tour caused him to miss Yorkshire's entire 1948 season and he failed to recover his form during the next two summers. He had better fortune with Leicestershire. He later combined appearances for Hertfordshire (1957–62) with coaching engagements, first at Caterham School and finally at Abingdon School.

MCC to West Indies, 1947–48: standing *G.A. Smithson, W. Place, H.J. Butler, M.F. Tremlett, J.C. Laker, J.H. Wardle, D. Brookes, J.D.B. Robertson;* seated *T.G. Evans, J. Hardstaff jr, S.C. Griffith, G.O.B. Allen (captain), K. Cranston, R. Howorth, J.T. Ikin.*

NOTABLE FEATS
- Scored 1351 runs in 1952.

Ref	Series	V	T	Venue	Result	Batting 1st No	Batting 1st R	Batting 1st HO	Batting 2nd No	Batting 2nd R	Batting 2nd HO	Ct
295/258	1947–48	WI	1	Bridgetown	D	6	0	c	–	–	–	–
296/259			2	Port of Spain	D	8	35	c	9	35	b	–

Career	M	I	NO	HS	R	Avge	100	50	Ct	St	Balls	R	W	Avge	BB	5w	10w	Rate
Test	2	3	0	35	70	23.33	–	–	–	–	–	–	–	–	–	–	–	–
F/c	200	333	27	169	6940	22.67	8	31	131	–	94	117	1	117.00	1-26	–	–	94.00

SNOW John Augustine

Sussex (1961 to 1977)

Wisden 1973
TOURS
A 1970–71; SA 1972–73 (Robins), 1973–74 (Robins); WI 1967–68, 1969–70 (Cav); P 1968–69; SL 1968–69; Z 1975–76 (Int XI)
Born Peopleton, Worcestershire 13 Oct 1941

Like most world-class fast bowlers, John Snow was a temperamental character whose fluctuating moods produced almost as many problems for cricket's administrators as they did for the opposing batsman. His distaste for both was easily apparent. Tall (6ft 1in) and extremely fit, he was a right-arm fast bowler who extracted a high degree of pace from a relatively abbreviated but smoothly accelerated run-up culminating in a superbly lithe body action. Slightly chest-on in delivery, he swung the ball in late and often made it break away on pitching. He never found it hard to exude hostility and his bouncer was a distinctly menacing device. He joined Sussex via Christ's Hospital and Culham Teacher Training College primarily as a batsman and frequently opened the innings in limited-overs games, particularly when helping Warwickshire win the Sunday league in 1980. Often a languid mover in the field, he had a strong flat throw. By 1970 he was the most dangerous fast bowler in world cricket but, needing to be inspired by an important occasion, he seldom stretched himself in county matches. Properly motivated he was the trump card in any attack and it was Ray Illingworth's sympathetic but astute handling of him in the 1970–71 Ashes campaign which proved decisive in a closely contested rubber. He might well have been the first to challenge Trueman's record of 307 Test wickets but for injury, Mr Packer and the brief suspension which followed his unfortunate collision with Gavaskar at Lord's (which Snow insists was purely accidental). His autobiography was aptly entitled *Cricket Rebel* and he is likely to remain the only international fast bowler to have had two volumes of verse published.

						Batting 1st			Batting 2nd				Bowling 1st			Bowling 2nd		
Ref	Series	V	T	Venue	Result	No	R	HO	No	R	HO	Ct	Balls	R	W	Balls	R	W
592/416	1965	NZ	2	Lord's	W-7w	11	2	*	–	–	–	1	66	27	2	144	53	2
595/419	1965	SA	2	Nottingham	L-94	9	3	ro	4	0	b	–	132	63	1	198	83	3
607/431	1966	WI	3	Nottingham	L-139	10	0	b	10	3	b	–	150	82	4	228	117	0
608/432			4	Leeds	L-I & 55	11	0	c	11	0	*	–	252	146	3	–	–	–
609/433			5	Oval	W-I & 34	11	59	*	–	–	–	–	125	66	2	78	40	3
618/434	1967	I	1	Leeds	W-6w	–	–	–	–	–	–	1	102	34	2	246	108	2
619/435			2	Lord's	W-I & 124	11	8	*	–	–	–	1	124	49	3	48	12	1
620/436			3	Birmingham	W-132	10	10	c	10	9	c	–	72	28	2	84	33	0
621/437	1967	P	1	Lord's	D	10	0	b	10	7	c	–	271	120	3	24	6	0
629/441	1967–68	WI	2	Kingston	D	10	10	b	–	–	–	–	126	49	7	162	91	1
630/442			3	Bridgetown	D	9	37	c	–	–	–	1	210	86	5	60	39	3
631/443			4	Port-of-Spain	W-7w	8	0	b	–	–	–	–	120	68	0	54	29	1
632/444			5	Georgetown	D	8	0	b	8	1	lbw	–	166	82	4	92	60	6
637/445	1968	A	1	Manchester	L-159	9	18	*	9	2	c	1	204	97	4	102	51	1
638/446			2	Lord's	D	9	0	*	–	–	–	–	54	14	1	72	30	1
639/447			3	Birmingham	D	10	19	c	–	–	–	–	102	46	1	54	32	1
640/448			4	Leeds	D	9	0	b	–	–	–	1	210	98	3	144	51	2
641/449			5	Oval	W-226	9	4	ro	9	13	c	1	210	67	3	66	22	0
648/451	1968–69	P	2	Dacca	D	9	9	c	–	–	–	1	150	70	4	72	15	0
649/452			3	Karachi	D	8	9	b	–	–	–	–	–	–	–	–	–	–
653/453	1969	WI	1	Manchester	W-10w	11	0	b	–	–	–	–	90	54	4	135	76	2
654/454			2	Lord's	D	11	9	*	–	–	–	–	234	114	5	132	69	1
655/455			3	Leeds	W-30	11	1	*	11	15	*	1	120	50	2	126	43	1
657/457	1969	NZ	2	Nottingham	D	10	4	*	–	–	–	–	144	61	0	36	19	0
658/458			3	Oval	W-8w	10	21	*	–	–	–	–	60	22	1	126	52	2
674/459	1970–71	A	1	Brisbane[2]	D	9	34	c	–	–	–	1	259	114	6	160	48	2
675/460			2	Perth	D	9	4	*	–	–	–	–	269	143	4	72	17	2
676/461			4	Sydney	W-299	8	37	c	–	–	–	–	112	23	1	141	40	7
677/462			5	Melbourne	D	8	1	b	–	–	–	1	232	94	2	96	21	2
678/463			6	Adelaide	D	8	38	b	–	–	–	–	168	73	2	136	60	1
679/464			7	Sydney	W-62	8	7	b	8	20	c	–	144	68	1	16	7	1
690/470	1971	I	1	Lord's	D	9	73	c	9	9	c	1	186	64	2	48	23	1
692/472			3	Oval	L-4w	9	3	c	9	0	c	–	144	68	2	66	14	1
698/473	1972	A	1	Manchester	W-89	9	3	b	9	0	lbw	1	120	41	4	162	87	4
699/474			2	Lord's	L-8w	9	37	b	9	0	c	–	192	57	5	48	15	0
700/475			3	Nottingham	D	10	6	c	–	–	–	–	186	92	5	144	94	3
701/476			4	Leeds	W-9w	9	48	st	–	–	–	–	78	11	2	60	26	0
702/477			5	Oval	L-5w	9	3	c	9	14	c	1	209	111	1	36	21	0
722/486	1973	NZ	1	Nottingham	W-38	9	8	b	9	7	b	–	78	21	3	258	104	2
723/487			2	Lord's	D	9	2	b	9	0	c	–	228	109	3	–	–	–
724/488			3	Leeds	W-I & 1	9	6	c	–	–	–	–	130	52	2	117	34	3
725/489	1973	WI	1	Oval	L-158	9	0	b	11	1	b	–	186	71	0	108	62	3
760/511	1975	A	1	Birmingham	L-I & 85	10	0	lbw	9	34	c	–	198	86	3	–	–	–
761/512			2	Lord's	D	9	11	c	–	–	–	–	126	66	4	114	82	0
762/513			3	Leeds	D	10	0	c	10	9	c	–	113	22	3	90	21	0
763/514			4	Oval	D	10	30	c	10	0	c	–	162	74	1	12	4	0
777/515	1976	WI	1	Nottingham	D	9	20	*	–	–	–	–	186	123	1	66	53	4
778/516			2	Lord's	D	9	0	b	10	6	*	2	114	68	4	42	22	0
780/518			4	Leeds	L-55	8	20	c	9	8	c	–	112	77	4	120	80	2

Career	M	I	NO	HS	R	Avge	100	50	Ct	St	Balls	R	W	Avge	BB	5w	10w	Rate
Test	49	71	14	73	772	13.54	–	2	16	–	12021	5387	202	26.66	7-40	8	1	59.50
F/c	346	451	110	73*	4832	14.17	–	11	125	–	60958	26675	1174	22.72	8-87	56	9	51.92

John Snow

J. A. SNOW – TEST BOWLING SUMMARY

Series	V	M	Balls	R	W	Avge	BB	5w	10w	Rate
1965	NZ	1	210	80	4	20.00	2-27	–	–	52.50
1965	SA	1	330	146	4	36.50	3-83	–	–	82.50
1966	WI	3	833	451	12	37.58	4-82	–	–	69.41
1967	I	3	676	264	10	26.40	3-49	–	–	67.60
1967	P	1	295	126	3	42.00	3-120	–	–	98.33
1967–68	WI	4	990	504	27	18.66	7-49	3	1	36.66
1968	A	5	1218	508	17	29.88	4-97	–	–	71.64
1968–69	P	2	222	85	4	21.25	4-70	–	–	55.50
1969	WI	3	837	406	15	27.06	5-114	1	–	55.80
1969	NZ	2	366	154	3	51.33	2-52	–	–	122.00
1970–71	A	6	805	708	31	22.83	7-40	2	–	58.22
1971	I	2	444	169	6	28.16	2-64	–	–	74.00
1972	A	5	1235	555	24	23.12	5-57	2	–	51.45
1973	NZ	3	811	320	13	24.61	3-21	–	–	62.38
1973	WI	1	294	133	3	44.33	3-62	–	–	98.00
1975	A	4	815	355	11	32.27	4-66	–	–	74.09
1976	WI	3	640	423	15	28.20	4-53	–	–	42.66
	A	20	5073	2126	83	25.61	7-40	4	–	61.12
	SA	1	330	146	4	36.50	3-83	–	–	82.50
	WI	14	3594	1917	72	26.62	7-49	4	1	49.91
	NZ	6	1387	554	20	27.70	3-21	–	–	69.35
	I	5	1120	433	16	27.06	3-49	–	–	70.00
	P	3	517	211	7	30.14	4-70	–	–	73.85
Home		37	9004	4090	140	29.21	5-57	2	–	64.31
Overseas		12	3017	1297	62	20.91	7-40	6	1	48.66
Totals		49	12021	5387	202	26.66	7-40	8	1	59.50

NOTABLE FEATS

- 50 wickets in 12th Test (*631*); 100 wickets in 26th Test (*674*); 150 wickets in 36th Test (*700*); 200 wickets in 49th Test (*780*).
- *609* Shared record E v WI 10th-wkt stand of 128 in 140 min with K. Higgs, both batsmen scoring their maiden first-class fifties. It remains the highest 10th-wkt stand for England at home.
- *629* Dismissed G.St A. Sobers first ball for the second time in successive encounters in Tests.
- *632* His 27 wickets remains the England record for a series in the Caribbean.
- Took 100 wickets in a season twice.

SOUTHERTON James

Surrey (1854 to 1879)
Sussex (1858 to 1872)
Hampshire (1861 to 1867)

TOUR A 1876–77
Born Petworth, Sussex 16 Nov 1827
Died Mitcham, Surrey 16 Jun 1880

At 49 years 119 days James Southerton remains the oldest man ever to begin a Test career. He was also the first Test cricketer to die (16 June 1880). Short but strongly built, he was a right-handed round-arm slow bowler who spun his off-breaks sharply. Gradually his easy action became higher, unlike that of most bowlers, as he converted towards an overarm delivery. He began his career as a batsman but steadily perfected the then little known art of slow round-arm bowling; within a few seasons he had thousands of imitators. A splendidly itinerant cricketer, he played for three counties in the same season (1867) before qualification rules were introduced. As a Sussex man then with Surrey, he was the only member of the English team in the inaugural Test who was not currently a professional with the county of his birth. He became landlord of 'The Cricketers' beside the famous ground at Mitcham Green. [*Illus. p.* 278]

NOTABLE FEATS

- Took 100 wickets in a season 10 times, including 210 in 1870.
- Took 9 for 30 for South v North at Lord's in 1875. His match figures of 16 for 51 were achieved in a single day.
- Took 4 wickets in 5 balls for Surrey v Lancashire at The Oval in 1869.
- Hat-trick for South v North at Sheffield in 1869.
- Bowled in an unchanged partnership throughout both completed innings of a match on 7 occasions, including 6 with James Lillywhite.

Ref	Series	V	T	Venue	Result	Batting 1st			Batting 2nd			Ct	Bowling 1st			Bowling 2nd		
						No	R	HO	No	R	HO		Balls	R	W	Balls	R	W
1/1	1876–77	A	1	Melbourne	L-45	11	6	c	11	1	*	2	148	61	3	–	–	–
2/2			2	Melbourne	W-4w	11	0	c	–	–	–	–	–	–	–	115	46	4

Career	M	I	NO	HS	R	Avge	100	50	Ct	St	Balls	R	W	Avge	BB	5w	10w	Rate
Test	2	3	1	6	7	3.50	–	–	2	–	263	107	7	15.28	4-46	–	–	37.57
F/c	286	480	130	82	3159	9.02	–	3	215	3	68648	24290	1681	14.44	9-30	192	59	40.83

SPOONER
Reginald Herbert

Lancashire (1899 to 1921)

Wisden 1905
Born Litherland, Lancashire 21 Oct 1880
Died Lincoln 2 Oct 1961

Reggie Spooner

A tall, slim opening batsman, Reggie Spooner embellished his regal strokeplay with an elegance of movement which few could approach even in cricket's Edwardian 'Golden Age'. His supreme skill was in playing the off-drive, especially off the faster bowlers. Strong wrists enabled him to strike the ball with surprising power for one of his limited physique, particularly off the back foot, and his straight driving had many a bowler leaping out of harm's way. An outstanding cricketer and rugby footballer during his schooldays at Marlborough, he was selected for his native county immediately he was available and marked his first appearance with innings of 44 and 83 against a Middlesex attack which included Albert Trott in his prime. A three-year absence involving military service in the Boer War failed to diminish his powers and he was soon making a record score at Trent Bridge. He was a fine fielder and made rare appearances in the guise of a right-arm slow bowler. His business commitments curtailed his appearances in most seasons and injury prevented him from accepting the captaincy of MCC's 1920–21 tour of Australia. His prowess as a rugby centre three-quarter for Liverpool earned him an England cap against Wales at Swansea in 1902–03.

NOTABLE FEATS

- Exceeded 1000 runs in a season 6 times, including 2312 in 1911.
- Scored 5 double centuries for Lancashire, notably 247 at Nottingham in 1903, then the record score v Nottinghamshire.
- Shared record Lancashire 1st-wkt stand of 368 with A.C. MacLaren v Gloucestershire at Liverpool in 1903.
- Scored 100 before lunch on 5 occasions.

TEST NOTES

- *87* Deputised for A.F.A. Lilley as wicket-keeper in 2nd inns and caught V.T. Trumper.
- *128* Deputised for E.J. Smith as wicket-keeper for most of the first session.

Ref	Series	V	T	Venue	Result	Batting 1st			Batting 2nd			Ct
						No	R	HO	No	R	HO	
86/83	1905	A	4	Manchester	W-I & 80	6	52	c	–	–	–	1
87/84			5	Oval	D	6	0	b	7	79	c	1
104/101	1909	A	4	Manchester	D	2	25	c	2	58	b	–
105/102			5	Oval	D	1	13	b	1	3	c	–
122/113	1912	SA	1	Lord's	W-I & 62	3	119	c	–	–	–	–
123/114		A	1	Lord's	D	3	1	c	–	–	–	–
124/115		SA	2	Leeds	W-174	3	21	c	3	82	b	1
126/116		A	2	Manchester	D	3	1	b	–	–	–	–
128/117		SA	3	Oval	W-10w	3	26	c	–	–	–	1
129/118		A	3	Oval	W-244	3	1	c	3	0	c	–

Career	M	I	NO	HS	R	Avge	100	50	Ct	St	Balls	R	W	Avge	BB	5w	10w	Rate
Test	10	15	0	119	481	32.06	1	4	4	–	–	–	–	–	–	–	–	–
F/c	237	393	16	247	13681	36.28	31	59	142	–	710	582	6	97.00	1-5	–	–	118.33

SPOONER
Richard Thompson

Warwickshire (1948 to 1959)

TOURS
WI 1953–54; I 1950–51 (Cwlth), 1951–52; P 1951–52; SL 1951–52
Born Stockton-on-Tees, Co. Durham 30 Dec 1919

NOTABLE FEATS

- Exceeded 1000 runs in a season 6 times, notably 1767 in 1951.
- Held 6 catches in an innings for Warwickshire v Nottinghamshire at Birmingham in 1957.

Graduating to Edgbaston after two years of minor counties cricket with Durham, Dick Spooner was an outstanding all-round cricketer. Just 5ft 7in high and compactly built, he was an extremely capable wicket-keeper and a very effective forceful left-handed opening batsman. He was 28 when he made his debut against Nottinghamshire at Trent Bridge in the first first-class match he ever saw. His high-class skills on either side of the stumps earned him three overseas tours but a rather useful contemporary called Evans restricted his home Test matches to one.

Dick Spooner successfully appeals for a catch off Raman Subba Row during Warwickshire's match against Surrey at The Oval in 1954.

						Batting 1st			Batting 2nd			Fielding 1st				Fielding 2nd			
Ref	Series	V	T	Venue	Result	No	R	HO	No	R	HO	Ct	St	Byes	Balls	Ct	St	Byes	Balls
339/292†	1951-52	I	1	Delhi	D	6	11	hw	6	1	b	1	–	12	1050	–	–	–	–
340/293†			2	Bombay[2]	D	4	46	lbw	4	5	*	2	–	0	834	1	–	6	499
341/294†			3	Calcutta	D	2	71	c	2	92	b	1	–	3	895	–	–	1	174
342/295†			4	Kanpur	W-8w	2	21	b	2	0	b	–	1	8	371	1	–	2	401
343/296†			5	Madras[1]	L-I & 8	2	66	c	2	6	lbw	2	1	8	918	–	–	–	–
385/309†	1953-54	WI	4	Port-of-Spain	D	7	19	b	2	16	c	–	–	6	1192	–	–	0	330
412/326†	1955	SA	5	Oval	W-92	8	0	b	8	0	b	2	–	0	390	–	–	0	526

Career	M	I	NO	HS	R	Avge	100	50	Ct	St	Balls	R	W	Avge	BB	5w	10w	Rate
Test	7	14	1	92	354	27.23	–	3	10	2	–	–	–	–	–	–	–	–
F/c	359	580	72	168*	13851	27.26	12	64	589	178	54	46	0	–	–	–	–	–

STANYFORTH
Lt-Col Ronald Thomas

Oxford University (1914)
Yorkshire (1928)

TOURS SA 1927–28; WI 1929–30
Born Chelsea, London 30 May 1892
Died Kirk Hammerton, Yorkshire 20 Feb 1964

Ronald Stanyforth enjoyed one of the more extraordinary cricket careers. He failed to make the 1st XI at Eton and was not awarded a blue at Oxford in the last few weeks before the First World War. As Captain Stanyforth his wicket-keeping blossomed in Army circles. 'Plum' Warner took him on his 1926 MCC tour to South America and, when Derbyshire's Guy Jackson had to decline the captaincy of the following winter's tour of South Africa because of ill health, he was an obvious and available deputy. Consequently he captained England in four Test matches before he had played in a single game of county cricket. When he amended this slight oversight the following summer by appearing in a grand total of three matches for Yorkshire, his Chelsea birthplace must have been a shade embarrassing. A strong personality never short of enthusiasm, he wrote a guide to wicket-keeping and was an MCC trustee in his last years.

MCC in South Africa, 1927–28: standing *W.R. Hammond, H. Eliiott, G.B. Legge, E.W. Dawson, H. Sutcliffe, W.E. Astill, G. Geary, I.A.R. Peebles;* seated *P. Holmes, G.E. Tyldesley, Captain R.T. Stanyforth (captain), G.T.S. Stevens, R.E.S. Wyatt;* in front *A.P. Freeman, S.J. Staples.*

TEST NOTES

• *171* A.P. Freeman deputised as wicket-keeper on the third day.

Ref	Series	V	T	Venue	Result	Batting 1st			Batting 2nd			Fielding 1st				Fielding 2nd			
						No	R	HO	No	R	HO	Ct	St	Byes	Balls	Ct	St	Byes	Balls
168/154*†	1927–28	SA	1	Johannesburg[1]	W-10w	9	1	c	–	–	–	–	–	0	411	1	–	5	416
169/155*†			2	Cape Town	W-87	8	4	b	8	1	b	1	–	2	606	–	–	6	607
170/156*†			3	Durban[2]	D	8	0	c	–	–	–	–	1	1	627	1	1	22	942
171/157*†			4	Johannesburg[1]	L-4w	10	1	b	10	6	*	3	–	8	555	1	–	16	296

Career	M	I	NO	HS	R	Avge	100	50	Ct	St	Balls	R	W	Avge	BB	5w	10w	Rate
Test	4	6	1	6*	13	2.60	–	–	7	2	–	–	–	–	–	–	–	–
F/c	61	79	16	91	1092	17.33	–	6	72	21	–	–	–	–	–	–	–	–

STAPLES
Samuel James

Nottinghamshire (1920 to 1934)

Wisden 1929
TOUR SA 1927–28
Born Newstead Colliery, Nottinghamshire 18 Sep 1892
Died Nottingham 4 Jun 1950

NOTABLE FEATS

• Took 100 wickets in a season 5 times.
• Took 9 for 141 for Nottinghamshire v Kent at Canterbury in 1927.

No one could challenge Sam Staples's Nottinghamshire qualification. He was born at Newstead Colliery and learned his cricket there. His run-up, a disjointed shambling affair, was rather like the progress of a pit wagon. The end product was a medley of off-breaks and cutters pitched on an immaculate length; his right-arm medium-paced cutters would move in either direction and the bona fide off-spin, usually bowled from round the wicket, would turn sharply on any surface that was damp or broken. On a rain-affected Southampton pitch in 1932, he returned the astonishing match figures of 10 for 21. The elder brother of his team-mate, Arthur Staples, he was an aggressive lower-order batsman who scored a century against Surrey and once shared a last-wicket stand of 140 in just over an hour. A fine fielder, he was a consistent wicket-taker on his tour of South Africa but his tour of Australia in 1928–29 ended disastrously: afflicted with muscular rheumatism soon after his arrival he returned home after weeks of illness in Melbourne without bowling a ball. He coached Hampshire in 1939 and, a decade later, stood as a first-class umpire for just one season before ill health compelled his retirement. [*Illus. above*]

Ref	Series	V	T	Venue	Result	Batting 1st			Batting 2nd			Ct	Bowling 1st			Bowling 2nd		
						No	R	HO	No	R	HO		Balls	R	W	Balls	R	W
170/156	1927–28	SA	3	Durban[2]	D	9	11	b	–	–	–	–	216	50	3	282	111	2
171/157			4	Johannesburg[1]	L-4w	9	39	b	9	6	b	–	195	81	3	126	67	3
172/158			5	Durban[2]	L-8w	9	2	b	9	7	b	–	264	96	3	66	30	1

Career	M	I	NO	HS	R	Avge	100	50	Ct	St	Balls	R	W	Avge	BB	5w	10w	Rate
Test	3	5	0	39	65	13.00	–	–	–	–	1149	435	15	29.00	3-50	–	–	76.60
F/c	385	475	95	110	6470	17.02	1	19	339	–	75688	30421	1331	22.85	9-141	72	11	56.86

STATHAM
John Brian CBE

Lancashire (1950 to 1968)

Wisden 1955

TOURS

A 1950–51, 1954–55, 1958–59, 1962–63; SA 1956–57, 1960–61 (Cav); WI 1953–54, 1959–60; NZ 1950–51, 1954–55; I 1951–52, 1967–68 (Pres XI); P 1951–52; SL 1951–52

Born Gorton, Manchester 17 Jun 1930

Brian Statham, like his right-arm fast bowling, was straight and honest. No professional cricketer has been more universally respected and his nickname, 'George', was a fitting tribute to his gentlemanly and scrupulously fair nature. His popularity in no way decreased his effectiveness as an extremely accurate and skilful pace bowler. Tall (6ft) and exceptionally lithe and supple (he was also called 'The Whippet'), he had a beautifully rhythmic and smoothly accelerated run-up, culminating in a high flowing action and follow through. His lissome movements were accentuated by his double-jointedness; when removing his sweater he would reach the back ribbing by coiling his right arm over his right shoulder more than half way down his spine. He was so accurate that on soft turf the marks where he pitched were usually grouped like rifle shots around a bull's-eye. Allied to this phenomenal control was his ability to move the ball either way off the seam. For almost a decade his partnerships with Tyson and Trueman enabled England to recover from the frequent shortfalls produced by erratic batting. His probing accuracy was the ideal foil for his partners' more varied and volatile pace and proved a major factor in their success. He was at his peak in 1954–55 and his speed in that Australian summer was not far short of Tyson's. He was the most undemonstrative of fast bowlers; a studious technician rather than a flamboyant artist. A superb mover in the field with a formidable throw, he seldom had the energy or opportunity to demonstrate his ability as a left-handed batsman. He was a shrewd and popular Lancashire captain for three seasons (1965–67).

NOTABLE FEATS

- 50 wickets in 20th Test (*393*); 100 wickets in 32nd Test (*434*); 150 wickets in 46th Test (*475*); 200 wickets in 57th Test (*508*); 250 wickets in 70th Test (*596*).
- *402* Took 3 for 9 as NZ were dismissed for 26 (record lowest score in Test cricket).
- *409* Dismissed D.J. McGlew twice in 3 balls for a 'pair' and bowled for 3 hrs 45 min to secure victory and his best Test analysis.
- *493* First 10-wkt analysis by an England fast bowler in post-war Tests.
- *538* Set world Test record of 237 wickets.
- *596* Second bowler after F.S. Trueman to take 250 wickets.
- Took 100 wickets in a season 13 times.
- Took 15 for 89 in the match for Lancashire v Warwickshire at Coventry in 1957, including his career-best 8 for 34; and 15 for 108 for Lancashire v Leicestershire at Leicester in 1964.
- Holds Lancashire career record for most wickets (1816).
- Three hat-tricks: 2 for Lancashire at Manchester (v Sussex in 1956 and v Leicestershire in 1958) and one for MCC v Transvaal at Johannesburg in 1956–57.

						Batting 1st			Batting 2nd				Bowling 1st			Bowling 2nd		
Ref	Series	V	T	Venue	Result	No	R	HO	No	R	HO	Ct	Balls	R	W	Balls	R	W
332/285	1950–51	NZ	1	Christchurch	D	11	9	b	–	–	–	–	144	47	1	–	–	–
335/288	1951	SA	2	Lord's	W-10w	10	1	b	–	–	–	–	36	7	0	108	33	2
336/289			3	Manchester	W-9w	11	1	c	–	–	–	–	42	8	1	102	30	1
339/292	1951–52	I	1	Delhi	D	9	4	b	–	–	–	–	126	49	1	–	–	–
340/293			2	Bombay[2]	D	9	27	c	–	–	–	–	174	96	4	120	30	1
341/294			3	Calcutta	D	8	1	b	–	–	–	–	162	46	1	24	8	0
342/295			4	Kanpur	W-8w	9	12	*	–	–	–	1	36	10	0	–	–	–
343/296			5	Madras[1]	L-I & 8	9	6	st	9	9	c	–	114	54	1	–	–	–
373/302	1953	A	2	Lord's	D	11	17	*	–	–	–	2	168	48	1	90	40	1
382/306	1953–54	WI	1	Kingston	L-140	9	8	b	9	1	lbw	–	216	90	4	102	50	2
383/307			2	Bridgetown	L-181	11	3	c	11	0	c	1	162	90	3	90	49	1
384/308			3	Georgetown	W-9w	11	10	*	–	–	–	–	162	64	4	132	86	2
385/309			4	Port-of-Spain	D	11	6	*	–	–	–	–	54	31	0	–	–	–
387/311	1954	P	1	Lord's	D	10	0	b	–	–	–	1	78	18	4	30	17	0
388/312			2	Nottingham	W-I & 129	–	–	–	–	–	–	2	108	38	2	120	66	3
389/313			3	Manchester	D	–	–	–	–	–	–	–	24	11	0	–	–	–
390/314			4	Oval	L-24	10	1	c	11	2	*	1	66	26	2	108	37	0
391/315	1954–55	A	1	Brisbane[2]	L-I & 154	10	11	b	11	14	c	–	272	123	2	–	–	–
392/316			2	Sydney	W-38	11	14	*	11	25	c	–	144	83	2	152	45	3
393/317			3	Melbourne	W-128	10	3	b	10	0	c	–	131	60	5	88	38	2
394/318			4	Adelaide	W-5w	11	0	c	–	–	–	1	152	70	0	96	38	3
395/319			5	Sydney	D	–	–	–	–	–	–	–	72	31	0	40	11	1
401/320	1954–55	NZ	1	Dunedin	W-8w	–	–	–	–	–	–	1	102	24	4	90	30	1
402/321			2	Auckland	W-I & 20	11	13	c	–	–	–	1	106	28	4	54	9	3

						Batting 1st			Batting 2nd				Bowling 1st			Bowling 2nd		
Ref	**Series**	**V**	**T**	**Venue**	**Result**	**No**	**R**	**HO**	**No**	**R**	**HO**	**Ct**	**Balls**	**R**	**W**	**Balls**	**R**	**W**
408/322	1955	SA	1	Nottingham	W-I & 5	10	20	c	–	–	–	–	150	47	1	60	16	0
409/323			2	Lord's	W-71	10	0	c	10	11	b	–	162	49	2	174	39	7
411/325			4	Leeds	L-224	10	4	b	10	3	hw	–	122	35	3	240	129	2
412/326			5	Oval	W-92	11	4	*	11	0	lbw	–	90	31	2	66	17	0
426/328	1956	A	2	Lord's	L-185	11	0	*	11	0	*	–	210	70	2	156	59	1
428/330			4	Manchester	W-I & 170	11	0	c	–	–	–	1	36	6	0	96	15	0
429/331			5	Oval	D	11	0	b	–	–	–	1	126	33	3	12	1	1
434/332	1956–57	SA	1	Johannesburg[3]	W-131	11	0	c	11	2	lbw	–	193	71	3	104	22	2
435/333			2	Cape Town	W-312	11	2	*	–	–	–	–	128	38	1	64	12	0
436/334			3	Durban[2]	D	11	6	b	11	9	c	–	176	56	2	88	32	1
437/335			4	Johannesburg[3]	L-17	11	12	*	11	4	*	1	184	81	2	104	37	3
439/337	1957	WI	1	Birmingham	D	11	13	b	–	–	–	1	234	114	3	12	6	0
440/338			2	Lord's	W-I & 36	11	7	b	–	–	–	1	108	46	1	175	71	3
441/339			3	Nottingham	D	–	–	–	–	–	–	–	172	78	1	248	118	5
457/345	1958	NZ	4	Manchester	W-I & 13	–	–	–	–	–	–	1	198	71	4	54	12	1
458/346			5	Oval	D	–	–	–	–	–	–	–	108	21	1	42	26	1
464/347	1958–59	A	1	Brisbane[2]	L-8w	10	2	c	10	3	c	1	160	57	1	48	13	0
465/348			2	Melbourne	L-8w	10	13	b	10	8	*	–	224	57	7	40	11	1
466/349			3	Sydney	D	11	0	*	–	–	–	1	128	48	0	16	6	0
467/350			4	Adelaide	L-10w	11	36	*	10	2	c	–	184	83	3	32	11	0
474/354	1959	I	1	Nottingham	W-I & 59	9	29	*	–	–	–	–	143	46	2	126	31	5
475/355			2	Lord's	W-8w	9	38	c	–	–	–	–	96	27	2	102	45	3
478/358			5	Oval	W-I & 27	10	3	*	–	–	–	–	99	24	2	108	50	3
488/360	1959–60	WI	2	Port-of-Spain	W-256	11	1	b	–	–	–	–	117	42	3	150	44	2
489/361			3	Kingston	D	11	13	b	11	12	lbw	1	193	76	3	108	45	1
490/362			4	Georgetown	D	11	20	*	–	–	–	–	216	79	1	–	–	–
492/364	1960	SA	1	Birmingham	W-100	11	14	*	10	22	c	1	168	67	2	108	41	3
493/365			2	Lord's	W-I & 73	10	2	*	–	–	–	–	120	63	6	126	34	5
494/366			3	Nottingham	W-8w	10	2	b	–	–	–	–	84	27	3	156	71	2
495/367			4	Manchester	D	11	0	b	–	–	–	–	132	32	3	24	3	0
496/368			5	Oval	D	10	13	*	10	4	c	–	228	96	1	72	57	2
507/369	1961	A	1	Birmingham	D	11	7	*	–	–	–	–	258	147	3	–	–	–
508/370			2	Lord's	L-5w	11	11	*	11	2	*	–	264	89	2	65	31	3
510/372			4	Manchester	L-54	10	4	c	10	8	b	1	126	53	5	264	106	1
511/373			5	Oval	D	10	18	b	10	9	*	–	233	75	3	–	–	–
530/382	1962	P	1	Birmingham	W-I & 24	–	–	–	–	–	–	–	126	54	4	114	32	2
532/384			3	Leeds	W-I & 117	11	26	*	–	–	–	2	120	40	2	120	50	4
533/385			4	Nottingham	D	–	–	–	–	–	–	1	109	55	2	132	47	2
535/387	1962–63	A	1	Brisbane[2]	D	11	8	*	–	–	–	2	128	75	1	128	67	1
536/388			2	Melbourne	W-7w	10	1	b	–	–	–	–	176	83	1	184	52	2
537/389			3	Sydney	L-8w	10	0	c	10	2	b	–	170	67	1	24	15	0
538/390			4	Adelaide	D	11	1	b	–	–	–	1	168	66	3	168	71	3
539/391			5	Sydney	D	11	17	*	–	–	–	–	144	76	1	32	8	0
543/395	1963	WI	1	Manchester	L-10w	11	0	b	11	7	b	–	222	121	0	–	–	–
547/399			5	Oval	L-8w	10	8	b	10	14	b	–	132	68	3	132	54	0
596/420	1965	SA	3	Oval	D	11	0	b	–	–	–	–	146	40	5	174	105	2

Career	**M**	**I**	**NO**	**HS**	**R**	**Avge**	**100**	**50**	**Ct**	**St**	**Balls**	**R**	**W**	**Avge**	**BB**	**5w**	**10w**	**Rate**
Test	70	87	28	38	675	11.44	–	–	28	–	16056	6261	252	24.84	7-39	9	1	63.71
F/c	559	647	145	62	5424	10.80	–	5	230	–	100985	36995	2260	16.36	8-34	123	11	44.68

J. B. STATHAM – TEST BOWLING SUMMARY

Series	**V**	**M**	**Balls**	**R**	**W**	**Avge**	**BB**	**5w**	**10w**	**Rate**
1950–51	NZ	1	144	47	1	47.00	1-47	–	–	144.00
1951	SA	2	288	78	4	19.50	2-33	–	–	72.00
1951–52	I	5	756	293	8	36.62	4-96	–	–	94.50
1953	A	1	258	88	2	44.00	1-40	–	–	129.00
1953–54	WI	4	918	460	16	28.75	4-64	–	–	57.37
1954	P	4	534	213	11	19.36	4-18	–	–	45.81
1954–55	A	5	1147	499	18	27.72	5-60	1	–	63.72

Brian Statham

J.B. STATHAM – TEST BOWLING SUMMARY *cont.*

Series	V	M	Balls	R	W	Avge	BB	5w	10w	Rate
1954–55	NZ	2	352	91	12	7.68	4-24	–	–	29.33
1955	SA	4	1064	363	17	21.35	7-39	1	–	62.58
1956	A	3	636	184	7	26.28	3-33	–	–	90.85
1956–57	SA	4	1041	349	14	24.92	3-37	–	–	74.35
1957	WI	3	949	433	13	33.30	5-118	1	–	73.00
1958	NZ	2	402	130	7	18.57	4-71	–	–	57.42
1958–59	A	4	832	286	12	23.83	7-57	1	–	69.33
1959	I	3	674	223	17	13.11	5-31	1	–	39.64
1959–60	WI	3	784	286	10	28.60	3-42	–	–	78.40
1960	SA	5	1218	491	27	18.18	6-63	2	1	45.11
1961	A	4	1210	501	17	29.47	5-53	1	–	71.17
1962	P	3	721	278	16	17.37	4-50	–	–	45.06
1962–63	A	5	1322	580	13	44.61	3-66	–	–	101.69
1963	WI	2	486	243	3	81.00	3-68	–	–	162.00
1965	SA	1	320	145	7	20.71	5-40	1	–	45.71
	A	22	5405	2138	69	30.98	7-57	3	–	78.33
	SA	16	3931	1426	69	20.66	7-39	4	1	56.97
	WI	12	3137	1422	42	33.85	5-118	1	–	74.69
	NZ	5	898	268	20	13.40	4-24	–	–	44.90
	I	8	1430	516	25	20.64	5-31	1	–	57.20
	P	7	1255	491	27	18.18	4-18	–	–	46.48
Home		37	8760	3370	148	22.77	7-39	7	1	59.18
Overseas		33	7296	2891	104	27.79	7-57	2	–	70.15
Totals		70	16056	6261	252	24.84	7-39	9	1	63.71

STEEL
Allan Gibson

Lancashire (1877 to 1893)
Cambridge University (1878 to 1881)

TOUR A 1882–83
Born West Derby, Liverpool
24 Sept 1858
Died Hyde Park, London 15 Jun 1914

Allan Steel

At his considerable peak, Allan Steel rated second only to W.G. Grace as an outstanding all-round cricketer. Just medium height (5ft 8in) and slightly built, he was a nimble-footed, aggressive middle-order batsman with a fine array of strokes and an extremely accurate right-arm slow bowler who could spin the ball either way. His bowling was based on exceptional accuracy, a wide range of pace changes which even included medium-fast swing, and a sharply spun leg-break. One of Marlborough's greatest cricketers, he also enjoyed unprecedented success at Cambridge where he spent four years as a blue, the third as captain, and also gained blues for rugby and racquets. As a freshman he spun the Light Blues to a dramatic victory at Lord's, following up his first innings analysis of 8 for 62 with 5 for 11 in 20.1 four-ball overs as Oxford were dispatched for 32. Three weeks later he played a major part in his university's historic two-day defeat of the Australians on the same ground and finished his first full season at the head of the national bowling averages. One of four brothers to play for Lancashire, he was still at Cambridge when he made his international debut in the inaugural Test in England. An inspired captain, he led England to victory against Australia in all three Tests of the 1886 rubber. His duties as a barrister severely limited his later career but his enthusiasm never dwindled and he was a popular and able MCC president in 1902.

NOTABLE FEATS

- Took 164 wickets (avge 9.43) in his first full season (1878).
- His match analysis of 13 for 73 at Lord's in 1878 remains the Cambridge record in Varsity matches.
- Held Cambridge career record for most wickets (198) until 1907 and only O.S. Wheatley has exceeded his 75 wickets (avge 7.42) of 1878.
- Took 9 for 63 for Lancashire v Yorkshire at Manchester in 1878.
- Hat-trick for Cambridge U v Oxford U at Lord's in 1879.
- Bowled in an unchanged partnership with A.H. Evans throughout both completed Players innings for the Gentlemen at The Oval in 1879.

Ref	Series	V	T	Venue	Result	Batting 1st No	R	HO	Batting 2nd No	R	HO	Ct	Bowling 1st Balls	R	W	Bowling 2nd Balls	R	W
4/4	1880	A		Oval	W-5w	7	42	c	–	–	–	1	116	58	3	124	73	2
9/9	1882	A		Oval	L-7	9	14	b	7	0	c	–	8	1	0	28	15	2
10/10	1882–83	A	1	Melbourne	L-9w	5	27	b	4	29	lbw	1	132	68	2	36	17	0
11/11			2	Melbourne	W-I & 27	4	39	c	–	–	–	–	–	–	–	–	–	–
12/12			3	Sydney	W-69	4	17	b	4	6	lbw	2	104	27	3	–	–	–
13/13			4	Sydney	L-4w	4	135	*	4	21	b	–	76	34	3	172	49	3
14/14	1884	A	1	Manchester	D	5	15	c	5	18	c	–	52	32	2	–	–	–
15/15			2	Lord's	W-I & 5	5	148	b	–	–	–	–	6	6	1	40	26	1
16/16			3	Oval	D	5	31	lbw	–	–	–	1	136	71	0	–	–	–
22/22*	1886	A	1	Manchester	W-4w	5	12	c	6	19	*	–	108	47	2	32	9	1
23/23*			2	Lord's	W-I & 106	5	5	lbw	–	–	–	–	84	34	2	64	14	0
24/24*			3	Oval	W-I & 217	6	9	st	–	–	–	–	–	–	–	28	20	1
28/28*	1888	A	1	Lord's	L-61	8	3	st	6	10	*	–	14	4	1	4	0	0

Career	M	I	NO	HS	R	Avge	100	50	Ct	St	Balls	R	W	Avge	BB	5w	10w	Rate
Test	13	20	3	148	600	35.29	2	–	5	–	1364	605	29	20.86	3-27	–	–	47.03
F/c	158	254	23	171	6767	29.29	7	35	130	–	30260	11480	783	14.66	9-63	64	20	38.64

STEELE
David Stanley

Northamptonshire (1963 to 1984)
Derbyshire (1979 to 1981)

Wisden 1976
TOURS
SA 1975–76 (Robins);
Z 1980–81 (Leics XI)
Born Bradeley, Staffordshire 29 Sep 1941

David Steele

David Steele was England's folk hero of the mid-seventies. Called up for Test duty against Australia in his 35th year, bespectacled and prematurely grey, he looked remarkably like a Home Guard character from 'Dad's Army'. Once he had found his way to the middle (he miscalculated the stairs and found himself in the Gents en route to his first Test innings), he quickly belied his appearance with a succession of staunch displays against Lillee, Thomson and Walker in their collective prime. Limitless courage, tenacity and concentration, plus a sound defence and a fine array of attacking strokes, brought him 365 runs and four fifties in his first three Tests. A careful man (known by his mates as 'Crime' because he seldom paid), he had struck a bet with his local butcher which duly stocked the Steele freezer with 365 lamb chops and four fillet steaks. He produced similar heroics against the 1976 West Indians and was desperately unlucky to be omitted from England's subsequent tour of India because of doubts about his technique against spin. An accurate left-arm leg-break bowler and a fine close field, he began his first Northamptonshire career after five seasons with his native Staffordshire (1958–62). Although he moved to Derbyshire when he was offered the captaincy, he resigned that office after only two months and returned to Northampton at the end of his three-year contract.

NOTABLE FEATS

- *761* Dismissed A.A. Mallett with his fourth ball in Test cricket.
- Exceeded 1000 runs in a season 10 times.
- Shared record Derbyshire 3rd-wkt stand of 291 with P.N. Kirsten v Somerset at Taunton in 1981.
- Hat-trick for Derbyshire v Glamorgan at Derby in 1980.
- Achieved the match 'double' (130 runs and 11 wickets) for Northamptonshire v Derbyshire at Northampton in 1978.
- Holds Northamptonshire career record for most catches by a non-wicket-keeper (469).

Ref	Series	V	T	Venue	Result	Batting 1st No	R	HO	Batting 2nd No	R	HO	Ct	Bowling 1st Balls	R	W	Bowling 2nd Balls	R	W
761/512	1975	A	2	Lord's	D	3	50	b	3	45	c	–	4	1	1	54	19	1
762/513			3	Leeds	D	3	73	c	3	92	c	2	–	–	–	–	–	–
763/514			4	Oval	D	3	39	b	3	66	c	2	12	1	0	–	–	–
777/515	1976	WI	1	Nottingham	D	3	106	c	3	6	c	1	–	–	–	–	–	–
778/516			2	Lord's	D	3	7	lbw	4	64	c	–	–	–	–	–	–	–
779/517			3	Manchester	L-425	3	20	lbw	3	15	c	1	–	–	–	–	–	–
780/518			4	Leeds	L-55	2	4	b	2	0	c	1	–	–	–	–	–	–
781/519			5	Oval	L-231	3	44	lbw	3	42	c	–	18	18	0	–	–	–

Career	M	I	NO	HS	R	Avge	100	50	Ct	St	Balls	R	W	Avge	BB	5w	10w	Rate
Test	8	16	0	106	673	42.06	1	5	7	–	88	39	2	19.50	1-1	–	–	44.00
F/c	500	812	124	140*	22346	32.47	30	117	546	–	36706	15511	623	24.89	8-29	26	3	58.91

STEVENS
Greville Thomas Scott

Middlesex (1919 to 1932)
Oxford University (1920 to 1923)

Wisden 1918
TOURS
SA 1922–23, 1927–28;
WI 1929–30, 1931–32 (Tennyson)
Born Hampstead, Middlesex 7 Jan 1901
Died Islington, London 19 Sep 1970

Apart from 'Boy' Collins (who whiled away five afternoons at Clifton collecting a modest undefeated 628), Greville Stevens must rank as the greatest English schoolboy cricketer of all time. A handy little batsman, in 1919 he notched up 466 in a University College School house match, caused some havoc with his leg-breaks and googlies and, that very same season, was precociously and sensationally selected for the Gentlemen against the Players at Lord's. Prior to that appearance he had celebrated his first-class debut by contributing ten wickets to a remarkable Middlesex victory. Not surprisingly he was a blue in all his four summers at Oxford and was still in residence when he first toured South Africa and began his Test career. His batting style was akin to that of Basil D'Oliveira half a century later; his strong arms overcoming a minimal backlift to lever the ball away with considerable force. A splendid close fielder, his opportunities for cricket after leaving university were severely restricted by his work. [*Illus. pp.* 297, 420]

NOTABLE FEATS

- *190* His match analysis of 10 for 195 remains the record by any overseas bowler in a Bridgetown Test.
- Exceeded 1000 runs in a season twice.
- Took 7 for 104 (10 for 136 in the match) on his first-class debut for Middlesex v Hampshire at Lord's in 1919.

Ref	Series	V	T	Venue	Result	Batting 1st No	R	HO	Batting 2nd No	R	HO	Ct	Bowling 1st Balls	R	W	Bowling 2nd Balls	R	W
148/134	1922–23	SA	1	Johannesburg[1]	L-168	8	11	b	10	2	c	–	–	–	–	24	19	0
166/152	1926	A	4	Manchester	D	6	24	c	–	–	–	1	192	86	3	–	–	–
167/153			5	Oval	W-289	6	17	c	6	22	c	2	174	85	1	18	13	1
168/154	1927–28	SA	1	Johannesburg[1]	W-10w	6	0	c	–	–	–	1	114	58	3	48	13	0
169/155			2	Cape Town	W-87	5	0	c	5	2	c	1	60	26	1	30	17	0
170/156			3	Durban[2]	D	6	69	b	–	–	–	1	24	12	0	66	58	0
171/157			4	Johannesburg[1]	L-4w	6	14	c	6	20	c	2	6	9	0	6	0	0
172/158*			5	Durban[2]	L-8w	6	13	c	6	18	c	–	12	11	0	–	–	–
190/176	1929–30	WI	1	Bridgetown	D	3	9	ro	3	5	c	1	162	105	5	160	90	5
191/177			2	Port-of-Spain	W-167	3	8	c	6	29	c	–	42	25	0	48	21	1

Career	M	I	NO	HS	R	Avge	100	50	Ct	St	Balls	R	W	Avge	BB	5w	10w	Rate
Test	10	17	0	69	263	15.47	–	1	9	–	1186	648	20	32.40	5-90	2	1	59.30
F/c	243	387	36	182	10376	29.56	12	55	213	–	32601	18364	684	26.84	8-38	29	5	47.66

STEVENSON Graham Barry

Yorkshire (1973 to 1986)
Northamptonshire (1987)

TOURS
A 1979–80; WI 1980–81; I 1979–80
Born Ackworth, Yorkshire 16 Dec 1955

NOTABLE FEATS

- Scored 115* at No. 11 for Yorkshire v Warwickshire at Birmingham in 1982 sharing record Yorkshire 10th-wkt stand of 149 with G. Boycott.

Graham Stevenson was an uncomplicated cricketer who struck the ball ferociously, bowled right-arm medium-fast, fielded enthusiastically and threw in hard. Tallish (5ft 11in) and strongly made, given a tiny percentage of Boycott's application and determination he would have been an outstanding all-rounder. It was ironic that, when he decided to play the innings of his life, the oracle of Fitzwilliam was left with the role of a sleeping partner. On that auspicious day 'Stevo' became one of only eight No. 11 batsmen to make a first-class hundred and finished with the fourth-highest score made in that position.

Graham Stevenson

						Batting 1st			Batting 2nd				Bowling 1st			Bowling 2nd		
Ref	Series	V	T	Venue	Result	No	R	HO	No	R	HO	Ct	Balls	R	W	Balls	R	W
876/556	1979–80	I		Bombay[3]	W-10w	10	27	*	–	–	–	–	84	59	2	30	13	0
898/565	1980–81	WI	4	St John's	D	10	1	b	–	–	–	–	198	111	3	–	–	–

Career	M	I	NO	HS	R	Avge	100	50	Ct	St	Balls	R	W	Avge	BB	5w	10w	Rate
Test	2	2	1	27*	28	28.00	–	–	–	–	312	183	5	36.60	3-111	–	–	62.40
F/c	188	229	34	115*	3965	20.33	2	16	73	–	26680	14075	488	28.84	8-57	18	2	54.67

STEWART Michael James

Surrey (1954 to 1972)

Wisden 1958
TOURS
SA 1962–63 (Cav);
WI 1955–56 (Swanton); I 1962–63 (Cav), 1963–64, 1967–68 (Int XI);
P 1967–68 (Int XI), 1970–71 (Cwlth);
SL 1967–68 (Int XI); Z 1959–60 (Surrey)
Born Herne Hill, Surrey 16 Sep 1932

A neat, alert opening batsman and brilliant close catcher, Micky Stewart began his long career in professional cricket with Surrey's all-conquering side of the 1950s. Of medium height (5ft 9in) and slightly built, he was an outstanding all-round sportsman at Alleyn's School. Superbly fit, his footballing prowess at inside-right won him an England amateur cap before he turned professional and joined Charlton Athletic. On 7 June 1957, fielding close to a Northampton pitch enlivened by rain, he held six catches at backward short-leg and one in the gully. Only Hammond, who held one more, has exceeded his total of 77 catches that season and his overall total of 634 is the sixth-highest for an entirely post-war career. An astute and enthusiastic captain of Surrey for ten seasons (1963–72),

Micky Stewart

he returned for a six-year stint as manager in 1979. He was appointed England's first professional team manager for three years from 1 April 1987.

NOTABLE FEATS

- Exceeded 1000 runs in a season 15 times, including 2045 in 1962.
- Scored 2 double centuries for Surrey at The Oval: 200* v Essex in 1962 and 227* v Middlesex in 1964.
- Held 7 catches in an innings to set a world record (later equalled) for Surrey v Northamptonshire at Northampton in 1957.
- Holds Surrey records for most catches by a fielder in a career (604) and in a season (77 in 1957). His 77 catches in 1957 (all for Surrey) is the second-highest total by a non-wicket-keeper. Held 61 catches in first-class cricket in 1958.

						Batting 1st			Batting 2nd			
Ref	Series	V	T	Venue	Result	No	R	HO	No	R	HO	Ct
531/383	1962	P	2	Lord's	W-9w	1	39	c	1	34	*	1
532/384			3	Leeds	W-I & 117	1	86	lbw	–	–	–	–
543/395	1963	WI	1	Manchester	L-10w	1	37	c	1	87	c	–
544/396			2	Lord's	D	1	2	c	1	17	c	3
545/397			3	Birmingham	W-217	2	39	lbw	2	27	c	–
546/398			4	Leeds	L-221	1	2	c	1	0	b	2
553/400	1963–64	I	1	Madras[2]	D	10	15	st	–	–	–	–
554/401			2	Bombay[2]	D	–	–	–	–	–	–	–

TEST NOTES

- *554* Retired from the match (and tour) with dysentery at tea on the first day.

Career	M	I	NO	HS	R	Avge	100	50	Ct	St	Balls	R	W	Avge	BB	5w	10w	Rate
Test	8	12	1	87	385	35.00	–	2	6	–	–	–	–	–	–	–	–	–
F/c	530	898	93	227*	26492	32.90	49	132	634	–	148	99	1	99.00	1-4	–	–	148.00

STODDART
Andrew Ernest

Middlesex (1885 to 1900)

Wisden 1893

TOURS

A 1887–88, 1891–92, 1894–95, 1897–98; WI 1896–97

Born Westoe, South Shields, Co. Durham 11 Mar 1863

Died St John's Wood, London 4 Apr 1915

Although Andrew Stoddart was a late developer as a cricketer, not playing seriously until he was 22, he rapidly regained any lost ground by being invited to play for Middlesex during an initial season in which he scored five hundreds for Hampstead. The following year, on 4 August 1886, he amassed the highest score then recorded in any class of cricket: 485 in 370 minutes out of Hampstead's 813 against Stoics. After playing poker all the previous night, he had freshened up with a swim before consuming a hearty breakfast. After his innings he played tennis and went to the theatre before finishing his epic day with a late-night supper party. 'Drewy', as he was known by his family ('Stoddy' by the sports world), was a supremely gifted and stylish opening batsman, a handy right-arm medium-pace change bowler and a high-class fielder anywhere. His exceptionally quick reactions enabled him to attack the fastest bowling even on fiery pitches; he was a powerful driver and a very lusty leg-side hitter. He organised and captained two of his four tours of Australia. The first, which began with a 10-run victory after England had followed on, produced one of the best contested of all Test series. Acknowledged as the finest three-quarter in the country, he also captained England at rugby, playing in ten internationals. Failing finances and health contributed to his suicide.

NOTABLE FEATS

- *39* Deputising for the injured W.G. Grace, he was the first captain to declare a Test innings closed.
- *43* His 173 in 320 min was then the highest score for England; it remained the highest by an England captain in Australia until 1974–75.
- *45* First England captain to invite the opposition to bat in a Test.
- Exceeded 1000 runs in a season 6 times, including 2072 in 1893.
- Scored 2 double centuries: 215* for Middlesex v Lancashire at Manchester in 1891 and 221 (in his final innings for Middlesex) v Somerset at Lord's in 1900.
- Carried his bat through a completed Middlesex innings twice.
- Achieved the match 'double' (143 runs and 10 wickets) for A. Priestley's XI v Jamaica at Kingston in 1896–97.

Andrew Stoddart

Ref	Series	V	T	Venue	Result	Batting 1st No	R	HO	Batting 2nd No	R	HO	Ct	Bowling 1st Balls	R	W	Bowling 2nd Balls	R	W
27/27	1887–88	A		Sydney	W-126	1	16	c	1	17	c	1	–	–	–	–	–	–
35/35	1891–92	A	1	Melbourne	L-54	4	0	c	2	35	b	–	30	10	0	–	–	–
36/36			2	Sydney	L-72	4	27	c	4	69	b	–	–	–	–	24	12	0
37/37			3	Adelaide	W-I & 230	3	134	lbw	–	–	–	1	–	–	–	–	–	–
39/39*	1893	A	1	Lord's	D	2	24	b	2	13	b	–	–	–	–	–	–	–
40/40			2	Oval	W-I & 43	2	83	b	–	–	–	–	–	–	–	–	–	–
41/41			3	Manchester	D	1	0	ro	1	42	c	–	–	–	–	–	–	–
42/42*	1894–95	A	1	Sydney	W-10	3	12	c	3	36	c	1	18	31	1	–	–	–
43/43*			2	Melbourne	W-94	3	10	b	3	173	b	1	–	–	–	–	–	–
44/44*			3	Adelaide	L-382	5	1	b	3	34	*	–	–	–	–	–	–	–
45/45*			4	Sydney	L-I & 147	4	7	st	3	0	c	–	–	–	–	–	–	–
46/46*			5	Melbourne	W-6w	3	68	st	3	11	lbw	–	–	–	–	–	–	–
50/50	1896	A	1	Lord's	W-6w	2	17	b	5	30	*	–	–	–	–	–	–	–
51/51			2	Manchester	L-3w	1	15	st	1	41	b	1	30	9	0	–	–	–
55/55*	1897–98	A	3	Adelaide	L-I & 13	8	15	c	8	24	c	–	24	10	1	–	–	–
56/56*			4	Melbourne	L-8w	8	17	c	6	25	b	1	36	22	0	–	–	–

Career	M	I	NO	HS	R	Avge	100	50	Ct	St	Balls	R	W	Avge	BB	5w	10w	Rate
Test	16	30	2	173	996	35.57	2	3	6	–	162	94	2	47.00	1-10	–	–	81.00
F/c	309	537	16	221	16738	32.12	26	85	257	–	14717	6571	278	23.63	7-67	10	2	52.93

STORER, William

Derbyshire (1887 to 1905)
London County (1900)

Wisden 1899
TOUR A 1897–98
Born Butterley, Derbyshire 25 Jan 1867
Died Derby 28 Feb 1912

Bill Storer, whose younger brother Harry was a contemporary Derbyshire player, was a fine utility cricketer. He enjoyed a lengthy county career as a highly skilled wicket-keeper and developed into a sound but enterprising middle-order batsman capable of scoring hundreds in each innings against Yorkshire. For good measure he would hand over his pads and gauntlets and break stubborn partnerships with his leg-breaks. He caused a sensation when he courageously stood up to the stumps to take the express fast bowling of Charles Kortright when MCC played the 1893 Australians. Strongly built, his footballing talents earned him appearances for Derby County. [*Illus. p.* 184]

TEST NOTES

- *54* Bowled in 1st inns: 1 for 55 (96 balls).
- *55* Bowled in 1st inns: 0 for 16 (18 balls).
- *56* Bowled in 1st inns: 1 for 24 (24 balls).
- *57* Bowled in 1st inns: 0 for 13 (30 balls).

NOTABLE FEATS

- Exceeded 1000 runs in a season 7 times.
- Scored 216* for Derbyshire v Leicestershire at Chesterfield in 1899.
- Scored hundreds in 3 consecutive innings for Derbyshire in 1896.
- Shared record Derbyshire 1st-wkt stand of 322 with J. Bowden v Essex at Derby in 1929.

Ref	Series	V	T	Venue	Result	Batting 1st No	R	HO	Batting 2nd No	R	HO	Fielding 1st Ct	St	Byes	Balls	Fielding 2nd Ct	St	Byes	Balls
53/53 †	1897–98	A	1	Sydney	W-9w	4	43	c	–	–	–	1	–	1	601	–	–	12	726
54/54 †			2	Melbourne	L-I & 55	6	51	c	5	1	c	1	–	14	1110	–	–	–	–
55/55 †			3	Adelaide	L-I & 13	4	4	b	5	6	c	3	–	16	1267	–	–	–	–
56/56 †			4	Melbourne	L-8w	6	2	c	7	26	c	3	–	3	610	–	–	0	238
57/57 †			5	Sydney	L-6w	5	44	b	5	31	c	3	–	5	601	–	–	6	376
60/60 †	1899	A	1	Nottingham	D	8	4	b	8	3	lbw	–	–	8	762	–	–	0	470

Career	M	I	NO	HS	R	Avge	100	50	Ct	St	Balls	R	W	Avge	BB	5w	10w	Rate
Test	6	11	0	51	215	19.54	–	1	11	–	168	108	2	54.00	1-24	–	–	84.00
F/c	289	490	41	216*	12966	28.87	17	63	376	55	11422	7863	232	33.89	5-20	4	–	49.23

STREET George Benjamin

Sussex (1909 to 1923)

TOUR SA 1922–23
Born Charlwood, Surrey 6 Dec 1889
Died Portslade, Sussex 24 Apr 1924

NOTABLE FEATS

- Holds Sussex record for most wicket-keeping dismissals in a season: 95 in 1923.

George Street was only 34 and had just enjoyed his best season as the Sussex wicket-keeper when, taking avoiding action against a truck at a crossroads, he crashed his motor-cycle into a wall and was instantly killed. He had succeeded Harry Butt two years before the First World War and quickly established himself as a sound keeper and useful lower-order batsman. When W.H. Livsey fractured a finger in the early weeks of MCC's 1922–23 tour of South Africa, he was sent out as a replacement and his four first-class matches there included the Third Test.

George Street

						Batting 1st			Batting 2nd			Fielding 1st				Fielding 2nd			
Ref	Series	V	T	Venue	Result	No	R	HO	No	R	HO	Ct	St	Byes	Balls	Ct	St	Byes	Balls
150/136†	1922–23	SA	3	Durban[2]	D	10	4	c	1	7	*	–	1	15	808	–	–	–	–

Career	M	I	NO	HS	R	Avge	100	50	Ct	St	Balls	R	W	Avge	BB	5w	10w	Rate
Test	1	2	1	7*	11	11.00	–	–	–	1	–	–	–	–	–	–	–	–
F/c	197	304	73	109	3984	17.24	1	12	308	121	105	66	3	22.00	3-26	–	–	35.00

STRUDWICK Herbert

Surrey (1902 to 1927)

Wisden 1912
TOURS
A 1903–04, 1911–12, 1920–21, 1924–25;
SA 1909–10, 1913–14
Born Mitcham, Surrey 28 Jan 1880
Died Shoreham, Sussex 14 Feb 1970

Bert Strudwick joined the Surrey staff in 1898 and served his county for 60 years. For half a century he held the world wicket-keeping record for most dismissals. His achievement was the more remarkable because he kept mostly to fast bowlers whereas his main challengers for that record, Ames and Huish, were provided with many more chances, particularly stumpings, by Kent's reliance on slow bowlers. Unobtrusive and exceptionally quick-footed, he had that certainty of touch and effortless timing which is the hallmark of the best wicket-keepers. He was 41 and had played in 15 Tests overseas before he was selected for England at home; the two Warwickshire stumpers, Lilley and 'Tiger' Smith, were preferred to him because of their superior batting skills. 'Struddy' at least had the compensation of the classic 1926 Ashes-winning finale as his farewell. One of the most popular and respected of cricketers, he spent his retirement years scoring for Surrey and coaching at the south London indoor school which he ran in partnership with Andy Sandham.

NOTABLE FEATS

- 50 dismissals in 19th Test (*158*).
- Until J.T. Murray claimed both honours in 1975, he held the world records for most catches and most dismissals in a first-class career. His Championship records of 964 catches and 1132 dismissals survived until R.W. Taylor overhauled them in 1980 and 1982 respectively.
- His 91 dismissals in 1903, his first full season, was then easily a first-class record.
- Holds Surrey career record for most wicket-keeping dismissals (1223).
- Held 6 catches in an innings for Surrey v Sussex at The Oval in 1914.

Ref	Series	V	T	Venue	Result	Batting 1st No	R	HO	Batting 2nd No	R	HO	Fielding 1st Ct	St	Byes	Balls	Fielding 2nd Ct	St	Byes	Balls
106/103†	1909–10	SA	1	Johannesburg[1]	L-19	11	7	b	11	1	*	1	1	1	378	1	–	2	684
107/104†			2	Durban[1]	L-95	11	1	hw	11	7	c	1	–	7	641	1	–	12	782
108/105†			3	Johannesburg[1]	W-3w	11	18	c	2	5	b	2	–	9	504	–	–	1	546
109/106†			4	Cape Town	L-4w	10	7	c	8	3	c	–	–	10	402	1	–	15	357
110/107			5	Cape Town	W-9w	10	2	c	–	–	–	–	–	–	–	–	–	–	–
116/108†	1911–12	A	1	Sydney	L-146	11	0	*	11	12	*	1	1	9	762	–	–	16	627
130/119†	1913–14	SA	1	Durban[1]	W-I & 157	11	2	*	–	–	–	2	–	6	340	1	–	6	314
131/120†			2	Johannesburg[1]	W-I & 12	10	14	c	–	–	–	2	2	10	377	2	1	9	502
132/121†			3	Johannesburg[1]	W-91	11	9	*	11	0	c	–	–	4	371	2	–	17	658
133/122†			4	Durban[1]	D	11	0	b	–	–	–	2	1	6	413	1	–	12	612
134/123†			5	Port Elizabeth	W-10w	3	3	b	–	–	–	2	1	2	394	1	1	6	571
135/124†	1920–21	A	1	Sydney	L-377	11	2	lbw	11	1	*	2	1	4	689	1	–	17	1155
136/125†			2	Melbourne	L-I & 91	9	21	*	9	24	c	2	–	1	825	–	–	–	–
137/126†			3	Adelaide	L-119	10	9	c	9	1	c	2	1	6	648	2	–	5	1115
139/128†			5	Sydney	L-9w	11	2	b	11	5	*	2	–	18	549	1	–	3	206
140/129†	1921	A	1	Nottingham	L-10w	9	0	c	9	0	b	–	–	8	468	–	–	0	37
141/130†			2	Lord's	L-8w	10	8	c	10	12	b	2	–	2	505	–	–	3	183
157/143†	1924	SA	5	Oval	D	10	2	*	–	–	–	1	–	4	744	–	–	–	–
158/144†	1924–25	A	1	Sydney	L-193	11	6	lbw	11	2	c	3	–	10	1218	2	–	2	1007
159/145†			2	Melbourne	L-81	11	4	b	3	22	lbw	3	–	18	899	1	–	11	477
160/146†			3	Adelaide	L-11	3	1	c	11	2	*	2	1	0	1224	–	–	4	545
161/147†			4	Melbourne	W-I & 29	11	7	*	–	–	–	1	–	13	507	2	–	15	597
162/148†			5	Sydney	L-307	11	1	*	11	0	c	2	–	2	821	–	1	6	947
163/149†	1926	A	1	Nottingham	D	–	–	–	–	–	–	–	–	–	–	–	–	–	–
164/150†			2	Lord's	D	–	–	–	–	–	–	2	–	12	929	–	–	5	528
165/151†			3	Leeds	D	11	1	c	–	–	–	1	–	2	990	–	–	–	–
166/152†			4	Manchester	D	–	–	–	–	–	–	1	–	2	902	–	–	–	–
167/153†			5	Oval	W-289	11	4	*	11	2	c	2	–	5	913	–	–	0	315

Career	M	I	NO	HS	R	Avge	100	50	Ct	St	Balls	R	W	Avge	BB	5w	10w	Rate
Test	28	42	13	24	230	7.93	–	–	60	12	–	–	–	–	–	–	–	–
F/c	675	836	244	93	6452	10.89	–	9	1242	255	138	102	1	102.00	1-9	–	–	138.00

Bert Strudwick in the score box at The Oval, 1958.

H. STRUDWICK – TEST SUMMARY

Series	V	M	I	NO	HS	R	Avge	100	50	Ct	St	Byes	Balls
1909–10	SA	5	9	1	18	51	6.37	–	–	7	1	57	4294
1911–12	A	1	2	2	12*	12	–	–	–	1	1	25	1389
1913–14	SA	5	6	2	14	28	7.00	–	–	15	6	78	4552
1920–21	A	4	8	3	24	65	13.00	–	–	12	2	54	5187
1921	A	2	4	–	12	20	5.00	–	–	2	–	13	1193
1924	SA	1	1	1	2*	2	–	–	–	1	–	4	744
1924–25	A	5	9	3	22	45	7.50	–	–	16	2	81	8242
1926	A	5	3	1	4*	7	3.50	–	–	6	–	26	4577
	A	17	26	9	24	149	8.76	–	–	37	5	199	20588
	SA	11	16	4	18	81	6.75	–	–	23	7	139	9590
Home		8	8	2	12	29	4.83	–	–	9	–	43	6514
Overseas		20	34	11	24	201	8.73	–	–	51	12	295	23664
Totals		28	42	13	24	230	7.93	–	–	60	12	338	30178

TEST NOTES

- *107* N.C. Tufnell deputised as wicket-keeper and became the first substitute to make a stumping in Test cricket.
- *110* N.C. Tufnell kept wicket.

STUDD
Charles Thomas

Middlesex (1879 to 1884)
Cambridge University (1880 to 1883)

TOUR A 1882–83
Born Spratton, Northamptonshire
2 Dec 1860
Died Ibambi, Belgian Congo 16 Jul 1931

NOTABLE FEATS

- Exceeded 1000 runs in a season twice and took 100 wickets twice, completing the 'double' in 1882 and 1883.
- Leading batsman of 1882 and second in 1883.
- Achieved the match 'double' (105 runs and 10 wickets) for Middlesex v Kent at Canterbury in 1883.

Charles (or 'CT') Studd was the most talented of the six brothers who played in the Eton XI and the youngest of the three who captained Cambridge in successive seasons. So swiftly did he develop his all-round talents as a classically stylish batsman, right-arm medium-fast bowler and agile fielder, that he appeared in five Test matches while still at university. He was a strong off-side batsman and used his height well in his bowling action. In 1882 he became only the second player after W.G. Grace to complete the 'double' of 1000 runs and 100 wickets in a season. Included in those figures were his contributions of 135 runs and eight wickets towards the Light Blues' historic win against the Australians. His career ended after the 1884 season when, deciding to become a missionary, he went to China until ill health forced him home ten years later. In 1900 he began similar work in India before devoting the rest of his life to overcoming illness and hardship in the Belgian Congo.

The three Studd brothers who captained Cambridge: J.E.K. (1884), C.T. (1883) and G.B. (1882).

						Batting 1st			Batting 2nd				Bowling 1st			Bowling 2nd		
Ref	Series	V	T	Venue	Result	No	R	HO	No	R	HO	Ct	Balls	R	W	Balls	R	W
9/9	1882	A		Oval	L-7	6	0	b	10	0	*	1	–	–	–	16	9	0
10/10	1882–83	A	1	Melbourne	L-9w	4	0	b	3	21	b	2	184	35	2	56	7	0
11/11			2	Melbourne	W-I & 27	2	14	b	–	–	–	1	16	22	0	–	–	–
12/12			3	Sydney	W-69	2	21	c	2	25	b	1	56	5	0	–	–	–
13/13			4	Sydney	L-4w	2	48	ro	2	31	c	–	24	12	0	32	8	1

Career	M	I	NO	HS	R	Avge	100	50	Ct	St	Balls	R	W	Avge	BB	5w	10w	Rate
Test	5	9	1	48	160	20.00	–	–	5	–	384	98	3	32.66	2-35	–	–	128.00
F/c	99	167	23	175*	4391	30.49	8	14	73	–	22659	7658	441+3	17.36	8-40	32	9	51.38

STUDD
George Brown

Cambridge University (1879 to 1882)
Middlesex (1879 to 1886)

TOUR A 1882–83
Born Netheravon, Wiltshire 20 Oct 1859
Died Pasadena, California, USA
13 Feb 1945

George Studd was the second-eldest of the three brothers who captained Cambridge in successive seasons after appearing in the same Eton XI. A stylish middle-order batsman, he favoured the drive and was a strong off-side player. Although his groundwork as a fielder was outstanding, he was an erratic catcher. In 1882 he played a captain's innings of 120 in the Varsity match and he was a tennis blue in his last two years. After joining his brother Charles on the Hon. Ivo Bligh's expedition to Australia and playing alongside him (with scant success) in all four Tests, he was called to the Bar. Before he could practise, severe illness compelled him to winter abroad and he followed CT's example by devoting the rest of his long life to missionary work, first in India and China, but mainly in one of the more squalid areas of California. [*Illus. above*]

Ref	Series	V	T	Venue	Result	Batting 1st			Batting 2nd			Ct
						No	R	HO	No	R	HO	
10/10	1882–83	A	1	Melbourne	L-9w	9	7	ro	9	0	c	–
11/11			2	Melbourne	W-I & 27	10	1	b	–	–	–	1
12/12			3	Sydney	W-69	9	3	b	10	8	c	3
13/13			4	Sydney	L-4w	10	3	ro	10	9	c	4

Career	M	I	NO	HS	R	Avge	100	50	Ct	St	Balls	R	W	Avge	BB	5w	10w	Rate
Test	4	7	0	9	31	4.42	–	–	8	–	–	–	–	–	–	–	–	–
F/c	87	142	10	120	2892	21.90	3	15	74	1	76	29	2	14.50	1-5	–	–	38.00

SUBBA ROW, Raman

Cambridge University (1951 to 1953)
Surrey (1953 to 1954)
Northamptonshire (1955 to 1961)

Wisden 1961
TOURS
A 1958–59; WI 1959–60; NZ 1958–59; I 1953–54 (Cwlth), 1961–62 (Int XI), 1967–68 (Pres XI); P 1961–62 (Int XI)
Born Streatham, Surrey 29 Jan 1932

Raman Subba Row during his century for England against Australia at Edgbaston, 1961; Wally Grout is keeping wicket.

TEST NOTES

• *491* Bowled in 2nd inns: 0 for 2 (6 balls).

Having enjoyed a highly successful sports career at Whitgift School, Raman Subba Row had little difficulty in gaining blues for cricket (all three years) and rugby fives at Cambridge. Tall (6ft 0½in) and slightly hunched, he was an extremely sound left-handed opening or middle-order batsman. Very on-side conscious in his early days, he strengthened his off-side technique and became a masterly placer of the speedy single. His slightly eccentric right-arm leg-breaks and googlies bore rich fruit when he took five Oxford wickets for 21 at Lord's in 1951. He was an excellent fielder, usually at slip but equally effective at gully or in the deep. He celebrated being captain of Northamptonshire (1958–61) by scoring 300 against his former county; it remains the record score for Northants and equalled the highest ever recorded against Surrey. He met with considerable success in Test cricket, scoring a valuable hundred in his first match overseas and adding other centuries in his first and last matches against Australia. He retired rather prematurely from first-class cricket after that season to devote himself to his public relations business but has seldom been far from cricket administration in the last two decades. In addition to managing the 1981–82 tour of India, he has served on MCC committees and been chairman of Surrey. As chairman of the TCCB since 1985, he has been splendidly progressive and his tireless, determined and skilful diplomacy was chiefly responsible for the ICC's unanimous agreement of a treaty to cover players' contact with South Africa.

NOTABLE FEATS

• *478* Shared record E v I 3rd-wkt stand of 169 with M.J.K. Smith.
• *490* Batted with a fractured knuckle in scoring 100 in his first Test v WI.
• *507* Twelfth England batsman to score 100 on debut v Australia.
• *511* Scored 137 in his final Test v Australia, the last 98 with a runner.
• Exceeded 1000 runs in a season 6 times, notably 1917 in 1959.
• Made record Northamptonshire score of 300 v Surrey at The Oval in 1958, sharing record Northants 6th-wkt stand of 376 with A. Lightfoot; it remains the County's highest partnership for any wicket.
• Scored 260* and shared record Northamptonshire 9th-wkt stand of 156 with S. Starkie v Lancashire at Northampton in 1955.

Ref	Series	V	T	Venue	Result	Batting 1st			Batting 2nd			Ct
						No	R	HO	No	R	HO	
457/345	1958	NZ	4	Manchester	W-I & 13	5	9	c	–	–	–	1
478/358	1959	I	5	Oval	W-I & 27	2	94	c	–	–	–	–
490/362	1959–60	WI	4	Georgetown	D	3	27	c	4	100	lbw	–
491/363			5	Port-of-Spain	D	4	22	c	5	13	lbw	–

Ref	Series	V	T	Venue	Result	Batting 1st No	R	HO	Batting 2nd No	R	HO	Ct
492/364	1960	SA	1	Birmingham	W-100	4	56	c	2	32	c	–
493/365			2	Lord's	W-I & 73	2	90	lbw	–	–	–	–
494/366			3	Nottingham	W-8w	1	30	b	1	16	*	1
495/367			4	Manchester	D	2	27	lbw	–	–	–	1
507/369	1961	A	1	Birmingham	D	2	59	c	2	112	b	–
508/370			2	Lord's	L-5w	2	48	lbw	2	8	c	–
509/371			3	Leeds	W-8w	2	35	lbw	2	6	b	–
510/372			4	Manchester	L-54	2	2	c	2	49	b	1
511/373			5	Oval	D	2	12	lbw	2	137	c	1

Career	M	I	NO	HS	R	Avge	100	50	Ct	St	Balls	R	W	Avge	BB	5w	10w	Rate
Test	13	22	1	137	984	46.85	3	4	5	–	6	2	0	–	–	–	–	–
F/c	260	407	65	300	14182	41.46	30	73	176	–	6243	3363	87	38.65	5-21	2	–	71.75

SUGG, Frank Howe

Yorkshire (1883)
Derbyshire (1884 to 1886)
Lancashire (1887 to 1899)

Wisden 1890
Born Ilkeston, Derbyshire 11 Jan 1862
Died Waterloo, Liverpool
29 May 1933

NOTABLE FEATS

- Exceeded 1000 runs in a season 5 times.
- Scored 220 for Lancashire v Gloucestershire at Bristol in 1896.

An uncomplicated all-round sportsman, Frank Sugg was a rugged middle-order batsman and a very sure-handed, fast-moving outfielder. Tall (6ft) and strongly built, he was a sharp-eyed natural hitter who relied mainly on the drive and the hoick over square-leg. He emulated James Southerton's feat, extremely rare in Victorian times, of playing for three counties. Derbyshire-born, he became yet another Test cricketer to make a dent in Yorkshire's boundary qualification. He then briefly assisted his native county before spending 13 summers with Lancashire. It was during his time at Old Trafford that he produced his best performances and gained two caps for England. Like Alan Oakman 68 years later, his entire Test career coincided with a brace of innings victories. In his quieter moments as a first-class umpire he could look back on a sporting kaleidoscope which encompassed captaining Sheffield Wednesday, Derby County and Burnley at soccer, weight-lifting, putting the shot, long distance swimming, reaching the final of the Liverpool amateur billiards championship, winning prizes galore for rifle shooting and holding the record for throwing a cricket ball.

Frank Sugg

Ref	Series	V	T	Venue	Result	Batting 1st No	R	HO	Batting 2nd No	R	HO	Ct
29/29	1888	A	2	Oval	W-I & 137	7	31	b	–	–	–	–
30/30			3	Manchester	W-I & 21	6	24	b	–	–	–	–

Career	M	I	NO	HS	R	Avge	100	50	Ct	St	Balls	R	W	Avge	BB	5w	10w	Rate
Test	2	2	0	31	55	27.50	–	–	–	–	–	–	–	–	–	–	–	–
F/c	305	515	30	220	11859	24.45	16	50	167	1	397	273	10	27.30	2-12	–	–	39.70

SUTCLIFFE, Herbert

Yorkshire (1919 to 1945)

Wisden 1920
TOURS
A 1924–25, 1928–29, 1932–33;
SA 1927–28; WI 1935–36 (Yorks);
NZ 1932–33
Born Summer Bridge, Harrogate,
Yorkshire 24 Nov 1894
Died Crosshills, Yorkshire 22 Jan 1978

NOTABLE FEATS

• 1000 runs in 9th Test (*161*) (12 inns); 2000 runs in 22nd Test (*174*) (33 inns); 3000 runs in 33rd Test (*194*) (52 inns); 4000 runs in 43rd Test (*223*) (68 inns).
• *153* Shared the first of 15 three-figure partnerships with J.B. Hobbs at the first attempt.
• *154* Shared stand of 268 with J.B. Hobbs which remains the 1st-wkt record for all Lord's Tests and was then the E v SA record.
• *158* His first opening stands against Australia with J.B. Hobbs realised 157 and 110.
• *159* With J.B. Hobbs achieved the first instance of a batting partnership enduring throughout a full day's Test match play; they remain the only England pair to achieve this feat. Their stand of 283 in 289 min remains the longest for the 1st wkt in this series. First to score 100 in each innings of a Test v Australia and the first Englishman to score 3 successive hundreds in Test cricket.
• *161* First to score 4 hundreds in one rubber of Test matches; it was his third 100 in successive Test innings at Melbourne. Completed 1000 runs in Tests in fewest innings (12) – since equalled.
• *162* His aggregate of 734 runs was the record for any rubber until 1928–29.
• *167* Shared 1st-wkt stand of 172 with J.B. Hobbs on a rain-affected pitch.
• *185* First to score hundreds in each innings of a Test twice.
• *220* His highest England innings of 194 overtook J.B. Hobbs's world record of 15 Test hundreds.
• Exceeded 1000 runs in a season 21 times – in succession (1919–39) – plus 3 times on tour, including 3000 on 3 occasions and 12 other instances of 2000.

Herbert Sutcliffe was an outstanding opening batsman whose remarkable technique and temperament enabled him to play long innings on the most difficult of pitches. It was his determination and unruffled calm that allowed him to achieve his record average for a season (96.96) in 1931, one of the wettest summers on record; the next highest average was the Nawab of Pataudi's 69.23. The greater the challenge the more resolute he became. He played every ball strictly on its merits, was always utterly composed and had a rare ability to shut out of his mind any disaster that might have occurred the previous ball. He played within his limits and possessed relentless concentration and an insatiable love of batting. His assessment of length was uncanny and he was an exceptional judge of a run. It was the latter skill which was such a feature of his partnerships with Hobbs; their extraordinary empathy frequently allowed them to sneak singles without calling. He lacked the classical elegance of 'The Master' but his pragmatic batting skills were second to none. Because of the First World War, during which he was commissioned in the Sherwood Foresters, he made his debut at the comparatively advanced age of 24. As if to reclaim lost time, he began by amassing the largest first-class aggregate ever achieved by a batsman in his first season, and went on to score at least 1000 runs in every season between the wars. In 14 consecutive summers (1922–35) he exceeded 2000 runs. He finished with the seventh-highest aggregate of runs and the sixth-highest tally of hundreds, including (much to Boycott's chagrin) the unassailable Yorkshire record of 112. His Test average of 60.73 is the highest by any England batsman playing 10 innings. He made his final appearances in 1945 before concentrating his mind with equal success on business. For three seasons (1959–61) he made a welcome return in the guise of an England selector. He was an avid reader and an extremely witty speaker.

Herbert Sutcliffe

NOTABLE FEATS *cont.*

- Leading batsman in 1930, 1931 (3006 runs, avge 96.96) and 1932 (3336 runs, avge 74.13). Amongst home batsmen his 1931 average has been exceeded only by G. Boycott.
- His 1839 runs in 1919 remains the record for a debut season.
- In 1932, when he made 14 hundreds, he scored 1193 runs in June and 1006 in August – the third of only 4 batsmen to score 1000 in separate months of same year.
- Scored 313 for Yorkshire v Essex at Leyton in 1932 sharing (then) world record 1st-wkt stand of 555 in 445 min with P. Holmes; it remains the highest stand for any wicket in Britain.
- Scored 15 other double centuries for Yorkshire and one for an England XI v The Rest.
- Shared in 6 1st-wkt stands of 300 and over (world record).
- Shared 69 three-figure 1st-wkt partnerships wih P. Holmes and 26 (15 in Tests) with J.B. Hobbs.
- Shared record Yorkshire 3rd-wkt stand of 323* with M. Leyland v Glamorgan at Huddersfield in 1928.
- Holds Yorkshire career records for most runs (38,561), most hundreds (112) and most instances of 1000 runs in a season (21); as well as their records for most runs (2883) and hundreds (12) in a season (1932).
- Scored hundreds in 4 consecutive innings twice (1931 and 1939), in addition to scoring 3 in successive innings in 1924–25, 1928 and 1931.
- Scored 100 in each innings of a match on 4 occasions: twice for England and twice for Yorkshire.
- Carried his bat through a completed innings on 7 occasions, including 6 for Yorkshire.
- Hit 10 sixes in his innings of 113 for Yorkshire v Northamptonshire at Kettering in 1933.

TEST NOTES

- *194* Retired hurt when 58* at 134–1 (2nd inns).

						Batting 1st			Batting 2nd			
Ref	Series	V	T	Venue	Result	No	R	HO	No	R	HO	Ct
153/139	1924	SA	1	Birmingham	W-I & 18	2	64	b	–	–	–	–
154/140			2	Lord's	W-I & 18	2	122	b	–	–	–	1
155/141			3	Leeds	W-9w	2	83	c	2	29	*	–
156/142			4	Manchester	D	–	–	–	–	–	–	–
157/143			5	Oval	D	2	5	c	–	–	–	1
158/144	1924–25	A	1	Sydney	L-193	2	59	c	2	115	c	–
159/145			2	Melbourne	L-81	2	176	b	2	127	b	–
160/146			3	Adelaide	L-11	6	33	c	2	59	c	1
161/147			4	Melbourne	W-I & 29	2	143	lbw	–	–	–	1
162/148			5	Sydney	L-307	2	22	c	2	0	b	–
163/149	1926	A	1	Nottingham	D	2	13	*	–	–	–	–
164/150			2	Lord's	D	2	82	b	–	–	–	5
165/151			3	Leeds	D	2	26	c	2	94	b	2
166/152			4	Manchester	D	2	20	c	–	–	–	–
167/153			5	Oval	W-289	2	76	b	2	161	b	1
168/154	1927–28	SA	1	Johannesburg[1]	W-10w	2	102	c	2	41	*	–
169/155			2	Cape Town	W-87	2	29	c	2	99	b	–
170/156			3	Durban[2]	D	2	25	b	2	8	c	–
171/157			4	Johannesburg[1]	L-4w	2	37	lbw	2	3	c	–
172/158			5	Durban[2]	L-8w	2	51	c	2	23	lbw	–
173/159	1928	WI	1	Lord's	W-I & 58	1	48	c	–	–	–	1
174/160			2	Manchester	W-I & 30	2	54	c	–	–	–	1
175/161			3	Oval	W-I & 71	2	63	b	–	–	–	–
176/162	1928–29	A	1	Brisbane[1]	W-675	2	38	c	2	32	c	–
177/163			2	Sydney	W-8w	2	11	c	–	–	–	–
178/164			3	Melbourne	W-3w	2	58	b	2	135	lbw	–
179/165			4	Adelaide	W-12	2	64	st	2	17	c	–
181/167	1929	SA	1	Birmingham	D	1	26	c	1	114	b	–
182/168			2	Lord's	D	1	100	c	1	10	c	–
183/169			3	Leeds	W-5w	1	37	c	1	4	c	1
184/170			4	Manchester	W-I & 32	1	9	b	–	–	–	1
185/171			5	Oval	D	2	104	b	2	109	*	–
194/180	1930	A	1	Nottingham	W-93	2	29	b	2	58	rh*	–
196/182			3	Leeds	D	2	32	c	2	28	*	–
197/183			4	Manchester	D	2	74	b	–	–	–	1
198/184			5	Oval	L-I & 39	2	161	c	2	54	c	1
210/191	1931	NZ	2	Oval	W-I & 26	1	117	st	–	–	–	–
211/192			3	Manchester	D	1	109	*	–	–	–	–
219/193	1932	I		Lord's	W-158	2	3	b	2	19	c	–
220/194	1932–33	A	1	Sydney	W-10w	1	194	lbw	1	1	*	–
221/195			2	Melbourne	L-111	1	52	c	1	33	b	1
222/196			3	Adelaide	W-338	1	9	c	1	7	c	–
223/197			4	Brisbane[2]	W-6w	2	86	lbw	2	2	c	–
224/198			5	Sydney	W-8w	2	56	c	–	–	–	–
225/199	1932–33	NZ	1	Christchurch	D	1	0	c	–	–	–	–
226/200			2	Auckland	D	1	24	c	–	–	–	–
227/201	1933	WI	1	Lord's	W-I & 27	2	21	c	–	–	–	1
228/202			2	Manchester	D	2	20	ro	–	–	–	1
233/207	1934	A	1	Nottingham	L-238	2	62	c	2	24	c	–
234/208			2	Lord's	W-I & 38	2	20	lbw	–	–	–	2
235/209			3	Manchester	D	2	63	c	2	69	*	–
237/211			5	Oval	L-562	2	38	c	2	28	c	–
242/216	1935	SA	1	Nottingham	D	1	61	lbw	–	–	–	–
243/217			2	Lord's	L-157	2	3	lbw	2	38	lbw	–

Career	M	I	NO	HS	R	Avge	100	50	Ct	St	Balls	R	W	Avge	BB	5w	10w	Rate
Test	54	84	9	194	4555	60.73	16	23	23	–	–	–	–	–	–	–	–	–
F/c	747	1088	123	313	50138	51.95	149	228	469	–	882	527	10	52.70	2-16	–	–	88.20

H. SUTCLIFFE – TEST BATTING SUMMARY

Series	V	M	I	NO	HS	R	Avge	100	50
1924	SA	5	5	1	122	303	75.75	1	2
1924–25	A	5	9	–	176	734	81.55	4	2
1926	A	5	7	1	161	472	78.66	1	3
1927–28	SA	5	10	1	102	418	46.44	1	2
1928	WI	3	3	–	63	165	55.00	–	2
1928–29	A	4	7	–	135	355	50.71	1	2
1929	SA	5	9	1	114	513	64.12	4	–
1930	A	4	7	2	161	436	87.20	1	3
1931	NZ	2	2	1	117	226	226.00	2	–
1932	I	1	2	–	19	22	11.00	–	–
1932–33	A	5	9	1	194	440	55.00	1	3
1932–33	NZ	2	2	–	24	24	12.00	–	–
1933	WI	2	2	–	21	41	20.50	–	–
1934	A	4	7	1	69*	304	50.66	–	3
1935	SA	2	3	–	61	102	34.00	–	1
	A	27	46	5	194	2741	66.85	8	16
	SA	17	27	3	122	1336	55.66	6	5
	WI	5	5	–	63	206	41.20	–	2
	NZ	4	4	1	117	250	83.33	2	–
	I	1	2	–	19	22	11.00	–	–
Home		33	47	7	161	2584	64.60	9	14
Overseas		21	37	2	194	1971	56.31	7	9
Totals		54	84	9	194	4555	60.73	16	23

SWETMAN, Roy

Surrey (1954 to 1961)
Nottinghamshire (1966 to 1967)
Gloucestershire (1972 to 1974)

TOURS
A 1958–59; SA 1962–63 (Cav/Cwlth); WI 1959–60; NZ 1958–59; I 1962–63 (Cwlth); P 1955–56; Z 1959–60 (Surrey)
Born Westminster, London 25 Oct 1933

NOTABLE FEATS

- Held 6 catches in an innings for Surrey twice in 1960: v Kent at The Oval and v Somerset at Taunton. Also dismissed 6 Rhodesian batsmen in an innings for the Cavaliers at Salisbury in 1962–63.

Just 5ft 6in high, Roy Swetman more than made up in confidence what he lacked in inches. An outstanding schoolboy wicket-keeper batsman, he made his debut for the Combined Services during his two years of conscription and his enthusiasm prompted Arthur McIntyre to take an early retirement. Like Jimmy Clitheroe, he managed to retain a totally undeserved appearance of boyish innocence into middle age. When he was selected for Australia in 1958, the interviewer who asked if his mother would miss him at Christmas was startled when he replied, 'Yes, I think my wife will too!' A restless and unpredictable spirit, he twice interrupted his retirement to become the second of five cricketers to be capped by three first-class counties.

Roy Swetman catches O'Neill off Laker during the Sydney Test, 1958–59.

Ref	Series	V	T	Venue	Result	Batting 1st			Batting 2nd			Fielding 1st				Fielding 2nd			
						No	R	HO	No	R	HO	Ct	St	Byes	Balls	Ct	St	Byes	Balls
466/349†	1958–59	A	3	Sydney	D	7	41	c	7	5	lbw	1	–	5	1026	–	–	6	200
468/351†			5	Melbourne	L-9w	7	1	c	7	9	lbw	2	–	5	805	–	–	0	103
472/352†	1958–59	NZ	1	Christchurch	W-I & 99	8	9	b	–	–	–	1	1	5	437	1	–	1	434
473/353†			2	Auckland	D	8	17	ro	–	–	–	2	–	7	537	–	–	–	–
476/356†	1959	I	3	Leeds	W-I & 173	8	19	*	–	–	–	4	–	0	413	1	–	0	334
477/357†			4	Manchester	W-171	9	9	c	10	21	*	1	–	0	474	1	–	8	871
478/358†			5	Oval	W-I & 27	8	65	c	–	–	–	2	–	1	513	2	–	4	570
487/359†	1959–60	WI	1	Bridgetown	D	8	45	c	–	–	–	1	–	8	1438	–	–	–	–
488/360†			2	Port-of-Spain	W-256	8	1	lbw	8	0	lbw	1	–	0	411	2	–	11	809
489/361†			3	Kingston	D	8	0	b	8	5	lbw	1	–	6	937	–	–	9	378
490/362†			4	Georgetown	D	8	4	lbw	9	3	c	1	1	4	1032	–	–	–	–

Career	M	I	NO	HS	R	Avge	100	50	Ct	St	Balls	R	W	Avge	BB	5w	10w	Rate
Test	11	17	2	65	254	16.93	–	1	24	2	–	–	–	–	–	–	–	–
F/c	286	411	73	115	6495	19.21	2	22	531	66	90	69	1	69.00	1-10	–	–	90.00

TATE
Frederick William

Sussex (1887 to 1905)

Born Brighton, Sussex 24 Jul 1867
Died Burgess Hill, Sussex 24 Feb 1943

It is ironic that, having provided yeoman service to Sussex as a stock bowler for almost two decades, Fred Tate should be remembered for his vital dropped catch and final dismissal in one of the closest finishes in Test history. A right-arm slow to medium-pace bowler then enjoying his most successful season, he was chosen on the morning of that fateful match, his 35th birthday, in preference to George Hirst because of the rain-affected conditions. A very safe slip, he was sent by MacLaren to the unaccustomed position of square-leg and promptly dropped Joe Darling, a miss which led to a crucial stand of 48. With heavy storms imminent, England needed 124 for the victory which would level the series. They fared badly on a treacherous surface and just one wicket remained with 8 runs still needed when Tate nervously joined Rhodes after a 45-minute break for rain. He edged a leg-side boundary off his first ball but was bowled by his fourth to give Australia what is still the narrowest victory by a team fielding last. In an understandably emotional prophecy, he said: 'I've a little lad at home who'll make up for that.' He was referring to the seven-year-old Maurice.

NOTABLE FEATS

- Took 100 wickets in a season 5 times, notably 180 in 1902.
- Took 9 for 73 for Sussex v Leicestershire at Leicester in 1902.
- Returned a match analysis of 15 for 68 for Sussex v Middlesex at Lord's in 1902.
- Hat-trick for Sussex v Surrey at The Oval in 1901.
- Bowled in an unchanged partnership throughout both completed innings of a match twice (1897 and 1902).

Fred Tate

					Batting 1st			Batting 2nd				Bowling 1st			Bowling 2nd		
Ref	Series	V	T Venue	Result	No	R	HO	No	R	HO	Ct	Balls	R	W	Balls	R	W
73/73	1902	A	4 Manchester	L-3	11	5	*	11	4	b	2	66	44	0	30	7	2

Career	M	I	NO	HS	R	Avge	100	50	Ct	St	Balls	R	W	Avge	BB	5w	10w	Rate
Test	1	2	1	5*	9	9.00	–	–	2	–	96	51	2	25.50	2-7	–	–	48.00
F/c	320	458	150	84	2952	9.58	–	6	236	–	67443	28691	1331	21.55	9-73	104	29	50.67

TATE
Maurice William

Sussex (1912 to 1937)

Wisden 1924
TOURS
A 1924–25, 1928–29, 1932–33;
SA 1930–31; NZ 1932–33; I/SL 1926–27
Born Brighton, Sussex 30 May 1895
Died Wadhurst, Sussex 18 May 1956

Maurice Tate more than compensated for his father's misfortune against the 1902 Australians by becoming one of England's greatest all-rounders. A genial, lion-hearted right-arm fast-medium bowler, his massive build, enormous feet, broad smile and open shirt made him a cartoonist's dream during his seven years as an automatic choice for England. Originally a slow off-spinner in the family mould, he developed his faster method after a chance net during which he bowled his captain, Arthur Gilligan, several times with a quicker ball. His short approach and smooth, economical action enabled him to undertake long spells. He swung the ball away devastatingly late and his powerful follow-through gave him deceptive nip off the pitch. He was the first bowler to exploit the use of the ball's seam, then much flatter and more thinly stitched than its modern counterpart. Besides maintaining an accurate length and being willing to toil away for hours, often in hot or unfavourable conditions, he managed to communicate his obvious enjoyment of being able to play cricket for a living. Alec Bedser, a very similar bowler in method and appearance, has often been compared to him. Those qualified to judge usually gave Tate the vote by a

Maurice Tate

narrow margin and it should be remembered that the Sussex man was also a front-line batsman capable of scoring 1713 runs and five hundreds in one season. A most entertaining player who delighted in six-hitting, his defensive technique allowed him successfully to open the Sussex innings and he shares the second-wicket record still. One of the most universally popular of cricketers, he appeared in 20 consecutive Tests against Australia.

NOTABLE FEATS

- 1000 runs in 33rd Test (*205*) (44 inns). 50 wickets in 9th Test (*161*); 100 wickets in 20th Test (*177*); 150 wickets in 37th Test (*210*).
- *153* Dismissed M.J. Susskind with his first ball in Test cricket and took 4 for 12 as South Africa were dismissed for 30 in 48 min off 75 balls; it remains the only Test innings in which no batsman reached double figures.
- *162* His total of 38 wickets remains the record for England in Australia.

NOTABLE FEATS *cont.*

- *205* Became the second player after W. Rhodes to complete the 'double' for England.
- Exceeded 1000 runs in a season 11 times (plus once on tour).
- Took 100 wickets in a season 13 times (plus once on tour), including 200 in 3 successive seasons. In 1925 he completed his 100 wickets on 17 June – the fifth-fastest on record.
- Completed the 'double' 8 times in successive years (1922–29) plus once on tour (MCC in India and Ceylon in 1926–27). They include three consecutive instances of 1000 runs and 200 wickets in a season (1923–25); A.E. Trott (twice) and A.S. Kennedy are the only others to have achieved this particular 'double'.
- Holds Sussex career records for most wickets (2211) and most instances of 100 wickets in a season (13); also the record for most wickets in a season (198 in 1925).
- Shared in two record Sussex stands v Northamptonshire at Hove: 385 (2nd wkt) with E.H. Bowley in 1921 (when he scored 203) and 255 (6th wkt) with K.S. Duleepsinhji in 1930.
- Scored hundreds in 3 consecutive innings for Sussex in 1927.
- Scored 100 before lunch 3 times.
- Took 9 for 71 for Sussex v Middlesex at Lord's in 1926.
- Three hat-tricks: two for Sussex, v Middlesex at Lord's in 1926 and v Northamptonshire at Peterborough in 1934; and one for the Rest of England v Lancashire at The Oval in 1926.
- Took 4 wickets in 5 balls for England v The Rest at Lord's in 1923.
- Bowled in an unchanged partnership with A.F. Wensley throughout both completed Glamorgan innings for Sussex at Hove in 1925.
- Achieved the match 'double' for Sussex twice (1920 and 1927).

						Batting 1st			Batting 2nd				Bowling 1st			Bowling 2nd		
Ref	Series	V	T	Venue	Result	No	R	HO	No	R	HO	Ct	Balls	R	W	Balls	R	W
153/139	1924	SA	1	Birmingham	W-I & 18	8	19	c	–	–	–	1	36	12	4	304	103	4
154/140			2	Lord's	W-I & 18	–	–	–	–	–	–	1	204	62	2	160	43	2
155/141			3	Leeds	W-9w	7	29	c	–	–	–	1	102	42	6	180	64	3
156/142			4	Manchester	D	–	–	–	–	–	–	–	144	34	3	–	–	–
157/143			5	Oval	D	7	50	b	–	–	–	–	174	64	3	–	–	–
158/144	1924–25	A	1	Sydney	L-193	8	7	c	8	0	c	–	441	130	6	271	98	5
159/145			2	Melbourne	L-81	9	34	b	11	0	b	–	360	142	3	267	99	6
160/146			3	Adelaide	L-11	2	27	c	8	21	b	1	144	43	2	80	17	0
161/147			4	Melbourne	W-I & 29	10	8	c	–	–	–	–	128	70	2	205	75	5
162/148			5	Sydney	L-307	9	25	b	9	33	c	–	317	92	4	315	115	5
163/149	1926	A	1	Nottingham	D	–	–	–	–	–	–	–	–	–	–	–	–	–
164/150			2	Lord's	D	–	–	–	–	–	–	–	300	111	2	150	38	1
165/151			3	Leeds	D	8	5	st	–	–	–	–	306	99	4	–	–	–
166/152			4	Manchester	D	–	–	–	–	–	–	–	218	88	2	–	–	–
167/153			5	Oval	W-289	9	23	b	9	33	*	1	223	40	3	54	12	1
173/159	1928	WI	1	Lord's	W-I & 58	8	22	c	–	–	–	–	162	54	2	132	28	2
174/160			2	Manchester	W-I & 30	7	28	b	–	–	–	1	210	68	1	54	10	1
175/161			3	Oval	W-I & 71	8	54	c	–	–	–	–	126	59	4	78	27	3
176/162	1928–29	A	1	Brisbane[1]	W-675	8	26	c	8	20	c	1	126	50	3	66	26	2
177/163			2	Sydney	W-8w	9	25	lbw	9	4	c	–	126	29	0	276	99	4
178/164			3	Melbourne	W-3w	9	21	c	7	0	ro	–	276	87	2	282	70	2
179/165			4	Adelaide	W-12	10	2	b	9	47	lbw	2	252	77	4	222	75	0
180/166			5	Melbourne	L-5w	10	15	c	8	54	c	2	372	108	0	228	76	0
181/167	1929	SA	1	Birmingham	D	8	40	c	–	–	–	–	264	65	3	96	43	0
182/168			2	Lord's	D	7	15	c	7	100	*	–	234	108	3	66	27	1
183/169			3	Leeds	W-5w	8	3	c	7	24	*	–	156	40	2	156	50	1
194/180	1930	A	1	Nottingham	W-93	9	13	b	7	24	c	–	114	20	3	300	69	3
195/181			2	Lord's	L-7w	8	54	c	8	10	c	–	384	148	1	78	21	1
196/182			3	Leeds	D	9	22	c	–	–	–	–	234	124	5	–	–	–
197/183			4	Manchester	D	7	15	c	–	–	–	–	180	39	1	–	–	–

Ref	Series	V	T Venue	Result	Batting 1st No	R	HO	Batting 2nd No	R	HO	Ct	Bowling 1st Balls	R	W	Bowling 2nd Balls	R	W
198/184			5 Oval	L-I & 39	8	10	st	8	0	ro	–	391	153	1	–	–	–
204/185	1930–31	SA	1 Johannesburg[1]	L-28	8	8	c	8	28	c	–	74	20	2	108	47	1
205/186			2 Cape Town	D	8	15	c	9	3	lbw	–	258	79	3	–	–	–
206/187			3 Durban[2]	D	–	–	–	–	–	–	–	162	33	2	54	12	1
207/188			4 Johannesburg[1]	D	10	26	c	6	38	c	–	162	46	2	132	52	2
208/189			5 Durban[2]	D	8	50	b	5	24	*	–	132	35	1	54	17	0
210/191	1931	NZ	2 Oval	W-I & 26	–	–	–	–	–	–	–	108	15	1	126	22	3
225/199	1932–33	NZ	1 Christchurch	D	9	10	*	–	–	–	–	222	42	2	18	5	0
245/219	1935	SA	4 Manchester	D	9	34	c	7	0	b	–	135	67	2	54	20	0

Career	M	I	NO	HS	R	Avge	100	50	Ct	St	Balls	R	W	Avge	BB	5w	10w	Rate
Test	39	52	5	100*	1198	25.48	1	5	11	–	12523	4055	155	26.16	6-42	7	1	80.79
F/c	679	970	103	203	21717	25.04	23	93	284	–	151149	50571	2784	18.16	9-71	195	44	54.29

M. W. TATE – TEST SUMMARY

Series	V	M	I	NO	HS	R	Avge	100	50	Balls	R	W	Avge	BB	5w	10w	Rate
1924	SA	5	3	–	50	98	32.66	–	1	1304	424	27	15.70	6-42	1	–	48.29
1924–25	A	5	9	–	34	155	17.22	–	–	2528	881	38	23.18	6-99	5	1	66.52
1926	A	5	3	1	33*	61	30.50	–	–	1251	388	13	29.84	4-99	–	–	96.23
1928	WI	3	3	–	54	104	34.66	–	1	762	246	13	18.92	4-59	–	–	58.61
1928–29	A	5	10	–	54	214	21.40	–	1	2226	697	17	41.00	4-77	–	–	130.94
1929	SA	3	5	2	100*	182	60.66	1	–	972	333	10	33.30	3-65	–	–	97.20
1930	A	5	8	–	54	148	18.50	–	1	1681	574	15	38.26	5-124	1	–	112.06
1930–31	SA	5	8	1	50	192	27.42	–	1	1136	341	14	24.35	3-79	–	–	81.14
1931	NZ	1	–	–	–	–	–	–	–	234	37	4	9.25	3-22	–	–	58.50
1932–33	NZ	1	1	1	10*	10	–	–	–	240	47	2	23.50	2-42	–	–	120.00
1935	SA	1	2	–	34	34	17.00	–	–	189	87	2	43.50	2-67	–	–	94.50
	A	20	30	1	54	578	19.93	–	2	7686	2540	83	30.60	6-99	6	1	92.60
	SA	14	18	3	100*	506	33.73	1	2	3601	1185	53	22.35	6-42	1	–	67.94
	WI	3	3	–	54	104	34.66	–	1	762	246	13	18.92	4-59	–	–	58.61
	NZ	2	1	1	10*	10	–	–	–	474	84	6	14.00	3-22	–	–	79.00
Home		23	24	3	100*	627	29.85	1	3	6393	2089	84	24.86	6-42	2	–	76.10
Overseas		16	28	2	54	571	21.96	–	2	6130	1966	71	27.69	6-99	5	1	86.33
Totals		39	52	5	100*	1198	25.48	1	5	12523	4055	155	26.16	6-42	7	1	80.79

TATTERSALL, Roy

Lancashire (1948 to 1960)

TOURS
A 1950–51; NZ 1950–51; I/SL 1951–52; P 1951–52
Born Tonge Moor, Bolton, Lancashire
17 Aug 1922

Roy Tattersall was a very tall (6ft 3in) and lean off-break bowler who was unfortunate to be an exact contemporary of a certain James Laker. Although not a robust tweaker of the ball, his immensely high action, allied to subtle changes of flight, pace and angle, posed searching problems and bore especially rich fruit in 1950 when he took the national averages by storm. Surprisingly omitted from the original party for that winter's tour to Australia, he was eventually summoned in an emergency. There he made his international debut, bowled economically and used his stubborn left-handed batting to great effect in sharing a decisive last-wicket stand of 74 with Reg Simpson in the final Test.

NOTABLE FEATS

- 50 wickets in 13th Test (*342*).
- *335* Took 9 of the 14 wickets which fell on the second day.
- *342* Took 3 wickets with his first 8 balls of the match.
- Took 100 wickets in a season 8 times, notably 193 at 13.59 in 1950 when he headed the national averages.
- Took 9 for 40 (including his only hat-trick) for Lancashire v Nottinghamshire at Manchester in 1953.
- Took 7 wickets in 19 balls for Lancashire v Nottinghamshire at Manchester in 1953.

Ref	Series	V	T	Venue	Result	Batting 1st No	R	HO	Batting 2nd No	R	HO	Ct	Bowling 1st Balls	R	W	Bowling 2nd Balls	R	W
330/283	1950–51	A	4	Adelaide	L-274	9	0	c	8	6	c	–	205	95	3	216	116	1
331/284			5	Melbourne	W-8w	11	10	b	–	–	–	1	88	40	0	40	6	0
332/285	1950–51	NZ	1	Christchurch	D	9	2	b	–	–	–	–	96	48	1	–	–	–
333/286			2	Wellington	W-6w	11	1	b	–	–	–	–	90	16	1	126	44	6
334/287	1951	SA	1	Nottingham	L-71	–	–	–	11	0	*	1	282	80	1	138	56	3
335/288			2	Lord's	W-10w	11	1	b	–	–	–	1	168	52	7	194	49	5
336/289			3	Manchester	W-9w	10	1	c	–	–	–	1	108	29	1	108	41	1
337/290			4	Leeds	D	10	4	c	–	–	–	1	360	83	1	96	13	0
338/291			5	Oval	W-4w	11	0	*	–	–	–	–	84	26	1	30	10	1
339/292	1951–52	I	1	Delhi	D	10	4	*	–	–	–	–	318	95	2	–	–	–
340/293			2	Bombay[2]	D	10	10	*	–	–	–	–	204	112	3	120	55	2
341/294			3	Calcutta	D	11	5	*	–	–	–	1	288	104	4	24	4	0
342/295			4	Kanpur	W-8w	11	2	st	–	–	–	–	126	48	6	167	77	2
343/296			5	Madras[1]	L-I & 8	11	2	*	11	0	*	–	234	94	2	–	–	–
372/301	1953	A	1	Nottingham	D	11	2	b	–	–	–	2	138	59	0	30	22	3
387/311	1954	P	1	Lord's	D	–	–	–	–	–	–	–	90	12	1	60	27	0

Career	M	I	NO	HS	R	Avge	100	50	Ct	St	Balls	R	W	Avge	BB	5w	10w	Rate
Test	16	17	7	10*	50	5.00	–	–	8	–	4228	1513	58	26.08	7-52	4	1	72.89
F/c	328	369	151	58	2040	9.35	–	1	146	–	70984	24692	1369	18.03	9-40	99	18	51.85

R. TATTERSALL – TEST BOWLING SUMMARY

Series	V	M	Balls	R	W	Avge	BB	5w	10w	Rate
1950–51	A	2	549	257	4	64.25	3-95	–	–	137.25
1950–51	NZ	2	312	108	8	13.50	6-44	1	–	39.00
1951	SA	5	1568	439	21	20.90	7-52	2	1	74.66
1951–52	I	5	1481	589	21	28.04	6-48	1	–	70.52
1953	A	1	168	81	3	27.00	3-22	–	–	56.00
1954	P	1	150	39	1	39.00	1-12	–	–	150.00
	A	3	717	338	7	48.28	3-22	–	–	102.42
	SA	5	1568	439	21	20.90	7-52	2	1	74.66
	NZ	2	312	108	8	13.50	6-44	1	–	39.00
	I	5	1481	589	21	28.04	6-48	1	–	70.52
	P	1	150	39	1	39.00	1-12	–	–	150.00
Home		7	1886	559	25	22.36	7-52	2	1	75.44
Overseas		9	2342	954	33	28.90	6-44	2	–	70.96
Totals		16	4228	1513	58	26.08	7-52	4	1	72.89

Roy Tatersall

TAVARÉ
Christopher James

Kent (1974 to 1988)
Oxford University (1975 to 1977)

TOURS
A 1982–83; NZ 1983–84; I/SL 1981–82; P 1983–84
Born Orpington, Kent 27 Oct 1954

In his formative years at Sevenoaks School and Oxford, Chris Tavaré was a graceful strokemaker with a very correct technique. Tall (6ft 1½in) and slim, he used his long reach to good effect and was a fluent driver and cutter. Soon after he resumed his regular career with Kent after three eminently successful years in The Parks, it was obvious that he had the potential to become an established Test batsman. His chance came against the all-conquering West Indies pace attack in 1980 when he was asked to fill the problem No. 3 spot in England's brittle order. His initial failure in this supreme task produced an overhaul of technique so drastic that, when he returned, he adopted a totally defensive approach which resulted in some ludicrously slow scoring. He celebrated his recall (Test *907*) by spending 710 minutes over a total of 147 runs; 287 minutes for 69 followed by 423

NOTABLE FEATS

- 1000 runs in 16th Test (*932*) (28 inns).
- *957* Shared record E v NZ 1st-wkt stand of 223 with G. Fowler – first instance since 1960 of England openers both scoring hundreds in the same inns.
- Exceeded 1000 runs in a season 12 times.
- Holds Kent record for most catches by a fielder in a season (48 in 1978).

TEST NOTES

- *907* Scored 78 in 423 min, including the slowest 50 in English first-class cricket (306 min).
- *916* Took 332 min to score 35. Bowled in 2nd inns: 0 for 11 (12 balls).
- *932* Recorded the second-slowest 50 in all first-class cricket (350 min). By taking 67 min to score his first run and another 60 min on 24 he became the first batsman in any grade of cricket to fail to score during 2 separate hours of an inns.
- *938* Spent 90 min on 66 in 1st inns and took 63 min to score first run in the 2nd inns.
- *957* Retired hurt when 22* at 73–3 (1st inns); resumed at 116–5.
- *994* Bowled in 2nd inns: 0 for 0 (18 balls).

Chris Tavaré hits out against India at The Oval, 1982; Kirmani is behind the stumps.

minutes for 78 formed the substance of nightmares. He even earned the accolade of becoming the only batsman in the entire charted history of cricket to include two runless periods of an hour or more in the same first-class innings. Hour upon hour of charting his metronomic half-cock defensive prods did, during one eminently forgettable display, allow the commitment to memory of the 50 states comprising America and in alphabetical order. Kent's committee earned no sympathy for his brutal dismissal after two years of captaincy (1983–84) but shrewdly he waited until after his benefit before moving to Somerset. It was significant that his new county had a higher regard for his qualities of leadership and appointed him vice-captain within a fortnight of his signing a contract.

						Batting 1st			Batting 2nd			
Ref	Series	V	T	Venue	Result	No	R	HO	No	R	HO	Ct
880/557	1980	WI	1	Nottingham	L-2w	3	13	b	3	4	c	1
881/558			2	Lord's	D	3	42	c	3	6	lbw	1
907/571	1981	A	5	Manchester	W-103	3	69	c	3	78	c	–
908/572			6	Oval	D	3	24	c	3	8	c	1
912/573	1981–82	I	1	Bombay[3]	L-138	3	56	c	3	0	c	2
913/574			2	Bangalore	D	3	22	lbw	3	31	c	–
914/575			3	Delhi	D	3	149	b	–	–	–	–
915/576			4	Calcutta	D	3	7	c	3	25	ro	2
916/577			5	Madras[1]	D	2	35	c	–	–	–	1
917/578			6	Kanpur	D	2	24	b	–	–	–	–
921/579	1981–82	SL		Colombo SO	W-7w	3	0	b	3	85	st	–
928/580	1982	I	1	Lord's	W-7w	2	4	c	2	3	b	1
929/581			2	Manchester	D	2	57	b	–	–	–	1
930/582			3	Oval	D	2	39	b	2	75	*	–
931/583	1982	P	1	Birmingham	W-113	2	54	b	2	17	c	1
932/584			2	Lord's	L-10w	2	8	b	2	82	c	1
933/585			3	Leeds	W-3w	1	22	c	1	33	c	1
938/586	1982–83	A	1	Perth	D	2	89	c	2	9	c	–
939/587			2	Brisbane[2]	L-7w	1	1	c	1	13	c	1
940/588			3	Adelaide	L-8w	1	1	c	1	0	c	–
941/589			4	Melbourne	W-3	3	89	c	3	0	b	1
942/590			5	Sydney	D	2	0	b	2	16	lbw	–
957/591	1983	NZ	1	Oval	W-189	2	45	ro	2	109	c	–
958/592			2	Leeds	L-5w	2	69	c	2	23	b	1
959/593			3	Lord's	W-127	1	51	b	1	16	c	–
960/594			4	Nottingham	W-165	1	4	c	1	13	c	1
975/595	1983–84	NZ	1	Wellington	D	1	9	b	1	36	*	–
976/596			2	Christchurch	L-I & 132	2	3	c	2	6	c	1
993/605	1984	WI	5	Oval	L-172	4	16	c	3	49	c	2
994/606	1984	SL		Lord's	D	3	14	c	–	–	–	–

Career	M	I	NO	HS	R	Avge	100	50	Ct	St	Balls	R	W	Avge	BB	5w	10w	Rate
Test	30	55	2	149	1753	33.07	2	12	20	–	30	11	0	–	–	–	–	–
F/c	328	552	59	168*	18539	37.60	35	102	328	–	665	525	5	105.00	1-3	–	–	133.00

C. J. TAVARÉ – TEST BATTING SUMMARY

Series	V	M	I	NO	HS	R	Avge	100	50
1980	WI	2	4	–	42	65	16.25	–	–
1981	A	2	4	–	78	179	44.75	–	2
1981–82	I	6	9	–	149	349	38.77	1	1
1981–82	SL	1	2	–	85	85	42.50	–	1
1982	I	3	5	1	75*	178	44.50	–	2
1982	P	3	6	–	82	216	36.00	–	2
1982–83	A	5	10	–	89	218	21.80	–	2
1983	NZ	4	8	–	109	330	41.25	1	2
1983–84	NZ	2	4	1	36*	54	18.00	–	–
1984	WI	1	2	–	49	65	32.50	–	–
1984	SL	1	1	–	14	14	14.00	–	–

Series	V	M	I	NO	HS	R	Avge	100	50
	A	7	14	–	89	397	28.35	–	4
	WI	3	6	–	49	130	21.66	–	–
	NZ	6	12	1	109	384	34.90	1	2
	I	9	14	1	149	527	40.53	1	3
	P	3	6	–	82	216	36.00	–	2
	SL	2	3	–	85	99	33.00	–	1
Home		16	30	1	109	1047	36.10	1	8
Overseas		14	25	1	149	706	29.41	1	4
Totals		30	55	2	149	1753	33.07	2	12

TAYLOR, Kenneth

Yorkshire (1953 to 1968)
Auckland (1963–64)

TOUR I 1963–64 (Swanton)
Born Primrose Hill, Huddersfield, Yorkshire 21 Aug 1935

NOTABLE FEATS

- Exceeded 1000 runs in a season 6 times.
- Scored 203* for Yorkshire v Warwickshire at Birmingham in 1961.

TEST NOTES

- *563* Bowled in 1st inns: 0 for 6 (12 balls).

A particularly esoteric conundrum would be: 'Which England Test cricketer completed his formal training as an artist at the Slade School of Fine Art?' The answer, as of course you knew, is Ken Taylor whose Yorkshire career spanned 15 years. A confident, fluent batsman, equally effective opening or in the middle-order, he surprisingly failed to make any impression during his three international outings. This deprived larger audiences of enjoying his outstanding ability as a swift outfielder with an exceptionally long and powerful throw. Although not rated by its perpetrator, his gentle right-arm medium-pace swing bowling once snared six victims in an innings. He played for Norfolk in 1972 while he was a master at Gresham's. Of average height (5ft 8in) and extremely fit, his footballing skills were put to good use in his early years first by Huddersfield Town and later by Bradford. Further family versatility was shown by his brother Jeff, who managed to combine the unlikely professions of pop guitarist and footballer, and his son Nick, who tried his talent as a fast bowler with three first-class counties before opting for a career in night-club management. [*Illus. p.* 329]

						Batting 1st			Batting 2nd			
Ref	Series	V	T	Venue	Result	No	R	HO	No	R	HO	Ct
474/354	1959	I	1	Nottingham	W-I & 59	2	24	lbw	–	–	–	1
475/355			2	Lord's	W-8w	2	6	c	2	3	lbw	–
563/407	1964	A	3	Leeds	L-7w	6	9	c	8	15	b	–

Career	M	I	NO	HS	R	Avge	100	50	Ct	St	Balls	R	W	Avge	BB	5w	10w	Rate
Test	3	5	0	24	57	11.40	–	–	1	–	12	6	0	–	–	–	–	–
F/c	313	524	36	203*	13053	26.74	16	68	150	–	10628	3763	131	28.72	6-75	1	–	81.12

TAYLOR, Leslie Brian

Leicestershire (1977 to date)
Natal (1981–82 to 1983–84)

TOURS
SA 1981–82 (SAB); WI 1985–86; Z 1980–81 (Leics XI)
Born Earl Shilton, Leicestershire 25 Oct 1953

NOTABLE FEATS

- Hat-trick for Leicestershire v Middlesex at Leicester in 1979.

Tall (6ft 3½in) and powerfully built, Les Taylor had the ideal physique for a right-arm fast-medium bowler, even a mining background. Although he was 23 when he made his first-class debut for Leicestershire, he soon made his mark as an accurate seam bowler who did enough with the ball to remove good batsmen. He headed his County's averages with 70 Championship wickets in 1981 but, ignored for England's winter tour, earned himself a three-year suspension from Test cricket by joining the clandestine expedition to South Africa. He bowled usefully in his two Tests against Australia in 1985, taking important wickets including the final Ashes-winning caught-and-bowled. A swarthy black-haired character with a sinister moustache, he was dubbed 'Lord Lucan' during his tour of the Caribbean, so rare and fleeting were his appearances.

Les Taylor

Ref	Series	V	T	Venue	Result	Batting 1st No	R	HO	Batting 2nd No	R	HO	Ct	Bowling 1st Balls	R	W	Bowling 2nd Balls	R	W
1021/616	1985	A	5	Birmingham	W-I & 118	–	–	–	–	–	–	–	156	78	1	78	27	0
1022/617			6	Oval	W-I & 94	11	1	*	–	–	–	1	78	39	1	69	34	2

Career	M	I	NO	HS	R	Avge	100	50	Ct	St	Balls	R	W	Avge	BB	5w	10w	Rate
Test	2	1	1	1*	1	–	–	–	1	–	381	178	4	44.50	2-34	–	–	95.25
F/c	203	181	78	60	1001	9.71	–	1	48	–	29803	13743	557	24.67	7-28	18	1	53.50

TAYLOR
Robert William MBE

Derbyshire (1961 to 1984)

Wisden 1977
TOURS
A 1970–71, 1971–72 (RW), 1974–75, 1978–79, 1979–80, 1982–83; SA 1975–76 (Int W); WI 1973–74; NZ 1970–71, 1974–75, 1977–78, 1983–84; I 1979–80, 1981–82; P 1977–78, 1983–84; SL 1969–70, 1981–82
Born Stoke-on-Trent, Staffordshire
17 Jul 1941

If a role model were required for the ideal sportsman, the complete professional who was supreme in his particular sporting niche and whose public and private image was beyond reproach, it would be hard to think of anyone to challenge Bob Taylor. As a wicket-keeper he was a perfectionist who maintained a consistency of form and fitness second to none. His technical expertise whether standing up to spin or back to the faster men never ceased to amaze. Such was his positioning that he seldom needed to dive and was rarely seen sprawled on the ground; his timing was so precise that fielders close to him rarely heard the ball meet his gloves. Graduating to the Derbyshire team via Staffordshire (1958–60) he quietly learned his craft and reached maturity just as a Kentish imp some five years his junior was receiving rave notices and, in due course, selection for England. For seven years Taylor was condemned to the role of understudy on winter tours; while there was little to choose between their keeping, the Kent player's brilliant batting gained preference. If Mr Packer had not suddenly appeared and waved his magic wand, Taylor's career might well have ended with the one consolation appearance he was given on Ray Illingworth's antipodean tour. When Knott had made himself ineligible for selection England were incredibly lucky to have in reserve a craftsman of such high standard. One of nature's gentlemen, he earned his nickname 'Chat' from his eagerness to socialise at functions and talk attentively to anyone. He was a competent lower-order batsman with a staunch defence and a repertoire of elegant strokes and, until he abandoned the role because he thought it was affect-

Bob Taylor catches Australia's Geoff Lawson off Bob Willis on the final day of the epic Leeds Test, 1981, and in the process breaks the world record for catches in first-class cricket.

Ref	Series	V	T	Venue	Result	Batting 1st No	R	HO	Batting 2nd No	R	HO	Fielding 1st Ct	St	Byes	Balls	Fielding 2nd Ct	St	Byes	Balls
685/465†	1970–71	NZ	1	Christchurch	W-8w	7	4	st	–	–	–	2	1	9	302	–	–	6	779
814/531†	1977–78	P	1	Lahore[2]	D	8	32	c	–	–	–	1	1	1	1064	1	–	0	224
815/532†			2	Hyderabad	D	7	0	b	–	–	–	1	–	4	694	1	–	13	652
816/533†			3	Karachi	D	7	36	lbw	7	18	*	1	–	2	760	–	–	–	–
817/534†	1977–78	NZ	1	Wellington	L-72	4	8	c	7	0	ro	4	–	12	702	–	–	2	355
818/535†			2	Christchurch	W-174	8	45	ro	–	–	–	1	–	4	743	1	–	0	216
819/536†			3	Auckland	D	7	16	b	–	–	–	1	–	5	846	2	–	6	944
825/537†	1978	P	1	Birmingham	W-I & 57	–	–	–	–	–	–	3	–	0	364	–	–	4	620
826/538†			2	Lord's	W-I & 120	8	10	c	–	–	–	1	–	0	216	3	–	1	401
827/539†			3	Leeds	D	7	2	c	–	–	–	1	–	0	634	–	–	–	–
828/540†	1978	NZ	1	Oval	W-7w	8	8	c	–	–	–	1	–	1	626	1	–	8	631
829/541†			2	Nottingham	W-I & 119	8	22	b	–	–	–	5	–	0	418	1	–	0	553
830/542†			3	Lord's	W-7w	7	1	lbw	–	–	–	1	1	4	859	3	–	0	223
834/543†	1978–79	A	1	Brisbane[2]	W-7w	4	20	lbw	–	–	–	5	–	0	295	–	–	9	934
835/544†			2	Perth	W-166	8	12	c	9	2	c	3	–	0	533	3	–	0	369
836/545†			3	Melbourne	L-103	8	1	b	8	5	c	1	–	0	713	1	1	4	570
837/546†			4	Sydney	W-93	8	10	c	8	21	*	–	–	2	864	–	–	0	394
838/547†			5	Adelaide	W-205	8	4	ro	8	97	c	2	–	1	428	–	–	0	536
839/548†			6	Sydney	W-9w	8	36	*	–	–	–	1	1	0	487	2	–	3	489
851/549†	1979	I	1	Birmingham	W-I & 83	–	–	–	–	–	–	–	–	1	697	1	–	7	574
852/550†			2	Lord's	D	9	64	c	–	–	–	3	–	0	335	–	–	2	888
853/551†			3	Leeds	D	9	1	c	–	–	–	1	–	11	660	–	–	–	–
868/553†	1979–80	A	1	Perth	L-138	8	14	b	8	15	b	3	–	4	600	3	1	4	851
870/554†			2	Sydney	L-6w	8	10	c	9	8	b	3	–	2	350	1	–	0	513
872/555†			3	Melbourne	L-8w	8	23	b	8	32	c	–	–	13	1079	–	–	0	232
876/556†	1979–80	I		Bombay[3]	W-10w	7	43	lbw	–	–	–	7	–	5	419	3	–	4	313
904/568†	1981	A	2	Lord's	D	9	0	c	9	9	b	3	–	6	712	1	–	0	293
905/569†			3	Leeds	W-18	8	5	c	8	1	c	3	–	4	932	4	–	0	217
906/570†			4	Birmingham	W-29	9	0	b	10	8	lbw	1	–	4	521	1	–	1	402
912/573†	1981–82	I	1	Bombay[3]	L-138	9	9	*	9	1	b	4	–	0	342	3	–	8	477
913/574†			2	Bangalore	D	10	33	c	–	–	–	2	–	2	900	–	–	–	–
914/575†			3	Delhi	D	8	0	lbw	–	–	–	1	1	20	961	–	–	–	–
915/576†			4	Calcutta	D	10	6	c	–	–	–	2	–	2	600	–	–	0	498
916/577†			5	Madras[1]	D	8	8	b	–	–	–	2	–	0	917	–	–	12	300
917/578†			6	Kanpur	D	8	0	b	–	–	–	1	–	1	732	–	–	–	–
921/579†	1981–82	SL		Colombo SO	W-7w	7	31	*	–	–	–	1	–	2	491	2	–	0	503
928/580†	1982	I	1	Lord's	W-7w	9	31	c	3	1	c	1	–	0	304	2	–	0	671
929/581†			2	Manchester	D	10	1	*	–	–	–	2	–	6	624	–	–	–	–
930/582†			3	Oval	D	9	3	lbw	–	–	–	1	–	3	776	3	–	0	216
931/583†	1982	P	1	Birmingham	W-113	10	1	lbw	10	54	c	2	–	5	476	3	–	0	340
932/584†			2	Lord's	L-10w	10	5	lbw	10	24	*	2	–	3	834	–	–	1	69
933/585†			3	Leeds	W-3w	9	18	c	9	6	*	2	–	1	605	3	–	0	486
938/586†	1982–83	A	1	Perth	D	9	29	*	7	31	b	1	–	4	791	1	–	0	132
939/587†			2	Brisbane[2]	L-7w	8	1	c	8	3	c	3	–	2	664	–	–	2	365
940/588†			3	Adelaide	L-8w	8	2	c	9	3	*	3	–	0	941	1	–	0	143
941/589†			4	Melbourne	W-3	9	1	c	9	37	lbw	1	–	0	474	1	–	5	577
942/590†			5	Sydney	D	8	0	lbw	9	28	*	1	–	3	690	1	–	0	789
957/591†	1983	NZ	1	Oval	W-189	9	0	lbw	–	–	–	1	–	0	342	4	–	3	661
958/592†			2	Leeds	L-5w	9	10	*	9	9	b	–	–	1	837	–	–	8	163
959/593†			3	Lord's	W-127	7	16	b	7	7	c	–	–	0	508	2	–	3	416
960/594†			4	Nottingham	W-165	8	21	b	8	0	b	–	–	0	492	4	–	2	774
975/595†	1983–84	NZ	1	Wellington	D	8	14	ro	–	–	–	3	–	4	562	2	–	4	1125
976/596†			2	Christchurch	L-I & 132	8	2	c	8	15	ro	4	–	8	433	–	–	–	–
977/597†			3	Auckland	D	6	23	st	–	–	–	–	–	0	1016	–	–	0	30
978/598†	1983–84	P	1	Karachi	L-3w	8	4	lbw	8	19	c	1	–	0	612	–	–	1	183
979/599†			2	Faisalabad	D	7	0	c	–	–	–	–	–	0	852	1	–	0	246
980/600†			3	Lahore[2]	D	8	1	lbw	10	5	b	1	–	0	768	–	–	0	351

Career	M	I	NO	HS	R	Avge	100	50	Ct	St	Balls	R	W	Avge	BB	5w	10w	Rate
Test	57	83	12	97	1156	16.28	–	3	167	7	12	6	0	–	–	–	–	–
F/c	639	880	167	100	12065	16.92	1	23	1473	176	117	75	1	75.00	1-23	–	–	117.00

ing his keeping, he was a popular Derbyshire captain (1975–76). Since his retirement he has combined work as a representative of a sports goods firm with public relations duties for Cornhill Insurance during the Test matches which they sponsor. It was while hosting a table during the lunch interval of the 1986 Lord's Test against New Zealand that he was summoned to substitute for the injured French. Even after nearly two years in retirement, he was able to demonstrate that his form and fitness were undiminished.

R. W. TAYLOR – TEST SUMMARY

Series	V	M	I	NO	HS	R	Avge	100	50	Ct	St	Byes	Balls
1970–71	NZ	1	1	–	4	4	4.00	–	–	2	1	15	1081
1977–78	P	3	4	1	36	86	28.66	–	–	5	1	20	3394
1977–78	NZ	3	4	–	45	69	17.25	–	–	9	–	29	3806
1978	P	3	2	–	10	12	6.00	–	–	8	–	5	2235
1978	NZ	3	3	–	22	31	10.33	–	–	12	1	13	3310
1978–79	A	6	10	2	97	208	26.00	–	1	18	2	19	6612
1979	I	3	2	–	64	65	32.50	–	1	5	–	21	3154
1979–80	A	3	6	–	32	102	17.00	–	–	10	1	23	3625
1979–80	I	1	1	–	43	43	43.00	–	–	10	–	9	732
1981	A	3	6	–	9	23	3.83	–	–	13	–	15	3077
1981–82	I	6	7	1	33	57	9.50	–	–	15	1	45	5727
1981–82	SL	1	1	1	31*	31	–	–	–	3	–	2	994
1982	I	3	4	1	31	36	12.00	–	–	9	–	9	2591
1982	P	3	6	2	54	108	27.00	–	1	12	–	10	2810
1982–83	A	5	10	3	31	135	19.28	–	–	13	–	16	5566
1983	NZ	4	7	1	21	63	10.50	–	–	11	–	17	4193
1983–84	NZ	3	4	–	23	54	13.50	–	–	9	–	16	3166
1983–84	P	3	5	–	19	29	5.80	–	–	3	–	1	3012
	A	17	32	5	97	468	17.33	–	1	54	3	73	18880
	NZ	14	19	1	45	221	12.27	–	–	43	2	90	15556
	I	13	14	2	64	201	16.75	–	1	39	1	84	12204
	P	12	17	3	54	235	16.78	–	1	28	1	36	11451
	SL	1	1	1	31*	31	–	–	–	3	–	2	994
Home		22	30	4	64	338	13.00	–	2	70	1	90	21370
Overseas		35	53	8	97	818	18.17	–	1	97	6	195	37715
Totals		57	83	12	97	1156	16.28	–	3	167	7	285	59085

NOTABLE FEATS

- 50 dismissals in 15th Test (*835*); 100 dismissals in 30th Test (*912*); 150 dismissals and 1000 runs in 47th Test (*942*) (67 inns).
- *834* First England wicket-keeper to catch 5 Australians in an innings.
- *876* Set world record with 10 catches in the match; his 7 catches in the 1st inns equalled Wasim Bari's world record. Shared record E v I 6th-wkt stand of 171 with I.T. Botham.
- *905* Exceeded J.T. Murray's world record of 1270 first-class catches.
- *931* Shared record E v P 10th-wkt stand of 79 with R.G.D. Willis.
- *942* Completed the fourth wicket-keepers' Test 'double' for England.
- Holds world records for most wicket-keeping dismissals and catches in a first-class career.
- Holds Championship records for most wicket-keeping dismissals (1222) and catches (1087) in a career.
- Holds Derbyshire career record for most dismissals (1304).
- Made 10 dismissals in a match twice: for Derbyshire v Hampshire at Chesterfield in 1963 and for England (above).
- Made 7 dismissals in an innings on 3 occasions (record): for England (above) and twice for Derbyshire (v Glamorgan at Derby 1966 and v Yorkshire at Chesterfield 1975); they equalled the world record until 1985. Made 6 dismissals in an innings on two other occasions for Derbyshire.

TEST NOTES

- *916* Bowled in 2nd inns: 0 for 6 (12 balls).

TENNYSON
3rd Lord (Hon. Lionel Hallam Tennyson)

Hampshire (1913 to 1935)

Wisden 1914
TOURS
SA 1913–14, 1924–25 (Joel); WI 1925–26, 1926–27†, 1927–28†, 1928–29 (Cahn), 1931–32†; I 1937–38†
(†Tennyson's own team)
Born Westminster, London 7 Nov 1889
Succeeded to title 1928
Died Bexhill-on-Sea, Sussex 6 Jun 1951

Lionel Tennyson was a cricketing gladiator who was at his best in adversity. There have been few more resolute or fearless sportsmen. When, at Leeds in 1921, he split his hand trying to stop a drive from Macartney which normal fielders would have avoided, he insisted on setting his side an example by wearing a basket guard over the injury and taking on the ferocious pace of Gregory and McDonald almost one-handed. Nor did he consider any situation, however bad, irretrievable. Only Tennyson could have rallied his Hampshire team to victory after they had been dismissed for 15 and followed on. By 1913, when he marked his first-class debut with a century for MCC, the skills as a right-arm fast bowler which had earned him a place in the Eton XI had largely deserted him. After First World War service in the Rifle Brigade during which he was wounded three times and mentioned in dispatches twice, it was his adventurous and often bucolic hitting which made his reputation. He was a most prodigious striker of the ball; one hit at Southampton was measured at 140 yards. What he lacked in consistency he more than compensated for in entertainment and life in the Hampshire team was never mundane during his 15-year reign as captain (1919–33). He

Lord Tennyson (left) and J.C.W. MacBryan going out to bat against the South Africans at Godalming in 1929.

was almost certainly the only county captain who employed his wicket-keeper as butler. A grandson of the poet, he succeeded his father to the title in 1928.

NOTABLE FEATS

- *142* After splitting his left hand fielding he scored 63 and 36 batting virtually with one hand.
- Exceeded 1000 runs in a season 7 times.
- Scored 110 on his first-class debut – for MCC v Oxford U at Lord's in 1913.
- Scored 217 for Hampshire v West Indians at Southampton in 1928.
- Scored 100 in 55 min for Hampshire v Gloucestershire at Southampton in 1927.

TEST NOTES

- *134* Bowled in 2nd inns: 0 for 1 (6 balls).

						Batting 1st			Batting 2nd			
Ref	Series	V	T	Venue	Result	No	R	HO	No	R	HO	Ct
130/119	1913–14	SA	1	Durban[1]	W-I & 157	4	52	lbw	–	–	–	–
131/120			2	Johannesburg[1]	W-I & 12	5	13	lbw	–	–	–	–
132/121			3	Johannesburg[1]	W-91	5	21	b	6	6	c	2
133/122			4	Durban[1]	D	5	1	c	6	0	b	2
134/123			5	Port Elizabeth	W-10w	8	23	lbw	–	–	–	–
141/130	1921	A	2	Lord's	L-8w	7	5	st	7	74	*	–
142/131*			3	Leeds	L-219	9	63	c	8	36	b	1
143/132*			4	Manchester	D	–	–	–	–	–	–	1
144/133*			5	Oval	D	7	51	b	–	–	–	–

Career	M	I	NO	HS	R	Avge	100	50	Ct	St	Balls	R	W	Avge	BB	5w	10w	Rate
Test	9	12	1	74*	345	31.36	–	4	6	–	6	1	0	–	–	–	–	–
F/c	477	759	38	217	16828	23.33	19	66	172	–	3756	2976	55	54.10	3-50	–	–	68.29

TERRY, Vivian Paul

Hampshire (1978 to date)

TOUR Z 1984–85 (Eng Co)
Born Osnabruck, West Germany
14 Jan 1959

Paul Terry, with his fractured arm in a sling, facing Joel Garner at the end of England's first innings at Manchester, 1984.

A tall (6ft) slim, square-shouldered opening batsman, Paul Terry graduated to the Hampshire team after a thorough apprenticeship first at Millfield and later as understudy to Gordon Greenidge and Chris Smith. A correct and confident player of fast bowling and a superb fielder, he seized his chance while Greenidge was absent with the 1984 West Indies tour to reap such a rich harvest of runs that the England selectors chose him for two Tests. Unfortunately the tourists' extra pace immediately exposed a weakness outside his off stump. When he was given a second chance he appeared to lose sight of a short ball from Winston Davis and sustained a fractured left ulna. He amazed everyone by reappearing when the fall of England's ninth wicket had left Allan Lamb marooned on 98. Few journeys have been as poignant as his stately progress to the wicket with his injured arm in a sling under his sweater. When advised to bat left-handed he had declined saying,'No thanks, I don't want my right arm broken as well!' Fortunately, Lamb completed his hard-earned century before Terry had to face a ball. When he did, a rampant Garner produced a mean yorker at his second attempt.

NOTABLE FEATS

- Exceeded 1000 runs in a season 5 times.
- Shared record Hampshire 1st-wkt stand of 347 with C.L. Smith v Warwickshire at Birmingham in 1987.

TEST NOTES

- *992* Retired hurt when 7* at 105–1 (1st inns); resumed at 278–9.

						Batting 1st			Batting 2nd			
Ref	Series	V	T	Venue	Result	No	R	HO	No	R	HO	Ct
991/603	1984	WI	3	Leeds	L-8w	3	8	c	3	1	lbw	1
992/604			4	Manchester	L-I & 64	3	7	b	–	–	–	1

Career	M	I	NO	HS	R	Avge	100	50	Ct	St	Balls	R	W	Avge	BB	5w	10w	Rate
Test	2	3	0	8	16	5.33	–	–	2	–	–	–	–	–	–	–	–	–
F/c	151	251	28	190	7694	34.50	16	45	156	–	89	39	0	–	–	–	–	–

THOMAS
John Gregory

Glamorgan (1979 to 1988)
Border (1983–84 to 1986–87)
Eastern Province (1987–88)

TOUR WI 1985–86
Born Trebanos, Glamorgan 12 Aug 1960

NOTABLE FEATS

- *1039* Shared England's highest 10th-wkt stand in the West Indies (72 with R.M. Ellison).

A lanky (6ft 3in) right-arm fast bowler, Greg Thomas is capable of bursts of high quality bowling at blistering pace. Unfortunately he is also likely to lose all control of his line, length and rhythm. The soft pitches of South Wales have never been ideal for a pace bowler who does little with the ball and in none of his ten seasons with Glamorgan did he manage to take 50 Championship wickets. In 1988 his promising lower-order batting developed to such an extent that he scored his first two hundreds. England's selectors will be hoping that a move to Northampton will inspire this softly spoken Welsh schoolteacher to realise his true potential as a strike bowler.

Greg Thomas

					Batting 1st			Batting 2nd				Bowling 1st			Bowling 2nd		
Ref	Series	V	T Venue	Result	No	R	HO	No	R	HO	Ct	Balls	R	W	Balls	R	W
1038/618	1985–86	WI	1 Kingston	L-10w	11	0	b	11	1	*	–	173	82	2	6	4	0
1039/619			2 Port-of-Spain	L-7w	11	4	b	11	31	*	–	120	86	2	30	21	0
1040/620			3 Bridgetown	L-I & 30	11	4	*	11	0	b	–	97	70	4	–	–	–
1041/621			4 Port-of-Spain	L-10w	11	5	*	11	0	b	–	90	101	0	–	–	–
1050/627	1986	NZ	2 Nottingham	L-8w	9	28	b	9	10	c	–	234	124	2	24	16	0

Career	M	I	NO	HS	R	Avge	100	50	Ct	St	Balls	R	W	Avge	BB	5w	10w	Rate
Test	5	10	4	31*	83	13.83	–	–	–	–	774	504	10	50.40	4-70	–	–	77.40
F/c	138	187	35	110	2550	16.77	2	5	53	–	19101	11297	359	31.46	6-68	10	1	53.20

THOMPSON
George Joseph

Northamptonshire (1905 to 1922)
Auckland (1911–12)

Wisden 1906
TOURS
A 1902–03; SA 1909–10; WI 1904–05; NZ 1902–03
Born Cogenhoe, Northampton 27 Oct 1877
Died Clifton, Bristol 3 Mar 1943

George Thompson was probably the best all-round cricketer to be produced by the county of Northamptonshire and it was almost solely through his efforts that they gained admission to the Championship after winning the Minor Counties title in successive years. Tall and heavily built, he was a bustling right-arm fast-medium bowler, a hard-hitting batsman with a sound defence and an agile close fielder. His bowling, similar in method to that of Bedser and Tate, was exceptionally accurate, gained nip off the pitch and included break and swerve. He toured Australia before 1905 when Northants gained first-class status. On the New Zealand leg of that expedition he took 177 wickets at 6 runs apiece, a performance which probably had something to do with the team winning all its 18 matches. He was appointed player-coach to Northamptonshire in 1919 but wounds received in the First World War effectively ended his career. He retired after three seasons and became an enthusiastic coach at Rugby, Clifton and Stowe. [*Illus. p.* 273]

NOTABLE FEATS

- Exceeded 1000 runs in a season 3 times and took 100 wickets 8 times, completing the 'double' twice (1906 and 1910). Headed the national averages in 1911 with 113 wickets at 16.80.
- Took 9 for 85 for Lord Hawke's XI v South Australia at Adelaide in 1902–03 and 9 for 64 for Northamptonshire v Derbyshire at Northampton in 1906.
- Returned a match analysis of 15 for 167 for Northamptonshire v Leicestershire at Northampton in 1906.
- Hat-trick for Northamptonshire v Lancashire at Manchester in 1907.
- Took 4 wickets in 5 balls for Northamptonshire v Leicestershire at Leicester in 1905.
- Caught all 3 victims of S.G. Smith's hat-trick for Northamptonshire v Warwickshire at Birmingham in 1914.
- Bowled in an unchanged partnership throughout both completed innings of a match for Northamptonshire on 4 occasions, including 2 with S.G. Smith.
- Achieved the match 'double' (136 runs and 10 wickets) for Northamptonshire v Somerset at Bath in 1913.

						Batting 1st			Batting 2nd				Bowling 1st			Bowling 2nd		
Ref	Series	V	T	Venue	Result	No	R	HO	No	R	HO	Ct	Balls	R	W	Balls	R	W
101/98	1909	A	1	Birmingham	W-10w	10	6	ro	–	–	–	2	–	–	–	24	19	0
106/103	1909–10	SA	1	Johannesburg[1]	L-19	6	16	lbw	6	63	b	–	66	25	0	168	100	1
107/104			2	Durban[1]	L-95	6	38	c	6	46	*	1	168	52	3	230	78	2
108/105			3	Johannesburg[1]	W-3w	4	21	c	1	10	lbw	2	102	74	2	138	54	3
109/106			4	Cape Town	L-4w	6	16	ro	6	6	c	–	96	50	4	123	62	3
110/107			5	Cape Town	W-9w	6	51	c	–	–	–	–	72	28	2	180	96	3

Career	M	I	NO	HS	R	Avge	100	50	Ct	St	Balls	R	W	Avge	BB	5w	10w	Rate
Test	6	10	1	63	273	30.33	–	2	5	–	1367	638	23	27.73	4-50	–	–	59.43
F/c	352	606	60	131*	12018	22.01	9	53	251	–	64032	30058	1591	18.89	9-64	147	40	40.24

THOMSON
Norman Ian

Sussex (1952 to 1972)

TOURS SA 1964–65; P 1955–56
Born Walsall, Staffordshire 23 Jan 1929

NOTABLE FEATS

- Took 100 wickets in a season 12 times.
- Took all 10 for 49 for Sussex v Warwickshire at Worthing in 1964 (15 for 75 in the match).

Ian Thomson's reward for maintaining a high degree of accuracy and fitness was a return of over 100 wickets for 12 successive seasons. A tall (6ft 1in) right-arm medium-pace bowler, he had an undistinguished shuffling approach but his high action enabled him to extract lift and movement if there was any life in the pitch. Basically he was an inswing bowler who moved the ball disconcertingly late but he also had a very good leg-cutter. An amateur who turned professional after his first season, he was the last bowler to take all 10 wickets in a first-class innings in Britain. Despite such ruthless exploitation of a rain-affected Worthing pitch, he was destined to finish on the losing side after Sussex were routed for 23 in their second innings. He retired after the 1965 season but reappeared for two matches in 1972.

Ian Thomson

						Batting 1st			Batting 2nd				Bowling 1st			Bowling 2nd		
Ref	Series	V	T	Venue	Result	No	R	HO	No	R	HO	Ct	Balls	R	W	Balls	R	W
571/410	1964–65	SA	1	Durban[2]	W-I & 104	–	–	–	–	–	–	1	90	23	1	78	25	1
572/411			2	Johannesburg[3]	D	10	27	*	–	–	–	1	138	47	1	96	36	0
573/412			3	Cape Town	D	10	0	c	–	–	–	–	270	89	2	84	31	1
574/413			4	Johannesburg[3]	D	10	3	c	–	–	–	–	186	91	0	114	43	0
575/414			5	Port Elizabeth	D	6	39	c	–	–	–	1	282	128	1	150	55	2

Career	M	I	NO	HS	R	Avge	100	50	Ct	St	Balls	R	W	Avge	BB	5w	10w	Rate
Test	5	4	1	39	69	23.00	–	–	3	–	1488	568	9	63.11	2-55	–	–	165.33
F/c	425	583	100	77	7120	14.74	–	13	135	–	88662	32867	1597	20.58	10-49	73	8	55.51

TITMUS
Frederick John MBE

Middlesex (1949 to 1982)
Surrey (1978)
Orange Free State (1975–76)

Wisden 1963
TOURS
A 1962–63, 1965–66, 1974–75; SA 1964–65, 1975–76 (Robins); WI 1967–68, 1969–70 (Cav); NZ 1962–63, 1974–75; I 1963–64; P 1955–56
Born St Pancras, London 24 Nov 1932

Fred Titmus

Fred Titmus made his debut for Middlesex at the age of 16 and his playing career spanned five decades. He was a high-class off-break bowler and a most effective middle-order batsman with a defensive technique worthy of his being employed to open an England innings on the first morning of a Test against Australia. From a neat, skipping run he commanded a vast range of variation; pace, angle and flight without any perceptible change of delivery and all achieved with a twinkling eye and endless stream of dry banter. He probably snared at least half his victims with the innocent looking quicker ball which suddenly drifted away late. A reliable slip fielder despite being endlessly conversational, he usually fielded on the outside of the cordon because of deafness on his right side. He was a courageous batsman as he proved against the 1963 West Indian pace attack of Hall and Griffith in their prime and he needed a great deal of that attribute after losing his four smaller toes to the propeller blade of a boat off the coast of Barbados. Within 10 weeks he was back captaining Middlesex for the fourth season and on his way to 924 first-class runs and 111 wickets. He retired after 1976 to coach at The Oval. There he made one first-class appearance for Surrey before resigning and returning to his Hertfordshire sub-post-office. Whenever Mike Brearley found him wandering around Lord's he would entice him back into the Middlesex team and it was not until 1982 that he played his final game. Well before then he had become one of only five players to score 20,000 runs and take 2500 wickets in first-class cricket. Just three bowlers, the fairly handy little trio of Rhodes, Shackleton and Freeman, have taken 100 wickets in a season more often. He was a cheerful pipe-smoking Test selector for three seasons (1986–88).

NOTABLE FEATS

- 1000 runs in 40th Test (*599*) (55 inns).
- 50 wickets in 17th Test (*553*); 100 wickets in 32nd Test (*591*); 150 wickets in 51st Test (*752*).
- *537* Took 4 wickets for 5 runs in 58 balls on the second day.
- *593* Took 4 wickets in his 21st over (W.WW.W).
- *599* Completed the Test 'double'.
- Exceeded 1000 runs in a season 8 times and took 100 wickets 16 times, notably 191 in 1955. He completed the 'double' 8 times.
- Holds Middlesex career records for most appearances (642), most wickets (2361) and most instances of 100 wickets in a season (11); also most wickets in a season (158 in 1955).
- Shared record Middlesex 6th-wkt stand of 227 with C.T. Radley v South Africans at Lord's in 1965.
- Twice took 9 wickets in an innings for Middlesex: 9 for 52 v Cambridge U at Fenner's in 1962 and 9 for 57 v Lancashire at Lord's in 1964.
- Returned a match analysis of 15 for 95 for Middlesex v Somerset at Bath in 1955.
- Hat-trick for Middlesex v Somerset at Weston-super-Mare in 1966.

						Batting 1st			Batting 2nd				Bowling 1st			Bowling 2nd		
Ref	Series	V	T	Venue	Result	No	R	HO	No	R	HO	Ct	Balls	R	W	Balls	R	W
409/323	1955	SA	2	Lord's	W-71	8	4	c	9	16	c	1	84	50	1	–	–	–
410/324			3	Manchester	L-3w	7	0	lbw	8	19	c	1	114	51	0	–	–	–
532/384	1962	P	3	Leeds	W-I&117	7	2	c	–	–	–	1	24	3	2	66	20	0
533/385			4	Nottingham	D	7	11	*	–	–	–	1	78	22	0	96	29	1

Ref	Series	V	T	Venue	Result	Batting 1st No	R	HO	Batting 2nd No	R	HO	Ct	Bowling 1st Balls	R	W	Bowling 2nd Balls	R	W
535/387	1962–63	A	1	Brisbane[2]	D	8	21	c	7	3	*	–	264	91	1	208	81	1
536/388			2	Melbourne	W-7w	7	15	c	–	–	–	–	120	43	4	112	25	1
537/389			3	Sydney	L-8w	7	32	b	7	6	c	1	296	79	7	–	–	–
538/390			4	Adelaide	D	7	59	*	–	–	–	1	161	88	2	192	69	0
539/391			5	Sydney	D	7	34	c	7	12	*	1	378	103	5	160	37	0
540/392	1962–63	NZ	1	Auckland	W-I & 215	8	26	st	–	–	–	1	150	44	2	36	2	1
541/393			2	Wellington	W-I & 47	7	33	ro	–	–	–	–	108	40	1	186	50	4
542/394			3	Christchurch	W-7w	8	4	c	–	–	–	–	180	45	1	126	46	4
543/395	1963	WI	1	Manchester	L-10w	7	0	c	8	17	b	1	240	105	1	–	–	–
544/396			2	Lord's	D	8	52	*	8	11	c	–	–	–	–	102	47	0
545/397			3	Birmingham	W-217	8	27	c	8	0	b	–	–	–	–	–	–	–
546/398			4	Leeds	L-221	8	33	lbw	8	5	st	1	150	60	1	114	44	4
553/400	1963–64	I	1	Madras[2]	D	8	14	c	6	10	b	–	300	116	5	119	46	4
554/401			2	Bombay[2]	D	5	84	*	–	–	–	2	216	56	2	276	79	3
555/402			3	Calcutta	D	9	26	b	–	–	–	–	90	46	1	276	67	2
556/403			4	Delhi	D	10	4	*	–	–	–	–	294	100	3	258	105	0
557/404			5	Kanpur	D	9	5	c	–	–	–	2	360	73	6	204	59	1
561/405	1964	A	1	Nottingham	D	2	16	c	2	17	lbw	–	24	6	1	–	–	–
562/406			2	Lord's	D	8	15	b	–	–	–	1	102	29	0	102	21	2
563/407			3	Leeds	L-7w	8	3	c	9	14	c	–	300	69	4	162	25	2
564/408			4	Manchester	D	7	9	c	–	–	–	–	264	100	0	6	0	0
565/409			5	Oval	D	8	8	c	4	56	b	–	252	51	1	–	–	–
571/410	1964–65	SA	1	Durban[2]	W-I & 104	–	–	–	–	–	–	–	120	20	1	275	66	5
572/411			2	Johannesburg[3]	D	8	2	b	–	–	–	–	239	73	4	270	101	1
573/412			3	Cape Town	D	8	4	c	–	–	–	–	302	133	2	36	21	0
574/413			4	Johannesburg[3]	D	8	1	lbw	2	13	c	–	174	68	1	186	98	1
575/414			5	Port Elizabeth	D	3	12	b	–	–	–	2	223	87	2	30	27	1
591/415	1965	NZ	1	Birmingham	W-9w	8	13	c	–	–	–	2	156	18	4	354	85	2
592/416			2	Lord's	W-7w	8	13	ro	3	1	c	1	90	25	2	234	71	2
593/417			3	Leeds	W-I & 187	–	–	–	–	–	–	1	36	16	0	156	19	5
594/418	1965	SA	1	Lord's	D	8	59	c	8	9	*	2	174	59	2	156	36	1
595/419			2	Nottingham	L-94	4	20	c	3	4	c	1	132	44	1	118	46	2
596/420			3	Oval	D	9	2	*	–	–	–	1	156	57	1	162	74	1
597/421	1965–66	A	1	Brisbane[2]	D	7	60	st	–	–	–	1	304	99	1	–	–	–
598/422			2	Melbourne	D	9	56	*	–	–	–	1	248	93	0	176	43	0
599/423			3	Sydney	W-I & 93	9	14	c	–	–	–	1	184	40	0	139	40	4
600/424			4	Adelaide	L-I & 9	8	33	lbw	8	53	c	1	296	116	3	–	–	–
601/425			5	Melbourne	D	8	42	*	–	–	–	1	336	86	1	–	–	–
605/429	1966	WI	1	Manchester	L-I & 40	7	15	b	7	12	c	–	210	83	5	–	–	–
606/430			2	Lord's	D	9	6	c	–	–	–	2	30	18	0	114	30	0
608/432			4	Leeds	L-I & 55	8	6	c	8	22	b	1	132	59	0	–	–	–
622/438	1967	P	2	Nottingham	W-10w	7	13	lbw	–	–	–	1	42	12	0	138	36	2
623/439			3	Oval	W-8w	7	65	c	–	–	–	–	78	21	2	175	64	2
628/440	1967–68	WI	1	Port-of-Spain	D	8	15	lbw	–	–	–	1	204	91	1	162	42	2
629/441			2	Kingston	D	8	19	lbw	8	4	c	–	–	–	–	42	32	1
751/504	1974–75	A	2	Perth	L-9w	8	10	c	8	61	c	–	224	84	2	–	–	–
752/505			3	Melbourne	D	8	10	c	8	0	b	–	176	43	2	232	64	2
753/506			4	Sydney	L-171	8	22	c	8	4	c	–	128	65	1	59	24	0
754/507			5	Adelaide	L-163	8	11	c	8	20	lbw	–	56	27	0	104	53	0

Career	M	I	NO	HS	R	Avge	100	50	Ct	St	Balls	R	W	Avge	BB	5w	10w	Rate
Test	53	76	11	84*	1449	22.29	–	10	35	–	15118	4931	153	32.22	7-79	7	–	98.81
F/c	792	1142	208	137*	21588	23.11	6	105	473	–	173585	63313	2830	22.37	9-52	168	26	61.33

F. J. TITMUS – TEST SUMMARY

Series	V	M	I	NO	HS	R	Avge	100	50	Balls	R	W	Avge	BB	5w	10w	Rate
1955	SA	2	4	–	19	39	9.75	–	–	198	101	1	101.00	1-50	–	–	198.00
1962	P	2	2	1	11*	13	13.00	–	–	264	74	3	24.66	2-3	–	–	88.00
1962–63	A	5	8	3	59*	182	36.40	–	1	1891	616	21	29.33	7-79	2	–	90.04
1962–63	NZ	3	3	–	33	63	21.00	–	–	786	227	13	17.46	4-46	–	–	60.46

Series	V	M	I	NO	HS	R	Avge	100	50	Balls	R	W	Avge	BB	5w	10w	Rate
1963	WI	4	8	1	52*	145	20.71	–	1	606	256	6	42.66	4-44	–	–	101.00
1963–64	I	5	6	2	84*	143	35.75	–	1	2393	747	27	27.66	6-73	2	–	88.62
1964	A	5	8	–	56	138	17.25	–	1	1212	301	10	30.10	4-69	–	–	121.20
1964–65	SA	5	5	–	13	32	6.40	–	–	1855	694	18	38.55	5-66	1	–	103.05
1965	NZ	3	3	–	13	27	9.00	–	–	1026	234	15	15.60	5-19	1	–	68.40
1965	SA	3	5	2	59	94	31.33	–	1	898	316	8	39.50	2-46	–	–	112.25
1965–66	A	5	6	2	60	258	64.50	–	3	1683	517	9	57.44	4-40	–	–	187.00
1966	WI	3	5	–	22	61	12.20	–	–	486	190	5	38.00	5-83	1	–	97.20
1967	P	2	2	–	65	78	39.00	–	1	433	133	6	22.16	2-21	–	–	72.16
1967–68	WI	2	3	–	19	38	12.66	–	–	408	165	4	41.25	2-42	–	–	102.00
1974–75	A	4	8	–	61	138	17.25	–	1	979	360	7	51.42	2-43	–	–	139.85
	A	19	30	5	61	716	28.64	–	6	5765	1794	47	38.17	7-79	2	–	122.65
	SA	10	14	2	59	165	13.75	–	1	2951	1111	27	41.14	5-66	1	–	109.29
	WI	9	16	1	52*	244	16.26	–	1	1500	611	15	40.73	5-83	1	–	100.00
	NZ	6	6	–	33	90	15.00	–	–	1812	461	28	16.46	5-19	1	–	64.71
	I	5	6	2	84*	143	35.75	–	1	2393	747	27	27.66	6-73	2	–	88.62
	P	4	4	1	65	91	30.33	–	1	697	207	9	23.00	2-3	–	–	77.44
Home		24	37	4	65	595	18.03	–	4	5123	1605	54	29.72	5-19	2	–	94.87
Overseas		29	39	7	84*	854	26.68	–	6	9995	3326	99	33.59	7-79	5	–	100.95
Totals		53	76	11	84*	1449	22.29	–	10	15118	4931	153	32.22	7-79	7	–	98.81

TOLCHARD Roger William

Leicestershire (1965 to 1983)

TOURS

A 1976–77, 1978–79; SA 1973–74 (Robins), 1974–75 (Robins/Int W), 1975–76 (Robins); I 1967–68 (Int XI), 1972–73, 1976–77, 1980–81 (Overseas XI); P 1967–68 (Int XI), 1972–73; SL 1967–68 (Int XI), 1972–73, 1976–77, 1977–78 (Robins); Z 1974–75 (Int W), 1975–76 (Int W), 1980–81 (Leics XI)

Born Torquay, Devon 15 Jun 1946

Roger Tolchard was an agile and aggressive wicket-keeper batsman with exceptionally nimble footwork. A brave hooker of fast bowling, he was also a very quick-footed improviser against spin and it was the latter quality which earned him his four Test caps on Tony Greig's tour of India. While Alan Knott kept wicket, 'Tolley's' lively fielding was put to good use in the covers or at short-leg. He justified his selection at the first opportunity, his vigil of nearly six hours on a breaking pitch contributing enormously towards England's eventual victory. It was a display totally out of character for a pugnacious strokemaker whose innings are built on well-judged singles and amazingly fast running between the wickets. He played for his native Devon for two seasons before starting his career with Leicestershire and returned there at the end of his three-year captaincy stint. He also went back to Malvern School – as cricket master. [*Illus. p.* 102]

NOTABLE FEATS

- Shared record Leicestershire 5th-wkt stand of 233 with N.E. Briers v Somerset at Leicester in 1979.
- Holds Leicestershire career record for most wicket-keeping dismissals (887) and match record for most catches in an innings (6 v Yorkshire at Leeds in 1973 and v Hampshire at Southampton in 1980). The 1973 instance involved the first 6 batsmen dismissed.

TEST NOTES

- *790* Retired hurt when 1* at 33–3 (1st inns); resumed at 209–7.

						Batting 1st			Batting 2nd			
Ref	Series	V	T	Venue	Result	No	R	HO	No	R	HO	Ct
789/521	1976–77	I	2	Calcutta	W-10w	5	67	b	–	–	–	2
790/522			3	Madras[1]	W-200	5	8	*	9	10	*	–
791/523			4	Bangalore	L-140	5	0	b	5	14	lbw	2
792/524			5	Bombay[3]	D	7	4	st	7	26	c	1

Career	M	I	NO	HS	R	Avge	100	50	Ct	St	Balls	R	W	Avge	BB	5w	10w	Rate
Test	4	7	2	67	129	25.80	–	1	5	–	–	–	–	–	–	–	–	–
F/c	483	680	189	126*	15288	31.13	12	86	912	125	48	34	1	34.00	1-4	–	–	48.00

TOWNSEND Charles Lucas

Gloucestershire (1893 to 1922)
London County (1900)

Wisden 1899
Born Clifton, Bristol 7 Nov 1876
Died Elton, Co. Durham 17 Oct 1958

As a 16-year-old Clifton schoolboy on holiday with Gloucestershire, Charlie Townsend achieved a unique first-class hat-trick when his sharp spin induced three stumpings from successive balls. Two years later, he created an even greater sensation when he joined the County at the end of his final term and proceeded to head the season's national bowling averages with 131 wickets at 13.94 apiece. Tall and very slim, he bowled right-handed with a slow round-arm action and could make the ball break either way. His sound left-handed batting rapidly took him into the all-rounder class and did most to earn him two Test caps in 1899 when he scored nine centuries. After one more summer he moved to Stockton-on-Tees and played only occasionally. His father played for Gloucestershire and his son played for England.

NOTABLE FEATS

- Exceeded 1000 runs in a season 3 times, including 2000 once, and took 100 wickets 4 times. He completed the 'double' twice, notably his 2440 runs and 101 wickets in 1899.
- 2 double centuries for Gloucestershire: 224* v Essex at Clifton in 1899 and 214 v Worcestershire at Cheltenham in 1906.
- Scored 100 before lunch for Gloucestershire 3 times.
- Twice took 9 wickets in an innings for Gloucestershire in 1898: 9 for 48 v Middlesex at Lord's and 9 for 128 v Warwickshire at Cheltenham.
- Took 15 or more wickets in a match for Gloucestershire on 5 occasions, notably 16 for 122 v Nottinghamshire at Nottingham in 1895.
- Hat-trick (all stumped by W.H. Brain) for Gloucestershire v Somerset at Cheltenham in 1893.
- Achieved the match 'double' (139 and 10 wickets) for Gloucestershire v Warwickshire at Birmingham in 1898.

England v Australia, Lord's, 1899: standing *T. Mycroft (umpire), T.W. Hayward, A.F.A. Lilley, W. Mead, W.A.J. West (umpire);* seated *C.B. Fry, F.S. Jackson, A.C. MacLaren (captain), K.S. Ranjitsinhji, C.L. Townsend;* in front *G.L. Jessop, W. Rhodes, J.T. Tyldesley.*

Ref	Series	V	T	Venue	Result	Batting 1st No	R	HO	Batting 2nd No	R	HO	Ct	Bowling 1st Balls	R	W	Bowling 2nd Balls	R	W
61/61	1899	A	2	Lord's	L-10w	4	5	st	4	8	b	–	75	50	3	–	–	–
64/64			5	Oval	D	6	38	b	–	–	–	–	25	16	0	40	9	0

Career	M	I	NO	HS	R	Avge	100	50	Ct	St	Balls	R	W	Avge	BB	5w	10w	Rate
Test	2	3	0	38	51	17.00	–	–	–	–	140	75	3	25.00	3-50	–	–	46.66
F/c	199	342	28	224*	9512	30.29	21	40	193	–	29794	16761	725	23.11	9-48	68	18	41.09

TOWNSEND David Charles Humphery

Oxford University (1933 to 1934)

TOUR WI 1934–35
Born Norton-on-Tees, Co. Durham
20 Apr 1912

Although he appeared in 37 first-class matches, making a spirited 72* against Yorkshire on his debut for Oxford in 1933 and ending his career with a return visit to The Parks in Free Foresters' colours 15 years later, David Townsend never appeared for a first-class county. He is the last 'stateless' cricketer to appear for England. Educated at Winchester, ill health prevented his playing as an Oxford freshman but he headed the University's averages as a senior, his 734 runs including three hundreds. The son of Charlie Townsend and grandson of Frank who played in W.G. Grace's Gloucestershire team, he was an entertaining opening batsman. An elegant cutter, he drove, pulled and hooked powerfully, founding this range of strokes on an extremely sound defensive technique. He was not so successful as a right-arm medium-pace change bowler. After finishing his studies he toured the Caribbean with R.E.S. Wyatt's MCC team. Most of his representative cricket was played for Durham (1935–50). [*Illus. p.* 510]

						Batting 1st			Batting 2nd				Bowling 1st			Bowling 2nd		
Ref	Series	V	T	Venue	Result	No	R	HO	No	R	HO	Ct	Balls	R	W	Balls	R	W
239/213	1934–35	WI	2	Port-of-Spain	L-217	2	5	lbw	2	36	c	–	–	–	–	–	–	–
240/214			3	Georgetown	D	1	16	lbw	1	1	lbw	–	–	–	–	6	9	0
241/215			4	Kingston	L-I & 161	2	8	c	2	11	b	1	–	–	–	–	–	–

Career	M	I	NO	HS	R	Avge	100	50	Ct	St	Balls	R	W	Avge	BB	5w	10w	Rate
Test	3	6	0	36	77	12.83	–	–	1	–	6	9	0	–	–	–	–	–
F/c	37	64	2	195	1801	29.04	4	6	16	–	1142	501	6	83.50	2-31	–	–	190.33

TOWNSEND Leslie Fletcher

Derbyshire (1922 to 1939)
Auckland (1934–35 to 1935–36)

Wisden 1934
TOURS WI 1929–30; I/SL 1933–34
Born Long Eaton, Derbyshire 8 Jun 1903

Leslie Townsend was an outstanding all-rounder and the first Derbyshire player to complete the 'double' in county matches alone. Although he played no cricket at his local council school, he would watch his local club and spend many hours at Trent Bridge studying the batting method of George Gunn. He made his debut at the age of 19, but it took five seasons before he began to flourish as an all-rounder. By nature a vigorous hitter, he had lacked patience or the art of selection. Gradually he developed a strong defence and became a fine off-driver. His right-arm medium-pace off-breaks delivered with an easy action made the ball break off the pitch with deceptive speed. He was an extremely agile fielder and played a prominent part in Derbyshire's lone Championship success in 1936. After the Second World War he emigrated to New Zealand and settled in Nelson, coaching until his retirement. When visited in 1984 he was in good health and his Derbyshire accent and range of anecdote were unimpaired. [*Illus. pp.* 126, 263]

NOTABLE FEATS

- Exceeded 1000 runs in a season 9 times, including 2000 once, and took 100 wickets 4 times, completing the 'double' on 3 occasions, notably his 2268 runs and 100 wickets in 1933.
- Scored 233 for Derbyshire v Leicestershire at Loughborough in 1933.
- Hat-trick for Derbyshire v Northamptonshire at Northampton in 1931.
- Achieved the match 'double' twice: for Derbyshire in 1934 and for Auckland in 1934–35.

Ref	Series	V	T	Venue	Result	Batting 1st No	R	HO	Batting 2nd No	R	HO	Ct	Bowling 1st Balls	R	W	Bowling 2nd Balls	R	W
192/178	1929–30	WI	3	Georgetown	L-289	6	3	c	6	21	b	2	96	48	2	45	25	2
230/204	1933–34	I	1	Bombay[1]	W-9w	7	15	c	–	–	–	–	54	25	0	72	33	0
231/205			2	Calcutta	D	9	40	c	–	–	–	–	48	19	0	48	22	2
232/206			3	Madras[1]	W-202	8	10	b	4	8	c	–	18	14	0	18	19	0

Career	M	I	NO	HS	R	Avge	100	50	Ct	St	Balls	R	W	Avge	BB	5w	10w	Rate
Test	4	6	0	40	97	16.16	–	–	2	–	399	205	6	34.16	2-22	–	–	66.50
F/c	493	786	75	233	19555	27.50	22	102	237	–	65573	22985	1088	21.12	8-26	51	16	60.26

TREMLETT
Maurice Fletcher

Somerset (1947 to 1960)
Central Districts (1951–52)

TOURS SA 1948–49; WI 1947–48
Born Stockport, Cheshire 5 Jul 1923
Died Southampton, Hampshire
30 Jul 1984

NOTABLE FEATS

- Exceeded 1000 runs in a season 10 times, including 2101 in 1951.

Tall (6ft 1in) and strongly built, Maurice Tremlett joined the Somerset staff in 1938 but had to wait nine years before his first-class debut. He made sure that first appearance would be remembered by contributing 8 wickets and a decisive 19* to a one-wicket victory over that season's champions. Although he possessed a good action and moved the ball at a lively pace, his right-arm fast-medium bowling gradually fell away and in 1950 he lost control of line and length completely. He became a specialist batsman for the final decade of his career, delighting spectators with his lofted straight hitting. The first professional to be appointed captain of Somerset (1956–59) he led them to third place in 1958 – still their highest position and one last reached in 1892. He retired to Southampton thus providing his son Tim with a Hampshire qualification.

Maurice Tremlett

Ref	Series	V	T	Venue	Result	Batting 1st No	R	HO	Batting 2nd No	R	HO	Ct	Bowling 1st Balls	R	W	Bowling 2nd Balls	R	W
295/258	1947–48	WI	1	Bridgetown	D	11	0	*	–	–	–	–	156	49	1	60	40	0
297/260			3	Georgetown	L-7w	10	0	c	11	18	*	–	84	35	1	–	–	–
298/261			4	Kingston	L-10w	11	0	b	11	2	c	–	186	98	2	6	4	0

Career	M	I	NO	HS	R	Avge	100	50	Ct	St	Balls	R	W	Avge	BB	5w	10w	Rate
Test	3	5	2	18*	20	6.66	–	–	–	–	492	226	4	56.50	2-98	–	–	123.00
F/c	389	681	49	185	16038	25.37	16	83	257	–	22093	10778	351	30.70	8-31	11	–	62.94

TROTT, Albert Edwin

Victoria (1892–93 to 1895–96)
Middlesex (1898 to 1910)
London County (1900 to 1904)
Hawke's Bay (1901–02)
Australia (1894–95)

Wisden 1899
TOURS A 1902–03; SA 1898–99
Born Abbotsford, Melbourne, Australia
6 Feb 1873
Died Harlesden, Middlesex 30 Jul 1914

Albert Trott

Albert Trott crowned the honour of his first Test cap for Australia by scoring 110 runs without being dismissed and bowling unchanged virtually throughout England's second innings to take 8 wickets. Consequently, he was somewhat miffed to find that he had been excluded from the Australian team to tour England 18 months later, especially as it was being led by his own brother. Still fuming, he paid his own fare, sailed to England, presented himself at Lord's and joined the MCC staff while he was spending two years qualifying for Middlesex. He soon made up for lost time and in his second and third summers achieved the first instances of a feat beyond even W.G. Grace: the 'double' of 1000 runs and 200 wickets. An immensely strong hitter, he was the first man to hit a ball over the present pavilion at Lord's. Playing for MCC and Ground against the 1899 Australians, he struck a ball from Monty Noble over the top of the roof and as far as one of the chimney pots above and behind it. His unusual bowling was basically off-spin but he relied on endless variations of pace rather than appreciable turn and his low action enabled him to conceal these changes. His yorker was devastatingly fast. When overweight and well past his prime, he had the sense of occasion to complete a brace of hat-tricks in the same innings of his benefit match. For good measure he was also a brilliant close catcher. A splendidly itinerant cricketer, apart from representing two countries at Test level, he also appeared for Hawke's Bay in New Zealand and achieved the match 'double' for them in 1901–02. He became an umpire (1911–13) until his ailing health deteriorated; when there appeared to be no hope of recovery he used his pistol.

NOTABLE FEATS

- *44* His innings analysis of 8 for 43 remains the record for all Tests at Adelaide.
- Exceeded 1000 runs in a season twice and took 100 wickets 7 times, including 200 twice, notably 239 at 17.09 in 1899 when he headed the national averages. Completed the 'double' twice (1899 and 1900), achieving the first instances of 1000 runs and 200 wickets – a feat later emulated by A.S. Kennedy and M.W. Tate.
- Took all 10 for 42 for Middlesex v Somerset at Taunton in 1900.
- Returned a match analysis of 15 for 187 for Middlesex v Sussex at Lord's in 1901.
- Bowled 8 batsmen in taking 8 for 43 for Middlesex v Gloucestershire at Clifton in 1900.
- Two hat-tricks in the same innings, a unique feat in first-class cricket in Britain: 4 wickets in 4 balls followed by a hat-trick, for Middlesex v Somerset at Lord's in 1907.
- Bowled in an unchanged partnership throughout both completed innings of a match for Middlesex twice (1899 and 1908).
- Achieved the match 'double' 5 times, including the first instance in South Africa (for Lord Hawke's XI v Transvaal at Johannesburg in 1898–99).

						Batting 1st			Batting 2nd				Bowling 1st			Bowling 2nd		
Ref	Series	V	T	Venue	Result	No	R	HO	No	R	HO	Ct	Balls	R	W	Balls	R	W
For Australia																		
44/41	1894–95	E	3	Adelaide	W-382	10	38	*	10	72	*	3	18	9	0	162	43	8
45/42			4	Sydney	W-I & 147	9	85	*	–	–	–	–	–	–	–	–	–	–
46/43			5	Melbourne	L-6w	9	10	c	9	0	b	1	180	84	1	114	56	0
For England																		
58/58	1898–99	SA	1	Johannesburg[1]	W-32	6	0	ro	6	6	c	–	151	61	4	166	49	5
59/59			2	Cape Town	W-210	6	1	c	6	16	b	–	102	69	4	55	19	4

Career	M	I	NO	HS	R	Avge	100	50	Ct	Balls	R	W	Avge	BB	5w	10w	Rate
Test (A)	3	5	3	85*	205	102.50	–	2	4	474	192	9	21.33	8-43	1	–	52.66
Test (E)	2	4	0	16	23	5.75	–	–	–	474	198	17	11.64	5-49	1	–	27.88
Combined	5	9	3	85*	228	38.00	–	2	4	948	390	26	15.00	8-43	2	–	36.46
F/c	375	602	53	164	10696	19.48	8	43	452	71549	35317	1674	21.09	10-42	131	41	42.74

TRUEMAN Frederick Sewards

Yorkshire (1949 to 1968)

Wisden 1953
TOURS
A 1958–59, 1962–63; SA 1960–61 (Cav); WI 1953–54, 1959–60, 1963–64 (Cav), 1964–65 (Cav); NZ 1958–59, 1962–63; I 1956–57 (Howard), 1967–68 (PM XI)
Born Stainton, Yorkshire 6 Feb 1931

Fred Trueman

Fred Trueman in his pomp was one of the most frightening sights known to any batsman and he has not improved much since becoming resident expert in the *Test Match Special* commentary box. A most hostile right-arm fast bowler, he quickly established himself as one of cricket's most outrageous characters, liberally distributing bouncers and bluster from his earliest days in the Yorkshire team. He began his Test career by reducing the terrified Indians to 0 for 4 wickets. By this time he was a national serviceman in the RAF. When he was chiefly instrumental in bowling India out twice in a day at Old Trafford he did himself out of an extra day's special leave. A few problems on his first tour sowed the seeds of his reputation for being a little tricky to handle and on occasions ever so slightly outspoken. It was a tragedy for English cricket that those early difficulties cost him many Tests and several tours. Even the odd hiatus could not prevent 'FS' from becoming the founder member of the now ever-growing 300 Test Wickets Club. Until Malcolm Marshall joined in 1988–89, he could claim the most economical cost per wicket and the fastest striking rate. He remained the leading Test wicket-taker until 1975–76 and held the England record until 1983–84. A little above average height (5ft 10½in) with a deep chest, immensely broad shoulders and strong legs ('Superbly built, Sunshine!'), he had a copy-book smoothly accelerated approach culminating in a classic action with an elongated final stride. Unruly black hair, ever-unfurling sleeves and a spice of invective completed the vision presented to the unfortunate batsman. He moved his outswinger impossibly late and could change to accurate off-cutters if the pitch suited them. His batting was typically flamboyant and he was a most entertaining and prolific hitter when his eye was in. He had a good defence and a fine array of bold but orthodox strokes. He usually fielded belligerently at backward short-leg and was a marvellous catcher. He proved an astute and forceful captain when he deputised as leader in Brian Close's absence. Before masterminding Yorkshire's innings defeat of the 1968 Australians at Sheffield, he came into the commentary box and described how he would dismiss each batsman. Without exception it went to plan. When he played Sunday league cricket for Derbyshire in 1972 he dismissed three of his former Yorkshire colleagues in a televised match. After each wicket he provided his own slow motion replay for the cameras.

(*Notable Feats see overleaf*)

						Batting 1st			Batting 2nd				Bowling 1st			Bowling 2nd		
Ref	Series	V	T	Venue	Result	No	R	HO	No	R	HO	Ct	Balls	R	W	Balls	R	W
351/297	1952	I	1	Leeds	W-7w	11	0	*	–	–	–	–	156	89	3	54	27	4
352/298			2	Lord's	W-8w	11	17	b	–	–	–	–	150	72	4	162	110	4
353/299			3	Manchester	W-I & 207	–	–	–	–	–	–	–	52	31	8	48	9	1
354/300			4	Oval	D	–	–	–	–	–	–	1	96	48	5	–	–	–
376/305	1953	A	5	Oval	W-8w	10	10	b	–	–	–	2	147	86	4	12	4	0
382/306	1953–54	WI	1	Kingston	L-140	10	18	c	10	1	b	–	208	107	2	36	32	0
385/309			4	Port-of-Spain	D	10	19	lbw	–	–	–	–	198	131	1	90	23	1
386/310			5	Kingston	W-9w	11	0	*	–	–	–	–	94	39	2	174	88	3
409/323	1955	SA	2	Lord's	W-71	11	2	*	11	6	*	–	96	73	2	114	39	0
426/328	1956	A	2	Lord's	L-185	10	7	c	10	2	b	1	168	54	2	168	90	5
427/329			3	Leeds	W-I & 42	11	0	c	–	–	–	3	48	19	1	66	21	1
439/337	1957	WI	1	Birmingham	D	10	29	*	–	–	–	1	180	99	2	30	7	2
440/338			2	Lord's	W-I & 36	10	36	*	–	–	–	2	75	30	2	138	73	2
441/339			3	Nottingham	D	–	–	–	–	–	–	–	180	63	5	210	80	4
442/340			4	Leeds	W-I & 5	10	2	*	–	–	–	2	102	33	2	66	42	2
443/341			5	Oval	W-I & 237	9	22	b	–	–	–	2	30	9	0	30	19	1

						Batting 1st			Batting 2nd				Bowling 1st			Bowling 2nd		
Ref	**Series**	**V**	**T**	**Venue**	**Result**	**No**	**R**	**HO**	**No**	**R**	**HO**	**Ct**	**Balls**	**R**	**W**	**Balls**	**R**	**W**
454/342	1958	NZ	1	Birmingham	W-205	9	0	b	–	–	–	1	126	31	5	102	33	1
455/343			2	Lord's	W-I & 148	9	8	b	–	–	–	3	24	6	1	66	24	2
456/344			3	Leeds	W-I & 71	–	–	–	–	–	–	1	66	18	1	84	22	0
457/345			4	Manchester	W-I & 13	10	5	b	–	–	–	1	179	67	3	12	11	0
458/346			5	Oval	D	10	39	*	–	–	–	–	96	41	2	36	3	0
466/349	1958–59	A	3	Sydney	D	9	18	c	8	0	st	–	144	37	1	32	9	0
467/350			4	Adelaide	L-10w	7	0	c	7	0	c	–	241	90	4	24	3	0
468/351			5	Melbourne	L-9w	9	21	c	9	36	b	3	200	92	4	55	45	0
472/352	1958–59	NZ	1	Christchurch	W-I & 99	9	21	lbw	–	–	–	3	65	39	1	48	20	1
473/353			2	Auckland	D	9	21	*	–	–	–	1	156	46	3	–	–	–
474/354	1959	I	1	Nottingham	W-I & 59	8	28	b	–	–	–	1	144	45	4	135	44	2
475/355			2	Lord's	W-8w	8	7	lbw	–	–	–	–	96	40	1	126	55	2
476/356			3	Leeds	W-I & 173	9	17	c	–	–	–	2	90	30	3	60	29	2
477/357			4	Manchester	W-171	10	0	b	8	8	c	1	90	29	1	139	75	2
478/358			5	Oval	W-I & 27	9	1	st	–	–	–	1	102	24	4	84	30	3
487/359	1959–60	WI	1	Bridgetown	D	9	3	c	–	–	–	1	282	93	4	–	–	–
488/360			2	Port-of-Spain	W-256	9	7	lbw	9	37	c	2	126	35	5	114	44	1
489/361			3	Kingston	D	9	17	c	9	4	lbw	–	198	82	2	108	54	4
490/362			4	Georgetown	D	10	6	b	–	–	–	1	240	116	3	–	–	–
491/363			5	Port-of-Spain	D	10	10	*	9	2	*	2	225	103	2	30	22	0
492/364	1960	SA	1	Birmingham	W-100	10	11	b	9	25	b	–	149	58	4	132	58	3
493/365			2	Lord's	W-I & 73	9	0	b	–	–	–	–	78	49	0	102	44	2
494/366			3	Nottingham	W-8w	9	15	b	–	–	–	1	87	27	5	132	77	4
495/367			4	Manchester	D	10	10	c	9	14	*	2	120	58	3	36	10	0
496/368			5	Oval	D	9	0	lbw	9	24	b	1	187	93	2	60	34	2
507/369	1961	A	1	Birmingham	D	10	20	c	–	–	–	1	221	136	2	–	–	–
508/370			2	Lord's	L-5w	10	25	b	10	0	c	–	204	118	4	60	40	2
509/371			3	Leeds	W-8w	8	4	c	–	–	–	–	132	58	5	95	30	6
510/372			4	Manchester	L-54	9	3	c	9	8	c	1	84	55	1	192	92	0
530/382	1962	P	1	Birmingham	W-I & 24	–	–	–	–	–	–	1	78	59	2	144	70	2
531/383			2	Lord's	W-9w	10	29	lbw	–	–	–	1	106	31	6	201	85	3
532/384			3	Leeds	W-I & 117	10	20	lbw	–	–	–	2	138	55	2	64	33	2
533/385			4	Nottingham	D	–	–	–	–	–	–	2	144	71	4	114	35	1
535/387	1962–63	A	1	Brisbane[2]	D	10	19	c	–	–	–	2	144	76	3	120	59	0
536/388			2	Melbourne	W-7w	9	6	c	–	–	–	1	184	83	3	160	62	5
537/389			3	Sydney	L-8w	9	32	b	9	9	c	2	160	68	0	48	20	2
538/390			4	Adelaide	D	10	38	c	–	–	–	1	152	54	1	187	60	4
539/391			5	Sydney	D	8	30	c	8	8	c	1	88	33	1	24	6	1
541/393	1962–63	NZ	2	Wellington	W-I & 47	9	3	b	–	–	–	–	120	46	4	108	27	1
542/394			3	Christchurch	W-7w	9	11	c	–	–	–	–	182	75	7	118	16	2
543/395	1963	WI	1	Manchester	L-10w	9	5	c	10	29	*	–	240	95	2	–	–	–
544/396			2	Lord's	D	9	10	b	9	0	c	–	264	100	6	156	52	5
545/397			3	Birmingham	W-217	9	4	b	9	1	c	1	156	75	5	87	44	7
546/398			4	Leeds	L-221	9	4	c	9	5	c	1	276	117	4	78	46	2
547/399			5	Oval	L-8w	8	19	b	8	5	c	1	157	65	3	6	0	0
561/405	1964	A	1	Nottingham	D	8	0	c	7	4	c	1	123	58	3	30	28	0
562/406			2	Lord's	D	9	8	b	–	–	–	–	150	48	5	108	52	1
563/407			3	Leeds	L-7w	9	4	c	10	12	*	–	147	98	3	42	28	1
565/409			5	Oval	D	9	14	c	–	–	–	2	201	87	4	–	–	–
591/415	1965	NZ	1	Birmingham	W-9w	10	3	c	–	–	–	1	108	49	1	196	79	3
592/416			2	Lord's	W-7w	9	3	b	–	–	–	–	119	40	2	156	69	0

Career	**M**	**I**	**NO**	**HS**	**R**	**Avge**	**100**	**50**	**Ct**	**St**	**Balls**	**R**	**W**	**Avge**	**BB**	**5w**	**10w**	**Rate**
Test	67	85	14	39*	981	13.81	–	–	64	–	15178	6625	307	21.57	8-31	17	3	49.43
F/c	603	713	120	104	9231	15.56	3	26	439	–	99858	42154	2304	18.29	8-28	126	25	43.34

NOTABLE FEATS

• 50 wickets in 10th Test (*426*); 100 wickets in 25th Test (*472*); 150 wickets in 37th Test (*492*); 200 wickets in 47th Test (*531*); 250 wickets in 56th Test (*542*); 300 wickets in 65th Test (*565*).
• *351* Reduced India to 0 for 4 in their 2nd inns by taking 3 wickets in 8 balls on his debut.
• *353* Achieved record E v I innings analysis of 8 for 31.
• *354* Set E v I series record with 29 wickets.
• *509* Took 5 for 0 with 24 off-cutters at a reduced pace.
• *531* Shared record E v P 9th-wkt stand of 76 with T.W. Graveney.
• *542* Passed J.B. Statham's world Test record of 242 wickets; his analysis of 7 for 75 remains the record for Christchurch Tests and for England in NZ.
• *545* Record match analysis (12 for 119) v WI in England and for any Birmingham Test. Ended with a 6 for 4 spell from 24 balls.
• *547* Set E v WI series record with 34 wickets.
• *565* First to take 300 wickets in Tests.
• Took 100 wickets in a season 12 times, notably 175 in 1960 and over 150 on 3 other occasions. Leading bowler in 1963 with 129 wickets at 15.15 apiece.
• Four hat-tricks for Yorkshire: three v Nottinghamshire (at Nottingham in 1951, Scarborough in 1955 and Bradford in 1963) and v MCC at Lord's in 1958.

F. S. TRUEMAN – TEST BOWLING SUMMARY

Series	V	M	Balls	R	W	Avge	BB	5w	10w	Rate
1952	I	4	718	386	29	13.31	8-31	2	–	24.75
1953	A	1	159	90	4	22.50	4-86	–	–	39.75
1953–54	WI	3	800	420	9	46.66	3-88	–	–	88.88
1955	SA	1	210	112	2	56.00	2-73	–	–	105.00
1956	A	2	450	184	9	20.44	5-90	1	–	50.00
1957	WI	5	1041	455	22	20.68	5-63	1	–	47.31
1958	NZ	5	791	256	15	17.06	5-31	1	–	52.73
1958–59	A	3	696	276	9	30.66	4-90	–	–	77.33
1958–59	NZ	2	269	105	5	21.00	3-46	–	–	53.80
1959	I	5	1066	401	24	16.70	4-24	–	–	44.41
1959–60	WI	5	1323	549	21	26.14	5-35	1	–	63.00
1960	SA	5	1083	508	25	20.32	5-27	1	–	43.32
1961	A	4	988	529	20	26.45	6-30	2	1	49.40
1962	P	4	989	439	22	19.95	6-31	1	–	44.95
1962–63	A	5	1267	521	20	26.05	5-62	1	–	63.35
1962–63	NZ	2	528	164	14	11.71	7-75	1	–	37.71
1963	WI	5	1420	594	34	17.47	7-44	4	2	41.76
1964	A	4	801	399	17	23.47	5-48	1	–	47.11
1965	NZ	2	579	237	6	39.50	3-79	–	–	96.50
	A	19	4361	1999	79	25.30	6-30	5	1	55.20
	SA	6	1293	620	27	22.96	5-27	1	–	47.88
	WI	18	4584	2018	86	23.46	7-44	6	2	53.30
	NZ	11	2167	762	40	19.05	7-75	2	–	54.17
	I	9	1784	787	53	14.84	8-31	2	–	33.66
	P	4	989	439	22	19.95	6-31	1	–	44.95
Home		47	10295	4590	229	20.04	8-31	14	3	44.95
Overseas		20	4883	2035	78	26.08	7-75	3	–	62.60
Totals		67	15178	6625	307	21.57	8-31	17	3	49.43

• Took 8 for 28 before lunch on the first day for Yorkshire v Kent at Dover in 1954.

TUFNELL
Col Neville Charsley

Cambridge University (1908 to 1910)
Surrey (1922)

TOURS SA 1909–10; NZ 1906–07
Born Simla, India 13 Jun 1887
Died Whitechapel, London 3 Aug 1951

Neville Tufnell was a talented wicket-keeper who toured New Zealand while still at Eton and visited South Africa during his final year at Cambridge. When, in the Second Test at Durban, he deputised for Strudwick after the Surrey keeper had been struck in the face, he proceeded to make the first stumping by a substitute in Test cricket. At the end of that rubber he made his only scheduled appearance in Test cricket but he had to wait another 12 years before playing in his first and only county match. When he did turn out for Surrey against Oxford University at The Oval in 1922, Strudwick was also in the team. [*Illus. p.* 273]

NOTABLE FEATS

• Stumped 5 batsmen in one innings off the bowling of J.H. Bruce-Lockhart for Cambridge U v Yorkshire at Fenner's in 1909.

						Batting 1st			Batting 2nd			Fielding 1st				Fielding 2nd			
Ref	Series	V	T	Venue	Result	No	R	HO	No	R	HO	Ct	St	Byes	Balls	Ct	St	Byes	Balls
110/107†	1909–10	SA	5	Cape Town	W-9w	9	14	c	–	–	–	–	–	0	233	–	1	25	594

Career	M	I	NO	HS	R	Avge	100	50	Ct	St	Balls	R	W	Avge	BB	5w	10w	Rate
Test	1	1	0	14	14	14.00	–	–	–	1	–	–	–	–	–	–	–	–
F/c	71	121	14	102	1514	14.14	1	4	59	40	84	118	1	118.00	1-54	–	–	84.00

TURNBULL Maurice Joseph Lawson

Glamorgan (1924 to 1939)
Cambridge University (1926 to 1929)

Wisden 1931
TOURS
A 1929–30; SA 1930–31; NZ 1929–30
Born Cardiff, Glamorgan 16 Mar 1906
Died near Montchamp, France
5 Aug 1944

Maurice Turnbull played cricket for England, rugby and hockey for Wales and was South Wales squash racquets champion. In his last year at Downside he scored 1323 runs at an average of 94.50; the previous summer he had top-scored with 40 against the formidable Lancashire attack on a difficult pitch in his first match for Glamorgan. He captained Cambridge in his final year and scored 1001 runs for them. The following season he began a ten-year term as captain of Glamorgan which was ended only by the Second World War. He was a high-class batsman who always looked to attack the bowling. From his early days as a predominantly on-side player, he developed a full range of orthodox strokes and improvised a few extra ones. His best innings were played in challenging situations, where either the side's position or the state of the pitch or a race against the clock inspired him. His contribution to Glamorgan cricket went far beyond the playing field. In 1930 he also took over the Club's administration when it was £5000 in the red – a colossal debt in those times. By 1939 with the aid of functions throughout Wales and membership drives he had turned the accounts into a surplus of £1000. As a major in the Welsh Guards he was killed instantly by a sniper's bullet during the Normandy landings.

NOTABLE FEATS
- Exceeded 1000 runs in a season 10 times.
- Scored 3 double centuries for Glamorgan, notably 233 v Worcestershire at Swansea in 1937.

MCC to Australia and New Zealand, 1929–30: standing *E.H. Bowley, W.L. Cornford, T.S. Worthington, M.S. Nichols, M.J.C. Allom, F. Barratt, M.J.L. Turnbull, G.B. Legge, E.T. Benson, W.S. Ferguson;* seated *E.W. Dawson, G.F. Earle, A.H.H. Gilligan (captain), F.E. Woolley, K.S. Duleepsinhji.*

Ref	Series	V	T	Venue	Result	Batting 1st No	R	HO	Batting 2nd No	R	HO	Ct
186/172	1929-30	NZ	1	Christchurch	W-8w	8	7	c	–	–	–	–
204/185	1930-31	SA	1	Johannesburg[1]	L-28	5	28	st	5	61	b	–
205/186			2	Cape Town	D	5	7	b	5	14	b	1
206/187			3	Durban[2]	D	–	–	–	–	–	–	–
207/188			4	Johannesburg[1]	D	6	25	st	9	0	*	–
208/189			5	Durban[2]	D	5	6	b	4	7	c	–
227/201	1933	WI	1	Lord's	W-I & 27	6	28	c	–	–	–	–
229/203			3	Oval	W-I & 17	5	4	b	–	–	–	–
252/221	1936	I	1	Lord's	W-9w	3	0	b	3	37	*	–

Career	M	I	NO	HS	R	Avge	100	50	Ct	St	Balls	R	W	Avge	BB	5w	10w	Rate
Test	9	13	2	61	224	20.36	–	1	1	–	–	–	–	–	–	–	–	–
F/c	388	626	37	233	17544	29.78	29	82	280	–	392	355	4	88.75	1-4	–	–	98.00

TYLDESLEY
George Ernest

Lancashire (1909 to 1936)

Wisden 1920
TOURS
A 1928–29; SA 1924–25 (Joel), 1927–28; WI 1926–27 (Tennyson)
Born Roe Green, Worsley, Lancashire
5 Feb 1889
Died Rhos-on-Sea, Denbighshire
5 May 1962

Ernest Tyldesley

Ernest Tyldesley reaped the benefit of being coached in childhood by J.T. (Johnny) Tyldesley, his elder brother by 15 years and one of Lancashire's greatest batsmen. So effective was the tuition that, by the end of his career, Ernest had amassed more runs and hundreds and at a higher average than his brother. He was an elegant, patient, courteous, clinical and quite ruthless slaughterer of bowling. A high quality touch player, his meagre ration of Test cricket was scant reward for his performances at either county or international level. Seven years passed between his England debut and his first Test appearance at Lord's and, although he saluted that occasion by scoring a century in 160 minutes, he was never again selected for a Test at Headquarters. He remains the only Lancashire player to score 100 centuries.

NOTABLE FEATS

- Exceeded 1000 runs in a season 18 times (plus once on tour), including 3024 in 1928 and 2000 on 5 other occasions. Scored 1024 runs in July 1926.
- Scored 7 double centuries, all for Lancashire, notably 256* v Warwickshire at Manchester in 1930.
- Set record for most fifties in consecutive first-class innings with 10 between 26 June and 27 July 1926 (later equalled by D.G. Bradman); his sequence included 7 hundreds.
- Holds Lancashire career records for most appearances (573), most runs (34,222) and most hundreds (90).
- Shared record Lancashire 2nd-wkt stand of 371 with F.B. Watson v Surrey at Manchester in 1928; it remains Lancashire's highest stand for any wicket.
- Scored hundreds in 4 consecutive innings in 1926, and in 3 consecutive innings on 2 other occasions (1928 and 1934).
- Scored 100 in each innings of a match for Lancashire twice.

TEST NOTES

- *172* Bowled in 2nd inns: 0 for 2 (3 balls).

						Batting 1st			Batting 2nd			
Ref	Series	V	T	Venue	Result	No	R	HO	No	R	HO	Ct
140/129	1921	A	1	Nottingham	L-10w	3	0	b	3	7	b	–
143/132			4	Manchester	D	5	78	*	–	–	–	1
144/133			5	Oval	D	3	39	c	–	–	–	–
155/141	1924	SA	3	Leeds	W-9w	6	15	ro	–	–	–	–
166/152	1926	A	4	Manchester	D	3	81	c	–	–	–	1
168/154	1927–28	SA	1	Johannesburg[1]	W-10w	3	122	lbw	–	–	–	–
169/155			2	Cape Town	W-87	3	0	b	3	87	lbw	–
170/156			3	Durban[2]	D	3	78	c	3	62	*	–
171/157			4	Johannesburg[1]	L-4w	3	42	lbw	3	8	c	–
172/158			5	Durban[2]	L-8w	3	100	c	3	21	c	–
173/159	1928	WI	1	Lord's	W-I & 58	3	122	c	–	–	–	–
174/160			2	Manchester	W-I & 30	3	3	b	–	–	–	–
175/161			3	Oval	W-I & 71	3	73	c	–	–	–	–
180/166	1928–29	A	5	Melbourne	L-5w	4	31	c	5	21	c	–

Career	M	I	NO	HS	R	Avge	100	50	Ct	St	Balls	R	W	Avge	BB	5w	10w	Rate
Test	14	20	2	122	990	55.00	3	6	2	–	3	2	0	–	–	–	–	–
F/c	648	961	106	256*	38874	45.46	102	191	293	–	421	346	6	57.66	3-33	–	–	70.16

TYLDESLEY John Thomas

Lancashire (1895 to 1923)

Wisden 1902
TOURS A 1901–02, 1903–04; SA 1898–99
Born Roe Green, Worsley, Lancashire 22 Nov 1873
Died Monton, Manchester 27 Nov 1930

An aggressive little dynamo just 5ft 6in high, Johnny Tyldesley was one of Lancashire's greatest batsmen. He learned his trade in the tough school of the league before establishing himself in the Lancashire team by scoring 152* in his second match. An extremely quick-footed attacking player in any conditions, he based his assaults on a well-organised defence and was particularly skilful on poor surfaces. Highly professional, he organised his innings like a campaign of battle. His talent for improvisation and ability to play strokes all round the wicket enabled him to overcome the leg-theory of Armstrong and the off-theory of McLeod in scoring his century against the 1905 Australians at Leeds. During cricket's 'Golden Age' of prolific amateur batsmen, 'JT' was the only professional batsman to retain his place in the England team. Another factor to influence his automatic Test selection for a decade was his brilliance in the outfield; exceptionally fast and sure-handed, he had a lethally accurate throw. He was Lancashire's coach from his retirement until 1929. The elder brother of Ernest by some 15 years, he collapsed and died as he was putting on his boots to go to work.

Johnny Tyldesley

NOTABLE FEATS

- 1000 runs in 20th Test (*83*) (35 inns).
- Exceeded 1000 runs in a season 19 times, including 3041 in 1901 and 2000 on 4 other occasions.
- Scored 13 double centuries for Lancashire, notably 295* v Kent at Manchester in 1906.
- Holds Lancashire record for the most runs in a season (2633 in 1901) and most instances of 1000 runs in a season (19).
- Shared record Lancashire 4th-wkt stand of 324 with A.C. MacLaren v Nottinghamshire at Nottingham in 1904.
- Scored hundreds in 3 consecutive innings for Lancashire on 2 occasions (1897 and 1904).

						Batting 1st			Batting 2nd			
Ref	Series	V	T	Venue	Result	No	R	HO	No	R	HO	Ct
58/58	1898–99	SA	1	Johannesburg[1]	W-32	3	17	ro	3	17	c	2
59/59			2	Cape Town	W-210	3	13	b	3	112	c	1
60/60	1899	A	1	Nottingham	D	7	22	c	7	10	c	–
61/61			2	Lord's	L-10w	7	14	c	7	4	c	–
65/65	1901–02	A	1	Sydney	W-I & 124	3	1	c	–	–	–	–
66/66			2	Melbourne	L-229	3	2	c	3	66	c	2
67/67			3	Adelaide	L-4w	3	0	c	3	25	ro	1
68/68			4	Sydney	L-7w	3	79	c	3	10	c	–
69/69			5	Melbourne	L-32	4	13	c	5	36	c	–
70/70	1902	A	1	Birmingham	D	5	138	lbw	–	–	–	–
71/71			2	Lord's	D	–	–	–	–	–	–	–
72/72			3	Sheffield	L-143	3	22	c	3	14	b	–
73/73			4	Manchester	L-3	3	22	c	3	16	c	1
74/74			5	Oval	W-1w	3	33	b	3	0	b	1
78/75	1903–04	A	1	Sydney	W-5w	3	53	b	3	9	c	–
79/76			2	Melbourne	W-185	3	97	c	3	62	c	1
80/77			3	Adelaide	L-216	3	0	c	4	10	c	1
81/78			4	Sydney	W-157	3	16	c	4	5	b	1
82/79			5	Melbourne	L-218	5	10	c	3	15	c	–
83/80	1905	A	1	Nottingham	W-213	3	56	c	3	61	c	–
84/81			2	Lord's	D	3	43	c	3	12	b	–
85/82			3	Leeds	D	3	0	b	3	100	st	–
86/83			4	Manchester	W-I & 80	3	24	b	–	–	–	1
87/84			5	Oval	D	3	16	b	4	112	*	–
93/90	1907	SA	1	Lord's	D	3	52	b	–	–	–	–
94/91			2	Leeds	W-53	3	12	b	3	30	c	1
95/92			3	Oval	D	3	8	b	3	11	c	–
101/98	1909	A	1	Birmingham	W-10w	3	24	b	–	–	–	1
102/99			2	Lord's	L-9w	3	46	lbw	3	3	st	–
103/100			3	Leeds	L-126	3	55	c	3	7	c	–
104/101			4	Manchester	D	3	15	c	3	11	b	2

- Scored 100 in each innings of a first-class match on 3 occasions.
- Scored 100 before lunch on 6 occasions.

Career	M	I	NO	HS	R	Avge	100	50	Ct	St	Balls	R	W	Avge	BB	5w	10w	Rate
Test	31	55	1	138	1661	30.75	4	9	16	–	–	–	–	–	–	–	–	–
F/c	608	994	62	295*	37897	40.66	86	193	355	–	296	211	3	70.33	1-4	–	–	98.66

J. T. TYLDESLEY – TEST BATTING SUMMARY

Series	V	M	I	NO	HS	R	Avge	100	50
1898–99	SA	2	4	–	112	159	39.75	1	–
1899	A	2	4	–	22	50	12.50	–	–
1901–02	A	5	9	–	79	232	25.77	–	2
1902	A	5	7	–	138	245	35.00	1	–
1903–04	A	5	10	–	97	277	27.70	–	3
1905	A	5	9	1	112*	424	53.00	2	2
1907	SA	3	5	–	52	113	22.60	–	1
1909	A	4	7	–	55	161	23.00	–	1
	A	26	46	1	138	1389	30.86	3	8
	SA	5	9	–	112	272	30.22	1	1
Home		19	32	1	138	993	32.03	3	4
Overseas		12	23	–	112	668	29.04	1	5
Totals		31	55	1	138	1661	30.75	4	9

TYLDESLEY
Richard Knowles

Lancashire (1919 to 1931)

Wisden 1925
TOUR A 1924–25
Born Westhoughton, Lancashire
11 Mar 1897
Died Over Hulton, Bolton, Lancashire
17 Sep 1943

Dick Tyldesley was the youngest of four brothers from Westhoughton, all of whom appeared for Lancashire. They were not related to Johnny and Ernest Tyldesley who came from a Worsley-based family. A former colliery worker, he was an extremely rotund right-arm slow bowler – specialising in leg-breaks and top-spinners – and a capable lower-order batsman. He was taught to bowl by his father who was the Westhoughton club's professional and through hours of dedicated practice became a master of length. When he added spin, flight and variations of angle and pace he was on his way to becoming the third-highest wicket-taker in Lancashire's history at the time of his retirement. A little above average height, he appeared untroubled by the ever-increasing vastness of his bulk and had immense stamina and concentration. Although he was Lancashire's leading bowler by some distance in 1931, that season marked the end of his career, the winter bringing an irreconcilable dispute with the committee over his terms of employment. [*Illus. p.* 161]

NOTABLE FEATS

- Took 100 wickets in a season 10 times, notably 184 in 1924. Headed the national averages in 1929 with 154 wickets at 15.57.
- Returned several outstanding analyses for Lancashire, notably 7 for 6 v Northamptonshire at Liverpool in 1924 and 5 for 0 v Leicestershire at Manchester in 1924.
- Took 4 wickets in 4 balls (separate innings) for Lancashire v Derbyshire at Derby in 1929.
- Bowled in an unchanged partnership with C.H. Parkin throughout both completed Warwickshire innings for Lancashire at Manchester in 1924.
- Equalled (then) world fielding record by holding 6 catches in an innings v Hampshire at Liverpool in 1921; it remains the Lancashire record.

					Batting 1st			Batting 2nd				Bowling 1st			Bowling 2nd		
Ref	Series	V	T Venue	Result	No	R	HO	No	R	HO	Ct	Balls	R	W	Balls	R	W
154/140	1924	SA	2 Lord's	W-I & 18	–	–	–	–	–	–	–	144	52	3	216	50	3
155/141			3 Leeds	W-9w	9	29	c	–	–	–	–	78	37	0	144	63	3
156/142			4 Manchester	D	–	–	–	–	–	–	–	71	11	1	–	–	–
157/143			5 Oval	D	9	1	*	–	–	–	1	132	36	2	–	–	–
159/145	1924–25	A	2 Melbourne	L-81	8	5	c	7	0	c	–	280	130	0	16	6	0
194/180	1930	A	1 Nottingham	W-93	10	1	c	10	5	b	–	126	53	2	210	77	3
196/182			3 Leeds	D	11	6	c	–	–	–	–	198	104	2	–	–	–

Career	M	I	NO	HS	R	Avge	100	50	Ct	St	Balls	R	W	Avge	BB	5w	10w	Rate
Test	7	7	1	29	47	7.83	–	–	1	–	1615	619	19	32.57	3-50	–	–	85.00
F/c	397	464	54	105	6419	15.65	1	15	337	–	66846	25980	1509	17.21	8-15	101	22	44.29

TYLECOTE Edward Ferdinando Sutton

Oxford University (1869 to 1872)
Kent (1875 to 1883)

TOUR A 1882–83
Born Marston Moretaine, Bedfordshire
23 Jun 1849
Died New Hunstanton, Norfolk
15 Mar 1938

Edward Tylecote was an outstanding batsman wicket-keeper who, as a schoolboy prodigy at Clifton, spent five years in the College XI, the last as captain. During that final summer he ruined a good game of cricket between Classical and Modern by scoring 404*, then the record score at any level. Opening the innings he carried his bat through an innings of 630 in six hours spread over three days. He gained the first of his four blues as a freshman and was captain in his last two summers. He played for Kent while he was a mathematical tutor at the Royal Military Academy and scored 100* against the 1882 Australians. Touring Australia with the Hon. Ivo Bligh's XI he made a decisive contribution to the match that recovered the Ashes for the first time. One of the first keepers to dispense with a long-stop, he was a most reliable and unobtrusive technician behind the stumps and an elegant off-side strokemaker in front of them. [*Illus. p.* 42]

NOTABLE FEATS

- *12* Scored the first half-century by a wicket-keeper in Test cricket.

						Batting 1st			Batting 2nd			Fielding 1st				Fielding 2nd			
Ref	Series	V	T	Venue	Result	No	R	HO	No	R	HO	Ct	St	Byes	Balls	Ct	St	Byes	Balls
10/10†	1882–83	A	1	Melbourne	L-9w	8	33	b	2	38	b	1	2	4	676	–	–	0	213
11/11†			2	Melbourne	W-I & 27	7	0	b	–	–	–	–	–	6	394	–	–	1	276
12/12†			3	Sydney	W-69	7	66	ro	7	0	c	–	1	6	717	–	–	6	278
13/13†			4	Sydney	L-4w	6	5	b	6	0	b	–	–	10	588	–	1	10	653
23/23†	1886	A	2	Lord's	W-I & 106	9	0	b	–	–	–	1	–	4	331	1	–	13	445
24/24†			3	Oval	W-I & 217	10	10	*	–	–	–	1	–	4	242	1	1	7	388

Career	M	I	NO	HS	R	Avge	100	50	Ct	St	Balls	R	W	Avge	BB	5w	10w	Rate
Test	6	9	1	66	152	19.00	–	1	5	5	–	–	–	–	–	–	–	–
F/c	93	158	10	107	3065	20.70	3	10	127	58	24	14	0	–	–	–	–	–

TYLER, Edwin James

Somerset (1891 to 1907)

TOUR SA 1895–96
Born Kidderminster, Worcestershire
13 Oct 1864
Died North Town, Taunton, Somerset
25 Jan 1917

Edwin Tyler was an extremely slow left-handed leg-break bowler who played a major part in elevating Somerset to first-class status in 1891. So slow was he that if he bowled a bad ball he had time to run down the pitch and retrieve it before it reached the batsman. In 1900 he was no-balled for throwing and his action came in for serious discussion but, as he was considered too slow to injure anybody, he was allowed to continue bowling without further harassment. A genial, popular character who also batted left-handed, he began his career with Kidderminster and appeared for Worcestershire in minor matches before joining Somerset. [*Illus. p.* 325]

NOTABLE FEATS

- Took 100 wickets in a season 3 times.
- His innings analysis of 10 for 49 v Surrey at Taunton in 1895 remains the Somerset record. Took 9 wickets in an innings for Somerset on 2 other occasions (1892 and 1907).
- Twice returned 15-wicket match analyses for Somerset at Taunton: 15 for 96 v Nottinghamshire in 1892 and 15 for 95 v Sussex in 1895.
- Hat-trick for Somerset v Yorkshire at Taunton in 1895.

						Batting 1st			Batting 2nd				Bowling 1st			Bowling 2nd		
Ref	Series	V	T	Venue	Result	No	R	HO	No	R	HO	Ct	Balls	R	W	Balls	R	W
49/49	1895–96	SA	3	Cape Town	W-I & 33	10	0	b	–	–	–	–	90	49	3	55	16	1

Career	M	I	NO	HS	R	Avge	100	50	Ct	St	Balls	R	W	Avge	BB	5w	10w	Rate
Test	1	1	0	0	0	0.00	–	–	–	–	145	65	4	16.25	3-49	–	–	36.25
F/c	185	310	52	66	2952	11.44	–	6	118	–	39309	19779	895	22.09	10-49	77	22	43.92

TYSON
Frank Holmes

Northamptonshire (1952 to 1960)

Wisden 1956
TOURS
A 1954–55, 1958–59; SA 1956–57, 1959–60 (Cwlth); WI 1955–56 (Swanton); NZ 1954–55, 1958–59
Born Farnworth, Lancashire 6 Jun 1930

Frank Tyson

For a handful of English seasons and one memorable antipodean summer Frank Tyson was the fastest bowler in world cricket. Tall (6ft) and immensely strong, he exuded hostility as he began his vast run-up. His premature baldness extended the high dome of his forehead and appeared to increase the sense of menace for the poor batsman. The sight of the slips and wicket-keeper retreating five yards after the first ball cannot have helped either. After he had reverted to his original reduced run-up following the debacle of Brisbane, he rediscovered his rhythm and for those few weeks attained a searing speed which, according to players who witnessed both series, was faster even than Jeff Thomson 20 years later. In 1968 he played in a benefit match despite a leg blackened by a contusion received the previous week. A little overweight and operating off a very truncated run, he gave a hint of the speed he could generate from that extremely powerful torso. His second ball flew from a length, took the bat's edge as the batsman protected his face and flew to this fielder at gully; only an instinctive protective reaction prevented a direct hit between the eyes and he was more than unlucky to be out. 'I'm glad you catch the easy ones,' bellowed the Typhoon, distinctly unimpressed. Two balls later the number three was stretchered off after a direct blow over the heart. Colin McDonald, the non-striker, consoled Frank: 'Don't worry about him. It'll show these club cricketers that we don't play for fun.' Heaven knows what it is was like when they were playing seriously. He was a capable and hard-hitting tail-end batsman and naturally had a powerful throw. An erudite graduate of Durham University, he emigrated to Australia and made a career in teaching (at one time he was a headmaster), writing and broadcasting before enjoying a long interlude as chief cricket coach to the Victorian Cricket Association.

NOTABLE FEATS

- 50 wickets in 9th Test (*408*).
- *393* Took 6 for 16 in 51 balls as Australia's last 8 wickets fell for 34 runs.
- Took 101 wickets in 1957.

Ref	Series	V	T	Venue	Result	Batting 1st No	Batting 1st R	Batting 1st HO	Batting 2nd No	Batting 2nd R	Batting 2nd HO	Ct	Bowling 1st Balls	Bowling 1st R	Bowling 1st W	Bowling 2nd Balls	Bowling 2nd R	Bowling 2nd W
390/314	1954	P	4	Oval	L-24	8	3	c	8	3	c	–	82	35	4	54	22	1
391/315	1954–55	A	1	Brisbane[2]	L-I & 154	7	7	b	7	37	*	–	232	160	1	–	–	–
392/316			2	Sydney	W-38	7	0	b	7	9	b	1	104	45	4	148	85	6
393/317			3	Melbourne	W-128	9	6	b	9	6	c	–	168	68	2	99	27	7
394/318			4	Adelaide	W-5w	9	1	c	–	–	–	–	209	85	3	120	47	3
395/319			5	Sydney	D	–	–	–	–	–	–	1	88	46	2	40	20	0
401/320	1954–55	NZ	1	Dunedin	W-8w	9	16	c	–	–	–	–	114	23	3	72	16	4
402/321			2	Auckland	W-I & 20	9	27	*	–	–	–	–	66	41	2	42	10	2
408/322	1955	SA	1	Nottingham	W-I & 5	9	0	c	–	–	–	–	144	51	2	129	28	6
410/324			3	Manchester	L-3w	10	2	b	9	8	b	–	264	124	3	81	55	3
429/331	1956	A	5	Oval	D	10	3	c	–	–	–	1	84	34	1	–	–	–
434/332	1956–57	SA	1	Johannesburg[3]	W-131	8	22	b	9	2	c	–	72	22	0	–	–	–
438/336			5	Port Elizabeth	L-58	9	1	c	9	23	c	1	136	38	2	184	40	6
467/350	1958–59	A	4	Adelaide	L-10w	9	0	c	9	33	c	–	224	100	1	–	–	–
468/351			5	Melbourne	L-9w	10	9	c	10	6	c	–	160	73	1	48	20	1
472/352	1958–59	NZ	1	Christchurch	W-I & 99	11	6	*	–	–	–	–	84	23	3	84	23	2
473/353			2	Auckland	D	–	–	–	–	–	–	–	120	20	1	–	–	–

Career	M	I	NO	HS	R	Avge	100	50	Ct	St	Balls	R	W	Avge	BB	5w	10w	Rate
Test	17	24	3	37*	230	10.95	–	–	4	–	3452	1411	76	18.56	7-27	4	1	45.42
F/c	244	316	76	82	4103	17.09	–	13	85	–	38079	16030	767	20.89	8-60	34	5	49.64

F. H. TYSON – TEST BOWLING SUMMARY

Series	V	M	Balls	R	W	Avge	BB	5w	10w	Rate
1954	P	1	136	57	5	11.40	4-35	–	–	27.20
1954–55	A	5	1208	583	28	20.82	7-27	2	1	43.14
1954–55	NZ	2	294	90	11	8.18	4-16	–	–	26.72
1955	SA	2	618	258	14	18.42	6-28	1	–	44.14
1956	A	1	84	34	1	34.00	1-34	–	–	84.00
1956–57	SA	2	392	100	8	12.50	6-40	1	–	49.00
1958–59	A	2	432	193	3	64.33	1-20	–	–	144.00
1958–59	NZ	2	288	96	6	16.00	3-23	–	–	48.00
	A	8	1724	810	32	25.31	7-27	2	1	53.87
	SA	4	1010	358	22	16.27	6-28	2	–	45.90
	NZ	4	582	186	17	10.94	4-16	–	–	34.23
	P	1	136	57	5	11.40	4-35	–	–	27.20
Home		4	838	349	20	17.45	6-28	1	–	41.90
Overseas		13	2614	1062	56	18.96	7-27	3	1	46.67
Totals		17	3452	1411	76	18.56	7-27	4	1	45.42

ULYETT, George

Yorkshire (1873 to 1893)

TOURS
A 1876–77, 1878–79, 1881–82, 1884–85, 1887–88; SA 1888–89
Born Crabtree, Pitsmoor, Sheffield, Yorkshire 21 Oct 1851
Died Pitsmoor, Sheffield 18 Jun 1898

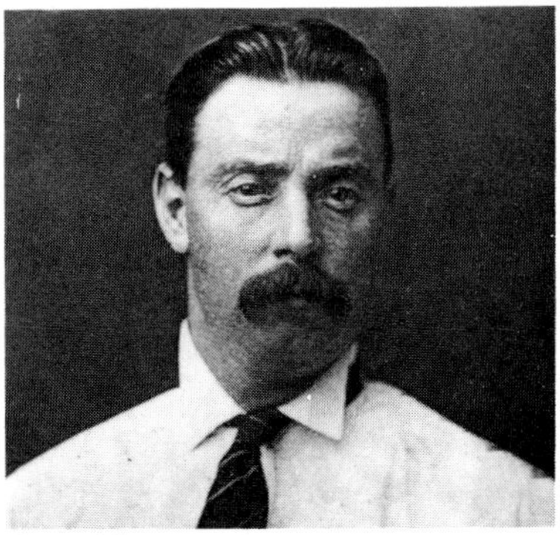

George Ulyett

Playing in the inaugural Test match, George Ulyett bowled the ball which coincided with a damaged part of Charlie Bannerman's glove, split the second finger of his right hand and compelled Test cricket's first century-maker also to become the first Test cricketer to retire hurt. He was a complete all-round cricketer. Acknowledged as the greatest Yorkshire batsman of the Victorian era, he remained in the front rank for almost two decades and was equally worth his place as a specialist right-handed round-arm fast bowler and outstanding fielder. A lively fun-loving character, he was known as 'Happy Jack' and his carefree approach to batting revolved around a policy of high, wide and handsome. Tall and strongly built, he was a prodigious striker of the ball and once cleared the roof of the old pavilion at Lord's. His opening partnerships with the patiently adhesive Louis Hall were a feature of Yorkshire cricket at that time. As a bowler, he was extremely rapid, extracting sharp break and lift from responsive surfaces. He died of pneumonia contracted while watching Yorkshire play Kent at Sheffield.

NOTABLE FEATS

- 50 wickets in 25th Test (*33*).
- *6* With R.G. Barlow shared the first century opening stand in Test cricket (122).
- *8* His 149 was the first Test hundred for England in Australia and the highest score for England on the first day of a Test in Australia until 1965–66.
- Exceeded 1000 runs in a season 10 times.
- Achieved the first instance of a bowler taking 4 wickets in 4 balls in a first-class match in Australia (for Lord Harris's XI v NSW at Sydney in 1878–79). Hat-trick for Yorkshire v Lancashire at Sheffield in 1883.
- Bowled in an unchanged partnership with A. Hill throughout both completed United South innings for Yorkshire at Bradford in 1874.

						Batting 1st			Batting 2nd				Bowling 1st			Bowling 2nd		
Ref	**Series**	**V**	**T**	**Venue**	**Result**	**No**	**R**	**HO**	**No**	**R**	**HO**	**Ct**	**Balls**	**R**	**W**	**Balls**	**R**	**W**
1/1	1876–77	A	1	Melbourne	L-45	4	10	lbw	6	24	b	1	100	36	0	76	39	3
2/2			2	Melbourne	W-4w	6	52	b	5	63	c	1	57	15	2	76	33	1
3/3	1878–79	A		Melbourne	L-10w	1	0	b	1	14	b	–	248	93	1	4	9	0
5/5	1881–82	A	1	Melbourne	D	2	87	c	2	23	st	–	80	41	2	60	30	1
6/6			2	Sydney	L-5w	1	25	c	1	67	lbw	–	90	11	2	60	48	2
7/7			3	Sydney	L-6w	1	0	b	1	23	b	1	12	10	0	–	–	–
8/8			4	Melbourne	D	1	149	c	1	64	c	2	96	40	1	–	–	–

Ref	Series	V	T	Venue	Result	Batting 1st No	R	HO	Batting 2nd No	R	HO	Ct	Bowling 1st Balls	R	W	Bowling 2nd Balls	R	W
9/9	1882	A		Oval	L-7	3	26	st	4	11	c	–	36	11	1	24	10	1
14/14	1884	A	1	Manchester	D	3	5	b	3	1	c	–	120	41	3	–	–	–
15/15			2	Lord's	W-I & 5	4	32	b	–	–	–	2	44	21	0	157	36	7
16/16			3	Oval	D	6	10	c	–	–	–	1	224	96	1	–	–	–
17/17	1884–85	A	1	Adelaide	W-8w	3	68	c	–	–	–	–	40	23	0	8	3	0
18/18			2	Melbourne	W-10w	8	0	b	–	–	–	–	60	23	0	32	19	1
19/19			3	Sydney	L-6	3	2	b	3	4	ro	2	50	17	1	156	42	2
20/20			4	Sydney	L-8w	1	10	b	1	2	c	1	216	91	3	–	–	–
21/21			5	Melbourne	W-I & 98	4	1	b	–	–	–	–	92	52	4	60	25	3
22/22	1886	A	1	Manchester	W-4w	7	17	b	7	8	c	2	145	46	4	27	7	1
23/23			2	Lord's	W-I & 106	8	19	b	–	–	–	1	–	–	–	32	13	0
24/24			3	Oval	W-I & 217	8	0	c	–	–	–	1	–	–	–	–	–	–
27/27	1887–88	A		Sydney	W-126	3	5	c	3	5	b	1	–	–	–	–	–	–
29/29	1888	A	2	Oval	W-I & 137	3	0	c	–	–	–	–	–	–	–	–	–	–
30/30			3	Manchester	W-I & 21	3	0	b	–	–	–	–	–	–	–	–	–	–
31/31	1888–89	SA	1	Port Elizabeth	W-8w	2	4	b	2	22	b	3	4	1	0	80	27	2
32/32			2	Cape Town	W-I & 202	2	22	b	–	–	–	–	16	0	0	–	–	–
33/33	1890	A	1	Lord's	W-7w	6	74	b	–	–	–	–	15	0	1	30	11	0

Career	M	I	NO	HS	R	Avge	100	50	Ct	St	Balls	R	W	Avge	BB	5w	10w	Rate
Test	25	39	0	149	949	24.33	1	7	19	–	2627	1020	50	20.40	7-36	1	–	52.54
F/c	533	922	40	199*	20629	23.38	18	99	365	–	31043	13113	650	20.17	7-30	23	3	47.75

G. ULYETT – TEST BOWLING SUMMARY

Series	V	M	Balls	R	W	Avge	BB	5w	10w	Rate
1876–77	A	2	309	123	6	20.50	3-39	–	–	51.50
1878–79	A	1	252	102	1	102.00	1-93	–	–	252.00
1881–82	A	4	398	180	8	22.50	2-11	–	–	49.75
1882	A	1	60	21	2	10.50	1-10	–	–	30.00
1884	A	3	545	194	11	17.63	7-36	1	–	49.54
1884–85	A	5	714	295	14	21.07	4-52	–	–	51.00
1886	A	3	204	66	5	13.20	4-46	–	–	40.80
1887–88	A	1	–	–	–	–	–	–	–	–
1888	A	2	–	–	–	–	–	–	–	–
1888–89	SA	2	100	28	2	14.00	2-27	–	–	50.00
1890	A	1	45	11	1	11.00	1-0	–	–	45.00
	A	23	2527	992	48	20.66	7-36	1	–	52.64
	SA	2	100	28	2	14.00	2-27	–	–	50.00
Home		10	854	292	19	15.36	7-36	1	–	44.94
Overseas		15	1773	728	31	23.48	4-52	–	–	57.19
Totals		25	2627	1020	50	20.40	7-36	1	–	52.54

UNDERWOOD
Derek Leslie MBE

Kent (1963 to 1987)

Wisden 1969

TOURS

A 1970–71, 1974–75, 1976–77, 1979–80; SA 1975–76 (Int W), 1981–82 (SAB); WI 1969–70 (Cav/Norfolk), 1973–74; NZ 1970–71, 1974–75; I 1967–68 (Int XI), 1972–73, 1976–77, 1979–80, 1981–82; P 1966–67 (MCC U-25), 1968–69, 1972–73; SL 1967–68 (Int XI), 1968–69, 1972–73, 1976–77, 1981–82

Born Bromley, Kent 8 Jun 1945

For two decades Derek Underwood was the leading spin bowler in England. A little above average height (5ft 11in) and left-handed, he operated from a longish splay-footed approach and was totally unlike any other post-war bowler. His pace was normally slow-medium but he could vary it a notch or two either way according to the conditions. Apart from his varied range of pace, angle and flight which he could tailor precisely for any particular conditions, he developed a quite astonishing degree of accuracy. His extra pace extracted awkward bounce and in no way inhibited his ability to swing or turn the ball. As a 17-year-old he took Kent's opponents by storm and became the youngest bowler in the history of first-class cricket to take 100 wickets in his first season. Many sages doubted he could repeat the feat and attributed his success to beginner's luck or inferior pitches. They soon grew silent as he repeated the performance season after season and dismissed top batsmen on bland surfaces all over the world. If there was anything in a pitch remotely in his favour he would seek it out and exploit it. Leaking covers at Lord's, Fusarium Oxysporum at Headingley, and drying pitches with a crust on which the ball could bite have been allies to unplayable spells of devilry. There was no better example of the latter than at The Oval in 1968 when, at the end of the performance which gave him most pleasure, he dismissed John Inverarity with just five minutes to spare to square the series. After that, Test captains tended to carry Underwood around like an umbrella in case of rain. But for his decision to join the Packer bandwagon and make an unauthorised tour of South Africa he would most probably have reached 400 Test wickets. A brave but ungainly batsman, he was involved in many rearguard actions and when, towards the end of his career, he achieved an unlikely century as a night-watchman the entire cricket world rejoiced.

						Batting 1st			Batting 2nd				Bowling 1st			Bowling 2nd		
Ref	**Series**	**V**	**T**	**Venue**	**Result**	**No**	**R**	**HO**	**No**	**R**	**HO**	**Ct**	**Balls**	**R**	**W**	**Balls**	**R**	**W**
607/431	1966	WI	3	Nottingham	L-139	11	12	*	11	10	*	2	12	5	0	258	86	0
608/432			4	Leeds	L-I & 55	10	0	c	10	0	c	–	144	81	1	–	–	–
622/438	1967	P	2	Nottingham	W-10w	–	–	–	–	–	–	–	30	17	1	156	52	5
623/439			3	Oval	W-8w	11	2	*	–	–	–	1	54	12	0	156	48	2
638/446	1968	A	2	Lord's	D	–	–	–	–	–	–	1	–	–	–	108	8	2
639/447			3	Birmingham	D	11	14	*	–	–	–	1	150	48	3	48	14	0
640/448			4	Leeds	D	11	45	*	–	–	–	–	166	41	4	271	52	2
641/449			5	Oval	W-226	10	9	*	10	1	*	–	327	89	2	189	50	7
647/450	1968–69	P	1	Lahore[2]	D	8	0	c	8	6	c	–	96	36	1	114	29	1
648/451			2	Dacca	D	10	22	c	–	–	–	–	162	45	1	264	94	5
649/452			3	Karachi	D	–	–	–	–	–	–	–	–	–	–	–	–	–
653/453	1969	WI	1	Manchester	W-10w	10	11	*	–	–	–	1	72	15	1	114	31	1
655/455			3	Leeds	W-30	9	4	c	9	16	b	2	–	–	–	132	55	4
656/456	1969	NZ	1	Lord's	W-230	10	1	c	10	4	b	–	177	38	4	186	32	7
657/457			2	Nottingham	D	9	16	c	–	–	–	–	132	44	1	18	5	0
658/458			3	Oval	W-8w	9	3	lbw	–	–	–	1	156	41	6	231	60	6
674/459	1970–71	A	1	Brisbane[2]	D	10	2	*	–	–	–	1	224	101	3	160	23	1
676/461			4	Sydney	W-299	10	0	c	–	–	–	2	176	66	4	64	17	0
677/462			5	Melbourne	D	10	5	c	–	–	–	–	152	78	1	96	38	1
678/463			6	Adelaide	D	10	1	*	–	–	–	–	168	45	1	280	85	1
679/464			7	Sydney	W-62	10	8	*	10	0	c	1	128	39	2	110	28	2
685/465	1970–71	NZ	1	Christchurch	W-8w	11	0	*	–	–	–	–	94	12	6	259	85	6
686/466			2	Auckland	D	11	1	*	11	8	*	3	304	108	5	16	0	0
687/467	1971	P	1	Birmingham	D	10	9	*	–	–	–	1	246	102	0	–	–	–
692/472	1971	I	3	Oval	L-4w	10	22	c	10	11	c	1	150	49	1	228	72	3
701/476	1972	A	4	Leeds	W-9w	10	5	c	–	–	–	–	186	37	4	126	45	6
702/477			5	Oval	L-5w	11	3	*	11	0	*	–	228	90	4	210	94	2
703/478	1972–73	I	1	Delhi	W-6w	10	6	c	–	–	–	–	54	16	0	180	56	4
704/479			2	Calcutta	L-28	10	0	c	10	4	c	–	124	43	2	84	36	1

Ref	Series	V	T	Venue	Result	Batting 1st No	R	HO	Batting 2nd No	R	HO	Ct	Bowling 1st Balls	R	W	Bowling 2nd Balls	R	W
706/481			4	Kanpur	D	10	0	*	–	–	–	1	306	90	3	156	46	2
707/482			5	Bombay[2]	D	4	9	c	–	–	–	2	156	100	1	228	70	2
719/483	1972–73	P	1	Lahore[2]	D	10	5	*	–	–	–	–	210	58	3	78	38	0
720/484			2	Hyderabad	D	10	20	*	–	–	–	–	288	119	0	–	–	–
724/488	1973	NZ	3	Leeds	W-I & 1	11	20	*	–	–	–	–	66	27	0	42	14	0
725/489	1973	WI	1	Oval	L-158	11	0	c	7	7	lbw	1	141	68	2	114	51	1
726/490			2	Birmingham	D	11	2	c	–	–	–	–	147	40	3	192	66	2
727/491			3	Lord's	L-I & 226	11	12	c	11	14	b	1	204	105	0	–	–	–
731/492	1973–74	WI	1	Port-of-Spain	L-7w	10	10	*	10	9	c	1	138	56	1	72	48	2
732/493			2	Kingston	D	9	24	c	7	12	c	–	216	98	0	–	–	–
734/495			4	Georgetown	D	11	7	*	–	–	–	–	107	36	1	–	–	–
735/496			5	Port-of-Spain	W-26	11	4	b	11	1	*	1	204	57	0	90	19	1
739/497	1974	I	1	Manchester	W-113	6	7	c	3	9	c	–	114	50	1	90	45	1
740/498			2	Lord's	W-I & 285	10	9	c	–	–	–	2	90	18	1	–	–	–
741/499			3	Birmingham	W-I & 78	–	–	–	–	–	–	–	90	30	1	18	3	0
742/500	1974	P	1	Leeds	D	10	9	ro	–	–	–	–	72	26	1	6	0	0
743/501			2	Lord's	D	10	12	*	–	–	–	–	84	20	5	209	51	8
744/502			3	Oval	D	3	43	lbw	–	–	–	–	264	106	2	48	15	1
750/503	1974–75	A	1	Brisbane[2]	L-166	9	25	c	9	30	c	–	160	54	2	208	63	2
752/505			3	Melbourne	D	9	9	c	9	4	c	–	176	62	0	152	43	0
753/506			4	Sydney	L-171	9	27	c	9	5	c	–	104	54	0	96	65	2
754/507			5	Adelaide	L-163	9	0	c	9	0	c	–	232	113	7	208	102	4
755/508			6	Melbourne	W-I & 4	9	11	b	–	–	–	–	–	–	–	144	39	0
758/509	1974–75	NZ	1	Auckland	W-I & 83	–	–	–	–	–	–	–	128	38	3	200	47	2
759/510			2	Christchurch	D	–	–	–	–	–	–	–	109	35	2	–	–	–
760/511	1975	A	1	Birmingham	L-I & 85	8	10	b	10	3	b	–	42	10	1	–	–	–
761/512			2	Lord's	D	10	0	*	–	–	–	–	78	29	1	186	64	0
762/513			3	Leeds	D	11	0	c	11	0	*	1	114	22	1	90	40	1
763/514			4	Oval	D	11	0	c	11	3	*	–	264	96	1	12	5	1
777/515	1976	WI	1	Nottingham	D	10	0	c	–	–	–	–	162	82	4	42	9	0
778/516			2	Lord's	D	10	31	b	11	2	b	–	112	39	5	147	73	2
779/517			3	Manchester	L-425	9	0	b	8	0	c	2	144	55	3	210	90	0
780/518			4	Leeds	L-55	9	1	c	7	0	c	–	108	80	0	–	–	–
781/519			5	Oval	L-231	7	4	b	9	2	c	1	365	165	3	54	38	0
788/520	1976–77	I	1	Delhi	W-I & 25	11	7	*	–	–	–	1	54	19	1	264	78	4
789/521			2	Calcutta	W-10w	10	4	c	–	–	–	–	78	24	1	197	50	3
790/522			3	Madras[1]	W-200	10	23	b	10	8	st	2	102	16	2	84	28	4
791/523			4	Bangalore	L-140	10	12	c	10	10	c	1	126	45	1	186	76	4
792/524			5	Bombay[3]	D	9	7	b	–	–	–	1	228	89	4	198	84	5
803/525	1976–77	A		Melbourne	L-45	3	7	c	10	7	b	–	94	16	3	96	38	1
804/526	1977	A	1	Lord's	D	10	11	*	10	12	*	–	150	42	0	60	16	2
805/527			2	Manchester	W-9w	10	10	b	–	–	–	2	122	53	1	197	66	6
806/528			3	Nottingham	W-7w	9	7	b	–	–	–	–	66	18	1	162	49	2
807/529			4	Leeds	W-I & 85	9	6	c	–	–	–	–	–	–	–	48	16	0
808/530			5	Oval	D	9	20	b	–	–	–	1	210	102	1	–	–	–
868/553	1979–80	A	1	Perth	L-138	10	13	lbw	10	0	c	1	78	33	1	246	82	3
870/554			2	Sydney	L-6w	11	12	c	5	43	c	1	80	39	2	156	71	3
872/555			3	Melbourne	L-8w	9	3	c	9	0	b	2	318	131	3	84	49	1
876/556	1979–80	I		Bombay[3]	W-10w	11	1	b	–	–	–	–	36	23	0	6	5	0
881/558	1980	WI	2	Lord's	D	7	3	lbw	–	–	–	–	176	108	1	–	–	–
912/573	1981–82	I	1	Bombay[3]	L-138	10	8	c	10	13	*	–	24	12	1	66	14	0
913/574			2	Bangalore	D	11	2	*	–	–	–	1	258	88	3	–	–	–
914/575			3	Delhi	D	10	2	*	–	–	–	–	288	97	2	–	–	–
915/576			4	Calcutta	D	7	13	c	–	–	–	–	174	45	3	186	38	0
916/577			5	Madras[1]	D	9	0	c	–	–	–	–	132	59	0	90	30	1
917/578			6	Kanpur	D	10	0	*	–	–	–	–	150	55	0	–	–	–
921/579	1981–82	SL		Colombo SO	W-7w	10	0	c	–	–	–	–	108	28	5	227	67	3

Career	M	I	NO	HS	R	Avge	100	50	Ct	St	Balls	R	W	Avge	BB	5w	10w	Rate
Test	86	116	35	45*	937	11.56	–	–	44	–	21862	7674	297	25.83	8-51	17	6	73.60
F/c	676	710	200	111	5165	10.12	1	2	261	–	139783	49993	2465	20.28	9-28	153	47	56.70

Inverarity lbw bowled Underwood at The Oval, 1968: the climax of a superb bowling performance by Underwood which squared the series against Australia. The rest of the England fielders are (left to right) R. Illingworth, T.W. Graveney, J.H. Edrich, E.R. Dexter, M.C. Cowdrey (captain), A.P.E. Knott, J.A. Snow, D.J. Brown, C. Milburn, B.L. D'Oliveira.

NOTABLE FEATS

- 50 wickets in 14th Test (*656*); 100 wickets in 23rd Test (*686*); 150 wickets in 40th Test (*734*); 200 wickets in 57th Test (*762*); 250 wickets in 69th Test (*803*).
- *640* His 45* remains the highest score by an England No. 11 v Australia.
- *656* His analysis of 7 for 32 is the record for either country in E v NZ Tests.
- *658* His match analysis of 12 for 101 is the record for E v NZ in England.
- *685* Took his 1000th first-class wicket; at 25 yrs 264 days he was the third-youngest to do so after G.A. Lohmann (1890) and W. Rhodes (1902). His match analysis of 12 for 97 is the record for any Test at Christchurch and for either country in E v NZ Tests.
- *743* The first 8-wicket analysis in E v P Tests included a spell of 6 for 2 from 51 balls.
- *754* His match analysis of 11 for 215 was England's best in Australia since 1928–29.
- *792* Equalled F.S. Trueman's E v I series record with 29 wickets.
- Took 100 wickets in a season 10 times, notably 157 in 1966 – the last instance of 150 wickets in any first-class season. Leading bowler 4 times (1966–67–78–79).
- Youngest (17) to take 100 wickets in first season (101 wickets in 1963) and the last of 11 bowlers to achieve this feat.
- Took 9 wickets in an innings for Kent on 3 occasions: 9 for 28 v Sussex at Hastings in 1964, 9 for 37 v Essex at Westcliff in 1966 and 9 for 32 v Surrey at The Oval in 1978.
- His 15 for 43 for an International XI v Ceylon President's XI at the Colombo Oval in 1967–68 is the record first-class match analysis in Sri Lanka.
- Hat-trick for Kent v Sussex at Hove in 1977.

D. L. UNDERWOOD – TEST BOWLING SUMMARY

Series	V	M	Balls	R	W	Avge	BB	5w	10w	Rate
1966	WI	2	414	172	1	172.00	1-81	–	–	414.00
1967	P	2	396	129	8	16.12	5-52	1	–	49.50
1968	A	4	1259	302	20	15.10	7-50	1	–	62.95
1968–69	P	3	636	204	8	25.50	5-94	1	–	79.50
1969	WI	2	318	101	6	16.83	4-55	–	–	53.00
1969	NZ	3	900	220	24	9.16	7-32	3	2	37.50
1970–71	A	5	1558	520	16	32.50	4-66	–	–	97.37
1970–71	NZ	2	673	205	17	12.05	6-12	3	1	39.58
1971	P	1	246	102	0	–	–	–	–	–
1971	I	1	378	121	4	30.25	3-72	–	–	94.50
1972	A	2	750	266	16	16.62	6-45	1	1	46.87
1972–73	I	4	1288	457	15	30.46	4-56	–	–	85.86
1972–73	P	2	576	215	3	71.66	3-58	–	–	192.00
1973	NZ	1	108	41	0	–	–	–	–	–
1973	WI	3	798	330	8	41.25	3-40	–	–	99.75
1973–74	WI	4	827	314	5	62.80	2-48	–	–	165.40
1974	I	3	402	146	4	36.50	1-18	–	–	100.50
1974	P	3	683	218	17	12.82	8-51	2	1	40.17
1974–75	A	5	1480	595	17	35.00	7-113	1	1	87.05
1974–75	NZ	2	437	120	7	17.14	3-38	–	–	62.42
1975	A	4	786	266	6	44.33	1-5	–	–	131.00
1976	WI	5	1344	631	17	37.17	5-39	1	–	79.05
1976–77	I	5	1517	509	29	17.55	5-84	1	–	52.31
1976–77	A	1	190	54	4	13.50	3-16	–	–	47.50
1977	A	5	1015	362	13	27.84	6-66	1	–	78.07
1979–80	A	3	962	405	13	31.15	3-71	–	–	74.00
1979–80	I	1	42	28	0	–	–	–	–	–
1980	WI	1	176	108	1	108.00	1-108	–	–	176.00
1981–82	I	6	1368	438	10	43.80	3-45	–	–	136.80
1981–82	SL	1	335	95	8	11.87	5-28	1	–	42.62
	A	29	8000	2770	105	26.38	7-50	4	2	76.19
	WI	17	3877	1656	38	43.57	5-39	1	–	102.02
	NZ	8	2118	586	48	12.20	7-32	6	3	44.12
	I	20	4995	1699	62	27.40	5-84	1	–	80.56
	P	11	2537	868	36	24.11	8-51	4	1	70.47
	SL	1	335	95	8	11.87	5-28	1	–	42.62
Home		42	9973	3515	145	24.24	8-51	10	4	68.77
Overseas		44	11889	4159	152	27.36	7-43	7	2	78.21
Totals		86	21862	7674	297	25.83	8-51	17	6	73.60

VALENTINE Bryan Herbert MC

Kent (1927 to 1948)
Cambridge University (1928 to 1929)

TOURS
SA 1938–39; WI 1931–32 (Tennyson); I/SL 1933–34
Born Blackheath, Kent 17 Jan 1908
Died Otford, Kent 2 Feb 1983

Bryan Valentine

Bryan Valentine seldom wasted time on playing himself in; a forceful batsman with a fine eye and quick feet, he was a firm believer in attack being the best form of defence. A fine all-round sportsman, he gained considerable acclaim as a lawn tennis player during his schooldays at Repton. It was there that he developed his front-foot technique and strong leg-side bias. He had begun his Kent career before going up to Cambridge, where, despite a 75-minute innings of 114 (retired) in the Freshmen's match, he had to wait until his second year before adding a cricket blue to the one he had gained for soccer. Not until 1931 did he improve his defensive technique against the turning ball sufficiently to assure his place in the Kent team. His on-driving became a feature of English cricket grounds in the 1930s but competition for Test places was so strong that he was never chosen for a home Test. He was joint captain of Kent in 1937 and after the War, in which he was badly wounded and won the MC, he returned to become sole leader for the next three summers. A popular and cheerful captain, he managed to extract a high level of enjoyment from his cricket while still playing it to win. He was a good fielder, a perpetrator of mild right-arm medium-pace outswingers and a most welcome choice as Kent president in 1967.

NOTABLE FEATS

- *230* Scored the first 100 in E v I Tests in his first innings for England.
- Exceeded 1000 runs in a season 9 times.
- Two double centuries for Kent, notably 242 v Leicestershire at Oakham in 1938.

						Batting 1st			Batting 2nd			
Ref	Series	V	T	Venue	Result	No	R	HO	No	R	HO	Ct
230/204	1933–34	I	1	Bombay[1]	W-9w	6	136	c	–	–	–	1
231/205			2	Calcutta	D	6	40	lbw	3	3	st	–
267/236	1938–39	SA	1	Johannesburg[1]	D	7	97	c	–	–	–	–
268/237			2	Cape Town	D	7	112	lbw	–	–	–	1
269/238			3	Durban[2]	W-I & 13	–	–	–	–	–	–	–
270/239			4	Johannesburg[1]	D	6	11	c	6	25	*	–
271/240			5	Durban[2]	D	7	26	st	7	4	*	–

Career	M	I	NO	HS	R	Avge	100	50	Ct	St	Balls	R	W	Avge	BB	5w	10w	Rate
Test	7	9	2	136	454	64.85	2	1	2	–	–	–	–	–	–	–	–	–
F/c	399	645	38	242	18306	30.15	35	90	289	–	1933	1125	27	41.66	3-58	–	–	71.59

VERITY, Hedley

Yorkshire (1930 to 1939)

Wisden 1932
TOURS
A 1932–33, 1936–37; SA 1938–39; WI 1935–36 (Yorks); NZ 1932–33, 1936–37; I/SL 1933–34
Born Headingley, Leeds, Yorkshire 18 May 1905
Died Caserta, Italy 31 Jul 1943

Following along the lengthy lineage of Yorkshire left-arm spinners, Hedley Verity was the world's outstanding exponent of the 1930s. Although he is best remembered for his feat of taking 14 Australian wickets in a day at Lord's in 1934, his successes were not restricted to pitches taking spin. His basic pace, like Derek Underwood's, was faster than for most bowlers of his type, but he varied it with great subtlety according to the conditions. So precise was his control of flight, line and length that he was extremely difficult to attack. A tall, thoughtful man, he was always composed and seemed completely unaffected by punishment. By the time he succeeded Wilfred Rhodes in the Yorkshire side, he was 25 and had matured through his experience in league and 2nd XI cricket into a high-class bowler. He acknowledged his coaching debt to his predecessor by naming his son Hedley Rhodes Verity. Yorkshire proceeded to win the Championship in

seven of his nine full summers, three of which saw him exceed 200 wickets. His most incredible performance was his 10 for 10 against Nottinghamshire which, perhaps not too surprisingly, remains the least expensive 10-wicket analysis in first-class cricket and the only one to include a hat-trick; 16 of his 19.4 overs were maidens. His determined batting took him within range of the 'double' in 1936 and he assisted Charlie Barnett in England's best opening stands of the 1936–37 series in Australia. He was a very capable fielder who specialised in the short-leg position. His death in an Italian POW camp from wounds received in Sicily when still near his prime as a bowler was a terrible loss to cricket.

Hedley Verity

						Batting 1st			Batting 2nd				Bowling 1st			Bowling 2nd		
Ref	Series	V	T	Venue	Result	No	R	HO	No	R	HO	Ct	Balls	R	W	Balls	R	W
210/191	1931	NZ	2	Oval	W-I & 26	–	–	–	–	–	–	–	133	52	2	75	33	2
211/192			3	Manchester	D	–	–	–	–	–	–	–	–	–	–	–	–	–
220/194	1932–33	A	1	Sydney	W-10w	7	2	lbw	–	–	–	–	78	35	0	24	15	0
222/196			3	Adelaide	W-338	9	45	c	8	40	lbw	1	96	31	0	120	26	1
223/197			4	Brisbane[2]	W-6w	10	23	*	–	–	–	1	162	39	0	114	30	2
224/198			5	Sydney	W-8w	10	4	c	–	–	–	1	102	62	3	114	33	5
225/199	1932–33	NZ	1	Christchurch	D	–	–	–	–	–	–	–	138	58	1	18	6	0
227/201	1933	WI	1	Lord's	W-I & 27	10	21	c	–	–	–	2	96	21	1	109	45	4
228/202			2	Manchester	D	9	0	*	–	–	–	1	192	47	2	78	40	0
230/204	1933–34	I	1	Bombay[1]	W-9w	9	24	c	–	–	–	–	162	44	3	120	50	1
231/205			2	Calcutta	D	10	55	*	–	–	–	1	172	64	4	186	76	4
232/206			3	Madras[1]	W-202	9	42	lbw	–	–	–	1	143	49	7	164	104	4
233/207	1934	A	1	Nottingham	L-238	9	0	b	9	0	*	2	204	65	1	102	48	1
234/208			2	Lord's	W-I & 38	9	29	st	–	–	–	2	216	61	7	135	43	8
235/209			3	Manchester	D	10	60	*	–	–	–	1	318	78	4	30	2	0
236/210			4	Leeds	D	9	2	*	–	–	–	–	281	113	3	–	–	–
237/211			5	Oval	L-562	9	11	b	8	1	c	–	258	123	0	84	43	0
242/216	1935	SA	1	Nottingham	D	–	–	–	–	–	–	1	246	52	3	–	–	–
243/217			2	Lord's	L-157	10	17	lbw	10	8	c	–	168	61	3	228	56	3
244/218			3	Leeds	D	10	1	c	–	–	–	–	72	5	2	78	4	0
245/219			4	Manchester	D	8	16	lbw	–	–	–	2	120	48	1	120	24	0
252/221	1936	I	1	Lord's	W-9w	11	2	*	–	–	–	1	109	42	2	96	17	4
253/222			2	Manchester	D	9	66	*	–	–	–	–	102	41	4	132	66	1
254/223			3	Oval	W-9w	8	4	c	–	–	–	–	150	30	3	96	32	1
255/224	1936–37	A	1	Brisbane[2]	W-322	10	7	c	10	19	lbw	–	224	52	1	–	–	–
256/225			2	Sydney	W-I & 22	8	0	*	–	–	–	1	24	17	2	152	55	1
257/226			3	Melbourne	L-365	10	0	c	9	11	c	2	112	24	2	303	79	3
258/227			4	Adelaide	L-148	1	19	c	1	17	b	–	128	47	0	296	54	0
259/228			5	Melbourne	L-I & 200	9	0	c	9	2	*	1	328	127	1	–	–	–
260/229	1937	NZ	1	Lord's	D	10	3	c	–	–	–	3	150	48	1	84	33	1
263/232	1938	A	1	Nottingham	D	8	3	b	–	–	–	–	45	36	1	372	102	3
264/233			2	Lord's	D	8	5	b	3	11	b	1	214	103	4	78	29	2
265/234			4	Leeds	L-5w	8	25	*	8	0	b	1	114	30	1	30	24	1
266/235			5	Oval	W-I & 579	9	8	*	–	–	–	–	30	15	0	42	15	2
267/236	1938–39	SA	1	Johannesburg[1]	D	8	26	b	–	–	–	1	353	61	4	128	17	0
268/237			2	Cape Town	D	8	29	b	–	–	–	–	294	70	5	80	13	0
269/238			3	Durban[2]	W-I & 13	–	–	–	–	–	–	–	64	9	0	280	71	3
270/239			4	Johannesburg[1]	D	8	8	c	–	–	–	1	301	127	3	–	–	–
271/240			5	Durban[2]	D	8	3	b	–	–	–	1	446	97	2	320	87	2
272/241	1939	WI	1	Lord's	W-8w	–	–	–	–	–	–	1	128	34	0	112	20	2

Career	M	I	NO	HS	R	Avge	100	50	Ct	St	Balls	R	W	Avge	BB	5w	10w	Rate
Test	40	44	12	66*	669	20.90	–	3	30	–	11173	3510	144	24.37	8-43	5	2	77.59
F/c	378	416	106	101	5605	18.08	1	13	269	–	84081	29146	1956	14.90	10-10	164	54	42.98

NOTABLE FEATS

- 50 wickets in 14th Test (*234*); 100 wickets in 26th Test (*256*).
- *234* Took 14 for 80 on the third day (6 of them in the final hour) to secure England's first win v Australia at Lord's since 1896. It remains the most wickets to fall to one bowler in a day of Test cricket in England. His match analysis of 15 for 104 was then the E v A record and has been surpassed only by J.C. Laker.
- Took 100 wickets in a season 9 times, including 200 in 3 successive years, notably 216 in 1936. Headed the national averages 4 times (1933–35–37–39).
- Achieved the world-record innings analysis for all first-class cricket: 10 for 10 for Yorkshire v Nottinghamshire at Leeds in 1932. It remains the only 10-wicket analysis to include a hat-trick. All 10 wickets were taken in the space of 52 balls and he ended the innings with a spell of 7 in 15 balls and 4 in 6.
- His 10 for 36 at Leeds in 1931 remains the best analysis achieved against Warwickshire and included 5 wickets in 8 balls; he took 9 wickets in an innings on 7 occasions – all for Yorkshire – notably 9 for 12 v Kent at Sheffield in 1936 (taking all 9 wickets in 39 balls).
- Holds Yorkshire record for the best match analysis: 17 for 91 v Essex at Leyton in 1933 – all achieved on the third day to equal the world record. Returned 15-wicket match analyses for Yorkshire on 3 other occasions.
- Two hat-tricks: v Notts in 1932 (above) and for MCC Australian XI v H.D.G. Leveson Gower's XI at Scarborough in 1937.

H. VERITY – TEST BOWLING SUMMARY

Series	V	M	Balls	R	W	Avge	BB	5w	10w	Rate
1931	NZ	2	208	85	4	21.25	2-33	–	–	52.00
1932–33	A	4	810	271	11	24.63	5-33	1	–	73.63
1932–33	NZ	1	156	64	1	64.00	1-58	–	–	156.00
1933	WI	2	475	153	7	21.85	4-45	–	–	67.85
1933–34	I	3	947	387	23	16.82	7-49	1	1	41.17
1934	A	5	1628	576	24	24.00	8-43	2	1	67.83
1935	SA	4	1032	250	12	20.83	3-56	–	–	86.00
1936	I	3	685	228	15	15.20	4-17	–	–	45.66
1936–37	A	5	1567	455	10	45.50	3-79	–	–	156.70
1937	NZ	1	234	81	2	40.50	1-33	–	–	117.00
1938	A	4	925	354	14	25.28	4-103	–	–	66.07
1938–39	SA	5	2266	552	19	29.05	5-70	1	–	119.26
1939	WI	1	240	54	2	27.00	2-20	–	–	120.00
	A	18	4930	1656	59	28.06	8-43	3	1	83.55
	SA	9	3298	802	31	25.87	5-70	1	–	106.38
	WI	3	715	207	9	23.00	4-45	–	–	79.44
	NZ	4	598	230	7	32.85	2-33	–	–	85.42
	I	6	1632	615	38	16.18	7-49	1	1	42.94
Home		22	5427	1781	80	22.26	8-43	2	1	67.83
Overseas		18	5746	1729	64	27.01	7-49	3	1	89.78
Totals		40	11173	3510	144	24.37	8-43	5	2	77.59

VERNON
George Frederick

Middlesex (1878 to 1895)

TOURS A 1882–83, 1887–88; I 1892–93
Born Marylebone, London 20 Jun 1856
Died Elmina, Gold Coast 10 Aug 1902

George Vernon was an entertaining hitter who swung down and sometimes across the line, connecting with immense strength more often than not. His technique was based entirely on robust driving and it served him well for Rugby, Middlesex and the MCC. He played in one Test on the Hon. Ivo Bligh's Ashes recovery tour and thereby became a double international having already gained his five England caps for rugby. He took a side to Australia in 1887–88 at the same time as one organised by Shaw and Shrewsbury; the result was financial disaster all round. Later he led the first tour by an English team to India in 1889–90 and returned three years later as a member of Lord Hawke's side which took part in the first season of first-class matches played on the sub-continent. He died of malarial fever. [*Illus. p.* 42]

					Batting 1st			Batting 2nd			
Ref	Series	V	T Venue	Result	No	R	HO	No	R	HO	Ct
10/10	1882–83	A	1 Melbourne	L-9w	11	11	*	11	3	lbw	–

Career	M	I	NO	HS	R	Avge	100	50	Ct	St	Balls	R	W	Avge	BB	5w	10w	Rate
Test	1	2	1	11*	14	14.00	–	–	–	–	–	–	–	–	–	–	–	–
F/c	239	391	21	160	7070	19.10	4	28	171	–	108	69	2	34.50	1-11	–	–	54.00

VINE, Joseph

Sussex (1896 to 1922)
London County (1901 to 1904)

Wisden 1906
TOUR A 1911–12
Born Willingdon, Sussex 15 May 1875
Died Aldrington, Hove, Sussex
25 Apr 1946

NOTABLE FEATS

• *120* Shared record E v A 7th-wkt stand of 143 with F.E. Woolley.
• Exceeded 1000 runs in a season 14 times and took 113 wickets in 1901 to complete the 'double'.
• Scored 202 for Sussex v Northamptonshire at Hastings in 1920.
• Carried his bat through a completed Sussex innings on 9 occasions.

By nature a forcing batsman, Joe Vine curbed his instincts when batting with Ranji and Fry. The latter was quite specific about his role and told him that his job was merely to defend one end and frustrate the bowlers while he murdered them at the other. Apart from occasionally breaking free of the shackles, such as in scoring a five-hour double century, he adopted the role of stonewaller with great effect. Although short and stockily built, he was an extremely rapid mover in the outfield and his tireless right-arm leg-break bowling enabled him to complete the 'double'. For many years he was coach to Brighton College. [*Illus. p.* 146]

NOTABLE FEATS *cont.*

• Returned a match analysis of 15 for 161 for Sussex v Nottinghamshire at Nottingham in 1901.
• Achieved the match 'double' (140 runs and 10 wickets) for Sussex v Oxford U at Eastbourne in 1906.
• Appeared in 399 consecutive Championship matches for Sussex and made 417 consecutive appearances for the County in all first-class matches between July 1900 and September 1914.

						Batting 1st			Batting 2nd			
Ref	Series	V	T	Venue	Result	No	R	HO	No	R	HO	Ct
119/111	1911–12	A	4	Melbourne	W-I & 225	9	4	*	–	–	–	–
120/112			5	Sydney	W-70	8	36	b	8	6	*	–

Career	M	I	NO	HS	R	Avge	100	50	Ct	St	Balls	R	W	Avge	BB	5w	10w	Rate
Test	2	3	2	36	46	46.00	–	–	–	–	–	–	–	–	–	–	–	–
F/c	547	920	79	202	25171	29.92	34	142	240	–	39299	19533	685	28.51	8-68	27	3	57.37

VOCE, William

Nottinghamshire (1927 to 1952)

Wisden 1933
TOURS
A 1932–33, 1936–37, 1946–47;
SA 1930–31; WI 1929–30; NZ 1932–33, 1936–37, 1946–47
Born Annesley Woodhouse, Nottinghamshire 8 Aug 1909
Died Nottingham 6 Jun 1984

NOTABLE FEATS

• 50 wickets in 12th Test (*220*).
• *256* Dismissed D.G. Bradman first ball during a spell of 3 wickets in 4 balls.
• Scored 1020 runs in 1933 and took 100 wickets in a season 6 times.
• Scored 100 in 45 min for Nottinghamshire v Glamorgan at Nottingham in 1931.

(*continued overleaf*)

A tall (6ft 1in) powerfully built left-arm bowler, Bill Voce was a central figure in the 'bodyline' controversy. Unlike Larwood and Jardine, he made his peace with the authorities and returned to Australia for two subsequent tours. He joined Nottinghamshire as a slow left-arm spinner but, within 18 months, he had remustered to left-arm fast-medium, bowling over the wicket. Opening England's bowling in the first series contested in the Caribbean, he took 11 wickets in his second Test. Three years later he adopted another form of attack and bowled fast-medium leg theory around the wicket in Australia as a foil to Larwood. There he was often considered as unpleasant to play as the expresses of his Nottinghamshire colleague because of the bounce he achieved on antipodean pitches. He was never chosen against Australia in England. Despite the 1934 Australians complaining about his short-pitched bowling for Notts against them, he was 'reinstated' in time for the next tour and responded by taking the wickets of O'Brien, Bradman and McCabe in four balls. Even though overweight, his form a decade later warranted a third tour but he failed to take a wicket in his last two Tests. He continued to serve Notts for another six seasons, reverting in his last summers to his original leg-spin. A very capable attacking batsman who made four hundreds in county matches, he had an incredibly strong throw from the boundary. Returning to Melbourne for the 1977 Centenary Test, he and Larwood were led out during an interval for a mid-pitch bow and received a tumultuous welcome from the vast crowd. 'Bit different from the last time we were here, Bill,' said Harold, with a wry grin.

NOTABLE FEATS *cont.*

- First fielder to hold 7 catches in a day in a first-class match in England (for Nottinghamshire v Glamorgan at Pontypridd in 1929).
- Bowled in an unchanged partnership with H. Larwood throughout both completed Leicestershire innings for Nottinghamshire at Nottingham in 1932.

						Batting 1st			Batting 2nd				Bowling 1st			Bowling 2nd		
Ref	Series	V	T	Venue	Result	No	R	HO	No	R	HO	Ct	Balls	R	W	Balls	R	W
190/176	1929–30	WI	1	Bridgetown	D	11	10	b	–	–	–	–	162	120	2	18	15	0
191/177			2	Port-of-Spain	W-167	11	2	*	–	–	–	2	168	79	4	224	70	7
192/178			3	Georgetown	L-289	11	1	*	11	2	lbw	–	156	81	2	96	44	0
193/179			4	Kingston	D	11	20	c	11	6	*	–	132	81	2	174	94	0
204/185	1930–31	SA	1	Johannesburg[1]	L-28	10	8	ro	9	0	c	–	156	45	4	164	59	4
205/186			2	Cape Town	D	9	30	c	10	1	*	–	198	95	0	–	–	–
206/187			3	Durban[2]	D	–	–	–	–	–	–	1	176	58	5	72	14	1
207/188			4	Johannesburg[1]	D	11	41	*	8	5	c	–	252	106	1	192	87	4
208/189			5	Durban[2]	D	9	0	c	–	–	–	–	162	51	2	132	46	2
209/190	1931	NZ	1	Lord's	D	11	1	*	–	–	–	1	60	40	0	192	60	0
219/193	1932	I		Lord's	W-158	10	4	*	10	0	*	–	102	23	3	72	28	2
220/194	1932–33	A	1	Sydney	W-10w	11	0	*	–	–	–	2	174	110	4	105	54	2
221/195			2	Melbourne	L-111	10	6	c	10	0	c	–	120	54	3	90	47	2
222/196			3	Adelaide	W-338	10	8	b	11	8	b	1	84	21	1	24	7	0
224/198			5	Sydney	W-8w	11	7	*	–	–	–	–	144	80	1	60	34	2
225/199	1932–33	NZ	1	Christchurch	D	8	66	c	–	–	–	1	103	27	3	24	13	0
226/200			2	Auckland	D	8	16	b	–	–	–	–	59	20	2	9	2	0
254/223	1936	I	3	Oval	W-9w	10	1	*	–	–	–	2	120	46	1	120	40	0
255/224	1936–37	A	1	Brisbane[2]	W-322	11	4	*	11	2	*	1	166	41	6	51	16	4
256/225			2	Sydney	W-I & 22	–	–	–	–	–	–	1	64	10	4	152	66	3
257/226			3	Melbourne	L-365	11	0	*	11	0	c	1	144	49	2	232	120	3
258/227			4	Adelaide	L-148	10	8	c	10	1	b	–	96	49	0	160	86	1
259/228			5	Melbourne	L-I & 200	10	3	st	10	1	c	1	232	123	3	–	–	–
260/229	1937	NZ	1	Lord's	D	9	27	c	–	–	–	–	146	74	2	113	41	3
277/245	1946	I	2	Manchester	D	8	0	b	–	–	–	–	120	44	1	36	2	0
279/247	1946–47	A	1	Brisbane[2]	L-I & 332	9	1	*	9	18	c	1	224	92	0	–	–	–
281/249			3	Melbourne	D	9	0	lbw	–	–	–	–	80	40	0	48	29	0

Career	M	I	NO	HS	R	Avge	100	50	Ct	St	Balls	R	W	Avge	BB	5w	10w	Rate
Test	27	38	15	66	308	13.39	–	1	15	–	6360	2733	98	27.88	7-70	3	2	64.89
F/c	426	525	130	129	7590	19.21	4	26	286	–	85350	35961	1558	23.08	8-30	84	20	54.78

Bill Voce

W. VOCE – TEST BOWLING SUMMARY

Series	V	M	Balls	R	W	Avge	BB	5w	10w	Rate
1929–30	WI	4	1130	584	17	36.35	7-70	1	1	66.47
1930–31	SA	5	1504	561	23	24.39	5-58	1	–	65.39
1931	NZ	1	252	100	0	–	–	–	–	–
1932	I	1	174	51	5	10.20	3-23	–	–	29.00
1932–33	A	4	801	407	15	27.13	4-110	–	–	53.40
1932–33	NZ	2	195	62	5	12.40	3-27	–	–	39.00
1936	I	1	240	86	1	86.00	1-46	–	–	240.00
1936–37	A	5	1297	560	26	21.53	6-41	1	1	49.88
1937	NZ	1	259	115	5	23.00	3-41	–	–	51.80
1946	I	1	156	46	1	46.00	1-44	–	–	156.00
1946–47	A	2	352	161	0	–	–	–	–	–
	A	11	2450	1128	41	27.51	6-41	1	1	59.75
	SA	5	1504	561	23	24.39	5-58	1	–	65.39
	WI	4	1130	584	17	36.35	7-70	1	1	66.47
	NZ	4	706	277	10	27.70	3-27	–	–	70.60
	I	3	570	183	7	26.14	3-23	–	–	81.42
Home		5	1081	398	12	33.16	3-23	–	–	90.08
Overseas		22	5279	2335	86	27.15	7-70	3	2	61.38
Totals		27	6360	2733	98	27.88	7-70	3	2	64.89

WADDINGTON Abraham

Yorkshire (1919 to 1927)

TOUR A 1920–21
Born Clayton, Thornton, Yorkshire 4 Feb 1893
Died Thraxenby, Scarborough, Yorkshire 28 Oct 1959

A highly competitive left-arm fast-medium bowler with bounding energy, Abe Warrington launched his career with 100 wickets in his very first season but at the advanced age of 26. His wholehearted efforts played an important part in the five Championships which Yorkshire won during his brief career. A forthright character, he had a fluent action, kept a good length and moved the ball in the air and off the pitch. Touring Australia after only two seasons of county cricket, he met with little success in his two Tests but headed the bowling averages for all matches. An all-round sportsman, he was a notable golfer and had kept goal for Bradford City and Halifax Town. [*Illus p.* 383]

NOTABLE FEATS

- Took 100 wickets in a season 5 times, including 100 (avge 18.74) in his debut season (1919).
- Hat-trick and 4 wickets in 5 balls for Yorkshire v Northamptonshire at Northampton in 1920.
- Bowled in an unchanged partnership with E. Robinson throughout both completed Northamptonshire innings of a match for Yorkshire twice (1920 and 1921).

					Batting 1st			Batting 2nd				Bowling 1st			Bowling 2nd		
Ref	Series	V	T Venue	Result	No	R	HO	No	R	HO	Ct	Balls	R	W	Balls	R	W
135/124	1920–21	A	1 Sydney	L-377	9	7	ro	9	3	b	1	108	35	1	138	53	0
138/127			4 Melbourne	L-8w	7	0	b	8	6	st	–	30	31	0	–	–	–

Career	M	I	NO	HS	R	Avge	100	50	Ct	St	Balls	R	W	Avge	BB	5w	10w	Rate
Test	2	4	0	7	16	4.00	–	–	1	–	276	119	1	119.00	1-35	–	–	276.00
F/c	266	265	69	114	2527	12.89	1	4	232	–	39842	16833	852	19.75	8-34	51	10	46.76

WAINWRIGHT Edward

Yorkshire (1888 to 1902)

Wisden 1894
TOUR A 1897–98
Born Tinsley, Sheffield, Yorkshire 8 Apr 1865
Died Sheffield 28 Oct 1919

Although Ted Wainwright met with little success during his abbreviated Test career, he produced some spectacular all-round performances in the high class company of Lord Hawke's Yorkshire team. A slow off-spinner, he was considered the deadliest bowler in the country on a sticky wicket. He was a big tweaker of the ball but sometimes it was to the detriment of his line and length. Oddly, he could make nothing of Australian conditions and looked an absolute novice when bowling there. He launched his county career with a hundred against the 1888 Australians in his first summer and added 18 more, including a hurricane double century at The Oval. [*Illus. p.* 184]

NOTABLE FEATS

- Exceeded 1000 runs in a season 3 times and took 100 wickets 5 times, completing the 'double' in 1897.
- Scored 228 for Yorkshire v Surrey at The Oval in 1899, sharing a record Yorkshire 5th-wkt stand of 340 with G.H. Hirst.
- Contributed 126 to Yorkshire's 887 in 10 hr 50 min v Warwickshire at Birmingham in 1896; the highest and longest innings in county cricket, it was the first first-class match to include hundreds by 4 batsmen.
- Took 9 for 66 for Yorkshire v Middlesex at Sheffield in 1894.
- Hat-trick and 5 wickets in 7 balls for Yorkshire v Sussex at Dewsbury in 1894 when he bowled in an unchanged partnership with R. Peel throughout both completed innings.
- Achieved the match 'double' (114 runs and 11 wickets) for Yorkshire v Sussex at Sheffield in 1892.

Ref	Series	V	T	Venue	Result	Batting 1st No	R	HO	Batting 2nd No	R	HO	Ct	Bowling 1st Balls	R	W	Bowling 2nd Balls	R	W
39/39	1893	A	1	Lord's	D	8	1	c	8	26	b	–	55	41	0	–	–	–
53/53	1897–98	A	1	Sydney	W-9w	8	10	b	–	–	–	–	–	–	–	–	–	–
54/54			2	Melbourne	L-I & 55	3	21	c	8	11	b	1	–	–	–	–	–	–
56/56			4	Melbourne	L-8w	2	6	c	2	2	c	–	18	11	0	54	21	0
57/57			5	Sydney	L-6w	2	49	c	2	6	b	1	–	–	–	–	–	–

Career	M	I	NO	HS	R	Avge	100	50	Ct	St	Balls	R	W	Avge	BB	5w	10w	Rate
Test	5	9	0	49	132	14.66	–	–	2	–	127	73	0	–	–	–	–	–
F/c	388	603	32	228	12475	21.84	19	48	346	–	45986	19331	1062	18.20	9-66	63	15	43.30

WALKER
Peter Michael

Glamorgan (1956 to 1972)
Transvaal (1956–57 to 1957–58)
Western Province (1962–63)

TOURS WI 1960–61 (Swanton), 1969–70 (Glam); P 1967–68 (Cwlth)
Born Clifton, Bristol 17 Feb 1936

Peter Walker was a very tall (6ft 4in), extremely articulate all-rounder who, since his retirement, has continued to serve Welsh cricket well as a writer and broadcaster. He was a world-class close catcher who would rank with the best of any generation and he fully deserved to amass the fourth highest total of catches by a fielder with an entirely post-war career. It is hard to remember any morsel escaping his long reach at short-leg and he was almost as infallible when he crossed to slip. An effective but slightly awkward right-handed batsman, he was vulnerable to pace early on. Originally a left-arm medium-pace swing bowler, he eventually converted to orthodox slow spin. Although he has been involved with Glamorgan's cricket and many of its other activities for more than three decades, he was born in Bristol and brought up in South Africa.

NOTABLE FEATS

- Exceeded 1000 runs in a season 11 times and took 100 wickets once, completing the 'double' in 1961.
- He also held 73 catches in 1961 and thus emulated P.G.H. Fender (1921) by completing the 'treble' of 1000 runs, 100 wickets and 50 catches.
- Held 69 catches in 1960; he and J. Tunnicliffe are alone in holding more than 65 catches in a season twice.
- Holds Glamorgan fielding records for most catches in a career (656) and in a season (67 in 1961 – the record for any county).
- Held 8 catches in the match v Derbyshire at Swansea in 1970 (Glamorgan record) and held 7 on 2 other occasions – no other fielder has held 7 in a match 3 times.
- Held 5 catches in an innings for Glamorgan 4 times (record).

Peter Walker batting against Surrey in 1964.

Ref	Series	V	T	Venue	Result	Batting 1st No	R	HO	Batting 2nd No	R	HO	Ct	Bowling 1st Balls	R	W	Bowling 2nd Balls	R	W
492/364	1960	SA	1	Birmingham	W-100	9	9	c	8	37	c	2	36	13	0	24	8	0
493/365			2	Lord's	W-I & 73	7	52	b	–	–	–	1	–	–	–	–	–	–
494/366			3	Nottingham	W-8w	8	30	c	–	–	–	2	–	–	–	18	13	0

Career	M	I	NO	HS	R	Avge	100	50	Ct	St	Balls	R	W	Avge	BB	5w	10w	Rate
Test	3	4	0	52	128	32.00	–	1	5	–	78	34	0	–	–	–	–	–
F/c	469	788	110	152*	17650	26.03	13	92	697	–	58125	23881	834	28.63	7-58	25	2	69.69

WALTERS Cyril Frederick

Glamorgan (1923 to 1928)
Worcestershire (1928 to 1935)
Wales (1927 to 1929)

Wisden 1934
TOURS
WI 1931–32 (Tennyson); I/SL 1933–34
Born Bedlinog, Glamorgan 28 Aug 1905

A former architect and surveyor, Cyril Walters left his native Glamorgan after six moderate seasons and constructed himself a flourishing career as secretary and opening batsman at Worcester. A consistent and stylish player, he compensated for his slight physique with elegant timing and wristy strokeplay. Captaincy introduced a new outlet for his talents and he proved an able leader for five summers (1931–35) until ill health and domestic pressures prompted his early retirement. Unlike so many players, he had easily bridged the gap between county and Test cricket, even to the extent of achieving a Test batting average 20 runs above his overall first-class one. He captained England in one match, his first against Australia (223), because Bob Wyatt had fractured his thumb. [*Illus. p.* 263]

NOTABLE FEATS

- Exceeded 1000 runs in a season 5 times, including 2000 twice, notably 2404 in 1933 – then the Worcestershire record.
- Scored 226 for Worcestershire v Kent at Gravesend in 1933.

						Batting 1st			Batting 2nd			
Ref	Series	V	T	Venue	Result	No	R	HO	No	R	HO	Ct
227/201	1933	WI	1	Lord's	W-I & 27	1	51	c	–	–	–	–
228/202			2	Manchester	D	1	46	lbw	–	–	–	–
229/203			3	Oval	W-I & 17	1	2	c	–	–	–	–
230/204	1933–34	I	1	Bombay[1]	W-9w	2	78	c	2	14	*	–
231/205			2	Calcutta	D	1	29	c	1	2	*	1
232/206			3	Madras[1]	W-202	2	59	lbw	2	102	c	–
233/207*	1934	A	1	Nottingham	L-238	1	17	lbw	1	46	b	–
234/208			2	Lord's	W-I & 38	1	82	c	–	–	–	1
235/209			3	Manchester	D	1	52	c	1	50	*	2
236/210			4	Leeds	D	1	44	c	1	45	b	–
237/211			5	Oval	L-562	1	64	c	1	1	b	2

Career	M	I	NO	HS	R	Avge	100	50	Ct	St	Balls	R	W	Avge	BB	5w	10w	Rate
Test	11	18	3	102	784	52.26	1	7	6	–	–	–	–	–	–	–	–	–
F/c	245	427	32	226	12145	30.74	21	55	101	–	425	380	5	76.00	2-22	–	–	85.00

WARD, Alan

Derbyshire (1966 to 1976)
Border (1971–72)
Leicestershire (1977 to 1978)

TOURS
A 1970–71; WI 1969–70 (Norfolk)
Born Dronfield, Derbyshire 10 Aug 1947

Although Derbyshire nursed him most carefully, Alan Ward's very promising career as a right-arm fast bowler crumbled on a succession of leg and back injuries. But for his dodgy undercarriage his exceptional pace would have guaranteed him rich pickings at Test level. Those injuries may have stemmed from his slightly ungainly action. Tall (6ft 3in) and on the lean side, he looked slightly precarious when running at full tilt but there was no denying the genuine pace of a bowler who could hurry the defensive strokes of a player of Roy Marshall's class on a slow pudding at Derby. He gained some notoriety for a splendid little contretemps which resulted in his being sent off the field by Brian Bolus for refusing to bowl against Yorkshire at Chesterfield in 1973. His one major tour ended in a premature flight home because of injury and he fared little better after moving to Leicester.

Alan Ward

Ref	Series	V	T Venue	Result	Batting 1st No	R	HO	Batting 2nd No	R	HO	Ct	Bowling 1st Balls	R	W	Bowling 2nd Balls	R	W
656/456	1969	NZ	1 Lord's	W-230	11	0	b	11	19	*	2	84	49	2	65	48	2
657/457			2 Nottingham	D	–	–	–	–	–	–	–	138	61	4	18	14	0
658/458			3 Oval	W-8w	11	21	c	–	–	–	–	30	10	0	108	28	2
687/467	1971	P	1 Birmingham	D	11	0	c	–	–	–	–	174	115	0	–	–	–
780/518	1976	WI	4 Leeds	L-55	10	0	lbw	10	0	c	1	90	103	2	54	25	2

Career	M	I	NO	HS	R	Avge	100	50	Ct	St	Balls	R	W	Avge	BB	5w	10w	Rate
Test	5	6	1	21	40	8.00	–	–	3	–	761	453	14	32.35	4-61	–	–	54.35
F/c	163	157	47	44	928	8.43	–	–	51	–	21910	10495	460	22.81	7-42	15	4	47.63

WARD, Albert

Yorkshire (1886)
Lancashire (1889 to 1904)

Wisden 1890
TOUR A 1894–95
Born Waterloo, Leeds, Yorkshire
21 Nov 1865
Died Bolton, Lancashire 6 Jan 1939

According to Lord Hawke, Albert Ward was poached from Yorkshire by their arch rivals. The facts were that, after an unsuccessful trial with his native county, he had taken a teaching engagement at Leyland which brought him into contact with the Lancashire committee. He was one of their more inspired selections, a tall (6ft) well-composed, patient opening batsman with a sound defensive technique who played within his capabilities. He was also a teasing right-arm slow bowler and a very safe outfielder. Although he was the leading scorer in Stoddart's epic 1894–95 series, he was never selected for another international. [*Illus. pp.* 184, 315]

NOTABLE FEATS

- *46* Shared 3rd-wkt stand of 210 with J.T. Brown – then a world Test record for any wicket.
- Exceeded 1000 runs in a season 9 times.
- Scored 219 for A.E. Stoddart's XI v S Australia at Adelaide in 1894–95.
- Carried his bat through a completed Lancashire innings on 5 occasions.

Ref	Series	V	T Venue	Result	Batting 1st No	R	HO	Batting 2nd No	R	HO	Ct
40/40	1893	A	2 Oval	W-I & 43	5	55	c	–	–	–	–
41/41			3 Manchester	D	5	13	c	5	0	b	–
42/42	1894–95	A	1 Sydney	W-10	2	75	c	2	117	b	–
43/43			2 Melbourne	W-94	2	30	c	2	41	b	1
44/44			3 Adelaide	L-382	4	5	c	1	13	b	–
45/45			4 Sydney	L-I & 147	2	7	c	2	6	c	–
46/46			5 Melbourne	W-6w	1	32	b	1	93	b	–

Career	M	I	NO	HS	R	Avge	100	50	Ct	St	Balls	R	W	Avge	BB	5w	10w	Rate
Test	7	13	0	117	487	37.46	1	3	1	–	–	–	–	–	–	–	–	–
F/c	385	642	51	219	17783	30.08	29	87	168	–	5036	2473	71	34.83	6-29	4	–	70.92

WARDLE, John Henry

Yorkshire (1946 to 1958)

Wisden 1954
TOURS
A 1954–55; SA 1956–57;
WI 1947–48, 1953–54; NZ 1954–55;
I 1967–68 (Pres XI)
Born Ardsley, Yorkshire 8 Jan 1923
Died Hatfield, Doncaster, Yorkshire
23 Jul 1985

One of cricket's more colourful characters, Johnny Wardle was an orthodox slow left-arm leg-break bowler who later developed the googly and Chinaman so well that he could bowl it with almost the same degree of accuracy. Tallish (5ft 10½in), strong and belligerent, he was an extremely valuable hard-hitting left-handed batsman. Although he had taken 4 for 7 when Australia collapsed to 35 for 8 at Old Trafford in 1953, the selectors preferred Tony Lock on English pitches and Wardle's only complete home series was against Pakistan in 1954. Once he had fine-tuned his unorthodox armoury, he became an automatic requirement for the harder surfaces overseas. Although highly popular with spectators, his relations with the Yorkshire team and captain were less harmonious and after his selection for the 1958–59 tour of Australia he was told that he would not be re-engaged for the following season. When he put his name to newspaper articles criticising his county captain and colleagues, he was sacked by Yorkshire and his tour invitation was withdrawn by MCC. The latter decision considerably weakened the balance of the England side on Australian pitches. He finished his playing days with Cambridgeshire (1963–69) and in the Lancashire league.

NOTABLE FEATS

- 50 wickets in 17th Test (*395*); 100 wickets in 27th Test (*437*).
- Took 100 wickets in a season 10 times, notably 195 in 1955.
- Took 90 wickets (avge 12.25) in South Africa in 1956–57.
- Took 9 for 25 for Yorkshire v Lancashire at Manchester in 1954.
- Returned match analysis of 16 for 112 (including 9 for 48) for Yorkshire v Sussex at Hull in 1954.

						Batting 1st			Batting 2nd				Bowling 1st			Bowling 2nd		
Ref	Series	V	T	Venue	Result	No	R	HO	No	R	HO	Ct	Balls	R	W	Balls	R	W
296/259	1947–48	WI	2	Port-of-Spain	D	10	4	c	10	2	*	–	18	9	0	–	–	–
324/277	1950	WI	2	Lord's	L-326	9	33	*	9	21	lbw	–	102	46	2	180	58	0
334/287	1951	SA	1	Nottingham	L-71	8	5	c	9	30	c	–	294	77	1	24	4	0
335/288			2	Lord's	W-10w	8	18	lbw	–	–	–	–	137	46	3	120	44	1
372/301	1953	A	1	Nottingham	D	9	29	*	–	–	–	–	210	55	1	72	24	0
373/302			2	Lord's	D	9	23	b	9	0	*	–	174	77	4	276	111	1
374/303			3	Manchester	D	5	5	b	–	–	–	–	171	70	3	30	7	4
384/308	1953–54	WI	3	Georgetown	W-9w	6	38	b	–	–	–	–	132	60	0	75	24	3
386/310			5	Kingston	W-9w	8	66	c	–	–	–	2	60	20	0	234	83	1
387/311	1954	P	1	Lord's	D	6	3	c	–	–	–	–	185	33	4	48	6	0
388/312			2	Nottingham	W-I & 129	8	14	*	–	–	–	–	36	9	1	192	44	3
389/313			3	Manchester	D	8	54	c	–	–	–	3	144	19	4	42	9	1
390/314			4	Oval	L-24	7	8	c	7	9	c	3	–	–	–	210	56	7
392/316	1954–55	A	2	Sydney	W-38	9	35	c	9	8	lbw	–	–	–	–	32	11	0
393/317			3	Melbourne	W-128	8	0	b	8	38	b	–	48	20	1	8	1	0
394/318			4	Adelaide	W-5w	8	23	c	–	–	–	–	152	59	0	34	8	1
395/319			5	Sydney	D	8	5	*	–	–	–	1	196	79	5	96	51	3
401/320	1954–55	NZ	1	Dunedin	W-8w	8	32	*	–	–	–	–	156	31	1	87	41	2
402/321			2	Auckland	W-I & 20	8	0	c	–	–	–	–	186	44	1	30	0	1
408/322	1955	SA	1	Nottingham	W-I & 5	8	2	lbw	–	–	–	–	192	24	4	174	33	1
409/323			2	Lord's	W-71	9	20	c	8	4	c	–	174	65	4	58	18	2
411/325			4	Leeds	L-224	9	24	c	8	21	c	–	54	33	0	342	100	4
426/328	1956	A	2	Lord's	L-185	9	0	c	9	0	b	–	120	40	1	42	19	0
434/332	1956–57	SA	1	Johannesburg[3]	W-131	9	6	*	4	0	lbw	–	160	52	3	24	18	0
435/333			2	Cape Town	W-312	8	3	st	–	–	–	1	190	53	5	152	36	7
436/334			3	Durban[2]	D	8	13	b	8	8	c	–	162	61	5	160	42	2
437/335			4	Johannesburg[3]	L-17	8	16	c	7	22	c	2	158	68	2	112	29	2
440/338	1957	WI	2	Lord's	W-I & 36	9	11	c	–	–	–	–	–	–	–	132	53	1

Career	M	I	NO	HS	R	Avge	100	50	Ct	St	Balls	R	W	Avge	BB	5w	10w	Rate
Test	28	41	8	66	653	19.78	–	2	12	–	6597	2080	102	20.39	7-36	5	1	64.67
F/c	412	527	71	79	7333	16.08	–	18	256	–	102367	35027	1846	18.97	9-25	134	29	55.45

Johnny Wardle bowling; Norman Yardley in the foreground.

J. H. WARDLE – TEST BOWLING SUMMARY

Series	V	M	Balls	R	W	Avge	BB	5w	10w	Rate
1947–48	WI	1	18	9	0	–	–	–	–	–
1950	WI	1	282	104	2	52.00	2-46	–	–	141.00
1951	SA	2	575	171	5	34.20	3-46	–	–	115.00
1953	A	3	933	344	13	26.61	4-7	–	–	71.76
1953–54	WI	2	501	187	4	46.75	3-24	–	–	125.25
1954	P	4	857	176	20	8.80	7-56	1	–	42.85
1954–55	A	4	566	229	10	22.90	5-79	1	–	56.60
1954–55	NZ	2	459	116	5	23.20	2-41	–	–	91.80
1955	SA	3	994	273	15	18.20	4-24	–	–	66.26
1956	A	1	162	59	1	59.00	1-40	–	–	162.00
1956–57	SA	4	1118	359	26	13.80	7-36	3	1	43.00
1957	WI	1	132	53	1	53.00	1-53	–	–	132.00
	A	8	1661	632	24	26.33	5-79	1	–	69.20
	SA	9	2687	803	46	17.45	7-36	3	1	58.41
	NZ	2	459	116	5	23.20	2-41	–	–	91.80
	WI	5	933	353	7	50.42	3-24	–	–	133.28
	P	4	857	176	20	8.80	7-56	1	–	42.85
Home		15	3935	1180	57	20.70	7-56	1	–	69.03
Overseas		13	2662	900	45	20.00	7-36	4	1	59.15
Totals		28	6597	2080	102	20.39	7-36	5	1	64.67

WARNER
Sir Pelham Francis

Oxford University (1894 to 1896)
Middlesex (1894 to 1920)

Wisden 1904
TOURS
A 1902–03, 1903–04, 1911–12;
SA 1898–99, 1905–06; WI 1896–97;
NZ 1902–03
Born The Hall, Port-of-Spain, Trinidad
2 Oct 1873
Knighted for services to cricket 1937
Died West Lavington, Sussex
30 Jan 1963

Few men have dedicated their lives to cricket to the extent that 'Plum' Warner did. Apart from his contributions as player, manager, writer and editor, he devoted some 60 years to serving on the MCC committee. Educated at Rugby and Oxford (where he was a blue in his last two summers), he was a slight, almost frail-looking figure, but he had great tenacity as a neat and efficient batsman who scored 60 first-class hundreds. In his very first Test match he scored 132* and carried his bat through the innings. He captained England ten times with mixed results (four wins and six defeats) and enjoyed a splendidly triumphant finale to his playing career when he crowned his long reign of Middlesex captaincy (1908–20) with a stirring victory which clinched the Championship. He was joint-manager of the controversial 'bodyline' tour but criticised Jardine's strategy rather more fiercely afterwards than he did at the time. In 1921 he began an 11-year tenure as cricket correspondent of the *Morning Post* and, in a few spare moments, founded *The Cricketer*, remaining its editor for almost 40 years. He was a Test selector in 1905 and 1911 before serving three spells as chairman: 1926, 1931–32 and 1935–39. During the Second World War he kept a fatherly eye on Lord's as deputy secretary of MCC before beginning a 15-year term as a trustee. He was the Club's president in 1950–51; a few years later a new stand bearing his name was constructed between the Lord's pavilion and the Grandstand.

NOTABLE FEATS

- *58* First to score 100 in his first Test, that match being v SA. First to carry his bat through a completed Test innings on debut for England.
- Exceeded 1000 runs in a season 14 times, including 2123 in 1911.
- Scored 3 double centuries, notably 244 for Rest of England v Warwickshire at The Oval in 1911.
- Carried his bat through a completed innings on 10 occasions, including 7 for Middlesex.

Ref	Series	V	T	Venue	Result	Batting 1st No	R	HO	Batting 2nd No	R	HO	Ct
58/58	1898–99	SA	1	Johannesburg[1]	W-32	2	21	c	2	132	*	–
59/59			2	Cape Town	W-210	2	31	c	2	23	b	–
78/75*	1903–04	A	1	Sydney	W-5w	2	0	c	2	8	b	–
79/76*			2	Melbourne	W-185	1	68	c	1	3	c	–
80/77*			3	Adelaide	L-216	1	48	c	1	79	c	–
81/78*			4	Sydney	W-157	1	0	b	9	31	*	–
82/79*			5	Melbourne	L-218	4	1	c	5	11	c	2
88/85*	1905–06	SA	1	Johannesburg[1]	L-1w	1	6	c	1	51	b	1
89/86*			2	Johannesburg[1]	L-9w	1	2	c	1	0	b	–
90/87*			3	Johannesburg[1]	L-243	1	19	b	1	2	b	–
91/88*			4	Cape Town	W-4w	6	1	c	1	4	b	–
92/89*			5	Cape Town	L-I & 16	2	0	b	7	4	c	–
104/101	1909	A	4	Manchester	D	1	9	b	1	25	b	–
122/113	1912	SA	1	Lord's	W-I & 62	5	39	st	–	–	–	–
123/114		A	1	Lord's	D	5	4	b	–	–	–	–

'Plum' Warner

Career	M	I	NO	HS	R	Avge	100	50	Ct	St	Balls	R	W	Avge	BB	5w	10w	Rate
Test	15	28	2	132*	622	23.92	1	3	3	–	–	–	–	–	–	–	–	–
F/c	519	875	75	244	29028	36.28	60	149	183	–	1128	636	15	42.40	2-26	–	–	75.20

WARR, John James

Cambridge University (1949 to 1952)
Middlesex (1949 to 1960)

TOURS
A 1950–51; WI 1955–56 (Swanton), 1956–57 (Norfolk); NZ 1950–51
Born Ealing, Middlesex 16 Jul 1927

John Warr

John Warr was a tireless and persevering right-arm fast-medium bowler who would try to bowl as rapidly at the end of an exhausting day as he had with the new ball in the freshness of morning. Tall and loose-limbed, he took a lengthy run and arched his back like a bow in his delivery. He was selected for Freddie Brown's tour while still at Cambridge. Although he proved effective in the state matches, injuries to Bailey and Wright led to him being over-bowled in his two Tests, both played on bland pitches. Consequently, he ended his brief career as the most expensive wicket-taker in Test cricket (1 for 281) and retained the privilege until 1985 when he was ousted by Roger Wijesuriya whose only wicket for Sri Lanka cost 294 runs. A highly entertaining and witty speaker, 'JJ' describes that dismissal: 'Ian Johnson, a bowler, got an inside edge and was caught by Godfrey Evans, standing up. It only just carried. The umpire didn't give it out but Ian walked. When I thanked him he said he wouldn't have done if it had been Victoria playing New South Wales!' He returned to complete his degree and captained Cambridge in his final year, handy training for his three astute and lively summers in charge of Middlesex (1958–60). He represented Australia on the ICC ('It was as a reward for my services to Australian cricket!') and was in great demand to attend dinners during his year as MCC president (1987–88).

NOTABLE FEATS

- Took 100 wickets in a season twice.
- Took 9 for 65 for Middlesex v Kent at Lord's in 1956.
- Hat-trick for Middlesex v Leicestershire at Loughborough in 1956.

Ref	Series	V	T Venue	Result	Batting 1st No	R	HO	Batting 2nd No	R	HO	Ct	Bowling 1st Balls	R	W	Bowling 2nd Balls	R	W
329/282	1950–51	A	3 Sydney	L-I & 13	10	4	b	10	0	b	–	288	142	0	–	–	–
330/283			4 Adelaide	L-274	10	0	b	9	0	b	–	128	63	0	168	76	1

Career	M	I	NO	HS	R	Avge	100	50	Ct	St	Balls	R	W	Avge	BB	5w	10w	Rate
Test	2	4	0	4	4	1.00	–	–	–	–	584	281	1	281.00	1-76	–	–	584.00
F/c	344	454	119	54*	3838	11.45	–	3	117	–	53000	21796	956	22.79	9-65	35	5	55.43

WARREN, Arnold

Derbyshire (1897 to 1920)

Born Codnor Park, Derbyshire
2 Apr 1875
Died Codnor, Derbyshire 3 Sep 1951

NOTABLE FEATS

- Took 100 wickets in a season 3 times.
- Shared world record first-class 9th-wkt stand of 283 with J. Chapman for Derbyshire v Warwickshire at Blackwell in 1910.
- Returned a match analysis of 15 for 112 for Derbyshire v Nottinghamshire at Welbeck in 1904.

Arnold Warren was a very tall, right-arm fast bowler and the first Derbyshire player to take 100 first-class wickets in a season. Operating off a long, bounding approach, he was one of the most rapid bowlers of his generation. Although he had a very rewarding first Test match, dismissing the cream of Australia's batting and bagging the prize wicket of Victor Trumper cheaply in both innings, he was not invited again. His batting brought the occasional spasm of dramatic success as when he went in at No. 10 with 111 needed to avert an innings defeat. In under three hours he had contributed his only first-class century to a ninth-wicket partnership of 283 which still survives as the world record.

Arnold Warren

Ref	Series	V	T Venue	Result	Batting 1st No	R	HO	Batting 2nd No	R	HO	Ct	Bowling 1st Balls	R	W	Bowling 2nd Balls	R	W
85/82	1905	A	3 Leeds	D	10	7	ro	–	–	–	1	116	57	5	120	56	1

Career	M	I	NO	HS	R	Avge	100	50	Ct	St	Balls	R	W	Avge	BB	5w	10w	Rate
Test	1	1	0	7	7	7.00	–	–	1	–	236	113	6	18.83	5-57	1	–	39.33
F/c	255	445	44	123	5507	13.73	1	11	195	–	42953	23061	939	24.55	8-69	72	15	45.74

WASHBROOK, Cyril

Lancashire (1933 to 1959)

Wisden 1947
TOURS
A 1946–47, 1950–51; SA 1948–49;
NZ 1946–47, 1950–51
Born Barrow, Blackburn, Lancashire
6 Dec 1914

Although the Second World War arrived just as Cyril Washbrook was being discussed as a possible Test opener, he survived the hostilities with his batting form intact to become the Lancashire half of a renowned Roses opening partnership with Len Hutton. A stocky figure of medium height (5ft 8¼in), with his cap always worn at a jaunty angle, he was a beautifully balanced player. His exceptional ability to handle fast bowling was fully tested by Lindwall, Miller and Johnston but they were not immune from the weight of his cutting and hooking. He was superbly quick on his feet and his fielding at cover-point was a delight to watch. Unfit towards the end of the 1950 season, he had a poor tour of the antipodes and his Test career appeared to have ended when he was appointed a selector in 1956.

After England had lost to Australia at Lord's, his colleagues persuaded him to return for the next match and bring some tenacity and experience to the middle order. More than five years after his last international appearance and aged 41, he joined Peter May with the scoreboard grimly showing 17 for 3. He responded by scoring 98 and their partnership of 187 in 287 minutes proved to be the turning point of the series. The first professional to be officially appointed captain of Lancashire (1954–59), he served two spells as a Test selector (1956–57 and 1971–72). His benefit of £14,000 in 1948 remained the record until 1971.

NOTABLE FEATS

- 1000 runs in 18th Test (*301*) (34 inns); 2000 runs in 27th Test (*324*) (49 inns).
- *282* Shared third consecutive century opening partnership with L. Hutton.
- *310* Shared (then) world-record 1st-wkt stand of 359 in 310 min with L. Hutton on the opening day of Test cricket at Ellis Park. It remains England's record opening stand in all Tests.
- *325* Shared record E v WI 1st-wkt stand of 212 with R.T. Simpson.
- Exceeded 1000 runs in a season 17 times (plus 3 times on tour), including 2000 twice, notably 2662 in 1947. Leading batsman in 1948. Scored 1079 runs in July 1946.
- Scored 7 double centuries, all for Lancashire, notably 251* v Surrey at Manchester in 1947.
- Shared 1st-wkt stand of 350* with W. Place for Lancashire v Sussex at Manchester in 1947.

Cyril Washbrook

						Batting 1st			Batting 2nd				Bowling 1st			Bowling 2nd		
Ref	**Series**	**V**	**T**	**Venue**	**Result**	**No**	**R**	**HO**	**No**	**R**	**HO**	**Ct**	**Balls**	**R**	**W**	**Balls**	**R**	**W**
262/231	1937	NZ	3	Oval	D	3	9	lbw	2	8	*	1	–	–	–	–	–	–
276/244	1946	I	1	Lord's	W-10w	2	27	c	2	24	*	–	–	–	–	–	–	–
277/245			2	Manchester	D	2	52	c	2	26	lbw	–	–	–	–	–	–	–
278/246			3	Oval	D	2	17	c	–	–	–	1	–	–	–	–	–	–
279/247	1946–47	A	1	Brisbane²	L-I & 332	2	6	c	2	13	c	–	–	–	–	–	–	–
280/248			2	Sydney	L-I & 33	2	1	b	2	41	c	1	–	–	–	–	–	–
281/249			3	Melbourne	D	2	62	c	2	112	b	1	–	–	–	–	–	–
282/250			4	Adelaide	D	2	65	c	2	39	c	–	–	–	–	–	–	–
283/251			5	Sydney	L-5w	2	0	b	2	24	b	–	–	–	–	–	–	–
284/252	1946–47	NZ		Christchurch	D	1	2	c	–	–	–	–	–	–	–	–	–	–
285/253	1947	SA	1	Nottingham	D	2	25	lbw	2	59	c	–	–	–	–	–	–	–
286/254			2	Lord's	W-10w	2	65	c	2	13	*	–	–	–	–	–	–	–
287/255			3	Manchester	W-7w	2	29	c	2	40	c	–	–	–	–	–	–	–
288/256			4	Leeds	W-10w	2	75	b	2	15	*	–	–	–	–	–	–	–
289/257			5	Oval	D	2	32	lbw	2	43	c	–	–	–	–	–	–	–
299/262	1948	A	1	Nottingham	L-8w	2	6	c	2	1	c	–	–	–	–	–	–	–
300/263			2	Lord's	L-409	2	8	c	2	37	c	1	–	–	–	–	–	–
301/264			3	Manchester	D	1	11	b	1	85	*	2	–	–	–	–	–	–
302/265			4	Leeds	L-7w	2	143	c	2	65	c	–	–	–	–	–	–	–
309/267	1948–49	SA	1	Durban²	W-2w	2	35	c	2	25	lbw	–	–	–	–	–	–	–
310/268			2	Johannesburg²	D	2	195	c	–	–	–	–	–	–	–	–	–	–
311/269			3	Cape Town	D	2	74	b	2	9	c	–	–	–	–	–	–	–
312/270			4	Johannesburg²	D	2	97	c	2	31	lbw	–	–	–	–	–	–	–
313/271			5	Port Elizabeth	W-3w	2	36	c	2	40	c	–	–	–	–	–	–	–
314/272	1949	NZ	1	Leeds	D	2	10	c	2	103	*	1	–	–	–	–	–	–
316/274			3	Manchester	D	2	44	c	–	–	–	1	–	–	–	12	8	0
324/277	1950	WI	2	Lord's	L-326	2	36	st	2	114	b	–	–	–	–	–	–	–
325/278			3	Nottingham	L-10w	2	3	c	2	102	c	–	–	–	–	–	–	–
327/280	1950–51	A	1	Brisbane²	L-70	2	19	c	2	6	c	–	–	–	–	–	–	–
328/281			2	Melbourne	L-28	2	21	lbw	2	8	b	–	–	–	–	–	–	–
329/282			3	Sydney	L-I & 13	2	18	c	2	34	b	–	–	–	–	–	–	–
330/283			4	Adelaide	L-274	2	2	c	2	31	lbw	–	–	–	–	–	–	–
331/284			5	Melbourne	W-8w	2	27	c	2	7	c	1	–	–	–	–	–	–

Ref	Series	V	T	Venue	Result	Batting 1st No	R	HO	Batting 2nd No	R	HO	Ct	Bowling 1st Balls	R	W	Bowling 2nd Balls	R	W
332/285	1950–51	NZ	1	Christchurch	D	2	58	c	–	–	–	–	–	–	–	24	25	1
427/329	1956	A	3	Leeds	W-I & 42	5	98	lbw	–	–	–	1	–	–	–	–	–	–
428/330			4	Manchester	W-I & 170	6	6	lbw	–	–	–	–	–	–	–	–	–	–
429/331			5	Oval	D	7	0	lbw	–	–	–	1	–	–	–	–	–	–

Career	M	I	NO	HS	R	Avge	100	50	Ct	St	Balls	R	W	Avge	BB	5w	10w	Rate
Test	37	66	6	195	2569	42.81	6	12	12	–	36	33	1	33.00	1-25	–	–	36.00
F/c	592	906	107	251*	34101	42.67	76	175	212	–	494	309	7	44.14	2-8	–	–	70.57

C. WASHBROOK – TEST BATTING SUMMARY

Series	V	M	I	NO	HS	R	Avge	100	50
1937	NZ	1	2	1	9	17	17.00	–	–
1946	I	3	5	1	52	146	36.50	–	1
1946–47	A	5	10	–	112	363	36.30	1	2
1946–47	NZ	1	1	–	2	2	2.00	–	–
1947	SA	5	10	2	75	396	49.50	–	3
1948	A	4	8	1	143	356	50.85	1	2
1948–49	SA	5	9	–	195	542	60.22	1	2
1949	NZ	2	3	1	103*	157	78.50	1	–
1950	WI	2	4	–	114	255	63.75	2	–
1950–51	A	5	10	–	34	173	17.30	–	–
1950–51	NZ	1	1	–	58	58	58.00	–	1
1956	A	3	3	–	98	104	34.66	–	1
	A	17	31	1	143	996	33.20	2	5
	SA	10	19	2	195	938	55.17	1	5
	WI	2	4	–	114	255	63.75	2	–
	NZ	5	7	2	103*	234	46.80	1	1
Home		20	35	6	143	1431	49.34	4	7
Overseas		17	31	–	195	1138	36.70	2	5
Totals		37	66	6	195	2569	42.81	6	12

WATKINS
Albert John
(known as Allan John Watkins)

Glamorgan (1939 to 1962)

TOURS
SA 1948–49; I 1951–52, 1953–54 (Cwlth); P 1951–52, 1955–56; SL 1951–52
Born Usk, Monmouthshire 21 Apr 1922

NOTABLE FEATS

- *339* Batted for 9 hrs and became first England player to bat throughout the day of a Test in India.
- Exceeded 1000 runs in a season 13 times and took 100 wickets twice, completing the 'double' in 1954 and 1955.
- Took 4 wickets in 5 balls for Glamorgan v Derbyshire at Chesterfield in 1954.
- Held 5 catches in an innings for MCC v South Zone at Bangalore in 1951–52.

'Allan' Watkins was the first Glamorgan player to appear for England against Australia. It was not a baptism he enjoyed recalling. England had been routed for 52 by a rampant Lindwall who, in addition to taking six wickets, had scored a direct hit on the Watkins shoulder and crippled him for the rest of the match. Just 5ft 6in high and comfortably built, he belied his physique and was an extremely energetic and talented left-handed all-rounder. An adventurous middle-order batsman with a solid defence and great determination, he battled for nine hours at Delhi in an epic match-saving rearguard action. His medium-fast swing bowling enabled him to complete the 'double' twice, and he was a fearless and skilful fielder at short-leg. His all-round contributions played a major part in Glamorgan's first Championship (1948). He played soccer for Plymouth Argyle and Cardiff City. His recent coaching engagements have included Framlingham and Oundle.

'Allan' Watkins

Ref	Series	V	T	Venue	Result	Batting 1st			Batting 2nd			Ct	Bowling 1st			Bowling 2nd		
						No	R	HO	No	R	HO		Balls	R	W	Balls	R	W
303/266	1948	A	5	Oval	L-I & 149	7	0	lbw	7	2	c	–	24	19	0	–	–	–
309/267	1948–49	SA	1	Durban[2]	W-2w	5	9	c	5	4	b	2	24	11	0	–	–	–
310/268			2	Johannesburg[2]	D	5	7	c	–	–	–	2	40	5	1	96	48	0
311/269			3	Cape Town	D	5	27	c	5	64	*	1	80	36	1	–	–	–
312/270			4	Johannesburg[2]	D	5	111	hw	6	10	b	–	16	9	0	24	16	2
313/271			5	Port Elizabeth	W-3w	5	14	c	9	5	*	1	40	24	0	–	–	–
315/273	1949	NZ	2	Lord's	D	5	6	c	5	49	*	1	18	11	0	–	–	–
339/292	1951–52	I	1	Delhi	D	5	40	c	4	137	*	–	186	60	0	–	–	–
340/293			2	Bombay[2]	D	6	80	c	–	–	–	1	192	97	0	78	20	3
341/294			3	Calcutta	D	4	68	c	4	2	b	1	126	31	0	–	–	–
342/295			4	Kanpur	W-8w	5	66	c	–	–	–	–	30	6	0	–	–	–
343/296			5	Madras[1]	L-I & 8	5	9	c	5	48	c	2	84	50	1	–	–	–
351/297	1952	I	1	Leeds	W-7w	6	48	lbw	–	–	–	3	66	21	0	66	32	0
352/298			2	Lord's	W-8w	6	0	b	–	–	–	1	102	37	3	48	20	0
353/299			3	Manchester	W-I & 207	6	4	c	–	–	–	2	–	–	–	24	1	0

Career	M	I	NO	HS	R	Avge	100	50	Ct	St	Balls	R	W	Avge	BB	5w	10w	Rate
Test	15	24	4	137*	810	40.50	2	4	17	–	1364	554	11	50.36	3-20	–	–	124.00
F/c	484	753	87	170*	20361	30.57	32	108	462	–	51422	20393	833	24.48	7-28	25	–	61.73

WATSON, William

Yorkshire (1939 to 1957)
Leicestershire (1958 to 1964)

Wisden 1954
TOURS
A 1958–59; WI 1953–54, 1956–57 (Norfolk); NZ 1958–59, 1960–61; I 1956–57 (Howard); Z 1962–63 (Cwlth)
Born Bolton upon Dearne, Yorkshire
7 Mar 1920

Willie Watson batting against South Africa on his England debut in 1951.

Willie Watson was better known as a tenacious left-half, who had won four soccer caps for England, than as a cricketer when he was selected for his first Test against Australia. After that epic contest his name was written indelibly in the game's chronicles for his part in saving a match which, at the start of the final day, looked doomed. His last-ditch stand with Trevor Bailey at Lord's in 1953 was one of Test cricket's most heroic feats. Enduring 257 minutes, the pair survived from 12.42pm until 5.50pm – 40 minutes from the close – and England went on to win the series and regain the Ashes after 19 years. Tallish (5ft 11in), he was a sound and stylish left-handed batsman and a very good outfielder. He moved to Leicestershire as captain and assistant secretary (1958–61) prior to becoming a Test selector (1962–64). His soccer clubs were Huddersfield Town, Sunderland and Halifax Town. In 1968 he emigrated to Johannesburg as coach and administrator of the Wanderers Club.

NOTABLE FEATS

- *373* Scored 109 in 346 min in his first Test against Australia.
- Exceeded 1000 runs in a season 14 times, including 2212 in 1959.
- Scored 3 double centuries, notably 257 for MCC v British Guiana at Georgetown in 1953–54 when he shared a 4th-wkt stand of 402 with T.W. Graveney which remains the record for any wicket by an English touring team.
- Shared record Leicestershire 3rd-wkt stand of 316* with A. Wharton v Somerset at Taunton in 1961.

Ref	Series	V	T	Venue	Result	Batting 1st			Batting 2nd			Ct
						No	R	HO	No	R	HO	
334/287	1951	SA	1	Nottingham	L-71	5	57	lbw	5	5	lbw	–
335/288			2	Lord's	W-10w	5	79	c	–	–	–	1
336/289			3	Manchester	W-9w	5	21	b	–	–	–	–
337/290			4	Leeds	D	5	32	b	–	–	–	–
338/291			5	Oval	W-4w	5	31	ro	5	15	c	–
354/300	1952	I	4	Oval	D	6	18	*	–	–	–	–
373/302	1953	A	2	Lord's	D	5	4	st	5	109	c	1
374/303			3	Manchester	D	6	16	b	–	–	–	–
375/304			4	Leeds	D	5	24	b	5	15	c	–

Ref	Series	V	T	Venue	Result	Batting 1st No	R	HO	Batting 2nd No	R	HO	Ct
382/306	1953–54	WI	1	Kingston	L-140	1	3	b	1	116	c	–
383/307			2	Bridgetown	L-181	2	6	st	2	0	c	–
384/308			3	Georgetown	W-9w	1	12	b	3	27	*	1
385/309			4	Port-of-Spain	D	5	4	c	1	32	c	–
386/310			5	Kingston	W-9w	5	4	c	2	20	*	2
412/326	1955	SA	5	Oval	W-92	5	25	c	6	3	b	1
425/327	1956	A	1	Nottingham	D	5	0	lbw	3	8	c	–
426/328			2	Lord's	L-185	5	6	c	4	18	b	–
457/345	1958	NZ	4	Manchester	W-I & 13	2	66	c	–	–	–	1
458/346			5	Oval	D	3	10	b	–	–	–	1
465/348	1958–59	A	2	Melbourne	L-8w	3	0	b	3	7	b	–
467/350			4	Adelaide	L-10w	6	25	b	2	40	c	–
472/352	1958–59	NZ	1	Christchurch	W-I & 99	2	10	c	–	–	–	–
473/353			2	Auckland	D	2	11	b	–	–	–	–

Career	M	I	NO	HS	R	Avge	100	50	Ct	St	Balls	R	W	Avge	BB	5w	10w	Rate
Test	23	37	3	116	879	25.85	2	3	8	–	–	–	–	–	–	–	–	–
F/c	468	753	109	257	25670	39.86	55	132	295	–	194	127	0	–	–	–	–	–

WEBBE
Alexander Josiah

Oxford University (1875 to 1878)
Middlesex (1875 to 1900)

TOUR A 1878–79
Born Bethnal Green, London
16 Jan 1855
Died Abinger Hammer, Surrey
19 Feb 1941

Alexander Webbe established his reputation as a high class batsman when captaining Harrow in the annual blood-lettings against Eton. A blue in all his four years at Oxford, he was elected captain in the last two, a rare privilege reserved for the most popular and gifted. While there he was selected for the Gentlemen and partnered W.G. Grace in a stand of 203 which brought high praise from the famous doctor. His stance was a crouching affair with feet apart like Jessop; there the similarity ended. 'Webbie' was a very patient player with an excellent defence, who revelled in that Harrow speciality, the crashing cover drive. For more than a decade he was the most reliable batsman in the Middlesex team. He was also an effective right-arm fast bowler, who frequently separated awkward partnerships, and an enthusiastic and safe fielder at mid-wicket. He enjoyed a long and memorable reign as captain of Middlesex (1885–98), served as president and remained closely involved with the Club's well-being until his death.
[*Illus. p.* 222]

NOTABLE FEATS

- Scored 1244 runs in 1887.
- Scored 243* for Middlesex v Yorkshire at Huddersfield in 1887.
- Carried his bat through a completed innings on 8 occasions, including 7 for Middlesex.
- Held 6 catches in an innings for Gentlemen v Players at Lord's in 1877; at the time it was the world record and it has been exceeded only twice.

Ref	Series	V	T	Venue	Result	Batting 1st No	R	HO	Batting 2nd No	R	HO	Ct
3/3	1878–79	A		Melbourne	L-10w	3	4	b	3	0	lbw	2

Career	M	I	NO	HS	R	Avge	100	50	Ct	St	Balls	R	W	Avge	BB	5w	10w	Rate
Test	1	2	0	4	4	2.00	–	–	2	–	–	–	–	–	–	–	–	–
F/c	370	641	58	243*	14465	24.81	14	60	227	10	7699	2748	109	25.21	5-23	2	–	70.63

WELLARD
Arthur William

Somerset (1927 to 1950)

Wisden 1936
TOUR I 1937–38 (Tennyson)
Born Southfleet, Kent 8 Apr 1902
Died Eastbourne, Sussex 31 Dec 1980

NOTABLE FEATS

- Exceeded 1000 runs in a season 4 times and took 100 wickets 8 times, completing the 'double' on 3 occasions. Took 131 wickets in his first full season (1929) after playing only 2 previous matches.
- Twice hit 5 sixes off successive balls for Somerset at Wells: off T.R. Armstrong v Derbyshire in 1936 and off F.E. Woolley v Kent in 1938.
- Hit over 50 sixes in 1933–35–36–38, including (then) record of 66 in 1935, and over 500 in his career.
- Returned match analysis of 15 for 101 for Somerset v Worcestershire at Bath in 1947.
- Holds Somerset record for most wickets in a season (169 in 1938).
- Hat-trick for Somerset v Leicestershire at Leicester in 1929.
- Achieved the match 'double' for Somerset twice (1929 and 1933).

Arthur Wellard developed late as a cricketer and played in no organised matches until his late teens. Thereafter his philosophy was simple: bowl as fast as possible and hit the ball out of sight. Tall and massively built he was a lion-hearted trier as a right-arm fast-medium bowler who developed a vicious break-back; and few batsmen have hit a ball further or more often. He delighted in the smaller Somerset grounds like Wells and Frome and was famous for his six-hitting which, it is estimated, accounted for a quarter of his runs. His bucket sized hands missed little at slip and he was still holding catches there in his early seventies. By then he had reverted to off-spin and drifters. He rarely betted but his appetite for playing cards resulted in one club drafting a new rule to prevent his bringing them to matches. He seldom lost.

Arthur Wellard

						Batting 1st			Batting 2nd				Bowling 1st			Bowling 2nd		
Ref	Series	V	T	Venue	Result	No	R	HO	No	R	HO	Ct	Balls	R	W	Balls	R	W
261/230	1937	NZ	2	Manchester	W-130	7	5	b	8	0	c	2	180	81	4	84	30	0
264/233	1938	A	2	Lord's	D	9	4	c	9	38	b	–	138	96	2	54	30	1

Career	M	I	NO	HS	R	Avge	100	50	Ct	St	Balls	R	W	Avge	BB	5w	10w	Rate
Test	2	4	0	38	47	11.75	–	–	2	–	456	237	7	33.85	4-81	–	–	65.14
F/c	417	679	46	112	12485	19.72	2	59	375	–	89597	39302	1614	24.35	8-52	108	24	55.51

WHARTON, Alan

Lancashire (1946 to 1960)
Leicestershire (1961 to 1963)

TOUR I 1956–57 (Howard)
Born Heywood, Lancashire 30 Apr 1923

Alan Wharton

Alan Wharton was a lively and erudite Lancastrian who enjoyed 15 productive summers at Old Trafford before continuing in the same vein throughout a three-year contract at Leicester. Tallish (5ft 11in) and very fit, he was a forceful left-handed batsman, an effective right-arm medium-pace bowler and a high class outfielder – as befits a Salford rugby league footballer. Although the War delayed his entry into county cricket, he was awarded his cap in his first season. He was a schoolmaster and a JP.

NOTABLE FEATS

- Exceeded 1000 runs in a season 11 times, including 2157 in 1959.
- Shared record Leicestershire 3rd-wkt stand of 316* with W. Watson v Somerset at Taunton in 1961.
- Scored 87* and 33*, sharing 1st-wkt stands of 166* and 66* with J. Dyson, when Lancashire beat Leicestershire by 10 wickets at Manchester in 1956 – the first instance in first-class cricket of a side winning without losing a wicket and the only one in Britain.

Ref	Series	V	T	Venue	Result	Batting 1st No	R	HO	Batting 2nd No	R	HO	Ct
314/272	1949	NZ	1	Leeds	D	5	7	lbw	5	13	b	–

Career	M	I	NO	HS	R	Avge	100	50	Ct	St	Balls	R	W	Avge	BB	5w	10w	Rate
Test	1	2	0	13	20	10.00	–	–	–	–	–	–	–	–	–	–	–	–
F/c	482	745	69	199	21796	32.24	31	110	288	–	16858	7488	237	31.59	7-33	2	–	71.13

WHITAKER John James

Leicestershire (1983 to date)

Wisden 1987
TOUR A 1986–87
Born Skipton, Yorkshire 5 May 1962

NOTABLE FEATS

- Exceeded 1000 runs in a season 5 times.
- Scored 200* for Leicestershire v Nottinghamshire at Leicester in 1986.

A little above medium height (5ft 10in), James Whitaker is an ambitious batsman who sets himself annual targets. In 1986 he achieved them with distinction. That season's tally of 1526 runs (avge 66.34 – the highest by an English batsman) earned him a winter in Australia. Despite a hundred against South Australia in his first match, his playing opportunities were few and far between. Botham's rib injury gave him a Test place at Adelaide but, short of match practice, he never found his normal rhythm and holed out to mid-off for just 11. If determination and courage earn success he should be a world beater. During 1986 he had become the first batsman to have bones broken in both hands by the same bowler (Malcolm Marshall) in the same innings. Four weeks later he returned straight to the county side after refusing a 'net' in the 2nd XI and scored 100* and 82* against his native Yorkshire.

James Whitaker being congratulated by Phil Edmonds after catching Australia's David Boon in the Adelaide Test, 1986–87.

Ref	Series	V	T	Venue	Result	Batting 1st No	R	HO	Batting 2nd No	R	HO	Ct
1060/631	1986–87	A	3	Adelaide	D	7	11	c	–	–	–	1

Career	M	I	NO	HS	R	Avge	100	50	Ct	St	Balls	R	W	Avge	BB	5w	10w	Rate
Test	1	1	0	11	11	11.00	–	–	1	–	–	–	–	–	–	–	–	–
F/c	131	199	28	200*	6713	39.25	16	35	84	–	122	168	1	168.00	1-41	–	–	122.00

WHITE
David William

Hampshire (1957 to 1971)
Glamorgan (1972)

TOURS
WI 1964–65 (Cav); I 1961–62; P 1961–62
Born Sutton Coldfield, Warwickshire
14 Dec 1935

NOTABLE FEATS

- Took 100 wickets in a season 4 times.
- Took 9 for 44 for Hampshire v Leicestershire at Portsmouth in 1966.
- Two hat-tricks for Hampshire v Sussex: at Portsmouth in 1961 (4 wickets in 5 balls) and at Hove in 1962. Also took 4 wickets in 5 balls for MCC v Services XI at Calcutta in 1961–62.
- Hit 4 sixes off consecutive balls from J.D. Piachaud for Hampshire v Oxford U at Oxford in 1960.

Describing 'Butch' White's approach to bowling on one occasion, Trevor Bailey said: 'He's got a heart as big as a lettuce!' Few who saw David White would argue with that assessment. Provided his captain did not rub him up the wrong way there was never a greater hearted trier even in the most unhelpful conditions. Off a run that many of the smaller grounds struggled to accommodate, this tall (6ft), massively built and exceptionally strong right-arm fast bowler would charge in like a one-man battering ram and bowl with every ounce of his energy for over after over. In attitude he was a pastoral Fred Trueman but the invective was always punctuated by a very big grin. He swung the ball in sharply and could also break it back off the pitch. His left-handed batting was based around variations on a single theme: right leg down the pitch and an almighty heave towards mid-wicket. If he connected there was generally a lengthy interval before the next ball. His nicknamer chose the wrong cartoon character; it should have been 'Desperate Dan'.

'Butch' White

Ref	Series	V	T	Venue	Result	Batting 1st No	R	HO	Batting 2nd No	R	HO	Ct	Bowling 1st Balls	R	W	Bowling 2nd Balls	R	W
512/374	1961–62	P	1	Lahore[2]	W-5w	10	0	b	–	–	–	–	132	65	3	72	42	0
519/381			3	Karachi	D	11	0	b	–	–	–	–	16	12	1	–	–	–

Career	M	I	NO	HS	R	Avge	100	50	Ct	St	Balls	R	W	Avge	BB	5w	10w	Rate
Test	2	2	0	0	0	0.00	–	–	–	–	220	119	4	29.75	3-65	–	–	55.00
F/c	337	395	104	58*	3080	10.58	–	5	106	–	58184	26913	1143	23.54	9-44	57	5	50.90

WHITE, John Cornish

Somerset (1909 to 1937)

Wisden 1929
TOURS A 1928–29; SA 1930–31
Born Holford, Somerset 19 Feb 1891
Died Combe Florey, Somerset 2 May 1961

Jack White was a greying 37-year-old, his ruddy complexion fully justifying his nickname of 'Farmer', when he won an Ashes series in Australia. His slow left-arm bowling relied more on subtle variations of pace, flight and angle than on leg-spin. Allied to his quite exceptional control of line and length this was sufficient to tie down such fine players as Woodfull, Kippax and even the young Bradman. He conceded only 760 runs in the series from the colossal output of 406.4 overs and took 25 wickets. A most capable batsman, he scored six first-class hundreds and twice achieved the 'double'. He captained Somerset for five seasons (1927–31), was their president in 1960 and served as a Test selector in 1929–30.

MCC in South Africa, 1930–31: standing *W. Sewell (manager), W.R. Hammond, W. Voce, T.W.J. Goddard, M.J.C. Allom, M.W. Tate, I.A.R. Peebles, T.H. Carlton Levick;* seated *E.H. Hendren, J.C. White (vice captain), A.P.F. Chapman (captain), R.E.S. Wyatt;* in front *A. Sandham, W. Farrimond, M. Leyland, G. Duckworth, M.J.L. Turnbull.*

NOTABLE FEATS

• Exceeded 1000 runs in a season twice and took 100 wickets 14 times, completing the 'double' twice.
• Holds Somerset career records for most wickets (2166), most instances of 100 wickets in a season (14) and most catches by a fielder (381).
• Shared record Somerset 5th-wkt stand of 235 with C.C.C. Case v Gloucestershire at Taunton in 1927.
• Took all 10 for 76 for Somerset v Worcestershire at Worcester in 1921 and took 9 wickets for Somerset on 4 other occasions.
• Returned the record Somerset match analysis of 16 for 83 v Worcestershire at Bath in 1919 – taking all 16 wickets on the same day. Took 15 wickets in Somerset matches on 2 other occasions.
• Hat-trick for Somerset v Middlesex at Lord's in 1923.
• Bowled in an unchanged partnership with E. Robson throughout both completed Derbyshire innings for Somerset at Derby in 1919.

TEST NOTES

• *174* Deputised for A.P.F. Chapman as captain throughout 2nd inns.

					Batting 1st			Batting 2nd				Bowling 1st			Bowling 2nd		
Ref	Series	V	T	Venue	Result	No	R	HO	No	R	HO	Ct	Balls	R	W	Balls	R	W
142/131	1921	A	3	Leeds	L-219	8	1	b	9	6	*	–	150	70	0	66	37	3
174/160	1928	WI	2	Manchester	W-I & 30	9	21	*	–	–	–	1	78	12	0	87	41	3
176/162	1928–29	A	1	Brisbane[1]	W-675	10	14	lbw	–	–	–	–	–	–	–	39	7	4
177/163			2	Sydney	W-8w	11	29	st	4	2	*	–	228	79	0	180	83	0
178/164			3	Melbourne	W-3w	11	8	*	–	–	–	–	342	64	1	341	107	5
179/165			4	Adelaide	W-12	11	0	c	10	4	*	1	360	130	5	389	126	8
180/166*			5	Melbourne	L-5w	11	9	*	10	4	c	–	453	136	2	108	28	0
181/167*	1929	SA	1	Birmingham	D	10	5	ro	–	–	–	1	192	28	0	78	23	0
182/168*			2	Lord's	D	10	8	b	10	18	*	–	210	61	2	54	11	0
183/169*			3	Leeds	W-5w	9	20	*	–	–	–	1	102	24	0	138	40	3
195/181	1930	A	2	Lord's	L-7w	10	23	*	10	10	ro	–	306	158	3	12	8	0
204/185	1930–31	SA	1	Johannesburg[1]	L-28	7	14	c	7	2	lbw	–	–	–	–	96	53	0
205/186			2	Cape Town	D	7	23	lbw	6	8	lbw	1	276	101	2	–	–	–
206/187			3	Durban[2]	D	–	–	–	–	–	–	–	96	21	3	108	33	3
208/189			5	Durban[2]	D	10	10	c	–	–	–	1	210	63	1	102	37	1

Career	M	I	NO	HS	R	Avge	100	50	Ct	St	Balls	R	W	Avge	BB	5w	10w	Rate
Test	15	22	9	29	239	18.38	–	–	6	–	4801	1581	49	32.26	8-126	3	1	97.97
F/c	472	765	102	192	12202	18.40	6	41	426	–	129288	43759	2356	18.57	10-76	193	58	54.87

WHYSALL
William Wilfrid

Nottinghamshire (1910 to 1930)

Wisden 1925
TOURS A 1924–25; WI 1928–29 (Cahn)
Born Woodborough, Nottinghamshire 31 Oct 1887
Died Nottingham 11 Nov 1930

Just a year after setting the record for the most prolific individual season in Nottinghamshire's history, 'Dodger' Whysall met with one of the more bizarre fates – even judged by the high standards set by England Test cricketers. He fell on a dance floor, grazed his elbow and septicaemia set in. Although he made little headway as a batsman wicket-keeper until after the Great War, from 1919 he blossomed into one of the most consistent opening batsmen in county cricket. Playing well within his limitations, he harnessed boundless patience to a rocklike defence. When set he had an array of strokes to challenge the best and his off-driving and pulling were superb. His pairing with George Gunn produced 40 three-figure opening partnerships in nine seasons. Although he was a very competent wicket-keeper – and a purveyor of right-arm medium-pace – and toured Australia as deputy to Strudwick, he was selected for his four Test matches as a specialist batsman. [*Illus. p.* 161]

NOTABLE FEATS

- Exceeded 1000 runs in a season 10 times, including 2000 on 5 occasions, notably 2716 in 1929.
- Scored 3 double centuries, all for Nottinghamshire, notably 248 v Northants at Nottingham in 1930.
- Holds Nottinghamshire records for most runs (2620 in 1929), most hundreds (9 in 1928 – since equalled) and most catches by a fielder (44 in 1929) in a season.
- Scored 100 in each inns for Nottinghamshire twice and, in 1930, scored hundreds in 4 consecutive inns.
- Carried his bat through a completed Nottinghamshire inns twice.

						Batting 1st			Batting 2nd				Bowling 1st			Bowling 2nd		
Ref	Series	V	T	Venue	Result	No	R	HO	No	R	HO	Ct	Balls	R	W	Balls	R	W
160/146	1924–25	A	3	Adelaide	L-11	1	9	b	5	75	c	2	16	9	0	–	–	–
161/147			4	Melbourne	W-I & 29	7	76	st	–	–	–	1	–	–	–	–	–	–
162/148			5	Sydney	L-307	7	8	lbw	7	18	st	4	–	–	–	–	–	–
198/184	1930	A	5	Oval	L-I & 39	3	13	lbw	3	10	c	–	–	–	–	–	–	–

Career	M	I	NO	HS	R	Avge	100	50	Ct	St	Balls	R	W	Avge	BB	5w	10w	Rate
Test	4	7	0	76	209	29.85	–	2	7	–	16	9	0	–	–	–	–	–
F/c	371	601	44	248	21592	38.76	51	103	316	16	201	200	6	33.33	3-49	–	–	33.50

WILKINSON
Leonard Litton

Lancashire (1937 to 1947)

TOUR SA 1938–39
Born Northwich, Cheshire 5 Nov 1916

After a marvellous first complete season, Len Wilkinson headed the first-class averages for MCC's 1938–39 tour of South Africa with 44 wickets at 18.86. But then the bubble burst. He enjoyed scant success in 1939 and played little first-class cricket after the War. He was a right-arm leg-break bowler with a frenetic action and a reliable close fielder; his batting would not come under the category of 'threatening'.

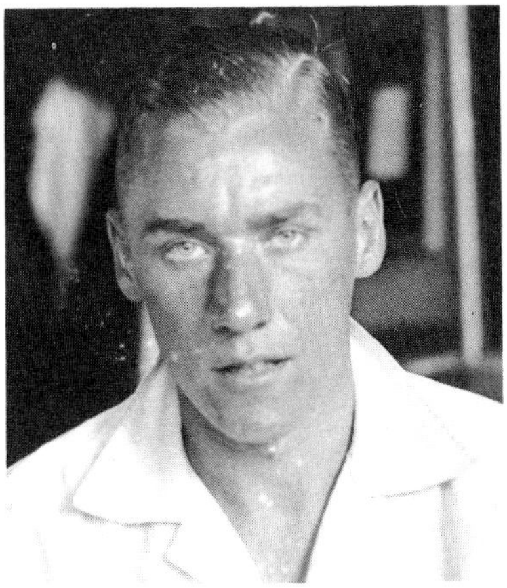

Len Wilkinson

NOTABLE FEATS

- Took 151 wickets (avge 23.38) in his first full season of county cricket (1938).
- Hat-trick for Lancashire v Sussex at Hove in 1938.

						Batting 1st			Batting 2nd				Bowling 1st			Bowling 2nd		
Ref	Series	V	T	Venue	Result	No	R	HO	No	R	HO	Ct	Balls	R	W	Balls	R	W
267/236	1938–39	SA	1	Johannesburg[1]	D	9	2	lbw	–	–	–	–	176	93	2	64	18	0
269/238			3	Durban[2]	W-I & 13	–	–	–	–	–	–	–	53	12	2	208	103	2
270/239			4	Johannesburg[1]	D	11	1	*	–	–	–	–	72	45	1	–	–	–

Career	M	I	NO	HS	R	Avge	100	50	Ct	St	Balls	R	W	Avge	BB	5w	10w	Rate
Test	3	2	1	2	3	3.00	–	–	–	–	573	271	7	38.71	2-12	–	–	81.85
F/c	77	69	27	48	321	7.64	–	–	53	–	14456	7121	282	25.25	8-53	17	3	51.26

WILLEY, Peter

Northamptonshire (1966 to 1983)
Eastern Province
(1982–83 to 1984–85)
Leicestershire (1984 to date)

TOURS
A 1979–80; SA 1972–73 (Robins), 1981–82 (SAB); WI 1980–81, 1985–86; I 1979–80; SL 1977–78 (Robins)
Born Sedgefield, Co. Durham
6 Dec 1949

Peter Willey is a tall (6ft 1in), strong, fearless Geordie whom England's selectors tend to call up for wartime exercises against the Caribbean pace battery but ignore for the more pacific opponents. He takes himself and his cricket very seriously but does indulge in the occasional laconic witticism. With the retirement of Fletcher and Gifford after the 1988 season, 'Wills' is the longest-serving county cricketer. He made his debut in 1966 as a 16-year-old and scored 78 in his first match. In those days he was a seam bowler but serious knee problems persuaded him to convert to slow off-spin and, at county level on turning pitches, he has been as effective as most. His innate toughness and natural gift of timing equip him ideally for dealing with the fastest bowling and he is immensely strong off his back foot. He is also the easiest batsman in the world to recognise from a vast distance because his stance is so extraordinarily square-on that he looks as if he is facing a bowler about to deliver from square-leg. It is a method he has carefully worked out as being the one best suited to his technique and, miraculously, he does have time to move into the right position to play his off-side strokes. He has recovered from both his contentious parting with Northamptonshire and an unhappy season as Leicestershire's captain (1987). Perhaps the most surprising aspect of the selections for the 1988 West Indies series was that he did not feature in a game of roulette involving 23 of his colleagues.

NOTABLE FEATS
- 1000 runs in 22nd Test (*1038*) (42 inns).
- *883* Shared match-saving 10th-wkt stand of 117* in 171 min with R.G.D. Willis – only England's third 10th-wkt century stand in 560 Tests.
- *898* Scored first Test hundred at Test cricket's 52nd ground.
- Exceeded 1000 runs in a season 8 times, notably 1783 in 1982.
- Shared record Northamptonshire 4th-wkt stand of 370 with R.T. Virgin v Somerset at Northampton in 1976.
- Shared record Leicestershire 4th-wkt stand of 290* with T.J. Boon v Warwickshire at Leicester in1984.
- Scored 227 for Northamptonshire v Somerset at Northampton in 1976.
- Scored 141* in his first match for Leicestershire (v Cambridge U at Fenner's in 1984).

Peter Willey

						Batting 1st			Batting 2nd				Bowling 1st			Bowling 2nd		
Ref	Series	V	T	Venue	Result	No	R	HO	No	R	HO	Ct	Balls	R	W	Balls	R	W
780/518	1976	WI	4	Leeds	L-55	5	36	lbw	5	45	c	–	6	4	0	–	–	–
781/519			5	Oval	L-231	5	33	c	5	1	c	–	18	11	0	–	–	–
854/552	1979	I	4	Oval	D	5	52	c	5	31	c	–	24	10	0	263	96	2
868/553	1979–80	A	1	Perth	L-138	3	9	c	3	12	lbw	1	–	–	–	6	1	0
870/554			2	Sydney	L-6w	4	8	c	3	3	b	–	6	2	0	24	17	0
872/555			3	Melbourne	L-8w	5	1	lbw	5	2	c	1	78	36	0	–	–	–
880/557	1980	WI	1	Nottingham	L-2w	7	13	b	7	38	b	–	30	4	0	12	12	0
881/558			2	Lord's	D	8	4	b	–	–	–	–	150	73	2	–	–	–
882/559			3	Manchester	D	7	0	b	7	62	*	–	–	–	–	–	–	–
883/560			4	Oval	D	6	34	c	8	100	*	1	66	22	0	–	–	–
884/561			5	Leeds	D	7	1	c	7	10	c	–	–	–	–	–	–	–
885/562	1980	A		Lord's	D	7	5	lbw	–	–	–	–	6	7	0	–	–	–

Ref	Series	V	T	Venue	Result	Batting 1st No	R	HO	Batting 2nd No	R	HO	Ct	Bowling 1st Balls	R	W	Bowling 2nd Balls	R	W
896/563	1980–81	WI	1	Port-of-Spain	L-I & 79	7	13	lbw	7	21	c	–	18	4	0	–	–	–
897/564			3	Bridgetown	L-298	7	19	*	7	17	lbw	–	–	–	–	36	23	0
898/565			4	St John's	D	7	102	*	5	1	*	–	120	30	0	–	–	–
899/566			5	Kingston	D	5	4	c	5	67	c	–	108	54	1	–	–	–
903/567	1981	A	1	Nottingham	L-4w	6	10	c	6	13	lbw	–	–	–	–	–	–	–
904/568			2	Lord's	D	6	82	c	7	12	c	–	–	–	–	–	–	–
905/569			3	Leeds	W-18	6	8	b	6	33	c	–	78	31	1	18	4	0
906/570			4	Birmingham	W-29	6	16	b	6	5	b	–	–	–	–	–	–	–
1017/612	1985	A	1	Leeds	W-5w	7	36	c	7	3	*	–	–	–	–	–	–	–
1038/618	1985–86	WI	1	Kingston	L-10w	7	0	c	4	71	b	–	24	15	1	–	–	–
1039/619			2	Port-of-Spain	L-7w	4	5	c	4	26	b	–	–	–	–	–	–	–
1040/620			3	Bridgetown	L-I & 30	4	5	c	4	17	lbw	–	–	–	–	–	–	–
1041/621			4	Port-of-Spain	L-10w	7	10	c	7	2	lbw	–	–	–	–	–	–	–
1049/626	1986	NZ	1	Lord's	D	6	44	lbw	6	42	b	–	–	–	–	–	–	–

Career	M	I	NO	HS	R	Avge	100	50	Ct	St	Balls	R	W	Avge	BB	5w	10w	Rate
Test	26	50	6	102*	1184	26.90	2	5	3	–	1091	456	7	65.14	2-73	–	–	155.85
F/c	502	823	108	227	21981	30.74	42	88	208	–	52570	20883	691	30.22	7-37	25	3	76.07

P. WILLEY – TEST BATTING SUMMARY

Series	V	M	I	NO	HS	R	Avge	100	50
1976	WI	2	4	–	45	115	28.75	–	–
1979	I	1	2	–	52	83	41.50	–	1
1979–80	A	3	6	–	12	35	5.83	–	–
1980	WI	5	9	2	100*	262	37.42	1	1
1980	A	1	1	–	5	5	5.00	–	–
1980–81	WI	4	8	3	102*	244	48.80	1	1
1981	A	4	8	–	82	179	22.37	–	1
1985	A	1	2	1	36	39	39.00	–	–
1985–86	WI	4	8	–	71	136	19.42	–	1
1986	NZ	1	2	–	44	86	43.00	–	–

Series	V	M	I	NO	HS	R	Avge	100	50
	A	9	17	1	82	258	16.12	–	1
	WI	15	29	5	102*	757	31.54	2	3
	NZ	1	2	–	44	86	43.00	–	–
	I	1	2	–	52	83	41.50	–	1
Home		15	28	3	100*	769	30.76	1	3
Overseas		11	22	3	102*	415	21.84	1	2
Totals		26	50	6	102*	1184	26.90	2	5

WILLIS
Robert George Dylan
MBE

Surrey (1969 to 1971)
Warwickshire (1972 to 1984)
Northern Transvaal (1972–73)

Wisden 1978
TOURS
A 1970–71, 1974–75, 1976–77, 1978–79, 1979–80, 1982–83; SA 1972–73 (Robins); WI 1973–74; NZ 1970–71, 1977–78, 1983–84; I 1976–77, 1979–80, 1981–82; P 1977–78, 1983–84; SL 1976–77, 1981–82
Born Sunderland, Co. Durham
30 May 1949

Bob Willis was an extremely tall (6ft 6in) and gangling, rather open-chested fast bowler. After an erratic start in county and Test cricket he developed into England's leading wicket-taker of all time and appeared in more Test matches than any other fast bowler (90). That statistic is astonishing considering that, for most of his career, he was able to keep going only at the expense of numerous bouts of surgery to his knees. Few expected him to continue playing after breaking down on the 1980–81 Caribbean tour before he had even played in a first-class match. But, within a few weeks, he was charging in from the Kirkstall End at Headingley to bowl England to a remarkable 18-run victory and return his best analysis in Test cricket – and that after England had followed on and were given bookmakers' odds of 500–1 against a win. What is more, he captained England in 18 Tests (7 wins, 5 defeats) after Brearley had retired (the second time) and Botham had been found unsuitable. Perhaps the selectors recalled his first match as captain of an England XI. On that memorable occasion at Pukekura Park, New Plymouth, in 1977–78, he had taken the last Central Districts wicket with the final ball of the match and with the scores level to record only the second tie in the history of New Zealand's first-class cricket. He was a better captain than many observers thought. If the action was sometimes run

TEST NOTES

• *819* Deputised for G. Boycott as captain on the last two days.

by committee when he was in one of his bowling trances, it seemed to work and he was an exceptionally fine motivator. However, like John Snow, he had great difficulty in arousing much interest in county matches. Although he captained Warwickshire for five seasons (1980–84), it was not the most inspired arrangement for either party. His batting consisted of great determination, variable patience and one stroke, which, depending on its momentum and timing, would either stun the ball like a spinning top or dispatch it vast distances anywhere. Prior to his disintegrating knees he had been an outstanding fielder at slip and a useful soccer goalkeeper for Guildford City. He added the forename 'Dylan' as a teenager in deference to folk singer Bob Dylan but was better known as 'Goose' because of his unique run-up with arms flapping like wings.

NOTABLE FEATS

• 50 wickets in 17th Test (*780*); 100 wickets in 28th Test (*807*); 150 wickets in 41st Test (*830*); 200 wickets in 58th Test (*903*); 250 wickets in 70th Test (*928*); 300 wickets in 81st Test (*958*).
• *883* Shared match-saving 10th-wkt stand of 117* in 171 min with P. Willey – only England's third 10th-wkt century stand in 560 Tests.
• *905* His 8 for 43 is the best analysis in Tests at Headingley.
• *907* 100 wickets v Australia during 3 wickets in his third over (W.4W.W).
• *908* Set new E v A record when he passed 109 wickets by W. Rhodes.
• *928* Shared record E v I 10th-wkt stand of 70 with P.J.W. Allott.
• *931* Shared record E v P 10th-wkt stand of 79 with R.W. Taylor.
• *975* Became E's leading wicket-taker when he exceeded 307 by F.S. Trueman.
• *991* Extended world Test record for most 'not out' innings to 55 and record number of wickets (then) by an England bowler to 325.
• Two hat-tricks for Warwickshire at Birmingham: v Derbyshire in 1972 and v West Indians in 1976.

						Batting 1st			Batting 2nd				Bowling 1st			Bowling 2nd		
Ref	Series	V	T	Venue	Result	No	R	HO	No	R	HO	Ct	Balls	R	W	Balls	R	W
676/461	1970–71	A	4	Sydney	W-299	11	15	*	–	–	–	1	72	26	0	24	1	1
677/462			5	Melbourne	D	11	5	*	–	–	–	–	160	73	3	80	42	1
678/463			6	Adelaide	D	11	4	c	–	–	–	1	96	49	2	104	48	1
679/464			7	Sydney	W-62	11	11	b	11	2	*	1	96	58	3	72	32	1
686/466	1970–71	NZ	2	Auckland	D	10	7	c	10	3	lbw	–	112	54	2	48	15	0
727/491	1973	WI	3	Lord's	L-I & 226	10	5	*	10	0	c	2	210	118	4	–	–	–
731/492	1973–74	WI	1	Port-of-Spain	L-7w	11	6	b	11	0	*	–	114	52	1	24	6	0
732/493			2	Kingston	D	11	6	*	11	3	*	2	144	97	3	–	–	–
733/494			3	Bridgetown	D	11	10	*	–	–	–	1	156	100	1	–	–	–
739/497	1974	I	1	Manchester	W-113	10	24	lbw	–	–	–	1	144	64	4	72	33	1
744/502	1974	P	3	Oval	D	11	1	*	–	–	–	–	168	102	2	42	27	0
750/503	1974–75	A	1	Brisbane[2]	L-166	10	13	*	10	3	*	–	173	56	4	120	45	3
751/504			2	Perth	L-9w	11	4	*	11	0	*	–	176	91	2	16	8	0
752/505			3	Melbourne	D	10	13	c	10	15	b	–	175	61	5	112	56	1
753/506			4	Sydney	L-171	10	2	b	10	12	b	–	144	80	0	88	52	1
754/507			5	Adelaide	L-163	11	11	*	11	3	b	1	80	46	1	40	27	0
780/518	1976	WI	4	Leeds	L-55	11	0	*	11	0	lbw	1	120	71	3	93	42	5
781/519			5	Oval	L-231	11	5	*	11	0	lbw	–	90	73	1	42	48	0
788/520	1976–77	I	1	Delhi	W-I & 25	10	1	c	–	–	–	2	42	21	0	54	24	1
789/521			2	Calcutta	W-10w	11	0	*	–	–	–	–	120	27	5	78	32	2
790/522			3	Madras[1]	W-200	11	7	ro	11	4	*	–	114	46	1	78	18	3
791/523			4	Bangalore	L-140	11	7	lbw	11	0	st	–	102	53	6	108	47	2
792/524			5	Bombay[3]	D	11	0	c	–	–	–	1	78	52	0	36	15	0
803/525	1976–77	A		Melbourne	L-45	11	1	*	11	5	*	1	64	33	2	176	91	0
804/526	1977	A	1	Lord's	D	11	17	b	11	0	c	1	181	78	7	60	40	2
805/527			2	Manchester	W-9w	11	1	*	–	–	–	–	126	45	2	96	56	2
806/528			3	Nottingham	W-7w	11	2	*	–	–	–	–	90	58	1	156	88	5
807/529			4	Leeds	W-I & 85	11	5	*	–	–	–	–	30	35	0	84	32	3
808/530			5	Oval	D	11	24	*	–	–	–	1	177	102	5	–	–	–
814/531	1977–78	P	1	Lahore[2]	D	11	14	c	–	–	–	–	136	67	0	56	34	2
815/532			2	Hyderabad	D	11	8	*	–	–	–	–	128	40	2	88	26	2
816/533			3	Karachi	D	11	5	lbw	–	–	–	1	64	23	1	–	–	–

Ref	Series	V	T	Venue	Result	Batting 1st No	R	HO	Batting 2nd No	R	HO	Ct	Bowling 1st Balls	R	W	Bowling 2nd Balls	R	W
817/534	1977–78	NZ	1	Wellington	L-72	11	6	*	11	3	c	–	200	65	2	120	32	5
818/535			2	Christchurch	W-174	11	6	*	–	–	–	–	160	45	1	56	14	4
819/536			3	Auckland	D	11	0	*	–	–	–	–	214	57	2	80	42	0
825/537	1978	P	1	Birmingham	W-I & 57	–	–	–	–	–	–	–	96	42	2	142	70	2
826/538			2	Lord's	W-I & 120	11	18	b	–	–	–	1	78	47	5	60	26	2
827/539			3	Leeds	D	–	–	–	–	–	–	–	156	48	2	–	–	–
828/540	1978	NZ	1	Oval	W-7w	11	3	*	–	–	–	–	122	42	5	78	39	1
829/541			2	Nottingham	W-I & 119	11	1	*	–	–	–	–	72	22	1	54	31	0
830/542			3	Lord's	W-7w	11	7	*	–	–	–	–	174	79	1	96	16	4
834/543	1978–79	A	1	Brisbane[2]	W-7w	11	8	c	–	–	–	1	112	44	4	222	69	3
835/544			2	Perth	W-166	10	2	c	10	3	*	–	149	44	5	96	36	1
836/545			3	Melbourne	L-103	10	19	c	10	3	c	–	104	47	0	56	21	0
837/546			4	Sydney	W-93	10	7	*	10	0	c	–	72	33	2	16	8	0
838/547			5	Adelaide	W-205	10	24	c	10	12	c	1	88	55	1	96	41	3
839/548			6	Sydney	W-9w	10	10	b	–	–	–	1	88	48	1	24	15	0
851/549	1979	I	1	Birmingham	W-I & 83	–	–	–	–	–	–	–	144	69	3	84	45	1
853/551			3	Leeds	D	10	4	*	–	–	–	–	108	42	2	–	–	–
854/552			4	Oval	D	10	10	*	–	–	–	–	108	53	3	168	89	1
868/553	1979–80	A	1	Perth	L-138	11	11	b	11	0	c	–	138	47	0	156	52	1
870/554			2	Sydney	L-6w	10	3	c	11	1	c	–	66	30	1	72	26	1
872/555			3	Melbourne	L-8w	11	4	c	11	2	c	–	126	61	0	30	8	0
880/557	1980	WI	1	Nottingham	L-2w	10	8	b	10	9	b	–	121	82	4	156	65	5
881/558			2	Lord's	D	10	14	b	–	–	–	–	186	103	3	–	–	–
882/559			3	Manchester	D	11	5	*	–	–	–	–	84	99	1	–	–	–
883/560			4	Oval	D	11	1	*	11	24	*	–	114	58	1	–	–	–
903/567	1981	A	1	Nottingham	L-4w	10	0	c	10	1	c	–	180	47	3	78	28	1
904/568			2	Lord's	D	11	5	c	–	–	–	1	166	50	3	72	35	1
905/569			3	Leeds	W-18	11	1	*	11	2	c	–	180	72	0	91	43	8
906/570			4	Birmingham	W-29	11	13	c	11	2	c	1	114	63	0	120	37	2
907/571			5	Manchester	W-103	11	11	c	11	5	*	–	84	63	4	185	96	3
908/572			6	Oval	D	10	3	b	–	–	–	–	186	91	4	60	41	0
912/573	1981–82	I	1	Bombay[3]	L-138	11	1	c	11	13	c	–	72	33	1	78	31	1
914/575			3	Delhi	D	–	–	–	–	–	–	–	156	99	2	–	–	–
915/576			4	Calcutta	D	11	11	*	–	–	–	–	84	28	2	36	21	0
916/577			5	Madras[1]	D	11	1	*	–	–	–	–	169	79	2	42	15	1
917/578			6	Kanpur	D	–	–	–	–	–	–	–	138	75	3	–	–	–
921/579	1981–82	SL		Colombo SO	W-7w	11	0	ro	–	–	–	2	114	46	2	54	24	1
928/580*	1982	I	1	Lord's	W-7w	11	28	b	–	–	–	–	96	41	3	168	101	6
929/581*			2	Manchester	D	11	6	c	–	–	–	–	102	94	2	–	–	–
930/582*			3	Oval	D	11	1	*	–	–	–	–	138	78	3	24	16	1
931/583*	1982	P	1	Birmingham	W-113	11	0	*	11	28	*	2	90	42	2	84	49	2
933/585*			3	Leeds	W-3w	11	1	*	–	–	–	1	156	76	3	114	55	3
938/586*	1982–83	A	1	Perth	D	10	26	c	10	0	b	2	191	95	3	36	23	2
939/587*			2	Brisbane[2]	L-7w	10	1	c	10	10	*	–	178	66	5	24	24	0
940/588*			3	Adelaide	L-8w	11	1	b	11	10	c	–	150	76	2	48	17	1
941/589*			4	Melbourne	W-3	10	6	*	10	8	*	1	90	38	3	102	57	0
942/590*			5	Sydney	D	10	1	c	–	–	–	1	120	57	1	60	33	1
957/591*	1983	NZ	1	Oval	W-189	10	4	c	–	–	–	2	120	43	4	72	26	2
958/592*			2	Leeds	L-5w	10	9	c	10	4	c	1	141	57	4	84	35	5
959/593*			3	Lord's	W-127	10	7	c	10	2	*	1	78	28	1	72	24	3
960/594*			4	Nottingham	W-165	10	25	*	10	16	b	–	60	23	0	114	37	1
975/595*	1983–84	NZ	1	Wellington	D	11	5	*	–	–	–	–	114	37	3	222	102	2
976/596*			2	Christchurch	L-I & 132	10	6	b	10	0	c	–	133	51	4	–	–	–
977/597*			3	Auckland	D	10	3	c	–	–	–	–	204	109	3	18	7	0
978/598*	1983–84	P	1	Karachi	L-3w	10	6	c	10	2	c	1	102	33	2	12	13	0
989/601	1984	WI	1	Birmingham	L-I & 180	11	10	*	10	22	c	1	150	108	2	–	–	–
990/602			2	Lord's	L-9w	11	2	b	–	–	–	–	114	48	2	90	48	0
991/603			3	Leeds	L-8w	11	4	*	11	5	*	–	108	123	2	48	40	0

Career	M	I	NO	HS	R	Avge	100	50	Ct	St	Balls	R	W	Avge	BB	5w	10w	Rate
Test	90	128	55	28*	840	11.50	–	–	39	–	17357	8190	325	25.20	8-43	16	–	53.40
F/c	308	333	145	72	2690	14.30	–	2	134	–	48056	22468	899	24.99	8-32	34	2	53.45

Bob Willis

R. G. D. WILLIS – TEST BOWLING SUMMARY

Series	V	M	Balls	R	W	Avge	BB	5w	10w	Rate
1970–71	A	4	704	329	12	27.41	3-58	–	–	58.66
1970–71	NZ	1	160	69	2	34.50	2-54	–	–	80.00
1973	WI	1	210	118	4	29.50	4-118	–	–	52.50
1973–74	WI	3	438	255	5	51.00	3-97	–	–	106.40
1974	I	1	216	97	5	19.40	4-64	–	–	43.20
1974	P	1	210	129	2	64.50	2-102	–	–	105.00
1974–75	A	5	1124	522	17	30.70	5-61	1	–	66.11
1976	WI	2	345	234	9	26.00	5-42	1	–	38.33
1976–77	I	5	810	335	20	16.75	6-53	2	–	40.70
1976–77	A	1	240	124	2	62.00	2-33	–	–	120.00
1977	A	5	1000	534	27	19.77	7-78	3	–	37.03
1977–78	P	3	472	190	7	27.14	2-26	–	–	67.42
1977–78	NZ	3	830	255	14	18.21	5-32	1	–	59.28
1978	P	3	532	233	13	17.92	5-47	1	–	40.92
1978	NZ	3	596	229	12	19.08	5-42	1	–	49.66
1978–79	A	6	1123	461	20	23.05	5-44	1	–	56.15
1979	I	3	612	298	10	29.80	3-53	–	–	61.20
1979–80	A	3	588	224	3	74.66	1-26	–	–	196.00
1980	WI	4	661	407	14	29.07	5-65	1	–	47.21
1981	A	6	1516	666	29	22.96	8-43	1	–	52.27
1981–82	I	5	775	381	12	31.75	3-75	–	–	64.58
1981–82	SL	1	168	70	3	23.33	2-46	–	–	56.00
1982	I	3	528	330	15	22.00	6-101	1	–	35.20
1982	P	2	444	222	10	22.20	3-55	–	–	44.40
1982–83	A	5	999	486	18	27.00	5-66	1	–	55.50
1983	NZ	4	741	273	20	13.65	5-35	1	–	37.05
1983–84	NZ	3	691	306	12	25.50	4-51	–	–	57.58
1983–84	P	1	114	46	2	23.00	2-33	–	–	57.00
1984	WI	3	510	367	6	61.16	2-48	–	–	85.00
	A	35	7294	3346	128	26.14	8-43	7	–	56.98
	WI	13	2164	1381	38	36.34	5-42	2	–	56.94
	NZ	14	3018	1132	60	18.86	5-32	3	–	50.30
	I	17	2941	1441	62	23.24	6-53	3	–	47.43
	P	10	1772	820	34	24.11	5-47	1	–	52.11
	SL	1	168	70	3	23.33	2-46	–	–	56.00
Home		41	8121	4137	176	23.50	8-43	10	–	46.14
Overseas		49	9236	4053	149	27.20	6-53	6	–	61.98
Totals		90	17357	8190	325	25.20	8-43	16	–	53.40

WILSON
Rev. Clement Eustace Macro

Cambridge University (1895 to 1898)
Yorkshire (1896 to 1899)

TOUR SA 1898–99
Born Bolsterstone, Yorkshire 15 May 1875
Ordained 1899
Died Calverhall, Shropshire 8 Feb 1944

By the time he was 18, Clem Wilson had developed into an extremely fine all-round cricketer and, on his performances for Uppingham, was rated very highly indeed. This seemed reasonable as he had just scored three successive hundreds and headed both batting and bowling averages. At Cambridge he managed to live up to these great expectations, gained a blue in each of his four years and made 118 in his last Varsity match. Three years later his brother Rockley scored a hundred to complete the only instance of brothers scoring centuries in that fixture. He had a strong defence but could attack when he wanted to. It was his bowling which made him memorable. Normally a right-arm fast-medium bowler, he could also bowl accurate left-arm spin and would sometimes change from one method to the other in the course of an innings. Against Surrey on one occasion, he ended a third-wicket partnership of 306 with a return catch from his left-arm slows. He retired from first-class cricket after his ordination in 1899. [*Illus. p.* 196]

Ref	Series	V	T	Venue	Result	Batting 1st No	R	HO	Batting 2nd No	R	HO	Ct
58/58	1898–99	SA	1	Johannesburg[1]	W-32	4	8	b	4	18	b	–
59/59			2	Cape Town	W-210	4	10	*	4	6	b	–

Career	M	I	NO	HS	R	Avge	100	50	Ct	St	Balls	R	W	Avge	BB	5w	10w	Rate
Test	2	4	1	18	42	14.00	–	–	–	–	–	–	–	–	–	–	–	–
F/c	51	78	10	115	1632	24.00	1	10	33	–	5719	2283	121	18.86	7-24	6	2	47.26

WILSON, Donald

Yorkshire (1957 to 1974)

TOURS
A 1970–71; NZ 1960–61, 1970–71; I 1963–64; SL 1969–70
Born Settle, Yorkshire 7 Aug 1937

Don Wilson was an extremely talented orthodox left-arm leg-break bowler who never fully realised his enormous potential. Tall (6ft 3in) with a model action, he varied his flight and pace cleverly and turned the ball enough. His height enabled him to extract more bounce than most of his type and, on his day, he was a very confident match-winner. He rather lost form once Close had left Yorkshire and reacted badly to the political in-fighting during Boycott's regime. His opportunities at international level were greatly diminished by Derek Underwood's presence. He was a flamboyant and hard-hitting left-handed batsman who could defend doggedly when the need arose. A supreme competitor, his large eyes and most expressive face left the unfortunate batsmen in no doubt about his opinions of their efforts to combat his wiles. He eventually lost all confidence at Yorkshire and spent three seasons with Lincolnshire (1975–77) before taking up residence at the Nursery End of Lord's as the MCC's head coach. Already highly regarded for his coaching of coloured boys in the Cape, he has created a marvellous atmosphere in the indoor school and beyond. One cannot imagine anyone being happier in that role or doing the job more efficiently or with greater enthusiasm.

NOTABLE FEATS

- Took 100 wickets in a season 5 times.
- Scored 30 runs (466266) off one over from R.N.S. Hobbs for Yorkshire v MCC at Scarborough in 1966.
- Three hat-tricks for Yorkshire: v Nottinghamshire (2) at Middlesbrough in 1959 and at Worksop in 1966, and v Kent at Harrogate in 1966.
- Held 5 catches in an innings for Yorkshire v Surrey at The Oval in 1969.

Don Wilson

Ref	Series	V	T	Venue	Result	Batting 1st No	R	HO	Batting 2nd No	R	HO	Ct	Bowling 1st Balls	R	W	Bowling 2nd Balls	R	W
553/395	1963	WI	1	Manchester	L-10w	4	42	c	–	–	–	–	144	67	1	24	2	1
554/396			2	Lord's	D	6	1	c	3	2	c	1	90	28	1	138	41	0
555/397			3	Birmingham	W-217	7	1	st	–	–	–	–	96	17	2	126	55	1
556/398			4	Leeds	L-221	4	6	c	–	–	–	–	132	41	1	246	74	2
557/399			5	Oval	L-8w	10	18	*	–	–	–	–	162	47	0	114	26	0
685/465	1970–71	NZ	1	Christchurch	W-8w	8	5	c	–	–	–	–	32	12	1	168	56	1

Career	M	I	NO	HS	R	Avge	100	50	Ct	St	Balls	R	W	Avge	BB	5w	10w	Rate
Test	6	7	1	42	75	12.50	–	–	1	–	1472	466	11	42.36	2-17	–	–	133.81
F/c	422	533	91	112	6230	14.09	1	10	250	–	69724	24977	1189	21.00	8-36	50	8	58.64

WILSON
Evelyn Rockley

Cambridge University (1899 to 1902)
Yorkshire (1899 to 1923)

TOUR WI 1901–02
Born Bolsterstone, Yorkshire 25 Mar 1879
Died Winchester, Hampshire 21 Jul 1957

The younger brother of Clem, Rockley Wilson was an outstanding right-arm slow bowler who could spin the ball either way and bat more than capably. In his final year at Rugby he had combined successful captaincy with an all-round performance which put him at the top of the batting and bowling lists. He scored a century against his university on his first-class debut and subsequently emulated his brother by scoring a hundred in the Varsity match and captaining Cambridge. After a few appearances for his native county during vacations, he embarked on duties as a master at Winchester College which were to span 40 years. Thereafter, his county cricket was mainly confined to the August holidays – he did not play for Yorkshire between 1903 and 1913. Several generations of Wykehamist cricketers had cause to be grateful for his sage advice. [*Illus. p.* 383]

NOTABLE FEATS

- Scored 117* on first-class debut – for A.J. Webbe's XI v Cambridge U at Cambridge in 1899.
- Hat-trick for Gentlemen v Players at Scarborough in 1919.

					Batting 1st			Batting 2nd				Bowling 1st			Bowling 2nd		
Ref	Series	V	T Venue	Result	No	R	HO	No	R	HO	Ct	Balls	R	W	Balls	R	W
139/128	1920–21	A	5 Sydney	L-9w	9	5	c	4	5	st	–	87	28	2	36	8	1

Career	M	I	NO	HS	R	Avge	100	50	Ct	St	Balls	R	W	Avge	BB	5w	10w	Rate
Test	1	2	0	5	10	5.00	–	–	–	–	123	36	3	12.00	2-28	–	–	41.00
F/c	136	190	28	142	3565	22.00	4	15	106	–	23840	8234	467	17.63	7-16	26	5	51.04

WOOD, Arthur

Yorkshire (1927 to 1946)

Wisden 1939
TOUR WI 1935–36 (Yorks)
Born Fagley, Bradford, Yorkshire
25 Aug 1898
Died Middleton, Ilkley, Yorkshire
1 Apr 1973

Arthur Wood was Yorkshire's wicket-keeper from 1927 until the Second World War and combined great expertise in that department with some high quality batting. He made his first appearance in Test cricket a few days before his 40th birthday when, on the editor of *Wisden*'s advice (as sought by Sir Pelham Warner, the chairman of selectors), he was selected as a last-minute replacement for Ames. He was so amazed at being chosen that he celebrated by travelling from Yorkshire to London by taxi. Going in to bat with England's score showing a fairly healthy position (770 for 6), he made a spirited 53. As he entered the England dressing room he remarked: 'I was always good in a crisis.'

NOTABLE FEATS

- Scored 1249 runs in 1935.

The Yorkshire side of 1936: standing *(players only) L. Hutton, H. Verity, W.E. Bowes, T.F. Smailes, C. Turner, A. Wood;* seated *W. Barber, H. Sutcliffe, A.B. Sellers (captain), M. Leyland, A. Mitchell.*

Ref	Series	V	T	Venue	Result	Batting 1st No	R	HO	Batting 2nd No	R	HO	Fielding 1st Ct	St	Byes	Balls	Fielding 2nd Ct	St	Byes	Balls
266/235†	1938	A	5	Oval	W-I & 579	8	53	c	–	–	–	2	–	4	313	1	–	1	205
272/241†	1939	WI	1	Lord's	W-8w	7	0	*	–	–	–	2	–	3	652	2	–	6	556
273/242†			2	Manchester	D	7	26	c	7	1	b	2	–	0	284	–	–	0	126
274/243†			3	Oval	D	8	0	b	–	–	–	1	1	0	813	–	–	–	–

Career	M	I	NO	HS	R	Avge	100	50	Ct	St	Balls	R	W	Avge	BB	5w	10w	Rate
Test	4	5	1	53	80	20.00	–	1	10	1	–	–	–	–	–	–	–	–
F/c	420	500	83	123*	8842	21.20	1	43	631	257	30	33	1	33.00	1-33	–	–	30.00

WOOD, Barry

Yorkshire (1964)
Lancashire (1966 to 1979)
Derbyshire (1980 to 1983)
Eastern Province
(1971–72 to 1973–74)

TOURS
NZ 1974–75; I/SL 1972–73; P 1972–73; Z 1975–76 (Int W)
Born Ossett, Yorkshire 26 Dec 1942

NOTABLE FEATS

- Exceeded 1000 runs in a season 8 times.
- Shared record Lancashire 5th-wkt stand of 249 with A. Kennedy v Warwickshire at Birmingham in 1975.

Barry Wood was a tough, resourceful opening batsman who relished the challenge imposed by fast bowling despite his lack of inches (5ft 6½in). He was an excellent cutter and hooker but was equally adept at playing defensively. His only obvious weakness was his inability to handle the Indian spinners on their own pitches but a few other batsmen from around the world have found similar difficulties. His technique tended to develop a flaw after jet-lag; in Test *758* he was bowled first ball three days after a 63-hour flight to New Zealand from the Caribbean. His right-arm medium-pace swing bowling was extremely successful in overcast conditions. An arch competitor, he was a superb fielder anywhere but particularly at gully. He captained Derbyshire briefly (1981–82) but was not re-engaged after the following season. A brilliant limited-overs exponent, he reappeared in Cheshire colours to lead their successful giant-killing of Northamptonshire in the 1988 NatWest Trophy.

Barry Wood

Ref	Series	V	T	Venue	Result	Batting 1st No	R	HO	Batting 2nd No	R	HO	Ct	Bowling 1st Balls	R	W	Bowling 2nd Balls	R	W
702/477	1972	A	5	Oval	L-5w	1	26	c	1	90	lbw	–	–	–	–	–	–	–
703/478	1972–73	I	1	Delhi	W-6w	1	19	c	1	45	c	–	–	–	–	12	13	0
704/479			2	Calcutta	L-28	1	11	b	1	1	b	1	–	–	–	–	–	–
705/480			3	Madras[1]	L-4w	1	20	c	1	5	c	2	–	–	–	–	–	–
721/485	1972–73	P	3	Karachi	D	1	3	c	1	5	c	–	–	–	–	–	–	–
758/509	1974–75	NZ	1	Auckland	W-I & 83	2	0	c	–	–	–	1	–	–	–	–	–	–
759/510			2	Christchurch	D	2	33	c	–	–	–	2	32	19	0	–	–	–
761/512	1975	A	2	Lord's	D	1	6	lbw	1	52	c	–	–	–	–	6	6	0
762/513			3	Leeds	D	1	9	lbw	1	25	lbw	–	30	10	0	–	–	–
763/514			4	Oval	D	1	32	b	1	22	lbw	–	–	–	–	–	–	–
778/516	1976	WI	2	Lord's	D	1	6	c	1	30	c	–	–	–	–	–	–	–
825/537	1978	P	1	Birmingham	W-I & 57	2	14	c	–	–	–	–	18	2	0	–	–	–

Career	M	I	NO	HS	R	Avge	100	50	Ct	St	Balls	R	W	Avge	BB	5w	10w	Rate
Test	12	21	0	90	454	21.61	–	2	6	–	98	50	0	–	–	–	–	–
F/c	357	591	75	198	17453	33.82	30	81	283	–	21571	9160	298	30.73	7-52	8	–	72.38

WOOD George Edward Charles

Cambridge University (1913 to 1920)
Kent (1919 to 1927)

Born Blackheath, Kent 22 Aug 1893
Died Christchurch, Hampshire 18 Mar 1971

George Wood was a most exciting wicket-keeper who stood up to the fastest bowlers in all his cricket for Cheltenham, Cambridge (where he was a blue three years either side of the Great War), Kent and England. He was no mean batsman, either opening or in the middle-order, and he could even provide a little right-arm medium-pace change bowling. In 1920 he had captained one of the strongest Cambridge sides in history. He had to decline an invitation to tour Australia in 1920–21 but was included in A.C. MacLaren's team of amateurs which defeated the 1921 Australians. A talented all-round sportsman, he also gained blues for rugby and hockey. *[Illus p. 336]*

						Batting 1st			Batting 2nd			Fielding 1st				Fielding 2nd			
Ref	Series	V	T	Venue	Result	No	R	HO	No	R	HO	Ct	St	Byes	Balls	Ct	St	Byes	Balls
153/139†	1924	SA	1	Birmingham	W-I & 18	10	1	b	–	–	–	–	–	1	75	1	–	4	862
154/140†			2	Lord's	W-I & 18	–	–	–	–	–	–	1	–	3	696	–	–	13	742
155/141†			3	Leeds	W-9w	10	6	ro	–	–	–	2	–	0	309	1	1	14	762

Career	M	I	NO	HS	R	Avge	100	50	Ct	St	Balls	R	W	Avge	BB	5w	10w	Rate
Test	3	2	0	6	7	3.50	–	–	5	1	–	–	–	–	–	–	–	–
F/c	101	157	18	128	2773	19.94	1	10	116	53	18	9	0	–	–	–	–	–

WOOD, Henry

Kent (1876 to 1882)
Surrey (1884 to 1900)

Wisden 1891
TOURS SA 1888–89, 1891–92
Born Dartford, Kent 14 Dec 1853
Died Waddon, Surrey 30 Apr 1919

Harry Wood was Surrey's third outstanding wicket-keeper following Lockyer and Pooley and preceding Strudwick. Selected by the Surrey committee for The Oval Test of 1888 (the home club usually picked England's teams prior to 1899), he justified their faith by keeping brilliantly. Victorian wicket-keeping gauntlets left a lot to be desired and his hands suffered terribly as a result of taking the fast deliveries of Lockwood and Richardson. He had little opportunity as a batsman but was a shrewd hitter with an adequate defence – as he proved in scoring his one and only first-class century in his final Test match. *[Illus. pp. 51, 201]*

NOTABLE FEATS

• *38* Scored the first 100 by a wicket-keeper in Test cricket; it was his only first-class century.

TEST NOTES

• *31* M.P. Bowden deputised as wicket-keeper after lunch on the second day and caught W.H. Milton.
• *38* W.L. Murdoch deputised as wicket-keeper throughout the 2nd inns.

						Batting 1st			Batting 2nd			Fielding 1st				Fielding 2nd			
Ref	Series	V	T	Venue	Result	No	R	HO	No	R	HO	Ct	St	Byes	Balls	Ct	St	Byes	Balls
29/29†	1888	A	2	Oval	W-I & 137	11	8	c	–	–	–	–	–	1	363	1	1	0	278
31/31†	1888–89	SA	1	Port Elizabeth	W-8w	5	3	c	–	–	–	–	–	8	302	–	–	7	361
32/32†			2	Cape Town	W-I & 202	6	59	c	–	–	–	–	–	2	189	–	–	2	114
38/38†	1891–92	SA		Cape Town	W-I & 189	8	134	*	–	–	–	1	–	5	292	–	–	–	–

Career	M	I	NO	HS	R	Avge	100	50	Ct	St	Balls	R	W	Avge	BB	5w	10w	Rate
Test	4	4	1	134*	204	68.00	1	1	2	1	–	–	–	–	–	–	–	–
F/c	316	422	96	134*	5523	16.94	1	17	556	118	65	42	0	–	–	–	–	–

WOOD, Reginald

Lancashire (1880 to 1884)
Victoria (1886–87)

TOUR A 1886–87
Born Woodchurch, Cheshire 7 Mar 1860
Died Manly, Sydney, Australia 6 Jan 1915

Reginald Wood emigrated to Australia from his native Cheshire and happened to be in the right place when the English team required a temporary understudy for Billy Barnes, who had damaged his hand when a punch aimed for the Australian captain, Percy McDonnell, had connected with a wall. Wood was a left-handed batsman and a left-arm medium-pace bowler who learned his cricket at Charterhouse and, prior to emigrating, had appeared in six matches as an amateur for Lancashire over a period of five summers. He had been playing as a professional for Victoria and was co-opted into the visitors' team for three matches including the Second Test. [*Not illustrated*]

						Batting 1st			Batting 2nd			
Ref	**Series**	**V**	**T**	**Venue**	**Result**	**No**	**R**	**HO**	**No**	**R**	**HO**	**Ct**
26/26	1886–87	A	2	Sydney	W-71	10	6	lbw	10	0	hw	–

Career	**M**	**I**	**NO**	**HS**	**R**	**Avge**	**100**	**50**	**Ct**	**St**	**Balls**	**R**	**W**	**Avge**	**BB**	**5w**	**10w**	**Rate**
Test	1	2	0	6	6	3.00	–	–	–	–	–	–	–	–	–	–	–	–
F/c	12	20	5	52	235	15.66	–	2	4	–	348	134	8	16.75	3-19	–	–	43.50

WOODS
Samuel Moses James

Cambridge University (1888 to 1891)
Somerset (1891 to 1910)

Wisden 1889
TOURS
Australia to E 1888; SA 1895–96;
WI 1896–97
Born Ashfield, Sydney, Australia
13 Apr 1867
Died Taunton, Somerset 30 Apr 1931

Sammy Woods was a magnificent all-rounder who learned his cricket in Sydney before coming to England in 1884 and going to Brighton College. He was still in attendance there when he was included in G.N. Wyatt's team and made his first-class debut against the 1886 Australians. A blue in each of his four years at Cambridge, he made his Test debut for the 1888 Australians. He then settled in Taunton and began a playing career with Somerset which was to endure for 20 seasons, the majority as captain (1894–1906). It was during this period that he appeared in three Tests for England in South Africa. He remained in Taunton for the rest of his life and continued as Somerset's secretary until 1923. Tall (6ft) and powerfully built, he weighed over 13 stone and was well suited to his role as an England rugby wing forward who gained 13 caps. He was a friendly, cheerful and very confident cricketer: an extremely forceful middle-order batsman who drove with tremendous power, an accurate right-arm fast bowler with a cleverly disguised slower ball, and a fine fielder.

Sammy Woods

NOTABLE FEATS

- Exceeded 1000 runs in a season 4 times and took 100 wickets twice, notably 153 in 1892.
- Scored 215 for Somerset v Sussex at Hove in 1895, completing his 200 in 135 min (then the world record).
- Shared record Somerset 7th-wkt stand of 240 with V.T. Hill v Kent at Taunton in 1898.
- Scored 100 before lunch on 3 occasions.
- Holds Cambridge U record for best innings (10 for 69) and match (15 for 88) analyses: v C.I. Thornton's XI at Fenner's in 1890.
- Returned a match analysis of 15 for 86 for Lord Hawke's XI v Philadelphians at Philadelphia in 1891–92.
- Hat-trick for Cambridge U v C.I. Thornton's XI at Fenner's in 1888.
- Bowled in an unchanged partnership with F.S. Jackson throughout both completed Players innings for Gentlemen at Lord's in 1894.

						Batting 1st			Batting 2nd				Bowling 1st			Bowling 2nd		
Ref	Series	V	T	Venue	Result	No	R	HO	No	R	HO	Ct	Balls	R	W	Balls	R	W
For Australia																		
28/28	1888	E	1	Lord's	W-61	6	18	c	6	3	c	1	16	6	1	–	–	–
29/29			2	Oval	L-I & 137	7	0	ro	7	7	c	–	128	80	2	–	–	–
30/30			3	Manchester	L-I & 21	7	4	c	7	0	b	–	73	35	2	–	–	–
For England																		
47/47	1895–96	SA	1	Port Elizabeth	W-288	6	7	b	8	53	c	–	–	–	–	–	–	–
48/48			2	Johannesburg[1]	W-I & 197	6	32	c	–	–	–	–	100	74	1	30	27	1
49/49			3	Cape Town	W-I & 33	5	30	b	–	–	–	4	–	–	–	65	28	3

Career	M	I	NO	HS	R	Avge	100	50	Ct	Balls	R	W	Avge	BB	5w	10w	Rate
Test (A)	3	6	0	18	32	5.33	–	–	1	217	121	5	24.20	2-35	–	–	43.40
Test (E)	3	4	0	53	122	30.50	–	1	4	195	129	5	25.80	3-28	–	–	39.00
Combined	6	10	0	53	154	15.40	–	1	5	412	250	10	25.00	3-28	–	–	41.20
F/c	401	690	35	215	15345	23.42	19	62	279	41207	21653	1040	20.82	10-69	77	21	39.62

WOOLLEY
Frank Edward

Kent (1906 to 1938)

Wisden 1911
TOURS
A 1911–12, 1920–21, 1924–25, 1929–30; SA 1909–10, 1913–14, 1922–23; NZ 1929–30
Born Tonbridge, Kent 27 May 1887
Died Halifax, Nova Scotia, Canada 18 Oct 1978

Frank Woolley was one of the greatest and most durable of all-rounders. His career with Kent spanned 32 years and by its end he had amassed a first-class treble that must for ever remain unique: 50,000 runs, 2000 wickets and 1000 catches. Tall and well-built, he was primarily an extremely elegant and fast-scoring left-handed batsman; only Jack Hobbs amassed a larger aggregate in first-class matches. It was not so much the vast quantity of his runs as the manner in which they were made which earned him special regard. Immensely dignified and assured, he swung the bat in a full, classical arc, timing the ball effortlessly and using his formidable reach to drive majestically and with great power. Coming into a Kent side in cricket's Golden Age probably influenced the young Woolley's style. Surprisingly for a player of such class and whose county form was so consistent, his record for England is very uneven and his final average disappointing. As a young man his left-arm slow bowling was an important feature of his cricket but it was seldom employed in the last decade of his career. He was a brilliant slip and holds the world record for most catches by a fielder, even with his total amended by several recent audits. He preserved his regal bearing until the end of his long life but, when complimented on the admirable straightness of his back, responded with the startling revelation that he had been unable to bend it for 15 years.

NOTABLE FEATS

• 1000 runs in 23rd Test (*135*) (34 inns); 2000 runs in 42nd Test (*157*) (63 inns); 3000 runs in 57th Test (*187*) (86 inns).
• 50 wickets in 28th Test (*140*).
• *120* Scored the first England 100 by a left-hander in Australia. Shared record E v A 7th-wkt stand of 143 with J. Vine.
• *129* Third after W. Bates and H. Trumble to score 50 and take 10 wickets in an E v A Test.
• *141* First England batsman to score 2 nineties in a Test.
• *167* Ended a (then) record sequence of 52 consecutive Tests.
• *184* Shared 3rd-wkt stand of 245 in 165 min with R.E.S. Wyatt.
• Exceeded 1000 runs in a season 28 times (equal record), including 3352 in 1928 and 2000 on 12 other occasions.
• Took 100 wickets in a season 8 times, notably 185 in 1920, each time completing the 'double', including most instances (4) of 2000 runs and 100 wickets.
• Scored 305* for MCC v Tasmania at Hobart in 1911–12, completing his 300 in 205 min (then the world record), and 8 other double centuries (6 for Kent).
• Shared record English first-class 10th-wkt stand of 235 with A. Fielder for Kent v Worcestershire at Stourbridge in 1909.
• Shared record Kent 2nd-wkt stand of 352 with W.H. Ashdown v Essex at Brentwood in 1934 – highest Kent stand for any wicket.
• Shared record Kent 5th-wkt stand of 277 with L.E.G. Ames v New Zealanders at Canterbury in 1931.
• Holds Championship career record for most catches by a fielder (710 in 707 matches).
• Holds Kent career records for most appearances (764), most runs (47,868), most hundreds (122), most instances of 1000 runs in a season (27) and most catches by a fielder (773). His 2894 runs (1928) and 10 hundreds (1928 and 1934) are Kent records for a season.
• Scored hundreds in 4 consecutive innings for Kent in 1929.
• Scored 100 before lunch on 13 occasions.
• Hat-trick for Kent v Surrey at Blackheath in 1919.
• Took 7 wickets in 24 balls for Kent v Surrey at The Oval in 1911.
• Bowled in an unchanged partnership with C. Blythe throughout both completed innings of a match twice (1910 and 1912).
• Achieved the match 'double' for Kent 6 times and for MCC (v Otago in Dunedin) once.
• Held 5 catches in an innings for Kent twice.

TEST NOTES

• *237* Recalled at the age of 47 he deputised for L.E.G. Ames as wicket-keeper and conceded the Test record total of byes (37). He remains the oldest to keep wicket in a Test.

Percy Chapman (left), 'Tich' Freeman and Frank Woolley.

						Batting 1st			Batting 2nd				Bowling 1st			Bowling 2nd		
Ref	Series	V	T	Venue	Result	No	R	HO	No	R	HO	Ct	Balls	R	W	Balls	R	W
105/102	1909	A	5	Oval	D	6	8	b	–	–	–	1	24	6	0	36	31	0
106/103	1909–10	SA	1	Johannesburg[1]	L-19	5	14	c	5	25	b	2	6	4	0	24	13	0
107/104			2	Durban[1]	L-95	5	22	c	5	4	c	2	90	23	1	60	34	1
108/105			3	Johannesburg[1]	W-3w	8	58	*	7	0	c	4	126	54	1	108	29	0
109/106			4	Cape Town	L-4w	5	69	c	4	64	b	1	36	23	1	18	24	0
110/107			5	Cape Town	W-9w	5	0	b	–	–	–	1	–	–	–	78	47	3

Ref	Series	V	T	Venue	Result	Batting 1st			Batting 2nd				Bowling 1st			Bowling 2nd		
						No	R	HO	No	R	HO	Ct	Balls	R	W	Balls	R	W
116/108	1911–12	A	1	Sydney	L-146	8	39	b	8	7	c	1	126	77	2	36	15	0
117/109			2	Melbourne	W-8w	8	23	c	–	–	–	–	1	0	1	18	21	0
118/110			3	Adelaide	W-7w	8	20	b	–	–	–	–	–	–	–	42	30	1
119/111			4	Melbourne	W-I & 225	7	56	c	–	–	–	–	66	22	1	12	7	0
120/112			5	Sydney	W-70	7	133	*	7	11	c	6	12	1	2	96	36	1
122/113	1912	SA	1	Lord's	W-I & 62	6	73	b	–	–	–	–	–	–	–	24	19	0
123/114		A	1	Lord's	D	6	20	c	–	–	–	–	–	–	–	–	–	–
124/115		SA	2	Leeds	W-174	6	57	b	6	4	c	–	36	13	1	–	–	–
126/116		A	2	Manchester	D	6	13	c	–	–	–	–	36	6	0	–	–	–
128/117		SA	3	Oval	W-10w	6	13	b	–	–	–	–	93	41	5	54	24	1
129/118		A	3	Oval	W-244	5	62	lbw	5	4	b	2	58	29	5	46	20	5
130/119	1913–14	SA	1	Durban[1]	W-I & 157	7	31	c	–	–	–	3	42	24	1	54	16	2
131/120			2	Johannesburg[1]	W-I & 12	7	0	b	–	–	–	1	18	5	1	126	45	0
132/121			3	Johannesburg[1]	W-91	7	7	lbw	7	37	st	1	30	13	0	42	24	0
133/122			4	Durban[1]	D	7	9	c	7	0	*	–	60	27	0	78	26	0
134/123			5	Port Elizabeth	W-10w	6	54	lbw	–	–	–	2	132	71	3	30	23	0
135/124	1920–21	A	1	Sydney	L-377	5	52	c	5	16	st	1	138	35	2	216	90	2
136/125			2	Melbourne	L-I & 91	6	5	b	6	50	b	2	162	87	2	–	–	–
137/126			3	Adelaide	L-119	5	79	c	5	0	b	1	126	47	0	228	91	0
138/127			4	Melbourne	L-8w	5	29	lbw	5	0	st	–	193	56	3	84	39	0
139/128			5	Sydney	L-9w	5	53	b	1	1	c	2	90	58	0	66	27	0
140/129	1921	A	1	Nottingham	L-10w	6	20	c	6	34	c	–	132	46	3	–	–	–
141/130			2	Lord's	L-8w	3	95	st	3	93	c	1	66	44	0	18	10	0
142/131			3	Leeds	L-219	1	0	b	4	37	b	3	30	34	1	108	45	1
143/132			4	Manchester	D	3	41	c	–	–	–	–	234	38	0	–	–	–
144/133			5	Oval	D	4	23	ro	–	–	–	2	66	31	2	–	–	–
148/134	1922–23	SA	1	Johannesburg[1]	L-168	3	26	lbw	4	15	c	1	–	–	–	96	33	0
149/135			2	Cape Town	W-1w	3	0	c	3	5	b	–	12	1	0	66	22	0
150/136			3	Durban[2]	D	3	0	c	–	–	–	3	90	47	0	–	–	–
151/137			4	Johannesburg[1]	D	3	15	c	3	115	*	1	36	10	0	36	26	0
152/138			5	Durban[2]	W-109	3	2	c	3	8	c	2	36	9	0	18	3	0
153/139	1924	SA	1	Birmingham	W-I & 18	3	64	c	–	–	–	–	–	–	–	60	41	0
154/140			2	Lord's	W-I & 18	3	134	*	–	–	–	1	–	–	–	24	9	0
155/141			3	Leeds	W-9w	4	0	b	–	–	–	–	–	–	–	54	21	0
156/142			4	Manchester	D	–	–	–	–	–	–	–	–	–	–	–	–	–
157/143			5	Oval	D	4	51	b	–	–	–	1	84	22	1	–	–	–
158/144	1924–25	A	1	Sydney	L-193	4	0	b	6	123	c	4	72	35	0	–	–	–
159/145			2	Melbourne	L-81	3	0	b	5	50	lbw	–	88	26	0	–	–	–
160/146			3	Adelaide	L-11	7	16	c	3	21	b	1	344	135	1	152	77	4
161/147			4	Melbourne	W-I & 29	4	40	st	–	–	–	2	72	53	1	48	17	1
162/148			5	Sydney	L-307	4	47	b	4	28	c	2	40	18	0	64	14	1
163/149	1926	A	1	Nottingham	D	–	–	–	–	–	–	–	–	–	–	–	–	–
164/150			2	Lord's	D	3	87	lbw	–	–	–	–	12	5	0	42	13	1
165/151			3	Leeds	D	3	27	ro	3	20	c	–	24	26	0	–	–	–
166/152			4	Manchester	D	4	58	c	–	–	–	1	12	19	0	–	–	–
167/153			5	Oval	W-289	3	18	b	3	27	lbw	2	–	–	–	–	–	–
183/169	1929	SA	3	Leeds	W-5w	5	83	b	4	95	*	–	–	–	–	79	35	3
184/170			4	Manchester	W-I & 32	4	154	c	–	–	–	1	54	22	0	108	51	1
185/171			5	Oval	D	4	46	hw	–	–	–	1	78	25	1	–	–	–
186/172	1929–30	NZ	1	Christchurch	W-8w	4	31	c	4	17	*	–	–	–	–	54	37	2
187/173			2	Wellington	D	4	6	c	4	23	b	–	171	76	7	138	48	2
188/174			3	Auckland	D	4	59	ro	–	–	–	–	–	–	–	–	–	–
189/175			4	Auckland	D	4	10	b	–	–	–	–	246	100	2	–	–	–
194/180	1930	A	1	Nottingham	W-93	4	0	st	4	5	b	–	–	–	–	18	3	0
195/181			2	Lord's	L-7w	2	41	c	2	28	hw	1	36	35	0	–	–	–
209/190	1931	NZ	1	Lord's	D	6	80	lbw	5	9	b	–	–	–	–	–	–	–
219/193	1932	I		Lord's	W-158	3	9	ro	3	21	c	–	–	–	–	–	–	–
237/211	1934	A	5	Oval	L-562	3	4	c	3	0	c	1	–	–	–	–	–	–

Career	M	I	NO	HS	R	Avge	100	50	Ct	St	Balls	R	W	Avge	BB	5w	10w	Rate
Test	64	98	7	154	3283	36.07	5	23	64	–	6495	2815	83	33.91	7-76	4	1	78.25
F/c	979	1532	85	305*	58969	40.75	145	295	1018	–	94955	41066	2068	19.85	8-22	132	28	45.91

F. E. WOOLLEY – TEST SUMMARY

Series	V	M	I	NO	HS	R	Avge	100	50	Balls	R	W	Avge	BB	5w	10w	Rate
1909	A	1	1	–	8	8	8.00	–	–	60	37	0	–	–	–	–	–
1909–10	SA	5	9	1	69	256	32.00	–	3	546	251	7	35.85	3-47	–	–	78.00
1911–12	A	5	7	1	133*	289	48.16	1	1	409	209	8	26.12	2-1	–	–	51.12
1912	SA	3	4	–	73	147	36.75	–	2	207	97	7	13.85	5-41	1	–	29.57
1912	A	3	4	–	62	99	24.75	–	1	140	55	10	5.50	5-20	2	1	14.00
1913–14	SA	5	7	1	54	138	23.00	–	1	612	274	7	39.14	3-71	–	–	87.42
1920–21	A	5	10	–	79	285	28.50	–	4	1303	530	9	58.88	3-56	–	–	144.77
1921	A	5	8	–	95	343	42.87	–	2	654	248	7	35.42	3-46	–	–	93.42
1922–23	SA	5	9	1	115*	186	23.25	1	–	390	151	0	–	–	–	–	–
1924	SA	5	4	1	134*	249	83.00	1	2	222	93	1	93.00	1-22	–	–	222.00
1924–25	A	5	9	–	123	325	36.11	1	1	880	375	8	46.87	4-77	–	–	107.25
1926	A	5	6	–	87	237	39.50	–	2	90	63	1	63.00	1-13	–	–	90.00
1929	SA	3	4	1	154	378	126.00	1	2	319	133	5	26.60	3-35	–	–	63.80
1929–30	NZ	4	6	1	59	146	29.20	–	1	609	261	13	20.07	7-76	1	–	46.84
1930	A	2	4	–	41	74	18.50	–	–	54	38	0	–	–	–	–	–
1931	NZ	1	2	–	80	89	44.50	–	1	–	–	–	–	–	–	–	–
1932	I	1	2	–	21	30	15.00	–	–	–	–	–	–	–	–	–	–
1934	A	1	2	–	4	4	2.00	–	–	–	–	–	–	–	–	–	–
	A	32	51	1	133*	1664	33.28	2	11	3590	1555	43	36.16	5-20	2	1	83.48
	SA	26	37	5	154	1354	42.31	3	10	2296	999	27	37.00	5-41	1	–	85.03
	NZ	5	8	1	80	235	33.57	–	2	609	261	13	20.07	7-76	1	–	46.84
	I	1	2	–	21	30	15.00	–	–	–	–	–	–	–	–	–	–
Home		30	41	2	154	1658	42.51	2	12	1746	764	31	24.64	5-20	3	1	56.32
Overseas		34	57	5	133*	1625	31.25	3	11	4749	2051	52	39.44	7-76	1	–	91.32
Totals		64	98	7	154	3283	36.07	5	23	6495	2815	83	33.91	7-76	4	1	78.25

WOOLMER
Robert Andrew

Kent (1968 to 1984)
Natal (1973–74 to 1975–76)
Western Province (1980–81)

Wisden 1976
TOURS
A 1976–77; SA 1973–74 (Robins), 1981–82 (SAB); I/SL 1976–77
Born Kanpur, India 14 May 1948

Tall (6ft) and comfortably built, Bob Woolmer was a stylish batsman who began his Kent career as a right-arm medium-pace swing bowler and lower-order batsman. His skill with a new ball was too useful for much consideration to be given to his batting in those early days. Undeterred, he worked hard on his method and inevitably copied the masterly technique of his captain, Colin Cowdrey. Many of his mannerisms were transferred too – and his patience. He had established his place in the England team with two fine hundreds against the 1977 Australians when he opted to join the Packer revolution but he failed to recover his form when he was picked after the truce. Married to a South African, he had spent several English winters in the Union coaching coloured and black children. He needed less persuasion than some to join the English rebel tour and promptly incurred a three-year ban. No sooner had he served his sentence than persistent back trouble compelled his premature retirement and his decision to emigrate permanently to Cape Town. He returned to Kent as their special coaching envoy for the 1987 season and would have been delighted with their performance the following year when, totally unfancied, they finished just one point behind the champions. His thought provoking autobiography was entitled *Pirate and Rebel?*

NOTABLE FEATS

- 1000 runs in 17th Test (*881*) (29 inns).
- *763* Took 394 min for the (then) slowest 100 in E v A Tests.
- Exceeded 1000 runs in a season 5 times, notably 1749 in 1976.
- Scored 203 for Kent v Sussex at Tunbridge Wells in 1982.
- Scored 100 before lunch on 3 occasions.
- Held 5 catches in an innings for Kent v Worcestershire at Worcester in 1976.

Bob Woolmer batting in the First Test against West Indies, 1980.

Ref	Series	V	T	Venue	Result	Batting 1st			Batting 2nd			Ct	Bowling 1st			Bowling 2nd		
						No	R	HO	No	R	HO		Balls	R	W	Balls	R	W
761/512	1975	A	2	Lord's	D	8	33	c	8	31	b	–	78	31	1	18	3	0
763/514			4	Oval	D	5	5	c	5	149	lbw	1	108	38	1	–	–	–
777/515	1976	WI	1	Nottingham	D	5	82	lbw	–	–	–	–	60	47	0	–	–	–
778/516			2	Lord's	D	5	38	c	6	29	c	2	–	–	–	–	–	–
779/517			3	Manchester	L-425	5	3	c	4	0	lbw	–	18	22	0	–	–	–
780/518			4	Leeds	L-55	1	18	c	1	37	lbw	–	36	25	1	42	26	0
781/519			5	Oval	L-231	1	8	lbw	1	30	c	–	54	44	0	30	30	0
788/520	1976–77	I	1	Delhi	W-I & 25	4	4	lbw	–	–	–	1	–	–	–	–	–	–
790/522			3	Madras[1]	W-200	2	22	c	2	16	lbw	2	6	2	0	–	–	–
803/525	1976–77	A		Melbourne	L-45	1	9	c	1	12	lbw	–	–	–	–	–	–	–
804/526	1977	A	1	Lord's	D	3	79	ro	3	120	c	1	30	20	0	–	–	–
805/527			2	Manchester	W-9w	3	137	c	3	0	*	1	–	–	–	–	–	–
806/528			3	Nottingham	W-7w	3	0	lbw	–	–	–	–	–	–	–	18	3	0
807/529			4	Leeds	W-I & 85	3	37	c	–	–	–	–	–	–	–	48	8	1
808/530			5	Oval	D	3	15	lbw	3	6	c	–	–	–	–	–	–	–
880/557	1980	WI	1	Nottingham	L-2w	4	46	c	4	29	c	–	–	–	–	–	–	–
881/558			2	Lord's	D	4	15	c	4	19	*	–	–	–	–	–	–	–
903/567	1981	A	1	Nottingham	L-4w	3	0	c	3	0	c	2	–	–	–	–	–	–
904/568			2	Lord's	D	3	21	c	3	9	lbw	–	–	–	–	–	–	–

Career	M	I	NO	HS	R	Avge	100	50	Ct	St	Balls	R	W	Avge	BB	5w	10w	Rate
Test	19	34	2	149	1059	33.09	3	2	10	–	546	299	4	74.75	1-8	–	–	136.50
F/c	350	545	75	203	15772	33.55	34	70	239	1	25767	10868	420	25.87	7-47	12	1	61.35

TEST NOTES

- *904* Retired hurt when 13* at 83–2 (1st inns); resumed at 284–5.

R. A. WOOLMER – TEST BATTING SUMMARY

Series	V	M	I	NO	HS	R	Avge	100	50
1975	A	2	4	–	149	218	54.50	1	–
1976	WI	5	9	–	82	245	27.22	–	1
1976–77	I	2	3	–	22	42	14.00	–	–
1976–77	A	1	2	–	12	21	10.50	–	–
1977	A	5	8	1	137	394	56.28	2	1
1980	WI	2	4	1	46	109	36.33	–	–
1981	A	2	4	–	21	30	7.50	–	–

Series	V	M	I	NO	HS	R	Avge	100	50
	A	10	18	1	149	663	39.00	3	1
	WI	7	13	1	82	354	29.50	–	1
	I	2	3	–	22	42	14.00	–	–
Home		16	29	2	149	996	36.88	3	2
Overseas		3	5	–	22	63	12.60	–	–
Totals		19	34	2	149	1059	33.09	3	2

WORTHINGTON Thomas Stanley

Derbyshire (1924 to 1947)

Wisden 1937

TOURS

A 1929–30, 1936–37; NZ 1929–30, 1936–37; I 1937–38 (Tennyson)

Born Bolsover, Derbyshire 21 Aug 1905

Died King's Lynn, Norfolk 31 Aug 1973

Like Woolmer, Stan Worthington began his cricketing career as a right-arm fast-medium bowler and lower-order batsman but he developed into a magnificent all-rounder whose playing days with Derbyshire spanned 23 years. His batting was often described as 'vigorous' and he certainly did not allow the grass to grow under his feet. Accuracy, particularly with regard to length, was the hallmark of his bowling. After playing for Northumberland (1949) and in the Lancashire league, he coached Lancashire for 11 years (1952–62). He died whilst on holiday in King's Lynn. [*Illus. pp.* 126, 167, 459]

NOTABLE FEATS

- *254* Shared record E v I 4th-wkt stand of 266 with W.R. Hammond.
- Exceeded 1000 runs in a season 10 times, notably 1774 in 1937.
- Scored 2 double centuries for Derbyshire, notably 238* v Sussex at Derby in 1937.
- Shared record Derbyshire 6th-wkt stand of 212 with G.M. Lee v Essex at Chesterfield in 1932.
- Scored 100 in 60 min for Derbyshire v Nottinghamshire at Ilkeston in 1933.

Ref	Series	V	T	Venue	Result	Batting 1st No	R	HO	Batting 2nd No	R	HO	Ct	Bowling 1st Balls	R	W	Bowling 2nd Balls	R	W
186/172	1929–30	NZ	1	Christchurch	W-8w	7	0	b	–	–	–	1	43	24	1	78	19	2
187/173			2	Wellington	D	7	32	st	–	–	–	1	132	63	2	60	44	1
188/174			3	Auckland	D	–	–	–	–	–	–	–	36	11	0	–	–	–
189/175			4	Auckland	D	7	0	b	–	–	–	–	90	25	1	–	–	–
253/222	1936	I	2	Manchester	D	4	87	c	–	–	–	1	24	15	1	78	27	0
254/223			3	Oval	W-9w	5	128	b	–	–	–	2	–	–	–	12	10	0
255/224	1936–37	A	1	Brisbane[2]	W-322	1	0	c	1	8	st	1	–	–	–	–	–	–
257/226			3	Melbourne	L-365	1	0	c	1	16	c	1	–	–	–	32	18	0
259/228			5	Melbourne	L-I & 200	2	44	hw	2	6	c	1	48	60	0	–	–	–

Career	M	I	NO	HS	R	Avge	100	50	Ct	St	Balls	R	W	Avge	BB	5w	10w	Rate
Test	9	11	0	128	321	29.18	1	1	8	–	633	316	8	39.50	2-19	–	–	79.12
F/c	453	720	59	238*	19221	29.07	31	94	340	–	49047	19939	682	29.23	8-29	16	2	71.91

WRIGHT
Charles William

Cambridge University (1882 to 1885)
Nottinghamshire (1882 to 1899)

TOURS SA 1895–96; I 1892–93
Born Harewood, Yorkshire 27 May 1863
Died Saxelby, Melton Mowbray, Leicestershire 10 Jan 1936

Charles Wright was a very sound opening batsman and a reliable wicket-keeper who learned his cricket at Charterhouse and was a blue for all four of his summers at Cambridge. He was coached by the Nottinghamshire professionals as a teenager and his defensive technique, particularly on treacherous pitches, was an admirable testimony to their teaching. At Bristol in 1893 he became the second of only three batsmen to be given out 'handled the ball' in a Championship match when the ball lodged in his pads and he picked it out. As acting captain of Nottinghamshire against Kent at Gravesend in 1890 he was the first ever to declare an innings closed. He retired after losing an eye during a partridge shoot but remained closely in touch with Nottinghamshire cricket, serving on the committee and as a trustee. [*Illus. p.* 325]

TEST NOTES

- *48* Deputised as wicket-keeper after H.R. Butt was injured in the 1st inns.

Ref	Series	V	T	Venue	Result	Batting 1st No	R	HO	Batting 2nd No	R	HO	Ct
47/47	1895–96	SA	1	Port Elizabeth	W-288	9	19	b	1	33	b	–
48/48			2	Johannesburg[1]	W-I & 197	8	71	b	–	–	–	–
49/49			3	Cape Town	W-I & 33	1	2	c	–	–	–	–

Career	M	I	NO	HS	R	Avge	100	50	Ct	St	Balls	R	W	Avge	BB	5w	10w	Rate
Test	3	4	0	71	125	31.25	–	1	–	–	–	–	–	–	–	–	–	–
F/c	265	461	21	114	6989	15.88	2	30	195	41	59	55	0	–	–	–	–	–

WRIGHT
Douglas Vivian Parson

Kent (1932 to 1957)

Wisden 1940
TOURS
A 1946–47, 1950–51; SA 1938–39, 1948–49; WI 1956–57 (Norfolk); NZ 1946–47, 1950–51
Born Sidcup, Kent 21 Aug 1914

Doug Wright bowled his rich assortment of leg-breaks and googlies at a bounding medium pace. On his day he was an absolute match winner, capable of turning the ball a prodigious amount. Although he was not particularly tall (5ft 10½in), he extracted a higher bounce than most leg-spinners and, bowling so briskly, could beat the best batsmen and become virtually unplayable. He could also provide a few searching questions for wicket-keepers as Tony Catt discovered at Northampton in 1955 when, seriously impeded by severe sunburn, he found the sharply spun lifting leg-breaks constantly flying over his scorched shoulders and conceded 48 byes. He was more prone than most leg-spinners to be erratic in length and direction but his successes more than outweighed those memories. A record collection of hat-tricks stands as testimony to his class and explains why the selectors were usually anxious to include him. His gentle unostentatious manner enabled him to become an outstandingly successful coach at Charterhouse.

						Batting 1st			Batting 2nd				Bowling 1st			Bowling 2nd		
Ref	Series	V	T	Venue	Result	No	R	HO	No	R	HO	Ct	Balls	R	W	Balls	R	W
263/232	1938	A	1	Nottingham	D	10	1	*	–	–	–	1	234	153	4	222	85	1
264/233			2	Lord's	D	10	6	b	10	10	*	1	96	68	1	48	56	1
265/234			4	Leeds	L-5w	9	22	c	9	0	c	–	90	38	2	30	26	3
268/237	1938–39	SA	2	Cape Town	D	9	33	c	–	–	–	–	208	83	2	96	62	0
269/238			3	Durban[2]	W-I & 13	–	–	–	–	–	–	–	96	37	2	120	56	0
271/240			5	Durban[2]	D	9	26	c	–	–	–	1	296	142	2	256	146	3
272/241	1939	WI	1	Lord's	W-8w	–	–	–	–	–	–	1	104	57	2	136	75	3
273/242			2	Manchester	D	8	1	*	8	0	*	–	40	20	0	24	9	1
274/243			3	Oval	D	9	6	lbw	–	–	–	1	104	53	0	–	–	–
276/244	1946	I	1	Lord's	W-10w	10	3	b	–	–	–	–	102	53	2	120	68	2
277/245			2	Manchester	D	11	0	lbw	–	–	–	–	12	12	0	12	17	0
279/247	1946–47	A	1	Brisbane[2]	L-I & 332	11	4	c	11	10	*	–	350	167	5	–	–	–
280/248			2	Sydney	L-I & 33	11	15	*	11	0	c	1	368	169	1	–	–	–
281/249			3	Melbourne	D	11	10	b	–	–	–	1	208	124	2	256	131	3
282/250			4	Adelaide	D	11	0	b	–	–	–	–	260	152	3	72	49	0
283/251			5	Sydney	L-5w	11	7	c	10	1	*	–	232	105	7	176	93	2
284/252	1946–47	NZ		Christchurch	D	–	–	–	–	–	–	–	78	61	0	–	–	–
286/254	1947	SA	2	Lord's	W-10w	–	–	–	–	–	–	–	234	95	5	194	80	5
287/255			3	Manchester	W-7w	10	4	*	–	–	–	–	54	30	0	60	32	3
288/256			4	Leeds	W-10w	–	–	–	–	–	–	–	120	24	2	84	31	0
289/257			5	Oval	D	10	14	b	–	–	–	–	174	89	2	180	103	2
300/263	1948	A	2	Lord's	L-409	11	13	*	11	4	c	–	129	54	1	114	69	1
309/267	1948–49	SA	1	Durban[2]	W-2w	11	0	c	–	–	–	–	72	29	1	208	72	4
310/268			2	Johannesburg[2]	D	11	1	*	–	–	–	–	208	104	3	112	35	1
311/269			3	Cape Town	D	11	11	c	–	–	–	–	72	58	0	16	18	0
317/275	1949	NZ	4	Oval	D	11	0	lbw	–	–	–	2	132	93	1	36	21	0
326/279	1950	WI	4	Oval	L-I & 56	11	4	lbw	11	6	*	–	318	141	5	–	–	–
327/280	1950–51	A	1	Brisbane[2]	L-70	–	–	–	11	2	c	–	128	81	1	–	–	–
328/281			2	Melbourne	L-28	11	2	lbw	11	2	lbw	–	64	63	0	72	42	1
329/282			3	Sydney	L-I & 13	11	0	ro	–	–	–	–	–	–	–	–	–	–
330/283			4	Adelaide	L-274	11	14	lbw	10	0	*	–	200	99	4	168	109	2
331/284			5	Melbourne	W-8w	10	3	lbw	–	–	–	–	72	50	0	120	56	3
332/285	1950–51	NZ	1	Christchurch	D	10	45	c	–	–	–	–	162	99	2	–	–	–
333/286			2	Wellington	W-6w	10	9	*	–	–	–	1	114	48	5	72	32	0

Career	M	I	NO	HS	R	Avge	100	50	Ct	St	Balls	R	W	Avge	BB	5w	10w	Rate
Test	34	39	13	45	289	11.11	–	–	10	–	8135	4224	108	39.11	7-105	6	1	75.32
F/c	497	703	225	84*	5903	12.34	–	16	182	–	92944	49307	2056	23.98	9-47	150	42	45.20

TEST NOTES

- *329* Tore a leg tendon as he was run out and was unable to bowl.

Doug Wright

NOTABLE FEATS

- 50 wickets in 16th Test (*283*); 100 wickets in 33rd Test (*332*).
- *263* Bowled J.H.W. Fingleton with his fourth ball in Test cricket.
- Took 100 wickets in a season 10 times, notably 177 in 1947.
- Took 9 for 47 for Kent v Gloucestershire at Bristol in 1939.
- Returned Kent match analyses of 16 for 80 v Somerset at Bath in 1939, 15 for 163 (including 9 for 51) for Kent v Leicestershire at Maidstone in 1949, and 15 for 173 v Sussex at Hastings in 1947.
- Seven hat-tricks (world record) – 6 for Kent (equalling record in England), plus one for MCC v Border at East London in 1938–39.

D. V. P. WRIGHT – TEST BOWLING SUMMARY

Series	V	M	Balls	R	W	Avge	BB	5w	10w	Rate
1938	A	3	720	426	12	35.50	4-153	–	–	60.00
1938–39	SA	3	1072	526	9	58.44	3-146	–	–	119.11
1939	WI	3	408	214	6	35.66	3-75	–	–	68.00
1946	I	2	246	150	4	37.50	2-53	–	–	61.50
1946–47	A	5	1922	990	23	43.04	7-105	2	–	83.56
1946–47	NZ	1	78	61	0	–	–	–	–	–
1947	SA	4	1100	484	19	25.47	5-80	2	1	57.89
1948	A	1	243	123	2	61.50	1-54	–	–	121.50
1948–49	SA	3	688	316	9	35.11	4-72	–	–	76.44
1949	NZ	1	168	114	1	114.00	1-93	–	–	168.00
1950	WI	1	318	141	5	29.60	5-141	1	–	63.60
1950–51	A	5	824	500	11	45.45	4-99	–	–	74.90
1950–51	NZ	2	348	179	7	25.57	5-48	1	–	49.71
	A	14	3709	2039	48	42.47	7-105	2	–	77.27
	SA	10	2860	1326	37	35.83	5-80	2	1	77.29
	WI	4	726	355	11	32.27	5-141	1	–	66.00
	NZ	4	594	354	8	44.25	5-48	1	–	74.25
	I	2	246	150	4	37.50	2-53	–	–	61.50
Home		15	3203	1652	49	33.71	5-80	3	1	65.36
Overseas		19	4932	2572	59	43.59	7-105	3	–	83.59
Totals		34	8135	4224	108	39.11	7-105	6	1	75.32

WYATT
Robert Elliott Storey

Warwickshire (1923 to 1939)
Worcestershire (1946 to 1951)

Wisden 1930
TOURS
A 1932–33, 1936–37; SA 1927–28, 1930–31; WI 1929–30, 1934–35; NZ 1932–33, 1936–37; I/SL 1926–27
Born Milford, Surrey 2 May 1901

Bob Wyatt was a very consistent and determined batsman whose long county career spanned 28 years. Application, a sound defence and a neat range of strokes provided him with a decade of regular Test cricket. In his early years his right-arm medium-pace swing bowling had brought him close to all-rounder status, particularly in 1926 when he had claimed 92 wickets. He captained Warwickshire for eight seasons (1930–37) before resigning after a disagreement with his committee. Towards the end of his first summer at the helm he was selected against Australia for the first time and appointed captain in place of the immensely popular Percy Chapman. It was through no fault of Wyatt's that England lost by an innings. Following a quiet interlude from Douglas Jardine, he expanded his reign to 16 Tests (3 wins, 5 defeats). After the Second World War he moved to Worcestershire for six seasons, skippering them jointly in 1949 and solely in 1950–51. A Test selector for four years (1950–53), he was chairman in his first season. He played in his final first-class match at the age of 56 and was still in fine fettle when he opened a new press box at Edgbaston 30 years later.

NOTABLE FEATS

- 1000 runs in 20th Test (*224*) (34 inns).
- *170* After bowling an opening spell of 11–10–1–1, he was not recalled until the total was 241–7 and then took 2 wickets in his next over.
- *184* Shared 3rd-wkt stand of 245 in 165 min with F.E Woolley.
- Exceeded 1000 runs in a season 17 times (plus once on tour) including 2000 on 5 occasions, notably 2630 in 1929.
- Scored 2 double centuries for Warwickshire, notably 232 v Derbyshire at Birmingham in 1937.
- Shared record Warwickshire 8th-wkt stand of 228 with A.J.W. Croom v Worcestershire at Dudley in 1925.
- Hat-trick for MCC v Ceylonese at Colombo in 1926–27, a match in which he also scored 124 (the fifth of only 10 such feats in first-class cricket).

TEST NOTES

- *172* Retired hurt when 4* at 49–3 (2nd inns); resumed at 89–5.

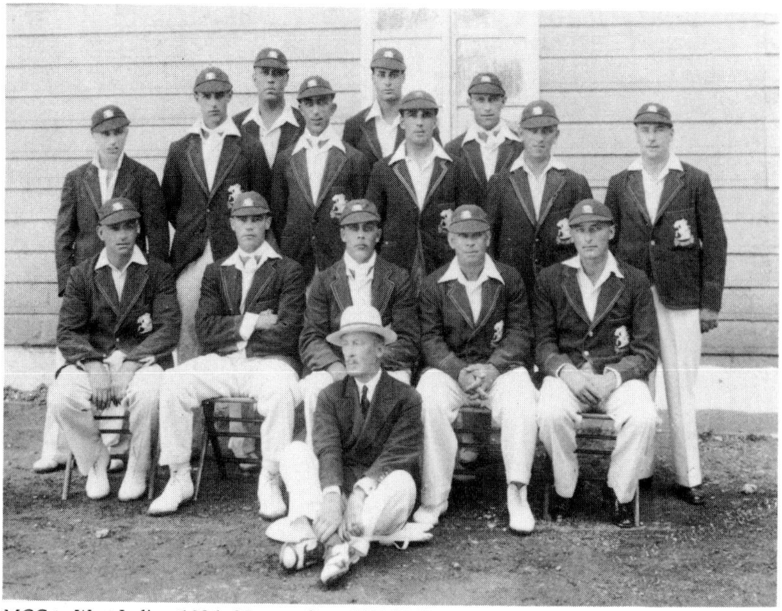

MCC to West Indies, 1934–35: standing *W.E. Hollies, D.C.H. Townsend, C.I.J. Smith, J. Iddon, K. Farnes, L.E.G. Ames, G.A.E. Paine, M. Leyland, W. Farrimond;* seated *W.R. Hammond, E.R.T. Holmes, R.E.S. Wyatt (captain), E.H. Hendren, W.E. Harbord;* in front *T.H. Carlton Levick (manager).*

						Batting 1st			Batting 2nd				Bowling 1st			Bowling 2nd		
Ref	Series	V	T	Venue	Result	No	R	HO	No	R	HO	Ct	Balls	R	W	Balls	R	W
168/154	1927–28	SA	1	Johannesburg[1]	W-10w	5	0	lbw	–	–	–	–	24	6	0	–	–	–
169/155			2	Cape Town	W-87	6	2	lbw	6	91	c	–	–	–	–	18	5	0
170/156			3	Durban[2]	D	5	0	lbw	–	–	–	–	78	4	3	90	31	0
171/157			4	Johannesburg[1]	L-4w	5	58	c	5	39	lbw	2	66	44	1	12	6	0
172/158			5	Durban[2]	L-8w	5	22	c	5	20	*	1	18	16	0	–	–	–
184/170	1929	SA	4	Manchester	W-I & 32	3	113	c	–	–	–	–	12	8	0	24	13	1
185/171			5	Oval	D	5	6	c	–	–	–	–	96	54	1	–	–	–
192/178	1929–30	WI	3	Georgetown	L-289	3	0	c	3	28	c	–	54	56	2	–	–	–
193/179			4	Kingston	D	3	58	c	2	10	c	–	24	11	0	147	58	2
198/184*	1930	A	5	Oval	L-I & 39	7	64	c	7	7	b	1	84	58	1	–	–	–
204/185	1930–31	SA	1	Johannesburg[1]	L-28	1	8	lbw	1	5	c	–	–	–	–	12	20	0
205/186			2	Cape Town	D	1	40	b	1	29	b	–	12	4	0	–	–	–
206/187			3	Durban[2]	D	1	54	c	–	–	–	1	–	–	–	–	–	–
207/188			4	Johannesburg[1]	D	1	37	lbw	1	7	lbw	–	12	10	0	–	–	–
208/189			5	Durban[2]	D	1	24	c	1	1	c	–	–	–	–	24	6	1
220/194	1932–33	A	1	Sydney	W-10w	2	38	lbw	2	0	*	–	–	–	–	–	–	–
221/195			2	Melbourne	L-111	2	13	lbw	7	25	lbw	–	–	–	–	–	–	–
222/196			3	Adelaide	W-338	6	78	c	3	49	c	–	–	–	–	–	–	–
223/197			4	Brisbane[2]	W-6w	4	12	c	–	–	–	–	–	–	–	–	–	–
224/198			5	Sydney	W-8w	6	51	c	2	61	*	2	12	12	0	–	–	–
225/199	1932–33	NZ	1	Christchurch	D	4	20	ro	–	–	–	1	–	–	–	–	–	–
226/200*			2	Auckland	D	2	60	b	–	–	–	–	–	–	–	–	–	–
228/202	1933	WI	2	Manchester	D	4	18	c	–	–	–	–	42	14	1	24	11	0
229/203*			3	Oval	W-I & 17	4	15	c	–	–	–	–	–	–	–	–	–	–
234/208*	1934	A	2	Lord's	W-I & 38	5	33	c	–	–	–	–	–	–	–	–	–	–
235/209*			3	Manchester	D	3	0	b	–	–	–	1	–	–	–	–	–	–
236/210*			4	Leeds	D	5	19	st	5	44	b	1	–	–	–	–	–	–
237/211*			5	Oval	L-562	5	17	b	6	22	c	–	24	28	0	–	–	–
238/212*	1934–35	WI	1	Bridgetown	W-4w	1	8	c	8	6	*	–	–	–	–	–	–	–
239/213*			2	Port-of-Spain	L-217	1	15	c	7	2	c	1	102	33	3	48	26	0
240/214*			3	Georgetown	D	2	21	c	2	71	b	–	60	10	0	24	7	1
241/215*			4	Kingston	L-I & 161	1	1	*rh	–	–	–	1	30	12	0	–	–	–

Ref	Series	V	T	Venue	Result	Batting 1st No	R	HO	Batting 2nd No	R	HO	Ct	Bowling 1st Balls	R	W	Bowling 2nd Balls	R	W
242/216*	1935	SA	1	Nottingham	D	2	149	c	–	–	–	–	–	–	–	–	–	–
243/217*			2	Lord's	L-157	1	53	c	1	16	b	1	24	9	0	24	2	0
244/218*			3	Leeds	D	1	0	c	5	44	c	–	24	1	1	36	12	0
245/219*			4	Manchester	D	5	3	lbw	8	15	*	–	24	12	0	–	–	–
246/220*			5	Oval	D	3	37	c	–	–	–	1	12	3	0	18	25	0
252/221	1936	I	1	Lord's	W-9w	5	0	c	–	–	–	1	18	7	0	42	8	0
258/227	1936–37	A	4	Adelaide	L-148	5	3	c	6	50	c	1	–	–	–	–	–	–
259/228			5	Melbourne	L-I & 200	6	38	c	6	9	ro	–	–	–	–	–	–	–

Career	M	I	NO	HS	R	Avge	100	50	Ct	St	Balls	R	W	Avge	BB	5w	10w	Rate
Test	40	64	6	149	1839	31.70	2	12	16	–	1395	642	18	35.66	3-4	–	–	77.50
F/c	739	1141	157	232	39405	40.04	85	207	415	1	59265	29597	901	32.84	7-43	31	2	65.77

R. E. S. WYATT – TEST BATTING SUMMARY

Series	V	M	I	NO	HS	R	Avge	100	50
1927–28	SA	5	8	1	91	232	33.14	–	2
1929	SA	2	2	–	113	119	59.50	1	–
1929–30	WI	2	4	–	58	96	24.00	–	1
1930	A	1	2	–	64	71	35.50	–	1
1930–31	SA	5	9	–	54	205	22.77	–	1
1932–33	A	5	9	2	78	327	46.71	–	3
1932–33	NZ	2	2	–	60	80	40.00	–	1
1933	WI	2	2	–	18	33	16.50	–	–
1934	A	4	6	–	44	135	22.50	–	–
1934–35	WI	4	7	2	71	124	24.80	–	1
1935	SA	5	8	1	149	317	45.28	1	1
1936	I	1	1	–	0	0	0.00	–	–
1936–37	A	2	4	–	50	100	25.00	–	1
	A	12	21	2	78	633	33.31	–	5
	SA	17	27	2	149	873	34.92	2	4
	WI	8	13	2	71	253	23.00	–	2
	NZ	2	2	–	60	80	40.00	–	1
	I	1	1	–	0	0	0.00	–	–
Home		15	21	1	149	675	33.75	2	2
Overseas		25	43	5	91	1164	30.63	–	10
Totals		40	64	6	149	1839	31.70	2	12

WYNYARD Edward George

Hampshire (1878 to 1908)

TOURS
SA 1905–06, 1909–10; WI 1904–05; NZ 1906–07
Born Saharanpur, Bengal, India 1 Apr 1861
Died Knotty Green, Beaconsfield, Buckinghamshire 30 Oct 1936

Over 6ft tall, Major Wynyard was an imposing figure on the cricket field and batted in an appropriately forcing style. Educated at Charterhouse and St Edward's, Oxford, he captained Hampshire (1896–99) after playing extensively in India during the 1880s. A splendidly abrasive character, he was bitterly offended when Ranji consumed some of his grapes. A slow lob bowler, he was a very mobile cover-point and equally adept at slip-catching. He won an FA Cup winner's medal with Old Carthusians in 1881 and was the only Test cricketer to be acknowledged as an expert figure skater. [*Illus. pp.* 268, 273]

NOTABLE FEATS

- Exceeded 1000 runs in a season twice.
- Scored 2 double centuries for Hampshire, notably 268 v Yorkshire at Southampton in 1896.
- Shared record English 6th-wkt stand of 411 with R.M. Poore for Hampshire v Somerset at Taunton in 1899.

Ref	Series	V	T	Venue	Result	Batting 1st No	R	HO	Batting 2nd No	R	HO	Ct	Bowling 1st Balls	R	W	Bowling 2nd Balls	R	W
52/52	1896	A	3	Oval	W-66	7	10	c	7	3	c	–	–	–	–	–	–	–
88/85	1905–06	SA	1	Johannesburg[1]	L-1w	4	29	st	4	0	b	–	–	–	–	18	15	0
89/86			2	Johannesburg[1]	L-9w	6	0	b	6	30	c	–	6	2	0	–	–	–

Career	M	I	NO	HS	R	Avge	100	50	Ct	St	Balls	R	W	Avge	BB	5w	10w	Rate
Test	3	6	0	30	72	12.00	–	–	–	–	24	17	0	–	–	–	–	–
F/c	154	272	20	268	8318	33.00	13	42	163	5	3790	2130	66	32.27	6-63	1	–	57.42

YARDLEY Norman Walter Dransfield

Cambridge University (1935 to 1938)
Yorkshire (1936 to 1955)

Wisden 1948
TOURS
A 1946–47; SA 1938–39; NZ 1946–47; I 1937–38 (Tennyson)
Born Gawber, Barnsley, Yorkshire
19 Mar 1915

NOTABLE FEATS

- *281* Dismissed D.G. Bradman in each innings.
- *285* Shared record E v SA 5th-wkt stand of 237 with D.C.S. Compton.
- Exceeded 1000 runs in a season 8 times, notably 1906 in 1947.
- Contributed 142 to the record total in South African first-class cricket: 676 by MCC v Griqualand West at Kimberley in 1938–39.

To Norman Yardley fell the impossible task of confronting Bradman's post-war Australians with an attack that began and ended with Alec Bedser. It was typical of his character that he should throw himself into the firing line but not in his wilder fantasies would he have expected to head the England bowling averages in consecutive Ashes series with his canny medium-pace and remove the great Don three times in succession. Tallish (5ft 10½in) and strongly built, he had made his reputation as an outstanding batsman with a sound defence during his university days at Cambridge. His four years as a blue brought scores of 90 and 101 in successive Varsity matches and he had a useful grounding in captaincy in his last term. He established himself in the Yorkshire team during the final pre-war summer and began his eight-year tenure on the captaincy in 1948. Considering the strength of the opposition he did well to gain four wins and suffer only seven defeats in his 14 Tests as leader. After his playing days, he combined his business interests in the wine trade with Test selection (1951–54), the Yorkshire presidency (1981–84), writing and radio broadcasting. In his youth he had been a fine all-round sportsman, gaining a hockey blue and becoming North of England squash champion six times.

Norman Yardley batting during England's innings in the 1948 Test trial; S.C. Griffith behind the stumps and Jack Crapp at slip for the Rest.

Ref	Series	V	T	Venue	Result	Batting 1st No	R	HO	Batting 2nd No	R	HO	Ct	Bowling 1st Balls	R	W	Bowling 2nd Balls	R	W
267/236	1938–39	SA	1	Johannesburg[1]	D	6	7	c	–	–	–	–	–	–	–	–	–	–
279/247	1946–47	A	1	Brisbane[2]	L-I & 332	7	29	c	7	0	c	1	104	47	0	–	–	–
280/248			2	Sydney	L-I & 33	7	25	c	7	35	b	–	72	23	1	–	–	–
281/249			3	Melbourne	D	7	61	b	7	53	*	1	160	50	2	160	67	3
282/250			4	Adelaide	D	8	18	*	8	18	c	–	248	101	3	104	69	1
283/251*			5	Sydney	L-5w	6	2	c	6	11	b	1	40	8	0	24	7	0
284/252	1946–47	NZ		Christchurch	D	2	22	b	–	–	–	–	24	12	1	–	–	–
285/253*	1947	SA	1	Nottingham	D	6	22	lbw	6	99	c	1	30	24	0	–	–	–
286/254*			2	Lord's	W-10w	6	5	c	–	–	–	2	–	–	–	–	–	–
287/255*			3	Manchester	W-7w	6	41	c	–	–	–	1	–	–	–	–	–	–
288/256*			4	Leeds	W-10w	6	36	c	–	–	–	2	–	–	–	–	–	–
289/257*			5	Oval	D	5	59	b	5	11	c	1	–	–	–	6	1	0
299/262*	1948	A	1	Nottingham	L-8w	7	3	lbw	7	22	c	–	102	32	2	–	–	–
300/263*			2	Lord's	L-409	6	44	b	6	11	b	1	90	35	2	78	36	2
301/264*			3	Manchester	D	7	22	c	–	–	–	–	24	12	0	–	–	–
302/265*			4	Leeds	L-7w	7	25	b	6	7	c	–	102	38	2	78	44	1
303/266*			5	Oval	L-I & 149	6	7	b	6	9	c	–	30	7	0	–	–	–
323/276*	1950	WI	1	Manchester	W-202	6	0	c	5	25	lbw	1	–	–	–	–	–	–
324/277*			2	Lord's	L-326	6	16	b	6	19	c	–	24	12	0	–	–	–
325/278*			3	Nottingham	L-10w	5	41	c	5	7	b	2	162	82	1	–	–	–

Career	M	I	NO	HS	R	Avge	100	50	Ct	St	Balls	R	W	Avge	BB	5w	10w	Rate
Test	20	34	2	99	812	25.37	–	4	14	–	1662	707	21	33.66	3-67	–	–	79.14
F/c	446	658	75	183*	18173	31.17	27	83	328	1	21220	8506	279	30.48	6-29	5	–	76.05

YOUNG, Harding Isaac

Essex (1898 to 1912)

TOUR WI 1910–11
Born Leyton, Essex 5 Feb 1876
Died Rochford, Essex 12 Dec 1964

'Sailor' Young was brought out of the Royal Navy by the Essex president, C.E. Green, to bowl his left-arm medium-pace with its confusing swerve. He suffered from muscular rheumatism and was unable to play regularly. After spending many years on the staff he became a first-class umpire (1921–31) and then a coach.

NOTABLE FEATS

- Took 139 wickets in 1899.
- Returned a match analysis of 15 for 154 for Essex v Warwickshire at Birmingham in 1899.
- Hat-trick for Essex v Leicestershire at Leyton in 1907.

'Sailor' Young

Ref	Series	V	T	Venue	Result	Batting 1st No	R	HO	Batting 2nd No	R	HO	Ct	Bowling 1st Balls	R	W	Bowling 2nd Balls	R	W
62/62	1899	A	3	Leeds	D	10	0	c	–	–	–	1	96	30	4	130	72	2
63/63			4	Manchester	D	9	43	b	–	–	–	–	145	79	4	185	81	2

Career	M	I	NO	HS	R	Avge	100	50	Ct	St	Balls	R	W	Avge	BB	5w	10w	Rate
Test	2	2	0	43	43	21.50	–	–	1	–	556	262	12	21.83	4-30	–	–	46.33
F/c	171	257	65	81	2303	11.99	–	4	80	–	26708	12014	514	23.37	8-54	27	4	51.96

YOUNG, John Albert

Middlesex (1933 to 1956)

TOUR SA 1948–49
Born Paddington, London 14 Oct 1912

Jack Young came from a theatrical background and had the deportment of a music hall artiste. Small (5ft 7in), neat and deliberate in his movements, he was a left-arm leg-break bowler of extraordinary accuracy who, to quote John Arlott, bowled 'those interminable maidens to the Australians'. He was a dogged but not very serious batsman and an expert fielder in the gully.

NOTABLE FEATS

- Took 100 wickets in a season 8 times, exceeding 150 in 4 occasions.
- Took 9 for 55 for an England XI v a Commonwealth XI at Hastings in 1951.
- Two hat-tricks for Middlesex: v Northamptonshire at Northampton in 1946 and v Lancashire at Lord's in 1951.

Jack Young

Ref	Series	V	T	Venue	Result	Batting 1st No	R	HO	Batting 2nd No	R	HO	Ct	Bowling 1st Balls	R	W	Bowling 2nd Balls	R	W
288/256	1947	SA	4	Leeds	W-10w	9	0	*	–	–	–	1	102	31	0	114	54	2
299/262	1948	A	1	Nottingham	L-8w	11	1	*	11	9	b	1	360	79	1	60	28	0
301/264			3	Manchester	D	11	4	c	–	–	–	–	84	36	1	126	31	1
303/266			5	Oval	L-I & 149	10	0	b	10	3	*	1	306	118	2	–	–	–
312/270	1948–49	SA	4	Johannesburg[2]	D	11	10	*	–	–	–	–	184	52	2	88	14	0
313/271			5	Port Elizabeth	W-3w	11	0	c	–	–	–	–	384	122	0	184	34	2
314/272	1949	NZ	1	Leeds	D	10	0	st	–	–	–	1	132	52	1	84	41	2
315/273			2	Lord's	D	10	1	*	–	–	–	1	160	65	3	–	–	–

Career	M	I	NO	HS	R	Avge	100	50	Ct	St	Balls	R	W	Avge	BB	5w	10w	Rate
Test	8	10	5	10*	28	5.60	–	–	5	–	2368	757	17	44.52	3-65	–	–	139.29
F/c	341	392	114	62	2485	8.93	–	1	148	–	79017	26795	1361	19.68	9-55	82	17	58.05

YOUNG
Richard Alfred

Cambridge University (1905 to 1908)
Sussex (1905 to 1925)

TOUR A 1907–08
Born Dharwar, India 16 Sep 1885
Died Hastings, Sussex 1 Jul 1968

Until M.J.K. Smith qualified, Dick Young was the only bespectacled sportsman to earn international caps at two sports and, by all accounts, the lenses in his glasses were thicker by far. He learned his cricket at Repton before going up to Cambridge where he was a blue in each of his four years. An extremely consistent middle-order batsman and a very capable wicket-keeper, he spent three decades as a maths master at Eton, playing for Sussex in the holidays. A noted soccer inside-right for Corinthians and Cambridge, where he gained a blue, he won an England amateur cap v Hungary. [*Illus. p.* 141]

NOTABLE FEATS

- Exceeded 1000 runs in a season twice, including 1170 in his debut season (1905) when 19.
- Scored 220 for Sussex v Essex at Leyton in 1905.

Ref	Series	V	T	Venue	Result	Batting 1st No	R	HO	Batting 2nd No	R	HO	Fielding 1st Ct	St	Byes	Balls	Fielding 2nd Ct	St	Byes	Balls
96/93†	1907–08	A	1	Sydney	L-2w	2	13	c	7	3	b	1	–	4	548	1	–	6	591
100/97†			5	Sydney	L-49	9	0	st	8	11	c	2	–	9	304	2	–	21	766

Career	M	I	NO	HS	R	Avge	100	50	Ct	St	Balls	R	W	Avge	BB	5w	10w	Rate
Test	2	4	0	13	27	6.75	–	–	6	–	–	–	–	–	–	–	–	–
F/c	139	242	11	220	6653	28.80	11	38	115	29	150	114	3	38.00	2-32	–	–	50.00

INDEX OF PHOTOGRAPHS

Other than Reginald Wood, each of England's 536 Test cricketers is illustrated at least once in the book. This selective index refers only to pages on which a player is identified in a caption. First-class career spans for each player are given in brackets.